MANAGERIAL ECONOMICS

MANAGERIAL ECONOMICS

SIXTH EDITION

S. Charles Maurice

Texas A & M University
Emeritus

Christopher R. Thomas

University of South Florida

Boston Burr Ridge, IL Dubuque, IA Madison, WI New York San Francisco St. Louis
Bangkok Bogotá Caracas Lisbon London Madrid
Mexico City Milan New Delhi Seoul Singapore Sydney Taipei Toronto

Irwin/McGraw-Hill

A Division of The **McGraw-Hill** *Companies*

Managerial Economics

This book is printed on acid-free paper.

1 2 3 4 5 6 7 8 9 0 DOC DOC 9 3 2 1 0 9 8

ISBN 0-256-17345-1

Editorial director: *Michael W. Junior*
Publisher: *Gary Burke*
Executive editor: *Paul Shensa*
Developmental editor: *Marilea Fried*
Marketing manager: *Nelson Black*
Project manager: *Terri Edwards*
Production supervisor: *Pam Augspurger*
Designer: *Lorna Lo*
Cover designer: *Amanda Kavanagh*
Supplements coordinators: *Louis Swaim and Florence Fong*
Editorial coordinator: *Katherine Mattison*
Compositor: *GAC/Shepard Poorman*
Typeface: *Palatino*
Printer: *R. R. Donnelley & Sons Company*

Cover art Joseph Stella, *Bridge,* 1936, oil on canvas, 50 1/8 x 30 1/8″ (127.3 x 76.5 cm), San Francisco Museum of Modern Art, WPA Federal Arts Project Allocation to San Francisco Museum of Art

Library of Congress Cataloging-in-Publication Data
Maurice, S. Charles.
Managerial economics / S. Charles Maurice, Christopher R. Thomas. — 6th ed.
p. cm.
Includes bibliographical references and index.
ISBN 0-256-17345-1
1. Managerial economics. I. Thomas, Christopher R. II. Title.
HD30.22.M39 1998
338.5′024′658—dc21 98-24973
CIP

http://www.mhhe.com

For my daughter
Brooke Michele Thomas
CRT

Tricia Ofczarzak
Like my daughter
SCM

BRIEF CONTENTS

CONTENTS

PREFACE

Why Managerial Economics?

Business students who wish to become successful managers of business enterprises should understand how the economic forces of the market create both opportunities and constraints for making profit. For this reason, business students—more than any other group of students—need to be trained in the application of microeconomic theory if they wish to become architects of business strategy rather than simply foremen or middle managers plodding along the beaten path of others. The primary goal of this book is to teach students the economic way of thinking about business decisions. We emphasize critical thinking skills and show students that *Managerial Economics* provides a logical way of analyzing business decisions. We strive to bring together those topics in microeconomic theory that can be applied to business decision making to create a powerful, timeless way of thinking about markets and business decisions—both today's decisions and tomorrow's.

Pedagogical Highlights

The Sixth Edition of *Managerial Economics* continues to emphasize the economic way of thinking about business decision making. While maintaining a rigorous style, we have designed this book to be one of the easiest books in managerial economics from which to teach *and* learn. Rather than parading students quickly through every interesting or new topic in microeconomics, we instead carefully develop and apply the most *useful* concepts in microeconomics for business decision making. Much of the detail that instructors may not have time to cover in class—or perhaps find tedious to cover in class—is clearly and completely developed for the reader.

To promote the development of analytical and critical thinking skills, which most students probably do not know how to accomplish on their own, we provide two different kinds of problem sets for each chapter. Much like the pedagogy in mathematics textbooks, which employ both "exercises" and "word problems," we provide both Technical Problems and Applied Problems:

Technical Problems—Each section of a chapter is keyed in the text to one or two Technical Problems specifically designed to build and reinforce a particular skill. The Technical Problems provide a step-by-step guide for students to follow in developing the analytical skills set forth in each chapter. The answers to *all* of the Technical Problems are provided at the end of the text, so the Technical Problems can serve as an integrated workbook within the text. The narrow focus of each Technical Problem allows students to pinpoint any areas of confusion so that interaction with the instructor—in the classroom or in the office—will be more productive. When students finish working the Technical Problems, they will have practiced all of the technical skills required to tackle the Applied Problems.

Applied Problems—Following the Technical Problems, each chapter has a set of Applied Problems which serve to build critical thinking skills as well as business decision-making skills. These problems, which are much like the "word problems" in a math textbook, are a mix of stylized business situations and real-world problems taken from *The Wall Street Journal*, *Business Week*, the *Economist*, and other business news publications. Business students frequently find classroom discussion of the Applied Problems to be among the most valuable lessons of their entire business training. Answers to Applied Problems are only available in the *Instructor's Manual.*

We believe the clarity of exposition, coupled with the integrated, step-by-step process of the Technical Problems, allows students to learn most of the technical skills before coming to class. To the extent that technical skills are indeed mastered before class, instructors can spend more time in class showing students how to *apply* the economic way of thinking to business decision making.

Audience

Managerial Economics has always been a self-contained book; no previous training in microeconomics is required. The Sixth Edition continues this tradition. Starting with only basic algebra and graph-reading skills, all other analytical tools employed in the book are developed within the text itself. Calculus is not a part of any chapter, but many of the chapter appendixes employ calculus to analyze mathematically some of the key topics covered in the chapter.

Managerial Economics is appropriate for undergraduate courses in managerial economics (or courses in applied microeconomics) and for MBA and Executive MBA level courses. The self-contained nature of the book can be especially valuable in night classes or Executive MBA programs where students may have limited opportunity to meet with an instructor for help outside class.

New Features in the Sixth Edition

The primary emphasis of this revision has been to make the Sixth Edition even easier to teach and learn from. Numerous changes, which are described below, make the book more user-friendly for *both* student and instructor by making the book a more self-contained learning resource. The new features of the Sixth Edition are:

- A new introductory chapter, "Managers, Firms, and Markets," teaches some of the introductory material of managerial economics, such as the concept of economic profit, the goals of a firm, principal-agent problems, and market structures. The Mathematical Appendix to Chapter 1 reviews the basic mathematics of present value.
- The analysis of decision making under risk now includes utility analysis and expected utility theory. The chapter on decision making under risk and uncertainty has been moved to the end of the book and is

now self-contained rather than spread throughout the text. (Putting risk analysis at the end of the book enables instructors to skip this material if they wish.)

- The chapter on oligopoly markets has been substantially revised to include more game theory analysis at a level suitable for business majors. We have resisted the temptation to present advanced game theoretic concepts that, while interesting, have little applicability in managerial decision making. The chapter remains an accessible treatment of game theoretic analysis of firms that are mutually interdependent.
- The Technical Problems at the end of each chapter have been redesigned to follow sequentially the individual sections of a chapter. Technical problems now provide a step-by-step progression of exercises to move students through an analytical progression of learned skills. At the end of the discussion of new analytical ideas in the text, a highlighted arrow in the margin points students to one or two Technical Problems designed to build a specific analytical skill. Students will be less dependent upon the instructor to master the technical skills of each chapter. When students do need help, they will be better able to pinpoint the area of difficulty.
- Every chapter has been updated and many have been rewritten to improve the presentation and flow of the material.
- Many new Applied Problems have been added, and all answers to Applied Problems are provided in the *Instructor's Manual.*
- Mathematical Appendixes have been revised and expanded in some chapters to provide a self-contained mathematical treatment of key topics for students who have some calculus background. Mathematical Exercises have been added to the math appendixes (with answers provided in the *Instructor's Manual*). As in previous editions, no calculus is employed in the body of the text. The book continues to focus on economic analysis rather than mathematical analysis. The *Student Workbook* provides a review of basic mathematical skills needed for the book in general (such as graph reading skills, linear equations, and slopes of lines and curves), as well as a review of simple differential calculus for the mathematical appendixes.
- Many new Illustrations—over 50 percent are new—have been added to replace outdated ones, and, where needed, Illustrations have been updated.
- The chapters employing statistical and quantitative analysis have been simplified. For tests of statistical significance, p-values are now reported along with test statistics. We continue to emphasize the use of statistical tests of significance, but do explain how p-values can be employed to determine exact levels of statistical significance. For quantitative problems, the use of units scaled in 100's or 1,000's has been discontinued in the Sixth Edition; all demand, production, and cost functions are expressed in units of one to avoid confusion for students.

Supplements

For this Sixth Edition of *Managerial Economics* we have carefully and thoroughly revised the three supplements for the text: the *Student Workbook*, the *Instructor's Manual*, and the *Testbank*. The *Student Workbook*, as noted, contains a tutorial on business mathematics. Each chapter of the *Workbook* has been carefully revised to match the style of the step-by-step Technical Problems in the textbook. As in previous editions, each chapter of the *Workbook* has four sections: Essential Concepts, Study

Problems, Multiple Choice/True-False, and Homework Exercises.

The *Instructor's Manual* contains a variety of old and new features: the Answers to Applied Problems, Answers to Mathematical Exercises (exercises found in the Mathematical Appendixes), and Answers to Homework Problems in the *Student Workbook*. In the Sixth Edition we are also including many of the old Illustrations that appeared in past editions but have since been replaced by more current, or more interesting, new Illustrations. Also new in this edition are Excel 97 spreadsheets for all of the Technical Problems involving numerical computations.

The *Testbank* for the Sixth Edition has been carefully revised and edited to make it match more closely the kinds of problems found at the end of each chapter (no problems from the Mathematical Appendixes are included). In addition to multiple choice questions (with answers), the Sixth Edition *Testbank* includes fill-in-the-blank questions that follow the style of the Technical Problems in each chapter.

A Word to Students

One of our primary objectives in writing this book is to provide you, the student, with a book that enhances your learning experience in managerial economics. We hope you will find this book to be so clearly written and the concepts so fundamentally important that you add this text to your business library for continued reference throughout your business career.

The degree of success you achieve in your managerial economics course will depend, in large measure, upon the effectiveness of your study. We would like to offer you this one tip on studying: Emphasize *active* study rather than *passive* study. Passive study activities are those that do not require you to think for yourself. Reading the text, reviewing class notes, and listening to lectures are "passive" in nature because the authors of your textbook or your instructor is providing the analytical guidance for you. You are simply following someone else's analytical thought process, working only hard enough to agree with the authors or instructor.

In contrast, "active" study techniques require you to think and reason for yourself. For example, when you close your book and put aside your lecture notes and try to explain a concept to yourself—perhaps sketching on a pad the graph or mathematical demonstration of a result—only then are you creating the path of logical analysis for yourself. The better you can explain the "how" and "why" of key concepts, the more thorough will be your understanding. Of course, some passive study is necessary to become familiar with the material, but genuine understanding and ability to use the decision-making skills of managerial economics require emphasis on active, rather than passive, study techniques.

Acknowledgments

Many of the improvements in this Sixth Edition are the result of suggestions by our colleagues and adopters at other universities. We would like to thank colleagues Joseph DeSalvo, Carole Green-Weishaupt, Kwabena Gyimah-Brempong, Dale Johnson, Brad Kamp, Gabriel Picone, Terry Sincich, and John Swinton at the University of South Florida and James Ullmer at Texas A&M University for numerous conversations concerning specific additions and changes to the text. This edition has also benefited substantially from the input and suggestions of our students. The critical eye of the doctors in the Executive MBA Program for Physicians at USF and the "real-world" managers in USF's traditional Executive MBA Program brought a number of pedagogical refinements to this edition.

We also received a number of valuable ideas for this edition from several reviewers:

Kwabena Gyimah-Brempong, *University of South Florida*
Paul Gabriel, *Loyola University Chicago*
Otis W. Gilley, *Louisiana Tech University*
Jack W. Hou, *California State University at Long Beach*
Fred Williams, *Montreal College*

We also wish to express our gratitude to Tricia Ofczarzak, who provided timely assistance in preparing the manuscript. Victoria Perk, at the Center for Urban Transportation Research, provided valuable assistance in the preparation of the *Testbank* and *Student Workbook.* And finally we thank Marilea Fried and Terri Edwards at McGraw-Hill for their dedication to this project. As always, we appreciate and encourage the comments and suggestions that we receive from students and faculty.

S. Charles Maurice
SCMaurice@aol.com

Christopher R. Thomas
CThomas@coba.usf.edu

CHAPTER 1

Managers, Firms, and Markets

> *Student of managerial economics: Will I ever use this?*
> *Professor: Only if your career is successful.*

Succeeding in the world of business, no matter how you slice it, means winning in the marketplace. From CEOs of large corporations to managers of small, privately held companies—and even nonprofit institutions such as hospitals and universities—managers cannot expect to succeed in business without a clear understanding of how market forces create both opportunities and constraints for business enterprises. Economic forces in the marketplace determine the demand for products, the prices of resources and costs of production, the number of rival firms, the nature of pricing strategies, and ultimately the profitability of business investments.

Publishers roll out dozens of new books each year touting the latest strategy *du jour* from one of the year's most "insightful" business gurus. The never-ending parade of new business "paradigms" and buzzwords might lead you to believe that successful managers must constantly replace outdated analytical methods with the latest fad in business decision making. While it is certainly true that managers must constantly be aware of new developments in the marketplace, the economic way of thinking about business decision making is timeless. Managerial economics provides a systematic, logical way of analyzing business decisions—both today's decisions and tomorrow's.

Instead of presenting a detailed list of rules for specific decision-making problems, such as how to design a successful automobile advertising campaign or how to obtain venture capital, managerial economics addresses the larger economic forces that shape both day-to-day operations and long-run planning

ILLUSTRATION 1.1

Managerial Economics
The Right ℞ for Doctors

The University of South Florida offers one of the nation's several M.B.A. programs designed specifically for medical doctors. The majority of the doctors enrolled in these specialized programs are seeking to develop the business decision-making skills they need to manage private and public medical clinics and hospitals.

As a group, doctors in these M.B.A. programs tend to be intelligent high-achievers who are in a hurry to learn something useful. They recognize their high opportunity costs of attending class rather than attending to patients, and they are understandably most interested in courses that will quickly teach them practical business skills. In managerial economics, they have found many valuable tools for business decision making and have been quick to apply the principles and tools of managerial economics to a variety of business problems in medicine. Some of the more interesting of these applications, all of which are topics you will learn about in this text, are discussed below:

- *Irrelevance of fixed costs in decision making:* Nearly all the physicians admitted to making some decisions based on fixed costs. A director of a radiation oncology department complained that many of her hospital's administrative costs are included as part of the incremental costs of treating additional patients. While the hospital prided itself in moving toward a marginal cost pricing structure for services, the accounting department's calculation of marginal cost was inflated by fixed administrative costs.
- *Price discrimination:* A doctor specializing in vasectomies wanted to increase revenue by engaging in price discrimination. After a lengthy discussion about the legality of charging different prices for medical services, he decided to promote his vasectomy clinic by placing a $40-off coupon in the local newspaper's TV guide. He believes that only lower-income patients will clip the coupon and pay the lower price.
- *Advertising dilemma:* After a class discussion on the advertising dilemma in oligopoly markets, a doctor who specializes in radial keratotomy (RK) surgery expressed her relief that none of the other three RK surgeons in her small town had shown any interest in advertising their services. She decided it would not be wise for her to begin running radio ads.
- *Linear trend forecasting:* Several physicians used linear trend analysis to forecast patient load. An administrator of a hospital's emergency room services found that using "day-of-week" dummy variables, he could offer hospital administrators statistical evidence—instead of his casual observation—that certain days of the week tend to be (statistically) significantly busier than others.

decisions. Managerial economics focuses on the application of *microeconomic* theory to business problems. Microeconomics is the study and analysis of the behavior of individual segments of the economy: individual consumers, workers and owners of resources, individual firms, industries, and markets for goods and services. Microeconomics is concerned with topics such as how consumers choose the goods and services they purchase and how firms make hiring, pricing, production, advertising, research and development, and investment decisions.

- *Strategic entry deterrence:* A doctor in New Orleans decided to open new clinics in Baton Rouge and Morgan City. No other clinics like his are currently operating in these two cities. In order to discourage other doctors from opening similar clinics, he plans to price his services just slightly above average total cost but significantly below the price that would maximize profit under monopoly.
- *Profit maximization vs. revenue maximization:* A doctor with a 25 percent ownership interest in a pharmaceutical supply firm realized during class that his sales manager is probably selling too many units, since the manager's compensation is based substantially on commissions. The doctor plans to recommend raising drug prices to sell fewer units and to begin paying the sales manager a percentage of profit.
- *Economies of scale and scope:* Hospital managers perceive the current trend toward "managed care" to be forcing hospitals to reduce costs without reducing quality. Economies of scale and scope, to the extent that such economies exist, offer an attractive solution to the need for cost reduction. Hospital administrators in the class were especially interested in empirical methods of measuring economies of scale in order to plan for future expansion or contraction.
- *Cost-minimizing input combination:* One doctor who owns and manages a chain of walk-in clinics decided to reduce the employment of M.D.s and increase the employment of R.N.s on the basis of classroom discussion of cost minimization. Apparently, for many of the procedures performed at the clinic, experienced nurses can perform the medical tasks approximately as well as the physicians, as long as the nurses are supervised by M.D.s. The doctor-manager reasoned that even though M.D.s have higher marginal products than R.N.s, the marginal product per dollar spent on R.N.s exceeded the marginal product per dollar spent on M.D.s.

The Wall Street Journal reported that doctors with M.B.A. degrees are becoming increasingly powerful in the medical profession as hospitals, health maintenance organizations, and other types of health care clinics hire them to manage the business aspect of health care.* Some doctors, as well as the American Medical Association, are opposed to blending business and medical values. The *WSJ* quotes one doctor's worries: "It's all too easy to become overly business-minded and begin seeing the world through green computer printouts." Given the nature of the applications of managerial economics cited above, it appears that a course in managerial economics offers doctors insights into the business of medicine that they would not usually get in medical school. Many doctors think this knowledge is good medicine.

*George Anders, "A New Breed of M.D.s Add M.B.A. to Vitae," *The Wall Street Journal,* Sept. 27, 1994, p. B1.

Business publications such as *The Wall Street Journal, Business Week, The Economist, Forbes,* and *Fortune* regularly cover the many stories of brilliant and disastrous decisions made by executive managers. Although luck often plays a role in the outcome of some of these stories, in many of them, the manager's understanding—or lack of understanding—of fundamental economic relations accounts for the difference between success and failure in business decision making. Although economic theory is not the only tool used by successful managers, it is a powerful and essential tool. The objective of this text is to show you how managers can use economic analysis in making decisions that will achieve the firm's goals—usually the maximization of profit.

1.1 MANAGERIAL ECONOMICS AND ECONOMIC THEORY

A large part of this text is devoted to the use of economic theory in addressing business decision-making problems. We want to explain briefly how and why economic theory is used to analyze business problems. No doubt you have heard statements such as, "That's OK in theory, but what about the real world?" or "I don't want ivory-tower theorizing, I want a practical solution." Practical solutions to challenging real-world problems are seldom found in cookbook formulas, superficial rules of thumb, or simple guidelines. Profitable solutions generally require that people understand how the real world functions, which is often far too complex to comprehend without making the simplifying assumptions used in theories. Theory allows people to gain insights into complicated problems by using simplifying assumptions to make sense out of confusion, to turn complexity into relative simplicity. By abstracting away from the irrelevant, managers can use the economic way of thinking about business problems to make predictions and explanations that are valid in the real world, even though the theory may ignore many of the actual characteristics of the real world.

Using economic theory is in many ways analogous to using a road map. A road map abstracts away from nonessential characteristics and concentrates on what is relevant for the task at hand. Suppose you want to drive from Tampa to Atlanta. If you have never made that trip before, you would probably want a map. Suppose you could have either an ordinary road map or a NASA satellite photograph of the region between Tampa and Atlanta. The satellite photograph is an exact representation of the real world; it shows every road, tree, building, cow, and river between Tampa and Atlanta. While the NASA photo would be amusing to look at, its inclusion of everything makes it inferior to a traditional road map in its ability to guide you to Atlanta. The road map abstracts from reality by eliminating nonessential information and showing only the important roads between Tampa and Atlanta. The simpler map gives a much clearer picture of how to get to Atlanta than the NASA photograph.

Likewise, the economic approach to understanding business decision making reduces business problems to their most essential components. Understanding the fundamentals of business decision making provides a way of thinking and analyzing problems that can be applied in a wide range of situations. The tools of analysis that you will learn in managerial economics will apply to today's decisions as well as to decisions you will face in the future.

1.2 MAXIMIZING PROFIT

In the standard economic theory of a firm, businesses are modeled as making pricing, employment, output, and investment decisions with the objective of maximizing profit. In practice, owners of firms, seeking to increase their personal wealth, generally do run a business primarily for the purpose of making as much profit as possible. Even when owners hire managers to run their businesses, the owners expect the managers to make decisions that will result in the greatest profit. Problems arise when owners cannot effectively monitor their managers, as the managers may choose to pursue goals other than profit maximization and thus reduce the value of the firm to its owners. Despite the possible problems of owners controlling managers, which we will discuss in greater detail later in this chapter, managers who fail to see the firm's role as earning profits for owners will quite likely be replaced either by the firm's current owners or, after a takeover of the firm, by new owners.

While this text focuses on making profitable business decisions, the principles and techniques set forth also offer valuable advice for managers of nonprofit organizations such as foundations, universities, hospitals, and government agencies. The manager of a hospital's indigent-care facility, for example, may wish to know how to minimize the cost of treating a community's indigent patients while maintaining a satisfactory level of care. A university president, facing a strict budget set by the state board of regents, may want to enroll and teach as many students as possible subject to meeting the budget constraint. Although profit maximization is the primary objective addressed in this text, the economic way of thinking about business decision making provides *all* managers with a powerful set of tools and insights for furthering the goals of their firms or organizations.

Economic Profit versus Accounting Profit

economic profit
The difference between total revenue and total economic cost, including both explicit and implicit costs: $\pi = TR - TC$.

Economic profit is the amount by which total revenue exceeds total economic cost, where total economic cost is the total opportunity cost of all resources used by the firm. As will be discussed in more detail in Chapter 9, the opportunity cost of using resources owned by others is equal to the dollar amount paid to the resource owners. For the resources used by the firm that are owned by the firm, the opportunity cost is equal to the largest payment that the owner could have received if those resources had been leased or sold in the market. If, for example, an owner manages her own firm, the greatest income she could have earned in alternative employment must be included as a cost of production. Or if the owner invested personal resources in purchasing the capital used in the firm's production process, the maximum return that could have been earned elsewhere if the capital had been sold or leased is an opportunity cost of production.

normal profit
The opportunity cost of owner-supplied resources.

Economists frequently refer to the opportunity cost of using the owner's own resources as **normal profit.** Normal profit is just another name for the implicit opportunity cost that a firm incurs when it employs owner-supplied resources such as financial capital and management services. In contrast to economic profit, which is computed by subtracting total cost from total revenue, normal profit is in no way related to total revenue. Normal profit is simply a part of total cost. As a part of total cost, normal profit does play a role in determining the economic profit of the firm:

$$\begin{aligned}\text{Economic profit} &= \text{Total revenue} - \text{Total economic cost} \\ &= \text{Total revenue} - \text{Explicit costs} - \text{Normal profit}\end{aligned}$$

Any return to the owner over and above a normal profit is economic profit. When total revenue just covers total economic cost, economic profit is zero and the firm's owner earns only a normal profit.

To illustrate these concepts, assume a firm has revenues of $5 million and explicit costs of $3 million. The owner of the firm has provided $1 million of capital to the firm. If the owner could have earned a 10 percent return on the $1 million in the best alternative investment (of similar risk), the normal profit is $100,000. Economic profit is $1.9 million (= $5 million − $3 million − $0.1 million). Sometimes normal profit is expressed as a rate of return. In this example, the normal rate of return is 10 percent. Suppose this same firm received a total revenue of only $3.1 million; then the firm would be earning only a normal profit (or just a **normal rate of return**), and economic profit is zero. In this text, when we use the term "profit," we mean economic profit.

normal rate of return
The rate of return earned by a firm when economic profit is zero and only a normal profit is being earned.

Relation Normal profit is the opportunity cost of the owner's resources, which are used by the firm. Normal profit is added to explicit costs to obtain the total economic cost of production. When economic profit is zero, the firm is just earning a normal profit or a normal rate of return. When economic profit is positive (negative), the firm earns a higher (lower) than normal rate of return.

When computing the profit of a business, accountants generally are not allowed to deduct normal profit as an expense because the Internal Revenue Service—as well as the Securities and Exchange Commission (SEC) in the case of publicly traded corporations—does not allow deduction of most types of implicit costs for the purposes of calculating taxable profit. **Accounting profit,** then, differs from economic profit because accounting profit does not subtract from total revenue the implicit costs of using resources and, consequently, exceeds economic profit by the amount of the firm's implicit costs or normal profit:

accounting profit
Total revenue minus explicit costs or economic profit plus normal profit.

$$\begin{aligned}\text{Accounting profit} &= \text{Total revenue} - \text{Explicit costs}\\ &= \text{Economic profit} + \text{Normal profit}\end{aligned}$$

Although accountants are required to ignore most kinds of implicit costs, owners of businesses must nevertheless bear *all* costs of using resources. Consequently, businesses are interested in maximizing economic profit rather than accounting profit.

Notice to students: The arrows in the left margin throughout this text are directing you to work the enumerated Technical Problems at the end of the chapter. Be sure to check the answers provided for you at the end of the book *before* proceeding to the next section of a chapter. We have carefully designed the Technical Problems to guide your learning in a step-by-step process.

Maximizing the Value of the Firm

Owners of a firm, whether the shareholders of a corporation or the owner of a single proprietorship, are best served by management decisions that seek to maximize the profit of the firm. In general, when managers maximize profit, they are also maximizing the value of the firm, which is the price someone will pay for the firm. How much will someone pay for a firm? Suppose you are going to buy a business on January 1 and sell it on December 31. If the firm is going to make an economic profit of $50,000 during the year, you are willing to pay no more than $50,000 (in monthly payments matching the flow of profit) to own the firm for that year. Since other potential buyers are *also* willing to pay up to $50,000, the firm likely sells for very nearly or exactly the amount of the economic profit earned in a year.

value of a firm
The price for which the firm can be sold, which equals the present value of future profits.

When a firm earns a stream of economic profit for a number of years in the future, the **value of a firm**—the price for which it can be sold—is the present value of the future economic profits expected to be generated by the firm:

$$\text{Value of a firm} = \frac{\pi_1}{(1 + r_1)} + \frac{\pi_2}{(1 + r_2)^2} + \cdots + \frac{\pi_T}{(1 + r_T)^T} = \sum_{t=1}^{T} \frac{\pi_t}{(1 + r_t)^t}$$

risk premium
An increase in the discount rate to compensate investors for uncertainty about future profits.

where π_t is the economic profit expected in period t, r_t is the risk-adjusted discount rate for period t, and T is the number of years in the life of a firm.[1] Since future profit is not known with certainty, the value of a firm is calculated using the profit *expected* to be earned in future periods. The greater the variation in possible future profits, the less a buyer is willing to pay for those risky future profits. The risk associated with not knowing future profits of a firm is accounted for by adding a **risk premium** to the (riskless) discount rate. A risk premium increases the discount rate, thereby decreasing the present value of profit received in the future, in order to compensate investors for the risk of not knowing with certainty the future value of profits. The more uncertain the future profits, the higher the risk premium used by investors in valuing a firm, and the more heavily future profits will be discounted.

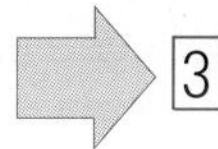
3

Relation The value of a firm is the price for which it can be sold, and that price is equal to the present value of the expected future profits of the firm. The larger (smaller) the risk associated with future profits, the higher (lower) the risk premium used to compute the value of the firm, and the lower (higher) will be the value of the firm.

The Equivalence of Value Maximization and Profit Maximization

Owners of a firm want the managers to make business decisions that will maximize the value of the firm, which, as we discussed in the previous subsection, is the sum of the discounted expected profits in current and future periods. As a general rule, then, a manager maximizes the value of the firm by making decisions that maximize expected profit in each period. That is, single-period profit maximization and maximizing the value of the firm are usually equivalent means to the same end: maximizing profit in each period will result in the maximum

[1]Since a dollar of profit received in the future is worth less than a dollar received now, multiperiod decision making employs the concept of present value. Present value is the value at the present time of a payment or stream of payments to be received (or paid) some time in the future. The appendix at the end of this chapter reviews the mathematics of present value computations, a topic usually covered in an introductory course in finance or accounting.

ILLUSTRATION 1.2

What Is the Value of a Firm?

The discussion of the value of a firm may have seemed a bit abstract, more suited for discussions in economic theory than for the use of sophisticated investors. Not so, as a "Smart Money" column in *Business Week* illustrates.

The column began by noting that investment analysts use a vast collection of tools to select stocks and one of their handier devices is the dividend discount model, or DDM: "The DDM works on the premise that an investment is worth the present value of its future cash flows. So to value a stock, you'll need the current annual dividend, a projected growth rate, and a 'discount rate.'"

The *Business Week* column used Exxon to illustrate the necessary calculation. At the time, the annual dividend was $2.20, which can be obtained from a newspaper. Exxon was expected to grow at a 7 percent annual rate, according to Value Line Investment Survey. This information could also be obtained from a broker. To calculate the discount rate, the column used the current rate on long-term government bonds, at the time about 9.2 percent. The column suggested adding an equity risk premium to compensate for the added risk of owning stocks. The premium was said to range between 2 and 5 percent, depending on the riskiness of the stock. For a blue chip such as Exxon, the column's author suggested about 3 percent, yielding a 12.2 percent discount factor.

To calculate the effective discount rate, subtract the 7 percent growth rate of the Exxon dividend from the discount rate of 12.2 percent to obtain 5.2 percent. Then convert 5.2 percent into decimal form (0.052) and divide the decimal value into the $2.20 dividend to obtain a present value of $42.30. The column pointed out that Exxon stock at the time was selling for $46 and, therefore, by this measure was overpriced. But the model is sensitive to the estimated values of discount and growth rates used in the calculation. A small change in the discount or growth rate produces a big difference in the present value of Exxon stock.

The DDM allows investors to ask "what-if" questions. For example, as the column's author pointed out, "If you think interest rates will fall, lower your discount rate by, say, a percentage point. That would value Exxon at $52, signaling a buy." Or, he went on to say, "if the discount rate is raised a point, that would value Exxon at $35, indicating you should wait for the price to fall."

According to the author, some pros recast the DDM by dividing the dividend by the stock price to get the current yield. Then they add the growth rate to get the stock's implied rate of return. (It was 11.8 percent for Exxon at the time.) The implied rates of return for several stocks can then be ranked by potential return, and only the growth rate must be estimated.

Before you plunge deeply into the market, we must warn you that the column pointed out that the DDM has limitations: "It works best on slow growing, mature companies that are consistent dividend payers." The model doesn't work well on high-flying biotech stocks, and it may make asset-rich stocks appear overpriced when takeover artists are willing to pay much more.

Source: Jeffrey Laderman, "Smart Money: Fast Figuring for Stock Handicappers," *Business Week*, Aug. 1, 1988, p. 103.

value of the firm, and maximizing the value of the firm requires maximizing profit in each period.

The equivalence of single-period profit maximization and maximizing the value of the firm holds only when the revenue and cost conditions in one time period are independent of revenue and costs in future time periods. When today's decisions affect profits in future time periods, price or output decisions that maximize profit in each (single) time period will not maximize the value of the firm. Two examples of these kinds of situations occur when (1) a firm's employees become more productive in future periods by producing more output in earlier periods—a case of learning by doing—and (2) current production has the effect of increasing cost in the future—as in extractive industries such as mining and oil production.

Despite these examples of inconsistencies between the two types of maximization, it is generally the case that there is little difference between the conclusions of single-period profit maximization (the topic of most of this text) and present value maximization. Thus, single-period profit maximization is generally the rule for managers to follow when trying to maximize the value of a firm.

4 **Principle** If cost and revenue conditions in any period are independent of decisions made in other time periods, a manager will maximize the value of a firm (the present value of the firm) by making decisions that maximize profit in every single time period.

1.3 SEPARATION OF OWNERSHIP AND CONTROL

When the manager of a firm is also the owner of a business, what is good for the owner is, of course, good for the manager. But most large business organizations are run by professional management teams that possess little or no equity ownership in the business. When the owners and managers are not the same people, conflicts can arise between the firm's owners and its managers.

These conflicts arise because of differences between the objectives of the owners and the managers. As already explained, owners want managers to maximize the value of the firm, which is usually accomplished by maximizing profit. Managers, when they have little or no ownership in a business, may pursue objectives that are not compatible with earning the maximum possible amount of profit for the owners. One profit-reducing objective managers are thought to pursue is the consumption of excessive or lavish perquisites. It is an unusual manager indeed who would not like to have the company pay for a lavish office, memberships in the most exclusive country clubs, extraordinary levels of life and health insurance, a limousine and chauffeur, and, if possible, a Challenger corporate jet. Another profit-reducing objective of managers is the pursuit of market share. Some managers are driven to have the firm be the largest, rather than the most profitable, firm in its industry. While maximizing the growth rate of a firm might be consistent with maximizing profit in some situations, as a general rule, pricing and output decisions that create the biggest, fastest-growing companies do not also maximize the value of the firm. In many industries, the most profitable firms are not the largest or fastest-growing ones, as Illustration 1.3 shows.

The Principal-Agent Problem

principal-agent problem
The conflict that arises when the goals of management (the agent) do not match the goals of the owner (the principal).

A principal in an agreement contracts with an agent to perform tasks designed to further the principal's objectives. A **principal-agent problem** arises when the agent has objectives different from those of the principal, and the principal either has difficulty enforcing the contract with the agent or finds it too difficult and costly to monitor the agent to verify that he or she is furthering the principal's objectives. Although there are a multitude of examples of the principal-agent problem in society, we are concerned here with the owner-manager

ILLUSTRATION 1.3

Managerial Strategy
Maximize Profit or Maximize Market Share?

Although sports and war metaphors are common in business conversation and management seminars, managers may be reducing the value of their firms by placing too much emphasis on beating their competitors out of market share rather than focusing on making the most profit for their shareholders. In a recent study of managerial strategy, Professors J. Scott Armstrong at the University of Pennsylvania's Wharton School and Fred Collopy at Case Western Reserve University advise CEOs to "keep their eyes on profits, not market share." Armstrong and Collopy discovered that, instead of maximizing profit, many managers make decisions with an eye toward performing well relative to their competitors—a decision-making point of view they refer to as "competitor-oriented."

In their nine-year study of over 1,000 experienced managers, Armstrong and Collopy found that managers are more likely to abandon the goal of profit maximization the greater the amount of information they have about the performance of their rivals. In the study, managers were asked to choose between two pricing plans for a new product—a low-price and a high-price strategy—and were told the five-year present value of expected profits associated with each strategy. The table in the next column presents two of the "treatments" which were administered to different groups of subjects.

Net Present Value of Expected Profit over Five Years

	Low-price strategy	High-price strategy
Base treatment:		
Your firm	$40 million	$ 80 million
Beat treatment:		
Your firm	40 million	80 million
Rival firm	20 million	160 million

The "base" treatment gives the manager no information about how a rival firm will fare under the two plans, while the "beat" treatment allows the manager to know how a decision will affect a rival. In the base treatment, almost all managers, as expected, chose the most profitable strategy (high price). When given information about the rival firm's profit, subjects could see the impact of their decision on their rival, and many managers abandoned profit maximization. In the beat treatment, 60 percent chose not to maximize profit (low price). To address the possibility that the subjects were considering longer-term profits, Armstrong and Collopy changed the payoffs to *20-year* present values. The results were the same.

Armstrong and Collopy believe the abandonment of profit as the firm's objective is a consequence of managers' having information about a competitor's performance. They discovered that exposing managers to techniques that focus on gaining market share increased the proportion of subjects who abandoned profit maximization. They also found that "executives who had taken strategic-management courses were more likely to make decisions that

problem, particularly as it applies to the corporate form of business organization. In corporations, shareholders are obviously the principals, and the managers are the agents.

moral hazard
Exists when either party to an agreement has an incentive not to abide by all provisions of the agreement.

The agency problem occurs because of moral hazard. **Moral hazard** exists when either party to an agreement has an incentive not to abide by all the provisions of the agreement *and* one party cannot cost-effectively find out if the other party is abiding by the agreement or cannot enforce the agreement even when that information is available. Although moral hazard arises in a large number of principal-agent agreements in business, we are concerned here only with moral hazard in the case of the firm's management working for shareholders.

You may be wondering why the shareholders don't simply tell the managers to maximize the value of the firm and, if they don't comply, replace them with harmed profitability." These results are impressive because they have been repeated in over 40 experiments with more than 1,000 subjects.

To see if firms that seek to maximize market share (competitor-oriented firms) tend to be less profitable *over the long run* than firms that pursue profit without concern for market share, Armstrong and Collopy tracked the performance of two groups of firms over a 54-year period. The group of firms that made pricing decisions based on competitor-oriented goals, such as increasing market share, were consistently less profitable over the 54-year period than the group that made pricing decisions to increase profit without regard to market share. Furthermore, companies pursuing market share were found to be less likely to survive: "Four of the six companies that focused strictly on market share (Gulf, American Can, Swift, and National Steel) did not survive. All four profit-oriented companies (DuPont, General Electric, Union Carbide, and Alcoa) did."

Armstrong and Collopy conclude that the use of competitor-oriented objectives is detrimental to profitability: "We believe that microeconomic theory, with its emphasis on profit maximization, is the most sensible course of action for firms; that is, managers should focus directly on profits." To encourage managers to keep their focus on profit and *not* on market share, they offer the following specific advice:

- Do not use market share as an objective.
- Avoid using sports and military analogies because they foster a competitor orientation.
- Do not use management science techniques that are oriented to maximizing market share, such as portfolio planning matrices and experience curve analysis.
- Design information systems to focus attention on the firm's performance, as measured by profits.
- Beware that improvements in the ability to measure market share—specifically through scanner data collected at checkouts—may lead to a stronger focus on market share and less focus on profitability.

As we emphasize in this chapter, shareholders wish to see the value of the firm maximized. A manager bent on being the biggest airline or biggest auto rental agency may fail to be the most profitable airline or auto rental agency. Between advances in shareholders' willingness and ability to fire CEOs and the active market for corporate control (mergers, acquisitions, and takeovers), a manager who fails to pursue primarily the maximization of profit may have a short career.

Sources: J. Scott Armstrong and Fred Collopy, "Competitor Orientation: Effects of Objectives and Information on Managerial Decisions and Profitability," *Journal of Marketing Research,* May 1996, pp. 188–99, and "The Profitability of Winning," *Chief Executive,* June 1, 1994, p. 60.

new managers. This process is a lot more complex and difficult than it appears at first glance. A large, modern corporation is an extremely complicated institution. The upper management of such a firm is much more familiar with the functioning of the corporation than most or even all of the stockholders. Stockholders would not even know, in many cases, whether management is or is not attempting to maximize the value of the firm or its profits, especially when business is good and the price of the stock is rising. Stockholders get most of their information about the performance of the firm from the managers themselves.

In the case of large corporations, any given shareholder typically holds a relatively small proportion of the total outstanding stock. Stockholders are generally broadly diversified and would have difficulty organizing into a group that could actually affect the firm's policies. Furthermore, an individual stockholder would probably not have the incentive to find the necessary information about the firm and then attempt to monitor management. The cost of obtaining and processing the required information would be huge, while the benefits to an individual shareholder would be small, even if the monitoring were successful. Shareholders usually have diversified portfolios in which no individual stock looms particularly large, relative to their total holdings. They frequently don't have much of an interest in one particular stock. Therefore, the owners of large corporations have a difficult time policing the managers.

Corporate Control Mechanisms

The discussion of agency problems is not meant to imply that shareholders are completely helpless in the face of managers who aren't doing what the shareholders expect them to do. Rules of corporate governance give shareholders rights that allow them to control managers directly through control measures and indirectly through the board of directors, whose responsibility it is to monitor management. Shareholders themselves, and in partnership with the board of directors, may choose from a variety of mechanisms for controlling agency problems. In addition to the governance methods available to shareholders, several forces outside the firm can also force managers to pursue maximization of the firm's value. We will review only briefly a few of the most important types of mechanisms that can intensify a manager's desire to maximize profit.

Stockholders often try to solve the agency problem by tying managers' compensation to fulfilling the goals of the shareholders. Managers have a greater incentive to make decisions that further the goals of shareholders when managers themselves are shareholders. Equity ownership is considered one of the most effective mechanisms for corporate control, so much so that some professional money managers and large institutional investors refuse to invest in firms whose managers hold little or no equity stake in the firms they manage.

The members of the board of directors are agents of the shareholders charged with monitoring the decisions of executive managers. But just as managers are agents for owners, so too are directors, and agency problems can arise between directors and shareholders. Many observers believe that the value of the board's monitoring services is enhanced by appointing outsiders—directors not serving on the firm's management team—and by linking directors' compensation to the value of the firm. The effectiveness of a board of directors is undermined when business decisions are so complex that the board cannot reliably judge whether a decision furthers shareholder interests and when the CEO plays a strong role in selection of the board members.

Another method of creating incentives for managers to make value-maximizing decisions involves corporate policy on debt financing. A policy that emphasizes financing corporate investments with debt rather than equity—selling shares of common stock to raise financial capital—can further the interests of shareholders in several ways. First, debt financing makes bankruptcy possible, since firms cannot go bankrupt if they have no debt. Thus, managers who value their employment have an additional incentive to increase profitability in order to lower the probability of bankruptcy. Second, managers face less pressure to generate revenues to cover the cost of investments if the payments are dividends to shareholders, which they can choose to defer or neglect altogether, rather than if the payments are installments on a loan. Finally, lenders have an incentive to monitor managers of firms that borrow money from them. Thus, banks and other lenders may make it difficult for managers to consume excessive perks or make unprofitable investments.

Corporate takeovers are also an important possible solution to the conflict between shareholders and managers who do not maximize the value of the firm. If the value of the firm is less with the present set of managers than it would be with another, there is a profit incentive for others to acquire the firm and replace the management team with a new set of managers. For example, if the firm has a poorly designed compensation scheme that fails to motivate managers to maximize profits, another company, or group of corporate raiders, believing its management could do a better job, might take over the firm by purchasing enough shares to take control. Even though most of the media, many politicians, and certainly the managers of the takeover targets dislike takeovers, frequently called "hostile," takeovers act as a check on the power of incompetent managers to create inefficiency and also on the power of managers who are less interested in maximizing profits, since they are not major owners, than they are in expanding their corporate domain. Thus, takeovers can sometimes resolve to some extent the conflict between managers and shareholders. Illustration 1.4 shows one well-known analyst's opinion on hostile takeovers.

1.4 MARKET STRUCTURE AND MANAGERIAL DECISION MAKING

As we mentioned earlier, managers cannot expect to succeed without understanding how market forces shape the firm's ability to earn profit. A particularly important aspect of managerial decision making is the pricing decision. The structure of the market in which the firm operates can limit the ability of a manager to raise the price of the firm's product without losing a substantial amount, possibly even all, of its sales.

Not all managers have the power to set the price of the firm's product. In some industries, each firm in the industry makes up a relatively small portion of total sales and produces a product that is identical to the output produced by all the rest of the firms in the industry. The price of the good in such a situation is not determined by any one firm or manager but, rather, by the impersonal forces of the marketplace—the intersection of market demand and supply, as you will see in the next chapter. If a manager attempts to raise the price above the market-determined price, the firm loses all its sales to the other firms in the industry. After all, buyers do not care from whom they buy this identical product, and they would be unwilling to pay more than the going market price for the product. In such a situation, the firm is a **price-taker** and cannot set the price of the product it sells. We will discuss price-taking firms in detail in Chapters 12 and 13, and you will see that the demand curve facing a price-taking firm is horizontal at the price determined by market forces.

price-taker
A firm that cannot set the price of the product it sells, since price is determined strictly by the market forces of demand and supply.

ILLUSTRATION 1.4

What's Wrong with Hostile Takeovers?

We briefly alluded to corporate takeovers as a possible solution to the conflict between shareholders and managers who do not maximize the corporation's present value. During the 1980s, there was a wave of hostile takeovers (hostile at least to the managers involved) along with a certain amount of illegal insider trading. The media and many politicians were outraged over this seeming affront to entrenched corporate managers. Robert J. Samuelson, a columnist for *Newsweek*, published two columns aimed at putting the takeover movement in perspective and showing how that movement was related to the conflict of shareholders and managers.

Samuelson began by noting that corporate raiders have been parodied as capitalism's juvenile delinquents, especially in the 1980s when many of the takeovers were financed by junk bonds. In contrast to the public's negative perception of takeovers, "hostile takeovers . . . represent a crude check on the power of corporate managers to waste wealth and create inefficiency. I doubt that those in Congress who condemn [T. Boone] Pickens [a prominent corporate raider at the time] and want to regulate takeovers understand [this]."

Samuelson also observed that, when corporate managers are not major owners of the companies they manage—and most are not—their loyalties become confused. Managers "may be less interested in maximizing profits than in preserving and expanding their corporate domain"—a central point of our discussion in the text.

"As long as a company's primary business is thriving, the conflict may lie dormant. Managers can maximize profits and expand simultaneously. But this happy marriage rarely lasts forever." Then as the business matures, management may diversify into a new business, where the company may have no special knowledge or talent. "Hostile takeovers arise mainly to exploit profit opportunities created when corporations cannot cope with their growth dilemma." Essentially, today's hostile takeovers represent a corrective for yesterday's abuses, as many corporations have become cumbersome empires that cannot motivate workers or be managed efficiently. These companies are the potential takeover targets. Even the distant threat of a takeover can be therapeutic. To ward off takeover attempts, "companies are furiously selling unwanted divisions and subsidiaries." According to these arguments, corporate raiders keep managers much more in line with the wishes of stockholders, and to the extent that they improve companies' efficiency, they benefit consumers and the public as well.

Samuelson reiterated the advantages and benefits of corporate takeovers in a later column: "Many companies are excessively bureaucratic or excessively diversified. They would operate more efficiently if broken up into their constituent businesses . . . or put under better management. . . . Fragmented shareholders are passive; directors are complacent." And, "short of bankruptcy, top executives have enjoyed huge job security. . . . Hostile takeovers shatter this security." The resulting stock market speculation over possible takeover candidates really reflects mismanagement. Suppose a company's stock sells at $10 and someone plans a takeover at $13 (takeover premiums average between 25 and 50 percent). The takeover group thinks better management can raise the stock's value to $17. "At a crude level, the gap between $10 and $17 (if attained) is mismanagement."

Then there enter traders with illegal inside information, such as Ivan Boesky, the most prominent inside trader in the 1980s. With a tip about the takeover, an inside trader can buy the stock at $10 and sell it at $13. Samuelson argues, however, "Nothing in Boesky's scam diminishes the real gains possible from replacing bad management with good." He also argues that even though the number of actual hostile takeovers is small, even the threat of a takeover spurs many managers to improve their efficiency. As noted in the text, takeovers can resolve to some extent the conflict between managers and shareholders.

Sources: Robert J. Samuelson, "In Praise of Boone," *Newsweek*, May 6, 1985, p. 59, and "The Super Bowl of Scandal," *Newsweek*, Dec. 1, 1986, p. 64.

price-setting firm
A firm that can raise its price without losing all of its sales.

In contrast to managers of price-taking firms, the manager of a **price-setting firm** does set the price of the product. A price-setting firm has the ability to raise its price without losing all sales because the product is somehow differentiated from rivals' products or perhaps because the geographic market area in which the product is sold has only one (or just a few) sellers of the product. At higher prices the firm sells less of its product, and at lower prices the firm sells more of its product. The ability to raise price without losing all sales is called **market power,** a subject we will examine more thoroughly in Chapters 14 through 17. Before we discuss some of the differing market structures to be analyzed in later chapters of this text, we first want you to consider the fundamental nature and purpose of a market.

market power
A firm's ability to raise price without losing all sales.

What Is a Market?

market
Any arrangement through which buyers and sellers exchange anything of value.

A **market** is any arrangement through which buyers and sellers exchange final goods or services, resources used for production, or, in general, anything of value. The "arrangement" may be a location and time, such as a commercial bank from 9 A.M. until 6 P.M. on weekdays only, an agricultural produce market every first Tuesday of the month, a trading "pit" at a commodity exchange during trading hours, or even the parking lot of a stadium an hour before game time when ticket scalpers sometimes show up to sell tickets to sporting events. An arrangement may also be something other than a physical location and time, such as a classified ad in a newspaper or a website on the Internet. You should view the concept of a market quite broadly, particularly since advances in technology create new ways of bringing buyers and sellers together.

Markets are arrangements that reduce the cost of making transactions. Buyers wishing to purchase something must spend valuable time and other resources finding sellers, gathering information about prices and qualities, and ultimately making the purchase itself. Sellers wishing to sell something must spend valuable resources locating buyers (or pay a fee to sales agents to do so), gathering information about potential buyers (for example, verifying creditworthiness or legal entitlement to buy), and finally closing the deal. These costs of making a transaction happen, which are additional costs of doing business over and above the price paid, are known as **transaction costs.** Buyers and sellers use markets to facilitate exchange because markets lower the transaction costs for both parties. To understand the meaning of this seemingly abstract point, consider two alternative ways of selling a used car that you own. One way to find a buyer for your car is to canvass your neighborhood, knocking on doors until you find a person willing to pay a price you are willing to accept. This will likely require a lot of your time and perhaps even involve buying a new pair of shoes. Alternatively, you could run an advertisement in the local newspaper describing your car and stating the price you are willing to accept for it. This method of selling the car involves a market—the newspaper ad. Even though

transaction costs
Costs of making a transaction happen, other than the price of the good or service itself.

you must pay a fee to run the ad, you choose to use this market because the transaction costs will be lower by advertising in the newspaper than by searching door to door.

Different Market Structures

market structure
Market characteristics that determine the economic environment in which a firm operates.

Market structure is a set of market characteristics that determines the economic environment in which a firm operates. As we will now explain, the structure of a market governs the degree of pricing power possessed by a manager, both in the short run and in the long run. The list of economic characteristics needed to describe a market is actually rather short:

- *The number and size of the firms operating in the market:* A manager's ability to raise the price of the firm's product without losing most, if not all, of its buyers depends in part upon the number and size of sellers in a market. If there are a large number of sellers with each producing just a small fraction of the total sales in a market, no single firm can influence market price by changing its production level. Alternatively, when the total output of a market is produced by one or a few firms with relatively large market shares, a single firm can cause the price to rise by restricting its output and to fall by increasing its output, as long as no other firm in the market decides to prevent the price from changing by suitably adjusting its own output level.
- *The degree of product differentiation among competing producers:* If sellers all produce products that consumers perceive to be identical, then buyers will never need to pay even a penny more for a particular firm's product than the price charged by the rest of the firms. By differentiating a product either through real differences in product design or through advertised image, a firm may be able to raise its price above its rivals' prices if consumers find the product differences sufficiently desirable to pay the higher price.
- *The likelihood of new firms entering a market when incumbent firms are earning economic profits:* When firms in a market earn economic profits, other firms will learn of this return in excess of opportunity costs and will try to enter the market. Once enough firms enter a market, price will be bid down sufficiently to eliminate any economic profit. Even firms with some degree of market power cannot keep prices higher than opportunity costs for long periods when entry is relatively easy.

Microeconomists have analyzed firms operating in a number of different market structures. Not surprisingly, economists have names for these market structures: perfect competition, monopoly, monopolistic competition, and oligopoly. Although each of these market structures is examined in detail later in this text, we will briefly discuss each one now to show you how market structure shapes a manager's pricing decisions.

In *perfect competition,* a large number of relatively small firms sell an undifferentiated product in a market with no barriers to the entry of new firms. Managers of firms operating in perfectly competitive markets are price-takers with no market power. At the price determined entirely by the market forces of demand and supply, they decide how much to produce in order to maximize profit. In the absence of entry barriers, any economic profit earned at the market-determined price will vanish as new firms enter and drive the price down to the average cost of production. Many of the markets for agricultural goods and other commodities traded on national and international exchanges closely match the characteristics of perfect competition.

In a *monopoly* market, a single firm, protected by some kind of barrier to entry, produces a product for which no close substitutes are available. A monopoly is a price-setting firm. The degree of market power enjoyed by the monopoly is determined by the ability of consumers to find imperfect substitutes for the monopolist's product. The higher the price charged by the monopolist, the more willing are consumers to buy other products. The existence of a barrier to entry allows a monopolist to raise its price without concern that economic profit will attract new firms. As you will see in Chapter 14, examples of true monopolies are rare.

In markets characterized by *monopolistic competition,* a large number of firms that are small relative to the total size of the market produce differentiated products without the protection of barriers to entry. The only difference between perfect competition and monopolistic competition is the product differentiation that gives monopolistic competitors some degree of market power; they are price-setters rather than price-takers. As in perfectly competitive markets, the absence of entry barriers ensures that any economic profit will eventually be bid away by new entrants. The toothpaste market provides one example of monopolistic competition. The many brands and kinds of toothpaste are close, but not perfect, substitutes. Toothpaste manufacturers differentiate their toothpastes by using different flavorings, abrasives, whiteners, fluoride levels, and other ingredients, along with a substantial amount of advertising designed to create brand loyalty.

In each of the three market structures discussed above, managers do not need to consider the reaction of rival firms to a price change. A monopolist has no rivals; a monopolistic competitor is small enough relative to the total market that its price changes will not usually cause rival firms to retaliate with price changes of their own; and, of course, a perfectly competitive firm is a price-taker and would not change its price from the market-determined price. In contrast, in the case of an *oligopoly* market, just a few firms produce most or all of the market output, so any one firm's pricing policy will have a significant effect on the sales of other firms in the market. This **mutual interdependence** of oligopolistic firms means that actions by any one firm in the market will have an effect on the sales of the other firms. As you will see in Chapter 15, the structure of oligopolies varies widely according to the degree of rivalry, product differentiation, and level of entry barriers. Automobile manufacturers, commercial jet aircraft makers, and farm tractor firms (for example, GM, Boeing, and John Deere) are typical oligopolists.

mutual interdependence
Condition in which actions by any one firm affect the sales of other firms in a market.

1.5 SUMMARY

Managerial economics provides a systematic, logical way of analyzing business decisions that focuses on the economic forces that shape both day-to-day decisions and long-run planning decisions. Managerial economics applies microeconomic theory—the study of the behavior of individual economic agents—to business problems in order to teach business decision makers how to use economic analysis to make decisions that will achieve the firm's goal—the maximization of profit.

Economic theory helps managers understand real-world business problems by using simplifying assumptions to abstract away from irrelevant ideas and information and turn complexity into relative simplicity. Like a road map, economic theory ignores everything irrelevant to the problem and reduces business problems to their most essential components.

Economic profit is the difference between a firm's total revenue and the total economic cost of using productive resources. The economic cost of using resources is the opportunity cost of using those resources. For resources owned by others, the opportunity cost of resource use is the dollar amount paid to the resource owners. For resources the firm uses that are owned by the firm, the opportunity cost is equal to the largest payment that the owner could have received if those resources had been leased or sold in the market.

The opportunity cost of using the owner's own resources is called normal profit. Normal profit is part of total cost. When economic profit is zero, the firm is just earning a normal profit or a normal rate of return. When economic profit is positive (negative), the firm earns a higher (lower) than normal rate of return. Since accountants are not allowed to deduct normal profit as a cost, accounting profit exceeds economic profit by the amount of the firm's implicit costs or normal profit:

$$\begin{aligned}\text{Accounting profit} &= \text{Total revenue} - \text{Explicit costs} \\ &= \text{Economic profit} + \text{Normal profit}\end{aligned}$$

Since all costs matter to owners of a firm, maximizing economic profit, rather than accounting profit, is the objective of the firm's owners.

The value of a firm is the price for which it can be sold, and that price is equal to the present value of the expected future profits of the firm. The risk associated with not knowing future profits of a firm is accounted for by adding a risk premium to the discount rate used to calculate the present value of the firm's future profits. The larger (smaller) the risk associated with future profits, the higher (lower) the risk premium used to compute the value of the firm, and the lower (higher) will be the value of the firm. In the absence of any agency problems, the objective of a manager is to maximize the value of the firm. A manager will maximize the value of a firm by making decisions that maximize profit in every single time period, unless cost and/or revenue conditions in any period depend upon decisions made in other time periods. If increasing current output has a positive effect on future revenue and profit, a value-maximizing manager selects an output level that is greater than the level chosen by a profit-maximizing manager. Alternatively, if current production has the effect of increasing cost in the future, maximizing the value of the firm will result in a lower current output than will maximizing single-period profit.

In firms where the managers are not also the owners, the managers are agents of the owners, or principals. A principal-agent problem exists when the agent has objectives different from those of the principal, and the principal either has difficulty enforcing agreements with the agent or finds it too difficult and costly to monitor the agent to verify that he or she is furthering the principal's objectives. Agency problems arise because of moral hazard. Moral hazard exists when either party to an agreement has an incentive not to abide by all the provisions of the agreement *and* one party cannot cost-effectively find out if the other party is abiding by the agreement or cannot enforce the agreement even when the information is available.

In order to address agency problems, shareholders can employ a variety of corporate control mechanisms. Shareholders can reduce or eliminate agency problems by (1) requiring that managers hold a stipulated amount of the firm's equity, (2) increasing the percentage of outsiders serving on the company's board of directors, and (3) financing corporate investments with debt instead of equity. Corporate takeovers also create an incentive for managers to make decisions that maximize the value of a firm.

The structure of the market in which a firm operates can limit the ability of managers to increase the price of the firm's products. In some markets, firms are price-takers. In these markets prices are determined not by managers but by market forces that cannot be controlled. In other markets, managers of price-setting firms possess some degree of market power and can raise price without losing all their sales.

A market is any arrangement that enables buyers and sellers to exchange goods and services, usually for money payments. A market may be a location at a certain time, a newspaper advertisement, a website on the Internet, or any other arrangement that works to bring buyers and sellers together. Markets exist to reduce transaction costs, the costs of making a transaction.

A market structure is a set of market characteristics that determines the economic environment in which a firm operates: (1) the number and size of the firms operating in the market, (2) the degree of product differentiation, and (3) the likelihood of new firms' entering. A perfectly competitive market has a large number of relatively small firms selling an undifferentiated product with no barriers to entry. A monopoly market is one in which a single firm, protected by barriers to entry, produces a product that has no close substitutes. In a monopolistically competitive market, a large number of relatively small firms produce differentiated products without any barriers to entry. Finally, in an oligopoly market, there are only a few firms experiencing mutual interdependence—each firm's pricing decision affects all other firms' profits—with varying degrees of product differentiation and barriers to entry.

TECHNICAL PROBLEMS

1. Fill in the blanks:
   a. ________ profit is a cost of doing business and is the amount by which ________ profit exceeds ________ profit.
   b. When a firm earns just a normal rate of return, ________ equals total economic cost and ________ profit is zero.
   c. When economic profit is positive, total revenue exceeds ________ and the firm earns a ________ (lower, higher) than normal rate of return.
   d. ________ profit best measures the performance of a firm because it considers all the costs to a firm of using resources.
2. During a year of operation, a firm collects $175,000 in revenue and spends $80,000 on raw materials, labor expense, utilities, and rent. The owners of the firm have provided $500,000 of their own money to the firm instead of investing the money and earning a 14 percent annual rate of return.
   a. The explicit costs of the firm are $________. The implicit costs are $________. Total economic cost is $________.
   b. The firm earns economic profit of $________. The firm's normal profit is $________, and the normal rate of return for the firm is ________ percent annually.
   c. The firm's accounting profit is $________.
   d. If the firm's costs stay the same but its revenue falls to $________, only a normal profit is earned.
   e. If the owners could earn 20 percent annually on the money they have invested in the firm, the economic profit of the firm would be ________ (when revenue is $175,000).
3. Over the next three years, a firm is expected to earn economic profits of $120,000 in the first year, $140,000 in the second year, and $100,000 in the third year. After the end of the third year, the firm will go out of business.
   a. If the risk-adjusted discount rate is 10 percent for each of the next three years, the value of the firm is $________. The firm can be sold today for a price of $________.

b. If the risk-adjusted discount rate is 8 percent for each of the next three years, the value of the firm is $________. The firm can be sold today for a price of $________.

4. Fill in the blanks:
   a. When current output has the effect of increasing future costs, the level of output that maximizes the value of the firm will be ________ (smaller, larger) than the level of output that maximizes profit in a single period.
   b. When current output has a positive effect on future profit, the level of output that maximizes profit in the current period will be ________ (smaller, larger) than the level of output that maximizes the value of the firm.

APPLIED PROBLEMS

1. The MidNight Hour, a local nightclub, earned $100,000 in accounting profit last year. This year the owner, who had invested $1 million in the club, decided to close the club. What can you say about the economic profit (and the rate of return) in the nightclub business?
2. A doctor spent two weeks doing charity medical work in Mexico. In calculating her taxable income for the year, her accountant deducted as business expenses her round-trip airline ticket, meals, and a hotel bill for the two-week stay. She was surprised to learn that the accountant, following IRS rules, could not deduct as a cost of the trip the $8,000 of income she lost by being absent from her medical practice for two weeks. She asked the accountant, "Since lost income is not deductible as an expense, should I ignore it when I make my decision next year to go to Mexico for charity work?" Can you give the doctor some advice on decision making?
3. For each of the firms below, identify the market structure that best matches the competitive characteristics found in that firm's market:
   a. International Harvester, a manufacturer of farm equipment
   b. The (single) cable television provider in Key West
   c. Sang Electronics, a Korean manufacturer of standard 32-megabyte random-access-memory (RAM) chips
   d. A firm producing laundry detergent

   Which of these firms could reasonably expect to earn a higher than normal rate of return over a relatively long period?
4. Taxicabs in New York City are licensed; in order to pick up passengers in the five boroughs of the city, you must have a medallion displayed on the hood of your taxi. There are no new medallions available. If you want a medallion, you have to buy it from someone who owns one.
   a. If you were to purchase an N.Y.C. taxicab company, what would you be purchasing?
   b. How would you calculate the value of the taxicab company?
   c. In October 1986, Mayor Ed Koch suggested that the number of N.Y.C. taxicab medallions be increased. What was the reaction to this suggestion? Why?
5. An article in *The Wall Street Journal* discusses a trend among some large U.S. corporations to base the compensation of outside members of their boards of directors partly on the performance of the corporation. "This growing practice more closely aligns the director to the company. [Some] companies link certain stock or

stock-option grants for directors to improved financial performance, using a measure such as annual return on equity."

How would such a linkage tend to reduce the agency problem between managers and shareholders as a whole? Why could directors be more efficient than shareholders in improving managerial performance and changing their incentives?

6. An article in *The Wall Street Journal* reported that large hotel chains, such as Marriott, are tending to reduce the number of hotels that they franchise to outside owners and increase the number the chain owns and manages itself. Some chains are requiring private owners or franchisees to make upgrades in their hotels, but they are having a difficult time enforcing the policy. Marriott says this upgrading is important because "we've built our name on quality."
   a. What type of agency problem is involved here?
   b. Why would Marriott worry about the quality of the hotels it doesn't own but franchises?
   c. Why would a chain such as Marriott tend to own its hotels in resort areas, such as national parks, where there is little repeat business, and franchise hotels in downtown areas, where there is a lot of repeat business? Think of the reputation effect and the incentive of franchises to maintain quality.

MATHEMATICAL APPENDIX Review of Present Value Calculations

The concept of present value is a tool used to determine the value of a firm, which is the present value of expected future profits to be earned. The last chapter of this text examines the investment decision of a firm, and you will find it useful there to be able to calculate present values. Even if you have not already studied present value analysis in your finance or accounting classes, this short presentation will provide you with the basic computational skills needed to calculate the present value of a stream of expected profit to be received in future periods.

Present Value of a Single Payment in the Future

The payment you would accept today rather than wait for a payment (or stream of payments) to be received in the future is called the *present value* (*PV*) of that future payment (or stream of payments). Suppose, for example, that a trustworthy person promises to pay you \$100 a year from now. Even though you are sure you will get the \$100 in a year, a dollar now is worth more than a dollar a year from now. How much money would you accept now rather than wait one year for a guaranteed payment of \$100? Because of the time value of money, you will be willing to accept less than \$100; that is, the present value of a \$100 payment one year from now is *less* than \$100. The process of calculating present value is sometimes referred to as *discounting* since the present value of a payment is less than the dollar amount of the future payment.

To properly discount the \$100 future payment, you must first determine the opportunity cost of waiting for your money. Suppose that, at no risk, you could earn a return of 6 percent by investing the money over a one-year period. This 6 percent return is called the *risk-free discount rate* since it determines the rate at which you will discount future dollars to determine their present value, assuming you bear no risk of receiving less than the promised amount. In Chapter 19, we will show you how to determine the appropriate risk premium to add to the risk-free discount rate when the future payment involves a degree of risk. For now, you need not be concerned about adjusting for risk.

Given that you can earn 6 percent (with no risk) on your money, how much money do you need now—let's denote this amount as $\$X$—in order to have exactly \$100 a year from now? Since $\$X(1.06)$ is the value of $\$X$ in one year, set this future value equal to \$100:

$$\$X(1.06) = \$100$$

It follows that the amount you must invest today ($\$X$) is \$94.34 (= \$100/1.06) in order to have \$100 in a year. Thus, the present value of \$100 to be received in one year is \$94.34 now. In other words, you would accept

$94.34 now, which will grow to $100 in one year (at a 6 percent annual discount rate).

Now suppose that the $100 payment comes not in one year but after two years. Investing $X at 6 percent would yield $X(1.06) at the end of year 1 and [$X(1.06)] (1.06) = $X(1.06)² at the end of year 2. For an investment to be worth $100 in two years,

$$\$X(1.06)^2 = \$100$$

The amount you must invest today in order to have $100 at the end of two years is $89 [= $100/(1.06)²]. Thus, the present value of $100 in two years with a discount rate of 6 percent is $89.

Clearly a pattern is emerging: The present value of $100 in one year at 6 percent is

$$PV = \frac{\$100}{(1.06)} = \$94.34$$

The present value of $100 in two years at 6 percent is

$$PV = \frac{\$100}{(1.06)^2} = \$89$$

Therefore, the present value of $100 to be received in t years (t being any number of years) with a discount rate of 6 percent is

$$PV = \frac{\$100}{(1.06)^t}$$

This relation can be made even more general to determine the present value of some net cash flow (NCF) to be received in t years at a discount rate of r. Net cash flow is the cash received in time period t, net of any costs or expenses that must be paid out of the cash inflow. Also note that if the discount rate is 6 percent, for example, r is expressed as 0.06, the decimal equivalent of 6 percent.

Relation The present value (PV) of $\$NCF$ to be received in t years at a discount rate of r is

$$PV = \frac{\$NCF}{(1 + r)^t}$$

As illustrated above, the present value of a cash flow declines the further in the future it is to be received—for example, the present value of $100 at 6 percent was $94.34 in one year and only $89 in two years. As should be evident from the more general statement of present value, the present value of a cash flow is inversely related to the discount rate—for example, the present value of $100 to be received in two years is $89 with a discount rate of 6 percent but only $85.73 [= $100/(1.08)²] with a discount rate of 8 percent.

Relation There is an inverse relation between the present value of a cash flow and the time to maturity: the present value of a cash flow to be received in t years is greater than that for the same cash flow to be received in $t + i$ years. There is an inverse relation between the present value of a cash flow and the discount rate.

Present Value of a Stream of Payments

So far we have considered the present value of a single payment. We now extend present value analysis to consider the value of a stream of payments in the future. Suppose your trustworthy friend promises to pay you $100 in one year and $100 in two years. Using 6 percent as the risk-free discount rate for the first year, the present value of the first payment would be

$$PV = \frac{\$100}{(1.06)} = \$94.34$$

Now suppose the opportunity cost in the second year is expected to be 7 percent because you believe interest rates will rise. At the 7 percent discount rate, the present value of the second payment would be

$$PV = \frac{\$100}{(1.07)^2} = \$87.34$$

Thus, the present value of the two-period stream of cash flows is

$$PV = \frac{\$100}{(1.06)} + \frac{\$100}{(1.07)^2} = \$181.68$$

From the preceding, you should be able to see that the present value of a stream of net cash flows is equal to the sum of the present values of the net cash flows. We can state this more precisely in the following:

Relation The present value of a stream of cash flows, where $\$NCF_t$ is the cash flow received or paid in period t, is given by

$$PV = \frac{\$NCF_1}{(1 + r_1)} + \frac{\$NCF_2}{(1 + r_2)^2} + \frac{\$NCF_3}{(1 + r_3)^3} + \cdots + \frac{\$NCF_T}{(1 + r_T)^T} = \sum_{t=1}^{T} \frac{\$NCF_t}{(1 + r_t)^t}$$

where r_t is the discount rate for period t, and T is the life span of the stream of cash flows.

To calculate the value of a firm, which is the present value of the firm's future stream of expected profits, treat the firm's expected profits as net cash flows and use the above relation. As you will see in Chapter 19, the present value of a future stream of payments provides important information for making investment decisions in such things as new plant, equipment, advertising campaigns, and even research and development projects.

MATHEMATICAL EXERCISES

In problems 1 and 2, use the following interest rates for U.S. Treasury securities for the risk-free discount rate:

Time to maturity (years)	Interest rate (percent)
1	5.75
2	6.00
3	6.25
4	6.50
5	6.75

1. Calculate the present value of a $1,000 payment to be received at the end of:
   a. One year
   b. Two years
   c. Three years
   d. Four years
   e. Five years
2. What is the present value of a firm with a five-year life span that earns the following stream of expected profit? (Treat all profits as being received at year-end.)

Year	Expected profit
1	$10,000
2	$20,000
3	$50,000
4	$75,000
5	$50,000

3. The *National Enquirer* reported that, in their divorce settlement, Burt Reynolds offered Loni Anderson $10 million spread evenly over 10 years but she demanded $5 million now. If the appropriate discount rate is 8 percent, which alternative is best for Burt and which for Loni? What if the discount rate is 20 percent?

Part I
Price Determination in Competitive Markets

CHAPTER 2

Demand, Supply, and Market Equilibrium

As we emphasized in Chapter 1, successful managers understand how market forces create both opportunities and constraints for profitable decision making. Such managers understand the way markets work, and they are able to predict the prices and production levels of the goods, resources, and services that are relevant to their businesses. The production manager of a soft-drink bottler could use new information about sugar production, such as government approval of a potent new fertilizer for growing sugar cane, to predict the future price of sugar and then make changes in syrup inventories. The owner-manager of a home-appliance manufacturing firm would want to use information about new home construction to make future production plans. This chapter presents one of the most powerful tools of economics for analyzing the way market forces determine prices and production in competitive markets—supply and demand analysis.

Even though supply and demand analysis is deceptively simple to learn and apply, it is widely used by highly experienced—and well-paid—market analysts and forecasters. You will see that such analysis provides a useful framework for processing market and other economic information to make decisions that affect the profitability of the business. And you will come across the concepts set forth in this chapter again and again throughout the rest of the text.

This chapter focuses primarily on the way markets for consumer goods and services function, although the basic concepts apply also to markets for resources, such as labor, land, raw materials, and capital equipment. Supply and demand analysis applies principally to markets characterized by many buyers and sellers and markets in which a homogeneous or relatively nondifferentiated good or service is sold. As we stated in the previous chapter, such markets are called competitive markets. However, as you will see later in the text, many of the principles of competitive markets apply to markets that do not meet all the exacting specifications of a competitive market.

We begin the analysis of competitive markets by describing the buyer side of the market—called the *demand side* of the market. Next we describe the seller side—called the *supply side.* We then combine the demand side with the supply side to show how prices and quantities sold are determined in a market. Finally, we show how forces on the demand side or the supply side of the market can change and thereby affect the price and quantity sold in a market.

2.1 DEMAND

quantity demanded The amount of a good or service consumers are willing and able to purchase during a given period of time (week, month, etc.).

The amount of a good or service that consumers in a market are willing and able to purchase during a given period of time (e.g., a week, a month) is called **quantity demanded.** Although economists emphasize the importance of price in purchasing decisions, as we will do, they also recognize that a multitude of factors other than price affect the amount of a good or service people will purchase. However, in order to simplify market analysis and make it manageable, economists ignore the many factors that have an insignificant effect on purchases and concentrate only on the most important factors. Indeed, only six factors are considered sufficiently important to be included in most studies of market demand.

This section develops two types of demand relations: (1) *generalized demand functions,* which show how quantity demanded is related to product price and five other factors that affect demand, and (2) *ordinary demand functions,* which show the relation between quantity demanded and the price of the product when all other variables affecting demand are held constant at specific values. As you will see in this chapter, ordinary demand functions are derived from generalized demand functions. Traditionally, economists have referred to ordinary demand functions simply as *demand functions* or *demand.* We shall follow this tradition.

The Generalized Demand Function

The six principal variables that influence the quantity demanded of a good or service are (1) the price of the good or service, (2) the incomes of consumers, (3) the prices of related goods and services, (4) the tastes or preference patterns of consumers, (5) the expected price of the product in future periods, and (6) the number of consumers in the market. The relation between quantity demanded and these six factors is referred to as the **generalized demand function** and is expressed as follows:

generalized demand function The relation between quantity demanded and the six factors that affect quantity demanded: $Q_d = f(P, M\ P_R, \mathcal{T}, P_e, N)$.

$$Q_d = f(P, M, P_R, \mathcal{T}, P_e, N)$$

where f means "is a function of" or "depends on," and

Q_d = quantity demanded of the good or service
P = price of the good or service
M = consumers' income (generally per capita)
P_R = price of related goods or services
$\mathcal{T}$ = taste patterns of consumers
P_e = expected price of the good in some future period
N = number of consumers in the market

The generalized demand function shows how all six variables *jointly* determine the quantity demanded. In order to discuss the *individual* effect that any one of these six variables has on Q_d, we must explain how changing just that one variable *by itself* influences Q_d. Isolating the individual effect of a single variable requires that all other variables that affect Q_d be held constant. Thus, whenever we speak of the effect that a particular variable has on quantity demanded, we mean the individual effect *holding all other variables constant.*

We now discuss each of the six variables to show how they are related to the amount of a good or service consumers buy. We begin by discussing the effect of changing the *price* of a good while holding the other five variables constant. As you would expect, consumers are willing and able to buy more of a good the lower the price of the good and will buy less of a good the higher the price of the good. Price and quantity demanded are negatively (inversely) related because when the price of a good rises, consumers tend to shift from that good to other goods that are now relatively cheaper. Conversely, when the price of a good falls, consumers tend to purchase more of that good and less of other goods that are now relatively more expensive. Price and quantity demanded are inversely related when all other factors are held constant. This relation between price and quantity demanded is so important that we will discuss it in more detail later in this chapter and again in Chapter 6.

Next, we consider changes in *income,* again holding constant the rest of the variables that influence consumers. An increase in income can cause the amount of a commodity consumers purchase either to increase or to decrease. If an increase in income causes consumers to demand more of a good, when all other variables in the generalized demand function are held constant, we refer to such a commodity as a **normal good.** A good is also a normal good if a decrease in income causes consumers to demand less of the good, all other things held constant. There are some goods and services for which an increase in income would reduce consumer demand, other variables held constant. This type of commodity is referred to as an **inferior good.** In the case of inferior goods, rising income causes consumers to demand *less* of the good, and falling income causes consumers to demand *more* of the good. Some examples of goods and services that might be inferior include mobile homes, shoe repair services, generic food products, and used cars.

normal good
A good or service for which an increase (decrease) in income causes consumers to demand more (less) of the good, holding all other variables in the generalized demand function constant.

inferior good
A good or service for which an increase (decrease) in income causes consumers to demand less (more) of the good, all other factors held constant.

Commodities may be *related in consumption* in either of two ways—as substitutes or as complements. In general, goods are *substitutes* if one good can be used in the place of the other; an example might be Toyotas and Chryslers. If two goods are substitutes, an increase in the price of one good will increase the demand for the other good. If the price of Toyotas rises while the price of Chryslers

substitutes
Two goods are substitutes if an increase (decrease) in the price of one of the goods causes consumers to demand more (less) of the other good, holding all other factors constant.

complements
Two goods are complements if an increase (decrease) in the price of one of the goods causes consumers to demand less (more) of the other good, all other things held constant

remains constant, we would expect consumers to purchase more Chryslers—holding all other factors constant. If an increase in the price of a related good causes consumers to demand more of a good, then the two goods are **substitutes.** Similarly, two goods are substitutes if a decrease in the price of one of the goods causes consumers to demand less of the other good, all other things constant.

Goods are said to be *complements* if they are used in conjunction with each other. Examples might be cameras and film, lettuce and salad dressing, or baseball games and hot dogs. A decrease in the price of tickets to the baseball game will increase demand for hot dogs at the game, all else constant. If the demand for one good decreases when the price of a related good increases, the two goods are **complements.** Similarly, two goods are complements if a decrease in the price of one of the goods causes consumers to demand more of the other good, all other things constant.[1]

Expectations of consumers also influence consumers' decisions to purchase goods and services. More specifically, consumers' expectations about the future price of a commodity can change their current purchasing decisions. If consumers expect the price to be higher in a future period, demand will probably rise in the current period. On the other hand, expectations of a price decline in the future will cause some purchases to be postponed—thus, demand in the current period will fall. An example of this can be seen in the automobile industry. Automakers often announce price increases for the next year's models several months before the cars are available in showrooms in order to stimulate demand for the current year's cars.

A change in consumer tastes can change demand for a good or service. Obviously, taste changes could either increase or decrease consumer demand. While consumer tastes are not directly measurable (as are the other variables in the generalized demand function), you may wish to view the variable $\mathcal{T}$ as an index of consumer tastes; $\mathcal{T}$ takes on larger values as consumers perceive a good becoming higher in quality, more fashionable, more healthful, or more desirable in any way. A decrease in $\mathcal{T}$ corresponds to a change in consumer tastes away from a good or service as consumers perceive falling quality, or displeasing appearance, or diminished healthfulness. Consequently, when all other variables in the generalized demand function are held constant, a movement in consumer tastes toward a good or service will increase demand and a movement in consumer tastes away from a good will decrease demand for the good. A change in consumer tastes or preferences occurs when, for example, the *New England Journal of Medicine* publishes research findings that show a higher incidence of cancer among people who regularly eat bacon. This causes the demand for bacon to decrease (the taste index $\mathcal{T}$ declines), all other factors remaining constant.

Finally, an increase in the number of consumers in the market will increase the demand for a good, and a decrease in the number of consumers will de-

[1]Not all commodities are either substitutes or complements in consumption. Many commodities are essentially independent. For example, we would not expect the price of lettuce to significantly influence the demand for automobiles. Thus, we can treat these commodities as independent and ignore the price of lettuce when evaluating the demand for automobiles.

crease the demand for a good, all other factors held constant. In markets that experience a growth in the number of buyers—such as the health care industry as the population matures or Florida during the tourist season—we would expect demand to increase.

The generalized demand function set forth above is expressed in the most general mathematical form. Economists and market researchers often express the generalized demand function in a more specific mathematical form in order to show more precisely the relation between quantity demanded and some of the more important variables that affect demand. They frequently express the generalized demand function in a linear functional form. The following equation is an example of a linear form of the generalized demand function:

$$Q_d = a + bP + cM + dP_R + e\mathcal{T} + fP_e + gN$$

where Q_d, P, M, P_R, $\mathcal{T}$, P_e, and N are as defined above, and a, b, c, d, e, f, and g are parameters.

slope parameters Parameters in a linear function that measure the effect on the dependent variable (Q_d) of changing one of the independent variables (P, M, P_R, $\mathcal{T}$, P_e, and N) while holding the rest of these variables constant.

The intercept parameter a shows the value of Q_d when the variables P, M, P_R, $\mathcal{T}$, P_e, and N are all simultaneously equal to zero. The other parameters, b, c, d, e, f, and g, are called **slope parameters:** they measure the effect on quantity demanded of changing one of the variables P, M, P_R, $\mathcal{T}$, P_e, or N while holding the rest of these variables constant. The slope parameter b, for example, measures the change in quantity demanded per unit change in price; that is, $b = \Delta Q_d/\Delta P$.[2] As stressed above, Q_d and P are inversely related, and b is negative because ΔQ_d and ΔP have opposite algebraic signs.

The slope parameter c measures the effect on the amount purchased of a one-unit change in income ($c = \Delta Q_d/\Delta M$). For normal goods, sales increase when income rises, so c is positive. If the good is inferior, sales decrease when income rises, so c is negative. The parameter d measures the change in the amount consumers want to buy per unit change in P_R ($d = \Delta Q_d/\Delta P_R$). If an increase in P_R causes sales to rise, the goods are substitutes and d is positive. If an increase in P_R causes sales to fall, the two goods are complements and d is negative. Since $\mathcal{T}$, P_e, and N are each directly related to the amount purchased, the parameters e, f, and g are all positive.[3]

Relation When the generalized demand function is expressed in linear form:

$$Q_d = a + bP + cM + dP_R + e\mathcal{T} + fP_e + gN$$

the slope parameters (b, c, d, e, f, and g) measure the effect on the amount of the good purchased of changing one of the variables (P, M, P_R, $\mathcal{T}$, P_e, and N) while holding the rest of the variables constant. For example, b ($= \Delta Q_d/\Delta P$) measures the change in quantity demanded per unit

[2]The symbol "Δ" means "change in." Thus if quantity demanded rises (falls), then ΔQ_d is positive (negative). Similarly, if price rises (falls), ΔP is positive (negative). In general, the ratio of the change in Y divided by the change in X ($\Delta Y/\Delta X$) measures the change in Y per unit change in X.

[3]Since consumer tastes are not directly measurable as are the other variables, you may wish to view $\mathcal{T}$ as an index of consumer tastes that ranges in value from 0, if consumers think a product is worthless, to 10 if they think the product is extremely desirable. In this case, the parameter e shows the effect on quantity of a one-unit change in the taste index ($\mathcal{T}$), and e is positive.

TABLE 2.1
Summary of the Generalized (linear) Demand Function
$Q_d = a + bP + cM + dP_R + e\mathcal{T} + fP_e + gN$

Variable	Relation to quantity demanded	Sign of slope parameter
P	Inverse	$b = \Delta Q_d/\Delta P$ is negative
M	Direct for normal goods	$c = \Delta Q_d/\Delta M$ is positive
	Inverse for inferior goods	$c = \Delta Q_d/\Delta M$ is negative
P_R	Direct for substitute goods	$d = \Delta Q_d/\Delta P_R$ is positive
	Inverse for complement goods	$d = \Delta Q_d/\Delta P_R$ is negative
$\mathcal{T}$	Direct	$e = \Delta Q_d/\Delta \mathcal{T}$ is positive
P_e	Direct	$f = \Delta Q_d/\Delta P_e$ is positive
N	Direct	$g = \Delta Q_d/\Delta N$ is positive

change in price holding M, P_R, $\mathcal{T}$, P_e, and N constant. When the slope parameter of a specific variable is positive (negative) in sign, quantity demanded is directly (inversely) related to that variable.

Table 2.1 summarizes this discussion of the generalized demand function. Each of the six factors that affect quantity demanded is listed, and the table shows whether the quantity demanded varies directly or inversely with each variable and gives the sign of the slope parameters. Again let us stress that these relations are in the context of all other things being equal. An increase in the price of the commodity will lead to a decrease in quantity demanded as long as the other variables—income, the price of related commodities, consumer tastes, price expectations, and the number of customers—remain constant.

A generalized demand function always includes price as a variable but may not always include every one of the other five variables shown in Table 2.1. Market analysts sometimes omit consumer tastes and price expectations, since these variables may not be important in every situation. The number of customers may also be disregarded in formulating a generalized demand equation when the number of consumers in a particular market does not change. For example, the demand for local telephone service is not likely to be sensitive to the expected price of telephone service. Households will not choose to disconnect their telephones this month on the basis of a belief that local telephone rates are going to fall next month. Consumer tastes may also have little impact on demand for local telephone service, since fashion generally plays little or no role in determining telephone demand. In a small town that experiences only an inconsequential change in the number of telephone customers, N does not play an important role in determining the variation in Q_d and need not be included in the generalized demand function. For these reasons, the generalized linear demand function can sometimes be simplified to include just three variables from Table 2.1:

$$Q_d = a + bP + cM + dP_R$$

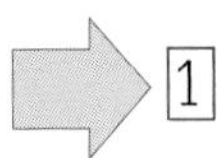

Although it is not always appropriate to use this simplified version of the generalized demand function, the three-variable demand function expressed above does provide a reasonable model of consumer demand in many applications.

Demand Functions

demand function (demand)
A table, graph, or an equation that shows how quantity demanded is related to product price, holding constant the five other variables that influence demand.

The relation between price and quantity demanded per period of time, when all other factors that affect consumer demand are held constant, is called a **demand function** or simply **demand.** Demand gives, for various prices of a good, the corresponding quantities that consumers are willing and able to purchase at each of those prices, all other things held constant. The "other things" that are held constant for a specific demand function are the five variables other than price that can affect demand. A demand function can be expressed as an equation, a schedule or table, or a graph. We begin with a demand equation.

A demand function can be expressed in the most general form as the equation

$$Q_d = f(P)$$

which means that the quantity demanded is a function of (depends on) the price of the good, holding all other variables constant. A demand function is obtained by holding all the variables in the generalized demand function constant except price. For example, using a three-variable demand function:

$$Q_d = f(P, M', P'_R) = f(P)$$

where the prime on the variables M and P_R means that those variables are held constant at some specified amount no matter what value the product price takes.

Relation A demand function expresses quantity demanded as a function of product price only: $Q_d = f(P)$. Demand functions—whether expressed as equations, tables, or graphs—give the quantity demanded at various prices, holding constant the effects of income, price of related goods, consumer tastes, expected price, and the number of consumers. Demand functions are derived from generalized demand functions by holding all the variables in the generalized demand function constant except price.

To illustrate the derivation of a demand function from the generalized demand function, suppose the generalized demand function is

$$Q_d = 1{,}800 - 20P + 0.6M - 50P_R$$

To derive a demand function, $Q_d = f(P)$, the variables M and P_R must be assigned fixed values. Suppose consumer income is \$20,000 and the price of a related good is \$250. To find the demand function, the fixed values of M and P_R are substituted into the generalized demand function:

$$\begin{aligned} Q_d &= 1{,}800 - 20P + 0.6(20{,}000) - 50(250) \\ &= 1{,}800 - 20P + 12{,}000 - 12{,}500 \\ &= 1{,}300 - 20P \end{aligned}$$

TABLE 2.2
The Demand Schedule for the Demand Function D_0: $Q_d = 1{,}300 - 20P$

Price	Quantity demanded
$65	0
60	100
50	300
40	500
30	700
20	900
10	1,100

Thus the demand function is expressed in the form of a linear demand equation, $Q_d = 1{,}300 - 20P$. The intercept parameter, 1,300, is the amount of the good consumers would demand if price is zero. The slope of this demand function ($= \Delta Q_d/\Delta P$) is -20 and indicates that a $1 increase in price causes quantity demanded to decrease by 20 units. Although not all demand functions are linear, you will see later in the text that the linear form is a frequently used specification for estimating and forecasting demand functions.

The above linear demand equation satisfies all the conditions set forth in the definition of demand. All variables other than product price are held constant—income at $20,000 and the price of a related good at $250. At each price, the equation gives the amount that consumers would purchase at that price. For example, if price is $50,

$$Q_d = 1{,}300 - (20 \times 50) = 300$$

or if price is $40,

$$Q_d = 1{,}300 - (20 \times 40) = 500$$

demand schedule
A table showing a list of possible product prices and the corresponding quantities demanded.

A **demand schedule** (or table) shows a list of several prices and the quantity demanded per period of time at each of the prices, again holding all variables other than price constant. Seven prices and their corresponding quantities demanded are shown in Table 2.2. Each of the seven combinations of price and quantity demanded is derived from the demand function exactly as shown above. (You may check this for yourself.)

demand curve
A graph showing the relation between quantity demanded and price when all other variables influencing quantity demanded are held constant.

As noted above, the final method of showing a demand function is a graph. A graphical demand function is called a **demand curve.** The seven price–quantity-demanded combinations in Table 2.2 are plotted in Figure 2.1, and these points are connected with the straight line D_0, which is the demand curve associated with the demand equation $Q_d = 1{,}300 - 20P$. This demand curve meets the specifications of the definition of demand. All variables other than price are held constant. The demand curve D_0 gives the value of quantity demanded (on the horizontal axis) for every value of price (on the vertical axis).

Note that in the graph of the demand equation, $Q_d = 1{,}300 - 20P$, the independent variable P is plotted along the vertical axis, and the dependent variable

FIGURE 2.1

A Demand Curve (Q_d = 1,300 − 20P)

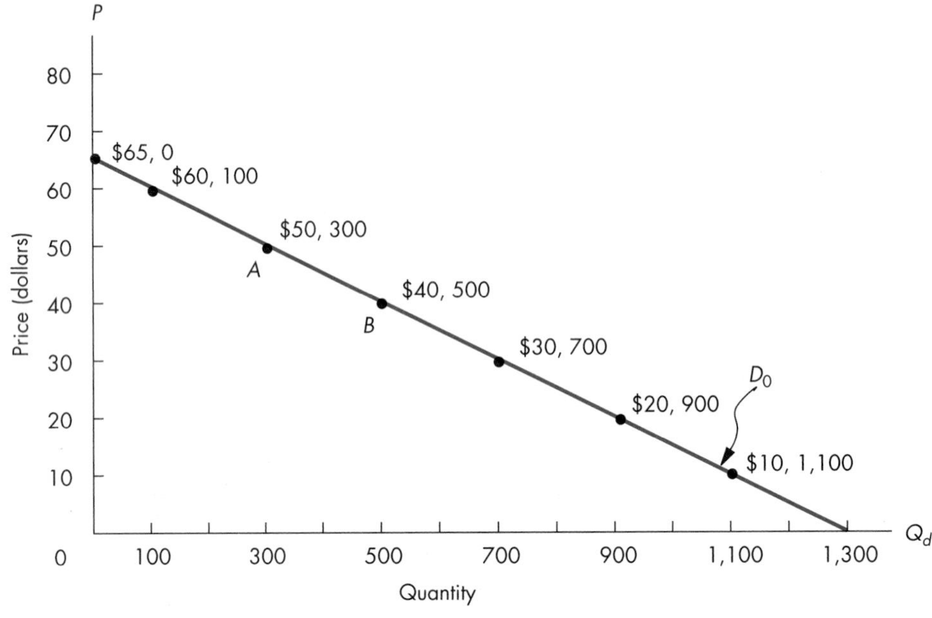

Q_d is plotted along the horizontal axis. This switch is traditional among economists. Thus the equation plotted in the figure is the inverse of the above demand equation: $P = 65 - 1/20Q_d$.[4] The vertical intercept is 65, indicating that at a price of $65, consumers will demand zero units of the good. The horizontal intercept is 1,300, which is the maximum amount of the good buyers will take when the good is given away ($P = 0$). The slope of the graphed inverse demand is $-1/20$, indicating that if quantity demanded rises by one unit, price must fall 1/20 of a dollar (or 5 cents). This inverse, as you can see, yields price-quantity combinations identical to those given by the above demand equation.

Although demand is generally interpreted as indicating the amount that consumers will buy at each price, sometimes managers and market researchers wish to know the highest price that can be charged for any given amount of the product. As it turns out, a point on a demand curve can be interpreted in either of two ways: (1) the maximum amount of a good that will be purchased if a given price is charged, or (2) the maximum price that consumers will pay for a specific amount of a good. Consider, for example, point *A* ($50, 300) on the demand curve in Figure 2.1. If the price of the good is $50, the maximum amount consumers will purchase is 300 units. Equivalently, $50 is the highest price that consumers

[4]Recall from high school algebra that the "inverse" of a function $Y = f(X)$ is the function $X = g(Y)$, which gives X as a function of Y, and the same pairs of Y and X values that satisfy $Y = f(X)$ also satisfy the inverse function $X = g(Y)$. In other words, both equations express the same relation between Y and X. For example, for the equation $Y = 10 + 2X$, the inverse function, $X = 1/2Y - 5$, is found by solving algebraically for X in terms of Y.

demand price
The maximum price consumers will pay for a specific amount of a good.

can be charged in order to sell 300 units. Sometimes $50 is called the **demand price** for 300 units, and each price on demand can be called the demand price for the corresponding quantity on the horizontal axis.

The Law of Demand

Before moving on to an analysis of changes in the variables that are held constant when deriving a demand function, we want to reemphasize the relation between price and quantity demanded, which was discussed earlier in this chapter. In the demand equation, the parameter on price is negative; in the demand schedule, price and quantity demanded are inversely related; and in the graph, the demand curve is negatively sloped. This inverse relation between price and quantity demanded is not simply a characteristic of the specific demand function discussed here. This inverse relation is so pervasive that economists refer to it as the **law of demand.** The law of demand states that quantity demanded increases when price falls and quantity demanded decreases when price rises, other things held constant.

law of demand
Quantity demanded increases when price falls, and quantity demanded decreases when price rises, other things held constant.

Economists refer to the inverse relation between price and quantity demanded as a law, not because this relation has been proved mathematically but because examples to the contrary have never been observed. If you have doubts about the validity of the law of demand, try to think of any goods or services that you would buy more of if the price were higher, other things being equal. Or can you imagine someone going to the grocery store expecting to buy one six-pack of Pepsi for $2.50, then noticing that the price is $5, and deciding to buy two or three six-packs? You don't see stores advertising higher prices when they want to increase sales or get rid of unwanted inventory.

The principal reason for the inverse relation between price and quantity demanded is that all goods have substitutes. When the price of one good rises, consumers can shift some of their purchases to other goods that serve a similar function. The only electric company in a city faces competition from the gas company in many uses. Even when AT&T was the only long-distance telephone company, people could substitute mail for telephone calls, and now AT&T faces intense competition from other long-distance phone companies. We believe it will be difficult for you to think of a product that you are now consuming for which there is absolutely no available substitute. We explore in much greater depth the concept of substitution and its relation to the law of demand in Chapter 6.

Once a demand function, $Q_d = f(P)$, is derived from a generalized demand function, a **change in quantity demanded** can be caused only by a change in price. The other five variables that influence demand in the generalized demand function (M, P_R, $\mathcal{T}$, P_e, and N) are fixed in value for any particular demand equation. A change in price is represented on a graph by a movement along a fixed demand curve. In Figure 2.1, if price falls from $50 to $40 (and the other variables remain constant), a change in quantity demanded from 300 to 500 units occurs and is illustrated by a movement along D_0 from point A to point B.

change in quantity demanded
A movement along a given demand curve that occurs when the price of the good changes, all else constant.

TABLE 2.3
Three Demand Schedules

(1) Price	(2) D_0 Quantity demanded (M = $20,000)	(3) D_1 Quantity demanded (M = $20,500)	(4) D_2 Quantity demanded (M = $19,500)
$65	0	300	0
60	100	400	0
50	300	600	0
40	500	800	200
30	700	1,000	400
20	900	1,200	600
10	1,100	1,400	800

Relation For a demand function $Q_d = f(P)$, a change in price causes a change in quantity demanded. The other five variables that influence demand in the generalized demand function (M, P_R, $\mathcal{T}$, P_e, and N) are fixed in value for any particular demand equation. On a graph, a change in price causes a movement along a demand curve from one price to another price.

Shifts in Demand

When any one of the five variables held constant when deriving a demand function from the generalized demand relation changes value, a new demand function results, causing the entire demand curve to *shift* to a new location. To illustrate this extremely important concept, we will show how a change in one of these five variables, such as income, affects a demand schedule.

We begin with the demand schedule from Table 2.2, which is reproduced in columns 1 and 2 of Table 2.3. Recall that the quantities demanded for various product prices were obtained by holding all variables except price constant in the generalized demand function. If income increases from $20,000 to $20,500, quantity demanded increases *at each and every price,* as shown in column 3. When the price is $30, for example, consumers will buy 700 units if their income is $20,000 but will buy 1,000 units if their income is $20,500. In Figure 2.2, D_0 is the demand curve associated with an income level of $20,000, and D_1 is the demand curve after income rises to $20,500. Since the increase in income caused quantity demanded to increase *at every price,* the demand curve shifts to the right from D_0 to D_1 in Figure 2.2. Everywhere along D_1 quantity demanded is greater than along D_0 for equal prices. This change in the demand function is called an **increase in demand.**

increase in demand
A change in the demand function that causes an increase in quantity demanded at every price and is reflected by a rightward shift in the demand curve.

decrease in demand
A change in the demand function that causes a decrease in quantity demanded at every price and is reflected by a leftward shift in the demand curve.

A **decrease in demand** occurs when a change in one or more of the variables M, P_R, $\mathcal{T}$, P_e, or N causes the quantity demanded to decrease at every price and the demand curve shifts to the left. Column 4 in Table 2.3 illustrates a decrease in demand caused by income falling to $19,500. At every price, quantity demanded in column 4 is less than quantity demanded when income is either $20,000 or $20,500 (columns 2 and 3, respectively, in Table 2.3). The demand curve in Figure 2.2 when income is $19,500 is D_2, which lies to the left of D_0 and D_1.

FIGURE 2.2
Shifts in Demand

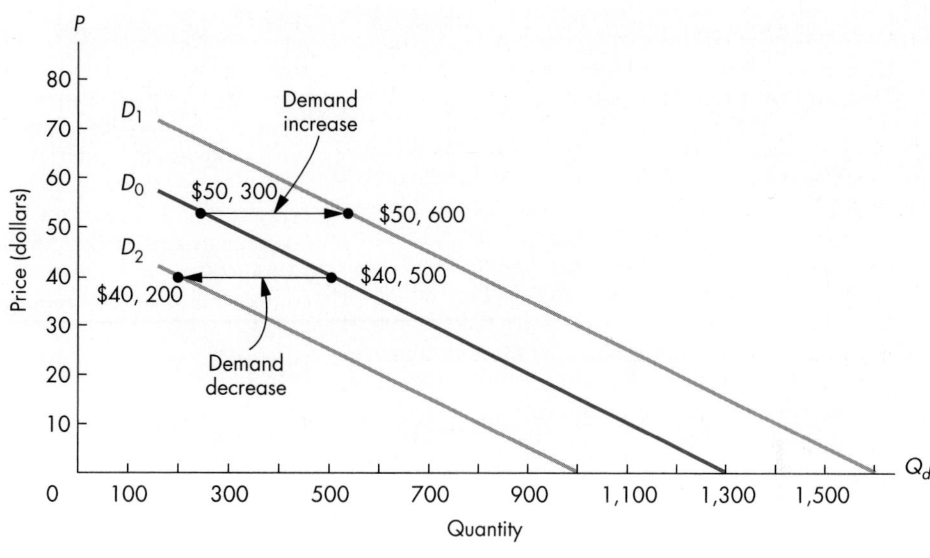

While we have illustrated shifts in demand caused by changes in income, a change in any one of the five variables that are held constant when deriving a demand function will cause a shift in demand. These five variables—M, P_R, $\mathcal{T}$, P_e, and N—are called the **determinants of demand** because they determine where the demand curve is located. A **change in demand** occurs when one or more of the determinants of demand change. Think of M, P_R, $\mathcal{T}$, P_e, and N as the five "demand-shifting" variables. The demand curve shifts to a new location only when one or more of these demand-shifting variables changes.

determinants of demand
Variables that change the quantity demanded at each price and that determine where the demand curve is located: M, P_R, $\mathcal{T}$, P_e, and N.

change in demand
A shift in demand, either leftward or rightward, that occurs only when one of the five determinants of demand changes.

Relation An increase in demand means that, at each price, more is demanded; a decrease in demand means that, at each price, less is demanded. Demand changes, or shifts, when one of the determinants of demand changes. These determinants of demand are income, prices of related goods, consumer tastes, expected future price, and the number of consumers.

The shifts in demand illustrated in Figure 2.2 were derived mathematically from the generalized demand function. Recall that the demand function D_0 ($Q_d = 1{,}300 - 20P$) was derived from the generalized demand function

$$Q_d = 1{,}800 - 20P + 0.6M - 50P_R$$

where income and the price of a related good were held constant at values of M = \$20,000 and P_R = \$250. When income increases from \$20,000 to \$20,500, the new demand equation at this higher income is found by substituting M = \$20,500 into the generalized demand function and solving for the new demand function:

ILLUSTRATION 2.1

Effects of Changes in Determinants of Demand on Price and Sales

Much of the discussion of demand in this chapter concerns the effects of changes in the determinants of demand, or demand-shifting variables, on demand functions, and the consequent effects of these shifts on prices and sales. Some actual examples of these effects, all of which were reported in *The Wall Street Journal*, should illustrate and reinforce this theoretical analysis. These examples illustrate the consequences of changes in income for normal goods, changes in the price of a related good (both substitutes and complements), changes in taste, and changes in price expectations. The examples also provide some insight into how managers can adjust to such changes in a way that benefits the firm.

Changes in Income

Ross Perot warned that free trade with Mexico would create a "giant sucking sound" as jobs moved from the United States to Mexico. Perot's prediction about job loss to Mexico proved to be incorrect, but in 1996 the *WSJ* reported that Perot may still be hearing a "giant sucking sound" but it may be the sound of goods, not jobs, being sucked from the United States into Mexico. Mexico, along with the rest of the so-called emerging markets worldwide, is booming. Rapidly increasing real income in Latin America is creating a boom in the demand for normal goods produced in the United States.

Managers of U.S. corporations selling normal goods (e.g., earthmovers, cellular phones, soft drinks, and cognac) are taking advantage of increased demand by foreign consumers. The *WSJ* quoted Joseph Quinlan, senior international economist at Dean Witter Reynolds, who observed that there is "a greater urgency in corporate America to sell more cigarettes and soft drinks to the emerging markets." For many firms, rising per capita incomes in foreign nations offer an opportunity to add a profitable new source of demand to keep sales rising.

Changes in Price of Related Goods

In June 1996, auto industry analyst Thomas M. Galvin, with Deutsche Morgan Grenfell/C. J. Lawrence in New York, downgraded his "buy" recommendation for auto stocks on the basis of what he and many other analysts believed to be the most reliable "warning signal" for predicting when the new-car market is likely to "go south." What cooled Galvin's interest in stocks of auto manufacturers was the downward spiral of retail prices for used cars. As we showed in this chapter, a decrease in the price of a substitute good, all other things constant, causes a decrease in the demand for a good. The *WSJ* reported that expiring leases in 1996 returned 4.6 million two- and three-year-old vehicles to dealerships as used vehicles—up from 3.9 million in 1995. The increase in the supply of used cars caused used-car prices to fall sharply in 1996. Facing lower prices for used cars, "the consumer starts to think more seriously about buying a used car in the future than a new car." Many consumers did buy used cars instead of new cars, and the demand for new cars decreased in 1996.

$$Q_d = 1{,}800 - 20P + (0.60 \times 20{,}500) - 12{,}500$$
$$= 1{,}600 - 20P$$

In Figure 2.2, this demand function is shown by the demand curve D_1. At every price, quantity demanded increases by 300 units (1,600 = 1,300 + 300). Each of the quantities in column 3 of Table 2.2 was calculated from the new demand equation $Q_d = 1{,}600 - 20P$. As you can see, every quantity in column 3 is 300 units larger than the corresponding quantity in column 2. Thus, the increase in income has caused an increase in demand.

When two goods are complements, an increase in the price of one causes a decrease in demand for the other good. In spring 1996, rising gasoline prices proved to be a mixed blessing for the many retail gasoline stations that are now also convenience stores. The *WSJ* reported that nearly 70 percent of the profit of gasoline station–convenience store combinations is generated by merchandise sales inside the stores. While rising gasoline prices may increase revenue from the gas pump, fewer gasoline buyers go into the stores for the convenience items, which carry relatively high profit margins.

Changes in Taste

As we stressed, consumer taste is an important determinant of demand. In 1996, the *WSJ* reported that, in a throwback to the 1950s, shiny chrome and aluminum products were fashionable again. Chrome blenders, toasters, and mixers became top-10 sellers at Williams-Sonoma in San Francisco. Demand for similar items with a white finish practically vanished.

Changes in Price Expectations

One would expect that expectations about the future price of a good would have an insignificant effect on the price of some goods, such as bread, movies, pizza, and other goods that are not durable or expensive. Price expectations would have a stronger effect on the demand for more durable, higher-priced goods, such as automobiles, jewelry, and major appliances. In a 1992 article about the bankruptcy of a huge Canadian real estate company, the *WSJ* stated, "More than any other business, real estate is dependent upon people's expectations about the future. When those expectations are hopeful, . . . the value of real estate soars. When those expectations turn gloomy, . . . real estate values crash."

Later in the article, the *WSJ* asked, "But where do these expectations come from? There is a tendency to dismiss them as irrational, mere 'animal spirits.' " The answer, "Most of the time, though, expectations come from the market's sifting of the best judgments of tens of thousands of highly intelligent people. And the best judgments are drab and dismal compared to those of the middle 1980s."

These illustrations should give you some idea of the way that changes in the determinants of demand actually shift the demand for goods and services and how such shifts affect the price and sales of the products. They should also give an insight into how managers can forecast and react to such changes in a manner that furthers the goals of the organization.

Sources: Bernard Wysocki, Jr., "Imports Are Surging in Developing Nations," *The Wall Street Journal,* July 8, 1996; Oscar Suris, "Used-Car Prices Cool, Chilling Detroit: Drop since Spring Is Bad Omen for New-Vehicle Sales," *The Wall Street Journal,* Oct. 1, 1996; Business Bulletin: "Convenience Stores That Sell Gas Find Higher Prices a Mixed Blessing," *The Wall Street Journal,* May 16, 1996; Louise Lee, "Consumers Are Taking a Shine to Products That Gleam," *The Wall Street Journal,* Aug. 8, 1996; David Frum, "Real Estate Victim of the '90s," *The Wall Street Journal,* Apr. 3, 1992.

When income falls from \$20,000 to \$19,500, demand shifts from D_0 to D_2. We leave the derivation of the demand function for D_2 as an exercise. The procedure, however, is identical to the process set forth above.

From the preceding discussion, you may have noticed that the direction in which demand shifts when one of the five demand determinants changes depends upon the sign of the slope parameter on that variable in the generalized demand function. The increase in income caused quantity demanded to rise for all prices because $\Delta Q_d/\Delta M$ (= +0.6) is positive, which indicates that a \$1 increase in income causes a 0.6-unit increase in quantity demanded at every price level. Since income increased by $500 in this example, quantity demanded increases by 300 units (= 500 × 0.6). Thus, when the slope parameter on M is positive in the generalized demand function, an increase in income causes an increase in demand. As explained earlier, when income and quantity demanded are positively related *in the generalized demand function,* the good is a normal good. If the parameter on M is negative, an increase in income causes a decrease in demand, and the good is an inferior good.[5]

Consider now the slope parameter on the price of a related good. Returning once more to the previous numerical example, recall that the slope parameter for P_R in the generalized demand function is equal to −50, which means that a $1 increase in the price of the related good causes quantity demanded to decrease by 50 units at every product price. In other words, an increase in the price of the related good causes the demand curve to shift to the left. As explained earlier, when P_R and Q_d are inversely related in the generalized demand function, the two goods are complements. Had the parameter for P_R been positive, the price of the related good and quantity demanded would be directly related, an increase in the price of the related good would shift demand to the right, and the two goods would be substitutes.

For $\mathcal{T}$, P_e, and N, the slope parameters are all positive in the generalized demand function, and an increase in any one of these variables causes demand to increase. A decrease in either $\mathcal{T}$, P_e, or N causes a decrease in demand. Table 2.4 (on page 41) summarizes this discussion for all five of the determinants of demand.

4 5 6

2.2 SUPPLY

quantity supplied
The amount of a good or service offered for sale during a given period of time (week, month, etc.).

The amount of a good or service offered for sale in a market during a given period of time (e.g., a week, a month) is called **quantity supplied,** which we will denote as Q_s. The amount of a good or service offered for sale depends upon an extremely large number of variables. As in the case of demand, economists ignore all the relatively unimportant variables in order to concentrate on those variables that have the greatest effect on quantity supplied. In general, economists assume that the quantity of a good offered for sale depends upon six major variables:

1. The price of the good itself
2. The price of the inputs used to produce the good
3. The prices of goods related in production
4. The level of available technology
5. The expectations of the producers concerning the future price of the good
6. The number of firms producing the good

[5]It is only correct to speak of a change in income affecting *quantity demanded* when referring to the generalized demand function. Once income has been held constant to derive a demand function, a change in income causes a change in demand (a shift in the demand curve), not a change in quantity demanded. The same distinction holds for the other determinants of demand P_R, $\mathcal{T}$, P_e, and N.

TABLE 2.4
Summary of Demand Shifts

Determinants of demand	Demand increases*	Demand decreases†	Sign of slope parameter‡
1. Income (M)			
Normal good	M rises	M falls	$c > 0$
Inferior good	M falls	M rises	$c < 0$
2. Price of related good (P_R)			
Substitute good	P_R rises	P_R falls	$d > 0$
Complement good	P_R falls	P_R rises	$d < 0$
3. Consumer tastes ($\mathcal{T}$)	$\mathcal{T}$ rises	$\mathcal{T}$ falls	$e > 0$
4. Expected price (P_e)	P_e rises	P_e falls	$f > 0$
5. Number of consumers (N)	N rises	N falls	$g > 0$

*Demand increases when the demand curve shifts rightward.
†Demand decreases when the demand curve shifts leftward.
‡This column gives the sign of the corresponding slope parameter in the generalized demand function.

The Generalized Supply Function

generalized supply function The relation between quantity supplied and the six factors that jointly affect quantity supplied: $Q_s = g(P, P_I, P_r, T, P_e, F)$.

The **generalized supply function** shows how all six of these variables *jointly* determine the quantity supplied. The generalized supply function is expressed mathematically as

$$Q_s = g(P, P_I, P_r, T, P_e, F).$$

The quantity of a good or service offered for sale (Q_s) is determined not only by the price of the good or service (P) but also by the prices of the inputs used in production (P_I), the prices of goods that are related in production (P_r), the level of available technology (T), the expectations of producers concerning the future price of the good (P_e), and the number of firms (F). The symbol g is used as "a function of" to distinguish the supply relation from the generalized demand function.

Now we consider how each of the six variables is related to the quantity of a good or service firms produce. We begin by discussing the effect of a change in the price of a good while holding the other five variables constant. Typically, the higher the price of the product, the greater the quantity firms wish to produce and sell, all other things being equal. Conversely, the lower the price, the smaller the quantity firms will wish to produce and sell. Producers are induced by higher prices to produce and sell more, while lower prices tend to discourage production. Thus, price and quantity supplied are, in general, directly related.

An increase in the price of one or more of the inputs used to produce the product will obviously increase the cost of production. If the cost rises, the good becomes less profitable and producers will want to supply a smaller quantity at each price. Conversely, a decrease in the price of one or more of the inputs used to produce the product will decrease the cost of production. When cost falls, the good becomes more profitable and producers will want to supply a larger amount at each price. Therefore, an increase in the price of an input causes a decrease in production, while a decrease in the price of an input causes an increase in production.

Changes in the prices of goods that are related in production may affect producers in either one of two ways, depending on whether the goods are substitutes or complements in production. Two goods, X and Y, are **substitutes in production** if an increase in the price of good X relative to good Y causes producers to increase production of good X and decrease production of good Y. For example, if the price of corn increases while the price of wheat remains the same, some farmers may change from growing wheat to growing corn, and less wheat will be supplied. In the case of manufactured goods, firms can switch resources from the production of one good to the production of a substitute (in production) commodity when the price of the substitute rises. Alternatively, two goods, X and Y, are **complements in production** if an increase in the price of good X causes producers to supply more of good Y. For example, crude oil and natural gas often occur in the same oil field, making natural gas a by-product of producing crude oil, or vice versa. If the price of crude oil rises, petroleum firms produce more oil, so the output of natural gas also increases. Other examples of complements in production include nickel and copper (which occur in the same deposit), beef and leather hides, and bacon and pork chops.

substitutes in production
Goods for which an increase in the price of one good relative to the price of another good causes producers to increase production of the now higher-priced good and decrease production of the other good.

complements in production
Goods for which an increase in the price of one good, relative to the price of another good, causes producers to increase production of both goods.

Next, we consider changes in the level of available technology. **Technology** is that state of knowledge concerning how to combine resources to produce goods and services. An improvement in the state of technology would lower the costs of production, which would increase the supply of the good to the market, all other things remaining the same. Even though measuring technology is rather complicated, you can view advances in technology as leading to lower costs and greater supply of the good.

technology
The state of knowledge concerning the combination of resources to produce goods and services.

A firm's decision about its level of production depends not only on the current price of the good but also upon the firm's *expectation* about the future price of the good. If firms expect the price of a good they produce to rise in the future, they may withhold some of the good, thereby reducing supply of the good in the current period. Finally, if the number of firms in the industry increases, more of the good or service will be supplied at each price. Conversely, a decrease in the number of firms in the industry decreases the supply of the good, all other things remaining constant.

As in the case of demand, economists often find it useful to express the generalized supply function in linear functional form:

$$Q_s = h + kP + lP_I + mP_r + nT + rP_e + sF$$

where Q_s, P, P_I, P_r, T, P_e, and F are defined as above, h is an intercept parameter, and k, l, m, n, r, and s are slope parameters. Table 2.5 summarizes this discussion of the generalized supply function. Each of the six factors that affect production is listed along with the relation to quantity supplied (direct or inverse). Let us again stress that, just as in the case of demand, these relations are in the context of all other things being equal.

TABLE 2.5
Summary of the Generalized (linear) Supply Function
$Q_s = h + kP + lP_I + mP_r + nT + rP_e + sF$

Variable	Relation to quantity supplied	Sign of slope parameter
P	Direct	$k = \Delta Q_s/\Delta P$ is positive
P_I	Inverse	$l = Q_s/\Delta P_I$ is negative
P_r	Inverse for substitutes in production (wheat and corn)	$m = \Delta Q_s/\Delta P_r$ is negative
	Direct for complements in production (oil and gas)	$m = \Delta Q_s/\Delta P_r$ is positive
T	Direct	$n = \Delta Q_s/\Delta T$ is positive
P_e	Inverse	$r = \Delta Q_s/\Delta P_e$ is negative
F	Direct	$s = \Delta Q_s/\Delta F$ is positive

Supply Functions

supply function
A table, a graph, or an equation that shows how quantity supplied is related to product price, holding constant the five other variables that influence supply.

determinants of supply
Variables that cause a change in supply (i.e., a shift in the supply curve).

change in quantity supplied
A movement along a given supply curve that occurs when the price of a good changes.

Just as demand functions are derived from the generalized demand function, supply functions are derived from the generalized supply function. A **supply function** shows the relation between Q_s and P holding the **determinants of supply** (P_I, P_r, T, P_e, and F) constant:

$$Q_s = g(P, P_I', P_r', T', P_e', \text{and } F') = g(P)$$

where the prime means the determinants of supply are held constant at some specified value. Once a supply function $Q_s = g(P)$ is derived from a generalized supply function, a **change in quantity supplied** can be caused only by a change in price.

Relation A supply function expresses quantity supplied as a function of product price only: $Q_s = g(P)$. Supply functions give the quantity supplied for various prices, holding constant the effects of input prices, prices of goods related in production, the state of technology, expected price, and the number of firms in the industry. Supply functions are derived from generalized supply functions by holding all the variables in the generalized supply function constant except price.

To illustrate the derivation of a supply function from the generalized supply function, suppose the generalized supply function is

$$Q_s = 50 + 10\text{P} - 8P_I + 5F$$

Technology, the prices of goods related in production, and the expected price of the product in the future have been omitted to simplify this illustration. Suppose the price of an important input is \$50, and there are currently 90 firms in the industry producing the product. To find the supply function, the fixed values of P_I and F are substituted into the generalized supply function:

$$\begin{aligned} Q_s &= 50 + 10P - 8(50) + 5(90) \\ &= 100 + 10P \end{aligned}$$

The linear supply function gives the quantity supplied for various product prices, holding constant the other variables that affect supply. For example, if the price of the product is $20,

$$Q_s = 100 + 10(20) = 300$$

or if the price is $50,

$$Q_s = 100 + 10(50) = 600$$

supply schedule
A table showing a list of possible product prices and the corresponding quantities supplied.

supply curve
A graph showing the relation between quantity supplied and price, when all other variables influencing quantity supplied are held constant.

A **supply schedule** (or table) shows a list of several prices and the quantity supplied at each of the prices, again holding all variables other than price constant. Table 2.6 shows seven prices and their corresponding quantities supplied. Each of the seven price–quantity-supplied combinations is derived, as shown above, from the supply equation $Q_s = 100 + 10P$, which was derived from the generalized supply function by setting $P_I = \$50$ and $F = 90$. Figure 2.3 graphs the **supply curve** associated with this supply equation and supply schedule. As with demand curves, price is shown on the vertical axis and quantity on the horizontal axis. Thus the equation plotted in the figure is the inverse of the supply equation: $P = -10 + 1/10Q$. The slope of this inverse supply equation graphed in Figure 2.3 is $\Delta P/\Delta Q_s$, which equals $1/10$ and is the reciprocal of the slope parameter k $(= \Delta Q_s/\Delta P = 10)$.

In the supply equation $Q_s = 100 + 10P$, the intercept parameter is a positive number, which would seem to indicate that producers are willing to offer 100 units to consumers when the price is zero. As we will show in a later chapter, and as your intuition tells you now, producers usually quit producing if price falls below some minimum level. You can think of $10 in Figure 2.3 as the lowest price for which production will occur. Mathematically speaking, we might say the supply equation describes supply only over the range of prices $10 or greater ($P \geq \$10$). We will show in later chapters how to find the price level below which production ceases.[6]

supply price
The minimum price necessary to induce producers voluntarily to offer a given quantity for sale.

Any particular combination of price and quantity supplied on a supply curve can be interpreted in either of two equivalent ways. A point on the supply schedule indicates either (1) the maximum amount of a good or service that will be offered for sale at a specific price or (2) the minimum price necessary to induce producers voluntarily to offer a given quantity for sale. This minimum price is sometimes referred to as the **supply price** for that level of output.

change in quantity supplied
A movement along a given supply curve that occurs when the price of the good changes, all else constant.

As in the case of a demand function, once a supply equation, $Q_s = g(P)$, is derived from a generalized supply function, a **change in quantity supplied** can be caused only by a change in price. A change in quantity supplied represents a movement along a given supply curve. Consider the supply curve S_0 in Figure 2.3. If product price rises from $20 to $30, the quantity supplied increases from 300 to 400 units, a movement from point R to point S along the supply curve S_0.

[6]When the intercept parameter is negative in a supply function, the supply curve intersects the price axis at a price greater than zero. (You will verify this in Technical Problem 7.) In such cases, the price at which the supply curve intersects the price axis represents the minimum price below which production ceases.

TABLE 2.6
The Supply Schedule for the Supply Function S_0: $Q_s = 100 + 10P$

Price	Quantity supplied
$65	750
60	700
50	600
40	500
30	400
20	300
10	200

FIGURE 2.3
A Supply Curve ($Q_s = 100 + 10P$)

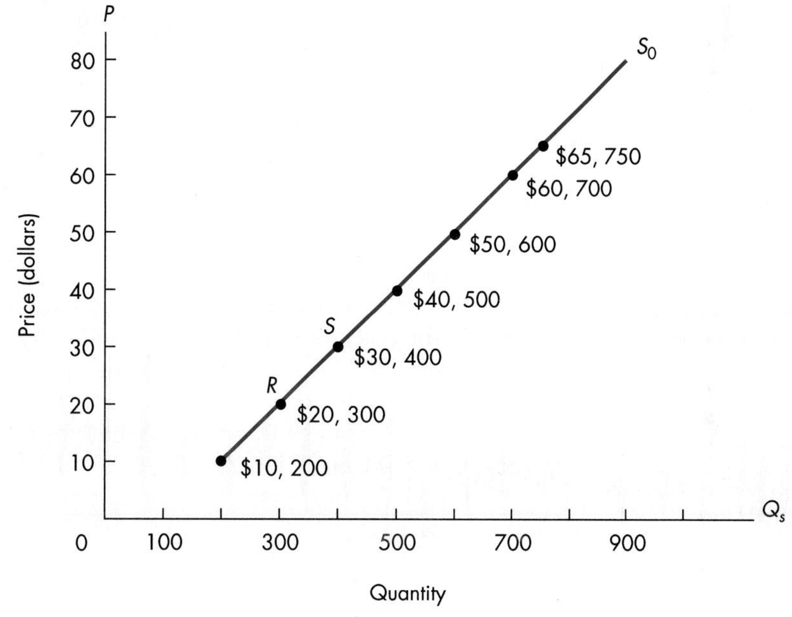

Relation For a supply function $Q_s = g(P)$, a change in price causes a change in quantity supplied. The other five variables that affect supply in the generalized supply function (P_I, P_r, T, P_e, F) are fixed in value for any particular supply function. On a graph, a change in price causes a movement along a supply curve from one price to another price.

Shifts in Supply

As we differentiate between a change in quantity demanded because of a change in price and a shift in demand because of a change in one of the determinants of demand, we must make the same distinction with supply. A shift in supply

TABLE 2.7
Three Supply Schedules

(1) Price	(2) S_0 Quantity supplied $Q_s = 100 + 10P$ (P_I = \$50, F = 90)	(3) S_1 Quantity supplied $Q_s = 250 + 10P$ (P_I = \$31.25, F = 90)	(4) S_2 Quantity supplied $Q_s = -200 + 10P$ (P_I = \$50, F = 30)
\$65	750	900	450
60	700	850	400
50	600	750	300
40	500	650	200
30	400	550	100
20	300	450	0
10	200	350	0

occurs only when one of the five determinants of supply (P_I, P_r, T, P_e, F) changes value. An increase in the number of firms in the industry, for example, causes the quantity supplied to increase at every price so that the supply curve shifts to the right, and this circumstance is called an **increase in supply.** A decrease in the number of firms in the industry causes a **decrease in supply,** and the supply curve shifts to the left. We can illustrate shifts in supply by examining the effect on the supply function of changes in the values of the determinants of supply.

increase in supply
A change in the supply function that causes an increase in quantity supplied at every price, and is reflected by a rightward shift in the supply curve.

decrease in supply
A change in the supply function that causes a decrease in quantity supplied at every price, and is reflected by a leftward shift in the supply curve.

Table 2.6 is reproduced in columns 1 and 2 of Table 2.7. If the price of the input falls to \$31.25, the new supply function is $Q_s = 250 + 10P$, and the quantity supplied increases *at each and every price* as shown in column 3. This new supply curve when the price of the input falls to \$31.25 is shown as S_1 in Figure 2.4 and lies to the right of S_0 at every price. Thus, the decrease in P_I causes the supply curve to shift rightward, illustrating an increase in supply. To illustrate a decrease in supply, suppose the price of the input remains at \$50 but the number of firms in the industry decreases to 30 firms. The supply function is now $Q_s = -200 + 10P$, and quantity supplied decreases *at every price* as shown in column 4. The new supply curve in Figure 2.4, S_2, lies to the left of S_0 at every price. Thus, the decrease in the number of firms causes a decrease in supply, which is represented by a leftward shift in the supply curve.

Relation An increase in supply means that, at each price, more of the good is supplied; a decrease in supply means that, at each price, less is supplied. Supply changes (or shifts) when one of the determinants of supply changes. These determinants of supply are the price of inputs, the price of goods related in production, the state of technology, the expected price in the future, and the number of firms in the industry.

As in the case of demand, the direction in which a supply curve shifts when one of the determinants of supply changes value depends upon the sign of the slope parameter in the generalized supply function. In the above example, when the input price falls to \$31.25, quantity supplied increases for every price because the slope parameter for P_I is negative ($l = -8$). Thus, a fall in the price of the input causes an increase in supply. Table 2.8 summarizes this discussion of shifts in supply.

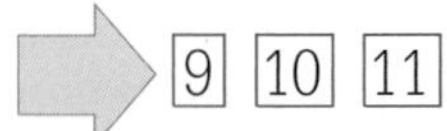
9 10 11

FIGURE 2.4
Shifts in Supply

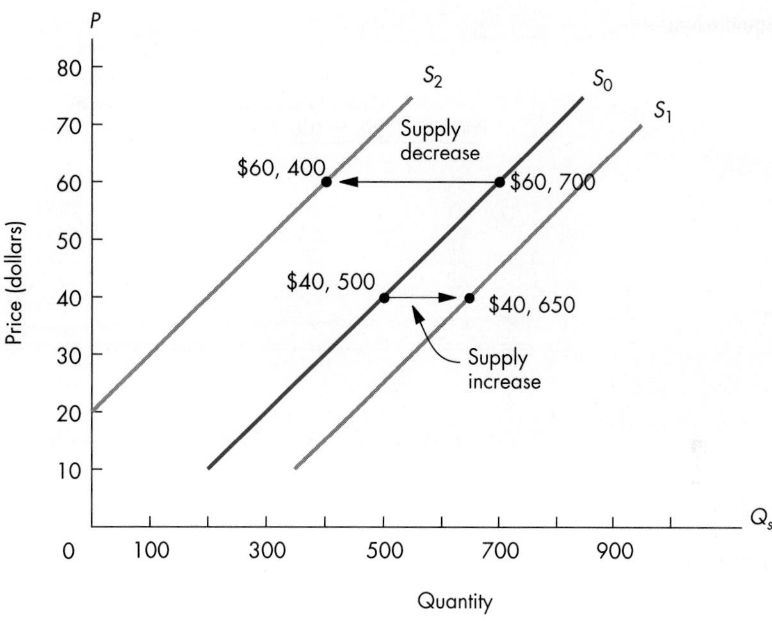

TABLE 2.8
Summary of Supply Shifts

Determinants of supply	Supply increases*	Supply decreases†	Sign of slope parameter‡
1. Price of inputs (P_I)	P_I falls	P_I rises	$l < 0$
2. Price of goods related in production (P_r)			
Substitute good	P_r falls	P_r rises	$m < 0$
Complement good	P_r rises	P_r falls	$m > 0$
3. State of technology (T)	T rises	T falls	$n > 0$
4. Expected price (P_e)	P_e falls	P_e rises	$r < 0$
5. Number of firms in industry (F)	F rises	F falls	$s > 0$

*Supply increases when the supply curve shifts rightward.
†Supply decreases when the supply curve shifts leftward.
‡This column gives the sign of the corresponding slope parameter in the generalized supply function.

2.3 MARKET EQUILIBRIUM

Demand and supply provide an analytical framework for the analysis of the behavior of buyers and sellers in markets. Demand shows how buyers respond to changes in price and other variables that determine quantities buyers are willing

TABLE 2.9
Market Equilibrium

(1) Price	(2) S_0 Quantity supplied ($Q_s = 100 + 10P$)	(3) D_0 Quantity demanded ($Q_d = 1{,}300 - 20P$)	(4) Excess supply (+) or excess demand (−) ($Q_s - Q_d$)
$65	750	0	+750
60	700	100	+600
50	600	300	+300
40	500	500	0
30	400	700	−300
20	300	900	−600
10	200	1,100	−900

market equilibrium A situation in which, at the prevailing price, consumers can buy all of a good they wish and producers can sell all of the good they wish. The price at which $Q_d = Q_s$.

equilibrium price The price at which $Q_d = Q_s$.

equilibrium quantity The amount of a good bought and sold in market equilibrium.

excess supply (surplus) Exists when quantity supplied exceeds quantity demanded.

excess demand (shortage) Exists when quantity demanded exceeds quantity supplied.

market clearing price The price of a good at which buyers can purchase all they want and sellers can sell all they want at that price. This is another name for the equilibrium price.

and able to purchase. Supply shows how sellers respond to changes in price and other variables that determine quantities offered for sale. The interaction of buyers and sellers in the marketplace leads to **market equilibrium.** Market equilibrium is a situation in which, *at the prevailing price,* consumers can buy all of a good they wish and producers can sell all of the good they wish. In other words, equilibrium occurs when price is at a level for which quantity demanded equals quantity supplied. In equilibrium, the price is called **equilibrium price** and the quantity sold is called **equilibrium quantity.**

To illustrate how market equilibrium is achieved, we can use the demand and supply schedules set forth in the preceding sections. Table 2.9 shows both the demand schedule for D_0 (given in Table 2.2) and the supply schedule for S_0 (given in Table 2.6). As the table shows, equilibrium in the market occurs when price is $40 and both quantity demanded and quantity supplied are equal to 500 units. At every price above $40, quantity supplied is greater than quantity demanded. **Excess supply** or a **surplus** exists when the quantity supplied exceeds the quantity demanded. The first three entries in column 4 of Table 2.9 show the excess supply or surplus at each price above $40. At every price below $40, quantity supplied is less than quantity demanded. A situation in which quantity demanded exceeds quantity supplied is called **excess demand** or a **shortage.** The last three entries in column 4 of the table show the excess demand or shortage at each price below the $40 equilibrium price. Excess demand and excess supply equal zero only in equilibrium. In equilibrium the market "clears" in the sense that buyers can purchase all they want and sellers can sell all they want at the equilibrium price. Because of this clearing of the market, equilibrium price is sometimes called the **market clearing price.**

Before moving on to a graphical analysis of equilibrium, we want to reinforce the concepts illustrated in Table 2.9 by using the demand and supply functions from which the table was derived. To this end, recall that the demand equation is $Q_d = 1{,}300 - 20P$ and the supply equation is $Q_s = 100 + 10P$. Since equilibrium requires that $Q_d = Q_s$, in equilibrium,

$$1{,}300 - 20P = 100 + 10P$$

FIGURE 2.5
Market Equilibrium

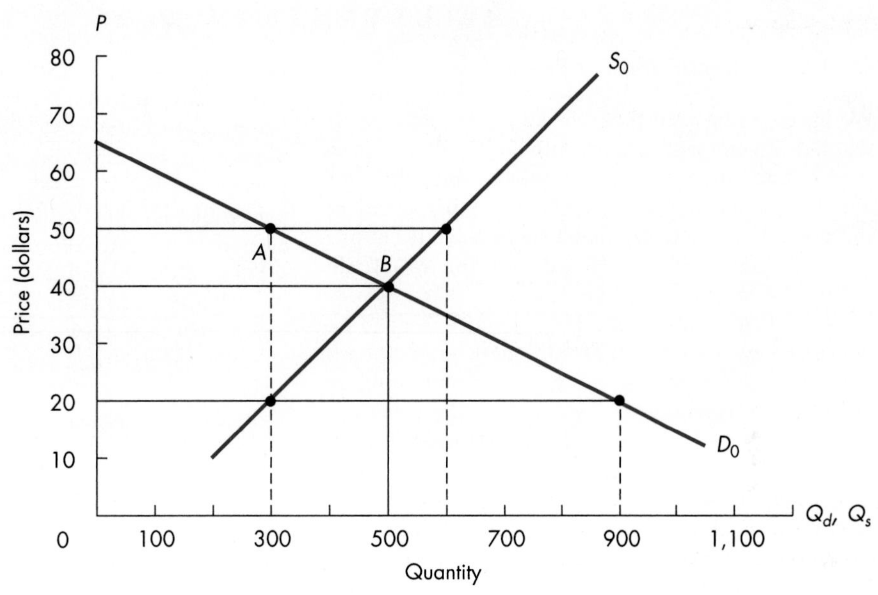

Solving this equation for equilibrium price,

$$1{,}200 = 30P$$
$$P = \$40$$

At the market clearing price of $40,

$$Q_d = 1{,}300 - (20 \times 40) = 500$$
$$Q_s = 100 + (10 \times 40) = 500$$

As expected, these mathematically derived results are identical to those presented in Table 2.9.

According to Table 2.9, when price is $50, there is a surplus of 300 units. Using the demand and supply equations, when $P = 50$,

$$Q_d = 1{,}300 - (20 + 50) = 300$$
$$Q_s = 100 + (10 \times 50) = 600$$

Therefore, when price is $50,

$$Q_s - Q_d = 600 - 300 = 300$$

which is the result shown in column 4.

To express the equilibrium solution graphically, Figure 2.5 shows the demand curve D_0 and the supply curve S_0 associated with the schedules in Table 2.9. These are also the demand and supply curves previously shown in

ILLUSTRATION 2.2

Do Buyers Really Bid Up Prices?

We have emphasized that when a surplus exists, unwanted inventories accumulate and sellers lower prices. And when there is a shortage, consumers, unable to buy all they want at the going price, bid up the price. It's easy to see that a surplus would induce sellers to lower the price. But do consumers actually bid up the price during a shortage?

Since 1986, housing markets in the U.S. have experienced two periods of rapidly increasing demand that created temporary shortages accompanied by episodes of consumers' bidding up the prices of homes. The predictable nature of consumer bidding wars is illustrated by two newspaper reports.

In spring 1986, an article in *The Wall Street Journal* described how the bidding process actually took place first in housing markets in Boston and upstate New York, then appeared later in most of the Northeast, suburbs of Chicago, Detroit, Minneapolis, parts of Ohio, and major California cities. Lured by lower mortgage interest rates, a huge influx of home buyers began offering sellers $100 to $45,000 extra for scarce houses in desirable suburbs or prestigious urban neighborhoods. The *WSJ* reported that bidding contests were breaking out in a growing number of hot housing markets for the first time since the late 1970s. While overbidding wasn't the norm, it occurred in 25 percent of home sales in some booming areas. As the *WSJ* noted, "Its pervasiveness is helping to drive house prices sky high," and "there is too much overbidding to hold down prices."

The article reported several specific examples. A New York couple offered $2,000 above the $181,000 asking price for a New Jersey home that needed a new furnace, a new paint job in the garage, and extensive bathroom repairs. They made the offer to win a bidding war with two other buyers. And they said they were happy because they knew people who had paid as much as $10,000 above the asking price.

A Washington, D.C., couple paid $4,500 above the asking price for a home in a fashionable neighborhood, after simply driving by. Many people were even giving up some purchase conditions, such as having a structural inspection for hidden flaws, in order to win bidding contests. A California couple reported paying $135,000 for a two-bedroom house priced at $120,000. An Alexandria, Virginia, lawyer, after she was outbid for another home, paid $170,000 for a $167,000 house that needed $25,000 in repairs. A real estate agent in Albany, New York, said that one-fourth of the homes in the area priced between $65,000 and $170,000 sold for more than the asking price.

In August 1997, an article in *The New York Times* reported that relatively low mortgage interest rates and growing stock portfolios were combining to promote the return of bidding wars in affluent areas of northern New Jersey, Los Angeles, the San Francisco Bay area, and Boston: "Competing buyers [are] push[ing] selling prices well beyond the asking price." One 30-something couple chose to pay $17,600 more than the asking price for a Bergen County, New Jersey, home rather than let another couple get the home for just $10,000 over the asking price. As another buyer put it, "I knew we had to come in with a good offer or we would run the risk of losing it."

Translated into demand and supply, when interest rates fell and stock market portfolios swelled in value, the demand for homes in many areas of the U.S. increased substantially. Quantity demanded exceeded quantity supplied at the old equilibrium price. Consumers, not able to get all the houses they wanted at that price, bid the price up. Not until the new price reaches the new higher equilibrium will overbidding cease.

Sources: Charles Bagli, "Home Buyers Find the Bidding Wars Are Back," *The New York Times*, Aug. 13, 1997; Joann S. Lublin, "Eager Home Buyers Bid Up Prices in Rising Numbers of Hot Markets," *The Wall Street Journal*, Mar. 7, 1986.

Figures 2.1 and 2.3. Clearly, \$40 and 500 units are the equilibrium price and quantity. Only at a price of \$40 does quantity demanded equal quantity supplied.

Market forces will drive price toward \$40. If price is \$50, producers want to supply 600 units while consumers only demand 300 units. An excess supply of 300 units develops. Producers must lower price in order to keep from accumulating unwanted inventories. At any price above \$40, excess supply results, and producers will lower price.

If price is \$20, consumers are willing and able to purchase 900 units, while producers offer only 300 units for sale. An excess demand of 600 units results. Since their demands are not satisfied, consumers bid the price up. Any price below \$40 leads to an excess demand, and the shortage induces consumers to bid up the price.

Given no outside influences that prevent price from being bid up or down, an equilibrium price and quantity is attained. This equilibrium price is the price that clears the market; both excess demand and excess supply are zero in equilibrium. Equilibrium is attained in the market because of the following:

Principle The equilibrium price is that price at which quantity demanded is equal to quantity supplied. When the current price is above the equilibrium price, quantity supplied exceeds quantity demanded. The resulting excess supply induces sellers to reduce price in order to sell the surplus. If the current price is below equilibrium, quantity demanded exceeds quantity supplied. The resulting excess demand causes the unsatisfied consumers to bid up price. Since prices below equilibrium are bid up by consumers and prices above equilibrium are lowered by producers, the market will converge to the equilibrium price-quantity combination.

A final point about market equilibrium should be made before moving on to changes in equilibrium in the next section. It is crucial for you to understand that in the analysis of demand and supply there will never be either a permanent shortage or a permanent surplus as long as price is allowed to adjust freely to the equilibrium level. In other words, assuming that market price adjusts *quickly* to the equilibrium level, surpluses or shortages do not occur in free markets. In the absence of impediments to the adjustment of prices (such as government-imposed price ceilings or floors), the market is always assumed to clear. This assumption greatly simplifies demand and supply analysis. Indeed, how many instances of surpluses or shortages have you seen in markets where prices can adjust freely? The duration of any surplus or shortage is generally short enough that we can reasonably ignore the adjustment period for purposes of demand and supply analysis.

2.4 CHANGES IN MARKET EQUILIBRIUM

If demand and supply never changed, equilibrium price and quantity would remain the same forever, or at least for a very long time, and market analysis would be extremely uninteresting and totally useless for managers. In reality, the variables held constant when deriving demand and supply curves do change. Consequently, demand and supply curves shift, and equilibrium price and quantity change. Using demand and supply, managers may make either qualitative

qualitative forecast A forecast that predicts only the direction in which an economic variable will move.

quantitative forecast A forecast that predicts both the direction and the magnitude of the change in an economic variable.

forecasts or quantitative forecasts. A **qualitative forecast** predicts only the *direction* in which an economic variable, such as price or quantity, will move. A **quantitative forecast** predicts both the *direction* and the *magnitude* of the change in an economic variable.

For instance, if you read in *The Wall Street Journal* that Congress is considering a tax cut, demand and supply analysis enables you to forecast whether the price and sales of a particular product will increase or decrease. If you forecast that price will rise and sales will fall, you have made a qualitative forecast about price and quantity. Alternatively, you may have sufficient data on the exact nature of demand and supply to be able to predict that price will rise by $1.10 and sales will fall by 7,000 units. This is a quantitative forecast. Obviously, a manager would get more information from a quantitative forecast than from a qualitative forecast. But managers may not always have sufficient data to make quantitative forecasts. In many instances, just being able to predict correctly whether price will rise or fall can be extremely valuable to a manager.

Thus, an important function and challenging task for managers is predicting the effect, especially the effect on market price, of specific changes in the variables that determine the position of demand and supply curves. We will first discuss the process of adjustment when something causes demand to change while supply remains constant, then the process when supply changes while demand remains constant.

Changes in Demand (supply constant)

To illustrate the effects of changes in demand when supply remains constant, we have reproduced D_0 and S_0 in Figure 2.6. Equilibrium occurs at $40 and 500 units, shown as point *A* in the figure. The demand curve D_1, showing an increase in demand, and the demand curve D_2, showing a decrease in demand, are reproduced from Figure 2.2. Recall that the shift from D_0 to D_1 was caused by an increase in income from $20,000 to $20,500. The shift from D_0 to D_2 resulted from the decrease in income from $20,000 to $19,500.

Begin in equilibrium at point *A*. Now let demand increase to D_1 as shown. At the original $40 price consumers now demand 800 units with the new demand. Since firms are still willing to supply only 500 units at $40, a shortage of 300 units results. As described in the previous section, the shortage causes the price to rise to a new equilibrium, where quantity demanded equals quantity supplied. This new equilibrium, where D_1 crosses S_0, occurs when price is $50 and quantity sold is 600 units (point *B*). Therefore the increase in demand increases both equilibrium price and quantity.

To illustrate the effect of a decrease in demand, supply held constant, we return to the original equilibrium at point *A* in the figure. Now we decrease the demand to D_2. At the original equilibrium price of $40, firms still want to supply 500 units, but now consumers want to purchase only 200 units. Thus, there is a surplus of 300 units at $40. As already explained, a surplus causes price to fall. In this example, the market returns to equilibrium only when price decreases to $30 and quantity sold is 400 (point *C*). Therefore the decrease in demand

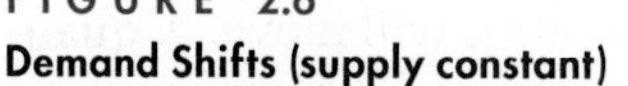

FIGURE 2.6
Demand Shifts (supply constant)

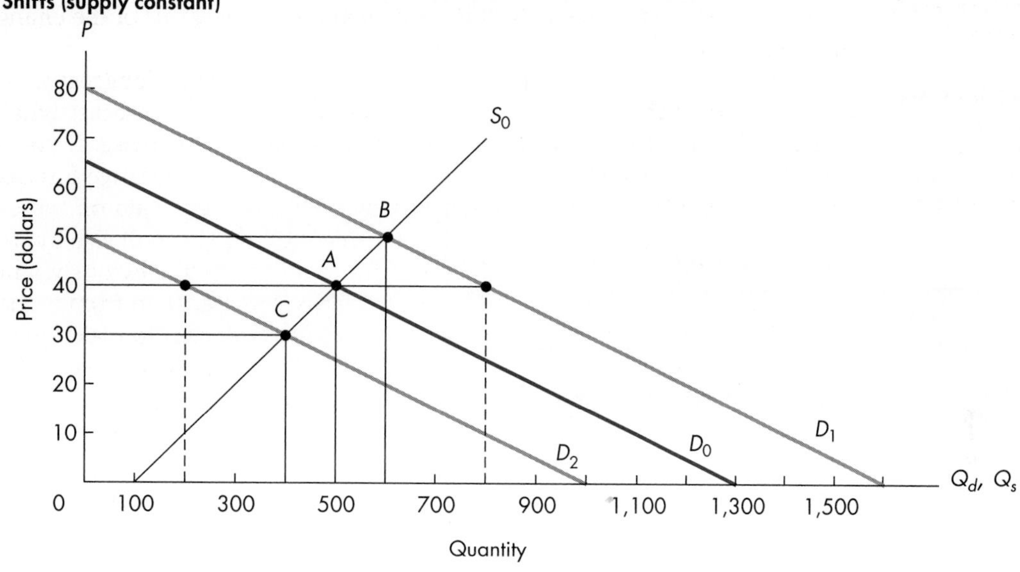

decreases both equilibrium price and quantity. We have now established the following principle:

Principle When demand increases and supply is constant, equilibrium price and quantity both rise. When demand decreases and supply is constant, equilibrium price and quantity both fall.

Changes in Supply (demand constant)

To illustrate the effects of changes in supply when demand remains constant, we reproduce D_0 and S_0 in Figure 2.7. The supply curve S_1, showing an increase in supply, and the supply curve S_2, showing a decrease in supply, are reproduced from Figure 2.4. Recall that the shift from S_0 to S_1 was caused by a decrease in the price of an input from \$50 to \$31.25. The shift from S_0 to S_2 resulted from a decrease in the number of firms in the industry from 90 to 30.

Begin in equilibrium at point *R*. Let supply first increase to S_1 as shown. At the original \$40 price consumers still want to purchase 500 units, but sellers now wish to sell 650 units, causing a surplus or excess supply of 150 units. The surplus causes price to fall, which induces sellers to supply less and buyers to demand more. Price continues to fall until the new equilibrium is attained at a price of \$35 and a quantity sold of 600 units (point *S*). At this new equilibrium, quantity demanded equals quantity supplied. Thus, when supply increases and demand remains constant, equilibrium price will fall and equilibrium quantity will increase.

To demonstrate the effect of a supply decrease, we return to the original input price, \$50, to obtain the original supply curve S_0 and the original equilib-

ILLUSTRATION 2.3

For Sale by Owner: One Kidney, Like-New Condition . . .

An acute shortage of human organs for transplantation has recently focused international attention on what appears to be an urgent need to increase charitable organ donations worldwide. The root of the current crisis can be traced, at least in part, to the development in 1986 of cyclosporine, a drug designed to inhibit organ and tissue rejection. Combined with increasing sophistication in tissue matching and advances in surgical techniques, the introduction of cyclosporine dramatically increased the success rates for many kinds of organ transplants. As survival rates increased and prices for transplants began to fall, demand for donated organs increased to levels that greatly exceeded the number of organs supplied through voluntary organ donations.

In 1995, U.S. doctors performed 2,400 heart transplant operations while 4,000 patients waited for hearts to be donated, 731 of whom died waiting. The situation was worse for kidneys: 10,000 kidney transplants were performed, 30,000 patients waited, and 1,375 died waiting for a kidney donation. For lung and liver transplants, 290 and 674 patients, respectively, died waiting for organs. In the United States and in most western European nations, the shortage of organs has placed the tremendous ethical burden of deciding who most deserves transplants squarely on the shoulders of the medical profession. The futile liver transplant for baseball legend Mickey Mantle highlighted the ethical dilemma in the United States.

Until recently, most medical professionals believed the best solution to the worsening shortage of organs was to encourage governments to promote vigorously an increase in the supply of organ donations. Educating citizens about the need to carry donor cards, strengthening laws to enforce the donation wishes of the deceased (families frequently overrule a deceased family member's organ donation decision), legalizing elective ventilation to increase organ-harvest rates (keeping brain-dead people alive with respirator machines), and even using animal organs are some of the options doctors hope will increase the supply of organs for transplantation. Unfortunately, the supply of organs appears stuck at

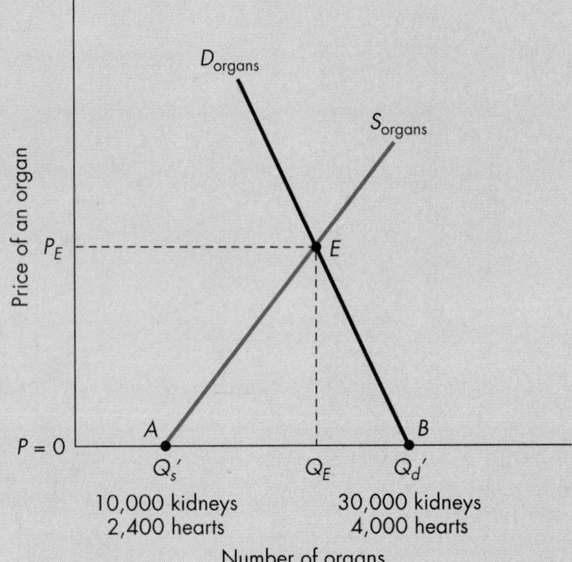

inadequate levels while demand for organs continues to rise rapidly, and the shortage worsens each year.

As we explained in this chapter, shortages of any good arise when the price of the good is not allowed to rise to the market clearing level. Try not to squirm as we treat human organs as economic goods no different from wheat. This Illustration shows how the laws of demand and supply can explain why there is a shortage of human organs and how to eliminate the shortage. Gary Becker, the 1992 Nobel laureate in economics proposed in a recent *Business Week* column, "There aren't enough livers, hearts, and kidneys to go around, so why not increase the [quantity] suppl[ied] by offering money to donors?" In the United States, the Transplant Act of 1984 makes it a felony to buy or sell organs. America's medical policymakers are now ready to consider relaxing the law to allow some form of financial incentives for organ donation. Despite this new willingness to try financial incentives, doctors remain fearful that cash payments for organs could backfire and decrease the quantity of organs supplied. *The Wall Street Journal* reports that physicians who in the past refused to consider financial reimbursement are now having second thoughts. One doctor is quoted: "Frankly, I'm against financial incentives. But I'm for saving lives, and therefore I'm for whatever it takes to save lives."

The accompanying figure shows an upward-sloping supply of donated organs, reflecting the observation that as the financial incentives for organ donation rise, so too does the number of organs donated. At a price of zero, the quantity of organs donated is Q_s' (point *A*) and the quantity demanded is Q_d' (point *B*). The shortage of human organs is measured by the distance between points *A* and *B* in the figure. In 1995, as noted above, "conscientious" citizens donated 10,000 kidneys as 30,000 patients waited for organs, and a shortage of 20,000 kidneys resulted. For heart transplants, a shortage of 1,600 hearts existed in 1995. As organ demand continues to shift rightward and organ supply remains stagnant, the shortage of organs (as measured by the distance between *A* and *B*) will only get much larger.

If millions of people die each year, why isn't point *A* located to the *right* of point *B* instead of to the *left* of it? In every country where citizens have been polled, surveys find an overwhelming willingness to donate organs. But as Kurtz and Saks report in their 1996 study, "The public has yet to put its 'organs' where its mouth is." Efforts to encourage organ donation as the "right thing to do" have so far caused only minimal rightward shifts in the organ supply curve. People's reluctance to designate themselves legally as organ donors can be attributed partly to procrastination and partly to anxiety harbored by some potential donors that, in the event of an accident, emergency room medical treatment might be less aggressive for accident victims whose driver's licenses are stamped "organ donor." In matters of one's own life, most people tend to be quite reluctant to take risks for free. As we show in a later chapter, people who have an aversion to risk require compensation in order to accept voluntarily a risky proposition. The higher the price offered for donated organs, the greater the number of people willing to stamp "organ donor" on their drivers' licenses.

At a price of P_E in the figure, the market for organs clears. Anyone willing and able to pay the market clearing price P_E will get an organ without a lengthy wait. When the price of donated organs rises to P_E, doctors and health care administrators no longer must make the dreadful decision of which patients get organs and which patients remain on the waiting list. The impersonal forces of the market allocate the scarce organs to the recipients most willing and able to pay for a donated organ. In the figure, those patients with demand prices—the maximum price a consumer would be willing and able to pay for a donated organ—at or above P_E choose to buy an organ at the market-determined price. Those patients between Q_E and point *B* with demand prices below P_E will not choose to buy an organ.

Many doctors, and indeed all compassionate citizens, are concerned that relying on market prices to allocate scarce organs leaves some patients without organs. Some patients choose not to pay for a new organ because even with a new organ, they judge their posttransplant life expectancy to be too short and tenuous to justify the price and discomfort of the transplant operation. Some patients between Q_E and *B* would have higher demand prices, and thus purchase an organ, if only their incomes were higher. Not all these people are poverty cases; some are simply people unwilling to strap their families with large medical bills. For potential recipients who truly represent poverty cases, compassionate donors could be allowed to designate that their organs go to the pool of indigent patients, where organs are allocated by a lottery system.

As long as the number of desired organs exceeds the number of donated organs—the quantity demanded exceeds the quantity supplied at a price of zero—the shortage of organs can be eliminated by letting the price of donated organs rise to the market clearing price. While not everyone who wants an organ for nothing will get one, at the market clearing price, more people get organs than would be the case if no financial incentives were offered (Q_E is greater than Q_s').

Sources: Gary Becker, "How Uncle Sam Could Ease the Organ Shortage," *Business Week*, Jan. 20, 1997, p. 18; "Buddy Can You Spare a Lung?" *The Economist*, Jan. 25, 1997, p. 19; Prerna Mona Khanna, "Scarcity of Organs for Transplant Sparks a Move to Legalize Financial Incentives," *The Wall Street Journal*, Sept. 8, 1992, p. B1; Sheldon F. Kurtz and Michael J. Saks, "The Transplant Paradox: Overwhelming Public Support for Organ Donation v. Under-Supply of Organs," *The Journal of Corporation Law*, Summer 1996, pp. 768–803.

FIGURE 2.7
Supply Shifts (demand constant)

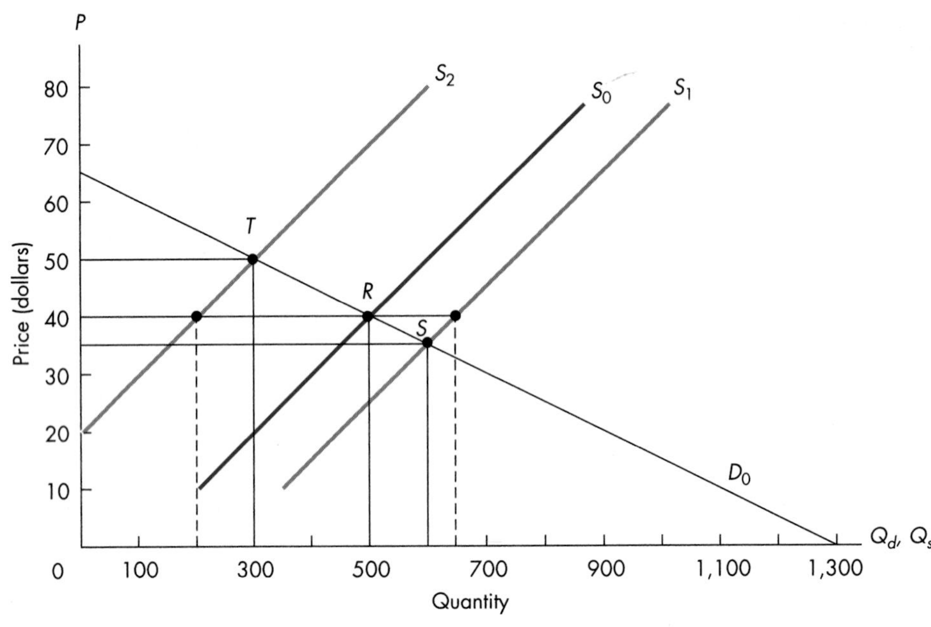

rium at P = \$40 and Q = 500 units (point R). Let the number of firms in the industry decrease from 90 to 30, causing supply to shift from S_0 to S_2 in Figure 2.7. At the original \$40 price, consumers still want to buy 500 units, but now sellers wish to sell only 200 units, as shown in the figure. This leads to a shortage or excess demand of 300 units. Shortages cause price to rise. The increase in price induces sellers to supply more and buyers to demand less, thereby reducing the shortage. Price will continue to increase until it attains the new equilibrium at a price of \$50 and 300 units of output being sold (point T). At the new equilibrium, S_2 intersects D_0 and quantity supplied equals quantity demanded. Therefore, when supply decreases while demand remains constant, price will rise and quantity sold will decrease. We have now established the following principle:

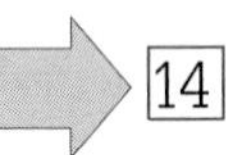

14 **Principle** When supply increases and demand is constant, equilibrium price falls and equilibrium quantity rises. When supply decreases and demand is constant, equilibrium price rises and equilibrium quantity falls.

Simultaneous Shifts in Both Demand and Supply

To this point, we have examined changes in demand or supply holding the other curve constant. In both cases, the effect on equilibrium price and quantity can be predicted. In situations involving both a shift in demand and a shift in supply,

FIGURE 2.8
Simultaneous Shifts in Demand and Supply: Demand and Supply Both Increase

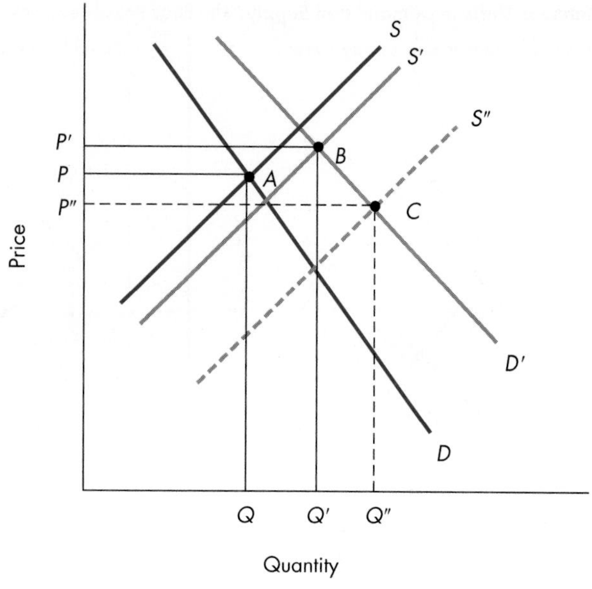

it is possible to predict either the direction in which price changes or the direction in which quantity changes, *but not both.* When it is not possible to predict the direction of change in a variable, the change in that variable is said to be **indeterminate.** The change in either equilibrium price or quantity will be indeterminate when the direction of change depends upon the relative magnitudes of the shifts in the demand and supply curves.

indeterminate
Term referring to the unpredictable change in either equilibrium price or quantity when the direction of change depends upon the relative magnitude of the shifts in the demand and supply curves.

In Figure 2.8, D and S are, respectively, demand and supply, and equilibrium price and quantity are P and Q (point A). Suppose demand increases to D' and supply increases to S'. Equilibrium quantity increases to Q', and equilibrium price rises from P to P' (point B). Suppose, however, that supply had increased even more to the dashed supply S'' so that the new equilibrium occurs at point C instead of at point B. Comparing point A to point C, equilibrium quantity still increases (Q to Q''), but now equilibrium price *decreases* from P to P''. In the case where both demand and supply increase, a *small* increase in supply relative to demand causes price to rise, while a *large* increase in supply relative to demand causes price to fall. In the case of a simultaneous increase in both demand and supply, equilibrium output always increases, but the change in equilibrium price is indeterminate.

When both demand and supply shift together, either (1) the change in quantity can be predicted and the change in price is indeterminate or (2) the change in quantity is indeterminate and the change in price can be predicted. Figure 2.9 summarizes the four possible outcomes when demand and supply both shift. In each of the four panels in Figure 2.9, point C shows an alternative point of

FIGURE 2.9

Summary of Simultaneous Shifts in Demand and Supply: The Four Possible Cases

Panel A — Demand increases and supply increases

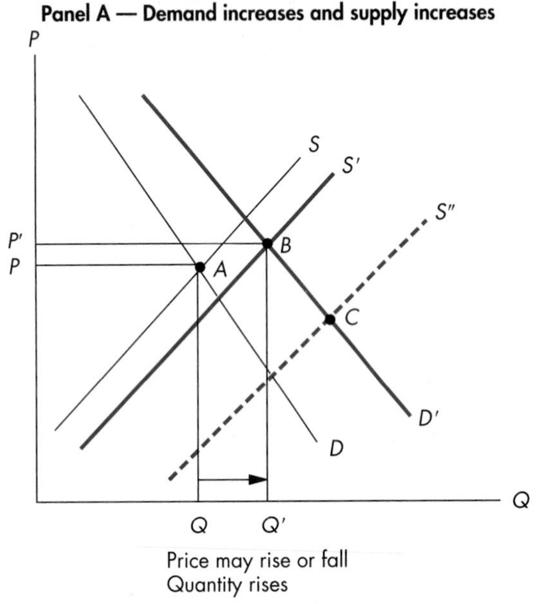

Price may rise or fall
Quantity rises

Panel B — Demand decreases and supply increases

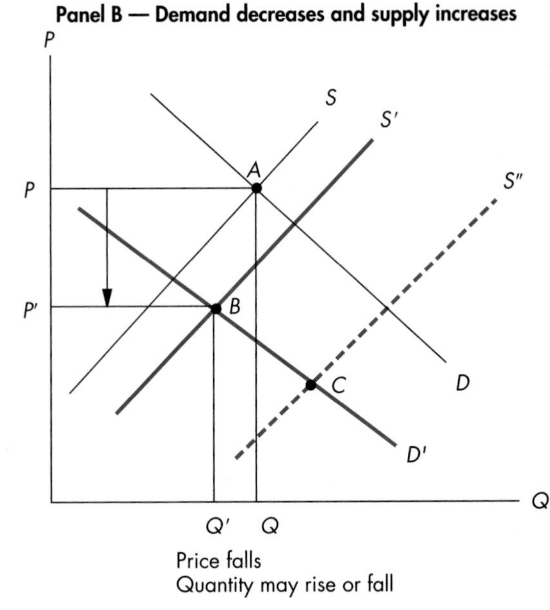

Price falls
Quantity may rise or fall

Panel C — Demand increases and supply decreases

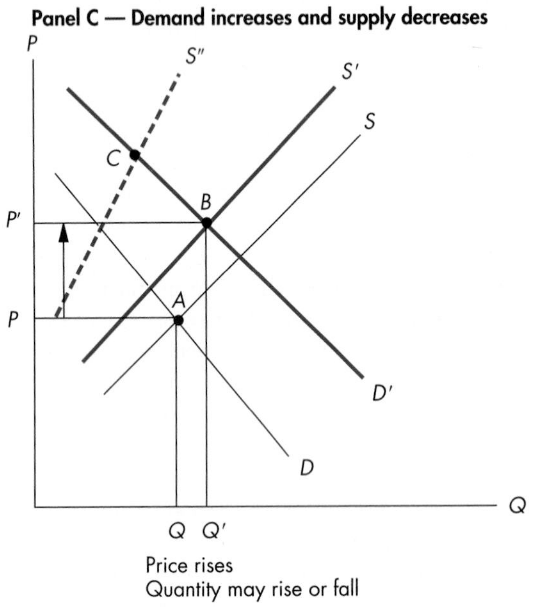

Price rises
Quantity may rise or fall

Panel D — Demand decreases and supply decreases

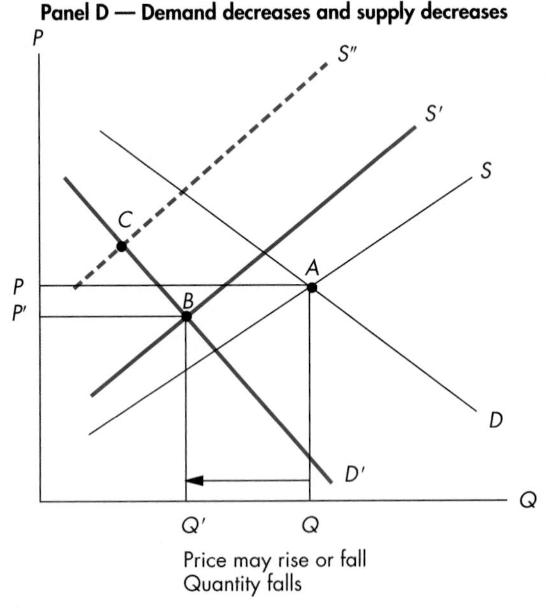

Price may rise or fall
Quantity falls

equilibrium that reverses the direction of change in one of the variables, price or quantity. You should use the reasoning process set forth above to verify the conclusions presented for each of the four cases. We have established the following principle:

Principle When demand and supply both shift simultaneously, if the change in quantity (price) can be predicted, the change in price (quantity) is indeterminate. The change in equilibrium quantity or price is indeterminate when the variable can either rise or fall depending upon the relative magnitudes by which demand and supply shift.

Predicting the Direction of Change in Airfares: A Qualitative Analysis

Suppose you manage the travel department for a large U.S. corporation and your sales force makes heavy use of air travel to call on customers. The president of the corporation wants you to reduce travel expenditures for 1999. The extent to which you will need to curb air travel in 1999 will depend upon what happens to the price of air travel. If airfares fall in 1999, you can satisfy the wants of both the president, who wants expenditures cut, and the sales personnel, who would be hurt by travel restrictions. Clearly, you need to predict what will happen to airfares in 1999. You have recently read in *The Wall Street Journal* about the following two events that you expect will affect the airline industry in 1999:

1. A number of new, small airlines have recently entered the industry and others are expected to enter in 1999.
2. Teleconferencing is becoming a popular, cost-effective alternative to business travel for many U.S. corporations. The trend is expected to accelerate in 1999 as telecommunications firms begin cutting prices on teleconferencing rates.

We can use Figure 2.10 to analyze how these events would affect the price of air travel in 1999. The current demand and supply curves in the domestic market are D_{1998} and S_{1998}. Equilibrium airfare in 1998 is denoted P_{1998} at point A in Figure 2.10.

An increase in the number of airlines causes supply to increase. The increase in supply is shown in Figure 2.10 by the shift in supply to S_{1999}. Since teleconferencing and air travel are substitutes, a reduction in the price of teleconferencing causes a decrease in demand. The decrease in demand is shown in Figure 2.10 by the shift in demand to D_{1999}. Thus, you must analyze a situation in which demand and supply shift simultaneously. The decrease in demand combined with the increase in supply leads you to predict a fall in airfares in 1999 to P_{1999} (point B in Figure 2.10). While you can predict that airfares will definitely fall when demand decreases and supply increases, you cannot predict whether equilibrium quantity will rise or fall in this situation (supply could instead shift to S'_{1999} in Figure 2.10). The change in quantity is indeterminate. The predicted fall in airfares is good news for you but bad news for the financially troubled airline industry.

This analysis of the air travel market is an example of qualitative analysis. You predicted only the *direction* of the price change, not the magnitude of the

FIGURE 2.10
Demand and Supply for Air Travel

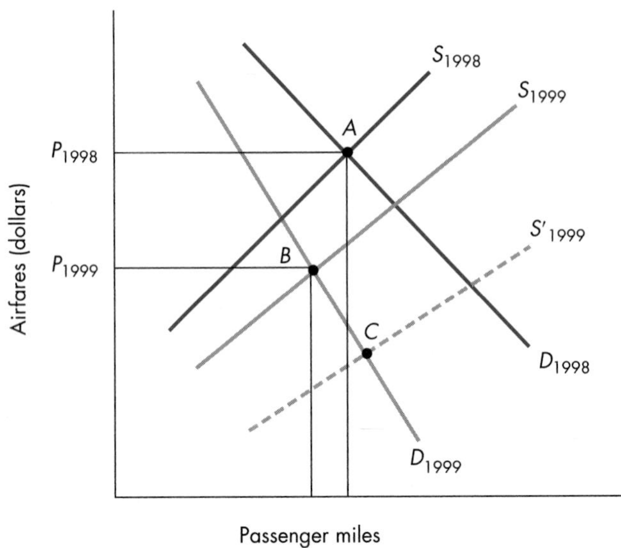

change. Managers are certainly interested in whether price will increase or decrease. They are also interested in *how much* price will increase or decrease. Determining how much price will rise involves quantitative analysis. In order to carry out quantitative analysis, either you must be given the exact specification of the market demand and supply equations or you must estimate them from market data. In later chapters we will show you how to estimate demand and supply from market data. We will look now at an example of quantitative analysis

15 where the demand and supply equations have already been estimated for you.

Advertising and the Price of Potatoes: A Quantitative Analysis

The Potato Growers Association of America estimates that next year the demand and supply functions facing U.S. potato growers will be

$$Q_d = 28 - 0.04\,P$$
$$Q_s = -2 + 0.16\,P$$

where quantity demanded and quantity supplied are measured in trillions of hundredweight (a measure equal to 100 pounds) per year, and price is measured in cents per hundredweight. First, we will predict the price of potatoes next year and how many potatoes will be sold. The market clearing price is easily determined by setting quantity demanded equal to quantity supplied and solving algebraically for equilibrium price:

$$
\begin{aligned}
Q_d &= Q_s \\
28 - 0.04\,P &= -2 + 0.16\,P \\
30 &= 0.20\,P \\
150 &= P_E
\end{aligned}
$$

Thus the equilibrium price of potatoes next year will be 150 cents ($1.50) per hundredweight. The equilibrium level of potato production is determined by substituting the market price of 150 cents into either the demand or the supply function to get Q_E:

$$
\begin{gathered}
Q_d = Q_s = Q_E \\
28 - (0.04 \times 150) = -2 + (0.16 \times 150) = 22
\end{gathered}
$$

Thus the equilibrium output of potatoes will be 22 trillion hundredweight per year.

Even though that's a lot of potatoes, the Potato Growers Association plans to begin a nationwide advertising campaign to promote potatoes by informing consumers of the nutritional benefits of potatoes. The association estimates that the advertising campaign, which will make consumers want to eat more potatoes, will increase demand to

$$Q_d = 40 - 0.05\,P$$

Assuming that supply is unaffected by the advertising, you would obviously predict that the market price of potatoes will rise as a result of the advertising and the resulting increase in demand. However, to determine the actual market clearing price, you must equate the new quantity demanded with the quantity supplied:

$$
\begin{aligned}
40 - 0.05\,P &= -2 + 0.16\,P \\
P_E &= 200
\end{aligned}
$$

The price of potatoes will increase to 200 cents ($2.00) with the advertising campaign. Consequently, the prediction is that the national advertising campaign will increase the market price of potatoes by 50 cents per hundredweight. This is an example of a quantitative forecast since the forecast involves both the magnitude and the direction of change in price. To make a quantitative forecast about the impact of the ads on the level of potato sales, you simply substitute the new market price of 200 cents into either the demand or the supply function to obtain the new Q_E:

16

$$
\begin{gathered}
Q_d = Q_s = Q_E \\
40 - (0.05 \times 200) = -2 + (0.16 \times 200) = 30
\end{gathered}
$$

2.5 CEILING AND FLOOR PRICES

Shortages and surpluses *can* occur after a shift in demand or supply, but as we have stressed, these shortages and surpluses are sufficiently short in duration that they can reasonably be ignored in demand and supply analysis. In other words, markets are assumed to adjust fairly rapidly, and we concern ourselves

FIGURE 2.11
Ceiling and Floor Prices

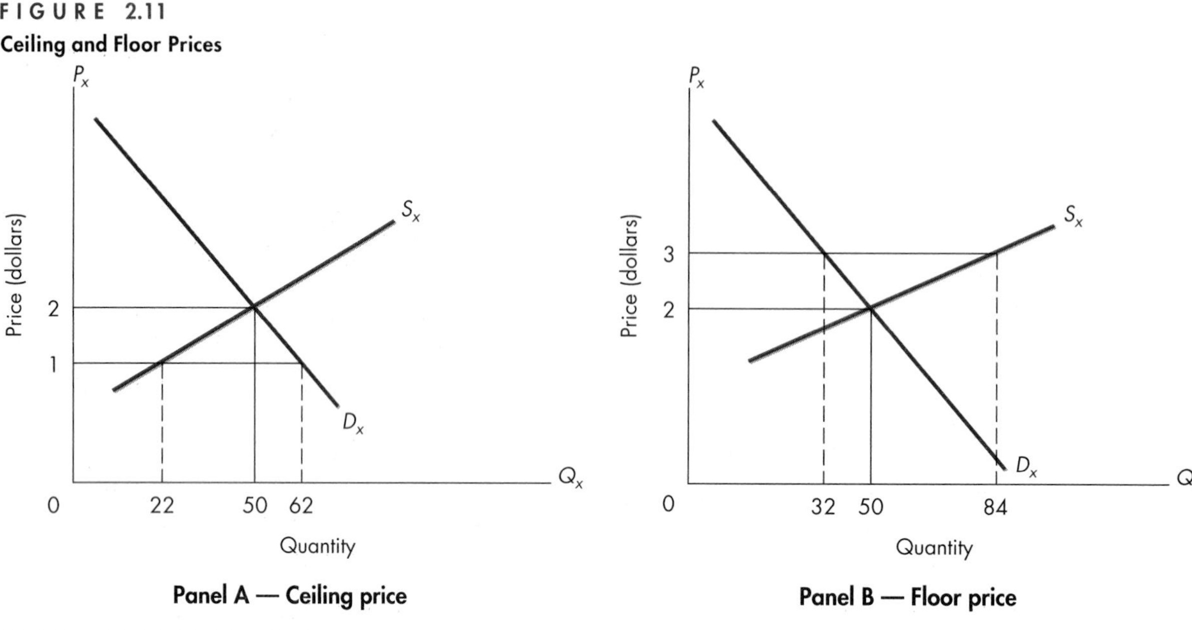

only with the comparison of equilibriums before and after a shift in supply or demand. There are, however, some types of shortages and surpluses that market forces do not eliminate. These are more permanent in nature and result from government interferences with the market mechanism, which prevent prices from freely moving up or down to clear the market.

Typically these more permanent shortages and surpluses are caused by government imposing legal restrictions on the movement of prices. Shortages and surpluses can be created simply by legislating a price below or above equilibrium. Governments have decided in the past, and will surely decide in the future, that the price of a particular commodity is "too high" or "too low" and will proceed to set a "fair price." Without evaluating the desirability of such interference, we can use demand and supply curves to analyze the economic effects of these two types of interference: the setting of minimum and maximum prices.

ceiling price
The maximum price the government permits sellers to charge for a good. When this price is below equilibrium, a shortage occurs.

If the government imposes a maximum price, or **ceiling price,** on a good, the effect is a shortage of that good. In Panel A of Figure 2.11, a ceiling price of \$1 is set on some good *X*. No one can legally sell *X* for more than \$1, and \$1 is less than the equilibrium (market clearing) price of \$2. At the ceiling price of \$1, the maximum amount that producers are willing to supply is 22 units. At \$1, consumers wish to purchase 62 units. A shortage of 40 units results from the imposition of the \$1 price ceiling. Market forces will not be permitted to bid up the price to eliminate the shortage because producers cannot sell the good for more than \$1. This type of shortage will continue until government eliminates the price ceiling or until shifts in either supply or demand cause the equilibrium price to fall to \$1 or lower. It is worth noting that "black" (illegal) markets usually arise in such cases. Some consumers are willing to pay more than \$1 for good *X* rather than do without it, and some producers are willing to sell good *X* for more than \$1 rather than forgo the extra sales. In most cases the law is not a sufficient deterrent to the illegal trade of a good at prices above the ceiling.

floor price
The minimum price the government permits sellers to charge for a good. When this price is above equilibrium, a surplus occurs.

Alternatively, the government may believe that the suppliers of the good are not earning as much income as they deserve and, therefore, sets a minimum price or **floor price.** You can see the results of such actions in Panel B of Figure 2.11. Dissatisfied with the equilibrium price of \$2 and equilibrium quantity of 50, the government sets a minimum price of \$3. Since the government cannot repeal the law of demand, consumers reduce the amount they purchase to 32 units. Producers, of course, are going to increase their production of *X* to 84 units in response to the \$3 price. Now a surplus of 52 units exists. Because the government is not allowing the price of *X* to fall, this surplus is going to continue until it is either eliminated by the government or demand or supply shifts cause market price to rise to \$3 or higher. In order for the government to ensure that producers do not illegally sell their surpluses for less than \$3, the government must either restrict the production of *X* to 32 units or be willing to buy (and store or destroy) the 52 surplus units.

This section can be summarized by the following principle:

Principle When the government sets a ceiling price below the equilibrium price, a shortage or excess demand results because consumers wish to buy more units of the good than producers are willing to sell at the ceiling price. If the government sets a floor price above the equilibrium price, a surplus or excess supply results because producers offer for sale more units of the good than buyers wish to consume at the floor price.

For managers to make successful decisions by watching for changes in economic conditions, they must be able to predict how these changes will affect the market. As we hope you have seen, this is precisely what economic analysis is designed to do. This ability to use economics to make predictions is one of the topics we will emphasize throughout the text.

2.6 SUMMARY

In this chapter we presented the basic framework of demand and supply analysis. The market was divided into two different groups of participants—consumers and producers. Demand analysis focuses on the behavior of consumers, while supply analysis examines the behavior of producers. The demand and supply curves together determine the price and output that occur in a market. The impact of changing market circumstances upon equilibrium price and output is determined by making the appropriate shifts in either demand or supply and comparing equilibriums before and after the change.

The generalized demand function specifies how the quantity demanded of a good is related to six variables that jointly determine the amount of a good or service consumers are willing and able to buy. By holding constant the five determinants of demand—income, the price of related goods, consumer tastes, expected price, and the number of consumers—and letting only the

FIGURE 2.12
Summary of Demand Shifts (supply constant) and Supply Shifts (demand constant)

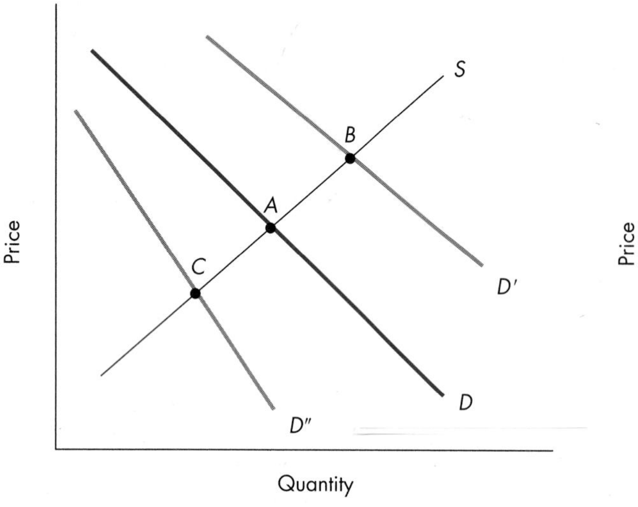

Panel A — Shifts in demand (supply constant)

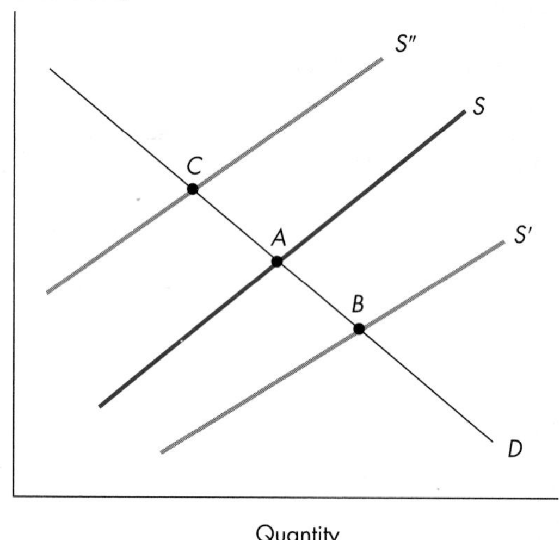

Panel B — Shifts in supply (demand constant)

price of the good vary, a demand function is derived. The law of demand states that quantity demanded and price are inversely related, all other variables influencing demand held constant. Whenever the price of a good changes, a "change in quantity demanded" occurs, which is represented by a movement along a fixed demand curve. A point on the demand curve shows either the maximum amount of a good that will be purchased if a given price is charged or the maximum price consumers will pay for a specific amount of the good.

The five determinants of demand (M, P_R, $\mathcal{T}$, P_e, and N) are also called the demand-shifting variables because their values determine the location of the demand curve. If any of these five variables changes, the demand curve shifts either leftward (demand decreases) or rightward (demand increases), and a change in demand is said to have occurred. Table 2.4 summarizes how demand curves shift when each of the determinants of demand changes value.

For producers, the generalized supply function shows how six variables—the price of the product, the price of inputs, the prices of goods related in production, the state of technology, the expected price of the good, and the number of firms—jointly determine the amount of a good or service producers are willing to supply. Quantity supplied and price are directly related, all other variables influencing supply held constant. When the price of a good changes, a change in quantity supplied occurs, which is represented by a movement along a fixed supply curve. A point on the supply curve shows either the maximum amount of a good that will be offered for sale at a given price or the minimum price (the supply price) necessary to induce producers voluntarily to offer a particular quantity for sale.

The five determinants of supply (P_I, P_r, T, P_e, and F) are also called the supply-shifting variables because their values determine the location of the supply curve. If any one of these five variables changes, the supply curve shifts either leftward (supply decreases) or rightward (supply increases), and a change in supply is said to have occurred. Table 2.8 summarizes how supply curves shift when each of the determinants of supply changes value.

The equilibrium price and quantity in a market are determined by the intersection of demand and supply curves. At the point of intersection, quantity demanded equals quantity supplied, and the market clears. Since the location of the demand and supply curves is determined by the five determinants of demand and the five determinants of supply, a change in any one of these 10 variables will result in a new equilibrium point. Figure 2.12 summarizes the results when either demand or supply shifts while the other curve remains constant. When demand increases and supply remains constant, price and quantity sold both rise, as shown by the movement from point *A* to *B* in Panel A of Figure 2.12. A decrease in demand, supply constant, causes both price and quantity sold to fall, as shown by the movement from point *A* to *C*. When supply increases and demand remains constant, price falls and quantity sold rises, as shown by the movement from point *A* to *B* in Panel B of Figure 2.12. A decrease in supply, demand constant, causes price to rise and quantity sold to fall, as shown by the movement from point *A* to *C* in Panel B.

When both supply and demand shift simultaneously, it is possible to predict either the direction in which price changes or the direction in which quantity changes, but not both. The change in equilibrium quantity or price is said to be indeterminate when the direction of change depends upon the relative magnitudes by which demand and supply shift. The four possible cases for simultaneous shifts in demand and supply are summarized in Figure 2.9.

Demand and supply analysis allows managers to make either qualitative or quantitative forecasts. A forecast is qualitative in nature when only the direction of change in market equilibrium is predicted. If enough quantitative information is available, managers can make quantitative forecasts to predict both the direction and magnitude of changes in equilibrium values of price and quantity. Never underestimate the value of qualitative forecasts. Correctly predicting the direction of change in price or sales can be an extremely valuable skill for any manager.

Sometimes the government imposes either a ceiling price or a floor price, which interferes with the market mechanism and prevents price from freely moving up or down to clear the market. When government sets a ceiling price below the equilibrium price, a shortage results because consumers wish to buy more of the good than producers are willing to sell at the ceiling price. If government sets a floor price above the equilibrium price, a surplus results because producers offer for sale more of the good than buyers wish to purchase at the higher floor price.

In this chapter we had two purposes. The first was to show you how managers can use economic theory to make predictions about the effect of exogenous events upon prices. We attempted to show what to expect about price and quantity in specific markets when certain variables change or are expected to change. As we will show in later chapters, the ability to make correct forecasts under difficult conditions separates good (successful) managers from those who are not so good (unsuccessful).

The second purpose was to prepare you for the material we will present in the following chapters. These chapters will show how demand and supply functions are derived from the behavior of consumers and firms and how these functions can be estimated. A thorough understanding of the material set forth in this chapter is essential to developing the ability to use and interpret demand and supply estimations and make accurate forecasts about the future.

TECHNICAL PROBLEMS

1. The generalized demand function for good *A* is

$$Q_d = 600 - 4P_A - 0.03\,M - 12P_B + 15\,\mathcal{T} + 6P_e + 1.5N$$

where Q_d = quantity demanded of good *A* each month, P_A = price of good *A*, M = average household income, P_B = price of related good *B*, $\mathcal{T}$ = a consumer taste index ranging in value from 0 to 10 (the highest rating), P_e = price consumers expect to pay next month for good *A*, and N = number of buyers in the market for good *A*.

a. Interpret the intercept parameter in the generalized demand function.

b. What is the value of the slope parameter for the price of good *A*? Does it have the correct algebraic sign? Why?

c. Interpret the slope parameter for income. Is good *A* normal or inferior? Explain.

d. Are goods *A* and *B* substitutes or complements? Explain. Interpret the slope parameter for the price of good *B*.

e. Are the algebraic signs on the slope parameters for $\mathcal{T}$, P_e, and N correct? Explain.
f. Calculate the quantity demanded of good A when $P_A = \$5$, $M = \$25{,}000$, $P_B = \$40$, $\mathcal{T} = 6.5$, $P_e = \$5.25$, and $N = 2{,}000$.

2. Consider the generalized demand function:

$$Q_d = 8{,}000 - 16P + 0.75M + 30P_R$$

a. Derive the equation for the demand function when $M = \$30{,}000$ and $P_R = \$50$.
b. Interpret the intercept and slope parameters of the demand function derived in part *a*.
c. Sketch a graph of the demand function in part *a*. Where does the demand function intersect the quantity-demanded axis? Where does it intersect the price axis?
d. Using the demand function from part *a*, calculate the quantity demanded when the price of the good is \$1,000 and when the price is \$1,500.
e. Derive the inverse of the demand function in part *a*. Using the inverse demand function, calculate the demand price for 24,000 units of the good. Give an interpretation of this demand price.

3. The demand curve for good X passes through the point $P = \$2$ and $Q_d = 35$. Give two interpretations of this point on the demand curve.
4. Recall that the generalized demand function for the demand curves in Figure 2.2 is

$$Q_d = 1800 - 20P + 0.6M - 50P_R$$

a. Derive the demand function for D_2 in Figure 2.2. Recall that for D_2 income is \$19,500 and the price of the related good is \$250.
b. Beginning with the demand curve D_2, suppose a decrease in income causes consumers to be willing and able to purchase 300 fewer units at each price. Sketch this new demand curve and label it D_3. What is the equation for D_3? By how much must income fall to cause the shift from D_2 to D_3?

5. Using a graph, explain carefully the difference between a movement along a demand curve and a shift in the demand curve.
6. What happens to *demand* when the following changes occur?
a. The price of the commodity falls.
b. Income increases and the commodity is normal.
c. Income increases and the commodity is inferior.
d. The price of a substitute good increases.
e. The price of a substitute good decreases.
f. The price of a complement good increases.
g. The price of a complement good decreases.

7. Consider the generalized supply function:

$$Q_s = 60 + 5P - 12P_I + 10F$$

where Q_s = quantity supplied, P = price of the commodity, P_I = price of a key input in the production process, and F = number of firms producing the commodity.
a. Interpret the slope parameters on P, P_I, and F.
b. Derive the equation for the supply function when $P_I = \$90$ and $F = 20$.
c. Sketch a graph of the supply function in part *b*. At what price does the supply

curve intersect the price axis? Give an interpretation of the price intercept of this supply curve.

d. Using the supply function from part *b*, calculate the quantity supplied when the price of the commodity is $300 and $500.

e. Derive the inverse of the supply function in part *b*. Using the inverse supply function, calculate the supply price for 680 units of the commodity. Give an interpretation of this supply price.

8. Suppose the supply curve for good X passes through the point $P = \$25$, $Q_s = 500$. Give two interpretations of this point on the supply curve.

9. The following generalized supply function shows the quantity of good X that producers offer for sale (Q_s):

$$Q_s = 19 + 20P_x - 10P_I + 6T - 32P_r - 20P_e + 5F$$

where P_x is the price of X, P_I is the price of labor, T is an index measuring the level of technology, P_r is the price of a good R that is related in production, P_e is the expected future price of good X, and F is the number of firms in the industry.

a. Determine the equation of the supply curve for X when $P_I = 8$, $T = 4$, $P_r = 4$, $P_e = 5$, and $F = 47$. Plot this supply curve on a graph.

b. Suppose the price of labor increases from 8 to 9. Find the equation of the new supply curve. Plot the new supply curve on a graph.

c. Is the good related in production a complement or a substitute in production? Explain.

d. What is the correct way to interpret each of the coefficients in the generalized supply function given above?

10. Using a graph, explain carefully the difference between a movement along a supply curve and a shift in the supply curve.

11. Other things remaining the same, what would happen to the *supply* of a particular commodity if the following changes occur?

a. The price of the commodity decreases.

b. A technological breakthrough enables the good to be produced at a significantly lower cost.

c. The prices of inputs used to produce the commodity increase.

d. The price of a commodity that is a substitute in production decreases.

e. The managers of firms that produce the good expect the price of the good to rise in the near future.

12. The table below presents the demand and supply schedules for apartments in a small U.S. city:

Monthly rental rate (dollars per month)	Quantity demanded (number of units per month)	Quantity supplied (number of units per month)
$300	130,000	35,000
350	115,000	37,000
400	100,000	41,000
450	80,000	45,000
500	72,000	52,000
550	60,000	60,000
600	55,000	70,000
650	48,000	75,000

a. If the monthly rental rate is \$600, excess ________ of ________ apartments per month will occur and rental rates can be expected to ________.
b. If the monthly rental rate is \$350, excess ________ of ________ apartments per month will occur and rental rates can be expected to ________.
c. The equilibrium or market clearing rental rate is \$________ per month.
d. The equilibrium number of apartments rented is ________ per month.

13. Suppose that the demand and supply functions for good X are

$$Q_d = 50 - 8P$$
$$Q_s = -17.5 + 10P$$

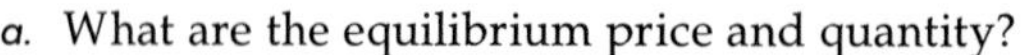

a. What are the equilibrium price and quantity?
b. What is the market outcome if price is \$2.75? What do you expect to happen? Why?
c. What is the market outcome if price is \$4.25? What do you expect to happen? Why?
d. What happens to equilibrium price and quantity if the demand function becomes $Q_d = 59 - 8P$?
e. What happens to equilibrium price and quantity if the supply function becomes $Q_s = -40 + 10P$ (demand is $Q_d = 50 - 8P$)?

14. Determine the effect upon equilibrium price and quantity sold if the following changes occur in a particular market:
a. Consumers' income increases and the good is normal.
b. The price of a substitute good (in consumption) increases.
c. The price of a substitute good (in production) increases.
d. The price of a complement good (in consumption) increases.
e. The price of inputs used to produce the good increases.
f. Consumers expect that the price of the good will increase in the near future.
g. It is widely publicized that consumption of the good is hazardous to health.
h. Cost-reducing technological change takes place in the industry.

15. Suppose that a pair of events from problem 14 occur simultaneously. For each of the pairs of events indicated below, perform a qualitative analysis to predict the direction of change in either the equilibrium price or the equilibrium quantity. Explain why the change in one of these two variables is indeterminate.
a. Both *a* and *h* in problem 14 occur simultaneously.
b. Both *d* and *e* in problem 14 occur simultaneously.
c. Both *d* and *h* in problem 14 occur simultaneously.
d. Both *f* and *c* in problem 14 occur simultaneously.

16. Suppose that the generalized demand function for good X is

$$Q_d = 60 - 2P_x + 0.01M + 7P_R$$

where

Q_d = quantity of X demanded
P_x = price of X
M = (average) consumer income
P_R = price of a related good R

a. Is good X normal or inferior? Explain.
b. Are goods X and R substitutes or complements? Explain.
Suppose that M = \$40,000 and P_R = \$20.

c. What is the demand function for good X?
Suppose the supply function is

$$Q_s = -600 + 10P_x$$

d. What are the equilibrium price and quantity?
e. What happens to equilibrium price and quantity if other things remain the same as in part *d* but income increases to $52,000?
f. What happens to equilibrium price and quantity if other things remain the same as in part *d* but the price of good R decreases to $14?
g. What happens to equilibrium price and quantity if other things remain the same, income and the price of the related goods are at their original levels, and supply shifts to $Q_s = -360 + 10P_x$?

17. In problem 12, suppose the city council decides rents are too high and imposes a rent ceiling of $400.
    a. The ceiling on rent causes a ________ of ________ apartments per month.
    b. How many *more* renters would have found an apartment in this city if the ceiling had not been imposed?
    Suppose that instead of imposing a ceiling price, the city council places a floor price of $600 on rental rates.
    c. The floor price on rent causes a ________ of ________ apartments per month.
18. Use the graph below to answer the following questions.

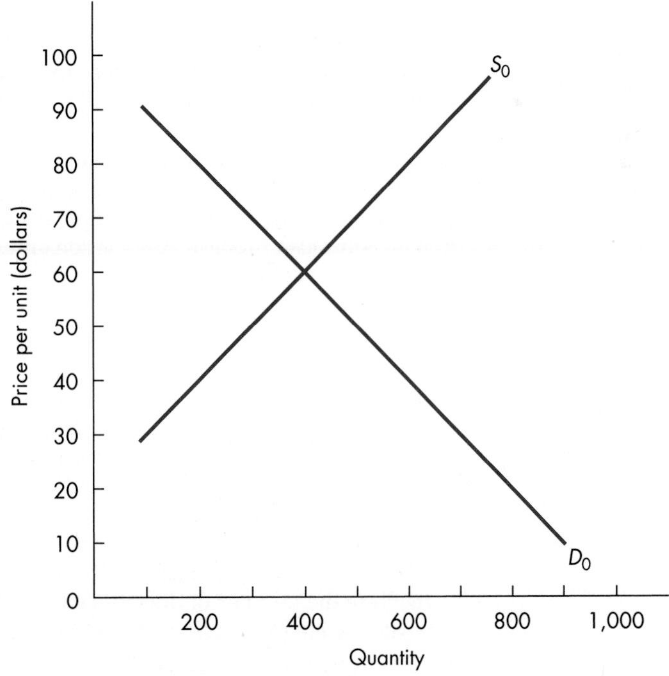

a. What is the equilibrium price and quantity?
b. What is the effect of a ceiling price of $40?
c. What is the effect of a floor price of $50? A floor price of $70?

d. Suppose income increases and consumers are willing and able to buy 100 more units at each price. Construct the new demand curve and label it D_1. What is the new equilibrium price and quantity?

e. Suppose input prices fall and suppliers are willing to offer for sale 200 more units at each price. Construct the new supply curve, and label it S_1. Suppose instead that when input prices fall, supply price falls by $20 for each level of output. Verify that the new supply curve is exactly the same in either case. What are the new equilibrium price and output when the supply and demand curves are Q_1 and S_1?

APPLIED PROBLEMS

1. Suppose you are the manager of a California winery. How would you expect the following events to affect the price you receive for a bottle of wine?
   a. The price of comparable French wines decreases.
   b. One hundred new wineries open in California.
   c. The unemployment rate in the United States decreases.
   d. The price of cheese increases.
   e. The price of a glass bottle increases significantly due to new government antishatter regulations.
   f. Researchers discover a new wine-making technology that reduces production costs.
   g. The price of wine vinegar, which is made from the leftover grape mash, increases.
   h. The average age of consumers increases, and older people drink less wine.
2. Citrus Speculation and Forecasting, Inc., has been hired by a private consortium of orange growers to predict what will happen to the price and output of oranges under the conditions below. What are your predictions?
   a. A major freeze destroys a large number of the orange trees in Florida.
   b. The scientists in the agricultural extension service of the University of Florida discover a way to double the number of oranges produced by each orange tree.
   c. The American Medical Association announces that orange juice can reduce the risk of heart attack.
   d. The price of grapefruit falls.
3. Morgan Realty is considering investing in an apartment complex in Tampa. After considerable research, managers at Morgan Realty discover some events that may influence their decision to buy. Tampa is growing steadily. Inflation is running at about 5 to 7 percent, but wages in Tampa are not keeping up. The rate of interest has risen to about 10 percent, but, because of the easy money policy undertaken by the Federal Reserve System, most authorities expect the interest rate to fall. Various new service-oriented industries, which will employ a large proportion of white-collar workers, are moving to the city. Finally, the University of South Florida in Tampa is undertaking a massive dormitory construction project, which is expected to increase the number of dormitory rooms by 45 percent over the next two years. Analyze the effect of each of these influences on the demand for apartments in Tampa.
4. Several economics faculty members were standing in line in the student union cafeteria for lunch. One was heard to say, "I sure wish the union would raise their food prices." The others agreed. What in the world would motivate such a wish?

5. In October 1990, rising jet fuel prices led most major U.S. airlines to raise fares by a total of 15.3 percent after the August invasion of Kuwait by Saddam Hussein. Explain how this substantial increase in airfares would affect the following:
   a. The demand for air travel
   b. The demand for hotels
   c. The demand for rental cars
   d. The supply of overnight mail
6. Toys-Were-Us, a toy retailing company, has just filed for protection under Chapter 11 bankruptcy law. Apparently management frequently raised toy prices when they should have been reduced and cut prices when they should have been raised. How would managers know when the firm's prices are too high? How would they know if the prices were too low?
7. Some firms experience extreme seasonal fluctuations in the demand for their goods or services. Some examples are air-conditioning repair services, toy retailers, and tax accounting firms.
   a. What problems would evolve from such seasonal fluctuations in demand?
   b. What can managers of such types of firms do to help solve these problems?
   c. Would the problem and/or solutions be different if the extreme fluctuations in demand were not seasonal or regular? An example might be a firm that manufactures a product for which demand is extremely sensitive to general economic conditions.
8. Suppose you are a stock market analyst specializing in the stocks of theme parks, and you are examining Disneyland's stock. *The Wall Street Journal* reports that tourism has slowed down in the United States. At Six Flags Magic Mountain in Valencia, California, a new Viper roller coaster is now operating and another new ride, Psyclone, will be opening this year. Using demand and supply analysis, predict the impact of these events on ticket prices and attendance at Disneyland. As reported in *The Wall Street Journal,* Disneyland slashed ticket prices and admitted that attendance was somewhat lower. Is this consistent with your prediction using demand and supply analysis? In light of the fact that both price and output were falling at Disneyland, is the law of demand being violated in the world of fantasy?
9. The Council on Economic Priorities recently published "Shopping for a Better World," a guide that rates 168 companies on their social performance. The aim of the council is to "make progressive policies profitable" by informing consumers about such questions as which pasta producer also makes cigarettes, which companies have women in executive management positions, which companies give to charity, and so on. Using demand and supply analysis, explain how disseminating this type of information can translate into higher profits for "socially responsible" firms.
10. California voters, in an attempt to halt the rapid increase in the state's automobile insurance rates, approved Proposition 103. The measure proposes to roll back auto insurance rates by 20 percent and freeze them for at least a year. Using a graph, show the impact of Proposition 103 on the market for automobile insurance in California. As the costs of providing insurance continue to rise, what do you predict will happen over time in the California market for auto insurance? How would your prediction change if Proposition 103 is defeated?
11. In January 1993, *The Wall Street Journal* reported that recent law school graduates were having a very difficult time obtaining jobs in the legal profession. Many law

schools said that 10 to 20 percent of their 1992 graduates still had not found jobs. The historical average had been 6 to 8 percent. Many recent graduates were taking jobs outside law at much lower wages than were typically paid to beginning lawyers. Based on this information, what would be your prediction about lawyers' salaries for the future? The next year? The next six years?

12. Construct a graph showing equilibrium in the market for movie tickets. Label both axes and denote the initial equilibrium price and quantity as P_0 and Q_0. For each of the following events, draw an appropriate new supply or demand curve for movies, and predict the impact of the event on the market price of a movie ticket and the number of tickets sold in the new equilibrium situation:
    a. Movie theaters double the price of soft drinks and popcorn.
    b. A national video rental chain cuts its rental rate by 25 percent.
    c. Cable television begins offering pay-per-view movies.
    d. The screenwriters' guild ends a 10-month strike.
    e. Kodak reduces the price it charges Hollywood producers for motion picture film.
13. An article in *Business Week* (May 19, 1997) reported the discovery of a new processing technology which makes it economically feasible to turn natural gas into a liquid petroleum that yields superclean gasoline, diesel fuel, or any other product derived from crude oil. This discovery represents 770 billion barrels of oil equivalent, "enough to slake the world's thirst for oil for 29 years."
    a. Using demand and supply analysis, explain why this new process will *not* cause a surplus of crude oil. If no surplus is created, then what will be the impact of this process on the market for crude oil?
    b. Had this process *not* been discovered, explain why we still would have had "enough" crude oil to meet the growing worldwide demand for crude oil.
14. According to an article in *The Wall Street Journal,* many cities were reporting a substantial decrease in the amount of garbage being collected after they changed from levying a tax on each household to pay for the pickup to charging a fee for each bag or can picked up. Would this have been the result of a change in demand? If so why, or if not, why not? If not, what was the probable reason?
15. Firewood prices in places from northern California to Boston and suburban New Jersey have remained steady even though the supply of firewood has been diminished by environmental restrictions on cutting. *The Wall Street Journal* (January 4, 1996) reports that sales of gas fireplaces are outpacing sales of wood-burning hearths and that "people are burning less and less wood." Use supply and demand analysis to show why firewood prices are not rising while the quantity of firewood burned is declining. (*Hint:* Allow for simultaneous shifts in the demand and supply of firewood.)

MATHEMATICAL APPENDIX Demand and Supply—The Linear Case

This appendix presents a mathematical analysis of demand and supply when both demand and supply are linear functions. The analytic tools required in this appendix, as well as in the mathematical appendixes in later chapters, are basic high school algebra and some fundamental concepts from calculus. The student workbook that accompanies this textbook provides a brief review of the mathematical tools employed in the mathematical appendixes in this book.

The Generalized Linear Demand Function

The linear form of the generalized demand function can be expressed as

(1) $$Q_d = a + bP + cM + dP_R$$

where Q_d is the quantity demanded per unit of time, P is the price per unit of the good or service, M is a measure of consumer income, and P_R is the price of the good or service related in consumption. To keep mathematical notation and expressions as simple as possible, only two of the five demand-shifting variables discussed in Chapter 2 are included in equation (1). The parameters a, b, c, and d have the following algebraic signs:

- *a:* The intercept parameter gives the value of Q_d if P, M, and P_R are all equal to zero simultaneously. Since quantity demanded must be a nonnegative value, a is restricted to being greater than or equal to zero ($a \geq 0$).
- *b:* The slope parameter for the price of the good, b, measures the rate of change in Q_d as price changes, holding the other variables that affect Q_d constant. Consequently, b can be interpreted as the partial derivative $\partial Q_d/\partial P$. The law of demand stipulates that Q_d and P are inversely related, thus b must be negative ($b < 0$).
- *c:* The slope parameter for consumer income, c, measures the rate of change in Q_d as income changes, holding all other variables constant. If the good or service is normal (inferior), then $\partial Q_d/\partial M$ will be positive (negative).
- *d:* The slope parameter for the price of a related good or service, d, measures the rate of change in Q_d as P_R changes, all else constant. If the related good or service is a substitute (complement), then $\partial Q_d/\partial P_R$ will be positive (negative).

Each of the partial derivatives (b, c, and d) is constant because the demand function is linear in functional form.

The Generalized Linear Supply Function

The linear form of the generalized supply function can be expressed as

(2) $$Q_s = h + kP + lP_I + sF$$

where Q_s is the quantity supplied per unit of time, P is the price per unit of the good, P_1 is the price of an input used in producing the good, and F is the number of firms in the industry. Again to keep mathematical expressions simple, we include only two of the five supply-shifting variables discussed in Chapter 2. The parameters h, k, l, and s have the following signs:

- *h:* The intercept parameter gives the value of Q_s if P, P_I, and F are all equal to zero simultaneously. The intercept parameter for the generalized supply curve (h) does not have any particular economic interpretation and can be positive, negative, or zero.
- *k:* The slope parameter for the price of the good, k, measures the rate of change in Q_s as price changes, holding the other variables that affect Q_s constant. Consequently, k can be interpreted as the partial derivative $\partial Q_s/\partial P$, and k cannot be negative ($k \geq 0$).
- *l:* The slope parameter for the price of an input, l, measures the rate of change in Q_s as the price of the input changes, holding all other variables constant. All other things equal, an increase (decrease) in input prices causes producers to decrease (increase) the amount of the good offered for sale, and thus $\partial Q_s/\partial P_I$ is negative.*
- *s:* The slope parameter for the number of firms, s, measures the rate of change in Q_s as the number of firms changes, holding all other variables constant. All other things equal, an increase in the number of firms causes the amount of the good offered for sale to increase, and thus $\partial Q_s/\partial F$ is positive.

As for the linear demand function, each of the partial derivatives (k, l, and s) is constant because the supply function is linear in form.

Derivation of Demand and Supply Functions

When all variables other than P are held constant in the generalized demand and supply functions, the ordinary demand and supply functions can be expressed as a function of price only:

---

*In most cases, more than one input price influences quantity supplied. For example, if three inputs are used in production, the generalized linear supply function can be expressed as $Q_s = h + kP + l_1P_{I1} + l_2P_{I2} + l_3P_{I3} + sF$. The slope parameters l_1, l_2, and l_3 are all negative.

(3) $$Q_d = f(P)$$

(4) $$Q_s = g(P)$$

To obtain demand and supply equations (3) and (4), respectively, all the variables other than P—often referred to as "shift variables"—are set equal to constant values (M', P'_R, P'_I, and F') in the generalized demand and supply functions:

$$Q_d = a + bP + cM' + dP'_R$$
$$Q_s = h + kP + lP'_I + sF'$$

The constant terms in each function may be grouped together as

(5), (6) $$A = a + cM' + dP'_R \quad \text{and} \quad H = h + lP'_I + sF'$$

which form the intercept parameters of the ordinary demand and supply functions:

(3′) $$Q_d = f(P) = A + bP$$

(4′) $$Q_s = g(P) = H + kP$$

When a change in M or P_R causes the value of A to change, a new demand equation results, and the graph of the demand equation—called the demand curve—shifts parallel to the original demand curve. (Why is the shift parallel?) For supply, a change in P_I or F causes H to change, and the supply curve shifts parallel to the original supply curve. It should be clear from inspecting equations (5) and (6) that shifts in demand or supply curves happen when changes in the values of one (or more) of the shift variables occur.

Inverse Demand and Supply Functions

The inverse of a function $y = f(x)$ can be expressed as $x = f^{-1}(y)$. Using this notation, the inverse demand and supply functions can be expressed as

(7) $$P = f^{-1}(Q_d) = -\frac{A}{b} + \frac{1}{b}Q_d$$

(8) $$P = g^{-1}(Q_s) = -\frac{H}{k} + \frac{1}{k}Q_s$$

When following the convention in economics of plotting P on the vertical axis and Q_d and Q_s on the horizontal axis, the demand and supply curves represent the *inverse* demand and supply equations. When price is graphed on the vertical axis and quantity on the horizontal axis, $-A/b$ and $-H/k$ are the price (vertical) intercepts for the demand and supply curves, respectively. The slopes of the demand and supply curves, when P is on the vertical axis and Q_d and Q_s are on the horizontal axis, are $1/b$ and $1/k$, respectively.

Market Equilibrium

The price at which the market reaches equilibrium or "clears" is the price for which $Q_d = Q_s$. To find equilibrium price, set $Q_d = Q_s$ and solve for P_E:

(9) $$A + bP_E = H + kP_E$$
$$P_E = \frac{A - H}{k - b} = P_E(b, k, A, H)$$

To solve for equilibrium output, Q_E, substitute P_E into either $Q_d = f(P)$ or $Q_s = g(P)$. Substituting equation (9) into (3′) yields the solution for Q_E:

(10) $$Q_E = A + bP_E = A + b\left(\frac{A - H}{k - b}\right)$$
$$= \frac{Ak - bH}{k - b} = Q_E(b, k, A, H)$$

The equilibrium values of both price and quantity are determined by the slopes of both demand and supply as well as the values of *all* the shift parameters in demand *and* supply.

Calculating the Change in P_E and Q_E

In this section, changes in equilibrium price and quantity are examined using the total differentials of P_E and Q_E. Three situations are examined: (1) demand shifts while supply remains unchanged, (2) supply shifts while demand remains unchanged, and (3) both demand and supply shift simultaneously. All three situations can be analyzed using the following total differentials of equations (9) and (10):

(11) $$dP_E = \frac{\partial P_E}{\partial A}\frac{\partial A}{\partial M'}dM' + \frac{\partial P_E}{\partial A}\frac{\partial A}{\partial P'_R}dP'_R + \frac{\partial P_E}{\partial H}\frac{\partial H}{\partial P'_I}dP'_I + \frac{\partial P_E}{\partial H}\frac{\partial H}{\partial F'}dF$$

(12) $$dQ_E = \frac{\partial Q_E}{\partial A}\frac{\partial A}{\partial M'}dM' + \frac{\partial Q_E}{\partial A}\frac{\partial A}{\partial P'_R}dP'_R + \frac{\partial Q_E}{\partial H}\frac{\partial H}{\partial P'_I}dP'_I + \frac{\partial Q_E}{\partial H}\frac{\partial H}{\partial F'}dF$$

A shift in demand (supply constant)

When one of the two demand-shifting variables in equation (3) changes value, demand shifts and new equilibrium values for price and quantity result. Suppose a change in income causes demand to shift while supply remains constant. This situation can be imposed on the differentials of P_E and Q_E by noting that $dP'_R = dP'_I = dF' = 0$, and thus for the linear demand and supply equations

$$(13) \qquad dP_E = \frac{\partial P_E}{\partial A}\frac{\partial A}{\partial M'}dM' = \frac{1}{k-b}c\,dM'$$

$$(14) \qquad dQ_E = \frac{\partial Q_E}{\partial A}\frac{\partial A}{\partial M'}dM' = \frac{k}{k-b}c\,dM'$$

Since $k - b$ is positive, dP_E and dM' have the same sign when the good is normal ($c > 0$). If the good is inferior, ($c < 0$), dP_E and dM' have opposite signs. Similarly for dQ_E, $k/(k - b)$ is positive, and thus Q_E and M' move in the same (opposite) direction when the good is normal (inferior).

Recall that the shift in demand from D_0 to D_1 in Figure 2.6 is caused by an increase in income from \$20,000 to \$20,500. Thus, $dM' = 500$. Substituting the values of the slope parameters for price from the demand and supply equations ($b = -20$ and $k = 10$) and the slope parameter for income ($c = 0.6$) into the differentials (13) and (14) yields

$$dP_E = \frac{1}{10-(-20)}\cdot 0.6\cdot 500 = +10$$

$$dQ_E = \frac{10}{10-(-20)}\cdot 0.6\cdot 500 = +100$$

Moving from point A to B in Figure 2.6 requires an increase in equilibrium price of \$10 and an increase in equilibrium quantity of 100 units.

A shift in supply (demand constant)

When one of the two supply-shifting variables in equation (4) changes value, supply shifts and new equilibrium values for price and quantity result. Suppose a change in the price of an input causes supply to shift while demand remains constant. This situation can be imposed on the differentials of P_E and Q_E by setting $dP'_R = dM' = dF' = 0$, and thus for the linear demand and supply equations

$$(15) \qquad dP_E = \frac{\partial P_E}{\partial H}\frac{\partial H}{\partial P'_I}dP'_I = -\frac{1}{k-b}l\,dP'_I$$

$$(16) \qquad dQ_E = \frac{\partial Q_E}{\partial H}\frac{\partial H}{\partial P'_I}dP'_I = -\frac{b}{k-b}l\,dP'_I$$

Since $-\frac{1}{k-b}$ is negative and l is negative, dP_E and dP'_I always have the same sign. When demand is constant, an increase (decrease) in the price of an input price always increases (decreases) the equilibrium price of the good or service. The opposite result holds for the change in Q_E. Since $-\frac{b}{k-b}$ is positive and l is negative, Q_E and P'_I move in opposite directions.

Simultaneous changes in both demand and supply

In this section one demand-shifting variable and one supply-shifting variable both change values simultaneously. Examination of the appropriate total differentials reveals that the direction of change in one of the equilibrium variables P_E or Q_E can be determined (with information about whether a good is normal or inferior or a substitute or complement good), but the direction of change in the other equilibrium variable cannot be determined—its change is indeterminate.

Turning first to a general analysis, suppose income increases while the price of a key ingredient falls, and all other things remain constant. The appropriate total differentials are found by setting $dP'_R = dF' = 0$ in equations (11) and (12):

$$(17) \qquad dP_E = \frac{\partial P_E}{\partial A}\frac{\partial A}{\partial M'}dM' + \frac{\partial P_E}{\partial H}\frac{\partial H}{\partial P'_I}dP'_I = \frac{1}{k-b}\cdot c\cdot dM' + -\frac{1}{k-b}\cdot l\cdot dP'_I$$

$$(18) \qquad dQ_E = \frac{\partial Q_E}{\partial A}\frac{\partial A}{\partial M'}dM' + \frac{\partial Q_E}{\partial H}\frac{\partial H}{\partial P'_I}dP'_I = \frac{k}{k-b}\cdot c\cdot dM' + -\frac{b}{k-b}\cdot l\cdot dP'_I$$

To illustrate the application of these two differentials, consider the generalized demand and supply functions presented in Chapter 2 and graphed in Figures 2.4 and 2.6. Let income increase from \$20,000 to \$20,500 ($dM' = 500$). Also let the price of the input decrease from \$50 to \$31.25 ($dP'_I = -18.75$). You know from reading Chapter 2 that when both demand and supply increase (as they do here), the change in equilibrium price will be indeterminate and the change in equilibrium quantity will be positive.

To verify that the change in P_E depends upon the magnitude of the changes in M' and P'_I, first find the signs of the coefficients for dM' and dP'_I. Since the good is normal in this example, c is positive, $\frac{c}{k-b}$ is positive, and the expression $\frac{c}{k-b}\,dM'$ is positive. Since l is negative, $-\frac{l}{k-b}$ is positive, and the expression $-\frac{l}{k-b}\,dP'_I$ is

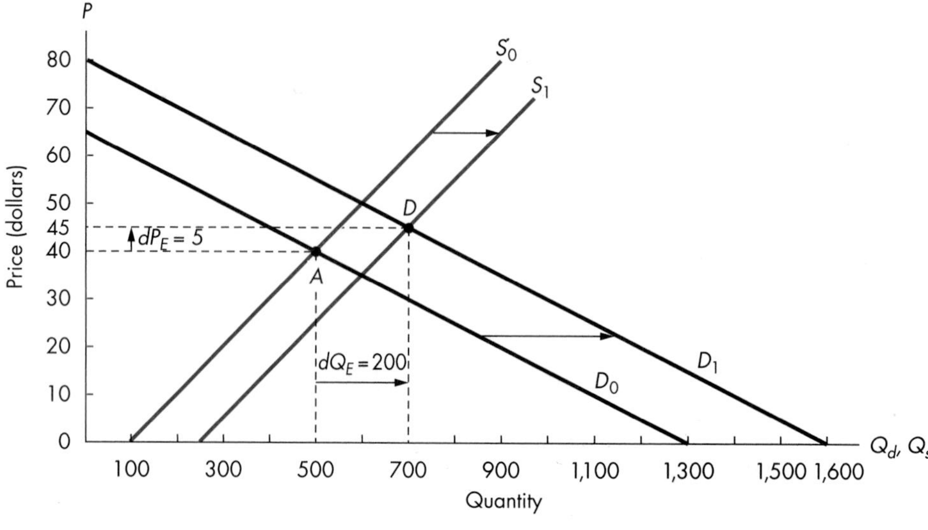

FIGURE 2A.1
Simultaneous Shifts in Demand and Supply: $dM' = 500$ and $dP_I' = -18.75$

negative. The two terms in the differential have opposite signs, and the differential dP_E cannot be signed. It follows that the change in P_E is indeterminate and depends upon the relative magnitudes of dM' and dP_I'.

It is easy to verify that the change in Q_E is definitely positive. Since c is positive, $\frac{ck}{k-b}$ is positive, and the expression $\frac{ck}{k-b}\,dM'$ is positive. Since l is negative, $-\frac{lb}{k-b}$ is negative, and the expression $-\frac{lb}{k-b}\,dP_I'$ is positive. Both terms in dQ_E are positive, so dQ_E is definitely positive regardless of the magnitudes of the changes in M' and P_I'.

Using the parameter values from D_0 and S_0, the changes in P_E and Q_E can be calculated as

$$dP_E = \frac{0.6}{10-(-20)}(500) + -\left(\frac{-8}{10-(-20)}\right)(-18.75)$$
$$= 10 + -5 = 5$$

$$dQ_E = \frac{0.6 \cdot 10}{10-(-20)}(500) + -\left(\frac{-8 \cdot -20}{10-(-20)}\right)(-18.75)$$
$$= 100 + 100 = 200$$

Figure 2A.1 shows the initial equilibrium point A and the simultaneous shifts in demand and supply that result in new equilibrium point D. As the figure shows, the simultaneous shifts from D_0 to D_1 and from S_0 to S_1 result in a \$5 increase in equilibrium price and a 200-unit increase in equilibrium quantity.

MATHEMATICAL EXERCISES

1. For linear demand and supply functions, changes in the values of any of the determinants of demand (M, P_R, $\mathcal{T}$, P_e, N) or determinants of supply (P_I, P_r, T, P_e, F) cause *parallel* shifts in demand or supply, respectively. Explain why these shifts are always parallel for linear demand and supply functions.
2. The generalized demand and supply functions for a good are determined to be

$$Q_d = 400 - 25P + 0.4M + 24P_R$$
$$Q_s = 48 + 12P - 20P_I + 20F$$

a. Initially $M = \$61{,}140$ and $P_R = \$6$. Find the equation for the demand function, D_0.
b. Find the inverse demand function.
c. Initially $P_I = \$25$ and $F = 22$. Find the equation for the supply function, S_0.
d. Find the inverse supply function.
e. If a price ceiling of $600 is imposed, does a shortage or surplus result? How much?
f. Solve for P_E and Q_E.

Now let the number of firms increase to 133.

g. Find the new supply function. What is the new equilibrium?
h. Calculate the change in P_E and Q_E using differentials. Comparing parts *f* and *g*, do the values of dP_E and dQ_E match the change in equilibrium values of price and output?

3. Consider the generalized demand and supply functions for good X:

$$Q_d = 800 - 2P - 0.01M + 16P_y$$
$$Q_s = 50 + 4P - 40P_I + 51F$$

a. Good X is a(n) ______ good. Goods X and Y are ______.

Suppose income is initially $20,000, the price of good Y is $10, the price of the input is $25, and the number of firms producing good X is 20.

b. Write the equations for demand and supply. What are price and quantity in initial equilibrium?

Now let the price of the related good Y increase to $50 and the price of the input increase to $36. Assume these two events occur simultaneously.

c. Find algebraic expressions for dP_E and dQ_E. Determine the algebraic signs of dP_E and dQ_E. Which panel in Figure 2.9 represents this situation?
d. Calculate numerical values for the change in P_E and Q_E using the differentials from part *c*. Now find the new equilibrium price and quantity. Do the computed values of dP_E and dQ_E match the change in price and quantity between parts *b* and *c*?

CHAPTER 3

Elasticity and Demand

Most managers agree that the toughest decision they face is the decision to raise or lower the price of their firms' products. In 1997 Walt Disney Company decided to raise ticket prices at its theme parks in Anaheim, California, and Orlando, Florida. Even though the price hike caused attendance at the Disney parks to fall, the price increase was a success because it boosted Disney's revenue—the price of a ticket multiplied by the number of tickets sold.[1] For Disney, the higher ticket price more than offset the smaller number of tickets purchased, and revenue increased. You might be surprised to learn that price increases do not always increase a firm's revenue. For example, suppose just one gasoline producer, Exxon, were to increase the price of its brand of gasoline while rival gasoline producers left their gasoline prices unchanged. Exxon would likely experience falling revenue, even though it increased its price, because many Exxon customers would switch to one of the many other brands of gasoline. In this situation, the reduced amount of gasoline sold would more than offset the higher price of gasoline, and Exxon would find its revenue falling.

When managers *lower* price to attract more buyers, revenues may either rise or fall, again depending upon how responsive consumers are to a price reduction. For example, in its 1997 marketing strategy, called "Campaign 55," McDonald's Corporation lowered the price of its Big Mac and Quarter Pounders to 55 cents in an effort to increase revenue. The price reduction resulted in *lower* revenue, and McDonald's abandoned the low-price strategy for all but its breakfast meals—lower prices did increase breakfast revenues.[2] Obviously, managers need to know how a price increase or decrease is going to affect the revenue of the firm. In this chapter you will learn how to use the concept of demand elasticity to predict how revenue will be affected by a change in the price of the product.

Managers recognize that quantity demanded and price are inversely related. When they are making pricing decisions, as you saw in the examples of Disney, Exxon, and McDonald's, it is even more important for managers to know *by how*

---

[1]See Stacy Kravetz, "Disney's Earnings, Boosted by Park, Top Expectations," *The Wall Street Journal*, July 23, 1997, p. B5.

[2]See Richard Gibson, "With Egg on Its Face, McDonald's Cuts the 55-Cent Specials to Breakfast Only," *The Wall Street Journal*, June 4, 1997, p. B7.

much sales will change for a given change in price. A 10 percent decrease in price that leads to a 2 percent increase in quantity demanded differs greatly in effect from a 10 percent decrease in price that causes a 50 percent increase in quantity demanded. There is a substantial difference in the effect on total revenue to the firm between these two responses to a change in price. Certainly, when making pricing decisions, managers should have a good idea about how responsive consumers will be to any price changes and whether revenues will rise or fall.

The majority of this chapter is devoted to the concept of *demand elasticity,* a measure of the responsiveness of quantity demanded to a change in price along a demand curve and an indicator of the effect of a price change on total consumer expenditure on a product. The concept of demand elasticity provides managers, economists, and policymakers with a framework for understanding why consumers in some markets are extremely responsive to changes in price while consumers in other markets are not. This understanding is useful in many types of managerial decisions. As noted, demand elasticity is so crucial to managerial decision making that we have devoted most of this chapter to examining this concept.

We will begin by defining the coefficient of demand elasticity and then show how to use demand elasticities to find the percentage changes in price or quantity that result from movements along a demand curve. Next, the relation between elasticity and the total revenue received by firms from the sale of a product is examined in detail. Then we discuss three factors that determine the degree of responsiveness of consumers, and hence the elasticity of demand. We also show how to compute the elasticity of demand either over an interval or at a point on demand and how to compute and use two other important elasticities—income and cross-price elasticities. The last section of this chapter introduces the concept of marginal revenue and demonstrates the relation among demand, marginal revenue, and elasticity.

3.1 THE COEFFICIENT OF DEMAND ELASTICITY

demand elasticity
A measure of the responsiveness of consumers to changes in the price of a good.

coefficient of demand elasticity (*E*)
The percentage change in quantity demanded, divided by the percentage change in price. *E* is always a negative number because *P* and *Q* are inversely related.

As noted above, **demand elasticity** measures the responsiveness or sensitivity of consumers to changes in the price of a good or service. Demand elasticity is sometimes referred to as *price elasticity* or *own-price elasticity* to distinguish this elasticity from income and cross-price elasticities—two other elasticities we will examine later in this chapter. We will begin this section by presenting a formal (mathematical) definition of demand elasticity and then show how demand elasticity can be used to predict the change in sales when price rises or falls or to predict the percentage reduction in price needed to stimulate sales by a given percentage amount.

Consumer responsiveness to a price change is measured by the **coefficient of demand elasticity (*E*)**, defined as

$$E = \frac{\%\Delta Q}{\%\Delta P} = \frac{\text{Percentage change in quantity demanded}}{\text{Percentage change in price}}$$

TABLE 3.1

The Coefficient of Demand Elasticity (E)

$$E = \frac{\%\Delta Q}{\%\Delta P}$$

Elasticity	Responsiveness	Coefficient of demand elasticity
Elastic	$\lvert\%\Delta Q\rvert > \lvert\%\Delta P\rvert$	$\lvert E\rvert > 1$
Unitary elastic	$\lvert\%\Delta Q\rvert = \lvert\%\Delta P\rvert$	$\lvert E\rvert = 1$
Inelastic	$\lvert\%\Delta Q\rvert < \lvert\%\Delta P\rvert$	$\lvert E\rvert < 1$

Note: The symbol "| |" denotes the absolute value.

Since price and quantity demanded are inversely related by the law of demand, the numerator and denominator always have opposite algebraic signs, and the coefficient of demand elasticity is always negative. The elasticity coefficient is calculated for movements along a given demand curve (or function) as price changes and all other factors affecting quantity demanded are held constant. Suppose a 10 percent price decrease ($\%\Delta P = -10\%$) causes consumers to increase their purchases by 30 percent ($\%\Delta Q = +30\%$). The coefficient of demand elasticity is equal to -3 ($= +30\%/-10\%$) in this case. In contrast, if the 10 percent decrease in price causes only a 5 percent increase in sales, the elasticity coefficient would equal -0.5 ($= +5\%/-10\%$). Clearly, the smaller (absolute) value of E indicates less sensitivity on the part of consumers to a change in price.

elastic
Segment of demand for which $|E| > 1$.

inelastic
Segment of demand for which $|E| < 1$.

unitary elastic
Segment of demand for which $|E| = 1$.

When a change in price causes consumers to respond so strongly that the percentage by which they adjust their consumption *exceeds* (in absolute value) the percentage change in price, demand is said to be **elastic** over that price interval. In mathematical terms, demand is elastic when $|\%\Delta Q|$ exceeds $|\%\Delta P|$, and thus $|E|$ is greater than 1. When a change in price causes consumers to respond so weakly that the percentage by which they adjust their consumption is *less than* (in absolute value) the percentage change in price, demand is said to be **inelastic** over that price interval. In other words, demand is inelastic when the numerator is smaller than the denominator (in absolute value), and thus $|E|$ is less than 1. In the special instance in which the percentage change in quantity *just equals* the percentage change in price (in absolute value), demand is said to be **unitary elastic,** and $|E|$ is equal to 1. Table 3.1 summarizes this discussion.

Suppose a manager knows the coefficient of demand elasticity for a company's product is equal to -2.5 over the range of prices currently being considered by the firm's marketing department. The manager is considering decreasing price by 8 percent and wishes to predict the percentage by which quantity demanded will increase. From the definition of the coefficient of demand elasticity, it follows that

$$-2.5 = \frac{\%\Delta Q}{-8\%}$$

so

$$-2.5 \times -8\% = \%\Delta Q$$

and

$$\%\Delta Q = +20\%$$

Thus, the manager can increase sales by 20 percent by lowering price 8 percent.

Alternatively, suppose a manager of a different firm faces a coefficient of demand elasticity equal to −0.5 over the range of prices the firm would consider charging for its product. This manager wishes to stimulate sales by 15 percent. The manager is willing to lower price to accomplish the increase in sales but needs to know the percentage amount by which price must be lowered to obtain the 15 percent increase in sales. Again using the definition of the coefficient of demand elasticity, it follows that

$$-0.5 = \frac{+15\%}{\%\Delta P}$$

so

$$\begin{aligned}\%\Delta P &= 15\%/-0.5 \\ &= -30\%\end{aligned}$$

Thus, this manager must lower price by 30 percent in order to increase sales by 15 percent.

As you can see, the concept of demand elasticity is rather simple. Demand elasticity is nothing more than a mathematical measure of how sensitive quantity demanded is to changes in price. We will now apply the concept of demand elasticity to a crucial question facing managers. How does a change in the price of the firm's product affect the total revenue received?

3.2 ELASTICITY AND TOTAL REVENUE

total revenue (*TR*) The total amount paid to producers for a good or service ($TR = P \times Q$).

Managers of firms, as well as industry analysts, government policymakers, and academic researchers, are frequently interested in how total revenue changes when there is a movement along the demand curve. **Total revenue (*TR*)**, which also equals the total expenditure by consumers on the commodity, is simply the price of the commodity times quantity demanded, or

$$TR = P \times Q$$

As we have emphasized, price and quantity demanded move in opposite directions along a demand curve: if price rises, quantity falls; if price falls, quantity rises. The change in price and the change in quantity have opposite effects on total revenue. The relative strengths of these two effects will determine the overall effect on *TR*. We will now examine these two effects, called the price effect and the quantity effect, along with the elasticity of demand to establish the relation between changes in price and total revenue.

Demand Elasticity and Changes in Total Revenue

price effect
The effect on total revenue of changing price, holding output constant.

quantity effect
The effect on total revenue of changing output, holding price constant.

When a manager raises the price of a product, the increase in price, by itself, would increase total revenue if the quantity sold remained constant. Conversely, when a manager lowers price, the decrease in price would decrease total revenue if the quantity sold remained constant. This effect on total revenue of changing price, for a given level of output, is called the **price effect.** When price changes, the quantity sold does not remain constant; it moves in the opposite direction of price. When quantity increases in response to a decrease in price, the increase in quantity, by itself, would increase total revenue if the price of the product remained constant. Alternatively, when quantity falls after a price increase, the reduction in quantity, by itself, would decrease total revenue if product price remained constant. The effect on total revenue of changing the quantity sold, for a given price level, is called the **quantity effect.** The price and quantity effects always push total revenue in opposite directions. Total revenue moves in the direction of the stronger of the two effects. If the two effects are equally strong, no change in total revenue can occur.

Suppose a manager increases price, causing quantity to decrease. The price effect, represented below by an upward arrow above P, and the quantity effect, represented by a downward arrow above Q, show how the change in TR is affected by opposing forces:

$$TR = \overset{\uparrow}{P} \times \overset{\downarrow}{Q}$$

To determine the direction of movement in TR, information about the relative strengths of the price effect and output effect must be known. The elasticity of demand tells a manager which effect, if either, is dominant.

If demand is elastic, $|E|$ is greater than one, the numerator ($|\%\Delta Q|$) is greater than the denominator ($|\%\Delta P|$), and the quantity effect dominates the price effect. To better see how the dominance of the quantity effect determines the direction in which TR moves, you can represent the dominance of the quantity effect by drawing the arrow above Q longer than the arrow above P. The direction of the dominant effect—the quantity effect here—tells a manager that TR will fall when price rises and demand is elastic:

$$\overset{\downarrow}{TR} = \overset{\uparrow}{P} \times \overset{\big\downarrow}{Q}$$

If a manager *decreases* price when demand is elastic, the arrows in the above diagram reverse directions. The arrow above Q is still the longer arrow since the quantity effect always dominates the price effect when demand is elastic.

Now consider a price increase when demand is *inelastic.* When demand is inelastic, $|E|$ is less than one, the numerator ($|\%\Delta Q|$) is less than the denominator ($|\%\Delta P|$), and the price effect dominates the quantity effect. The dominant price

TABLE 3.2
Relations between Demand Elasticity and Total Revenue (*TR*)

	Elastic $\lvert\%\Delta Q\rvert > \lvert\%\Delta P\rvert$ *Q*-effect dominates	Unitary elastic $\lvert\%\Delta Q\rvert = \lvert\%\Delta P\rvert$ No dominant effect	Inelastic $\lvert\%\Delta Q\rvert < \lvert\%\Delta P\rvert$ *P*-effect dominates
Price rises	*TR* falls	No change in *TR*	*TR* rises
Price falls	*TR* rises	No change in *TR*	*TR* falls

effect can be represented by an upward arrow above *P* which is longer than the downward arrow above *Q*. The direction of the dominant effect tells the manager that *TR* will rise when price rises and demand is inelastic:

$$\overset{\uparrow}{TR} = \overset{\big\uparrow}{P} \times \overset{\downarrow}{Q}$$

When a manager decreases price and demand is inelastic, the arrows in the above diagram would reverse directions. A downward arrow above *P* would be a long arrow since the price effect always dominates the quantity effect when demand is inelastic.

When demand is unitary elastic, $|E|$ is equal to one, and neither the price effect nor the quantity effect dominates. The two effects exactly offset each other, so price changes have no effect on total revenue when demand is unitary elastic.

Relation The effect of a change in price on total revenue ($TR = P \times Q$) is determined by the elasticity of demand. When demand is elastic (inelastic), the quantity (price) effect dominates. Total revenue always moves in the same direction as the variable (*P* or *Q*) having the dominant effect. When demand is unitary elastic, neither effect dominates, and changes in price leave total revenue unchanged.

Table 3.2 summarizes the relation between price changes and revenue changes under the three elasticity conditions.

Changing Price at Borderline Music Emporium: A Numerical Example

The manager at Borderline Music Emporium faces the demand curve for compact discs shown in Figure 3.1. At the current price of \$18 per compact disc, Borderline can sell 600 CDs each week. The manager can lower price to \$16 per compact disc and increase sales to 800 CDs per week. In Panel A of Figure 3.1, over the interval *a* to *b* on demand curve *D* the coefficient of demand elasticity is equal to −2.43. (You will learn how to make this calculation in Section 3.4 of this chapter.) Since the demand for compact discs is elastic over this range of prices ($|-2.43| > 1$), the manager knows the quantity effect dominates the price effect. Lowering price from \$18 to \$16 results in an increase in the quantity of CDs sold, so the manager knows that total revenue, which always moves in the direction of the dominant effect, must increase.

FIGURE 3.1

Changes in Total Revenue of Borderline Music Emporium

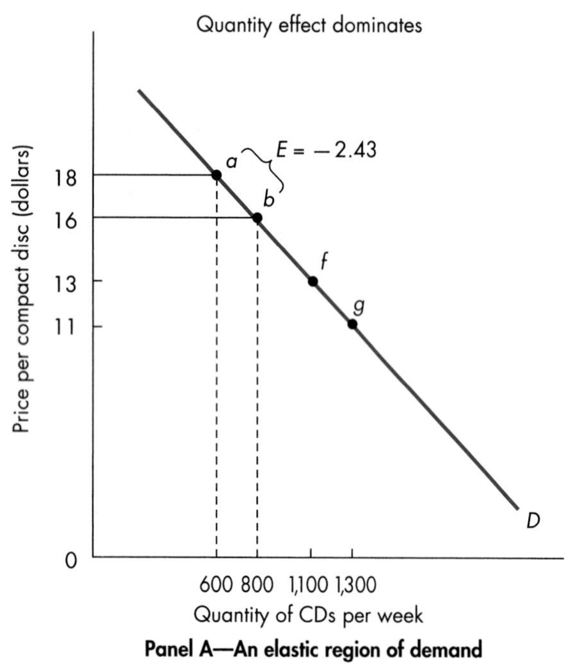

Panel A—An elastic region of demand

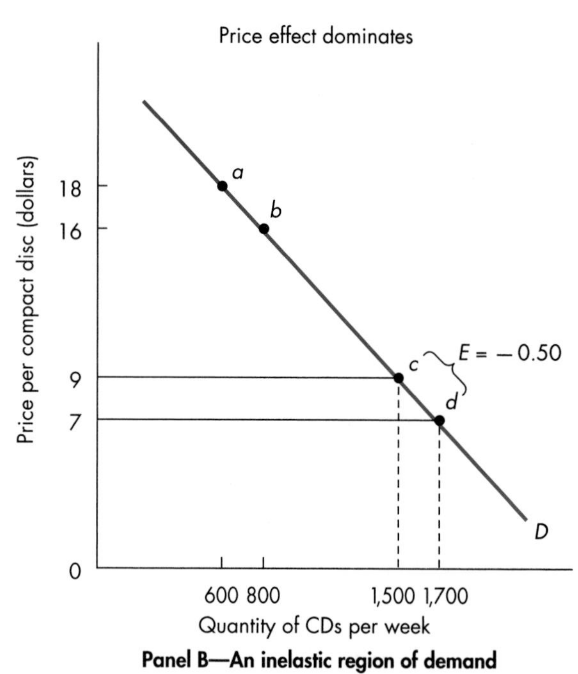

Panel B—An inelastic region of demand

To verify that revenue indeed rises when the manager at Borderline lowers the price over an elastic region of demand, you can calculate total revenue at the two prices, \$18 and \$16:

Point a: $TR = \$18 \times 600 = \$10{,}800$
Point b: $TR = \$16 \times 800 = \$12{,}800$

Total revenue rises by \$2,000 (= 12,800 − 10,800) when price is reduced over this elastic region of demand. While Borderline earns less revenue on each CD sold, the number of CDs sold each week rises enough to more than offset the downward price effect, causing total revenue to rise.

Now suppose the manager at Borderline is charging just \$9 per compact disc and sells 1,500 CDs per week (see Panel B). The manager can lower price to \$7 per disc and increase sales to 1,700 CDs per week. Over the interval c to d on demand curve D, the elasticity of demand equals −0.5. Over this range of prices for CDs, the demand is inelastic ($|-0.5| < 1$), and Borderline's manager knows the price effect dominates the quantity effect. If the manager lowers price from \$9 to \$7, total revenue, which always moves in the direction of the dominant effect, must decrease.

To verify that revenue falls when the manager at Borderline lowers price over an inelastic region of demand, you can calculate total revenue at the two prices, $9 and $7:

$$\text{Point } c\text{:} \quad TR = \$9 \times 1{,}500 = \$13{,}500$$
$$\text{Point } d\text{:} \quad TR = \$7 \times 1{,}700 = \$11{,}900$$

Total revenue falls by $1,600 ($\Delta TR = \$11{,}900 - \$13{,}500 = -\$1{,}600$). Total revenue always falls when price is reduced over an inelastic region of demand. Borderline again earns less revenue on each CD sold, but the number of CDs sold each week does not increase enough to offset the downward price effect and total revenue falls.

If the manager decreases (or increases) the price of compact discs over a unitary-elastic region of demand, total revenue does not change. You should verify that demand is unitary elastic over the interval f to g in Panel A of Figure 3.1.

Note in Figure 3.1 that demand is elastic over the $16 to $18 price range but inelastic over the $7 to $9 price range. In general, the elasticity of demand varies along any particular demand curve, even one that is linear. It is usually incorrect to say a demand curve is either elastic or inelastic. You can say only that a demand curve is elastic or inelastic over a particular price range. For example, it is correct to say that demand curve D in Figure 3.1 is elastic over the $16 to $18 price range and inelastic over the $7 to $9 price range.

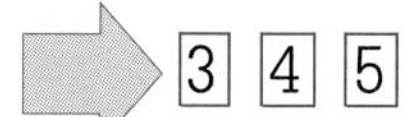

3.3 FACTORS AFFECTING DEMAND ELASTICITY

Demand elasticity plays such an important role in business decision making that managers should understand not only how to use the concept to obtain information about the demand for the products they sell but also how to recognize the factors that affect demand elasticity. We will now discuss the three factors that make the demand for some products more elastic than the demand for other products.

Availability of Substitutes

The availability of substitutes is by far the most important determinant of demand elasticity. The better the substitutes for a given good or service, the more elastic the demand for that good or service. When the price of a good rises, consumers will substantially reduce consumption of that good if they perceive that close substitutes are readily available. Naturally, consumers will be less responsive to a price increase if they perceive that only poor substitutes are available.

Some goods for which demand is rather elastic include fruit, corporate jets, and cafeteria meals. Alternatively, goods for which consumers perceive few or no good substitutes have low elasticities of demand. Wheat, salt, and gasoline tend to have low elasticities because there are only poor substitutes available—for instance, corn, pepper, and diesel fuel, respectively.

The definition of the market for a good greatly affects the number of substitutes and thus the good's elasticity of demand. For example, if all the grocery stores in a city raised the price of milk by 25 cents per gallon, total sales of milk would undoubtedly fall—but probably not by much. If, on the other hand, only the Food King chain of stores raised price by 25 cents, the sales of Food King milk would probably fall substantially. There are many good substitutes for Food King milk, but there are not nearly as many substitutes for milk in general.

Percentage of Consumer's Budget

The percentage of the consumer's budget that is spent on the commodity is also important in the determination of price elasticity. All other things equal, we would expect the price elasticity to be directly related to the percentage of consumers' budgets spent on the good. For example, the demand for refrigerators is probably more price elastic than the demand for toasters, since the expenditure required to purchase a refrigerator would make up a larger percentage of the budget of a "typical" consumer.

Time Period of Adjustment

The length of the time period used in measuring the price elasticity affects the magnitude of the elasticity coefficient. In general, the longer the time period of measurement, the larger (the more elastic) the coefficient of demand elasticity will be. This relation is the result of consumers' having more time to adjust to the price change.

Consider, again, the way consumers would adjust to an increase in the price of milk. Suppose the dairy farmers' association is able to convince all producers of milk nationwide to raise their milk prices by 15 percent. During the first week the price increase takes effect, consumers come to the stores with their grocery lists already made up. Shoppers notice the higher price of milk but have already planned their meals for the week. While a few of the shoppers will react immediately to the higher milk prices and reduce the amount of milk they purchase, many shoppers will go ahead and buy the same amount of milk as they purchased the week before. If the dairy association collects sales data and measures the elasticity of demand for milk after the first week of the price hike, they will be happy to see that the 15 percent increase in the price of milk caused only a modest reduction in milk sales.

Over the coming weeks, however, consumers begin looking for ways to consume less milk. They substitute foods that have similar nutritional composition to milk; consumption of cheese, eggs, and yogurt all increase. Some consumers will even switch to powdered milk for some of their less urgent milk needs—perhaps to feed the cat or to use in cooking. Six months after the price increase, the dairy association again measures the demand elasticity of milk. Now the coefficient of demand elasticity is probably much larger (more elastic) since it is measured over a six-month time period instead of a one-week time period.

For most goods and services, given a longer time period to adjust, the demand for the commodity exhibits more responsiveness to changes in price—the demand becomes more elastic. Of course, we can treat the effect of time on elasticity within the framework of the effect of available substitutes. The greater the

FIGURE 3.2
Calculating Arc Elasticity

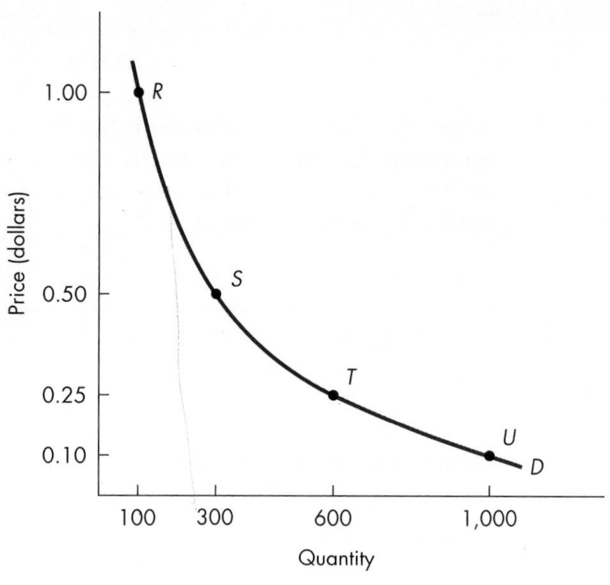

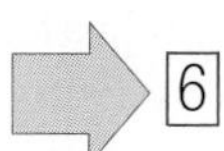
6

time period available for consumer adjustment, the more substitutes become available and economically feasible. As we stressed above, the more available are substitutes, the more elastic is demand.

3.4 CALCULATING DEMAND ELASTICITY

The coefficient of demand elasticity can be calculated either (1) over an interval (or arc) along demand or (2) at a point on a demand curve. The choice of whether to measure demand elasticity at a point on demand or over an interval depends upon the particular application. In both cases, E still measures the sensitivity of consumers to changes in the price of the commodity.

Computing Elasticity over an Interval

arc elasticity
The coefficient of demand elasticity calculated over an interval of a demand curve.

When the coefficient of demand elasticity is calculated over an interval of a demand curve or schedule, the coefficient is called the **arc elasticity.** For example, in Figure 3.2, the elasticities measured over the intervals *RS, ST, TU*—or any other *price range* that might be of interest—are all referred to as arc elasticities.[3] Between any two points on demand, the percentage changes in quantity demanded and price are calculated as

[3]The arc between any two points on a demand *curve* corresponds to a movement between any two prices in a demand *schedule.* Thus, the elasticity coefficient calculated between two prices in a demand schedule is also called an arc elasticity.

$$\%\Delta Q = \frac{\Delta Q}{Q_{\text{base}}} \times 100$$

$$\%\Delta P = \frac{\Delta P}{P_{\text{base}}} \times 100$$

where Q_{base} and P_{base} represent the "base" upon which the percentage changes are computed. When taking the ratio of the two percentage changes, the factor of 100 cancels out of the numerator and denominator, and the arc elasticity of demand can be expressed as

$$E = \frac{\dfrac{\Delta Q}{Q_{\text{base}}}}{\dfrac{\Delta P}{P_{\text{base}}}}$$

The only thing that could possibly complicate the above calculation is the choice of the base price and base quantity. The mathematical convention is to use the "initial" values of P and Q as the base upon which to measure the percentage changes. This convention, however, requires a minor modification in the way arc elasticities are computed. If we use the initial price and quantity as base values for computing elasticity, we get two different values of E for the same interval, depending on whether the movement is up or down over the interval. In fact, the interval may be so wide that moving up demand (price rises) produces one value of E that indicates demand is elastic while moving down demand (price falls) produces another value of E that indicates demand is inelastic.[4]

The correct approximation of arc elasticity is obtained by using the average (or midpoint) values of quantity and price as the base for computing percentage changes.[5] When arc elasticities are being measured over an interval of a demand curve, the following arc formula should be used:

$$E = \frac{\%\Delta Q}{\%\Delta P} = \frac{\dfrac{\Delta Q}{Q_{\text{base}}}}{\dfrac{\Delta P}{P_{\text{base}}}} = \frac{\dfrac{\Delta Q}{\text{Average } Q}}{\dfrac{\Delta P}{\text{Average } P}}$$

We will use this formula (here and throughout the rest of the text) to compute the arc elasticity of demand over the interval RS as shown in Figure 3.2:

$$E = \frac{\dfrac{100 - 300}{200}}{\dfrac{1.00 - .50}{.75}} = \frac{-1}{\dfrac{2}{3}} = -\frac{3}{2} = -1.5$$

[4]If you doubt this statement, calculate the elasticity over the interval RS in Figure 3.2. Using R as the base point and moving down to S will result in a calculated arc elasticity of -4. Beginning at point S and moving up to R produces an elasticity of $-\frac{2}{3}$.

[5]The average values of P and Q are also the midpoint values between the initial values and the new values. For example, if Q is initially 300 units and the new value is 100, the midpoint value is 200, which is also the average value [(300 + 100)/2 = 200].

TABLE 3.3
Computing Arc Elasticities

Interval	Price falls from	Total revenue (when P falls)	Arc elasticity (E)
RS	\$1 to \$0.50	TR rises	$\frac{(100-300)/200}{(1.00-.50)/.75} = -1.5$
ST	\$0.50 to \$0.25	TR unchanged	$\frac{(300-600)/450}{(.50-.25)/.375} = -1$
TU	\$0.25 to \$0.10	TR falls	$\frac{(600-1{,}000)/800}{(.25-.10)/.175} = -0.583$

The arc elasticity equals -1.5 whether the computation is made moving up or down interval *RS*. Table 3.3 shows the computations for the three intervals *RS*, *ST*, and *TU* in Figure 3.2. We have established the following principle:

Principle When calculating the elasticity of demand over an interval of demand, use the arc elasticity formula:

$$E = \frac{\Delta Q}{\text{Average } Q} \Big/ \frac{\Delta P}{\text{Average } P}$$

Computing Elasticity at a Point

point elasticity
A measurement of demand elasticity calculated at a point on the demand curve rather than over an interval.

As noted, it is sometimes useful to measure elasticity at a point on the demand curve rather than over an interval. When elasticity is computed at a point on demand it is called **point elasticity** of demand. Computing elasticity at a point on demand is no more difficult than computing arc elasticity. We begin with the case of a linear demand.

If the demand curve is linear, it can be expressed in intercept-slope form as $P = a + bQ$, where a is the P-intercept and b is the inverse slope of the demand function ($\Delta P/\Delta Q$), which is negative because P and Q are negatively related along demand. The elasticity of demand at a given point on demand is

$$E = \%\Delta Q/\%\Delta P = P/(P - a)$$

where P is the value of price at the given point on demand.[6] Now consider the

[6]The proof of this formula is relatively simple. Let the inverse of the demand function be expressed as $P = a + bQ$; and, solving for demand, $Q = -a/b + (1/b)P$. Since we do not have to worry about averaging the bases P and Q at a *point* on demand, the elasticity formula can be written as

$$E = \frac{\Delta Q/Q}{\Delta P/P} = \frac{\Delta Q}{\Delta P} \cdot \frac{P}{Q}$$

The slope of demand, $\Delta Q/\Delta P$ equals $1/b$. Therefore,

$$E = \frac{1}{b} \cdot \frac{P}{Q} = \frac{1}{b} \cdot \frac{P}{\left(-\frac{a}{b} + \frac{1}{b}P\right)} = \frac{P}{P - a}$$

See the appendix at the end of this chapter for a derivation of this result using calculus.

ILLUSTRATION 3.1

Texas Calculates Elasticity

In addition to its regular license plates, the state of Texas, as do other states, sells personalized or "vanity" license plates. To raise additional revenue, the state will sell a vehicle owner a license plate saying whatever the owner wants as long as it uses six letters (or numbers), no one else has the same license as the one requested, and it isn't obscene. For this service, the state charges a higher price than the price for standard licenses. Many people are willing to pay the higher price rather than display a license of the standard form such as 387 BRC.

For example, an ophthalmologist announces his practice with the license MYOPIA. Others tell their personalities with COZY-1 and ALL MAN. A rabid *Star Trek* fan has BM ME UP.

In 1986, Texas increased the price for such plates from \$25 to \$75. The *Houston Post* (October 19, 1986) reported that before the price increase about 150,000 cars in Texas had personalized licenses. After the increase in price, only 60,000 people ordered the vanity plates. As it turned out, demand was rather inelastic over this range. As you can calculate, the own-price elasticity is −0.86. Thus revenue rose after the price increase, from \$3,750,000 to \$4,500,000.

But the *Houston Post* article quoted the assistant director of the Texas Division of Motor Vehicles as saying, "Since the demand dropped* the state didn't make money from the higher fees, so the price for next year's personalized plates will be \$40." If the objective of the state is to make money from these licenses and if the numbers in the article are correct, this is the wrong thing to do. It's hard to see how the state lost money by increasing the price from \$25 to \$75—the revenue increased and the cost of producing plates must have decreased since fewer were produced. So the move from \$25 to \$75 was the right move.

Moreover, let's suppose that the elasticity between \$75 and \$40 is essentially the same as that calculated for the movement from \$25 to \$75 (−0.86). We can use this estimate to calculate what happens to revenue if the state drops the price to \$40. We must first find what the new quantity demanded will be at \$40. Using the arc elasticity formula and the elasticity of −0.86,

$$E = \frac{\Delta Q/\text{Average } Q}{\Delta P/\text{Average } P} = \frac{(60{,}000 - Q)/[(60{,}000 + Q)/2]}{(75 - 40)/[(75 + 40)/2]} = -0.86$$

where Q is the new quantity demanded. Solving this equation for Q, the estimated sales are 102,000 (rounded) at a price of \$40. With this quantity demanded and price, total revenue would be \$4,080,000 representing a decrease of \$420,000 from the revenue at \$75 a plate. If the state's objective is to raise revenue by selling vanity plates, it should increase rather than decrease price.

This application actually makes two points. First, even decision makers in organizations that are not run for profit, such as government agencies, should be able to use economic analysis. Second, managers whose firms are in business to make a profit should make an effort to know (or at least have a good approximation for) the elasticity of demand for the products they sell. Only with this information will they know what price to charge.

*It was, of course, quantity demanded that decreased, not demand.

Source: Barbara Boughton, "A License for Vanity," *Houston Post*, Oct. 19, 1986, pp. 1G, 10G.

linear demand curve in Panel A of Figure 3.3. At a price of \$100 (point L), the elasticity of demand is -5 [$= 100/(100 - 120)$] since the intercept, a, equals 120. At a price of \$60 (point M), demand is unitary elastic [$E = -1 = 60/(60 - 120)$]. When price is \$40 (point N), demand is inelastic [$E = -0.5 = 40/(40 - 120)$].

We now use Panel B of Figure 3.3 to show how to compute demand elasticity at a point on a *curvilinear* demand. To compute elasticity of demand for a price

FIGURE 3.3
Calculating Point Elasticity

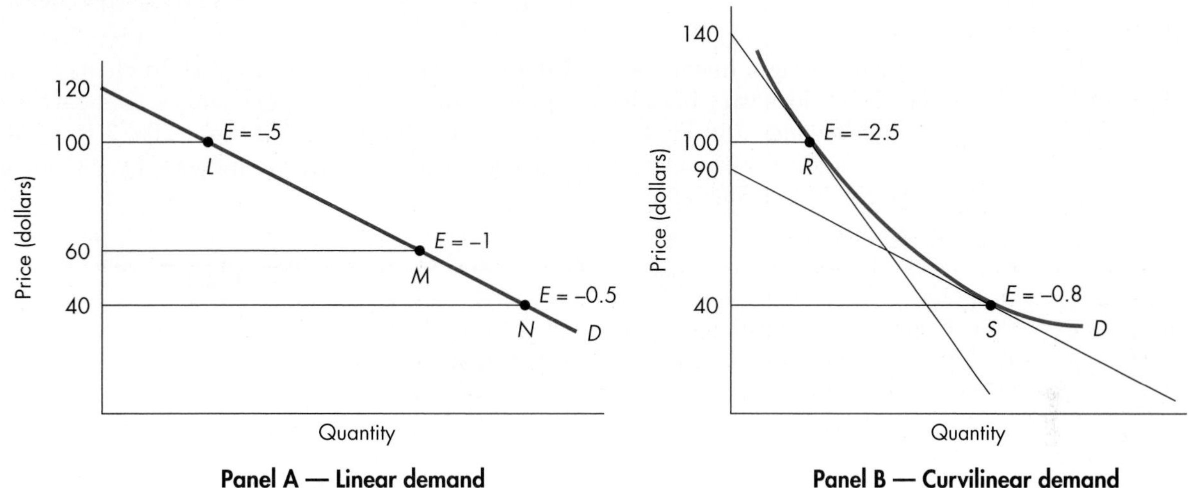

Panel A — Linear demand **Panel B — Curvilinear demand**

of \$100, first construct the line tangent to point R on the demand curve, extending the tangent line until it touches the price axis. Since P, Q, and slope are identical for the linear demand and the curvilinear demand at R, their elasticities are identical at R. Therefore, to calculate the elasticity of the curved demand at R, compute the point elasticity as for a linear demand curve, using the price intercept of the tangent line as the value of a. At \$100, the elasticity of demand is -2.5 [$= 100/(100 - 140)$]. At \$40, the elasticity of demand is -0.8 [$= 40/(40 - 90)$].

For calculating demand elasticity, the point elasticity method is generally used only when the price change of interest is small. If the anticipated price change spans a sizable arc along the demand curve, the interval measure of elasticity should be used.

Elasticity (generally) Varies along a Demand Curve

In general, different intervals or points along the same demand curve have differing elasticities of demand, even when the demand curve is linear. When demand is linear, the slope of the demand curve is constant. Even though the *absolute* rate at which quantity demanded changes as price changes ($\Delta Q/\Delta P$) remains constant, the *proportional* rate of change in Q as P changes ($\%\Delta Q/\%\Delta P$) varies along a linear demand curve. To see why, rewrite the coefficient of elasticity as

$$E = \frac{\Delta Q/Q}{\Delta P/P}$$

or

$$E = \frac{\Delta Q}{\Delta P} \cdot \frac{P}{Q}$$

Moving along a linear demand does not cause the term $\Delta Q/\Delta P$ to change, but elasticity does vary because the proportionality term P/Q changes. Compare intervals *ab* and *cd* in Figure 3.1. Over both intervals, $\Delta Q/\Delta P = -200/2 = -100$; that is, a $1 decrease in price causes quantity demanded to increase by 100 units. The computed elasticities,

$$E_{ab} = -100 \cdot \frac{17}{700} = -2.43 \qquad \text{and} \qquad E_{cd} = -100 \cdot \frac{8}{1{,}600} = -0.5$$

differ because the proportionality term P/Q becomes smaller when moving down the demand curve. Note that demand elasticity decreases when moving down a linear demand curve, *regardless* of whether elasticity is measured over an interval or at a point (see Panel A, Figure 3.3). Thus, price and demand elasticity vary *directly* along a linear demand curve.

In the case of curvilinear demand, price and demand elasticity also vary, except in one special case. When the demand equation takes the form $Q = aP^b$, the elasticity is *constant* along the demand curve and is equal to b.[7] We mention
7 8 9 this special case here simply to be complete.

Relation In general, the elasticity of demand varies along a demand curve. For a linear demand, price and elasticity vary directly: the higher the price, the more elastic the demand. For a curvilinear demand, there is no general rule about the relation between price and elasticity, except for the special case of $Q = aP^b$, which has a constant demand elasticity (equal to b) for all prices.

3.5 OTHER ELASTICITIES

income elasticity (E_M) A measure of the responsiveness of quantity demanded to changes in income, holding all other variables in the generalized demand function constant.

cross-price elasticity (E_{XY}) A measure of the responsiveness of quantity demanded to changes in the price of a related good, when all the other variables in the generalized demand function remain constant.

Sometimes economists and business decision makers are interested in measuring the sensitivity of consumers to changes in either income or the price of a related good. **Income elasticity** measures the responsiveness of quantity demanded to changes in income, holding all other variables in the generalized demand function constant. **Cross-price elasticity** measures the responsiveness of quantity demanded to changes in the price of a related good, when all the other variables in the generalized demand function remain constant. In this section we show how to calculate and interpret these two elasticities.

Income Elasticity

As noted, income elasticity measures the responsiveness of quantity purchased when income changes, all else constant. Income elasticity, E_M, is the percentage change in quantity demanded divided by the percentage change in income, holding all other variables in the generalized demand function constant, including the good's own price:

---

[7] See the appendix at the end of this chapter for a proof of this result.

FIGURE 3.4
Calculating Income Elasticity of Demand

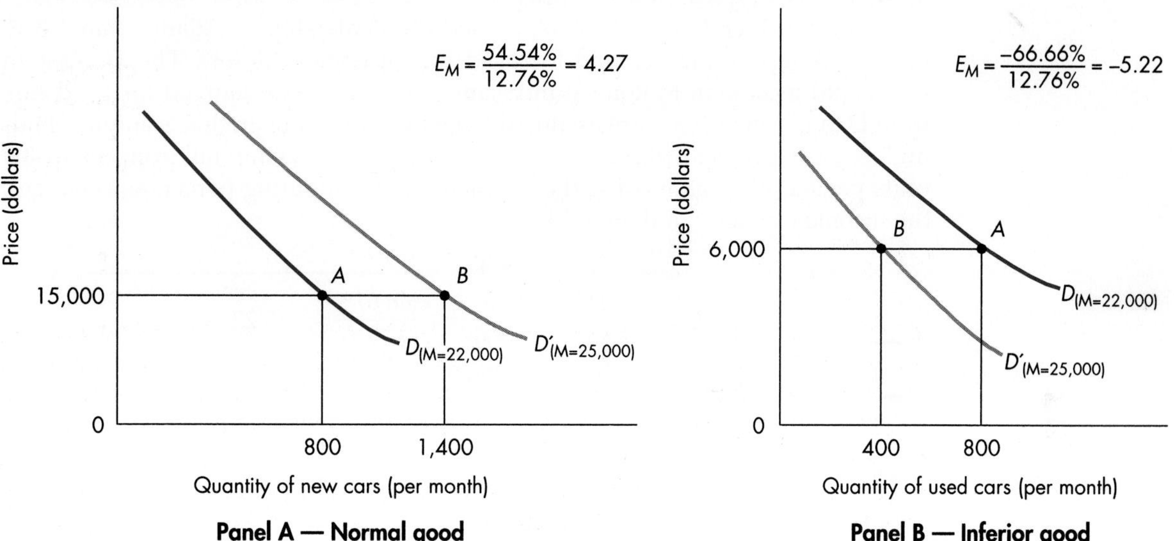

$$E_M = \frac{\%\Delta Q}{\%\Delta M} = \frac{\Delta Q/Q}{\Delta M/M} = \frac{\Delta Q}{\Delta M} \cdot \frac{M}{Q}$$

As you can see, the sign of E_M depends upon the sign of $\Delta Q/\Delta M$, which may be positive (if the good is normal) or negative (if the good is inferior). Thus, if the good is normal, the income elasticity is positive. If the good is inferior, the income elasticity is negative.

To illustrate the use of income elasticity, consider Metro Ford, a new-car dealership in Atlanta. The manager of Metro Ford expects average household income in Fulton County to increase from \$22,000 to \$25,000 annually when the current recession ends, causing an increase in the demand for new cars. At a constant average price of \$15,000 per car, the increase in income will cause sales to rise from 800 to 1,400 units per month. Panel A in Figure 3.4 illustrates this situation. The increase in income shifts the demand for new cars rightward—a new car is a normal good. To calculate the income elasticity of demand, we use the arc elasticity method of computing percentage changes over an interval. The income elasticity of demand in Panel A is

$$E_M = \frac{\%\Delta Q}{\%\Delta M} = \frac{\frac{600}{1{,}100}}{\frac{3{,}000}{23{,}500}} = \frac{54.55\%}{12.77\%} = 4.27$$

We should mention that the choice of \$15,000 as the price at which to measure income elasticity is arbitrary. The manager at Metro Ford probably chose a price of \$15,000 as a typical new-car price.

Now consider Lemon Motors, a used-car dealership in Atlanta. Panel B in Figure 3.4 depicts the demand for used cars at Lemon Motors. The increase in household income in Fulton County causes a decrease in demand for used cars from D to D'—used cars are assumed to be inferior goods in this example. Holding used-car prices at \$6,000, sales at the used-car dealership fall from 800 to 400 units per month. Again using the arc method of computing percentage changes, the income elasticity of demand is

$$E_M = \frac{\%\Delta Q}{\%\Delta M} = \frac{\dfrac{-400}{600}}{\dfrac{3{,}000}{23{,}500}} = \frac{-66.67\%}{12.77\%} = -5.22$$

As expected, the income elasticity is negative for an inferior good.

Relation The income elasticity measures the responsiveness of consumers to changes in income when the price of the good and all other determinants of demand are held constant. The income elasticity is positive (negative) for normal (inferior) goods.

Cross-Price Elasticity

The cross-price elasticity of a good, as already noted, measures the responsiveness of quantity demanded of one good to changes in the price of another good, when all the other variables in the generalized demand function remain constant. The cross-price elasticity between the good in question (X) and another good (Y)—denoted E_{XY}—is calculated by taking the ratio of the percentage change in the quantity demanded of good X ($\%\Delta Q_X$) and dividing by the percentage change in the price of the other good Y ($\%\Delta P_Y$):

$$E_{XY} = \frac{\%\Delta Q_X}{\%\Delta P_Y} = \frac{\Delta Q_X/Q_X}{\Delta P_Y/P_Y} = \frac{\Delta Q_X}{\Delta P_Y} \cdot \frac{P_Y}{Q_X}$$

Note that the sign of E_{XY} depends upon the sign of $\Delta Q_X/\Delta P_Y$, which can be positive or negative. Recall from Chapter 2 that if an increase in the price of one good causes the quantity purchased of another good to increase, the goods are substitutes (i.e., $\Delta Q_X/\Delta P_Y > 0$). If the rise in the price of one good causes the quantity purchased of another good to fall, the goods are complements (i.e., $\Delta Q_X/\Delta P_Y < 0$). If there is no change in the quantity purchased of the other good, the two goods are independent (i.e., $\Delta Q_X/\Delta P_Y = 0$). Thus, E_{XY} is positive when X and Y are substitutes; E_{XY} is negative when X and Y are complements.[8]

Suppose the commissioner of the Tampa Sports Authority is studying the pricing of Tampa Bay Buccaneer football tickets. Of particular concern is the sensitivity of football fans to the price of hockey tickets (P_H) and the price of

[8]We should note that the cross-price elasticity of X for Y need not equal the cross-price elasticity of Y for X, although the two will generally have the same signs.

FIGURE 3.5
Calculating Cross-Price Elasticity of Demand

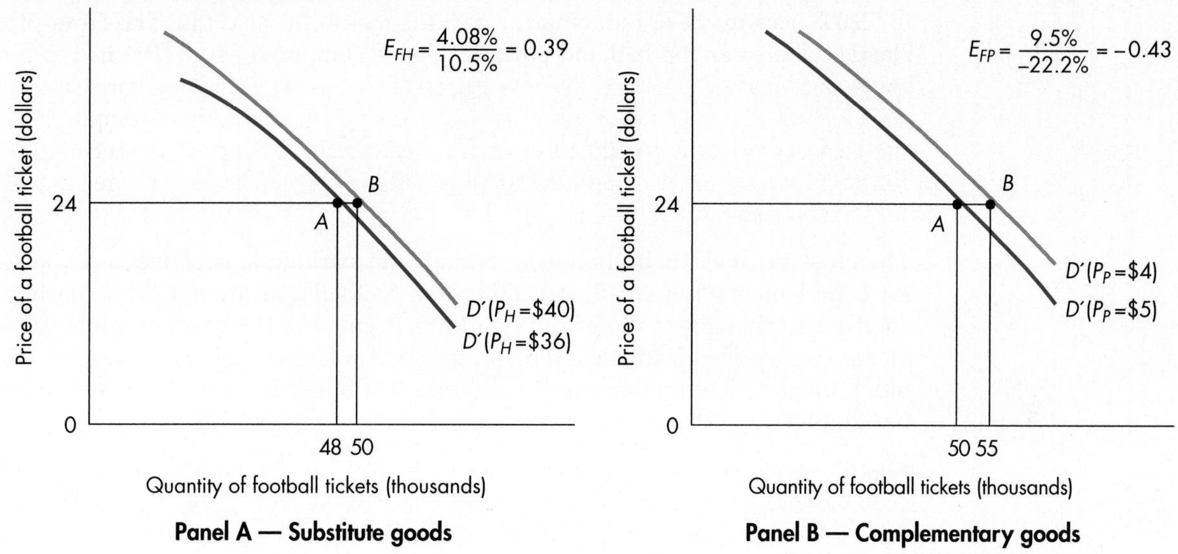

parking at Houhlihan's Stadium (P_P), a substitute good and a complementary good, respectively, for football games. If Buccaneer fans are quite responsive to changes in the prices of hockey and parking, the commissioner may be able to improve attendance at Bucs' home games by recommending to the Sports Authority an increase in the price of hockey and a decrease in the price of parking at the stadium. If football fans are rather insensitive to both the price of hockey and the price of parking, there is not much the commissioner of the Sports Authority can do to stimulate sales—only improved performance of the team or a reduction in the price of football tickets is likely to enhance attendance.

As illustrated in Panel A in Figure 3.5, an increase from \$36 to \$40 in the price of Lightning tickets (Tampa's hockey team) will cause the demand for football tickets to shift rightward from D to D'. At a constant price of \$24 for football tickets, sales of football tickets (Q_F) increase from 48,000 to 50,000 (point A to point B). The cross-price elasticity between football and hockey (E_{FH}) is computed using the arc formula:

$$E_{FH} = \frac{\%\Delta Q_F}{\%\Delta P_H} = \frac{\frac{2,000}{49,000}}{\frac{4}{38}} = \frac{4.08\%}{10.53\%} = 0.39$$

Note that the cross-price elasticity between football and hockey is positive (for substitutes) but rather small, indicating football and hockey are rather weak substitutes.

Panel B in Figure 3.5 shows that decreasing the price of parking (P_P) from \$5 to \$4 causes an increase in the demand for football tickets from D to D'. At a constant \$24 price of football tickets, sales of football tickets increase from 50,000 to 55,000, as a result of reducing the parking fees at the stadium. The cross-price elasticity between football and parking (E_{FP}) is computed as

$$E_{FP} = \frac{\%\Delta Q_F}{\%\Delta P_P} = \frac{\frac{5{,}000}{52{,}500}}{\frac{-1}{4.5}} = \frac{9.52\%}{-22.22\%} = -0.43$$

The cross-price elasticity between football and parking is negative (as expected for complements) but small, indicating that football fans are not particularly responsive to changes in the price of parking. Because of the small absolute values of the cross-price elasticities, the Tampa Sports Authority is not likely to have much impact on attendance at Bucs games if it raises hockey prices and lowers

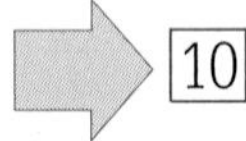

10 parking fees.

Relation The cross-price elasticity measures the responsiveness of the quantity demanded of one good when the price of another good changes, holding the price of the good and all other determinants of demand constant. Cross-price elasticity is positive (negative) when the two goods are substitutes (complements).

3.6 MARGINAL REVENUE, DEMAND, AND ELASTICITY

The responsiveness of consumers to changes in the price of a good must be considered by managers when making pricing and output decisions. The elasticity of demand gives managers essential information about how total revenue will be affected by a change in price. As it turns out, an equally important concept for pricing and output decisions is *marginal revenue.* **Marginal revenue (*MR*)** is the addition to total revenue attributable to selling 1 additional unit of output:

marginal revenue (*MR*) The addition to total revenue attributable to selling one additional unit of output.

$$MR = \Delta TR/\Delta Q$$

Marginal revenue is related to demand elasticity because marginal revenue, like demand elasticity, involves changes in total revenue caused by movements along a demand curve.

Marginal Revenue and Demand

As noted, marginal revenue is related to the way changes in price and output affect total revenue along a demand curve. To see the relation between marginal revenue and price, consider the following numerical example. The demand schedule for a product is presented in columns 1 and 2 of Table 3.4. Price times quantity gives the total revenue obtainable at each level of sales, shown in column 3.

Marginal revenue, shown in column 4, indicates the change in total revenue from an additional unit of sales. Note that marginal revenue equals price only for the first unit sold. For the first unit sold, total revenue is the demand price

ILLUSTRATION 3.2

Empirical Elasticities of Demand*

Using the appropriate data and statistical techniques, it is possible to estimate own-price, income, and cross-price elasticities from actual demand schedules. We have collected a sample of estimated demand elasticities from a variety of sources and present them in the accompanying table. In the chapter on empirical demand functions, we will show how to estimate actual demand elasticities.

Looking at the own-price elasticities presented in the table, note that the demand for basic agricultural products such as beef and eggs is inelastic. Fruit, for which consumers can find many substitutes, has a much more elastic demand than beef or eggs. For any particular make and model of automobile, consumers can find plenty of readily available substitutes. Consequently, the demand elasticity for General Motors' Pontiac Catalina is very large. Another factor affecting own-price elasticity is the length of time consumers have to adjust to a price change. It is interesting that gasoline demand is inelastic in the short run but elastic in the long run.

We explained in the text that cross-price elasticities are positive for substitutes and negative for complements. All three pairs of goods in the table are substitutes ($E_{XY} > 0$). Beef and chicken are weak substitutes, while margarine and butter seem to be rather strong substitutes. The extremely high cross-price elasticity of demand between Pontiac Catalinas and Chevrolet Impalas suggests that these two cars were virtually identical in the eyes of consumers.

Normal goods have positive income elasticities of demand (E_M), and inferior goods have negative income elasticities. Potatoes are inferior goods since E_M is negative. Beef is more strongly normal than chicken, indicating that a given percentage increase in income causes an almost fourfold greater increase in beef consumption than chicken consumption. The high income elasticity of demand for foreign travel indicates that consumer demand for foreign travel is quite responsive to changes in income. Furniture demand, on the other hand, appears to be rather insensitive to changes in income.

Table of Empirical Elasticities of Demand

Own-price elasticities of demand (E):	
Beef	−0.956
Eggs	−0.263
Fruit	−3.021
GM Pontiac Catalina	−16.99
Gasoline (short run)	−0.43
Gasoline (long run)	−1.50
Cross-price elasticities of demand (E_{XY}):	
Beef and chicken	0.350
Margarine and butter	1.526
Catalinas and Impalas	19.3
Income elasticities of demand (E_M):	
Beef	1.27
Chicken	0.33
Potatoes	−0.81
Foreign travel by US citizens	3.09
Furniture	0.53

*For own-price, cross-price, and income elasticities for all agricultural products, see Dale Heien, "The Structure of Food Demand: Interrelatedness and Duality," *American Journal of Agricultural Economics,* May 1982. For automobile own-price and cross-price elasticities, see F. Owen Irvine, Jr., "Demand Equations for Individual New Car Models Estimated Using Transaction Prices with Implications for Regulatory Issues," *Southern Economic Journal,* January 1983. For short-run and long-run gasoline elasticities, see, respectively, Robert Archibald and Robert Gillingham, "An Analysis of Short-Run Consumer Demand for Gasoline Using Household Survey Data," *Review of Economics and Statistics,* November 1980, and James Griffin and Henry Steele, *Energy Economics and Policy,* Academic Press, 1980, p. 232. For foreign travel and furniture income elasticities, see Hendrik Houthakker and Lester Taylor, *Consumer Demand in the United States; Analyses and Projections,* Harvard University Press, 1970.

for 1 unit. The first unit sold adds \$4—the price of the first unit—to total revenue, and the marginal revenue of the first unit sold equals \$4; that is, $MR = P$ for the first unit. If 2 units are sold, the second unit should contribute \$3.50 (the price of the second unit) to total revenue. But total revenue for 2 units is only \$7, indicating that the second unit adds only \$3 (= \$7 − \$4) to total revenue. Thus the

TABLE 3.4
Demand and Marginal Revenue

(1) Unit sales	(2) Price	(3) Total revenue	(4) Marginal revenue ($\Delta TR/\Delta Q$)
0	$4.50	$ 0	—
1	4.00	4.00	$4.00
2	3.50	7.00	3.00
3	3.10	9.30	2.30
4	2.80	11.20	1.90
5	2.40	12.00	0.80
6	2.00	12.00	0
7	1.50	10.50	−1.50

marginal revenue of the second unit is not equal to price, as it was for the first unit. Indeed, examining columns 2 and 4 in Table 3.4 indicates that $MR < P$ for all but the first unit sold.

Marginal revenue is less than price ($MR < P$) for all but the first unit sold because price must be lowered in order to sell more units. Not only is price lowered on the marginal (additional) unit sold, but price is also lowered for all the inframarginal units sold. The **inframarginal units** are those units that could have been sold at a higher price had the firm not lowered price to sell the marginal unit. Marginal revenue for any output level can be expressed as

inframarginal units Units of output that could have been sold at a higher price had a firm not lowered its price to sell the marginal unit.

$$MR = \text{Price} - \frac{\text{Revenue lost by lowering price}}{\text{on the inframarginal units}}$$

The second unit of output sells for $3.50. By itself, the second unit contributes $3.50 to total revenue. But marginal revenue is not equal to $3.50 for the second unit because in order to sell the second unit, price on the first unit is lowered from $4 to $3.50. In other words, the first unit is an inframarginal unit, and the $0.50 lost on the first unit must be subtracted from the price. The net effect on total revenue of selling the second unit is $3 (= $3.50 − $0.50), the same value as shown in column 4 of Table 3.4.

If the firm is currently selling 2 units and wishes to sell 3 units, it must lower price from $3.50 to $3.10. The third unit increases total revenue by its price, $3.10. In order to sell the third unit, the firm must lower price on the 2 units that could have been sold for $3.50 if only 2 units were offered for sale. The revenue lost on the 2 inframarginal units is $0.80 (= $0.40 × 2). Thus the marginal revenue of the third unit is $2.30 (= $3.10 − $0.80), and marginal revenue is less than the price of the third unit.

It is now easy to see why $P = MR$ for the first unit sold. For the first unit sold, price is not lowered on any inframarginal units. Since price must fall in order to sell additional units, marginal revenue must be less than price at every other level of sales (output).

FIGURE 3.6
Demand, Marginal Revenue, and Total Revenue

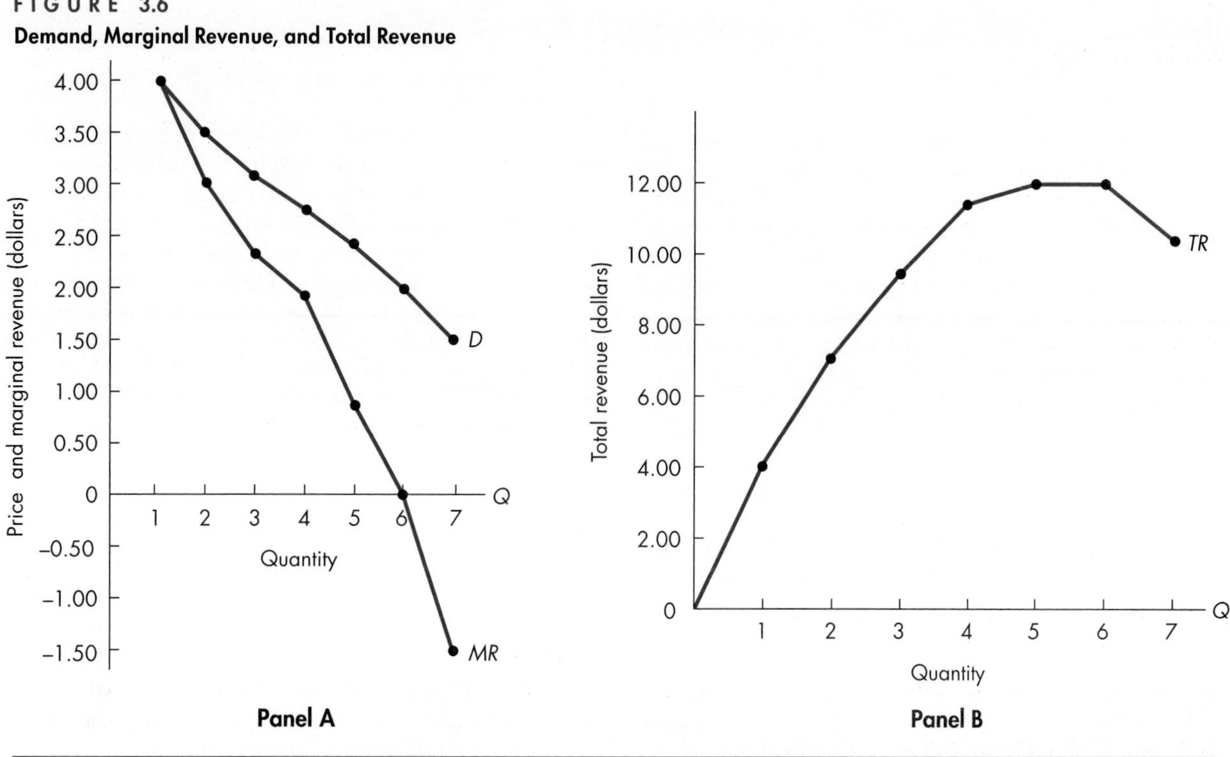

As shown in column 4, marginal revenue declines for each additional unit sold. Notice that it is positive for each of the first 5 units sold. However, marginal revenue is zero for the sixth unit sold, and it becomes negative thereafter. That is, the seventh unit sold actually causes total revenue to decline. Marginal revenue is positive when the effect of lowering price on the inframarginal units is less than the revenue contributed by the added sales at the lower price. Marginal revenue is negative when the effect of lowering price on the inframarginal units is greater than the revenue contributed by the added sales at the lower price.

Relation Marginal revenue must be less than price for all units sold after the first, because the price must be lowered in order to sell more units. When marginal revenue is positive, total revenue increases when quantity increases. When marginal revenue is negative, total revenue decreases when quantity increases. Marginal revenue is zero when total revenue is maximized.

Figure 3.6 shows graphically the relations among demand, marginal revenue, and total revenue for the demand schedule in Table 3.4. As noted above, *MR* is below price (in Panel A) at every level of output except the first. When total revenue (in Panel B) begins to decrease, marginal revenue becomes negative. Demand and marginal revenue are both negatively sloped.

ILLUSTRATION 3.3

Cigarette Taxes and Demand Elasticity

In 1993, President Clinton appeared to be leaning toward a large tax increase on cigarettes, and possibly alcohol, to finance part of his proposed health care plan. *The Wall Street Journal* (April 14, 1993) pointed out a problem with such "sin taxes." The chairwoman of the President's Council of Economic Advisors noted that such taxes are designed to do two things at once: (1) raise revenue for the government, and (2) discourage drinking, smoking, and other activities considered harmful to people's health. As the *WSJ* pointed out, the two goals may conflict. If the administration proves too successful in discouraging alcohol and tobacco consumption, there might not be enough money to pay for the health plan.

The director of the Congressional Budget Office believed that if the White House imposed a tobacco tax of $1 to $2 per pack, the tendency would be to "overestimate the amount of revenue that would come in." An industry analysis of the federal liquor tax in 1985 concluded that the government had expected to raise $14 billion in revenue over three years but only $11 billion came in. The president of the Distilled Spirits Council stated that after the tax on liquor was raised in 1991, the government actually collected 2.3 percent less in tax revenue.

On the other hand, the director of the Alcohol Policies Project at the Center for Science in the Public Interest argued that the falloff in revenue after the last tax increase was temporary, and stated, "To say that raising taxes doesn't raise more money is nonsense." A lawyer with the Nonsmokers' Rights Association of Canada pointed to the Canadian experience with "sin taxes" by arguing that tax increases on tobacco over the past decade had lifted the average price of a pack of cigarettes in Canada to $4.43 (U.S.) from $1.74. At the same time Canadians were smoking 40 percent fewer cigarettes and yet, overall tobacco tax revenue soared to $5.6 billion from $1.6 billion.

As you probably realize, the effect on government revenue from an excise tax on tobacco, alcohol, or any other good depends in large part on the elasticity of demand for that good. Consider the above statement saying the idea that raising taxes doesn't raise more money is just total nonsense. Obviously, if the government imposes a tax on a good that had not been previously taxed, tax receipts must rise if sales do not fall to zero after the price increase resulting from the tax. However, a tax increase over an existing tax may either increase or decrease tax revenue, depending on demand elasticity.

The accompanying figure illustrates this point. Assume that in this cigarette market there is already a tax on cigarettes of $1 per pack. The relevant current supply is shown by the supply curve labeled $S_{\$1\ tax}$. Two possible demand curves in equilibrium are D_1 and D_2. At the point of equilibrium, D_1 is more elastic than D_2, since any given percentage change in price will cause a larger percentage change in quantity demanded along D_1 than along D_2. When a $1-per-pack tax is levied, equilibrium price is $2 and sales are 700 million packs per month. Government's tax receipts from the $1-per-pack tax are therefore $700 million.

Now let the tax increase to $2 per pack, and the cigarette supply curve shifts upward (a decrease in supply) to the curve labeled $S_{\$2\ tax}$. If D_2 (the less elastic demand) is the relevant demand curve, price rises to approximately $2.75 and sales fall to 530 million packs per month. After the tax increase, tax receipts *rise* to $1,060 million (= $2 × 530 million packs). Also note that the elasticity of demand over the range of the price increase is

$$E = \frac{\Delta Q/\text{Average } Q}{\Delta P/\text{Average } P} = \frac{-170/615}{.75/2.375} = -0.875$$

Demand is inelastic over this range.

Sometimes the interval over which marginal revenue is measured is greater than 1 unit of output. After all, managers don't necessarily increase output by just 1 unit at a time. Suppose in Table 3.4 that we want to compute marginal revenue when output increases from 2 units to 5 units. Over the interval, the

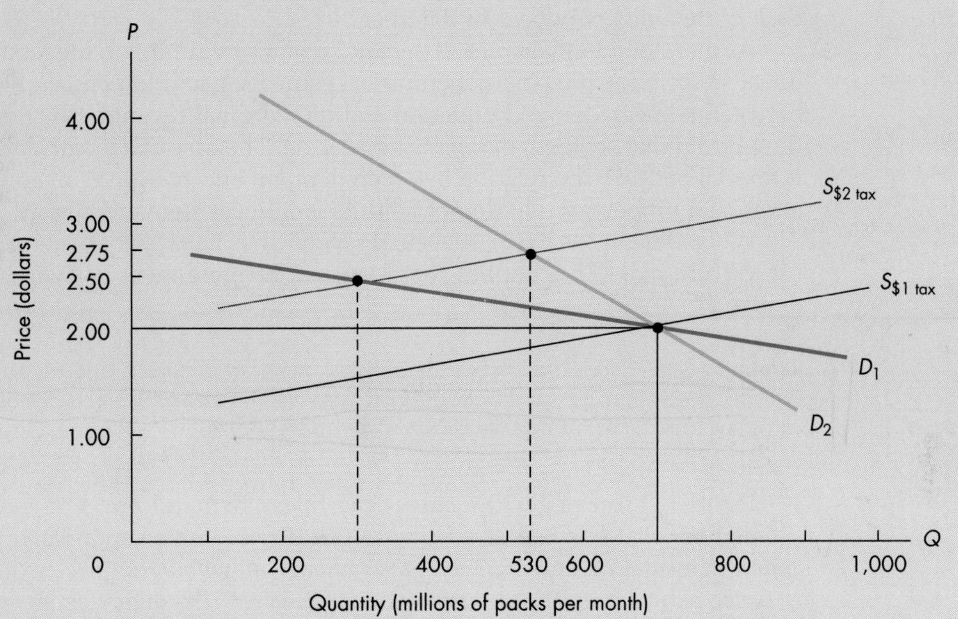

Now assume that D_1 (the more elastic demand) is the relevant demand curve. The shift in supply after the tax increase causes price to increase to $2.50 and sales to decrease to 300 million. Tax receipts now *fall* from $700 million at the $1 tax to $600 million (= $2 × 300 million packs) at the $2 tax. Demand elasticity over this range is

$$E = \frac{\Delta Q/\text{Average } Q}{\Delta P/\text{Average } P} = \frac{-400/500}{.50/2.25} = -3.60$$

This time demand is quite elastic over the range.

This exercise demonstrates two points: (1) The effect on government tax revenue of an increase in taxes on cigarettes or alcohol depends on the demand elasticity for the good, and (2) if demand is sufficiently elastic—not just elastic—the tax increase could actually *decrease,* not increase, government revenue.

There is substantial empirical evidence that demand for cigarettes is relatively inelastic (see Grossman et al., 1993). Elasticity estimates vary by age group: −1.20 for youths age 12 to 17, −0.74 for young smokers age 20 to 25, −0.44 for smokers between 26 and 35 years old, and −0.15 for smokers over 35 years old. Virtually all studies of federal cigarette tax revenues assume an inelastic demand for cigarettes, and therefore they predict higher tax revenues from tax hikes. In a recent study, a tax rate of $1.26 a pack was predicted to maximize tax revenue at $16 billion, while a $2 tax hike was predicted to yield only $11 billion in tax revenues.

Sources: Rick Wartzman, "Clinton's Proposal for 'Sin Taxes' May Stumble by Turning Too Many Americans into Saints," *The Wall Street Journal,* Apr. 14, 1993. Michael Grossman, Jody Sindelar, John Mullahy, and Richard Andersen, "Alcohol and Cigarette Taxes," *Journal of Economic Perspectives,* Fall 1993.

change in total revenue is $5 (= $12 − $7), and the change in output is 3 units. Marginal revenue is $1.67 (= $\Delta TR/\Delta Q$ = $5/3) per unit change in output; that is, each of the 3 units contributes (on average) $1.67 to total revenue. As a general rule, whenever the interval over which marginal revenue is being measured is more than a single unit, divide ΔTR by ΔQ to obtain the marginal revenue for each of the units of output in the interval.

As mentioned in Chapter 2, demand equations are frequently specified to be linear in form for purposes of empirical estimation and forecasting. The relation between a linear demand equation and its marginal revenue function is no different from that set forth in the above relation. The case of a linear demand curve is special because the relation between demand and marginal revenue has some additional properties that do not hold for nonlinear demand curves.

When demand is linear, marginal revenue lies halfway between demand and the vertical axis. This implies that marginal revenue must be twice as steep as demand.[9]

Relation When demand is linear, $P = a + bQ$, marginal revenue is also linear, intersects the vertical (price) axis at the same point demand does, and is twice as steep as demand. The equation of the linear marginal revenue curve is $MR = a + 2bQ$.

Figure 3.7 (on page 103) shows the linear demand curve $P = 6 - 0.05Q$. (Remember that b is negative because P and Q are inversely related.) The associated marginal revenue curve is also linear, intersects the price axis at \$6, and is twice as steep as the demand curve. Because it is twice as steep, marginal revenue intersects the quantity axis at 60 units, which is half the output level for which demand intersects the quantity axis. The equation for marginal revenue has the same vertical intercept but twice the slope: $MR = 6 - 0.10Q$.

Marginal Revenue and Elasticity

Using Figure 3.7, we now examine the relation of own-price elasticity to demand and marginal revenue. Recall that if total revenue increases when price falls and quantity rises, demand is elastic; if total revenue decreases when price falls and quantity rises, demand is inelastic. When marginal revenue is positive in Panel A, from a quantity of zero to 60, total revenue increases as price declines in Panel B; thus demand is elastic over this range. Conversely, when marginal revenue is negative, at any quantity greater than 60, total revenue declines when price falls; thus demand must be inelastic over this range. Finally, if marginal revenue is zero, at a quantity of 60, total revenue does not change when quantity changes, so the elasticity of demand is unitary at 60.

Except for marginal revenue being linear and twice as steep as demand, all the above relations hold for nonlinear demands. Thus for all demand curves the following relation must hold:

Relation Marginal revenue is less than price at every level of output after the first unit. When MR is positive (negative), total revenue increases (decreases) as quantity increases, and demand is elastic (inelastic). When MR is zero, the elasticity of demand is unitary.

[9]The mathematical relation between demand and marginal revenue in the case of a linear demand is derived in the appendix to this chapter.

FIGURE 3.7
Linear Demand, Marginal Revenue, and Elasticity

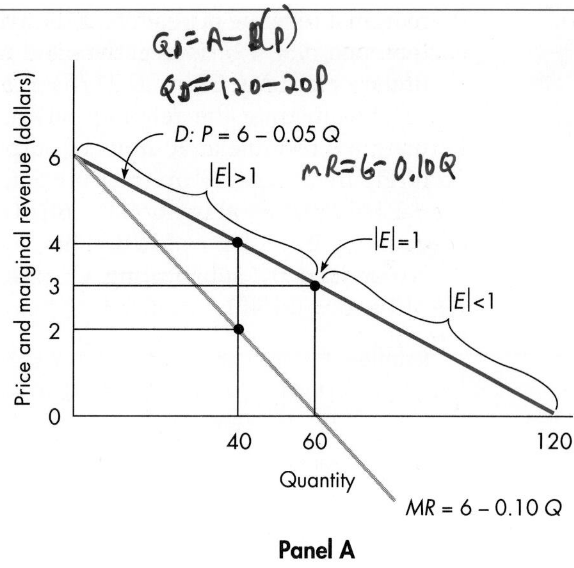

Panel A

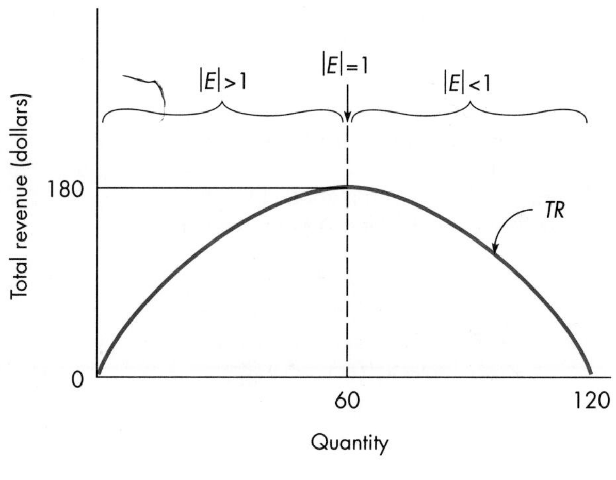

Panel B

The relation among marginal revenue, elasticity of demand, and price at any quantity can be expressed still more precisely. As shown in this chapter's appendix the relation between marginal revenue, price, and elasticity, *for linear or curvilinear demands,* is

$$MR = P\left(\frac{1}{E} + 1\right)$$

where E is the own-price elasticity of demand and P is product price. When demand is elastic ($|E| > 1$), $|1/E|$ is less than one, $(1/E) + 1$ is positive, and marginal revenue is positive. When demand is inelastic ($|E| < 1$), $|1/E|$ is greater than one, $1 + 1/E$ is negative, and marginal revenue is negative. In the case of unitary elasticity ($|E| = 1$), $(1/E) + 1$ is zero, and marginal revenue is zero.

To illustrate the relation between *MR*, *P*, and *E* numerically, we calculate marginal revenue at 40 units of output for the demand curve shown in Panel A of Figure 3.7. At 40 units of output, the point elasticity of demand is equal to -2 [$= P/(P - a) = 4/(4 - 6)$]. Using the formula presented above, *MR* is equal to 2 [$= 4(1 - 1/2)$]. This is the same value for marginal revenue that is obtained by substituting $Q = 40$ into the equation for marginal revenue: $MR = 6 - 0.1(40) = 2$.

Relation For any demand curve, when demand is elastic ($|E| > 1$), marginal revenue is positive. When demand is inelastic ($|E| < 1$), marginal revenue is negative. When demand is unitary elastic ($|E| = 1$), marginal revenue is zero. For all demand and marginal revenue curves:

$$MR = P\left(\frac{1}{E} + 1\right)$$

11 12 13 where E is the own-price elasticity of demand.

3.7 SUMMARY

Demand elasticity—the own-price elasticity of demand—measures the responsiveness or sensitivity of consumers to changes in the price of a good. The elasticity of demand is the ratio of the percentage change in quantity demanded to the percentage change in the price of the good. Over a specified price range, demand is said to be either elastic, unitary elastic, or inelastic according to whether the absolute value of the elasticity coefficient is greater than, equal to, or less than one, respectively. In the case of linear demand, moving down the demand curve causes the absolute value of the demand elasticity to get smaller.

An extremely important relation in economic analysis relates the change in total revenue (due to a change in price) and the elasticity of demand. If demand is elastic for a given change in price, an increase in price causes total revenue to fall. A decrease in price causes total revenue to rise if demand is elastic over the price range. If demand is inelastic for a given price change, an increase in price causes total revenue to rise, while a decrease in price causes total revenue to fall.

Several factors affect the own-price elasticity of demand. The most important of these is the availability of close substitutes. The better and more numerous the substitutes for a good, the more elastic the demand for the good. Demand elasticity is directly related to the percentage of the consumers' budgets spent on the good. Also, the longer the time period that consumers have to adjust to price changes, the more responsive they will be, and the more elastic is demand.

Demand elasticities are calculated either for intervals along the demand curve or at points on the demand curve. The arc elasticity formula is used to calculate elasticity along an arc (or interval) of demand. The arc elasticity formula uses the average or midpoint values of price and quantity, rather than the initial values, for the purpose of computing percentage changes. Specifically, the arc elasticity of demand (E) is

$$E = \frac{\Delta Q}{\text{Average } Q} \bigg/ \frac{\Delta P}{\text{Average } P}$$

In contrast to the arc elasticity, the point elasticity of demand measures elasticity at a point. When demand is linear, the point elasticity is calculated as

$$E = P/(P - a)$$

where a is the price intercept of the demand curve. The point elasticity of demand for a curvilinear demand is computed by constructing the tangent line to the curve at the point of measure. Extend the tangent line until it intersects the price axis. Compute the point elasticity as for a linear demand, using the price intercept of the tangent line as the value of a.

When elasticities are compared along a particular demand curve, the absolute value of demand elasticity generally varies directly with price: demand is more elastic at higher prices and less elastic at lower prices. An exception to this rule is the special demand curve $Q = aP^b$, which has a constant elasticity equal to the value of b throughout its entire range of prices.

Two other important elasticities are income elasticity, which measures the responsiveness of quantity purchased to changes in income, and cross-price elasticity, which measures the responsiveness of quantity purchased to changes in the price of related goods (substitutes or complements). Both of these elasticities are measured using the arc (averaging) method to compute percentage changes. In the case of income elasticity, the elasticity measure is positive if the good is normal, negative if the good is inferior. In the case of cross-price elasticity, the elasticity measure is positive if the two goods are substitutes, negative if they are complements.

Marginal revenue is the change in total revenue resulting from the sale of an additional unit of output. Marginal revenue declines as output increases and is less than price for every quantity except the first unit, in which case marginal revenue equals price. When MR is positive, TR is rising as price falls and quantity demanded increases. When MR is negative, TR is falling. When MR is zero, TR is neither rising nor falling: it is at its maximum value. In the case of linear demand, where demand is expressed as $P = a + bQ$, marginal revenue is also linear and is expressed as $MR = a + 2bQ$. In other words, marginal revenue is linear, intersects the price axis at the same point as demand, and is twice as steep as demand.

For any demand, linear or curvilinear, marginal revenue can be expressed as $MR = P[(1/E) + 1]$, where E is the own-price elasticity of demand. Hence, if demand is elastic, marginal revenue is positive. If demand is inelastic, marginal revenue is negative. When demand is unitary elastic, marginal revenue is equal to zero.

TECHNICAL PROBLEMS

1. Moving along a demand curve, quantity demanded decreases 8 percent when price increases 10 percent.
   a. The coefficient of demand elasticity is calculated to be ______.
   b. Given the demand elasticity calculated in part *a*, demand is ______ (elastic, inelastic, unitary elastic) along this portion of the demand curve.
   c. For this interval of demand, the percentage change in quantity is ______ (greater than, less than, equal to) the percentage change in price.
2. The coefficient of demand elasticity for a firm's product is equal to −1.5 over the range of prices being considered by the firm's manager.
   a. If the manager decreases the price of the product by 6 percent, the manager predicts that quantity demanded will ______ by ______ percent.
   b. If the manager wishes to increase sales by 30 percent, the manager predicts the price of the product must be ______ by ______ percent.
3. Fill in the blanks:
   a. When demand is elastic, the ______ effect dominates the ______ effect.
   b. When demand is inelastic, the ______ effect dominates the ______ effect.
   c. When demand is unitary elastic, ______ effect dominates.
   d. When a change in price causes a change in quantity demanded, total revenue always moves in the ______ direction as the variable (P or Q) having the ______ effect.
4. Fill in the blanks:
   a. When demand is elastic, an increase in price causes quantity demanded to ______ and total revenue to ______.

b. When demand is inelastic, a decrease in price causes quantity demanded to ________ and total revenue to ________.
c. When demand is unitary elastic, an increase in price causes quantity demanded to ________ and total revenue to ________.
d. If price falls and total revenue falls, demand must be ________.
e. If price rises and total revenue stays the same, demand must be ________.
f. If price rises and total revenue rises, demand must be ________.

5. In Panel A of Figure 3.1, verify that demand is unitary elastic over the price range of \$11 to \$13 without calculating the coefficient of demand elasticity.
6. For each pair of elasticities, which elasticity (in absolute value) is larger? Why
   a. The demand elasticity for carbonated soft drinks or the demand elasticity for Coca Cola
   b. The demand elasticity for socks (men's or women's) or the demand elasticity for business suits (men's or women's)
   c. The demand elasticity for electricity in the short run or the demand elasticity for electricity in the long run
7. Use the graph below to answer the following questions:

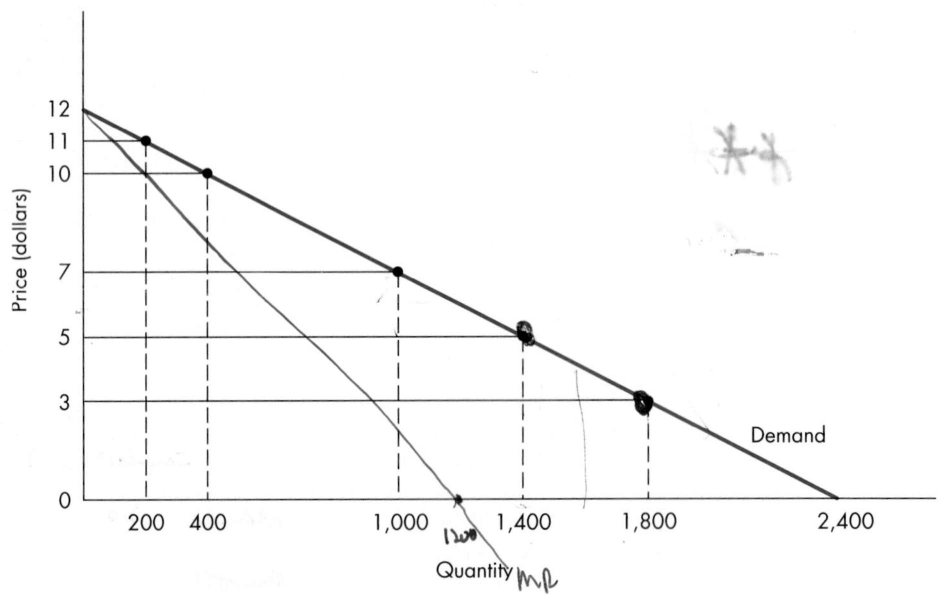

   a. The arc elasticity of demand over the price range \$3 to \$5 is ________.
   b. The arc elasticity of demand over the price range \$10 to \$11 is ________.
   c. The arc elasticity of demand over the price range \$5 to \$7 is ________.
8. Use the linear demand curve shown below to answer the following questions:

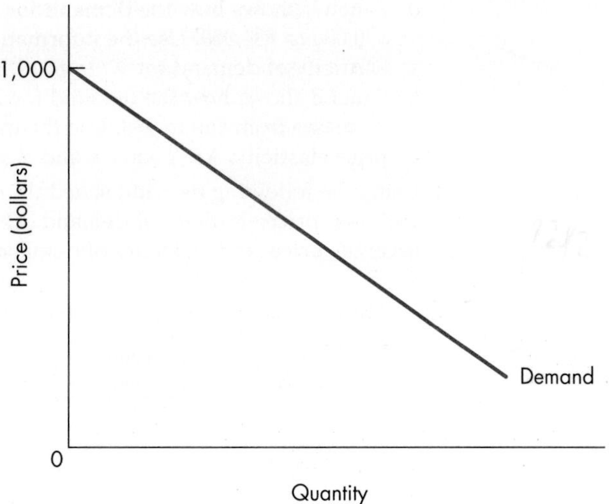

a. The point elasticity of demand at a price of $800 is ________.
b. The point elasticity of demand at a price of $200 is ________.
c. Demand is unitary elastic at a price of $________.
d. As price rises, $|E|$ ________ (gets larger, gets smaller, stays the same) for a linear demand curve.

9. Suppose the demand for good X is $Q = 20/P$.
   a. When P = $1, total revenue is ________.
   b. When P = $2, total revenue is ________.
   c. When P = $4, total revenue is ________.
   d. The elasticity of demand is equal to ________. Why?

10. In the two panels shown below, the demand for good X shifts due to a change in income (Panel A) and a change in the price of a related good Y (Panel B). Holding the price of good X constant at $50, calculate the following elasticities:

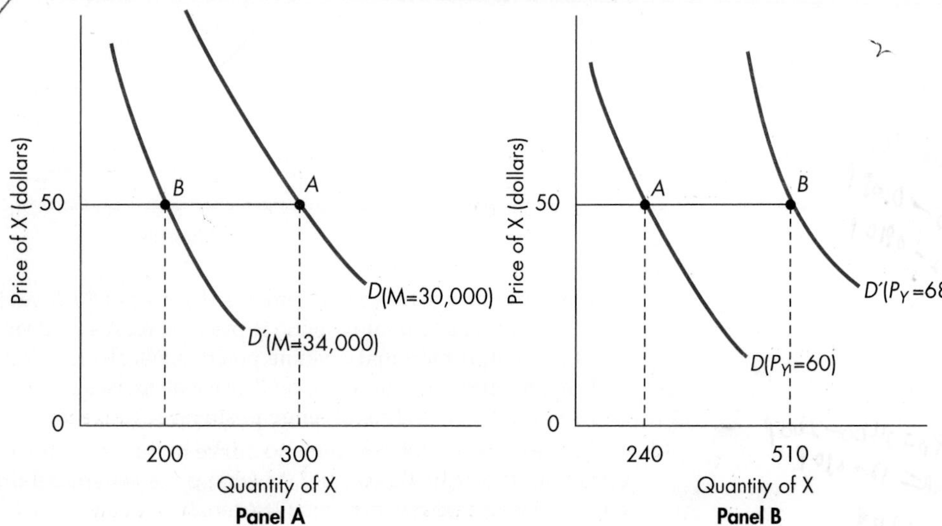

a. Panel A shows how the demand for X shifts when income increases from \$30,000 to \$34,000. Use the information in Panel A to calculate the income elasticity of demand for X. Is good X normal or inferior?

b. Panel B shows how the demand for X shifts when the price of related good Y increases from \$60 to \$68. Use the information in Panel B to calculate the cross-price elasticity. Are goods X and Y substitutes or complements?

11. Using the following demand schedule, calculate total revenue, marginal revenue, and own-price elasticity of demand. Then show the relation among marginal revenue, price, and elasticity of demand.

Price	Quantity demanded	Total revenue	Marginal revenue	Elasticity of demand
\$60	8	______		
50	16	______	______	______
40	24	______	______	______
30	32	______	______	______
20	40	______	______	______
10	48	______	______	______

12. Use the graph below to answer the following questions:

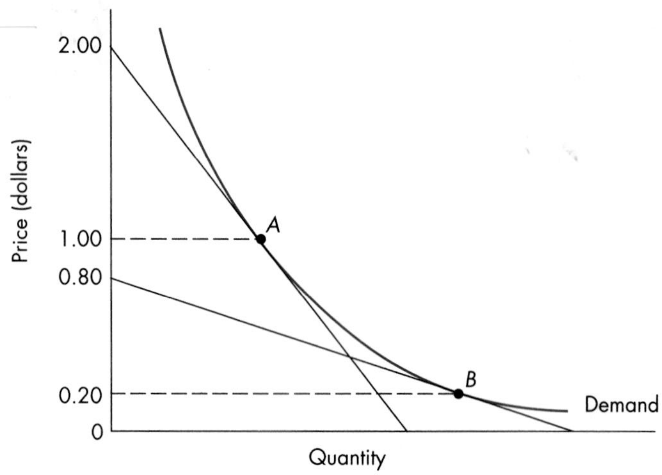

a. What are the elasticities of demand at prices of \$0.20 and \$1.00?

b. What happens to total revenue if price increases by a small amount at point A? At point A, is marginal revenue positive, negative, or zero?

c. What happens to total revenue if price decreases by a small amount at point B? At point B, is marginal revenue positive, negative, or zero?

13. Write the equation for the demand curve in the graph for problem 7. What is the equation for marginal revenue? At what price is demand unitary elastic? At what output is marginal revenue equal to zero?

APPLIED PROBLEMS

1. In an article about the financial problems of *USA Today*, *Newsweek* (April 27, 1992) reported that the paper was losing about $20 million a year. A Wall Street analyst said that the paper should raise its price from 50 cents to 75 cents, which he estimated would bring in an additional $65 million a year. The paper's publisher rejected the idea, saying that circulation could drop sharply after a price increase, citing *The Wall Street Journal*'s experience after it increased its price to 75 cents. What implicit assumptions are the publisher and the analyst making about demand elasticity?
2. Assume that the demand for plastic surgery is price inelastic. Are the following statements true or false? Explain.
   a. When the price of plastic surgery increases, the number of operations decreases.
   b. The percentage change in the price of plastic surgery is less than the percentage change in quantity demanded.
   c. Changes in the price of plastic surgery do not affect the number of operations.
   d. Quantity demanded is quite responsive to changes in price.
   e. If more plastic surgery is performed, expenditures on plastic surgery will decrease.
   f. The marginal revenue of another operation is negative.
3. What effect, if any, does each of the following events have on the own-price elasticity of demand for corporate jets?
   a. Reduced corporate earnings lead to cuts in travel budgets and increase the share of expenditures on private jet travel.
   b. Further deregulation of the commercial airlines industry substantially increases the variety of departure times and destinations offered by commercial airlines.
   c. The cost of manufacturing corporate jets rises.
   d. A new, much more fuel-efficient corporate jet is introduced.
4. Aztec Enterprises depends heavily upon advertising to sell its products. Management at Aztec is allowed to spend $2 million monthly on advertising, but no more than this amount. Each month, Aztec spends exactly $2 million on advertising. What is Aztec's elasticity of demand for advertising? Can you write the equation for Aztec's demand for advertising?
5. You are assistant to the president of a large state university. The university, faced with declining enrollment, is considering a large decrease in tuition. You are asked to forecast the effect. What factors would you have to consider? Explain.
6. The own-price elasticity of demand for imported whiskey is estimated to be −0.20 over a wide interval of prices. The federal government decides to raise the import tariff on foreign whiskey, causing its price to rise by 20 percent. Will sales of whiskey rise or fall, and by what percentage amount?
7. As manager of Citywide Racquet Club, you must determine the best price to charge for locker rentals. Assume that the (marginal) cost of providing lockers is zero. The monthly demand for lockers is estimated to be

$$Q = 100 - 2P$$

   where P is the monthly rental price, and Q is the number of lockers rented per month.
   a. What price would you charge?

b. How many lockers are rented monthly at this price?
c. Explain why you chose this price.

8. The demand curve for haircuts at Terry Bernard's Hair Design is

$$P = 15 - 0.15Q$$

where Q is the number of cuts per week, and P is the price of a haircut. Terry is considering raising her price above the current price of $9. Terry is unwilling to raise price if the price hike will cause revenues to fall.
a. Should Terry raise the price of haircuts above $9? Why or why not?
b. Suppose demand for Terry's haircuts increases to $P = 22 - 0.22Q$. At a price of $9, should Terry raise the price of her haircuts? Why or why not?

9. As part of his plan to reduce the budget deficit, President Clinton proposed raising the excise tax on gasoline by 50 cents per gallon. While passage of this proposal was blocked by Congress, what would have happened to the sales of gasoline if the price of gasoline were to rise by 45 cents per gallon? (Producers cannot pass the entire 50-cent tax increase on to consumers.) Assume that the average price of gasoline is now $1.30 per gallon and use the short-run price elasticity for gasoline presented in Illustration 3.2 to answer this question. Would you have expected total expenditure on gasoline by consumers to have risen or fallen had Clinton's proposed 50-cent-per-gallon excise tax been enacted? Explain.

10. *The Wall Street Journal* (February 13, 1992) reported that movie attendance dropped 8 percent in 1991 as ticket prices rose a little more than 5 percent. What is the elasticity of demand for movie tickets? Could demand elasticity be somewhat overestimated from these figures? That is, could other things have changed, accounting for some of the decline in attendance?

MATHEMATICAL APPENDIX Demand Elasticity

The Coefficient of Demand Elasticity

Let the demand function be expressed as $Q = Q(P)$, where the law of demand requires that quantity demanded and price be inversely related: $dQ/dP = Q'(P) < 0$, so the demand curve is downward-sloping. The slope of the demand curve measures the *absolute* rate of change in Q as P changes. The value of the absolute rate of change depends upon the units of measure of both P and Q. A measure of the *proportional* rate of change is invariant to the units of measure of P and Q. The coefficient of demand elasticity, E, measures the proportional rate of change in quantity demanded as price changes:

$$E = \frac{\dfrac{dQ}{Q}}{\dfrac{dP}{P}} = \frac{dQ}{dP}\frac{P}{Q} = Q'(P)\frac{P}{Q} \qquad (1)$$

As shown above, the elasticity coefficient can also be expressed as the slope of demand, $Q'(P)$, times a proportionality factor, P/Q. Since the slope of demand is negative and the proportionality factor is always positive, E is always a negative number.

When demand is linear, $Q'(P)$ is constant. E, however, is *not* constant as changes in price cause movements along a linear demand function. Moving down a linear demand, P falls and Q increases, causing the proportionality factor to decrease. Thus, as P decreases, E diminishes in absolute value; that is, $|E|$ decreases.

Demand Elasticity and Changes in Total Revenue

In this section it will be useful to employ the inverse demand function, $P = P(Q)$, so that total revenue can be conveniently expressed as a function of Q. Total revenue for a firm is the price of the product times the number of units sold:

$$\text{Total revenue} = TR = R(Q) = P(Q)Q \qquad (2)$$

In order to examine how total revenue changes as sales

increase with lower prices, the derivative of total revenue, known as marginal revenue, is defined as

(3) $$\text{Marginal revenue} = MR = R'(Q) = P'(Q)Q + P(Q)$$

where $P'(Q) = (dP/dQ) < 0$. Marginal revenue is positive, negative, or zero as total revenue is rising, falling, or at its maximum value, respectively.

To derive the relation between elasticity and changes in total revenue (i.e., marginal revenue), marginal revenue can be expressed as a function of E as follows: First, factor P out of the expression for MR in (3):

(4) $$MR = R'(Q) = P\left(P'(Q)\frac{Q}{P} + 1\right)$$

Notice that $P'(Q) \cdot (Q/P)$ is the inverse of E. Substituting $1/E$ into expression (4) results in a useful relation between MR, P, and E:

(5) $$MR = R'(Q) = P\left(\frac{1}{E} + 1\right)$$

Several important relations can be derived from equation (5):

1. When Q is continuous and $Q > 0$, MR is less than P.* In the special case of a horizontal demand curve, $E = \infty$, $MR = P$. You will see this special case in a later chapter.
2. When demand is unitary elastic ($E = -1$), $MR = 0$ and an infinitesimally small change in Q causes no change in TR. Therefore, TR is at its maximum value when demand is unitary elastic and $MR = 0$.
3. When demand is elastic (inelastic), MR is positive (negative), a decrease in P causes an increase in Q, and total revenue rises (falls).

Linear Demand, Marginal Revenue, and Point Elasticity

Let the straight-line demand be expressed as an inverse demand function:

(6) $$P = P(Q) = a + bQ$$

where a is the positive price intercept, and $b = dP/dQ$ is the negative slope of the inverse demand line. The total revenue received by the firm for a given level of sales, Q, is

(7) $$TR = R(Q) = P(Q)Q = (a + bQ)Q = aQ + bQ^2$$

Notice that a linear demand function has a quadratic total revenue function which graphs as a ∩-shaped curve.

Marginal revenue associated with a linear demand function can be found by taking the derivative of total revenue:

(8) $$MR = R'(Q) = a + 2bQ$$

In absolute value, the slope of MR, $2b$, is twice as great as the slope of demand, b. Both curves have the same vertical intercept, a. This relation is shown in Figure 3A.1.

To derive the point elasticity for a linear demand, it is convenient to employ the demand function expressed as $Q = Q(P)$, rather than the inverse demand in equation (6). The demand function associated with the inverse demand in equation (6) is

(9) $$Q = Q(P) = -\frac{a}{b} + \frac{1}{b}P = \frac{1}{b}(-a + P)$$

The slope of the demand function, dQ/dP, is $1/b$. Substituting $1/b$ for dQ/dP and expression (9) for Q in the elasticity equation (1) provides a rather simple algebraic expression for the point elasticity of demand when demand is linear:

(10) $$E = \frac{1}{b}\frac{P}{\frac{1}{b}(-a + P)} = \frac{P}{(P - a)}$$

Equation (10) makes it clear that E is not constant for linear demands. The elasticity of demand varies inversely with price along a linear demand curve:

(11) $$\frac{dE}{dP} = \frac{-a}{(P - a)^2} < 0$$

As price falls along a linear demand, E gets larger algebraically (i.e., less negative), $|E|$ gets smaller, and demand becomes less elastic. Similarly, as price rises, $|E|$ gets larger and demand becomes more elastic.

The Special Case of Constant Elasticity of Demand: $Q = aP^b$

When demand takes the form $Q = aP^b$, the elasticity of demand is constant and equal to b:

(12) $$E = \frac{dQ}{dP} \cdot \frac{P}{Q} = baP^{b-1}\left(\frac{P}{aP^b}\right) = b$$

For example, when $Q = aP^{-1}$, demand is unitary elastic for all prices.

---

*When quantity is a discrete variable, rather than a continuous variable, $P = MR$ for the first unit sold. For the first unit sold, there are no inframarginal units, so no revenue is lost by lowering price to sell the first unit. After the first unit sold, $P > MR$.

FIGURE 3A.1
Linear Demand and Marginal Revenue

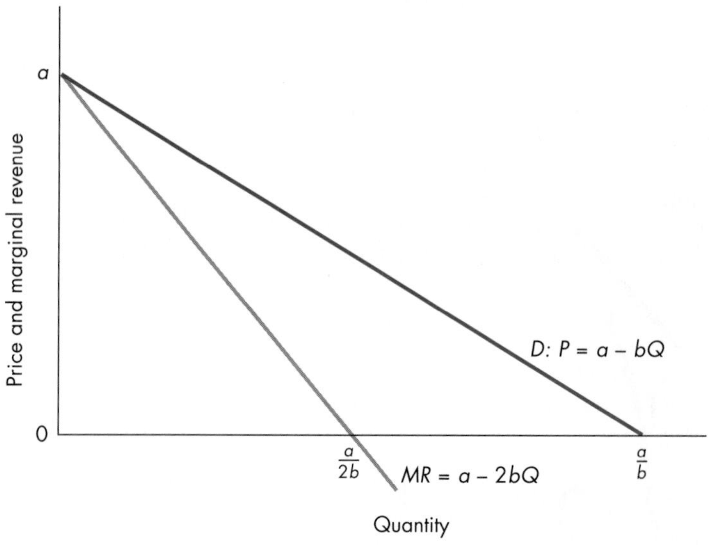

MATHEMATICAL EXERCISES

1. Consider the linear demand function $Q = 20 - 0.5P$.
   a. Write the inverse demand function.
   b. Write the total revenue function.
   c. Using calculus, find the level of output, Q_{rmax}, where total revenue reaches its maximum value. What price, P_{rmax}, maximizes total revenue? What is the value of TR at its maximum point?
   d. Write the equation for marginal revenue. Using MR, verify that Q_{rmax} derived in part c maximizes total revenue.
   e. Calculate the point elasticity of demand at P_{rmax}. Does E have the expected value? Explain briefly.
2. Let a linear demand function be expressed as $Q = A + BP$, where $B < 0$.
   a. Express the point elasticity of demand as a function of Q and A only.
   b. Take the derivative dE/dQ and verify that demand becomes less elastic moving down the demand curve.
3. Suppose demand takes the form $Q = 36P^{-1}$.
   a. Show that the point elasticity of demand is constant and equal to -1.
   b. Write the total and marginal revenue functions.

Part II
Some Preliminaries

CHAPTER 4

Fundamentals of Managerial Decision Making

The Theory of Optimization

One of the most important tasks of managers, perhaps the most important, is making decisions that further the goals of the firm. The ability to make decisions that will lead to the best outcome under a given set of circumstances is the distinguishing characteristic of a good manager. As we will show in this chapter, finding the best solution involves applying the fundamental principles of the theory of optimization.

Consider, for example, the optimization problem facing a store manager who wishes to determine how many store detectives to hire in order to reduce shoplifting. One may think at first that the manager should hire enough detectives to eliminate shoplifting altogether. However, since detectives cost money, this would generally not be the best choice. As an example, suppose the store was experiencing average shoplifting losses of $20 a day, and another detective could eliminate this loss but would cost the store $100 a day. Clearly the additional detective would cost $80 a day more than would be saved. There is some optimal number of detectives, and we will show you how that number is determined. A similar type of decision might involve a manager who must decide how much output his or her firm should produce. The answer is not "as much as is possible." More production adds to the firm's revenues, but producing more also adds to costs. We will develop a simple analytical process for choosing the "best" level of output.

A slightly different type of optimizing decision, involving a production manager, is choosing the best combination of workers, machinery, and raw materials in order to produce a specified level of output at the lowest possible cost. Another example, for an advertising manager, is determining how to allocate a given advertising budget among TV, radio, and newspaper advertising so as to obtain the highest level of sales possible within the budget. We will set forth a simple rule that leads to the best solution for these types of decisions.

This chapter develops the rules of optimizing behavior that are the underpinnings of managerial decision making. These rules form the foundation of the theories of profit maximization, production, input choice, and consumer behavior that are developed throughout the text. The rules of optimization are pervasive in the study of economics; managers should know and understand these basic principles because this knowledge will enable them to make better decisions.

We should emphasize from the beginning that although we will use numerical examples of the benefits and costs related to optimizing decisions, we are not going to show you how to actually measure the benefits and costs in this chapter. This chapter is designed only to show the techniques of optimization, so the numbers are purely hypothetical. Later in the text we will describe how to measure the benefits and costs associated with various decision problems facing managers.

We begin the analysis of optimization theory by explaining some terminology that you will encounter in this chapter and throughout a large part of the text. We then derive two rules for making optimal decisions. If you thoroughly understand both rules, you should have little difficulty with the theories that are developed later in the text.

4.1 CONCEPTS AND TERMINOLOGY

Before we begin to develop the theory of optimizing behavior, we must present some concepts and terminology that you should be familiar with in order to understand the development and application of the principles of optimization. In addition to their use in this chapter, these concepts are used throughout the text when setting forth theoretical concepts.

Objective Functions

objective function
The function the decision maker seeks to maximize or minimize.

Optimizing behavior on the part of a decision maker involves trying to maximize or minimize an **objective function.** For a manager of a firm, the objective function is usually profit, which is to be maximized. For a consumer, the objective function is the satisfaction derived from consumption of goods, which is to be maximized. For a city manager seeking to provide adequate law enforcement services, the objective function might be cost, which is to be minimized. For the manager of the marketing division of a large corporation, the objective function is usually sales, which are to be maximized. In other words, the objective function measures whatever it is that the particular decision maker wishes to either maximize or minimize.

maximization problem
An optimization problem that involves maximizing the objective function.

minimization problem
An optimization problem that involves minimizing the objective function.

If the decision maker seeks to *maximize* an objective function, the optimization problem is called a **maximization problem.** Alternatively, if the objective function is to be minimized, the optimization problem is called a **minimization problem.** As a general rule, when the objective function measures a benefit, the decision maker seeks to maximize this benefit and is solving a maximization problem. When the objective function measures a cost, the decision maker seeks to minimize this cost and is solving a minimization problem. As you will see, the rules for solving maximization and minimization problems are identical.

Activities or Choice Variables

activities or **choice variables** Determine the value of the objective function.

The value of the objective function is determined by the level of one or more **activities** or **choice variables.** For example, the value of profit depends upon the number of units of output produced and sold. The production of units of the good is the activity that determines the value of the objective function, which in this case is profit. The decision maker controls the value of the objective function by choosing the level of the activities or choice variables.

Objective functions may be a function of more than one activity. Consider the cost of producing a good or service. If just two inputs—labor and capital—are used in production, the cost function (objective function) can be expressed as

$$\begin{aligned} C &= wL + rK \\ &= f(L, K) \end{aligned}$$

where C is the cost of production, w is the price of a unit of labor services, L is the amount of labor services employed, r is the price of a unit of capital services, and K is the amount of capital services employed. The cost function has two choice variables, L and K. For any given level of output, a manager will choose L and K to minimize the cost of production.

discrete choice variable A choice variable that can take only specific integer values.

continuous choice variable A choice variable that can take on any value between two end points.

The choice variables in the optimization problems discussed in this text will at times vary discretely and at other times vary continuously. A **discrete choice variable** can take on only specified integer values, such as 1, 2, 3, . . . or 10, 20, 30, ... An example of a discrete choice variable is in Table 3.4 in Chapter 3, in which quantity sold varies in units of one. All examples of discrete choice variables will be presented in tables.

A **continuous choice variable** can take on any value between two end points. For example, a continuous variable that can vary between zero and 10 can take on the value 2, 2.345, 7.9, 8.999, or any one of the infinite number of values between the two limits. An example of a continuous choice variable is in Figure 3.7 in Chapter 3, in which quantity sold can take on any value along the horizontal axis between zero and 120 units. Examples of continuous choice variables will usually be presented graphically but will sometimes be shown by equations. As it turns out, the optimization rules differ only slightly in the discrete and continuous cases.

Unconstrained and Constrained Optimization

unconstrained optimization An optimization problem in which the decision maker can choose the level of activity from an unrestricted set of values.

In addition to being categorized as either maximization or minimization problems, optimization problems are also categorized according to whether the decision maker can choose the values of the choice variables in the objective function from an *unconstrained* or *constrained* set of values. **Unconstrained optimization** problems occur when a decision maker can choose the level of activity from an unrestricted set of values in order to maximize the objective function. In this text, we show how to solve only unconstrained *maximization* problems because all the *unconstrained* decision problems we address are maximization problems.[1] In managerial decision making, the most important type of unconstrained maximization problem arises when an activity generates both benefits and costs, and the decision maker must maximize the net benefit of the activity, where the net benefit is the difference between the total benefit and the total cost of the activity.

An example of an unconstrained optimization problem that you will encounter throughout this text is that of a firm that chooses the level of sales—or resource usage or advertising—to maximize its profit. Increased sales increase the firm's revenues, which is the benefit. Increased sales also increase the firm's costs, because the inputs used to produce the increased output must be paid. Profit, which is calculated as the difference between total revenue and total cost, is the net benefit from the firm's sales. The firm chooses the level of sales that gives the maximum net benefits or profits. The profit maximization problem is considered an *unconstrained* optimization problem because the manager can choose any level of output in order to maximize net benefit. In the pursuit of the highest possible profit, the manager is bound by no external restrictions on how much output the firm may produce.[2]

constrained optimization
An optimization problem in which the decision maker chooses values for the choice variables from a restricted set of values.

constrained maximization
A maximization problem where the activities must be chosen to satisfy a side constraint that the total cost of the activities be held to a specific amount.

Constrained optimization problems involve choosing the levels of two or more activities that generate both benefits and costs to a decision maker. In this text, we examine both constrained maximization and constrained minimization problems. A **constrained maximization** problem occurs when a decision maker chooses the levels of two or more activities so as to maximize the total benefits, subject to the side constraint that the total (combined) cost of these activities be held to a specific amount. The objective function is the total benefit function, and the constraint is the total cost function. Since total cost is held to a specific level, the choice of activity levels is constrained to the various combinations of activity levels, whose combined cost just equals the specified constraint on cost. An example of a constrained maximization problem involves a corporate advertising director who can spend only $10,000 per month, in total, on advertising in various media. The advertising director must choose, for example, the level of advertising on radio, newspapers, and billboards in order to maximize monthly sales. The maximization problem is a constrained problem because the combined cost of radio, newspaper, and billboard advertising cannot exceed $10,000.

---

[1]As it turns out, all unconstrained minimization problems can be transformed into unconstrained maximization problems just by multiplying the objective function by -1. The value of the choice variable that minimizes the objective function is exactly equal to the value of the choice variable that maximizes the objective function (after it has been multiplied by -1).

[2]As long as there exists a range of output over which the firm can earn positive profit, a rational manager will obviously avoid the ranges where profit is negative. Since the decision maker *chooses* not to select values of the choice variable in the range of negative profit, no *external* constraint is present, and the optimization problem is an unconstrained one.

constrained minimization
A minimization problem where the activities must be chosen to satisfy a side constraint that the total benefit of the activities be held to a specific amount.

A **constrained minimization** problem occurs when a decision maker chooses the levels of two or more activities so as to minimize the total costs from the activities, subject to the side constraint that the total (combined) benefits of these activities are held to a specific amount. In this case, the objective function is the total cost function, and the total benefit function is now the constraint. Holding total benefits constant restricts the choice of activity levels. An example of a constrained minimization problem involves a manager who wishes to find the combination of inputs to hire in order to produce 300 units of output per week at the lowest possible total cost. The objective function is the total cost of the combination of inputs chosen to produce 300 units of output. While there are many combinations of inputs that can be used to produce 300 units of the good, the decision maker must choose from the subset of all input combinations that will produce exactly 300 units of output, which is the constraint.

As we will show later in this chapter, the constrained maximization and the constrained minimization problems have one simple rule for the solution. Therefore, you will only have one rule to learn for all constrained optimization problems.

marginal analysis
An analytical tool for solving optimization problems that involves changing the value(s) of the choice variable(s) by a small amount to see if the objective function can be further increased (for maximization problems) or further decreased (for minimization problems).

Marginal Analysis

Even though there are a huge number of possible maximizing or minimizing decisions, you will see that all optimization problems can be solved using a powerful analytical tool called **marginal analysis.** Marginal analysis involves changing the value(s) of the choice variable(s) by a small amount to see if the objective function can be further increased (in the case of maximization problems) or further decreased (in the case of minimization problems). If so, the manager continues to make incremental adjustments in the choice variables until no further improvements are possible. Marginal analysis leads to two simple rules for solving optimization problems, one for unconstrained decisions and one for constrained decisions. We turn first to the unconstrained decision.

4.2 UNCONSTRAINED MAXIMIZATION

As noted above, an unconstrained maximization problem arises when a decision maker chooses the level of an activity so as to obtain the maximum possible net benefit from the activity, where net benefit (NB) is the difference between total benefit (TB) and total cost (TC):

$$NB = TB - TC$$

As we mentioned, the most frequently encountered unconstrained maximization problem for managers is choosing the levels of activities such as output, advertising, and input usage that maximize the firm's profit. In all such cases the total benefit is the total revenue from the activities, the total cost is how much the activities cost the firm, and the net benefit is the total profit. Because the same rules apply to all such unconstrained problems, we introduce the concept by considering the most general form of the problem.

TABLE 4.1
Unconstrained Maximization: The Case of a Discrete Choice Variable

(1) Level of activity (*A*)	(2) Total benefit of activity (*TB*)	(3) Total cost of activity (*TC*)	(4) Net benefit of activity (*NB*)	(5) Marginal benefit (*MB*)	(6) Marginal cost (*MC*)
0	$ 0	$ 0	$ 0	—	—
1	16	2	14	16	2
2	30	6	24	14	4
3	40	11	29	10	5
4	48	20	28	8	9
5	54	30	24	6	10
6	58	45	13	4	15
7	61	61	0	3	16
8	63	80	−17	2	19

optimal level of the activity
The level of activity that maximizes net benefit.

The level of activity that maximizes net benefit is called the **optimal level of the activity.** In this section we develop the simple rule for finding the optimal level of an activity: Increase the activity when another unit of the activity creates greater *additional* benefits than *additional* costs, and decrease the level of the activity when 1 less unit of the activity creates a greater reduction in costs than in benefits.

Maximization with a Discrete Choice Variable

We begin the analysis of unconstrained maximization with a very general discrete choice variable problem. Table 4.1 shows a schedule of total benefits and total costs for various levels of some activity, called *A*, expressed in integers between 0 and 8. Note that both total benefit (column 2) and total cost (column 3) increase as the activity is increased. The net benefit for each level of activity is computed by subtracting column 3 from column 2. Clearly, the net benefit changes as the level of the activity changes. In this optimization problem, the activity level (*A*) is the choice variable because it is the variable that determines the level of net benefit.

It is obvious from column 4, Table 4.1, that the optimal level of the activity is 3 units, because the net benefit associated with 3 units ($29) is higher than that associated with any other level. Therefore, if the level of the activity is less than 3, an increase in *A* increases the net benefit. If the level of the activity is greater than 3, a decrease in *A* also increases the net benefit. Note that at the optimal level of the activity, the total benefit is not maximized nor is the total cost minimized. The solution to an unconstrained maximization problem maximizes the *net* benefit.

We also can find the optimal level of the activity by using *marginal analysis.* As noted earlier, marginal analysis involves examining the effects of small changes in the level of an activity to see if such changes increase or decrease the net benefit of the activity. Marginal analysis is based on the following simple principle:

Principle If, at a given level of activity, a small increase or decrease in the level of that activity causes *net benefit* to increase, then that level of the activity is not optimal. The activity is increased or decreased in order to obtain the highest net benefit. The optimal level of the activity is attained when no further increases in net benefit are possible for any changes in the activity.

marginal benefit (*MB*) The addition to total benefit attributable to increasing the activity by a small amount.

marginal cost (*MC*) The addition to total cost attributable to increasing the activity by a small amount.

The marginal analysis solution to optimization problems involves comparing the **marginal benefit (*MB*)** of a change in an activity and the **marginal cost (*MC*)** of the change. Marginal benefit is the addition to total benefit that occurs when the level of an activity is increased by a small amount. Marginal benefit also measures the *reduction* in total benefit when the activity level is *decreased* by a small amount. Marginal cost is the increase in total cost that occurs when the level of an activity is increased by a small amount. Marginal cost also measures the decrease in total cost when the level of the activity is decreased by a small amount. Expressed more formally, marginal benefit and marginal cost are defined as

$$MB = \frac{\text{Change in total benefit}}{\text{Change in activity}} = \frac{\Delta TB}{\Delta A}$$

and

$$MC = \frac{\text{Change in total cost}}{\text{Change in activity}} = \frac{\Delta TC}{\Delta A}$$

where the symbol "Δ" means "the change in" and A denotes the level of the activity. Thus, marginal benefit and marginal cost are the changes in benefits and costs *per unit* change in the activity.

Columns 5 and 6 in Table 4.1 show the marginal benefit and marginal cost for each change in the level of the activity. The marginal benefit of the third unit of the activity is $10 because increasing A from 2 to 3 units increases total benefit from $30 to $40. The marginal benefit also indicates how much total benefit decreases if A is reduced by a small amount. Reducing A from 3 to 2 units decreases total benefit by $10. Thus $10 is the amount that the third unit adds to the total benefit and is also the amount by which the total benefit falls when the third unit is given up.

You can determine whether net benefit (*NB*) is rising or falling simply by comparing marginal benefit (*MB*) and marginal cost (*MC*), without even computing net benefit. Begin by assuming that at some current level of the activity, an increase in the activity causes marginal benefit to exceed marginal cost ($MB > MC$). If A increases by 1 unit, two things occur. Total benefit (*TB*) rises and total cost (*TC*) rises. Whether or not net benefit (*NB*) rises depends on how much total benefit rises relative to how much total cost rises. Since by assumption marginal benefit exceeds marginal cost, total benefit must rise by more than total cost rises; thus, net benefit must rise. In Table 4.1, the marginal benefit of

TABLE 4.2
Relations between Marginal Benefit (*MB*), Marginal Cost (*MC*), and Net Benefit (*NB*)

	$MB > MC$	$MB < MC$
Increase activity	*NB* rises	*NB* falls
Decrease activity	*NB* falls	*NB* rises

the third unit of the activity is $10, and the marginal cost is $5. Since the third unit adds $10 to total benefit and only $5 to total cost, net benefit rises by $5 (from $24 to $29, as shown in column 4). Suppose the decision maker mistakenly decreases the activity when *MB* exceeds *MC*. In this case, total benefit falls by more than total cost, and net benefit declines. For example, at 3 units of the activity, reducing the activity level to 2 units causes total benefit to fall by $10 (*MB*) and total cost to fall by $5 (*MC*). Net benefit falls by $5 (from $29 to $24) when *A* is decreased from 3 to 2 units.

Now suppose marginal benefit is less than marginal cost ($MB < MC$). Increasing *A* causes total benefit to rise by less than total cost, and net benefit *falls.* In Table 4.1 the marginal benefit from adding the fifth unit is $6, and the marginal cost is $10. Increasing *A* from 4 to 5 units causes total benefit to rise by only $6, while total cost rises by $10; net benefit must fall by $4 (from $28 to $24). *Decreasing A* from 5 to 4 units will cause net benefit to *rise.* Total benefit falls by only $6, while total cost falls by $10, causing net benefit to rise by $4 (from $24 to $28). The relation between marginal benefit, marginal cost, and net benefit is summarized in Table 4.2.

The relation between marginal benefit, marginal cost, and net benefit provides the keys to finding the optimal level of an activity using marginal analysis. If marginal benefit exceeds marginal cost, increasing the activity results in higher net benefits. The decision maker continues to increase the activity until the last unit is reached for which marginal benefit exceeds marginal cost (any further increase in activity causes *MC* to exceed *MB*). Refer again to Table 4.1. When considering the first unit of the activity, the decision maker increases the activity from zero to 1 because $16 (*MB*) is greater than $2 (*MC*). The decision maker should also add the second unit of activity, because the second unit adds $14 to total benefit and only $4 to total cost. Since the marginal benefit of the third unit ($10) is greater than the marginal cost ($5), the third unit will be added. The fourth unit of activity should not be added since it adds only $8 to total benefit, while adding $9 to total cost. If the decision maker mistakenly undertakes the fourth unit of activity, net benefit falls by $1. Thus, the optimal level of the activity is 3 units. Marginal analysis leads to the conclusion that 3 units of activity maximize net benefit without ever having to calculate net benefit at each level of the activity. Even more important, you obtain the same solution to the optimization problem by using either the total benefit approach or the marginal analysis approach, and marginal analysis is simpler and more general.

Up to this point, we have discussed unconstrained maximization problems in which the choice variable is discrete. The results are summarized in the following principle:

Principle When a decision maker faces an unconstrained maximization problem and must choose among discrete levels of an activity, the activity should be increased if $MB > MC$ and decreased if $MB < MC$. Thus, the optimal level of the activity is attained—net benefit is maximized—when the level of the activity is the last level for which marginal benefit exceeds marginal cost.

Maximization with a Continuous Choice Variable

When a choice variable can vary continuously, marginal analysis is used in exactly the same manner as it is when the choice variable is discrete. However, when the choice variable is continuous, the incremental adjustments in the activity can be extremely small, and the decision maker will need to adjust the level of activity until marginal benefit *exactly equals* marginal cost. Figure 4.1 illustrates the situation graphically.

Assume that increasing the level of some activity, A, increases total benefit and total cost, both of which are expressed in dollars. Thus, marginal benefit and marginal cost are positive for each increase in the activity. Panel A of the figure shows the net benefit (total benefit minus total cost) for all relevant levels of the activity. As you can see, the maximum net benefit ($300) is obtained from using 100 units of the activity. Now we will show that marginal analysis (comparing marginal benefit and marginal cost) leads to the identical solution for the optimal level of activity.

In Panel B, the positively sloped marginal cost curve shows the marginal cost from small increases in the activity over the relevant range. The negatively sloped marginal benefit curve shows the marginal benefit for small increases in the activity. As emphasized above, a decision maker should increase the activity level as long as each additional unit of the activity adds more to total benefit than to total cost. From the graph, for each additional unit of the activity from zero to 100 units, the marginal benefit exceeds the marginal cost. For example, the 45th unit of the activity provides a marginal benefit of $16 but is obtained at a marginal cost of only $9. Thus, the 45th unit added $7 (= $16 − $9) to net benefit. Similarly, the 46th unit would add slightly less than $16 to total benefit, slightly more than $9 to total cost, and, as a result, slightly less than $7 to net benefit. By an identical argument, every unit up to 100 units adds more to benefit than to cost and, therefore, should be added.

Alternatively, suppose the decision maker mistakenly chooses to use 170 units of the activity, at which marginal cost ($16) exceeds marginal benefit ($7). Reducing the activity level by 1 unit (from 170 to 169) reduces total benefit by $7 but reduces total cost by $16. This 1-unit reduction causes net benefit to increase $9 ($16 − $7). For every 1-unit decrease in the activity back to 100 units, net benefit rises because MB is less than MC over this range.

FIGURE 4.1
Unconstrained Maximization: The Case of a Continuous Choice Variable

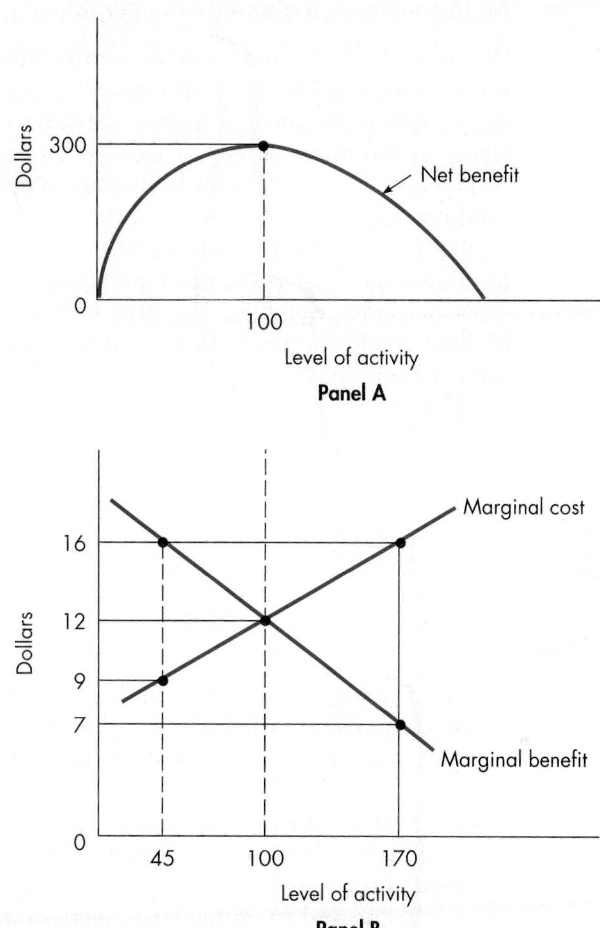

Therefore, by showing that *NB* can be further increased at every other level of activity, we have shown that only 100 units, where marginal benefit equals marginal cost at $12, results in the maximum level of net benefit. It is important to note that to find the optimal level of an activity, the decision maker needs to have information only on *marginal* benefit and *marginal* cost. Information on net benefit is not necessary.

Thus we have established the following principle:

Principle When a decision maker wishes to obtain the maximum net benefit from an activity that is continuously variable, the optimal level of the activity is that level at which the marginal benefit equals the marginal cost ($MB = MC$).

Profit Maximization at Austin Semiconductor: An Unconstrained Maximization Problem

We turn now to a more specific optimization problem. Suppose you have been hired to manage Austin Semiconductor, a medium-size electronics manufacturing firm that produces a highly specialized semiconductor device used exclusively in the manufacture of laptop computers. Your first goal is to adjust the production level of the firm to maximize profit, the difference between the firm's total revenue (what it takes in) and total cost (what it pays out). Austin Semiconductor is currently producing 2,999 semiconductor units per month. You want to determine if this is the optimal (profit-maximizing) level of output. If not, you must determine whether the firm should increase or decrease production and by how much. You know that these questions can be easily answered if you have information on the firm's marginal revenue (benefit) and marginal cost of production.

You ask your marketing research department to estimate the marginal revenue from sales of additional units and your production engineers to estimate the marginal cost of producing additional units. Figure 4.2 shows the marginal revenue (MR) and marginal cost (MC) curves they give you. From the graph, you see that the 3,000th semiconductor produced each month would add \$1 to monthly total revenue, while the 3,000th unit adds \$0.36 to monthly total cost.[3] Obviously, Austin Semiconductor can increase profit by \$0.64 by increasing production from 2,999 to 3,000 units per month. And the firm should continue to increase production until marginal revenue just equals marginal cost. In Figure 4.2, marginal revenue equals marginal cost at 5,000 units per month. Note that you found the profit-maximizing level of output without knowing either total revenue, total cost, or profit. To determine how much profit the firm makes at 5,000 units per month, you would need to know the total revenue and the total cost. We will develop these functions later in the text.

Had your marketing department and production engineers given you marginal revenue and marginal cost *equations* instead of graphs, you still could find the optimal level of semiconductor production. The equations for marginal revenue and marginal cost shown in Figure 4.2 are, respectively,

$$MR = 1.60 - 0.00020Q$$
$$MC = 0.00012Q$$

where Q is the number of semiconductor units produced each month. To determine the profit-maximizing level of output, you set marginal revenue equal to marginal cost and solve for Q^* (the profit-maximizing level of output):

[3]When interpreting numerical values for marginal benefit and marginal cost, remember that the values refer to, or are associated with, a particular unit of activity. In this example, marginal cost is equal to \$0.36 for the *3,000th* unit. Strictly speaking, it is incorrect to say "marginal cost is \$0.36 for *3,000 units.*" At 3,000 units of production, the marginal cost is \$0.36 *for the last unit produced* (i.e., the 3,000th unit).

FIGURE 4.2
Marginal Revenue and Marginal Cost at Austin Semiconductor

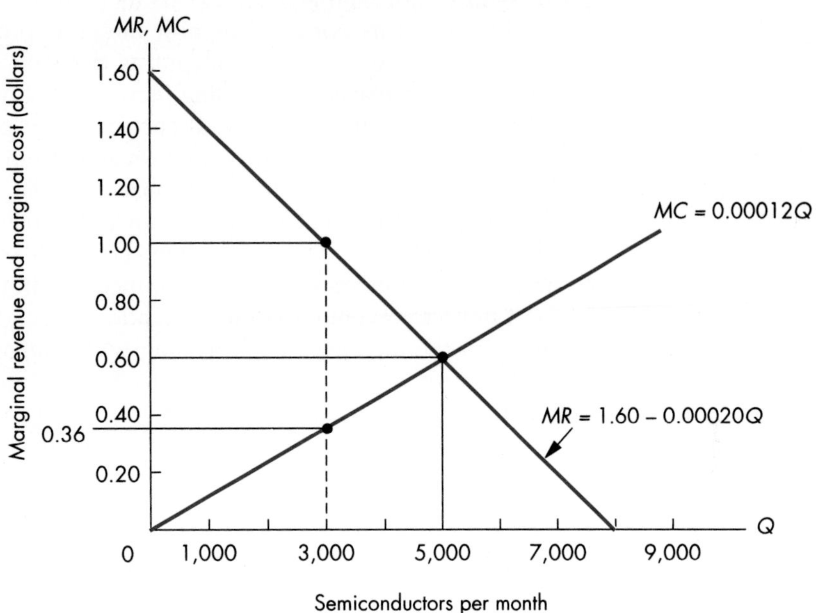

$$1.60 - 0.00020Q = 0.00012Q$$
$$Q^* = 5{,}000 \text{ units}$$

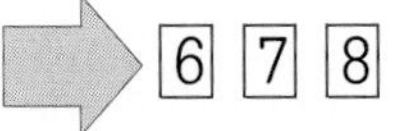

As expected, this is the same level of output obtained by finding the intersection of the *MR* and *MC* curves in Figure 4.2.

More Than One Choice Variable

To this point, we have considered cases in which managers choose the level of only one variable to maximize net benefits. Many times managers can choose the levels of two or more variables. For example, in the chapter introduction, a manager chose only the number of store detectives to reduce shoplifting. We could easily expand this problem by letting the manager choose simultaneously the number of both detectives and surveillance cameras. The manager of Austin Semiconductor could choose the amount of output, the expenditure on advertising, and the number of salespeople that maximize profit. Or a manager might want to determine the output levels of several of the firm's products.

When decision makers wish to maximize the net benefits from several activities, precisely the same principle applies: The firm maximizes net benefits when the marginal benefit from each activity equals the marginal cost of that activity. The problem is somewhat more complicated because the marginal benefit or return from increasing one activity may depend on the levels of the other activities. The same can be said for the marginal cost. This complication, however, does not change the fundamental principle that, at the optimal choice, the marginal benefit from each activity equals its marginal cost.

To illustrate this point, let us now alter the profit-maximization problem to include advertising as well as output as decision variables that are chosen simultaneously. Increased advertising increases the quantity of a good demanded, and hence the revenue obtained, at each price. Suppose that, at a given level of output and advertising, the marginal revenue from an increase in output equals its marginal cost ($MR_Q = MC_Q$). Suppose also that, at these levels of output and advertising, the marginal revenue from an increase in advertising exceeds its marginal cost ($MR_A > MC_A$). The firm should clearly increase its level of advertising in order to increase its profits. (Since additional expenditures on advertising add more to revenue than to cost, additional advertising will lead to higher profits.) But the increase in advertising will change the firm's level of sales and output because increased advertising leads to an increase in demand. When output changes, the marginal revenue and marginal cost associated with output are no longer equal. For instance, with the increase in output, it may be that $MR_Q < MC_Q$, so the firm would want to decrease output. Then, if output is decreased, the marginal revenue and marginal cost associated with advertising may again change. The point is that the firm will have to adjust both output and advertising until the marginal benefits equal the marginal costs in both activities; the firm will have to equate marginal revenue and marginal cost for output and advertising simultaneously.

In another example of unconstrained optimization, consider a profit-maximizing firm that uses several inputs in the production process (i.e., the level of output depends on the levels of usage of several inputs). The firm would hire the amount of each input at which the marginal benefit (increased revenue) from each input equals its marginal cost (e.g., the wage rate in the case of labor). The complication is that the marginal revenue generated by any one input depends on the level of usage of the other inputs. Therefore, if for any one input, marginal revenue is not equal to marginal cost, the firm will have to adjust (increase or decrease) its usage of that input. Since this change in the usage of that input will change the marginal revenues from the other inputs, their levels of usage must also be adjusted until equilibrium is reached. Again, the complication of multiple choice variables does not change the principle of unconstrained optimization. Each choice variable is determined such that $MR = MC$. The only difference is that the several optimization conditions must be met simultaneously.

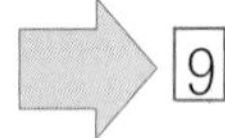
9

Sunk Costs and Fixed Costs Are Irrelevant

sunk costs
Costs that have previously been paid.

fixed costs
Costs that are constant and must be paid no matter what level of the activity is chosen.

In our discussion of optimization problems, we never mentioned sunk costs or fixed costs. **Sunk costs** are costs that have previously been paid. **Fixed costs** are costs that are constant and must be paid no matter what level of an activity is chosen. Such costs are totally irrelevant in decision making. They either have already been paid, in the case of sunk costs, or must be paid no matter what a manager or any other decision maker decides to do, in the case of fixed costs.

Suppose you have paid \$1 million for a piece of machinery. Any output produced by the machine will require labor and raw material, the payments for which are marginal costs. Then, using the above maximization rule, you determine that 1,000 units produced and sold per day yields the maximum profit or net benefit. If 1,000 units per day was the profit-maximizing choice when you paid \$1 million for the machine, it must also be the profit-maximizing choice if the machine had cost \$2 million, \$500,000, or any other amount. Since a sunk cost has already been paid, a decision maker should take it as given and then make the best decision about what should be done.

Converting this example to a fixed cost, suppose that you financed the machine using borrowed funds and must pay off the loan at the rate of \$10,000 a month. This amount is a fixed payment and must be paid no matter how much is produced, even if production is zero. If, as above, 1,000 units a day is the profit-maximizing output, you should produce this amount. If the payments had been \$15,000 a month rather than \$10,000, the profit-maximizing output would be the same even though monthly profit would be \$5,000 lower. If the monthly payment had been \$6,000, monthly profit would be \$4,000 higher, but the profit-maximizing output remains 1,000 units a day.

Therefore, when making decisions, you should consider only costs and benefits that you can do something about. Things that you have no control over should not affect a decision. Some economic experiments do, however, indicate that many people do not ignore fixed or sunk costs when making decisions. They say things like, "I've already got so much invested in this project, I have to go on with it." As you are aware, they should weigh the costs and benefits of going on before going on. Then, if the benefits are greater than the *additional* costs, they should go on; if the *additional* costs are greater than the benefits, they should not go on. As the Illustration 4.2 on pages 130–131 shows, not ignoring fixed or sunk costs is a bad policy even in everyday decision making.

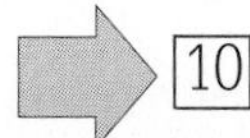

4.3 CONSTRAINED OPTIMIZATION

While many of the decisions facing a manager involve unconstrained choice of an activity (or activities) in order to maximize net benefit, on many occasions a manager will face situations in which the choice of activity levels is constrained by the circumstances surrounding the maximization or minimization problem. These constrained optimization problems can be solved, as in the case of unconstrained maximization, using the logic of marginal analysis. As noted in Section 4.1, even though constrained optimization problems can be either maximization or minimization problems, the optimization rule is the same for both types.

A crucial concept for solving constrained optimization problems is the concept of marginal benefit per dollar spent on an activity. Before you can understand how to solve constrained optimization problems, you must first understand how to interpret the ratio of the marginal benefit of an activity divided by the price of the activity. We turn now to a discussion of marginal benefit per dollar and then show how to use this concept to find the optimal levels of the activities in constrained optimization problems.

ILLUSTRATION 4.1

How Much Sulfur Dioxide Emission Is Optimal?

A Benefit-Cost Analysis

The Clean Air Act of 1990, signed into law by President Bush on November 15, 1990, represented the nation's first major reform of laws in two decades governing the control of pollution. One of the provisions of the bill, which addressed the acid rain problem, required reduction of sulfur dioxide (SO_2) emissions by 10 million tons annually by the year 2000. The bill identified 111 electric power plants with the worst SO_2 emissions. These plants had to meet an intermediate pollution reduction goal by 1995 and fully comply by 2000.

"Acid rain" refers to the elevated level of acidity in rain caused primarily by emissions of SO_2 from coal-burning electric utility plants. Sulfur dioxide reacts with hydrogen peroxide in clouds to form sulfuric acid, which is dissolved in raindrops.* Originally, policymakers and environmentalists thought acid rain was killing aquatic life in many of the lakes in northeastern United States and in parts of Canada. Additionally, environmentalists were concerned over damage to forests, agricultural land, and buildings. Emissions of SO_2 also were thought to affect atmospheric visibility and human health.

To assess the damage of acid rain, Congress commissioned a 10-year, $500 million study in 1980 called the National Acid Precipitation Assessment Program (NAPAP). According to NAPAP, the impact and costs of acid rain were much smaller than environmentalists had originally thought. Fewer lakes had been damaged by acid rain, agriculture appeared to be unaffected by acid rain, and damage to forests was minimal. Several studies found aesthetic benefits from reducing the level of SO_2 emissions. While it appears that controlling SO_2 has some benefits, the magnitude of such benefits is not widely agreed upon. Paul Portney estimated that the benefits from controlling SO_2, as set forth by the Clean Air Act, would be in the range of $2 billion to $9 billion annually.†

Portney also estimated that the costs of compliance with the Clean Air Act would exceed $30 billion annually (and would rise substantially by the year 2000). The compliance expenditures did not include other indirect social costs of pollution control, such as job losses, higher prices, and lower product quality. Given these costs and benefits, Portney noted, "If these estimates are even close to correct, . . . costs may exceed benefits by a considerable margin." Why is this so? Could it be that government policymakers do not understand marginal analysis? After all, at the level of SO_2 emissions allowed under the Clean Air Act, not only is the marginal cost of pollution abatement much greater than marginal benefit, but total cost exceeds total benefit—that is, net benefit from pollution control is negative.

Marginal Benefit per Dollar Spent on an Activity

Retailers frequently advertise that their products give "more value for your money." People don't usually interpret this as meaning the best product in its class or the one with the highest value. Neither do they interpret it as meaning the cheapest. The advertiser wants to get across the message that customers will get more for their money or more value for each dollar spent on the product. When product rating services (such as *Consumer Reports*) rate a product a "best buy," they don't mean it is the best product or the cheapest; they mean that consumers will get more value per dollar spent on that product. When firms want to fill a position, they don't necessarily hire the person who would be the

Portney believed that this nonoptimal level of pollution control results from misperceptions about both the benefits and costs of controlling SO_2 emissions. Regardless of how a policymaker perceives costs and benefits, the optimal level of SO_2 emissions is the level at which spending one more dollar on reducing SO_2 generates exactly one more dollar of additional benefits. Policymakers would avoid being lured into possibly buying too much pollution control by mistakenly considering only the increase in total benefits of reduced emissions if they (correctly) compared marginal benefits and marginal costs. This is only one example of government policy that could have benefited from the use of marginal benefit-cost analysis.

By April 1992, the government had made some progress in using optimization principles in its efforts to reduce air pollution. On April 14, 1992, *The Wall Street Journal* reported, "A growing number of regulators believe conventional 'command and control' regulation—which allows each plant to pollute so much but no more—is failing to stop destruction of the environment. These authorities, encouraged by economists, want to harness the Earth's atmosphere to financial markets and let the markets rid the world of acid rain and global warming."‡ Under a new plan, "utilities, refineries, and manufacturers would buy and sell pollution rights, which are supposed to ease the transition to increasingly stringent emission limits."

There was opposition to the new plan from environmentalists and others, but proponents won over some opposition by arguing that traditional regulation gives polluters no incentive to reduce emissions lower than what is allowed. They said markets will create strong competition among companies to find the cheapest and most technologically advanced ways to cut pollution. At that time, offset trades had occurred in several states, but mostly in California. The result was "less pollution in the air over California." The net effect, according to a vice president of a company that helps firms manage Clean Air Act reductions, was "cleaner air. This changes the whole calculus of what companies are going to do: how they fuel their plants, the capital improvements they'll make, how much they operate plants, everything."

In short, it is more efficient for government to set the amount of emission and then let firms, using optimization principles, determine the most cost-effective way to achieve the goal. One would hope also that government would use some type of cost-benefit calculation when setting the goal.

*Laurence Kulp, "Acid Rain: Causes, Effects, and Control," *Regulation,* Winter 1990.

†Paul R. Portney, "Economics and the Clean Air Act," *Journal of Economic Perspectives,* Fall 1990.

‡"New Rules Harness Power of Free Markets to Curb Air Pollution," *The Wall Street Journal,* Apr. 14, 1992.

most productive in the job—that person may cost too much. Neither do they necessarily hire the person who would work for the lowest wages—that person may not be very productive. They want the employee who can do the job and give the highest productivity for the wages paid.

In the above examples, phrases such as "most value for your money" and "best buy" mean that a particular activity yields the highest marginal benefit per dollar spent. To illustrate this concept, suppose you are the office manager for an expanding law firm and you find that you need an extra copy machine in the office—the one copier you have is being overworked. You shop around and find three brands of office copy machines (brands *A*, *B*, and *C*) that have virtually identical features. The three brands do differ, however, in price and in the num-

ILLUSTRATION 4.2

Is Cost-Benefit Analysis Really Useful?

We have extolled the usefulness of optimization theory—often referred to as *cost-benefit analysis*—in business decision making as well as decision making in everyday life. This process involves weighing the marginal benefits and marginal costs of an activity while ignoring all previously incurred or sunk costs. The principal rule is to increase the level of an activity if marginal benefits exceed marginal costs and decrease the level if marginal costs exceed marginal benefits. This simple rule, however, flies in the face of many honored traditional principles such as "Never give up" or "Anything worth doing is worth doing well" or "Waste not, want not." So you might wonder if cost-benefit analysis is as useful as we have said it is.

It is, at least according to an article in *The Wall Street Journal* titled "Economic Perspective Produces Steady Yields." In this article, a University of Michigan research team concludes, "Cost-benefit analysis pays off in everyday living." This team quizzed some of the university's seniors and faculty members on such questions as how often they walk out on a bad movie, refuse to finish a bad novel, start over on a weak term paper, or abandon a research project that no longer looks promising. They believe that people who cut their losses this way are following sound economic rules: calculating the net benefits of alternative courses of action, writing off past costs that can't be recovered, and weighing the opportunity to use future time and effort more profitably elsewhere.*

The findings: Among faculty members, those who use cost-benefit reasoning in this fashion had higher salaries relative to their age and departments. Economists were more likely to apply the approach than professors of humanities or biology. Among students, those who have learned to use cost-benefit analysis frequently are apt to have far better grades than their SAT scores would have predicted. The more economics courses the students had taken, the more likely they were to apply cost-benefit analysis outside the classroom. The director of the University of Michigan study did concede that for many Americans, cost-benefit rules often appear to conflict with traditional principles such as those we previously mentioned. Notwithstanding these probable conflicts, the study provides evidence that decision makers can indeed prosper by following the logic of marginal analysis and benefit-cost analysis.

College students aren't the only ones who have found cost-benefit analysis useful in everyday decision making. As *The Wall Street Journal* reported (January 30, 1995), "Rapist and murderer Roger Bjorklund is no economist, but he knows a good cost-benefit analysis when he sees one."† In 1993 he was

ber of copies the machines will make before they wear out. Brand *A*'s copy machine costs $2,500 and will produce about 500,000 copies before it wears out. The marginal benefit of this machine is 500,000 ($MB_A = 500{,}000$) since the machine provides the law office with the ability to produce 500,000 additional copies. To find the marginal benefit *per dollar spent* on copy machine *A*, marginal benefit is divided by price ($P_A = 2{,}500$):

$$
\begin{aligned}
MB_A/P_A &= 500{,}000 \text{ copies}/2{,}500 \text{ dollars} \\
&= 200 \text{ copies}/\text{dollar}
\end{aligned}
$$

You get 200 copies for each of the dollars spent to purchase copy machine *A*.

Now compare machine *A* with machine *B*, which will produce 600,000 copies and costs $4,000. The marginal benefit is greater, but so is the price. To determine facing a choice between letting his case proceed fairly or tampering with the jury. If he was convicted, he could be sentenced to death. If he got away with tampering, and was acquitted, he would be free. If he was caught tampering, he would face no more than a $1,000 fine and six months in jail. Even if the tampering was discovered after he was acquitted, he could not be retried. He did what his cost-benefit calculus demanded and sent threatening letters to five jurors. He was convicted anyway but still thought the gambit was worth the try. On death row Mr. Bjorklund reflected, "With the penalty I was facing, you don't tend to worry about what punishment a person could receive for tampering."

This was no isolated case. Prosecutors warned that incidents of jury tampering were on the rise and had broken out of the organized crime arena where they were once confined. Law enforcement officers believed the reason was that tough new sentencing laws had raised the cost of being convicted of serious crimes. Both federal and state courts had increased sentences and removed opportunities for parole. State courts were increasingly imposing the death penalty and minimum mandatory sentences for gun-related crimes. The penalties for tampering remained low.

As repellent as it may be, sometimes tampering works. Twenty defendants in a racketeering case went free; then two of them later confessed to tampering but could not be retried. The foreman of the jury that acquitted reputed mob chieftain John Gotti was later convicted of accepting a bribe to sell his vote and influence the jury. Mr. Gotti could not be retried on those charges. The attorney who formerly ran the prosecutor's office in Brooklyn, New York, noted, "Tampering is not something you ordinarily find out about. . . . It happens more often than we know." Many other prosecutors agreed.

As the *WSJ* noted, to law and economics scholars it is the most logical thing in the world. One such professor at the University of Chicago Law School stated, "Prisoners, like everyone else, are usually rational about how they act. Prisoners and their families and friends appear to be doing exactly what you would predict they'd be doing." As the cost of being convicted rose, the possible benefits from jury tampering increased while the cost of tampering remained constant. Thus it was logical to choose more of the activity—jury tampering.

We have shown a broad spectrum of people, from students and faculty to prisoners, who have found cost-benefit analysis useful. We think that you as business managers will find it useful also.

*"Economic Perspective Produces Steady Yield," *The Wall Street Journal*, Mar. 31, 1992.

†"Tampering with Juries Appeals to Defendants Facing Steep Sentences," *The Wall Street Journal*, Jan. 30, 1995.

how "good a deal" you get with machine *B*, compute the marginal benefit per dollar spent on machine *B*:

$$\begin{aligned} MB_B/P_B &= 600{,}000 \text{ copies}/4{,}000 \text{ dollars} \\ &= 150 \text{ copies/dollar} \end{aligned}$$

Even though machine *B* provides a higher marginal benefit, its marginal benefit per dollar spent is lower than that for machine *A*. Machine *A* is a better deal than machine *B* because it yields higher marginal benefit per dollar. The third copy machine produces 580,000 copies over its useful life and costs $2,600. Machine C is neither the best machine (580,000 < 600,000 copies) nor is it the cheapest machine ($2,600 > $2,500), but of the three machines, machine C provides the greatest marginal benefit per dollar spent:

$$MB_C/P_C = 580{,}000 \text{ copies}/2{,}600 \text{ dollars}$$
$$= 223 \text{ copies/dollar}$$

You would rank machine *C* first, machine *A* second, and machine *B* third.

When choosing among different activities, a decision maker compares the marginal benefits per dollar spent on each of the activities, *not* the marginal benefits of the activities. Marginal benefit, by itself, does not provide sufficient information for decision-making purposes. It is marginal benefit per dollar spent that

11 matters in decision making.

Constrained Maximization

In the general constrained maximization problem, a manager or decision maker must choose the levels of two or more activities in order to maximize a total benefit (objective) function subject to a constraint in the form of a budget that restricts the amount that can be spent. To illustrate how marginal analysis can be employed to find the optimal levels of activities for a constrained maximization problem, consider a situation in which there are two activities, *A* and *B*. Each unit of activity *A* costs $4 to undertake, and each unit of activity *B* costs $2 to undertake. The manager faces a constraint that allows a total expenditure of only $100 on activities *A* and *B* combined. The manager wishes to allocate the $100 between activities *A* and *B* so that the total benefit from both activities combined is maximized.

The manager is currently choosing to employ 20 units of activity *A* and 10 units of activity *B*. The constraint is met for the combination 20*A* and 10*B* since ($4 × 20) + ($2 × 10) = $100. For this combination of activities, suppose that the marginal benefit of the last unit of activity *A* is 40 units of additional benefit and the marginal benefit of the last unit of *B* is 10 units of additional benefit. In this situation, the marginal benefit per dollar spent on activity *A* exceeds the marginal benefit per dollar spent on activity *B*:

$$MB_A/P_A = 40/4 = 10 > 5 = 10/2 = MB_B/P_B$$

Spending an additional dollar on activity *A* increases total benefit by 10 units, while spending an additional dollar on activity *B* increases total benefit by 5 units. Since the marginal benefit per dollar spent is greater for activity *A*, it provides "more for the money" or is a better deal at this combination of activities.

To take advantage of this fact, the manager can increase activity *A* by 1 unit and decrease activity *B* by 2 units (now, $A = 21$ and $B = 8$). This combination of activities still costs $100 [($4 × 21) + ($2 × 8) = $100]. Purchasing 1 more unit of activity *A* causes total benefit to rise by 40 units, while purchasing 2 less units of activity *B* causes total benefit to fall by 20 units. The combined total benefit from activities *A* and *B* *rises* by 20 units (= 40 − 20) *and* the new combination of activities ($A = 21$ and $B = 8$) costs the same amount, \$100, as the old combination ($A = 20$ and $B = 10$). The decision maker has succeeded in increasing total benefit without spending any more than \$100 on the activities.

Naturally, the manager will continue to increase spending on activity A and reduce spending on activity B as long as MB_A/P_A exceeds MB_B/P_B. In most situations, the marginal benefit of an activity declines as the activity increases.[4] Consequently, as activity A is increased, MB_A gets smaller. As activity B is decreased, MB_B gets larger. Thus, as spending on A rises and spending on B falls, MB_A/P_A falls and MB_B/P_B rises. As the manager increases activity A and decreases activity B, a point is eventually reached at which activity A is no longer a better deal than activity B; that is, MB_A/P_A equals MB_B/P_B. At this point, total benefit is maximized subject to the constraint that only \$100 is spent on the two activities.

If the original allocation of spending on activities A and B had been such that

$$MB_A/P_A < MB_B/P_B$$

the manager would recognize that activity B is the better deal. In this case, total benefit could be increased by spending more on activity B and less on activity A while maintaining the \$100 budget. Activity B would be increased by 2 units for every 1-unit decrease in activity A (in order to satisfy the \$100 spending constraint) until the marginal benefit per dollar spent is equal for both activities:

$$MB_A/P_A = MB_B/P_B$$

We have developed the following rule for finding the optimal activity levels for constrained maximization problems:

Principle In order to maximize total benefits subject to a constraint on the level of activities, choose the level of each activity so that the marginal benefit per dollar spent is equal for all activities.

$$MB_A/P_A = MB_B/P_B$$

12 13 and at the same time, the chosen level of activities must also satisfy the constraint.

The Optimal Allocation of Advertising Expenditures: A Constrained Maximization Problem

To illustrate how a firm can use the technique of constrained maximization to allocate its advertising budget, suppose a manager of a small retail firm wants

[4] Decreasing marginal benefit is quite common. As you drink several cans of Coke in succession, you get ever smaller amounts of additional satisfaction from successive cans. As you continue studying for an exam, each additional hour of study increases your expected exam grade by ever smaller amounts. In such cases, marginal benefit is inversely related to the level of the activity. Increasing the activity causes marginal benefit to fall, and decreasing the activity level causes marginal benefit to rise.

to maximize the effectiveness (in total sales) of the firm's weekly advertising budget of $2,000. The manager has the option of advertising on the local television station or on the local AM radio station. As a class project, a marketing class at a nearby college estimated the impact on the retailer's sales of varying levels of advertising in the two different media. The manager wants to maximize the number of units sold; thus the total benefit is measured by the total number of units sold. The estimates of the *increases* in weekly sales (the marginal benefits) from increasing the levels of advertising on television and radio are as follows:

	Increase in units sold	
Number of ads	MB_{TV}	MB_{radio}
1	400	360
2	300	270
3	280	240
4	260	225
5	240	150
6	200	120

Television ads are more "powerful" than radio ads in the sense that the marginal benefits from additional TV ads tend to be larger than those for more radio ads. However, since the manager is constrained by the limited advertising budget, the relevant measure is not simply marginal benefit but, rather, marginal benefit per dollar spent on advertising. The price of television ads is $400 per ad, and the price of radio ads is $300 per ad. Although the first TV ad dominates the first radio ad in terms of its marginal benefit (increased sales), the marginal benefit per dollar's worth of expenditure for the first radio ad is greater than that for the first television ad:

	Marginal benefit/price	
	Television	Radio
Ad 1	400/400 = 1.00	360/300 = 1.2

This indicates that sales rise by 1 unit per dollar spent on the first television ad and 1.2 units on the first radio ad. Therefore, when the manager is allocating the budget, the first ad she selects will be a radio ad—the activity with the largest marginal benefit per dollar spent. Following the same rule, the $2,000 advertising budget would be allocated as follows:

Decision	MB/P	Ranking of MB/P	Cumulative expenditures
Buy radio ad 1	360/300 = 1.20	1	$ 300
Buy TV ad 1	400/400 = 1.00	2	700
Buy radio ad 2	270/300 = 0.90	3	1,000
Buy radio ad 3	240/300 = 0.80	4	1,300
Buy TV ad 2	300/400 = 0.75	5 (tie)	1,700
Buy radio ad 4	225/300 = 0.75	5 (tie)	2,000

By selecting two television ads and four radio ads, the manager of the firm has maximized sales subject to the constraint that only $2,000 can be spent on advertising activity. Note that for the optimal levels of television and radio ads (two TV and four radio):

$$\frac{MB_{\text{TV}}}{P_{\text{TV}}} = \frac{MB_{\text{radio}}}{P_{\text{radio}}} = 0.75$$

The fact that the preceding application used artificially simplistic numbers shouldn't make you think that the problem is artificial. If we add a few zeros to the prices of TV and radio ads, we have the real-world situation faced by advertisers.

Constrained Minimization

Constrained minimization problems involve minimizing a total cost function (the objective function) subject to a constraint that the levels of activities be chosen such that a given level of total benefit is achieved. To illustrate how marginal analysis is applied to constrained minimization problems, consider a manager who must minimize the total cost of two activities, *A* and *B*, subject to the constraint that 3,000 units of benefit are to be generated by those activities. The price of activity *A* is $5 per unit, and the price of activity *B* is $20 per unit. Suppose the manager is currently using 100 units of activity *A* and 60 units of activity *B* and this combination of activity generates total benefit equal to 3,000. At this combination of activities, the marginal benefit of the last unit of activity *A* is 30 and the marginal benefit of the last unit of activity *B* is 60. In this situation, the marginal benefit per dollar spent on activity *A* exceeds the marginal benefit per dollar spent on activity *B:*

$$MB_A/P_A = 30/5 = 6 > 3 = 60/20 = MB_B/P_B$$

Since the marginal benefit per dollar spent is greater for activity *A* than for activity *B,* activity *A* gives "more for the money."

To take advantage of activity *A,* the manager can reduce activity *B* by 1 unit, causing total benefit to fall by 60 units and reducing cost by $20. To hold total benefit constant, the 60 units of lost benefit can be made up by increasing activity *A* by 2 units with a marginal benefit of 30 each. The additional units of activity *A* cause total cost to rise by $10. By reducing activity *B* by 1 unit and increasing activity *A* by 2 units, the manager *reduces* total cost by $10 (= $20 − $10) without reducing total benefit.

As long as $MB_A/P_A > MB_B/P_B$, the manager will continue to increase activity *A* and decrease activity *B* at the rate that holds *TB* constant until

$$MB_A/P_A = MB_B/P_B$$

This is the same condition that must be met in the case of constrained maximization. If there are more than two activities in the objective function, the condition is expanded to require that the marginal benefit per dollar spent be equal for all activities:

$$MB_A/P_A = MB_B/P_B = MB_C/P_C = \cdots = MB_Z/P_Z$$

We can express the principle of constrained optimization as follows:

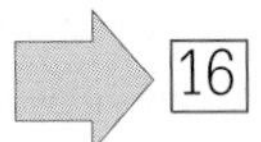
16 **Principle** An objective function is maximized or minimized subject to a constraint if, for all the activities in the objective function, the ratios of marginal benefit to price are equal and the constraint is satisfied.

The Optimal Combination of Inputs: A Constrained Minimization Problem

Cyber Corporation is currently producing 10,000 units of output using two inputs, capital and labor. At the existing input usage level, the marginal product of capital is 300 (the last unit of capital increased output by 300 units), and the marginal product of labor is 150 (the last worker hired increased output by 150 units per year). Cyber wishes to produce 10,000 units at the lowest possible total cost.

The current wage rate (w) is \$30,000 per year, and the annual cost of using a unit of capital (r) is \$80,000 per year. Comparing the marginal benefits per dollar spent on labor and capital reveals that Cyber Corporation is currently using too much capital and too little labor:

$$\frac{MP_K}{r} = \frac{300}{\$80{,}000} < \frac{150}{\$30{,}000} = \frac{MP_L}{w}$$

If Cyber reduces capital usage by 1 unit, output would fall by 300 units per year, and annual cost would decline by \$80,000. Then, to hold output at 10,000 units per year, the 300 units per year lost from the reduction in capital could be produced by employing two more workers, at a cost of only \$60,000, because the marginal product of each worker is approximately 150 units of output and each of the two additional workers costs the firm \$30,000. The following table summarizes the transaction:

Action	Cost	Output
Reduce capital by 1 unit	−\$80,000	−300
Employ two additional workers	+60,000	+300
Net change	−\$20,000	0

As this example indicates, the firm can save \$20,000 while continuing to produce 10,000 units per year by replacing some of its capital with labor. Cyber would continue reducing its capital and adding labor, holding output constant, as long

ILLUSTRATION 4.3

Constrained Maximization in the Toy Business and Why Frisbees Are Called Frisbees

When Mattel Inc. offered Hasbro Inc. $5.2 billion in a takeover bid that would have created one huge company out of the two largest toy manufacturers, Hasbro, in rebuffing the offer, warned that "competition for new toy ideas would be substantially reduced" if the two companies merged.* Many industry observers agreed. So did the two market leaders introduce a lot of new toys? Not according to an article in *The Wall Street Journal.*

The article reported that at the big Toy Fair exposition in New York neither company exhibited many new toys but both seemed to have adopted the strategy of repackaging old toys such as Barbie, G.I. Joe, and *Star Wars* action figures. "The vast bulk of the 5,000 'new' items at Toy Fair were either retreads—line extensions, as the trade prefers to call them—or figurines and tie-ins from movies and other media. Of the 15 top-selling toys and games on the market today, only three are toy-company inventions that originated within the past year." The editors of an industry magazine wondered if the toy makers were running out of ideas, but that doesn't seem to be the reason for the lack of new toys. The situation seems to be the result of a reemphasis on marketing and repackaging familiar old toys rather than developing new ones. This change in emphasis appears to have been a rational, constrained optimization decision.

Hasbro was spending about one-third as much on toy research and development as it was on marketing. Mattel was spending five times as much on marketing as on product development and design. A Mattel spokesman said, "Mattel's strategy is partly an outcome of watching too many high fliers flame out. . . . [Now] marketing is the name of the game in the toy industry. Our success has been concentrating on time-tested products that endure from year to year." The emphasis on marketing over development had not always been the case, however.

Previously, "products were made to appeal to parents, and manufacturers had the luxury of designing sophisticated toys because they could count on the department stores, where most were sold, to demonstrate new products for consumers." Then discounters such as Kmart and Wal-Mart took over toy retailing, and their salespeople didn't have the time to demonstrate and explain toys. According to the *WSJ*, the burden of product promotion shifted to the manufacturers, which obviously resorted to television. A game inventor, who had worked at Hasbro and Mattel, said that the day he came to work at Mattel, he was told two things: Invent games with the head buyer at Toys "R" Us in mind, not the consumer; and don't create games that can't be explained in a 30-second commercial on TV. In fact, nearly half of all U.S. toy sales were coming from licensed products based on movies and TV shows.

As the *WSJ* pointed out, the change in the marketing process "means the invention process is different too. Hits of yesteryear often were serendipitous strokes of ingenuity, idle time and a vigilant eye." For example, the Frisbee originated at Yale University, where students, after eating pies from a local bakery, started tossing around the empty pie tins. A carpenter invented a plastic variation and called it the "Pluto Platter" but sold the rights to Wham-O, which renamed it after the local bakery—Frisbie's. (This story doesn't really add very much to the analysis, but we found it interesting and thought you might too.)

So what does this illustration illustrate? Toy manufacturers have two ways of promoting their products: bringing out new toys and marketing. When retailing changed its methods of selling, the benefits from inventing new toys fell and the benefits from marketing rose. With limited resources for promotion, the toy manufacturers increased marketing expenditure, where the marginal benefits per dollar were higher, and decreased expenditure on developing new toys, where the marginal benefits per dollar were lower. This is a lesson that any manager should learn.

*"Toy Business Focuses More on Marketing and Less on New Ideas," *The Wall Street Journal*, Feb. 29, 1996.

as the above inequality held. As capital is reduced, MP_K rises; as labor increases, MP_L falls. Eventually a point is reached where MP_L/w equals MP_K/r, and no further reallocations will lower cost.

Alternatively, if the firm had originally been using levels of capital and labor at which $MP_K/r > MP_L/w$, the firm could reduce total cost by substituting some capital for labor at a rate that keeps output constant. Only in the case in which $MP_K/r = MP_L/w$ is there no reallocation between capital and labor that would reduce cost.

4.4 SUMMARY

In this chapter we have given you the key to the kingdom of economic decision making: marginal analysis. Virtually all of microeconomics involves solutions to optimization problems. The most interesting and challenging problems facing a manager involve trying either to maximize or to minimize particular objective functions. Regardless of whether the optimization involves maximization or minimization, or constrained or unconstrained choice variables, all optimization problems are solved by using marginal analysis. No other tool in managerial economics is more powerful than the ability to attack problems by using the logic of marginal analysis.

The results of this chapter fall neatly into two categories: the solution to unconstrained and the solution to constrained optimization problems. When the values of the choice variables are *not* restricted by constraints such as limited income, limited expenditures, or limited time, the optimization problem is said to be unconstrained. One of the most important unconstrained optimization problems facing managers is selecting the set of variables that will maximize the profit of the firm. This problem and all other unconstrained maximization problems can be solved by following this simple rule: To maximize an objective function, the value of which depends on certain activities or choice variables, each activity is carried out until the marginal benefit from an increase in the activity equals the marginal cost of the increased activity:

$$MB_A = MC_A, MB_B = MC_B, \cdots, MB_Z = MC_Z$$

When the choice variables are not continuous but discrete, it may not be possible to precisely equate benefit and cost at the margin. For discrete choice variables, the decision maker simply carries out the activity up to the point where *any further* increases in the activity result in marginal cost exceeding marginal benefit.

In many instances, managers face limitations on the range of values that the choice variables can take. For example, budgets may limit the amount of labor and capital managers may purchase. Time constraints may limit the number of hours managers can allocate to certain activities. Such constraints are common and require modifying the solution to optimization problems. To maximize or minimize an objective function subject to a constraint, the ratios of the marginal benefit to price must be equal for all activities,

$$\frac{MB_A}{P_A} = \frac{MB_B}{P_B} = \cdots = \frac{MB_Z}{P_Z}$$

and the values of the choice variables must meet the constraint. One of the most important constrained optimization problems facing a manager is the task of producing a given output at the least possible total cost.

The two decision rules presented in this chapter will be used throughout this text. If you remember these rules, economic analysis will be clear and straightforward. These two rules, although simple, are the essential tools for making economic decisions. And, as the rules emphasize, *marginal changes* are the keys to optimization decisions.

TECHNICAL PROBLEMS

1. For each of the following decision-making problems, determine whether the problem involves constrained or unconstrained optimization; what the objective function is and, for each constrained problem, what the constraint is; and what the choice variables are.
   a. We have received a foundation grant to purchase new PCs for the staff. You decide what PCs to buy.
   b. We aren't earning enough profits. Your job is to redesign our advertising program and decide how much TV, direct-mail, and magazine advertising to use. Whatever we are doing now isn't working very well.
   c. We have to meet a production quota but think we are going to spend too much doing so. Your job is to reallocate the machinery, the number of workers, and the raw materials needed to meet the quota.
   d. We have saved $2,000 to spend on our vacation next month. You decide whether we go to New York, the beach, or Mexico.
   e. We have an opening for a new salesperson and have received applications for the job from more individuals than we want to interview. You decide how many we should interview.
2. Fill in the blanks below. In an unconstrained maximization with discrete choice variables:
   a. The activity should be increased if ________ exceeds ________.
   b. The activity should be decreased if ________ exceeds ________.
   c. The optimal level of the activity is the last unit of the activity for which ________ exceeds ________.
   d. At the optimal level of the activity ________ is maximized.
3. Fill in the blanks in the following table. Then use the table to answer the questions:

X	*TB*	*TC*	*NB*	*MB*	*MC*
0	$ 0	$__	$ 0		
1	__	__	27	$35	$__
2	65	__	__	__	10
3	85	30	__	__	__
4	__	__	51	__	14
5	__	60	__	8	__
6	__	__	__	5	20

   a. If activity *X* is increased from 2 to 3 units, total benefit ________ by $________.
   b. If *X* is increased from 2 to 3 units, total cost ________ by $________, and net benefit ________ by $________.
   c. If *X* is decreased from 5 to 4 units, total benefit ________ by $________.
   d. If *X* is decreased from 5 to 4 units, total cost ________ by $________, and net benefit ________ by $________.
   e. The optimal level of activity is ________ units of this activity, and net benefit is $________.

4. Use the graph below to answer the following questions:

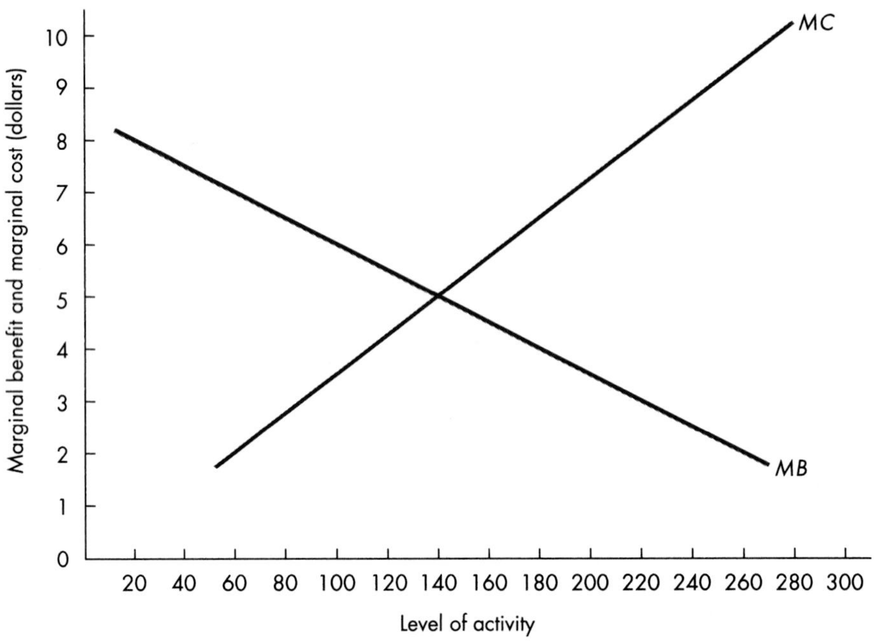

   a. At 60 units of the activity, marginal benefit is $______ and marginal cost is $______.
   b. Adding the 60th unit of the activity causes net benefit to ______ (increase, decrease) by $______.
   c. At 180 units of the activity, marginal benefit is $______ and marginal cost is $______.
   d. Subtracting the 180th unit of the activity causes net benefit to ______ (increase, decrease) by $______.
   e. The optimal level of the activity is ______ units. At the optimal level of the activity, marginal benefit is $______ and marginal cost is $______.

5. Fill in the blanks in the following statement:

   If marginal benefit exceeds marginal cost, then increasing the level of activity by one unit ______ (increases, decreases) ______ (total, marginal, net) benefit by more than it ______ (increases, decreases) ______ (total, marginal) cost. Therefore, ______ (increasing, decreasing) the level of activity by one unit must increase net benefit. The manager should continue to ______ (increase, decrease) the level of activity until marginal benefit and marginal cost are ______ (zero, equal).

6. Activity A has the following marginal benefit (MB) and marginal cost (MC) functions:

$$MB = 50 - 0.025A$$

and

$$MC = 40 + 0.025A$$

where MB and MC are measured in dollars.

a. The 100th unit of the activity increases total benefit by $______ and increases total cost by $______. Since marginal benefit is ______ (greater, less) than marginal cost, adding the 100th unit of the activity ______ (increases, decreases) net benefit by $______.

b. The 400th unit of the activity increases total benefit by $______ and increases total cost by $______. Since marginal benefit is ______ (greater, less) than marginal cost, subtracting the 400th unit of the activity ______ (increases, decreases) net benefit by $______.

c. The optimal level of the activity is ______ units. At the optimal level of activity, marginal benefit is $______ and marginal cost is $______.

The total benefit (*TB*) and total cost (*TC*) functions for the activity are:

$$TB = 50A - 0.0125A^2$$

and

$$TC = 40A + 0.0125A^2$$

where *TB* and *TC* are measured in dollars.

d. For the optimal level of the activity in part *c*, the total benefit is $______, the total cost is $______, and the net benefit is $______.

7. Correct this statement: "The optimal level of any activity is that level for which marginal benefit exceeds marginal cost by the greatest possible amount."
8. "At the optimal level of the activity, further increases in the activity necessarily decrease *total* benefit." Evaluate.
9. A decision maker can choose the levels of two activities, *A* and *B*, so as to maximize net benefits. The marginal benefit functions of *A* and *B* are

$$MB_A = 20A - 10B$$
$$MB_B = -6A + 30B$$

A costs $40 per unit and *B* costs $42 per unit. What are the optimal amounts of *A* and *B*?

10. Analyze the following statements.
    a. This is a lousy vacation resort, and it's been raining the whole time. I'd leave but I've already paid for the hotel for the week, so I guess I will stay.
    b. My business is losing money every month, but I have so much invested in it already that I'm going to keep on with it.
    c. I hate golf, but I paid so much for the clubs that I can't give it up.
    d. The cost of my yearly business license has doubled, so I'm going to sell the business because the profits will fall.
    e. The cost of my yearly business license has doubled, but I guess I'll keep on operating the business even though profits will fall, because it's the best I can do.
11. You are interviewing three people for one sales job. On the basis of your experience and insight, you believe Jane can sell 600 units a day, Joe can sell 450 units a day, and Joan can sell 400 units a day. The daily salary each person is asking is as follows: Jane, $200; Joe, $150; and Joan, $100. How would you rank the three applicants?
12. Fill in the blanks. When choosing the levels of two activities, *A* and *B*, in order to maximize total benefits within a given budget:
    a. If at the given levels of *A* and *B*, MB/P of *A* is ______ MB/P of *B*, increasing *A*

and decreasing B while holding expenditure constant will increase total benefits.

b. If at the given levels of A and B, MB/P of A is ________ MB/P of B, increasing B and decreasing A while holding expenditure constant will increase total benefits.

c. The optimal levels of A and B are the levels at which ________ equals ________.

13. A decision maker is choosing the levels of two activities, A and B, so as to maximize total benefits under a given budget. The prices and marginal benefits of the last units of A and B are denoted P_A, P_B, MB_A, and MB_B.

a. If $P_A = \$20$, $P_B = \$15$, $MB_A = 400$, and $MB_B = 600$, what should the decision maker do?

b. If $P_A = \$20$, $P_B = \$30$, $MB_A = 200$, and $MB_B = 300$, what should the decision maker do?

c. If $P_A = \$20$, $P_B = \$40$, $MB_A = 300$, and $MB_B = 400$, how many units of A can be obtained if B is reduced by one unit? How much will benefits increase if this exchange is made?

d. If the substitution in part *c* continues to equilibrium and MB_A falls to 250, what will MB_B be?

14. A decision maker wishes to maximize the total benefit associated with three activities, X, Y, and Z. The price per unit of activities X, Y, and Z is \$1, \$2, and \$3, respectively. The following table gives the ratio of the marginal benefit to the price of the activities for various levels of each activity:

Level of activity	$\frac{MB_X}{P_X}$	$\frac{MB_Y}{P_Y}$	$\frac{MB_Z}{P_Z}$
1	10	22	14
2	9	18	12
3	8	12	10
4	7	10	9
5	6	6	8
6	5	4	6
7	4	2	4
8	3	1	2

a. If the decision maker chooses to use one unit of X, one unit of Y, and one unit of Z, the total benefit that results is \$________.

b. For the fourth unit of activity Y, each dollar spent increases total benefit by \$________. The fourth unit of activity Y increases total benefit by \$________.

c. Suppose the decision maker can spend a total of only \$18 on the three activities. What is the optimal level of X, Y, and Z? Why is this combination optimal? Why is the combination 2X, 2Y, and 4Z not optimal?

d. Now suppose the decision maker has \$33 to spend on the three activities. What is the optimal level of X, Y, and Z? If the decision maker has \$35 to spend, what is the optimal combination? Explain.

15. Suppose a firm is considering two different activities, X and Y, which yield the total benefits presented in the schedule below. The price of X is \$2 per unit, and the price of Y is \$10 per unit.

Level of activity	Total benefit of activity X (TB_X)	Total benefit of activity Y (TB_Y)
0	\$ 0	\$ 0
1	30	100
2	54	190
3	72	270
4	84	340
5	92	400
6	98	450

a. The firm places a budget constraint of \$26 on expenditures on activities X and Y. What is the level of X and Y that maximizes total benefit subject to the budget constraint?
b. What is the total benefit associated with the optimal level of X and Y in part *a*?
c. Now let the budget constraint increase to \$58. What is the optimal level of X and Y now? What is the total benefit when the budget constraint is \$58?

16. *a.* If, in a constrained minimization problem, $P_A = \$10$, $P_B = \$10$, $MB_A = 600$, and $MB_B = 300$ and one unit of B is taken away, how many units of A must be added to keep benefits constant?
b. If the substitution in part *a* continues to equilibrium, what will be the equilibrium relation between MB_A and MB_B?

APPLIED PROBLEMS

1. Using optimization theory, analyze the following quotations:
a. "The optimal number of traffic deaths in the United States is zero."
b. "Any pollution is too much pollution."
c. "We cannot pull U.S. troops out of Bosnia. We have committed so much already."
d. "If Congress cuts out the NASA space station, we will have wasted all the resources that we have already spent on it. Therefore, we must continue funding it."
e. "If the 55-mile-per-hour speed limit has reduced traffic deaths, we should reduce the speed limit even more."

2. Appalachian Coal Mining believes that it can increase labor productivity and, therefore, net revenue by reducing air pollution in its mines. It estimates that the marginal cost function for reducing pollution by installing additional capital equipment is

$$MC = 40P$$

where P represents a reduction of one unit of pollution in the mines. It also feels that for every unit of pollution reduction the marginal increase in revenue (MR) is

$$MR = 1{,}000 - 10P$$

How much pollution reduction should Appalachian Coal Mining undertake?

3. The business section of the *International Herald Tribune* carried a story with the headline "Hark! The Herald Angels Sing of Teleconferencing" (Peter H. Lewis, New York Times Service). The story described how video teleconferencing—two-way telecasts—is gaining popularity with businesses. Indeed, it was reported that some firms are regarding teleconferencing as an effective substitute for in-person conferences. And the cost has been declining to the point where it is comparable to "having four or five executives jump on a plane to go to a common point."

   Your boss asked you to evaluate teleconferencing as an alternative to the six global conferences the firm is currently holding each year. In his instructions to you, he said that "it looks like we might be able to realize substantial savings without reducing the impact of the conferences."

   Set up a plan for solving this optimization problem. What are the benefits? What are the costs? Should this problem be treated as a constrained or unconstrained optimization problem? Why?

4. Twentyfirst Century Electronics has discovered a theft problem at its warehouse and has decided to hire security guards. The firm wants to hire the optimal number of security guards. The following table shows how the number of security guards affects the number of radios stolen per week.

Number of security guards	Number of radios stolen per week
0	50
1	30
2	20
3	14
4	8
5	6

   a. If each security guard is paid \$200 a week and the cost of a stolen radio is \$25, how many security guards should the firm hire?
   b. If the cost of a stolen radio is \$25, what is the most the firm would be willing to pay to hire the first security guard?
   c. If each security guard is paid \$200 a week and the cost of a stolen radio is \$50, how many security guards should the firm hire?

5. U.S. Supreme Court Justice Stephen Breyer's book *Breaking the Vicious Circle: Toward Effective Risk Regulation* (1993) examines government's role in controlling and managing the health risks society faces from exposure to environmental pollution. One major problem examined in the book is the cleanup of hazardous waste sites. Justice Breyer was extremely critical of policymakers who wish to see waste sites 100 percent clean.

a. Explain, using the theory of optimization and a graph, the circumstances under which a waste site could be made "too clean." (Good answers are dispassionate and employ economic analysis.)
b. Justice Breyer believes that society can enjoy virtually all the health benefits of cleaning up a waste site for only a "small fraction" of the total cost of completely cleaning a site. Using graphical analysis, illustrate this situation. (*Hint:* Draw *MB* and *MC* curves with shapes that specifically illustrate this situation.)

6. In Illustration 4.2 we noted that the rule for maximization set forth in the text contradicts some honored traditional principles such as "Never give up," "Anything worth doing is worth doing well," or "Waste not, want not." Explain the contradiction for each of these rules.
7. Janice Waller, the manager of the customer service department at First Bank of Jefferson County, can hire employees with a high school diploma for $20,000 annually and employees with a bachelor's degree for $30,000. She wants to maximize the number of customers served, given a fixed payroll. The table below shows how the total number of customers served varies with the number of employees:

Number of employees	Total number of customers served	
	High school diploma	Bachelor's degree
1	120	100
2	220	190
3	300	270
4	370	330
5	430	380
6	470	410

a. If Ms. Waller has a payroll of $160,000, how should she allocate this budget in order to maximize the number of customers served?
b. If she has a budget of $150,000 and currently hires three people with high school diplomas and three with bachelor's degrees, is she making the correct decision? Why or why not? If not, what should she do? (Assume she can hire part-time workers.)
c. If her budget is increased to $240,000, how should she allocate this budget?

8. Many candidates for political office, particularly in local elections, call for increased government spending on public education. Ignoring the politics of the issue:
a. Is it possible for government to spend too much on education? Explain.
b. How would you advise government officials to determine how much to spend on education?
c. If a city government has a given budget to spend on education, street repair, and police protection, using the principles set forth in this chapter, how would you advise the government to determine how to allocate these limited dollars, again politics aside?

9. Rob Spana, southeast sales manager for Manufacturer's Aluminum Supply, makes most of his outside sales by playing either golf or tennis with potential clients.

From much past experience, he estimates that various levels of playing golf and tennis generate the following amounts of additional sales (MB):

Number of rounds of golf (G)	Additional sales generated (MB_G)	Number of tennis matches (T)	Additional sales generated (MB_T)
1	$2,500	1	$2,400
2	2,000	2	2,250
3	1,750	3	2,100
4	1,375	4	1,800
5	1,250	5	1,500
6	1,200	6	1,050
7	1,125	7	750
8	1,100	8	600

One round of golf (18 holes) takes 5 hours to play (including a half-hour stop at the clubhouse), and one tennis match (best two out of three sets) takes 3 hours to complete. Rob can get away from the office tc play golf and tennis only 20 hours each week.

a. What is the optimal number of rounds of golf to play and the optimal number of tennis matches to play?

b. Suppose Rob gets sick one week and can get in only 12 hours of golf and tennis. What level of golf and tennis play is optimal?

10. Bavarian Crystal Works designs and produces lead crystal wine decanters for export to international markets. The production manager of Bavarian Crystal Works estimates total and marginal production costs to be

$$TC = 10{,}000 + 40Q + 0.0025Q^2$$

and

$$MC = 40 + 0.005Q$$

where costs are measured in U.S. dollars, and Q is the number of wine decanters produced annually. Because Bavarian Crystal Works is only one of many crystal producers in the world market, it can sell as many of the decanters as it wishes for $70 apiece. Total and marginal revenue are

$$TR = 70Q \quad \text{and} \quad MR = 70$$

where revenues are measured in U.S. dollars, and Q is annual decanter production.

a. What is the optimal level of production of wine decanters? What is the marginal revenue from the last wine decanter sold?

b. What is the total revenue, total cost, and net benefit (profit) from selling the optimal number of wine decanters?

c. At the optimal level of production of decanters, an extra decanter can be sold for $70, thereby increasing total revenue by $70. Why does the manager of this firm *not* produce and sell one more unit?

11. Joy Land Toys, a toy manufacturer, is experiencing quality problems on its assembly line. The marketing division estimates that each defective toy that leaves the plant costs the firm $10, on average, for replacement or repair. The engineering

department recommends hiring quality inspectors to sample for defective toys. In this way many quality problems can be caught and prevented before shipping. After visiting other companies, a management team derives the following schedule showing the approximate number of defective toys that would be produced for several levels of inspection:

Number of inspectors	Average number of defective toys (per day)
0	92
1	62
2	42
3	27
4	17
5	10
6	5

The daily wage of inspectors is $70.

a. How many inspectors should the firm hire?

b. What would your answer to *a* be if the wage rate is $90?

c. What if the average cost of a defective toy is $5 and the wage rate of inspectors is $70?

MATHEMATICAL APPENDIX A Brief Presentation of Optimization Theory

Theory of Unconstrained Maximization

This section sets forth a mathematical analysis of unconstrained maximization. We begin with a single-variable problem in its most general form. An activity, the level of which is denoted as x, generates both benefits and costs. The total benefit function is $B(x)$ and the total cost function is $C(x)$. The objective is to maximize net benefit, NB, defined as the difference between total benefit and total cost. Net benefit is itself a function of the level of activity and can be expressed as

$$NB = NB(x) = B(x) - C(x) \tag{1}$$

The necessary condition for maximization of net benefit is that the derivative of NB with respect to x equal zero:

$$\frac{dNB(x)}{dx} = \frac{dB(x)}{dx} - \frac{dC(x)}{dx} = 0 \tag{2}$$

Equation (2) can then be solved for the optimal level of x, denoted x^*. Net benefit is maximized when

$$\frac{dB(x)}{dx} = \frac{dC(x)}{dx} \tag{3}$$

Since dB/dx is the change in total benefit with respect to the level of activity, this term is marginal benefit. Similarly for cost, dC/dx is the change in total cost with respect to the level of activity, and this term is marginal cost. Thus net benefit is maximized at the level of activity where marginal benefit equals marginal cost.

This unconstrained optimization problem can be easily expanded to more than one choice variable or kind of activity. To this end, let total benefit and total cost be functions of two different activities, denoted by x and y. The net benefit function with two activities is expressed as

$$NB = NB(x, y) = B(x, y) - C(x, y) \tag{4}$$

Maximization of net benefit when there are two activities affecting benefit and cost requires both of the partial derivatives of NB with respect to each of the activities to be equal to zero:

$$\frac{\partial NB(x, y)}{\partial x} = \frac{\partial B(x, y)}{\partial x} - \frac{\partial C(x, y)}{\partial x} = 0 \tag{5a}$$

$$\frac{\partial NB(x, y)}{\partial y} = \frac{\partial B(x, y)}{\partial y} - \frac{\partial C(x, y)}{\partial y} = 0 \tag{5b}$$

Equations (5a) and (5b) can be solved simultaneously for the optimal levels of the variables, x^* and y^*. Maximization of net benefit thus requires

(6a) $$\frac{\partial B}{\partial x} = \frac{\partial C}{\partial x}$$

and

(6b) $$\frac{\partial B}{\partial y} = \frac{\partial C}{\partial y}$$

For each activity, the marginal benefit of the activity equals the marginal cost of the activity. The problem can be expanded to any number of choice variables with the same results.

Turning now to a mathematical example, consider the following specific form of the total benefit and total cost functions:

(7) $$B(x) = ax - bx^2$$

and

(8) $$C(x) = cx - dx^2 + ex^3$$

where the parameters, a, b, c, d, and e are all positive.

Now the net benefit function can be expressed as

(9) $$NB = NB(x) = B(x) - C(x) = ax - bx^2 - cx + dx^2 - ex^3$$

To find the optimal value of x, take the derivative of the net benefit function with respect to x and set it equal to zero:

(10) $$\frac{dNB}{dx} = a - 2bx - c + 2dx - 3ex^2 = (a - c) - 2(b - d)x - 3ex^2 = 0$$

This quadratic equation can be solved using the quadratic formula or by factoring.*

Suppose the values of the parameters are $a = 60$, $b = 0.5$, $c = 24$, $d = 2$, and $e = 1$. The net benefit function is

(11) $$NB = NB(x) = 60x - 0.5x^2 - 24x + 2x^2 - x^3$$

*Obviously, the solution to this quadratic equation yields two values for x. The maximization, rather than minimization, solution is the value of x at which the second-order condition is met:

$$\frac{d^2NB}{dx^2} = -2(b - d) - 6ex < 0$$

Now take the derivative of NB [or substitute parameter values into equation (10)] to find the condition for optimization:

(12) $$(60 - 24) - 2(0.5 - 2)x - 3(1)x^2 = 36 + 3x - 3x^2 = 0$$

This equation can be factored: $(12 - 3x)(3 + x) = 0$. The solutions are $x = 4$, $x = -3$. (*Note:* The quadratic equation can also be used to find the solutions.) The value of x that maximizes net benefit is $x^* = 4$.† To find the optimal, or maximum, value of net benefit, substitute $x^* = 4$ into equation (11) to obtain

$$NB^* = 60(4) - 0.5(4)^2 - 24(4) + 2(4)^2 - (4)^3 = 104$$

Theory of Constrained Maximization

In a constrained maximization problem a decision maker determines the level of the activities, or choice variables in order to obtain the most benefit under a given cost constraint. In a constrained minimization problem a decision maker determines the levels of the choice variables in order to obtain the lowest cost of achieving a given level of benefit. As we showed in the text, the solutions to the two types of problems are the same. We first consider constrained maximization.

Constrained maximization

We first assume a general total benefit function with two choice variables, the levels of which are denoted x and y: $B(x, y)$. The partial derivatives of this function represent the marginal benefit for each activity:

$$MB_x = \frac{\partial B(x, y)}{\partial x} \quad \text{and} \quad MB_y = \frac{\partial B(x, y)}{\partial y}$$

The constraint is that the total cost function must equal a specified level of cost, denoted as $\overline{C}$:

(13) $$C(x, y) = P_x x + P_y y = \overline{C}$$

where P_x and P_y are the prices of x and y. Now the Lagrangian function to be maximized can be written as

(14) $$\mathcal{L} = B(x, y) + \lambda(\overline{C} - P_x x - P_x y)$$

†This value of x is the one that satisfies the second-order condition for a maximum in the preceding footnote:

$$\frac{d^2NB}{dx^2} = -2(-1.5) - 6(1)(4) = -21 < 0$$

where λ is the Lagrangian multiplier. The first-order condition for a maximum requires the partial derivatives of the Lagrangian with respect to the variables x, y, and λ to be zero:

$$\frac{\partial \mathcal{L}}{\partial x} = \frac{\partial B}{\partial x} - \lambda P_x = 0 \tag{14a}$$

$$\frac{\partial \mathcal{L}}{\partial y} = \frac{\partial B}{\partial y} - \lambda Py = 0 \tag{14b}$$

$$\frac{\partial \mathcal{L}}{\partial \lambda} = \overline{C} - P_x x - P_y y = 0 \tag{14c}$$

Notice that satisfaction of the first-order condition (14c) requires that the cost constraint be met.

Rearranging the first two equations (14a) and (14b):

$$\frac{\partial B}{\partial x} = \lambda P_x \quad \text{or} \quad \frac{MB_x}{P_x} = \lambda$$

$$\frac{\partial B}{\partial y} = \lambda P_y \quad \text{or} \quad \frac{MB_y}{P_y} = \lambda$$

It therefore follows that the levels of x and y must be chosen so that

$$\frac{MB_x}{P_x} = \frac{MB_y}{P_y} \tag{15}$$

The marginal benefits per dollar spent on the last units of x and y must be equal.

The three equations in (14) can be solved by substitution or by Cramer's rule for the equilibrium values, x^*, y^*, and λ^*. Therefore, x^* and y^* give the values of the choice variables that yield the maximum benefit possible at the given level of cost.

Constrained minimization

For the constrained minimization problem we want to choose the levels of two activities, x and y, to obtain a given level of benefit at the lowest possible cost. Therefore, the problem is to minimize $C = P_x x + P_y y$, subject to $\overline{B} = B(x, y)$, where $\overline{B}$ is the specified level of benefit. The Lagrangian function is

$$\mathcal{L} = P_x x + P_y y + \lambda[\overline{B} - B(x, y)] \tag{16}$$

The first-order conditions are

$$\begin{aligned} \frac{\partial \mathcal{L}}{\partial x} &= P_x - \lambda \frac{\partial B}{\partial x} = 0 \\ \frac{\partial \mathcal{L}}{\partial y} &= P_y - \lambda \frac{\partial B}{\partial y} = 0 \\ \frac{\partial \mathcal{L}}{\partial \lambda} &= [\overline{B} - B(x, y)] = 0 \end{aligned} \tag{17}$$

As in the constrained maximization problem, the first two equations can be rearranged to obtain

$$\begin{aligned} \frac{\partial B}{\partial x} &= \frac{1}{\lambda} P_x \quad \text{or} \quad \frac{MB_x}{P_x} = \frac{1}{\lambda} \\ \frac{\partial B}{\partial y} &= \frac{1}{\lambda} P_y \quad \text{or} \quad \frac{MB_y}{P_y} = \frac{1}{\lambda} \end{aligned} \tag{18}$$

Once again the marginal benefits per dollar spent on the last units of x and y must be the same, because, from (18),

$$\frac{MB_x}{P_x} = \frac{MB_y}{P_y}$$

The three equations in (17) can be solved by substitution or by Cramer's rule for the equilibrium values, x^*, y^*, and λ^*. These are the values of the choice variables that attain the lowest cost of reaching the given level of benefit.

MATHEMATICAL EXERCISES

1. Assume the only choice variable is x. The total benefit function is $B(x) = 170x - x^2$, and the cost function is $C(x) = 100 - 10x + 2x^2$.
   a. What are the marginal benefit and marginal cost functions?
   b. Set up the net benefit function and then determine the level of x that maximizes net benefit.
   c. What is the maximum level of net benefit?
2. The only choice variable is x. The total benefit function is $B(x) = 100x - 2x^2$, and the total cost function is $C(x) = \frac{1}{3}x^3 - 6x^2 + 52x + 80$.
   a. What are the marginal benefit and marginal cost functions?

b. Set up the net benefit function and then determine the level of x that maximizes net benefit. (Use the positive value of x.)
c. What is the maximum level of net benefit?

3. A decision maker wishes to maximize total benefit, $B = 3x + xy + y$, subject to the cost constraint, $\overline{C} = 4x + 2y = 70$. Set up the Lagrangian and then determine the values of x and y at the maximum level of benefit, given the constraint. What are the maximum benefits?
4. A decision maker wishes to minimize the cost of producing a given level of total benefit, $B = 288$. The cost function is $C = 6x + 3y$ and the total benefit function is $B = xy$. Set up the Lagrangian and then determine levels of x and y at the minimum level of cost. What is the minimum value of cost?

CHAPTER 5

Basic Estimation Techniques

In order to implement the various techniques discussed in this text, managers must be able to determine the mathematical relation between the economic variables that make up the various functions used in managerial economics—demand functions, production functions, cost functions, and others. For example, managers often must determine the total cost of producing various levels of output. As you will see in Chapter 11, the relation between total cost (C) and quantity (Q) can be specified as

$$C = a + bQ + cQ^2 + dQ^3$$

parameters
The coefficients in an equation that determine the exact mathematical relation among the variables.

where a, b, c, and d are the *parameters* of the cost equation. **Parameters** are coefficients in an equation that determine the exact mathematical relation among the variables in the equation. Once the numerical values of the parameters are determined, the manager then knows the quantitative relation between output and total cost. For example, suppose the values of the parameters of the cost equation are determined to be $a = 1{,}262$, $b = 1.0$, $c = -0.03$, and $d = 0.005$. The cost equation can now be expressed as

$$C = 1{,}262 + 1.0Q - 0.03Q^2 + 0.005Q^3$$

This equation can be used to compute the total cost of producing various levels of output. If, for example, the manager wishes to produce 30 units of output, the total cost can be calculated as

parameter estimation
The process of finding estimates of the numerical values of the parameters of an equation.

$$C = 1{,}262 + 30 - 0.03(30)^2 + 0.005(30)^3 = \$1{,}400$$

Thus, in order for the cost function to be useful for decision making, the manager must know the numerical values of the parameters.

regression analysis
A statistical technique for estimating the parameters of an equation and testing for statistical significance.

The process of finding estimates of the numerical values of the parameters of an equation is called **parameter estimation.** Although there are several techniques for estimating parameters, the values of the parameters are often obtained by using a technique called **regression analysis.** Regression analysis uses data on economic variables to determine a mathematical equation that describes the relation between the economic variables. Regression analysis involves both the estimation of parameter values and testing for statistical significance.

In this chapter, we will set forth the *basics* of regression analysis. We want to stress that throughout the discussion of regression analysis, in this chapter and the chapters that follow, we are not as much interested in your knowing the ways the various statistics are calculated as we are in your knowing how these statistics can be interpreted and used. We will often rely on intuitive explanations, leaving formal derivations for the appendixes at the end of the chapter.

5.1 THE SIMPLE LINEAR REGRESSION MODEL

dependent variable The variable whose variation is to be explained.

explanatory variables The variables that are thought to cause the dependent variable to take on different values.

Regression analysis is a technique used to determine the mathematical relation between a **dependent variable** and one or more **explanatory variables.** The explanatory variables are the economic variables that are thought to affect the value of the dependent variable. In the *simple linear regression model,* the dependent variable Y is related to only *one* explanatory variable X, and the relation between Y and X is linear:

$$Y = a + bX$$

intercept parameter The parameter that gives the value of Y at the point where the regression line crosses the Y-axis.

slope parameter The slope of the regression line, $b = \Delta Y/\Delta X$, or the change in Y associated with a one-unit change in X.

This is the equation for a straight line, with X plotted along the horizontal axis and Y along the vertical axis. The parameter a is called the **intercept parameter** because it gives the value of Y at the point where the regression line crosses the Y-axis. (X is equal to zero at this point.) The parameter b is called the **slope parameter** because it gives the slope of the regression line. The slope of a line measures the rate of change in Y as X changes ($\Delta Y/\Delta X$); it is therefore the change in Y per unit change in X.

Note that Y and X are linearly related in the regression model; that is, the effect of a change in X on the value of Y is constant. More specifically, a one-unit change in X causes Y to change by a constant b units. The simple regression model is based on a linear relation between Y and X, in large part because estimating the parameters of a linear model is relatively simple statistically. As it turns out, assuming a linear relation is not overly restrictive. For one thing, many variables are actually linearly related or very nearly linearly related. For those cases where Y and X are instead related in a curvilinear fashion, you will see that a simple transformation of the variables often makes it possible to model nonlinear relations within the framework of the linear regression model. You will see how to make these simple transformations later in this chapter.

A Hypothetical Regression Model

true (or **actual**) **relation** The true or actual underlying relation between Y and X that is unknown to the researcher but is to be discovered by analyzing the sample data.

To illustrate the simple regression model, consider a statistical problem facing the Tampa Bay Travel Agents' Association. The association wishes to determine the mathematical relation between the dollar volume of sales of travel packages (S) and the level of expenditures on newspaper advertising (A) for travel agents located in the Tampa–St. Petersburg metropolitan area. Suppose that the **true (**or **actual) relation** between sales and advertising expenditures is

$$S = 10{,}000 + 5A$$

FIGURE 5.1
The True Regression Line: Relating Sales and Advertising Expenditures

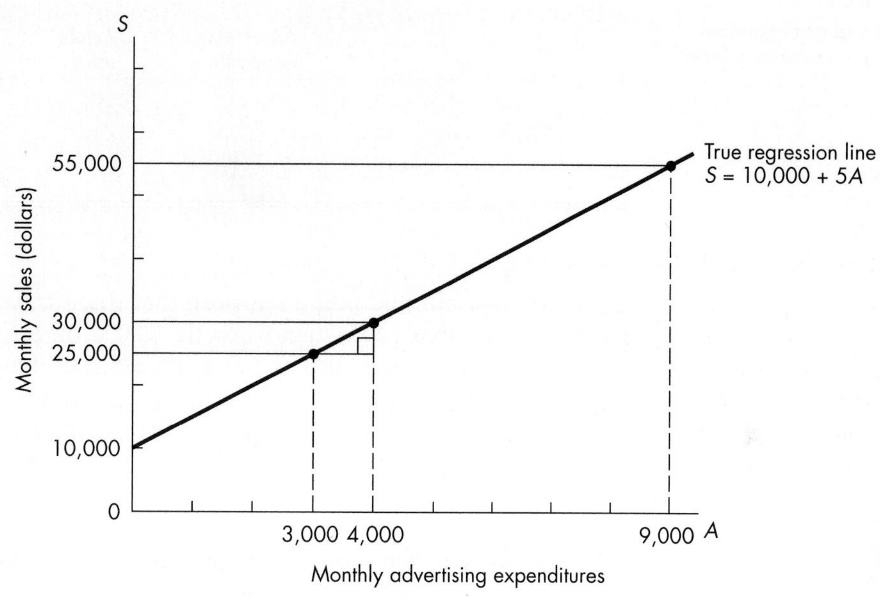

where S measures monthly sales in dollars, and A measures monthly advertising expenditures in dollars. The true relation between sales and advertising is unknown to the analyst; it must be "discovered" by analyzing data on sales and advertising. Researchers are never able to know with certainty the exact nature of the underlying mathematical relation between the dependent variable and the explanatory variable, but regression analysis does provide a method for estimating the true relation.

Figure 5.1 shows the true or actual relation between sales and advertising expenditures. If an agency chooses to spend nothing on newspaper advertising, its sales are expected to be \$10,000 per month. If an agency spends \$3,000 monthly on ads, it can expect sales of \$25,000 (= 10,000 + 5 × 3,000). Because $\Delta S/\Delta A$ equals 5, for every \$1 of additional expenditure on advertising, the travel agency can expect a \$5 increase in sales. For example, increasing outlays from \$3,000 to \$4,000 per month causes expected monthly sales to rise from \$25,000 to \$30,000, as shown in the figure.

The Random Error Term

The regression equation (or line) shows the level of expected sales for each level of advertising expenditure. As noted, if a travel agency spends \$3,000 monthly on ads, it can expect on average to have sales of \$25,000. We should stress that \$25,000 should be interpreted not as the exact level of sales that a firm will experience when advertising expenditures are \$3,000 but only as an average

TABLE 5.1
The Impact of Random Effects on January Sales

Firm	Advertising expenditure	Actual sales	Expected sales	Random effect
Tampa Travel Agency	\$3,000	\$30,000	\$25,000	\$5,000
Buccaneer Travel Service	3,000	21,000	25,000	−4,000
Happy Getaway Tours	3,000	25,000	25,000	0

level. To illustrate this point, suppose that three travel agencies in the Tampa–St. Petersburg area each spend exactly \$3,000 on advertising. Will all three of these firms experience sales of precisely \$25,000? This is *not* likely. While each of these three firms spends exactly the same amount on advertising, each firm experiences certain *random* effects that are peculiar to that firm. These random effects cause the sales of the various firms to deviate from the expected \$25,000 level of sales.

Table 5.1 illustrates the impact of random effects on the actual level of sales achieved. Each of the three firms in Table 5.1 spent \$3,000 on advertising in the month of January. According to the true regression equation, each of these travel agencies would be expected to have sales of \$25,000 in January. As it turns out, the manager of the Tampa Travel Agency used the advertising agency owned and managed by her brother, who gave better than usual service. This travel agency actually sold \$30,000 worth of travel packages in January—\$5,000 more than the expected or average level of sales. The manager of Buccaneer Travel Service was on a ski vacation in early January and did not start spending money on advertising until the middle of January. Buccaneer Travel Service's sales were only \$21,000—\$4,000 less than the regression line predicted. In January nothing unusual happened to Happy Getaway Tours, and its sales of \$25,000 exactly matched what the average travel agency in Tampa would be expected to sell when it spends \$3,000 on advertising.

Because of these random effects, the level of sales for a firm cannot be *exactly* predicted. The regression equation shows only the *average* or *expected* level of sales when a firm spends a given amount on advertising. The exact level of sales for any particular travel agency (such as the *i*th agency) can be expressed as:

$$S_i = 10{,}000 + 5A_i + e_i$$

where S_i and A_i are, respectively, the sales and advertising levels of the *i*th agency and e_i is the random effect experienced by the *i*th travel agency. Since e_i measures the amount by which the *actual* level of sales differs from the average level of sales, e_i is called an *error term,* or a *random error.* The **random error term** captures the effects of all the minor, unpredictable factors that cannot reasonably be included in the model as explanatory variables.

random error term
An unobservable term added to a regression model to capture the effects of all the minor, unpredictable factors that affect Y but cannot reasonably be included as explanatory variables.

Because the *true* regression line is unknown, the first task of regression analysis is to obtain estimates of a and b. To do this, data on monthly sales and advertising expenditures must be collected from Tampa Bay–area travel agents.

TABLE 5.2

Sales and Advertising Expenditures for a Sample of Seven Travel Agencies

Firm	Sales	Advertising expenditure
A	$15,000	$2,000
B	30,000	2,000
C	30,000	5,000
D	25,000	3,000
E	55,000	9,000
F	45,000	8,000
G	60,000	7,000

Using these data, a regression line is then fitted. Before turning to the task of fitting a regression line to the data points in a sample, we summarize the simple regression model in the following statistical relation:

Relation The simple linear regression model relates a dependent variable Y to a single independent explanatory variable X in a linear equation called the true regression line:

$$Y = a + bX$$

where a is the Y-intercept, and b is the slope of the regression line ($\Delta Y/\Delta X$). The regression line shows the average or expected value of Y for each level of the explanatory variable X.

5.2 FITTING A REGRESSION LINE

The purpose of regression analysis is twofold: (1) to estimate the parameters (a and b) of the true regression line, and (2) to test whether the estimated values of the parameters are statistically significant. (We will discuss the meaning of statistical significance later.) We turn now to the first task—the estimation of a and b. You will see that estimating a and b is equivalent to fitting a straight line through a scatter of data points plotted on a graph. Regression analysis provides a way of finding the line that "best fits" the scatter of data points.

time-series
A data set in which the data for the dependent and explanatory variables are collected over time for a specific firm.

cross-sectional
A data set in which the data on the dependent and explanatory variables are collected from many different firms or industries at a given point in time.

scatter diagram
A graph of the data points in a sample.

To estimate the parameters of the regression equation, an analyst first collects data on the dependent and explanatory variables. The data can be collected over time for a specific firm (or a specific industry); this type of data set is called a **time-series.** Alternatively, the data can be collected from several different firms or industries at a given time; this type of data set is called a **cross-sectional** data set. No matter how the data are collected, the result is a scatter of data points (called a **scatter diagram**) through which a regression line can be fitted.

To show how the parameters are estimated, we refer once again to the Tampa Bay Travel Agents' Association. Suppose the association asks 7 agencies (out of the total 475 agencies located in the Tampa–St. Petersburg area) for data on their sales and advertising expenditures during the month of January. These data (a cross-sectional data set) are presented in Table 5.2 and are plotted in a scatter diagram in Figure 5.2. Each dot in the figure refers to a specific sales-expenditure

FIGURE 5.2
The Sample Regression Line: Relating Sales and Advertising Expenditures

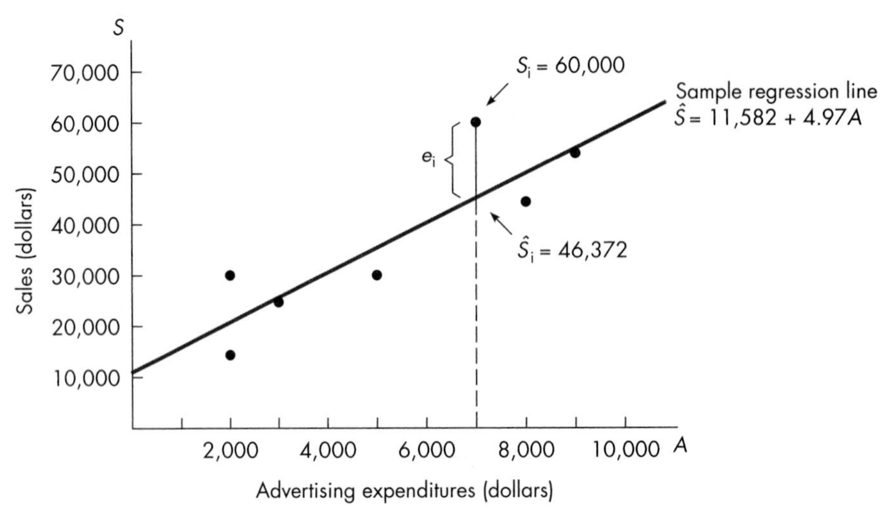

combination in the table. The data seem to indicate that a positive relation exists between sales and advertising—the higher the level of advertising, the higher (on average) the level of sales. The objective of regression analysis is to find the straight line that best fits the scatter of data points. Since fitting a line through a scatter of data points simply involves choosing values of the parameters a and b, fitting a regression line and estimation of parameters are conceptually the same thing.

population regression line
The equation or line representing the true (or actual) underlying relation between the dependent variable and the explanatory variable(s).

sample regression line
The line that best fits the scatter of data points in the sample and provides an estimate of the population regression line.

method of least-squares
A method of estimating the parameters of a linear regression equation by finding the line that minimizes the sum of the squared distances from each sample data point to the sample regression line.

The association wants to use the data in the sample to estimate the true regression line, also called the **population regression line.** The line that best fits the data in the sample is called the **sample regression line.** Since the sample contains information on only 7 out of the total 475 travel agencies, it is highly unlikely that the sample regression line will be exactly the same as the true regression line. The sample regression line is only an estimate of the true regression line. Naturally, the larger the size of the sample, the more accurately the sample regression line will estimate the true regression line.

In Figure 5.2, the sample regression line that best fits the seven sample data points presented in Table 5.2 is given by

$$\hat{S} = 11{,}582 + 4.97A$$

where $\hat{S}$ is called the fitted or predicted value of S. Regression analysis uses the **method of least-squares** to find the sample regression line that best fits the data in the sample. The principle of least-squares is based on the idea that the sample regression line that is most likely to match the *true* regression line is the line that minimizes the sum of the squared distances from each sample data point to the *sample* regression line.

fitted or **predicted value**
The predicted value of Y (denoted $\hat{Y}$) associated with a particular value of X, which is obtained by substituting that value of X into the sample regression equation.

residual
The difference between the actual value of Y and the fitted (or predicted) value of Y: $Y_i - \hat{Y}_i$.

estimators
The formulas by which the estimates of parameters are computed.

estimates
The estimated values of parameters obtained by substituting sample data into estimators.

Look at the sample data point for advertising expenditures of \$7,000 and sales of \$60,000 in Figure 5.2. The sample regression equation indicates that advertising expenditures of \$7,000 will result in \$46,372 (= 11,582 + 4.97 × 7,000) of sales. The value \$46,372 is called the **fitted** or **predicted value** of sales, which we denote as $\hat{S}_i$. The difference between the actual value of sales and the fitted (predicted) value, $S_i - \hat{S}_i$, is called the **residual** and is equal to the vertical distance between the data point and the fitted regression line (denoted e_i in Figure 5.2). The residual for the data point at (\$7,000, \$60,000) is \$13,628 (= \$60,000 − \$46,372). Regression analysis selects the straight line (i.e., chooses a and b), in order to minimize the sum of the squared residuals (Σe_i^2), which is why it is often referred to as least-squares analysis.

We are not concerned with teaching you the details involved in computing the least-squares estimates of a and b since computers are almost always used in regression analysis for this purpose. Nevertheless, it might be informative for you to see how the computer can calculate estimates of a and b. The formulas by which the estimates of a and b are computed are frequently called **estimators.** The formulas for computing the least-squares estimates of a and b (denoted $\hat{a}$ and $\hat{b}$ to indicate that these are **estimates** and not the true values) are

$$\hat{b} = \frac{\Sigma(X_i - \overline{X})(Y_i - \overline{Y})}{\Sigma(X_i - \overline{X})^2}$$

and

$$\hat{a} = \overline{Y} - \hat{b}\overline{X}$$

where $\overline{Y}$ and $\overline{X}$ are, respectively, the sample means of the dependent variable and independent variable, and X_i and Y_i are the observed values for the ith observation. While our central concern is that you understand how to interpret regression analysis, we have provided the mathematical derivation of the least-squares formulas for $\hat{a}$ and $\hat{b}$ in the appendix at the end of this chapter for those who wish to see a formal derivation. So you can appreciate the tedious nature of the arithmetic involved in computing least-squares estimates, this chapter's appendix illustrates the computations that will be done for you by a computer. We can now summarize least-squares estimation with the following statistical relation:

Relation Estimating the parameters of the true regression line is equivalent to fitting a line through a scatter diagram of the sample data points. The sample regression line, which is found using the method of least-squares, is the line that best fits the sample:

$$\hat{Y} = \hat{a} + \hat{b}X$$

where $\hat{a}$ and $\hat{b}$ are the least-squares estimates of the true (population) parameters a and b. The sample regression line estimates the true regression line.

We now turn to the task of testing hypotheses about the true values of a and b—which are unknown to the researcher—using the information contained in the sample. These tests involve determining whether the dependent variable

is truly related to the independent variable or whether the relation as estimated from the sample data is due only to the randomness of the sample.

5.3 TESTING FOR STATISTICAL SIGNIFICANCE

Once the parameters of an equation are estimated, the analyst must address the question of whether or not the parameter estimates ($\hat{a}$ and $\hat{b}$) are significantly different from zero. If the estimated coefficient is far enough away from zero—either sufficiently greater than zero (a positive estimate) or sufficiently less than zero (a negative estimate)—the estimated coefficient is said to be **statistically significant.** The question of statistical significance arises because the estimates are themselves random variables. The parameter estimates are random because they are calculated using values of Y and X that are collected in a random fashion (remember, the sample is a random sample). Since the values of the parameters are *estimates* of the true parameter values, the estimates are rarely equal to the true parameter values. In other words, the estimates calculated by the computer are almost always going to be either too large or too small.

statistically significant
There is sufficient evidence from the sample to indicate that the true value of the coefficient is not zero.

Because the estimated values of the parameters ($\hat{a}$ and $\hat{b}$) are unlikely to be the true values (a and b), it is possible that a parameter could truly be equal to zero even though the computer calculates a parameter estimate that is not equal to zero. Fortunately, statistical techniques exist that provide a tool for making probabilistic statements about the true values of the parameters. This tool is called **hypothesis testing.**

hypothesis testing
A statistical technique for making a probabilistic statement about the true value of a parameter.

To understand fully the concept of hypothesis testing, you would need to take at least one course, and probably two, in statistics. In this text we intend only to motivate through intuition the *necessity* and *process* of performing a test of statistical significance. Our primary emphasis will be to show you how to test the hypothesis that Y is truly related to X. If Y is indeed related to X, the true value of the slope parameter b will be either a positive or a negative number. (Remember, if $b = \Delta Y/\Delta X = 0$, no change in Y occurs when X changes.) Thus, the explanatory variable X has a statistically significant effect on the dependent variable Y when $b \neq 0$.[1]

We will now discuss the procedure for testing for statistical significance by describing how to measure the accuracy, or precision, of an estimate. Then we will introduce and explain a statistical test (called a t-test) that can be used to make a probabilistic statement about whether or not Y is truly related to the explanatory variable X—that is, whether or not the true value of the parameter b is zero.

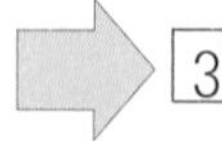

[1]Testing for statistical significance of the intercept parameter a is typically of secondary importance to testing for significance of the slope parameters. As you will see, it is the slope parameters rather than the intercept parameter that provide the most essential information for managerial decision making. Nevertheless, it is customary to test the intercept parameter for statistical significance in exactly the same manner as the slope parameter is tested.

FIGURE 5.3
Relative Frequency Distribution for $\hat{b}$ When $b = 5$

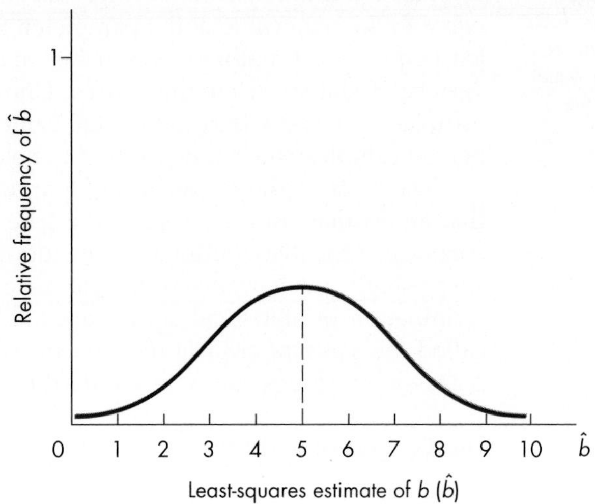

The Relative Frequency Distribution for $\hat{b}$

As noted, the necessity of testing for statistical significance arises because the analyst does not know the true values of a and b—they are estimated from a random sample of observations on Y and X. Consider again the relation between sales of travel packages and advertising expenditures estimated in the previous section. The least-squares estimate of the slope parameter b from the sample of seven travel agencies shown in Table 5.2 is 4.97. Suppose you collected a new sample by randomly selecting seven other travel agencies and use their sales and advertising expenditures to estimate b. The estimate for b will probably not equal 4.97 for the second sample. Remember, $\hat{b}$ is computed using the values of S and A in the sample. Because of randomness in sampling, different samples generally result in different values of S and A, and thus different estimates of b. Therefore, $\hat{b}$ is a random variable—its value varies in repeated samples.

relative frequency distribution
The distribution (and relative frequency) of values $\hat{b}$ can take because observations on Y and X come from a random sample.

The relative frequency with which $\hat{b}$ takes on different values provides information about the *accuracy* of the parameter estimates. Even though researchers seldom have the luxury of taking repeated samples, statisticians have been able to determine theoretically the **relative frequency distribution** of values that $\hat{b}$ would take in repeated samples. Figure 5.3 shows the relative frequency, or likelihood, that $\hat{b}$ takes on different values in repeated samples, *when the true value of* b *is equal to 5.*

Notice that the distribution of values that $\hat{b}$ might take in various samples is centered around the true value of 5. Even though the probability of drawing a sample for which $\hat{b}$ exactly equals 5 is extremely small, the average (mean or

unbiased estimator
An estimator that produces estimates of a parameter that are on average equal to the true value of the parameter.

expected) value of all possible values of $\hat{b}$ is 5. The estimator $\hat{b}$ is said to be an **unbiased estimator** if the average (mean or expected) value of the estimator is equal to the true value of the parameter. Statisticians have demonstrated that the least-squares estimators of a and b ($\hat{a}$ and $\hat{b}$) are unbiased estimators in a wide variety of statistical circumstances. Unbiasedness does not mean that any one estimate equals the true parameter value. Unbiasedness means only that, in repeated samples, the estimates tend to be centered around the true value.

The smaller the dispersion of $\hat{b}$ around the true value, the more likely it is that an estimate of $\hat{b}$ is close to the true value. In other words, the smaller the variance of the distribution of $\hat{b}$, the more accurate estimates are likely to be. Not surprisingly, the variance of the estimate of b plays an important role in the determination of statistical significance. The square root of the variance of $\hat{b}$ is called the *standard error of the estimate,* which we will denote $S_{\hat{b}}$.[2] All computer regression routines compute standard errors for the parameter estimates.

The Concept of a *t*-Ratio

When we regressed sales on advertising expenditures for the seven travel agencies in Table 5.2, we obtained an estimate of b equal to 4.97. Since 4.97 is not equal to zero, this seems to suggest that the level of advertising does indeed affect sales. (Remember that if $b = 0$, there is no relation between sales and advertising.) As explained above, the estimate of b calculated using a random sample may take on a range of values. Even though 4.97 is greater than zero, it is possible that the true value of b is zero. In other words, the analyst runs some risk that the true value of b is zero even when $\hat{b}$ is not calculated to be zero.

The probability of drawing a sample for which the estimate of b is much larger than zero is very small when the true value of b is actually zero. How large does $\hat{b}$ have to be for an analyst to be quite sure that b is not really zero (i.e., advertising does play a significant role in determining sales)? The answer to this question is obtained by performing a hypothesis test. The hypothesis that one normally tests is that $b = 0$. Statisticians use a ***t*-test** to make a probabilistic statement about the likelihood that the true parameter value b is not equal to zero. Using the t-test, it is possible to determine statistically how large $\hat{b}$ must be in order to conclude that b is not equal to zero.

***t*-test**
A statistical test used to test the hypothesis that the true value of a parameter is equal to zero ($b = 0$).

In order to perform a t-test for statistical significance, we form what statisticians call a ***t*-ratio:**

***t*-ratio**
The ratio of an estimated regression parameter divided by the standard error of the estimate.

$$t = \frac{\hat{b}}{S_{\hat{b}}}$$

where $\hat{b}$ is the least-squares estimate of b, and $S_{\hat{b}}$ is the standard error of the estimate, both of which are calculated by the computer. The numerical value of the t-ratio is called a ***t*-statistic.**

***t*-statistic**
The numerical value of the *t*-ratio.

[2] More correctly, the standard error of the estimate is the square root of the *estimated* variance of $\hat{b}$.

By combining information about the size of $\hat{b}$ (in the numerator) and the accuracy or precision of the estimate (in the denominator), the *t*-ratio indicates how much confidence one can have that the true value of b is actually larger than (significantly different from) zero. The larger the absolute value of the *t*-ratio, the more confident one can be that the true value of b is not zero. To show why this is true, we must examine both the numerator and the denominator of the *t*-ratio. Consider the numerator when the estimate $\hat{b}$ is positive. When b actually is zero, drawing a random sample that will produce an estimate of b that is much larger than zero is unlikely. Thus, the larger the numerator of the *t*-ratio, the less likely it is that b really does equal zero. Turning now to the denominator of the *t*-ratio, recall that $S_{\hat{b}}$, the standard error of the estimate, measures the accuracy of the estimate of b. The smaller the standard error of $\hat{b}$ (and thus the more accurate $\hat{b}$ is), the smaller the error in estimation is likely to be. Consequently, the farther from zero $\hat{b}$ is (i.e., the larger the numerator) and the smaller the standard error of the estimate (i.e., the smaller the denominator), the larger the *t*-ratio, and the more sure we are that the true value of b is greater than zero.

Now consider the situation when the estimate $\hat{b}$ is negative (for example, if we had estimated the relation between profits and shoplifting). In this case we would be more certain that b was really negative if the *t*-ratio had a more negative magnitude. Regardless of whether $\hat{b}$ is positive or negative, the following important statistical relation is established:

 4

Relation The larger the absolute value of $\frac{\hat{b}}{S_{\hat{b}}}$ (the *t*-ratio), the more probable it is that the true value of b is not equal to zero.

Performing a *t*-Test for Statistical Significance

critical value of *t*
The value that the *t*-statistic must exceed in order to reject the hypothesis that $b = 0$.

The *t*-statistic is used to test the hypothesis that the true value of b equals zero. If the calculated *t*-statistic or *t*-ratio is greater than the **critical value of *t*** (to be explained later), then the hypothesis that $b = 0$ is rejected in favor of the alternative hypothesis that $b \neq 0$. When the calculated *t*-statistic exceeds the critical value of *t*, b is significantly different from zero, or, equivalently, b is statistically significant. If the hypothesis that $b = 0$ cannot be rejected, then the sample data are indicating that X, the explanatory variable for which b is the coefficient, is not related to the dependent variable Y ($\Delta Y/\Delta X = 0$). Only when a parameter estimate is statistically significant should the associated explanatory variable be included in the regression equation.

Type I error
Error in which a parameter estimate is found to be statistically significant when it is not.

Although performing a *t*-test is the correct way to assess the statistical significance of a parameter estimate, there is always some risk that the *t*-test will indicate $b \neq 0$ when in fact $b = 0$. Statisticians refer to this kind of mistake as a **Type I error**—finding a parameter estimate to be significant when it is not.[3] The

[3]Statisticians also recognize the possibility of committing a Type II error, which occurs when an analyst *fails* to find a parameter estimate to be statistically significant when it *truly* is significant. In your statistics class you will study both types of errors, Type I and Type II. Because it is usually impossible to determine the probability of committing a Type II error, tests for statistical significance typically consider only the possibility of committing a Type I error.

level of significance
The probability of finding the parameter to be statistically significant when in fact it is not.

probability of making a Type I error when performing a t-test is referred to as the **level of significance** of the t-test. The level of significance associated with a t-test is the probability that the test will indicate $b \neq 0$ when in fact $b = 0$. Stated differently, the significance level is the probability of finding the parameter to be statistically significant when in fact it is not. As we are about to show you, an analyst can control or select the level of significance for a t-test. Traditionally, either a 0.01, 0.02, 0.05, or 0.10 level of significance is selected, which reflects the analyst's willingness to tolerate at most a 1, 2, 5, or 10 percent probability of finding a parameter to be significant when it is not. In practice, however, the significance level tends to be chosen arbitrarily. We will return to the problem of selecting the appropriate level of significance later in this discussion of t-tests.

level of confidence
The probability of correctly failing to reject the true hypothesis that $b = 0$; equals one minus the level of significance.

A concept closely related to the level of significance is the level of confidence. The **level of confidence** equals one minus the level of significance, and thus gives the probability that you will *not* make a Type I error. The confidence level is the probability a t-test will *correctly* find no relation between Y and X (i.e., $b = 0$). The lower the level of significance, the greater the level of confidence. If the level of significance chosen for conducting a t-test is 0.05 (5 percent), then the level of confidence for the test is 0.95 (95 percent), and you can be 95 percent confident that the t-test will correctly indicate lack of significance. The levels of significance and confidence provide the same information, only in slightly different ways: the significance level gives the probability of making a Type I error, while the confidence level gives the probability of *not* making a Type I error. A 5 percent level of significance and a 95 percent level of confidence mean the same thing.

Relation In testing for statistical significance, the level of significance chosen for the test determines the probability of committing a Type I error, which is the mistake of finding a parameter to be significant when it is not truly significant. The level of confidence for a test is the probability of not committing a Type I error. The lower (higher) the significance level of a test, the higher (lower) the level of confidence for the test.

degrees of freedom
The number of observations in the sample minus the number of parameters being estimated by the regression analysis ($n - k$).

The t-test is simple to perform. First, calculate the t-statistic (t-ratio) from the parameter estimate and its standard error, both of which are calculated by the computer. (In most statistical software, the t-ratio is also calculated by the computer.) Next, find the appropriate critical value of t for the chosen level of significance. (Critical values of t are provided in a t-table at the end of this book, along with explanatory text.) The critical value of t is defined by the level of significance and the appropriate degrees of freedom. The **degrees of freedom** for a t-test are equal to $n - k$, where n is the number of observations in the sample and k is the number of parameters estimated.[4] (In the advertising example, there

[4]Occasionally you may find other statistics books (or t-tables in other books) that define k as the "number of explanatory variables" rather than the "number of parameters estimated," as we have done in this text. When k is not defined to include the estimated intercept parameter, then the number of degrees of freedom must be calculated as $n - (k + 1)$. No matter how k is defined, the degrees of freedom for the t-test are always equal to the number of observations minus the number of parameters estimated.

are 7 − 2 = 5 degrees of freedom, since we have seven observations and estimated two parameters, a and b.)

Once the critical value of t is found for, say, the 5 percent level of significance or 95 percent level of confidence, the absolute value of the calculated t-statistic is compared with the critical value of t. If the absolute value of the t-statistic is greater than the critical value of t, we say that, at the 95 percent confidence level, the estimated parameter is (statistically) significantly different from zero. If the absolute value of the calculated t-statistic is less than the critical value of t, the estimated value of b cannot be treated as being significantly different from zero and X plays no statistically significant role in determining the value of Y.

Returning to the advertising example, we now test to see if 4.97, the estimated value of b, is significantly different from zero. The standard error of $\hat{b}$, which is calculated by the computer, is equal to 1.23. Thus, the t-statistic is equal to 4.04 (= 4.97/1.23). Next we compare 4.04 to the critical value of t, using a 5 percent significance level (a 95 percent confidence level). As noted above, there are 5 degrees of freedom. If you turn to the table of critical t-values at the end of the text, you will find that the critical value of t for 5 degrees of freedom and a 0.05 level of significance is 2.571. Since 4.04 is larger than 2.571, we reject the hypothesis that b is zero and can now say that 4.97 ($\hat{b}$) is significantly different from zero. This means that advertising expenditure is a statistically significant variable in determining the level of sales. If 4.04 had been less than the critical value, we would not have been able to reject the hypothesis that b is zero and we would not have been able to conclude that advertising plays a significant role in determining the level of sales.

The procedure for testing for statistical significance of a parameter estimate is summarized in the following statistical principle:

Principle In order to test for statistical significance of a parameter estimate $\hat{b}$, compute the t-ratio

$$t = \frac{\hat{b}}{S_{\hat{b}}}$$

where $S_{\hat{b}}$ is the standard error of the estimate $\hat{b}$. Next, for the chosen level of significance, find the critical t value in the t-table at the end of the text. Choose the critical t-value with $n - k$ degrees of freedom for the chosen level of significance. If the absolute value of the t-ratio is greater (less) than the critical t-value, then $\hat{b}$ is (is not) statistically significant.

Using *p*-Values to Determine Statistical Significance

Using a t-test to determine whether a parameter estimate is statistically significant requires that you select a level of significance at which to perform the test. In most of the situations facing a manager, choosing the significance level for the test involves making an arbitrary decision. We will now show you an alternative method of assessing the statistical significance of parameter estimates that does not require that you "preselect" a level of significance (or, equivalently, the level of confidence) or use a t-table to find a critical t-value. With this alternative method, the *exact degree* of statistical significance is determined by answering the question, "Given the t-ratio calculated for $\hat{b}$, what would be the lowest level of significance—or the highest level of confidence—that would allow the hypothesis $b = 0$ to be rejected in favor of the alternative hypothesis $b \neq 0$?"

Consider the t-test for the parameter estimate 4.97. In the previous section, the effect of advertising (A) on sales (S) was found to be statistically significant because the calculated t-ratio 4.04 exceeded 2.571, the critical t-value for a 5 percent level of significance (a 95 percent level of confidence). A t-ratio *only* as large as 2.571 would be sufficient to achieve a 5 percent level of significance that $b \neq 0$. The calculated t-ratio 4.04 is much larger than the critical t for the 5 percent significance level. This means a significance level *lower* than 5 percent (or a confidence level *higher* than 95 percent) would still allow one to reject the hypothesis of no significance ($b = 0$). What is the lowest level of significance or, equivalently, the greatest level of confidence that permits rejecting the hypothesis that $b = 0$ when the computer calculates a t-ratio of 4.04? The answer is given by the *p-value* for 4.04, which most statistical software, and even spreadsheets, can calculate.

p-value
The exact level of significance for a test statistic, which is the probability of finding significance when none exists.

The ***p*-value** associated with a calculated t-ratio gives the *exact* level of significance for a t-ratio associated with a parameter estimate.[5] In other words, the p-value gives the exact probability of committing a Type I error—finding significance when none exists—if you conclude that $b \neq 0$ on the basis of the t-ratio calculated by the computer. One minus the p-value is the exact degree of confidence that can be assigned to a particular parameter estimate.

The p-value for the calculated t-ratio 4.04 (= 4.97/1.23) is 0.010. A p-value of 0.010 means that the exact level of significance for a t-ratio of 4.04 is 1 percent and the exact level of confidence is 99 percent. Rather than saying $\hat{b}$ is statistically significant at the 5 percent level of significance (or the 95 percent level of confidence), using the p-value we can make a more precise, and stronger, statement: $\hat{b}$ is statistically significant at exactly the 1 percent level of significance. In other words, at the 99 percent confidence level advertising affects sales ($b \neq 0$); that is, there is only a 1 percent chance that advertising does *not* affect sales.

While t-tests are the traditional means of assessing statistical significance, most computer software packages now routinely print the p-values associated with t-ratios. Rather than preselecting a level of significance (or level of confidence) for t-tests, it is now customary to report the p-values associated with the estimated parameters—usually along with standard errors and t-ratios—and let the users of the statistical estimations decide whether the level of significance is acceptably low or the level of confidence is acceptably high.

5 **Relation** The exact level of significance associated with a t-statistic, its p-value, gives the exact (or minimum) probability of committing a Type I error—finding significance when none exists—if you conclude that $b \neq 0$ on the basis of the t-ratio calculated by the computer. One minus the p-value is the exact degree of confidence that can be assigned to a particular parameter estimate.

[5] Although this section discusses t-statistics, a p-value can be computed for any test statistic, and it gives the exact significance level for the associated test statistic.

ILLUSTRATION 5.1

How Confident Is "Confident Enough"?

When a hypothesis is true, the level of significance expresses the probability of making the wrong decision (rejection), and the level of confidence expresses the probability of making the correct decision (fail to reject). We have emphasized that the choice of significance level in a statistical analysis depends on the judgment of the analyst and the perceived consequences of making an error. While the choice of significance level also determines the confidence level—the two probabilities must sum to 1—decision makers tend to focus their attention on choosing a sufficiently high level of confidence, rather than thinking of choosing a sufficiently low level of significance. We want to tell you a story to better illustrate how the consequences of a wrong decision can affect the choice of confidence or significance levels.

During the first days of the Persian Gulf war, the world was stunned by the success rate of the bombing attacks against military targets in Iraq. In his first news briefing at the outbreak of the war, General Norman Schwarzkopf reported that 80 percent of the nearly 15,000 sorties flown had successfully hit their intended targets. Many of the correspondents in attendance were highly suspicious about such an extraordinary success rate, but two reporters, Barbara Smith and Heraldo Jones, decided to test the general's assertion that the true success rate was 80 percent. They obtained a list of the locations of 100 of the 15,000 targets, then enlisted the help of a pilot of a three-seater Stealth fighter to fly them over each of the 100 targets to see how many were damaged by bombs. Smith and Jones counted 65 bomb-damaged targets, indicating only a 65 percent success rate, as opposed to the reported 80 percent.

Each reporter had to decide whether 65 percent was far enough away from 80 percent to refute the Schwarzkopf assertion. Both realized the inherent randomness of sampling and that the 100 targets may not have exactly reflected the population of 15,000 targets, known only to the general and his staff.

Smith was tempted to report to her news director that she had discovered compelling evidence that General Schwarzkopf incorrectly reported the success rate of the air war. If correct, she would probably become famous and win a Pulitzer Prize; but if wrong, she would be ruined professionally. Smith was not willing to take more than a 5 percent chance of committing a Type I error: publicly rejecting the Schwarzkopf assertion of an 80 percent success rate when the assertion was correct. In other words, she had to be 95 percent confident that, if Schwarzkopf was correct, her "test" would not reject Schwarzkopf's assertion. Smith decided that 65 percent was not far enough below 80 percent to make her feel 95 percent confident that 80 percent was an exaggeration. Therefore, she did not report her findings.

Jones, in contrast to Smith, badly wanted to be an anchor. He was willing to bet his career by taking a 75 percent risk that he was wrong and the general was right; that is, he was comfortable with only a 25 percent level of confidence. At the 25 percent level of confidence, Jones viewed a 65 percent success rate as being far enough away from the asserted 80 percent success rate that he rejected the general's assertion. Jones called his news anchor with startling evidence that General Schwarzkopf had misinformed the public about the success of the air war. Jones's network reported his story on national news, and upon hearing this news report, General Schwarzkopf decided to reveal the list of the initial 15,000 sorties. Using the entire population of 15,000 targets, the Middle East press corps verified that 80 percent of the targets were indeed damaged by bombs. As it turned out, Barbara Smith was later promoted to anchor at her network. Heraldo Jones was fired and now hosts a talk show at an obscure radio station in College Station, Texas.

5.4 EVALUATION OF THE REGRESSION EQUATION

Once the individual parameter estimates $\hat{a}$ and $\hat{b}$ have been tested for statistical significance using *t*-tests, researchers often wish to evaluate the *complete* estimated regression equation, $\hat{Y} = \hat{a} + \hat{b}X$. Evaluation of the regression equation involves determining how well the estimated regression equation "explains" the variation in *Y*. Two statistics are frequently employed to evaluate the overall acceptability of a regression equation. The first is called the *coefficient of determination,* normally denoted as "R^2" and pronounced "*R*-square." The second is the *F-statistic,* which is used to test whether the *overall* equation is statistically significant.

The Coefficient of Determination (R^2)

coefficient of determination (R^2) The fraction of total variation in the dependent variable explained by the regression equation.

The **coefficient of determination (R^2)** measures the fraction of the total variation in the dependent variable that is explained by the regression equation. In terms of the example used earlier, it is the fraction of the variation in sales that is explained by variation in advertising expenditures. Therefore, the value of R^2 can range from 0 (the regression equation explains none of the variation in *Y*) to 1 (the regression equation explains all the variation in *Y*). While the R^2 is printed out as a decimal value by most computers, the R^2 is often spoken of in terms of a percentage. For example, if the calculated R^2 is 0.7542, we could say that approximately 75 percent of the variation in *Y* is explained by the model.

If the value of R^2 is high, there is high correlation between the dependent and independent variables; if it is low, there is low correlation. For example, in Figure 5.4, Panel A, the observations in the scatter diagram all lie rather close to the regression line. Since the deviations from the line are small, the correlation between *X* and *Y* is high and the value of R^2 will be high. In the extreme case when all of the observations lie on a straight line, R^2 will be equal to 1. In Panel B, the observations are scattered widely around the regression line. The correlation between *X* and *Y* in this case is much less than that in Panel A, so the value of R^2 is rather small.

We must caution you that high correlation between two variables (or even a statistically significant regression coefficient) does not necessarily mean the variation in the dependent variable *Y* is *caused by* the variation in the independent variable *X*. It might be the case that variation in *Y* is caused by variation in *Z*, but *X* happens to be correlated to *Z*. Thus *Y* and *X* will be correlated even though variation in *X* does not cause *Y* to vary. A high R^2 does not prove that *Y* and *X* are causally related, only that *Y* and *X* are correlated. We summarize this discussion with a statistical relation:

Relation The coefficient of determination (R^2) measures the fraction of the total variation in *Y* that is explained by the variation in *X*. R^2 ranges in value from 0 (the regression explains none of the variation in *Y*) to 1 (the regression explains all the variation in *Y*). A high R^2 indicates *Y* and *X* are highly correlated and the scatter diagram tightly fits the sample regression line.

FIGURE 5.4
High and Low Correlation

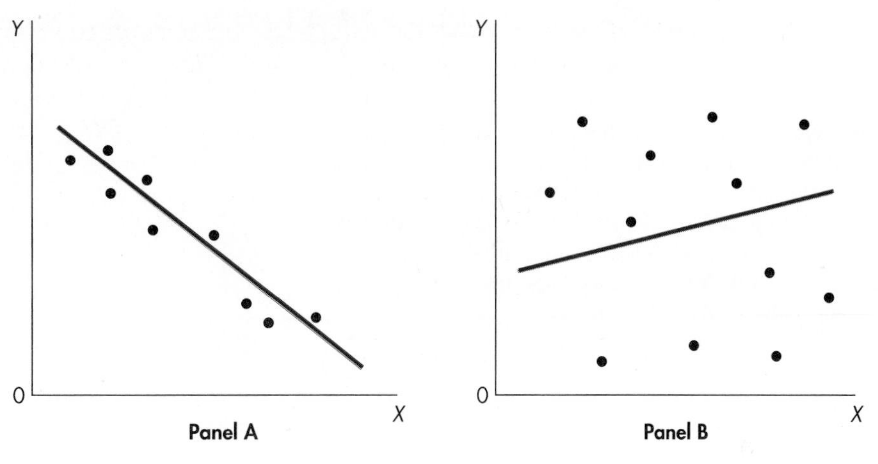

The *F*-Statistic

F-statistic
A statistic used to test whether the overall regression equation is statistically significant.

Although the R^2 is a widely used statistic, it is subjective in the sense of how much explained variation—explained by the regression equation—is enough to view the equation as being statistically significant. An alternative is the ***F*-statistic.** In very general terms, this statistic provides a measure of the ratio of explained variation (in the dependent variable) to unexplained variation. To test whether the overall equation is significant, this statistic is compared with a critical *F*-value obtained from an *F*-table (at the end of this text). The critical *F*-value is identified by two separate degrees of freedom and the significance level. The first of the degrees of freedom is $k - 1$ (i.e., the number of independent variables) and the second is $n - k$. If the value for the calculated *F*-statistic exceeds the critical *F*-value, the regression equation is statistically significant at the specified significance level. The discussion of the *F*-statistic is summarized in a statistical relation:

Relation The *F*-statistic is used to test whether the regression equation as a whole explains a significant amount of the variation in *Y*. The test involves comparing the *F*-statistic to the critical *F*-value with $k - 1$ and $n - k$ degrees of freedom and the chosen level of significance. If the *F*-statistic exceeds the critical *F*-value, the regression equation is statistically significant.

Rather than performing an *F*-test, which requires that you select arbitrarily a significance or confidence level, you may wish to report the exact level of significance for the *F*-statistic. The *p*-value for the *F*-statistic gives the exact level of significance for the regression equation as a whole. One minus the *p*-value is the exact level of confidence associated with the computed *F*-statistic.

ILLUSTRATION 5.2

R&D Expenditures and the Value of the Firm

In order to determine how much to spend on research and development (R&D) activities, a manager may wish to know how R&D expenditures affect the value of the firm. To investigate the relation between the value of a firm and the amount the firm spends on R&D, Wallin and Gilman* used simple regression analysis to estimate the model

$$V = a + bR$$

where the value of the firm (V) is measured by the price-to-earnings ratio, and the level of expenditures on R&D (R) is measured by R&D expenditures as a percentage of the firm's total sales.

Wallin and Gilman collected a cross-sectional data set on the 20 firms with the largest R&D expenditures in the 1981–1982 time period. The computer output from a regression program and a scatter diagram showing the 20 data points with the sample regression line are presented here:

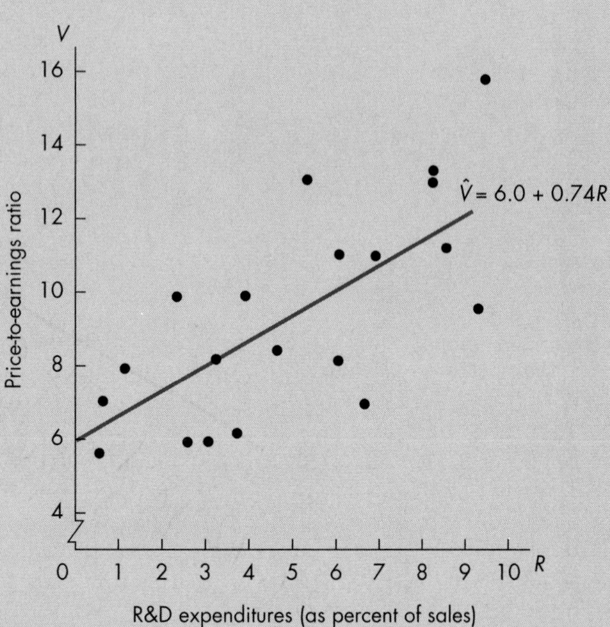

DEPENDENT VARIABLE: V		R-SQUARE	F-RATIO	P-VALUE ON F
OBSERVATIONS: 20		0.5274	20.090	0.0003

VARIABLE	PARAMETER ESTIMATE	STANDARD ERROR	T-RATIO	P-VALUE
INTERCEPT	6.00	0.917	6.54	0.0001
R	0.74	0.165	4.48	0.0003

All the statistics you will need in order to analyze a regression—the coefficient estimates, the standard errors, the t-ratios, R^2, the F-statistic, and the p-value—are automatically calculated and printed by most available regression programs. As mentioned before, our objective is not that you understand how these statistics are calculated. Rather, we want you to know how to set up a regression and interpret the results. We now provide you with a hypothetical example of a regression analysis that might be performed by a manager of a firm.

First, we test to see if the estimate of a is statistically significant. To test for statistical significance, use the t-ratio for $\hat{a}$, which the computer has calculated for you as the ratio of the parameter estimate to its standard error:

$$t_{\hat{a}} = \frac{6.00}{0.917} = 6.54$$

and compare this value with the critical value of t. We will use a 5 percent significance level (a 95 percent confidence level). Since there are 20 observations and two parameters are estimated, there are $20 - 2 = 18$ degrees of freedom. The table at the end of the text (critical t-values) gives us a critical value of 2.101. The calculated t-value for $\hat{a}$ is larger than 2.101, so we conclude that $\hat{a}$ is significantly different from zero. The p-value for $\hat{a}$ is so small (0.0001) that the probability of finding significance when none exists is virtually zero. In this case, the selection of a 5 percent significance level greatly underestimates the exact degree of significance associated with the estimate of a. The estimated value of a suggests that firms which spend nothing on R&D, on average, have price-to-earnings ratios of 6.

The estimate of b (0.74) is positive, which suggests V and R are directly related. The calculated t-ratio is 4.48, which is greater than the critical value of t. The p-value for $\hat{b}$ indicates the significance level of the t-test could have been set as low as 0.0003, or 0.03 percent, and the hypothesis that $b = 0$ could be rejected. In other words, with a t-statistic equal to 4.48, the probability of incorrectly concluding that R&D expenditures significantly affect the value of a firm is just 0.03 percent. Or stated equivalently in terms of a confidence level, we can be 99.97 percent confident that the t-test would *not* indicate statistical significance if none existed. The value of $\hat{b}$ implies that if a firm increases R&D expenditures by one percent (of sales), the firm can expect its value (as measured by the P/E ratio) to rise by 0.74.

The R^2 for the regression equation indicates that about 53 percent of the total variation in the value of a firm is explained by the regression equation; that is, 53 percent of the variation in V is explained by the variation in R. The regression equation leaves 47 percent of the variation in the value of the firm unexplained.

The F-ratio is used to test for significance of the entire equation. To determine the critical value of F (with a 5 percent significance level), it is necessary to determine the degrees of freedom. In this case, $k - 1 = 2 - 1 = 1$ and $n - k = 20 - 2 = 18$ degrees of freedom. In the table of values of the F-statistic at the end of the text, you can look down the $k - 1 = 1$ column until you get to the 18th row ($n - k = 18$) and read the value 4.41. Since the calculated F-value (20.090) exceeds 4.41, the regression equation is significant at the 5 percent significance level. In fact, the F-value of 20.090 is much larger than the critical F-value for a 5 percent level of significance, suggesting that the exact level of significance will be much lower than 0.05. The p-value for the F-statistic, 0.0003, confirms that the exact significance level is much smaller than 0.05.

*C. Wallin and J. Gilman, "Determining the Optimal Level for R&D Spending," *Research Management* 14, 5 (September/October 1986), pp. 19–24.

Source: Adapted from a regression problem presented in Terry Sincich, *A Course in Modern Business Statistics*, Dellen/Macmillan, 1994, p. 432.

Controlling Product Quality at SLM: A Regression Example

Specialty Lens Manufacturing (SLM) produces contact lenses for patients who are unable to wear standard contact lenses. These specialty contact lenses must meet extraordinarily strict standards. The production process is not perfect, however, and some lenses have slight flaws. Patients receiving flawed lenses almost always detect the flaws, and the lenses are returned to SLM for replacement. Returned lenses are costly, in terms of both redundant production costs and diminished corporate reputation for SLM. Every week SLM produces 2,400 lenses, and inspectors using high-powered microscopes have time to examine only a fraction of the lenses before they are shipped to doctors.

Management at SLM decided to measure the effectiveness of its inspection process using regression analysis. During a 22-week time period, SLM collected data each week on the number of lenses produced that week which were later returned by doctors because of flaws (F) and the number of hours spent that week examining lenses (H). The manager estimated the regression equation

$$F = a + bH$$

using the 22 weekly observations on F and H. The computer printed out the following output:

DEPENDENT VARIABLE: F		R-SQUARE	F-RATIO	P-VALUE ON F
OBSERVATIONS: 22		0.4527	16.54	0.001
VARIABLE	PARAMETER ESTIMATE	STANDARD ERROR	T-RATIO	P-VALUE
INTERCEPT	90.0	28.13	3.20	0.004
H	−0.80	0.32	−2.50	0.021

As expected, $\hat{a}$ is positive and $\hat{b}$ is negative. If no inspection is done ($H = 0$), SLM's management expects 90 lenses from each week's production to be returned as defective. The estimate of b ($\hat{b} = \Delta F/\Delta H = -0.80$) indicates that each additional hour per week spent inspecting lenses will decrease the number of flawed lenses by 0.8. Thus, it takes 10 extra hours of inspection to find eight more flawed lenses.

In order to determine if the parameter estimates $\hat{a}$ and $\hat{b}$ are significantly different from zero, the manager can conduct a t-test on each estimated parameter. The t-ratios for $\hat{a}$ and $\hat{b}$ are 3.20 and −2.50, respectively:

$$t_{\hat{a}} = 90.0/28.13 = 3.20 \qquad \text{and} \qquad t_{\hat{b}} = -0.80/0.32 = -2.50$$

The critical t-value is found in the table at the end of the book. There are 22 observations and two parameters, so the degrees of freedom are $n - k = 22 - 2 = 20$. Choosing the 5 percent level of significance (a 95 percent level of confidence), the critical t-value is 2.086. Since the absolute values of $t_{\hat{a}}$ and $t_{\hat{b}}$ both exceed 2.086, both $\hat{a}$ and $\hat{b}$ are statistically significant at the 5 percent significance level.

Instead of performing a t-test at a fixed level of significance, the manager could assess the significance of the parameter estimates by examining the p-values for $\hat{a}$ and $\hat{b}$. The exact level of significance for $\hat{a}$ is 0.004, or 0.4 percent, which indicates that the t-statistic of 3.20 is just large enough to reject the hypothesis that $\hat{a}$ is zero at a significance level of 0.004 (or a confidence level of 0.996). The p-value for $\hat{a}$ is so small that the manager almost certainly has avoided committing a Type I error (finding statistical significance where there is none). The exact level of significance for $\hat{b}$ is 0.021, or 2.1 percent. For both parameter estimates, the p-values provide a stronger assessment of statistical significance than could be established by satisfying the requirements of a t-test performed at a 5 percent level of significance.

Overall, because $R^2 = 0.4527$, the equation explains about 45 percent of the total variation in the dependent variable (F), with 55 percent of the variation in F remaining unexplained. To test for significance of the entire equation, the manager could use an F-test. The critical F-value is obtained from the table at the end of the book. Since $k - 1 = 2 - 1 = 1$, and $n - k = 22 - 2 = 20$, the critical F-value at the 5 percent significance level is 4.35. The F-statistic calculated by the computer, 16.54, exceeds 4.35, and the entire equation is statistically significant. The p-value for the F-statistic shows that the exact level of significance for the entire equation is 0.001, or 0.1 percent (a 99.9 percent level of confidence).

Using the estimated equation, $\hat{F} = 90.0 - 0.80H$, the manager can estimate the number of flawed lenses that will be shipped for various hours of weekly inspection. For example, if inspectors spend 60 hours per week examining lenses, SLM can expect 42 ($= 90 - 0.8 \times 60$) of the lenses shipped to be flawed.

5.5 MULTIPLE REGRESSION

Thus far we have discussed simple regressions involving a linear relation between the dependent variable Y and a *single* explanatory variable X. In many problems, however, the variation in Y depends upon more than one explanatory variable. There may be quite a few variables needed to explain adequately the variation in the dependent variable. **Multiple regression models** use two or more explanatory variables to explain the variation in the dependent variable. In this section we will show how to use and interpret multiple regression models.

multiple regression models
Regression models that use more than one explanatory variable to explain the variation in the dependent variable.

The Multiple Regression Model

A typical multiple regression equation might take the form

$$Y = a + bX + cW + dZ$$

In this equation, Y is the dependent variable; a is the intercept parameter; X, W, and Z are the explanatory variables; and b, c, and d are the slope parameters for each of these explanatory variables.

As in simple regression, the slope parameters b, c, and d measure the change in Y associated with a 1-unit change in one of the explanatory variables, holding the rest of the explanatory variables constant. If, for example, $c = 3$, then a 1-unit increase in W results in a 3-unit increase in Y, holding X and Z constant.

Estimation of the parameters of a multiple regression equation is accomplished by finding a linear equation that best fits the data. As in simple regression, a computer is used to obtain the parameter estimates, their individual standard errors, the F-statistic, the R^2, and the p-values. The statistical significance of the individual parameters and of the equation as a whole can be determined by t-tests and an F-test, respectively. The R^2 is interpreted as the fraction of the variation in Y explained by the *entire set* of explanatory variables taken together. Indeed, the only real complication introduced by multiple regression is that there are more t-tests to perform. Although (as you may know from courses in statistics) the *calculation* of the parameter estimates becomes much more difficult as additional independent variables are added, the manner in which they are *interpreted* does not change. Consider the following example.

A Multiple Regression Consumption Function

Suppose you work for the state legislature and you wish to project sales tax revenue for the coming year. Since a primary source of sales tax revenue comes from levies on household consumption, you will need to estimate a consumption function. Suppose you believe the variation in household consumption expenditures can be adequately explained by using two independent variables—family income and the number of children in the household. The multiple regression equation can be specified as

$$C = a + bI + cN$$

where C is monthly consumption expenditures, I is monthly income, and N is the number of children. Since income and consumption are expected to be positively related, you would expect b to be positive. Likewise, c is expected to be positive. Furthermore, you would also expect a to be positive since it reflects the consumption expenditures for a family with no children and no income. The intercept parameter is often referred to as the "minimum subsistence level of consumption."

In order to estimate a, b, and c, you could obtain data from a sample of families. Suppose that such data were obtained from 30 families and used in an available regression program. The output from the estimation of your simple consumption function is as follows:

DEPENDENT VARIABLE: C		R-SQUARE	F-RATIO	P-VALUE ON F
OBSERVATIONS: 30		0.5763	18.36	0.0001
VARIABLE	PARAMETER ESTIMATE	STANDARD ERROR	T-RATIO	P-VALUE
INTERCEPT	443.0	125.0	3.54	0.0015
I	0.810	0.296	2.74	0.0108
N	132.50	68.8	1.93	0.0640

As expected, the estimates of a, b, and c are all positive. The intercept parameter indicates that a family with no income ($I = 0$) and no children ($N = 0$) is expected to spend \$443 per month on consumption items. The estimate of b indicates that households will spend 81 cents on consumption out of each additional dollar of income received. (Presumably, the average household saves 19 cents of each additional dollar of income.) Each additional child is estimated to add \$132.50 to monthly consumption expenditures.

In order to determine if the parameter estimates are significantly different from zero, you can conduct t-tests on each of the three parameter estimates. The t-ratios for $\hat{a}$, $\hat{b}$, and $\hat{c}$ are calculated as the ratio of the estimated parameter to its standard error, a calculation which is made by most computer programs (see the "t-ratio" column in the computer printout). Since there are 30 observations and three parameters are estimated, the degrees of freedom are $n - k = 30 - 3 = 27$. For testing at the 5 percent level of significance (a 95 percent confidence level), the critical value of t is found in the table at the end of the book to be 2.052.

Comparing the calculated t-statistics shown in the computer printout with the critical t, you can see that the absolute values of $t_{\hat{a}}$ (= 3.54) and $t_{\hat{b}}$ (= 2.74) exceed the critical value of 2.052. Thus, the estimates of a and b are statistically significant. In fact, the p-values for $\hat{a}$ and $\hat{b}$ indicate exact significance levels lower than 5 percent (0.15 percent and 1.08 percent, respectively) and confidence levels higher than 95 percent (99.85 percent and 98.92 percent, respectively).

In the case of $\hat{c}$, however, the t-statistic (1.93) is not greater than 2.052, and you cannot conclude that c is not equal to zero. As you can confirm by examining its p-value, $\hat{c}$ is statistically significant at (exactly) the 6.4 percent level of significance (or 93.6 percent confidence level). In order to reject the hypothesis that $c = 0$, a higher level of significance must be acceptable. Thus, the statistical evidence that the number of children affects consumption expenditures is weaker than the evidence that income affects consumption expenditures.[6]

Turning now to the overall equation: The value of R^2 indicates that 57.6 percent of the total variation in consumption expenditures is explained by the regression equation (i.e., by the variation in I and N). To test for significance of the entire equation, you can compare the F-statistic with the critical F-value or examine the p-value on the F-statistic. To obtain the critical F-value, note there are $k - 1 = 3 - 1 = 2$ and $n - k = 30 - 3 = 27$ degrees of freedom. From the table of F-statistics at the end of the text, the critical F-value at the 5 percent level of significance is 3.35. Since the F-statistic (18.36) exceeds this value, you can say that the regression equation is statistically significant at the 5 percent significance level. Alternatively, you could have looked at the F-statistic's p-value of 0.01 percent to discover that the equation as a whole is statistically significant at an extremely high level of confidence.

 8 9

[6]When the p-value for a parameter estimate is not small enough to meet the researcher's tolerance for risk of committing a Type I error, the associated explanatory variable is typically dropped from the regression equation. A new equation is estimated with only the explanatory variables that have sufficiently small p-values.

ILLUSTRATION 5.3

Do Auto Insurance Premiums Really Vary with Costs?

In an article examining the impact of Proposition 103 on auto insurance rates in California, Benjamin Zycher noted that in 1988 an adult male with no citations or at-fault accidents who lived in Hollywood could expect to pay an annual insurance premium of $1,817. The same adult male driver would have to pay only $862 if he lived in Monrovia, only $697 in San Diego, and only $581 in San Jose. Zycher explains that this variability in premiums exists because insurers obviously determine premiums by considering the individual's driving record, type of car, sex, age, and various other factors that are "statistically significant predictors of an individual driver's future losses."

Also important in the determination of insurance premiums is the geographic location of the driver's residence. Future losses are likely to be smaller in rural areas compared with urban areas because of lower vehicle densities, reduced theft, smaller repair costs, and so on. Using data on bodily-injury premiums for 20 California counties, we investigated the relation between insurance premiums and two explanatory variables—the number of claims and the average dollar cost of a claim in the various counties. Specifically, we wanted to determine if the variation in premiums across counties can be adequately explained by cost differences across the counties.

Using the data shown in the accompanying table, we estimated the following multiple regression equation:

$$P = a + b_1 N + b_2 C$$

where P is the average bodily insurance premium paid per auto, N is the number of claims per thousand insured vehicles, and C is the average dollar amount of each bodily-injury claim. The computer

Bodily Injury in California: Claims, Costs, and Premiums

County	Claims* (N)	Cost† (C)	Annual premium‡ (P)
Los Angeles	23.9	$10,197	$319.04
Orange	19.5	9,270	255.00
Ventura	16.7	9,665	225.51
San Francisco	16.3	8,705	208.95
Riverside	15.2	8,888	200.16
San Bernardino	15.6	8,631	196.22
San Diego	16.0	8,330	191.80
Alameda	14.4	8,654	191.46
Marin	13.0	8,516	190.78
San Mateo	14.1	7,738	189.01
Sacramento	15.3	7,881	181.42
Santa Clara	14.4	7,723	179.74
Contra Costa	13.2	8,702	177.92
Santa Barbara	10.7	9,077	176.65
Sonoma	10.6	9,873	171.38
Fresno	14.7	7,842	168.11
Kern	11.9	7,717	160.97
Humboldt	12.2	7,798	151.02
Butte	11.1	8,783	129.84
Shasta	9.7	9,803	126.34

*Per thousand insured vehicles.
†Average per claim.
‡Average premium income per insured auto.
Source: Western Insurance information service.

5.6 NONLINEAR REGRESSION ANALYSIS

While linear regression models can be applied to a wide variety of economic relations, there are also many economic relations that are nonlinear in nature. Nonlinear regression models are used when the underlying relation between Y and X plots as a curve, rather than a straight line. An analyst generally chooses a nonlinear regression model when the scatter diagram shows a curvi-

output for this multiple regression equation is the following:

DEPENDENT VARIABLE: P		R-SQUARE	F-RATIO	P-VALUE ON F
OBSERVATIONS: 20		0.9116	87.659	0.0001
VARIABLE	PARAMETER ESTIMATE	STANDARD ERROR	T-RATIO	P-VALUE
INTERCEPT	−74.139	34.612	−2.14	0.0470
N	11.320	0.953	11.88	0.0001
C	0.011	0.004	2.75	0.0137

There is evidence from these parameter estimates that bodily-injury premiums in a particular county are positively related to both the number of claims in that county and the average cost of those claims. Specifically, an additional claim per thousand vehicles in a county ($\Delta N = 1$) tends to increase yearly premiums by $11.32. A $1,000 increase in the average cost of claims in a county ($\Delta C = 1{,}000$) tends to increase premiums by about $11 annually. The intercept in this regression has no meaningful interpretation.

The p-values for the individual parameter estimates indicate that all estimates are significant at less than the 0.05 level. You can confirm this by performing t-tests at the 5 percent significance level on each of the three estimated parameters.

Notice also that the R^2 is 0.9116, indicating that 91 percent of the variation in premiums is explained by variables N and C. The p-value on the F-ratio also provides more statistical evidence that the relation between the dependent variable P and the explanatory variables N and C is quite strong. The critical F-value for $F_{2,17}$ at a 5 percent level of significance is 3.59. Since the F-statistic exceeds this value by a large amount, the regression equation is statistically significant at a level below 0.01 percent.

It is interesting to note how well the level of premiums can be explained using only two explanatory variables. Indeed, this regression analysis supports Benjamin Zycher's claim that the substantial statewide variation in California auto insurance premiums can be attributed to geographic differences in the costs incurred by insurers.

Source: See Benjamin Zycher, "Automobile Insurance Regulation, Direct Democracy, and the Interests of Consumers," *Regulation*, Summer 1990.

linear pattern. In some cases, economic theory will strongly suggest that Y and X are related in a nonlinear fashion, and the analyst can expect to see a curvilinear pattern in the scatter of data points. Later in this text, we will introduce you to several important economic relations that are nonlinear in nature. You will need to know how to estimate the parameters of a nonlinear economic relation using the techniques of regression analysis.

In this section, we will show you two forms of nonlinear regression models for which the parameters can be estimated using *linear* regression analysis. The trick to using *linear* regression to estimate the parameters in *nonlinear* models is to transform the nonlinear relation into one that is linear and can be estimated by the techniques of least-squares. Two extremely useful forms of nonlinear models that you will encounter later in the text are (1) quadratic regression models and (2) log-linear regression models. As you will see, using either one of these two nonlinear models does not complicate the analysis much at all.

Quadratic Regression Models

quadratic regression model A nonlinear regression model of the form $Y = a + bX + cX^2$.

One of the most useful nonlinear forms for managerial economics is the **quadratic regression model,** which can be expressed as

$$Y = a + bX + cX^2$$

In a number of situations later in this book, theoretical relations between economic variables will graph as either a U-shaped or an inverted-U-shaped curve. You may recall from your high school algebra class that quadratic functions have graphs that are either U- or ∩-shaped, depending upon the signs of b and c. If b is negative and c is positive, the quadratic function is U-shaped. If b is positive and c is negative, the quadratic function is ∩-shaped. Thus, a U-shaped quadratic equation ($b < 0$ and $c > 0$) is appropriate when as X increases, Y first falls, eventually reaches a minimum, and then rises thereafter. Alternatively, an inverted-U-shaped quadratic equation ($b > 0$ and $c < 0$) is appropriate if as X increases, Y first rises, eventually reaches a peak, and then falls thereafter.

In order to estimate the three parameters of the quadratic relation (a, b, and c), the equation must be transformed into a linear form that can be estimated using linear regression analysis. This task is accomplished by creating a new variable Z, defined as $Z = X^2$, then substituting Z for X^2 to transform the quadratic model into a linear model:

$$\begin{aligned} Y &= a + bX + cX^2 \\ &= a + bX + cZ \end{aligned}$$

The slope parameter for Z (c) is identical to the slope parameter for X^2 (c).

This simple transformation is accomplished by having the computer create a new variable Z by squaring the values of X for each observation. You then regress Y on X and Z. The computer will generate an intercept parameter estimate ($\hat{a}$), a slope parameter estimate for X ($\hat{b}$), and a slope parameter estimate for Z ($\hat{c}$). The estimated slope parameter for Z is $\hat{c}$, which, of course, is the slope parameter on X^2. We illustrate this procedure with an example.

Figure 5.5 shows a scatter diagram for 12 observations on Y and X (shown by the table in the figure). Looking at the scatter of data points, it is clear that fitting a straight line through the data points would produce a "poor" fit but fitting a U-shaped curve will produce a much better fit. To estimate the parameters of a quadratic regression equation, a new variable Z ($= X^2$) is generated on the computer. The actual data used in the regression are presented in Figure 5.5. The computer printout from the regression of Y on X and Z is shown here:

DEPENDENT VARIABLE: Y		R-SQUARE	F-RATIO	P-VALUE ON F
OBSERVATIONS: 12		0.7445	13.11	0.0022

VARIABLE	PARAMETER ESTIMATE	STANDARD ERROR	T-RATIO	P-VALUE
INTERCEPT	140.0	17.14	8.17	0.0001
X	−20.0	4.14	−4.83	0.0009
Z	1.0	0.50	2.00	0.0770

FIGURE 5.5
A Quadratic Regression Equation

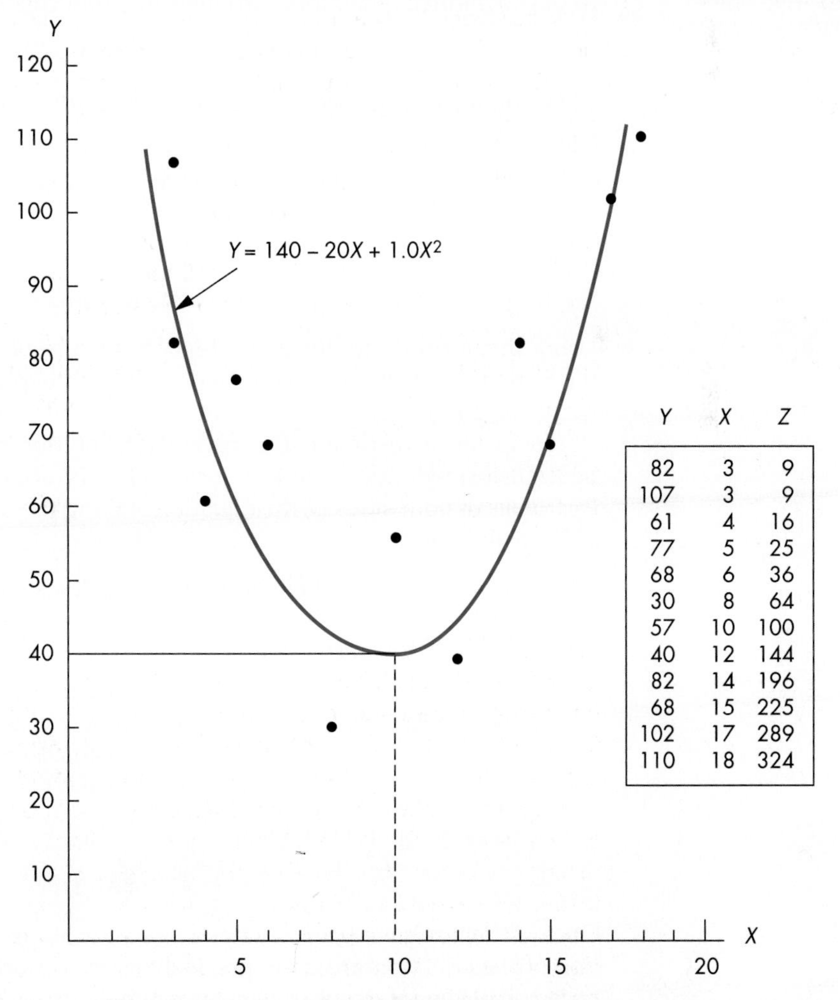

Thus, the estimated quadratic regression equation is

$$Y = 140 - 20X + 1.0X^2$$

The estimated slope parameter for Z is 1.0. As explained above, 1.0 is also the slope parameter estimate for X^2. The estimated equation can be used to estimate the value of Y for any particular value of X. For example, if X is equal to 10, the quadratic regression equation predicts that Y will be equal to 40 ($= 140 - 20 \times 10 + 10^2$). In any multiple regression equation, the estimated parameters are tested for statistical significance by performing the usual t-tests as discussed above.

Log-Linear Regression Models

log-linear regression model A nonlinear regression model of the form $Y = aX^bZ^c$.

Another kind of nonlinear equation that can be estimated by transforming the equation into a linear form is a **log-linear regression model** in which Y is related to one or more explanatory variables in a multiplicative fashion:

$$Y = aX^bZ^c$$

This nonlinear functional form is particularly useful because the parameters b and c are elasticities:

$$b = \frac{\text{Percentage change in } Y}{\text{Percentage change in } X}$$

$$c = \frac{\text{Percentage change in } Y}{\text{Percentage change in } Z}$$

Using this form of nonlinear regression, the elasticities are estimated directly—the parameter estimates associated with each explanatory variable are elasticities. (The parameter a, however, is not an elasticity.)

In order to estimate the parameters of this nonlinear equation, it must be transformed into a linear form. This is accomplished by taking *natural logarithms* of both sides of the equation. Taking the logarithm of the function $Y = aX^bZ^c$ results in

$$\ln Y = (\ln a) + b(\ln X) + c(\ln Z)$$

So, if we define

$$Y' = \ln Y$$
$$X' = \ln X$$
$$Z' = \ln Z$$
$$a' = \ln a$$

the regression equation is linear:

$$Y' = a' + bX' + cZ'$$

Once estimates have been obtained, tests for statistical significance and evaluation of the equation are done precisely as we described earlier. The only difference is that the intercept parameter estimate provided by the computer is not a;

rather it is equal to ln a. To obtain the parameter estimate for a, we must take the antilog of the parameter estimate $\hat{a}'$:

$$\text{antilog}\,(\hat{a}') = e^{\hat{a}'}$$

The antilog of a number can be found using the "e^x" key on most hand calculators. We illustrate the log-linear regression model with an example.

Panel A of Figure 5.6 shows a scatter diagram of 12 observations on Y and X. The scatter diagram in Panel A suggests that a curvilinear model will fit these data better than a linear model. Suppose we use a log-linear model with one explanatory variable: $Y = aX^b$. Since Y is positive at all points in the sample, the parameter a is expected to be positive. Since Y is decreasing as X increases, the parameter on X (b) is expected to be negative. The actual values of Y and X plotted in the scatter diagram in Panel A are shown in the box in Panel A.

To estimate the parameters a and b in the nonlinear equation, we transform the equation by taking logarithms:

$$\ln Y = \ln a + b \ln X$$

Thus, the curvilinear model in Panel A is transformed into an equivalent model that is linear when the variables are expressed in logarithms. In Panel B, the transformed variables, ln Y and ln X, are obtained by instructing the computer to take logarithms of Y and X, respectively. The 12 observations, in terms of logarithms, are displayed in Panel B. Regressing ln Y on ln X results in the following computer printout:

DEPENDENT VARIABLE: LNY		R-SQUARE	F-RATIO	P-VALUE ON F
OBSERVATIONS: 12		0.8750	70.0	0.0001
VARIABLE	PARAMETER ESTIMATE	STANDARD ERROR	T-RATIO	P-VALUE
INTERCEPT	11.06	0.48	23.04	0.0001
LNX	−0.96	0.11	−8.73	0.0001

As the F-ratio and R^2 indicate, a log-linear model does a quite reasonable job of explaining the variation in Y. The t-ratios for the intercept and slope parameters are 23.04 and −8.73, respectively. Both parameter estimates are statistically significant at the 1 percent level since both t-statistics exceed the critical t-value of 3.169. You can see by the p-values that the parameter estimates are significant at levels less than 0.0001.

Panel B of Figure 5.6 illustrates why this model is called a log-linear model. Notice that when the data points in Panel A are converted to logarithms (ln Y

FIGURE 5.6
A Log-Linear Regression Equation

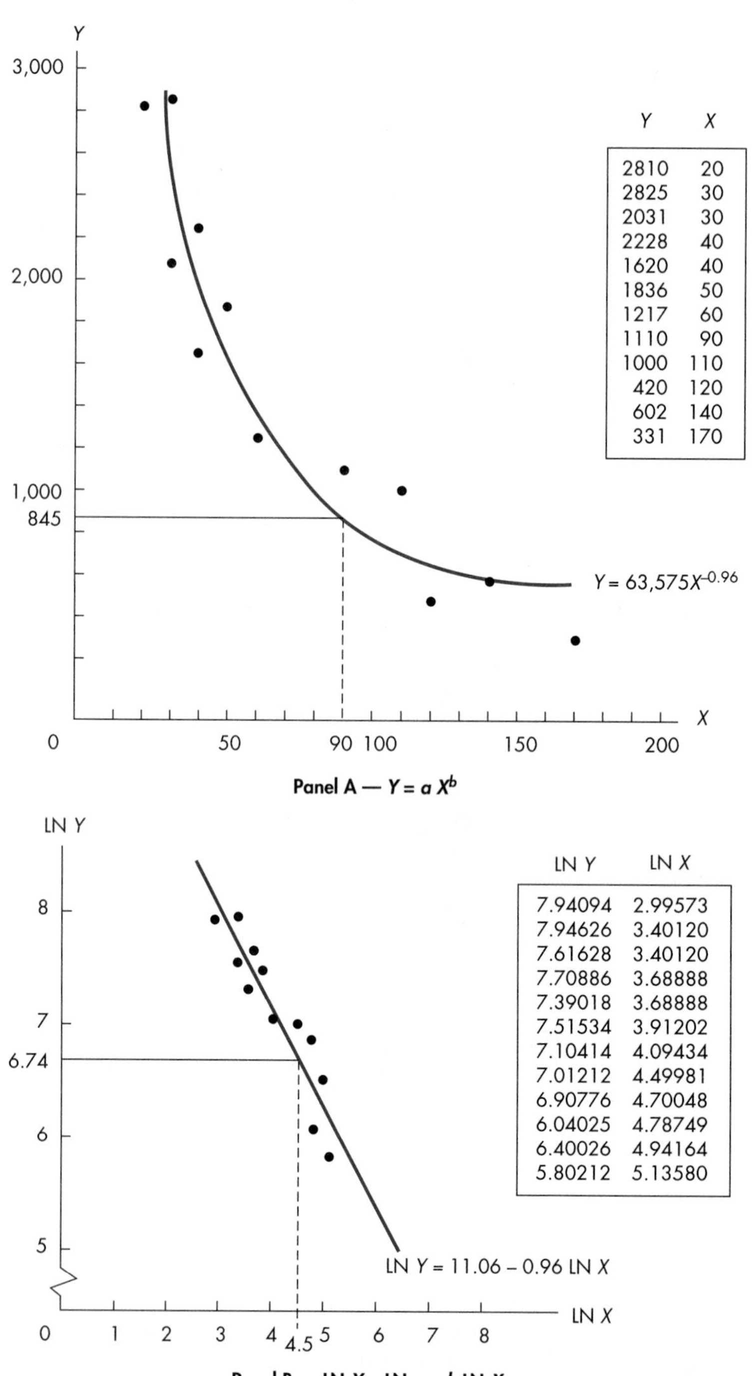

Y	X
2810	20
2825	30
2031	30
2228	40
1620	40
1836	50
1217	60
1110	90
1000	110
420	120
602	140
331	170

LN Y	LN X
7.94094	2.99573
7.94626	3.40120
7.61628	3.40120
7.70886	3.68888
7.39018	3.68888
7.51534	3.91202
7.10414	4.09434
7.01212	4.49981
6.90776	4.70048
6.04025	4.78749
6.40026	4.94164
5.80212	5.13580

and ln X), the *natural logarithms* of Y and X exhibit a linear relation, as indicated by the scatter diagram shown in Panel B. The estimated log-linear regression equation is plotted in Panel B to show you how a straight line fits the natural logarithms of Y and X.

To obtain the parameter estimates in the nonlinear equation $Y = aX^b$, note that the slope parameter on ln X is also the exponent on X in the nonlinear equation ($\hat{b} = -0.96$). Since b is an elasticity, the estimated elasticity is -0.96. Thus, a 10 percent increase in X results in a 9.6 percent decrease in Y. To obtain an estimate of a, we take the antilog of the estimated value of the intercept parameter:

$$\hat{a} = \text{antilog } (11.06) = e^{11.06} = 63{,}575$$

In order to show that the two models are mathematically equivalent, we have calculated the predicted value of ln Y when ln X is equal to 4.5. Using the estimated log-linear regression equation, we find that when ln $X = 4.5$, ln $Y = 6.74$ [$= 11.06 - 0.96(4.5)$]. Taking antilogs of ln Y and ln X, we get the point $X = 90$ and $Y = 845$ [$= 63{,}575(90)^{-0.96}$]. Thus, the two equations are equivalent representations of the mathematical relation between Y and X.

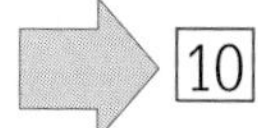

5.7 REGRESSION ANALYSIS IN MANAGERIAL DECISION MAKING

We hope you have seen from this brief overview that regression analysis is extremely useful because it offers managers a way of estimating the functions they need for managerial decision making. While we will have much more to say about specific applications of regression analysis in later chapters, at this point we want you simply to understand that regression techniques are actually used in managerial decision making.

As Robert F. Soergel (general marketing manager, E. L. Weingard Division, Emerson Electric Company) put it, "Regression analysis can be extremely helpful, and it's not as difficult as its name suggests."[7] Regression analysis is simply a tool to provide the information necessary for a manager to make decisions that maximize profits, or as Mr. Soergel observed, "The computer is a tool, not a master." We will use this tool to find estimates of the various functions we will describe later in the text. It's not that hard, and we agree with Mr. Soergel's conclusion of "the best part: it's not expensive."

The statistical analyses (or, if you wish, econometrics) that we are going to use in this text are really rather simple. Our two major objectives are also simple:

1. We want you to be able to set up a regression equation that could subsequently be estimated by using one of the readily available regression packages.
2. We want you to be able to use the output of a regression to examine those economic issues that are of interest to the manager of an enterprise.

[7]"Probing the Past for the Future," *Sales & Marketing Management,* Mar. 14, 1983.

Hence, in terms of the field of study known as econometrics, we will concentrate our attention on helping you avoid what are called *specification errors.* In simple terms, this means that we will show you how to set up an estimation equation that is appropriate for the use to which it is to be put. Specification errors—such as excluding important explanatory variables or using an inappropriate form for the equation—are serious; they can result in the estimates being *biased.*

In addition to specification errors, there are other problems that can be encountered in regression analysis. These problems, which are more difficult than the material we want to cover in this text, are reviewed briefly in the appendix to this chapter.

5.8 SUMMARY

This chapter set forth the basic principles of regression analysis—estimation and testing for statistical significance. The emphasis of the chapter was on explaining how to interpret the results of regression analysis, rather than on the mathematics of regression analysis. A mathematical derivation of the statistical techniques is presented in the appendix at the end of the chapter.

The simple linear regression model relates a dependent variable to a single explanatory variable in a linear fashion: $Y = a + bX$. The parameter a is the Y-intercept—the value of Y when X is zero. The parameter b is the slope of the regression line; it measures the rate of change in Y as X changes ($\Delta Y/\Delta X$). Because the variation in Y is affected not only by variation in X but also by various random effects, we cannot predict exactly the actual value of Y. Thus, you should interpret the regression equation as giving the average or expected value of Y for any particular value of X.

Parameter estimates are obtained by choosing values of a and b that minimize the sum of the squared residuals. The residual is the difference between the actual value of Y and the fitted value of Y ($Y_i - \hat{Y}_i$). This method of estimating a and b is called the method of least-squares. The estimated regression line, $Y = \hat{a} + \hat{b}X$, is called the *sample regression line.* The sample regression line is an estimate of the true regression line.

The estimates $\hat{a}$ and $\hat{b}$ do not, in general, equal the true values of a and b. Since $\hat{a}$ and $\hat{b}$ are computed from the data in the random sample, the estimates themselves are random variables. Statisticians have shown that the distribution of values that the estimates might take is centered around the true value of the parameter. An estimator is *unbiased* if the mean value of the estimator is equal to the true value of the parameter. The method of least-squares produces unbiased estimates of a and b.

It is the randomness of the parameter estimates that necessitates testing for statistical significance. Just because the estimate $\hat{b}$ is not equal to zero does *not* mean the true value of b is not actually equal to zero. Even when b *does* equal zero, it is still possible that the sample of Y and X values will produce a least-squares estimate $\hat{b}$ that is different from zero. It is necessary to determine statistically if there is sufficient evidence in the sample to indicate that Y is truly related to X (i.e., $b \neq 0$). This is called testing for statistical significance.

A t-test can be used to test for statistical significance of parameter estimates. To test for statistical significance of an individual parameter estimate, the researcher must first determine the level of significance for the test. The significance level of a test is the probability of finding a parameter estimate to be significantly different from zero when, in fact, b is zero (a Type I error). One minus the significance level is the level of confidence of the test. The choice of a significance or confidence level is in most cases rather arbitrary; lower (higher) levels of significance (confidence), other things equal, are more desirable. Traditionally, either a 0.01, 0.02, 0.05, or 0.10 level of significance is selected, which reflects the analyst's willingness to tolerate, at most, a 1, 2, 5, or 10 percent probability of finding a parameter to be significant when it is not truly significant. The appropriate significance level is determined by the analyst on the basis of the cost of making an error.

Once the level of significance (or confidence) is chosen, performing a t-test is straightforward. A t-test is based on the fact that the larger the absolute value of the

t-ratio, $t = \hat{b}/S_{\hat{b}}$, the more probable it is that the true value of b is not equal to zero ($S_{\hat{b}}$ is the standard error of the parameter estimate). So first compute the t-ratio as defined above. Then find the critical t-value in the t-table. Locate the critical t-value with $n - k$ degrees of freedom for the chosen level of significance. If the absolute value of the t-ratio is greater than the critical t-value, $\hat{b}$ is statistically significant at the chosen level of significance. If the absolute value is less than the critical t-value, $\hat{b}$ is not statistically significant. If $\hat{b}$ is significant at the 0.05 level of significance, either of two equivalent statements can be made: (1) the probability of incorrectly finding $\hat{b}$ to be significant is less than 5 percent, or (2) you can be at least 95 percent confident that the t-test will *not* find statistical significance when there is none ($b = 0$).

An alternative method of assessing the statistical significance of parameter estimates is to treat as statistically significant only those parameter estimates whose p-values are smaller than the maximum acceptable significance level. Most regression software now calculates a p-value for each parameter estimate. The p-value gives the exact (or minimum) level of significance for a parameter estimate.

To measure how well the sample regression line fits the data, the R^2 statistic (also called the coefficient of determination) is computed. The R^2 measures the fraction of the total variation in Y that is explained by the variation in X. The value of R^2 ranges from 0 (the regression equation explains none of the variation in Y) to 1 (the regression equation explains all the variation in Y). A high R^2 indicates Y and X are highly correlated, and the scatter diagram tightly fits the sample regression line.

The F-statistic is used to test whether the equation as a whole explains a significant amount of the variation in Y. To test whether the overall equation is significant, the F-statistic is compared to the critical F-value with $k - 1$ and $n - k$ degrees of freedom and the chosen level of significance. If the value for the calculated F-statistic exceeds the critical F-value, the regression equation is statistically significant. Alternatively, if the p-value for the F-statistic is smaller than the acceptable level of significance, then the equation as a whole is statistically significant.

Multiple regression models use two or more explanatory variables to explain the variation in the dependent variable. The coefficient on each of the explanatory variables measures the degree of variation in Y associated with variation in that explanatory variable, holding all other explanatory variables constant. As in the case of simple regression, each coefficient is tested for significance by using the t-test. The degree of significance for each coefficient is given by its p-value. The F-statistic is used to test the overall equation for significance. The R^2 measures the fit of the equation.

Many economic relations of interest to managers are *nonlinear* in nature. Two types of nonlinear models are presented in this chapter: (1) quadratic regression models and (2) log-linear regression models. The quadratic regression model is appropriate when the curve fitting the scatter diagram is either U-shaped or inverted-U-shaped. The quadratic equation, $Y = a + bX + cX^2$, is transformed into a linear form by computing a new variable, $Z = X^2$, and substituting for X^2 to get a linear form: $Y = a + bX + cZ$. A second type of nonlinear model presented in this chapter is the log-linear model. In this nonlinear model, the dependent variable is related to one or more explanatory variables in a multiplicative fashion. The log-linear model for two explanatory variables takes the form $Y = aX^bZ^c$. A particularly useful feature of this specification is that the parameters b and c are elasticities. For example, b measures the percent change in Y that results when X changes by one percent. By taking natural logarithms, the logarithm of Y can be expressed as a linear function of the logarithms of the explanatory variables: $\ln Y = \ln a + b \ln X + c \ln Z$. Once this transformation is made, estimation and tests of statistical significance proceed as usual.

We must emphasize again that all the statistics needed for regression analysis are automatically computed when using a computerized regression routine. The purpose of this chapter was to show you how to interpret and use the regression statistics produced by the computer.

TECHNICAL PROBLEMS

1. A simple linear regression equation relates R and W as follows:

$$R = a + bW$$

   a. The explanatory variable is ______, and the dependent variable is ______.

b. The slope parameter is ________, and the intercept parameter is ________.
c. When W is zero, R equals ________.
d. For each one unit increase in W, the change in R is ________ units.

2. Regression analysis is often referred to as least-squares regression. Why is this name appropriate?
3. Regression analysis involves estimating the values of parameters and testing the estimated parameters for significance. Why must parameter estimates be tested for statistical significance?
4. Evaluate the following statements:
   a. "The smaller the standard error of the estimate, $S_{\hat{b}}$, the more accurate the parameter estimate."
   b. "If $\hat{b}$ is an unbiased estimate of b, then $\hat{b}$ equals b."
   c. "The more precise the estimate of $\hat{b}$ (i.e., the smaller the standard error of $\hat{b}$), the higher the t-ratio."
5. The linear regression in problem 1 is estimated using 26 observations on R and W. The least-squares estimate of b is 40.495, and the standard error of the estimate is 16.250. Perform a t-test for statistical significance at the 5 percent level of significance.
   a. There are ________ degrees of freedom for the t-test.
   b. The value of the t-statistic is ________. The critical t-value for the test is ________.
   c. Is $\hat{b}$ statistically significant? Explain.
   d. The p-value for the t-statistic is ________. (*Hint:* In this problem, the t-table provides the answer.) The p-value gives the probability of rejecting the hypothesis that ________ ($b = 0$, $b \neq 0$) when b is truly equal to ________. The confidence level for the test is ________ percent.
   e. What does it mean to say an estimated parameter is statistically significant at the 5 percent significance level?
   f. What does it mean to say an estimated parameter is statistically significant at the 95 percent confidence level?
   g. How does the level of significance differ from the level of confidence?
6. Ten data points on Y and X are employed to estimate the parameters in the linear relation $Y = a + bX$. The computer output from the regression analysis is the following:

DEPENDENT VARIABLE: Y		R-SQUARE	F-RATIO	P-VALUE ON F
OBSERVATIONS: 10		0.5223	8.747	0.0182
VARIABLE	PARAMETER ESTIMATE	STANDARD ERROR	T-RATIO	P-VALUE
INTERCEPT	800.0	189.125	4.23	0.0029
X	−2.50	0.850	−2.94	0.0187

a. What is the equation of the sample regression line?
b. Test the intercept and slope estimates for statistical significance at the 1 percent significance level. Explain how you performed this test, and present your results.
c. Interpret the p-values for the parameter estimates.
d. Test the overall equation for statistical significance at the 1 percent significance level. Explain how you performed this test, and present your results. Interpret the p-value for the F-statistic.
e. If X equals 140, what is the fitted (or predicted) value of Y?
f. What fraction of the total variation in Y is explained by the regression?

7. A simple linear regression equation, $Y = a + bX$, is estimated by a computer program, which produces the following output:

DEPENDENT VARIABLE: Y		R-SQUARE	F-RATIO	P-VALUE ON F
OBSERVATIONS: 25		0.7482	68.351	0.0001
VARIABLE	PARAMETER ESTIMATE	STANDARD ERROR	T-RATIO	P-VALUE
INTERCEPT	325.24	125.09	2.60	0.0160
X	0.8057	0.2898	2.78	0.0106

a. How many degrees of freedom does this regression analysis have?
b. What is the critical value of t at the 5 percent level of significance?
c. Test to see if the estimates of a and b are statistically significant.
d. Discuss the p-values for the estimates of a and b.
e. How much of the total variation in Y is explained by this regression equation? How much of the total variation in Y is unexplained by this regression equation?
f. What is the critical value of the F-statistic at a 5 percent level of significance? Is the overall regression equation statistically significant?
g. If X equals 100, what value do you expect Y will take? If X equals zero?

8. Evaluate each of the following statements:
a. "In a multiple regression model, the coefficients on the explanatory variables measure the percent of the total variation in the dependent variable Y explained by that explanatory variable."
b. "The more degrees of freedom in the regression, the more likely it is that a given t-ratio exceeds the critical t-value."
c. "The coefficient of determination (R^2) can be exactly equal to 1 only when the sample regression line passes through each and every data point."

9. A multiple regression model, $R = a + bW + cX + dZ$, is estimated by a computer package, which produces the following output:

DEPENDENT VARIABLE: R		R-SQUARE	F-RATIO	P-VALUE ON F
OBSERVATIONS: 34		0.3179	4.660	0.00865

VARIABLE	PARAMETER ESTIMATE	STANDARD ERROR	T-RATIO	P-VALUE
INTERCEPT	12.6	8.34	1.51	0.1413
W	22.0	3.61	6.09	0.0001
X	−4.1	1.65	−2.48	0.0188
Z	16.3	4.45	3.66	0.0010

a. How many degrees of freedom does this regression analysis have?
b. What is the critical value of t at the 2 percent level of significance?
c. Test to see if the estimates of a, b, c, and d are statistically significant at the 2 percent significance level. What are the exact levels of significance for each of the parameter estimates?
d. How much of the total variation in R is explained by this regression equation? How much of the total variation in R is unexplained by this regression equation?
e. What is the critical value of the F-statistic at the 1 percent level of significance? Is the overall regression equation statistically significant at the 1 percent level of significance? What is the exact level of significance for the F-statistic?
f. If W equals 10, X equals 5, and Z equals 30, what value do you predict R will take? If W, X, and Z are all equal to zero?

10. Suppose Y is related to R and S in the following nonlinear way:

$$Y = aR^bS^c$$

a. How can this nonlinear equation be transformed into a linear form that can be analyzed by using multiple regression analysis?

Sixty-three observations are used to obtain the following regression results:

DEPENDENT VARIABLE: LNY		R-SQUARE	F-RATIO	P-VALUE ON F
OBSERVATIONS: 63		0.8151	132.22	0.0001

VARIABLE	PARAMETER ESTIMATE	STANDARD ERROR	T-RATIO	P-VALUE
INTERCEPT	−1.386	0.83	−1.67	0.1002
LNR	0.452	0.175	2.58	0.0123
LNS	0.30	0.098	3.06	0.0033

b. Test each estimated coefficient for statistical significance at the 5 percent level of significance. What are the exact significance levels for each of the estimated coefficients?
c. Test the overall equation for statistical significance at the 5 percent level of significance. Interpret the p-value on the F-statistic.
d. How well does this nonlinear model fit the data?
e. Using the estimated value of the intercept, compute an estimate of a.
f. If $R = 200$ and $S = 1{,}500$, compute the expected value of Y.
g. What is the estimated elasticity of R? Of S?

APPLIED PROBLEMS

1. The director of marketing at Vanguard Corporation believes that sales of the company's Bright Side laundry detergent (S) are related to Vanguard's own advertising expenditure (A), as well as the combined advertising expenditures of its three biggest rival detergents (R). The marketing director collects 36 weekly observations on S, A, and R to estimate the following multiple regression equation:

$$S = a + bA + cR$$

where S, A, and R are measured in dollars per week.
a. What sign does the marketing director expect a, b, and c to have?
b. Interpret the coefficients a, b, and c.

The regression output from the computer is as follows:

DEPENDENT VARIABLE: S	R-SQUARE	F-RATIO	P-VALUE ON F
OBSERVATIONS: 36	0.2247	4.781	0.0150

VARIABLE	PARAMETER ESTIMATE	STANDARD ERROR	T-RATIO	P-VALUE
INTERCEPT	175086.0	63821.0	2.74	0.0098
A	0.8550	0.3250	2.63	0.0128
R	−0.284	0.164	−1.73	0.0927

c. Does Vanguard's advertising expenditure have a statistically significant effect on the sales of Bright Side detergent? Explain, using the appropriate p-value.
d. Does advertising by its three largest rivals affect sales of Bright Side detergent in a statistically significant way? Explain, using the appropriate p-value.
e. What fraction of the total variation in sales of Bright Side remains unexplained? What can the marketing director do to increase the explanatory power of the sales equation? What other explanatory variables might be added to this equation?

f. What is the expected level of sales each week when Vanguard spends $40,000 per week and the combined advertising expenditures for the three rivals is $100,000 per week?

2. In his analysis of California's Proposition 103 (see Illustration 5.3), Benjamin Zycher notes that one of the most important provisions of this proposition is eliminating the practice by insurance companies of basing premiums (in part) on the geographic location of drivers. Prohibiting the use of geographic location to assess the risk of a driver creates a substantial implicit subsidy from low-loss counties to high-loss counties, such as Los Angeles, Orange, and San Francisco counties. Zycher hypothesizes that the percent of voters favoring Proposition 103 in a given county (V) is inversely related to the (average) percentage change in auto premiums (P) that the proposition confers upon the drivers of that county.

   The data in the table below were presented by Zycher to support his contention that V and P are inversely related:

County	Percent for Proposition 103 (V)	Change in average premium (P)
Los Angeles	62.8	−21.4
Orange	51.7	−8.2
San Francisco	65.2	−0.9
Alameda	58.9	+8.0
Marin	53.5	+9.1
Santa Clara	51.0	+11.8
San Mateo	52.8	+12.6
Santa Cruz	54.2	+13.0
Ventura	44.8	+1.4
San Diego	44.1	+10.7
Monterey	41.6	+15.3
Sacramento	39.3	+16.0
Tulare	28.7	+23.3
Sutter	32.3	+37.1
Lassen	29.9	+46.5
Siskiyou	29.9	+49.8
Modoc	23.2	+57.6

Sources: California Department of Insurance and Office of the California Secretary of State.

Using the data in the table, we estimated the regression equation

$$V = a + bP$$

to see if voting behavior is related to the change in auto insurance premiums in a statistically significant way. Here is the regression output from the computer:

DEPENDENT VARIABLE: V	R-SQUARE	F-RATIO	P-VALUE ON F
OBSERVATIONS: 17	0.7399	42.674	0.0001

VARIABLE	PARAMETER ESTIMATE	STANDARD ERROR	T-RATIO	P-VALUE
INTERCEPT	53.682	2.112	25.42	0.0001
P	−0.528	0.081	−6.52	0.0001

a. Does this regression equation provide evidence of a statistically significant relation between voter support for Proposition 103 in a county and changes in average auto premiums affected by Proposition 103 in that county? Perform an *F*-test at the 95 percent level of confidence.

b. Test the intercept estimate for significance at the 95 percent confidence level. If Proposition 103 has no impact on auto insurance premiums in any given county, what percent of voters do you expect will vote for the proposition?

c. Test the slope estimate for significance at the 95 percent confidence level. If P increases by 10 percent, by what percent does the vote for Proposition 103 decline?

3. A security analyst specializing in the stocks of the motion picture industry wishes to examine the relation between the number of movie theater tickets sold in December and the annual level of earnings in the motion picture industry. Time-series data for the last 15 years are used to estimate the regression model

$$E = a + bN$$

where E is total earnings of the motion picture industry measured in dollars per year, and N is the number of tickets sold in December. The regression output is as follows:

DEPENDENT VARIABLE: E	R-SQUARE	F-RATIO	P-VALUE ON F
OBSERVATIONS: 15	0.8311	63.96	0.0001

VARIABLE	PARAMETER ESTIMATE	STANDARD ERROR	T-RATIO	P-VALUE
INTERCEPT	25042000.0	20131000.0	1.24	0.2369
N	32.31	8.54	3.78	0.0023

a. How well do movie ticket sales in December explain the level of earnings for the entire year? Present statistical evidence to support your answer.
b. On average, what effect does a 100,000-ticket increase in December sales have on the annual earnings in the movie industry?
c. Sales of movie tickets in December are expected to be approximately 950,000. According to this regression analysis, what do you expect earnings for the year to be?

4. The manager of Collins Import Autos believes the number of cars sold in a day (Q) depends upon two factors: (1) the number of hours the dealership is open (H), and (2) the number of salespersons working that day (S). After collecting data for two months (53 days), the manager estimates the following log-linear model:

$$Q = aH^bS^c$$

a. Explain how to transform this log-linear model into a linear form that can be estimated using multiple regression analysis.

The computer output for the multiple regression analysis is shown below:

DEPENDENT VARIABLE: LNQ		R-SQUARE	F-RATIO	P-VALUE ON F
OBSERVATIONS: 53		0.5452	29.97	0.0001
VARIABLE	PARAMETER ESTIMATE	STANDARD ERROR	T-RATIO	P-VALUE
INTERCEPT	0.9162	0.2413	3.80	0.0004
LNH	0.3517	0.1021	3.44	0.0012
LNS	0.2550	0.0785	3.25	0.0021

b. How do you interpret coefficients b and c? If the dealership increases the number of salespersons by 20 percent, what will be the percentage increase in daily sales?
c. Test the overall model for statistical significance at the 5 percent significance level.
d. What percent of the total variation in daily auto sales is explained by this equation? What could you suggest to increase this percentage?
e. Test the intercept for statistical significance at the 5 percent level of significance. If H and S both equal zero, are sales expected to be zero? Explain why or why not.
f. Test the estimated coefficient b for statistical significance. If the dealership decreases its hours of operation by 10 percent, what is the expected impact on daily sales?

STATISTICAL APPENDIX Further Development

Least-Squares Parameter Estimation

Consider the sample regression line

(1) $$\hat{Y}_i = a + \hat{b}X_i$$

where $\hat{a}$ and $\hat{b}$ are estimates of the population parameters a and b. The goal of least-squares regression is to find estimates of $\hat{a}$ and $\hat{b}$ that minimize the sum of the squared residuals (denoted *ESS*) for the sample of n observations on Y and X:

(2) $$ESS = \sum_{i=1}^{n} e_i^2 = \sum_{i=1}^{n} (Y_i - \hat{Y}_i)^2 = \sum_{i=1}^{n} (Y_i - \hat{a} - \hat{b}X_i)^2$$

Notice that *ESS* is a function of the estimates $\hat{a}$ and $\hat{b}$. To find the values of the estimates that minimize *ESS*, partially differentiate equation (2) with respect to $\hat{a}$ and $\hat{b}$, and then set the two partial derivatives equal to zero:

(3) $$\frac{\partial ESS}{\partial \hat{a}} = -2\sum (Y_i - \hat{a} - \hat{b}X_i) = 0$$

(4) $$\frac{\partial ESS}{\partial \hat{b}} = -2\sum X_i (Y_i - \hat{a} - \hat{b}X_i) = 0$$

Multiplying and rearranging terms:

(3a) $$\sum Y_i = n\hat{a} + \hat{b}\sum X_i$$

(4a) $$\sum Y_i X_i = \hat{a}\sum X_i + \hat{b}\sum X_i^2$$

Now solve (3a) and (4a) simultaneously for $\hat{a}$ and $\hat{b}$. To do this, multiply (3a) by $\sum X_i$ and (4a) by n:

(3b) $$\sum X_i \sum Y_i = n\hat{a}\sum X_i + \hat{b}\,(\sum X_i)^2$$

(4b) $$n\sum Y_i \sum X_i = n\hat{a}\sum X_i + \hat{b}\,n\sum X_i^2$$

Next, subtract (3b) from (4b):

(5) $$n\sum Y_i X_i - \sum X_i \sum Y_i = \hat{b}\,[n\sum X^2 - (\sum X_i)^2]$$

and it follows that:

(6) $$\hat{b} = \frac{n\sum X_i Y_i - \sum X_i \sum Y_i}{n\sum X_i^2 - (\sum X_i)^2}$$

where $\overline{X}$ and $\overline{Y}$ are the sample means of X and Y. After finding $\hat{b}$, $\hat{a}$ is calculated as

(7) $$\hat{a} = \overline{Y} - \hat{b}\overline{X}$$

To illustrate how the computer uses equations (6) and (7) to estimate a and b, Table 5A.1 shows the computations that will be done for you by a computer.

TABLE 5A.1
Computing the Least-Squares Estimates $\hat{a}$ and $\hat{b}$ for the Sample of Seven Travel Agencies

Sales (Y_i)	Advertising expenditure (X_i)	$X_i - \overline{X}$	$(X_i - \overline{X})^2$	$Y_i - \overline{Y}$	$(X_i - \overline{X})(Y_i - \overline{Y})$
15,000	2,000	−3,143	9,878,449	−22,143	69,595,449
30,000	2,000	−3,143	9,878,449	−7,143	22,450,449
30,000	5,000	−143	20,449	−7,143	1,021,449
25,000	3,000	−2,143	4,592,449	−12,143	26,022,449
55,000	9,000	3,857	14,876,449	17,857	68,874,449
45,000	8,000	2,857	8,162,449	7,857	22,447,449
60,000	7,000	1,857	3,448,449	22,857	42,445,449
Σ 260,000	36,000		50,857,143		252,857,143

$\overline{Y} = 260{,}000/7 = 37{,}143$.
$\overline{X} = 36{,}000/7 = 5{,}143$.
$\hat{b} = \sum(X_i - \overline{X})(Y_i - \overline{Y})/\sum(X_i - \overline{X})^2 = 252{,}857{,}143/50{,}857{,}143 = 4.97$.
$\hat{a} = \overline{Y} - \hat{b}\overline{X} = 37{,}143 - (4.97 \times 5{,}143) = 11{,}582$.

FIGURE 5A.1
Decomposition of Total Variation in Y

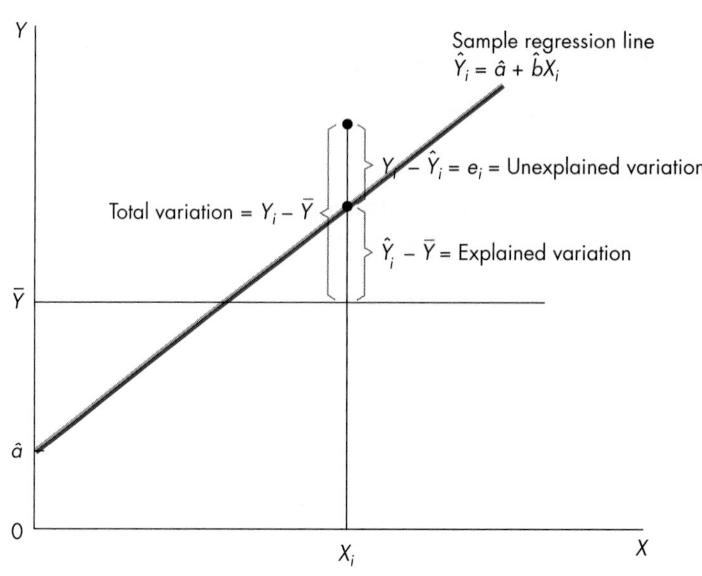

Table 5A.1 calculates the parameter estimates for the sample regression line that best fits the data in Table 5.2.

Derivation of the Coefficient of Determination (R^2)

The coefficient of determination, denoted R^2, measures how well the overall equation explains the variation in the dependent variable Y. The total variation in Y can be attributed to one of two things: variation due to changes in the explanatory variable(s) or variation due to random influences. R^2 is derived by decomposing the variation in Y into these two component parts.

Statisticians measure the variation in the dependent variable as $Y_i - \bar{Y}$, the variation in Y about the sample mean ($\bar{Y}$). To motivate why the sample mean is used, recall that if Y_i does not vary at all in the sample (i.e., Y_i is constant for all observations), Y_i equals Y for every observation in the sample. The sample mean, then, provides a point of reference about which the variation in Y_i can be measured. The amount by which the value of Y predicted by the regression ($\hat{Y}_i$) deviates from the sample mean ($\bar{Y}$) is referred to as the explained variation and is denoted $\hat{Y}_i - \bar{Y}$. The unexplained variation in Y_i is the residual amount, $Y_i - \hat{Y}_i$. Figure 5A.1 shows how the variation in Y_i is decomposed for one particular observation in the sample.

The total variation in Y_i in the sample is computed by squaring the total variation in Y_i and summing across all observations in the sample:

$$\text{Total variation} = \Sigma(Y_i - \bar{Y})^2$$

Given the decomposition discussed above, the total variation in Y can also be expressed as the sum of the explained and unexplained variation in Y:

$$\begin{matrix}\text{Total} & & \text{Total} & & \text{Total}\\ \text{variation} & = & \text{explained} & + & \text{unexplained}\\ \text{in } Y & & \text{variation} & & \text{variation}\end{matrix}$$

$$\Sigma(Y_i - \bar{Y})^2 = \Sigma(\hat{Y}_i - \bar{Y})^2 + \Sigma(Y_i - \hat{Y}_i)^2$$

The coefficient of determination measures the fraction of total variation explained by the regression:

$$R^2 = \frac{\text{Total explained variation}}{\text{Total variation in } Y} = \frac{\Sigma(\hat{Y}_i - \bar{Y})^2}{\Sigma(Y_i - \bar{Y})^2}$$

Thus it follows that R^2 can vary from 0 to 1 in value.

Some Additional Problems in Regression Analysis

Multicollinearity

When using regression analysis, we assume that the explanatory (right-hand side) variables are linearly independent of one another. If this assumption is violated, we have the problem of *multicollinearity.* Under normal circumstances, multicollinearity will result in the estimated standard errors being larger than their true values. This means, then, that if multicollinearity exists, finding statistical significance will be more difficult. More specifically, if moderate multicollinearity is present, the estimate of the coefficient, $\hat{b}$, will be unbiased but the estimated standard error, $S_{\hat{b}}$, will be increased. Thus, the *t*-coefficient, $t = \hat{b}/S_{\hat{b}}$, will be reduced, and it will be more difficult to find statistical significance.

Multicollinearity is not unusual. The question is what to do about it. As a general rule, the answer is *nothing.* To illustrate, consider the following function that denotes some true relation:

$$Y = a + bX + cZ$$

If X and Z are not linearly independent—if X and Z are collinear—the standard errors of the estimates for b and c will be increased. Shouldn't we just drop one? Not in the normal instance. If Z is an important explanatory variable, the exclusion of Z would be a *specification error* and would result in biased estimates of the coefficients—a much more severe problem.

Heteroscedasticity

The problem of *heteroscedasticity* is encountered when the variance of the error term is not constant. It can be encountered when there exists some relation between the error term and one or more of the explanatory variables—for example, when there exists a positive relation between X and the errors (i.e., large errors are associated with large values of X).

In such a case, the estimated parameters are still unbiased, but the standard errors of the coefficients are biased; so the calculated *t*-ratios are unreliable. This problem, most normally encountered in cross-section studies, can sometimes be corrected by performing a transformation on the data or equation. Otherwise, it becomes necessary to employ a technique called weighted least-squares estimation.

Autocorrelation

The problem of *autocorrelation,* associated with time-series data, occurs when the errors are not independent over time. For example, it could be the case that a high error in one period tends to promote a high error in the following period.

With autocorrelation (sometimes referred to as *serial correlation*) the estimated parameters are unbiased, but the standard errors are again biased, resulting in unreliability of the calculated *t*-ratios. Tests for determining if autocorrelation is present (most notably the Durbin-Watson test) are included in most of the available regression packages. Furthermore, most packages also include techniques for estimating an equation in the presence of autocorrelation.

Part III

Demand

Theory and Empirical Analysis

CHAPTER 6

Theory of Consumer Behavior

The willingness of consumers to purchase a product or service is the fundamental source of profit for any business. No matter how efficiently production is accomplished, a firm cannot earn a profit unless buyers believe they can benefit by consuming the firm's product rather than buying a rival's product or even saving their money for future consumption. Understanding consumer behavior, then, is the first step in making profitable pricing, advertising, product design, and production decisions.

Firms spend a great deal of time and money trying to estimate and forecast the demand for their products. Obtaining accurate estimates of demand requires more than a superficial understanding of the underpinnings of demand functions. While we are sympathetic to students who find the level of abstraction in this chapter somewhat daunting, we nevertheless encourage you to meet the challenge of learning these fundamental concepts of consumer behavior. A manager's need for practical analysis of demand—both estimation of demand and demand forecasting—requires an economic model of consumer behavior to guide the analysis.

This chapter presents only the most important aspects of the theory of consumer behavior. The theory follows directly from the theory of constrained maximization described in Chapter 4. (As you read this chapter, you may want to look back at Chapter 4 to see how closely the analysis here follows that general framework.)

Few, if any, people have incomes sufficient to buy as much as they desire of every good or service. Because consumers are constrained by the amount of their incomes, they attempt to maximize their satisfaction from the goods and services they purchase, given this constraint.

When you finish this chapter, you will have a good understanding of why consumers choose to purchase one bundle of products rather than some other bundle. You will also discover that the theory of consumer behavior, as presented in this chapter, is an important tool in other business courses you take, particularly in marketing and finance. Even though a full appreciation of the value of this chapter may not come with a single course in managerial economics, you will begin to see its value in the next two chapters when we show you how to estimate and forecast consumer demand.

6.1 CONSUMER PREFERENCES AND UTILITY

As with all economic models, the theory of consumer behavior employs some simplifying assumptions. These assumptions permit us to go directly to the fundamental determinants of consumer behavior and to abstract away from the less important aspects of the consumer's decision process. Let us briefly describe these assumptions.

Complete Information

We assume for now that consumers have complete information pertaining to their consumption decisions. They know the full range of goods and services available and the capacity of each to provide utility. Further, the price of each good is known exactly, as is each consumer's income during the time period in question. Admittedly, to assume perfect knowledge is an abstraction from reality, but the assumption of complete information does not distort the relevant aspects of real-world consumer decisions. It allows us to concentrate on how real consumption choices are made without becoming bogged down with extraneous details.

Preference Ordering

The second assumption is that consumers are able to rank all conceivable bundles of commodities. When confronted with two or more bundles of goods, consumers can determine their order of preference among them. As an example, suppose a consumer is confronted with two bundles consisting of different combinations of two goods. Bundle *A* consists of five candy bars and one soft drink. Bundle *B* consists of three candy bars and three soft drinks. Ranking the two bundles, the person can make one of three possible responses: (1) I prefer bundle *A* to bundle *B*, (2) I prefer bundle *B* to bundle *A*, or (3) I would be equally satisfied with either.

The same is true when ranking any two bundles of goods and services. The consumer either prefers one bundle to the other or is indifferent between the two. A consumer who is indifferent between two bundles clearly feels that either bundle would yield the same level of satisfaction. A preferred bundle would yield more satisfaction than the other, less-preferred bundle. We should also note that price has nothing to do with preferences. Preference is a theoretical concept about how people can rank bundles of goods.

We also assume that the consumer is rational in the following sense: If there are three bundles of goods, *A*, *B*, and *C*, and if the consumer prefers *A* to *B* and *B* to *C*, then bundle *A* must be preferred to bundle *C*. Or if the consumer is indifferent between *A* and *B* and prefers *B* to *C*, then *A* must be preferred to *C*. We can extend this assumption to any number of combinations; if consumers can rank any two bundles of goods, they can rank all conceivable combinations of goods and services.

Finally, we assume consumers always prefer to have more of a good rather than less of the good. We do recognize that people may consume so much of something that they become satiated with it and do not want any more; however, no one would purchase so much of a good that they would be happier to have less of it. We summarize this discussion with a principle:

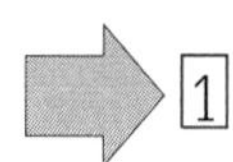

Principle Consumers have a preference pattern that (1) establishes a rank ordering of all bundles of goods and (2) compares all pairs of bundles, indicating that bundle *A* is preferred to bundle *B*, *B* is preferred to *A*, or the consumer is indifferent between *A* and B. In a three- (or more) way comparison, if *A* is preferred (indifferent) to *B*, and *B* is preferred (indifferent) to *C*, *A* must be preferred (indifferent) to *C*. Consumers prefer more of a good to less of that good.

The Utility Function

utility
Benefits consumers obtain from the goods and services they consume.

Economists name the benefits consumers obtain from the goods and services they consume **utility.** This is not completely descriptive. Utility implies usefulness, and many of the products most of us consume may not be particularly useful. Many people are willing to pay a lot more for a Mercedes or BMW than they would pay for a Geo, which may well be just as useful. And people can differ drastically over what is and is not useful. A child would probably consider a Nintendo game more useful than new clothes, while the parents would have the opposite opinion. Most people probably buy a lot of things that others would not consider particularly useful. Nonetheless, we will follow tradition and refer to the benefits obtained from goods and services as utility.

Settling on a name for the benefits does not solve the problem of how to measure these benefits from consumption. Who could say how many units of benefit, or how much utility, they receive from consuming an ice cream cone or a pizza or from going to the dentist? After all, it is not possible to plug a "utility meter" into a consumer's ear and measure the amount of utility generated by consuming some good or service. And even if we could measure utility, what units or denomination would we use? In class, we have used terms such as "utils," which is too serious, "globs," which is too frivolous, "bushels," which is too precise, and others we need not mention. Over time, we have settled on the phrase "units of utility," which is certainly pedestrian and dull, but it seems as good a name as any.

utility function
An equation that shows an individual's perception of the level of utility that would be attained from consuming each conceivable bundle of goods: $U = f(X, Y)$.

Consumer preferences can be represented as a **utility function.** A utility function shows an individual's perception of the level of utility that would be attained from consuming each conceivable bundle or combination of goods and services. A simple form of a utility function for a person who consumes only two goods, *X* and *Y*, might be

$$U = f(X, Y)$$

where X and Y are, respectively, the amounts of goods X and Y consumed, f means "a function of" or "depends upon," and U is the amount of utility the person receives from each combination of X and Y. Thus, utility depends upon the quantities consumed of X and Y.

The actual numbers assigned to the levels of utility are arbitrary. It is inconceivable that anyone could actually assign specific numbers for the amount of utility received from consuming every possible combination of goods. Therefore, a utility function is a theoretical concept that proves useful in analysis. We need only say that if a consumer prefers one combination of goods, say, $20X$ and $30Y$, to some other combination, say, $15X$ and $32Y$, the amount of utility derived from the first bundle is greater than the amount from the second. It makes no difference if the amount of utility assigned to the first bundle is 150 and the amount to the second is 100 or if the first number is 90 and the second is 80. The only thing that matters is that

$$U = f(20,30) > U = f(15,32)$$

For analytical simplicity and graphical convenience we will analyze the case of a consumer choosing between only two goods or services. The utility function will therefore be specified as above. We could express a utility function with any number of goods and services. Such a utility function would be

$$U = f(X_1, X_2, X_3, \ldots, X_n)$$

where X_i is the amount of the ith good or service, and U is an index of utility depending on the quantities consumed of goods $X_1, X_2, X_3, \ldots, X_n$. We should emphasize, however, that the two-good approach enables us to derive every important theoretical concept that can be derived from the n-good model and is far less complex analytically.

6.2 INDIFFERENCE CURVES

indifference curve
A locus of points representing different bundles of goods and services, each of which yields the same level of total utility.

Consumers are willing to make tradeoffs or substitute among different goods. This willingness to substitute is determined by the form of that person's utility function. A fundamental tool for analyzing consumer behavior is an **indifference curve,** which is a locus of points representing different combinations of goods and services, each of which provides an individual with the same level of utility. Therefore the consumer is indifferent among all combinations of goods shown on an indifference curve—hence the name. The above assumption that a consumer chooses among bundles consisting of only *two* goods enables us to analyze consumer behavior using two-dimensional graphs of indifference curves without any loss of explanatory capability.

Properties

Figure 6.1 shows a representative indifference curve with the typically assumed shape. The quantity of good X is plotted along the horizontal axis; the quantity of good Y is plotted along the vertical axis.

FIGURE 6.1
A Typical Indifference Curve

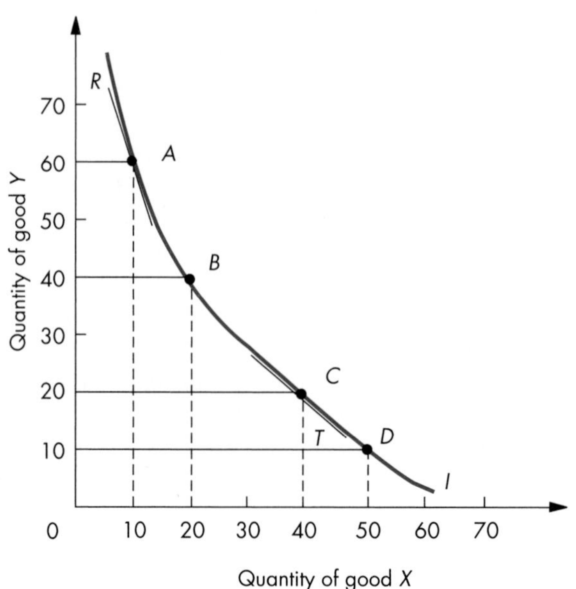

All combinations of goods X and Y along indifference curve I yield the consumer the same level of utility. In other words, the consumer is indifferent among all points, such as point A, with 10 units of X and 60 units of Y; point B, with $20X$ and $40Y$; point C, with $40X$ and $20Y$; and so on. At any point on I, it is possible to take away some amount of X and add some amount of Y (though not necessarily the same amount) and leave the consumer with the same level of utility. Conversely, we can add X and take away just enough Y to make the consumer indifferent between the two combinations.

An indifference curve is downward-sloping. This assumption reflects the fact that the consumer obtains utility from both goods. Thus, if more X is added, some Y must be taken away in order to maintain the same level of utility. If the curve in Figure 6.1 were to begin sloping upward at, say, 70 units of X, this would mean that the consumer has so much X that any additional X would reduce utility if the quantity of Y remains constant. In such a case, to keep the consumer at the same level of utility when X is added, more Y would have to be added to compensate for the lost utility from having more X. Likewise, if the curve were to begin bending backward at, say, 75 units of Y, this would mean that the consumer experiences reduced levels of utility with increases in Y.

Indifference curves are convex. This shape requires that as the consumption of X is increased relative to consumption of Y, the consumer is willing to accept a smaller reduction in Y for an equal increase in X, in order to stay at the same level of utility. This property is apparent in Figure 6.1. Begin at point A, with 10 units of X and 60 units of Y. In order to increase the consumption of X by

10 units, to 20, the consumer is willing to reduce the consumption of Y by 20 units, to 40. Given indifference curve I, the consumer will be indifferent between the two combinations represented by A and B. Next begin at C, with $40X$ and $20Y$. From this point, to gain an additional 10 units of X (move to point D), the consumer is willing to give up only 10 units of Y, much less than the 20 units willingly given up to obtain 10 more units at point A. The convexity of indifference curves implies a diminishing marginal rate of substitution, to which we now turn.

Marginal Rate of Substitution

marginal rate of substitution (MRS) A measure of the number of units of Y that must be given up per unit of X added so as to maintain a constant level of utility.

An important concept in indifference curve analysis is the marginal rate of substitution. The **marginal rate of substitution (*MRS*)** measures the number of units of Y that must be given up per unit of X added so as to maintain a constant level of utility. Returning to Figure 6.1, you can see that the consumer is indifferent between combinations A ($10X$ and $60Y$) and B ($20X$ and $40Y$). Thus the rate at which the consumer is willing to substitute is

$$\frac{\Delta Y}{\Delta X} = \frac{60 - 40}{10 - 20} = -\frac{20}{10} = -2$$

The marginal rate of substitution is 2, meaning that the consumer is willing to give up 2 units of Y for each unit of X added. Since it would be cumbersome to have the minus sign on the right side of the equation, the marginal rate of substitution is defined as

$$MRS = -\frac{\Delta Y}{\Delta X} = 2$$

For the movement from C to D along I, the marginal rate of substitution is

$$MRS = -\frac{\Delta Y}{\Delta X} = -\frac{(20 - 10)}{(40 - 50)} = \frac{10}{10} = 1$$

In this case the consumer is willing to give up only 1 unit of Y per additional unit of X added.

Therefore, the marginal rate of substitution diminishes along an indifference curve. When consumers have a small amount of X relative to Y, they are willing to give up a lot of Y to gain another unit of X. When they have less Y relative to X, they are willing to give up less Y in order to gain another unit of X.

We have, thus far, calculated the marginal rate of substitution for relatively large changes in the quantities of the two goods; that is, over *intervals* along an indifference curve. In Figure 6.1 the *MRS* over the interval from A to B is 2, and the *MRS* over the interval from C to D is 1. Now consider measuring the *MRS* at a *point* on an indifference curve; that is, let the changes in X and Y along the indifference curve be extremely small. The marginal rate of substitution at a point can be closely approximated by (the absolute value of) the slope of a line tangent to the indifference curve at the point. For example, consider point C in Figure 6.2 A line tangent to indifference curve I at point C, TT', has a slope of

FIGURE 6.2
The Slope of an Indifference Curve and the *MRS*

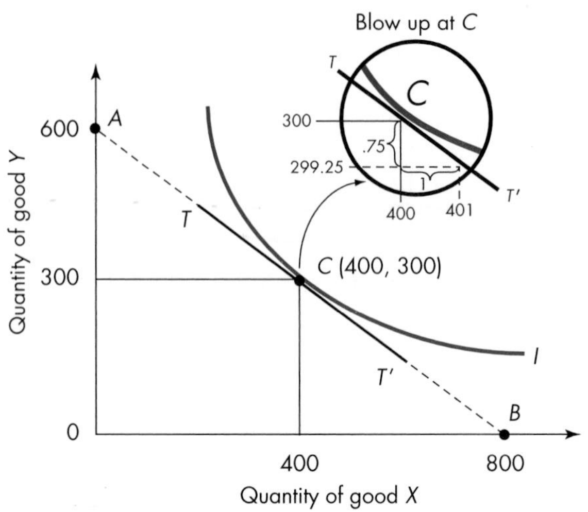

-0.75 (= $\Delta Y/\Delta X = -\ 600/800$). The (absolute value of the) slope of the tangent line gives a good *estimate* of the amount of Y that must be given up to keep utility constant when one more unit of X is consumed. Suppose the consumer moves along the indifference curve by adding one more unit of X, from 400 to 401 units. Using the slope of the tangent line as an approximation, the change in Y needed to keep utility constant is -0.75; in other words, a one-unit increase in X requires a 0.75-unit decrease in Y to remain indifferent. But as the blowup in Figure 6.2 shows, if the movement is along the indifference curve, only a little *less* than 0.75 units of Y must be sacrificed to remain indifferent. Nevertheless, the (absolute value of the) slope of the tangent line is a fairly close approximation of the exact *MRS*. As the changes in X and Y become smaller and smaller, the (absolute value of the) tangent line becomes a better and better approximation of the *MRS* at that point.

In Figure 6.1 the (absolute values of the) slopes of tangent lines R and T give the marginal rates of substitution at points A and C, respectively. Looking at these tangents, it is easy to see that the (absolute value of the) slope of the indifference curve, and hence the *MRS*, decreases as X increases and Y decreases along the indifference curve. This results from the assumption that indifference curves are convex.

Relation Indifference curves are negatively sloped and convex. Moving along an indifference curve, when the consumption of one good is increased, consumption of the other good is necessarily reduced by the amount required to maintain a constant level of utility. For a unit increase (decrease) in X, the marginal rate of substitution measures the decrease (increase) in Y needed to keep utility constant ($MRS = -\Delta Y/\Delta X$). For very small changes in X, the marginal rate of substitution is the negative of the slope of the indifference curve at a point. The marginal rate of substitution decreases as the consumer moves down an indifference curve.

2 3

FIGURE 6.3
Indifference Map

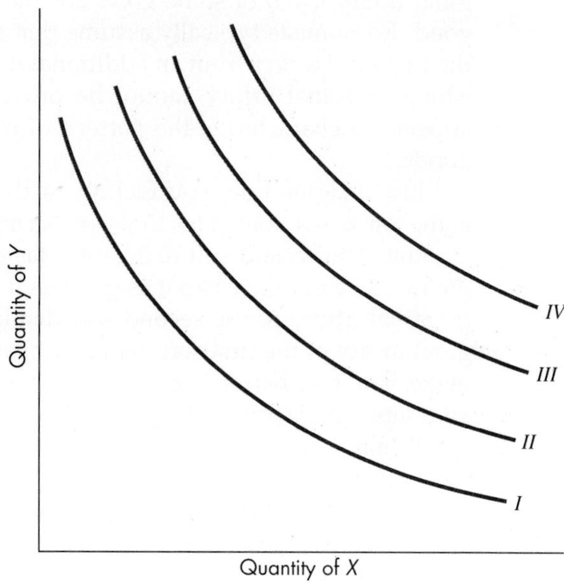

Indifference Maps

An indifference map is made up of two or more indifference curves. Figure 6.3 shows a typical indifference map, with four indifference curves, *I*, *II*, *III*, and *IV*. Any indifference curve lying above and to the right of another represents a higher level of utility. Thus any combination of *X* and *Y* on *IV* is preferred to any combination on *III*, any combination on *III* is preferred to any on *II*, and so on. All bundles of goods on the same indifference curve are equivalent; all combinations lying on a higher curve are preferred.

The indifference map in Figure 6.3 consists of only four indifference curves. We could have drawn many, many more. In fact, the *X*-*Y* space actually contains an infinite number of indifference curves. Each point in the space lies on one and only one indifference curve. That is, the same combination of goods cannot give two levels of utility. Thus indifference curves cannot intersect.

Relation An indifference map consists of several indifference curves. The higher (or further to the right) an indifference curve, the greater the level of utility associated with the curve. Combinations of goods on higher indifference curves are preferred to combinations on lower curves.

marginal utility
The addition to total utility that is attributable to the addition of one unit of a good to the current rate of consumption, holding constant the amounts of all other goods consumed.

A Marginal Utility Interpretation of *MRS*

The concept of *marginal utility* can give additional insight into the properties of indifference curves, particularly the slope of indifference curves. **Marginal utility** is the addition to total utility that is attributable to consuming one more unit of a good, holding constant the amounts of all other goods consumed. Thus marginal utility (MU) of some good equals $\Delta U/\Delta Q$, where Q is the quantity of the good. Economists typically assume that as the consumption of a good increases, the marginal utility from an additional unit of the good diminishes. While diminishing marginal utility cannot be proved theoretically, falling marginal utility appears to characterize the pattern of consumption for most people with most goods.

Just imagine how you feel about the soft drinks you consume at a football game on a hot day. The first soft drink boosts your utility by a substantial amount. The second soft drink does taste good, and it increases your utility, but the increase in utility is not as great as it was for the first soft drink. So while the marginal utility of the second soft drink is positive, it is smaller than the marginal utility of the first soft drink. Similarly, the third and fourth soft drinks also make you feel better (i.e., increase your utility), but by successively smaller amounts. This demonstrates the concept of diminishing marginal utility.

While some economists object to the concept of marginal utility on the grounds that utility is not measurable, many other economists find it useful to relate marginal utility to the marginal rate of substitution along an indifference curve. The change in total utility that results when both X and Y change by small amounts is related to the marginal utilities of X and Y as

$$\Delta U = (MU_x \times \Delta X) + (MU_y \times Y)$$

where MU_x and MU_y are the marginal utilities of X and Y, respectively.[1] To illustrate this relation, suppose a consumer increases consumption of X by two units ($\Delta X = 2$) and decreases consumption of Y by one unit ($\Delta Y = -1$). Further suppose the marginal utility of X is 25 for each additional unit of X, and the marginal utility of Y is 10. The amount by which utility changes is computed as

$$\Delta U = (25 \times 2) + (10 \times -1) = 40$$

Consuming two more X and one less Y causes total utility to rise by 40 units of utility.

For points on a given indifference curve, all combinations of goods yield the same level of utility, so ΔU is zero for all changes in X and Y that would keep the consumer on the same indifference curve. From the above equation, if $\Delta U = 0$, it follows that

$$\Delta U = 0 = (MU_x \times \Delta X) + (MU_y \times \Delta Y)$$

Therefore, solving for $-\Delta Y/\Delta X$,

$$-\frac{\Delta Y}{\Delta X} = \frac{MU_x}{MU_y}$$

---

[1]Note that we have stretched one of the assumptions in this analysis. Recall that marginal utility is the increase in utility from a one-unit increase in the rate of consumption in a good, holding the consumption of all other goods constant. In this example, we speak of marginal utility while letting the consumption of both goods change at the same time. However, if the change in each is small, this presents little or no problem.

ILLUSTRATION 6.1

To Fly Fast or to Fly Far:

Tradeoffs in the Market

In 1996 Cessna Aircraft Corp. and Gulfstream Aircraft Inc. each introduced a new business jet—the Cessna Citation X and the Gulfstream V. *The Wall Street Journal* noted at the time that the two planes "aren't directly competitive, but their reception in the marketplace will indicate the relative importance to buyers of speed and range."* The Citation X, with a speed up to 600 miles per hour, was the fastest civilian plane short of the Concord. The Gulfstream V, with a range up to 7,500 miles, was the longest-range business jet. Cessna boasted that its jet could fly moguls from New York to California for breakfast, then back to New Jersey in time for cocktails. Gulfstream cited its jet's ability to fly 14 hours nonstop, from California to Spain or India.

Industry analysts differed in their predictions about the success in the market of the two planes. Some predicted consumers would value the range of Gulfstream more; others said that Cessna's speed would prevail. Obviously the Gulfstream also flies pretty fast, and the Cessna also flies pretty far, but the two manufacturers chose to emphasize different features. In terms of indifference curves, Cessna viewed the indifference map of corporate jet buyers as being something like the curves shown in Panel A of the graph in the next column. It believed that consumers would be willing to trade off a lot of range for more speed. In this case, the marginal rate of substitution between range and speed is high. Gulfstream viewed the indifference map as being like the curves shown in Panel B. That is, consumers would not be willing to trade off as much range for more speed. In this view, the marginal rate of substitution between range and speed is low.

A great deal of money rode on these decisions, since the start-up cost of a new airplane is very high and it often takes the market a long time to render a verdict. A Canadian firm planning to introduce a competitor to the Gulfstream estimated that its start-up costs would be about $1 billion U.S. dollars.

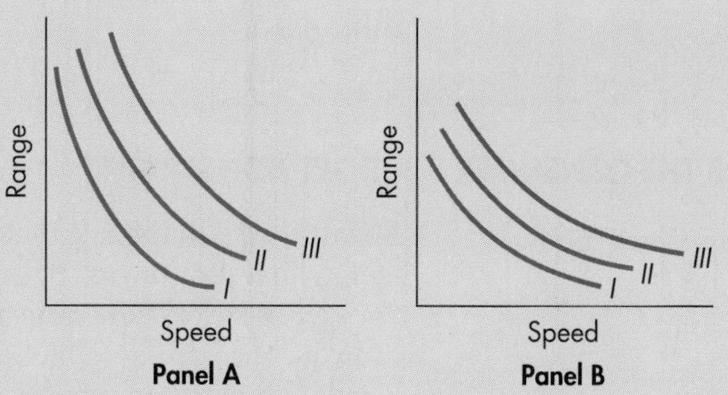

This situation illustrates the importance of predicting tradeoffs in business decision making. Products have many different characteristics. Managers making long-range decisions often try to determine the relative values that consumers place on these different characteristics, and one product generally cannot incorporate all the desirable characteristics.

For example, an ice cream manufacturer must decide how much fat to put into a new product. Fat makes ice cream taste good, but for dietary reasons many consumers value low-fat, low-cholesterol food. The manufacturer must evaluate consumer tradeoffs between taste and health. Automobile manufacturers must predict the willingness of consumers to trade off performance, styling, and reliability in their cars. According to some observers, U.S. auto manufacturers made the wrong decision several years ago when they emphasized size and style over reliability. As it turned out, consumers valued reliability more than the U.S. automakers had predicted, and the firms subsequently lost considerable sales to foreign producers.

It is not the actual estimation and graphing of indifference curves that is useful to decision makers. It is the *concept* of these curves that is useful. All products have some substitutes, and consumers are willing to trade one product for another at some rate. The important thing is estimating the rate at which they are willing to make the tradeoff.

*"The Fastest Jet May Not Win the Race," *The Wall Street Journal,* Aug. 1, 1996.

where $-\Delta Y/\Delta X$ is the negative of the slope of the indifference curve, or the marginal rate of substitution. Thus, the marginal rate of substitution can be interpreted as the ratio of the marginal utility of X divided by the marginal utility of Y:

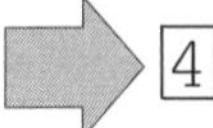

$$MRS = MU_x/MU_y$$

6.3 THE CONSUMER'S BUDGET CONSTRAINT

Recall from Chapter 2 that demand functions indicate what consumers are both *willing and able* to do. Because indifference curves are derived from the preference patterns of consumers, they show what consumers are willing to do. They indicate the rate at which consumers are willing to substitute among different goods. They give no indication of the consumer's income or the prices that must be paid for the goods. Consumers are, however, constrained as to what they are able to do—what bundles of goods they can purchase—by the market-determined prices of the goods and by their incomes. We now turn to an analysis of the income constraint faced by consumers.

Budget Lines

If consumers had unlimited money incomes or if goods were free, there would be no problem of economizing. People could buy whatever they wanted and would have no problem of choice. But this is not generally the case.

Consumers normally have limited incomes and goods are not free. Their problem is how to spend the limited income in a way that gives the maximum possible utility. The constraint faced by consumers can be illustrated graphically.

Continue to assume the consumer buys only two goods, bought in quantities X and Y. The consumer has a fixed money income of \$1,000, which is the maximum amount that can be spent on the two goods in a given period.[2] For simplicity, assume the entire income is spent on X and Y. If the price of X is \$5 per unit and the price of Y is \$10 per unit, the amount spent on X (\$5 × X) plus the amount spent on Y (\$10 × Y) must equal the \$1,000 income:

$$\$5X + \$10Y = \$1{,}000$$

Alternatively, solving for Y in terms of X,

$$Y = \frac{\$1{,}000}{\$10} - \frac{\$5}{\$10}X = 100 - \frac{1}{2}X$$

budget line
The locus of all bundles of goods that can be purchased at given prices if the entire money income is spent.

The graph of this equation, shown in Figure 6.4, is a straight line called the *budget line.* A **budget line** is the locus of all combinations or bundles of goods that can be purchased at given prices if the entire money income is spent.

To purchase any one of the bundles of X and Y on the budget line AB in Figure 6.4, the consumer spends exactly \$1,000. If the consumer decides to spend all \$1,000 on good Y and spend nothing on good X, 100 (=\$1,000/\$10) units of Y

[2]More advanced theories permit consumers to save and borrow between periods.

FIGURE 6.4
A Consumer's Budget Constraint

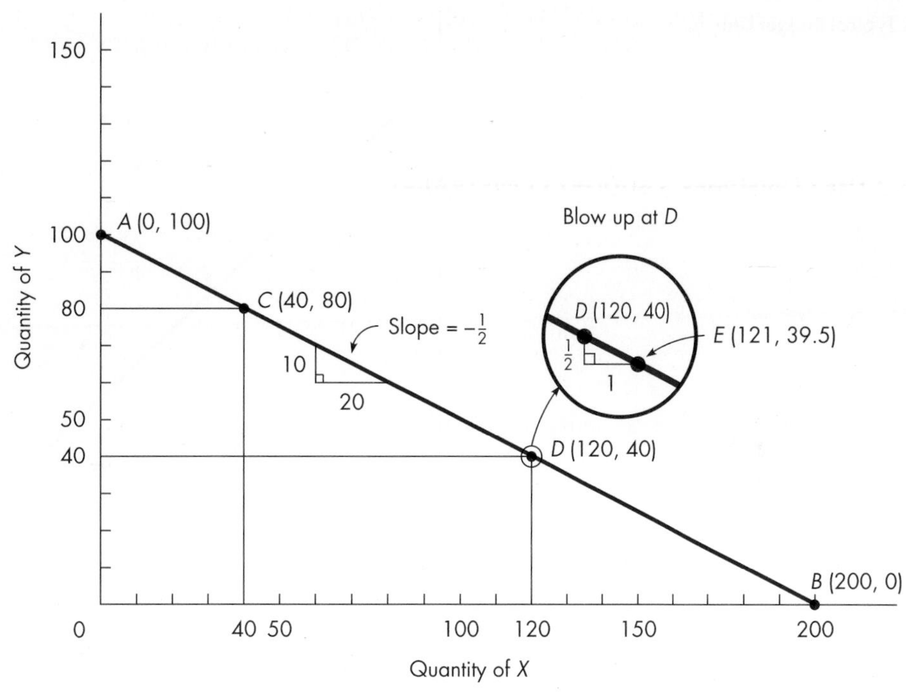

can be purchased (point A in Figure 6.4). If the consumer spends all \$1,000 on X and buys no Y, 200 (= \$1,000/\$5) units of X can be purchased (point B). In Figure 6.4, consumption bundles C, with $40X$ and $80Y$, and D, with $120X$ and $40Y$, represent two other combinations of goods X and Y that can be purchased by spending exactly \$1,000, because $(80 \times \$10) + (40 \times \$5) = \$1{,}000$ and $(40 \times \$10) + (120 \times \$5) = \$1{,}000$.

The slope of the budget line, $-1/2$ (= $\Delta Y/\Delta X$), indicates the amount of Y that must be given up if one more unit of X is purchased. For every additional unit of X purchased, the consumer must spend \$5 more on good X. To continue meeting the budget constraint, \$5 less must be spent on good Y; thus the consumer must give up 1/2 unit of Y. To illustrate this point, suppose the consumer is currently purchasing bundle D but wishes to move to bundle E, which is composed of one more unit of X and 1/2 unit less of Y (see the blowup in Figure 6.4). Bundles D and E both cost \$1,000 to purchase, but the consumer must trade off 1/2 unit of good Y for the extra unit of good X in bundle E. Note also that if the consumer buys one less unit of X, then an *additional* 1/2 unit of Y can be purchased with the same money income.

The rate at which the consumer can trade off Y for one more unit of X is equal to the price of good X (here \$5) divided by the price of good Y (here \$10); that is,

$$\text{Slope of the budget line} = -P_x/P_y$$

FIGURE 6.5
A Typical Budget Line

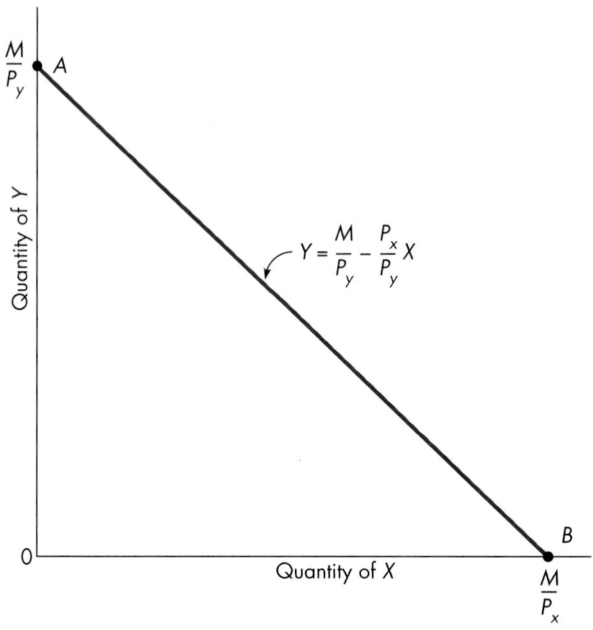

where P_x and P_y are the prices of goods X and Y, respectively. In Figure 6.4, the slope of the budget line is $-1/2$, which equals $-\$5/\$10$.

The relation between money income (M) and the amount of goods X and Y that can be purchased can be expressed in general as

$$M = P_xX + P_yY$$

This equation can be rewritten in the form of a straight line:

$$Y = \frac{M}{P_y} - \frac{P_x}{P_y}X$$

The first term, M/P_y, gives the amount of Y the consumer can buy if no X is purchased. As noted, $-P_x/P_y$ is the slope of the budget line and indicates how much Y must be given up for an additional unit of X.

The general form of a typical budget line is shown in Figure 6.5. The line AB shows all combinations of X and Y that can be purchased with the given money income (M) and given prices of the goods (P_x and P_y). The intercept on the Y axis, A, is M/P_y; the horizontal intercept, B, is M/P_x. The slope of the budget line is $-P_x/P_y$. Note that this slope can be derived by the typical "rise-over-run" formula $[(M/P_y \div M/P_x) = -P_x/P_y]$.

FIGURE 6.6
Shifting Budget Lines

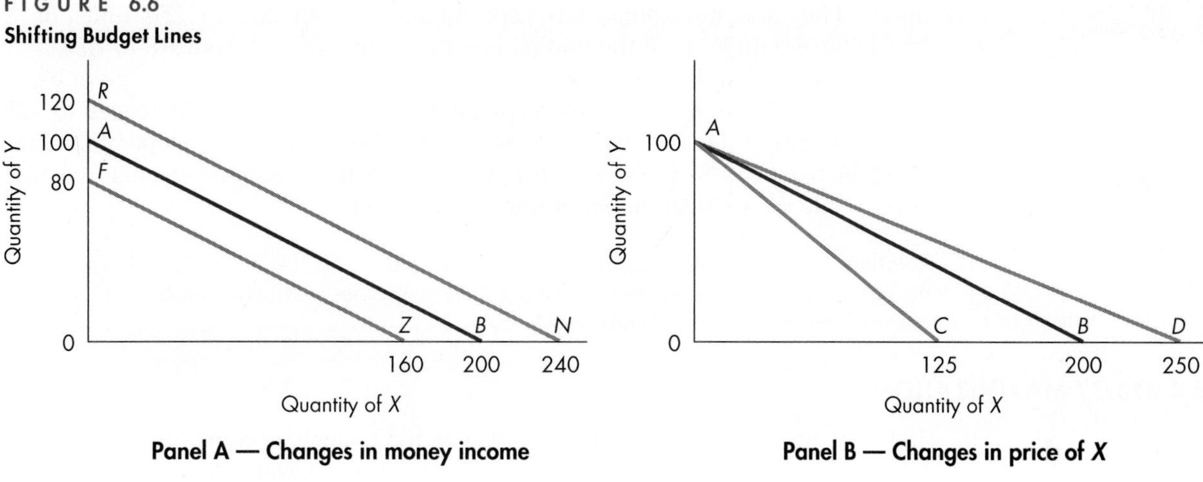

Panel A — Changes in money income

Panel B — Changes in price of X

Shifting the Budget Line

If money income (M) or the price ratio (P_x/P_y) changes, the budget line must change. Panel A of Figure 6.6 shows the effect of changes in income. Begin with the original budget line shown in Figure 6.4, AB, which corresponds to $1,000 money income and prices of X and Y of $5 and $10, respectively. Next let money income increase to $1,200, holding the prices of X and Y constant. Since the prices do not change, the slope of the budget line remains the same ($-1/2$). But since money income increases, the vertical intercept (M/P_y) increases (shifts upward) to 120 (= $1,200/$100). That is, if the consumer now spends the entire income on good Y, 20 more units of Y can be purchased than was previously the case. The horizontal intercept (M/P_x) also increases, to 240 (= $1,200/$5). The result of an increase in income is, therefore, a parallel shift in the budget line from AB to RN. The increase in income increases the set of combinations of the goods that can be purchased.

Alternatively, begin once more with budget line AB and then let money income decrease to $800. In this case the set of possible combinations of goods decreases. The vertical and horizontal intercepts decrease to 80 (= $800/$10) and 160 (= $800/$5), respectively, causing a parallel shift in the budget line to FZ, with intercepts of 80 and 160.

Panel B shows the effect of changes in the price of good X. Begin as before with the original budget line AB and then let the price of X fall from $5 to $4 per unit. Since M/P_y does not change, the vertical intercept remains at B (100 units of Y). However, when P_x decreases, the absolute value of the slope (P_x/P_y) falls to 4/10 (= $4/$10). In this case, the budget line becomes less steep. After the price of X falls, more X can be purchased if the entire money income is spent on X. Thus the horizontal intercept increases from 200 to 250 units of X (= \$1,000/\$4). In Panel B the budget line pivots (or rotates) from AB to AD.

An increase in the price of good X to \$8 causes the budget line to pivot backward, from AB to AC. The intercept on the horizontal axis decreases to 125 (= \$1,000/\$8). When P_x increases to \$8, the absolute value of the slope of the line, P_x/P_y, increases to 8/10 (= \$8/\$10). The budget line becomes steeper when P_x rises, while the vertical intercept remains constant.

5 **Relation** An increase (decrease) in money income causes a parallel outward (backward) shift in the budget line. An increase (decrease) in the price of X causes the budget line to pivot backward (outward) around the original vertical intercept.

6.4 UTILITY MAXIMIZATION

To this point we have set forth the tools needed to analyze consumer choice. The budget line shows all bundles of commodities that are available to the consumer, given the limited income and market-determined prices. The indifference map shows the preference ordering of all conceivable bundles of goods. In order to make marketing decisions, managers need to know how consumers choose the bundle of goods and services they actually purchase from all the possible bundles that they could purchase. Managers should be aware of the consumer-choice process when estimating the demand for their firms' products, forecasting future demand, and making advertising decisions. We will now use these tools to show how consumers choose, from all possible combinations of goods, the combination that yields the highest level of utility.

Maximizing Utility Subject to a Limited Money Income[3]

We will illustrate the maximization process graphically with the use of a rather far-fetched example. Joan Johnson is a young, overworked, underpaid management trainee working for a large corporation. Johnson's monthly food budget is \$400, which, because she works such long hours, is spent only on pizzas and burgers. The price of a pizza is \$8, and the price of a burger is \$4. The water, with which she washes down the burgers and pizzas, is free. Johnson's task is to determine the combination of pizzas and burgers that yields the highest level of utility possible from the \$400 food budget at the given prices.

The maximization process is shown graphically in Figure 6.7. Indifference curves I through IV represent a portion of Johnson's indifference map between pizzas, plotted along the vertical axis, and burgers, plotted along the horizontal axis. Her budget line, from 50 pizzas to 100 burgers, shows all combinations of the two fast foods that Johnson can consume during a month. If she spends the entire \$400 on pizzas at \$8 each, she can consume 50 pizzas. If she spends the entire \$400 on burgers at \$4 each, she can consume 100 burgers. Or she can

[3]A mathematical approach to constrained utility maximization is provided in the appendix to this chapter.

FIGURE 6.7
Constrained Utility Maximization

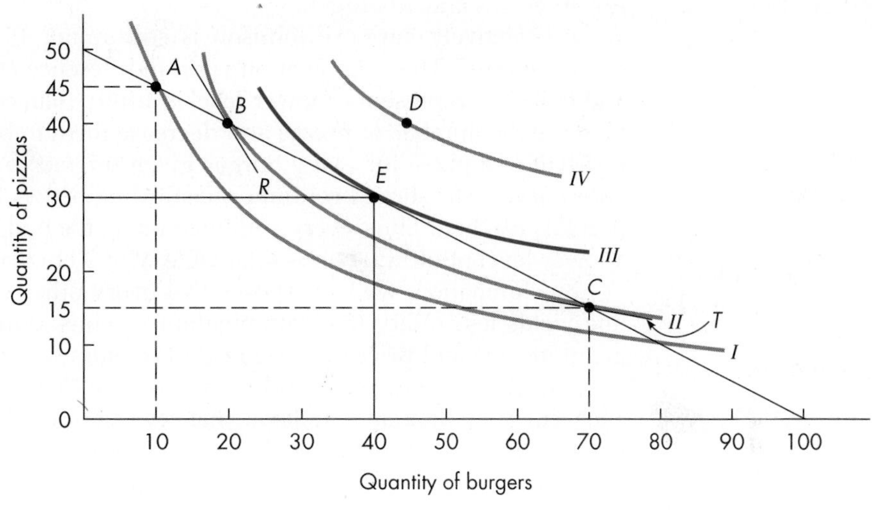

consume any other combination on the line. The absolute value of the slope of the budget line is the price of burgers divided by the price of pizzas, or $P_B/P_P =$ \$4/\$8 = 1/2. This indicates that to consume one additional \$4 burger, Johnson must give up half of an \$8 pizza. Alternatively, one more pizza can be bought at a cost of two burgers.

As is clear from the graph, the highest possible level of utility is reached when Johnson purchases 30 pizzas and 40 burgers a month. This combination is represented by point *E,* at which the budget line is tangent to indifference curve *III.* Many other combinations of the two fast foods, such as 40 pizzas and 45 burgers at point *D* on indifference curve *IV,* are preferable to the combination at *E,* but these other combinations cannot be purchased at the given prices and the \$400 income. For example, 40 pizzas and 45 burgers would cost \$500. All such bundles lie outside Johnson's budget constraint.

Johnson can purchase many combinations along her budget line other than the one at point *E.* These other combinations all lie on lower indifference curves and are therefore less preferred. Consider the combination at point *A,* consisting of 45 pizzas and 10 burgers. This combination can be purchased with the \$400 income but, because it is on indifference curve *I,* it clearly gives a lower level of utility than combination *E* on indifference curve *III.* If Johnson is consuming the combination at point *A,* she can increase the number of burgers, decrease the number of pizzas at the rate of one more burger for one-half less pizza, and move down the budget line. This substitution leads to higher and higher levels of utility—for example, 40 pizzas and 20 burgers (combination *B*) are on indifference curve *II* and therefore provide more utility than combination *A* on curve *I.* Johnson should not stop at *B.* She should continue substituting pizzas for burgers until point *E* on curve *III* is attained. Thus, every combination on the budget line above point E represents a lower level of utility than can be attained by consuming 30 pizzas and 40 burgers.

Alternatively, suppose Johnson is consuming 15 pizzas and 70 burgers—combination C. This combination is on indifference curve *II*, which is below *III* and therefore represents a lower level of utility than combination E. Johnson can increase the number of pizzas and decrease the number of burgers at the rate of one-half of a pizza for every burger given up and can move to higher indifference curves. She should continue substituting pizzas for burgers until combination E is reached. Thus, every combination on the budget line below E represents a lower level of utility than is attainable with 30 pizzas and 40 burgers.

By elimination, we have shown that every other combination on the budget line yields less utility than combination E. Thus, utility is maximized with the given income and prices when Johnson consumes at point E, the point at which the budget line is tangent to indifference curve *III*, the highest attainable indifference curve. It therefore follows that the highest attainable level of utility is reached by consuming the combination at which the marginal rate of substitution (the absolute value of the slope of the indifference curve) equals the price ratio (the absolute value of the slope of the budget line).

We can use this relation between the *MRS* and the price ratio to provide more insight into why every other combination on the budget line yields less utility than the combination at point E. Consider again the combination at B, with 40 pizzas and 20 burgers. At this combination, the *MRS* (the absolute value of the slope of indifference curve *II*) is greater than the absolute value of the slope of the budget line, $P_B/P_P = 1/2$. Suppose the *MRS* at B is 2 (the slope of tangent R equals 2). This means that Johnson, in order to obtain one more burger, is *just willing* to exchange two pizzas. Exchanging two pizzas for one more burger leaves Johnson at the same level of utility—she is made no better and no worse off by this exchange. If Johnson could get one burger and give up *less* than two pizzas, she would be better off. Since burgers cost only half as much as pizzas, the market allows Johnson to obtain one more burger while only giving up half a pizza. Giving up half a pizza to get one more burger is a much more favorable exchange rate than the exchange rate she is just willing to make (giving up two pizzas for one burger). Thus, Johnson moves to a higher indifference curve by trading only half a pizza for an additional burger.

As you can see, at every other combination on the budget line above E, the absolute value of the slope of the indifference curve—the *MRS*—must be greater than the absolute value of the slope of the budget line. Therefore, at each of these combinations, Johnson, by the same argument, can raise her utility by adding a burger and giving up less pizza than she would be willing to give up in order to gain the additional burger. Thus, all combinations above E, at which the *MRS* is greater than 1/2, leads to less utility than combination E.

At any combination on the budget line below E, the *MRS* is obviously less than the price ratio. Suppose the *MRS* at combination C is 1/10 (the absolute value of the slope of tangent T equals 1/10), meaning that Johnson is just willing to give up 10 burgers in order to obtain an additional pizza. Since the absolute value of the slope of the budget line is 1/2, she can obtain the additional pizza by giving up only two burgers. She clearly becomes better off by sacrificing the two burgers for the additional pizza.

At every point on the budget line below *E*, the *MRS* is less than 1/2, and Johnson can obtain the additional pizza by giving up fewer burgers than the amount she is just willing to give up. Thus, she should continue reducing the number of burgers and increasing the number of pizzas until utility is maximized at *E* with 30 pizzas and 40 burgers. Again we have shown that all combinations other than *E* yield less utility from the given income.

The marginal rate of substitution is the rate at which the consumer is *willing* to substitute one good for another. The price ratio is the rate at which the consumer is *able* to substitute one good for another in the market. Thus, equilibrium occurs where the rate at which the consumer is willing to substitute equals the rate at which he or she is able to substitute. We can summarize the concept of consumer utility maximization with the following:

Principle A consumer maximizes utility subject to a limited money income at the combination of goods for which the indifference curve is just tangent to the budget line. At this combination, the marginal rate of substitution (the absolute value of the slope of the indifference curve) is equal to the price ratio (the absolute value of the slope of the budget line):

6 7 8

$$-\frac{\Delta Y}{\Delta X} = MRS = \frac{P_X}{P_Y}$$

Marginal Utility Interpretation of Equilibrium

As noted in the beginning of this chapter, the theory of constrained utility maximization is a straightforward application of the theory of constrained maximization developed in Chapter 4. Recall from Chapter 4 that a decision maker attains the highest level of benefits possible within a given cost constraint when the marginal benefit per dollar spent on each activity is the same and the cost constraint is met.

As shown above, a consumer attains the highest level of utility from a given income when the marginal rate of substitution for any two goods, say, goods *X* and *Y*, is equal to the ratio of the prices of the two goods: that is, $-\Delta Y/\Delta X = MRS = P_x/P_y$. Recall that the marginal rate of substitution is equal to the ratio of the marginal utilities of the two goods. Therefore, utility-maximizing equilibrium occurs when the entire income is spent and

$$MRS = -\frac{\Delta Y}{\Delta X} = \frac{MU_x}{MU_y} = \frac{P_x}{P_y}$$

or, by rearranging this equation,

$$\frac{MU_x}{P_x} = \frac{MU_y}{P_y}$$

This second expression means that the marginal utility per dollar spent on the last unit of good *X* equals the marginal utility per dollar spent on the last unit of good *Y*. For example, if $MU_x = 10$ and $P_x = \$2$, $MU_x/P_x = 5$, meaning that one

ILLUSTRATION 6.2

"We're Number One" (in *MU/P*) and That's Not Bad

In 1990, Buick advertised extensively that a survey of over 26,000 new-car buyers had revealed that Buick was the only American car line ranked in the top 10 in initial quality—according to owner-reported problems during the first 90 days. Buick featured in its ads a list of the top-10 automobiles in the survey, in which it was ranked fifth: behind Lexus, Mercedes-Benz, Toyota, and Infiniti and ahead of Honda, Nissan, Acura, BMW, and Mazda. All nine of these other car lines are Japanese or German.

In his nationally syndicated column, "High Five Is Goodbye Wave, not the Symbol of Quality," August 23, 1990, columnist George Will somewhat berated Buick for bragging about *only* being fifth. He stated that the "We're Number One" boasts of winning college football players and their fans may be "mistaken, and the passion may be disproportionate to the achievement, but at least it is better than chanting 'We're Number Five.' "

Mr. Will noted that such ads imply, "Don't expect us to measure up to the big boys—the ones overseas." He wanted Americans to become "impatient and censorious about lax standards (We're Number 5) that are producing pandemic shoddiness in everything from cars to art to second graders' homework." Mr. Will ended his column: "Americans would feel better, and might be more inclined to buy Buick, if they saw an ad reprinting the list above, but with a text that says: 'Fifth place is not nearly good enough for Americans to brag about. And until we do better, we apologize!' "

Mr. Will may well have been correct that many U.S. firms were not producing products up to the quality standards of many foreign firms. We want to point out, however, that his criticism of Buick's boast of being number five as indicative of shoddy American quality may not have been quite valid. In fact, it may be great to be "Number Five."

The annual auto issue of *Consumer Reports,* April 1990, gave the following list prices of the top-10 automobile lines for their medium-size models, the category of most Buick models:

1. Lexus $35,000
2. Mercedes-Benz $48,000 (avg.)
3. Toyota $21,500
4. Infiniti $38,000

additional dollar spent on X (which buys one-half of a \$2 unit of X) increases utility by 5 units, or one less dollar spent on X decreases utility by 5 units.

To see why marginal utilities per dollar spent must be equal for the last unit consumed of both goods, suppose the condition did not hold and

$$\frac{MU_x}{P_x} < \frac{MU_y}{P_y}$$

The marginal utility per dollar spent on good X is less than the marginal utility per dollar spent on Y. The consumer can take dollars away from X and spend them on Y. As long as the inequality holds, the lost utility from each dollar taken away from X is less than the added utility from each additional dollar spent on Y, and the consumer continues to substitute Y for X. As the consumption of X decreases, we would expect the marginal utility of X to rise. As Y in-

5. Buick $15,000 (avg.)
6. Honda $14,500 (compact)
7. Nissan $18,000
8. Acura $26,000
9. BMW $37,000 (avg.)
10. Mazda $25,000

Buick was priced lower than all the other cars except the Honda Accord, a compact car listed because Honda did not produce a medium-size car. This Honda, which was ranked below Buick, was only $500 less than Buick despite being a smaller car. All the other models were priced higher, some more than double. Of the cars ranked above Buick, Toyota's price was 40 percent higher, and the prices of the other three were two to three times Buick's price.

Following the approach used in the theory of consumer behavior, consider the quality-per-dollar cost of a car:

$$\frac{\text{Quality of the brand}}{\text{Price of the brand}}$$

For the top-ranked automobile, Lexus, to have more quality per dollar, that is,

$$\frac{\text{Quality of Lexus}}{\text{Price of Lexus}} > \frac{\text{Quality of Buick}}{\text{Price of Buick}}$$

Lexus would have to have $2\frac{1}{3}$ more or better quality than Buick, because its price was $2\frac{1}{3}$ higher. Mercedes-Benz would have to have 3.2 times the quality of Buick; Infiniti, 2.5 times the quality; and Toyota, 1.4 times Buick's quality. Because the cars ranked 7 through 10 were higher-priced and ranked lower in quality, they could not have more quality per dollar. Since Buick's price was only 3 percent higher than Honda's, Buick would have to have only a bit more than 3 percent more quality to be ranked higher in quality per dollar.

Based upon a measure of quality per dollar of cost, Buick could easily have been ranked higher than fifth. Quite possibly, it was really number one, and should not have been disparaged. Perhaps Buick should not have apologized in its ads as suggested but, instead, should have said, "We're Number One (or maybe Number Two) in quality per dollar."

"High Five Is Goodbye Wave, not the Symbol of Quality," George Will, Aug. 23, 1990, *The San Diego Tribune,* p. B-11.

creases, its marginal utility would decline. The consumer continues substituting until MU_x/P_x equals MU_y/P_y.

A simple numerical example should make this concept more concrete: Suppose a customer with an income of $140 is spending it all on 20 units of X priced at $4 each and 30 units of Y priced at $2 each: ($4 × 20) + ($2 × 30) = $140. Further suppose that the marginal utility of the last unit of X is 20 and the marginal utility of the last unit of Y is 16. The ratio of marginal utilities per dollar spent on X and Y is

$$\frac{MU_x}{P_x} = \frac{20}{4} = 5 < 8 = \frac{16}{2} = \frac{MU_y}{P_y}$$

The consumer should reallocate spending on X and Y because it is possible to increase utility while still spending only $140. To see how this can be done, let the consumer spend one more dollar on Y. Buying another dollar's worth of good Y causes utility to increase by 8 units.[4] In order to stay within the \$140 budget, the consumer must also reduce spending on good X by one dollar. Spending one dollar less on good X causes utility to fall by 5 units. Since the consumer loses 5 units of utility from reduced consumption of good X but gains 8 units of utility from the increased consumption of good Y, the consumer experiences a net gain in utility of 3 units while still spending only \$140. Note that it is not marginal utility per se that matters; it is marginal utility per dollar. In this example, the marginal utility of X was higher than that of Y. But the consumer is made better off by giving up some X and buying more Y.

The consumer should continue transferring dollars from X to Y as long as $MU_x/P_x < MU_y/P_y$. Because MU_x increases as less X is purchased and MU_y decreases as more Y is purchased, the consumer will reach utility-maximizing equilibrium when $MU_x/P_x = MU_y/P_y$, and no further changes should be made.

Alternatively, if

$$\frac{MU_x}{P_x} > \frac{MU_y}{P_y}$$

the marginal utility per dollar spent on X is greater than the marginal utility per dollar spent on Y. The consumer takes dollars away from Y and buys additional X, continuing to substitute until the equality holds.

9 **Principle** To obtain maximum satisfaction from a limited money income, a consumer allocates money income so that the marginal utility per dollar spent on each good is the same for all commodities purchased, and all income is spent.

Finding the Optimal Bundle of Hot Dogs and Cokes

The following numerical example will illustrate the points made in this section. Suppose your boss decides that you have been working too hard and gives you the rest of the day off and a ticket to the afternoon baseball game. After getting seated at the stadium, you discover that you have only \$20, and the concessionaire won't take American Express (or Visa, for that matter). Hot dogs and Cokes are the only snack items you plan to consume while at the game, but it's a hot day, you missed lunch, and \$20 is not going to be enough money to buy all the Cokes and hot dogs you would want to consume. The only rational thing to do is to maximize your utility subject to your \$20 budget constraint.

On the back of your baseball program you make a list of the marginal utility you expect to receive from various levels of hot dog and Coke consumption. You then divide the marginal utilities by the prices of hot dogs and Cokes, \$2.50 and \$2, respectively. The back of your baseball program looks like this:

[4]Even though one extra dollar of expenditure on Y allows the consumer to purchase only half a unit of Y, and producers may be willing to sell only integer amounts (i.e., you can't buy half a burger at most fast-food restaurants), Y is in fact measuring the *rate* of consumption of good Y per unit of time and can include fractional units. If, for example, 12 burgers are consumed weekly, the number of burgers consumed daily is a fraction—1.71 (= 12/7) burgers per day.

Units per game	Marginal utility of hot dogs (MU_H)	$\frac{MU_H}{P_H}$	Marginal utility of Cokes (MU_C)	$\frac{MU_C}{P_C}$
1	20	8	60	30
2	15	6	40	20
3	12.5	5	20	10
4	10	4	16	8
5	7.5	3	8	4
6	5	2	4	2

Using this information, you can now figure out how to get the most satisfaction from consuming hot dogs and Cokes, given your budget constraint.

Should you buy a Coke or a hot dog first? The first unit of Coke increases total utility by 30 units for each dollar spent (on the first Coke), while the first hot dog increases total utility by only 8 units per dollar spent (on the first hot dog). You buy the first Coke and have $18 left. After finishing the first Coke, you consider whether to buy the first hot dog or the second Coke. Since 8 (= MU_H/P_H) < 20 (= MU_C/P_C), you buy the second Coke and have $16 left. Using similar reasoning, you buy the third Coke.

The fourth Coke and the first hot dog both increase total utility by 8 units per dollar spent. You buy both of them and note that the marginal utilities per dollar spent both equal 8. This is not yet optimal, however, because you have spent only $10.50 (one hot dog and four Cokes). You continue using marginal analysis until you end up buying four hot dogs and five Cokes, at which $MU_H/P_H = 4 = MU_C/P_C$. You have spent the entire $20 on the four hot dogs and five Cokes. No other combination of Cokes and hot dogs that you could have

10 purchased for $20 would have yielded more total utility.

A General Graphical Summary of Consumer Utility Maximization

Figure 6.8 summarizes graphically the fundamental principles of utility maximization under a budget constraint. A consumer purchases two goods, X and Y, with a given income, M. The prices of X and Y are, respectively, P_x and P_y. The budget line is the line AB, from M/P_y (the maximum amount of Y attainable if no X is purchased) to M/P_x (the maximum amount of X attainable if no Y is purchased). The slope of the budget line is $-P_x/P_y$, which gives the rate at which X can be substituted for Y in the market, holding the level of spending constant.

The marginal rate of substitution measures the number of units of Y the consumer is willing to give up per additional unit of X, holding the level of utility constant. MRS is equal to the absolute value of the slope of the indifference curve:

$$MRS = -\Delta Y/\Delta X = -\text{ slope of line tangent to indifference curve}$$

The highest level of utility with the given budget line is achieved with $\overline{X}$ units of X and $\overline{Y}$ units of Y. At this combination, budget line AB is tangent to indifference curve II at point E, which is the highest curve with at least one combination

FIGURE 6.8
Utility Maximization with a Budget Constraint

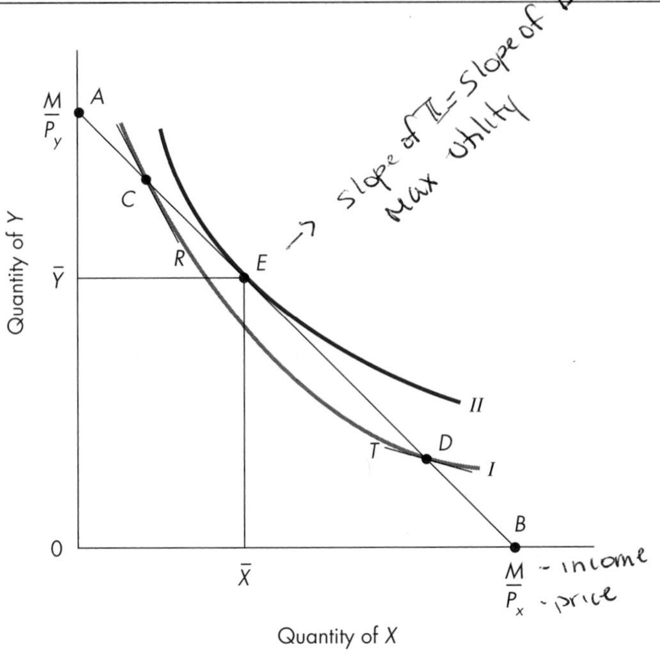

on the budget line. At this combination, the slope of the indifference curve equals the slope of the budget line:

$$MRS = P_x/P_y$$

and

$$P_x\overline{X} + P_y\overline{Y} = M$$

At any combination on the budget line above the point of equilibrium (point *E*), the indifference curve through that combination crosses the budget line from above, and thus is steeper than the budget line. This implies

$$MRS > P_x/P_y$$

At point *C*, for example, tangent line *R* is steeper than the budget line, so $MRS > P_x/P_y$ at this point. If the consumer gives up *MRS* units of *Y* to get an extra unit of *X*, the consumer is made no better (or worse) off. In market transactions, the consumer must give up only P_x/P_y units of *Y* to get one more unit of *X*. Consequently, buying one unit more of *X* and P_x/P_y fewer units of *Y* in the marketplace leaves the consumer on the budget line, while increasing utility because the consumer gives up less *Y* than the amount that would leave the consumer just indifferent. The consumer would continue to give up *Y* and increase *X*, moving down the budget line, until the point of tangency is reached.

At any combination on the budget line below the equilibrium combination E, the budget line is steeper than the indifference curve. At point D, for example, the budget line is steeper than tangent line T. At points on AB below E, $MRS < P_x/P_y$. If the consumer gives up one unit of X, P_x/P_y more units of Y can be purchased in the market and still satisfy the budget constraint. The consumer is just willing to give up one unit of X in exchange for MRS additional units of Y. Buying one less unit of X and P_x/P_y more units of Y leaves the consumer on the budget line, while increasing consumer satisfaction because the consumer gets more Y than the amount that would leave the consumer just indifferent. The consumer would continue to give up X and increase Y, moving up the budget line, until the point of tangency is reached.

The marginal utility interpretation of consumer equilibrium provides an alternative way to show that equilibrium must occur at point E by comparing the marginal utilities per dollar spent on each of the two goods X and Y. Since MRS equals MU_x/MU_y along an indifference curve, the equilibrium condition can also be expressed as

$$\frac{MU_x}{P_x} = \frac{MU_y}{P_y}$$

This equilibrium condition implies that the marginal utility per dollar spent on the last unit of each good is the same.

At any combination on the budget line above point E, $MRS > P_x/P_y$ and hence,

$$\frac{MU_x}{P_x} > \frac{MU_y}{P_y}$$

Good X gives the consumer greater additional utility per dollar spent than does good Y. By spending one more dollar on good X, the consumer gains MU_x/P_x additional units of utility. In order to remain on the budget line, the consumer must spend one less dollar on good Y, causing utility to fall by MU_y/P_y units. Since $MU_x/P_x > MU_y/P_y$, the net effect of reallocating a dollar of the budget from Y to X is an increase in utility. The consumer continues to reallocate spending to good X away from good Y until the marginal utilities per dollar spent are equal for the last units consumed of X and Y. This occurs at point E.

At any combination on the budget line below point E, $MRS < P_x/P_y$, and hence,

$$\frac{MU_x}{P_x} < \frac{MU_y}{P_y}$$

Good Y gives the consumer more additional utility per dollar spent than does good X. By spending one more dollar on good Y, the consumer gains MU_y/P_y additional units of utility. In order to remain on the budget line, the consumer must spend one less dollar on good X, causing utility to fall by MU_x/P_x units. Since $MU_x/P_x < MU_y/P_y$, the net effect of reallocating a dollar of the budget from X to Y is an increase in utility. The consumer continues to reallocate spending to good Y away from good X until the marginal utilities per dollar spent are equal for the last units consumed of X and Y. Again, this occurs at point E.

Thus far, for graphical purposes, we have assumed that the consumer purchases only two goods. The analysis is easily extended, although not graphically, to any number of goods. Since the above equilibrium conditions must apply to *any* two goods in a consumer's consumption bundle, they must apply to all goods in the bundle. Therefore, if a consumer purchases N goods, $X_1, X_2, X_3, \ldots, X_N$ with prices $P_1, P_2, P_3, \ldots, P_N$ from a given income M, utility maximization requires

$$P_1X_1 + P_2X_2 + P_3X_3 + \cdots + P_NX_N = M$$

and

$$-\frac{\Delta X_i}{\Delta X_j} = MRS = \frac{P_j}{P_i}$$

for any two goods, X_i and X_j. Alternatively, in terms of marginal utilities per dollar spent,

$$\frac{MU_1}{P_1} = \frac{MU_2}{P_2} = \frac{MU_3}{P_3} = \cdots = \frac{MU_N}{P_N}$$

In this way the maximization principle is expanded to cover any number of goods.

Before ending this section, we should note that we have assumed thus far that a consumer purchases some positive amount of each good considered. We have not analyzed why someone chooses not to buy any amount of some goods. This can be easily shown within the framework of the theory. Suppose that in the previous discussion all income is spent on goods 1 through N but the consumer chooses to purchase zero units of some good, Z. Then it must be the case that the marginal utility per dollar that would have been spent on the *first* unit of Z is less than the marginal utility per dollar spent on the last unit of all the other goods purchased:

$$MU_Z/P_Z < MU_1/P_1 = MU_2/P_2 = \cdots = MU_N/P_N$$

The first unit of good Z was not worth taking dollars away from the goods that are purchased. Perhaps if the price of Z goes down, this person might choose to buy some.

6.5 AN INDIVIDUAL CONSUMER'S DEMAND CURVE

Of major interest to a manager is how consumer choice or consumer behavior relates to the demand for a product. We can now use the theory of consumer utility maximization to derive a demand curve for a consumer. In this way we will provide a complete analysis of the underpinnings of demand, which were briefly discussed in Chapter 2. Recall from Chapter 2 that demand was defined as the quantity of a good the consumer is willing and able to purchase at each price in a list of prices, holding other things constant. You have just seen that

FIGURE 6.9
Deriving a Demand Curve

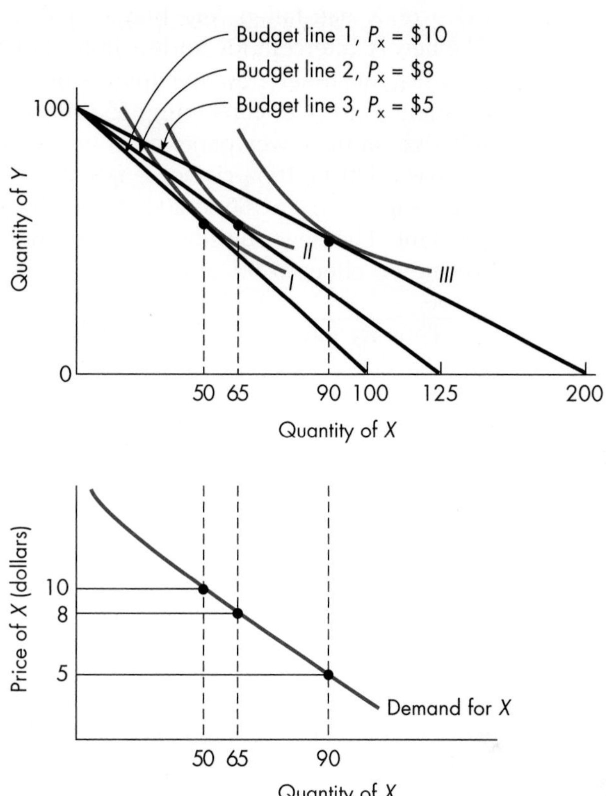

consumers maximize utility when the rate at which they are *willing* to substitute one good for another just equals the rate at which they are *able* to substitute. It would seem, therefore, that the two theories are closely related, and they are. The theory of demand can be easily developed from the theory of consumer behavior.

We use Figure 6.9 to show this relation and how an individual consumer's demand curve is obtained. Begin with a money income of $1,000 and prices of good *X* and good *Y* both equal to $10. The corresponding budget line is given by budget line 1, from 100*Y* to 100*X*, in the upper panel of the figure. From the previous analysis, you know the consumer maximizes utility where budget line 1 is tangent to indifference curve *I*, consuming 50 units of *X*. Thus, when income is $1,000, one point on this consumer's demand for *X* is $10 and 50 units of *X*. This point is illustrated on the price-quantity graph in the lower panel of Figure 6.9.

Following the definition of demand, we hold money income and the price of the other good, *Y*, constant, while letting the price of *X* fall from $10 to $8. The new budget line is the less steep budget line 2. Since money income and the price of Y remain constant, the vertical intercept does not change, but because the price of X has fallen, the budget line must pivot outward along the X-axis. The new X-intercept for budget line 2 is 125 (= \$1,000/\$8). With this new budget line, the consumer now maximizes utility where budget line 2 is tangent to indifference curve *II*, consuming 65 units of X. Thus another point on the demand schedule in the lower panel must be \$8 and 65 units of X.

Next, letting the price of X fall again, this time to \$5, the new budget line is budget line 3, from 100 to 200. Again the price of Y and money income are held constant. The new equilibrium is on indifference curve *III*. At the price \$5, the consumer chooses 90 units of X, another point on this consumer's demand curve.

Thus we have derived the following demand schedule for good X:

Price	Quantity demanded
\$10	50
8	65
5	90

This schedule, with other points so generated, is graphed as a demand curve in price-quantity space in the lower part of Figure 6.9. This demand curve is downward-sloping. As the price of X falls, the quantity of X the consumer is willing and able to purchase increases, following the rule of demand. Furthermore, we followed the definition of demand, holding money income and the price of the other good (goods) constant. Thus an individual's demand for a good is derived from a series of utility-maximizing equilibrium points. We used only three such points, but we could easily have used more in order to obtain more points on the demand curve. We can summarize this section with the following:

11 **Principle** The demand curve of an individual for a specific commodity relates utility-maximizing equilibrium quantities purchased to market prices, holding constant money income and the prices of all other goods. The slope of the demand curve illustrates the law of demand: quantity demanded varies inversely with price.

6.6 SUBSTITUTION AND INCOME EFFECTS

As emphasized in Chapter 2, when the price of a good decreases, consumers tend to substitute more of that good for other goods, since the good in question has become cheaper relative to other goods. Conversely, when the price of a good rises, it becomes more expensive relative to other goods, and consumers tend to substitute some additional amounts of the other goods for some of the good with the now higher price. This is called the *substitution effect.*

There is also another effect, called the *income effect.* If a good becomes cheaper, people who are consuming that good are made better off. Since the price of that good has fallen, people can consume the same amount as before, but because of the reduced price, they have some income left over which can be spent on the good with the now lower price and on other goods as well. The opposite happens when the price of a good increases. Consumers are worse off in the sense that they now cannot afford the bundle they originally chose. They must consume less of the now more expensive good, less of the other good, or less of both. Before presenting a complete graphical analysis, we will begin with a simple numerical demonstration of the two effects.

A Numerical Illustration

We begin this illustration with a consumer of two goods, *X* and *Y*; with prices of P_x = \$10 and P_y = \$20; and with an income of \$500. The consumer is in utility-maximizing equilibrium, spending \$500 on 20 units of *X* and 15 units of *Y*. In equilibrium the marginal utility of the last unit of *X* is 60, and the marginal utility of the last unit of *Y* is 120. Thus in equilibrium

$$P_xX + P_yY = (\$10 \times 20) + (\$20 \times 15) = \$500$$

and

$$MU_x/P_x = 60/\$10 = 6 = MU_y/P_y = \$120/20 = 6$$

Next let the price of *X* fall to \$5. Now, at the original combination of *X* and *Y*,

$$P_xX + P_yY = (\$5 \times 20) + (\$20 \times 15) = 400 < \$500$$

and

$$MU_x/P_x = 60/\$5 = 12 > MU_y/P_y = 120/\$20 = 6$$

This consumer is no longer in equilibrium. The original combination of goods costs \$100 less than income, so there is leftover income to spend on more of both goods. Furthermore, the marginal utility per dollar spent on the last unit of *X*, 12, is now greater than the marginal utility per dollar spent on the last unit of *Y*, 6. On the basis of the previous analysis, dollars should be taken from *Y* and added to *X* until the marginal utility per dollar is the same for both goods. The first effect of the price decrease is an income effect: the consumer is better off and can buy more of both goods. The second effect is a substitution effect: the marginal utility per dollar is not the same for the two goods, so the consumer should take dollars away from *Y* and buy more *X* to return to equilibrium. While we have examined these two effects separately, a consumer would carry out the two types of reallocation simultaneously.

For a price increase, the income and substitution effects are similar to those just discussed for a price decrease, but they go in the opposite direction. For example, if the price of *X* increases, the consumer cannot buy the original bundle of goods with the \$500 income, so is made worse off. Also, the marginal utility per dollar spent on the last unit of *X* is now less than the marginal utility per dollar spent on the last unit of *Y*. The consumer should take dollars away from *X* and spend them on *Y* until the marginal utility per dollar is the same for both goods. We will now analyze each effect in turn with a slightly more formal
12 graphical analysis.

FIGURE 6.10
The Substitution Effect

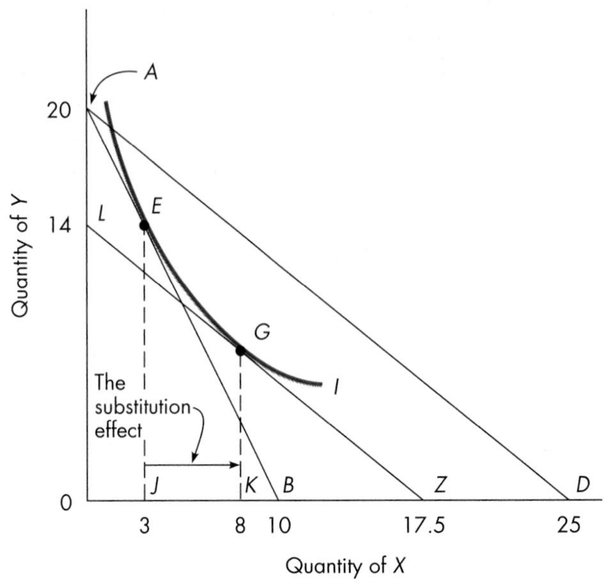

Substitution Effect

substitution effect The change in the consumption of a good that would result if the consumer remained on the same indifference curve after the price of the good changed.

We begin the analysis of the substitution effect with a precise definition. The **substitution effect** is the change in the consumption of a good that would result if the consumer remained on the original indifference curve after the price of the good changes.

We develop the substitution effect formally in Figure 6.10. Begin with the original budget line *AB*, which corresponds to money income of \$150, P_y = \$7.50, and P_x = \$15. The consumer is originally in equilibrium where budget line *AB* is tangent to indifference curve *I* at three units of *X* (point *E*). Now let the price of *X* decrease to \$6 so that the new budget line pivots outward to *AD*, because \$150/\$6 = 25.

The consumer, being better off because more choices are now available, can move to an indifference curve higher than *I*. But the substitution effect concerns changes along the *same* indifference curve. To this end, we theoretically take away just enough of the consumer's income to force a new budget line, with the same slope as *AD* to reflect the lower price of *X*, to become tangent to the original indifference curve *I*. This is shown as the parallel shift of the budget line *AD* to the adjusted budget line *LZ*. It is important to note that the slope of *LZ*, 4/5 (= \$6/\$7.50), reflects the new, lower price of *X*, but is associated with a lower money income than is the original budget line *AB*. Since budget line *LZ* is tangent to indifference curve *I* at point *G*, the consumer now chooses to purchase eight units of *X*. Note that the consumer's adjustment from point *E* to point *G*, which takes place along the original indifference curve *I*, is a theoretically conceived (or hypothetical) adjustment in consumption. It is the change in the optimal consumption that would occur when the price of *X* relative to the price of *Y* falls from 2 (= 15/7.50) to .8 (= 6/7.50) *and* the consumer is forced by a *hypothetical* reduction in income to remain on the same indifference curve.

The substitution effect is shown as the distance *JK* (five additional units of *X*), resulting from the movement along *I* from *E* to *G*. It is clear that this effect is negative—a decrease in price must result in an increase in consumption of the good when utility is held constant. This must always be the case, given the shape of indifference curves. When the price of *X* falls from $15 to $6, the budget line becomes flatter; so the budget line, after taking away some income, must be tangent to the original indifference curve at a point with a less steep slope (*MRS*) than was the case at the original equilibrium. This can occur only with increased consumption of *X*.

Principle The substitution effect is the change in the consumption of a good after a change in its price, when the consumer is forced by a change in money income to consume at some point on the original indifference curve. Considering the substitution effect only, the amount of the good consumed must vary inversely with its price.

Income Effect

income effect
The change in the consumption of a good resulting strictly from a change in purchasing power after the price of a good changes.

The direction of the income effect is not unambiguous, as was the case for the substitution effect. Before we analyze the income effect, let us define it. The **income effect** from a price change is the change in the consumption of a good resulting strictly from the change in purchasing power.

We noted earlier that a decrease in the price of a good makes a consumer of that good better off in the sense of being able to purchase the same bundle of goods and have income left over; that is, the consumer can move to a higher indifference curve. An increase in the price of a good makes a consumer worse off because he or she is unable to purchase the original bundle; that is, the consumer must move to a lower indifference curve. Since the consumer moves to a higher or lower indifference curve, depending upon the direction of the price change, and the substitution effect takes place along the original indifference curve, the income effect is simply the difference between the total effect of the price change—the movement from one indifference curve to another—and the substitution effect.

Figure 6.11 illustrates how to isolate the substitution and income effects for a decrease in the price of *X*. First consider (in Panel A) the case of a normal good. The consumer initially faces the budget line *AB* (M = $150, P_x = $15, and P_y = $7.50), and maximizes utility subject to budget line *AB* at point *E* on indifference curve *I*. Let the price of *X* fall from $15 to $6, so that the budget line pivots to *AD*. The new equilibrium is at point *F* on indifference curve *II*. The total effect of the price decrease is an increase in the consumption of *X* from 3 units to 12.

As explained earlier, the substitution effect is the change in consumption of *X* that would result if the consumer remained on the same indifference curve

FIGURE 6.11
Income and Substitution Effects: A Decrease in P_x

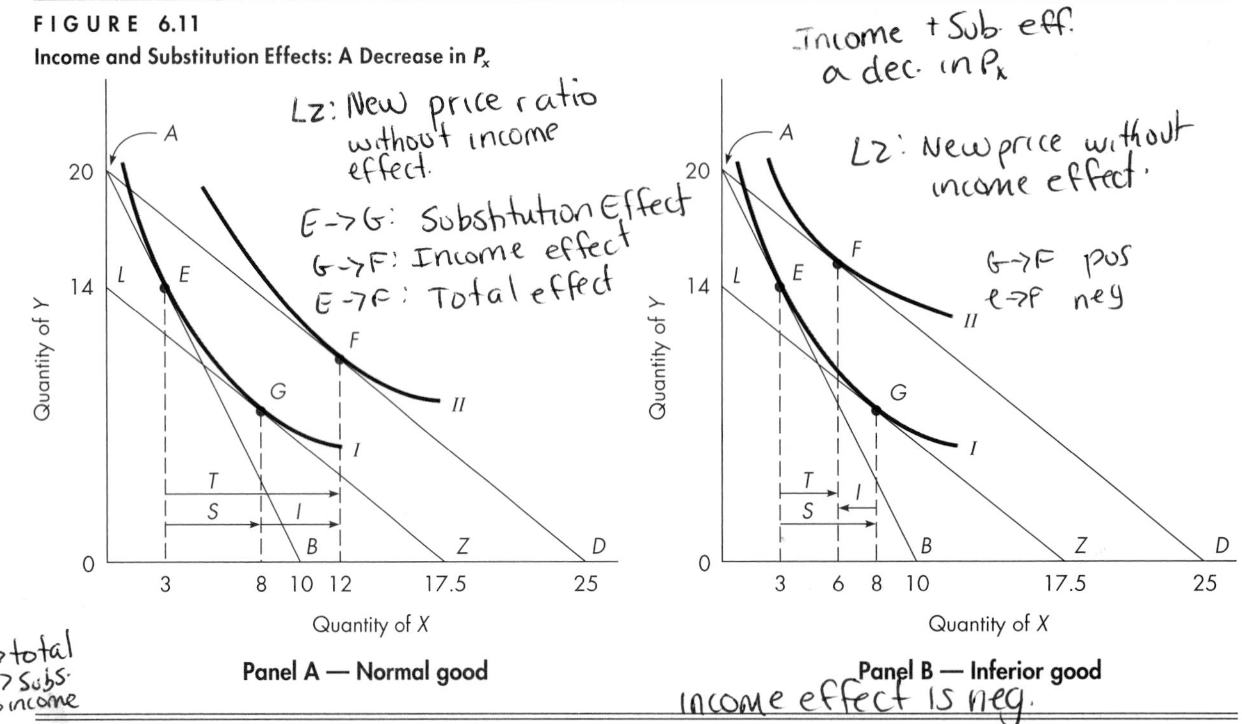

Panel A — Normal good

Panel B — Inferior good

after the change in price. At the new price ratio $P_x/P_y = \$6/\$7.50 = 0.8$, we again temporarily take away just enough income to keep the consumer on the original indifference curve. This reduction in income causes the budget line to shift downward to *LZ*. In this example, income must be reduced to \$105 (= \$7.50 × 14 = \$6 × 17.5) to isolate the substitution effect. On the adjusted budget line *LZ*, $MRS = P_x/P_y$ at point *G*. The substitution effect of the price *reduction* is an *increase* in consumption of *X* by 5 units. For the substitution effect alone, the price and consumption of *X* move in opposite directions.

Recall from Chapter 2 that consumption of a normal good increases when income increases, prices held constant. This is exactly what happens when the hypothetical reduction in income is restored and the budget line shifts from *LZ* back to *AD*. When the income that was hypothetically taken away to isolate the substitution effect is returned, the consumer increases the consumption of *X* by 4 units. You can see in Panel A that good *X* is a normal good because the increase in income from \$105 to \$150 (*LZ* to *AD*) causes consumption of *X* to increase from 8 to 12.

total effect
The sum of the substitution and income effects.

When the price of *X falls,* both the substitution effect and the income effect cause the consumer to purchase *more* of the good—the income effect reinforces the substitution effect. Both of these effects cause consumption of *X* to move in the opposite direction of the change in price. The **total effect** of the decrease in price is equal to the sum of the substitution and income effects:

$$\begin{array}{ccc} \text{Total effect of} \\ \text{price decrease} \end{array} = \begin{array}{c} \text{Substitution} \\ \text{effect} \end{array} + \begin{array}{c} \text{Income} \\ \text{effect} \end{array}$$

$$9 = 5 + 4$$

The situation is different for an inferior good. Recall from Chapter 2 that if a good is inferior, an increase in income (holding prices constant) causes less of the good to be consumed. The case of an inferior good is illustrated in Panel B of Figure 6.11. Begin, as before, with budget line *AB*. Equilibrium is at *E* on indifference curve *I* with 3 units of *X* being consumed. Let the price of *X* fall from \$15 to \$6, which causes the budget line to pivot outward to *AD*. The new equilibrium is at *F* on indifference curve *II*, with 6 units of *X* being consumed. The total effect of the price decrease is an increase of 3 units in the consumption of *X*.

In Panel B, the substitution effect is isolated in exactly the same way as in Panel A and is again equal to 5 units of *X*. Note that the substitution effect is greater than the total effect. It is apparent that the income effect has partially offset the substitution effect. This will always be true for inferior goods because the income effect for inferior goods moves in the opposite direction from the substitution effect. When the budget line moves back to *AD* from *LZ*, the increase in income causes the consumption of *X* to *fall* from 8 to 6 units of *X*, and thus the income effect is −2 units of *X*. The total effect of the decrease in the price of *X* is

$$\begin{array}{c} \text{Total effect of} \\ \text{price decrease} \end{array} = \begin{array}{c} \text{Substitution} \\ \text{effect} \end{array} + \begin{array}{c} \text{Income} \\ \text{effect} \end{array}$$

$$3 = 5 + (-2)$$

Figure 6.12 shows the substitution, income, and total effects for an increase in the price of good *X*. Panel A illustrates the case of a normal good. The initial budget line is *AR* ($M = \$60$, $P_x = \$2.40$, and $P_y = \$4$), and the consumer initially maximizes utility at point *E* on indifference curve *II*. When the price of *X* increases from \$2.40 to \$6, the budget line pivots to *AS* and the new equilibrium is at point *F* on indifference curve *I*. The substitution effect is isolated by temporarily increasing income to \$84 (the adjusted budget line is *LZ*). The substitution effect of the price *increase* is a *reduction* in the consumption of *X* by 5 units. When income is returned to \$60, the adjusted budget line shifts back to *AS*, and the consumer reduces consumption by 2 more units of *X*. The total effect of the increase in price is

$$\begin{array}{c} \text{Total effect of} \\ \text{price increase} \end{array} = \begin{array}{c} \text{Substitution} \\ \text{effect} \end{array} + \begin{array}{c} \text{Income} \\ \text{effect} \end{array}$$

$$-7 = -5 + (-2)$$

Note that the income and substitution effects reinforce each other since *X* is a normal good.

In Panel B, good *X* is inferior. The substitution effect is the same as in Panel A, but now the income effect partially offsets the substitution effect. When the budget line shifts backward from *LZ* to *AS*, income falls from \$84 to \$60, and consumption of the inferior good *X* increases from 5 to 6 units. The total effect of the increase in price is

FIGURE 6.12

Income and Substitution Effects: An Increase in P_x

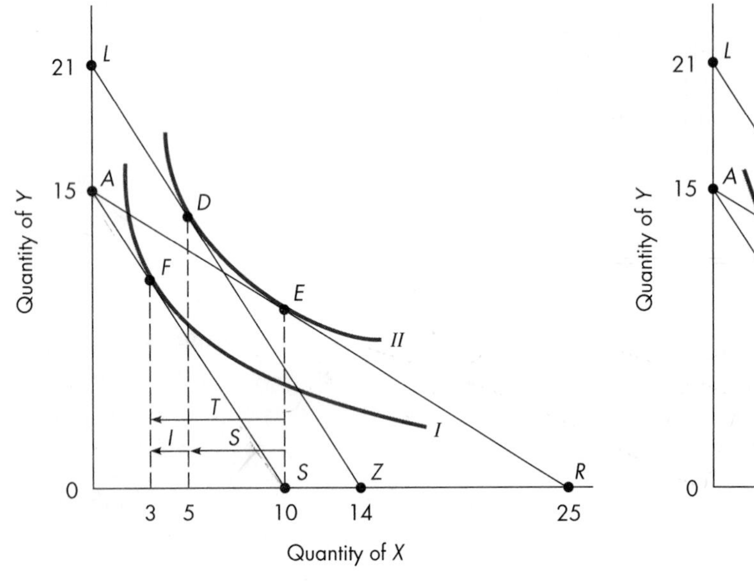

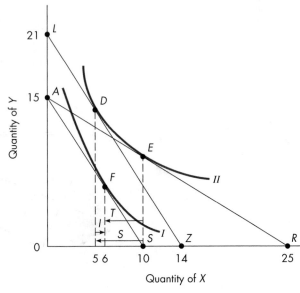

Panel A — Normal good **Panel B — Inferior good**

$$\text{Total effect of price increase} = \text{Substitution effect} + \text{Income effect}$$
$$-4 = -5 + 1$$

Because X is inferior in Panel B, the substitution and income effects move in opposite directions. These effects are summarized in Table 6.1 and the following relation:

Relation Considering the substitution effect alone, an increase (decrease) in the price of a good causes less (more) of the good to be demanded. For a normal good, the income effect—from the consumer's being made better or worse off by the price change—adds to or reinforces the substitution effect. The income effect in the case of an inferior good offsets or takes away from the substitution effect.

Why Demand Slopes Downward

In the case of a normal good, it is clear why price and quantity demanded are negatively related along demand. From the substitution effect alone, a decrease in price is accompanied by an increase in quantity demanded. (An increase in price decreases quantity demanded.) For a normal good, the income effect must add to the substitution effect. Since both effects move quantity demanded in the same direction, demand must be negatively sloped.

TABLE 6.1
Summary of Substitution and Income Effects for a Change in the Price of *X*

	Substitution effect	Income effect
Price of *X* decreases:		
Normal good	*X* rises	*X* rises
Inferior good	*X* rises	*X* falls
Price of *X* increases:		
Normal good	*X* falls	*X* falls
Inferior good	*X* falls	*X* rises

In the case of an inferior good, the income effect does not move in the same direction, and to some extent it offsets the substitution effect. However, looking at Panel B in Figures 6.11 and 6.12 again, you can see that the income effect only *partially* offsets the substitution effect, so quantity demanded still varies inversely with price. This is generally the case: even if the commodity is inferior, the substitution effect almost always dominates the income effect and the demand curve still slopes downward.

Giffen good
A good for which the demand curve is upward-sloping.

It is *theoretically* possible that the income effect for an inferior good could dominate the substitution effect. In this case—the case of a so-called **Giffen good**—quantity demanded would vary directly with price and the demand curve would be upward-sloping. However, in this text, we will ignore Giffen goods. While experimental economists have suggested that a Giffen good may exist for an individual, we have as yet seen no convincing evidence of the existence of a Giffen good for a group of consumers.

6.7 MARKET DEMAND CURVES

market demand
A list of prices and the quantities consumers are willing and able to purchase at each price in the list, other things being held constant.

Managerial decision makers are typically more interested in the market demand for a product than in the demand of an individual consumer. Nonetheless, the behavior of individual consumers in the market determines market demand. Recall that in Chapter 2 we defined **market demand** as a list of prices and the corresponding quantity consumers are willing and able to purchase at each price in the list, holding constant money income, the prices of other goods, tastes, price expectations, and the number of consumers. When deriving individual demand in this chapter, we pivoted the budget line around the vertical intercept, therefore holding income and the prices of other goods constant. Since the indifference curves remained constant, tastes were unchanged.

Thus the discussion here conforms to the conditions of market demand. To obtain the market demand function, we need only to aggregate the individual demand functions of all potential customers in the market. We now demonstrate this aggregation.

Suppose there are only three individuals in the market for a particular commodity. In Table 6.2, the quantities demanded by each consumer at each price in

TABLE 6.2
Aggregating Individual Demands

Price	Quantity demanded: Consumer 1	Consumer 2	Consumer 3	Market demand
$6	3	0	0	3
5	5	1	0	6
4	8	3	1	12
3	10	5	4	19
2	12	7	6	25
1	13	10	8	31

FIGURE 6.13
Derivation of Market Demand

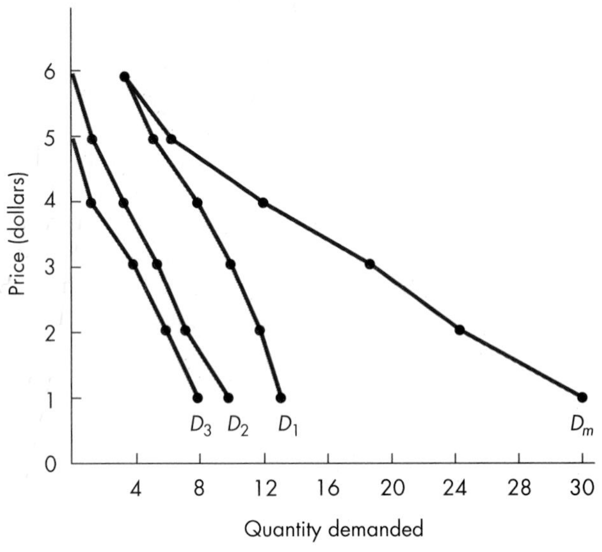

column 1 are shown in columns 2, 3, and 4. Column 5 shows the sum of these quantities demanded at each price and is therefore the market demand. Since the demand for each consumer is negatively sloped, market demand is negatively sloped also. Quantity demanded is inversely related to price.

Figure 6.13 shows graphically how a market demand curve can be derived from the individual demand curves. The individual demands of consumers 1, 2, and 3 from Table 6.2 are shown graphically as D_1, D_2, and D_3, respectively. The market demand curve, D_m, is simply the sum of the quantities demanded at each price. At $6, consumer 1 demands 3 units. Since the others demand nothing, 3 is the quantity demanded by the market. At every other price, D_m is the horizontal summation of the quantities demanded by the three consumers. And if other consumers came into the market, their demand curves would be added to D_m to obtain the new market demand.

Relation The market demand curve is the horizontal summation of the demand curves of all consumers in the market. It therefore shows how much all consumers demand at each price over the relevant range of prices.

6.8 IMPERFECT INFORMATION ABOUT PRICE AND QUANTITY

Thus far in this chapter, we have assumed that consumers have complete information about the price and quality of the goods and services available in the market. Although this is a useful approach for understanding consumer behavior, in most cases, consumers probably do not have complete information about the prices of all the products that are available, and they may not be fully aware of the amount of utility they will receive from these products—that is, they may not know about product quality. Because information is not complete, consumers must engage in search activities to gather information. Consumers gather information about prices and quality in many ways—for example, by reading research or trade magazines (such as *Consumer Reports, Car & Driver, PC Computing,* etc.), visiting stores and talking with salesclerks, talking to friends, and watching the newspapers for advertisements that convey information about prices and quality.

All these search activities take time and sometimes money. Even if no monetary expenditure is involved with the search, the time itself required to search for information has value to consumers. Economists refer to the costs of gathering information about price and quality as **search costs.** It is important for managers to understand how and why consumers search for price and quality information. To the extent that managers can reduce the search costs associated with buying their firms' products, they can expect to sell more units.

search costs
The costs of gathering information about product prices or product quality.

When consumers engage in search activities for information about product prices and quality, they incur both benefits and costs. As it turns out, the theory of searching for information is essentially the same regardless of whether it is price or quality information. To illustrate how consumers determine how much search activity to undertake, we will consider a consumer who wants information about product price. The results of this discussion can be directly applied to determining how much time to spend searching for quality information. Since search activity involves both costs and benefits, and there is no constraint on the amount of search activity undertaken, the consumer's search problem is an unconstrained maximization problem. Using the theory of optimization developed in Chapter 4, the optimal level of search occurs at the point where the marginal benefit of search just equals the marginal cost of search.

The marginal benefit from searching one more hour is the reduction in the price the consumer must pay for the good. We will assume the consumer knows with certainty the marginal benefit associated with various levels of search activity, even though consumers usually do not know exactly how much lower a price they will find if they search an extra hour. To illustrate the search decision, consider the problem facing Mark Smith, who is shopping for a Pentium personal

FIGURE 6.14
Finding the Optimal Level of Search

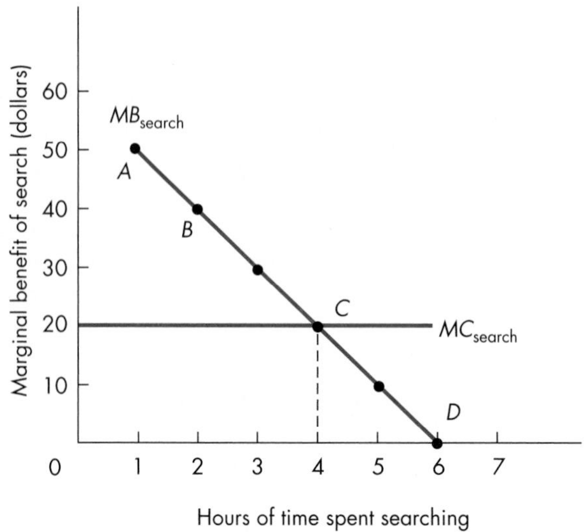

computer. Mark knows exactly what features he needs in a PC (i.e., quality is known) and is going to buy the cheapest brand of PC with these features he can find in the amount of time he decides to spend shopping. Figure 6.14 shows the (known) marginal benefit curve for the additional hours Mark spends searching for a lower-priced Pentium PC.

Mark knows he can buy a PC from a mail-order firm that advertises in *PC Computing* magazine and pay a price of $2,000 with no search activity. As shown by point *A* in Figure 6.14, Mark can spend one hour shopping at various stores and can get a personal computer with the same features for $50 less than the mail-order price (i.e., the no-search price). If Mark wants to shop for a second hour, he can save another $40 (point *B*) and get a computer for $90 (= $50 + $40) less than the mail-order price. Mark can continue finding a lower price by searching up to six hours. Once Mark has spent six hours shopping, he will have found the lowest price in town (point *D*). While it might seem optimal to search for the lowest price, consumers generally quit shopping before they have found the lowest possible price because search is costly.

Mark recognizes that searching for a lower price is using up some of his valuable leisure time, which he values at $20 per hour. Thus, Mark's marginal cost of search is $20 per hour. For the first hour of search that Mark undertakes, he saves $50 by finding a lower price for the computer but he spends $20 worth of his time. Clearly, Mark is better off by using $20 worth of time to save $50. For the second hour spent shopping, Mark can reduce price by another $40, but again he gives up $20 worth of his time. This extra hour of search makes Mark better off. Mark will continue searching until the marginal cost of an extra hour of search exceeds the marginal benefit. In Figure 6.14, Mark will increase his search time up to four hours, the point at which the marginal benefit of search equals the marginal cost of search (point C). This example treats search time as a continuous variable. Had search time been a discrete variable, Mark would have continued to increase the search up to the last level for which the marginal benefit exceeded the marginal cost of search. We can summarize the rule for consumer search in the following principle:

Principle When the marginal benefit of search is known with certainty, the consumer maximizes the net benefit by increasing search activity up to the point where the marginal benefit of search equals the marginal cost of search. If the consumer must choose among discrete levels of activity, the consumer maximizes net benefit by increasing search activity up to the last level of search for which the marginal benefit of search exceeds the marginal cost of search.

6.9 IMPERFECT INFORMATION AND ADVERTISING

Advertising is big business. A number of U.S. corporations spend more than $1 billion annually on advertising. While many consumers may feel that they are bombarded with superficial and sometimes annoying advertising, a significant amount of advertising actually improves knowledge about product prices and quality. Some advertising even succeeds in convincing people that certain goods or services are more desirable than they had previously believed. Indeed, advertising does increase sales; otherwise, firms wouldn't advertise.

To illustrate how advertising improves and alters the information that consumers use in making consumption decisions, we classify advertising as either (1) purely informative or (2) image advertising. **Purely informative advertising** is designed primarily to convey information about product quality and product price. **Image advertising** conveys an image about a product that is designed to alter and enhance consumers' perception of the good.

purely informative advertising Advertising designed primarily to convey price, quality, or availability information about a product.

image advertising Advertising that conveys an image about a product.

Purely Informative Advertising

Examples of purely informative advertising are newspaper ads for grocery stores and drugstores, catalog ads, and ads in technical publications. If consumers had complete information about both product price and the ability of goods to satisfy their wants, there would be no need for informative advertising. As noted in the previous section, consumers do not always have full information about prices or the quality of all products and may decide to engage in activities that increase their knowledge about prices and qualities.

Recall from our discussion of utility maximization that the higher the marginal utility per dollar spent on a good (MU/P), the more of the good a consumer will wish to purchase for any given level of income. Informative advertising can affect either marginal utility or price, or both. Marginal utility can be increased by providing information on product quality, and the average price paid can be lowered by giving shoppers information about prices.

First, consider the effect of informative advertising on marginal utility. When informative ads convey information to buyers about the desirable attributes of a

ILLUSTRATION 6.3

Some Perils of Image Advertising

On March 13, 1996, *The Wall Street Journal* reported that Time Warner had hired a new advertising agency to craft its first-ever corporate image campaign.* Time Warner was "poring over the thousands of cultural icons it produces—from characters in Loony Tunes cartoons to those in the hit show 'Friends'—searching for images that will strike a rich chord with the public." The ads would be designed to promote an emotional response, reminding people how often they are moved by Time Warner songs, books, movies, cartoons, and TV shows. The *WSJ* noted that Time Warner's corporate persona had never reflected the glory of its parts, which include some of the world's choicest entertainment properties—Warner Brothers Studio, Warner Music, and Time Inc. magazines—with some of the most popular brand names.

Instead, the company's image on Wall Street and in corporate America had been influenced more by its huge debt, depressed stock price, and seemingly perpetual management crises. It had been picketed by rap-music opponents at its annual meeting and subjected to lawsuits by former executives, having to pay more than $100 million in severance pay. And Time Warner was involved in a court dispute with a former partner over whether the company could go ahead with its planned purchase of Turner Broadcasting. Obviously something had to be done. But there was disagreement over what.

The *WSJ* noted, "Some studies show that corporate ad campaigns help attract new employees and even boost a company's stock price. But experts disagreed on the effectiveness of image advertising, particularly when a company is troubled or involved in controversy." A corporate-identity consultant stated, "It's the wrong time to stick your head over the bunker. There is a real risk that with so much hanging in the balance, particularly with the Turner situation, it could backfire." Time Warner and the advertising agency declined to comment. As of fall 1997, the huge campaign had not been put into effect.

When it succeeds, image advertising can be an extremely powerful and cost-effective method of persuading consumers to buy a company's product. Image advertising campaigns can, however, fail spectacularly. Since the advertised image is intended literally to become a characteristic of the product or the company, the success or failure of an image advertising campaign depends crucially upon finding and projecting an image that people will want "to buy." Even highly paid advertising agencies cannot guarantee that an image advertising campaign will be successful, for it can backfire if the projected image turns out to be unpopular.

Subaru of America learned just how perilous image advertising can be when it launched a bold advertising campaign designed to link Subaru cars with the image of practicality and reverse snobbery.† According to the Subaru ad, "A car is a car. If it

product, the consumers' perception of product quality may rise, causing the perceived marginal utility to increase. For a given price, an increase in marginal utility causes MU/P to rise, and consumers will buy more of the product.

Next, consider the effect of informative advertising on the price paid by consumers for the product. As emphasized above, searching for price and quality information is costly. Not only do consumers spend valuable time in the search of information, but many decide to purchase magazines such as *Consumer Reports* and *Motor Trend* for information on automobiles and other durable goods, *The Wall Street Journal* for information on financial products and services, or various catalogs, computer databases, and so on. When consumers incur search costs, the price they consider in making their consumption decision is *full price.* The **full price (P_F)** a consumer pays for a unit of a product equals the

full price
The money price per unit purchased plus the search costs per unit.

improves your standing with the neighbors, then you live among snobs with distorted values. A car is steel, electronics, rubber, plastic, and glass. A machine." Subaru believed a trend was under way in the United States of rejecting "1980s-style greed" in favor of practicality and basic values. When the first ad appeared in fall 1991, advertising critics thought it was sensational. Six months later, however, Subaru sales had fallen sharply and began a lengthy decline.

According to *The Wall Street Journal,* Subaru "misjudged how important status is for car buyers willing to fork over $13,000 or more, and underestimated the powerful emotions involved in choosing a car." Subaru's image of practicality just didn't sell. By May 1992, Subaru abandoned its unsuccessful image advertising in favor of an informative advertising campaign that emphasized the special features of Subaru cars.

Image ads frequently employ celebrities to enhance the image of a company or product; however, this can be risky since celebrity images often change over time. Corporations may spend millions designing an image advertising campaign around a celebrity only to see the celebrity's popularity fade or, in some cases, even become negative or undesirable. Executives at Pepsi undoubtedly lost a lot of sleep over the alleged misdeeds of Madonna and Michael Jackson. The Florida Department of Citrus, which employed Burt Reynolds to promote Florida orange juice, decided to cancel its television commercials because his highly publicized divorce from Loni Anderson was tarnishing Reynolds' image and had reduced the effectiveness of his commercials.

The risk of using celebrities in image advertising can be substantially reduced by resurrecting celebrities who are dead.‡ Some companies, such as PepsiCo, the Gap, and McDonald's, used deceased celebrities in their ads in order (practically) to eliminate the risk of embarrassment. The Gap featured Humphrey Bogart, Orson Wells, Rock Hudson, Sammy Davis Jr., and Marilyn Monroe in its ads for khaki trousers. Pepsi used a Buddy Holly look-alike in television ads overseas.

While this illustration shows that image advertising can, and does, backfire on occasion, you should not conclude that purely informative advertising is somehow better, or less risky, than image advertising. Both forms of advertising involve some degree of risk, and neither type of advertising can be guaranteed to increase demand.

*"Time Warner Mulls Image Ads Starring Its Icons," *The Wall Street Journal,* Mar. 13, 1996.

†Joanne Lipman, "Subaru's New Ad Campaign Isn't Working" *The Wall Street Journal,* Mar. 31, 1992.

‡Kevin Goldman, "Dead Celebrities Are Resurrected as Pitchmen," *The Wall Street Journal,* Jan. 7, 1994.

money price per unit purchased (P) plus the search costs per unit (S):

$$P_F = P + S$$

For example, if the money price of a good is $5 per unit and a consumer spends $2 worth of resources searching for price and quality information about that good before making a purchase, the full price of the good is equal to $7 (= $5 + $2), and the marginal utility per dollar spent on the good is $MU/\$7$.

Managers use informative advertising to reduce the search costs (S) for their firms' products. To the extent that informative ads reduce the full price consumers pay for a product, full price falls, MU/P_F rises, and consumers buy more of that product. In addition, informative ads can lower the marginal costs of search. As discussed above, the lower the marginal cost of additional search, the greater the amount of time spent searching for a lower price and the more likely that the actual money price paid (P) is lower. Thus, informative ads can lower both P and S, causing P_F to fall, MU/P_F to rise, and sales to increase.

Image Advertising

Image advertising is designed to change consumers' preference patterns in order to make a good seem more desirable, more useful, or more valuable. For example, Cadillac ads give an image of elegance, making Cadillac owners seem successful and accomplished. Ads for Land Rovers try to present an image of adventuresome, daring owners. Nike ads suggest that Nike wearers have great athletic ability. Calvin Klein ads imply that people who wear Calvin Klein clothing are chic, modern, and "in the know." Of course, some advertising simply tells you that a product tastes best, looks best, makes you feel best, or is best for your health.

The purpose of all image advertising is to cause consumers to perceive a higher marginal utility associated with the product. Such advertising would therefore raise consumers' valuation of the product and hence increase the marginal rate of substitution with other products, making the advertised product more desirable relative to these other goods. Therefore, image advertising tries to affect the indifference curves of potential consumers, allowing the firm to charge a higher price, sell more, or perhaps both. As explained earlier, an increase in marginal utility increases MU/P and thus causes an increase in the demand for the good. In contrast to informative advertising, image advertising does not affect the full price of a good. It only affects preferences.

6.10 SUMMARY

This chapter has provided the theoretical underpinnings for demand analysis. We began with the assumption that consumers can rank various bundles of goods as to whether they prefer one bundle to another or are indifferent between the two. We then constructed an indifference curve showing all combinations of two commodities among which a consumer is indifferent. The collection of all indifference curves—the consumer's indifference map—shows what the consumer is willing to purchase. On a more technical level, we discussed why the marginal rate of substitution diminishes as more of good X is consumed and why the slope of the indifference curve—the marginal rate of substitution—is equal to the ratio of the marginal utilities of the two commodities:

$$MRS = MU_x/MU_y$$

The consumers' budget line determines what the consumer is able to consume. The budget line is a straight line with a slope equal to the ratio of the prices of the two commodities:

$$Y = (M/P_y) - (P_x/P_y)X$$

As income changes, the budget line shifts. As price changes, the budget line rotates.

The consumer maximizes utility subject to the constraint of a limited income by consuming that combination of the two commodities at which the budget line is tangent to an indifference curve. At that point, the slope of the budget line is equal to the slope of the highest attainable indifference curve, so the equilibrium condition can be expressed as

$$MRS = MU_x/MU_y = P_x/P_y$$

or

$$\frac{MU_x}{P_x} = \frac{MU_y}{P_y}$$

An individual consumer's demand curve can be derived by holding income and the prices of all other commodities constant and then altering the price of one commodity and observing how the constrained utility-maximizing consumption of that commodity changes. Price changes have two effects: a substitution effect and an income effect. The substitution effect of a price change upon the consumption of a good is always negative; that is, quantity demanded varies inversely with price, holding utility constant and considering the substitution effect only. If the good is normal, the income effect reinforces the substitution effect. If the good is inferior, the income effect offsets to some extent the substitution effect.

The market demand curve is the horizontal summation of the demand curves of all consumers in the market. It shows how much all consumers demand at each price in the relevant range of prices.

When consumers have imperfect information about prices and product quality, they engage in a search for information. The optimal level of search is found by considering both the benefits from searching for more information and the search costs associated with gathering price or quality information. When the marginal benefit from search and the marginal cost of search are both known with certainty, the consumer will continue to search up to the point where

$$MB_{\text{search}} = MC_{\text{search}}$$

The purpose of advertising is to increase sales. Advertising can be classified as either purely informative advertising or image advertising. Informative advertising conveys information about the product price and product quality. The higher the marginal utility per dollar spent on a good (MU/P), the more of the good the consumer will buy. Information about product quality can enhance the perceived marginal utility of a good, increasing MU/P and increasing sales. Informative advertising can also lower consumer information search costs. This, in turn, lowers the full price (money price plus the search costs) of the good or service and increases sales. Image advertising conveys an image about a product that is designed to increase the consumer's perception of the marginal utility of the good. Increasing marginal utility causes MU/P to increase for the good. Thus, successful image advertising increases demand.

TECHNICAL PROBLEMS

1. Answer the following questions about consumer preferences:
   a. If Julie prefers Diet Coke to Diet Pepsi and Diet Pepsi to regular Pepsi but is indifferent between Diet Coke and Classic Coke, what are her preferences between Classic Coke and regular Pepsi?
   b. If James purchases a Ford Mustang rather than a Ferrari, what are his preferences between the two cars?
   c. If Julie purchases a Ferrari rather than a Ford Mustang, what are her preferences between the two cars?
   d. James and Jane are having a soft drink together. Coke and Pepsi are the same price. If James orders a Pepsi and Jane orders a Coke, what are the preferences of each between the two colas?
2. Suppose that two units of X and eight units of Y give a consumer the same utility as four units of X and two units of Y. Over this range:
   a. If the consumer obtains one more unit of X, how many units of Y must be given up in order to keep utility constant?
   b. If the consumer obtains one more unit of Y, how many units of X must be given up in order to keep utility constant?
   c. What is the marginal rate of substitution?
3. Use the graph on the next page of a consumer's indifference curve to answer the questions:

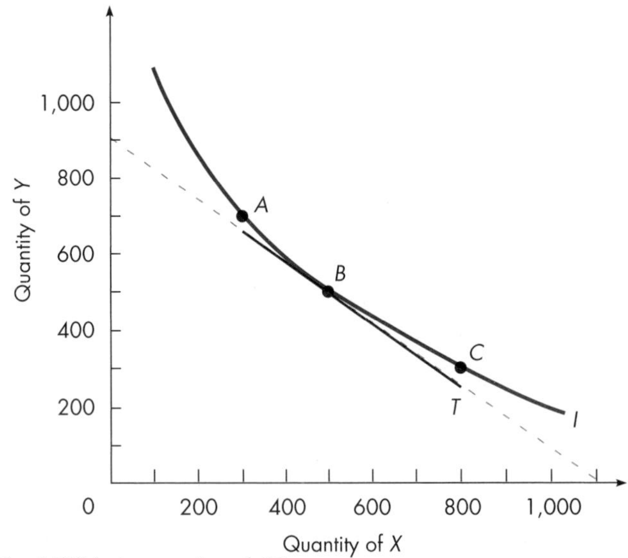

a. What is the *MRS* between *A* and *B*?
b. What is the *MRS* between *B* and *C*?
c. What is the *MRS* at *B*?

4. A consumer buys only two goods, *X* and *Y*.
   a. If the *MRS* between *X* and *Y* is 2 and the marginal utility of *X* is 20, what is the marginal utility of *Y*?
   b. If the *MRS* between *X* and *Y* is 3 and the marginal utility of *Y* is 3, what is the marginal utility of *X*?
   c. If a consumer moves downward along an indifference curve, what happens to the marginal utilities of *X* and *Y*? What happens to the *MRS*?
5. Use the following figure to answer the questions:

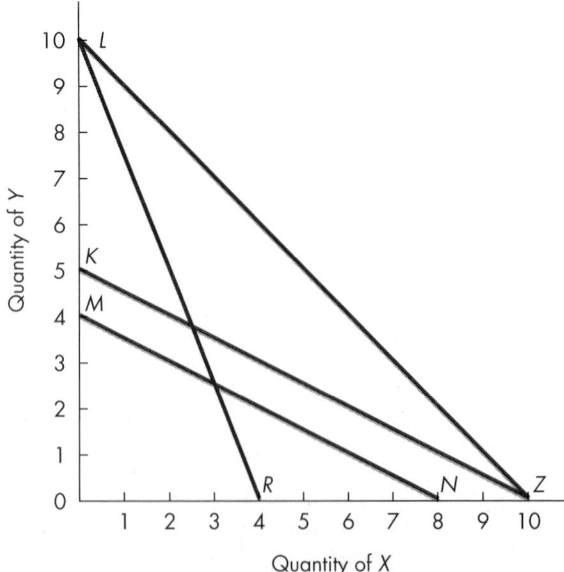

a. The equation of budget line LZ is Y = _______ − _______ X.
b. The equation of budget line LR is Y = _______ − _______ X.
c. The equation of budget line KZ is Y = _______ − _______ X.
d. The equation of budget line MN is Y = _______ − _______ X.
e. If the relevant budget line is LR and the consumer's income is \$200, what are the prices of X and Y? At the same income, if the budget line is LZ, what are the prices of X and Y?
f. If the budget line is MN, P_y = \$40, and P_x = \$20, what is income? At the same prices, if the budget line is KZ, what is income?

6. Suppose a consumer has the indifference map shown in the following graph. The relevant budget line is LZ. The price of good Y is \$10.

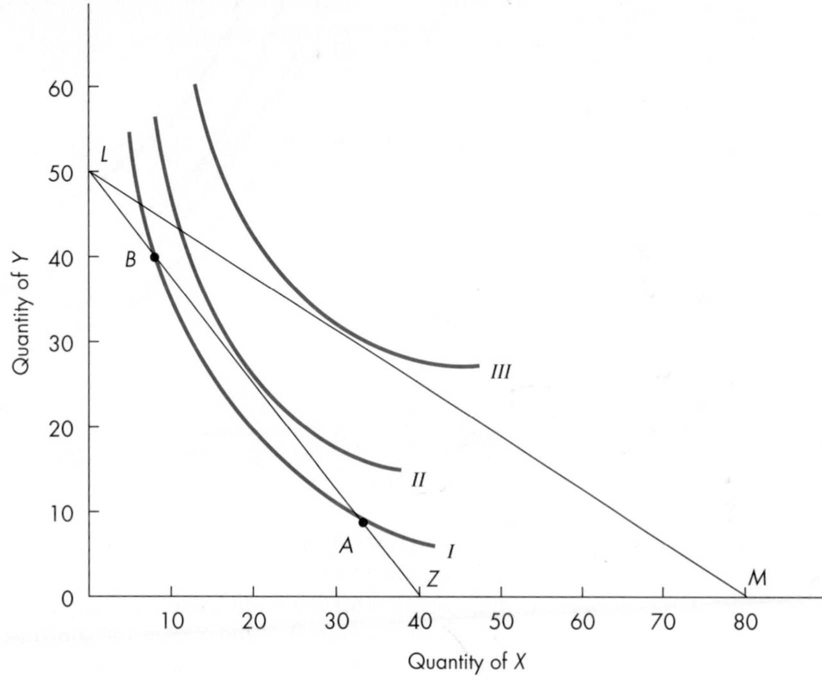

a. What is the consumer's income?
b. What is the price of X?
c. Write the equation for the budget line LZ.
d. What combination of X and Y will the consumer choose? Why?
e. What is the marginal rate of substitution at this combination?
f. Explain in terms of the MRS why the consumer would not choose combinations designated by A or B.
g. Suppose the budget line pivots to LM, money income remaining constant. What is the new price of X? What combination of X and Y is now chosen?
h. What is the new MRS?

7. Suppose that the marginal rate of substitution is 2, the price of X is \$3, and the price of Y is \$1.
a. If the consumer obtains one more unit of X, how many units of Y must be given up in order to keep utility constant?

b. If the consumer obtains one more unit of Y, how many units of X must be given up in order to keep utility constant?
c. What is the rate at which the consumer is *willing* to substitute X for Y?
d. What is the rate at which the consumer is *able* to substitute X for Y?
e. Is the consumer making the utility-maximizing choice? Why or why not? If not, what should the consumer do? Explain.

8. The following graph shows a portion of a consumer's indifference map. The consumer faces the budget line LZ, and the price of X is \$20.

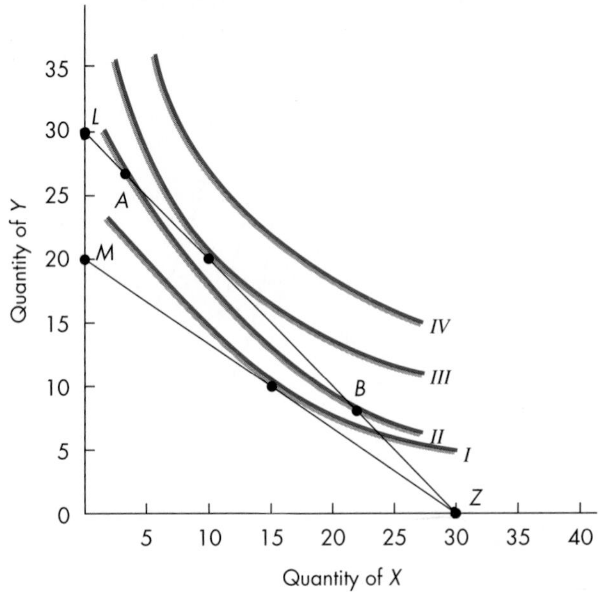

a. The consumer's income = \$________.
b. The price of Y is \$________.
c. The equation for the budget line LZ is ________.
d. What combination of X and Y does the consumer choose? Why?
e. The marginal rate of substitution for this combination is ________.
f. Explain in terms of *MRS* why the consumer does not choose either combination A or B.
g. What combination is chosen if the budget line is MZ?
h. What is the price of Y?
i. What is the price of X?
j. What is the *MRS* in equilibrium?

9. Sally purchases only pasta and salad with her income of \$160 a month. Each month she buys 10 pasta dinners at \$6 each and 20 salads at \$5 each. The marginal utility of the last unit of each is 30. What should Sally do? Explain.

10. Assume that an individual consumes three goods, X, Y, and Z. The marginal utility (assumed measurable) of each good is independent of the rate of consumption of other goods. The prices of X, Y, and Z are, respectively, \$1, \$3, and \$5. The total income of the consumer is \$65, and the marginal utility schedule is as follows:

Units of good	Marginal utility of X (units)	Marginal utility of Y (units)	Marginal utility of Z (units)
1	12	60	70
2	11	55	60
3	10	48	50
4	9	40	40
5	8	32	30
6	7	24	25
7	6	21	18
8	5	18	10
9	4	15	3
10	3	12	1

a. Given a $65 income, how much of each good should the consumer purchase to maximize utility?

b. Suppose income falls to $43 with the same set of prices; what combination will the consumer choose?

c. Let income fall to $38; let the price of *X* rise to $5 while the prices of *Y* and *Z* remain at $3 and $5. How does the consumer allocate income now? What would you say if the consumer maintained that *X* is not purchased because he or she could no longer afford it?

11. The following graph shows a portion of a consumer's indifference map and three budget lines. The consumer has an income of $1,000.

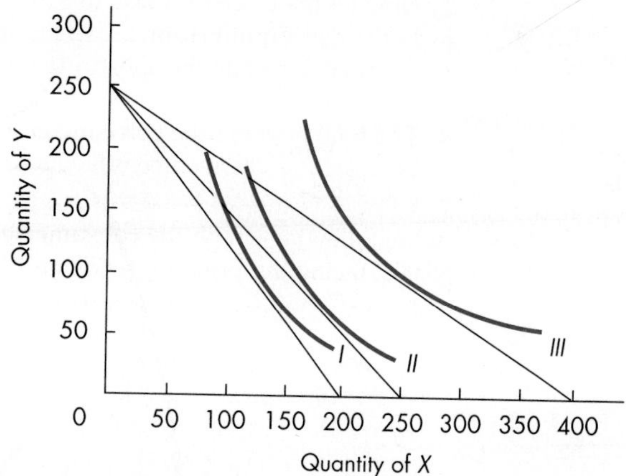

What is the price of *Y*? What are three price-quantity combinations on this consumer's demand curve?

12. Sam is buying 20 units of *X* at $20 each and 30 units of *Y* at $10 each with his income of $700. The marginal utility of the last *X* is 30 and of the last *Y*, 15.

a. Is Sam maximizing utility under these conditions? Why or why not?

b. The price of *X* falls to $15. What happens to his purchasing power at this combination of goods? How will this effect probably change his purchases?

c. After the price decrease, what happens to the relative marginal utilities per dollar for the two goods? How will this effect probably affect his purchases?
d. When Sam reaches a new equilibrium, what will be the new ratio of the two marginal utilities? Explain.

13. In the following graph the consumer begins in equilibrium with an income of \$2,000, facing prices of P_x = \$5 and P_y = \$10.

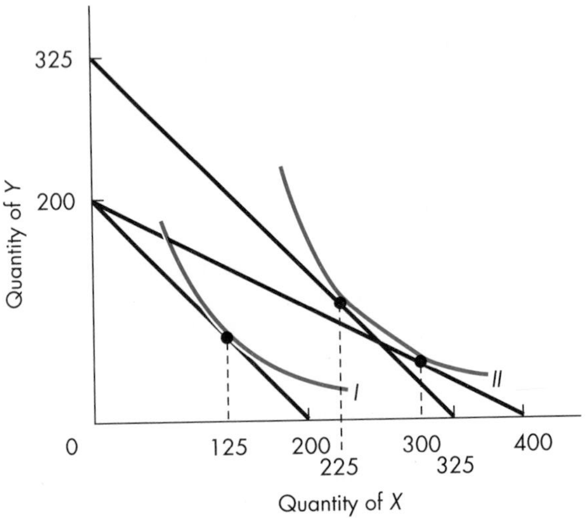

a. In equilibrium, ________ units of X are consumed.
Now let the price of X rise to \$10.
b. In the new equilibrium, ________ units of X are consumed.
c. In order to isolate the substitution effect, \$________ must be given to the consumer.
d. The total effect of the price increase is ________. The substitution effect is ________. The income effect is ________.
e. Good X is a ________ good.

14. In the following graph the consumer begins in equilibrium with an income of \$5,000, facing the prices P_x = \$50 and P_y = \$25.

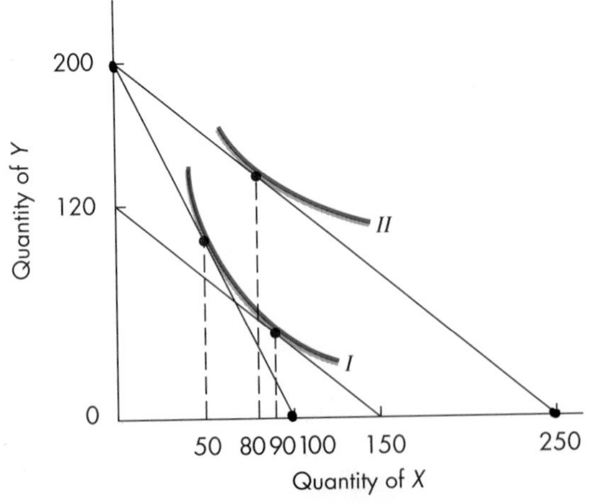

a. In equilibrium, ______ units of X are consumed.
Now let the price of X fall to \$20, income and the price of Y remaining constant.

b. In the new equilibrium, ______ units of X are consumed.

c. In order to isolate the substitution effect, \$______ must be taken away from the consumer.

d. The total effect of the price decrease is ______. The substitution effect is ______. The income effect is ______.

15. Suppose there are only three consumers in the market for good X. The quantities demanded by each consumer at each price between \$1 and \$9 are shown in the table below:

	Quantity demanded			
Price of X	Consumer 1	Consumer 2	Consumer 3	Market demand
\$9	0	5	10	______
8	0	10	20	______
7	10	15	30	______
6	20	20	40	______
5	30	25	50	______
4	40	30	60	______
3	50	35	70	______
2	60	40	80	______
1	70	45	90	______

a. Using the following axes, draw the demand curve for each of the three consumers. Label the three curves D_1, D_2, and D_3, respectively.

b. Fill in the blanks in the table for the market quantity demanded at each price.

c. Construct the market demand curve in the graph, and label it D_m.

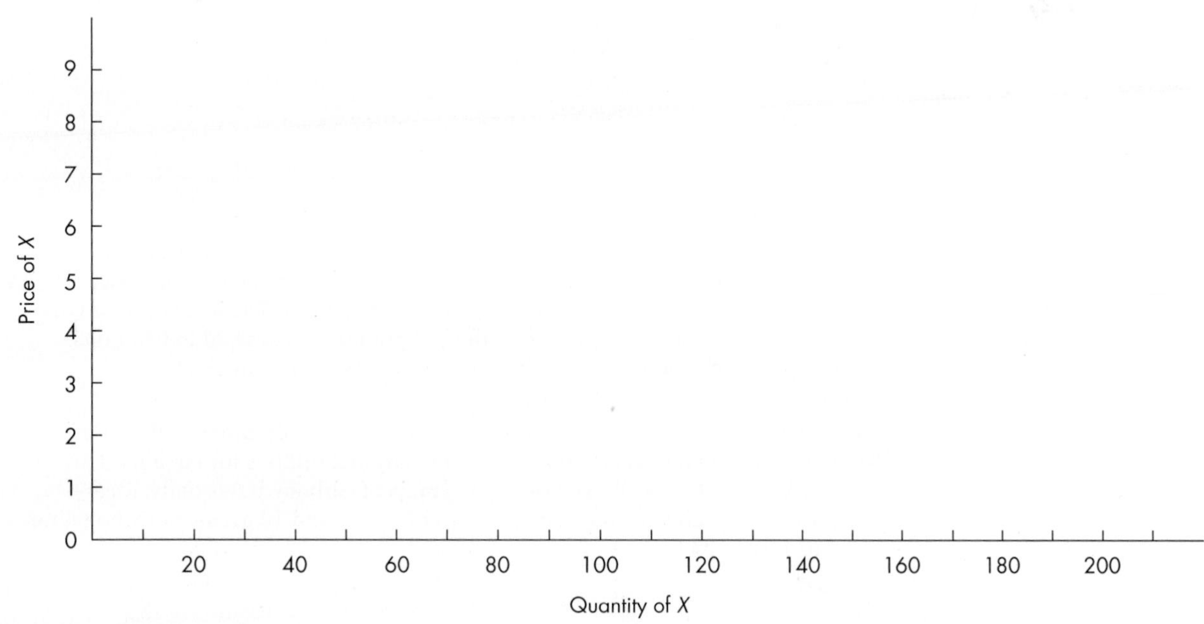

16. The following graph shows the (known) marginal benefit curve for a consumer searching for price information. The consumer's leisure time is worth $15 per hour.

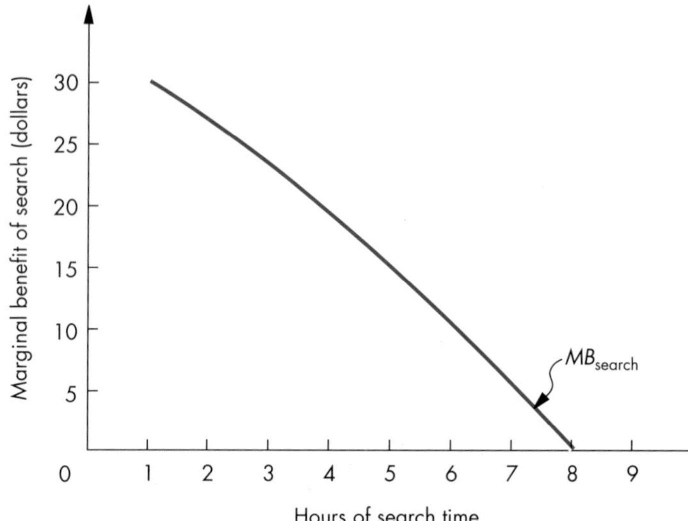

   a. If the consumer wishes to obtain the lowest possible price, ________ hours should be spent searching for a lower price.
   b. On the graph above, draw the marginal cost curve for search.
   c. The consumer maximizes the net benefit of search by spending ________ hours searching for a lower price. The optimal level of search is the level for which ________ equals ________.
   d. If the consumer's leisure time is worth only $5 per hour, the optimal level of search is ________ hours.

APPLIED PROBLEMS

1. Gigi has a limited income and consumes only wine and cheese; her current consumption choice is 4 bottles of wine and 10 pounds of cheese. The price of wine is $10 per bottle, and the price of cheese is $4 per pound. The last bottle of wine added 50 units to Gigi's utility, while the last pound of cheese added 40 units.
   a. Is Gigi making the utility-maximizing choice? Why or why not?
   b. If not, what should she do instead? Why?
2. Suppose Bill is on a low-carbohydrate diet. He can eat only three foods: Rice Krispies, cottage cheese, and popcorn. The marginal utilities for each food are tabulated below. Bill is allowed only 167 grams of carbohydrates daily. Rice Krispies, cottage cheese, and popcorn provide 25, 6, and 10 grams of carbohydrates per cup, respectively.

Units of food (cups/day)	Marginal utility of Rice Krispies	Marginal utility of cottage cheese	Marginal utility of popcorn
1	175	72	90
2	150	66	80
3	125	60	70
4	100	54	60
5	75	48	50
6	50	36	40
7	25	30	30
8	25	18	20

a. Given that Bill can consume only 167 grams of carbohydrates daily, how many cups of each food will he consume daily? Show your work.

b. Suppose Bill's doctor tells him to further reduce his carbohydrate intake to 126 grams per day. What combination will he consume?

3. Increasingly, employees are being allowed to choose benefit packages from a menu of items. For instance, workers may be given a package of benefits that includes basic and optional items. Basics might include modest medical coverage, life insurance equal to a year's salary, vacation time based on length of service, and some retirement pay. But then employees can use credits to choose among such additional benefits as full medical coverage, dental and eye care, more vacation time, additional disability income, and higher company payments to the retirement fund. How do you think flexible benefit packages would affect an employee's choice between higher wages and more benefits?
4. Grocery store ads are examples of informative advertising. They generally contain nothing more than price and availability information. Why is no quality information presented? For what kind of products would we be likely to find no quality information in the ad? What kind of products require that quality information be presented?
5. Have you ever made mistakes such as the following: studying too long for a test that turned out to be easy, not studying long enough for a test that turned out to be extremely hard, agreeing to go on a blind date that turned out to be miserable, buying a package of cookies that were so bad you threw most of them away, and not buying enough potato chips and soft drinks for a party? Does the possibility that people make mistakes necessarily contradict or negate the theory of consumer behavior? Discuss.
6. The beef association, dairy farmers, the potato growers association, the U.S. textile industry, and the Florida citrus growers often run ads designed to increase the demand for a product. Why are trade associations, rather than individual firms, placing these ads?
7. The manager-owner of Good Guys Enterprises obtains utility from income (profit) and from having the firm behave in a socially conscious manner, such as making charitable contributions or civic expenditures. Can you set up the problem and

derive the equilibrium conditions if the manager-owner wishes to obtain a specific level of utility at the lowest possible cost? Do these conditions differ from the utility-maximizing conditions?

8. Joan Quant decides to buy a used car. She is known for carefully and intelligently making her consumption decisions. After carefully considering a number of various makes of autos, she has decided to buy a compact car driven no more than 75,000 miles. Joan lives in a rather large urban area that has several newspapers, as well as a publication specializing in used cars. Given that search is costly, how could Joan determine the amount of time to spend searching for the best price? In what sense is this the best price?

9. After Iraq invaded Kuwait, gasoline prices rose dramatically—up to 50 percent. There were many effects of the increased price of gasoline. Explain the following effects in terms of the income effect, or the substitution effect, or both effects:
   a. People drove less and purchased less gas.
   b. People ate out less often.
   c. People had more tune-ups done on their cars.
   d. Bike sales went up.
   e. The sale of lottery tickets fell.
   f. People took vacations closer to home.

10. In terms of the consumer theory set forth in this chapter, can you explain the meaning of the following statements?
    a. "I think you get more for your money from Nike than from Reebok."
    b. "I wanted to buy an RX-7 rather than a Mazda 626, but it just wasn't worth it."
    c. "I'd like to go to Mexico over Spring break, but I just can't afford it," said Don. Jill asked, "Don't you have enough money in your account?" Don replied, "Yeah, but I can't afford to go."
    d. "I'll have to flip a coin to decide whether to buy chocolate chip or vanilla fudge ice cream."

11. On April 23, 1991, the Air Force awarded a $93 billion (or more) contract to a group led by Lockheed, Boeing, and General Dynamics to build the new fighter plane for the 21st century, the YF-22 Lightning 2. A group headed by Northrop and McDonnell Douglas, which had spent over $1 billion on development for their alternative YF-23, lost out on the contract. That evening on CNN's *Crossfire,* Secretary of Defense Cheney explained that the Lockheed group got the contract because their "quality for the price per plane was higher." He didn't elaborate. In terms of the theory set forth in this chapter, did he mean
    a. The Lockheed quality was higher?
    b. The Lockheed price was lower?
    If neither, what did he mean?

12. *The Wall Street Journal* (January 22, 1992) reported that the "laws of economics often don't apply in (the) health-care field," citing numerous examples of consumers that paid higher prices than necessary for health care and, in some cases, received lower quality care at the higher price. Despite widely varying prices and qualities, patients rarely comparison shop among doctors and hospitals. Using consumer search theory, explain why patients may spend little or no time searching for price and quality information when seeking medical help.

MATHEMATICAL APPENDIX: A Brief Presentation of Consumer Theory

This appendix provides a mathematical analysis of the theory of consumer behavior and the derivation of demand functions from a consumer's utility-maximization conditions. The analytical tools required are the fundamentals of constrained maximization.

The Relation between the Marginal Rate of Substitution and Marginal Utility

A consumer has a general utility function with two goods of

$$U = U(X, Y)$$

The marginal utilities are defined as

$$MU_x = \partial U/\partial X \qquad \text{and} \qquad MU_y = \partial U/\partial Y$$

The marginal rate of substitution (*MRS*), showing the rate at which the consumer is willing to substitute one good for the other while holding utility constant, is

$$MRS = -dY/dX$$

The minus sign is included to keep *MRS* positive since $dY/dX < 0$ along an indifference curve.

To derive the relation between *MRS* and marginal utilities, take the total differential of the utility function and set $dU = 0$ to hold utility constant along a given indifference curve:

$$dU = \frac{\partial U}{\partial X}dX + \frac{\partial U}{\partial Y}dY = 0 \tag{1}$$

Solving equation (1) for $MRS = -dY/dX$,

$$MRS = -\frac{dY}{dX} = \frac{\partial U/\partial X}{\partial U/\partial Y} = \frac{MU_x}{MU_y}$$

Since MU_x decreases and MU_y increases as X increases and Y decreases when moving downward along an indifference curve, the indifference curve is convex; that is, $-d^2Y/dX^2 < 0$.

Utility Maximization Subject to an Income Constraint: The General Case

We now derive mathematically the consumer's utility-maximizing equilibrium conditions, set forth graphically and algebraically in the text, using the tools of differential calculus.

The consumer maximizes utility

$$U = U(X, Y)$$

subject to an income (budget) constraint

$$M = P_xX + P_yY$$

The Lagrangian function to be maximized is

$$\mathcal{L} = U(X, Y) + \lambda(M - P_xX - P_yY)$$

where P_x and P_y are the prices of goods X and Y, M is income, and λ is the Lagrangian multiplier. Maximization of the function with respect to the levels of X and Y requires the following first-order conditions:

$$\frac{\partial \mathcal{L}}{\partial X} = \frac{\partial U}{\partial X} - \lambda P_x = 0 \tag{2a}$$

$$\frac{\partial \mathcal{L}}{\partial Y} = \frac{\partial U}{\partial Y} - \lambda P_y = 0 \tag{2b}$$

Setting $\partial\mathcal{L}/\partial\lambda$ equal to zero forces the budget constraint to be met:

$$M - P_xX - P_yY = 0 \tag{3}$$

Combining equations (2a) and (2b), the necessary conditions for maximizing utility subject to the budget constraint are

$$\frac{\partial U/\partial X}{\partial U/\partial Y} = \frac{P_x}{P_y} \tag{4}$$

Note that $\partial U/\partial X$ and $\partial U/\partial Y$ are the marginal utilities of the two goods; their ratio is the marginal rate of substitution. The ratio P_x/P_y is the absolute value of the slope of the budget line. Hence, the necessary condition for income-constrained utility maximization is that the marginal rate of substitution between the two commodities be equal to the ratio of their prices. That is, from equation (4),

$$\frac{\partial U/\partial X}{\partial U/\partial Y} = \frac{MU_x}{MU_y} = \frac{P_x}{P_y}$$

or

$$\frac{MU_x}{P_x} = \frac{MU_y}{P_y} \tag{5}$$

The marginal utilities per dollar spent on the last units of X and Y are equal.

Derivation of the Consumer's Demand Function

The equilibrium conditions shown in equations (2) and (3) form a system of three equations that can be solved for the equilibrium values of λ^*, X^*, and Y^* in terms of the parameters M, P_x, and P_y. The demand functions from this solution are

$$X^* = X^*(M, P_x, P_y)$$

(6) and

$$Y^* = Y^*(M, P_x, P_y)$$

These demands are functions of the good's own price, the price of the related good, and income, as discussed in this chapter and in Chapter 2. To conform to the law of demand,

$$\frac{\partial X^*}{\partial P_x} < 0 \quad \text{and} \quad \frac{\partial Y^*}{\partial P_y} < 0$$

The derivatives $\frac{\partial X^*}{\partial P_y}$, $\frac{\partial X^*}{\partial M}$, $\frac{\partial Y^*}{\partial P_x}$, and $\frac{\partial Y^*}{\partial M}$ can be of any sign, although $\frac{\partial X^*}{\partial M}$ and $\frac{\partial Y^*}{\partial M}$ cannot both be negative. That is, both goods cannot be inferior because more income would lead to less expenditure, which violates the assumptions of consumer theory.

The own-price elasticities of demand in equilibrium are

$$E_x = \frac{\partial X^*}{\partial P_x} \cdot \frac{P_x}{X^*} \quad \text{and} \quad E_y = \frac{\partial Y^*}{\partial P_y} \cdot \frac{P_y}{Y^*}$$

Derivation of Demand from a Specific Utility Function

We now assume a consumer with the simple utility function

$$U = U(X, Y) = XY$$

As above, the income constraint is

$$M = P_x X + P_y Y$$

so that the Lagrangian to be maximized is

$$\mathcal{L} = XY + \lambda(M - P_x X - P_y Y)$$

The first-order maximization conditions are

(7a) $$\frac{\partial \mathcal{L}}{\partial X} = Y - \lambda P_x = 0$$

(7b) $$\frac{\partial \mathcal{L}}{\partial Y} = X - \lambda P_y = 0$$

and

(8) $$M - P_x X - P_y Y = 0$$

Thus from equations (7a) and (7b):

(9) $$\frac{MU_x}{MU_y} = \frac{Y}{X} = \frac{P_x}{P_y}$$

Solving (9) for Y,

(10) $$Y = \left(\frac{P_x}{P_y}\right) X$$

then, using (8) to solve for X in terms of Y, equation (10) is

$$Y = \frac{P_x}{P_y}\left(\frac{M}{P_x} - \frac{P_y}{P_x} Y\right) = \frac{M}{P_y} - Y$$

or

(11) $$Y^* = \frac{M}{2P_y}$$

Similarly, using (10) and substituting into the budget constraint,

$$X = \frac{P_y}{P_x} Y = \frac{P_y}{P_x}\left(\frac{M}{P_y} - \frac{P_x}{P_y} X\right)$$

Thus

(12) $$X^* = \frac{M}{2P_x}$$

Equations (11) and (12) are the demand functions for goods Y and X. These demands are both negatively sloped because

$$\partial Y^*/\partial P_y = -M/2P_y^2 \quad \text{and} \quad \partial X^*/\partial P_x = -M/2P_x^2$$

The two goods are normal because

$$\partial Y^*/\partial M = 1/2P_y \quad \text{and} \quad \partial X^*/\partial M = 1/2P_x$$

Both $\partial Y^*/\partial P_x$ and $\partial X^*/\partial P_y$ equal zero, so the two goods are independent. With this specific form of the utility function, the consumer spends half of the income on good X [$P_x X^* = (1/2)M$] and half on Y [$P_y Y = (1/2)M$] regardless of the level of income and the price of the other good. Since the same amount is spent on each good at any price of that good, the own-price elasticity of each is unitary. This can be verified as follows:

$$E_x = \frac{\partial X^*}{\partial P_x}\frac{P_x}{X^*} = -\frac{M}{2P_x^2}\frac{P_x}{X^*} = -\frac{M}{2P_x^2}\frac{P_x}{(M/2P_x)} = -1$$

and

$$E_y = \frac{\partial Y^*}{\partial P_y}\frac{P_y}{Y^*} = -\frac{M}{2P_y^2}\frac{P_y}{Y^*} = -\frac{M}{2P_y^2}\frac{P_y}{(M/2P_y)} = -1$$

MATHEMATICAL EXERCISES

1. Assume a consumer with the utility function

$$U = U(X, Y) = X^2Y^2$$

and the typical budget constraint

$$M = P_xX + P_yY$$

a. Set up the constrained maximization problem and derive the first-order conditions.

b. Derive the consumer's demand for X and Y in terms of the parameters.

c. Derive the own-price elasticities of demand. Do the demand functions obey the law of demand?

2. To demonstrate that a utility function that is a monotonic transformation of another utility function gives the same first-order conditions and hence the same demand functions, multiply the utility function $U = U(X, Y)$ by a constant term, k, and show that the two yield the same first-order conditions.

3. Assume a consumer with the utility function

$$U = U(X, Y) = (X + 2)(Y + 1)$$

and the budget constraint

$$M = P_xX + P_yY$$

a. Set up the constrained maximization problem, and derive the first-order conditions.

b. Derive the demand for X and Y.

c. Derive the own-price elasticities of demand. Do the demands obey the law of demand?

d. Are the products substitutes or complements?

4. Demonstrate that if income and both prices change by exactly the same proportions, this does not change the equilibrium conditions and therefore the equilibrium quantities of the two goods do not change.

CHAPTER 7

Empirical Demand Functions

Information about demand is essential for making pricing and production decisions. General Motors, Ford, Chrysler, Nissan, and other large automobile manufacturers all use empirical estimates of demand in making decisions about how many units of each model to produce and what prices to charge for different car models. Managers at the national headquarters of Domino's Pizza need to estimate how pizza demand in the United States is affected by a downturn in the economy—take-out food businesses tend to prosper during recessions. At the Columbia/HCA Hospital chain, short-run and long-run estimates of patient load (demand) in its various geographic markets are crucial for making expansion plans. Virtually all large electric utilities employ economists and statisticians to estimate demand for electricity.

Large business enterprises pioneered the use of empirical demand functions and econometric price forecasts in business pricing decisions. When thousands, even millions, of units are to be priced, managers are understandably uncomfortable making "seat-of-the-pants" guesses about the optimal price to charge. Furthermore, businesses, large and small, know that changing prices is a costly practice. New price lists must be disseminated both to the sales force and to customers. Changing prices may give loyal buyers a reason to shop around again. Most managers wish to avoid, or at least reduce, the substantial anxiety that accompanies pricing decisions. Indeed, many managers admit that they avoid, as much as they possibly can, making pricing decisions for fear of making enormously costly mistakes. As a general rule, managers intensely dislike "throwing darts" until they find the right price (the bull's eye); they covet any information or technique of analysis that can help them make profitable pricing decisions. We cannot, in fairness, tell you that econometric analysis and forecasting of demand solves all of management's pricing problems. It can, however, provide managers with valuable information about demand, which should improve any manager's price-setting skills.

Like all tools used in decision making, statistical demand analysis has some important limits, which we discuss at the end of Chapter 8. Profitable pricing decisions require skillful use of both judgment and quantitative analysis. While large firms generally have been more willing to employ statistical demand analysis, significant improvement in the sophistication, availability, and ease of use of econometric software—coupled with falling prices on powerful desktop computers—is now luring more medium- and small-size firms into the use of statistical demand analysis and forecasting.

empirical demand functions
Demand equations derived from actual market data.

The fundamental building block of statistical demand analysis is the empirical demand function. **Empirical demand functions** are demand equations derived from actual market data. From empirical demand functions, managers can get quantitative estimates of the impact on sales of changes in the price of the product, changes in the level of consumer income, and changes in the price of competing products and products that are complements in consumption. As you will see in later chapters, empirical demand functions can be extremely useful in making pricing and production decisions.

We begin our discussion of empirical demand analysis with a description of some of the more direct methods of demand estimation—consumer interviews and market studies. We deal rather briefly with these methods, attempting only to point out the strengths and weaknesses in each. The primary topic of the chapter is the use of regression analysis to estimate demand functions and associated demand elasticities—own-price, income, and cross-price elasticities. As always, our fundamental concern is how an analyst can use regression analysis and interpret the results, rather than the precise statistical concepts underlying the estimation. To this end, we will provide some examples to show how actual demand functions have been estimated and interpreted.

This chapter about demand estimation and the next chapter about demand forecasting are intended to provide you with an introductory treatment of empirical demand analysis. While our discussion of statistical demand estimation (and statistical demand forecasting) is limited to the simpler methods, these methods are widely used in business to analyze market demand. Almost all the more advanced techniques of empirical demand analysis that you will encounter in your marketing research, advanced statistics, and econometrics courses are extensions of, or related to, the methods we will present in this chapter and the next one.

7.1 DIRECT METHODS OF DEMAND ESTIMATION

Direct methods of demand estimation are techniques that do not involve regression analysis. After reading about some of these direct methods of estimation, you may get the impression that direct estimation techniques are quite simple and straightforward. This is far from correct. Many of the techniques used in making direct estimates of demand are quite sophisticated and require a great deal of experience and expertise in order to estimate demand accurately. This section is designed only to give an overview of some of the methods that can be used and is not meant to teach you how to make these types of estimates. Such instruction is left to more advanced marketing courses.

Consumer Interviews

Since consumers themselves should be the most knowledgeable about their individual demand functions for particular commodities, the most straightforward method of demand estimation would be simply to ask potential buyers how much of the commodity they would buy at different prices with alternative values for the determinants of demand (i.e., the price of substitute commodities, the price of complement commodities, and so on). At the simplest level, this might be accomplished by stopping shoppers and asking them how much of the product they would buy at various prices. At a more sophisticated level, this procedure would entail administering detailed questionnaires to a selected sample of the population by professional interviewers. While this procedure appears very simple, there exist several substantial problems. Among these problems are (1) the selection of a representative sample, (2) response bias, and (3) the inability of the respondent to answer accurately. Let's look at each of these problems briefly.

When selecting a sample of the population for a survey, the resulting demand estimation is reliable only if the survey uses a representative sample. A **representative sample** has the same characteristics of the population as a whole. A representative sample is typically obtained by *randomly* selecting members for the sample from the general population. For example, if 52 percent of the population is female, and if 35 percent have annual incomes over $65,000, then a representative sample should have approximately 52 percent females and 35 percent persons with incomes over $65,000. In actuality, it is very difficult to obtain a truly representative sample.

representative sample
A sample, usually drawn randomly, that has characteristics that accurately reflect the population as a whole.

A classic illustration of what can happen if the sample is not random occurred during the presidential campaign of 1948. A survey was performed that predicted an overwhelming victory for Thomas Dewey. In fact, Harry Truman won the election. The problem with the survey was that the sample was drawn from the subscription list of a particular magazine. The subscribers were not representative of the entire population of the United States; they were instead a subgroup of the voting population and had some important characteristics in common. Thus, the biased sample led to biased results. In 1936, in a similar but less celebrated election forecast error, a popular magazine predicted Franklin Roosevelt would lose the election, but it was wrong because the pollsters used a telephone survey and only wealthy people were able to afford phones at that time. Today, election forecasting has become so accurate—in large part due to the advanced sampling techniques now employed by pollsters—that television networks are not allowed to project winners until the polls are all closed on election day.

Another example of a biased sample yielding misleading results occurred at a home-building convention, during which Owens-Corning Fiberglas Corporation commissioned a survey to determine the industry's outlook for future sales. The results were startling. The survey indicated that builders were planning to increase housing starts by an amazing 30 percent. When asked to interpret the bullish forecast, Michael Sumichrast, chief economist for the National Association of Home Builders, replied that "it shows when you ask stupid questions, you get stupid answers." Apparently, the survey did not use a representative sample. According to *The Wall Street Journal,* the survey was taken only among the builders who attended the convention, and these builders tend to be the larger and more aggressive companies which would naturally be more bullish in their outlook.[1]

response bias
The difference between the response given by an individual to a hypothetical question and the action the individual takes when the situation actually occurs.

A **response bias** can result simply from the fact that those interviewed are giving hypothetical answers to hypothetical questions. The answers do not necessarily reflect what the individual will do; rather, they may reflect intentions or desires. More importantly, however, the responses may be biased by the manner in which the question is asked. In many cases, the questions may be such that the respondents give what they view as a more socially acceptable response, rather than reveal their true preferences.

One example of response bias is found in a survey by an automobile manufacturer taken many years ago—during a time of cheap gasoline. Potential consumers were asked if they would be interested in buying small, economical cars (i.e., fuel-efficient cars) which were not flashy, fast, or showy. A large number of people said they would indeed buy such a car. On the basis of this survey, the manufacturer introduced a small, fuel-efficient car—with disastrous results. Perhaps had the respondents—who indicated that they wanted economy cars—been asked whether their *neighbors* would buy such cars, they might have provided more valid responses. It's easier to say that your neighbor wants a flashy car than to admit that you do. The point is that the wrong question was asked. The way the question was asked induced a response bias.

Past surveys by food manufacturers have yielded bad results because of response bias. The food industry has a lot riding on the claims that people make about what they eat. Food companies have, in the past, conducted their market research by asking people what they eat. On the basis of the results of these surveys, the food manufacturers would develop new products. But, as noted in *The Wall Street Journal,* there is one big problem: "People don't always tell the truth."[2] As Harry Balzer, the vice president of a market research firm, said: "Nobody likes to admit he likes junk food." In other words, a response bias exists in such surveys. Instead of answering truthfully, a consumer is likely to give a socially acceptable answer. Asking a sweets-eater how many Twinkies he eats "is like asking an alcoholic if he drinks much."

[1]See "Stupid Questions," *The Wall Street Journal,* Feb. 7, 1984.

[2]See Betsy Morris, "Study to Detect True Eating Habits Finds Junk-Food Fans in Health-Food Ranks," *The Wall Street Journal,* Feb. 3, 1984.

Finally, it is quite possible that the respondent is *simply unable to answer accurately the question posed.* Conceptually, the firm performing the survey may want to know about the elasticity of demand for its products. Thus, the firm is interested in the response of consumers to incremental changes in price and some other variable. For example, the firm needs to know how the consumers would react to such things as a 1, 2, or 3 percent increase (or decrease) in price or a 5 percent increase (decrease) in advertising expenditures. Obviously, most people interviewed are not able to answer such questions precisely.

Although the survey technique is plagued with these inherent difficulties, it can still be an extremely valuable tool for a manager to use in quantifying demand. The trick in doing a survey is to avoid the pitfalls, and, as the following discussion indicates, that can be done.

Market Studies and Experiments

A somewhat more expensive and difficult technique for estimating demand and demand elasticity is the controlled market study or experiment. The analyst attempts to hold everything constant during the study except for the price of the good.

Those carrying out such market studies normally display the products in several different stores, generally in areas with different characteristics, over a period of time. They make certain that there are always sufficient amounts available in every store at each price to satisfy demand. In this way the effect of changes in supply is removed. There is generally no advertising. During the period of the experiment, price is changed in relatively small increments over a range, and sales are recorded at each price. In this way, many of the effects of changes in other things can be removed, and a reasonable approximation of the actual demand curve can be estimated.

An example of such an approach is a study conducted by M&M/Mars using 150 stores over a 12-month period to determine the optimal weights for its candy bars.[3] Instead of altering the price from store to store, the company kept price constant and altered the size of the product. As the director of sales development reported, in stores where the size was increased, "sales went up 20 percent to 30 percent almost overnight." As a result, M&M/Mars decided to change much of its product line.

A relatively new technique for estimating demand is the use of experiments performed in a laboratory or in the field. Such experiments are a compromise between market studies and surveys. In some types of laboratory experiments, volunteers are paid to simulate actual buying conditions without going through real markets. Volunteer consumers are given money to go on simulated market trips. The experimenter changes relative prices between trips. After many shopping trips by many consumers an approximation of demand is obtained. The volunteers have the incentive to act as though they are really shopping, because there is a probability that they may keep their purchases.

---

[3]See John Koten, "Why Do Hot Dogs Come in Packs of 10 and Buns in 8s or 12s?" *The Wall Street Journal*, Sept. 21, 1984.

Going a step further, some economists have conducted experiments about consumer behavior—with the help of psychologists—in mental institutions and in drug centers, by setting up token economies (which incidentally are supposed to have therapeutic value). Patients receive tokens for jobs performed. They can exchange these tokens for goods and services. The experimenters can change prices and incomes and thus generate demand curves, the properties of which are compared with the theoretical properties of such curves.

In field experiments, the researchers want to be able to change the price of goods and actually observe the behavior of the consumers. Let us give you an example of this type of experiment. Some economists at Texas A&M were interested in estimating the own-price elasticity of the demand for electric energy.[4] They recruited a sample of 100 households to participate in their experiment. The objective of the study was to observe these households' weekly consumption of electric power. After first establishing the households' baseline levels of usage, the researchers experimentally changed the price of electric power for part of their sample by paying rebates for reductions in weekly electricity usage.

For example, in one of their subgroups, the researchers paid the household 1.3 cents for every kilowatt-hour (kwh) reduction in weekly usage. At the time this study was conducted, the cost of electric power to the residential consumers was 2.6 cents per kwh. Therefore, for this subgroup, the price of consuming an additional kwh was increased: to consume an additional kwh, the household not only had to *pay* 2.6 cents but also had to *forgo* the rebate of 1.3 cents it could have received had it conserved rather than consumed electricity. Hence, for this subgroup, the price of electricity increased by 50 percent, from 2.6 to 3.9 cents per kwh.

Other subgroups were given other rebate schedules. And one subgroup—the control group—was given no rebate. The researchers could then actually measure the reduction in electricity consumption due to the experimentally imposed price increase by comparing the change in the consumption of the subgroup receiving the rebate with the change in the consumption of the control group.

The results of this experimental study indicated that the maximum own-price elasticity of the residential demand for electricity was 0.32. That is, the experiment indicated that the residential demand for electricity was price inelastic. However, as the researchers indicated, this study measured an extremely short-run elasticity. (As we noted in Chapter 3, we would expect the price elasticity to increase as the time period for adjustment gets longer.)

1 The experimental approach to estimating the demand for products has rapidly moved out of the laboratories and off the college campuses to the real-world applications more of interest to Wall Street and Main Street. The rapid growth of microcomputers and cable television systems has made possible market experiments that could only have been dreamed of a few years ago.

[4]This example is taken from Raymond C. Battalio, John H. Kagel, Robin C. Winkler, and Richard A. Wineh, "Residential Electricity Demand: An Experimental Study," *Review of Economics and Statistics,* May 1979, pp. 180–189.

7.2 SPECIFICATION OF THE EMPIRICAL DEMAND FUNCTION

Managers can use the techniques of regression analysis outlined in Chapter 5 to obtain estimates of the demand for their firms' products. The theoretical foundation for specifying and analyzing empirical demand functions is provided by the theory of consumer behavior, which was presented in Chapter 6. In this section, we will show you two possible specifications of the demand function to be estimated. Again, we do not intend to teach you statistics or econometrics. Instead, we want to give you an idea of how these techniques of demand estimation can provide useful information for managerial decision making.

As we will discuss later in this chapter (Section 7.3), the statistical method used to estimate the parameters of a market demand function differs depending on whether the price of the product is determined by the simultaneous forces of demand and supply or is set directly by the manager. Despite the differences in the way the parameters are estimated, the way that empirical demand functions are specified and interpreted is essentially the same.

A General Empirical Demand Specification

In order to estimate a demand function for a product, it is necessary to use a specific functional form. Here we will consider both linear and nonlinear forms. Before proceeding, however, we must simplify the general demand relation. Recall that quantity demanded depends on the price of the product, consumer income, the price of related goods, consumer tastes or preferences, expected price, and the number of buyers. Given the difficulties inherent in quantifying taste and price expectations, we will ignore these variables—as is commonly done in many empirical demand studies—and write the general demand function as

$$Q = f(P, M, P_R, N)$$

where

Q = quantity purchased of a good or service
P = price of the good or service
M = consumers' income
P_R = price(s) of related good(s)
N = number of buyers

While this general demand specification seems rather simple and straightforward, the task of defining and collecting the data for demand estimation requires careful consideration of numerous factors. For example, it is important to recognize the geographic boundaries of the product market. Suppose a firm sells its product only in California. In this case, the consumer income variable (M) should measure the buyers' incomes in the state of California. Using average household income in the United States would be a mistake unless California's household income level matches nationwide income levels and trends. It is also crucial to include the prices of all substitute and complement goods that affect sales of the firm's product in California. While we will illustrate empirical demand functions using just one related good (either a substitute or a complement), there are often numerous related goods whose prices should be included in the specification of an empirical demand function. Whether the market is growing (or shrinking) in size is another consideration. Researchers frequently include a measure of population in the demand specification as a proxy variable for the number of buyers. As you can see from this brief discussion, defining and collecting data to estimate even a simple general demand function requires careful consideration.

A Linear Empirical Demand Specification

The simplest demand function is one that specifies a linear relation. In linear form, the empirical demand function is specified as

$$Q = a + bP + cM + dP_R + eN$$

In this equation, the parameter b measures the change in quantity demanded that would result from a one-unit change in price. That is, $b = \Delta Q/\Delta P$, which is assumed to be negative. Also,

$$c = \Delta Q/\Delta M \gtrless 0 \text{ if the good is } \begin{cases} \text{normal} \\ \text{inferior} \end{cases}$$

and

$$d = \Delta Q/\Delta P_R \gtrless 0 \text{ if commodity } R \text{ is a} \begin{cases} \text{substitute} \\ \text{complement} \end{cases}$$

Using the techniques of regression analysis, this linear demand function can be estimated to provide estimates of the parameters a, b, c, d, and e. Then t-tests are performed, or p-values examined, to determine if these parameters are statistically significant.

As stressed in Chapter 3, the elasticity of demand is an important aspect of demand. The elasticities of demand—with respect to own price, income, and the prices of related commodities—can be calculated from a linear demand function without much difficulty. Consider first the own-price elasticity, defined as

$$E = \frac{\Delta Q}{\Delta P} \cdot \frac{P}{Q}$$

In a linear specification, $b = \Delta Q/\Delta P$, so the *estimated* own-price elasticity is

$$\hat{E} = \hat{b} \cdot \frac{P}{Q}$$

As you know from the discussion of demand elasticity in Chapter 3, the elasticity depends upon where it is measured along the demand curve (note the P/Q term in the formula above). The elasticity should be evaluated at the price and quantity values that correspond to the point on the demand curve being analyzed.

In similar manner, the income elasticity may be estimated as

$$\hat{E}_M = \hat{c} \cdot \frac{M}{Q}$$

Likewise, the estimated cross-price elasticity is

$$\hat{E}_{XR} = \hat{d} \cdot \frac{P_R}{Q}$$

2 where the X in the subscript refers to the good for which demand is being estimated.

A Nonlinear Empirical Demand Specification

The most commonly employed nonlinear demand specification is the log-linear (or constant elasticity) form. A log-linear demand function is written as

$$Q = aP^b M^c P_R^d N^e$$

The obvious potential advantage of this form is that it provides a better estimate if the true demand function is indeed nonlinear. Furthermore, as you may recall from Chapter 5, this specification allows for the direct estimation of the elasticities. Specifically, the value of parameter b measures the own-price elasticity of demand. Likewise, c and d, respectively, measure the income elasticity and cross-price elasticity of demand.[5]

As you learned in Chapter 5, to obtain estimates from a log-linear demand function, you must convert it to natural logarithms. Thus, the function to be estimated is linear in the logarithms:

3

$$\ln Q = \ln a + b \ln P + c \ln M + d \ln P_R + e \ln N$$

Choosing a Demand Specification

Although we have presented only two functional forms (linear and log-linear) as possible choices for specifying the empirical demand equation, there are many possible functional forms from which to choose. Unfortunately, the exact functional form of the demand equation generally is not known to the researcher. As noted in Chapter 5, choosing an incorrect functional form of the equation to be estimated results in biased estimates of the parameters of the equation. Selecting the appropriate functional form for the empirical demand equation warrants more than a toss of a coin on the part of the researcher.

In practice, choosing the functional form to use is, to a large degree, a matter of judgment and experience. Nevertheless, there are some things a manager can do to suggest the best choice of functional form. When possible, a manager

[5]The appendix to this chapter shows the derivation of the elasticities associated with the log-linear demand specification.

ILLUSTRATION 7.1

Demand for Imported Goods in Trinidad and Tobago:
A Log-Linear Estimation

Trinidad and Tobago, two small developing countries in the Caribbean, rely heavily on imports from other nations to provide their citizens with consumer and capital goods. Policymakers in these two countries need estimates of the demand for various imported goods to aid them in their trade-related negotiations and to make forecasts of trade balances in Trinidad and Tobago. The own-price elasticities and income elasticities of demand are of particular interest.

In a recent empirical study, John S. Gafar estimated the demand for imported goods in the two countries, using a log-linear specification of demand.* According to Gafar, the two most common functional forms used to estimate import demand are the linear and log-linear forms. As we noted, the choice of functional form is often based on the past experience of experts in a particular area of empirical research. Gafar chose to use the log-linear specification because a number of other import studies "have shown that the log-linear specification is preferable to the linear specification."† Gafar noted that he experimented with both the linear and log-linear forms and found the log-linear model had the higher R^2.

In his study, Gafar estimated the demand for imports of eight groups of commodities. The demand for any particular group of imported goods is specified as

$$Q_d = aP^bM^c$$

where Q_d is the quantity of the imported good demanded by Trinidad and Tobago, P is the price of the imported good (relative to the price of a bundle of domestically produced goods), and M is an income variable. Taking natural logarithms of the demand equation results in the following demand equation to be estimated:

$$\ln Q_d = \ln a + b \ln P + c \ln M$$

Recall from the discussion in the text that b is the own-price elasticity of demand and c is the income elasticity of demand. The sign of $\hat{b}$ is expected to be negative and the sign of $\hat{c}$ can be either positive or negative. The results of estimation are presented in the accompanying table.

Estimated Own-Price and Income Elasticities in Trinidad and Tobago

Product group	Own-price elasticity estimates ($\hat{b}$)	Income elasticity estimates ($\hat{c}$)
Food	−0.6553	1.6411
Beverages and tobacco	-0.0537^n	1.8718
Crude materials (except fuel)	−1.3879	4.9619
Animal and vegetable oils and fats	−0.3992	1.8688
Chemicals	−0.7211	2.2711
Manufactured goods	0.2774^n	3.2085
Machinery and transport equipment	−0.6159	2.9452
Miscellaneous manufactured articles	−1.4585	4.1997

Only two of the estimated parameters are *not* statistically significant at the 5 percent level of significance (denoted by "*n*" in the table). Note that all the product groups have the expected sign for $\hat{b}$, except manufactured goods, for which the parameter estimate is not statistically significant. The estimates of $\hat{c}$ suggest that all eight product groups are normal goods ($\hat{c} > 0$). As you can see, with the log-linear specification, it is much easier to estimate demand elasticities than it is with a linear specification.

*This illustration is based on John S. Gafar, "The Determinants of Import Demand in Trinidad and Tobago: 1967–84," *Applied Economics* 20 (1988).

†Ibid.

should consider the functional form used in similar empirical studies of demand. If a linear specification has worked well in the past or has worked well for other products that are similar, specifying a linear demand function may be justified. In some cases a manager may have information or experience that indicates whether the demand function is either linear or curvilinear, and this functional form is then used to estimate the demand equation.

Sometimes researchers employ a series of regressions to settle on a suitable specification of demand. If the estimated coefficients of the first regression specification have the wrong signs, or if they are not statistically significant, the specification of the model may be wrong. Researchers may then estimate some new specifications, using the same data, to search for a specification that gives significant coefficients with the expected signs.[6]

For the two specifications we have discussed here, a choice between them should consider whether the sample data to be used for estimating demand are best represented by a demand function with varying elasticities (linear demand) or by one with constant elasticity (log-linear demand). When price and quantity observations are spread over a wide range of values, elasticities are more likely to vary, and a linear specification with its varying elasticities is usually a more appropriate specification of demand. Alternatively, if the sample data are clustered over a narrow price (and quantity) range, a constant-elasticity specification of demand, such as a log-linear model, may be a better choice than a linear model. Again we stress that experience in estimating demand functions and additional training in econometric techniques are needed in order to become skilled at specifying the empirical demand function.

We now discuss how to estimate the parameters of the empirical demand function. As it turns out, not only must you choose the proper functional form for the empirical demand equation, but you must also choose the correct method of estimation.

7.3 DEMAND ESTIMATION: MARKET-DETERMINED VERSUS MANAGER-DETERMINED PRICES

As noted above, estimating the parameters of the empirical demand function can be accomplished using regression analysis, and the method of estimating the parameters depends upon whether the price of the product is determined by the intersection of demand and supply curves (a *market-determined* price) or is set by the manager of a firm (a *manager-determined* price). As we have stressed throughout the text, our goal is to show you how to *use* estimated values of parameters in decision making, rather than to show you the statistical details involved in computing the estimates. In this section, we will briefly discuss *why* the parameters of a demand function in which price is market-determined cannot be correctly estimated using the same estimation method that is appropriate for

[6]In a strict statistical sense, it is incorrect to estimate more than one model specification with the same set of data. This practice is common, however, given the high costs often associated with collecting sample data.

estimating parameters of a demand function in which price is manager-determined. While it is not important for the purposes of managerial decision making to understand the computational procedure required to estimate correctly demand curves with market-determined prices, it is quite important that you know which statistical estimation procedure is the appropriate one for your firm. As you will see, the statistical problems that sometimes arise in demand estimation can be routinely handled by "asking" the computer to use the correct estimation procedure.

For some firms, a manager does not set the price of the firm's product; rather, as you saw in Chapter 2, price is determined by the point where the industry's supply curve crosses its demand curve. Recall from Chapter 1 that firms in this situation are called *price-taking* firms. For example, firms producing agricultural commodities must generally accept market-determined prices for their products. When price is determined by the simultaneous interaction of demand and supply, price is being "set" within a system of demand and supply equations. When a variable is determined by a system of equations, it is said to be an **endogenous variable** in that system. For price-taking firms, managers must accept the price of the product as it is determined by market forces in a system of demand and supply equations.

endogenous variable
A variable whose value is determined by a system of equations.

When a firm produces a differentiated product or competes with a relatively small number of rivals, the firm can choose the price of its product and the associated quantity along the firm's downward-sloping demand curve. Recall from our discussion in Chapter 1 that firms such as these are called *price-setting* firms and possess market power. For price-setting firms, price is not determined by the simultaneous forces of demand and supply. Price is an **exogenous variable** when it is manager-determined rather than being determined within a system of demand and supply equations. While price is exogenously determined when a firm is a price-setting firm, another situation in which price is exogenous occurs when a government agency determines the price a firm can charge, as when public service commissions set the price utilities can charge for electricity. We can summarize our discussion with a relation:

exogenous variable
A variable in a system of equations that is determined outside the system.

Relation Managers of price-taking firms do not set the price of the product they sell; rather, prices are endogenous or market-determined by the intersection of demand and supply. Managers of price-setting firms set the price of the product they sell by producing the quantity associated with the chosen price on the downward-sloping demand curve facing the firm. Since price is manager-determined rather than market-determined, price is exogenous for price-setting firms.

The distinction between price-taking firms and price-setting firms plays an important role in determining how the parameters of an empirical demand function must be estimated in order to obtain estimates that are not biased. In order for the least-squares method of estimating the parameters of a regression equation to yield unbiased estimates of the regression parameters, the explanatory variables cannot be correlated with the random error term of the equation. We did not mention this fact in our discussion of regression analysis in Chapter 5 because virtually all the applications covered in this book involve explanatory variables that are not likely to be correlated with the random error term in the equation. There is one important exception, however, and it involves the estimation of demand when the price of the product or service—an explanatory variable in all demand functions—is endogenously determined by demand and supply. In the next section, we discuss estimation of demand when price is endogenous and show how to use a method of estimation called *two-stage least-squares* that is appropriate for estimating the industry demand for price-taking firms. Then in Section 7.5 we show how to use the "ordinary" least-squares method of estimation to estimate empirical demand functions for price-setting firms.

7.4 ESTIMATING DEMAND FOR PRICE-TAKING FIRMS

As we discussed in the last section, a fundamental difficulty arises in estimating industry demand for price-taking firms because the observed quantity and price data used in a regression analysis of demand are determined simultaneously by the intersection of demand and supply. Consequently, the observed variation in equilibrium quantity and price is caused by all the factors that can shift either demand or supply. Because market quantity and price are simultaneously determined by both demand and supply, estimation of industry demand for price-taking firms involves a bit more challenge than estimation of demand curves for price-setting firms (discussed in Section 7.5). The problem of estimating demand when price is market-determined is frequently referred to as the **simultaneity problem**.

simultaneity problem The problem in estimating market demand that arises because variation in observed values of market quantity and price are simultaneously determined by changes in both demand *and* supply.

To understand the nature of the simultaneity problem, consider the following simple model of industry demand and supply curves for gasoline (say, unleaded 89 octane grade):

$$\text{Demand:} \quad Q = a + bP + cM + \epsilon_d$$
$$\text{Supply:} \quad Q = h + kP + lP_c + \epsilon_s$$

where Q is the number of gallons of gasoline sold in a month (i.e., equilibrium Q), P is the average price of gasoline (before taxes are added), M is consumer income, P_c is the average price of crude oil (a key ingredient input for gasoline production), and ϵ_d and ϵ_s are the random error terms representing random influences on demand and supply, respectively. These two equations make up a system of two simultaneous equations with two *endogenous* variables: Q and P. The values of the other economic variables in the system, M and P_c, are determined outside this system of equations and are exogenous.

Panel A of Figure 7.1 shows how four monthly observations, from January through April, on P and Q are generated by the demand and supply curves for gasoline. The demand and supply equations in Panel A can be represented as

$$\text{Demand:} \quad Q = A + bP, \quad \text{where } A = a + cM + \epsilon_d$$
$$\text{Supply:} \quad Q = H + lP, \quad \text{where } H = h + lP_c + \epsilon_s$$

The location of the demand curve in any one of the four months is determined by the value of the demand intercept, A, for that month. The demand intercept is itself determined by the value of the exogenous variable M and the random

FIGURE 7.1
The Nature of Simultaneity

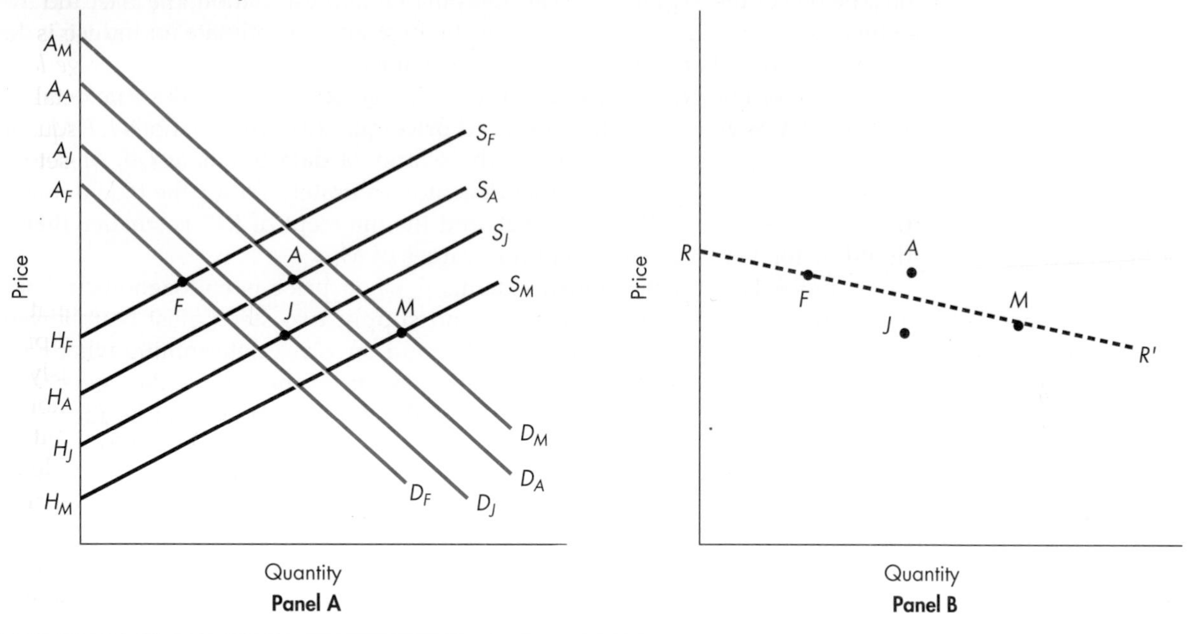

error term ϵ_d, which accounts for random variation in monthly gasoline demand. Similarly, the location of monthly supply is determined by the values of P_c and ϵ_s. The four monthly values of the demand and supply intercepts are shown as A_J, A_F, A_M, A_A, and H_J, H_F, H_M, H_A, respectively. The observed values of price and quantity at points *J*, *F*, *M*, and *A* in Panel A of Figure 7.1 are determined solely by the values of the exogenous variables of the system and the random errors in both demand and supply. Consequently, the equilibrium values of price and quantity, P_E and Q_E, can be expressed as functions of *M*, P_c, ϵ_d, and ϵ_s:

$$P_E = f(M, P_c, \epsilon_d, \epsilon_s) \qquad \text{and} \qquad Q_E = g(M, P_c, \epsilon_d, \epsilon_s)$$

reduced-form equations
Equations expressing each endogenous variable as functions of all exogenous variables and random errors in the system

These equations, which express the endogenous variables as functions of the exogenous variables and the random error terms, are called the **reduced-form equations** of the system. The reduced-form equations show two things clearly: (1) The observed values of *P* and *Q* are each determined by *all* the exogenous variables and random errors in both the demand *and* the supply equations, and (2) the observed values of price are correlated with the random errors in both demand and supply. The first point shows why, in estimating industry demand, information about variation in supply-shifting variables is required to properly explain the observed variation in quantity demanded (which is Q_E). The second point explains why price is correlated with the random errors. As we mentioned, when explanatory variables are correlated with the random error term of the equation to be estimated, the ordinary method of least-squares estimation will produce biased estimates of the parameters of a demand equation. Since price must be one of the explanatory variables in demand estimation, the least-squares method presented in Chapter 5 is not the best way to estimate an industry demand equation when price is market-determined.

Panel B of Figure 7.1 illustrates the challenge of estimating the true demand equation that is generating the observed price-quantity combinations *J*, *F*, *M*, and *A*. Fitting a regression line through the scatter of data points at *J*, *F*, *M*, and *A* produces a regression line RR' that does not accurately reflect the true demand function. The slope of RR' is too flat, and the intercept of RR' is smaller than it should be for any of the four monthly values of *M*.

To properly estimate industry demand when price is endogenously determined by the intersection of demand and supply, two steps must be followed. The first step, called **identification of demand**, involves determining whether it is possible to trace out the true demand curve from the sample data generated by the underlying system of equations. If the demand curve can be identified from sample data—as it can be in most cases—then the second step involves using the method of **two-stage least-squares (2SLS)** to estimate the parameters of the industry demand equation. A complete discussion of the identification of demand and the use of two-stage least-squares is quite complex and unnecessary for our purpose, which, throughout the book, is to show you how to use and interpret the parameters estimated using regression analysis. We turn now to a brief intuitive discussion of identification and then to the use of two-stage least-squares regression.

identification of demand
The process of making sure the sample data will trace out the true demand curve.

two-stage least-squares (2SLS)
A method of estimating parameters of demand when price is endogenous or market-determined.

Identification of Industry Demand

The observed quantities sold and the observed prices are not simply points on a specific demand curve but, rather, points of market equilibrium that occur at the intersection of the demand and supply curves. As you saw in Panel B of Figure 7.1, the observed price-quantity combinations (*J*, *F*, *M*, *A*) may not trace out a picture of the underlying industry demand curve. Before a researcher runs a regression analysis to estimate an industry demand equation, the researcher must be sure that the data generated by the underlying system of demand and supply equations will trace out the true demand equation.

There are several ways to identify a demand equation, but we will show you only the most widely used method here. Figure 7.2 illustrates this method of identifying demand. When the supply equation contains an exogenous supply-shifting variable that does not also cause the demand curve to shift, then changes in this exogenous variable shift the supply curve along a stationary demand curve. The resulting points of intersection along the demand curve generate observable points of equilibrium that trace out the true underlying demand curve; demand is identified.

Typically, the identification problem is solved when, in addition to the price of the product, quantity supplied is a function of at least one of the supply-shifting variables discussed in Chapter 2 (technology, input prices, prices of goods related in production, price expectations, or the number of sellers). Since

FIGURE 7.2
Identification of Demand

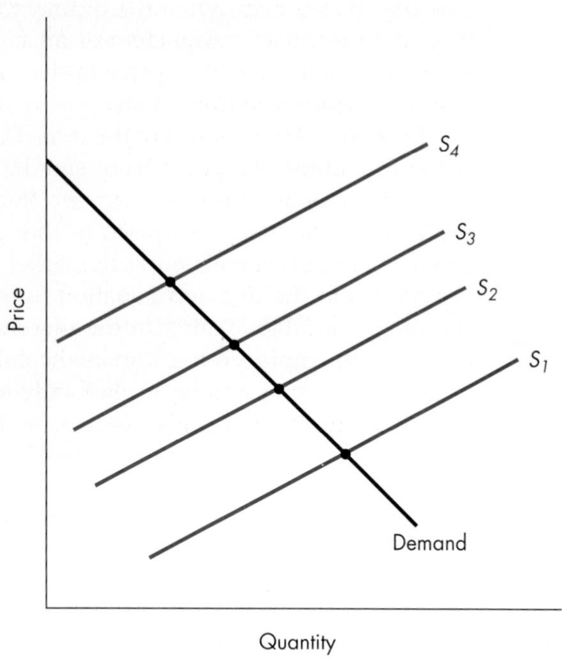

a supply-shifting variable will not generally also be a demand-shifting variable, the demand function is identified in most commonly occurring situations. We can summarize this method of identifying demand in a relation:

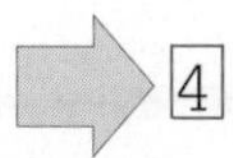

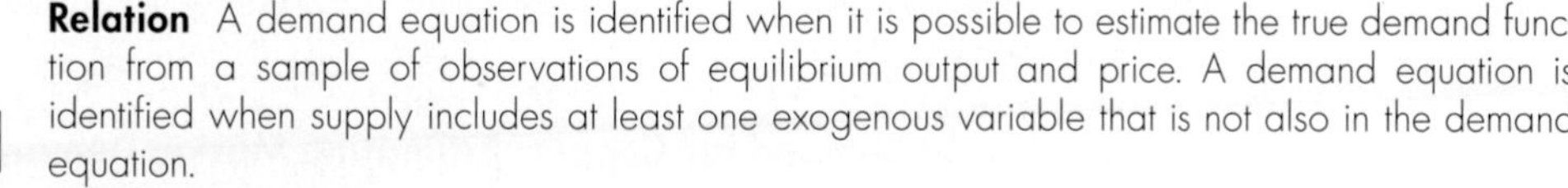
Relation A demand equation is identified when it is possible to estimate the true demand function from a sample of observations of equilibrium output and price. A demand equation is identified when supply includes at least one exogenous variable that is not also in the demand equation.

Estimation of Demand Using Two-Stage Least-Squares (2SLS)

In order for the ordinary least-squares method of estimating the parameters of a regression equation to yield unbiased estimates of the regression parameters, the right-hand-side explanatory variables cannot be correlated with the random error term of the equation. Since all demand functions will have price as one of the explanatory variables, ordinary least-squares estimation is not a suitable method of estimating industry demand when price is an endogenous variable. As can be seen by examining the reduced-form equations, random variations in either the demand or the supply equations will cause variation in price, and, consequently, price will be correlated with the random error term in the demand (and supply) equation(s). Thus, when price is market-determined—as it will be for price-taking firms—price will be correlated with the random error term in the demand equation, and the least-squares estimates of the parameter of the demand equation will be biased. Recall that a parameter estimate is biased if the average (or expected) value of the estimate does not equal the true value of the parameter. The bias that occurs when the ordinary least-squares estimation method is employed to estimate parameters of an equation for which one, or more, of the right-hand-side variables (price in this case) is an endogenous variable is called a **simultaneous equations bias.**

simultaneous equations bias
Bias in estimation that occurs when the ordinary least-squares estimation method is used to estimate the parameters of an equation for which one, or more, of the explanatory variables is an endogenous variable.

Econometricians employ the two-stage least-squares (2SLS) estimation technique to address the problem of simultaneous equations bias. As its name suggests, the estimation proceeds in two steps. In the first stage, a proxy variable for the endogenous variable (price in this case) is created in such a way that the proxy variable is correlated with market price but uncorrelated with the random error term in the demand equation. In the second stage, price is replaced with the proxy variable created in the first stage, and the usual least-squares procedure is then employed to estimate the parameters of the demand equation.[7] Two-stage least-squares can be applied only to demand equations that are identified. If demand is not identified, there is no estimation technique that will correctly estimate the parameters of the demand equation.

Many regression programs are available, even for personal computers, that have a two-stage least-squares routine, and these 2SLS packages perform the two stages of estimation automatically. It is normally necessary for the user to specify only which variables are endogenous and which are exogenous in the system of equations. Once the estimates for the parameters of a demand equation have been obtained from the second stage of the regression, their significance can be evaluated using either a t-test or the p-values in precisely the same manner as for any other regression equation.[8] We summarize this discussion in a principle:

5

Principle When market price is an endogenous variable, price will be correlated with the random error term in the demand equation causing a simultaneous equations bias if the ordinary least-squares (OLS) method of estimation is applied. To avoid simultaneous equations bias, the two-stage least-squares method of estimation (2SLS) can be employed if the demand equation is identified.

The World Demand for Copper: Estimating Market Demand Using 2SLS

To illustrate how a market demand function is estimated using two-stage least-squares, we estimate the world demand for copper (i.e., the market demand for all countries buying copper). In its simplest form, the world demand for copper is a function of the price of copper, income, and the price of any related commodities. Using aluminum as the related commodity, because it is the primary substitute for copper in manufacturing, the demand function can be written in linear form as

$$Q_{\text{copper}} = a + bP_{\text{copper}} + cM + dP_{\text{aluminum}}$$

It is tempting to simply regress copper consumption on the price of copper, income, and the price of aluminum. Because the price of copper and the quantity

[7]A more complete presentation of 2SLS estimation is presented in the appendix to this chapter.

[8]Due to the manner in which 2SLS estimates are calculated, the R^2 and F-statistics are not particularly meaningful.

of copper consumed are determined simultaneously by the intersection of industry demand and supply, it is necessary first to determine if copper demand is identified; then, if it is, the empirical demand function for copper can be estimated using 2SLS. The copper demand function is identified if it is reasonable to believe that the copper supply equation includes at least one exogenous variable not found in the copper demand function. We turn now to the specification of copper supply.

Begin by letting the quantity supplied of copper depend on the price of copper and the level of available technology. Next consider inventories, which play a particularly important role in the market for copper. When inventories rise, current production usually falls. To measure *changes* in copper inventory, define a variable denoted by X to be the ratio of consumption to production in the preceding period. As consumption declines relative to production, X will fall, and current production is expected to decline. Thus, the supply function can be reasonably specified in linear form as

$$Q_{\text{copper}} = e + fP_{\text{copper}} + gT + hX$$

Since the supply function includes two exogenous variables that are excluded from the demand equation (T and X), the demand function is identified and may be estimated using 2SLS.

The data needed to estimate demand are (1) the world consumption (sales) of copper in 1,000 metric tons, (2) the price of copper and aluminum in cents per pound, deflated by a price index to obtain the real (i.e., constant-dollar) prices, (3) an index of real per capita income, and (4) the world production of copper (in order to calculate the inventory variable, X). Time serves as a proxy for available technology (this assumes that the level of technology increased steadily over time). The resulting data set is presented in Table A of the appendix at the end of this chapter.

Using these data, the demand function is estimated using 2SLS. The results of these estimations are presented below:

Two-Stage Least-Squares Estimation

DEPENDENT VARIABLE: QC	R-SQUARE	F-RATIO	P-VALUE ON F
OBSERVATIONS: 25	0.5763	118.033	0.0001

VARIABLE	PARAMETER ESTIMATE	STANDARD ERROR	T-RATIO	P-VALUE
INTERCEPT	−6837.800	1264.500	−5.408	0.0001
PC	−66.495	31.534	−2.109	0.0472
M	13997.000	1306.300	10.715	0.0001
PA	107.660	44.510	2.419	0.0247

ILLUSTRATION 7.2

Estimating the Demand for Corporate Jets

Given the success that many of our former students have experienced in their careers and the success we predict for you, we thought it might be valuable for you to examine the market for corporate aircraft. Rather than dwell on the lackluster piston-driven and turboprop aircraft, we instead focus this illustration on the demand for corporate jets. In a recent empirical study of general aviation aircraft, McDougall and Cho estimated the demand using techniques that are similar to the ones in this chapter.* Let's now look at how regression analysis can be used to estimate the demand for corporate jets.

In order to estimate the demand for corporate jets, McDougall and Cho specified the variables that affect jet aircraft sales and the general demand relation as follows:

$$Q_J = f(P, P_R, M, D)$$

when

Q_J = number of new corporate jets purchased
P = price of a new corporate jet
P_R = price of a used corporate jet
M = income of the buyers
D = so-called dummy variable to account for seasonality of jet sales

Since the market for used jets is extensively used by corporations, the price of used jets (a substitute) is included in the demand equation. We should note that P and P_R are not the actual prices paid for the aircraft but are instead the user costs of an aircraft. A jet aircraft provides many miles of transportation, not all of which are consumed during the first period of ownership. The user cost of a jet measures the cost per mile (or per hour) of operating the jet by spreading the initial purchase price over the lifetime of jet transportation services and adjusting for depreciation in the value of the aircraft.

The income of the buyers (M) is approximated by corporate profit since most buyers of small jet aircraft are corporations. The data used to estimate the demand equation are quarterly observations (1981I-1985III). Many corporations purchase jets at year-end for tax purposes. Consequently, jet sales tend to be higher in the fourth quarter, all else constant, than in the other three quarters of any given year. Adjusting for this pattern of seasonality is accomplished by adding a variable called a "dummy variable," which takes on values of 1 for observations in the fourth quarter and 0 for observations in the other three quarters. In effect, the dummy variable shifts the estimated demand equation rightward during the fourth quarter. A complete explanation of the use of dummy variables to adjust for seasonality in data is presented in Chapter 8 of this text.

The following linear model of demand for corporate jets is estimated:

$$Q_J = a + bP + cP_R + dM + eD_4$$

McDougall and Cho estimated this demand equation using least-squares estimation rather than two-stage least-squares because they noted that the supply curve for aircraft is almost perfectly elastic or horizontal. If the supply of jets is horizontal, the supply price of new jets is constant no matter what the level of output. Since the market price of jets is determined by the position of the (horizontal) jet supply curve, and the position of supply is fixed by the exogenous determinants of supply, the price of jets is itself exogenous. If jet price (P) is exogenous, least-squares regression is appropriate. The computer output obtained by McDougall and Cho from estimating this equation follows:

Before estimating the demand equation, we determined whether the estimated coefficients $\hat{b}$, $\hat{c}$, and $\hat{d}$ should be positive or negative based on theoretical considerations. We expected that (1) due to a downward-sloping demand curve for copper, $b < 0$; (2) since copper is a normal good, $c > 0$; and (3) since copper and aluminum are substitutes, $d > 0$. The estimated coefficients do conform to this sign pattern. Examining the p-values for the parameter estimates shows that

DEPENDENT VARIABLE: QJ		R-SQUARE	F-RATIO	P-VALUE ON F
OBSERVATIONS: 18		0.8623	20.35	0.0001
VARIABLE	PARAMETER ESTIMATE	STANDARD ERROR	T-RATIO	P-VALUE
INTERCEPT	17.33	43.3250	0.40	0.6956
P	−0.00016	0.000041	−3.90	0.0018
PR	0.00050	0.000104	4.81	0.0003
M	−0.85010	0.7266	−1.17	0.2630
D4	31.99	8.7428	3.66	0.0030

Theoretically, the predicted signs of the estimated coefficients are (1) $\hat{b} < 0$, since demand for corporate jets is expected to be downward-sloping; (2) $\hat{c} > 0$, since new and used jets are substitutes; (3) $\hat{d} > 0$, because corporate jets are expected to be normal goods; and (4) $\hat{e} > 0$, because the tax effect at year-end should cause jet demand to increase (shift rightward) during the fourth quarter. All the estimates, except $\hat{d}$, match the expected signs.

The p-values for the individual parameter estimates indicate that all the variables in the model play a statistically significant role in determining sales of jet aircraft, except corporate profits. The model as a whole does a good job of explaining the variation in sales of corporate jets—86 percent of this variation is explained by the model ($R^2 = 0.8623$). The F-ratio indicates that the model as a whole is significant at the 0.01 percent level.

McDougall and Cho estimated the own-price and cross-price elasticities of demand using the values of Q_J, P, and P_R in the third quarter of 1985:

$$E = \hat{b}\frac{P_{1985III}}{Q_{1985III}} = -3.95$$

$$E_{NU} = \hat{c}\frac{P_{R,1985III}}{Q_{1985III}} = 6.41$$

where E_{NU} is the cross-price elasticity between new-jet sales and the price of used jets. The own-price elasticity estimate suggests that the quantity demanded of new corporate jets is quite responsive to changes in the price of new jets ($|E| > 1$). Furthermore, a 10 percent decrease in the price of used jets is estimated to cause a 64.1 percent decrease in sales of new corporate jets. Given this rather large cross-price elasticity, used jets appear to be viewed by corporations as extremely close substitutes for new jets, and for this reason, we advise all of our managerial economics students to look closely at the used-jet market before buying a new corporate jet.

*The empirical results in this illustration are taken from Gerald S. McDougall and Dong W. Cho, "Demand Estimates for New General Aviation Aircraft: A User-Cost Approach," *Applied Economics* 20 (1988).

all parameter estimates are statistically significant at the 5 percent level, or better.

Now, we calculate estimates of the demand elasticities. While the elasticity can be evaluated at any point on the demand curve, we choose to estimate the elasticities for the values of P_c, M, and P_A in the last year of the sample. From Table A in the appendix, we obtain, for the 25th observation in the sample, the values $P_c = 36.33$, $M = 1.07$, and $P_A = 22.75$. At the point associated with the 25th observation on the estimated demand curve, the estimated quantity of copper demanded is calculated to be 8,172.49 ($= -6{,}837.8 - 66.495 \times 36.33 + 13{,}997 \times 1.07 + 107.66 \times 22.75$). The own-price elasticity of demand is estimated to be

$$\hat{E} = \hat{b}\frac{P_c}{Q_c} = -66.495 \cdot \frac{36.33}{8{,}172.49} = -0.296$$

Similarly, the estimated income elasticity of demand is

$$\hat{E}_M = \hat{c}\frac{M_c}{Q_c} = 13{,}997 \cdot \frac{1.07}{8{,}172.49} = 1.833$$

and the estimated cross-price elasticity of demand is

$$\hat{E}_{CA} = \hat{d}\frac{P_A}{Q_c} = 107.66 \cdot \frac{22.75}{8{,}172.49} = 0.300$$

Thus, the demand for copper—when evaluated at the point associated with the 25th observation in the sample—is inelastic ($|E| < 1$), copper is a normal good ($E_M > 0$), and copper is a substitute for aluminum ($E_{CA} > 0$). Note that copper is a rather poor substitute for aluminum since a 10 percent increase in the price of aluminum increases the quantity demanded of copper by only 3 percent.

7.5 ESTIMATING DEMAND FOR PRICE-SETTING FIRMS

When a manager sets the price of a product, price is an *exogenous* variable because its value is determined by forces other than those of demand and supply—namely, by the "force" of the manager. When price is set by a manager, no simultaneity problem exists. Demand is identified because the manager's price changes can trace out the firm's underlying demand function. Ordinary least-squares estimation is appropriate since price is not correlated with the random error terms, because it is exogenously determined by the manager. We summarize this important point with a principle:

Principle When a firm is a price-setting firm, the problem of simultaneity vanishes, and the demand curve for the firm can be estimated using the ordinary least-squares method of estimation.

Estimating the Demand for Pizzas: An Example

We will now illustrate how a firm with price-setting power can estimate the demand equation for its output. Consider Checkers Pizza, one of only two home delivery pizza firms serving the Westbury neighborhood of Houston. The manager and owner of Checkers Pizza, Ann Chovie, knows that her customers are rather price-conscious. Pizza buyers in Westbury pay close attention to the price she charges for a home-delivered pizza and the price her competitor, Al's Pizza Oven, charges for a similar home-delivered pizza.

Ann decides to estimate the empirical demand function for her firm's pizza. She collects data on the last 24 months of pizza sales from her own company records. She knows the price she charged for her pizza during that time period, and she also has kept a record of the prices charged at Al's Pizza Oven. Ann is able to obtain average household income figures from the Westbury Small Business Development Center. The only other competitor in the neighborhood is the local branch of McDonald's. Ann is able to find the price of a Big Mac for the last 24 months from advertisements in old newspapers. She adjusts her price and income data for the effects of inflation by deflating the dollar figures, using a deflator she obtained from the *Survey of Current Business.* (She had to make a trip to the University of Houston library.) To measure the number of buyers in the market area (N), Ann collected data on the number of residents in Westbury. As it turned out, the number of residents had not changed during the last 24 months, so Ann dropped N from her specification of demand. The data she collected are presented in Table B in the appendix at the end of this chapter.

Since the price of pizza at Checkers Pizza is set by Ann, and therefore is an exogenous variable, she can estimate the empirical demand equation using the standard techniques of regression analysis—2SLS is not required. Ann first estimates the following linear specification of demand using the 24 monthly observations she collected:

$$Q = a + bP + cM + dP_{\text{Al}} + eP_{\text{BMac}}$$

where

Q = sales of pizza at Checkers Pizza
P = price of a pizza at Checkers Pizza
M = average annual household income in Westbury
P_{Al} = price of a pizza at Al's Pizza Oven
P_{BMac} = price of a Big Mac at McDonald's

The following computer printout shows the results of her least-squares regression:

DEPENDENT VARIABLE: Q		R-SQUARE	F-RATIO	P-VALUE ON F
OBSERVATIONS: 24		0.9699	153.17	0.0001
VARIABLE	PARAMETER ESTIMATE	STANDARD ERROR	T-RATIO	P-VALUE
INTERCEPT	−346.856	413.886	−0.84	0.4124
P	−196.000	11.036	−17.76	0.0001
M	0.075	0.010	7.50	0.0001
PAL	174.500	31.698	5.50	0.0001
PBMAC	81.086	22.155	3.66	0.0017

Ann tests the four estimated slope parameters ($\hat{b}$, $\hat{c}$, $\hat{d}$, and $\hat{e}$) for statistical significance at the 1 percent level of significance. The critical t-value for 19 degrees of freedom ($n - k = 24 - 5$) at the 1 percent significance level is 2.861. The t-ratios for all four slope parameters exceed 2.861, and thus the coefficients are all statistically significant. Ann sees the p-values for the four slope parameters and realizes the exact level of significance is much lower than the 1 percent level used in her t-tests (and the level of confidence is higher than 99 percent). She is pleased to see that the model explains nearly 97 percent of the variation in her pizza sales ($R^2 = 0.9699$) and that the model as a whole is highly significant, as indicated by the p-value on the F-statistic of 0.0001.

Ann decides to calculate estimated demand elasticities at values of P, M, P_{Al}, and P_{BMac} that she feels "typify" the pizza market in Westbury for the past 24 months. These values are $P = 9.05$, $M = 26{,}614$, $P_{\text{Al}} = 10.12$, and $P_{\text{BMac}} = 1.15$. At this "typical" point on the estimated demand curve, the quantity of pizza demanded is

$$\begin{aligned}\hat{Q} &= -346.856 - 196 \times 9.05 + 0.075 \times 26{,}614 + 174.5 \times 10.12 + 81.086 \times 1.15 \\ &= 1{,}734.58\end{aligned}$$

The elasticities for the linear demand specification are estimated in the now familiar fashion:

$$\begin{aligned}\hat{E} &= \hat{b}(P/Q) = (-196)(9.05/1{,}734) = -1.023 \\ \hat{E}_M &= \hat{c}(M/Q) = 0.075(26{,}614/1{,}734) = 1.151 \\ \hat{E}_{\text{Al}} &= \hat{d}(P_{\text{Al}}/Q) = 174.5(10.12/1{,}734) = 1.018 \\ \hat{E}_{\text{BMac}} &= \hat{e}(P_{\text{BMac}}/Q) = 81.086(1.15/1{,}734) = 0.054\end{aligned}$$

Ann's estimated elasticities show that she prices her pizzas just slightly higher than the price at which demand is unit elastic. A one percent increase in average household income will cause sales to rise by 1.15 percent—pizzas are a normal good in Westbury. The estimated cross-price elasticity E_{Al} suggests that if Al's Pizza Oven raises its pizza price by one percent, sales of Checkers' pizzas will increase by 1.02 percent. While the price of a Big Mac does play a statistically significant role in determining sales of Checkers' pizzas, the impact is estimated to be quite small. Indeed, a 10 percent decrease in the price of a Big Mac will decrease sales of Checkers' pizzas only by one-half of one percent (0.54 percent). Apparently families in Westbury aren't very willing to substitute a Big Mac for a home-delivered pizza from Checkers Pizza.

While Ann is satisfied that a linear specification of demand for her firm's pizza does an outstanding job of explaining the variation in her pizza sales, she decides to estimate a nonlinear model just for comparison. Ann chooses a log-linear demand specification of the form

$$Q = aP^{b}M^{c}P_{\text{Al}}^{d}P_{\text{BMac}}^{e}$$

which can be transformed (by taking natural logarithms) into the following estimable form:

$$\ln Q = \ln a + b \ln P + c \ln M + d \ln P_{\text{Al}} + e \ln P_{\text{BMac}}$$

The regression results from the computer are presented below:

DEPENDENT VARIABLE: LNQ		R-SQUARE	F-RATIO	P-VALUE ON F
OBSERVATIONS: 24		0.9600	114.25	0.0001
VARIABLE	PARAMETER ESTIMATE	STANDARD ERROR	T-RATIO	P-VALUE
INTERCEPT	−2.442	0.823	−2.94	0.0084
LNP	−0.981	0.065	−15.09	0.0001
LNM	1.194	0.187	6.39	0.0001
LNPAL	1.304	0.215	6.07	0.0001
LNPBMAC	0.055	0.015	3.67	0.0016

While the *F*-ratio and R^2 for the log-linear model are just slightly smaller than those for the linear specification, the log-linear specification certainly performs just as well. Recall that the slope parameter estimates in a log-linear model are elasticities. While the elasticity estimates from the log-linear model come extremely close to the elasticity estimates from the linear model, linear and log-linear specifications may not always produce such similar elasticity estimates. In general, the linear demand is appropriate when elasticities are likely to vary, and a log-linear specification is appropriate when elastiticies are constant. In this case, Ann could use either one of the empirical demand functions for business decision making.

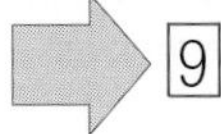

7.6 SUMMARY

This chapter presented the basic techniques of estimating demand functions. Consumer interviews and market studies are direct methods of estimating demand. In consumer interviews, interviewers administer detailed questionnaires to a selected sample of the population in order to determine how much of the commodity the respondents would buy at different prices with alternative values for the determinants of demand. When estimating demand using consumer interviews, managers may encounter problems with the selection of a representative sample, with biases in the responses of consumers, and with the inability of consumers to answer questions accurately. An alternative method of directly estimating demand involves controlled market studies or experiments. In a typical market study, a product is displayed at a number of different stores, each store having its own particular characteristics. Price is varied over time and sales are recorded for each price, thereby producing an approximation of the actual demand curve for the product. In some cases, experiments are used to simulate consumer choice in a laboratory (controlled) environment.

While consumer interviews and market studies can provide managers with valuable information about consumer demand, actual estimation of demand functions is most often accomplished using the technique of regression analysis. Two specifications for demand, linear and log-linear, are presented in this chapter. When demand is specified to be linear in form, the coefficients on each of the explanatory variables measure the rate of change in quantity demanded as that explanatory variable changes, holding all other explanatory variables constant. In linear form, the empirical demand specification is

$$Q = a + bP + cM + dP_R$$

where Q is the quantity demanded, P is the price of the good or service, M is consumer income, and P_R is the price of some related good R. The slope parameter estimates are interpreted as follows: $b = \Delta Q/\Delta P$, $c = \Delta Q/\Delta M$, and $d = \Delta Q/\Delta P_R$. The expected signs of the parameter estimates are given by consumer theory. Given the law of demand, b is expected to be negative. If the good is normal (inferior), c is expected to be positive (negative). If the two goods X and R are substitutes (complements), d is expected to be positive (negative). The estimated demand elasticities are computed as

$$\hat{E} = \hat{b} \cdot \frac{P}{Q} \qquad \hat{E}_M = \hat{c} \cdot \frac{M}{Q} \qquad \text{and} \qquad \hat{E}_{XR} = \hat{d} \cdot \frac{P_R}{Q}$$

As in any regression analysis, the statistical significance of the parameter estimates can be assessed by performing t-tests or examining p-values.

When demand is specified as log-linear, the demand function is written as

$$Q = aP^bM^cP_R^d$$

In order to estimate the log-linear demand function, it is converted to natural logarithms:

$$\ln Q = \ln a + b \ln P + c \ln M + d \ln P_R$$

In log-linear form, the elasticities of demand are constant, and the estimated elasticities are

$$\hat{E} = \hat{b}, \qquad \hat{E}_M = \hat{c}, \qquad \text{and} \qquad \hat{E}_{XR} = \hat{d}$$

To choose between these two specifications of demand, a researcher should consider whether the sample data to be used for estimating demand are best represented by a demand function with varying elasticities (linear demand) or by one with constant elasticity (log-linear demand). When price and quantity observations are spread over a wide range of values, elasticities are likely to vary, and a linear specification with its varying elasticities is usually a more appropriate specification of demand. Alternatively, if the sample data are clustered over a narrow price (and quantity) range, a constant-elasticity specification of demand, such as a log-linear model, may be a better choice than a linear model.

The method of estimating the parameters of an empirical demand function depends upon whether the price of the product is market-determined or manager-determined. Managers of price-taking firms do not set the price of the product they sell; rather, prices are endogenous or "market-determined" by the intersection of demand and supply. Managers of price-setting firms set the price of the product they sell by producing the quantity associated with the chosen price on the downward-sloping demand curve facing the firm. Since price is manager-determined rather than market-determined, price is exogenous for price-setting firms.

When estimating industry demand for price-taking firms, complications arise because of the problem of simultaneity. The simultaneity problem refers to the fact that the observed variation in equilibrium output and price is the result of changes in the determinants of both demand and supply. Because output and price are determined jointly by the forces of supply and demand, two econometric problems arise when a researcher tries to estimate the coefficients of demand: the identification problem and the simultaneous equations bias problem.

The identification problem involves determining whether it is possible to trace out the true demand curve from the sample data. Demand is identified when supply includes at least one exogenous variable that is not also in the demand equation. The problem of simultaneous equations bias arises when price is an endogenous variable, as it is when price is market-determined for price-taking firms. In order for the standard or ordinary least-squares (OLS) regression procedure to yield unbiased parameter estimates, all explanatory variables must be uncorrelated with the random error term in the demand equation. An endogenous variable is always correlated with the error term in both the demand and supply equations. (This can be verified by examining the reduced form equation for Q, which shows how Q is related to all the exogenous variables and error terms in the system.) Since price is an explanatory variable in the demand equation, and an endogenous variable in the case of price-taking firms, a simultaneous equations bias will result when the OLS procedure is used to estimate demand. The simultaneous equations bias is eliminated by estimating the parameters of the empirical demand equation using 2SLS.

When estimating the demand curve facing a price-setting firm—a firm that can control or set the price of its product by varying its own level of production—the problem of simultaneity does not arise. The demand curve for price-setting firms can be estimated using the ordinary least-squares method of estimation.

TECHNICAL PROBLEMS

1. Cite the three major problems with consumer interviews or surveys and provide an example of each.
2. The estimated market demand for good X is

$$\hat{Q} = 70 - 3.5P - 0.6M + 4P_Z$$

where $\hat{Q}$ is the estimated number of units of good X demanded, P is the price of the good, M is income, and P_Z is the price of related good Z. (All parameter estimates are statistically significant at the 1 percent level.)

   a. Is X a normal or an inferior good? Explain.
   b. Are X and Z substitutes or complements? Explain.
   c. At $P = 10$, $M = 30$, and $P_Z = 6$, compute estimates for the own-price, income, and cross-price elasticities.

3. The empirical demand function for good X is estimated in log-linear form as

$$\ln\hat{Q} = 11.74209 - 1.65 \ln P + 0.8 \ln M - 2.5 \ln P_Y$$

where $\hat{Q}$ is the estimated number of units of good X demanded, P is the price of X, M is income, and P_Y is the price of related good Y. (All parameter estimates are significantly different from zero at the 5 percent level.)

   a. Is X a normal or an inferior good? Explain.
   b. Are X and Y substitutes or complements? Explain.
   c. Express the empirical demand function in the alternative (nonlogarithmic) form: $\hat{Q} =$ ________ .
   d. At $P = 50$, $M = 36{,}000$, and $P_Y = 25$, what are the estimated own-price, income, and cross-price elasticities? What is the predicted number of units of good X demanded?

4. For each of the following sets of demand and supply functions, determine if the demand function is identified and explain why or why not:
   a. Demand: $Q = a + bP$
   Supply: $Q = e + fP$
   b. Demand: $Q = a + bP + cM$
   Supply: $Q = e + fP$
   c. Demand: $Q = a + bP + cW$
   Supply: $Q = e + fP + gW$
   d. Demand: $Q = a + bP + cM$
   Supply: $Q = e + fP + gT + hP_I$
5. Evaluate the following statement: "If a demand equation is not identified, then two-stage least-squares (2SLS) must be used to estimate the demand equation."
6. With the data in Table A of the appendix, the world demand for copper can be estimated by using ordinary least-squares, rather than by using 2SLS, as done in the text example. The estimation results using OLS are as follows:

DEPENDENT VARIABLE: QC		R-SQUARE	F-RATIO	P-VALUE ON F
OBSERVATIONS: 25		0.9646	190.846	0.0001
VARIABLE	PARAMETER ESTIMATE	STANDARD ERROR	T-RATIO	P-VALUE
INTERCEPT	−6150.039	931.924	−6.60	0.0001
PC	−12.517	14.37	−0.87	0.3936
M	12065.00	720.48	16.74	0.0001
PA	65.379	29.782	2.20	0.0395

Compare the OLS parameter estimates to the 2SLS estimates presented in this chapter. Do you see any problems with using OLS to estimate the parameters of world copper demand? Explain.

7. In the text example dealing with the world demand for copper, we estimated the demand elasticities. Using these estimates, evaluate the impact on the world consumption of copper of:
   a. The formation of a worldwide cartel in copper that increases the price of copper by 10 percent
   b. The onset of a recession that reduces world income by 5 percent
   c. A technical breakthrough that is expected to reduce the price of copper by 6 percent
   d. A 10 percent reduction in the price of aluminum
8. A linear demand function of the form

$$Q = a + bP + cM + dP_R$$

was estimated using 2SLS. (The demand function was first identified by specifying the supply function.) The results of this estimation are as follows:

Two-Stage Least-Squares Estimation

DEPENDENT VARIABLE: Q		R-SQUARE	F-RATIO	P-VALUE ON F
OBSERVATIONS: 30		0.8075	36.35	0.0001
VARIABLE	PARAMETER ESTIMATE	STANDARD ERROR	T-RATIO	P-VALUE
INTERCEPT	68.38	12.65	5.41	0.0001
P	−6.50	3.15	−2.06	0.0492
M	0.13926	0.0131	10.63	0.0001
PR	−10.77	2.45	−4.40	0.0002

a. Are the signs of $\hat{b}$ and $\hat{c}$ as would be predicted theoretically?
b. What does the sign of $\hat{d}$ imply about the relation between the commodity and the related good R?
c. Are the parameter estimates $\hat{a}$, $\hat{b}$, $\hat{c}$, and $\hat{d}$ statistically significant?
d. Using the values $P = 225$, $M = 24{,}000$, and $P_R = 60$, calculate estimates of:
(1) The own-price elasticity of demand
(2) The income elasticity of demand
(3) The cross-price elasticity

9. The following log-linear demand curve for a price-setting firm is estimated using the ordinary least-squares method:

$$Q = aP^bM^cP_R^d$$

Following are the results of this estimation:

DEPENDENT VARIABLE: LNQ		R-SQUARE	F-RATIO	P-VALUE ON F
OBSERVATIONS: 25		0.8587	89.165	0.0001
VARIABLE	PARAMETER ESTIMATE	STANDARD ERROR	T-RATIO	P-VALUE
INTERCEPT	6.77	4.01	1.69	0.0984
LNP	−1.68	0.70	−2.40	0.0207
LNM	−0.82	0.22	−3.73	0.0005
LNPR	1.35	0.75	1.80	0.0787

a. The estimated demand equation can be expressed in natural logarithms as $\ln Q =$ ________.
b. Does the parameter estimate for b have the expected sign? Explain.
c. Given these parameter estimates, is the good a normal or an inferior good? Explain. Is good R a substitute or a complement? Explain.
d. Which of the parameter estimates are statistically significant at the 5 percent level of significance?
e. Find the following elasticities:
(1) The own-price elasticity of demand
(2) The cross-price elasticity of demand
(3) The income elasticity of demand
f. A 10 percent decrease in household income, holding all other things constant, will cause quantity demanded to ________ (increase, decrease) by ________ percent.
g. All else constant, a 10 percent increase in price causes quantity demanded to ________ (increase, decrease) by ________ percent.
h. A 5 percent decrease in the price of R, holding all other variables constant, causes quantity demanded to ________ (increase, decrease) by ________ percent.

APPLIED PROBLEMS

1. Sharp Econometrics, a consulting firm in San Francisco, has been hired by Nitax Cameras, Inc., to estimate the demand for its single-lens-reflex (SLR) cameras. Nitax provides the econometricians at Sharp with data from 45 states during 1998 on the quantity of Nitax SLRs purchased, the price of a Nitax in each state, the average household income in each state, and the average price of 35mm film in each state.
   a. Is this data set sufficient to identify the demand function? Why or why not? Sharp Econometrics is also employed by Knoxville Slugger Baseball Bats to estimate the demand for baseball bats. Sharp has data for the last five years on the quantity of Knoxville Slugger baseball bats sold, the price of bats, consumers' income, the price of baseballs, and the price of lumber.
   b. Is this data set sufficient to identify the demand function? Why or why not?
2. The manager of We-Rent-All, a tool rental business, wants to estimate the demand for the firm's airless paint sprayers, using data from last year. The manager, while collecting the needed data, discovers that during the past year, the store had only three sprayers to rent and the three units were rented all the time. Consequently, the supply curve for airless sprayers was perfectly inelastic over the range of prices We-Rent-All charged to rent these machines. Can the manager estimate the demand for airless sprayers using data from last year? Why or why not? Explain by using a graph.
3. Wilpen Company, a price-setting firm, produces nearly 80 percent of all tennis balls purchased in the United States. Wilpen estimates the U.S. demand for its tennis balls by using the following linear specification:

$$Q = a + bP + cM + dP_R$$

where Q is the number of cans of tennis balls sold quarterly, P is the wholesale price Wilpen charges for a can of tennis balls, M is the consumers' average household income, and P_R is the average price of tennis rackets. The regression results are as follows:

DEPENDENT VARIABLE: Q		R-SQUARE	F-RATIO	P-VALUE ON F
OBSERVATIONS: 20		0.8435	28.75	0.001
VARIABLE	PARAMETER ESTIMATE	STANDARD ERROR	T-RATIO	P-VALUE
INTERCEPT	425120.0	220300.0	1.93	0.0716
P	−25930.6	8774.0	−2.96	0.0093
M	1.024	0.251	4.08	0.0009
PR	−2478.0	785.0	−3.16	0.0061

a. Discuss the statistical significance of the parameter estimates $\hat{a}$, $\hat{b}$, $\hat{c}$, and $\hat{d}$ using the *p*-values. Are the signs of $\hat{b}$, $\hat{c}$, and $\hat{d}$ consistent with the theory of demand?

Wilpen plans to charge a wholesale price of $1.65 per can. The average price of a tennis racket is $110, and consumers' average household income is $24,600.

b. What is the estimated number of cans of tennis balls demanded?

c. At the values of P, M, and P_R given, what are the values of the own-price, income, and cross-price elasticities of demand?

d. What will happen, in percentage terms, to the number of cans of tennis balls demanded if the price of tennis balls decreases 15 percent?

e. What will happen, in percentage terms, to the number of cans of tennis balls demanded if average household income increases by 20 percent?

f. What will happen, in percentage terms, to the number of cans of tennis balls demanded if the average price of tennis rackets increases 25 percent?

4. In the examination of world demand for copper, we used a linear specification. However, we could have estimated a log-linear specification. That is, we could have specified the copper demand function as

$$Q_c = aP_c^b M^c P_A^d$$

or

$$\ln Q_c = \ln a + b \ln P_c + c \ln M + d \ln P_A$$

The results of such an estimation, using the data in Table A of the appendix, are presented below:

Two-Stage Least-Squares Estimation

DEPENDENT VARIABLE: LNQC	R-SQUARE	F-RATIO	P-VALUE ON F
OBSERVATIONS: 25	0.8845	53.599	0.0001

VARIABLE	PARAMETER ESTIMATE	STANDARD ERROR	T-RATIO	P-VALUE
INTERCEPT	9.738976	1.734675	5.61	0.0001
LNPC	−0.913921	0.616026	−1.48	0.1528
LNM	2.734251	0.551151	4.96	0.0001
LNPA	0.793509	0.330947	2.40	0.0259

a. Using the p-values, discuss the statistical significance of the parameter estimates $\hat{a}$, $\hat{b}$, $\hat{c}$, and $\hat{d}$. Are the signs of $\hat{b}$, $\hat{c}$, and $\hat{d}$ consistent with the theory of demand?

b. What are the values of the own-price, income, and cross-price elasticities of demand? Compare these elasticity estimates with the estimated elasticities for the linear specification of copper demand (estimated in this chapter).

c. Which specification of copper demand, the linear or log-linear, appears to be more appropriate?

5. In a recent article, a researcher reported that he had found that the demand curve for kerosene sloped upward—as the price of kerosene rose, the quantity demanded of kerosene increased. What questions might you have for this researcher?

6. The sales director of Nutra Dinner, Inc., a company producing high-nutrition, low-fat, low-salt microwave dinners, wishes to estimate demand for one of the firm's latest additions—asparagus gumbo. The sales director sets up a booth at a health food convention in order to conduct consumer interviews to estimate demand for the asparagus gumbo dinner. Among the questions asked are these two: (1) How many times a day do you actually eat asparagus? and (2) Would you rather eat a dinner of liver, asparagus, and herbal tea or a turkey dinner with mashed potatoes, corn-on-the-cob, and wine? What three problems are likely to affect the validity of the consumer interview method of estimating demand? Explain each one.

MATHEMATICAL APPENDIX — Empirical Elasticities and Two-Stage Least-Squares Estimation

Derivation of Elasticity Estimates for Linear and Log-Linear Demands

As demonstrated in Chapter 3, the own-price elasticity of demand is

$$E = \frac{\partial Q}{\partial P} \cdot \frac{P}{Q}$$

With the linear specification of the demand function,

$$Q = a + bP + cM + dP_R$$

the parameter b is an estimate of the partial derivative of quantity demanded with respect to the price of the product,

$$\hat{b} = \text{Estimate of} \left(\frac{\partial Q}{\partial P} \right)$$

Hence for any price–quantity demanded combination (P, Q), the estimated own-price elasticity of that point on the demand function is

$$\hat{E} = \hat{b} \cdot \frac{P}{Q}$$

With the log-linear specification of the demand function,

$$Q = aP^b M^c P_R^d$$

the partial derivative of quantity demanded with respect to own price is

$$\frac{\partial Q}{\partial P} = baP^{b-1} M^c P_R^d = \frac{bQ}{P}$$

Hence, $\hat{b}$ is an estimate of own-price elasticity

$$\hat{E} = \frac{\hat{b}Q}{P} \cdot \frac{P}{Q} = \hat{b}$$

Using the same methodology, estimates of income and cross-price elasticities can be obtained. The estimates are summarized in the following table:

Elasticity	Definition	Estimate from linear specification	Estimate from log-linear specification
Own-price	$E = \frac{\partial Q}{\partial P} \cdot \frac{P}{Q}$	$\hat{b} \cdot \frac{P}{Q}$	$\hat{b}$
Income	$E_M = \frac{\partial Q}{\partial M} \cdot \frac{M}{Q}$	$\hat{c} \cdot \frac{M}{Q}$	$\hat{c}$
Cross-price	$E_{XR} = \frac{\partial Q}{\partial P_R} \cdot \frac{P_R}{Q}$	$\hat{d} \cdot \frac{P_R}{Q}$	$\hat{d}$

Note that the elasticity estimates from the linear specification depend on the point on the demand curve at which the elasticity estimate is evaluated. In contrast, the log-linear demand curve exhibits constant elasticity estimates.

Simultaneous Equations Bias and Two-Stage Least-Squares Estimation

Simultaneous equations bias

Consider the following system of demand and supply equations

$$\text{Demand: } Q = a + bP + cM + \epsilon_d$$
$$\text{Supply: } Q = d + eP + fP_I + \epsilon_s$$

where P and Q are the endogenous variables, M and P_I are the exogenous variables, and ϵ_d and ϵ_s are the random error terms for demand and supply. We now solve for the *reduced-form equations,* which show how the values of the endogenous variables are determined by the exogenous variables and the random error terms. First we set $Q_d = Q_s$ and solve for P^*:

$$a + bP + cM + \epsilon_d = d + eP + fP_I + \epsilon_s$$
$$P(b - e) = d - a + fP_I - cM + \epsilon_s - \epsilon_d$$
$$P^* = \frac{d - a}{b - e} + \frac{f}{b - e}P_I + \frac{-c}{b - e}M + \frac{\epsilon_s - \epsilon_d}{b - e}$$

Next, we substitute P^* into either demand or supply and solve for Q^*:

$$Q^* = \frac{bd - ae}{b - e} + \frac{bf}{b - e}P_I + \frac{-ce}{b - e}M + \frac{b\epsilon_s - e\epsilon_d}{b - e}$$

The reduced-form equations for P^* and Q^* can be expressed in a simpler, more general form as follows:

$$P^* = f(P_I, M, \epsilon_d, \epsilon_s)$$
$$Q^* = g(P_I, M, \epsilon_d, \epsilon_s)$$

The reduced-form equations show:

1. *The problem of simultaneity:* Each one of the endogenous variables, P^* and Q^* in this case, is clearly determined by all the exogenous variables in the system and by all the random error terms in the system. Thus the observed variations in both P and Q are reflecting variations in both demand- and supply-side determinants.
2. *The simultaneous equations bias:* In order for the ordinary least-squares estimation procedure to produce unbiased estimates of a, b, and c in the demand equation, the explanatory variables (P and M) must *not* be correlated with the error term in the demand equation, ϵ_d (for a proof of this statement, see Gujarati*). The reduced-form equations show us clearly that all endogenous variables are functions of all random error terms in the system. P is an endogenous variable, and we have seen that P is a function of ϵ_d. Thus, P will be correlated with the error term in the demand equation, and the estimates of a, b, and c will be biased if the ordinary least-squares procedure is employed. The bias that results because P is an endogenous explanatory variable is called simultaneous equations bias.

*Damodar N. Gujarati, *Basic Econometrics,* McGraw-Hill, 1988.

Two-stage least-squares estimation

If a market demand equation is identified, it can be estimated using any number of available techniques. Perhaps the most widely used of these techniques—and the one that is most likely to be preprogrammed into the available regression packages—is two-stage least-squares (2SLS).

As shown above, the estimates of the parameters of the demand equation will be biased if ordinary least-squares is employed because price is an endogenous variable that is on the right-hand side of the demand equation. Because price is endogenous, it will be correlated with the error term in the demand equation, causing simultaneous equations bias.

Conceptually, the endogenous right-hand-side variable (in this case, price) must be made to behave as if it is exogenous; traditional regression techniques are used to obtain estimates of the parameters. In the linear example we have been using, we have a system of two simultaneous equations:

$$\text{Demand: } Q = a + bP + cM + \epsilon_d$$
$$\text{Supply: } Q = d + eP + fP_I + \epsilon_s$$

In these equations, P is an endogenous variable. To obtain unbiased estimates of a, b, and c, the estimation of the demand function proceeds in two steps or stages, which is why the technique is called two-stage least-squares:

Stage 1: The endogenous right-hand-side variable is regressed on all the exogenous variables in the system:

$$P = \alpha + \beta M + \gamma P_I$$

From this estimation, we obtain estimates of the parameters, that is, $\hat{\alpha}$, $\hat{\beta}$, and $\hat{\gamma}$. Using these estimates and the *actual values* of the exogenous variables, we generate a *new* price series—predicted price—as follows:

$$\hat{P} = \hat{\alpha} + \hat{\beta}M + \hat{\gamma}P_I$$

Note how the predicted price, $\hat{P}$, is obtained. $\hat{P}$ is simply a linear combination of the exogenous variables, so it follows that $\hat{P}$ is now also exogenous. However, given the way that the predicted price series is obtained, the values of $\hat{P}$ will correspond closely to the original values of P. In essence, this first stage forces price to behave as if it were exogenous.

Stage 2: We then use the predicted price variable ($\hat{P}$) in the demand function we wish to estimate. That is, in the second stage, we estimate the regression equation:

$$Q = a + b\hat{P} + cM$$

Note that this estimation uses the exogenous variable constructed in the first stage. We use predicted price, $\hat{P}$, rather than the actual price variable, P, in the final regression.

MATHEMATICAL EXERCISES

1. Let demand be specified as

$$Q = 200\ P^{-1.5}\ M^{0.8}\ P_R^{\ -1.2}$$

where Q is quantity demanded of the good, P is the price, M is disposable income, and P_R is the price of good R.

a. Using partial derivatives, find the own-price, income, and cross-price elasticities. Verify that the own-price, income, and cross-price elasticities are constant and equal to the exponents of P, M, and P_R, respectively.

b. Calculate quantity demanded when P = \$10, M = \$15,000, and P_R = \$4.

c. Write the log-linear specification of demand: ln Q = ________.

d. Using logarithms and the expression in part *c*, find the value of Q when P = \$10, M = \$15,000, and P_R = \$4. Does your answer using logarithms match your answer in part *b*?

2. Consider the following system of demand and supply equations:

$$\text{Demand: } Q = 400 - 3P + 0.1M + \epsilon_d$$
$$\text{Supply: } Q = 20 + 2P + 4P_I + \epsilon_s$$

where P and Q are endogenous variables, M and P_I are exogenous variables, and ϵ_d and ϵ_s are the random error terms for demand and supply, respectively.

a. Solve algebraically for the reduced-form equations for price and quantity.

b. Using the reduced-form equations, explain why ordinary least-squares is not the appropriate method for estimating the parameters of *either* the demand or the supply function.

c. Demonstrate that the structural parameters for the slopes of demand and supply (−3 and 2, respectively) can be identified from the coefficients in the two reduced-form equations. (*Hint:* Examine the algebraic expressions for the reduced-form equations in this appendix to find a way to solve for the coefficients on P in the demand and supply equations by using some of the coefficients in the reduced-form equations.)

Data Appendix: Data Used in Chapter 7 Examples

TABLE A

The World Copper Market*

Year	World consumption (Q_C)	Real price, copper (P_C)	Index of real income (M)	Real price, aluminum (P_A)	X	T
1	3,173.0	26.56	0.70	19.76	0.97679	1
2	3,281.1	27.31	0.71	20.78	1.03937	2
3	3,135.7	32.95	0.72	22.55	1.05153	3
4	3,359.1	33.90	0.70	23.06	0.97312	4
5	3,755.1	42.70	0.74	24.93	1.02349	5
6	3,875.9	46.11	0.74	26.50	1.04135	6
7	3,905.7	31.70	0.74	27.24	0.97686	7
8	3,957.6	27.23	0.72	26.21	0.98069	8
9	4,279.1	32.89	0.75	26.09	1.02888	9
10	4,627.9	33.78	0.77	27.40	1.03392	10
11	4,910.2	31.66	0.76	26.94	0.97922	11
12	4,908.4	32.28	0.79	25.18	0.99679	12
13	5,327.9	32.38	0.83	23.94	0.96630	13
14	5,878.4	33.75	0.85	25.07	1.02915	14
15	6,075.2	36.25	0.89	25.37	1.07950	15
16	6,312.7	36.24	0.93	24.55	1.05073	16
17	6,056.8	38.23	0.95	24.98	1.02788	17
18	6,375.9	40.83	0.99	24.96	1.02799	18
19	6,974.3	44.62	1.00	25.52	0.99151	19
20	7,101.6	52.27	1.00	26.01	1.00191	20
21	7,071.7	45.16	1.02	25.46	0.95644	21
22	7,754.8	42.50	1.07	22.17	0.96947	22
23	8,480.3	43.70	1.12	18.56	0.98220	23
24	8,105.2	47.88	1.10	21.32	1.00793	24
25	7,157.2	36.33	1.07	22.75	0.93810	25

*The data presented are actual values for 1951–1975.
Q_c = world consumption (sales) of copper in 1000's of metric tons,
P_c = price of copper in cents per pound (inflation adjusted),
M = index of real per capita income (1970 = 1.00),
P_A = price of aluminum in cents per pound (inflation adjusted),
X = ratio of consumption in the previous year to production in the previous year, and
T = technology (time period is a proxy).

TABLE B
Data for Checkers Pizza

Observation	Q	P	M	P_{Al}	P_{BMac}
1	1,773	8.65	25,500	10.55	1.25
2	1,863	8.65	25,600	10.45	1.35
3	1,798	8.65	25,700	10.35	1.55
4	1,775	8.65	25,970	10.30	1.05
5	1,796	8.65	25,970	10.30	0.95
6	1,786	8.65	25,750	10.25	0.95
7	1,916	7.50	25,750	10.25	0.85
8	1,997	7.50	25,950	10.15	1.15
9	2,008	7.50	25,950	10.00	1.25
10	2,012	7.50	26,120	10.00	1.75
11	1,864	8.50	26,120	10.25	1.75
12	1,884	8.50	26,150	10.25	1.85
13	1,762	8.50	26,200	9.75	1.50
14	1,398	9.99	26,350	9.75	1.10
15	1,480	9.99	26,450	9.65	1.05
16	1,458	9.99	26,350	9.60	1.25
17	1,469	9.99	26,850	10.00	0.55
18	1,525	10.25	27,350	10.25	0.55
19	1,587	10.25	27,350	10.20	1.15
20	1,554	10.25	27,950	10.00	1.15
21	1,622	9.75	28,159	10.10	0.55
22	1,717	9.75	28,264	10.10	0.55
23	1,755	9.75	28,444	10.10	1.20
24	1,731	9.75	28,500	10.25	1.20

CHAPTER 8

Demand Forecasting

A knowledge of future demand conditions can be extremely useful to managers when they are planning production schedules, inventory control, advertising campaigns, output in future periods, and investment, among other things. This chapter will describe some techniques that managers can use to forecast future demand conditions. The range of forecasting techniques is so wide that a complete discussion is quite beyond the scope of this text. Therefore, we confine ourselves to a brief description of some of the more widely used techniques. For convenience, we divide forecasting methods into two groups—qualitative models and statistical models.

qualitative model
A model that does not employ explicit models or methods that can be replicated by another analyst.

Qualitative models are more difficult to describe than statistical models since there exists no explicit model or method that can serve as a reference point. There is no model that can be used to replicate the initial forecast with a given set of data, and this feature, above all others, distinguishes this approach. It has been said by some that a qualitative model is essentially a "rule-of-thumb" technique. However, you should not infer from this description that qualitative forecasts are naive or unsophisticated. Indeed, it is the very complexity of this method that makes replication so difficult, since such forecasts are typically based on at least some subjective factors. In the final analysis, qualitative forecasts are often based on *expert opinion.* The forecaster examines the available data, solicits the advice of others, and then sifts through this amalgamation of evidence to formulate a forecast. The weights assigned to the various bits and pieces of information are subjectively determined and, we might add, separate the neophyte from the expert.

statistical model
A model that employs explicit models or methods that can be replicated by other analysts.

In contrast, a **statistical model** employs explicit models or methods that can be replicated by another analyst. The results of statistical models can be reproduced by different researchers. An additional advantage of this approach is the existence of reasonably well-defined standards for evaluating such models. The final advantage of statistical models is the ability to use them in simulation models. (Basically, *simulation models* are models in which a researcher can obtain alternative forecasts for the future values of the endogenous variable, given alternative future trends in the exogenous variables.) Statistical models can be further subdivided into two categories—time-series models and econometric models.

We begin with a discussion of qualitative forecasts. Next, we describe some basic time-series techniques. We then introduce econometric models and show how to examine the impact on future demand of changes in the exogenous variables of the model. We close this chapter with a note on some of the more important problems involved in forecasting.

8.1 QUALITATIVE FORECASTING TECHNIQUES

As noted, qualitative forecasting methods are rather difficult to describe due to the subjective elements involved. Forecasters combine available data with their knowledge of the firm and industry and, assigning subjective weights to these pieces of evidence, obtain a forecast. While qualitative forecasting may indeed be the best technique, it is difficult, if not impossible, to teach this approach. In truth, we do not actually know how people are successful at qualitative forecasting. We can say only that those who are successful understand economics and know a great deal about their industries.

Skillful forecasters do use data to make qualitative forecasts. While it is impossible to set forth the manner in which their subjective weights are assigned to the data they use, we can describe some of the data that forecasters may observe and use.

It is possible that the analyst has observed through experience (or, perhaps, by using regression techniques) that a relation exists between the sales of the firm and the movement in certain aggregate economic variables over time. More specifically, the managers know that changes in certain economic variables lead the changes in the firm's sales. If managers know the variables, they can use these leading indicators as a barometer to predict changes in the sales of the firm. The problem, then, is the isolation of these indicators and the collection of appropriate data.

The problem of data identification and collection has been simplified immensely through the work of the Bureau of Economic Analysis (BEA), which is a branch of the U.S. Department of Commerce, and the Conference Board. The Conference Board, which is a private, not-for-profit organization, was appointed by the BEA in 1996 to maintain the Business Cycle Indicators database, a set of over 200 economic data series that includes leading-indicator series and the various composite indexes of economic activity. The Conference Board publishes,

TABLE 8.1
The 10 Leading Indicators

1. Average weekly hours, manufacturing
2. Average weekly initial claims for unemployment insurance
3. Manufacturers' new orders, consumer goods and materials
4. Vendor performance, slower-deliveries diffusion index
5. Manufacturers' new orders, nondefense capital goods
6. Building permits, new private-housing units
7. Stock prices, 500 common stocks
8. Money supply, M2
9. Interest rate spread, 10-year Treasury bonds less federal funds
10. Index of consumer expectations

Source: The Conference Board, Business Cycle Indicators, www.tcb-indicators.org.

monthly, *Business Cycle Indicators,* which contains data on a large number of indicators, both individually and in composite form.

leading indicator
An economic variable that changes direction ahead of a change in the direction of the business cycle.

composite index
A group of indicators averaged to get a single index.

Of the more than 200 economic variables tracked by the Conference Board, 10 have been identified as particularly important leading indicators. A **leading indicator** is an economic variable whose direction changes ahead of a change in the direction of the business cycle. No one economic variable can accurately track movements in overall business activity, so it is useful to analyze a group of indicators known as a **composite index.** Table 8.1 presents a list of the 10 leading indicators that currently are "averaged" to get the widely reported and watched Composite Index of Leading Indicators.

If a forecaster can relate the firm's sales to one or more of the leading indicators, or a composite of leading indicators, it can then try to generate short-term forecasts on the basis of these published data. For example, a firm that manufactures dishwashers would be interested in the index of new building permits. An increase in building permits precedes housing starts, which precede the purchase of dishwashers. An experienced forecaster could combine this information with personal knowledge about the firm (e.g., its share of the market) and about the market (e.g., the percentage of new houses that have dishwashers) to provide a forecast of sales for the firm.

There are also more complex situations in which more than one indicator is used. In some instances, the different indicators could provide conflicting forecasts. To handle this difficulty, two multiple-indicator methods are commonly employed. One method, already mentioned, is to calculate a composite index, that is, a weighted average of individual indicators. Indeed, the Conference Board itself publishes several composite indicators, one of which is the weighted average of the 10 leading indicators. In Figure 8.1, we have provided a graph of the behavior of this composite index over the period 1964–1996. In this figure it is easy to see why the variables included are leading indicators. Note how the index turned down prior to the recessions of 1969–1970, 1973–1975, 1980, 1981–1983, and 1991–1992. Likewise, the upturn in this composite index preceded—led—the upturn in general economic activity.

FIGURE 8.1
Composite Index of the 10 Leading Indicators (1964–1996)

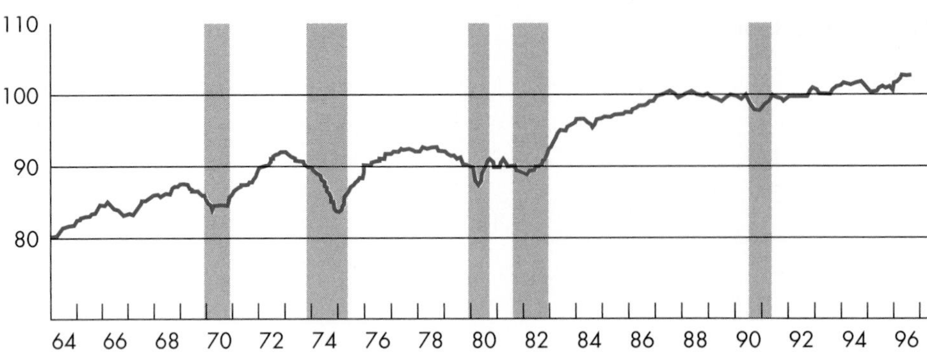

Note: Periods shaded are periods of recession as determined by the Bureau of Economic Analysis (e.g., the 1969–1970 recession covered the period December 1969 through November 1970).
Sources: Bureau of Economic Analysis and the Conference Board.

diffusion index
An index measuring the proportion of indicators in a composite index that are rising over a six-month span.

A second method of using multiple indicators involves calculating a *diffusion index.* A **diffusion index** measures the proportion of indicators in a composite index that are *rising* over a six-month span. Thus, a diffusion index reflects the degree to which all indicators in a group are pointing in the same direction. For example, if 7 of the 10 leading indicators were continuously rising over a particular six-month period, the diffusion index would be 7/10, or 70 percent. Using a diffusion index, one normally defines a critical percentage (usually 50 percent) above which one would say that economic activity is rising. Likewise, if the diffusion index is below the critical value, economic activity is said to be declining. In Figure 8.2 we have provided a graph of the diffusion index for the 10 leading indicators for the period 1964–1996 and compared it with periods of recession.

Again, let us stress that the procedures outlined above require a great many subjective decisions by forecasters. The analyst must determine the appropriate indicators and then interpret them in light of the conditions that will exist in their particular markets and firms. First, these indicators do not always indicate changes in another economic variable (and there also exists some random month-to-month variation in the indicators). Second, the lead times are not necessarily constant. Third, and most important, since these leading indicators predict the direction rather than the magnitude of changes, the responsibility for assigning a magnitude rests with the forecaster.

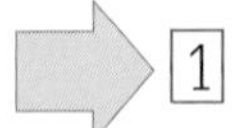
1

8.2 TIME-SERIES FORECASTS OF SALES AND PRICE

Statistical forecasting is more analytical than qualitative forecasting because the models can be replicated by another researcher. Statistical forecasting uses empirical data in basic statistical models to generate forecasts about economic variables. There are two categories of statistical methods: time-series models and econometric models. We begin with time-series models.

FIGURE 8.2
Diffusion Index for the 10 Leading Indicators: Percentage of Components Rising over a Six-Month Span

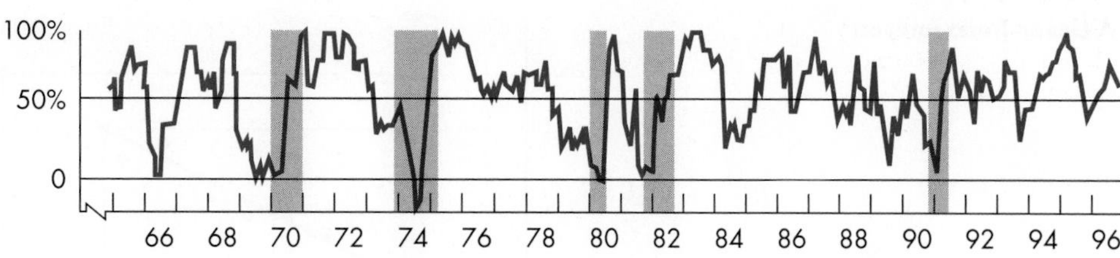

Sources: Bureau of Economic Analysis and the Conference Board.

time-series model
A statistical model that shows how a time-ordered sequence of observations on a variable is generated.

As noted in Chapter 5, a *time series* is simply a time-ordered sequence of observations on a variable. In general, a **time-series model** uses only the time-series history of the variable of interest to predict future values. Time-series models describe the process by which these historical data were generated. Thus, to forecast using time-series analysis, it is necessary to specify a mathematical model that represents the generating process. We will first discuss a general forecasting model and then give examples of price and sales forecasts.

Linear Trend Forecasting

A linear trend is the simplest time-series forecasting method. Using this type of model, one could posit that sales or price increases or decreases linearly over time. For example, a firm's sales for the period 1989–1998 are shown by the 10 data points in Figure 8.3. The straight line that best fits the data scatter, calculated using simple regression analysis, is illustrated by the solid line in the figure. The fitted line indicates a positive trend in sales. Assuming that sales in the future will continue to follow the same trend, sales in any future period can be forecast by extending this line and picking the forecast values from this *extrapolated* dashed line for the desired future period. We have illustrated sales forecasts for 1999 and 2004 ($\hat{Q}_{1999}$ and $\hat{Q}_{2004}$) in Figure 8.3.

Summarizing this procedure, we assumed a linear relation between sales and time:

$$Q_t = a + bt$$

Using the 10 observations for 1989–1998, we regressed time (t = 1989, 1990, . . . , 1998), the independent variable expressed in years, on sales, the dependent variable expressed in dollars, to obtain the estimated trend line:

$$\hat{Q}_t = \hat{a} + \hat{b}t$$

This line best fits the historical data. It is important to test whether there is a statistically significant positive or negative trend in sales. As shown in Chapter 5, it is easy to determine if $\hat{b}$ is significantly different from zero either by using a t-test for statistical significance or by examining the p-value for $\hat{b}$. If $\hat{b}$ is positive and statistically significant, sales are trending upward over time. If $\hat{b}$ is negative

FIGURE 8.3
A Linear Trend Forecast

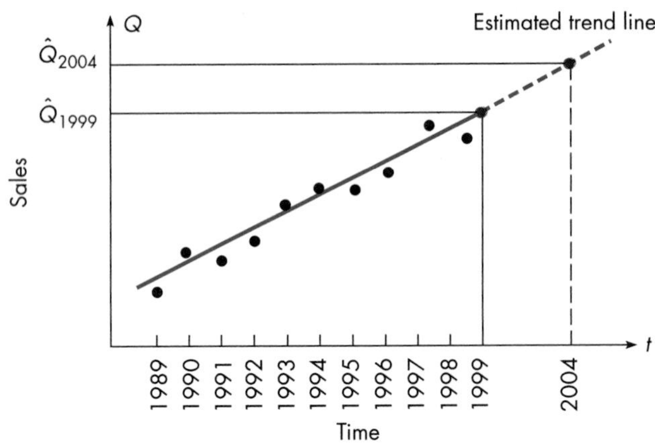

and statistically significant, sales are trending downward over time. However, if $\hat{b}$ is not statistically significant, one would assume that $b = 0$, and sales are constant over time. That is, there is no relation between sales and time, and any variation in sales is due to random fluctuations.

If the estimation indicates a statistically significant trend, you can then use the estimated trend line to obtain forecasts of future sales. For example, if a manager wanted a forecast for sales in 1999, the manager would simply insert 1999 into the estimated trend line:

$$\hat{Q}_{1999} = \hat{a} + \hat{b} \times (1999)$$

A Sales Forecast for Terminator Pest Control

In January 1999, Arnold Schwartz started Terminator Pest Control, a small pest-control company in Atlanta. Terminator Pest Control serves mainly residential customers citywide. At the end of March 2000, after 15 months of operation, Arnold decides to apply for a business loan from his bank to buy another pest-control truck. The bank is somewhat reluctant to make the loan, citing concern that sales at Terminator Pest Control did not grow significantly over its first 15 months of business. In addition, the bank asks Arnold to provide a forecast of sales for the next three months (April, May, and June).

Arnold decides to do the forecast himself using a time-series model based on past sales figures. He collects the data on sales for the last 15 months—sales are measured as the number of homes serviced during a given month. Since data are collected monthly, Arnold creates a continuous time variable by numbering the months consecutively as January 1999 = 1, February 1999 = 2, and so on. The data for Terminator and a scatter diagram are shown in Figure 8.4.

FIGURE 8.4
Forecasting Sales for Terminator Pest Control

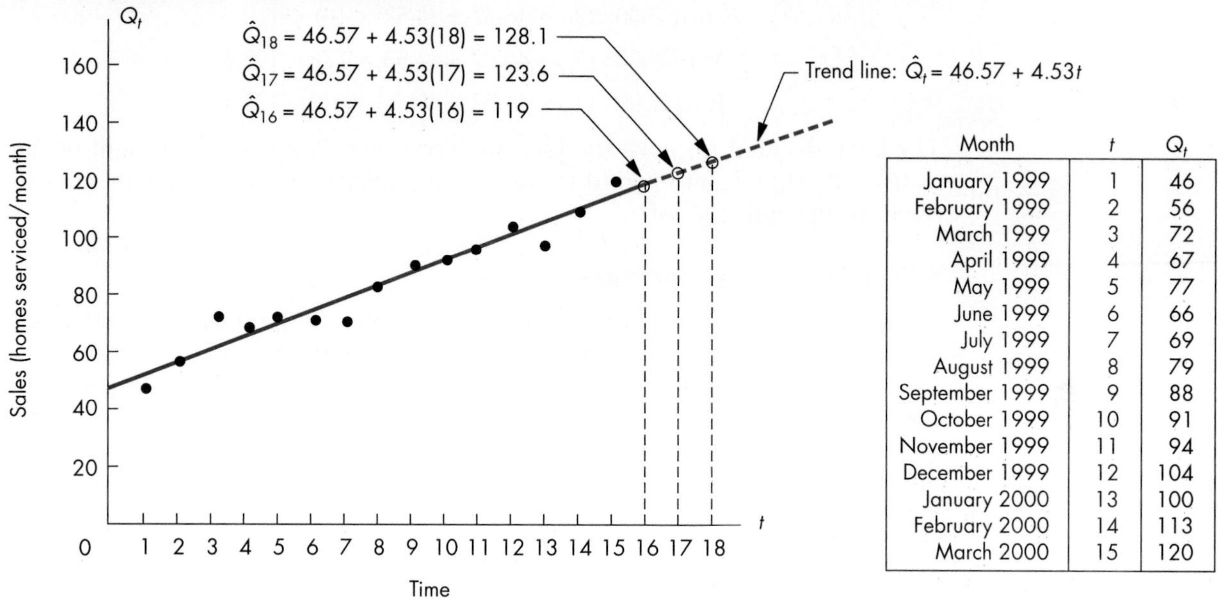

Month	t	Q_t
January 1999	1	46
February 1999	2	56
March 1999	3	72
April 1999	4	67
May 1999	5	77
June 1999	6	66
July 1999	7	69
August 1999	8	79
September 1999	9	88
October 1999	10	91
November 1999	11	94
December 1999	12	104
January 2000	13	100
February 2000	14	113
March 2000	15	120

Arnold estimates the linear trend model

$$Q_t = a + bt$$

and gets the following printout from the computer:

```
DEPENDENT VARIABLE:  Q   R-SQUARE      F-RATIO     P-VALUE ON F

      OBSERVATIONS:  15  0.9231        156.11      0.0001

                          PARAMETER    STANDARD
    VARIABLE              ESTIMATE     ERROR       T-RATIO    P-VALUE

    INTERCEPT             46.57        3.29        14.16      0.0001
    T                     4.53         0.36        12.58      0.0001
```

The t-ratio for the time variable, 12.58, exceeds the critical t of 3.012 for 13 degrees of freedom (= 15 − 2) at the 1 percent level of significance. The exact level of significance for the estimate 4.53 is less than 0.0001, as indicated by the

p-value. Thus, the sales figures for Terminator suggest a statistically significant upward trend in sales. The sales forecasts for April, May, and June of 2000 are

$$\text{April 2000: } \hat{Q}_{16} = 46.57 + (4.53 \times 16) = 119$$
$$\text{May 2000: } \hat{Q}_{17} = 46.57 + (4.53 \times 17) = 123.6$$
$$\text{June 2000: } \hat{Q}_{18} = 46.57 + (4.53 \times 18) = 128.1$$

The bank decided to make the loan to Terminator Pest Control in light of the statistically significant upward trend in sales and the forecast of higher sales in the three upcoming months.

A Price Forecast: Lumber Prices in Miami

In December 1992, after hurricane Andrew demolished the small town of Homestead, Florida, as well as severely damaging parts of Miami and the surrounding areas, the price of all types of lumber products began to increase sharply. Suppose, at the time, you worked for a large lumber producer in south Florida, and your manager wants you to forecast the price of lumber for the next two quarters. Information about the price of a ton of lumber is readily available. Using 8 quarterly observations on lumber prices since 1992 (III), you estimated a linear trend line for lumber prices through the 1994 (II) time period. Your computer output for the linear time trend model on lumber price was as follows:

DEPENDENT VARIABLE: Q	R-SQUARE	F-RATIO	P-VALUE ON F	
OBSERVATIONS: 8	0.7572	18.71	0.0050	
VARIABLE	PARAMETER ESTIMATE	STANDARD ERROR	T-RATIO	P-VALUE
INTERCEPT	2066.0	794.62	2.60	0.0407
T	25.00	8.62	2.90	0.0273

Both parameter estimates, $\hat{a}$, and $\hat{b}$, are significant at the 5 percent significance level since both t-ratios exceed 2.447, the critical t for the 5 percent significance level. (Notice also that both p-values are less than 0.05.) Thus, the real (inflation-adjusted) price for a ton of lumber exhibited a statistically significant trend upward since the third quarter of 1992. Lumber prices have risen, on average, \$25 per ton each quarter over the range of this sample period (1992 III through 1994 II).

To forecast the price of lumber for the next two quarters, you make the following computations:

$$\hat{P}_{1994\ (III)} = 2066 + (25 \times 9) = \$2{,}291 \text{ per ton}$$
$$\hat{P}_{1994\ (IV)} = 2066 + (25 \times 10) = \$2{,}316 \text{ per ton}$$

FIGURE 8.5
Sales with Seasonal Variation

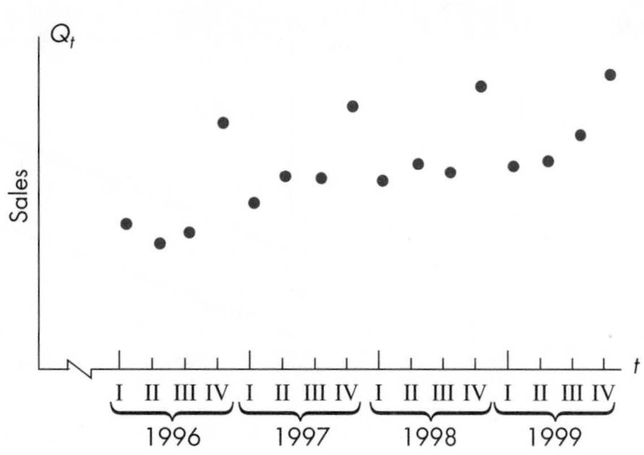

As you can see by the last two hypothetical examples, the linear trend method of forecasting is a simple procedure for generating forecasts for either sales or price. Indeed, this method can be applied to forecast any economic variable for which a time series of observations is available.

8.3 SEASONAL (OR CYCLICAL) VARIATION

seasonal or **cyclical variation**
The regular variation that time-series data frequently exhibit.

Time-series data may frequently exhibit regular, **seasonal** or **cyclical variation** over time, and the failure to take such regular variations into account when estimating a forecasting equation would bias the forecast. Frequently, when quarterly or monthly sales are being used to forecast sales, seasonal variation may occur—the sales of many products vary systematically by month or by quarter. For example, in the retail clothing business, sales are generally higher before Easter and Christmas. Thus, sales would be higher during the second and fourth quarters of the year. Likewise, the sales of hunting equipment would peak during early fall, the third quarter. In such cases, you would definitely wish to incorporate these systematic variations when estimating the equation and forecasting future sales. We shall describe the technique most commonly employed to handle cyclical variation.

Correcting for Seasonal Variation by Using Dummy Variables

Consider the simplified example of a firm producing and selling a product for which sales are consistently higher in the fourth quarter than in any other quarter. A hypothetical data scatter is presented in Figure 8.5. In each of the four years, the data point in the fourth quarter is much higher than in the other three. While a time trend clearly exists, if the analyst simply regressed sales against time, without accounting for the higher sales in the fourth quarter, too large a trend would be estimated (i.e., the slope would be too large). In essence, there is an upward shift of the trend line in the fourth quarter. Such a relation is

FIGURE 8.6
The Effect of Seasonal Variation

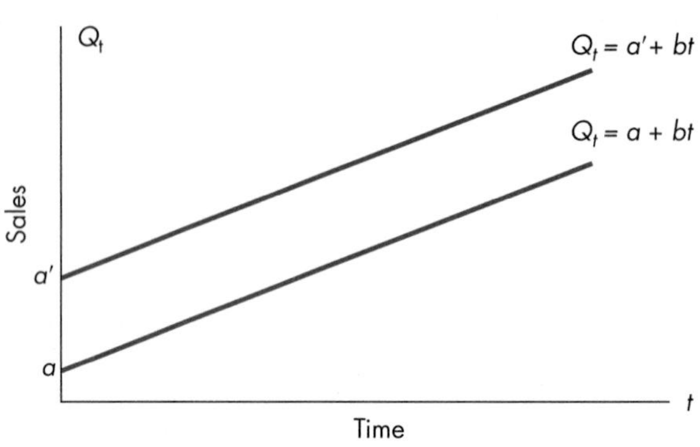

presented in Figure 8.6. In the fourth quarter, the intercept is higher than in the other quarters. In other words, a', the intercept of the trend line for the fourth-quarter data points, exceeds a, the intercept of the trend line for the data points in the other quarters. One way of specifying this relation is to define a' as $a' = a + c$, where c is some positive number. Therefore, the regression line we want to estimate will take the form

$$\hat{Q}_t = a + bt + c$$

where $c = 0$ in the first three quarters.

dummy variable
A variable that takes only values of 0 and 1.

To estimate the preceding equation, statisticians use what is commonly referred to as a *dummy variable* in the estimating equation. A **dummy variable** is a variable that can take on only the values of *zero* or *one.* In this case, we would assign the dummy variable (D) a value of 1 if the sales observation is from the fourth quarter and zero in the other three quarters. The data are shown in Table 8.2, where Q_t represents the sales figure in the tth period and $D = 1$ for quarter IV and zero otherwise. Since quarterly data are being used, time is converted into integers to obtain a continuous time variable. Using these data, the following equation is estimated:

$$\hat{Q}_t = a + bt + cD$$

The above specification produces two equations like those shown in Figure 8.6. The estimated slope of the two equations would be the same ($\hat{b}$). For quarters I, II, and III the estimated intercept is $\hat{a}$, while for the fourth quarter the estimated intercept is $\hat{a} + \hat{c}$. This estimation really means that for any future period t, the sales forecast would be

$$\hat{Q}_t = \hat{a} + \hat{b}t$$

unless period t occurs in the fourth quarter, in which case the sales forecast would be

$$\hat{Q}_t = \hat{a} + \hat{b}t + \hat{c} = (\hat{a} + \hat{c}) + \hat{b}t$$

TABLE 8.2
Creating a Dummy Variable

Q_t	t	D
$Q_{1996(I)}$	1	0
$Q_{1996(II)}$	2	0
$Q_{1996(III)}$	3	0
$Q_{1996(IV)}$	4	1
$Q_{1997(I)}$	5	0
$Q_{1997(II)}$	6	0
$Q_{1997(III)}$	7	0
$Q_{1997(IV)}$	8	1
$Q_{1998(I)}$	9	0
$Q_{1998(II)}$	10	0
$Q_{1998(III)}$	11	0
$Q_{1998(IV)}$	12	1
$Q_{1999(I)}$	13	0
$Q_{1999(II)}$	14	0
$Q_{1999(III)}$	15	0
$Q_{1999(IV)}$	16	1

For example, referring to the data in Table 8.2, when a manager wishes to forecast sales in the third quarter of 2000, the manager uses the equation

$$\hat{Q}_{2000(III)} = \hat{a} + \hat{b}\,(19)$$

If a manager wishes to forecast sales in the fourth quarter of 2000, the forecast is

$$\hat{Q}_{2000(IV)} = (\hat{a} + \hat{c}) + \hat{b}\,(20)$$

In other words, when the forecast is for quarter IV, the forecast equation adds the amount $\hat{c}$ to the sales that would otherwise be forecast.[1]

Going a step further, it could be the case that there exist quarter-to-quarter differences in sales (i.e., in Figure 8.6 there would be four trend lines). In this case, three dummy variables are used: D_1 (equal to one in the first quarter and zero otherwise), D_2 (equal to one in the second quarter and zero otherwise), and D_3 (equal to one in the third quarter and zero otherwise).[2] Then, the manager estimates the equation

$$Q_t = a + bt + c_1D_1 + c_2D_2 + c_3D_3$$

[1]Throughout this discussion, we have assumed that trend lines differ only with respect to the intercepts—the slope is the same for all the trend lines. Dummy variables can also be used to reflect differences in slopes. This technique is beyond the scope of this text, and we refer the interested reader to the references cited at the end of this text.

[2] Likewise, if there were month-to-month differences, 11 dummy variables would be used to account for the monthly change in the intercept. Note that in using dummy variables, you must always use one less dummy variable than the number of periods being considered.

TABLE 8.3

Quarterly Sales Data for Statewide Trucking Company (1996–1999)

(1) Year	(2) Quarter	(3) Sales	(4) t	(5) D_1	(6) D_2	(7) D_3
	I	$ 72,000	1	1	0	0
	II	87,000	2	0	1	0
1996	III	87,000	3	0	0	1
	IV	150,000	4	0	0	0
	I	82,000	5	1	0	0
	II	98,000	6	0	1	0
1997	III	94,000	7	0	0	1
	IV	162,000	8	0	0	0
	I	97,000	9	1	0	0
	II	105,000	10	0	1	0
1998	III	109,000	11	0	0	1
	IV	176,000	12	0	0	0
	I	105,000	13	1	0	0
	II	121,000	14	0	1	0
1999	III	119,000	15	0	0	1
	IV	180,000	16	0	0	0

In quarter I the intercept is $a + c_1$, in quarter II it is $a + c_2$, in quarter III it is $a + c_3$, and in quarter IV it is a only.

To obtain a forecast for some future quarter, it is necessary to include the coefficient for the dummy variable for that particular quarter. For example, predictions for the third quarter of a particular year would take the form

$$\hat{Q}_t = \hat{a} + \hat{b}t + \hat{c}_3$$

Perhaps the best way to explain how dummy variables can be used to account for cyclical variation is to provide an example.

The Dummy-Variable Technique: An Example

Jean Reynolds, the sales manager of Statewide Trucking Company, wishes to predict sales for all four quarters of 2000. The sales of Statewide Trucking are subject to seasonal variation and also have a trend over time. Reynolds obtains sales data for 1996–1999 by quarter. The data collected are presented in Table 8.3. Note that since quarterly data are used, time is converted into a continuous variable by numbering quarters consecutively in column 4 of the table.

Reynolds knows, from a college course in managerial economics, that obtaining the desired sales forecast requires that she estimate an equation containing three dummy variables—one less than the number of time periods in the annual cycle. She chooses to estimate the following equation:

$$Q_t = a + bt + c_1D_1 + c_2D_2 + c_3D_3$$

where D_1, D_2, and D_3 are, respectively, dummy variables for quarters I, II, and III.[3] Using the data in Table 8.3, she estimates the preceding equation, and the results of this estimation are shown here:

DEPENDENT VARIABLE:	QT	R-SQUARE	F-RATIO	P-VALUE ON F
OBSERVATIONS:	16	0.9965	794.126	0.0001

VARIABLE	PARAMETER ESTIMATE	STANDARD ERROR	T-RATIO	P-VALUE
INTERCEPT	139625.0	1743.5	80.08	0.0001
T	2737.5	129.96	21.06	0.0001
D1	−69788.0	1689.5	−41.31	0.0001
D2	−58775.0	1664.3	−35.32	0.0001
D3	−62013.0	1649.0	−37.61	0.0001

Upon examining the estimation results, Reynolds notes that a positive trend in sales is indicated ($\hat{b} > 0$). In order to determine whether the trend is statistically significant, either a *t*-test can be performed on $\hat{b}$ or the *p*-value for $\hat{b}$ can be assessed for significance. The calculated *t*-value for $\hat{b}$ is $t_{\hat{b}} = 21.06$. With $16 - 5 = 11$ degrees of freedom, the critical value of t (using a 5 percent significance level) is 2.201. Since $21.06 > 2.201$, $\hat{b}$ is statistically significant. The *p*-value for $\hat{b}$ is so small (0.01 percent) that the chance of making a Type I error—incorrectly finding significance—is virtually zero. Thus, Reynolds has strong evidence suggesting a positive trend in sales.

[3]This is only one of the specifications that is appropriate. Equally appropriate is

$$Q_t = a + bt + c_2D_2 + c_3D_3 + c_4D_4$$
$$Q_t = a + bt + c_1D_1 + c_3D_3 + c_4D_4$$

or

$$Q_t = a + bt + c_1D_1 + c_2D_2 + c_4D_4$$

It is necessary only to have *any three* of the quarters represented by the dummy variables.

Next, Reynolds calculates the estimated intercepts of the trend line for each of the four quarters. In the first quarter,

$$\hat{a} + \hat{c}_1 = 139{,}625 - 69{,}788$$
$$= 69{,}837$$

in the second quarter

$$\hat{a} + \hat{c}_2 = 139{,}625 - 58{,}775$$
$$= 80{,}850$$

in the third quarter

$$\hat{a} + \hat{c}_3 = 139{,}625 - 62{,}013$$
$$= 77{,}612$$

and in the fourth quarter

$$\hat{a} = 139{,}625$$

These estimates indicate that the intercepts, and thus sales, are lower in quarters I, II, and III than in quarter IV. The question that always must be asked is: Are these intercepts *significantly* lower?

To answer this question, Reynolds decides to compare quarters I and IV. In quarter I, the intercept is $\hat{a} + \hat{c}_1$; in quarter IV, it is $\hat{a}$. Hence, if $\hat{a} + \hat{c}$ is significantly lower than $\hat{a}$, it is necessary that $\hat{c}_1$ be significantly less than zero. That is, if

$$\hat{a} + \hat{c}_1 < \hat{a}$$

it follows that $\hat{c}_1 < 0$. Reynolds already knows that $\hat{c}_1$ is negative; to determine if it is significantly negative, she can perform a t-test. The calculated value of t for $\hat{c}_1$ is -41.31. Since $|-41.31| > 2.201$, $\hat{c}_1$ is significantly less than zero. This indicates that the intercept—and the sales—in the first quarter is less than that in the fourth. The t-values for $\hat{c}_2$ and $\hat{c}_3$, -35.32 and -37.61, respectively, are both greater (in absolute value) than 2.201 and are significantly negative. Thus, the intercepts in the second and third quarters are also significantly less than the intercept in the fourth quarter. Hence, Reynolds has evidence that there is a significant increase in sales in the fourth quarter.

She can now proceed to forecast sales by quarters for 2000. In the first quarter of 2000, $t = 17$, $D_1 = 1$, $D_2 = 0$, and $D_3 = 0$. Therefore, the forecast for sales in 2000 would be

$$
\begin{aligned}
\hat{Q}_{2000(\text{I})} &= \hat{a} + \hat{b} \times 17 + \hat{c}_1 \times 1 + \hat{c}_2 \times 0 + \hat{c}_3 \times 0 \\
&= \hat{a} + \hat{b} \times 17 + \hat{c}_1 \\
&= 139{,}625 + 2{,}737.5 \times 17 - 69{,}788 \\
&= 116{,}374.5
\end{aligned}
$$

Using precisely the same method, the forecasts for sales in the other three quarters of 2000 are as follows:

$$
\begin{aligned}
2000(\text{II})\text{: } \hat{Q}_{2000(\text{II})} &= \hat{a} + \hat{b} \times 18 + \hat{c}_2 \\
&= 139{,}625 + 2{,}737.5 \times 18 - 58{,}775 \\
&= 130{,}125
\end{aligned}
$$

$$
\begin{aligned}
2000(\text{III})\text{: } \hat{Q}_{2000(\text{III})} &= \hat{a} + \hat{b} \times 19 + \hat{c}_3 \\
&= 139{,}625 + 2{,}737.5 \times 19 - 62{,}013 \\
&= 129{,}624.5
\end{aligned}
$$

$$
\begin{aligned}
2000(\text{IV})\text{: } \hat{Q}_{2000(\text{IV})} &= \hat{a} + \hat{b} \times 20 \\
&= 139{,}625 + 2{,}737.5 \times 20 \\
&= 194{,}375
\end{aligned}
$$

In this example, we have confined our attention to quarterly variation. However, exactly the same techniques can be used for monthly data or any other type of seasonal or cyclical variation. In addition to its application to situations involving seasonal or cyclical variation, the dummy-variable technique can be used to account for changes in sales (or any other economic variable that is being forecast) due to forces such as wars, bad weather, or even strikes at a competitor's production facility. We summarize the dummy-variable technique with the following:

Relation When seasonal variation causes the intercept of the demand equation to vary systematically from season to season, dummy variables can be added to the estimated forecasting equation to account for the cyclical variation. If there are N seasonal time periods to be accounted for, $N - 1$ dummy variables are added to the demand equation. Each of these dummy variables accounts for one of the seasonal time periods by taking a value of 1 for those observations that occur during that season, and a value of 0 otherwise. Used in this way, dummy variables allow the intercept of the demand equation to vary across seasons.

Before leaving the discussion of time-series models, we should mention that the linear trend model is just one—and probably the simplest—of many different types of time-series models that can be used to forecast economic variables. More advanced time-series models fit cyclical patterns, rather than straight lines, to the scatter of data over time. These techniques, which involve moving-average models, exponential smoothing models, and Box-Jenkins models, go well beyond the scope of a managerial textbook. In fact, you can take entire courses in

ILLUSTRATION 8.1

Forecasting New-Home Sales: A Time-Series Forecast

Suppose that in January 1991, the market analyst of a national real estate firm wanted to forecast the total number of new homes that would be sold in the United States in March 1991. Let's examine how this analyst could have used time-series techniques to forecast sales of new homes. The actual data on the total number of new homes sold monthly during the years 1989–1990 are presented in the table (columns 1–3) and are shown by the line (Q_t) in the graph.

Suppose the market analyst forecasts sales using a linear trend, and the following linear specification is estimated:

$$Q_t = a + bt$$

where Q_t is the number of new homes sold in the tth month, and $t = 1, 2, \ldots, 24$. Note that because these are monthly data, the analyst must convert time into integers, as shown in column 4 of the table (ignore column 5 for now). When the analyst runs a regresxsion analysis on the 24 time-series observations on new-home sales, the following computer output results:

DEPENDENT VARIABLE:	QT	R-SQUARE	F-RATIO	P-VALUE ON F
OBSERVATIONS:	24	0.5675	28.871	0.0001

VARIABLE	PARAMETER ESTIMATE	STANDARD ERROR	T-RATIO	P-VALUE
INTERCEPT	61336.90	2544.70	24.10	0.0001
T	−957.0	178.10	−5.37	0.0001

business forecasting that will teach how to implement some of these more sophisticated time-series forecasting techniques.

8.4 ECONOMETRIC MODELS

econometric model A statistical model that employs an explicit structural model to explain the underlying economic relations.

Another method used in statistical forecasting and decision making is econometric modeling. The primary characteristic of **econometric models,** which differentiates this approach from the preceding approaches, is the use of an explicit structural model that attempts to *explain* the underlying economic relations. More specifically, if we wish to employ an econometric model to forecast future sales, we must develop a model that incorporates the variables that actually determine the level of sales (e.g., income, the price of substitutes, and so on). This

Monthly Sales of New Homes in the United States (1989–1990)

(1) Year	(2) Month	(3) Sales	(4) t	(5) D_1
1989	1	52,000	1	0
	2	51,000	2	0
	3	58,000	3	1
	4	60,000	4	1
	5	61,000	5	1
	6	58,000	6	1
	7	62,000	7	1
	8	61,000	8	1
	9	49,000	9	0
	10	51,000	10	0
	11	47,000	11	0
	12	40,000	12	0
1990	1	45,000	13	0
	2	50,000	14	0
	3	58,000	15	1
	4	52,000	16	1
	5	50,000	17	1
	6	50,000	18	1
	7	46,000	19	1
	8	46,000	20	1
	9	38,000	21	0
	10	37,000	22	0
	11	34,000	23	0
	12	29,000	24	0

Source: U.S. Department of Housing and Urban Development.

The estimated forecast equation, $\hat{Q}_t = 61{,}336.90 - 957t$, is labeled $\hat{Q}_t$ in the figure.

The estimate of b is negative ($\hat{b} = -957$), indicating sales were decreasing over the time period 1989–1990. The analyst needs to assess the statistical significance of $\hat{b}$. The p-value for $\hat{b}$ is less than 0.01 percent, which strongly indicates a negative trend in new-home sales over the period 1989–1990. Note also that the R^2 indicates a rather loose fit, as can be seen in the figure as well, even though the model as a whole is statistically significant (the p-value for the F-statistic is 0.0001).

Using the estimated linear trend line, the market analyst can forecast sales for March 1991 ($t = 27$) by substituting the value 27 for t:

$$\hat{Q}_{\text{March 1991}} = 61{,}336.90 - 957 \times 27 = 35{,}500$$

Using linear trend analysis, the number of new homes sold in March 1991 is forecast to be 35,500. The number of homes actually sold in March 1991 turned out to be 51,000. The analyst's forecast, using a trend-line technique, underestimates the actual number of homes sold by 30.4 percent, a rather sizable error.

The market analyst could improve the forecast by modifying the forecast equation to reflect the seasonality of new-home sales: in the spring and summer months, new-home sales tend to be higher than in other months as families try to relocate while school is out of session. Let's examine how adding a dummy variable to account for this seasonality can substantially improve the market analyst's sales forecast.

approach is in marked contrast to the qualitative approach, in which a loose relation was posited between sales and some leading indicators, and the time-series approach, in which sales are assumed to behave in some regular fashion over time.

The use of econometric models has several advantages. First, econometric models require analysts to define explicit causal relations. This specification of an explicit model helps eliminate problems such as spurious (false) correlation between normally unrelated variables and may make the model more logically consistent and reliable.

Second, this approach allows analysts to consider the sensitivity of the variable to be forecasted to changes in the exogenous variables. Using estimated elasticities, forecasters can determine which of the variables are most important in

ILLUSTRATION 8.1

(continued)

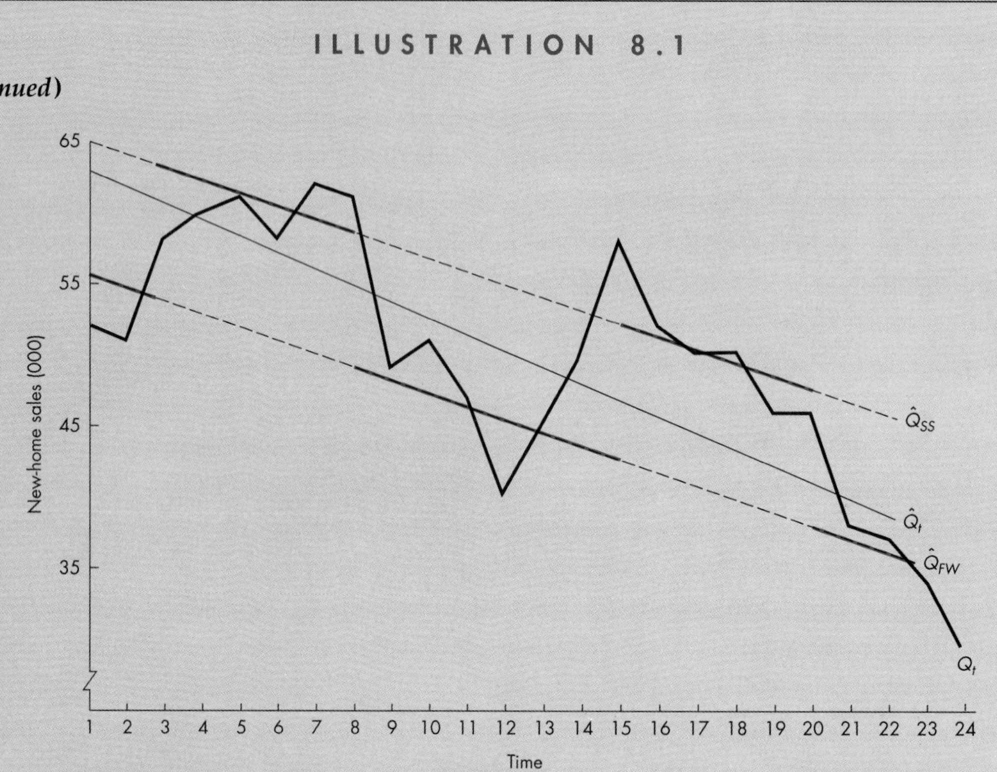

To account for the seasonal increase in new-home sales during the spring and summer months (March through August), the analyst can define a dummy variable, D_t, to be equal to 1 when $t = 3, 4, 5, 6, 7, 8,$ and 15, 16, 17, 18, 19, 20. The dummy variable is equal to zero for all other months. The values of the dummy variable are shown in column 5 of the table. Adding this dummy variable to the trend line results in the following equation to be estimated:

$$Q_t = a + bt + cD_t$$

Again using the sales data for 1989–1990, a regression analysis results in the following computer output:

DEPENDENT VARIABLE:	QT	R-SQUARE	F-RATIO	P-VALUE ON F
OBSERVATIONS:	24	0.8763	74.379	0.0001

VARIABLE	PARAMETER ESTIMATE	STANDARD ERROR	T-RATIO	P-VALUE
INTERCEPT	55111.10	1637.10	33.66	0.0001
T	−853.9	98.51	−8.67	0.0001
D	9875.5	1364.10	7.24	0.0001

As was the case when no adjustment was made for seasonality, a statistically significant downward trend in sales is present ($\hat{b} < 0$). The p-value for each of the parameter estimates in the model with a dummy variable is so small that there is less than a 0.01 percent chance of making a Type I error (mistakenly finding significance). Note that after accounting for seasonal variation, the trend line is less steep ($|-853.9| < |-957|$).

The estimated intercept for the trend line is 55,111.1 for fall and winter months ($D_t = 0$). During the spring and summer buying season, the estimated intercept of the trend line is

$$\hat{a} + \hat{c} = 55{,}111.1 + 9{,}875.5$$
$$= 64{,}986.6$$

To check for statistical significance of $\hat{c}$, we note that the p-value for $\hat{c}$ indicates less than a 0.01 percent chance that $c = 0$. Thus the statistical evidence suggests that there is a significant increase in sales of new homes during the spring and summer months. The increase in the average number of new homes sold in March through August compared with September through February is about 9,875 more homes per month.

The estimated trend lines representing the spring and summer months ($\hat{Q}_{SS}$) and the fall and winter months ($\hat{Q}_{FW}$) are shown in the figure. Note that the spring and summer trend line is parallel to the fall and winter line, but the sales intercept is higher during spring and summer months. The estimated trend line for the fall and winter months is the solid portion of the lower trend line. For the spring and summer months, the estimated trend line is the solid portion of the upper trend line. Note how much better the line fits when it is seasonally adjusted. Indeed, the R^2 increased from 0.5675 to 0.8763.

We now determine whether adding the dummy variable improves the accuracy of the market analyst's forecast of sales in March 1991. Using the estimated trend line accounting for seasonal variation in sales, the sales forecast for March 1991 ($t = 27$) is now

$$\hat{Q}_{\text{March 1991}} = 55{,}111.1 - 853.9 \times 27 + 9{,}875.5 = 41{,}931$$

Clearly, this forecast is an improvement over the unadjusted forecast. The sales forecast that accounts for seasonality underestimates the actual level of sales by 9,070 homes, or 17.8 percent. Compare this with the previous forecast of 35,500, which underestimated actual sales by 30.4 percent. In order to further improve the accuracy of the forecast, the analyst might try using one of the more complicated time-series techniques, which fit cyclical curves to the data, thereby improving the fit (R^2) and the forecast. As already noted, these techniques are well beyond the scope of this text.

determining changes in the variable to be forecasted. Therefore, the analyst can examine the behavior of these variables more closely.

Forecasting the Demand Function

In addition to wanting to know the current demand for their firms' products, managers frequently want to forecast what demand will be during some future period. After all, decisions about price and output are generally made prior to actual production and sales. Such pricing and output decisions require a prior knowledge about what demand will be when production and sales actually take place.

Suppose that the estimated general demand relation for a firm's product is

$$\hat{Q} = \hat{a} + \hat{b}P + \hat{c}M + \hat{d}P_R$$

where Q is quantity demanded, P is price, M is income, and P_R is the price of a good related in consumption. For specific values of the exogenous variables, $M = M'$and $P_R = P_R'$, the estimated demand function is

$$\hat{Q} = (\hat{a} + \hat{c}M' + \hat{d}P_R') + \hat{b}P = \hat{a}' + \hat{b}P$$

The intercept term, $\hat{a}'$, captures the effect of all the exogenous variables and the constant term; that is, changes in either or both of the exogenous variables cause the intercept term $\hat{a}'$ to change value. This is just another way of saying that the demand curve shifts when either M or P_R, or both, change value.

Assume that the above demand equation is estimated in 1999 but the manager wants to forecast what demand will be in 2001. Assume also that the manager believes that the parameters of the demand function ($\hat{a}$, $\hat{b}$, $\hat{c}$, and $\hat{d}$) will not change significantly between 1999 and 2001. The manager does, however, believe that income and the price of the related good will change over this time period. In order to forecast the demand in 2001, the manager must obtain forecast values for both the exogenous variables in 2001, M_{01} and $P_{R,01}$. Forecasted values of the exogenous variables are generally obtained from one of two sources: (1) the firm's own time-series forecast of the exogenous variables, or (2) commercial vendors' forecasts from macroeconomic (econometric) models that forecast the values of many aggregate economic variables.[4]

Once forecasts for the exogenous variables are obtained, the "location" of the demand curve in 2001 can be determined by substituting the values of the forecasted exogenous variables into the estimated demand relation:

$$\begin{aligned}\hat{Q}_{01} &= (\hat{a} + \hat{c}M_{01} + \hat{d}P_{R,01}) + \hat{b}P \\ &= \hat{a}'_{01} + \hat{b}P\end{aligned}$$

[4]Numerous private firms are in the business of selling macroeconomic forecasts of dozens of economic variables to businesses. While businesses wish to forecast the price and sales of their own products, they do not wish to undertake the formidable task of building a large, simultaneous equations model of the U.S. or world economy in order to forecast for the next four quarters such exogenous variables as the rate of inflation, interest rates, or the level of household income.

The forecasted values of the exogenous variables determine where the demand curve intersects the quantity axis (i.e., the "location" of demand).

To illustrate this process of forecasting future demand, we turn to a numerical example. Suppose a firm estimates its general demand relation to be

$$\hat{Q} = 250 - 15P + 0.01M - 4P_R$$

Since $\hat{c}$ is positive, the good is normal; and since P_R is negative, the related good is a complementary good. The firm obtains forecasts of the exogenous variables, M and P_R, 18 months in the future. The forecasts are $M' = \$50{,}000$ and $P_R{}' = \$100$. the forecasted demand equation 18 months from now is

$$\begin{aligned}\hat{Q} &= [250 + (0.01 \times 50{,}000) + (-4 \times 100)] - 15P \\ &= 350 - 15P\end{aligned}$$

Again let us emphasize that it is changes in the future values of the exogenous variables that cause the demand function in the future to be different from the demand function in the current time period. The parameters of the demand function are assumed to be constant; that is, a, b, c, and d do not change value; rather, it is M and P_R that change demand.

Simultaneous Equations Forecasts

Using econometric models to forecast future price and sales in a market is slightly more complicated and requires more information than forecasting future demand. To forecast price and sales, an analyst must have an estimate not only of demand but also of supply. Nonetheless, the idea behind simultaneous equations forecasting is really quite simple.

We introduce and illustrate the methodology to be used to forecast price and sales with Figure 8.7. Suppose that, using regression analysis, we have estimated the demand function

$$Q = \hat{a} + \hat{b}P + \hat{c}M + \hat{d}P_R$$

and the supply function

$$Q = \hat{e} + \hat{f}P + \hat{g}P_I$$

where Q is quantity, P is the price, M is income, P_R is the price of a good related in consumption, and P_I is the price of an input used in production. (Note again that the "hats" on the parameters indicate that these are estimates.) Suppose we know the actual 1999 values for the exogenous variables M_{99} and $P_{R,99}$. Therefore, we know where the demand function is located in 1999. Likewise, if $P_{I,99}$ is also known, we know where the supply function is located in 1999. These demand and supply functions are illustrated in Figure 8.7. Note that their intersection indicates price and sales in 1999.

Suppose that in 1999 we want to forecast sales for 2001. To obtain this sales forecast, we must know where the demand and supply functions will be located in 2001; that is, we must determine the values of the exogenous variables in 2001.

FIGURE 8.7
Simultaneous Equations Forecasting

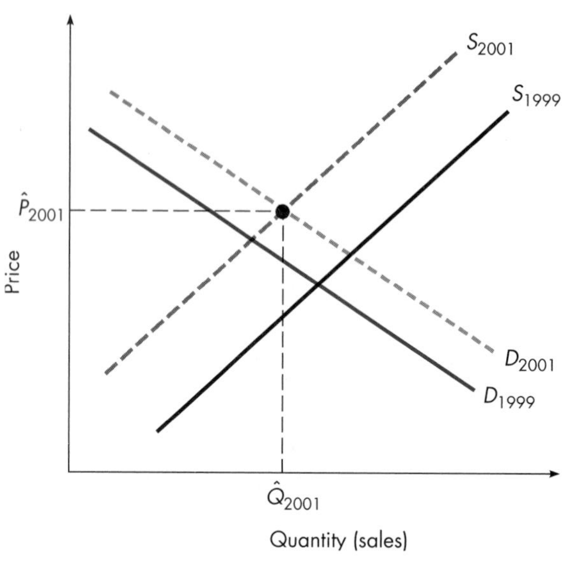

In the case of the estimated demand function, the values of income and the price of the related good in 2001 will determine the location of the 2001 demand function. For simplicity, suppose that over the period 1999–2001, the price of the related good is expected to remain unchanged,

$$P_{R,01} = P_{R,99}$$

but income is expected to rise,

$$M_{01} > M_{99}$$

Because the good is a normal good, demand would increase and the location of the demand curve in 2001 would be as indicated in Figure 8.7.

In the case of the supply function, its location in 2001 is determined by the predicted value of P_I. Suppose P_I is expected to rise:

$$P_{I,01} > P_{I,99}$$

The increase in the input price will cause a decrease in supply, as illustrated by the 2001 supply curve in Figure 8.7.

Finding the location of the future demand and supply functions requires the future, or forecasted, values of the exogenous variables for the time period of the forecast. As already mentioned, a manager can obtain forecasted values of exogenous variables by either using time-series techniques to generate predicted values of the exogenous variables or purchasing forecasts of the exogenous variables from forecasting firms.

Once forecasts for the exogenous variables are obtained, the locations of the 2001 demand and supply functions are determined from their specifications. The intersection of the 2001 demand and supply curves then provides the forecasted values of price and sales (output) in 2001. In Figure 8.7, these forecasts are denoted as $\hat{P}_{2001}$ and $\hat{Q}_{2001}$.

Relation The technique of forecasting with simultaneous equations involves three steps. First, the current (or prevailing) demand and supply functions are estimated using currently available data. Then, future (forecasted) variables of the exogenous variables are substituted into the current demand and supply equations to obtain the demand and supply functions in the forecast time period. Finally, the intersection of future demand and supply provides the forecast of future price and sales (output).

The World Market for Copper: A Simultaneous Equations Forecast

As an example of forecasting with simultaneous equations, we use the copper data presented in Chapter 7 to forecast future copper sales in year 26. To this end, we will follow the three steps outlined in the discussion of simultaneous equations forecasting:

Step 1: Estimate the current demand and supply equations. We begin with the demand and supply functions for copper. The world demand function for copper was specified as

$$Q_{\text{copper}} = a + bP_{\text{copper}} + cM + dP_{\text{aluminum}}$$

and the world supply function as

$$Q_{\text{copper}} = e + fP_{\text{copper}} + gT + hX$$

where time (T) is a proxy for the level of available technology and X is the ratio of consumption of copper to production of copper in the preceding period to reflect inventory changes. Both of these functions are identified and were estimated in Chapter 7 using two-stage least-squares. The estimated demand for copper is

$$Q_{\text{copper}} = -6{,}837.8 - 66.495\,P_{\text{copper}} + 13{,}997M + 107.66\,P_{\text{aluminum}}$$

and the estimated supply function is

$$\hat{Q}_{\text{copper}} = 149.104 + 18.154\,P_{\text{copper}} + 213.88T + 1{,}819.8X$$

Step 2: Locate the demand and supply functions for the time period 26. To locate demand and supply in year 26, we obtain forecast values for the exogenous variables in year 26. Since time is a proxy for technology, the period-26 value for T is simply $T_{26} = 26$. As previously noted, the value of X in any period is the ratio of consumption to production in the preceding period. Since both of these values are known (consumption was 7,157.2 and production was 8,058.0), $\hat{X}_{26} = 0.88821$ (= 7,157.2/8,058.0). For the other two exogenous variables, M and P_R, values must be obtained using time-series forecasting.

To obtain values for $\hat{M}_{26}$ and $\hat{P}_{R,26}$, a linear trend method of forecasting was used to obtain

$$\hat{M}_{26} = 1.13 \text{ and } \hat{P}_{R,26} = 23.79$$

Using $\hat{M}_{26}$ and $\hat{P}_{R,26}$, the demand function in time period 26 is

$$\begin{aligned}\hat{Q}_{\text{copper},26} &= -6{,}837.8 - 66.495\, P_{\text{copper},26} + 13{,}997(1.13) + 107.66(23.79) \\ &= 11{,}540.04 - 66.495\, P_{\text{copper},26}\end{aligned}$$

Likewise, using $\hat{T}_{26} = 26$ and $\hat{X}_{26} = 0.88821$, the supply function in time period 26 is

$$\begin{aligned}\hat{Q}_{\text{copper},26} &= 149.104 + 18.154\, P_{\text{copper},26} + 213.88(26) + 1{,}819.8(0.88821) \\ &= 7{,}326.348 + 18.154\, P_{\text{copper},26}\end{aligned}$$

Step 3: Calculate the intersection of the demand and supply functions. We set quantity demanded equal to quantity supplied and solve for equilibrium price:

$$\begin{aligned}11{,}540.04 - 66.495\, P_{\text{copper},26} &= 7{,}326.348 + 18.154\, P_{\text{copper},26} \\ P_{\text{copper},26} &= 49.78\end{aligned}$$

The sales forecast is then found by substituting $P_{\text{copper},26}$ into either the demand or the supply equation. Using the demand function,

$$\begin{aligned}Q_{\text{copper},26} &= 11{,}540.04 - 66.495\,(49.78) = 7{,}326.348 + 18.154\,(49.78) \\ &= 8{,}230.0\end{aligned}$$

Thus, we forecast that sales of copper in year 26 will be 8,230.0 (thousand) metric tons.[5] The price of copper in year 26 is forecast to be 49.8 cents per pound.

8.5 SOME FINAL WARNINGS

We have often heard it said about forecasting that "he who lives by the crystal ball ends up eating ground glass." While we do not make nearly so dire a judgment, we do feel that you should be aware of the major limitations of and problems inherent in forecasting. Basically, our warnings are concerned with three issues—confidence intervals, specification, and change of structure.

To illustrate the issue of confidence intervals in forecasting, consider once again the simple linear trend model,

$$Q_t = a + bt$$

[5]As we noted in Chapter 7, the data we used for the copper market illustration are the actual data for the period 1951–1975. Hence, our forecast for year 26 can be interpreted as the forecast for 1976. The actual value for copper consumption in 1976 was 8,174.0, so the forecast error in this example was 0.54 percent—about one-half of 1 percent.

FIGURE 8.8
Confidence Intervals

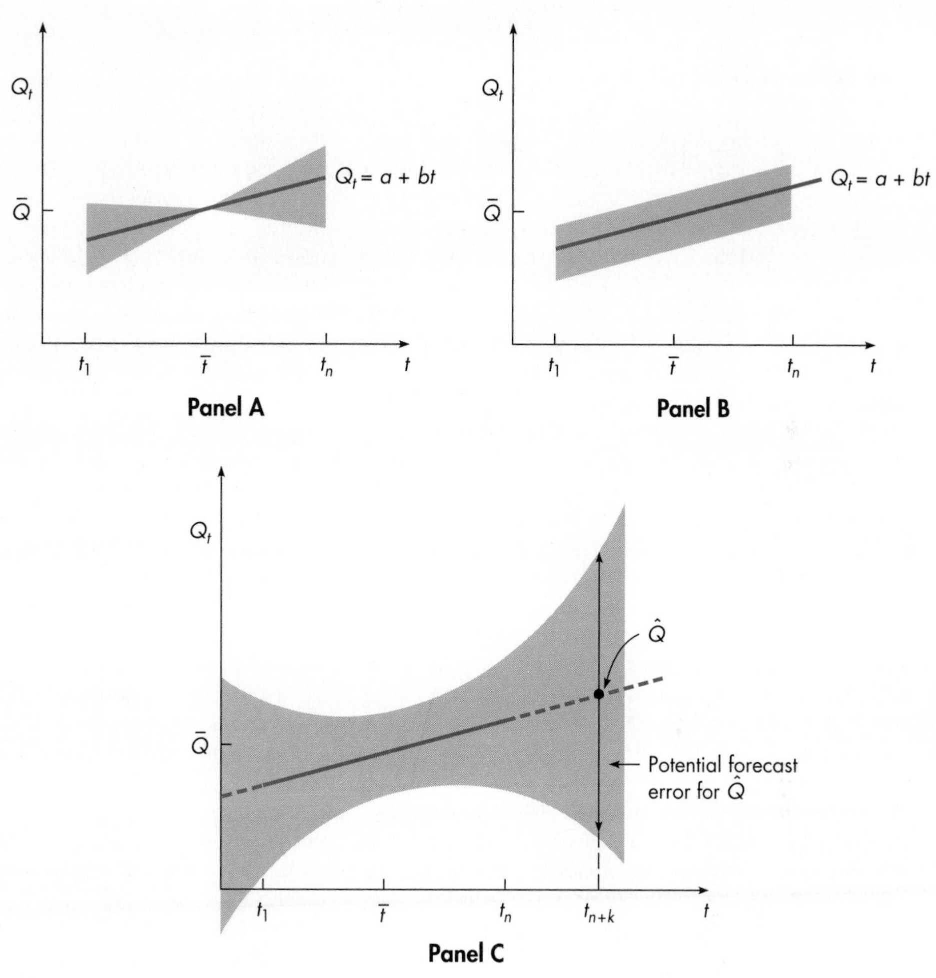

In order to obtain the prediction model, we must estimate two coefficients, *a* and *b*. Obviously, we cannot estimate these coefficients with certainty. Indeed, the estimated standard errors reflect the magnitude of uncertainty (i.e., potential error) about the values of the parameters.

In Figure 8.8, we have illustrated a situation in which there are observations on sales for periods t_1 through t_n. Due to the manner in which it was calculated, the regression line will pass through the sample mean of the data points ($\overline{Q}$, $\bar{t}$). In Panel A, we have illustrated as the shaded area our confidence region if there exist errors only in the estimation of the slope, *b*. In Panel B, the shaded area represents the confidence region if an error exists only in the estimation of the intercept, *a*. These two shaded areas are combined in Panel C. As you can see,

ILLUSTRATION 8.2

The Perils of Forecasting

As we have noted, the forecasting of sales and price is not as precise and scientific as it might appear when one is learning the techniques. An article in *The Wall Street Journal* (December 9, 1992) illustrated some of the pitfalls involved with forecasting retail sales.

"During November and December, many retailers ring up a third of their annual sales and half of their profits. Yule receipts can turn a good year . . . into a great one. And a bad season can stop the show." Most chains begin planning for Christmas by early February, when merchants make their holiday sales forecasts. They base their forecasts on, among other things, their hunches, based on last year's results and the future economic outlook. They place their orders four to eight months in advance, leaving some flexibility for possible changes in orders and unexpected delays in shipping. It is important to have enough of what customers want because running out of stock early would cost many lost sales. On the other hand, stores don't want to have too much stock either. Either carrying over large inventories or resorting to huge markdowns can ruin profits for the entire year.

In five out of the past ten years, the early forecast for Christmas sales turned out to be rather close to what actually occurred. In the other five years, the forecasts were the *opposite* of what actually happened—in some cases drastically missing the mark. According to the *WSJ*, there are several factors that help determine just how full Santa's bag will be for retailers.

The first is economics. In several seasons, unexpected changes in the economy—outside the control of retailers—had a substantial effect on sales. For example, Christmas 1991 was a disaster for many merchants because they weren't expecting the slump in the economy. By fall, when consumer demand dropped, they had already stocked up inventories, forcing them to discount prices heavily in December. The 1985 season was much smoother. Even though many chains had flat holiday sales, profits were good because there were few emergency markdowns. Even though sales were not great, retailers made money because their forecasts turned out to be right.

Good planning, based on economic forecasts, is the second factor. The chief economist at J.C. Penney noted that anticipating what consumer demand will be is critical. Since stores must order so far in advance, they must forecast what merchandise to order even if they are right about what the state of the economy will be. This complicates the problem even more.

The third factor is timing. Even though retailers urge consumers to shop early, they must generally wait until the two weeks before Christmas for 40 percent of their holiday sales. Thus successful forecasts must predict not only the correct magnitude but also the timing of sales.

Timing is important because of the fourth factor, the so-called "panic button." Many retailers have slashed prices too early when sales slip a little. Profits are therefore needlessly reduced. The *WSJ* points out that the decision to go into "alarm-bell" mode is usually made at the highest level of the management structure.

Finally, even though forecasters have done the best job possible, there are numerous factors that are beyond their control. For example, the stock market crash in October 1987 and the Iraqi invasion of Kuwait in the summer of 1991 both sent consumer confidence plunging. And there is always the weather. Merrill Lynch & Co. contends that a 2-degree temperature difference, plus or minus, from the norm is enough to affect sales. Retailers say that this is especially true during the Christmas season.

So forecasting is not always as scientific as it seems. Unexpected things can and do happen. Of course, if you make a forecast and miss, you can always blame unforeseen events. As noted in the *WSJ*, "Retailers have been known to blame slow sales on unseasonably warm weather or unseasonably cold weather, rain, sleet, and snow."

the further the value of t is from the mean value of t, the wider the zone of uncertainty becomes.

Now consider what happens when we use the estimated regression line to predict future sales. At a future time period, t_{n+k}, the prediction for sales will be a point on the extrapolated regression line (i.e., $\hat{Q}$). However, note what happens to the region of uncertainty about this estimate. The further one forecasts into the future, the wider is this region of uncertainty, and this region increases geometrically rather than arithmetically.

This warning applies not just to time-series models. It applies to all statistical techniques. The further the variables used in the forecasts are from the mean values used in the regression, the wider will be the region of uncertainty and, therefore, the less precise the forecast will be. For example, consider the econometric forecasting model for copper. If we attempt to forecast copper sales using a value of per capita income that is much higher than the mean in the data set, the confidence interval for the forecast will be much wider than would be the case if the value of income used in the forecast was close to the mean value in the data set.

We mentioned the problem of incorrect specification in our discussion of demand estimation, but we feel that it is important enough to deserve another mention here. In order to generate reliable forecasts, the model used must incorporate the appropriate variables. The quality of the forecast can be severely reduced if important explanatory variables are excluded or if an improper functional form is employed (e.g., using a linear form when a nonlinear form is appropriate).

We have saved what we feel to be the most important problem for last. This problem stems from potential changes in structure. Forecasts are widely, and often correctly, criticized for failing to predict turning points—sharp changes in the variable under consideration. If it were the case that these changes were only the result of radical changes in the exogenous variables, the simulation approach should be able to handle the problem. However, it is often the case that such changes are the result of changes in the structure of the market itself.

For example, in our consideration of the copper market, there exists the potential for a major change in structure. A major consumer of copper is the telecommunications industry. This industry has been replacing copper transmitting cables with glass fibers. As this change occurs, the demand for copper will be affected significantly. More specifically, any temporal or econometric relation estimated using data before such a change occurred would be incapable of correctly forecasting quantity demanded after the change. In the context of a demand function, the coefficients would be different before and after the change.

Unfortunately, we know of no satisfactory method of handling this problem of "change in structure." Instead, we must simply leave you with the warning that changes in structure are likely. The further you forecast into the future, the
5 6 more likely it is that you will encounter such a change.

8.6 SUMMARY

This chapter set forth some of the basic methods of forecasting demand. The purpose of the chapter was to show some of the simpler techniques that can be used to forecast demand in future time periods. A complete treatment of demand forecasting is a course in itself. The emphasis in this chapter was on understanding the nature of the forecasting problem and on how to interpret the results of demand forecasts. You can learn more about demand forecasting by taking advanced courses in marketing, statistics, and econometrics.

Forecasting models are either qualitative models or statistical models. Qualitative forecasting involves combining the available data with a heavy dose of expert opinion about the firm and industry. Qualitative forecasting is complex and not easily replicated. It is difficult to teach qualitative forecasting techniques because the subjective or judgment component of the forecast depends upon the experience and knowledge of the forecaster.

Statistical forecasting models can be subdivided into two categories—time-series models and econometric models. Time-series forecasts use the time-ordered sequence of historical observations on a variable to develop a model for predicting future values of that variable. Time-series models specify a mathematical model representing the generating process, then use statistical techniques to fit the historical data to the mathematical model.

The simplest time-series forecast is a linear trend forecast where the generating process is assumed to be the linear model $Q_t = a + bt$. Using time-series data on Q, regression analysis is used to estimate the trend line that best fits the data. If b is greater (less) than zero, sales are increasing (decreasing) over time. If b equals zero, sales are constant over time.

When data exhibit cyclical variation, such as seasonal patterns, dummy variables can be added to the time-series model to account for the seasonality. If there are N seasonal time periods to be accounted for, $N - 1$ dummy variables are added to the demand equation. Each dummy variable accounts for one of the seasonal time periods. The dummy variable takes a value of 1 for those observations that occur during the season assigned to that dummy variable and a value of 0 otherwise. This type of dummy variable allows the intercept of the demand equation to take on different values for each season—the demand curve can shift up and down from season to season.

In contrast to time-series models, econometric models use an explicit structural model to *explain* the underlying economic relations. Simultaneous equations forecasting uses both a demand and a supply equation to model price and output (sales) determination. The technique of forecasting with simultaneous equations involves three steps. First, the current (or prevailing) demand and supply functions are estimated using currently available data. Then, future (forecasted) values of the exogenous variables are substituted into the current demand and supply equations to obtain the demand and supply functions in the forecast time period. Finally, the intersection of future demand and supply provides the forecast of future price and sales (output).

When making forecasts, analysts must be careful to recognize that the further into the future the forecast is made, the wider the confidence interval or region of uncertainty. Incorrect specification of the demand equation (as well as supply in the case of simultaneous equations forecasts) can seriously undermine the quality of a forecast. An even greater problem for accurate forecasting is posed by the occurrence of structural changes that cause turning points in the variable being forecast. Forecasts often fail to predict turning points. While there is no satisfactory way to account for unexpected structural changes, forecasters should note that the further into the future you forecast, the more likely it is that a structural change will occur.

This chapter concludes Part III of the text on demand analysis. In Part IV of the text, we will present the theory of production and cost. We also will describe the empirical techniques used to estimate production functions and the various cost equations used by managers to make output and investment decisions.

TECHNICAL PROBLEMS

1. Contrast and compare qualitative and statistical forecasting methods.
2. A linear trend equation for sales of the form

$$Q_t = a + bt$$

was estimated for the period 1985–1999 (i.e., t = 1985, 1986, . . . , 1999). The results of the regression are as follows:

DEPENDENT VARIABLE: QT	R-SQUARE	F-RATIO	P-VALUE ON F
OBSERVATIONS: 15	0.7660	42.561	0.0001

VARIABLE	PARAMETER ESTIMATE	STANDARD ERROR	T-RATIO	P-VALUE
INTERCEPT	73.71460	34.08	2.16	0.0498
T	3.7621	1.0363	3.63	0.0030

a. Evaluate the statistical significance of the estimated coefficients. Does this estimation indicate a significant trend?
b. Using this equation, forecast sales in 2000 and 2001.
c. Comment on the precision of these two forecasts.

3. Consider a firm subject to quarter-to-quarter variation in its sales. Suppose that the following equation was estimated using quarterly data for the period 1990–1998 (the time variable goes from 1 to 36). The variables D_1, D_2, and D_3 are, respectively, dummy variables for the first, second, and third quarters (e.g., D_1 is equal to 1 in the first quarter and zero otherwise).

$$Q_t = a + bt + c_1D_1 + c_2D_2 + c_3D_3$$

The results of the estimation are presented below:

DEPENDENT VARIABLE: QT	R-SQUARE	F-RATIO	P-VALUE ON F
OBSERVATIONS: 36	0.9899	761.133	0.0001

VARIABLE	PARAMETER ESTIMATE	STANDARD ERROR	T-RATIO	P-VALUE
INTERCEPT	51.234	7.16	7.15	0.0001
T	3.127	0.524	5.97	0.0001
D1	−11.716	2.717	−4.31	0.0002
D2	−1.424	0.836	−1.70	0.0985
D3	−17.367	2.112	−8.22	0.0001

a. At the 1 percent level of significance, perform t- and F-tests to check for statistical significance of the coefficients and the equation. Discuss also the significance of the coefficients and equation in terms of p-values.
b. Calculate the intercept in each of the four quarters. What do these values imply?

c. Use this estimated equation to forecast sales in the four quarters of 1999.

4. Supply and demand functions were specified for commodity X:

$$\text{Demand: } Q = a + bP + cM + dP_R$$
$$\text{Supply: } Q = e + fP + gP_I$$

Using quarterly data for the period 1992(I) through 1999(IV), these functions were estimated via 2SLS. The resulting parameter estimates are presented in the following estimated equations. (All estimated coefficients are statistically significant.)

$$\text{Demand: } Q = 500 - 300P + 1.0M - 200P_R$$
$$\text{Supply: } Q = -400 + 200P - 100P_I$$

The predicted values for the exogenous variables (M, P_R, and P_I) for the first quarter of 2001 were obtained from a macroeconomic forecasting model. These predicted values are:

Income (M) = 10,000
The price of the commodity related in consumption (P_R) = 20
The price of inputs (P_I) = 6.

a. Are the signs of the estimated coefficients as would be predicted theoretically? Explain.
b. Predict the sales of commodity X in the first quarter of 2001.
c. Perform a simulation analysis to determine the sales of commodity X in 2001(I) if income were $9,000 and $12,000.

5. Describe the major shortcomings of time-series models.
6. In the final section of this chapter we provided warnings about three problems which frequently arise. List, explain, and provide an example of each.

APPLIED PROBLEMS

1. Freeze Tech, a manufacturer of refrigerators and freezers, is concerned about near-term economic conditions and wishes to obtain a qualitative forecast of sales in the upcoming quarter. If you are the market analyst for Freeze Tech and you plan to use the 10 leading indicators published by the Conference Board to formulate your qualitative forecast, explain how each of these indicators might affect future sales. (For example, if the average workweek of production workers in manufacturing increased, explain the effect on Freeze Tech's sales.) Which of these indicators would be most important in formulating your qualitative forecast?
2. Cypress River Landscape Supply is a large wholesale supplier of landscaping materials in Georgia. Cypress River's sales vary seasonally; sales tend to be higher in the spring months than in other months.
   a. Suppose Cypress River estimates a linear trend *without* accounting for this seasonal variation. What effect would this omission have on the estimated sales trend?
   b. Alternatively, suppose there is, in fact, no seasonal pattern to sales, and the trend line is estimated using dummy variables to account for seasonality. What effect would this have on the estimation?

3. Rubax, a U.S. manufacturer of athletic shoes, estimates the following linear trend model for shoe sales:

$$Q_t = a + bt + c_1D_1 + c_2D_2 + c_3D_3$$

where

Q_t = sales of athletic shoes in the tth quarter
t = 1, 2, . . . , 28[1992(I), 1992(II), . . . , 1998(IV)]
D_1 = 1 if t is quarter I (winter); 0 otherwise
D_2 = 1 if t is quarter II (spring); 0 otherwise
D_3 = 1 if t is quarter III (summer); 0 otherwise

The regression analysis produces the following results:

DEPENDENT VARIABLE: QT	R-SQUARE	F-RATIO	P-VALUE ON F
OBSERVATIONS: 28	0.9651	159.01	0.0001

VARIABLE	PARAMETER ESTIMATE	STANDARD ERROR	T-RATIO	P-VALUE
INTERCEPT	184500	10310	17.90	0.0001
T	2100	340	6.18	0.0001
D1	3280	1510	2.17	0.0404
D2	6250	2220	2.82	0.0098
D3	7010	1580	4.44	0.0002

a. Is there sufficient statistical evidence of an upward trend in shoe sales?
b. Do these data indicate a statistically significant seasonal pattern of sales for Rubax shoes? If so, what is the seasonal pattern exhibited by the data?
c. Using the estimated forecast equation, forecast sales of Rubax shoes for 1999(III) and 2000(II).
d. How might you improve this forecast equation?

4. The automobile industry relies heavily on sales forecasts. If an automobile firm produces too many cars, the costs of holding them in inventory are substantial. If too few cars are produced, sales are lost and substantial profits are forgone. As is evident from the recent experience of U.S. automobile manufacturers, such forecasting is not yet precise.

a. If you were to provide a qualitative forecast, which of the 10 leading indicators would be most relevant? Why?
b. How well would you expect time-series forecasting to work in forecasting the automobile market?

Suppose you decide to use an econometric forecasting model for this market.

c. Specify the demand and supply functions you think would be appropriate and explain why.
d. In our examination of the copper market, the values of the exogenous variables were forecast using historical trends. Such an approach might not be advisable in

the automobile market—particularly in the case of the complementary good, gasoline. The real (deflated) price of gasoline fell during most of the 1960s. Only after the mid-1970s did gasoline prices begin to rise rapidly with its subsequent decline through most of the 1980s. Then, the Persian Gulf war caused gasoline prices to rise rather significantly for a few months in the fall of 1990, after which prices again declined. With this history in mind, suggest a methodology for forecasting automobile sales in the future.

5. Suppose you are the market analyst for a major U.S. bank and the bank president asks you to forecast the median price of new homes and the number of new homes that will be sold in 2002. You specify the following demand and supply functions for the U.S. housing market:

$$\text{Demand: } Q_H = a + bP_H + cM + dP_A + eR$$
$$\text{Supply: } Q_H = f + gP_H + hP_M$$

where the endogenous variables are measured in the following way:

Q_H = thousands of units sold quarterly
P_H = median price of a new home in thousands of dollars

The exogenous variables are median income in dollars (M), average price of apartments (P_A), mortgage interest rate as a percent (R), and the price of building materials as an index (P_M).

a. Is the demand equation identified? Explain.
b. What signs do you expect each of the estimated coefficients to have? Explain.
Using quarterly data for the period 1990(I) through 1999(I), you estimate these equations using two-stage least-squares. All the coefficients are statistically significant and the estimated equations are

$$\text{Demand: } Q_H = 504.5 - 10.0P_H + 0.01M + 0.5P_A - 11.75R$$
$$\text{Supply: } Q_H = 326.0 + 15P_H - 1.8P_M$$

The predicted values for the exogenous variables for the first quarter of 2002 are obtained from a private econometrics firm. The predicted values are:

Median income (M) = 26,000
Average price of apartments (P_A) = 400
Mortgage interest rate (R) = 14
Price of building materials (P_M) = 320 (an index)

c. Using these predicted values of the exogenous variables, forecast the median price and sales of new homes in 2002.
d. Suppose you feel that the predicted mortgage interest rate for 2002, 14 percent, is much too high. Determine how changing the forecast interest rate to 10 percent affects the forecast price and sales for 2002.

6. A number of prominent economic forecasters believe the price of scrap metal—leftover copper from pipes, steel from wrecked cars, and aluminum from old beverage cans—is more useful in predicting the future path of the economy than many government statistics (*The Wall Street Journal*, April 27, 1992). Why would scrap-metal prices be a useful leading indicator? In what type of forecasts would these prices be valuable?

Part IV

Production and Cost

Theory and Empirical Analysis

CHAPTER 9

Theory of Production and Cost in the Short Run

No doubt almost all managers know that profit is determined not only by the revenue a firm generates but also by the costs associated with production of the firm's good or service. Many managers, however, find managing the revenue portion of the profit equation more interesting and exciting than dealing with issues concerning the costs of production. After all, revenue-oriented decisions may involve such tasks as choosing the optimal level and mix of advertising media, determining the price of the product, and making decisions to expand into new geographic markets or new product lines. Even the decision to buy or merge with other firms may be largely motivated by the desire to increase revenues. When revenue-oriented tasks are compared with those involved in production issues—spending time with production engineers discussing productivity levels of workers or the need for more and better capital equipment, searching for lower-cost suppliers of production inputs, adopting new technologies to reduce production costs, and perhaps even engaging in a downsizing plan—it is not surprising that managers may enjoy time spent on revenue decisions more than time spent on production and cost decisions.

As barriers to trade weakened or vanished in the 1990s, the resulting globalization of markets and heightened competition made it much more difficult to increase profits by simply selling more units or charging higher prices. Global competition has intensified the need for managers to increase productivity and reduce costs in order to satisfy stockholders' desire for greater profitability. As one management consultant recently interviewed in *The Wall Street Journal* put it, "Cost-cutting has become the holy-grail of corporate management" in the 1990s. As we will discuss further in Chapter 10, managers must understand the theory of production and cost in order to reduce costs successfully. Many costly errors have been made by managers seeking to "reengineer" or "restructure" production. Most of these errors could have been avoided by managers possessing an understanding of the fundamentals of production and cost that we will now set forth. This chapter and Chapter 10 show how the structure of a firm's costs is determined by the nature of the production process that transforms inputs into goods and services and by the prices of the inputs used in producing the goods or services. In Chapter 11, we show you how to employ regression analysis to estimate the parameters of the production and cost functions for a firm.

Managers make production decisions in two different decision-making time frames: short-run production decisions and long-run production decisions. In short-run decision-making situations, a manager must produce with at least some inputs that are fixed in quantity. In a typical short-run situation, the manager has a fixed amount of plant and equipment with which to produce the firm's output. The manager can change production levels by hiring more or less labor and purchasing more or less raw materials, but the size of the plant is viewed by the manager as essentially unchangeable or fixed for the purposes of making production decisions in the short run.

Long-run decision making concerns the same types of decisions as the short run with one important distinction—the usage of all inputs can be either increased or decreased. In the long run, a manager can choose to operate in any size plant with any amount of capital equipment. Once a firm builds a new plant or changes the size of an existing plant, the manager is once more in a short-run decision-making framework. Sometimes economists think of the short run as the time period during which production actually takes place and the long run as the planning horizon during which future production will take place. As it turns out, the structure of costs differs in rather crucial ways depending upon whether production is taking place in the short run or whether the manager is planning for a particular level of production in the long run.

This chapter presents the fundamentals of the theory of production and the theory of cost in the short run. We will show how the theory of short-run cost is based upon the theory of short-run production. Using production theory, managers determine how much of the variable input(s) to use in combination with the fixed input(s) to produce a particular level of output. After we set forth the theory of production in the short run, we derive the structure of the firm's costs in the short run. By applying the concepts of production theory, the manager can determine the combination of inputs to use to produce a given amount of output at the lowest total cost. Given input prices and the amount of each input that will be purchased, it is a straightforward task to determine the total cost of production.

9.1 SOME BASIC CONCEPTS OF PRODUCTION THEORY

production
The creation of goods and services from inputs or resources.

Production is the creation of goods and services from inputs or resources, such as labor, machinery and other capital equipment, land, raw materials, and so on. Obviously, when a company such as Ford makes a truck or car or when Exxon refines a gallon of gasoline, the activity is production. But production goes much further than that. A doctor produces medical services, a teacher produces education, and a singer produces entertainment. So production involves services as well as making the goods people buy. Production is also undertaken by governments and nonprofit organizations. A city police department produces protection, a public school produces education, and a hospital produces health care.

In the following chapters, as in most of this text, we will analyze production within the framework of business firms using inputs to produce goods, rather than services. Such an approach is more simple and straightforward than the study of the production of services or production by agencies of the government. It is conceptually easier to visualize the production of cars, trucks, or refrigerators than the production of education, health, or security, which are hard to measure and even harder to define. Nonetheless, throughout the discussion, remember that the concepts developed here apply to services as well as goods and to government production as well as firm production.

Production Functions

A production function is the link between levels of input usage and attainable levels of output. That is, the production function formally describes the relation between physical rates of output and physical rates of input usage. With a given state of technology, the attainable quantity of output depends on the quantities of the various inputs employed in production. A **production function** is a schedule (or table or mathematical equation) showing the maximum amount of output that can be produced from any specified set of inputs, given the existing technology or state of the art of production.

production function
A schedule (or table or mathematical equation) showing the maximum amount of output that can be produced from any specified set of inputs, given the existing technology.

Many different inputs are used in production. So, in the most general case, we can define maximum output, Q, to be a function of the level of usage of the various inputs, X. That is,

$$Q = f(X_1, X_2, \ldots, X_n)$$

But in our discussion we will generally restrict attention to the simpler case of a product whose production entails only one or two inputs. We will normally use capital and labor as the two inputs. Hence the production function we will usually be concerned with is

$$Q = f(L, K)$$

where L and K represent, respectively, the amounts of labor and capital used in production. However, we must stress that the principles to be developed apply to situations with more than two inputs and, as well, to inputs other than capital and labor.

Technical Efficiency and Economic Efficiency

Before proceeding, we want to distinguish between *technical efficiency* and *economic efficiency*. **Technical efficiency** is achieved when the maximum possible amount of output is being produced with a given combination of inputs. The definition of a production function assumes that technical efficiency is being achieved because the production function gives the *maximum* output level that can be achieved for any particular combination of inputs. Thus, technical efficiency is implied by the production function.

technical efficiency
Production of the maximum level of output that can be obtained from a given combination of inputs.

To illustrate the concept of technical efficiency, consider a firm that manufactures electric generators using an assembly-line process that begins with workers manually performing five steps before the generator reaches a computer-controlled drill press. At this stage, the computer-controlled drill press makes 36 holes that are required for final assembly. In the process of drilling 36 holes almost 2 pounds of iron is removed. Using this production process, the firm employs 10 assembly-line workers and 1 computer-controlled drill press and produces 140 generators each day. A production engineer studying this process discovers that moving the computer-controlled drill press to the beginning of the assembly line, ahead of five steps that are performed manually, will save laborers energy each day—the generators weigh 2 pounds less when they get to the workers on the assembly line. By moving the drilling to the beginning of the production process, the same 10 workers and 1 drill press can produce 150 generators per day. The production engineer is unable to find any other change in the production process that would further increase output. Now the firm is operating in a technically efficient manner; 150 generators is the maximum number of generators that can be produced daily using 10 laborers and 1 drill press.

economic efficiency
Production of a given amount of output at the lowest possible cost.

Economic efficiency is achieved when the firm is producing a given amount of output at the lowest possible cost. As you will recall from Chapter 4, this is a constrained optimization problem. The optimization rules discussed there and those to be developed in Chapter 10 lead a producer to an economically efficient method of production.

One should be careful about labeling a particular production process inefficient. Certainly a process would be technically inefficient if another process can produce the same amount of output using less of one or more inputs and the same amounts of all others. If, however, the second process uses less of some inputs but more of others, the economically efficient method of producing a given level of output depends on the prices of the inputs. Even when both are technically efficient, one process might cost less—be economically efficient—under one set of input prices while the other may be economically efficient at other input prices.

Short Run and Long Run

fixed input
An input for which the level of usage cannot readily be changed.

variable input
An input for which the level of usage may be changed quite readily.

When analyzing the process of production, it is convenient to introduce the classification of inputs as *fixed* or *variable.* A **fixed input** is one for which the level of usage cannot readily be changed. To be sure, no input is ever absolutely fixed, no matter how short the period of time under consideration. However, the cost of immediately varying the use of an input may be so great that, for all practical purposes, the input is fixed. For example, buildings, major pieces of machinery, and managerial personnel are inputs that generally cannot be rapidly augmented or diminished. A **variable input,** on the other hand, is one for which the level of usage may be changed quite readily in response to desired changes in output. Many types of labor services as well as certain raw and processed materials would be in this category.

short run
That period of time in which the level of usage of one or more of the inputs is fixed.

As mentioned in the introduction, economists distinguish between the *short run* and the *long run.* The **short run** refers to that period of time in which the level of usage of one or more of the inputs is fixed. Therefore, in the short run, changes in output must be accomplished exclusively by changes in the use of the variable inputs. Thus, if producers wish to expand output in the short run, they must do so by using more hours of labor (a variable service) and other variable inputs, with the existing plant and equipment. Similarly, if they wish to reduce output in the short run, they may discharge only certain inputs. They cannot immediately "discharge" a building or a blast furnace (even though its use may fall to zero). In the context of our simplified production function, we might consider capital to be the fixed input and write the resulting short-run production function as

$$Q = f(L, \overline{K})$$

where the bar over capital means that it is fixed. Furthermore, since capital is fixed, output depends only on the level of usage of labor, so we could write the short-run production function as simply

$$Q = f(L)$$

long run
That period of time (or planning horizon) in which all inputs are variable.

The **long run** is defined as that period of time (or planning horizon) in which all inputs are variable. The long run refers to that time in the future when output changes can be accomplished in the manner most advantageous to the producers. For example, in the short run a producer may be able to expand output by operating the existing plant for more hours per day. In the long run, it may be more economical to install additional productive facilities and return to the normal workday.

3 4

Fixed or Variable Proportions

Most of the discussion in this chapter and Chapter 10 refers to production functions that allow at least some substitution of one input for another in reaching an output target. When substitution is possible, we say inputs may be used in *variable proportions.* As a consequence, producers must determine not only the optimal level of output to produce but also the optimal combination of inputs. **Variable proportions production** means that output can be changed in the short run by changing the variable inputs without changing the fixed inputs. And it means that the same output can be produced using different combinations of inputs.

variable proportions production
Production in which a given level of output can be produced with more than one combination of inputs.

Most economists regard production under conditions of variable proportions as typical of both the short and the long run. There is certainly no doubt that proportions are variable in the long run. When making an investment decision, for instance, a producer may choose among a wide variety of different production processes. As an example of polar-opposite processes, an automobile can be practically handmade or it can be made by assembly-line techniques. In the short run, however, there may be some cases where there is little opportunity for substitution among inputs.

fixed proportions production
Production in which one, and only one, ratio or mix of inputs can be used to produce a good.

Fixed proportions production means that there is one, and only one, ratio or mix of inputs that can be used to produce a good. If output is expanded or contracted, all inputs must be expanded or contracted at the same rate to maintain the fixed input ratio. At first glance, this might seem the usual condition: one worker and one shovel produce a ditch; two parts hydrogen and one part oxygen produce water. Adding a second shovel or a second part of oxygen will not augment the rate of production. In such cases, the producer has little discretion about what combination of inputs to employ. The only decision is how much to produce.

In actuality, examples of fixed proportions production are hard to come by. Certainly some "ingredient" inputs are often used in relatively fixed proportions to output. Otherwise, the quality of the product would change. There is so much leather in a pair of shoes of a particular size and style. Use less leather, and we have a different type of shoe. There is so much tobacco in a cigarette. And so on. In these cases, the producer has little choice over the quantity of input per unit of output. But fixed-ingredient inputs are really only a short-run problem. Historically, when these necessary ingredients have become very expensive, businesses have invented new processes, discovered new ingredients, or somehow overcome the problem of a given production function and increasingly scarce ingredients. As a consequence, we will direct attention here to production in which the producer has some control over the mix of inputs and will concentrate on production with variable proportions.

9.2 PRODUCTION IN THE SHORT RUN

We begin the analysis of production in the short run with the simplest kind of short-run situation—only *one* variable input and *one* fixed input:

$$Q = f(L, \bar{K})$$

The firm has chosen the level of capital (made its investment decision), so capital is fixed in amount. Once the level of capital is fixed, the only way the firm can change its output is by changing the amount of labor it employs.

Total Product

Suppose a firm with a production function of the form $Q = f(L, K)$ can, in the long run, choose levels of both labor and capital between 0 and 10 units. A production function giving the maximum amount of output that can be produced from every possible combination of labor and capital is shown in Table 9.1. For example, from the table, 4 units of labor combined with 3 units of capital can produce a maximum of 325 units of output; 6 labor and 6 capital can produce a maximum of 655 units of output; and so on. Note that with zero capital, no output can be produced regardless of the level of labor usage. Likewise, with zero labor, there can be no output.

Once the level of capital is fixed, the firm is in the short run, and output can be changed only by varying the amount of labor employed. Assume now that the capital stock is fixed at 2 units of capital. The firm is in the short run and can

TABLE 9.1

A Production Function

Units of labor (L)	Units of capital (K): 0	1	2	3	4	5	6	7	8	9	10
0	0	0	0	0	0	0	0	0	0	0	0
1	0	25	52	74	90	100	108	114	118	120	121
2	0	55	112	162	198	224	242	252	258	262	264
3	0	83	170	247	303	342	369	384	394	400	403
4	0	108	220	325	400	453	488	511	527	535	540
5	0	125	258	390	478	543	590	631	653	663	670
6	0	137	286	425	523	598	655	704	732	744	753
7	0	141	304	453	559	643	708	766	800	814	825
8	0	143	314	474	587	679	753	818	857	873	885
9	0	141	318	488	609	708	789	861	905	922	935
10	0	137	314	492	617	722	809	887	935	953	967

TABLE 9.2

Total, Average, and Marginal Products of Labor (with capital fixed at 2 units)

(1) Number of workers (L)	(2) Total product (Q)	(3) Average product ($AP = Q/L$)	(4) Marginal product ($MP = \Delta Q/\Delta L$)
0	0	—	—
1	52	52	52
2	112	56	60
3	170	56.7	58
4	220	55	50
5	258	51.6	38
6	286	47.7	28
7	304	43.4	18
8	314	39.3	10
9	318	35.3	4
10	314	31.4	−4

vary output only by varying the usage of labor (the variable input). The column in Table 9.1 under 2 units of capital gives the total output, or total product of labor, for 0 through 10 workers. This column, for which $K = 2$, represents the short-run production function when capital is fixed at 2 units.

These total products are reproduced in column 2 of Table 9.2 for each level of labor usage in column 1. Thus, columns 1 and 2 in Table 9.2 define a production function of the form $Q = f(L, \bar{K})$, where $\bar{K} = 2$. In this example, total product (Q) rises with increases in labor up to a point (9 workers) and then declines. While total product does eventually *fall* as more workers are employed, managers would not (knowingly) hire additional workers if they knew output would fall. In Table 9.2, for example, a manager can hire either 8 workers or 10 workers to produce 314 units of output. Obviously, the economically efficient amount of labor to hire to produce 314 units is 8 workers.

Average and Marginal Products

Average and marginal products are obtained from the production function and may be viewed merely as different ways of looking at the same information. The **average product of labor (*AP*)** is the total product divided by the number of workers:

average product of labor (*AP*)
Total product (output) divided by the number of workers ($AP = Q/L$).

$$AP = Q/L$$

In our example, average product, shown in column 3, first rises, reaches a maximum at 56.7, then declines thereafter.

The **marginal product of labor (*MP*)** is the additional output attributable to using one additional worker with the use of all other inputs fixed (in this case, at 2 units of capital). That is,

marginal product of labor (*MP*)
The additional output attributable to using one additional worker with the use of all other inputs fixed ($MP = \Delta Q/\Delta L$).

$$MP = \Delta Q/\Delta L$$

where Δ means "the change in." The marginal product schedule associated with the production function in Table 9.2 is shown in column 4 of the table. Because no output can be produced with zero workers, the first worker adds 52 units of output; the second adds 60 units (that is, increases output from 52 to 112); and so on. Note that increasing the amount of labor from 9 to 10 actually decreases output from 318 to 314. Thus the marginal product of the 10th worker is negative. In this example, marginal product first increases as the amount of labor increases, then decreases, and finally becomes negative. This is a pattern frequently assumed in economic analysis.

In this example, the production function assumes that labor, the variable input, is increased one worker at a time. But we can think of the marginal product of an input when more than 1 unit is added. At a fixed level of capital, suppose that 20 units of labor can produce 100 units of output and that 30 units of labor can produce 200 units of output. In this case, output increases by 100 units as labor increases by 10. Thus

$$MP = \frac{\Delta Q}{\Delta L} = \frac{100}{10} = 10$$

Output increases by 10 units for each additional worker hired.

We might emphasize that we speak of the marginal product of labor, not the marginal product of a particular laborer. We assume that all workers are the same, in the sense that if we reduce the number of workers from 8 to 7 in Table 9.2, total product falls from 314 to 304 regardless of which of the 8 workers is released. Thus the order of hiring makes no difference; a third worker adds 58 units of output no matter who is hired.

Figure 9.1 shows graphically the relations among the total, average, and marginal products set forth in Table 9.2. In Panel A, total product increases up to

FIGURE 9.1

Total, Average, and Marginal Products ($\bar{K} = 2$)

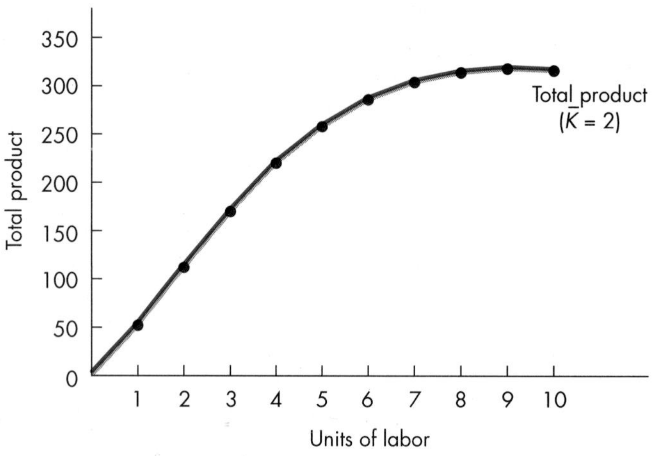

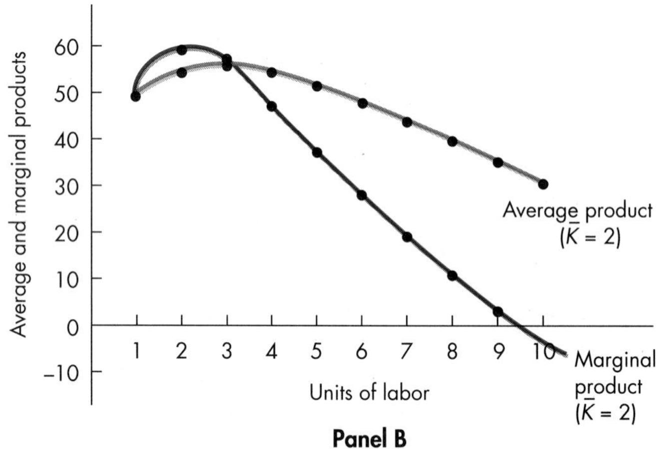

nine workers, then decreases. Panel B incorporates a common assumption made in production theory: average product first rises then falls. When average product is increasing, marginal product is greater than average product (after the first worker, at which they are equal). When average product is decreasing, marginal product is less than average product.[1] This result is not peculiar to this particular production function; it occurs for any production function for which average product first increases then decreases.

An example might help demonstrate that for any average and marginal schedule, the average must increase when the marginal is above the average and

[1]This relation is demonstrated in the appendix to this chapter.

decrease when the marginal is below the average. If you have taken two tests and made grades of 70 and 80, your average grade is 75. If your third test grade is higher than 75, the marginal grade is above the average, so your average grade increases. Conversely, if your third grade is less than 75—the marginal grade is below the average—your average falls. In production theory, if each additional worker adds more than the average, average product rises; if each additional worker adds less than the average, average product falls.

As shown in Figure 9.1, marginal product first increases then decreases, becoming negative after nine workers. The maximum marginal product occurs before the maximum average product is attained. When marginal product is *increasing*, total product increases at an *increasing* rate. When marginal product begins to *decrease* (after two workers), total product begins to increase at a *decreasing* rate. When marginal product becomes negative (10 workers), total product declines.

We should note another important relation between average and marginal product that is not obvious from the table or the graph, but does follow directly from the discussion. If labor is allowed to vary continuously rather than in discrete units of one, as in the example, marginal product equals average product when average is at its maximum. This follows because average product must increase when marginal is above average and decrease when marginal is below average. The two, therefore, must be equal when average is at its maximum.

Law of Diminishing Marginal Product

law of diminishing marginal product
The principle that as the number of units of the variable input increases, other inputs held constant, a point will be reached beyond which the marginal product decreases.

The slope of the marginal product curve in Panel B of Figure 9.1 illustrates an important principle, the **law of diminishing marginal product.** As the number of units of the variable input increases, other inputs held constant, there exists a point beyond which the marginal product of the variable input declines. When the amount of the variable input is small relative to the fixed inputs, more intensive utilization of fixed inputs by variable inputs may initially increase the marginal product of the variable input as this input is increased. Nonetheless, a point is reached beyond which an increase in the use of the variable input yields progressively less additional output. Each additional unit has, on average, fewer units of the fixed inputs with which to work.

To illustrate the concept of diminishing marginal returns, consider the kitchen at Mel's Hot Dogs, a restaurant that sells hot dogs, french fries, and soft drinks. Mel's kitchen has one gas range for cooking the hot dogs, one deep-fryer for cooking french fries, and one soft-drink dispenser. One cook in the kitchen can prepare 15 meals (consisting of a hot dog, fries, and soft drink) per hour. Two cooks can prepare 35 meals per hour. The marginal product of the second cook is 20 meals per hour, 5 more than the marginal product of the first cook. One cook possibly concentrates on making fries and soft drinks while the other cook prepares hot dogs. Adding a third cook results in 50 meals per hour being produced, so the marginal product of the third worker is 15 (= 50 − 35) additional meals per hour.

Therefore, after the second cook, the marginal product of additional cooks begins to decline. The fourth cook, for example, can increase the total number of meals prepared to 60 meals per hour—a marginal product of just 10 additional meals. A fifth cook adds only 5 extra meals per hour, an increase to 65 meals. While the third, fourth, and fifth cooks increase the total number of meals prepared each hour, their marginal contribution is diminishing because the amount of space and equipment in the kitchen is fixed (i.e., capital is fixed). Mel could increase the size of the kitchen or add more cooking equipment to increase the productivity of all workers. The point at which diminishing returns set in would then possibly occur at a higher level of employment.

The marginal product of additional cooks can even become negative. For example, adding a sixth cook reduces the number of meals from 65 to 60. The marginal product of the sixth cook is -5. Do not confuse *negative* marginal product with *diminishing* marginal product. Diminishing marginal product sets in with the third cook, but marginal product does not become negative until the sixth cook is hired. Obviously, the manager would not want to hire a sixth cook, since output would fall. The manager would hire the third, or fourth, or fifth cook, even though marginal product is decreasing, if more than 35, 50, or 60 meals must be prepared. As we will demonstrate, managers do in fact employ variable inputs beyond the point of diminishing returns but not to the point of negative marginal product.

The law of diminishing marginal product is a simple statement concerning the relation between marginal product and the rate of production that comes from observing real-world production processes. While the eventual diminishing of marginal product cannot be proved or refuted mathematically, it is worth noting that a contrary observation has never been recorded. That is why the relation is called a law.

Changes in Fixed Inputs

The production function shown in Figure 9.1 and also in Table 9.2 was derived from the production function shown in Table 9.1 by holding the capital stock fixed at 2 units ($\overline{K} = 2$). As can be seen in Table 9.1, when different amounts of capital are used, total product changes for each level of labor usage. Indeed, each column in Table 9.1 represents a different short-run production function, each corresponding to the particular level at which capital stock is fixed. Because the output associated with every level of labor usage changes when capital stock changes, a change in the level of capital causes a *shift* in the total product curve for labor. Since total product changes for every level of labor usage, average product and marginal product of labor also must change at every level of labor usage.

Referring once more to Table 9.1, notice what happens when the capital stock is increased from 2 to 3 units. The total product of three workers increases from 170 to 247, as shown in column 3. The average product of three workers increases from 56.7 to 82.3 (= 247/3). The marginal product of the third worker increases from 58 to 85 [$\Delta Q/\Delta L = (247 - 162)/1 = 85$]. Table 9.3 shows the total, average, and marginal product schedules for two levels of capital stock, $\overline{K} = 2$ and $\overline{K} = 3$. As you can see, *TP, AP,* and *MP* all increase at each level of labor usage as *K* increases from 2 to 3 units. Figure 9.2 shows how a change in the fixed amount

TABLE 9.3
The Effect of Changes in Capital Stock

	$\overline{K} = 2$			$\overline{K} = 3$		
L	*Q*	*AP*	*MP*	*Q*	*AP*	*MP*
0	0	—	—	0	—	—
1	52	52	52	74	74	74
2	112	56	60	162	81	88
3	170	56.7	58	247	82.3	85
4	220	55	50	325	81.3	78
5	258	51.6	38	390	78	65
6	286	47.7	28	425	70.8	35
7	304	43.4	18	453	64.7	28
8	314	39.3	10	474	59.3	21
9	318	35.3	4	488	54.2	14
10	314	31.4	−4	492	49.2	4

of capital shifts the product curves. In Panel A, increasing $\overline{K}$ causes the total product curve to shift upward, and in Panel B, the increase in $\overline{K}$ causes both *AP* and *MP* to shift upward.

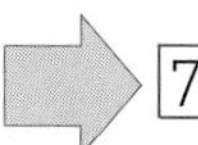
7

9.3 SUMMARY OF SHORT-RUN PRODUCTION

The production function gives the maximum amount of output that can be produced from any given combination of inputs, given the state of technology. The production function assumes technological efficiency in production, because technological efficiency occurs when the firm is producing the maximum possible output with a given combination of inputs. Economic efficiency occurs when a given output is being produced at the lowest possible total cost.

In the short run, at least one input is fixed. In the long run, all inputs are variable. This chapter examines the short-run situation when only one input is variable and one fixed. Panel A of Figure 9.3 shows a typical total product curve when labor is the only variable input. This curve gives the maximum amount of output that can be produced by each amount of labor when combined with the fixed inputs. The total product curve reflects the following relations:

1. No output can be produced with zero workers.
2. Output increases at an increasing rate until L_0 workers are employed producing Q_0 units of output. Over this range marginal product is increasing.
3. Total product then increases but at a decreasing rate when the firm hires between L_0 and L_2 workers. Over this range *MP* is decreasing.
4. Average product reaches its maximum value at L_1, where *AP* equals *MP*.
5. Finally a point will be reached beyond which output will decline, indicating a negative marginal product. In Figure 9.3 this occurs for employment levels greater than L_2. The maximum possible total product is thus Q_2.

FIGURE 9.2

Shifts in Total, Average, and Marginal Product Curves

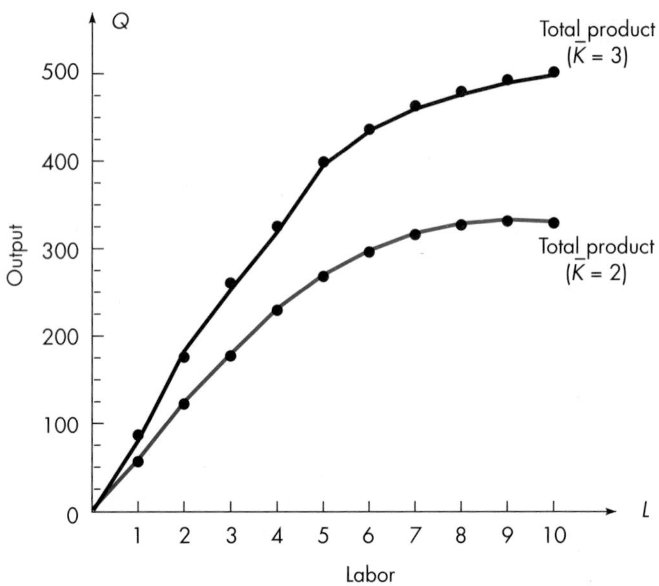

Panel A — Shift in total product when *K* increases

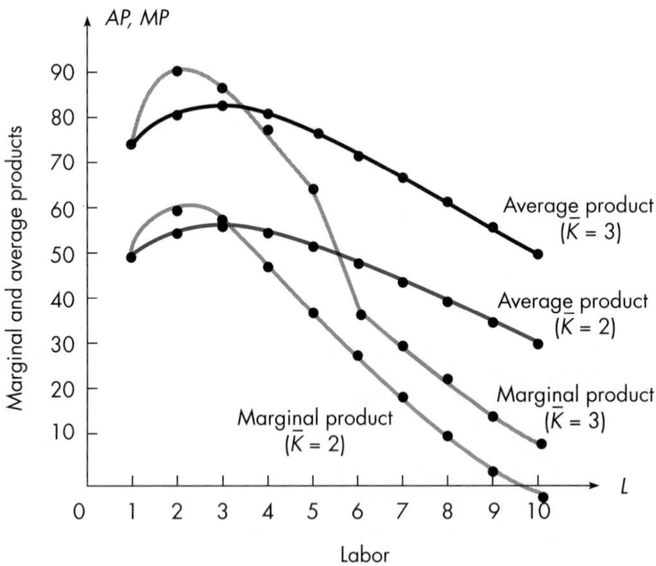

Panel B — Shifts in *MP* and *AP* when *K* increases

FIGURE 9.3
Total, Average, and Marginal Product Curves

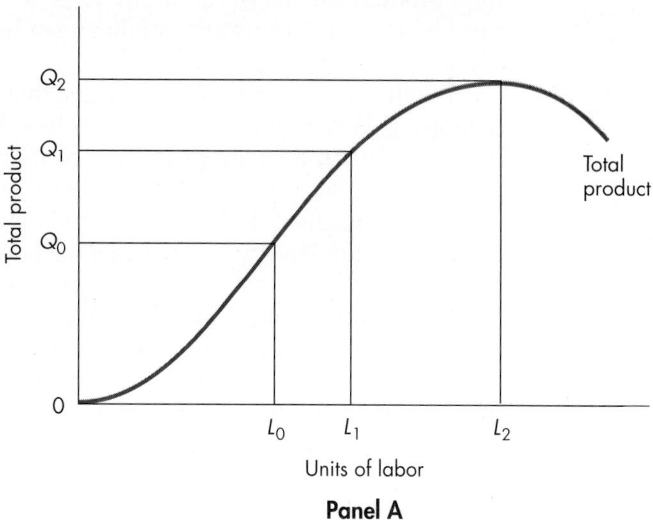

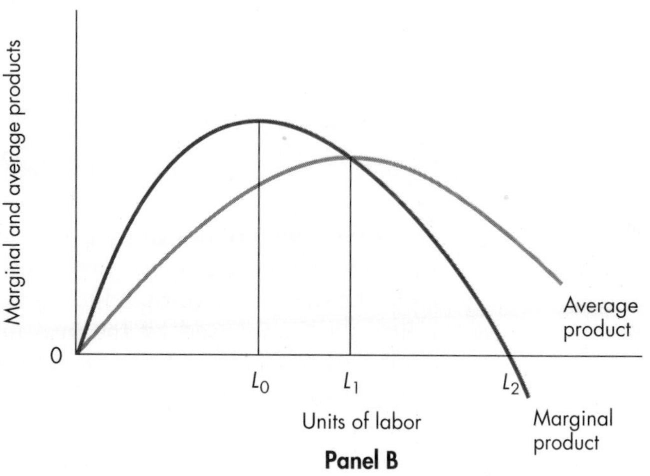

The corresponding average and marginal product curves are shown in Panel B. Note that both curves first rise, reach a maximum, then decline. Marginal product attains a maximum (at L_0) at a lower input level than the level at which average product attains its maximum (at L_1). While average product is always positive, marginal product is zero at L_2 units of labor and is negative thereafter. Beyond L_2, the firm is using so much labor (relative to the fixed inputs) that output actually falls with the addition of more units. Possibly so much labor is being used that additional workers simply get in each other's way and therefore reduce the total output that can be produced. The falling portion of the total product curve (*MP* is negative) is not economically efficient since any output for which total product is falling can be produced using less labor and thus at a lower cost.

When marginal product is greater than average product, average product is increasing. When marginal product is less than average product, average product is falling. When average product is at its maximum, that is, neither rising nor falling, marginal product equals average product. The reason for this was discussed previously. The concepts of average and marginal product will become quite important later, when we analyze how firms decide how much of an input to hire.

We are now ready to derive the cost structure of the firm in the short run. For any level of output the manager wishes to produce, the economically efficient amount of labor to combine with the fixed amount of capital is found from the total product curve. In Figure 9.3, if the manager wishes to produce Q_0 units of output, the amount of labor that will produce Q_0 units at the lowest total cost is L_0 units. The total cost of producing Q_0 units is found by multiplying the price of labor per unit times L_0 to get the total expenditure on labor; then this amount is added to the cost of the fixed input. This computation can be done for every level of output to get the short-run total cost of production. We turn now to the costs of production in the short run.

9.4 THE NATURE OF ECONOMIC COSTS

Recall from the discussion of economic profit in Chapter 1 that the economic cost to a firm of using resources in the production of goods or services is correctly measured by the total opportunity cost of all resources used by the firm. We told you in Chapter 1 that the opportunity cost of using resources owned by others is equal to the dollar amount paid to the resource owners. For resources owned by the firm itself and used by the firm in production, the opportunity cost is equal to the largest payment that the owner(s) could have received if those resources had been leased or sold in the market. Because the concept of economic cost is so crucial in decision making, and yet so widely misunderstood, we will now present a more complete explanation of economic costs.

Explicit and Implicit Costs

opportunity cost
What the firm's owners give up to use a resource; the sum of explicit and implicit costs.

The cost of using resources to produce a good or service is the **opportunity cost** to the owners of the firm using those resources. The opportunity cost is what the owners must give up to use a resource. All costs of production are opportunity costs, and for decision-making purposes, it is opportunity costs that matter.

ILLUSTRATION 9.1

High Productivity Rescues U.S. Petroleum Producers

During the early to mid-1980s, the price of a barrel of crude oil (measured in 1996 dollars) fell dramatically from a historic high price of $58 per barrel down to around $13 per barrel, where crude oil prices remain as we go to press. As an article in *Business Week* pointed out, crude oil is now cheaper, indeed much cheaper, than bottled water.* Despite the precipitous fall in oil prices, petroleum firms in the United States have managed to become profitable at the $13-per-barrel price level. The current profitability of crude-oil producers in the face of falling crude-oil prices has been made possible by tremendous gains in the productivity of exploration operations (the process of finding underground and undersea oil deposits) and development and production operations (the process of getting the oil to the earth's surface).

As we explain in this chapter, productivity and costs are inversely related. To achieve lower costs, oil-producing firms in the United States responded to falling crude-oil prices in the 1980s by investing heavily in new technologies that promised to lower both the cost of finding oil deposits and the cost of getting oil out of the ground. Douglas Bohi, in a recent study of the U.S. petroleum industry conducted by Resources for the Future, reported that the new technologies that are now bringing higher productivity and lower costs to exploration and development of oil deposits "rival in imagination and expense those used to explore outer space."† Bohi discussed three of the most important new technologies: three-dimensional seismology, horizontal drilling, and new deepwater drilling technologies.

Three-dimensional (3D) views of underground rock formations provide a tremendous advantage over two-dimensional (2D) seismology techniques. Even though 3D seismological analysis costs twice as much as 2D analysis, the success rate in exploration is more than doubled and average costs of exploration decrease over 20 percent. *Business Week* reported that Exxon Corporation cut its exploration costs by 85 percent in the last 10 years. In production of crude oil, 3D seismology, coupled with horizontal drilling techniques and so-called "geosteering drill bits," makes it possible to recover more of the oil in the newly discovered deposits.

Deepwater drilling, which on average yields five times as much crude oil as onshore drilling does, is booming now. Advances in deepwater drilling platform technology—such as computer-controlled thrusters using coordinate readings from satellites to keep floating platforms in place—have made deep deposits in the Gulf of Mexico accessible. British-Borneo Chief Executive Alan J. Gaynor stated, in the *Business Week* article, "We've wholly changed the cost structure of doing business in deep water." Some deep deposits in the Gulf of Mexico are as large as some of the oil fields in the Middle East.

Productivity increases are also pushing higher the amount of oil that can be recovered from deposits. While "the average field gives up just 35 percent of its contents as the pressure naturally lifting the oil dissipates," new air-injection technologies are recovering up to 70 percent of the oil in some reservoirs.

As a result of these productivity advances, costs have fallen to the point that U.S. producers can now make a profit producing oil at prices as low as $13 per barrel. Producers in Norway claim they can make a profit at just $12 per barrel. While it has become fashionable in the 1990s to criticize drivers of sport utility vehicles (SUVs) for "wasting" gasoline, the article in *Business Week* predicted that productivity increases "will pull more (oil) from the ground than people ever dreamed possible"—good news for both environmentalists and manufacturers of SUVs.

*Peter Coy, Gary McWilliams, and John Rossant, "The New Economics of Oil," *Business Week,* Nov. 3, 1997.

†Douglas Bohi, "High-Tech Leads to Uptick in U.S. Petroleum Supply," *Resources* (Resources for the Future, Washington, D.C.), Fall 1997, p. 17.

explicit cost
An out-of-pocket monetary payment for the use of a resource.

The opportunity cost of using an input or a resource is classified as either an *explicit cost* or an *implicit cost.* **Explicit costs** are what most people mean when they think of the cost of something. An explicit cost is the monetary payment made by a firm for the use of an input owned or controlled by other individuals. Explicit costs are also referred to as *accounting costs.* For example, if a firm purchases 40 hours of unskilled labor services for $8 per hour, an explicit (accounting) cost of $320 is incurred by the firm. The $320 payment is the amount the firm's owners give up to use the 40 hours of labor. Other types of explicit costs include the costs of purchasing raw materials, leasing a building, purchasing advertising, and leasing a plot of land.

implicit cost
The forgone return the firm's owners could have received had they used their own resources in their best alternative use.

Firms frequently use some resources that do not involve explicit monetary payments. Even though the firm does not make an explicit monetary payment for the use of such an input, the opportunity cost of using the input is not zero.[2] Such nonmonetary opportunity costs are called **implicit costs.** An implicit cost is the opportunity cost of using resources that are owned by the owners of the firm. The implicit cost is the foregone return the owners of the firm could have received had they used their own resources in their best alternative use rather than using the resources for their own firm's production. Implicit costs typically take two forms: (1) the opportunity cost of using land or capital owned by the firm, or (2) the opportunity cost of the owner's time spent managing the firm or working for the firm in some other capacity. These implicit costs are just as real and important in decision making as the firm's out-of-pocket explicit costs.

normal profit
The implicit cost of using owner-supplied resources.

As we explained in Chapter 1, economists also refer to the implicit cost of using owner-supplied resources as **normal profit.** Normal profit is just an alternative name for the implicit costs of using owner-supplied resources. Consequently, normal profit is a part of the total cost of using resources. We will have more to say about normal profit when we discuss profit maximization in Parts V and VI.

To illustrate the implicit cost of using capital owned by the firm, suppose Alpha Corporation and Beta Corporation are two manufacturing firms that produce a particular good and are in every way identical, with one exception: the owner of Alpha Corporation rents the building in which the good is produced; the owner of Beta Corporation inherited the building the firm uses and therefore pays no rent. Which firm has the higher costs of production? The costs are the same, even though Beta makes no explicit payment for rent. The reason the costs are the same is that using the building to produce goods costs the owner of Beta the amount of income that could have been earned had the building been leased at the prevailing rent. Since these two buildings are the same, presumably the market rentals would be the same. In other words, Alpha incurred an explicit cost for the use of its building, whereas Beta incurred an implicit cost for the use of its building. Regardless of whether the payment is explicit or implicit, the opportunity cost of using the building resource is the same for both firms.

---

[2]The opportunity cost to a firm of using a resource is only equal to zero if the market value of the resource is zero, that is, if no other firm would be willing to pay anything for the use of that resource.

The opportunity cost or implicit cost of using capital equipment or land that is owned by the firm (that is, owned by the firm's owners) is the return that could have been received if this resource had not been used by the firm but, instead, been employed in its best alternative use. This sacrificed return can be measured in one of two ways. As in the above example, the sacrificed return is what could have been earned from leasing or renting the resource to some other firm. Alternatively, the sacrificed return can be measured as the amount the owner could earn if the resource, such as the building, were sold and the payment invested at the market rate of interest. The sacrificed interest is the implicit cost. These two measures of implicit cost are frequently the same, but if they are not equal, the true opportunity cost is the *best* alternative return.[3]

We should note that the opportunity cost of using land or capital owned by the firm may not bear any relation to the amount the firm paid for the land or capital. The opportunity cost reflects the current market value of the resource. If the firm paid $1 million for a plot of land two years ago, but the market value of the land has since fallen to $500,000, the implicit cost is the best return that could be earned if the land is sold for $500,000, not $1 million (which would be impossible under the circumstances), and the proceeds are invested. Similarly, if the market value has risen to $2 million, the implicit cost is the best possible return on $2 million, not $1 million. If the value of the land has fallen to zero, the implicit cost of using it is zero—there is no alternative return. Note that the implicit cost is not what the resource could be sold for but the best return that could be earned by selling the resource and investing this amount in the best way possible. In the above example, if the $2 million could be invested at 10 percent, the implicit cost is $200,000.

Another example of an implicit cost is the value of a firm owner's time that is used to manage the business. Presumably, if the owners of firms are not managing their businesses or working for their firms in another capacity, they could obtain a job with some other firm, possibly as managers. The salary that could be earned in this alternative occupation is an implicit cost that should be considered as part of the total cost of production, because it is an opportunity cost to these owners.

The implicit cost of an owner's time spent managing a firm or working for the firm in some other capacity is frequently, though not always, the same as the payment that would be necessary to hire an equivalent manager or worker if the owner does not work for the firm. As an extreme example of a case in which these amounts would not be the same, suppose Shaquille O'Neal retires from basketball and opens a sporting-goods store that he manages himself. Presumably, he could hire an equivalent manager for about $50,000 to $70,000 a year. Mr. O'Neal's opportunity cost, however, is the $10 million to $12 million he could earn from playing basketball and endorsing products. In most other cases that are not so far-fetched, the two amounts would be similar.

[3]The implicit cost of an owner's land or capital is frequently the same as the amount the firm would have to pay if it leased an identical piece of land or capital, although this is not always the case.

The total cost of using resources for production is the sum of all explicit costs and all implicit costs. Both are real opportunity costs. Throughout the remainder of this chapter and in later chapters, when we refer to a firm's cost, we include both explicit and implicit costs, even though we will not explicitly divide them into two separate categories. In all cases, "cost" will mean the entire opportunity cost.

Principle The opportunity cost to a firm of using resources is the amount the firm gives up by using these resources. Opportunity costs are explicit or implicit. An explicit opportunity cost is the payment the firm makes to a resource owner to hire, rent, or lease that resource. Implicit opportunity costs are the forgone earnings from using resources owned by the firm in the firm's own production process. These resources are typically any land or capital owned by the firm and an owner's time spent working for the firm. The implicit cost is the return that could have been earned in the best alternative use of the resources.

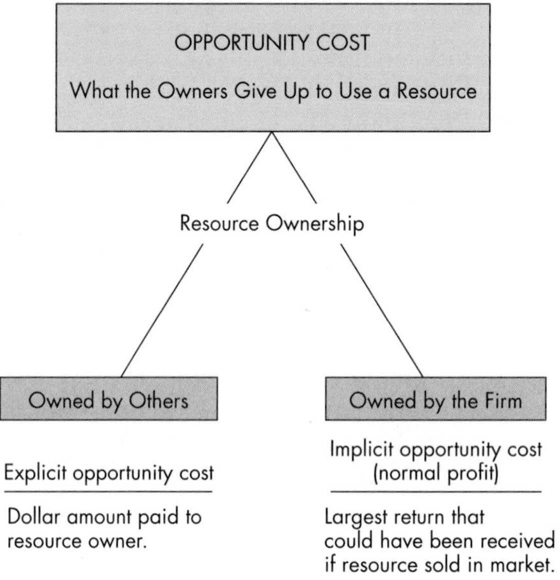

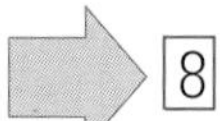

Fixed and Variable Costs

In the short run some inputs are fixed. Since these inputs have to be paid for regardless of the level of output produced, payments for fixed inputs remain constant no matter what level of output is produced. Such payments are called *fixed costs.* An example of a fixed cost is a machine that is leased for one year at a cost of $500 per month. The cost of the machine is $500 every month for one year regardless of how many units of output are produced using the machine. Even if the firm shuts down for a month and does not use the machine, the firm still must pay $500 for the machine that month.

Payments for variable inputs are called *variable costs.* Producing more output requires more variable inputs. Thus, variable costs increase as the level of output increases. Examples of variable costs are payments for many types of labor, ingredient inputs or raw materials, or the energy used in production.

ILLUSTRATION 9.2

Implicit Costs and Household Decision Making

As we explained in the text, the implicit opportunity cost to the firm of using a resource owned by the firm equals the best possible forgone payment the firm could have received if it had rented or leased the resource to another firm or had chosen to sell the resource in the market and invest the returns from the sale rather than retain the input for its own use. Producers decide how much of a resource to use on the basis of the opportunity cost of the resource, regardless of whether that opportunity cost is an explicit cost or an implicit cost. You should not get the impression that opportunity costs, particularly implicit costs, are relevant only to decisions about production. All decision makers, including household decision makers, must consider both explicit and implicit costs in order to get the most from their limited resources.

Consider homeowners who pay off their mortgages early. Suppose a homeowner wins the state lottery and decides to pay off a $100,000 balance on a home mortgage. After "burning the mortgage," the homeowner no longer must make monthly mortgage payments, an explicit cost of homeownership. Ignoring maintenance costs and changes in the market value of the home, is the cost of owning the home now zero? Certainly not. By using his or her own financial resources to pay off the mortgage, the homeowner must forgo the income that could have been earned if the $100,000 had been invested elsewhere. If the homeowner could earn 7.5 percent on a certificate of deposit, the implicit cost (opportunity cost) of paying off the mortgage is $7,500 per year. Smart lottery winners do not pay off their mortgages if the interest rate on the mortgage is less than the rate of interest they can earn by putting their money into investments no more risky than homeownership. They do pay off their mortgages if the rate on the mortgage is higher than the rate they can earn by making investments no more risky than homeownership.

Another example of how implicit costs affect decisions made by households involves a story in *The St. Petersburg Times* about Jamie Lashbrook, an 11-year-old boy from Brooksville, Florida.* Jamie won two tickets to Super Bowl XXV by kicking a field goal before a Tampa Bay Buccaneers game. Jamie quickly discovered that using the two "free" tickets does in fact involve an opportunity cost. Less than one day after winning the tickets, Jamie's father had received more than a dozen requests from people who were willing to pay as much as $1,200 for each ticket. While the boy *obtained* the tickets at little or no cost, *using* these tickets involved an implicit cost—the payment Jamie could have received if he had sold the tickets in the marketplace rather than using them himself. We don't know if Jamie actually went to the Super Bowl or not, but even this 11-year-old decision maker knew better than to ignore the implicit cost of using a resource.

*Bill Adair, "Wanted: The Hottest Ticket in Town," *The St. Petersburg Times,* Jan. 6, 1991.

9.5 SHORT-RUN TOTAL COSTS

total fixed cost (*TFC*) The total amount paid for fixed inputs. Total fixed cost does not vary with output.

total variable cost (*TVC*) The amount paid for variable inputs. Total variable cost increases with increases in output.

As noted above, in the short run the levels of use of some inputs are fixed, and the costs associated with these fixed inputs must be paid regardless of the level of output produced. Other costs vary with the level of output. **Total fixed cost (*TFC*)** is the sum of the short-run fixed costs that must be paid regardless of the level of output produced. **Total variable cost (*TVC*)** is the sum of the amounts spent for each of the variable inputs used. Total variable cost increases as output increases. Short-run **total cost (*TC*),** which also increases as output increases, is the sum of total variable and total fixed cost:

$$TC = TVC + TFC$$

TABLE 9.4
Short-Run Total Cost Schedules

(1) Output (*Q*)	(2) Total fixed cost (*TFC*)	(3) Total variable cost (*TVC*)	(4) Total cost (*TC*) $TC = TFC + TVC$
0	$6,000	$ 0	$ 6,000
100	6,000	4,000	10,000
200	6,000	6,000	12,000
300	6,000	9,000	15,000
400	6,000	14,000	20,000
500	6,000	22,000	28,000
600	6,000	34,000	40,000

total cost (*TC*)
The sum of total fixed cost and total variable cost. Total cost increases with increases in output ($TC = TFC + TVC$).

A Numerical Example

To show the relation between output (*Q*) and total cost in the short run, we present the simplest case. A firm uses two inputs, capital and labor, to produce output. The total fixed cost paid for capital is $6,000 per period. In Table 9.4, column 2, the total fixed cost (*TFC*) for each of seven possible levels of output is $6,000, including zero units of output. Column 3 shows the total variable cost (*TVC*) for each level of output. Total variable cost is zero when output is zero because the firm hires none of the variable input, labor, if it decides not to produce. As the level of production rises, more labor must be hired, and total variable cost rises, as shown in column 3. Total cost (*TC*) is obtained by adding total fixed cost and total variable cost. Column 4 in Table 9.4, which shows the total cost of production for various levels of output, is the sum of columns 2 and 3.

Figure 9.4 shows the total cost curves associated with the total cost schedules in Table 9.4. The total-fixed-cost curve is horizontal at $6,000, indicating that *TFC* is constant for all levels of output. Total variable cost starts at the origin, since the firm incurs no variable costs if production is zero; *TVC* rises thereafter as output increases, because to produce more the firm must use more resources, thereby increasing cost. Since total cost is the sum of *TFC* and *TVC*, the *TC* curve lies above the *TVC* curve by an amount exactly equal to $6,000 (*TFC*) at each output level. Consequently, *TC* and *TVC* are parallel and have identical shapes.

Average and Marginal Costs

A more useful way of depicting the firm's cost structure is through the behavior of short-run average and marginal costs. Table 9.5 presents the average and marginal costs derived from the total cost schedules in Table 9.4. First, consider average fixed cost, given in column 2. **Average fixed cost (*AFC*)** is total fixed cost divided by output:

average fixed cost (*AFC*)
Total fixed cost divided by output ($AFC = TFC/Q$).

$$AFC = TFC/Q$$

Average fixed cost is obtained by dividing the fixed cost (in this case $6,000) by output. Thus *AFC* is high at relatively low levels of output; since the denom-

FIGURE 9.4
Total Cost Curves

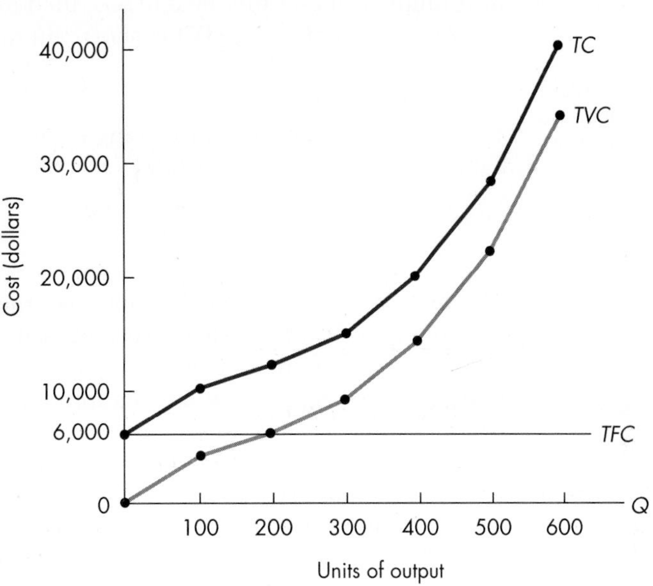

TABLE 9.5
Average and Marginal Cost Schedules

(1) Output (*Q*)	(2) Average fixed cost (*AFC*) *AFC* = *TFC*/*Q*	(3) Average variable cost (*AVC*) *AVC* = *TVC*/*Q*	(4) Average total cost (*ATC*) *ATC* = *TC*/*Q*	(5) Marginal cost (*SMC*) *SMC* = Δ*TC*/Δ*Q*
0	—	—	—	
				$ 40
100	$60	$40	$100	
				20
200	30	30	60	
				30
300	20	30	50	
				50
400	15	35	50	
				80
500	12	44	56	
				120
600	10	56.7	66.7	

inator increases as output increases, *AFC* decreases over the entire range of output. If output were to continue increasing, *AFC* would approach zero as output became extremely large.

average variable cost (*AVC*)
Total variable cost divided by output ($AVC = TVC/Q$).

Average variable cost (*AVC*) is total variable cost divided by output:

$$AVC = TVC/Q$$

The average variable cost of producing each level of output in Table 9.5 is shown in column 3. *AVC* at first falls to \$30, then increases thereafter.

average total cost (*ATC*)
Total cost divided by output or the sum of average fixed cost plus average variable cost ($ATC = TC/Q = AFC + AVC$).

Average total cost (*ATC*) is short-run total cost divided by output:

$$ATC = TC/Q$$

The average total cost of producing each level of output is given in column 4 of Table 9.5. Since total cost is total variable cost plus total fixed cost,

$$ATC = \frac{TC}{Q} = \frac{TVC + TFC}{Q} = AVC + AFC$$

The average total cost in the table has the same general structure as average variable cost. It first declines, reaches a minimum at \$50, then increases thereafter. The minimum *ATC* is attained at a larger output (between 300 and 400) than that at which *AVC* attains its minimum (between 200 and 300). This result is not peculiar to the cost schedules in Table 9.5; as we shall show later, it follows for all average cost schedules of the general type shown here.

short-run marginal cost (*SMC*)
The change in either total variable cost or total cost per unit change in output ($\Delta TVC/\Delta Q = \Delta TC/\Delta Q$).

Finally, **short-run marginal cost (*SMC*)** is defined as the change in either total variable cost or total cost per unit change in output:

$$SMC = \frac{\Delta TVC}{\Delta Q} = \frac{\Delta TC}{\Delta Q}$$

The two definitions are the same because when output increases, total cost increases by the same amount as the increase in total variable cost. Thus, since $TC = TFC + TVC$,

$$SMC = \frac{\Delta TC}{\Delta Q} = \frac{\Delta TFC}{\Delta Q} + \frac{\Delta TVC}{\Delta Q} = 0 + \frac{\Delta TVC}{\Delta Q} = \frac{\Delta TVC}{\Delta Q}$$

The short-run marginal cost is given in column 5 of Table 9.5. It is the per-unit change in cost resulting from a change in output when the use of the variable input changes. For example, when output increases from 0 to 100, both total and variable costs increase by \$4,000. The change in cost per unit of output is, therefore, \$4,000 divided by the increase in output, 100, or \$40. Thus the marginal cost over this range is \$40. It can be seen that *MC* first declines, reaches a minimum of \$20, then rises. Note that minimum marginal cost is attained at an output (between 100 and 200) below that at which either *AVC* or *ATC* attains its minimum. Marginal cost equals *AVC* and *ATC* at their respective minimum levels. We shall return to the reason for this result below.

The average and marginal cost schedules in columns 3, 4, and 5 are shown graphically in Figure 9.5. Average fixed cost is not graphed because it is a curve that simply declines over the entire range of output and because, as you will see, it is irrelevant for decision making. The curves in Figure 9.5 depict the properties of the cost schedules we have discussed. All three curves decline at first and then rise. Marginal cost equals *AVC* and *ATC* at each of their minimum levels. Marginal cost is below *AVC* and *ATC* when they are declining and above them when they are increasing. Since *AFC* decreases over the entire range of output

FIGURE 9.5
Average and Marginal Cost Curves

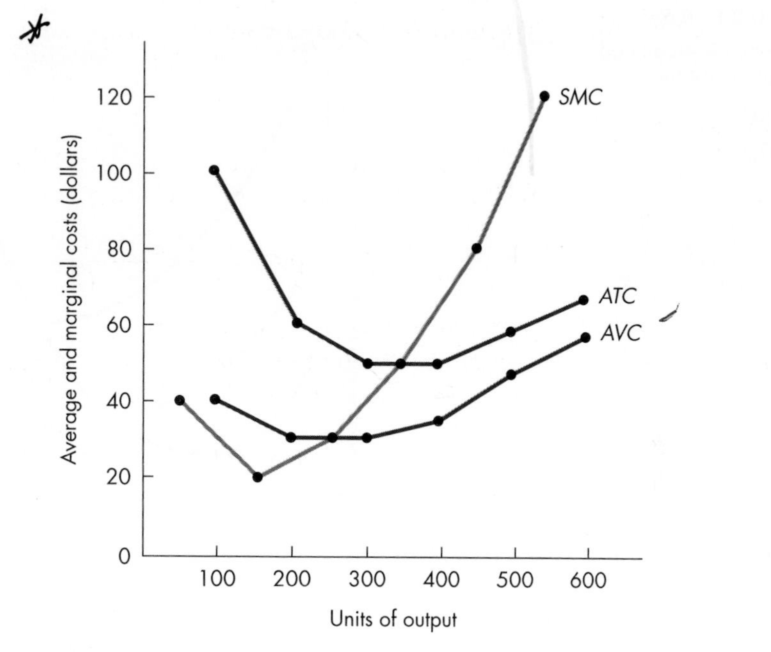

and since $ATC = AVC + AFC$, *ATC* becomes increasingly close to *AVC* as output increases. As we show below, these are the general properties of typically assumed average and marginal cost curves.

General Short-Run Average and Marginal Cost Curves

Most of the properties of cost curves set forth thus far in this section were derived by using the specific cost schedules in Tables 9.4 and 9.5. These properties also hold for general cost curves when output and therefore cost vary continuously rather than discretely. These typical average and marginal cost curves are shown in Figure 9.6. These curves show the following:

Relations (1) *AFC* declines continuously, approaching both axes asymptotically (as shown by the decreasing distance between *ATC* and *AVC*). (2) *AVC* first declines, reaches a minimum at Q_2, and rises thereafter. When *AVC* is at its minimum, *SMC* equals *AVC*. (3) *ATC* first declines, reaches a minimum at Q_3, and rises thereafter. When *ATC* is at its minimum, *SMC* equals *ATC*. (4) *SMC* first declines, reaches a minimum at Q_1, and rises thereafter. *SMC* equals both *AVC* and *ATC* when these curves are at their minimum values. Furthermore, *SMC* lies below both *AVC* and *ATC* over the range for which these curves decline; *SMC* lies above them when they are rising.

In general, the reason marginal cost crosses *AVC* and *ATC* at their respective minimum points follows from the definitions of the cost curves. If marginal cost is below average variable cost, each additional unit of output adds less to cost than the average variable cost of that unit. Thus, average variable cost must

FIGURE 9.6
Short-Run Average and Marginal Cost Curves

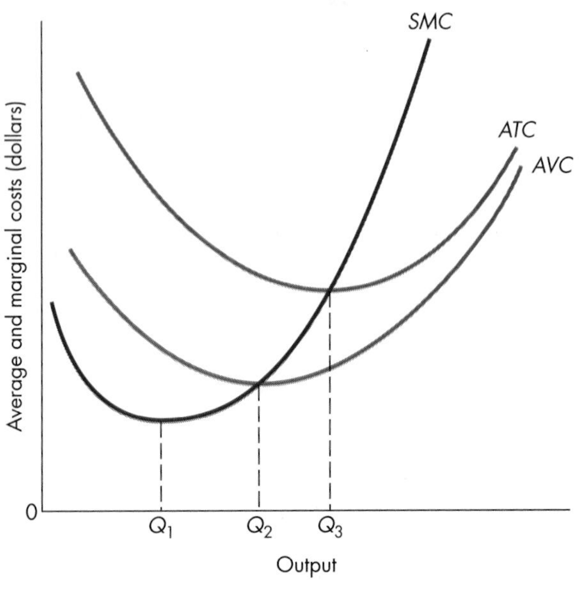

decline over this range. When *SMC* is above *AVC*, each additional unit of output adds more to cost than *AVC*. In this case, *AVC* must rise.

So when *SMC* is less than *AVC*, average variable cost is falling; when *SMC* is greater than *AVC*, average variable cost is rising. Thus *SMC* must equal *AVC* at the minimum point on *AVC*. Exactly the same reasoning can be used to show that *SMC* crosses *ATC* at the minimum point on the latter curve.[4]

9.6 RELATIONS BETWEEN SHORT-RUN COSTS AND PRODUCTION

We will now describe, in some detail, exactly how the short-run cost curves set forth in the preceding section are derived. As you will recall, once the total variable cost (*TVC*) and the total fixed cost (*TFC*) are developed, all the other costs—*TC, ATC, AVC, AFC*, and *MC*—can be derived directly from the simple formulas that define these costs. Total fixed cost is simply the sum of the payments for the fixed inputs. As we will now show, total variable cost is derived directly from the short-run production function. In addition to deriving *TVC* from the total product curve, we also show how average variable cost can be derived from average product and how marginal cost can be derived from marginal product.

Total Costs and the Short-Run Production Function

We begin with the short-run production function shown in columns 1 and 2 in Table 9.6. If 4 units of labor are employed, the firm can produce (a maximum of) 100 units; if 6 units of labor are employed, the firm's maximum output is 200

[4]This relation is derived in the appendix to this chapter.

TABLE 9.6
Short-Run Production and Short-Run Total Costs

Short-run production		Short-run total costs		
(1) Labor (L)	(2) Output (Q)	(3) Total variable cost ($TVC = wL$)	(4) Total fixed cost ($TFC = rK$)	(5) Total cost ($TC = wL + rK$)
0	0	0	$6,000	$ 6,000
4	100	$ 4,000	6,000	10,000
6	200	6,000	6,000	12,000
9	300	9,000	6,000	15,000
14	400	14,000	6,000	20,000
22	500	22,000	6,000	28,000
34	600	34,000	6,000	40,000

units; and so on. (Remember, the production function assumes technical efficiency.) For this example, we assume the wage rate—the price of a unit of labor services (w)—is $1,000. Total variable cost for any given level of output is simply the amount of labor employed multiplied by the wage rate:

$$TVC = w \times L$$

Column 3 shows the total variable costs associated with the various levels of output. Obviously, *TVC* is derived directly from the short-run production function. Note that *TVC* is derived for a particular wage rate. If the wage rate increases, *TVC* must increase at each level of output.

To see how total fixed cost is determined, assume that the short-run production function in columns 1 and 2 is derived for a firm using 3 units of capital in the short run ($\overline{K} = 3$) and that capital costs $2,000 per unit to employ. Thus, the total fixed cost is

$$TFC = r \times K = \$2,000 \times 3 = \$6,000$$

where r is the price of a unit of capital services. Column 4 shows the total fixed cost for each level of output.

Short-run total cost (*TC*) is the sum of the total variable cost and total fixed costs of production:

$$TC = wL + rK$$

Column 5 in Table 9.6 shows the total cost of producing each level of output in the short run when the firm's level of capital is fixed at 3 units. Note that these total cost schedules are the same as the ones in Table 9.4. Using the formulas set forth earlier in this chapter, we could easily derive *AVC* and *MC* from the *TVC* schedule and *ATC* from the *TC* schedule. However, we can give you more of an understanding of the reasons for the typical shape of these curves by showing the relation between *AVC* and *AP* and *MC* and *MP*, which we discuss next.

TABLE 9.7
Average and Marginal Relations between Cost and Production

Short-run production				Short-run costs	
(1) Labor	(2) Q	(3) AP (Q/L)	(4) MP $(\Delta Q/\Delta L)$	(5) AVC (w/AP)	(6) SMC (w/MP)
0	0	—	—	—	—
			25		$ 40
4	100	25		$40	
			50		20
6	200	33.33		30	
			33.33		30
9	300	33.33		30	
			20		50
14	400	28.57		35	
			12.50		80
22	500	22.73		44	
			8.33		120
34	600	17.65		56.67	

Average Variable Cost and Average Product

Table 9.7 reproduces the production function in columns 1 and 2 of Table 9.6. The average product of labor ($AP = Q/L$) is calculated in column 3 of Table 9.7. The relation between AVC and AP can be seen as follows: Consider the 100 units of output that can be produced by four workers. The total variable cost of using four workers is found by multiplying \$1,000—the wage rate—by the four workers employed:

$$TVC = \$1{,}000 \times 4$$

The 100 units of output produced by the four workers can be found by multiplying 25—the average product—by the four workers employed:

$$Q = 25 \times 4$$

Since AVC is TVC divided by Q,

$$AVC = \frac{TVC}{Q} = \frac{\$1{,}000 \times 4}{25 \times 4} = \frac{\$1{,}000}{25} = \frac{w}{AP} = \$40$$

From this numerical illustration, you can see that AVC can be calculated as either TVC/Q or w/AP. It is easy to show that this relation holds in general for any production function with one variable input. In general,

$$AVC = \frac{TVC}{Q} = \frac{w \times L}{AP \times L} = \frac{w}{AP}$$

In Table 9.7, column 5 shows the value of average variable cost calculated by dividing \$1,000 by average product at each level of output. You should verify that the computation of *AVC* in Table 9.7 ($AVC = w/AP$) yields the same values for *AVC* as the values obtained for *AVC* in Table 9.5 ($AVC = TVC/Q$).

Marginal Cost and Marginal Product

The relation between marginal cost and marginal product is also illustrated in Table 9.7. Column 4 shows the marginal product associated with the additional labor employed to increase production in 100-unit intervals. For example, to increase production from 100 to 200 units, two additional workers are required (an increase from 4 to 6 units of labor), so the marginal product is 50 units per additional worker. The change in total variable cost associated with going from 100 to 200 units of output is \$2,000—\$1,000 for each of the two extra workers. So,

$$SMC = \frac{\Delta TVC}{\Delta Q} = \frac{\$1{,}000 \times 2}{50 \times 2} = \frac{w}{MP} = \$20$$

Repeating this calculation for each of the 100-unit increments to output, you can see that the marginal cost at each level of output is the wage rate divided by the marginal product, and this will be true for any production function with one variable input, since

$$SMC = \frac{\Delta TVC}{\Delta Q} = \frac{\Delta(w \times L)}{\Delta Q} = w\frac{\Delta L}{\Delta Q} = \frac{w}{MP}$$

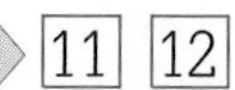

You can verify that the values for marginal cost calculated as w/MP in
11 12 Table 9.7 are identical to the values for marginal cost calculated as $\Delta TC/\Delta Q$ in
Table 9.5.

The Graphical Relation between *AVC*, *MC*, *AP*, and *MP*

Figure 9.7 illustrates the relation between cost curves and product curves. We have constructed a typical set of product and cost curves in Panels A and B, respectively. Assume the wage rate is \$21, and consider first the product and cost curves over the range of labor usage from zero to 500 units of labor. In Panel A, marginal product lies above average product over this range, so average product is rising. Since marginal cost is inversely related to marginal product ($MC = w/MP$) and average variable cost is inversely related to average product ($AVC = w/AP$), and since both *MP* and *AP* are rising, both *MC* and *AVC* are falling as output rises when labor usage increases (up to points *A* and *B* in Panel A). Marginal product reaches a maximum value of 9 at 500 units of labor usage (point *A*). The level of output that corresponds to using 500 units of labor is found by using the relation $AP = Q/L$. Since $AP = 6.5$ and $L = 500$, *Q* must be 3,250 (= 6.5×500). Thus, marginal product reaches its *maximum* value at 3,250 units of output, and, consequently, marginal cost must reach its *minimum* value at 3,250 units of output. At 3,250 units, marginal cost is equal to \$2.33 ($= w/MP = \$21/9$), and average variable cost is equal to \$3.23 ($= w/AP = \$21/6.5$). Points *A* and *B* in Panel A correspond to points *a* and *b* in Panel B of Figure 9.7.

One of the most important relations between production and cost curves in the short run involves the effect of the law of diminishing marginal product

FIGURE 9.7
Short-Run Production and Cost Relations

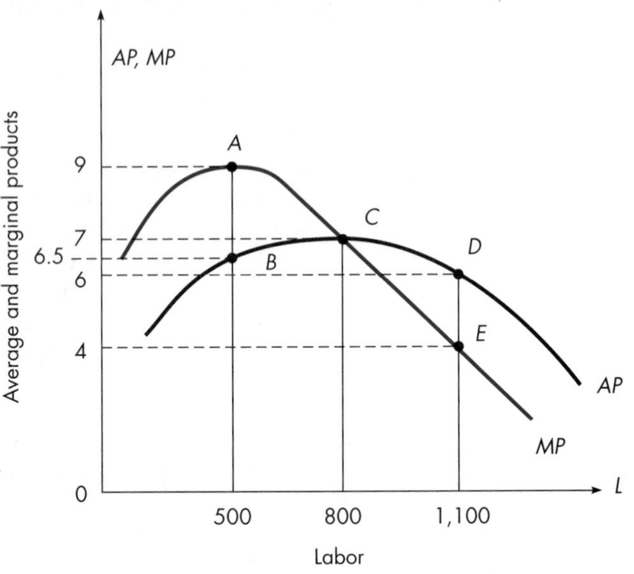

Panel A — Product curves

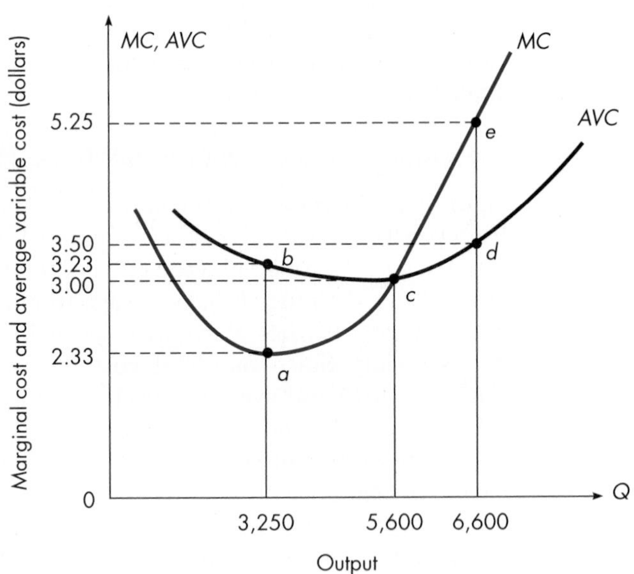

Panel B — Cost curves

on the marginal cost of production. While marginal product generally rises at first, the law of diminishing marginal product states that when capital is fixed, a point will eventually be reached beyond which marginal product must begin to fall. As marginal product begins to fall, marginal cost begins to rise. In Figure 9.7, marginal product begins to fall beyond 500 units of labor (beyond point A in Panel A). Marginal cost begins to rise beyond 3,250 units of output (beyond point a in Panel B).

Consider the range of labor usage between 500 and 800 units of labor. Marginal product is falling, but while marginal product still lies above average product, average product continues to rise up to point C, where $MP = AP$. At point C, average product reaches its maximum value at 800 units of labor. When 800 units of labor are employed, 5,600 units of output are produced ($5{,}600 = AP \times L = 7 \times 800$). Thus, at 5,600 units of output, marginal cost and average variable cost are both equal to \$3:

$$MC = w/MP = \$21/7 = \$3$$
$$AVC = w/AP = \$21/7 = \$3$$

So, at 5,600 units of output, average variable cost reaches its minimum and is equal to marginal cost.

Finally, consider the cost and product relations as labor usage increases beyond 800 units. Marginal product is below average product, and average product continues to decrease but never becomes negative. Marginal product will eventually become negative, but a manager who wishes to minimize costs would never hire an amount of labor that would have a negative marginal product. If marginal product is negative, the manager could *increase* output by *decreasing* labor usage, and this would also decrease the firm's expenditure on labor. Points D and E in Panel A correspond to points d and e in Panel B. At 1,100 units of labor, average product is 6, and output is 6,600 units ($= AP \times L = 6 \times 1{,}100$). You should verify for yourself that marginal cost is \$5.25 and average variable cost is \$3.50 when 6,600 units are produced.

We can now summarize the discussion of the relation between production and cost by restating the two fundamental relations between product and cost variables:

$$SMC = w/MP \qquad \text{and} \qquad AVC = w/AP$$

Thus the following relations must hold:

Relations When marginal product (average product) is increasing, marginal cost (average variable cost) is decreasing. When marginal product (average product) is decreasing, marginal cost (average variable cost) is increasing. When marginal product equals average product at maximum *AP*, marginal cost equals average variable cost at minimum *AVC*.

As we explained in Section 9.2, when the fixed inputs are allowed to change, all the product curves, *TP, AP,* and *MP,* shift. This, of course, will shift the short-run cost curves.

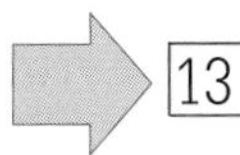

9.7 SUMMARY OF SHORT-RUN COST

In the short run when some inputs are fixed, short-run total cost (*TC*) is the sum of total variable cost (*TVC*) and total fixed cost (*TFC*):

$$TC = TVC + TFC$$

Average fixed cost is total fixed cost divided by output:

$$AFC = TFC/Q$$

Average variable cost is total variable cost divided by output:

$$AVC = TVC/Q$$

Average total cost is total cost divided by output:

$$ATC = TC/Q = AVC + AFC$$

Short-run marginal cost (*SMC*) is the change in either total variable cost or total cost per unit change in output:

$$SMC = \Delta TVC/\Delta Q = \Delta TC/\Delta Q$$

A typical set of short-run cost curves is characterized by the following features: (1) *AFC* decreases continuously as output increases, (2) *AVC* is U-shaped, (3) *ATC* is U-shaped, (4) *SMC* is U-shaped and crosses both *AVC* and *ATC* at their minimum points, and (5) *SMC* lies below (above) both *AVC* and *ATC* over the output range for which these curves fall (rise).

The link between product curves and cost curves in the short run when one input is variable is reflected in the following relations:

$$SMC = w/MP \qquad \text{and} \qquad AVC = w/AP$$

When *MP* (*AP*) is increasing, *SMC* (*AVC*) is decreasing. When *MP* (*AP*) is decreasing, *SMC* (*AVC*) is increasing. When *MP* equals *AP* at *AP*'s maximum value, *SMC* equals *AVC* at *AVC*'s minimum value. Similar but not identical relations hold when more than one input is variable.

TECHNICAL PROBLEMS

1. "When a manager is using a technically efficient input combination, the firm is also producing in an economically efficient manner." Evaluate this statement.
2. Firms *A* and *B* both produce good *X*, and each firm plans to produce 1,000 units per day of good *X*. The firms can choose either of the two following production processes (i.e., input combinations) to produce 1,000 units daily:

	Process 1	Process 2
Labor	10	8
Capital	20	25

a. Is it possible for both process 1 and process 2 to be technically efficient? Explain why or why not.
b. Firm *A* must pay \$200 per day for a unit of labor and \$100 per day for a unit of capital. For Firm *A*, process ______ is economically efficient.
c. Firm *B* must pay \$250 per day for a unit of labor and \$75 per day for a unit of capital. For Firm *B*, process ______ is economically efficient.

3. Economists frequently say that the firm plans in the long run and operates in the short run. Explain.
4. For each of the following situations, determine whether the manager is concerned with a short-run or a long-run production decision. Explain briefly in each case.
   a. A petroleum drilling supervisor on an offshore drilling platform decides to add an extra 6-hour shift each day in order to keep the drill rig running 24 hours per day.
   b. The vice president of offshore petroleum drilling operations in the Gulf of Mexico chooses to deploy three more offshore drilling platforms in the Gulf.
   c. A manufacturing engineer plans the production schedule for the month.
   d. After studying a demographic report on future increases in birthrates, a hospital administrator decides to add a new pediatric wing to the hospital.
5. Fill in the blanks in the following table:

		Q/L	ΔQ/ΔL
Units of labor	Total product	Average product	Marginal product
1	40	40	______
2	88	44	48
3	138	46	50
4	176	44	38
5	200	40	24
6	210	35	10
7	203	29	-7
8	176	22	−27

6. Refer to Table 9.2 and explain precisely why using 10 units of labor and 2 units of capital is not economically efficient.
7. The following table shows the amount of total output produced from various combinations of labor and capital:

Units of labor	Units of capital 1	2	3	4
1	50	120	160	180
2	110	260	360	390
3	150	360	510	560
4	170	430	630	690
5	160	480	710	790

a. Calculate the marginal product and average product of labor when capital is held constant at 2 units. When the average product of labor is increasing, what is the relation between the average product and the marginal product? What about when the average product of labor is decreasing?

b. Calculate the marginal product of labor for each level of the capital stock. How does the marginal product of the second unit of labor change as the capital stock increases? Why?

8. In a week, the manager-owner of a manufacturing firm spends $1,000 on raw materials, $500 on utilities, $750 leasing tools, and $400 on rent. The manager-owner earned $1,000 per week before quitting her job to start this manufacturing enterprise.

   a. The firm has explicit costs of $________ and implicit costs of $________.

   b. The normal profit for this firm is $________ per week.

9. Fill in the blanks in the following table:

Output	Total cost	Total fixed cost	Total variable cost	Average fixed cost	Average variable cost	Average total cost	Marginal cost
100	260	200	60				
200		200	90				.30
300		200	150		.50		
400		200	220			1.05	
500		200	360				
600		200	660				3.00
700		200	1120		1.60		
800	2,040	200	1840				

10. Assume average variable cost is constant over a range of output. What is marginal cost over this range? What is happening to average total cost over this range?

11. Suppose that a firm is currently employing 20 workers, the only variable input, at a wage rate of $60. The average product of labor is 30, the last worker added 12 units to total output, and total fixed cost is $3,600.

   a. What is marginal cost?

   b. What is average variable cost?

   c. How much output is being produced?

   d. What is average total cost?

   e. Is average variable cost increasing, constant, or decreasing? What about average total cost?

12. The first two columns in the following table give a firm's short-run production function when the only variable input is labor, and capital (the fixed input) is held constant at 5 units. The price of capital is $2,000 per unit, and the price of labor is $500 per unit.

Units of labor	Units of output	Average product	Marginal product	Cost: Fixed	Cost: Variable	Cost: Total	Average cost: Fixed	Average cost: Variable	Average cost: Total	Marginal cost
0	0	xx	xx	____	____	____	xx	xx	xx	xx
20	4,000	____	____	____	____	____	____	____	____	____
40	10,000	____	____	____	____	____	____	____	____	____
60	15,000	____	____	____	____	____	____	____	____	____
80	19,400	____	____	____	____	____	____	____	____	____
100	23,000	____	____	____	____	____	____	____	____	____

a. Complete the table.
b. What is the relation between average variable cost and marginal cost? Between average total cost and marginal cost?
c. What is the relation between average product and average variable cost? Between marginal product and marginal cost?

13. Assume that labor—the only variable input of a firm—has the average and marginal product curves shown in the graph below. Labor's wage is $2 per unit.

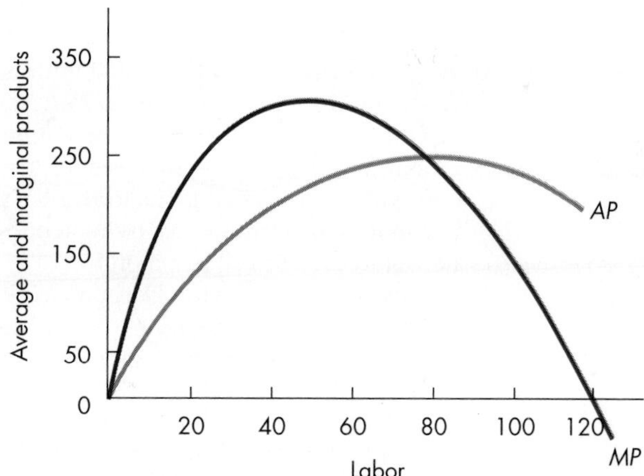

a. When the firm attains minimum average variable cost, how many units of labor is it using?
b. What level of output is associated with minimum average variable cost?
c. What is the average variable cost of producing this output?
d. Suppose the firm is using 100 units of labor. What is output? What is marginal cost? What is average variable cost?

APPLIED PROBLEMS

1. At a management luncheon, two managers were overheard arguing about the following statement: "A manager should never hire another worker if the new person causes diminishing returns." Is this statement correct? If so, why? If not, explain why not.
2. Explain why it would cost Pete Sampras or Steffi Graf more to leave the professional tennis tour and open a tennis shop than it would for the coach of a university tennis team to do so.
3. You are the adviser to the president of a university. A wealthy alumnus buys and then gives to the university a plot of land for use as an athletic field. The president says that as far as the land is concerned, it does not cost the university anything to use the land as an athletic field. What do you say?
4. Suppose that you manage a business and have to make business trips of two to four days at least once a month. What factors determine the total cost of a trip? What factors would you consider when deciding whether your salespeople should travel by automobile or airplane? Are these necessarily the same factors that determine the cost of your own travel?
5. Until recently you worked as an accountant, earning $30,000 annually. Then you inherited a piece of commercial real estate bringing in $12,000 in rent annually. You decided to leave your job and operate a video rental store in the office space you inherited. At the end of the first year, your books showed total costs of $30,000 for video purchases, utilities, taxes, and supplies. What is your economic cost for the year? What is your normal profit?
6. When Burton Denson graduated with honors from the American Trucking Academy, his father gave him a $350,000 tractor-trailer rig. Recently, Burton was boasting to some fellow truckers that his revenues were typically $25,000 per month, while his operating costs (fuel, maintenance, and depreciation) amounted to only $18,000 per month. Tractor-trailer rigs identical to Burton's rig rent for $15,000 per month. If Burton was driving trucks for one of the competing trucking firms, he would earn $5,000 per month.
   a. How much are Burton Denson's explicit costs per month? How much are his implicit costs per month?
   b. What is the dollar amount of the opportunity cost of the resources used by Burton Denson each month?
   c. Burton is proud of the fact that he is generating a net cash flow of $7,000 (= $25,000 − $18,000) per month, since he would be earning only $5,000 per month if he were working for a trucking firm. What advice would you give Burton Denson?
7. The famous financial analyst Jane Bryant Quinn, in her *Newsweek* column (February 8, 1993), gave the following advice:

   > But you can't "buy and forget" the new stocks any more than you could the old . . . you have to make continuous judgments on when to hold and when to sell. You also need a fix on companies other than the ones you own. Stocks need to be judged not just for themselves but in relation to what you could earn by switching money somewhere else.

   According to Quinn, what is the implicit opportunity cost of holding a stock share? State her advice in terms of opportunity cost. If her advice is sound, and it is, why don't the most astute investors evaluate, buy, and sell stocks continuously? Answer in terms of opportunity cost and information costs.

8. Engineers at a national research laboratory built a prototype automobile that could be driven 180 miles on a single gallon of unleaded gasoline. They estimated that in mass production the car would cost $40,000 per unit to build. The engineers argued that Congress should force U.S. automakers to build this energy-efficient car.
   a. Is energy efficiency the same thing as economic efficiency? Explain.
   b. Under what circumstances would the energy-efficient automobile described above be economically efficient?
   c. If the goal of society is to get the most benefit from its limited resources, then why not ignore economic efficiency and build the energy-saving automobile?
9. After two quarters of increasing levels of production, the CEO of Canadian Fabrication & Design was upset to learn that, during this time of expansion, productivity of the newly hired sheet metal workers declined with each new worker hired. Believing that the new workers were either lazy or ineffectively supervised (or possibly both), the CEO instructed the shop foreman to "crack down" on the new workers to bring their productivity levels up.
   a. Explain carefully in terms of production theory why it might be that no amount of "cracking down" can increase worker productivity at CF&D.
   b. Provide an alternative to cracking down as a means of increasing the productivity of the sheet metal workers.
10. An article in *Business Week* (November 10, 1997) warned of the dangers of deflation as the collapse of numerous Asian economies was creating worries that Asia might try to "export its way out of trouble" by oversupplying everything from automobiles to semiconductors. Evidence that deflation had become a genuine concern for managers was provided by a statement in the article by John Smith, chairman and CEO of General Motors Corporation: "Fundamentally, something has changed in the economy. In today's age, you cannot get price increases." The article offers the following advice to managers: "Productivity growth lets companies boost profits even as prices fall." Using production theory, comment on this advice.
11. *Business Week*, in an article dealing with management (October 22, 1984, p. 156), wrote, "When he took over the furniture factory three years ago . . . [the manager] realized almost immediately that it was throwing away at least $100,000 a year worth of wood scrap. Within a few weeks, he set up a task force of managers and workers to deal with the problem. And within a few months, they reduced the amount of scrap to $7,000 worth." Was this necessarily an *economically efficient* move?

MATHEMATICAL APPENDIX Short-Run Production and Cost Relations

This appendix uses calculus to derive several useful relations in short-run production and cost analysis. We consider only the two-input case; however, all results hold for any number of inputs in production. Define the production function as

$$Q = f(L, K) \tag{1}$$

where Q is the maximum possible output attainable when L units of labor and K units of capital are employed to produce a good or service. Thus, the production function is characterized by technical efficiency. Assume that production requires positive amounts of both inputs:

$$Q = f(0, K) = f(L, 0) = 0 \tag{2}$$

If the usage of either input is zero, output is zero. In the short run, at least one input is fixed. Assume capital is the fixed input. By holding capital constant at $\bar{K}$ units, the short-run production function can be expressed as

$$Q = f(L, \bar{K}) = g(L) \tag{3}$$

Thus, $g(L)$ is the short-run production function when capital is fixed at $\overline{K}$ units.

Average Product and Marginal Product

The relation between average and marginal product plays an important role in understanding the nature of production and the shape of short-run cost curves. Average product is defined as

$$AP = AP(L) = Q/L \tag{4}$$

and marginal product is defined as the rate of change in output as the variable input labor changes:

$$MP = MP(L) = \frac{dQ}{dL} = \frac{dg(L)}{dL} = g'(L) \tag{5}$$

Recall from this chapter that *when* AP *is increasing (decreasing),* MP *is greater (less) than* AP. *When* AP *reaches its maximum value,* MP = AP. This relation can be demonstrated by differentiating AP with respect to L to find the condition under which AP increases or decreases:

$$\begin{aligned} \frac{d(AP)}{dL} &= \frac{d(Q/L)}{dL} = \frac{(dQ/dL)L - Q}{L^2} \\ &= \frac{1}{L}(MP - AP) \end{aligned} \tag{6}$$

Thus, the sign of $d(AP)/dL$ is positive (negative) when MP is greater (less) than AP. So AP rises (falls) when MP is greater (less) than AP. The peak of AP occurs where the slope of AP is zero; that is, $d(AP)/dL$ is zero. Thus, the maximum point on AP is reached where $MP = AP$.

The Cost Relations: *ATC, AVC,* and *SMC*

Begin by defining short-run total cost, TC, to be a function of the level of production, Q:

$$TC = TC(Q) = TVC(Q) + TFC$$

where $TVC(Q)$ is total variable cost and TFC is total fixed cost. Since $dTFC/dQ = 0$, short-run marginal cost is the rate of change in either TC or TVC as output changes:

$$SMC = \frac{dTC}{dQ} = \frac{dTVC}{dQ} \tag{7}$$

Recall that TC and TVC are parallel, so their slopes are identical at any level of production. Average total cost, ATC, can be expressed as

$$\begin{aligned} ATC = ATC(Q) &= \frac{TC(Q)}{Q} = \frac{TVC(Q)}{Q} + \frac{TFC}{Q} \\ &= AVC(Q) + AFC(Q) \end{aligned} \tag{8}$$

Note that *average* fixed cost is a function of Q, while *total* fixed cost is not a function of Q.

Recall from this chapter that *when* ATC *is increasing (decreasing),* MC *is greater (less) than* ATC. *When* ATC *reaches its minimum value,* SMC = ATC. This relation can be demonstrated by differentiating ATC with respect to Q to find the condition under which ATC increases or decreases:

$$\begin{aligned} \frac{d(ATC)}{dQ} &= \frac{d[TVC(Q)/Q + TFC/Q]}{dQ} \\ &= \frac{\frac{dTVC(Q)}{dQ}Q - TVC \cdot 1 + 0 \cdot Q - TFC \cdot 1}{Q^2} \end{aligned}$$

Factoring the term $1/Q$ simplifies the expression:

$$\begin{aligned} \frac{d(ATC)}{dQ} &= \frac{1}{Q}\left(\frac{dTVC}{dQ} - \frac{TVC}{Q} - \frac{TFC}{Q}\right) \\ &= \frac{1}{Q}(SMC - AVC - AFC) \\ &= \frac{1}{Q}(SMC - ATC) \end{aligned} \tag{9}$$

Thus, the sign of $d(ATC)/dQ$ is positive (negative) when SMC is greater (less) than ATC. The minimum point on ATC occurs where its slope is zero, which is where $SMC = ATC$.

Relations between Production and Cost

The structure of a firm's cost curves is determined by the production function. To show that the shapes of the cost curves are determined by the production function, we now derive the relations between (1) MP and SMC and (2) AP and AVC.

Relation between *MP* and *SMC*

Recall that $SMC = dTVC/dQ$. Since $TVC = wL$ and w is a constant, SMC can be expressed as

$$SMC = \frac{d(wL)}{dQ} = w\frac{dL}{dQ} = w\frac{1}{MP} = \frac{w}{MP} \tag{10}$$

SMC and MP are inversely related. As labor productivity rises (falls) in the short run, SMC falls (rises). Over the range of input usage characterized by diminishing returns (MP is falling), marginal cost is rising in the short run.

Relation between *AP* and *AVC*

Recall also that $AVC = TVC/Q$. Again substituting wL for TVC:

(11) $$AVC = \frac{wL}{Q} = w\frac{L}{Q} = w\frac{1}{AP} = \frac{w}{AP}$$

From expression (11), it is clear that when average product is rising (falling), average variable cost is falling (rising). Average variable cost reaches its minimum value where average product reaches its maximum value, which, as we demonstrated above, is where $MP = AP$.

MATHEMATICAL EXERCISES

1. Consider the production function $Q = 20K^{1/2}L^{1/2}$. The firm operates in the short run with 16 units of capital.
   a. The firm's short-run production function is $Q =$ ________.
   b. The average product of labor function is $AP =$ ________.
   c. The marginal product of labor function is $MP =$ ________.
   d. Show that marginal product diminishes for all levels of labor usage.
2. Total cost (TC) and total variable cost (TVC) are parallel, yet average total cost (ATC) and average variable cost (AVC) are *not* parallel.
   a. Demonstrate mathematically that ATC and AVC are not parallel.
   b. Show mathematically that when both ATC and AVC are falling, ATC falls faster than AVC, and when both are rising, AVC rises faster than ATC.
3. For the short-run production function in question 1, let the wage be $20.
   a. Derive $AVC(Q)$.
   b. When 160 units are produced, ________ units of labor are employed, and the average product is ________. Average variable cost is $________.
   c. Derive $SMC(Q)$.
   d. Using the marginal product (MP) function derived in part *c*, the marginal product is ________ when 160 units are produced. SMC is $________. Verify that $SMC(Q)$ evaluated at $Q = 4$ is identical to calculating SMC by using the ratio w/MP.

CHAPTER 10

Theory of Production and Cost in the Long Run

Long-run production decisions involve changing the level of employment of inputs that are fixed in the short run. A firm may wish to increase its scale of operation by building a larger production facility, which typically requires a substantial lead time for planning the new facility; getting various government permits, licenses, and environmental approvals; building the facility; and testing the new equipment before production begins. Managers involved in the planning of a new plant are engaged in long-run decision making and will be interested in knowing something about the long-run cost of production—the cost of producing in the future when any scale of production facility can be employed. In many cases, the desirability of increasing the size of operations in the long run is driven by a need to achieve economies of scale in production. As you will see in this chapter, it may be possible to reduce unit costs by expanding the production levels in the long run.

Other interesting managerial decisions involve long-run analysis of costs. For example, when economies of scope exist, it may be possible to reduce the cost of producing one good by becoming a producer of other goods related in production. Adding new products generally involves changing the types and amounts of various inputs and, consequently, is a long-run decision. Restructuring by either upsizing or downsizing a firm may be a long-run decision if it requires changing the amount of fixed inputs employed in the short run. Restructuring at a hospital could involve adding a new wing to the building; at an electric utility, a new coal-fired generator may be needed. Restructuring production may also involve moving production facilities to new geographic locations, perhaps overseas to reduce labor costs.

During the 1990s, an historically unprecedented amount of merger and acquisition activity has been transforming numerous industries. Some corporate strategists have attempted to achieve economies of scale by merging with other companies producing similar products. In other cases, acquisitions have been designed to take advantage of cost savings associated with multiproduct production—economies of scope. And in some cases, such as the surprising 1995 divestiture by AT&T of its computer and electronic equipment divisions, divestitures and spin-offs have been undertaken to avoid diseconomies of scope or scale. The analysis of cost in the long run is essential in making these decisions.

In all the examples mentioned above, managers are trying to find and exploit opportunities to reduce costs in the long run by changing the employment of inputs that are fixed in the short run. In this chapter, we will analyze the situation in which there are two or more variable inputs, a situation that is both more complex and more interesting than production with only one variable input. The analysis of production set forth here can be considered long run if capital and labor are the only inputs the firm employs—no inputs are fixed. In the short run, however, when two or more inputs are variable, the economically efficient choice of variable inputs is also determined using the same analytical techniques presented in this chapter. It is crucial for you to keep in mind that while we will typically refer to production in this chapter as "long-run" production, the material also applies to the short-run situation when a firm combines more than one variable input with its fixed inputs to produce a good or service.[1]

We first develop some tools to be used later in the analysis; then we derive and set forth the principles of cost minimization at a given level of output. As will become apparent, these principles follow directly from the principles of constrained minimization and constrained maximization set forth in Chapter 4. Once we show how the economically efficient input combination is found for producing various levels of output, it is a straightforward task to derive the long-run total cost schedule or curve. We then analyze several important concepts concerning costs of production in the long run.

10.1 PRODUCTION ISOQUANTS

isoquant
A curve showing all possible combinations of inputs physically capable of producing a given fixed level of output.

An important tool of analysis when two inputs are variable is the *production isoquant* or simply *isoquant.* An **isoquant** is a curve (or locus of points) showing all possible combinations of the inputs physically capable of producing a given (fixed) level of output. Each point on an isoquant is technically efficient; that is, for each combination on the isoquant, the maximum possible output is that associated with the given isoquant. The concept of an isoquant implies that it is possible to substitute some amount of one input for some of the other, say, labor for capital, while keeping output constant. Therefore, if the two inputs are continuously divisible, as we will assume, there are an infinite number of input combinations capable of producing each level of output.

[1]The appendix to this chapter demonstrates mathematically that the efficient combination of inputs, when two or more inputs are variable, is chosen in the same way in both the short run and the long run.

To understand the concept of an isoquant, return for a moment to Table 9.1 in the preceding chapter. This table shows the maximum output that can be produced by combining different levels of labor and capital. Now note that several levels of output in this table can be produced in two ways. For example, 108 units of output can be produced using either 6 units of capital and 1 worker or 1 unit of capital and 4 workers. Thus these two combinations of labor and capital are two points on the isoquant associated with 108 units of output. And if we assumed that labor and capital were continuously divisible, there would be many more combinations on this isoquant.

Other input combinations in Table 9.1 that can produce the same level of output are:

$Q = 258$: using $K = 2, L = 5$ or $K = 8, L = 2$
$Q = 400$: using $K = 9, L = 3$ or $K = 4, L = 4$
$Q = 453$: using $K = 5, L = 4$ or $K = 3, L = 7$
$Q = 708$: using $K = 6, L = 7$ or $K = 5, L = 9$
$Q = 753$: using $K = 10, L = 6$ or $K = 6, L = 8$

Each pair of combinations of K and L is two of the many combinations associated with each specific level of output. Each demonstrates that it is possible to increase capital and decrease labor (or increase labor and decrease capital) while keeping the level of output constant. For example, if the firm is producing 400 units of output with 9 units of capital and 3 units of labor, it can increase labor by 1, decrease capital by 5, and keep output at 400. Or if it is producing 453 units of output with $K = 3$ and $L = 7$, it can increase K by 2, decrease L by 3, and keep output at 453. Thus, an isoquant shows how one input can be substituted for another while keeping the level of output constant.

Characteristics of Isoquants

We now set forth the typically assumed characteristics of isoquants when labor, capital, and output are continuously divisible. Figure 10.1 illustrates three such isoquants. Isoquant Q_1 shows all the combinations of capital and labor that will yield 100 units of output. As shown, the firm can produce 100 units of output by using 10 units of capital and 75 of labor, or 50 units of capital and 15 of labor, or any other combination of capital and labor on isoquant Q_1. Similarly, isoquant Q_2 shows the various combinations of capital and labor that can be used to produce 200 units of output. And isoquant Q_3 shows all combinations that can produce 300 units of output. Each capital-labor combination can be on only one isoquant. That is, isoquants cannot intersect.

Isoquants Q_1, Q_2, and Q_3 are only three of an infinite number of isoquants that could be drawn. A group of isoquants is called an *isoquant map.* In an isoquant map, all isoquants lying above and to the right of a given isoquant indicate higher levels of output. Thus in Figure 10.1 isoquant Q_2 indicates a higher level of output than isoquant Q_1, and Q_3 indicates a higher level than Q_2.

We should also note that combinations other than those on a given isoquant can be used to produce the given level of output, but such combinations would

FIGURE 10.1
Typical Isoquants

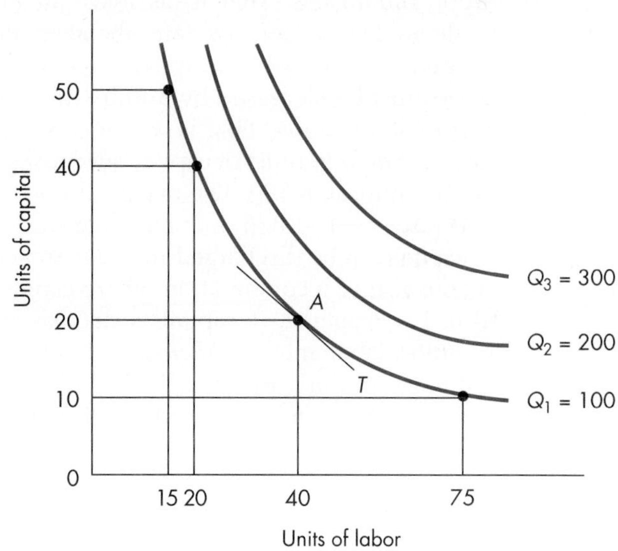

not reflect the "maximum-amount-of-output" concept we introduced in the definition of a production function. Clearly, 100 units of output *could* be produced using *more than* 10 units of capital and *more than* 75 units of labor, but such production would involve wasting some inputs. In contrast, it is impossible to produce 100 units of output using less than 10 units of capital with 75 units of labor, or vice versa. For any combination along an isoquant, if the usage level of either input is reduced and the other is held constant, output must decline.

Marginal Rate of Technical Substitution

As depicted in Figure 10.1, isoquants slope downward over the relevant range of production. This negative slope indicates that if the firm decreases the amount of capital employed, more labor must be added in order to keep the rate of output constant. Or if labor use is decreased, capital usage must be increased to keep output constant. Thus, the two inputs can be substituted for one another to maintain a constant level of output.

Great theoretical and practical importance is attached to the rate at which one input must be substituted for another in order to keep output constant. This rate at which one input is substituted for another along an isoquant is called the **marginal rate of technical substitution (*MRTS*)**, and is defined as

marginal rate of technical substitution (*MRTS*)
The rate at which one input is substituted for another along an isoquant $\left(-\frac{\Delta K}{\Delta L}\right)$.

$$MRTS = -\frac{\Delta K}{\Delta L}$$

The minus sign is added in order to make *MRTS* a positive number, since $\Delta K/\Delta L$, the slope of the isoquant, is negative.

Over the relevant range of production the marginal rate of technical substitution diminishes. That is, as more and more labor is substituted for capital while holding output constant, the absolute value of $\Delta K/\Delta L$ decreases. This can be seen in Figure 10.1. If capital is reduced from 50 to 40 (a decrease of 10 units), labor must be increased by 5 units (from 15 to 20) in order to keep the level of output at 100 units. That is, when capital is plentiful relative to labor, the firm can discharge 10 units of capital but must substitute only 5 units of labor in order to keep output at 100. The marginal rate of technical substitution in this case is $-\Delta K/\Delta L = -(-10)/5 = 2$, meaning that for every unit of labor added, 2 units of capital can be discharged in order to keep the level of output constant. However, consider a combination where capital is more scarce and labor more plentiful. For example, if capital is decreased from 20 to 10 (again a decrease of 10 units), labor must be increased by 35 units (from 40 to 75) to keep output at 100 units. In this case the *MRTS* is 10/35, indicating that for each unit of labor added, capital can be reduced by slightly more than one-quarter of a unit.

Thus, as capital decreases and labor increases along an isoquant, the amount of capital that can be discharged for each unit of labor added declines. Or, put another way, the amount of labor that must be added for each unit of capital eliminated, holding output constant, must increase. This relation is seen in Figure 10.1. As the change in labor and the change in capital become extremely small around a point on an isoquant, the absolute value of the slope of a tangent to the isoquant at that point is the *MRTS* ($-\Delta K/\Delta L$) in the neighborhood of that point. For example, in Figure 10.1, the absolute value of the slope of tangent T to isoquant Q_1 at point A shows the marginal rate of technical substitution at that point. Thus, the slope of the isoquant reflects the rate at which labor can be substituted for capital. It is easy to see that the isoquant becomes less and less steep with movements downward along the isoquant. Thus *MRTS* declines along an isoquant as labor increases and capital decreases.

Relation of *MRTS* to Marginal Products

For very small movements along an isoquant, the marginal rate of technical substitution equals the ratio of the marginal products of the two inputs. We will demonstrate why this comes about.

The level of output, Q, depends upon the use of the two inputs, L and K. Since Q is constant along an isoquant, ΔQ must equal zero for any change in L and K that would remain on a given isoquant. Suppose that, at a point on the isoquant, the marginal product of capital (MP_K) is 3 and the marginal product of labor (MP_L) is 6. If we add 1 unit of labor, output would increase by 6 units. To keep Q at the original level, capital must decrease just enough to offset the 6-unit increase in output generated by the increase in labor. Because the marginal product of capital is 3, 2 units of capital must be discharged in order to reduce output by 6 units. In this case the $MRTS = -\Delta K/\Delta L = -(-2)/1 = 2$, which is exactly equal to $MP_L/MP_K = 6/3 = 2$.

Or if we were to increase capital by 1 unit, output would rise by 3. Labor must decrease by one-half a unit to offset the increase of 3 units of output and keep output constant, since $MP_L = 6$. In this case, the $MRTS = -\Delta K/\Delta L = -(1)/(-1/2) = 2$, which is again equal to MP_L/MP_K.

In more general terms, we can say that when L and K are allowed to vary slightly, the change in Q resulting from the change in the two inputs is the marginal product of L times the amount of change in L plus the marginal product of K times its change. Put in equation form,

$$\Delta Q = (MP_L)(\Delta L) + (MP_K)(\Delta K)$$

In order to remain on a given isoquant, it is necessary to set ΔQ equal to zero. Then, solving for the marginal rate of technical substitution, yields[2]

$$MRTS = -\frac{\Delta K}{\Delta L} = \frac{MP_L}{MP_K}$$

Using this relation, the reason for diminishing $MRTS$ is easily explained. As additional units of labor are substituted for capital, the marginal product of labor diminishes. Two forces are working to diminish labor's marginal product: (1) less capital causes a downward shift of the marginal product of labor curve, and (2) more units of the variable input (labor) cause a downward movement along the marginal product curve. Thus, as labor is substituted for capital, the marginal product of labor must decline. For analogous reasons the marginal product of capital increases as less capital and more labor are used. The same two forces are present in this case: a movement along a marginal product curve and a shift in the location of the curve. In this situation, however, both forces work to increase the marginal product of capital. Thus, as labor is substituted for capital, the marginal product of capital increases. Combining these two conditions, as labor is substituted for capital, MP_L decreases and MP_K increases, so MP_L/MP_K will decrease.[3]

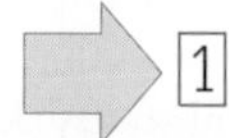

10.2 ISOCOST CURVES

isocost curves
Lines that show the various combinations of inputs that may be purchased for a given level of expenditure at given input prices.

Producers must consider relative input prices in order to find the least-cost combination of inputs to produce a given level of output. An extremely useful tool for analyzing the cost of purchasing inputs is an *isocost curve*. An **isocost curve** shows all combinations of inputs that may be purchased for a given level of total expenditure at given input prices. As you will see in the next section, isocost curves play a key role in finding the combination of inputs that produce a given output level at the lowest possible total cost.

Before we develop the concept of isocost curves, we need to discuss briefly how input prices are determined. For most managers, the price of each input is

---

[2]This relation is demonstrated mathematically in the appendix to this chapter.

[3]Note that we have violated our assumption about marginal product somewhat. The marginal product of an input is defined as the change in output per unit change in the input, the use of other inputs held constant. In this case we allow the usage of both inputs to change; thus the marginal product is really an approximation. But we are speaking only of slight or very small changes in use. Thus, violation of the assumption is small and the approximation approaches the true variation for small changes.

determined in the market for that input by the intersection of the demand for the input and the supply of the input. In such cases, the manager simply takes the market-determined price of the input as given when deciding how much of the input to purchase for production. In some cases, however, managers may be large enough buyers of resources that they can bargain with sellers of the resource to get a better price. They may, for example, get a lower price on an input if they buy a greater quantity of that input. In this case, the price of the input is not constant but, rather, declines as more of the input is purchased. While some managers may have the ability to negotiate lower prices for their inputs, we concentrate upon producers who are relatively small purchasers, so we treat input prices as constant.

Characteristics of Isocost Curves

Suppose a manager must pay \$25 for each unit of labor services and \$50 for each unit of capital services employed. The manager wishes to know what combinations of labor and capital can be purchased for \$400 total expenditure on inputs. Figure 10.2 shows the isocost curve for \$400 when the price of labor is \$25 and the price of capital is \$50. Each combination of inputs on this isocost curve costs \$400 to purchase. Point *A* on the isocost curve shows how much capital could be purchased if no labor is employed. Since the price of capital is \$50, the manager can spend all \$400 on capital alone and purchase 8 units of capital and zero units of labor. Similarly, point *D* on the isocost curve gives the maximum amount of labor—16 units—that can be purchased if labor costs \$25 per unit and \$400 is spent on labor alone. Points *B* and *C* also represent input combinations that cost \$400. At point *B*, for example, \$300 (= \$50 × 6) is spent on capital and \$100 (= \$25 × 4) is spent on labor, which represents a total cost of \$400.

If we continue to denote the quantities of capital and labor by K and L, and denote their respective prices by r and w, total cost, C, is $C = wL + rK$. Total cost is simply the sum of the cost of L units of labor at w dollars per unit and of K units of capital at r dollars per unit:

$$C = wL + rK$$

In the example above, the total cost function is $400 = 25L + 50K$. Solving this equation for K, you can see the combinations of K and L that can be chosen: $K = \frac{400}{50} - \frac{25}{50}L = 8 - \frac{1}{2}L$. More generally, if a fixed amount $\overline{C}$ is to be spent, the firm can choose among the combinations given by

$$K = \frac{\overline{C}}{r} - \frac{w}{r}L$$

If $\overline{C}$ is the total amount to be spent on inputs, the most capital that can be purchased (if no labor is purchased) is $\overline{C}/r$ units of capital, and the most labor that can be purchased (if no capital is purchased) is $\overline{C}/w$ units of labor.

FIGURE 10.2
An Isocost Curve (w = \$25 and r = \$50)

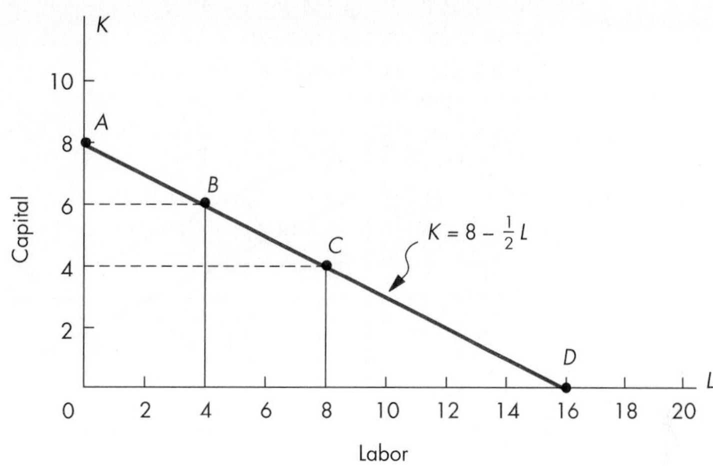

The slope of the isocost curve is equal to the negative of the relative input price ratio, $-w/r$. This ratio is important because it tells the manager how much capital must be given up if 1 more unit of labor is purchased. In the example given above and illustrated in Figure 10.2, $-w/r = -\$25/\$50 = -1/2$. If the manager wishes to purchase 1 more unit of labor at \$25, 1/2 unit of capital, which costs \$50, must be given up in order to keep the total cost of the input combination constant. If the price of labor happens to rise to \$50 per unit, r remaining constant, the slope of the isocost curve is $-\$50/\$50 = -1$, which means the manager must give up 1 unit of capital for each additional unit of labor purchased in order to keep total cost constant.

Shifts in Isocost Curves

If the constant level of total cost associated with a particular isocost curve changes, the isocost curve shifts parallel. Figure 10.3 shows how the isocost curve shifts when the total expenditure on resources ($\overline{C}$) increases from \$400 to \$500. The isocost curve shifts out parallel, and the equation for the new isocost curve is

$$K = 10 - \frac{1}{2}L$$

The slope is still $-1/2$ because $-r/w$ does not change. The K-intercept is now 10, indicating that a maximum of 10 units of capital can be purchased if no labor is purchased and \$500 is spent.

In general, an increase in cost, holding input prices constant, leads to a parallel upward shift in the isocost curve. A decrease in cost, holding input prices constant, leads to a parallel downward shift in the isocost curve. An infinite number of isocost curves exist, one for each level of total cost.

FIGURE 10.3
Shift in an Isocost Curve

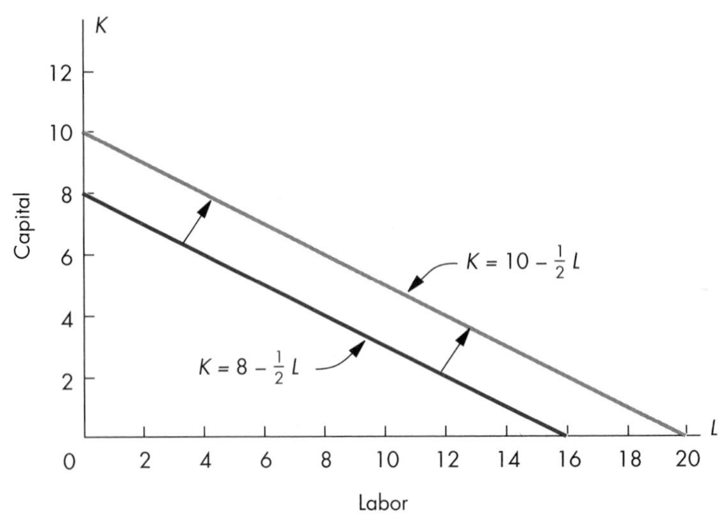

Relation At constant input prices, w and r for labor and capital, a given expenditure on inputs ($\overline{C}$) will purchase any combination of labor and capital given by the following equation, called an isocost curve:

$$K = \frac{\overline{C}}{r} - \frac{w}{r}L$$

10.3 FINDING THE OPTIMAL COMBINATION OF INPUTS

A manager who wishes to maximize profit must first decide how much output to produce and then how to produce that amount at the lowest possible total cost. We have shown that any given level of output can be produced by many combinations of inputs—as illustrated by isoquants. When a manager wishes to produce a given level of output at the lowest possible total cost, the manager chooses the combination on the desired isoquant that costs the least. This is a constrained minimization problem that a manager can solve by following the rule for constrained optimization set forth in Chapter 4. The ability to find the cost-minimizing combination of inputs is a fundamental skill a manager must master if profit is to be maximized.

While managers whose goal is profit maximization are generally and primarily concerned with searching for the least-cost combination of inputs to produce a given (profit-maximizing) output, managers of nonprofit organizations may face an alternative situation. In a nonprofit situation, a manager may have a budget or fixed amount of money available for production and wish to maximize the amount of output that can be produced. As we have shown using isocost curves, there are many different input combinations that can be purchased for a given (or fixed) amount of expenditure on inputs. When a manager wishes to maximize output for a given level of total cost, the manager must choose the input combination on the isocost curve that lies on the highest isoquant. This is a constrained maximization problem; the rule for solving it was set forth in Chapter 4.

Whether the manager is searching for the input combination that minimizes cost for a given level of production or maximizes total production for a given level of expenditure on resources, the optimal combination of inputs to employ is found using the same rule. We first illustrate the fundamental principles of cost minimization with an output constraint; then we will turn to the case of output maximization given a cost constraint.

Production of a Given Output at Minimum Cost[4]

The principle of minimizing the total cost of producing a given level of output is illustrated in Figure 10.4. The manager wants to produce 10,000 units of output at the lowest possible total cost. All combinations of labor and capital capable of producing this level of output are shown by isoquant Q_1. The price of labor (w) is \$40 per unit, and the price of capital (r) is \$60 per unit.

Consider the combination of inputs 60*L* and 100*K*, represented by point *A* on isoquant Q_1. At point *A*, 10,000 units can be produced at a total cost of \$8,400, where the total cost is calculated by adding the total expenditure on labor and the total expenditure on capital:[5]

$$C = wL + rK = (\$40 \times 60) + (\$60 \times 100) = \$8{,}400$$

The manager can lower the total cost of producing 10,000 units by moving down along the isoquant and purchasing input combination *B*, because this combination of labor and capital lies on a lower isocost curve ($K''L''$) than input combination *A*, which lies on $K'L'$. The blowup in Figure 10.4 shows that combination *B* uses 66*L* and 90*K*. Combination *B* costs \$8,040 [= (\$40 × 66) + (\$60 × 90)]. Thus, the manager can decrease the total cost of producing 10,000 units by \$360 (= \$8,400 − \$8,040) by moving from input combination *A* to input combination *B* on isoquant Q_1.

Since the manager's objective is to choose the combination of labor and capital on the 10,000-unit isoquant that can be purchased at the lowest possible cost, the manager will continue to move downward along the isoquant until the lowest possible *isocost* curve is reached. Examining Figure 10.4 reveals that the lowest cost of producing 10,000 units of output is attained at point *E* by using 90 units of labor and 60 units of capital on isocost curve $K'''L'''$, which shows all

[4]Conditions for minimizing total cost subject to an output constraint are derived mathematically in the appendix to this chapter.

[5]Alternatively, you can calculate the cost associated with an isocost curve as the maximum amount of labor that could be hired at \$40 per unit if no capital is used. For $K'L'$, 210 units of labor could be hired (if $K = 0$) for a cost of \$8,400. Or 140 units of capital can be hired at \$60 (if $L = 0$) for a cost of \$8,400.

FIGURE 10.4
Optimal Input Combination to Minimize Cost for a Given Output

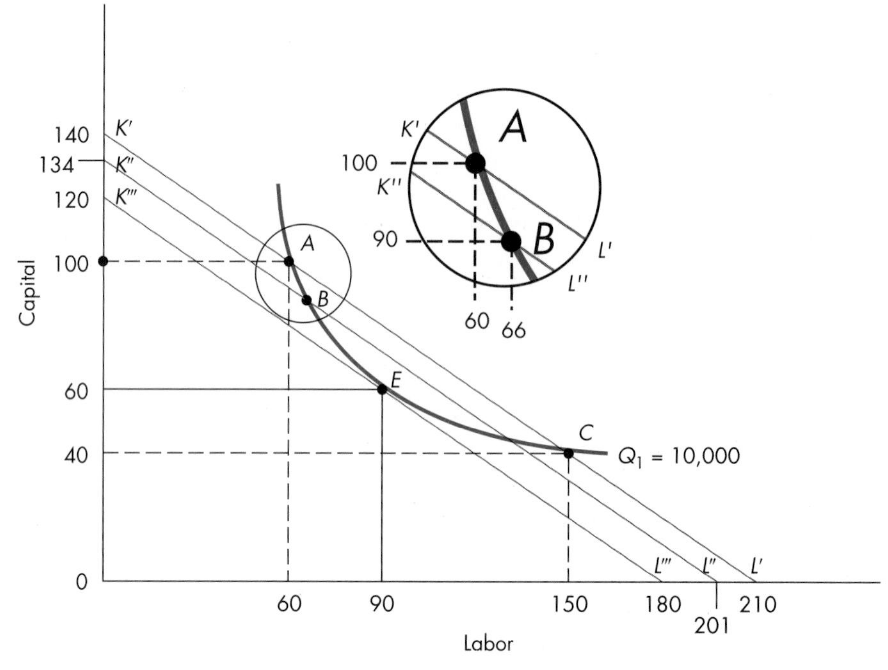

input combinations that can be purchased for $7,200. Note that at this cost-minimizing input combination:

$$C = wL + rK = (\$40 \times 90) + (\$60 \times 60) = \$7{,}200$$

No input combination on an isocost curve below the one going through point E is capable of producing 10,000 units of output. The total cost associated with input combination E is the lowest possible total cost for producing 10,000 units when $w = \$40$ and $r = \$60$.

Suppose the manager chooses to produce using 40 units of capital and 150 units of labor—point C on the isoquant. The manager could now increase capital and reduce labor along isoquant Q_1, keeping output constant and moving to lower and lower isocost curves, and hence lower costs, until point E is reached. Regardless of whether a manager starts with too much capital and too little labor (such as point A) or too little capital and too much labor (such as point C), the manager can move to the optimal input combination by moving along the isoquant to lower and lower isocost curves until input combination E is reached.

At point E, the isoquant is tangent to the isocost curve. Recall that the slope (in absolute value) of the isoquant is the *MRTS*, and the slope of the isocost curve (in absolute value) is equal to the relative input price ratio, w/r. Thus, at point E,

MRTS equals the ratio of input prices. In cost minimizing equilibrium,

$$MRTS = \frac{w}{r}$$

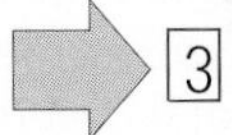

3 To minimize the cost of producing a given level of output, the manager employs the input combination for which $MRTS = w/r$.

The Marginal Product Approach to Cost Minimization

Recall from the discussion in Chapter 4 that finding the optimal levels of two activities *A* and *B* in a constrained optimization problem involved equating the marginal benefit per dollar spent on each of the activities (MB/P). A manager compares the marginal benefit per dollar spent on each activity to determine which activity is the "better deal"; that is, which activity gives the highest marginal benefit per dollar spent. In constrained equilibrium, both activities are equally good deals ($MB_A/P_A = MB_B/P_B$) and the constraint is met.

The tangency condition for cost minimization, $MRTS = w/r$, is equivalent to the condition of equal marginal benefit per dollar spent set forth in Chapter 4. Recall that $MRTS = MP_L/MP_K$; thus the cost-minimizing condition can be expressed in terms of marginal products:

$$MRTS = MP_L/MP_K = w/r$$

After a bit of algebraic manipulation, the equilibrium condition may be expressed as

$$\frac{MP_L}{w} = \frac{MP_K}{r}$$

The marginal benefits of hiring extra units of labor and capital are the marginal products of labor and capital. Dividing each marginal product by its respective input price tells the manager the additional output that will be forthcoming if one more dollar is spent on that input. Thus, at point *E* in Figure 10.4, the marginal product per dollar spent on labor is equal to the marginal product per dollar spent on capital, and the constraint is met ($Q = 10{,}000$ units).

To illustrate how a manager uses information about marginal products and input prices to find the least-cost input combination, we return to point *A* in Figure 10.4, where *MRTS* is greater than w/r. Assume that at point *A*, $MP_L = 160$ and $MP_K = 80$; thus $MRTS = 2$ ($= MP_L/MP_K = 160/80$). Since the slope of the isocost curve is 2/3 ($= w/r = 40/60$), *MRTS* is greater than w/r, and

$$\frac{MP_L}{w} = \frac{160}{40} = 4 > 1.33 = \frac{80}{60} = \frac{MP_K}{r}$$

The firm should substitute labor, which has the higher marginal product per dollar, for capital, which has the lower marginal product per dollar. For example, an additional unit of labor would increase output by approximately 160 units while increasing labor cost by \$40.[6] To keep output constant, 2 units of capital must be released, causing output to fall 160 units (the marginal product of each unit of capital released is approximately 80), but the cost of capital would fall by \$120, which is \$60 for each of the 2 units of capital released. Output remains constant at 10,000 because the higher output from 1 more unit of labor is just offset by the lower output from 2 fewer units of capital. However, because labor cost rises by only \$40 while capital cost falls by \$120, the total cost of producing 10,000 units of output falls by \$80 (= \$120 − \$40).

This example shows that when MP_L/w is greater than MP_K/r, the manager can reduce cost by increasing labor usage while decreasing capital usage just enough to keep output constant. Since $MP_L/w > MP_K/r$ for every input combination along Q_1 from point *A* to point *E*, the firm should continue to substitute labor for capital until it reaches point *E*. As more labor is used, MP_L falls because of diminishing marginal product. As less capital is used, MP_K rises for the same reason. As the manager substitutes labor for capital, *MRTS* falls until equilibrium is reached.

Now consider point *C*, where *MRTS* is less than w/r, and consequently MP_L/w is less than MP_K/r. The marginal product per dollar spent on the last unit of labor is less than the marginal product per dollar spent on the last unit of capital. In this case, the manager can reduce cost by increasing capital usage and decreasing labor usage in such a way as to keep output constant. To see this, assume that at point *C*, $MP_L = 40$ and $MP_K = 240$, and thus $MRTS = 40/240 = 1/6$, which is less than w/r (= 2/3). If the manager uses 1 more unit of capital and 6 fewer units of labor, output stays constant while total cost falls by \$180. (You should verify this yourself.) The manager can continue moving upward along isoquant Q_1, keeping output constant but reducing cost until point *E* is reached. As capital is increased and labor decreased, MP_L rises and MP_K falls until, at point *E*, MP_L/w equals MP_K/r. We have now derived the following:

Principle In order to produce a given level of output at the lowest possible cost when two inputs (*L* and *K*) are variable and the prices of the inputs are, respectively, *w* and *r*, a manager chooses the combination of inputs for which

$$MRTS = \frac{MP_L}{MP_K} = \frac{w}{r}$$

which implies that

$$\frac{MP_L}{w} = \frac{MP_K}{r}$$

In cost-minimizing equilibrium, the isoquant associated with the desired level of output (the slope of which is the *MRTS*) is tangent to the isocost curve (the slope of which is w/r) at the optimal combination of inputs. This equilibrium condition also means that the marginal product per dollar spent on the last unit of each input is the same.

[6] Note that we use "approximately" because we have ignored the possibility of diminishing marginal product.

Production of Maximum Output with a Given Level of Cost

As discussed earlier, in most cases managers choose the firm's level of production then choose the input combination that permits production of that output at least cost. There may be times, however, when managers can spend only a fixed amount on production and wish to attain the highest level of production consistent with that amount of expenditure. This is a constrained maximization problem, and as we showed in Chapter 4, the equilibrium condition for constrained maximization is the same as that for constrained minimization.[7] In other words, the input combination that maximizes the level of output for a given level of total cost of inputs is that combination for which

$$MRTS = w/r \qquad \text{or} \qquad \frac{MP_L}{w} = \frac{MP_K}{r}$$

This is the same condition that must be satisfied by the input combination that minimizes the total cost of producing a given output level.

This situation is illustrated in Figure 10.5 on page 372. The isocost line KL shows all possible combinations of the two inputs that can be purchased for the level of total cost (and input prices) associated with this isocost curve. Suppose the manager chooses point R on the isocost curve and is thus meeting the cost constraint. While 500 units of output are produced using L_R units of labor and K_R units of capital, the manager could produce more output at no additional cost by using less labor and more capital.

This can be accomplished, for example, by moving up the isocost curve to point S. Point S and point R lie on the same isocost curve and consequently cost the same amount. Point S lies on a higher isoquant, Q_2, allowing the manager to produce 1,000 units without spending any more than the given amount on inputs (represented by isocost curve KL). The highest level of output attainable with the given level of cost is 1,700 units (point E), which is produced by using L_E labor and K_E capital. At point E, the highest attainable isoquant, isoquant Q_3, is just tangent to the given isocost, and $MRTS = w/r$ or $MP_L/w = MP_K/r$—the same conditions that must be met to minimize the cost of producing a given output level.

To see why MP_L/w must equal MP_K/r in order to maximize output for a given level of expenditures on inputs, suppose that this optimizing condition does not hold. Specifically, assume that $w = \$2$, $r = \$3$, $MP_L = 6$, and $MP_K = 12$, so that

$$\frac{MP_L}{w} = \frac{6}{2} = 3 < 4 = \frac{12}{3} = \frac{MP_K}{r}$$

The last unit of labor adds 3 units of output per dollar spent; the last unit of capital adds 4 units of output per dollar. If the firm wants to produce the maximum output possible with a given level of cost, it could spend $1 less on labor,

[7] Conditions for output maximization subject to a cost constraint are derived mathematically in the appendix.

ILLUSTRATION 10.1

Downsizing or Dumbsizing
Optimal Input Choice Should Guide Restructuring Decisions

As we stressed in the introduction to this chapter and in the previous chapter, successful managers know how to manage costs. Increased competition, both domestically, as a result of deregulation in many industries, and globally, as trade barriers fall and free markets emerge in many parts of the world, is pressuring managers to reduce costs to remain profitable. One of the most disparaged strategies for cost cutting in the 1990s has been corporate "downsizing" or synonymously, corporate "restructuring." Managers downsize or restructure a firm by permanently laying off a sizable fraction of their workforce. In many cases, managers achieve the targeted level of reduction in workforce using across-the-board layoffs.

If a firm employs more than the efficient amount of labor, reducing the amount of labor employed can lead to lower costs for producing the same amount of output. The value of a firm, measured by the market value of its common stock, often rises when corporate executives announce plans for downsizing or restructuring the firm. Sometimes the enthusiasm of investors over a downsizing plan fades once managers begin to implement the labor cuts. During the 1990s, business publications documented dozens of restructuring plans that failed to realize the promised cost savings. Apparently, a successful restructuring requires more than "meat-ax," across-the-board cutting of labor. *The Wall Street Journal* recently reported that "despite warnings about downsizing becoming dumbsizing, many companies continue to make flawed decisions—hasty, across-the-board cuts—that come back to haunt them."*

The reason that across-the-board cuts in labor do not generally deliver the desired lower costs can be seen by applying the efficiency rule for choosing inputs that we have developed in this chapter. In order either to minimize the total cost of producing a given level of output or to maximize the output for a given level of cost, a manager must base employment decisions on the marginal product per dollar spent on labor, MP/w. Across-the-board downsizing, when no consideration is given to productivity or wages, cannot lead to an efficient reduction in the amount of labor employed by the firm. Workers with the lowest MP/w ratios must be cut first if the manager is to realize the greatest possible cost savings.

Consider this example: A manager is ordered to cut the firm's labor force by as many workers as it takes to lower its labor costs by $10,000 per month. The manager wishes to meet the lower level of labor costs with as little loss of output as possible. The manager examines the employment performance of six workers: workers *A* and *B* are senior employees, and workers *C, D, E,* and *F* are junior employees. The

thereby reducing labor by one-half a unit and hence output by 3 units. It could spend this dollar on capital, thereby increasing output by 4. Cost would be unchanged, and total output would rise by 1 unit. And the firm would continue taking dollars out of labor and adding them to capital as long as the inequality holds. But as labor is reduced, its marginal product will increase, and as capital is increased, its marginal product will decline. Eventually the marginal product per dollar spent on each input will be equal.

We have established the following:

Principle In the case of two variable inputs, labor and capital, the manager of a firm maximizes output for a given level of cost by using the amounts of labor and capital such that the marginal rate of technical substitution ($MRTS$) equals the input price ratio (w/r). In terms of a graph, this condition is equivalent to choosing the input combination where the slope of the given isocost table shows the productivity and wages paid monthly to each of these six workers. The senior workers (*A* and *B*) are paid more per month than the junior workers (*C, D, E,* and *F*), but the senior workers are more productive than the junior workers. Per dollar spent on wages, each senior worker contributes 0.50 units of output per month, while each dollar spent on junior workers contributes 0.40 units per month. Consequently, the senior workers provide the firm with more "bang per buck," even though their wages are higher. The manager, taking an across-the-board approach to cutting workers, could choose to lay off $5,000 worth of labor in each category: lay off worker *A* and workers *C* and *D*. This across-the-board strategy saves the required $10,000, but output falls by 4,500 units per month (= 2,500 + 2 × 1,000). Alternatively, the manager could rank the workers according to the marginal product per dollar spent on each worker. Then, the manager could start by sequentially laying off the workers with the smallest marginal product per dollar spent. This alternative approach would lead the manager to lay off four junior workers. Laying off workers *C, D, E,* and *F* saves the required $10,000 but reduces output by 4,000 units per month (= 4 × 1,000). Sequentially laying off the workers that give the least bang for the buck results in a smaller reduction in output while achieving the required labor savings of $10,000.

Worker	Marginal product (*MP*)	Wage (*w*)	*MP/w*
A	2,500	$5,000	0.50
B	2,500	$5,000	0.50
C	1,000	$2,500	0.40
D	1,000	$2,500	0.40
E	1,000	$2,500	0.40
F	1,000	$2,500	0.40

This illustration shows that restructuring decisions should be made on the basis of the production theory presented in this chapter. Input employment decisions cannot be made efficiently without using information about both the productivity of an input *and* the price of the input. A manager must consider marginal product per dollar spent. Across-the-board approaches to restructuring cannot, in general, lead to efficient reorganizations because these approaches do not consider information about worker productivity per dollar spent when making the layoff decision. Reducing the amount of labor employed is not "dumbsizing" if a firm is employing more than the efficient amount of labor. *Dumbsizing* occurs only when a manager lays off the wrong workers or too many workers.

*Alex Markels and Matt Murray, "Call It Dumbsizing: Why Some Companies Regret Cost-Cutting," *The Wall Street Journal*, May 14, 1996.

curve equals the slope of the highest attainable isoquant. This equilibrium condition implies that the marginal product per dollar spent on the last unit of each input is the same.

10.4 OPTIMIZATION AND COST

Using Figure 10.4 we showed how a manager can choose the optimal (least-cost) combination of inputs to produce a given level of output. We also showed how the total cost of producing that level of output is calculated. When the optimal input combination for each possible output level is determined and total cost is calculated for each one of these input combinations, a total cost curve (or schedule) is generated. In this section, we illustrate how any number of optimizing points can be combined into a single graph and how these points are related to the firm's cost structure.

FIGURE 10.5
Output Maximization for a Given Level of Cost

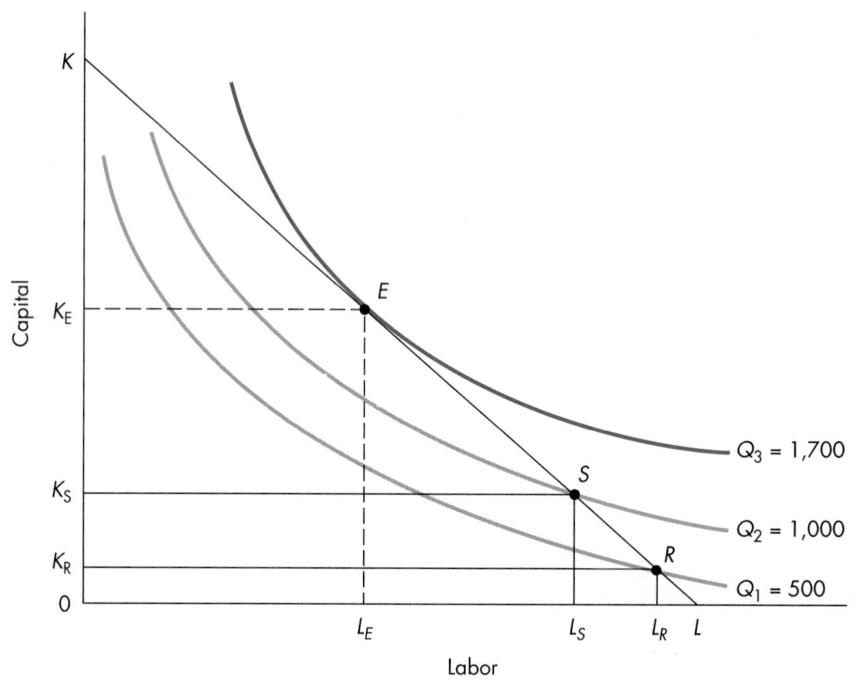

An Expansion Path

In Figure 10.4 we illustrated one optimizing point for a firm. This point shows the optimal (least-cost) combination of inputs for a given level of output. However, as you would expect, there exists an optimal combination of inputs for every level of output the firm might choose to produce. And the proportions in which the inputs are used need not be the same for all levels of output. To examine several optimizing points at once, we use the *expansion path*.

expansion path
The curve or locus of points that shows the cost-minimizing input combination for each level of output with the input/price ratio held constant.

The **expansion path** shows the cost-minimizing input combination for each level of output with the input/price ratio held constant. It therefore shows how input usage changes as output changes. Figure 10.6 illustrates the derivation of an expansion path. Isoquants Q_1, Q_2, and Q_3 show, respectively, the input combinations of labor and capital that are capable of producing 500, 700, and 900 units of output. The price of capital (r) is \$20 and the price of labor (w) is \$10. Thus any isocost curve would have a slope of $10/20 = 1/2$.

The three isocost curves KL, $K'L'$, and $K''L''$, each of which has a slope of 1/2, represent the minimum costs of producing the three levels of output, 500, 700, and 900, because they are tangent to the respective isoquants. That is, at equilibrium points A, B, and C, $MRTS = w/r = 1/2$. In the figure, the expansion path connects these points of equilibrium and all other points so generated.

FIGURE 10.6
An Expansion Path

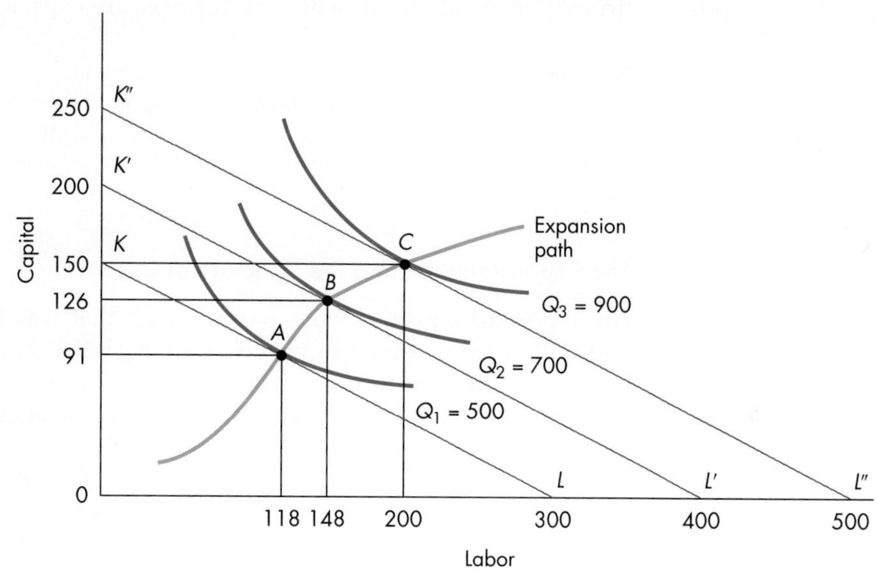

Note that points *A*, *B*, and *C* are also points indicating the combinations of inputs that can produce the maximum output possible at each level of cost given by isocost curves *KL*, *K'L'*, and *K''L''*. The optimizing condition, as emphasized, is the same for cost minimization with an output constraint and output maximization with a cost constraint. For example, to produce 500 units of output at the lowest possible cost, the firm would use 91 units of capital and 118 units of labor. The lowest cost of producing this output is therefore \$3,000 (from the vertical intercept, \$20 × 150 = \$3,000). Likewise, 91 units of capital and 118 units of labor is the input combination that can produce the maximum possible output (500 units) under the cost constraint given by \$3,000 (isocost curve *KL*). Each of the other points of equilibrium along the expansion path also shows an input combination that is the cost-minimizing combination for the given output or the output-maximizing combination for the given cost. At every point along the expansion path,

$$MRTS = \frac{MP_L}{MP_K} = \frac{w}{r}$$

and

$$\frac{MP_L}{w} = \frac{MP_K}{r}$$

Therefore, the expansion path is the curve or locus of points along which the marginal rate of technical substitution is constant and equal to the input price ratio. It is a curve with a special feature: It is the curve or locus along which the firm will expand output when input prices are constant.[8]

6 **Relation** The expansion path is the curve along which a firm expands (or contracts) output when input prices remain constant. Each point on the expansion path represents an efficient (least-cost) input combination. Along the expansion path, the marginal rate of technical substitution equals the constant input price ratio. The expansion path indicates how input usage changes when output or cost changes.

The Expansion Path and the Structure of Cost

An important aspect of the expansion path that was implied in this discussion and will be emphasized in the remainder of this chapter is that the expansion path gives the firm its cost structure. The lowest cost of producing any given level of output can be determined from the expansion path. Thus, the structure of the relation between output and cost is determined by the expansion path.

Recall from the discussion of Figure 10.6 that the lowest cost of producing 500 units of output is $3,000, which was calculated as the price of capital, $20, times the vertical intercept of the isocost curve, 150. Alternatively, the cost of producing 500 units can be calculated by multiplying the price of labor by the amount of labor used plus the price of capital by the amount of capital used:

$$wL + rK = (\$10 \times 118) + (\$20 \times 91) = \$3{,}000$$

Using the same method, we calculate the lowest cost of producing 700 and 900 units of output, respectively, as

$$(\$10 \times 148) + (\$20 \times 126) = \$4{,}000$$

and

$$(\$10 \times 200) + (\$20 \times 150) = \$5{,}000^{9}$$

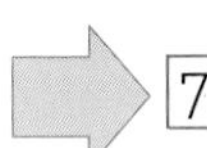
Similarly, the sum of the quantities of each input used times the respective input prices gives the minimum cost of producing every level of output along the expansion path. As you will see later in this chapter, this allows the firm to relate
7 its cost to the level of output used.

[8]We should note that thus far in our discussion of the expansion path we have assumed that as the firm expands output, it increases its usage of all inputs. This need not be the case. It is possible that as a firm expands, it actually decreases the usage of one or more—though not all—inputs over the relevant range. For example, in the two-input case, a firm may increase output by using more capital and less labor. In this case, labor would be called an *inferior input.* An input is said to be inferior if, over a range, increased output causes less of the input to be used. In such cases, the expansion path curves backward if the quantity of the inferior input is plotted along the horizontal axis or curves downward if the quantity of the interior input is plotted along the vertical. Since this phenomenon is not of particular theoretical or empirical importance, we will not consider it further in our analysis.

[9]As you can verify, these are the same costs that would be obtained by multiplying the price of capital (labor) times the vertical (horizontal) intercept of the relevant isocost curve.

FIGURE 10.7
Returns to Scale

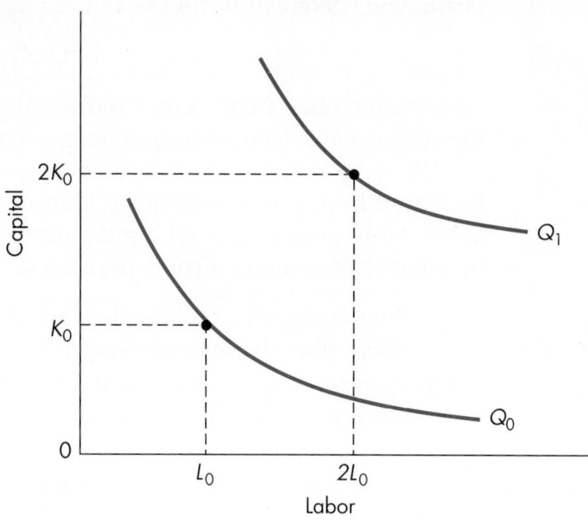

10.5 RETURNS TO SCALE

We will now describe the effect of a proportional increase in all inputs on the level of output produced. For example, if the firm's usage of all inputs doubles, output would increase. The question is: By how much? The answer to this question depends upon the concept of returns to scale.

constant returns to scale
Condition in which all inputs are increased by the same proportion and output also increases by that exact proportion.

increasing returns to scale
Condition in which all inputs are increased by the same proportion and output increases by more than that proportion.

decreasing returns to scale
Condition in which all inputs are increased by the same proportion and output increases by less than that proportion.

Assume the usage of all inputs increases by 25 percent. If output increases by exactly 25 percent, the production function exhibits **constant returns to scale.** If, however, output increases by more than 25 percent, the production function exhibits **increasing returns to scale.** Alternatively, if output increases by less than 25 percent, the production function is characterized by **decreasing returns to scale.**

These relations can be illustrated using Figure 10.7. Begin with an arbitrary level of capital and labor at K_0 and L_0. This combination of capital and labor produces some level of output, Q_0. For purposes of illustration, we define Q_0 to be 100 units. Now, double the level of input usage to $2K_0$ and $2L_0$. Output increases to Q_1. The question is the magnitude of the increase. Input usage has increased by 100 percent. If Q_1 is equal to 200, output would have exactly doubled (increased by 100 percent) in response to the doubling of input usage, so constant returns to scale are indicated. If Q_1 is greater than 200 units (for example, 215), increasing returns to scale are indicated. If Q_1 is less than 200 units (for example, 180), the production function exhibits decreasing returns to scale.

Returns to scale are defined more analytically by writing the production function in functional form:

$$Q = f(L,K)$$

If input usage increases by a constant proportion (for example, c) and the proportionate change in output is z,

$$f(cL,cK) = zQ$$

Again remember that c and z represent proportionate increases in the level of input usage and level of output, respectively.

We have noted, in the case of constant returns to scale, that if inputs are increased by a given percentage, output rises by the same percentage, that is, $z = c$. More generally, if all inputs increase by a factor of c and output goes up by a factor of z, then a firm experiences:

1. Increasing returns to scale if $z > c$ (Output goes up proportionately more than the increase in input usage.)
2. Constant returns to scale if $z = c$ (Output goes up by the same proportion as the increase in input usage.)
3. Decreasing returns to scale if $z < c$ (Output goes up proportionately less than the increase in input usage.)

Do not deduce from this discussion of returns to scale that firms with variable proportions production functions actually expand output by increasing their usage of every input in exactly the same proportion. As you have seen, the very concept of variable proportions means that the firms do not necessarily expand inputs in the same proportions. The expansion path may twist and turn in many directions. However, the concept of returns to scale does enter into some aspects

8 of production and cost theory, and you should be familiar with this term.

10.6 SUMMARY OF LONG-RUN PRODUCTION

In the long run, all inputs are variable. Figure 10.8 summarizes graphically the long-run production decision. In the figure, isoquants Q_1, Q_2, and Q_3 show all possible combinations of labor and capital capable of producing three of the infinite number of output levels that the firm may choose to produce. Isoquants are downward-sloping to reflect the fact that if larger amounts of labor are used, less capital is required to produce the same output level. The marginal rate of technical substitution (*MRTS*) is the absolute value of the slope of an isoquant and measures the rate at which the two inputs can be substituted for one another while maintaining a constant level of output: $MRTS = -\Delta K/\Delta L$. The marginal rate of technical substitution can be expressed as the ratio of the two marginal products:

$$-\frac{\Delta K}{\Delta L} = MRTS = \frac{MP_L}{MP_K}$$

As labor is substituted for capital, MP_L declines and MP_K rises, causing *MRTS* to diminish along the isoquant.

The isocost curves show the various combinations of inputs that may be purchased for a given dollar outlay. The equation of an isocost curve is given by

FIGURE 10.8
Summary of Cost Minimization and Output Maximization

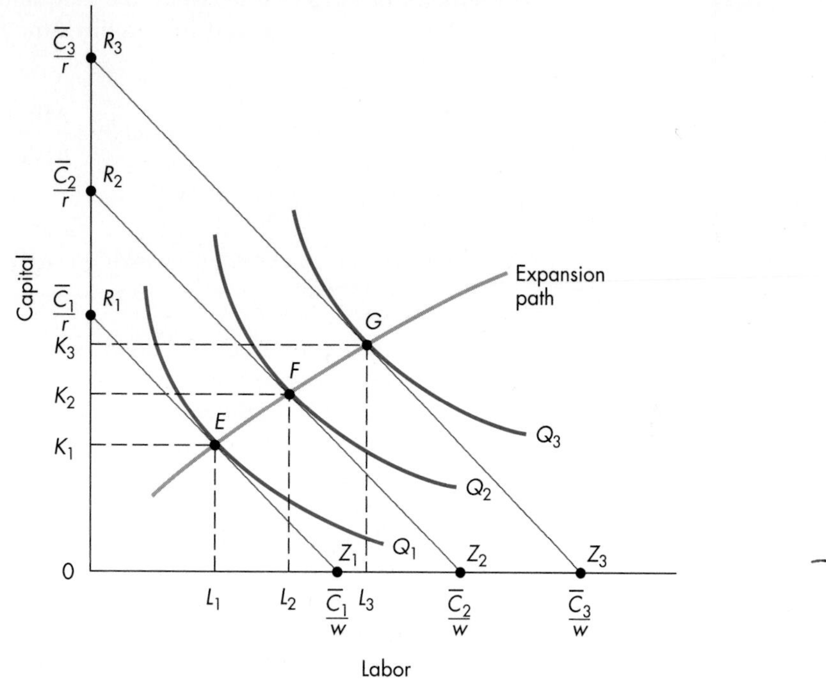

$$K = \frac{\overline{C}}{r} - \frac{w}{r}L$$

where $\overline{C}$ is the cost of any of the input combinations on this isocost curve; and w and r are the prices of labor and capital, respectively. The slope of an isocost curve is the negative of the input/price ratio ($-w/r$). The isocost curve intersects the capital (or vertical) axis at $\overline{C}/r$, which represents the amount of capital that may be purchased when all $\overline{C}$ dollars are spent on capital and no labor is purchased. The isocost curve intersects the labor (or horizontal) axis at $\overline{C}/w$. The cost associated with any particular isocost curve can be determined by multiplying the price of capital by $\overline{C}/r$ or the price of labor by $\overline{C}/w$.

A manager minimizes the total cost of producing a given level of output or maximizes output for a given level of cost (expenditure on inputs) by choosing an input combination at the point of tangency between the relevant isoquant and isocost curves. Points E, F, and G are points of tangency between each of the three isoquants and the *lowest* isocost curve that includes an input combination that is capable of producing the output level given by that isoquant. Alternatively, these points of tangency indicate the combination of inputs on each isocost curve that can produce the largest output (the highest isoquant) that is attainable from any combination on the given isocost curve.

Since the cost-minimizing or output-maximizing input combination occurs at the point of tangency between the isoquant and the isocost curve, the slopes of the two curves are equal in equilibrium. The equilibrium condition may be expressed as

$$MRTS = \frac{MP_L}{MP_K} = \frac{w}{r}$$

or

$$\frac{MP_L}{w} = \frac{MP_K}{r}$$

Thus, the marginal product per dollar spent on the last unit of each input is the same. Equating marginal product per dollar spent on all variable inputs is the rule managers should follow both in the long run when all inputs are variable and in the short run when two or more inputs are variable.

The expansion path shows the equilibrium (or optimal) input combination for every level of output. Figure 10.8 shows a typical expansion path. An expansion path is derived for a specific price of labor (w) and price of capital (r). An expansion path shows how input usage changes when output changes, input prices remaining constant. Along the expansion path the marginal rate of technical substitution is constant, since the ratio of input prices (w/r) is constant.

All points on the expansion path are both cost-minimizing and output-maximizing combinations of labor and capital. For example, consider the input combination consisting of K_2 units of capital and L_2 units of labor (combination F in Figure 10.8). Combination F lies on the lowest possible isocost curve for which Q_2 units of output can be produced. Thus, the minimum cost for producing Q_2 units of output is $\overline{C}_2$ ($= wL_2 + rK_2$). Similarly, the minimum cost of producing Q_1 units is $\overline{C}_1$, and the minimum cost for Q_3 units is $\overline{C}_3$.

Input combination F also lies on the highest possible isoquant (Q_2) costing only $\overline{C}_2$. Thus, L_2 units of labor and K_2 units of capital is the input combination that maximizes output when only $\overline{C}_2$ can be spent on inputs. Similarly, Q_1 and Q_3 are the maximum levels of output that can be produced when only $\overline{C}_1$ and $\overline{C}_3$, respectively, can be spent on inputs.

Returns to scale, a long-run concept, involves the effect on output of changing all inputs by equiproportionate amounts. If all inputs are increased by a factor of c and output goes up by a factor of z, then a firm experiences increasing returns to scale if $z > c$, constant returns to scale if $z = c$, and decreasing returns to scale if $z < c$.

Now that we have demonstrated how a manager can find the cost-minimizing input combination when more than one input is variable, we can derive the cost curves facing a manager in the long run. The structure of long-run cost curves is determined by the structure of long-run production, as reflected in the expansion path.

FIGURE 10.9
Long-Run Expansion Path

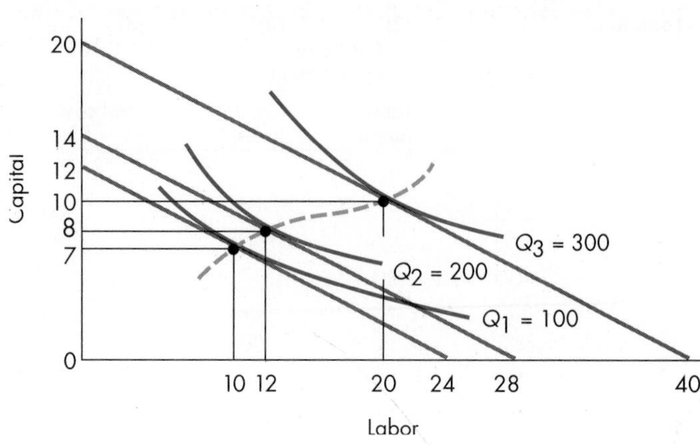

10.7 LONG-RUN COSTS

Recall from Chapter 9 that the long run is not some particular date in the future. The long run simply means that all inputs are variable to the firm. One of the first decisions to be made by the firm is to determine the scale of operations, that is, the size of the firm. To make this decision, a manager must know the cost of producing each relevant level of output. As emphasized above, just as short-run cost is derived from the short-run production function, long-run cost is derived from the long-run expansion path, to which we now turn.

Derivation of Cost Schedules from a Production Function

As we have throughout this chapter, we assume that the firm's levels of usage of the inputs do not affect the prices that must be paid for the inputs—the manager takes input prices as given. We also continue to assume that the only two inputs used in production are labor and capital. We begin the discussion with a situation in which the price of labor (w) is \$5 per unit and the price of capital (r) is \$10 per unit. Figure 10.9 shows a portion of the firm's expansion path. Isoquants Q_1, Q_2, and Q_3 are associated, respectively, with 100, 200, and 300 units of output.

For the given set of input prices, the isocost curve with intercepts of 12 units of capital and 24 units of labor, which clearly has a slope of $-5/10$ $(= -w/r)$, shows the least-cost method of producing 100 units of output: use 10 units of labor and 7 units of capital. If the firm wants to produce 100 units, it spends \$50 (\$5 $\times$ 10) on labor and \$70 (\$10 $\times$ 7) on capital, giving it a total cost of \$120.

TABLE 10.1
Derivation of a Long-Run Cost Schedule

(1)	(2)	(3)	(4)	(5)	(6)
	Least-cost combination of				
Output	Labor (units)	Capital (units)	Total cost ($w = \$5$, $r = \$10$)	Average cost (*LAC*)	Marginal cost (*LMC*)
100	10	7	$120	$1.20	$1.20
200	12	8	140	0.70	0.20
300	20	10	200	0.67	0.60
400	30	15	300	0.75	1.00
500	40	22	420	0.84	1.20
600	52	30	560	0.93	1.40
700	60	42	720	1.03	1.60

long-run average cost (*LAC*)
Long-run total cost divided by output ($LAC = LTC/Q$).

long-run marginal cost (*LMC*)
The change in long-run total cost per unit change in output ($LMC = \Delta LTC/\Delta Q$).

Similar to the short run, we define **long-run average cost (*LAC*)** as

$$LAC = \frac{\text{Long-run total cost } (LTC)}{\text{Output } (Q)}$$

and **long-run marginal cost (*LMC*)** as

$$LMC = \frac{\Delta LTC}{\Delta Q}$$

Therefore at an output of 100,

$$LAC = \frac{LTC}{Q} = \frac{\$120}{100} = \$1.20$$

Since there are no fixed inputs in the long run, there is no fixed cost when output is zero. Thus, the long-run marginal cost of producing the first 100 units is

$$LMC = \frac{\Delta LTC}{\Delta Q} = \frac{\$120 - 0}{100 - 0} = \$1.20$$

The first row of Table 10.1 gives the level of output (100), the least-cost combination of labor and capital that can produce that output, and the long-run total, average, and marginal costs when output is 100 units.

Returning to Figure 10.9, you can see that the least-cost method of producing 200 units of output is to use 12 units of labor and 8 units of capital. Thus, producing 200 units of output costs \$140 (= \$5 × 12 + \$10 × 8). The average cost is \$0.70 (= \$140/200) and, since producing the additional 100 units increases total cost from \$120 to \$140, the marginal cost is \$0.20 (= \$20/100). These figures are shown in the second row of Table 10.1, and they give additional points on the firm's long-run total, average, and marginal cost curves.

Figure 10.9 shows that the firm will use 20 units of labor and 10 units of capital to produce 300 units of output. Using the same method as before, we

FIGURE 10.10

Long-Run Total, Average, and Marginal Cost

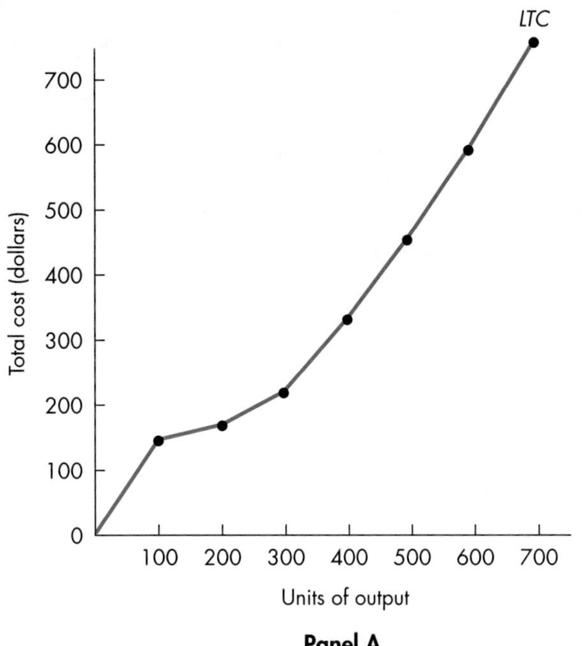

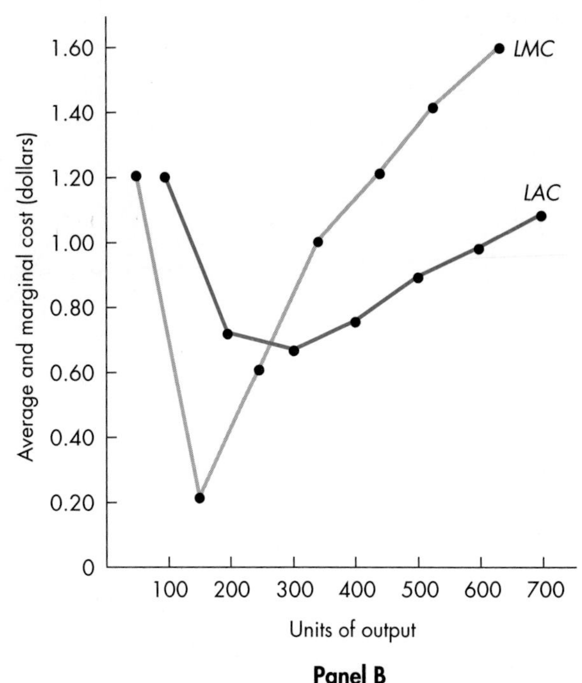

calculate total, average, and marginal costs, which are given in row 3 of Table 10.1.

Figure 10.9 shows only three of the possible cost-minimizing choices. But, if we were to go on, we could obtain additional least-cost combinations, and in the same way as above, we could calculate the total, average, and marginal costs of these other outputs. This information is shown in the last four rows of Table 10.1 for output levels from 400 through 700.

Thus, at the given set of input prices and with the given technology, column 4 shows the long-run total cost schedule, column 5 the long-run average cost schedule, and column 6 the long-run marginal cost schedule. The corresponding long-run total cost curve is given in Panel A, Figure 10.10. This curve shows the least cost at which each quantity of output in Table 10.1 can be produced when no input is fixed. Its shape depends exclusively on the production function and the input prices.

This curve reflects three of the commonly assumed characteristics of long-run total cost. First, because there are no fixed costs, *LTC* is zero when output is zero. Second, cost and output are directly related; that is, *LTC* has a positive slope. It costs more to produce more, which is to say that resources are scarce or that one never gets something for nothing. Third, *LTC* first increases at a

FIGURE 10.11
Long-Run Average and Marginal Cost Curves

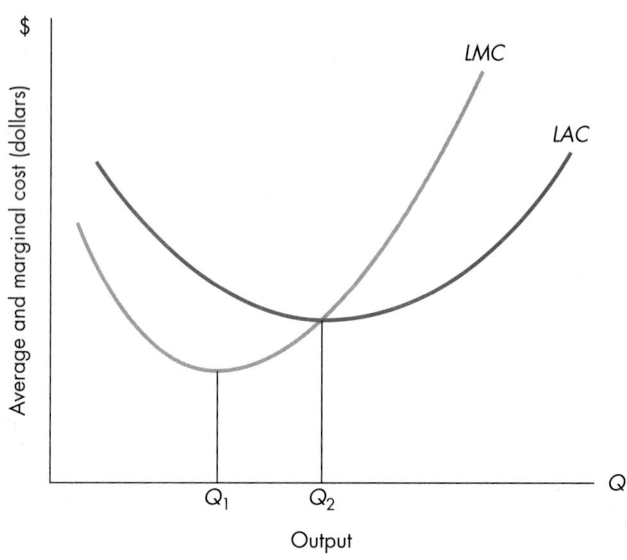

decreasing rate then increases at an increasing rate. This implies that marginal cost first decreases then increases.

Turn now to the long-run average and marginal cost curves derived from Table 10.1 and shown in Panel B of Figure 10.10. These curves reflect the characteristics of typical *LAC* and *LMC* curves. They have essentially the same shape as they do in the short run—but, as we shall show below, for different reasons. Long-run average cost first decreases, reaches a minimum (at 300 units of output), then increases. Long-run marginal cost first declines, reaches its minimum at a lower output than that associated with minimum *LAC* (between 100 and 200 units), and then increases thereafter.

In Figure 10.10, marginal cost crosses the average cost curve at approximately the minimum of average cost. As we will show below, when output and cost are allowed to vary continuously, *LMC* crosses *LAC* at exactly the minimum point on the latter. (It is only approximate in Figure 10.10 because output varies discretely by 100 units in the table.)

The reasoning is the same as that given for short-run average and marginal cost curves. When marginal cost is less than average cost, each additional unit produced adds less than average cost to total cost, so average cost must decrease. When marginal cost is greater than average cost, each additional unit of the good produced adds more than average cost to total cost, so average cost must be increasing over this range of output. Thus, marginal cost must be equal to average cost when average cost is at its minimum.

Figure 10.11 shows long-run marginal and average cost curves that reflect the typically assumed characteristics when output and cost can vary continuously.

Relations As illustrated in Figure 10.11, (1) long-run average cost, defined as

$$LAC = \frac{LTC}{Q}$$

first declines, reaches a minimum (here at Q_2 units of output), and then increases. (2) When *LAC* is at its minimum, long-run marginal cost, defined as

$$LMC = \frac{\Delta LTC}{\Delta Q}$$

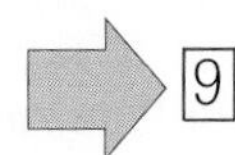

equals *LAC*. (3) *LMC* first declines, reaches a minimum (here at Q_1, less than Q_2), and then increases. *LMC* lies below *LAC* over the range in which *LAC* declines; it lies above *LAC* when *LAC* is rising.

Economies and Diseconomies of Scale

economies of scale The range of output over which long-run average cost (*LAC*) falls as output increases.

diseconomies of scale The range of output over which long-run average cost (*LAC*) rises as output increases.

The economic forces that explain the shape of long-run cost curves are economies and diseconomies of scale. **Economies of scale** occur when long-run average cost falls as output increases. In Figure 10.11, economies of scale exist over the range of output from zero units up to Q_2 units of output. **Diseconomies of scale** occur when long-run average cost rises as output increases. Diseconomies of scale set in beyond Q_2 units of output in Figure 10.11. We first discuss why economists believe economies of scale exist, and then we present some reasons why firms may eventually experience diseconomies of scale.

Probably the most fundamental reason for economies of scale is that larger-scale firms are able to take greater advantage of opportunities for specialization and division of labor. Consider, for example, a small-scale automobile brake and muffler shop. With only a few mechanics and a small number of customers each day, each mechanic must be able to perform *both* brake and muffler repairs. As the number of customers grows larger, the shop can have some mechanics specialize in brake repair and other mechanics specialize in muffler repair. Thus, in the long run, when workers and equipment are expanded together to create larger-scale operations, very substantial gains may be reaped by division of jobs and the specialization of workers in one job or another.

Technological factors constitute a second force contributing to economies of scale. We now discuss three important ways in which they can do so. First, if several different machines, each with a different rate of output, are required in a production process, the operation may have to be quite sizable to permit proper meshing of equipment. Suppose only two types of machines are required, one that produces the product and one that packages it. If the first machine can produce 30,000 units per day and the second can package 45,000 units per day, output will have to be 90,000 units per day in order to utilize fully the capacity of each type of machine.

A second technological source of scale economies is the fact that the cost of purchasing and installing larger machines is usually proportionately less than the cost of smaller machines. For example, a printing press that can run 200,000 papers per day does not cost 10 times as much as one that can run 20,000 per day—nor does it require 10 times as much building space, 10 times as many people to operate it, and so forth. Again, expanding size tends to reduce the unit cost of production.

The final technological element is perhaps the most important technological factor of all: As the scale of operation expands, there is usually a qualitative, as well as a quantitative, change in equipment. Consider ditchdigging: The smallest scale of operation is one worker and one shovel. But as the scale expands beyond a certain point, the firm does not simply continue to add workers and shovels. Shovels and most workers are replaced by a modern ditchdigging machine. In like manner, expansion of scale normally permits the introduction of various types of automation devices, all of which tend to reduce the unit cost of production.

Thus two broad forces, (1) specialization and division of labor and (2) technological factors, enable producers to reduce unit cost by expanding the scale of operation.[10] These forces give rise to the negatively sloped portion of the long-run average cost curve.

You may wonder why the long-run average cost curve would ever rise. After all possible economies of scale have been realized, why doesn't the curve become horizontal?

The rising portion of *LAC*, or diseconomies of scale, is generally attributed to limitations to efficient management. Managing any business entails controlling and coordinating a wide variety of activities—production, transportation, finance, sales, and so on. To perform these managerial functions efficiently, a manager must have accurate information; otherwise, the essential decision making is done in ignorance.

As the scale of plant expands beyond a certain point, top management necessarily has to delegate responsibility and authority to lower-echelon employees. Contact with the daily routine of operation tends to be lost, and efficiency of operation declines. Red tape and paperwork expand; management is generally not as efficient. Thus, the cost of the managerial function increases, as does the unit cost of production.

It is difficult to determine just when diseconomies of scale set in and when they become strong enough to outweigh the economies of scale. In businesses where economies of scale are negligible, diseconomies may soon become of paramount importance, causing *LAC* to turn up at a relatively small volume of output. Panel A of Figure 10.12 shows a long-run average cost curve for a firm of this type. In other cases, economies of scale are extremely important. Even after the efficiency of management begins to decline, technological economies of scale may offset the diseconomies over a wide range of output. Thus the *LAC* curve may not turn upward until a very large volume of output is attained. This case is illustrated in Panel B of Figure 10.12.

[10]This discussion of economies of scale has concentrated on physical and technological forces. There are financial reasons for economies of scale as well. Large-scale purchasing of raw and processed materials may enable the buyer to obtain more favorable prices (quantity discounts). The same is frequently true of advertising. As another example, financing large-scale businesses is normally easier and less expensive: a nationally known business has access to organized security markets, so it may place its bonds and stocks on a more favorable basis. Bank loans also usually come easier and at lower interest rates to large, well-known corporations.

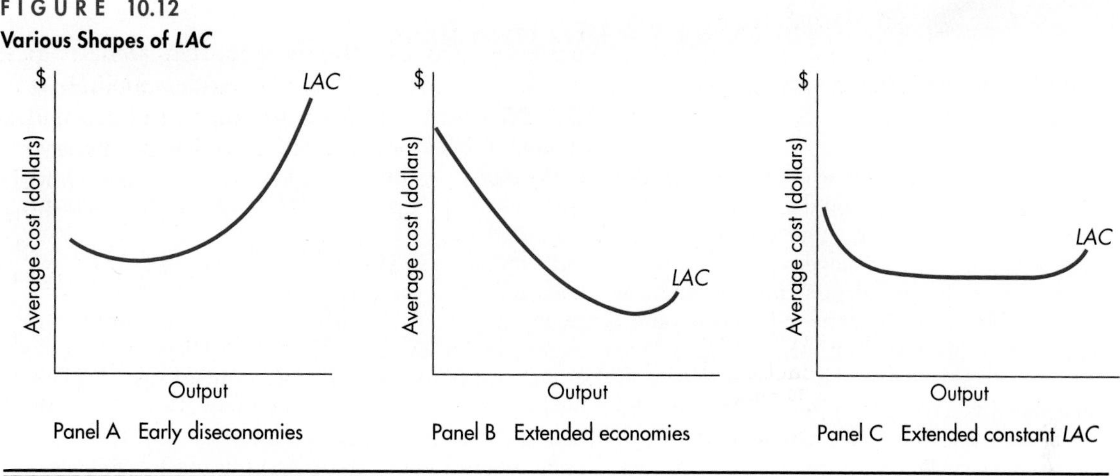

FIGURE 10.12
Various Shapes of *LAC*

10

In many actual situations, however, neither of these extremes describes the behavior of *LAC*. A very modest scale of operation may enable a firm to capture all the economies of scale, and diseconomies may not be incurred until the volume of output is very great. In this case, *LAC* would have a long horizontal section, as shown in Panel C of Figure 10.12. Some economists and business executives feel that this type of *LAC* curve describes many production processes in the American economy. For analytical purposes, however, we will assume a representative *LAC*, such as that illustrated earlier in Figure 10.11.

Economies of Scope

economies of scope The situation in which the joint cost of producing two or more goods is less than the sum of the separate costs of producing the goods.

Many firms produce a number of different products. These multiproduct firms use inputs that contribute simultaneously to the production of two or more goods—a citrus orchard produces both oranges and grapefruit, an oil well produces both crude oil and natural gas, an automotive plant produces both cars and trucks, and commercial banks use the same assets to provide a variety of different financial services. Whenever it is less costly for a single firm to produce two or more products together than for separate firms to produce the same level of output for each product, **economies of scope** are said to exist.

For example, consider Precision Mufflers, a firm that installs replacement mufflers and also repairs brakes. This firm uses inputs that simultaneously contribute to the production of two different services. Precision Mufflers can replace 25 mufflers and perform 10 brake jobs a day for a total cost of $1,400. A firm that specializes in muffler replacement can install only 25 replacement mufflers at a total cost of $1,000. Another firm that specializes in brake repair can perform 10 brake jobs for a total cost of $600. Since the joint cost of replacing 25 mufflers and fixing the brakes on 10 cars ($1,400) is less than the total cost of two separate

ILLUSTRATION 10.2

Managing Economies and Diseconomies of Scale

Our discussion of why economies and diseconomies of scale exist may have given you the impression that economies and diseconomies are unavoidable and beyond the control of a firm's management. To some extent this is correct: the production function and the state of technology determine the range of economies and diseconomies of scale. The manager of a firm does, however, choose the size of the firm which, in turn, determines where the firm will operate on the long-run average cost curve. The manager's choice of firm size is often subject to a great deal of uncertainty, since the precise shape of *LAC* is not known with certainty. Management sometimes makes decisions about firm size that turn out to be incorrect, choosing a size or scale that is either too small or too large. Two business articles in *The Wall Street Journal* illustrate how firms have been affected by past decisions about firm size. Some of these decisions turned out well; others did not.

What can firms too small to compete effectively with larger firms in the market do to enhance their competitive position? For two personal computer manufacturers the answer was to merge their businesses. In May 1993, AST Research, the eighth-largest U.S. PC producer, agreed to acquire the personal computer business of Tandy Corporation, the seventh-largest U.S. producer. This merger would move AST into fourth place in the industry. Recent price wars had hurt the two firms, and according to one industry analyst, "Computer makers like AST have been forced to look to high volume sales for profit [with the] focus on turning out [units] more efficiently and at lower cost."

According to the *WSJ*, the acquisition of Tandy's business would provide some innovative new products and better economies of scale for AST. The economies would come from AST's acquired ability to expand into new markets and increase its market share. The merger would help it establish a direct consumer sales channel through Tandy's 6,600 Radio Shack stores and other chains of computer stores. In essence, AST wanted Tandy's sales capacity in order to achieve previously unattainable economies of scale, thereby leading to lower costs and enhanced ability to compete by reducing prices.

Sometimes firms are actually too big to compete successfully with smaller rivals that have lower per-unit costs. *The Wall Street Journal* reported that many of Japan's biggest steel producers had become too

firms producing the same level of outputs ($1,600 = $1,000 + $600), economies of scope exist.

Let $C(X)$ be the total cost of producing a given level of some good X by a single-product firm and $C(Y)$ be the total cost of producing a given level of another good Y by a single-product firm. If $C(X, Y)$ represents the cost of a single firm's jointly producing the same levels of X and Y, economies of scope exist when

$$C(X, Y) < C(X) + C(Y)$$

The degree to which economies of scope exist (SC) can be measured by the fraction

$$SC = \frac{C(X) + C(Y) - C(X, Y)}{C(X, Y)}$$

large and were being outperformed by smaller, more efficient firms. Nippon Steel Corporation, the biggest steelmaker in the world's number-one steel-producing country, symbolizes the problem facing firms that grow too large. Close to Nippon's largest mill, the little Tokyo Steel Company opened a plant that was 1/20 the size of traditional Japanese steel mills but five times as efficient. The new mill undercut the prices of Nippon and other big steelmakers by 39 percent. According to the *WSJ*, Tokyo Steel planned to build two more "minimills." Other small Japanese steel producers were following suit with more small mills. "Big Steel" in Japan was beginning to look like Big Steel in the U.S. had a decade before. Net profits for Japan's largest three steel producers were down between 77 and 92 percent. And, according to a study by Paine-Webber, Nippon's largest mill did not even rank among the 40 lowest-cost steel producers in the world.

The trend was worldwide: "Large, high-volume 'integrated' plants with disjointed production lines are giving way to small plants with faster, cheaper production methods that can adjust quickly to demand variations." The president of the world's second-largest steelmaker said, "It's quite sure that in the future the largest part of steel will be produced in smaller mills." The chairman of another large steel firm observed, "If the integrated [plants] take this chance to restructure, they can keep their position. If not, newcomers will take it." But the *WSJ* was less optimistic for the huge firms: "Unlike nimbler mini-mill operators, however, many old-line makers remain saddled with slow-moving corporate cultures, bloated staffs, and huge investments in increasingly outdated mills." It appears then that the largest steelmakers had become too large and inflexible because of, among other things, serious managerial diseconomies of scale.

These two examples are intended to show the crucial role played by the shape of the long-run average cost curve in promoting or hindering a firm's ability to compete. As we mentioned in the introduction to this chapter, successful managers must recognize and exploit opportunities to reduce unit costs either by increasing the scale of operation when economies of scale exist or by decreasing scale in the presence of diseconomies of scale. In the appendix to the next chapter, we will show you how to estimate empirically the long-run average cost curve for your firm.

Sources: Ken Yamada and Kyle Pope, "AST to Acquire PC Business of Tandy Corporation," *The Wall Street Journal*, May 27, 1993; Dana Milbank, "Big Steel Is Threatened by Low-Cost Rivals, Even in Japan, Korea," *The Wall Street Journal*, Feb. 2, 1993.

When production involves economies of scope, the sum of the separate costs of producing X and Y by separate firms exceeds the cost of producing X and Y jointly by the same firm, and SC is positive. If diseconomies of scope exist, the sum of producing X and Y by separate firms is less than producing X and Y jointly by the same firm, and SC is negative. The greater the economies of scope, the larger the value of SC.

The reasons for the existence of economies of scope are varied. Economies of scope frequently arise when inputs can be jointly used to produce more than one product. The shared resources that lead to economies of scope may be the inputs used in the manufacture of the product, whereas in some cases it may involve only the administrative and marketing resources of the firm. In other cases, the production process may involve joint products for which the production of one good results in the production of another good at little or no extra cost. Examples of joint products are beef and leather, wool and mutton, chickens and fertilizer, and sometimes crude oil and natural gas.

ILLUSTRATON 10.3

Economies of Scale and Scope in Banking

During the 1980s, the banking industry in the United States experienced an unprecedented period of deregulation. One of the key results of this deregulation has been widespread legislative changes by state legislatures allowing interstate banking activities. By 1990, only three states completely prohibited interstate banking. One of the most controversial effects of interstate banking was the consolidation that took place through mergers and acquisitions of local banks by large, out-of-state banks. According to Robert Goudreau and Larry Wall, the primary incentives for interstate expansion appear to be to gain market power, to diversify earnings, and to exploit economies of scale and scope.* To the extent that significant economies of scale exist in banking, large banks will have a cost advantage over small banks. If there are economies of scope in banking, then banks offering more banking services (products) will have lower costs than banks that provide a small number of services.

Two empirical studies attempted to measure economies of both scale and scope in the financial services industry. John Murray and Robert White studied 61 credit unions in British Columbia.† They found significant economies of scale in the credit union industry. Larger credit unions had lower long-run average costs than smaller ones. They also found evidence of economies of scope for credit unions offering a full line of consumer loans and mortgage loans. Thus, credit unions that offered automobile loans as well as home mortgage loans could provide mortgage loans and automobile loans at a lower cost than credit unions specializing only in home mortgages or only in automobile loans.

In another study, Thomas Gilligan, Michael Smirlock, and William Marshall examined 714 commercial banks to determine the extent of economies of scale and scope in commercial banking.‡ They concluded that economies of scale in banking are exhausted at relatively low output levels. In other words, the long-run average cost curve (*LAC*) for commercial banks is shaped like *LAC* in Panel C of Figure 10.12. When *LAC* reaches its minimum value at relatively low levels of output, small banks are not necessarily at a cost disadvantage when they compete with large banks. Economies of scope also appear to be present for banks producing the traditional set of bank products (various types of loans and deposits). Given their empirical evidence that economies of scale do not extend over a wide range of output, Gilligan, Smirlock, and Marshall argued that public policymakers should not encourage bank mergers on the basis of cost savings. They also pointed out that government regulations restricting the types of loans and deposits that a bank may offer can lead to higher costs, given their evidence of economies of scope in banking.

*Robert Goudreau and Larry Wall, "Southeastern Interstate Banking and Consolidation: 1984–90," *Economic Review* (Federal Reserve Bank of Atlanta), November/December 1990, pp. 32–41.

†John Murray and Robert White, "Economies of Scale and Economies of Scope in Multiproduct Financial Institutions: A Study of British Columbia Credit Unions," *Journal of Finance,* June 1983, pp. 302–321.

‡Thomas Gilligan, Michael Smirlock, and William Marshall, "Scale and Scope Economies in the Multi-Product Banking Firm," *Journal of Monetary Economics* 13 (1984), pp. 393–405.

Relation Economies of scope exist when the joint cost of producing two or more goods is less than the sum of the separate costs of producing the goods. In the case of two goods *X* and *Y*, economies of scope are measured by

$$SC = \frac{C(X) + C(Y) - C(X, Y)}{C(X, Y)}$$

11 where *SC* is greater (less) than zero when (dis)economies of scope exist.

FIGURE 10.13
Long-Run and Short-Run Average Cost Curves

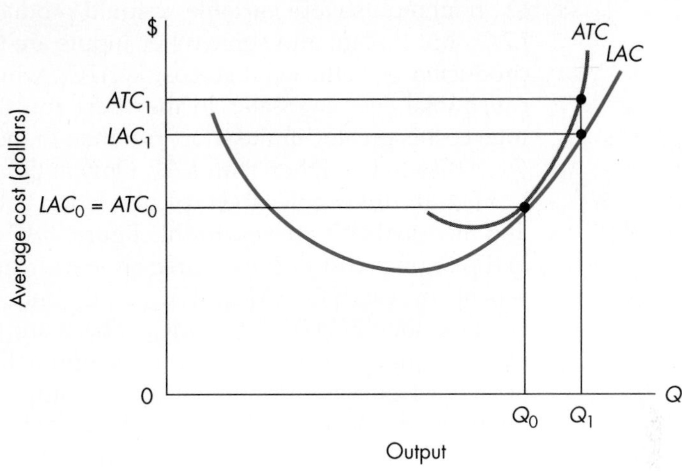

10.8 RELATIONS BETWEEN SHORT-RUN AND LONG-RUN COSTS

We can summarize the discussion of cost thus far by noting that firms *plan* in the long run and *operate* in the short run. Indeed, we call the long run the firm's planning horizon. The long-run cost function gives the most efficient (the least-cost) method of producing any given level of output, because all inputs are variable. But once a particular firm size is chosen and the firm begins producing, the firm is in the short run. Plant and equipment have already been constructed. Now if the firm wishes to change its level of output, it can't vary the usage of all inputs. Some inputs, the plant and so forth, are fixed to the firm. Thus the firm cannot vary all inputs optimally and therefore cannot produce this new level of output at the lowest possible cost.

Such a situation is shown in Figure 10.13, where *LAC* is the firm's long-run average cost curve. Suppose that when making its plans, the firm decided that it wanted to produce Q_0 units of output per period. It chooses the optimal combination of inputs to produce this output at the lowest possible cost. At this least cost, the average cost of producing Q_0 units is LAC_0 in the figure. Since the firm would not wish to vary any of its inputs as long as it continues to produce Q_0—and as long as input prices and technology remain the same—the short-run average total cost of producing Q_0 is the same as the long-run average cost ($ATC_0 = LAC_0$).

Thus the short-run average total cost curve, *ATC*, equals and is tangent to *LAC* at Q_0. But, since some inputs are fixed in the short run, if the firm wants to vary its output in the short run, it cannot produce this new output at the lowest possible cost. At any output other than Q_0, the short-run input combination is not the least-cost combination; it would result in a higher total cost and average cost than the combination that would be chosen if all inputs were variable.

Suppose, for example, that the firm wants to increase its output from Q_0 to Q_1. If all inputs were variable, it could produce this output at an average cost of LAC_1. But if plant and some other inputs are fixed, ATC gives the average cost of producing Q_1. This average cost is ATC_1, which is clearly higher than LAC_1 because total cost is greater in the short run than in the long run. And because total cost is greater in the short run than in the long run at any output other than Q_0, ATC will be higher than LAC. Only at Q_0 are the two average costs the same.

Figure 10.14 shows the typical relation between short- and long- run average and marginal cost curves. In this figure, LAC and LMC are the long-run average and marginal cost curves. Three short-run situations are indicated by the three sets of curves: ATC_1, SMC_1; ATC_2, SMC_2; and ATC_3, SMC_3.

First look at ATC_1 and SMC_1. These are the short-run curves for the plant size designed to produce output Q_S optimally. The long-run and short-run average cost curves are tangent at this output. Since marginal cost, $\Delta C/\Delta Q$, is given by the slope of the total cost curve, long-run marginal cost equals short-run marginal cost at the output given by the point of tangency, Q_S. Finally, short-run marginal cost crosses short-run average cost at the latter's minimum point. Note that because Q_S is on the decreasing portion of LAC, ATC_1 must also be decreasing at the point of tangency.

ATC_3 and SMC_3 show another short-run situation—a different plant size. Here tangency occurs at Q_L on the increasing part of LAC. Thus, ATC_3 is increasing at this point also. Again the two marginal curves are equal at Q_L, and SMC_3 crosses ATC_3 at the minimum point on the latter.

Finally, ATC_2 is the short-run average cost curve corresponding to the output level—plant size—at which long-run average cost is at its minimum. At output level Q_M, the two average cost curves are tangent. The two marginal cost curves, SMC_2 and LMC, are also equal at this output. And since both average cost curves attain their minimum at Q_M, the two marginal cost curves must intersect the two average cost curves. Thus, all four curves are equal at output Q_M. That is, at Q_M, $LAC = ATC_2 = SMC_2 = LMC$.

If the firm is limited to producing with only one of the three short-run cost structures shown in Figure 10.14, it would choose the cost structure—plant size—given by ATC_1 to produce outputs from zero to Q_1, because the average cost, and hence the total cost, of producing each output over this range is lower under this cost specification. If it wishes to produce any output between Q_1 and Q_2, it would choose the plant size given by ATC_2. This average cost curve lies below either of the other two for any output over this range. It would choose the cost structure shown by ATC_3 for any level of output greater than Q_2.

But typically the firm is not limited to three sizes—large, medium, or small. In the long run it can build the plant of the size that leads to lowest average cost at whatever level of output is chosen. The long-run average cost curve is a planning device, because this curve shows the least cost of producing each possible output. Managers therefore are normally faced with a choice among a wide variety of plant sizes.

The long-run planning curve, LAC, is a locus of points representing the lowest possible unit cost of producing the corresponding output. The manager

FIGURE 10.14
Long-Run and Short-Run Average and Marginal Costs

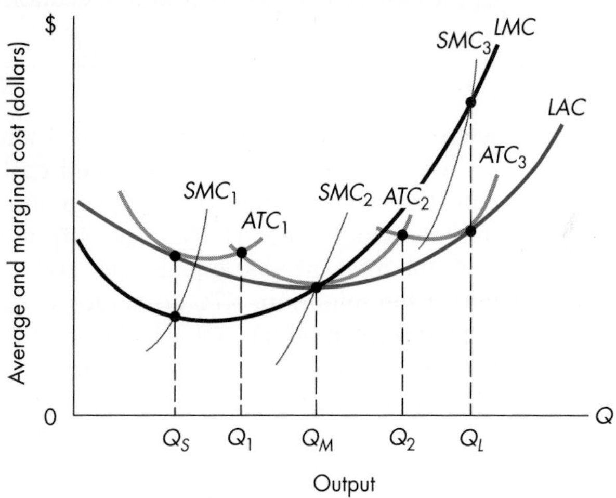

determines the desired size of plant by reference to this curve, selecting the short-run plant that yields the lowest unit cost of producing the volume of output desired.

Relations (1) *LMC* intersects *LAC* when the latter is at its minimum point. There exists some short-run plant size for which the minimum *ATC* coincides with minimum *LAC*. (2) At each output where a particular *ATC* is tangent to *LAC*, the relevant SMC equals LMC. At outputs below (above) the tangency output, the relevant *SMC* is less (greater) than *LMC*. (3) For all *ATC* curves, the point of tangency with *LAC* is at an output less (greater) than the output of minimum *ATC* if the tangency is at an output less (greater) than that associated with minimum *LAC*.

10.9 SUMMARY OF LONG-RUN COST

The long-run cost curves are derived from the expansion path. Since the expansion path gives the efficient combination of labor and capital used to produce any particular level of output, the long-run total cost of producing that output level is the sum of the optimal amounts of labor and capital times their prices. Long-run average cost (*LAC*) is defined as

$$LAC = LTC/Q$$

and is U-shaped. Long-run marginal cost (*LMC*) is defined as

$$LMC = \Delta LTC/\Delta Q$$

and is also U-shaped. *LMC* lies below (above) *LAC* over the output range for which *LAC* is decreasing (increasing). *LMC* crosses *LAC* at the minimum point on *LAC*. When *LAC* is decreasing, economies of scale are present. When *LAC* is increasing, diseconomies are present.

When a firm produces more than one good or service, economies of scope may be present. Economies of scope exist when the joint cost of producing two or more goods is less than the sum of the separate costs of producing the goods. In the case of two goods X and Y, economies of scope are measured by

$$SC = \frac{C(X) + C(Y) - C(X, Y)}{C(X, Y)}$$

where SC is greater (less) than zero when (dis)economies of scope exist.

We have distinguished between cost in the short run and cost in the long run. The relations between long-run and short-run costs can be summarized by the following points: (1) At each output at which a particular ATC is tangent to LAC, the relevant SMC equals LMC; (2) there exists some short-run plant size for which the minimum ATC coincides with minimum LAC; and (3) except for the output level at which $ATC = LAC$, cost is always higher in the short run than in the long run for every short-run situation.

While the cost of production is important to business firms and to the economy as a whole, it is only half the story. Cost gives one aspect of economic activity; it is the obligation to pay out funds. The other aspect is revenue or demand. To the individual manager, revenue constitutes the flow of funds from which the obligation may be met.

Thus, both demand and cost must be taken into consideration. After discussing empirical estimation of production and cost in the next chapter, we will combine our theories of demand and cost to analyze firms' supply decisions.

TECHNICAL PROBLEMS

1. The figure shows the isoquant for producing 1,000 units.

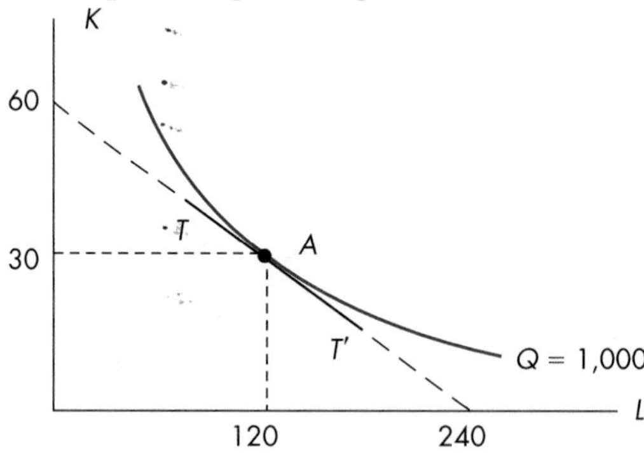

   a. At point A in the figure, the marginal rate of technical substitution ($MRTS$) is ________.
   b. At point A in the figure, increasing labor usage by 1 unit requires that the manager ________ (increase, decrease) capital usage by (approximately) ________ units in order to keep the level of production at exactly 1,000 units.
   c. If the marginal product of the 30th unit of capital is 80, then the marginal product of the 120th unit of labor is ________.
2. The price of capital is \$50 per unit. Use the figure below, which shows an isocost curve, to answer the questions that follow:

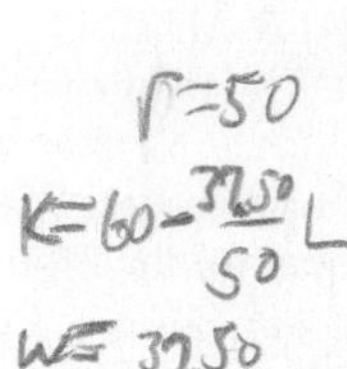

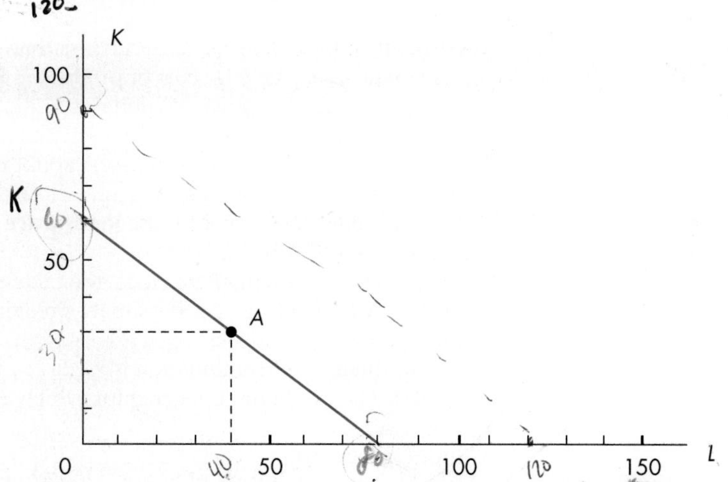

a. The equation for the isocost curve shown in the figure is $K =$ ________. The price of labor is $________ per unit. The total cost associated with this isocost curve is $________.

b. Input combination A is ________ units of labor and ________ units of capital. The total cost of input combination A is $ ________. Verify that point A satisfies the isocost equation in part *a*.

c. For the input prices used in parts *a* and *b*, construct the isocost curve for input combinations costing $4,500. For the $4,500 isocost curve, the capital intercept is ________ and the labor intercept is ________. The equation of the isocost curve is $K =$ ________. If 40 units of labor are employed, then ________ units of capital can be employed for a total cost of $4,500.

3. In the figure below, labor costs $100 per unit. The manager wants to produce 2,500 units of output. Answer the following questions:

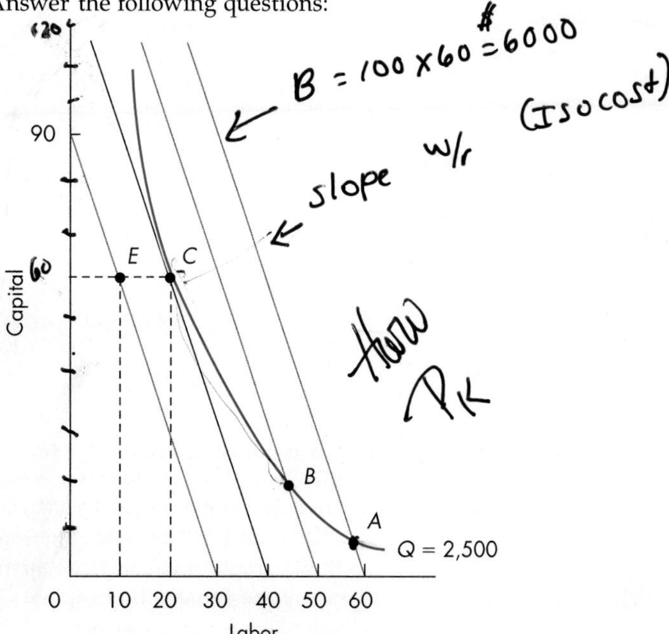

a. At point A, the $MRTS$ is ________ (less than, greater than, equal to) the input price ratio w/r. The total cost of producing 2,500 units with input combination A is $________. The price of capital is $________ per unit.
b. By moving from A to B, the manager ________ (decreases, increases) labor usage and ________ (decreases, increases) capital usage. The move from A to B decreases ________ but leaves ________ unchanged. At B, $MRTS$ is ________ (less than, greater than, equal to) the input price ratio w/r. The total cost of producing at B is $________.
c. At point C, the manager ________ the ________ cost of producing 2,500 units of output. $MRTS$ is ________ (less than, greater than, equal to) the input price ratio w/r.
d. The optimal input combination is ________ units of labor and ________ units of capital. The minimum total cost for which 2,500 units can be produced is $________.
e. Input combination E costs $________. Explain why the manager does not choose input combination E.

4. Suppose a firm is currently using 500 laborers and 325 units of capital to produce its product. The wage rate is $25, and the price of capital is $130. The last laborer adds 25 units to total output, while the last unit of capital adds 65 units to total output. Is the manager of this firm making the optimal input choice? Why or why not? If not, what should the manager do?
5. In the following graph, LZ is the isocost curve and Q_1 is an isoquant.

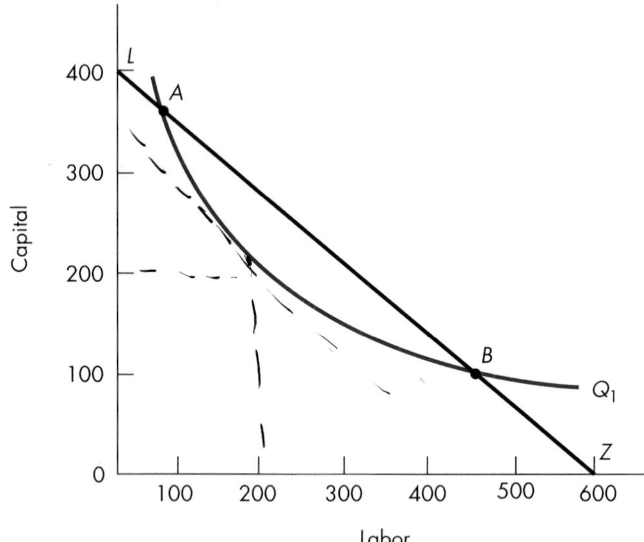

a. For input combination A, MP_L/w is ________ than MP_K/r. Explain, in terms of MP_L/w and MP_K/r, why combination A is not efficient.
b. For input combination B, MP_L/w is ________ than MP_K/r. Explain, in terms of MP_L/w and MP_K/r, why combination B is not efficient.
c. In the graph, find and label the optimal input combination for producing the output designated by isoquant Q_1. (*Hint*: You need to use the straight edge of a ruler.)

6. An expansion path can be derived under the assumption either that the manager attempts to produce each output at minimum cost or that the manager attempts to produce the maximum output at each level of cost. The paths are identical in both cases. Explain why.
7. In the following graph, the price of capital is \$100 per unit.

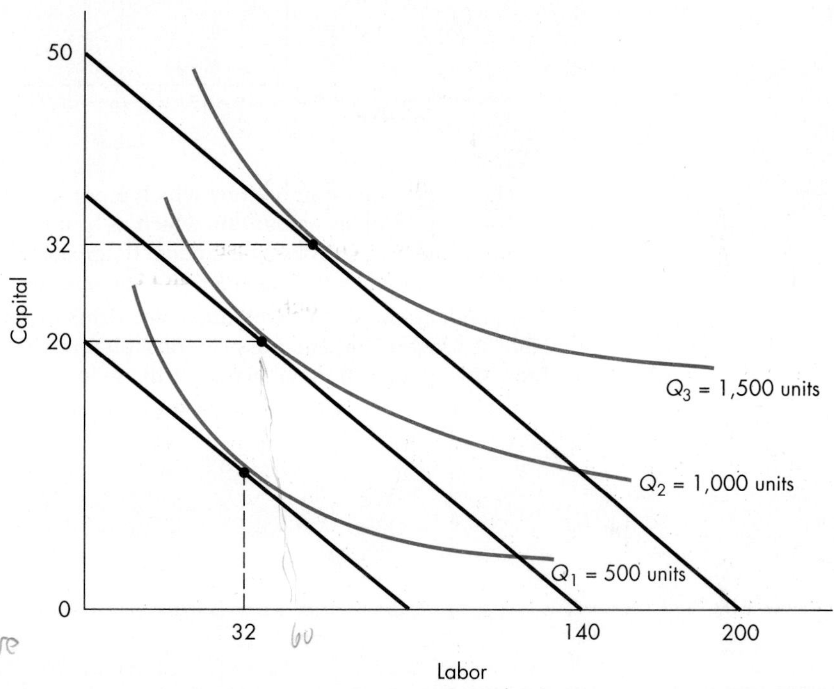

a. The price of labor is \$________.
b. To produce 500 units efficiently, a manager would use ________ units of labor and ________ units of capital. The minimum cost of producing 500 units is \$________.
c. To produce 1,000 units efficiently, a manager would use ________ units of labor and ________ units of capital. The minimum cost of producing 1,000 units is \$________.
d. To produce 1,500 units efficiently, a manager would use ________ units of labor and ________ units of capital. The minimum cost of producing 1,500 units is \$________.
e. In the graph, construct the expansion path.
f. Along the expansion path constructed in part *e*, the marginal rate of technical substitution is equal to ________.

8. The figure below shows two points of production, *A* and *B*, and the levels of output for each input combination. Assume a manager moves from *A* to *B*.

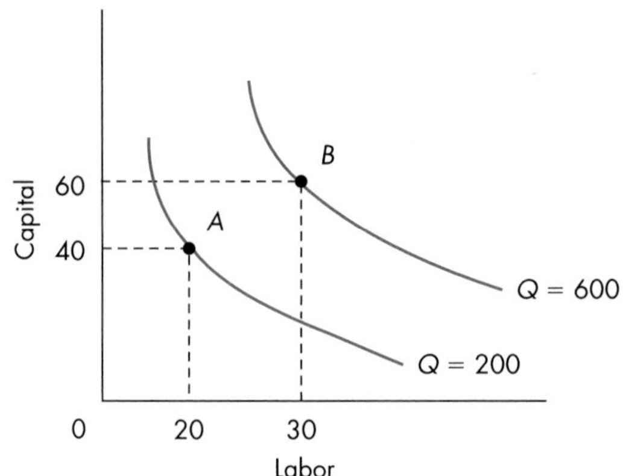

a. The proportionate amount by which input usage increases, c, is ________.
b. The proportionate amount by which output increases, z, is ________.
c. Since c is ________ (less than, equal to, greater than) z, ________ returns to scale are present when the manager adjusts input usage from point A to point B.

9. The graph below shows five points on a firm's expansion path when the price of labor is $25 per unit and the price of capital is $100 per unit.
From this graph, fill in the blanks in the following table:

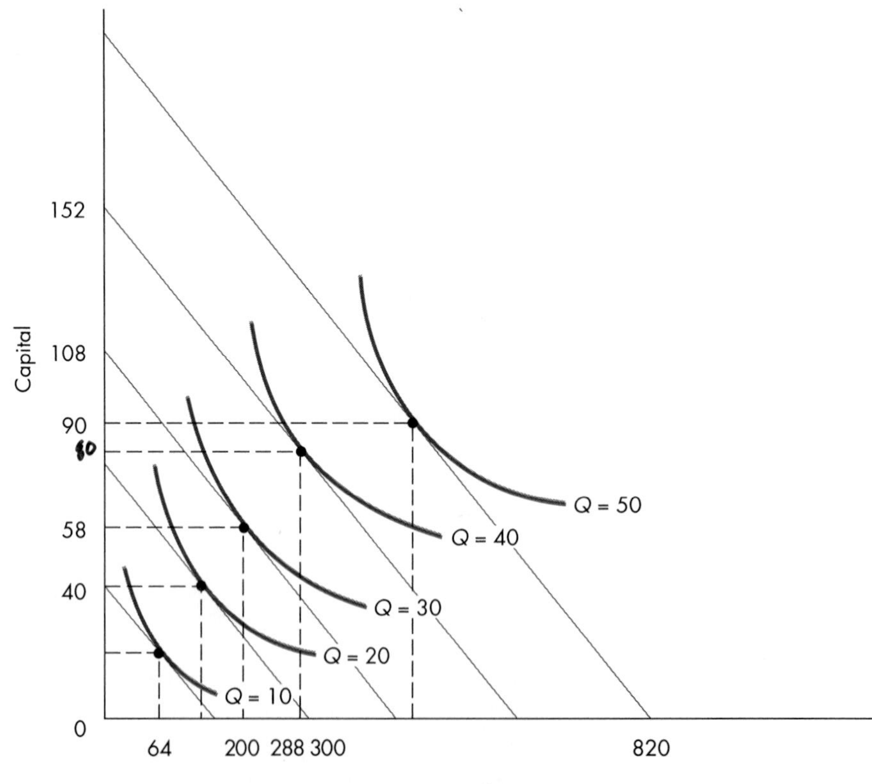

Q	L	K	LTC	LAC	LMC
10					
20					
30					
40					
50					

10. In problem 9, economies of scale exist over the range of output ______ to ______ units. Diseconomies of scale exist over the range of output ______ to ______ units.
11. Using the example in the text concerning Precision Muffler, calculate the degree to which economies of scope exist (*SC*) when the firm is producing 25 muffler replacements and 10 brake jobs. Are there economies or diseconomies of scope?

APPLIED PROBLEMS

1. A study by the Computer Manufacturers Association of America analyzed the significant increase in the usage of computers by business firms in the United States over the last two decades. In terms of production theory, one might say the computer-labor ratio has risen.
   a. Using production theory, provide a rationale for this trend.
   b. Given the falling prices of business computers, what types of changes in business offices would you expect to have occurred?
2. The Largo Publishing House uses 400 printers and 200 printing presses to produce books. A printer's wage rate is $20, and the price of a printing press is $5,000. The last printer added 20 books to total output, while the last press added 1,000 books to total output. Is the publishing house making the optimal input choice? Why or why not? If not, how should the manager of Largo Publishing House adjust input usage?
3. How does the theory of efficient production apply to managers of government bureaus or departments that are not run for profit? How about nonprofit clubs that collect just enough dues from their members to cover the cost of operation?
4. The MorTex Company assembles garments entirely by hand even though a textile machine exists which can assemble garments faster than a human can. Workers cost $50 per day, and each additional laborer can produce 200 more units per day (i.e., marginal product is constant and equal to 200). Installation of the first textile machine on the assembly line will increase output by 1,800 units daily. Currently the firm assembles 5,400 units per day.
   a. The financial analysis department at MorTex estimates that the price of a textile machine is $600 per day. Can management reduce the cost of assembling 5,400 units per day by purchasing a textile machine and using less labor? Why or why not?
   b. The Textile Workers of America is planning to strike for higher wages. Management predicts that if the strike is successful, the cost of labor will increase to $100 per day. If the strike is successful, how would this affect the decision in question *a* to purchase a textile machine? Explain.

5. Gamma Corporation, one of the firms that retains you as a financial analyst, is considering buying out Beta Corporation, a small manufacturing firm that is now barely operating at a profit. You recommend the buyout because you believe that new management could substantially reduce production costs, and thereby increase profit to a quite attractive level. You collect the following product information in order to convince the CEO at Gamma Corporation that Beta is indeed operating inefficiently:

$$MP_L = 10 \qquad P_L = \$20$$
$$MP_K = 15 \qquad P_K = \$15$$

   Explain how these data provide evidence of inefficiency. How could the new manager of Beta Corporation improve efficiency?

6. Government at all levels sometimes imposes regulations on business firms, such as pollution controls on the amount of emissions, safety regulations for workers, and requirements on access for handicapped workers or customers.
   a. How might such regulations be thought of as being negative technological change—that is, technological deterioration rather than technological improvement?
   b. What effect would such regulations be expected to have?
   c. Given your answer to part *b* of this question, is it still possible for such regulations to be efficient from the point of view of society? Explain.

7. We frequently hear the following terms used by businesspersons. What does each mean in economic terminology?
   a. Spreading the overhead
   b. A break-even level of production
   c. The efficiency of mass production

8. The production engineers at Impact Industries have derived the expansion path shown in the following figure. The price of labor is $100 per unit.

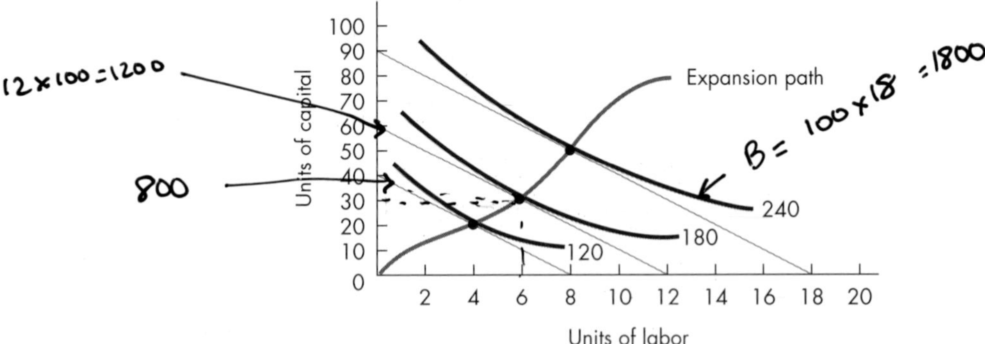

   a. What price does Impact Industries pay for capital?
   b. If the manager at Impact decides to produce 180 units of output, how much labor and capital should be used in order to minimize total cost?
   c. What is the total cost of producing 120, 180, and 240 units of output in the long run?
   d. Impact Industries originally built the plant (i.e., purchased the amount of capital) designed to produce 180 units optimally. *In the short run with capital fixed,* if the manager decides to expand production to 240 units, what is the amount of

labor and capital that will be used? (*Hint:* How must the firm expand output in the short run when capital is fixed?)

e. Given your answer to part *d*, calculate average variable, average fixed, and average total cost in the short run.

9. Commercial bakeries typically sell a variety of products (breads, rolls, muffins, cakes, etc.) to local grocery stores. There are substantial economies of scale in the production of each one of the bakery products, which makes it cost effective for bakeries to specialize in the production of just one product. Grocery stores, however, prefer to buy from multiproduct bakeries that sell a full line of bakery products. How might managers organize production to take advantage of the economies of scale and scope in production and marketing that exist in the baking industry?

10. The Qwik Serve Walk-In Clinic always has three M.D.s and eight R.N.s working at its 24-hour clinic, which serves customers with minor emergencies and ailments. The clinic has hired an efficiency expert to examine its operations and make suggestions for reducing costs.

    For some of the medical procedures done at the clinic, experienced nurses can perform the medical tasks approximately as well as the physicians can, as long as the nurses are supervised by M.D.s. Since M.D.s are more highly trained than nurses, the marginal product of M.D.s is higher than the marginal product of R.N.s.

    The manager of the clinic is confused by the efficiency consultant's report because the report recommends using more R.N.s and fewer M.D.s in order to lower the cost of providing a given level of medical services. Under what circumstances would it be economically efficient for this clinic to use more R.N.s and fewer M.D.s (given $MP_{MD} > MP_{RN}$)? Explain.

11. The speed at which data are transmitted in a computer chip can be dramatically increased by deep-freezing the "interconnects"—wires that connect computer chips—to temperatures in the range of 75 to 125 degrees below zero centigrade. *The Wall Street Journal* (January 31, 1997, p. 1) reported that "such cooling (technology) was considered 10 years ago, but was rejected as too costly and cumbersome in light of easier chip advancements." Now, according to the *WSJ*, improvements in cooling technology have created widespread interest. A vice president of research at IBM says, "The technology may [now be able to] as much as double processor performance," while the cost of the technology has "less-than-doubled." Explain in terms of the marginal product per dollar spent on this cooling technology:

    a. Why the cooling technology was *not* adopted by computer manufacturers 10 years ago

    b. Why "the whole industry is looking at it again" 10 years later

12. Ross Perot added his memorable "insight" to the debate over the North American Free Trade Agreement (NAFTA) when he warned that passage of NAFTA would create a "giant sucking sound" as U.S. employers shipped jobs to Mexico, where wages are lower than wages in the United states. As it turned out, many U.S. firms chose *not* to produce in Mexico despite the much lower wages there. Explain why it may not be economically efficient to move production to foreign countries, even ones with substantially lower wages.

MATHEMATICAL APPENDIX Production and Cost Relations with Two Variable Inputs

Production with Two Variable Inputs

This appendix examines the manager's choice of the optimal input combination for variable proportions production, and it relates this choice of inputs to the costs of production. Two situations are examined. In the first, a long-run decision framework is developed. We specify the production function as $Q = f(L, K)$ and assume both L and K are variable inputs. Since all inputs in the production function are variable, this is a long-run production decision. We derive mathematically the rules for cost minimization given an output constraint and for output maximization given a cost constraint. We then show how to derive the input demand functions for L and K and how to derive the expansion path in the long run. We also demonstrate the relation between the long-run average and marginal costs. We end our discussion of the long run with a derivation of long-run costs for the specific production function $Q = AL^aK^{1-a}$.

In the second situation, we briefly show how the optimization rules are identical for short-run decisions in which three inputs are employed, $Q = f(L, M, K)$. Two of these inputs, labor (L) and raw materials (M), are variable inputs, while the third input, capital (K), is fixed in the short run. In this short-run situation, we examine only the optimal choice for minimizing the cost of producing a given output.

Cost Minimization When All Inputs Are Variable

Define a two-input production function as

$$Q = f(L, K) \tag{1}$$

The marginal products of the two inputs are the partial derivatives

$$MP_L = \frac{\partial Q}{\partial L} \quad \text{and} \quad MP_K = \frac{\partial Q}{\partial K}$$

Before we begin discussing optimization, let's establish that the slope of an isoquant (in absolute value) can be expressed as the ratio of the marginal products. Begin by taking the total differential of the production function in equation (1) above:

$$dQ = \frac{\partial f}{\partial L}dL + \frac{\partial f}{\partial K}dK = MP_L dL + MP_K dK$$

Along an isoquant dL and dK must be such that dQ is zero. Thus we set $dQ = 0$ and solve for the $MRTS$:

$$MP_L dL + MP_K dK = 0$$

$$MP_K dK = -MP_L dL$$

$$MRTS \equiv -\frac{dK}{dL} = \frac{MP_L}{MP_K}$$

Now consider a manager who plans to produce a specific level of output, denoted as $\bar{Q}$. The manager's optimization problem is to choose L and K to minimize the long-run total cost (C) of producing $\bar{Q}$ units of output. Given input prices for L and K, denoted as w and r, respectively, the long-run total cost of employing any input combination (L, K) is $C = wL + rK$. The constrained minimization problem is solved by minimizing the following Lagrangian function:

$$\mathcal{L} = wL + rK + \lambda[\bar{Q} - f(L, K)]$$

where λ is the Lagrangian multiplier. Minimization of the Lagrangian equation, which is a function of three variables L, K, and λ, requires that L, K, and λ be chosen such that the first-order necessary conditions in the following system are simultaneously satisfied:

$$\frac{\partial \mathcal{L}}{\partial L} = w - \lambda\frac{\partial Q}{\partial L} = 0 \tag{2a}$$

$$\frac{\partial \mathcal{L}}{\partial K} = r - \lambda\frac{\partial Q}{\partial K} = 0 \tag{2b}$$

$$\frac{\partial \mathcal{L}}{\partial \lambda} = \bar{Q} - f(L, K) = 0 \tag{2c}$$

Combining conditions (2a) and (2b) in ratio form, it follows that the necessary condition for minimizing the cost of producing $\bar{Q}$ units of output is

$$\frac{w}{r} = \frac{\partial Q/\partial L}{\partial Q/\partial K} = \frac{MP_L}{MP_K} = MRTS \quad \text{or} \quad \frac{MP_L}{w} = \frac{MP_K}{r} \tag{3}$$

Necessary condition (3) for minimization requires that the manager chooses an input combination such that the slope of the isocost line is equal to the slope of the isoquant, which is the tangency solution derived in this chapter. Thus, conditions (2a) and (2b) require that the manager selects input combinations that lie on the expansion path. Alternatively, the conditions for minimization require that the marginal products per dollar spent on each input be equal. Finally, to ensure that $\bar{Q}$ units of output are produced, the manager must not only be on the expansion path but also be on the $\bar{Q}$ isoquant. Necessary condition (2c) forces the manager to be on the $\bar{Q}$ isoquant.

Output Maximization When All Inputs Are Variable

Now let the manager choose L and K to maximize output for a given level of total cost, $\overline{C}$. This constrained maximization problem is solved by maximizing the following Lagrangian function:

$$\mathcal{L} = f(L, K) + \lambda(\overline{C} - wL - rK)$$

Maximization of the Lagrangian equation, which is a function of three variables, L, K, and λ, requires that L, K, and λ be chosen so that the following partial derivatives simultaneously equal zero:

(4a) $$\frac{\partial \mathcal{L}}{\partial L} = \frac{\partial Q}{\partial L} - \lambda w = 0$$

(4b) $$\frac{\partial \mathcal{L}}{\partial K} = \frac{\partial Q}{\partial K} - \lambda r = 0$$

(4c) $$\frac{\partial \mathcal{L}}{\partial \lambda} = \overline{C} - wL - rK = 0$$

Combining conditions (4a) and (4b) in ratio form, it follows that the necessary condition for maximizing output for a given level of cost is the same as that in expression (3), the conditions for cost minimization.

Thus, as we showed in this chapter, both cost minimization or output maximization require that the manager chooses the input combination where the isoquant is tangent to the isocost line. The tangency requirement can also be interpreted as requiring the marginal product per dollar spent on the last unit of each input to be the same. [*Note:* Maximization condition (4c) forces the manager to select L and K from the $\overline{C}$ isocost line.]

The Expansion Path and Efficient Input-Usage Functions

We now derive the expansion line when L and K are both variable inputs. Then, using the expansion path, the efficient levels of L and K can be expressed as functions of Q, w, and r. Recall from the chapter that the expansion path is the locus of L and K combinations for which the marginal rate of technical substitution equals the (constant) input/price ratio. Thus, the expansion path can be expressed as

(5) $$K^* = K^*(L^*; w, r)$$

where K^* and L^* are the efficient levels of input usage for producing various levels of output, *given* fixed input prices w and r. The expansion path in expression (5) is obtained from expression (3) by solving algebraically for K^* in terms of L^*, w, and r. For each value of L^* in (5), there is a single value of K^*.

From the expansion path, it is possible to express the optimal levels of input usage as functions of $\overline{Q}$ given the fixed input prices w and r:

(6a) $$L^* = L^*(\overline{Q}; w, r)$$

(6b) $$K^* = K^*(\overline{Q}; w, r)$$

To derive the efficient input-usage functions (6a) and (6b), substitute the values of labor and capital (L^*, K^*), which solve the system of first-order necessary conditions (2a to 2c) for the cost-minimization problem in expression (2c):

(7) $$\overline{Q} - f(L^*, K^*) = 0$$

To find $L^*(\overline{Q}; w, r)$, substitute the expansion path equation (5) into (7) and solve for L^* in terms of $\overline{Q}$, w, and r. To find $K^*(\overline{Q}; w, r)$, substitute the expression $L^*(\overline{Q}; w, r)$ into the expansion path equation (5) to get $K^*(\overline{Q}; w, r)$. The efficient input functions, which are derived from the expansion path, are used to derive the long-run cost functions for a firm. Later in this appendix, we show how this is done for the production function $Q = AL^aK^{1-a}$.

Cost Relations in the Long Run

As noted above, the efficient input-usage functions are employed to derive the cost functions for a firm in the long run. Long-run total cost, *LTC*, for each level of output, can be expressed as

(8) $$LTC = LTC(Q; w, r) = wL^*(Q; w, r) + rK^*(Q; w, r)$$

Since *LTC* is expressed as a function of *efficient* input usage, the *LTC* function embodies economic efficiency. That is, for any level of output, and a given set of input prices w and r, *LTC* is the lowest possible cost for producing that output level when a manager is able to vary the levels of input usage for all inputs in the long run.

Long-run average cost (*LAC*) and long-run marginal cost (*LMC*) are defined as

(9) $$LAC = \frac{LTC(Q; w, r)}{Q}$$

and

(10) $$LMC = \frac{\partial LTC(Q; w, r)}{\partial Q}$$

The relation between LAC and LMC is identical to the relation between ATC (and AVC) and SMC in the short-run situation. *When* LAC *is decreasing (increasing),* LMC *is less (greater) than* LAC. *When* LAC *reaches its minimum value,* LMC = LAC. The mathematical derivation of these results follows precisely the procedure set forth for the short-run situation in the appendix to Chapter 9.

The Expansion Path and Long-Run Costs: $Q = AL^aK^{1-a}$

Let the production function be defined as $Q = AL^aK^{1-a}$, where a is restricted by $0 < a < 1$. Begin by finding the two marginal product functions:

$$\text{(11a)} \qquad MP_L = \frac{\partial Q}{\partial L} = aAL^{a-1}K^{1-a}$$

$$\text{(11b)} \qquad MP_K = \frac{\partial Q}{\partial K} = (1-a)AL^aK^{-a}$$

The $MRTS$ can be expressed as the ratio of the marginal products:

$$\text{(12)} \qquad MRTS = \frac{MP_L}{MP_K} = \frac{aAL^{a-1}K^{1-a}}{(1-a)AL^aK^{-a}} = \frac{a}{(1-a)}\frac{K}{L}$$

Since the $MRTS$ is a function of the capital-labor ratio (K/L), the $MRTS$ will be constant along a straight line out of the origin in K-L space. Thus, the expansion path must be linear in this case. (Why?) The expansion path, given fixed input prices w and r, is derived from the tangency condition:

$$\text{(13)} \qquad \frac{aK^*}{(1-a)L^*} = \frac{w}{r}$$

Substituting for K^*, the expansion path is expressed as

$$\text{(14)} \qquad K^* = K^*(L^*; w, r) = \frac{w}{r}\frac{(1-a)}{a}L^*$$

As noted above, the expansion path for this production function is a straight line out of the origin: $K^* = mL^*$, where $m = w(1-a)/ra > 0$.

Now we derive the efficient input-usage functions. For L^*, substitute (14) into (2c):

$$\text{(15)} \qquad \overline{Q} - f(L^*, K^*) = \overline{Q} - A(L^*)^a\left(\frac{w}{r}\frac{1-a}{a}L^*\right)^{1-a} = 0$$

Solving implicit function (15) for L^* yields the following efficient usage function for labor:

$$\text{(16)} \qquad L^* = L^*(\overline{Q}; w, r) = \frac{\overline{Q}}{A}\left(\frac{w(1-a)}{ra}\right)^{-(1-a)}$$

To find the efficient usage function for capital, substitute (16) into (14):

$$\text{(17)} \qquad \begin{aligned} K^* = K^*(\overline{Q}; w, r) &= \frac{w}{r}\frac{1-a}{a}\left[\frac{\overline{Q}}{A}\left(\frac{w(1-a)}{ra}\right)^{-(1-a)}\right] \\ &= \left(\frac{w}{r}\frac{1-a}{a}\right)^{1-(1-a)}\frac{\overline{Q}}{A} \\ &= \left(\frac{w}{r}\frac{1-a}{a}\right)^{a}\frac{\overline{Q}}{A} \end{aligned}$$

The efficient input-usage functions (16) and (17) are single-valued functions; that is, for any $\overline{Q}$, there is a single L^* and a single K^*. The long-run cost functions are derived using the efficient input-usage functions for L^* and K^*:

$$\text{(18)} \qquad \begin{aligned} LTC(Q; w, r) &= wL^* + rK^* \\ &= \frac{Q}{A}w^ar^{1-a}\left[\left(\frac{a}{1-a}\right)^{1-a} + \left(\frac{1-a}{a}\right)^a\right] \end{aligned}$$

$$\text{(19)} \qquad \begin{aligned} LAC(Q; w, r) &= \frac{LTC}{Q} \\ &= \frac{1}{A}w^ar^{1-a}\left[\left(\frac{a}{1-a}\right)^{1-a} + \left(\frac{1-a}{a}\right)^a\right] \end{aligned}$$

$$\text{(20)} \qquad \begin{aligned} LMC(Q; w, r) &= \frac{\partial LTC}{\partial Q} \\ &= \frac{1}{A}w^ar^{1-a}\left[\left(\frac{a}{1-a}\right)^{1-a} + \left(\frac{1-a}{a}\right)^a\right] \end{aligned}$$

Notice that, for this production function, LAC and LMC are constant (i.e., not functions of Q) and are the same ($LAC = LMC$).

Short-Run Production and Costs with Two Variable Inputs

Let the firm produce in the short run with two variable inputs, labor (L) and raw materials (M), and one fixed input, capital (K). The short-run production function in this situation can be expressed as

$$\text{(21)} \qquad Q = f(L, M, \overline{K}) = g(L, M)$$

With fixed input prices, w, i, and r, the short-run total cost of production is $TC = TVC + TFC$, where $wL + iM$ is TVC and $r\overline{K}$ is TFC. The short-run constrained minimization problem is solved by minimizing the following Lagrangian function:

$$\mathcal{L} = wL + iM + r\overline{K} + \lambda[\overline{Q} - g(L, M)]$$

Minimization of the Lagrangian equation, which is a function of three variables L, M, and λ, requires that L, M, and λ be chosen such that the first-order necessary conditions in the following system are simultaneously satisfied:

(22a) $$\frac{\partial \mathcal{L}}{\partial L} = w - \lambda \frac{\partial g(L, M)}{\partial L} = 0$$

(22b) $$\frac{\partial \mathcal{L}}{\partial M} = i - \lambda \frac{\partial g(L, M)}{\partial M} = 0$$

(22c) $$\frac{\partial \mathcal{L}}{\partial \lambda} = \overline{Q} - g(L, M) = 0$$

Combining conditions (22a) and (22b) in ratio form, it follows that the necessary condition for minimizing the cost of producing $\overline{Q}$ units of output is

(23) $$\frac{w}{i} = \frac{\partial Q/\partial L}{\partial Q/\partial M} = \frac{MP_L}{MP_M} \quad \text{or} \quad \frac{MP_L}{w} = \frac{MP_M}{i}$$

Necessary condition (23) shows that the manager chooses *variable* inputs in exactly the same way regardless of whether it is the short run or long run.

MATHEMATICAL EXERCISES

1. The production function is $Q = AL^aK^b$, where $a > 0$ and $b > 0$.
   a. The marginal product of labor is $MP_L =$ ________.
   b. The marginal product of capital is $MP_K =$ ________.
   c. The marginal rate of technical substitution is $MRTS =$ ________.
   d. Show that the isoquants for this production function are convex. [*Hint:* Show that $MRTS$ diminishes as L increases. (Why?)]
   e. Derive the equation for the long-run expansion path.
2. For the production function in exercise 1, let the price of labor be w and the price of capital be r.
   a. The efficient usage function for labor is $L^* =$ ________.
   b. The efficient usage function for capital is $K^* =$ ________.
   c. Find the long-run cost functions: LTC, LAC, and LMC.
   d. Show that both LAC and LMC increase at any Q when either w or r increases.
3. The production function for a firm is $Q = 24L^{.5}K^{.5}$. In the shortrun, the firm has a fixed amount of capital, $\overline{K} = 121$. The price of labor is \$10 per unit, and the price of capital is \$20 per unit.
   a. The short-run production function is $Q =$ ________.
   b. The marginal product of labor is $MP_L =$ ________. Show that the marginal product of labor diminishes for all levels of labor usage.
   c. Write the equation for the short-run expansion path.
   d. Derive the short-run TVC, TFC, and TC functions.
   e. Derive SMC, AVC, ATC, and AFC.
4. For the production function in exercise 3:
   a. Find the long-run expansion path.
   b. Derive the efficient input-usage functions for labor and capital.
   c. Derive the long-run cost functions: LTC, LAC, and LMC.
   d. Show that neither economies nor diseconomies of scale exist at any level of production.

CHAPTER 11

Empirical Analysis of Production and Cost

Managers use estimates of production and cost functions to make output, pricing, hiring, and investment decisions. Chapters 9 and 10 set forth the basic theories of production and cost. We will now show you some statistical techniques that can be used to estimate production and cost functions. The focus will be on estimating short-run production functions and short-run cost functions. These are the functions that managers need to make a firm's pricing, output, and hiring decisions. Although long-run production and cost functions can help managers make long-run decisions about investments in plant and equipment, most of the analysis in this text concerns short-run operational decisions. Application of regression analysis to the estimation of short-run production and cost functions is a rather straightforward task. However, because of difficult problems with the data that are required to estimate long-run production and cost functions—as well as the more complex regression equations required—managers typically restrict their use of regression analysis to estimation of short-run production and cost functions.

We begin by showing how to use regression analysis to estimate short-run production functions. The first step in estimating a production function and the associated product curves (such as average product and marginal product) is to specify the **empirical production function,** which is the exact mathematical form of the equation to be estimated. We discuss how to specify a cubic equation to estimate short-run production functions when only one input, labor, is variable. As you will see, the cubic equation has the properties of the theoretical short-run production function discussed in Chapter 9. Next, we explain how to estimate the parameters of the short-run production function and test for statistical significance.

empirical production function
The mathematical form of the production function to be estimated.

After developing the techniques of empirical production analysis, we turn to estimation of short-run cost equations. The cubic specification is also employed to estimate the short-run cost functions. The analysis of empirical cost functions begins with a brief discussion of some general issues concerning the nature of estimating cost functions, such as adjusting for inflation and measurement of economic cost. We then explain how to estimate the various short-run cost functions derived in Chapter 9: the average variable cost (*AVC*), marginal cost (*MC*), and total variable cost (*TVC*) curves. Then we demonstrate how to estimate and test the parameters of these cost functions.

We must stress at the outset that the purpose here is not so much to teach you how to do the actual estimations of the functions but, rather, to show how to use and interpret the estimates of production and cost equations. As emphasized in Chapter 5, the computer will do the tedious calculations involved with estimation. However, you must tell it what to estimate. Therefore, you should learn how to choose the particular function that is best suited for the purpose at hand.

As already noted, this chapter focuses primarily on short-run production and cost estimation. However, we have set forth the techniques used to estimate long-run production and cost functions in the appendix at the end of this chapter. Once you see that application of regression analysis to short-run functions is rather easy, you may wish to tackle this more difficult appendix treating long-run empirical analysis.

11.1 SPECIFICATION OF THE SHORT-RUN PRODUCTION FUNCTION

Before describing how to estimate short-run production functions, we will first specify an appropriate functional form for the long-run production function. Recall from Chapter 9 that the short-run production function is derived from the long-run production function when holding the levels of some inputs constant. Once the fixed inputs are held constant at some predetermined levels and only one input is allowed to vary, the production equation to be estimated should have the theoretical characteristics set forth in Chapter 9.

In this chapter, we will continue to consider the case of two variable inputs, labor and capital. The most general form of such a production function is

$$Q = f(L, K)$$

long-run production function
A production function in which all inputs are variable.

short-run production function
A production function in which at least one input is fixed.

In this form, the production function can be viewed as a **long-run production function** since both labor (L) and capital (K) are variable inputs. In the short run, when the level of capital usage is fixed at $\overline{K}$, the **short-run production function** is expressed in general form as

$$Q = f(L, \overline{K}) = g(L)$$

The exact mathematical form of this production function is frequently referred to as the *estimable form* of the production function. In general, an *estimable form* of an equation—whether it is a production equation, cost equation, or any other type of equation—is the exact mathematical form of the equation that can be estimated using regression analysis. We will now specify an estimable form for the production function. We will first show why a linear specification of the estimable form is inappropriate; then we will describe an appropriate nonlinear specification of the long-run and short-run production functions.

Shortcomings of a Linear Specification

Given our earlier discussion of regression techniques, the mathematical form for the *long-run* production function that might first come to mind is a simple linear form:

$$Q = aK + bL$$

There are, however, two major problems with using this linear functional form for the long-run production function. First, in this form, it is not necessary to use positive amounts of both inputs in order to produce a positive level of output. For instance, let K equal zero. Output would then be equal to bL, which is greater than zero when any (positive) amount of labor is employed. Thus, production can take place without using any capital. (The same is true for labor.) A second problem arises because the isoquants are straight lines. While the isoquants would slope downward, they would not be convex, so the marginal rate of technical substitution (*MRTS*) is not diminishing.[1] These two problems indicate that a linear specification does not conform to the necessary theoretical characteristics of a long-run production function.

Consider also the linear specification for the *short-run* production function. Since capital is constant in the short run, the short-run production function is

$$\begin{aligned} Q = f(L, \overline{K}) &= a\overline{K} + bL \\ &= c + bL \end{aligned}$$

where $c = a\overline{K}$. Two problems make this linear production function an unsuitable specification of a *short-run production function.* First, when no labor is used, positive output is produced (when $L = 0$, $Q = c$). Second, because the marginal product of labor in this specification is

$$MP = \frac{\Delta Q}{\Delta L} = b$$

---

[1]For any given level of output, Q', the various combinations of L and K which will produce exactly Q' units are given by

$$Q' = aK + bL$$

Thus, the equation for the Q' isoquant is

$$K = \frac{Q'}{a} - \frac{b}{a}L$$

which is linear with a constant slope of $-b/a$.

the marginal product of labor is constant. Hence, the law of diminishing marginal product is violated. As in the long-run specification, the linear form also fails to conform to the theoretical characteristics of a short-run production function. These problems render the simple linear specification unsuitable as a functional form for estimating either a long-run or a short-run production function.

A Cubic Production Function

Although a linear specification of a production function is not tractable, many other specifications are theoretically suitable. A particularly useful *nonlinear* functional form, which can be transformed into a linear form for easy estimation, is the **cubic production function**:

cubic production function
A production function of the form $Q = aK^3L^3 + bK^2L^2$.

$$Q = aK^3L^3 + bK^2L^2$$

For this form of the production function, both inputs are required in order to produce output. If either capital or labor usage equals zero, no output is produced. Furthermore, the cubic production function has convex isoquants, so the marginal rate of technical substitution diminishes as required by the theory of production. (All the mathematical properties of cubic production functions set forth in this chapter are mathematically derived in this chapter's appendix.)

short-run cubic production function
A production function of the form $Q = AL^3 + BL^2$.

Holding capital constant at $\overline{K}$ units ($K = \overline{K}$), the **short-run cubic production function** is

$$\begin{aligned} Q &= a\overline{K}^3L^3 + b\overline{K}^2L^2 \\ &= AL^3 + BL^2 \end{aligned}$$

where $A = a\overline{K}^3$ and $B = b\overline{K}^2$, and both A and B are constant when $\overline{K}$ is constant. The average and marginal products for the cubic short-run production function are, respectively,

$$AP = \frac{Q}{L} = AL^2 + BL$$

and

$$MP = \frac{\Delta Q}{\Delta L} = 3AL^2 + 2BL$$

As shown in the appendix, for the average and marginal products to first rise, reach a maximum, and then fall (as illustrated in Chapter 9), A must be negative and B must be positive. This requires that, in the above production function, $a < 0$ and $b > 0$. It is also shown in the appendix that the level of labor usage beyond which marginal product begins to fall, and diminishing returns set in, is

$$L_m = -\frac{B}{3A}$$

FIGURE 11.1
Marginal and Average Product Curves for the Short-Run Cubic Production Function: $Q = AL^3 + BL^2$

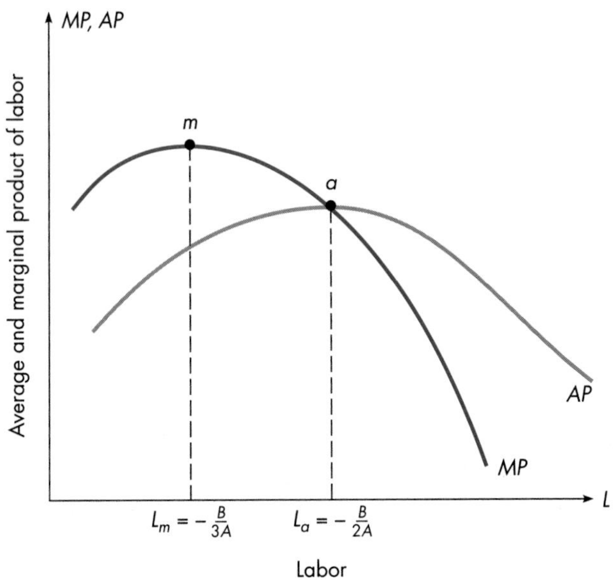

When marginal product equals average product and average product is at its maximum (as discussed in Chapter 9),[2]

$$L_a = -\frac{B}{2A}$$

Recall that A is negative ($A < 0$) and B is positive ($B > 0$), so both L_m and L_a are positive. These relations are shown in Figure 11.1.

Note that when the fixed level of capital changes, both A ($= a\overline{K}^3$) and B ($= b\overline{K}^2$) change in value and all three product curves (*TP, AP,* and *MP* shift.[3] Also note that once estimates of A and B are obtained for any one of the three product equations (*TP, AP,* and *MP*), the other two have also been estimated; that is, A and B are the only two parameters that need to be estimated to get all three equations.

[2]The level of labor usage at which *AP* reaches its maximum value, L_a, can be found algebraically. First, set *AP* equal to *MP*:

$$AL^2 + BL = 3AL^2 + 2BL$$

or

$$0 = 2AL^2 + BL$$

Solving for L, the level of labor usage at which average product is maximized is $L_a = -B/2A$.

[3]Recall from Tables 9.1 and 9.3 in Chapter 9 that capital is held constant in any given column. The entire marginal and average product schedules change when capital usage changes.

TABLE 11.1
Summary of the Short-Run Cubic Production Function

	Short-run cubic production function
Total product	$Q = AL^3 + BL^2$ where $A = a\overline{K}^3$ $B = b\overline{K}^2$
Average product	$AP = AL^2 + BL$
Marginal product	$MP = 3AL^2 + 2BL$
Diminishing marginal returns	Beginning at $L_m = -\dfrac{B}{3A}$
Diminishing average product	Beginning at $L_a = -\dfrac{B}{2A}$
Restrictions on parameters	$A < 0$ $B > 0$

3 The short-run cubic production function exhibits all the theoretical properties discussed in Chapter 9. Table 11.1 summarizes the cubic specification of the short-run production function.

11.2 ESTIMATION OF A SHORT-RUN CUBIC PRODUCTION FUNCTION

Now that we have specified a cubic form for the short-run production function, we can discuss how to estimate this production function. As you will see, only the simple techniques of regression analysis presented in Chapter 5 are needed to estimate the cubic production function in the short run when capital is fixed. We illustrate the process of estimating the production function with an example.

Suppose a small plant uses labor with a fixed amount of capital to assemble a product. There are 40 observations on labor usage (hours per day) and output (number of units assembled per day). The manager wishes to estimate the production function and the marginal product of labor. Figure 11.2 presents a scatter diagram of the 40 observations.

The scatter diagram suggests that a cubic specification of short-run production is appropriate because the scatter of data points appears to have an S-shape, similar to the theoretical total product curve set forth in Chapter 9. For such a curve, the slope first increases and then decreases, indicating that the marginal product of labor first increases, reaches a maximum, and then decreases. Both the marginal product and average product curves should take on the inverted-U-shape described in Chapter 9 and shown in Figure 9.3.

Since it seems appropriate to estimate a cubic production function in this case, we specify the following estimable form:

$$Q = AL^3 + BL^2$$

Following the procedure discussed in Chapter 5, we transform the cubic equation into a linear form for estimation:

$$Q = AX + BW$$

FIGURE 11.2
Scatter Diagram for a Cubic Production Function

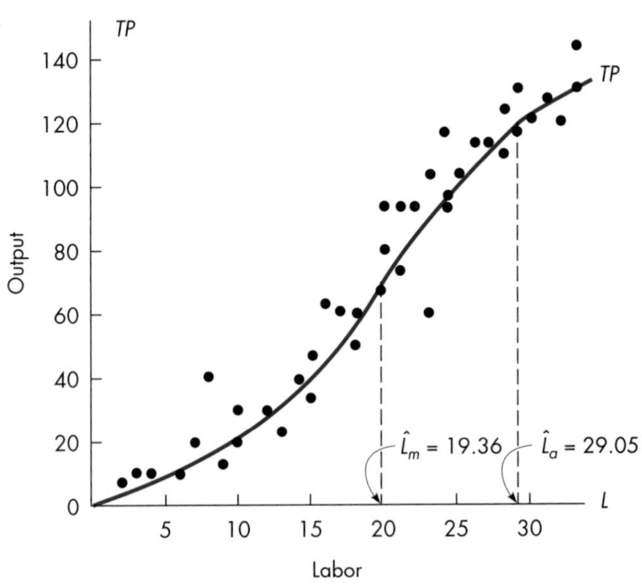

regression through the origin
A regression in which the intercept term is forced to equal zero.

where $X = L^3$ and $W = L^2$. In order to correctly estimate the cubic equation, we must account for the fact that the cubic equation does not include an intercept term. In other words, the estimated regression line must pass through the origin; that is, when $L = 0$, $Q = 0$. **Regression through the origin** simply requires that the analyst specify in the computer routine that the intercept term be "suppressed." Most computer programs for regression analysis provide the user with a simple way to suppress the intercept term. After using a regression routine to estimate a cubic equation for the 40 observations on output and labor usage (and suppressing the intercept), the following computer output is forthcoming:

DEPENDENT VARIABLE: Q		R-SQUARE	F-RATIO	P-VALUE ON F
OBSERVATIONS: 40		0.9837	1148.83	0.0001
VARIABLE	PARAMETER ESTIMATE	STANDARD ERROR	T-RATIO	P-VALUE
L3	−0.0047	0.0006	−7.833	0.0001
L2	0.2731	0.0182	15.005	0.0001

The F-ratio and the R^2 for the cubic specification are quite good.[4] The critical value of F with $k - 1 = 1$ and $n - k = 38$ degrees of freedom is 4.1 at the 5 percent significance level. The p-values for both estimates $\hat{A}$ and $\hat{B}$ are so small that there is less than a 0.01 percent chance of making a Type I error (mistakenly concluding that $A \neq 0$ and $B \neq 0$). The following parameter estimates are obtained from the printout:

$$\hat{A} = -0.0047 \qquad \text{and} \qquad \hat{B} = 0.2731$$

The estimated short-run cubic production function is

$$\hat{Q} = -0.0047L^3 + 0.2731L^2$$

The parameters theoretically have the correct signs; $\hat{A} < 0$ and $\hat{B} > 0$. We must test to see if $\hat{A}$ and $\hat{B}$ are significantly negative and positive, respectively. The computed t-ratios allow us to test for statistical significance:

$$t_{\hat{a}} = -7.83 \qquad \text{and} \qquad t_{\hat{b}} = 15.00$$

The absolute values of both t-statistics exceed the critical t-value for 38 degrees of freedom at a 5 percent level of significance (2.021). Hence, $\hat{A}$ is significantly negative, and $\hat{B}$ is significantly positive. Both estimates satisfy the theoretical characteristics of a cubic production function.

The estimated marginal product of labor is

$$\begin{aligned}\widehat{MP} &= 3\hat{A}L^2 + 2\hat{B}L \\ &= 3(-0.0047)L^2 + 2(0.2731)L \\ &= -0.0141L^2 + 0.5462L\end{aligned}$$

The level of labor usage beyond which diminishing returns set in (after MP_L reaches its maximum) is estimated as

$$\hat{L}_m = -\frac{\hat{B}}{3\hat{A}} = -\frac{0.2731}{3(-0.0047)} = 19.36$$

Note in Figure 11.2 that L_m is at the point where total product no longer increases at an increasing rate but begins increasing at a decreasing rate. The estimated average product of labor is

$$\begin{aligned}\widehat{AP} &= \hat{A}L^2 + \hat{B}L \\ &= (-0.0047)L^2 + (0.2731)L\end{aligned}$$

The maximum average product is attained when $AP = MP$ at the estimated level of labor usage:

$$\hat{L}_a = -\frac{\hat{B}}{2\hat{A}} = -\frac{0.2731}{2(-0.0047)} = 29.05$$

[4]For purposes of illustration, the hypothetical data used in this example were chosen to fit closely an S-shaped cubic equation. In most real-world applications, you will probably get smaller values for the F-ratio, R^2, and t-statistics.

Maximum AP, as expected, occurs at a higher level of labor usage than maximum MP (see Figure 11.2). The evidence indicates that the cubic estimation of the production function from the data points in Figure 11.2 provides a good fit and has all the desired theoretical properties.

11.3 SHORT-RUN COST ESTIMATION: SOME PROBLEMS WITH MEASURING COST

The techniques of regression analysis can also be used to estimate cost functions. Cost depends upon the level of output being produced, as well as the prices of the inputs used in production. This relation can be expressed mathematically as

$$TC = TC(Q; w, r)$$

where we continue to let w denote the price of a unit of labor services and r the price of a unit of capital services. Before describing procedures used in estimating short-run cost functions, we must discuss two important considerations that arise when measuring the cost of production—the problem of inflation and that of measuring economic cost.

When short-run cost functions are being estimated, the data will necessarily be such that the level of usage of one (or more) of the inputs is fixed. In the context of the two-input production function employed in Chapter 9, this restriction could be interpreted to mean that the firm's capital stock is fixed while labor usage is allowed to vary. In most cases, a manager will be using a time-series set of observations on cost, output, and input prices to estimate the short-run cost function. The time period over which the data are collected should be short enough so that at least one input remains fixed. For instance, an analyst might collect monthly observations over a two-year period in which the firm did not change its basic plant (i.e., capital stock). Thus, the analyst could obtain 24 observations on cost, output, and input prices. When using a time-series data set of this type, an analyst should be careful to adjust the cost and input price data (which are measured in dollars) for inflation and to make sure the cost data measure economic cost. We now discuss these two possible problems.

Correcting Data for the Effects of Inflation

nominal cost data
Data that have not been corrected for the effects of inflation.

While output is expressed in physical units, cost and input prices are expressed in nominal dollars. Hence, the **nominal cost data** would include the effect of inflation. That is, over time, inflation could cause reported costs to rise, even if output remained constant. Such a situation is depicted in Figure 11.3. As you can see in this figure, estimation based on a data set affected by inflation will indicate that cost rises more steeply than it would if inflation did not exist in the data. In order to accurately measure the real increase in cost caused by increases in output, it is necessary to eliminate the effects of inflation.

deflating
Correcting for the influence of inflation by dividing nominal cost data by a price index.

Correcting for the effects of inflation is easily accomplished by **deflating** nominal cost data into constant (or real) dollars using a price index. To convert nominal cost into a constant-dollar amount, the nominal cost data are divided by the appropriate price index for the period under consideration. Price indexes can

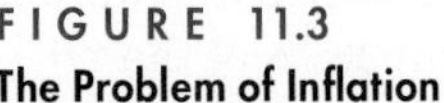
FIGURE 11.3
The Problem of Inflation

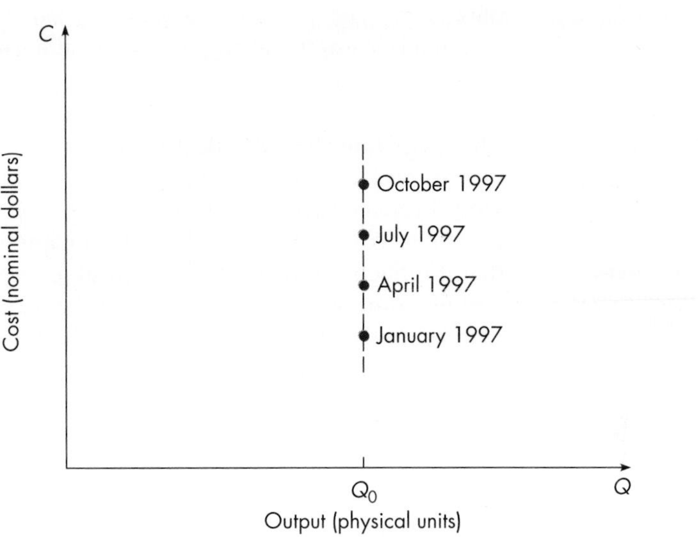

be obtained from the *Survey of Current Business,* published by the U.S. Department of Commerce. We will illustrate the process of deflating nominal cost data later in this chapter.

Inflation also can affect input prices, but for short-run cost estimation this is seldom a problem. As long as inflation affects all input prices and cost equally—that is, all input prices and cost rise equiproportionately—the effect of inflation on cost estimation is fully corrected for by deflating nominal cost. For example, if there is a 4 percent increase in cost and in the prices of both labor and capital, deflating cost by 4 percent will remove the effect of inflation, even when the prices of the inputs are not included in the cost equation. Therefore, it is a fairly common practice to omit input prices in short-run cost estimation because the span of the time-series data set is generally short enough that changes in the real input prices do not occur or are quite small. Thus, we will concentrate on showing how to adjust for inflation in the cost data and not be concerned with the effects of inflation on input prices.

Problems Measuring Economic Cost

Another potentially troublesome problem can result from the difference between the accounting definition of cost and the economic definition of cost. As stressed in Chapter 9, the cost of using resources in production is the opportunity cost of using the resources. Since accounting data are of necessity based on expenditures, opportunity cost may not be reflected in the firm's accounting records. To illustrate this problem, suppose a firm owns its own machinery. The opportunity cost of this equipment is the income that could be derived if the machinery were leased to another firm, but this cost would not be reflected in the accounting data.

In a two-input setting, total cost at a given level of outputs is

$$C = wL + rK$$

user cost of capital The firm's opportunity cost of using capital.

The wage rate should reflect the opportunity cost of labor to the firm; so expenditures on labor, wL (including any additional compensation not paid as wages), would reflect opportunity cost. The problem is the calculation of the firm's opportunity cost of capital. The cost of capital, r, must be calculated in such a way that it reflects the **user cost of capital.** User cost includes not only the acquisition cost of a unit of capital but also (1) the return foregone by using the capital rather than renting it, (2) the depreciation charges resulting from the use of the capital, and (3) any capital gains or losses associated with holding the particular type of capital. Likewise, the measurement of the capital stock, K, must be such that it reflects the stock actually owned by the firm. For example, you might want the capital variable to reflect the fact that given piece of capital has depreciated physically or embodies a lower technology than a new piece of capital. While these problems are difficult, they are not insurmountable. The main thing to remember is that such opportunity-cost data would be expected to differ greatly from the reported cost figures in accounting data.

11.4 ESTIMATION OF A SHORT-RUN COST FUNCTION

As is the case when estimating a production function, specification of an appropriate equation for a cost function must necessarily precede the estimation of the parameters using regression analysis. The specification of an empirical cost equation must ensure that the mathematical properties of the equation reflect the properties and relations described in Chapter 9. Figure 11.4 illustrates again the typically assumed total variable cost, average variable cost, and marginal cost curves.

Since the shape of any one of the three cost curves determines the shape of the other two, we begin with the average variable cost curve. Because this curve is U-shaped, the simplest possible form, the linear specification, $AVC = a + bQ$, cannot be used. Because the simple linear form won't work, we use the slightly more complex specification,

$$AVC = a + bQ + cQ^2$$

As explained earlier, input prices are not included as explanatory variables in the cost equation because the input prices (adjusted for inflation) are assumed to be constant over the relatively short time span of the time-series data set. In order for the AVC curve to be U-shaped, a must be positive, b must be negative, and c must be positive; that is, $a > 0$, $b < 0$, and $c > 0$.[5]

Given the specification for average variable cost, the specifications for total variable cost and marginal cost are straightforward. Since $AVC = TVC/Q$, it

[5]The appendix to this chapter derives the mathematical properties of a cubic cost function.

FIGURE 11.4
Representative Short-Run Cost Curves

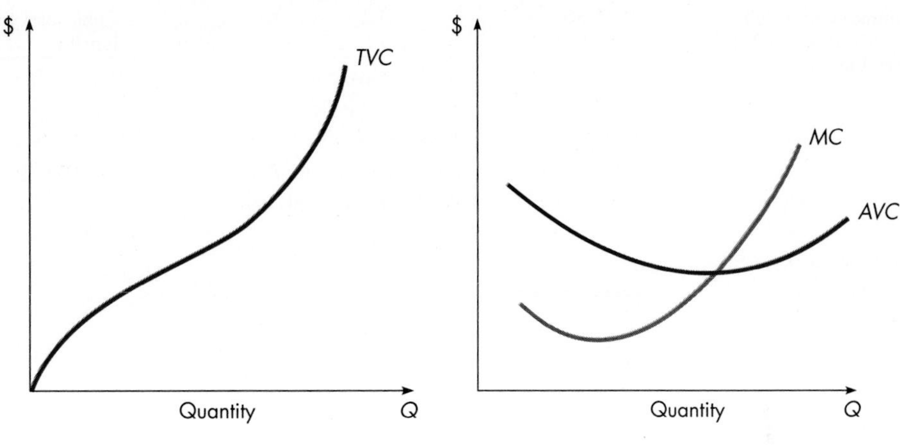

follows that

$$TVC = AVC \times Q = (a + bQ + cQ^2)Q = aQ + bQ^2 + cQ^3$$

Note that this equation is a cubic specification of *TVC,* which conforms to the S-shaped *TVC* curve in Figure 11.4.

The equation for marginal cost is somewhat more difficult to derive. It can be shown, however, that the marginal cost equation associated with the above *TVC* equation is

$$MC = a + 2bQ + 3cQ^2$$

If, as specified for *AVC,* $a > 0$, $b < 0$, and $c > 0$, the marginal cost curve will also be U-shaped.

Because all three of the cost curves, *TVC, AVC,* and *MC,* employ the same parameters, it is necessary to estimate only one of these functions in order to obtain estimates of all three. For example, estimation of *AVC* provides estimates of a, b, and c, which can then be used to generate the marginal and total variable cost functions. The total cost curve is trivial to estimate; simply add the constant fixed cost to total variable cost.

As for the estimation itself, ordinary least-squares estimation of the total (or average) variable cost function is usually sufficient. Once the estimates of a, b, and c are obtained, it is necessary to determine whether the parameter estimates are of the hypothesized signs and statistically significant. The tests for significance are again accomplished using either t-tests or p-values.

Using the estimates of a total or average variable cost function, we can also obtain an estimate of the output at which average cost is a minimum. Remember that when average variable cost is at its minimum, average variable cost and marginal cost are equal. Thus we can define the minimum of average variable cost as the output at which

$$AVC = MC$$

TABLE 11.2
Summary of a Cubic Specification for Total Variable Cost

	Cubic total variable cost function
Total variable cost	$TVC = aQ + bQ^2 + cQ^3$
Average variable cost	$AVC = a + bQ + cQ^2$
Marginal cost	$MC = a + 2bQ + 3cQ^2$
AVC reaches minimum point	$Q_m = -b/2c$
Restrictions on parameters	$a > 0$ $b < 0$ $c > 0$

FIGURE 11.5
A Potential Data Problem

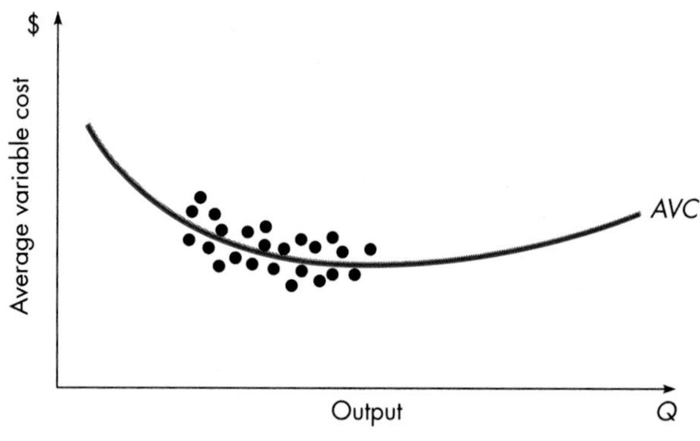

Using the specifications of average variable cost and marginal cost presented above, we can write this condition as

$$a + bQ + cQ^2 = a + 2bQ + 3cQ^2$$

or

$$bQ + 2cQ^2 = 0$$

Solving for Q, the level of output at which average variable cost is minimized is

$$Q_m = -b/2c$$

Table 11.2 summarizes the mathematical properties of a cubic specification for total variable cost.

Before estimating a short-run cost function, we want to mention a potential problem that can arise when the data for average variable cost are clustered around the minimum point of the average cost curve, as shown in Figure 11.5. If the average variable cost function is estimated using data points clustered as shown in the figure, the result is that while $\hat{a}$ is positive and $\hat{b}$ is negative, a t-test or a p-value would indicate that $\hat{c}$ is not statistically different from zero. This result does not mean that the average cost curve is not U-shaped. The problem is that because there are no observations for the larger levels of output, the estimation simply cannot determine whether or not average cost is rising over that range of output.

Estimation of Short-Run Costs at Rockford Enterprises: An Example

In October 1997, the manager at Rockford Enterprises decided to estimate the total variable, average variable, and marginal cost functions for the firm. The capital stock at Rockford has remained unchanged since the third quarter of 1995. The manager collected quarterly observations on cost and output over this period and the resulting data were as follows:

Quarter	Output	Average variable cost ($)
1995 (III)	300	$39.23
1995 (IV)	100	40.54
1996 (I)	150	29.62
1996 (II)	250	29.61
1996 (III)	400	49.97
1996 (IV)	200	34.98
1997 (I)	350	47.39
1997 (II)	450	62.02
1997 (III)	500	69.69

Average variable cost was measured in nominal (i.e., current) dollars, and the cost data were subject to the effects of inflation. Over the period for which cost was to be estimated, costs had increased due to the effects of inflation. The manager's analyst decided to eliminate the influence of inflation by deflating the nominal costs. Recall that such a deflation involves converting nominal cost into constant-dollar cost by dividing the nominal cost by an appropriate price index. The analyst used the Consumer Price Index (CPI) published in the *Survey of Current Business.* The following values for the CPI were used to deflate the nominal cost data:

Quarter	Consumer Price Index (1992 = 1.00)
1995 (III)	1.082
1995 (IV)	1.086
1996 (I)	1.093
1996 (II)	1.101
1996 (III)	1.108
1996 (IV)	1.116
1997 (I)	1.122
1997 (II)	1.125
1997 (III)	1.129

To obtain the average variable cost (measured in constant dollars) for the 300 units produced in the third quarter of 1995, \$39.23 is divided by 1.082, which gives \$36.26. Repeating this computation for each of the cost figures, the manager obtained the following data set:

Quarter	Output	Deflated average variable cost (\$)
1995 (III)	300	\$36.26
1995 (IV)	100	37.33
1996 (I)	150	27.10
1996 (II)	250	26.89
1996 (III)	400	45.10
1996 (IV)	200	31.34
1997 (I)	350	42.24
1997 (II)	450	55.13
1997 (III)	500	61.73

Given these inflation-adjusted data, the manager estimated the cost functions. As shown above, it is sufficient to estimate any one of the three cost curves in order to obtain the other two because each cost equation is a function of the same three parameters—*a*, *b*, and *c*. The manager decided to estimate the average variable cost function:

$$AVC = a + bQ + cQ^2$$

and obtained the following printout from the estimation of this equation:

DEPENDENT VARIABLE: AVC		R-SQUARE	F-RATIO	P-VALUE ON F
OBSERVATIONS: 9		0.9382	45.527	0.0002
VARIABLE	PARAMETER ESTIMATE	STANDARD ERROR	T-RATIO	P-VALUE
INTERCEPT	44.473	6.487	6.856	0.0005
Q	−0.143	0.0482	−2.967	0.0254
Q2	0.000362	0.000079	4.582	0.0037

After the estimates were obtained, the manager determined that the estimated coefficients had the theoretically required signs: $\hat{a} > 0$, $\hat{b} < 0$, and $\hat{c} > 0$. To determine whether these coefficients are statistically significant, the *p*-values were examined, and the exact level of significance for each of the estimated coefficients was acceptably low (all the *t*-ratios are significant at better than the 5 percent level of significance).

The estimated average variable cost function for Rockford Enterprises is, therefore,

$$\widehat{AVC} = 44.473 - 0.143Q + 0.000362Q^2$$

which conforms to the shape of the average variable cost curve in Figure 11.4. As emphasized above, the marginal cost and total variable cost equations are easily determined from the estimated parameters of *AVC*, and no further regression analysis is necessary. In this case,

$$\begin{aligned}\widehat{MC} &= \hat{a} + 2\hat{b}Q + 3\hat{c}Q^2 \\ &= 44.473 - 0.286Q + 0.0011Q^2\end{aligned}$$

and

$$\begin{aligned}\widehat{TVC} &= \hat{a}Q + \hat{b}Q^2 + \hat{c}Q^3 \\ &= 44.473Q - 0.143Q^2 + 0.000362Q^3\end{aligned}$$

To illustrate the use of the estimated cost equations, suppose the manager wishes to calculate the marginal cost, average variable cost, and total variable cost when Rockford is producing 350 units of output. Using the estimated marginal cost equation, the marginal cost associated with 350 units is

$$\begin{aligned}MC &= 44.473 - 0.286(350) + 0.0011(350)^2 \\ &= 44.473 - 100.10 + 134.75 \\ &= \$79.12\end{aligned}$$

Average variable cost for this level of output is

$$\begin{aligned}AVC &= 44.473 - 0.143(350) + 0.000362(350)^2 \\ &= 44.473 - 50.05 + 44.345 \\ &= \$38.77\end{aligned}$$

and total variable cost for 350 units of output is

$$\begin{aligned}TVC &= AVC \times Q \\ &= 38.77 \times 350 \\ &= \$13{,}569\end{aligned}$$

The total cost of 350 units of output would, of course, be $13,569 plus fixed cost.

Finally, the output level at which average variable cost is minimized can be computed as

$$Q_m = -b/2c$$

In this example,

$$\hat{Q}_m = \frac{0.143}{2 \times 0.000362} = 197$$

At Rockford Enterprises, average variable cost reaches its minimum at an output level of 197 units, when

$$\begin{aligned} AVC &= 44.473 - 0.143(197) + 0.000362(197)^2 \\ &= 44.473 - 28.17 + 14.05 \\ &= \$30.35 \end{aligned}$$

5 As you can see from this example, estimation of short-run cost curves is just a straightforward application of cost theory and regression analysis. Many firms do, in fact, use regression analysis to estimate their costs of production.

11.5 SUMMARY

This chapter showed how to specify and estimate a popular form of production and cost functions—the cubic specification. We discussed how to use the results of the estimations to investigate a variety of production and cost issues that are relevant to managerial decision making, such as finding the point of diminishing returns and estimating the values of marginal products and marginal costs.

As we demonstrated, simple linear specifications are not appropriate for the estimation of production functions or cost functions because linear models do not conform to the various theoretical characteristics of long-run or short-run production and cost functions. Instead, we employed a slightly more complicated nonlinear specification, the cubic specification. The mathematical properties of the short-run cubic production and cost specification are summarized again for you in Table 11.3.

Estimation of the short-run cubic production function involves estimating the two parameters A and B. This is accomplished by regressing output on L^3 and L^2 using the technique of regression through the origin. Once A and B are estimated, the estimated t-ratios or p-values are examined to test that A is significantly negative and B is significantly positive. Once estimates of A and B are obtained for any one of the three product equations (TP, AP, and MP), the other two product equations will also have been estimated, since A and B are the only two parameters in all three equations. The cubic production function exhibits all the theoretical properties discussed in Chapter 9.

When estimating cost equations, researchers must be careful to adjust for the effects of inflation. The effects of inflation are removed from the data by "deflating" using price indexes, which can be obtained from a variety of sources including the *Survey of Current Business*, published by the U.S. Department of Commerce and available at most libraries (U.S. government documents section). Researchers must also be careful to use economic costs, rather than accounting costs, to measure the cost of production.

A suitable specification for estimating a set of short-run cost curves (TVC, AVC, and MC) is a cubic TVC equation with the associated AVC and MC equations summarized in Table 11.3. If $a > 0$, $b < 0$, and $c > 0$, the total variable cost curve has the typical S-shape and average variable cost and marginal cost are U-shaped. Average variable cost reaches its minimum value at an output level of $Q_m = -b/2c$.

This chapter concludes Part IV of this text, which discussed production and cost. Now that revenue and cost relations have been presented, we are ready to proceed with the analysis of managerial decision making in the context of a profit-maximizing firm. In Parts V and VI of this text, you will learn how output, price, and investment decisions are made by managers. The crucial consideration in all decisions made by the manager is economic profit. You now have the tools to estimate both the revenue and cost equations needed for business decision making.

TABLE 11.3
Summary of the Short-Run Cubic Production and Cost Specification

	Short-run cubic production equations
Total product	$Q = AL^3 + BL^2$
Average product of labor	$AP = AL^2 + BL$
Marginal product of labor	$MP = 3AL^2 + 2BL$
Diminishing marginal returns	Beginning at $L_m = -B/3A$
Restrictions on parameters	$A < 0$ $B > 0$

	Short-run cubic cost equations
Total variable cost	$TVC = aQ + bQ^2 + cQ^3$
Average variable cost	$AVC = a + bQ + cQ^2$
Marginal cost	$MC = a + 2bQ + 3cQ^2$
Average variable cost reaches minimum at	$Q_m = -\frac{b}{2c}$
Restrictions on parameters	$a > 0, b < 0, c > 0$

TECHNICAL PROBLEMS

1. Consider the linear long-run production function:

$$Q = aK + bL$$

   Calculate the marginal rate of technical substitution, and explain why this functional form does not conform to the theoretical properties of a production function.

2. Consider the multiplicative production function:

$$Q = aLK$$

   a. Does production require positive amounts of both inputs?
   b. What are the marginal products? Do they diminish?
   c. Does the marginal rate of technical substitution diminish?

3. The following cubic equation is a long-run production function for a firm:

$$Q = -0.002K^3L^3 + 6K^2L^2$$

   Suppose the firm employs 10 units of capital.
   a. What are the equations for the total product, average product, and marginal product of labor curves?
   b. At what level of labor usage does the marginal product of labor begin to diminish?
   c. Calculate the marginal product and average product of labor when 10 units of labor are being employed.

   Now suppose the firm doubles capital usage to 20 units.
   d. What are the equations for the total product, average product, and marginal product of labor curves?

e. What happened to the marginal and average product of labor curves when capital usage increased from 10 to 20 units? Calculate the marginal and average products of labor for 10 units of labor now that capital usage is 20 units. Compare your answer to part *c*. Did the increase in capital usage affect marginal and average product as you expected?

4. A firm estimates its cubic production function of the following form

$$Q = AL^3 + BL^2$$

and obtains the following estimation results:

DEPENDENT VARIABLE: Q		R-SQUARE	F-RATIO	P-VALUE ON F
OBSERVATIONS: 25		0.8457	126.10	0.0001
VARIABLE	PARAMETER ESTIMATE	STANDARD ERROR	T-RATIO	P-VALUE
L3	−0.002	0.0005	−4.00	0.0005
L2	0.400	0.080	5.00	0.0001

a. What are the estimated total, average, and marginal product functions?
b. Are the parameters of the correct sign, and are they significant at the 1 percent level?
c. At what level of labor usage is average product at its maximum?

Now recall the following formulas derived in Chapter 9: $AP = Q/L$, $AVC = w/AP$, and $MC = w/MP$. Assume that the wage rate for labor (w) is \$200.

d. What is output when average product is at its maximum?
e. At the output level for part *d*, what are average variable cost and marginal cost?
f. When the rate of labor usage is 120, what is output? What are *AVC* and *MC* at that output?
g. Conceptually, how could you derive the relevant cost curves from this estimate of the production functions?

5. Consider estimation of a short-run average variable cost function of the form

$$AVC = a + bQ + cQ^2$$

Using time-series data, the estimation procedure produces the following computer output:

DEPENDENT VARIABLE: AVC		R-SQUARE	F-RATIO	P-VALUE ON F
OBSERVATIONS: 15		0.4135	4.230	0.0407
VARIABLE	PARAMETER ESTIMATE	STANDARD ERROR	T-RATIO	P-VALUE
INTERCEPT	30.420202	6.465900	4.70	0.0005
Q	−0.079952	0.030780	−2.60	0.0232
Q2	0.000088	0.000032	2.75	0.0176

a. Do the parameter estimates have the correct signs? Are they statistically significant at the 5 percent level of significance?
b. At what level of output do you estimate average variable cost reaches its minimum value?
c. What is the estimated marginal cost curve?
d. What is the estimated marginal cost when output is 700 units?
e. What is the estimated average variable cost curve?
f. What is the estimated average variable cost when output is 700 units?

APPLIED PROBLEMS

1. You are planning to estimate a short-run production function for your firm, and you have collected the following data on labor usage and output:

Labor usage	Output
3	1
7	2
9	3
11	5
17	8
17	10
20	15
24	18
26	22
28	21
30	23

Does a cubic equation appear to be a suitable specification given these data? You may wish to construct a scatter diagram to help you answer this question.

2. Dimex Fabrication Co., a small manufacturer of sheet-metal body parts for a major U.S. automaker, estimates its long-run production function to be

$$Q = -0.015625K^3L^3 + 10K^2L^2$$

where Q is the number of body parts produced daily, K is the number of sheet-metal presses in its manufacturing plant, and L is the number of labor-hours per day of sheet-metal workers employed by Dimex. Dimex is currently operating with 8 sheet-metal presses.

   a. What is the total product function for Dimex? The average product function? The marginal product function?

   b. Managers at Dimex can expect the marginal product of additional workers to fall beyond what level of labor employment?

   c. Dimex plans to employ 50 workers. Calculate total product, average product, and marginal product.

3. The chief economist for Argus Corporation, a large appliance manufacturer, estimated the firm's short-run cost function for vacuum cleaners using an average variable cost function of the form

$$AVC = a + bQ + cQ^2$$

where AVC = dollars per vacuum cleaner and Q = number of vacuum cleaners produced each month. Total fixed cost each month is $180,000. The following results were obtained:

DEPENDENT VARIABLE: AVC		R-SQUARE	F-RATIO	P-VALUE ON F
OBSERVATIONS: 19		0.7360	39.428	0.0001
VARIABLE	PARAMETER ESTIMATE	STANDARD ERROR	T-RATIO	P-VALUE
INTERCEPT	191.93	54.65	3.512	0.0029
Q	−0.0305	0.00789	−3.866	0.0014
Q2	0.0000024	0.00000098	2.449	0.0262

   a. Are the estimates $\hat{a}$, $\hat{b}$, and $\hat{c}$ statistically significant at the 2 percent level of significance?

   b. Do the results indicate that the average variable cost curve is U-shaped? How do you know?

   c. If Argus Corporation produces 8,000 vacuum cleaners per month, what is the estimated average variable cost? Marginal cost? Total variable cost? Total cost?

   d. Answer part *c*, assuming that Argus produces 10,000 vacuum cleaners monthly.

   e. At what level of output will average variable cost be at a minimum? What is minimum average variable cost?

MATHEMATICAL APPENDIX Empirical Production and Cost Relations

The Cubic Production Function

In Chapter 11, the cubic production function was introduced:

$$Q = aK^3L^3 + bK^2L^2$$

This functional form is best suited for short-run applications, rather than long-run applications. When capital is fixed ($K = \overline{K}$), the short-run cubic production function is

$$Q = a\overline{K}^3L^3 + b\overline{K}^2L^2$$
$$= AL^3 + BL^2$$

where $A = a\overline{K}^3$ and $B = b\overline{K}^2$. This section of the appendix presents the mathematical properties of the short-run cubic production function.

Input usage

In order to produce output, some positive amount of labor is required:

$$Q(0) = A(0)^3 + B(0)^2 = 0$$

Marginal product

The marginal product function for labor is

$$\frac{dQ}{dL} = Q_L = 3AL^2 + 2BL$$

The slope of marginal product is

$$\frac{d^2Q}{dL^2} = Q_{LL} = 6AL + 2B$$

In order for marginal product of labor to first rise, then fall, Q_{LL} must first be positive and then negative. Q_{LL} will be positive, then negative (as more labor is used) when A is negative and B is positive. These are the only restrictions on the short-run cubic production function:

$$A < 0 \quad \text{and} \quad B > 0$$

Marginal product of labor reaches its maximum value at L_m units of labor usage. This occurs when $Q_{LL} = 0$. Setting $Q_{LL} = 0$, and solving for L_m,

$$L_m = -B/3A$$

Average product

The average product function for labor is

$$AP = \frac{Q}{L} = AL^2 + BL$$

Average product reaches its maximum value at L_a units of labor usage. This occurs when $dAP/dL = 2AL + B = 0$. Solving for L_a,

$$L_a = -\frac{B}{2A}$$

The Cubic Cost Function

The cubic cost function,

$$TVC = aQ + bQ^2 + cQ^3$$

generates average and marginal cost curves that have the typical U-shapes set forth in Chapter 9. Since $AVC = TVC/Q$,

$$AVC = a + bQ + cQ^2$$

The slope of the average variable cost function is

$$\frac{dAVC}{dQ} = b + 2cQ$$

Average variable cost is at its minimum value when $dAVC/dQ = 0$, which occurs when $Q = -b/2c$. To guarantee a minimum, the second derivative,

$$\frac{d^2AVC}{dQ^2} = 2c$$

must be positive, which requires c to be positive.

When $Q = 0$, $AVC = a$, which must be positive. In order for average variable cost to have a downward-sloping region, b must be negative. Thus, the parameter restrictions for a short-run cubic cost function are

$$a > 0, \quad b < 0, \quad \text{and} \quad c > 0$$

The marginal cost function is

$$MC = \frac{dTVC}{dQ} = a + 2bQ + 3cQ^2$$

The Cobb-Douglas Production Function

In Chapter 11, we used a cubic specification for estimating the production function. In this appendix, we show you another nonlinear specification of the production function that has been widely used in business economics applications. We will describe the mathematical properties of both the long-run and the short-run Cobb-Douglas production function and explain how to estimate the parameters using regression analysis. In order to help you distinguish between the Cobb-Douglas form and the cubic form, we will use Greek letters to represent the parameters of the Cobb-Douglas functions.

The long-run Cobb-Douglas production function: $Q = \gamma K^{\alpha} L^{\beta}$

INPUT USAGE In order to produce output, both inputs are required:

$$Q(0, L) = \gamma 0^{\alpha} L^{\beta} = Q(K, 0) = \gamma K^{\alpha} 0^{\beta} = 0$$

MARGINAL PRODUCTS The marginal product functions for capital and labor are

$$\frac{\partial Q}{\partial K} = Q_K = \alpha \gamma K^{\alpha - 1} L^{\beta} = \alpha \frac{Q}{K}$$

and

$$\frac{\partial Q}{\partial L} = Q_L = \beta \gamma K^{\alpha} L^{\beta - 1} = \beta \frac{Q}{L}$$

In order that the marginal products be positive, α and β must be positive. The second derivatives,

$$\frac{\partial^2 Q}{\partial K^2} = Q_{KK} = \alpha(\alpha - 1)\ \gamma K^{\alpha - 2} L^{\beta}$$

and

$$\frac{\partial^2 Q}{\partial L^2} = Q_{LL} = \beta(\beta - 1)\ \gamma K^{\alpha} L^{\beta - 2}$$

demonstrate that, if the marginal products are diminishing (i.e., Q_{KK} and $Q_{LL} < 0$), α and β must be less than one.

MARGINAL RATE OF TECHNICAL SUBSTITUTION From Chapter 10, the *MRTS* of L for K is Q_L/Q_K. In the context of the Cobb-Douglas function,

$$MRTS = \frac{Q_L}{Q_K} = \frac{\beta}{\alpha} \cdot \frac{K}{L}$$

Note first that the *MRTS* is invariant to output,

$$\frac{\partial MRTS}{\partial Q} = 0$$

Hence, the Cobb-Douglas production is *homothetic*—the production function has a straight-line expansion path and changes in the output level have no effect on relative input usage. Moreover, the *MRTS* demonstrates that the Cobb-Douglas production function is characterized by convex isoquants. Taking the derivative of the *MRTS* with respect to L,

$$\frac{\partial MRTS}{\partial L} = -\frac{\beta}{\alpha} \cdot \frac{K}{L^2}$$

Hence, the *MRTS* diminishes as capital is replaced with labor: the isoquants are convex.

OUTPUT ELASTICITIES Output elasticities are defined as

$$E_K = \frac{\partial Q}{\partial K} \cdot \frac{K}{Q} = Q_K \cdot \frac{K}{Q}$$

and

$$E_L = \frac{\partial Q}{\partial L} \cdot \frac{L}{Q} = Q_L \cdot \frac{L}{Q}$$

Using the Cobb-Douglas specification,

$$E_K = \left(\alpha \frac{Q}{K}\right) \cdot \frac{K}{Q} = \alpha$$

and

$$E_L = \left(\beta \frac{Q}{L}\right) \cdot \frac{L}{Q} = \beta.$$

THE FUNCTION COEFFICIENT Begin with a production function, $Q = Q(K, L)$. Suppose that the levels of usage of both inputs are increased by the same proportion (λ); i.e., $Q = Q(\lambda K, \lambda L)$. The definition of the function coefficient ($\mathscr{E}$) is

$$\mathscr{E} = \frac{dQ/Q}{d\lambda/\lambda}$$

Take the total differential of the production function

$$dQ = Q_K dK + Q_L dL$$

and rewrite this as

$$dQ = Q_K K \frac{dK}{K} + Q_L L \frac{dL}{L}$$

Since K and L were increased by the same proportion, $dK/K = dL/L = d\lambda/\lambda$. Thus,

$$dQ = \frac{d\lambda}{\lambda}(Q_K K + Q_L L)$$

Using this expression, the function coefficient is

$$\mathcal{E} = Q_K \cdot \frac{K}{Q} + Q_L \cdot \frac{L}{Q} = E_K + E_L$$

In the context of the Cobb-Douglas production function, it follows that

$$\mathcal{E} = \alpha + \beta$$

Estimating the long-run Cobb-Douglas production function

The mathematical properties of the Cobb-Douglas production function make it a popular specification for estimating long-run production functions. After converting to natural logarithms, the estimable form of the Cobb-Douglas function ($Q = \gamma K^{\alpha} L^{\beta}$) is

$$\ln Q = \ln \gamma + \alpha \ln K + \beta \ln L$$

Recall from the previous discussion that $\hat{\alpha}$ and $\hat{\beta}$ are estimates of the output elasticities of capital and labor, respectively. Recall also that the estimated marginal products,

$$\widehat{MP}_K = \hat{\alpha}\frac{Q}{K} \quad \text{and} \quad \widehat{MP}_L = \hat{\beta}\frac{Q}{L}$$

are significantly positive and decreasing (the desired theoretical property) if the t-tests or p-values on $\hat{\alpha}$ and $\hat{\beta}$ indicate that these coefficients are significantly positive but less than 1 in value.

The function coefficient is estimated as

$$\hat{\xi} = \hat{\alpha} + \hat{\beta}$$

and provides a measure of returns to scale. In order to determine whether $\hat{\alpha} + \hat{\beta}$ is significantly greater (less) than 1, a t-test is performed. If $\hat{\alpha} + \hat{\beta}$ is not significantly greater (less) than 1, we cannot reject the existence of constant returns to scale. To determine whether the sum, $\hat{\alpha} + \hat{\beta}$, is significantly different from 1, we use the following t-statistic:

$$t_{\hat{\alpha}+\hat{\beta}} = \frac{(\hat{\alpha} + \hat{\beta}) - 1}{S_{\hat{\alpha}+\hat{\beta}}}$$

where the value 1 indicates that we are testing "different from" and $S_{\hat{\alpha}+\hat{\beta}}$ is the estimated standard error of the sum of the estimated coefficients ($\hat{\alpha} + \hat{\beta}$). After calculating this t-statistic, it is compared to the critical t-value from the table. Again note that since the calculated t-statistic can be negative (when $\hat{\alpha} + \hat{\beta}$ is less than 1), it is the absolute value of the t-statistic that is compared with the critical t-value. Some statistical software can give p-values for this test.

The only problem in performing this test involves obtaining the estimated standard error of $\hat{\alpha} + \hat{\beta}$. All regression packages can provide the analyst, upon request, with variances and covariances of the regression coefficients, $\hat{\alpha}$ and $\hat{\beta}$, in a variance-covariance matrix.* Traditionally, variances of $\hat{\alpha}$ and $\hat{\beta}$ are denoted as Var($\hat{\alpha}$) and Var($\hat{\beta}$) and the covariance between $\hat{\alpha}$ and $\hat{\beta}$ as Cov($\hat{\alpha}$, $\hat{\beta}$). As you may remember from a statistics course,

$$\text{Var}(\hat{\alpha} + \hat{\beta}) = \text{Var}(\hat{\alpha}) + \text{Var}(\hat{\beta}) + 2\,\text{Cov}(\hat{\alpha}, \hat{\beta})$$

The estimated standard error of $\hat{\alpha} + \hat{\beta}$ is

$$S_{\hat{\alpha}+\hat{\beta}} = \sqrt{\text{Var}(\hat{\alpha}) + \text{Var}(\hat{\beta}) + 2\,\text{Cov}(\hat{\alpha}, \hat{\beta})}$$

The short-run Cobb-Douglas production function

When capital is fixed in the short run at $\bar{K}$, the short-run Cobb-Douglas production function is

$$Q = \gamma \bar{K}^{\alpha} L^{\beta} = \delta L^{\beta}$$

where $\delta = \gamma \bar{K}^{\alpha}$. Note that if L is 0, no output is forthcoming. In order for output to be positive, δ must be positive. The marginal product of labor is

$$Q_L = \delta \beta L^{\beta - 1}$$

In order for marginal product to be positive, β must be positive. The second derivative

$$Q_{LL} = \beta(\beta - 1)\delta L^{\beta - 2}$$

reveals that if the marginal product of labor is diminishing, β must be less than 1. Thus, the restrictions for the Cobb-Douglas production in the short run are

$$\delta > 0 \quad \text{and} \quad 0 < \beta < 1$$

*The variance-covariance matrix is a listing (in the form of a matrix on the computer printout) of the estimated variances and covariances of all the estimated coefficients. For example, in the regression of $Y = \alpha + \beta X$, the variance-covariance matrix provides estimates of Var($\hat{\alpha}$), Var($\hat{\beta}$), and Cov($\hat{\alpha}$, $\hat{\beta}$). As noted in Chapter 5, the variance of a regression coefficient provides a measure of the dispersion of the variable about its mean. The covariance of the regression coefficients provides information about the joint distribution, that is, the relation between the two regression coefficients.

Estimating the short-run Cobb-Douglas production function

As in the case of the long-run Cobb-Douglas production function, the short-run Cobb-Douglas production function must also be transformed into a linear form by converting it to natural logarithms. The equation actually estimated is

$$\ln Q = \tau + \beta \ln L$$

where $\tau = \ln \delta$. Recall that β must be positive for the marginal product of labor to be positive and less than 1 for the marginal product to be decreasing (i.e., $0 < \beta < 1$). It is common practice to test that $\beta > 0$ and $\beta < 1$ using a *t*-test.

Estimation of a Long-Run Cost Function

Since the general form for the long-run cost function with two inputs is

$$LTC = f(Q, w, r)$$

and since cross-sectional data are generally used for long-run estimation, the empirical specification of a long-run cost function must, as emphasized above, include the prices of inputs as explanatory variables. At first glance, it would appear that the solution would be simply to add the input prices as additional explanatory variables in the cost function developed above and express total cost as

$$LTC = aQ + bQ^2 + cQ^3 + dw + er$$

This function, however, fails to satisfy a basic characteristic of cost functions. A total cost function can be written as $LTC = wL + rK$. If both input prices double, holding output constant, input usage will not change but total cost will double. Letting LTC' denote total cost after input prices double,

$$\begin{aligned} LTC' &= (2w)L + (2r)K \\ &= 2(wL + rK) \\ &= 2LTC \end{aligned}$$

The long-run cost function suggested above does not satisfy this requirement. For a given output, if input prices double,

$$\begin{aligned} LTC' &= aQ + bQ^2 + cQ^3 + d(2w) + e(2r) \\ &= aQ + bQ^2 + cQ^3 + dw + er + (dw + er) \\ &= LTC + dw + er \end{aligned}$$

and LTC' is not equal to $2LTC$.

Therefore, an alternative form for estimating a long-run cost function must be found. The most commonly employed form is a log-linear specification such as the Cobb-Douglas specifications. With this type of specification, the total cost function is expressed as

$$LTC = \alpha Q^{\beta} w^{\gamma} r^{\delta}$$

Using this functional form, when input prices double while holding output constant:

$$\begin{aligned} LTC' &= \alpha Q^{\beta}(2w)^{\gamma}(2r)^{\delta} \\ &= 2^{(\gamma+\delta)}(\alpha Q^{\beta} w^{\gamma} r^{\delta}) \\ &= 2^{(\gamma+\delta)} LTC \end{aligned}$$

If $\gamma + \delta = 1$, doubling input prices indeed doubles the total cost of producing a given level of output—the required characteristic of a cost function. Hence, it is necessary to *impose* this condition on the proposed log-linear cost function by defining δ as $1 - \gamma$; so

$$\begin{aligned} LTC &= \alpha Q^{\beta} w^{\gamma} r^{1-\gamma} \\ &= \alpha Q^{\beta} w^{\gamma} r^{-\gamma} r \\ &= \alpha Q^{\beta} (w/r)^{\gamma} r \end{aligned}$$

The parameter restrictions are $\alpha > 0$, $\beta > 0$, and $0 < \gamma < 1$, which ensure that total cost is positive and increases when output and input prices increase.

To estimate the above total cost equation, it must be converted to natural logarithms:

$$\ln LTC = \ln \alpha + \beta \ln Q + \gamma \ln\left(\frac{w}{r}\right) + 1 \ln r$$

While we can estimate the parameters α, β, and γ, this formulation requires that the coefficient for $\ln r$ be *precisely* equal to one. If we were to estimate this equation, such a value cannot be guaranteed. To impose this condition on the empirical cost function, we simply move $\ln r$ to the left-hand side of the equation to obtain

$$\ln LTC - \ln r = \ln \alpha + \beta \ln Q + \gamma \ln (w/r)$$

which, using the rules of logarithms, can be rewritten as

$$\ln\left(\frac{LTC}{r}\right) = \ln \alpha + \beta \ln Q + \gamma \ln (w/r)$$

This equation is then estimated in order to obtain an estimate of the long-run cost function.

As noted earlier, the primary use of the long-run cost function is in the firm's investment decision. Therefore, once the above cost equation is estimated, its most important use is determining the extent of economies of scale. From the discussion of log-linear functions in Chapter 5, the coefficient β indicates the *elasticity of total cost* with respect to output; that is,

$$\beta = \frac{\text{Percentage change in total cost}}{\text{Percentage change in output}}$$

When $\beta > 1$, cost is increasing more than proportionately to output (e.g., if the percentage change in output is 25 percent and the percentage change in cost is 50 percent, β would be equal to 2); therefore long-run average cost would be increasing. Hence if $\beta > 1$, the estimates indicate diseconomies of scale. If $\beta < 1$, total cost increases proportionately less than the increase in output and economies of scale would be indicated. Furthermore, note that the magnitude of the estimate of β indicates the "strength" of the economies or diseconomies of scale. Finally, if $\beta = 1$, there are constant returns to scale. The statistical significance of β is tested in the manner outlined earlier. Table 11A.1 summarizes the mathematical properties of the Cobb-Douglas specification for long-run total cost.

TABLE 11A.1

Summary of the Cobb-Douglas Specification for Long-Run Total Cost

Long-run total cost	$LTC = \alpha Q^{\beta} w^{\gamma} r^{1-\gamma}$ $= \alpha Q^{\beta}\left(\frac{w}{r}\right)^{\gamma} r$
Estimable form	$\ln\left[\frac{LTC}{r}\right] = \ln\alpha + \beta\ln Q + \gamma\ln\left(\frac{w}{r}\right)$
Elasticity of total cost	$\beta = \frac{\%\Delta LTC}{\%\Delta Q}$
If $\begin{Bmatrix}\beta < 1\\ \beta = 1\\ \beta > 1\end{Bmatrix}$ there exist $\begin{Bmatrix}\text{economies of}\\ \text{constant returns to}\\ \text{diseconomies of}\end{Bmatrix}$ scale	
Restrictions on parameters	$\alpha > 0$ $\beta > 0$ $0 < \gamma < 1$

MATHEMATICAL EXERCISES

1. Why would the restrictions $A > 0$ and $B < 0$ be inappropriate for a short-run cubic production function?
2. For the short-run cubic production function, show that increasing $\bar{K}$ always results in an increase in the level of labor usage at which diminishing returns begin.
3. Consider the Cobb-Douglas production function $Q = 36K^{0.5}L^{1.0}$.
   a. Find the marginal product functions.
   b. Write equations for the *MRTS* and the output elasticities.
   c. The function coefficient is equal to ________, so the production function is characterized by ________ returns to scale.
4. Let the long-run total cost function be $LTC = (1/12)Qw^{0.5}r^{0.5}$.
   a. Demonstrate that a doubling of input prices causes *LTC* to double.

b. Find the elasticity of total cost. This long-run total cost function is characterized by ________ scale.

c. Let $w = \$16$ and $r = \$25$, and find *LMC* and *LAC*. Graph the *LMC* and *LAC* curves. Are these curves consistent with part *b?*

d. Is your answer to part *b* consistent with your answer to part *d* in Mathematical Exercise 4 in Chapter 10?

Part V
Perfect Competition

CHAPTER 12

Managerial Decision Making in Perfectly Competitive Markets

Now we are ready to get to the bottom line. Literally. Up to this point in the text, we have developed several tools—optimization theory, demand analysis and forecasting, and production and cost analysis—that you may have found interesting enough as single topics. But now, and for the rest of the text, we bring these tools together to build a framework for making the most important decisions affecting the profitability of the firm—how much to produce and what price to charge. We are going to analyze how managers make price and output decisions to maximize the profit of the firm.

As it turns out, the nature of the price and output decision is strongly influenced by the structure of the market in which the firm sells its product. Recall from Chapter 1 that we discussed the characteristics of several market structures. Market structure determines whether a manager will be a price-setter or a price-taker. The theoretical market structure in which firms take the market price as given is called perfect competition. We begin our discussion of pricing and output decisions by examining how managers of price-taking, perfectly competitive firms should make production decisions in order to maximize profit. We will develop a number of important ideas that will carry over and apply to managers who are price-setters. For example, we will demonstrate that output decisions should never be based on considerations of fixed costs, that a firm may find it desirable to continue producing even though the firm is losing money, that a manager should not stop hiring labor just because labor productivity begins to fall, and that in the absence of entry barriers a firm can be expected to earn zero economic profit in the long run.

As we begin our discussion of profit maximization for price-taking firms, you may wonder how many managers are really price-takers, rather than price-setters. In a recent survey of one of our executive M.B.A. classes, even we were surprised to find that 34 of the 38 manager-students felt that their firms had little or no control over the price they could charge for their products; their prices were determined by market forces beyond their control. Although the assumptions of perfect competition, to be set forth in the next section, may seem quite narrowly focused, many managers face market conditions that closely approximate the model of perfect competition. And even if you are a manager of a price-setting firm, you will find the analysis of profit maximization under conditions of perfect competition to be a valuable framework for making profitable decisions.

We assume in this chapter and the following five chapters that the goal of the manager is to maximize the firm's profit. It has been suggested that a manager may have other goals: to maximize the firm's sales, or rate of growth of sales; to maximize the manager's own utility by using the firm's resources for personal benefit; to promote the manager's favorite social causes. As we discussed in Chapter 1, such goals can lead to conflicts between owners and managers. It is our goal in this book to show how to make decisions that will make you a more effective manager, which generally means maximizing the profit of the firm. If you choose a different goal, you do so at your own risk.

As Chapter 1 discussed in some detail, when we assume that a firm maximizes its profit, we refer to its economic profit. Economic profit is the firm's total revenue minus its total cost. Recall that total cost is the sum of explicit or accounting costs, which are payments to outside owners of resources used by the firm, plus implicit cost or normal profit, which is the opportunity cost of using resources owned by the firm owners. Thus

$$\begin{aligned}\text{Economic profit} &= \text{Total revenue} - \text{Total cost}\\ &= \text{Total revenue} - \text{Explicit cost} - \text{Implicit cost (normal profit)}\end{aligned}$$

As you might expect, the manager's profit-maximizing decision is a direct application of the theory of unconstrained maximization, set forth in Chapter 4. Managers of firms that are price-takers look at price and cost conditions to answer three fundamental questions: (1) Should the firm produce or shut down? (2) If the firm produces, what is the optimal level of production? (3) What are the optimal levels of inputs to employ? Since the manager of a perfectly competitive firm takes product price as given, there is obviously no pricing decision.

After briefly setting forth all the characteristics of perfect competition, we first analyze how a manager determines the firm's output or level of production that maximizes profit. We address the short-run decision, when some inputs are fixed, and then the long-run decision, when all inputs are variable. Finally, we discuss how a manager chooses the levels of input usage that maximize profit. We will show that the output and the input decisions each lead to the same results.

12.1 CHARACTERISTICS OF PERFECT COMPETITION

perfect competition
A market structure that exists when (1) all firms produce a homogeneous product, (2) each firm is so small it cannot affect price, (3) entry and exit are unrestricted, and (4) each firm has complete knowledge about production and prices.

As discussed in the introduction to this chapter, the most important characteristic of perfectly competitive markets is that each firm takes the market price of the product it sells as given. We now set forth all the characteristics of **perfect competition:**

1. The product of each firm in a perfectly competitive market is identical to the product of every other firm. This condition ensures that buyers are indifferent as to the firm from which they purchase. Product differences, whether real or imaginary, are precluded under perfect competition. Thus, the market is characterized by a homogeneous (or perfectly standardized) commodity.
2. Each firm in the industry must be so small relative to the total market that it cannot affect the market price of the good it produces by changing its output. If all producers act together, changes in quantity will definitely affect market price. But if perfect competition prevails, each producer is so small that individual changes will go unnoticed. Also, no individual firm is able to affect the price of any input by its usage of that input. Again, all producers could, under certain conditions, change their usage of an input and affect its price. In other words, the actions of any individual firm do not affect the market supply of the product produced or the market demand for any input.
3. There exists unrestricted entry and exit into and out of the industry. Hence, there can be no artificial restrictions on the number of firms in the industry. New firms do not require huge amounts of capital equipment and investment to enter perfectly competitive industries.
4. Each firm has full and complete knowledge about the product and the market. Thus each firm knows the best—least-cost—method of production, the price of output, and input prices. Even potential entrants know whether or not firms in the industry are making economic profits. This assumption of complete information is made for analytical convenience only and is not necessary for the development of the theory.

Because firms in perfectly competitive markets produce identical products and face a given market price, the essence of the theory is that producers do not recognize any competitiveness among themselves; that is, no direct competition among firms exists. Therefore, the theoretical concept of competition in these markets is diametrically opposed to the generally accepted concept of competition. We could say that the automobile industry or the personal computer industry is quite competitive since each firm in these industries must consider what its rivals will do before it makes a decision about advertising campaigns, design changes, quality improvements, and so forth. However, that type of market is far removed from the theory of perfect competition, which permits no personal rivalry. ("Personal" rivalry is personal in the sense that firms consider the reactions of other firms in determining their own policy.) In perfect competition all relevant economic magnitudes are determined by impersonal market forces.

12.2 DEMAND FACING A PERFECTLY COMPETITIVE FIRM

Suppose you are the owner-manager of a small citrus orchard that specializes in the production of oranges, which your firm then processes to be sold as frozen concentrate. You wish to determine the maximum price you can charge for various levels of output of frozen concentrate; that is, you wish to find the demand schedule facing your firm. After consulting *The Wall Street Journal*, you find that the market-determined price of orange juice concentrate is $1.20 per pound. You have 50,000 pounds of concentrate to sell, which makes your output minuscule compared with the tens of millions of pounds of orange juice concentrate sold in the market as a whole. On top of that, you realize that buyers of orange juice concentrate don't care whom they buy from since all orange juice concentrate is virtually identical (homogeneous).

All at once it hits you like a ton of oranges: You can sell virtually all the orange juice concentrate you wish at the going market price of $1.20 per pound. Even if you increased your output tenfold to 500,000 pounds, you could still find buyers willing to pay you $1.20 per pound for the entire 500,000 pounds because your output, by itself, is not going to affect (shift) market supply in any perceptible way. Indeed, if you lowered the price to sell more oranges, you would be needlessly sacrificing revenue. You also realize that you cannot charge a price higher than $1.20 per pound because buyers will simply buy from one of the thousands of other citrus producers that produce orange juice concentrate identical to your own.

By this reasoning, you realize that the demand curve facing your citrus grove can be drawn as shown in Figure 12.1. The demand for your firm's product is horizontal at a price of $1.20 per pound of orange juice concentrate. The demand price for any level of orange juice concentrate is $1.20, no matter how many pounds you produce. This means that every extra pound sold contributes $1.20 to total revenue, and hence the market price of $1.20 is also the marginal revenue for every pound of orange juice concentrate sold. The demand curve facing the citrus producer is also its marginal revenue curve.

We can generalize the above discussion to apply to *any* firm that is perfectly competitive. When a market is characterized by a large number of (relatively) small producers, each producing a homogeneous product, the demand curve facing the manager of each individual firm is horizontal at the price determined by the intersection of the *market* demand and supply curves. In addition, the horizontal demand curve is also the marginal revenue curve facing the manager.

Figure 12.2 illustrates the derivation of demand for a perfectly competitive firm. Note, in the figure, that the *market* demand curve D in Panel A is downward-sloping, which the law of demand always requires of a demand curve. It is the demand curve faced by a single firm that is horizontal, as shown in Panel B of Figure 12.2. Recall from Chapter 2 that demand price is the maximum price buyers can be charged for a given amount of the good. The demand

FIGURE 12.1
Demand and Marginal Revenue Facing a Citrus Producer

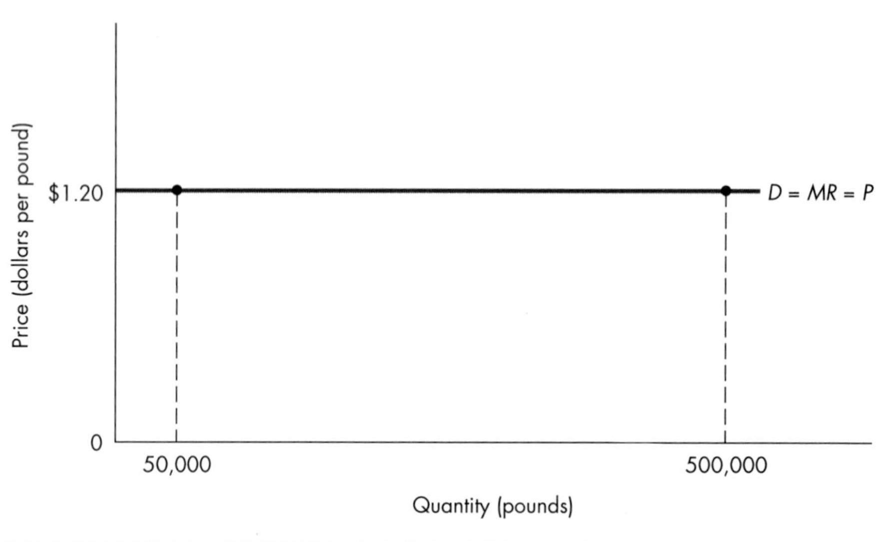

FIGURE 12.2
Derivation of Demand for a Perfectly Competitive Firm

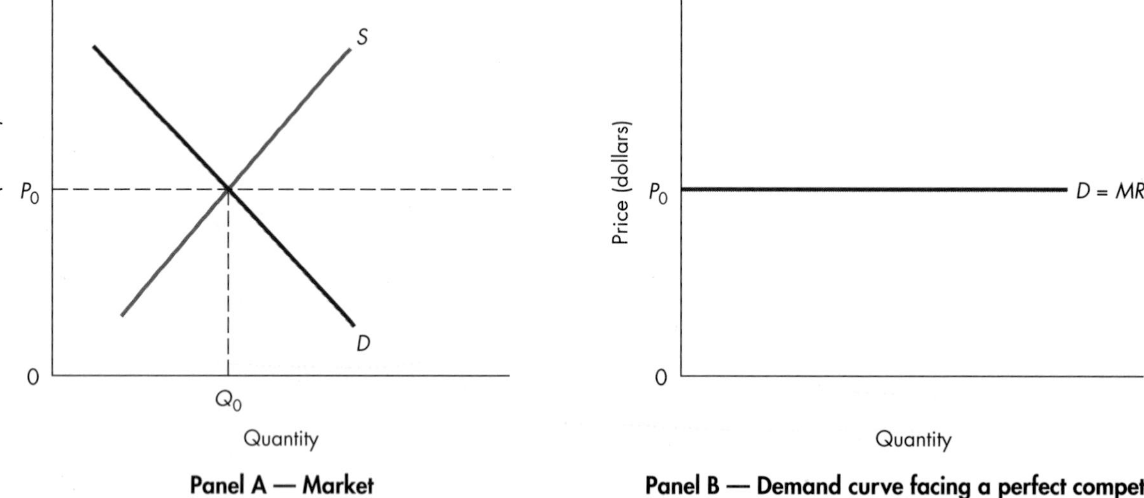

price is constant, and equal to P_0, for any level of output produced by the firm. Since each additional unit sold adds exactly P_0 to total revenue, marginal revenue equals P_0 for all output levels for the firm, as shown in Panel B in Figure 12.2.

The horizontal demand curve facing an individual firm selling in a perfectly competitive market is frequently called a *perfectly* (or infinitely) *elastic demand.* Recall from Chapter 3 that the point elasticity of demand is measured by $E = P/(P - a)$, where a is the price intercept of the demand curve. Measured at any given price, as demand becomes flatter, $|P - a|$ becomes smaller and $|E|$ becomes larger. In the limit when demand is horizontal, $P - a = 0$, and $|E| = \infty$. Thus, for a horizontal demand, demand is said to be infinitely elastic or perfectly elastic.

Looked at another way, the product sold by a perfectly competitive firm has a large number of *perfect* substitutes—the identical (homogeneous) products sold by the other firms in the industry. As we stressed in Chapter 3, the better the substitutes for a product, the more elastic the demand for the product. The perfectly competitive firm's product, with many perfect substitutes, therefore has a perfectly elastic demand.

Again, we emphasize that the fact that perfectly competitive firms face a perfectly elastic or horizontal demand does not mean that the law of demand does not apply to perfectly competitive markets. It does. The *market demand* for the product is downward-sloping.

Relation The demand curve facing the manager of an individual perfectly competitive firm is horizontal or perfectly elastic at the price determined by the intersection of the *market* demand and supply curves. Since marginal revenue equals price for a perfectly competitive firm, the demand curve is also simultaneously the marginal revenue curve under perfect competition (i.e., $D = MR$). The firm can sell all it wants at the market price. Each additional unit of sales adds an amount equal to price to the firm's total revenue.

12.3 PROFIT MAXIMIZATION IN THE SHORT RUN

We now turn to the output decision facing the manager of a firm in a perfectly competitive industry in the short run. Recall that the short run is that time period of decision making during which the firm has at least one of its inputs fixed in quantity. In the short-run period of analysis, the manager has fixed costs that must be paid regardless of the level of output and variable costs that vary with the level of output.

shut down
Condition in which a firm produces zero output but must still pay for fixed inputs.

In the short run, a manager must make two decisions. The first decision is whether to produce or shut down during the period. By **shut down,** we mean the manager decides to produce zero output and to hire none of the variable inputs. When production is zero, the only costs incurred by the firm are the fixed costs. If the first decision is to produce (rather than shut down), the second decision is the choice of the optimal level of output. As noted earlier, when a firm is in a perfectly competitive industry, the manager has no control over price and therefore does not have a pricing decision.

In this section, we first discuss the firm's output decision, assuming that the decision to produce rather than shut down has been made. We then give the conditions under which the manager should choose to shut down rather than produce. Next, a numerical example is presented to emphasize that fixed costs are completely irrelevant for managerial decision making. After briefly summarizing the firm's output decision in the short run, we derive the supply curve for a perfectly competitive firm.

FIGURE 12.3
Finding the Profit-Maximizing Output Level: $P = MC$

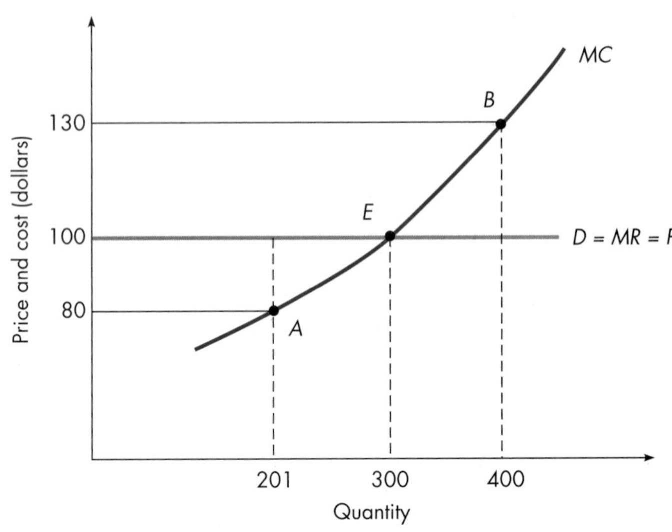

The Manager's Output Decision

We begin by assuming the manager has already decided to produce rather than shut down and must now find the optimal level of output to produce. Using the terminology presented in Chapter 4, the optimal level of output is the level of output that maximizes the objective function, which is economic profit (π):

$$\pi = TR - TC$$

where TR is total revenue and TC is total cost. Under some circumstances, which we discuss later, a firm will choose to incur losses (i.e., profit is negative) yet continue to produce rather than shut down. In such a situation, the manager chooses the level of output that *minimizes* the loss of the firm. Since minimizing a loss is equivalent to maximizing a (negative) profit, the decision rule for finding the optimal level of output is exactly the same regardless of whether profit is positive or negative. For this reason, we will speak of profit maximization in deriving the rule for finding the optimal level of output even though the same rule applies to the firm that is minimizing a loss.

A manager of a profit-maximizing firm will increase its output as long as the marginal revenue (which is equal to price) from selling another unit exceeds the marginal cost of producing that unit. Figure 12.3 illustrates the output decision of a manager. The firm faces a market-determined price of $100, which is the marginal revenue, and the marginal cost curve is MC. Suppose that the firm is producing 200 units of output, which it can sell for a price of $100 per unit, and the marginal cost of the 201st unit is $80 (see point A in Figure 12.3). By choosing to produce and sell the 201st unit, the manager adds $100 to revenue and only \$80 to cost, thereby adding \$20 to the firm's profit. By this same reasoning, the manager would continue to increase production as long as MR (= P) is greater than MC. In Figure 12.3, output would be increased to 300 units, the output level for which $P = MR = MC = \$100$ (point E in Figure 12.3).

If, on the other hand, a mistake has been made and the firm is producing an output of 400 units, at which marginal revenue (price) is less than marginal cost, the manager can increase the firm's profit by reducing output. For example, the marginal cost of producing the 400th unit is \$130, while the price remains \$100 (see point B in Figure 12.3). The manager could decrease output by 1 unit and reduce the firm's cost by \$130 (the cost of the extra resources needed to produce the 400th unit). The lost sale of that unit would reduce revenue by only \$100, so the firm's profit would increase by \$30. By the same reasoning, the manager would continue to decrease production as long as MR (= P) is less than MC (up to point E in Figure 12.3). It follows, then, that the manager maximizes profit by choosing that level of output where MR (= P) = MC. This rule is, of course, the rule for unconstrained maximization set forth in Chapter 4 ($MB = MC$).

We obviously don't mean to imply that the firm begins with zero output and then expands by actually producing and selling the first unit, then the second, and so on, until it produces and sells the last unit, at which MR equals MC. The manager makes the short-run production decision after looking at price and the firm's cost structure. He or she then chooses the optimal level of output to produce.

The Output Decision: Positive Economic Profit

Figure 12.4 shows a typical set of short-run cost curves—marginal cost (MC), average total cost (ATC), and average variable cost (AVC). (Average fixed cost is omitted for convenience and because, as we will demonstrate, it is irrelevant for the output decision.) Suppose that the market-determined price, and therefore the marginal revenue, is \$15 per unit. Marginal revenue equals marginal cost at point E, with 700 units of output being produced and sold.

The firm would not produce less than 700 units. At any lower output, an additional unit sold would add \$15 to the firm's revenue, but since marginal cost is less than \$15 for this unit of output, the cost of producing this additional unit is less than the additional revenue. Thus, at any output lower than 700 units, producing and selling an additional unit of output would increase profit. Likewise, the firm would not produce more than 700 units. Beyond 700 units, a reduction in output would increase profit, because 1 less unit of output would reduce cost by more than \$15, the lost revenue. Thus, producing any output less than or greater than 700 units is not profit-maximizing.

Therefore the firm maximizes profit by producing and selling 700 units of output per period of time. The average total cost of producing 700 units is \$10 per unit, as shown from ATC in the figure. Thus, the total cost of production is average total cost times quantity, or $\$10 \times 700 = \$7{,}000$. Total revenue, price times quantity, is $\$15 \times 700 = \$10{,}500$. The maximum possible profit is, therefore, $\$10{,}500 - \$7{,}000 = \$3{,}500$.

FIGURE 12.4
Profit Maximization in the Short Run

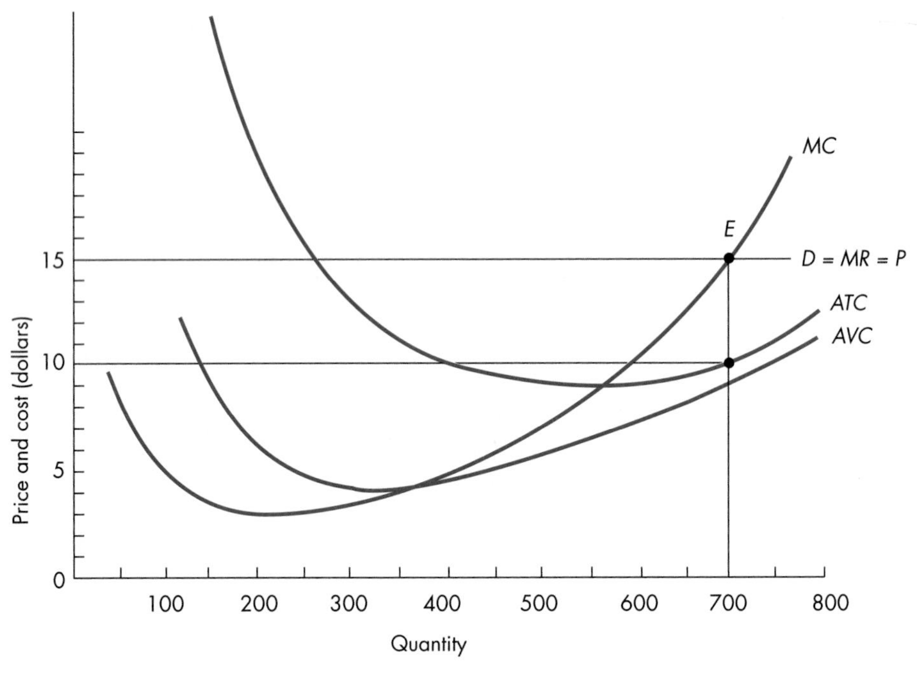

Since the \$7,000 total cost includes the normal profit or opportunity cost of the resources provided by the firm's owners, the owners are earning \$3,500 more than they could if they had employed their resources in their best alternative use. The \$3,500 economic profit is a return to the owners *in excess* of what they could have earned in their best alternative. As explained earlier, when a firm earns positive economic profit, it is earning more than a normal profit or more than a normal rate of return.

The Output Decision: The Firm Operates at a Loss

In the short run, when the manager of a perfectly competitive firm faces a market-determined price that is less than average total cost ($P < ATC$) at every level of output, total revenue must be less than total cost at every level of output and the firm will incur a loss no matter what output it produces. Therefore, the manager must decide whether to produce the output that leads to the smallest loss or to shut down the firm, produce zero output, and lose all its fixed costs. The decision rule is simple: The firm should produce a positive output and suffer a loss only if that loss is smaller than the loss the firm would incur by producing nothing (shutting down). The firm should shut down and produce nothing if the loss at zero output is less than the smallest loss it could incur by producing a positive level of output. When a firm produces nothing, it loses an amount equal

FIGURE 12.5
Loss Minimization in the Short Run

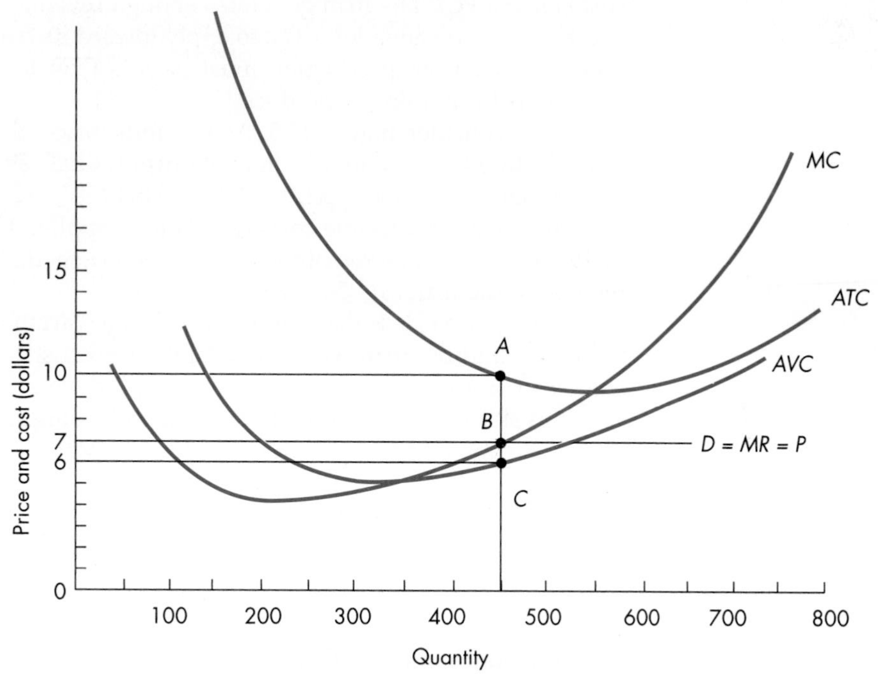

to its total fixed cost ($\pi = -TFC$). The firm's total revenue is zero, and its total cost is equal to its fixed cost since variable cost is zero.

Figure 12.5 illustrates the manager's decision to produce or to shut down. Suppose the manager faces a price of \$7. The firm must suffer a loss at every output level because \$7 is less than average total cost ($P < ATC$) at all levels of output. If the manager does decide to produce, rather than shut down, the firm should produce 450 units where MR (= P) = MC = \$7. At 450 units of output, total revenue is \$3,150 (= \$7 × 450), total cost is \$4,500 (= \$10 × 450), and the firm earns a (negative) profit equal to −\$1,350 (= \$3,150 − \$4,500). The manager should choose to produce 450 units at a loss of \$1,350 only if the firm would lose more than \$1,350 by producing nothing.

To compute the total fixed cost (the loss when $Q = 0$), recall that $TFC = AFC \times Q$. Also recall that $AFC = ATC - AVC$. You can see in Figure 12.5 that AFC = \$4 (the distance from A to C, or \$10 − \$6), so TFC = \$4 × \$450 = \$1,800. The manager should produce 450 units at a loss of \$1,350 rather than produce zero units (shut down) and lose \$1,800.

In a short-run situation when a firm cannot earn positive economic profit ($P < ATC$), a manager should make the decision to produce or shut down production using the following rule: If the price exceeds the average variable cost ($P > AVC$), the firm should produce the level of output where $P = MC$ rather than produce nothing at all. When $P > AVC$, total revenue exceeds total variable cost ($TR > TVC$). The firm generates enough revenue to pay all its variable costs and has some revenue left over to apply toward its fixed costs. Consequently, the loss incurred from production must be less than total fixed cost, which is the amount lost if nothing is produced.

Again consider Figure 12.5. At 450 units, price ($7) exceeds average variable cost ($6) by $1. Thus, on 450 units of output, total revenue ($3,150) exceeds total variable cost ($6 × 450 = $2,700) by $450 ($3,150 − $2,700). The $450 revenue left over after paying variable costs can then be applied toward paying a part of the $1,800 fixed cost. The remainder of the fixed costs that are not covered represent the loss to the firm ($1,350 = $1,800 − $450).

When price is less than minimum average variable cost ($P < AVC$), TR is less than TVC, and the firm would lose all its fixed costs plus the portion of its variable costs not covered by revenues if it produces. The firm could improve its earnings situation by producing nothing and losing only fixed cost. We can summarize the manager's decision to produce or not to produce with a principle:

Principle In the short run, the manager of a firm will choose to produce, rather than shut down, as long as total revenue more than covers the total variable costs of production ($TR > TVC$) or, equivalently, price exceeds average variable cost ($P > AVC$). If price is less than average variable cost ($P < AVC$), the manager will produce nothing and lose only fixed costs.

The Irrelevance of Fixed Costs

When managers make production decisions, they decide how much to produce (if they do produce) by choosing the level of output where price equals marginal cost. They decide whether or not to produce that output by comparing price with average variable cost. If $P > AVC$, the firm should produce (even at a loss) the output level at which $P = MC$. Thus, fixed costs or sunk costs play absolutely no role in the manager's output decision.

To provide you with more insight into why fixed costs do not matter in decision making, we remind you that the marginal cost curve is unaffected by changes in fixed cost. Recall from Chapter 9 that the U-shape of the marginal cost curve is determined by the S-shape of the total variable cost curve or the ∩-shape of the marginal product curve. In Figure 12.5, for example, any change whatsoever in fixed cost has no effect on the marginal cost curve. If total fixed costs double, MC does not shift or change shape, and marginal revenue still intersects marginal cost at the same level of output. No matter what the level of fixed costs, 450 units is the profit-maximizing (loss-minimizing) level of output when price is $7.

To illustrate that fixed costs do not affect the decision to produce or not to produce, we chose five different levels of total fixed costs and examined the shutdown decision for a firm with the MC and AVC curves shown in Figure 12.5. Keeping market price at $7, Table 12.1 shows all the relevant revenue, cost, and profit information for each of the five levels of fixed cost. First note that the optimal level of production for any of the five levels of fixed cost is 450 units because MC equals $7 at 450 units, no matter what the level of fixed costs. In all

TABLE 12.1
The Irrelevance of Fixed Costs

(1) Total fixed costs	(2) Price	(3) Output	(4) Total revenue	(5) Total variable costs	(6) Revenue remaining after paying variable costs	(7) Profit (loss) if Q = 450	(8) Profit (loss) if Q = 0
$ 200	$7	450	$3,150	$2,700	$450	$ 250	$ −200
1,800	7	450	3,150	2,700	450	−1,350	−1,800
3,000	7	450	3,150	2,700	450	−2,550	−3,000
10,000	7	450	3,150	2,700	450	−9,550	−10,000
100,000	7	450	3,150	2,700	450	−99,550	−100,000

cases shown in Table 12.1, total revenue is $3,150, total variable cost is $2,700, and, after all variable costs are paid, $450 remains to apply toward the fixed costs.

When fixed cost is only $200, economic profit is positive because revenue exceeds all costs. Obviously the manager chooses to produce and earn a profit, rather than produce nothing and lose the fixed cost. For each of the other four cases, the revenue remaining after paying variable cost is not enough to pay all the fixed cost, and profit is negative. Columns 7 and 8, respectively, show the loss if the firm produces 450 units (where $P = MC$) and the loss if the firm produces nothing and loses its fixed cost.

Note that in all cases when the firm makes a loss, the loss from producing 450 units is $450 less than the loss if the firm shuts down. No matter how high the total fixed cost, the firm loses $450 less by producing a positive amount of output than by producing nothing (shutting down). The level of fixed cost has

5 no effect on the firm's decision to produce.

Summary of the Manager's Output Decision in the Short Run

Figure 12.6 summarizes three possible short-run situations for the firm. First, if the market-established price is P_1, the demand and marginal revenue facing the firm are D_1 and MR_1. The optimal output for the firm to produce is at point *A*, where $MC = P_1$, and the firm will produce q_1 units of output. Since *ATC* is less than price at q_1, the firm makes an economic profit.

Next let the market price fall to P_2. Price equals *MC* at point *C*. Because average total cost is greater than price at this output, total cost is greater than total revenue, and the firm suffers a loss. The amount of loss is the loss per unit (*CR*) times the number of units produced (q_2).

When price is P_2 and demand is $D_2 = MR_2$, there is simply no way the firm can earn a profit. At every output level, average total cost exceeds price. The firm will continue to produce if, and only if, it loses less by producing than by closing the plant entirely. If the firm produced zero output, total revenue would also be zero and total cost would be the total fixed cost. The loss would thus be equal to total fixed cost. If the firm produces where $MC = MR_2$ (point *C*), total

FIGURE 12.6
Profit, Loss, or Shutdown in the Short Run

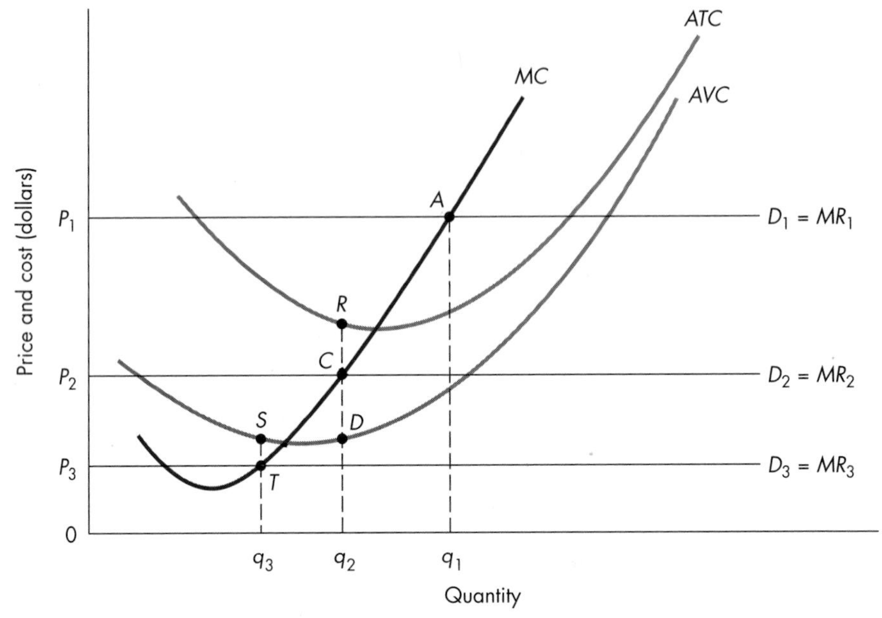

revenue is greater than total variable cost, because $P_2 > AVC$ at q_2 units of output. The firm covers all its variable costs and still has *CD* times the number of units produced (q_2) left over to pay part of its fixed cost. A smaller loss is suffered when production takes place than would be the case if the firm were shut down. The loss is that part of fixed cost not covered by revenue and is clearly less than the entire fixed cost.

Finally, in Figure 12.6, suppose that the market price is P_3. Demand is given by $D_3 = MR_3$. If the firm were to produce, its equilibrium would be at *T*, where $MC = P_3$. Output would be q_3 units per period of time. However, since the average variable cost of production exceeds price, not only would the firm lose all its fixed costs but it would also lose *ST* dollars per unit on its variable costs as well. The firm could improve its earnings situation by producing nothing and losing only fixed cost. Thus when price is below average variable cost at every level of output, the short-run, loss-minimizing output is zero.

As discussed in Chapter 9 and as shown in Figure 12.6, average variable cost reaches its minimum at the point at which marginal cost and average variable cost intersect. If price is less than the minimum average variable cost, the loss-minimizing output is zero. For any price equal to or greater than minimum average variable cost, equilibrium output is determined by the intersection of marginal cost and price.[1]

[1]This result is demonstrated mathematically in the appendix to this chapter.

ILLUSTRATION 12.1

Do R&D Expenditures Affect Drug Prices?

In August 1997, the Clinton administration announced that drug companies will be required to test whether the medicines they sell for adults are also safe and effective for children and to put the pediatric dosages on the labels. It was estimated that the new requirement would increase the cost of drug development by more than $200 million annually. A former official with the Food and Drug Administration (FDA), in an editorial in *The Wall Street Journal,* noted that this regulation would delay the introduction of new drugs and that "government regulation imposes enormous costs on drug development that must be passed along to consumers in higher prices."*

A well-known economist, in a follow-up letter to the *WSJ,* agreed that more stringent requirements would increase expected research costs per product introduction.[†] However, he disagreed that increased costs of drug development would be passed along to consumers in higher prices. He pointed out, "Nearly all pharmaceutical research and development costs are borne prior to FDA approval and before the first dose is ever sold." Such costs would be fixed or sunk costs and would not affect a firm's price or output decisions: "The value of a product depends on its acceptance in the marketplace and the costs of producing another unit of output, but not at all on whether it was discovered either after a long and arduous effort or fortuitously at the first attempt."

According to the letter, price setting depends on anticipated future conditions and not on those in the past, even though expected research costs may affect research budgets and thereby the number of new products in the future. These costs would not influence prices charged for products already discovered.

This response reinforces our emphasis in this text that sunk costs, already borne, and fixed costs, which must be paid no matter what decision is made, should not be taken into account in price and output decisions. There is, however, more to this story, which we will continue in Illustration 12.2 after we set forth the theory of the firm in the long run.

*Henry I. Miller, "FDA Loves Kids So Much, It'll Make You Sick," *The Wall Street Journal,* Aug. 18, 1997.

†William S. Comanor, "Higher Price Means Better Medicine," *The Wall Street Journal,* Sept. 9, 1997.

Principle (1) Average variable cost tells whether to produce; the firm ceases to produce—shuts down—if price falls below minimum *AVC.* (2) Marginal cost tells how much to produce; if $P >$ minimum *AVC,* the firm produces the output at which $MC = P$. (3) Average total cost tells how much profit or loss is made if the firm decides to produce; profit equals the difference between *P* and *ATC* multiplied by the quantity produced and sold.

12.4 SHORT-RUN SUPPLY FOR THE FIRM AND INDUSTRY

Using the concepts developed in the preceding discussion, it is possible to derive the short-run supply curve for an individual firm in a perfectly competitive market. Figure 12.7 illustrates the process. In Panel A, points *a, b,* and *c* are the profit-maximizing equilibrium points for the firm at prices of $5, $9, and $17, respectively. That is, the marginal cost curve above average variable cost indicates the quantity the firm would be willing and able to supply at each price, which is the definition of supply. Panel B shows 80, 110, and 150 units of output as the quantities supplied from Panel A when market price is $5, $9, and $17, respectively. For a market price lower than minimum average variable cost, quantity supplied is zero.

FIGURE 12.7
Derivation of a Short-Run Supply Curve for an Individual Firm

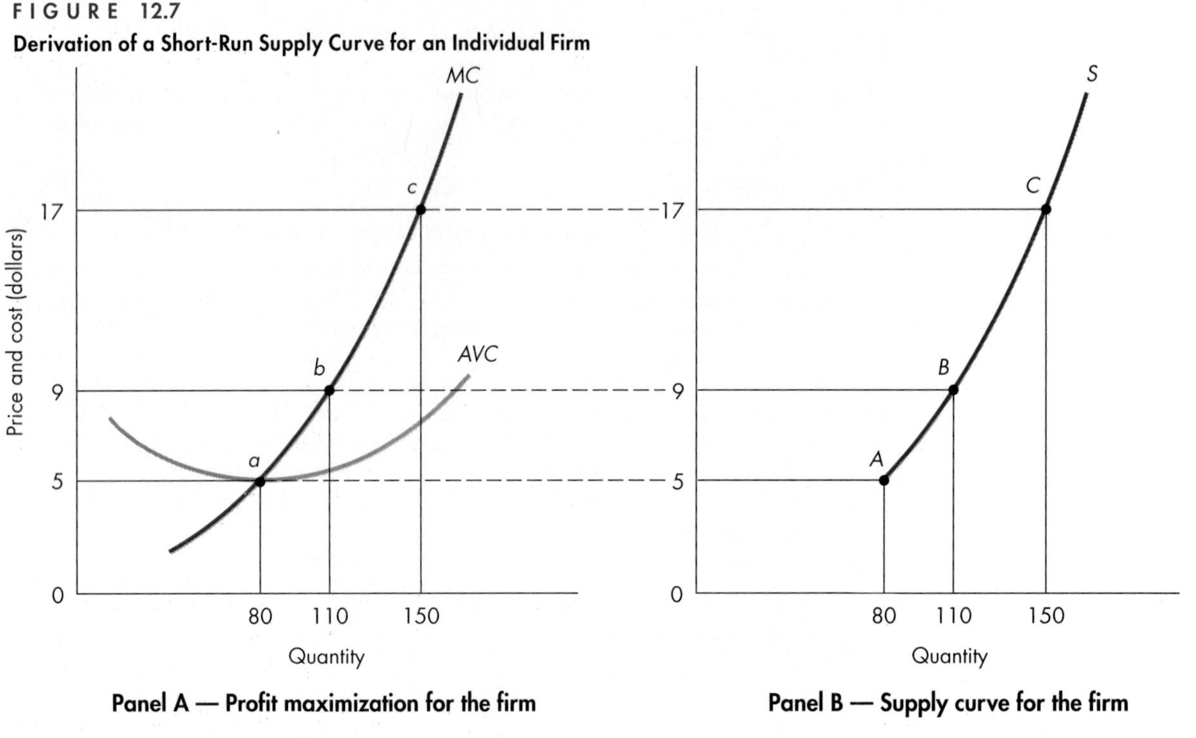

Relation The short-run supply curve for an individual firm in a perfectly competitive market is the portion of the firm's marginal cost curve above minimum average variable cost. For market prices less than minimum average variable cost, quantity supplied is zero.

In contrast to market demand curves of consumers, described in Chapter 6, the industry supply curve cannot always be obtained by simply summing (horizontally) the marginal cost curves of each producer. The reason is that the short-run supply curve for each firm is derived assuming that the prices of variable inputs are constant. No change in input usage by an individual firm acting alone can change an input's unit cost to the firm, because a single competitive firm is so small relative to all users of the resource. But if all producers in an industry *simultaneously* expand output and thereby their usage of inputs, there may be a noticeable increase in the demand for some inputs. When all firms attempt to increase output, the prices of some variable inputs may be bid up, and the increase in these input prices causes an increase in all firms' cost curves, including marginal cost. Consequently, the industry's short-run supply curve usually is somewhat more steeply sloped and somewhat less elastic when input prices increase in response to an increase in industry output than when input prices remain constant (as would be the presumption if we simply summed the marginal cost curves). In any case, in the short run, quantity supplied by the industry varies directly with price.

Before concluding this discussion of supply, we should note that any change that shifts the firm's marginal cost curve shifts each firm's supply curve and hence the industry's supply curve. For example, an increase in the wage rate would increase (shift upward) each firm's marginal cost curve, since labor is usually a variable input. With the higher wage the marginal cost of producing each additional unit of output would rise, so each firm would supply less at each price of the product.

Relation The short-run supply curve for a competitive industry cannot, in general, be obtained by horizontally summing the supply curves of all the individual firms in the industry. Since increases in industry output may cause input prices to rise, which in turn shifts each firm's marginal cost curve upward, the industry supply curve tends to be more steeply sloped (less elastic) than the horizontal summation would be. Short-run supply for a perfectly competitive industry is always upward-sloping.

This concludes our analysis of a perfectly competitive firm's short-run profit-maximizing output decision. As you saw, the firm can make an economic profit or a loss in the short run, depending on market price. Certainly a firm would not go on indefinitely suffering a loss in each period. In the long run, a firm would exit from the industry if it could not cover its total cost with its revenue. Or even if the firm is making a profit in the short run, it may wish to change its plant size or capacity in the long run in order to earn even more profit. We will now analyze the profit-maximizing output decision of perfectly competitive firms in the long run when all inputs, and therefore all costs, are variable.

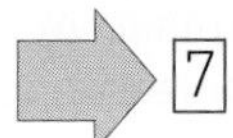 7

12.5 PROFIT MAXIMIZATION IN THE LONG RUN

In the short run, the manager's production decisions are limited because some of the inputs used by the firm are fixed for the short-run period of production. Typically, the key input that a manager views as fixed in the short run is the amount of capital available to the firm in the form of plant or equipment. In the long run, all inputs are variable, and a manager can choose to employ any size plant—amount of capital—required to produce most efficiently the level of output that will maximize profit. The choice of plant size is often referred to as the "scale of operation." The scale of operation may be fixed in the short run, but in the long run it can be altered as economic conditions warrant.

The long run can also be viewed as the planning stage, prior to a firm's entry into an industry. In this stage the firm is trying to decide how large a production facility to construct, that is, the optimal scale of operation. Once the plans have congealed (a particular-size plant is built), the firm operates in a short-run situation. Recall that a fundamental characteristic of perfect competition is unrestricted entry and exit of firms into and out of the industry. As you will see in this section, the entry of new firms, which is possible only in the long run, plays a crucial role in long-run analysis of competitive industries.

FIGURE 12.8
Profit-Maximizing Equilibrium in the Long Run

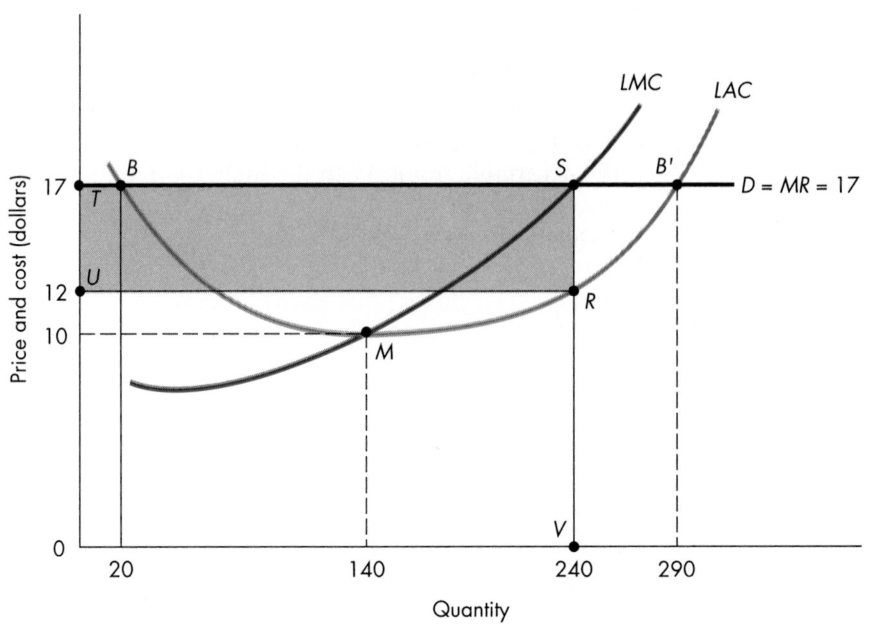

P = MR

In the long run, just as in the short run, the firm attempts to maximize profits. Exactly the same approach is used, except in this case there are no fixed costs; all costs are variable. As before, the firm takes a market-determined price as given. This market price is again the firm's marginal revenue. As in the preceding section, the firm would increase output as long as the marginal revenue from each additional unit is greater than the marginal cost of that unit. It would decrease output when marginal cost exceeds marginal revenue. The firm maximizes profit by equating marginal cost and marginal revenue.

Profit-Maximizing Equilibrium for the Firm in the Long Run

Suppose that an entrepreneur is considering entering a competitive industry in which the firms already in the industry are making economic profits. The prospective entrant, knowing the long-run costs and the product price, expects to make an economic profit also. Since all inputs are variable, the entrant can choose the scale or the plant size for the new firm. We examine the decision graphically.

In Figure 12.8, *LAC* and *LMC* are the long-run average and marginal cost curves. The firm's perfectly elastic demand, *D*, indicates the equilibrium price ($17) and is the same as marginal revenue. As long as price is greater than long-run average cost, the firm can make a profit. Thus, in Figure 12.8, any output between 20 and 290 units yields some economic profit. The points of output

ILLUSTRATION 12.2

Do R&D Expenditures Affect Drug Prices? The Rest of the Story

Recall from Illustration 12.1 a *Wall Street Journal* editorial that argued that new regulations on drugs would raise the cost of drug development, thus causing delays in drug introduction and higher drug prices to consumers. In a letter to the editor, an economist pointed out that the research and development costs are sunk or fixed costs and therefore would have *no effect on prices for drugs already discovered*. This is correct. But because the previous illustration was in the context of our discussion of the firm's short-run decision making, we did not focus there on the long-run implications of the analysis. Now that we have discussed the long run, we can address these long-run implications here.

Note that the above statement that R&D costs would have no effect on the prices of drugs already discovered is short-run analysis. Although we cannot know for certain, it appears that the editorial writer was analyzing possible long-run effects of drug regulation. Obviously, research and development expenses are a sunk cost once they have been made. However, if a firm is in the planning stage of developing a new drug or modifying a drug to comply with new regulations, these potential development costs would be variable. As such, they would affect a firm's decision about how much to spend on development or whether to spend at all.

Suppose, for example, that a drug manufacturer is considering developing a new drug and, if the decision is made to do it, is determining how much to spend. In making this decision, the manager would weigh the expected additional costs of research and development plus the expected costs of production and sales along with the expected additional revenues to be generated. This is a long-run marginal cost–marginal benefit decision. The manager would have some idea about the price that could be charged for the new drug if it is introduced. Suppose new FDA regulations are expected to increase these expected R&D costs. That could tip the balance against development of the new drug if expected additional costs are now greater than expected additional revenues. If such is the case, there would be a little less competition among related drugs than would have been the case with the new drug, possibly resulting in higher prices of similar drugs.

We do not mean to imply that such a scenario would occur in all cases. Certainly some new drugs would be profitable even after the increased development costs necessary to comply with new regulations. But some probably would not. Depending on how many would not, the supply of new drugs on the market would decrease, prices would rise, and fewer drugs would be available.

In the long run all costs are variable. In order to undertake any new investment project, including R&D expenditure, managers must expect that these costs will be covered by revenue. Anything that raises these costs is likely to raise prices.

So in the case of drug regulations raising drug prices, both writers were correct. In the short run, additional development costs would not increase the price of drugs already on the market. In the long run, additional development costs would be likely to raise drug prices.*

*We will analyze the firm's investment decision in more detail in Chapter 19.

B and *B′* are sometimes called the break-even points. At these two points, price equals long-run average cost, economic profit is zero, and the owners of the firm earn only a normal profit (or rate of return).

Maximum profit occurs at 240 units of output (point *S*), where marginal revenue equals long-run marginal cost. The firm would want to select the plant size to produce 240 units of output. Note that the firm would not, under these circumstances, want to produce 140 units of output at point *M*, the minimum point of long-run average cost. At *M*, marginal revenue exceeds marginal cost, so the firm can gain by producing more output. As shown in Figure 12.8, at point *S* total revenue (price times quantity) at 240 units of output is equal to $4,080 (= $17 × 240), which is the area of the rectangle 0*TSV*. The total cost (average cost times quantity) is equal to $2,880 (= $12 × 240), which is the area of the rectangle 0*URV*. The total profit is $1,200 [= ($17 − $12) × 240], which is the area of the rectangle *UTSR*.

Thus the firm would plan to operate at a scale (or plant size) such that long-run marginal cost equals price. This would be the most profitable situation under the circumstances. But, as we shall show, these circumstances will change. If the firm illustrated in Figure 12.8 is free to enter the industry, so are other prospective entrants. And this entry will drive down the market price. We will now show how this occurs.

Long-Run Competitive Equilibrium for the Industry

While the individual firm is in long-run profit-maximizing equilibrium when $MR = LMC$ (as shown in Figure 12.8), the *industry* will not be in long-run equilibrium until there is no incentive for new firms to enter or incumbent firms to exit. The economic force that induces firms to enter into an industry or that drives firms out of an industry is the existence of economic profits or economic losses, respectively.

Economic profits attract new firms into the industry, and entry of these new firms increases industry supply. This increased supply drives down price. As price falls, all firms in the industry adjust their output levels in order to remain in profit-maximizing equilibrium. New firms continue to enter the industry, price continues to fall, and existing firms continue to adjust their outputs until all economic profits are eliminated. There is no longer an incentive for new firms to enter, and all firms in the industry earn only a normal rate of return.

Economic losses motivate some existing firms to exit, or leave, the industry. The exit of these firms decreases industry supply. The reduction in supply drives up market price. As price is driven up, all firms in the industry must adjust their output levels in order to remain in profit-maximizing equilibrium. Firms continue to exit until economic losses are eliminated, and economic profit is zero; that is, firms earn only a normal rate of return.

long-run competitive equilibrium
Condition in which all firms are producing where $P = LMC$ and economic profits are zero ($P = LAC$).

Long-run competitive equilibrium, then, requires not only that all firms be in profit-maximizing equilibrium, but also that economic profits be zero. These two conditions are satisfied when price equals marginal cost ($P = LMC$), so that firms are in profit-maximizing equilibrium, and price also equals average cost ($P = LAC$), so that no entry or exit occurs. These two conditions for equilibrium can be simultaneously satisfied only when price equals minimum *LAC*, at which point $LMC = LAC$.

FIGURE 12.9
Long-Run Equilibrium for a Firm in a Perfectly Competitive Industry

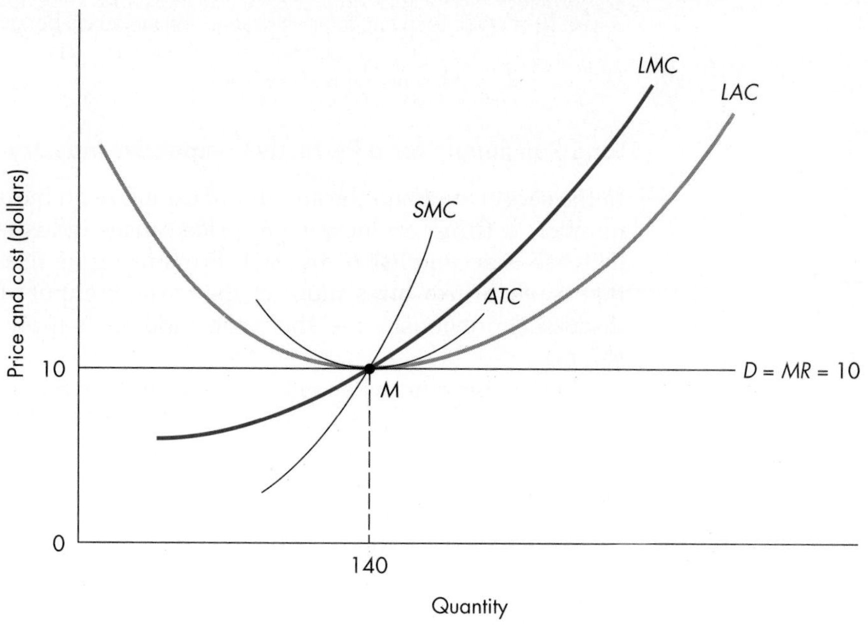

Figure 12.9 shows a typical firm in long-run competitive equilibrium.[2] The long-run cost curves in Figure 12.9 are similar to those in 12.8. The difference between the two figures is that in Figure 12.8 the *firm* is in profit-maximizing equilibrium, but the industry is not yet in zero-profit equilibrium. In Figure 12.9, the firm is in profit-maximizing equilibrium (P equals LMC), and the industry is also in long-run competitive equilibrium because economic profit is zero ($P = LAC$).

Long-run equilibrium occurs at a price of $10 and output of 140, at point M. Each (identical) firm in the industry makes neither economic profit nor loss. There is no incentive for further entry because the rate of return in this industry is the normal rate of return, which is equal to the firm's best alternative. For the same reason, there is no incentive for a firm to leave the industry. The number of firms stabilizes, and each firm operates with a plant size represented by short-run marginal and average cost, SMC and ATC, respectively. We can now summarize long-run competitive equilibrium with a principle:

[2]We will assume that all firms in the industry have identical cost curves. For example, Figures 12.8 and 12.9 show the cost curves of a typical firm. While it is not necessary to assume identical costs for all firms, this assumption substantially simplifies the theoretical analysis without affecting the conclusions.

Principle In long-run competitive equilibrium, all firms are in profit-maximizing equilibrium ($P = LMC$), and there is no incentive for firms to enter or exit the industry because economic profit is zero ($P = LAC$). Long-run competitive equilibrium occurs because of the entry of new firms into the industry or the exit of existing firms from the industry. The market adjusts so that $P = LMC = LAC$, which is at the minimum point on LAC.

Long-Run Supply for a Perfectly Competitive Industry

In the short run when the amount of capital in an industry is fixed, as well as the number of firms, an increase in price causes industry output to increase. This increase is accomplished by each firm's using its fixed capital more intensively, that is, each firm hires more of the variable inputs to increase output. As we discussed previously, the short-run industry supply curve is always upward-sloping.

In the long run, when entry of new firms is possible, the industry's response to an increase in price takes on a new dimension: The industry's supply adjustment to a change in price is not complete until entry or exit results in zero economic profit. This means that for all points on the long-run industry supply curve, economic profit must be zero.

increasing-cost industry
An industry in which input prices rise as all firms in the industry expand output.

constant-cost industry
An industry in which input prices remain constant as all firms in the industry expand output.

To derive the industry supply curve in the long run, we must differentiate between two types of industries: (1) an increasing-cost industry, and (2) a constant-cost industry. An industry is an **increasing-cost industry** if, as all firms in the industry expand output and thus input usage, the prices of some inputs used in the industry rise. For example, if the personal computer industry expands production by 15 percent, the price of many specialized inputs (such as microprocessor chips, RAM boards, disk drives, and so on) will increase, causing marginal and average cost for all firms to shift upward. An industry is a **constant-cost industry** if, as industry output and input usage increase, all prices of inputs used in the industry remain constant.[3] For example, the rutabaga industry is probably so small that its usage of inputs such as fertilizer, farm labor, and machinery have no effect on the prices of these inputs. This industry is therefore probably a constant-cost industry.

Figure 12.10 shows the relation between a typical firm (Panel A) in a constant-cost industry and the long-run industry supply curve (Panel B) for a constant-cost industry. Note that the supply price in the long run is constant and equal to \$10 for all levels of industry output. This result follows from the long-run equilibrium condition that economic profit must be zero. The long-run supply price, \$10, is equal to minimum long-run average cost for every level of output produced by the industry because the entry of new firms always bids price down to the point of zero economic profit (point M in Figure 12.10). Because the industry is a constant-cost industry, expansion of industry output does

[3]Theoretically it is possible that input prices might fall as industry output rises, in which case there is a decreasing-cost industry. Decreasing-cost industries are so extremely rare that we will not consider them in this text.

FIGURE 12.10
Long-Run Industry Supply for a Constant-Cost Industry

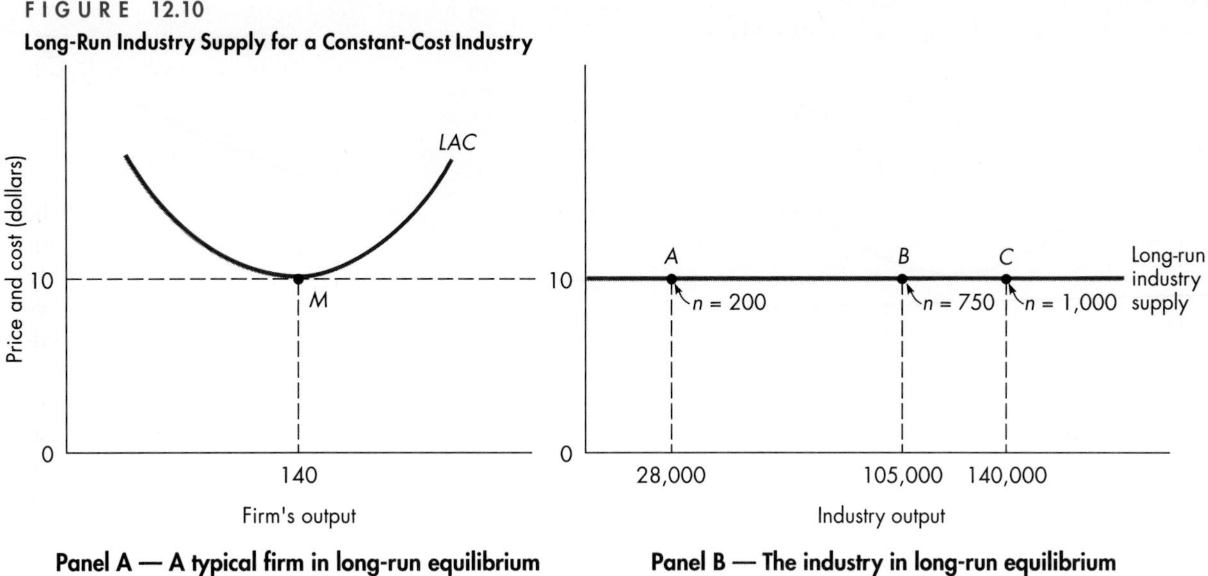

Panel A — A typical firm in long-run equilibrium **Panel B — The industry in long-run equilibrium**

not cause minimum *LAC* (point *M*) to rise. Therefore, long-run supply price (= minimum *LAC*) is constant.

For example, if industry output expands from 28,000 units to 105,000 units through the entry of new firms, each firm (old and new) ends up producing 140 units of output at the minimum *LAC* of $10. No single firm expands output in the long run; output expands because there are more firms, each producing 140 units. When the industry produces 28,000, 105,000, and 140,000 units, the industry is in long-run equilibrium with 200, 750, and 1,000 firms, respectively. Finally, note that at all points on long-run industry supply (*A, B,* and *C,* for example), economic profit is zero. For a constant-cost industry, long-run industry supply is perfectly elastic.

Next consider an increasing-cost industry. Figure 12.11 illustrates the relation between a typical firm (Panel A) in an increasing-cost industry and the long-run industry supply curve (Panel B). In contrast to the constant-cost case, the supply price for an increasing-cost industry rises as industry output increases.

Since the industry is an increasing-cost industry, as the industry expands output, resource prices rise, causing the long-run average cost in Panel A to shift upward. LAC_A, LAC_B, and LAC_C represent the increasingly higher long-run average costs associated with industry output levels of 28,000, 105,000, and 140,000 units, respectively. For example, when the industry output increases from 28,000 units, produced by 200 firms, to 105,000 units, input prices rise, causing minimum *LAC* to rise to *M′* (in Panel A). Each firm in the industry still produces 140

FIGURE 12.11

Long-Run Industry Supply for an Increasing-Cost Industry

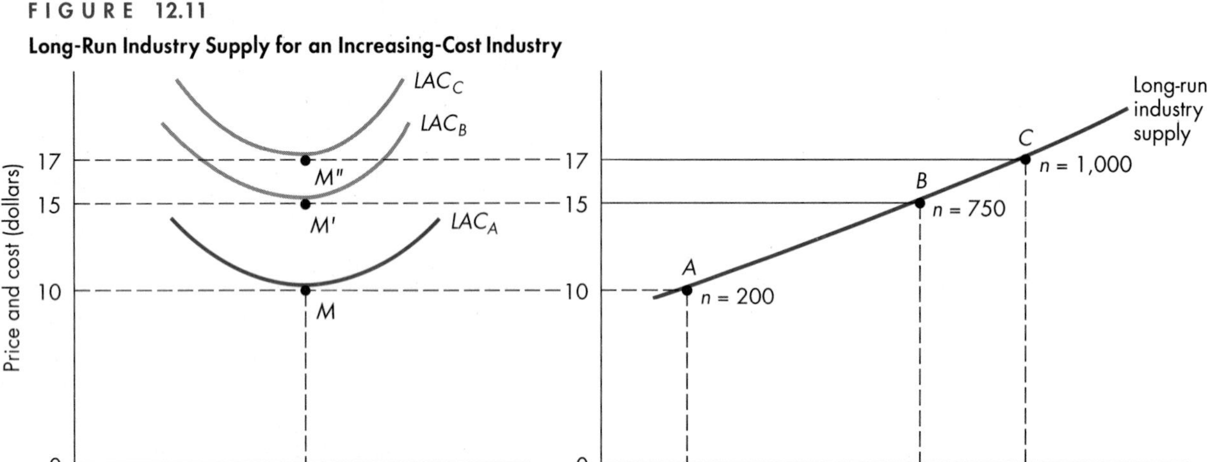

Panel A — A typical firm in long-run equilibrium

Panel B — The industry in long-run equilibrium

units, but there are now 750 firms producing a total industry output of 105,000 units at an average cost of \$15.[4] Just as in the case of a constant-cost industry, economic profit is zero at all points along the long-run supply curve. And similarly, when industry output increases from 105,000 to 140,000 units, input prices rise further, causing minimum *LAC* to rise to *M''*. At point *C*, 1,000 firms each produce 140 units at an average cost of \$17 per unit and earn zero economic profit.

Relations For a constant-cost industry, as industry output expands, input prices remain constant, and the minimum point on long-run average cost (*LAC*) is unchanged. Since long-run supply price equals minimum *LAC*, the long-run industry supply curve is perfectly elastic (horizontal) for a constant-cost industry. For an increasing-cost industry, as industry output expands, input prices are bid up, causing minimum *LAC* to rise and long-run supply price to rise. The long-run industry supply curve for an increasing-cost industry is upward-sloping. Economic profit is zero at all points on the long-run industry supply curve for both constant- and increasing-cost industries, and each firm earns just a normal profit or normal rate of return.

Managers of firms in industries that have the characteristics of perfect competition (in particular, low barriers to entry and homogenous product) should

[4]In Figure 12.11 we have assumed that the minimum points on the higher *LAC* curves, LAC_B and LAC_C remain at 140 units of output. Actually, *M'* and *M''* could also be at output levels either larger or smaller than 140 units; in this case, we would simply have to adjust the number of firms associated with points *B* and *C* in Panel B.

expect to see economic profit competed away in the long run by the entry of new firms, regardless of whether constant or increasing costs characterize the industry. Likewise, managers should expect that losses in the short run will be eliminated in the long run as firms exit the industry and the price of the product rises. Managers can also expect to see entry of new firms driving up the prices they pay for inputs if they are operating in an increasing-cost industry that is expanding.

We should note that in our discussion of long-run competitive equilibrium we have assumed that the adjustment process goes smoothly. That is, when economic profits are being earned, expansion takes place just as long as it takes to drive price down to minimum long-run average cost and to reduce economic profits to zero, where each firm earns a normal profit. Industry expansion ceases when this point is reached. In reality this process may not be so smooth. The industry can overexpand and drive price below minimum average cost, where firms cannot earn even a normal profit. In this case the losses would cause firms to exit until price is driven back up to where the losses are eliminated and firms do earn a normal profit. Sometimes this process may not be completed until a long period of time has elapsed. Illustration 12.3 describes one such situation.

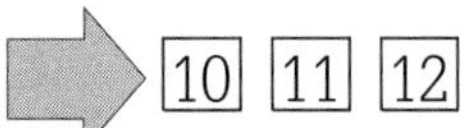

Rent and Long-Run Competitive Equilibrium

The fact that economic profit is zero in long-run competitive equilibrium does not mean that "nobody gets rich" in a competitive industry. Obviously, those with skills or talent that are greatly in demand can make a lot of money if the market salary or wage for people with those skills is high. Resource owners can earn a substantial return over and above owners of similar types of resources if their resources are more productive than the others employed in the industry.

An example of such a situation is a restaurant managed by Marcel Le Beau, who is paid a salary of $50,000 a year. His recipes, known only to him, are so marvelous that the restaurant owners earn $150,000 each year over their explicit costs, including Le Beau's salary. The opportunity cost to the owners of using their capital in the restaurant is only $70,000 a year, leaving them an $80,000 economic profit. Without Le Beau and his fabulous recipes, no other restaurant in town is earning more than a normal profit.

One day at lunch we suggested to Monsieur Le Beau that he should demand a raise, perhaps as much as $80,000 more a year. The owners would still earn a normal profit, which, presumably, is as much as they could make without him. We said that if they didn't give him the raise, some other restaurant surely would. He replied that asking for a raise is considered rude in the province he grew up in. So the owners continue to make economic profits because of their unique, more productive, and polite resource, Marcel Le Beau.

To illustrate the concept of more productive, scarce resources a bit more concretely, now suppose that you are an experienced construction supervisor for a builder of median-priced homes and you are exceptionally talented at organizing subcontractors—concrete workers, carpenters, bricklayers, plumbers,

ILLUSTRATION 12.3

For Perfect Competitors a Boom Can Be a Dangerous Thing

The U.S. farm belt was riding a grain boom in the spring of 1996. According to *The Wall Street Journal*, corn and wheat prices had risen to their highest levels in two decades*: "Sales of pickups, tractors and combines are surging. Growers are making plans to put long-idled fields back into production. Land prices are moving up." But, as the *WSJ* noted, all this good fortune was making the fortunate uneasy. One grower said, "We all know a boom can be a dangerous thing." He was alluding to the "Grain Belt's last big party," in the 1970s, one that ended badly.

Soaring land prices had made many area farmers millionaires. Consequently, they spent a great deal on consumption goods. But "above all, they bought land, bidding up prices wildly for the scarce supply of good soil that was for sale. [The farmer quoted above] went deep into debt to buy new equipment and triple the size of his operation."

According to the *WSJ*, "Then grain stockpiles ballooned. Crop prices fell. Land purchases leveraged at the high interest rates of those days were exposed as blatantly uneconomical, and the price of land plunged. The rural Midwest sank into a 1980s debt crisis that nearly wiped out a generation of farmers." The article asked, "Will it happen again?"

Many economists at the time thought that the upturn had a better chance of avoiding such a fate. One reason given was that exports were more firmly rooted and not as likely to fall as much as they did in the 1980s. There was less competition from European grain exports because of recent trade agreements. But a large percentage of grain sales were to Asia's growing economies, many of which experienced sharp downturns in 1997. The U.S. market had, however, expanded.

Furthermore, farmers, scared by the bust in the 1980s, had become more conservative and more sophisticated in business. One example given was a 34-year-old farmer who, right after high school, had borrowed $228,000 to buy farmland. After watching the value of his land fall by two-thirds, he went to college, where he studied what had gone wrong, then went on to earn an M.B.A. at the University of Chicago. He returned to the family farm in 1993, and using business practices he had learned, was earning a 30 percent return on equity by 1995. He had lost a lot of his appetite for land, saying, "I learned my lesson." Because so many young people had left agriculture after the bust, a large percentage of farmland was owned by people over 60, who were interested in avoiding risk. Much of the new investment was being made in cash rather than through debt. Farmers were being more cautious because they expected government subsidies to be gradually eliminated. Bankers had become more reluctant to make loans—debt as a percentage of farm assets was 16 percent compared with the 1985 high of 23 percent.

We conclude this illustration with a prediction made in *The Wall Street Journal* article: "Nobody here thinks the changes made by farmers have buried the boom-and-bust cycle. Today's high crop prices will inevitably boost production enough to rebuild the nation's depleted stockpiles and knock prices down again."

This is the point of this illustration. Perfectly competitive firms and industries have ups and downs—the very nature of perfect competition is cyclical. No one farmer, acting alone, would be able to prevent falling prices before they came. When prices are high and people are earning above-normal profit, production always expands. Price will fall. Profits will return to normal or, as in the above case, to far below normal when there is too much investment. The one thing the farmers discussed here could do, and seemed to be doing at the time, was restrain some of their previous exuberance during good times so as to moderate their own losses when the market inevitably turns down. Oh, there is one other point: As in the case of the teenage land speculator turned successful businessman, a good education in economics and business is very useful in any profession.

*High Grain Price Lifts Farmers, but Will They Overexpand as Before?" *The Wall Street Journal*, Mar. 21, 1996.

FIGURE 12.12
Economic Rent in Long-Run Competitive Equilibrium

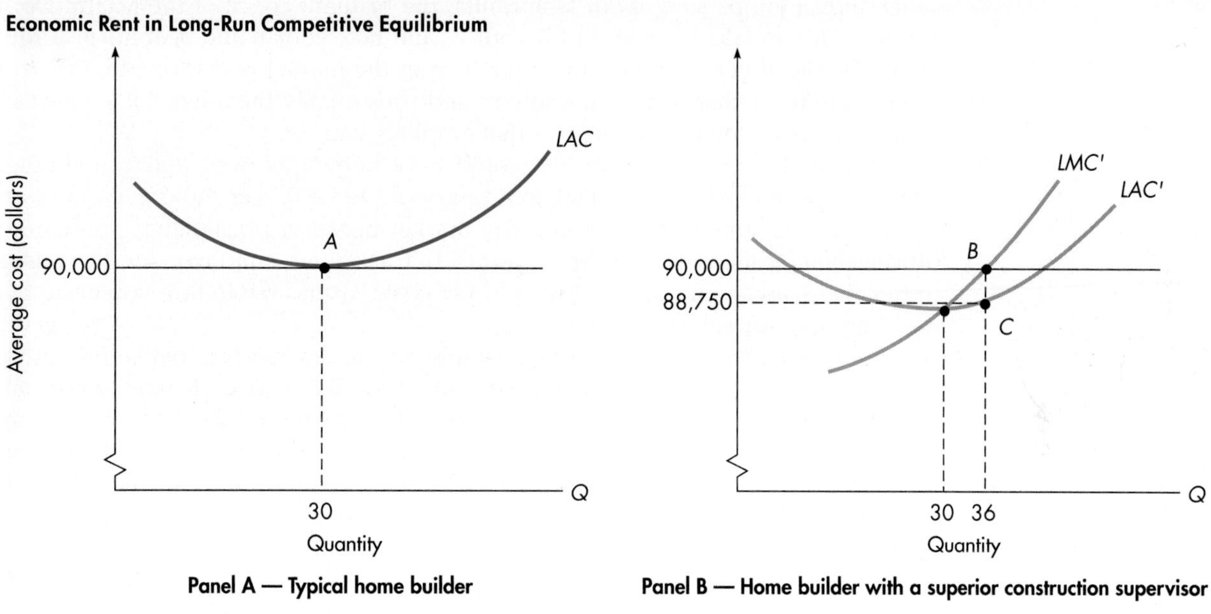

Panel A — Typical home builder

Panel B — Home builder with a superior construction supervisor

painters, and so forth. You can build a house in 10 percent less time than the typical experienced construction supervisor in the industry, and this saving of time reduces the average costs of constructing a house by $2,000.

The home construction industry in your market is in long-run equilibrium. Each firm in the market, including yours, is selling homes at the going market price of $90,000, which is the minimum long-run average cost for every other firm but your employer. Each of the other firms builds 30 houses a year and earns only a normal profit at the $90,000 price. Panel A of Figure 12.12 illustrates the situation for every other contractor in the market. Each of these produces at point *A* in the figure. Assume that an experienced construction contractor is typically paid $80,000 a year, which is what you are paid.

The situation for the firm that employs you is illustrated in Panel B. *LAC'* and *LMC'* are your firm's long-run average and marginal cost curves. At each level of output, *LAC'* is $2,000 below the long-run average cost for every other firm (*LAC* in Panel A) because you can construct a house for $2,000 less than any other contractor. Your firm produces where *LMC'* equals price ($90,000), building 36 houses per year, as shown by point *B* in Panel B. Your firm makes an economic profit, a return over and above the normal profit included in cost, of $1,250 per house, or $45,000 (= $1,250 × 36). You are solely responsible for the $45,000 economic profit. Your firm is identical in every way to every other firm except for your superior skills. (As the famous football coach and philosopher Bum Phillips said about Don Shula, the brilliant coach of the Miami Dolphins, "He can take his'n and beat your'n, and take your'n and beat his'n.") You could be the supervisor for any other firm in the market and earn $45,000 economic profit for that firm. You know it, and presumably the other firms know it also, as does the owner of the firm that employs you.

You know now, and probably would have known anyway, that you should ask for a raise of around $45,000, to a salary of $125,000. You could get a raise of about $45,000 from other firms in the market because, presumably, you could lower their costs as well. Even if you didn't ask your employer for the raise, other firms, aware of your ability to lower costs, would try to lure you away by bidding up your salary.

Your employer, and any other employer in the market, really has little choice. A firm could pay you the additional $45,000 and earn only a normal profit because all economic profit would go toward your salary. Or your firm could refuse to pay the additional $45,000, causing you to move to another firm or perhaps start your own. Your original employer would find that its costs had shifted back to *LAC* after you left and would consequently earn only a normal profit because it would be in the situation shown in Panel A. Thus, each firm in the market would earn only a normal profit whether it hires you at $125,000 or not. But you would earn a premium because of your superior skills.

economic rent (or **rent**) A payment in excess of a resource's opportunity cost (the highest payment a resource could earn in an alternative occupation).

The additional payment you receive above the typical salary of $80,000 is called **economic rent** or simply **rent.** Rent is the payment to a superior or more productive resource over and above its opportunity cost (what the resource could earn in its best alternative occupation). The opportunity cost for experienced supervisors is what they could earn in their best alternative occupation—such as selling insurance or supervising a factory. If this opportunity cost is around $80,000, the other supervisors are earning zero rent and you are earning $45,000 rent after your salary increase.

This same type of analysis holds for any resource that, if compensated at only its opportunity cost, would result in the firm's earning economic profit in long-run competitive equilibrium. The return to that resource will be bid up as in the above example. Therefore, even in a competitive industry, owners of particularly productive resources can earn substantial premiums even though economic profit is zero. While this example examined rents to superior skills of a manager, resources such as superior land, superior location, superior craftsmanship, or superior capital (that cannot be easily duplicated) can also earn economic rent for their owners.

You might be wondering about a situation in which the owner of a competitive firm is also the owner of the superior resource that causes the long-run average cost to be lower than the costs of other firms in the industry. Would this firm owner earn an economic profit when the industry is in long-run competitive equilibrium? The answer is no. The firm owner's opportunity cost rises because presumably the owner could sell the superior resource to another firm, and, consequently, *the firm's implicit cost increases.* The owner earns a premium (rent) as the resource owner but earns only a normal profit as the firm's owner. This classification is only a technicality that economists make in order to be consistent. The resource and firm owner makes no distinction as to what income is called when it is deposited in the bank.

Relation Economic rent is a payment to the owner of a resource in excess of the resource's
opportunity cost. Firms that employ such exceptionally productive resources earn only a normal
13 profit (economic profit is zero) in long-run competitive equilibrium because the potential economic
profit from employing a superior resource is paid to the resource as rent.

12.6 PROFIT-MAXIMIZING INPUT USAGE

Thus far, we have analyzed the firm's profit-maximizing decision in terms of the output decision. But, as noted in the introduction, we can also consider profit maximization from the input side. Of course, when we determine the profit-maximizing level of output, we implicitly have determined the economically efficient level of input usage of the firm. Recall from Chapters 9 and 10 that the cost function is directly related to the production function. Thus, when we determine a unique profit-maximizing level of output, we also determine the cost-minimizing quantity of each input that is used in the production process.

It is possible, however, to determine a profit-maximizing equilibrium directly from the input decision. In this way, we can develop the theory of a competitive firm's demand for inputs or factors of production.

Marginal Revenue Product

The principle of choosing input usage to maximize profits is simple and follows directly from the theory of unconstrained maximization set forth in Chapter 4. The firm should expand its usage of any input (or factor of production) as long as additional units of the input add more to the firm's revenue than to its cost. The firm would not increase the usage of any input if hiring more units increases the firm's cost more than its revenue.

marginal revenue product (*MRP*) (*MRP* = Δ*TR*/Δ*I*)
The additional revenue earned when the firm hires 1 more unit of the input.

The additional revenue added by another unit of the input is called the **marginal revenue product (*MRP*)** of that input:

$$MRP = \Delta TR/\Delta I$$

where TR is the firm's total revenue and I is the level of usage of a particular input. Thus if the additional revenue generated by, say, the tenth worker is $150, the additional output attributable to hiring the tenth worker adds $150 to the firm's revenue when it is sold.

The marginal revenue product of an input is equal to the marginal revenue from selling the output produced times the marginal product of the input:[5]

$$MRP = \frac{\Delta TR}{\Delta I} = MR \times MP$$

[5]The appendix at the end of this chapter demonstrates mathematically that $MRP = MR \times MP$.

TABLE 12.2

Finding the Profit-Maximizing Level of Input Usage

(1) Units of variable input (I)	(2) Output (Q)	(3) Marginal product $\left(\frac{\Delta Q}{\Delta I}\right)$	(4) Marginal revenue product ($P \times MP$)	(5) Marginal cost $\left(\frac{w}{MP}\right)$	(6) Marginal revenue (= P)
1	20	20	$200	$ 5	$10
2	50	30	300	3.33	10
3	90	40	400	2.50	10
4	120	30	300	3.33	10
5	138	18	180	5.55	10
6	150	12	120	8.33	10
7	155	5	50	20	10
8	158	3	30	33.33	10
9	154	−4	−40	—	10

For a competitive firm, the marginal revenue from the additional production of an input is equal to the price of the product, which *is* marginal revenue for a perfectly competitive firm, times the marginal product of the input:

$$MRP = P \times MP$$

For example, if 1 additional unit of an input, say, labor, has a marginal product of 10 and the price at which the product can be sold is $5, the marginal revenue product for that unit of the input is $50 (= $P \times MP$ = $5 × 10). In other words, hiring the extra unit of labor adds 10 extra units of output which can each be sold for $5 each, and thus the addition to total revenue attributable to hiring this extra unit of labor is $50.[6]

As shown in Chapter 9, the "typical" marginal product curve first increases, reaches a maximum, then declines thereafter. Therefore, the *MRP* curve, which is simply price times marginal product, also rises then declines. At the level of input usage at which marginal product becomes negative, the marginal revenue product becomes negative also. Since an input's marginal product depends on the usage of other inputs, the marginal revenue product also changes at each level of the input when the quantities of other inputs change.

A typical *MRP* schedule for a single variable input (I) is given in Table 12.2, assuming that the price of the product is $10. Columns 1 and 2 show the firm's

[6]In the case of a perfectly competitive industry, the marginal revenue product of an input is sometimes referred to as the *value of marginal product (VMP)* since the additional revenue attributable to hiring an extra unit of the input is simply the market value of the additional output produced by the additional unit of the input. *MRP* and *VMP* are just different names for precisely the same concept—both are measures of the increase in revenue attributable to hiring an extra unit of the input.

production function for 1 through 9 units of input usage. Column 3 shows that the marginal product of the input first rises through 3 units of input usage, then decreases, becoming negative at 9 units of the input. The marginal revenue product ($10 × *MP*) in column 4 also increases through 3 units of the input, then decreases, becoming negative at 9 units of the input. We will return to columns 5 and 6 later in this section. If the price of the product increases, *MRP* will increase for each level of input usage. If the price of the product falls, *MRP* falls also.

Marginal Revenue Product and the Hiring Decision

The quantity of an input a manager chooses to hire depends on the marginal revenue product and the marginal cost of the input. Assume that a manager can hire as much of an input as is desired at a constant price—that is, the price that must be paid for the input is the same no matter how much or how little is hired. Thus, the marginal cost is equal to the price of the input.[7]

Suppose that labor is the input for which the *MRP* schedule is shown in Table 12.2. If the wage rate of labor is $100 per unit of labor, each additional unit of labor hired through the sixth adds more to revenue (*MRP* > $100) than it adds to cost. Each unit after the sixth adds less to revenue (*MRP* < $100) than it adds to cost; that is, each unit after the sixth adds less than the wage rate to revenue. Thus, with the given *MRP* schedule and wage rate, the manager hires 6 units of labor.

If the firm is hiring only 5 units, it could add the sixth unit of labor, and revenue would rise by $120 while cost would increase by $100; thus profit would increase $20. If the firm makes a mistake and employs 7 workers, it could increase profit by reducing labor usage by 1 unit. Eliminating the seventh worker would decrease revenue $50 as cost falls $100; profit would increase $50.

A general rule for a continuously variable input is illustrated graphically in Figure 12.13. In this example, labor is the only variable input, and only the decreasing portion of *MRP* is shown. The *MRP* curve is simply the *MP* curve multiplied by the market price of the product produced at each level of labor usage over the relevant range. Therefore, if at a labor usage of $\overline{L}$ the marginal product is $\overline{MP}$, $\overline{MRP} = \overline{P} \times \overline{MP}$, where $\overline{P}$ is product price. This means that the $\overline{L}$th worker adds $\overline{MRP}$ to total revenue. If the wage rate is w_1, the manager would wish to hire L_1 units of labor. The manager would not stop short of L_1, because up to employment level L_1 an additional unit of labor would add more to revenue than to cost. The manager would not hire more than L_1, because beyond L_1 the added cost would exceed the added revenue. If the wage rate falls to w_2, the manager would increase labor usage to L_2 units. Hence, if labor is the firm's only variable input, the manager maximizes profits or minimizes loss by employing

[7]In some instances, the price of an input may either rise or fall as a firm hires more of the input. When the price is not constant, marginal cost will not be equal to the price of the input.

FIGURE 12.13
A Competitive Firm's Demand for Labor

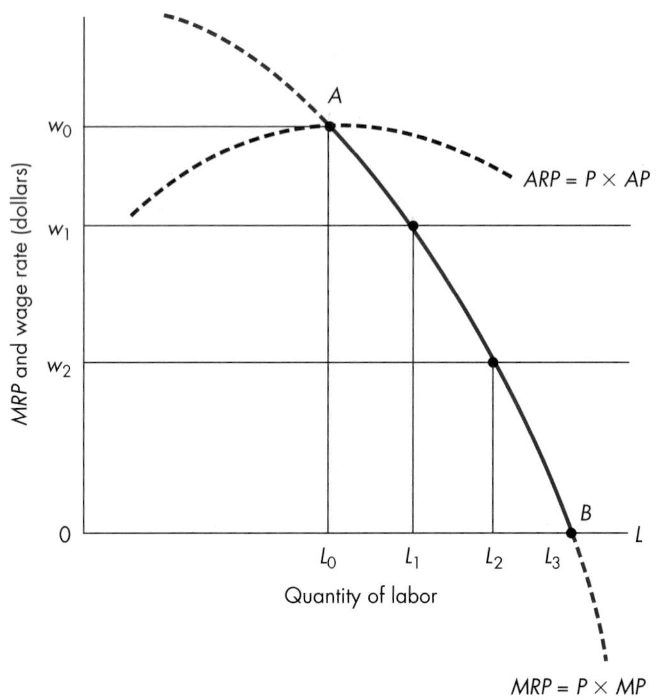

the amount of labor for which the marginal revenue product of labor equals the wage rate:

$$MRP = w$$

This result holds for any variable input.[8]

Principle If the *MRP* of an additional unit of a variable input is greater than the price of that input, that unit should be hired. If the *MRP* of an additional unit adds less than its price, that unit should not be hired. If the usage of the variable input varies continuously, the manager should employ the amount of the input at which

$$MRP = \text{Input price}$$

The above principle is equivalent to the condition that the profit-maximizing, perfectly competitive firm will produce the level of output at which

[8]As noted, we did not include the upward-sloping portion of the *MRP* curve because this segment is not relevant to the hiring decision. If the wage equals *MRP* and *MRP* is increasing, the manager could hire additional units, and the marginal revenue product of these inputs would be greater than the wage. Therefore, this level of input use would not be profit-maximizing. Later in this section we show that the relevant portion of *MRP* is that range of input usage for which $AP > MP$ and MP is positive.

$P = MC$. Recall from Chapter 9 that cost minimization at any level of output requires that

$$MC = \frac{w}{MP}$$

Recall also that the profit-maximizing level of output is where

$$P = MC$$

But, from the cost-minimization condition, when one input is variable,

$$P = MC = \frac{w}{MP}$$

or

$$P \times MP = w$$

which gives the profit-maximizing level of input usage. Thus the profit-maximizing, output-choice equilibrium condition, $P = MC$, is equivalent to the profit-maximizing, input-choice equilibrium condition, $MRP = w$. Each leads to the same level of output and the same level of input usage.

To illustrate numerically that the profit-maximizing decision for the manager is invariant to choosing either input usage or output, we now return to Table 12.2, in which we showed that 6 units of labor is the level of labor usage that maximizes profit. Marginal cost (column 5) is computed by dividing the wage rate ($100) by the marginal product for each unit of labor from 1 through 9. For example, the first 20 units of output are produced, using 1 unit of labor costing $100. Thus, the marginal cost per unit of the first 20 units of output is $5 ($= w/MP_L =$ $100/20). The other values for marginal cost in column 5 are calculated in the same way. The marginal revenue is equal to the price received for each unit of output, which is $10 in this example. Using the usual rules of marginal analysis for the output decision, a manager would increase production up to the 150th unit of output because *MR* exceeds *MC*. Beyond 150 units of output, marginal cost exceeds marginal revenue. Since the manager maximizes profit by hiring 6 units of labor to produce 150 units, it does not matter if the manager chooses input usage or output to maximize profit; the outcomes are identical.

We now want to be more precise about the range of *MRP* over which a manager would actually operate. Clearly, a manager never hires labor beyond the point at which *MRP* becomes negative—when *MRP* is negative, hiring more labor *decreases* total revenue. Furthermore, we will now demonstrate that a manager shuts down operations (i.e., hires no labor) if the wage rate rises above the *average revenue product* of labor. The **average revenue product (*ARP*)** of labor is the average revenue per worker, $ARP = TR/L$, and it is easy to see that *ARP* can be calculated as price times average product:

average revenue product (*ARP*)
The average revenue per worker ($ARP = TR/L$).

$$ARP = \frac{TR}{L} = \frac{PQ}{L} = P\frac{Q}{L} = P \times AP$$

To see why a manager shuts down when $w > ARP$, suppose $MRP = w$—as necessary for profit maximization—at a level of labor usage where ARP is less than the wage rate:

$$w > ARP$$

Substituting TR/L for ARP into this inequality results in the following expression:

$$w > TR/L$$

Now multiply both sides of the inequality by L, and you can see that

$$wL > TR \quad \text{or} \quad TVC > TR$$

Thus total variable cost exceeds total revenue when $w > ARP$. From previous analysis, you know that the manager should shut down when total revenue does not cover total variable costs.[9] Therefore, no labor would be hired if the average revenue product is less than the wage rate.

In Figure 12.13, the firm's demand for labor is the MRP curve over the range of labor usage L_0 to L_3 (between points A and B). To maximize profit, the manager chooses the level of labor usage for which $MRP = w$. When wages rise above w_0 in Figure 12.13 at the level of labor usage for which $MRP = w$, the wage rate exceeds the average revenue product ($w > ARP$) and the manager will shut the firm down and hire no labor at all. At all wage rates above point A, the firm shuts down. Below point B, MRP is negative, and the manager would never hire more than L_3 units of labor. We now summarize the discussion in a principle:

Principle The demand for a single variable input by a perfectly competitive firm is the positive portion of the MRP curve over the range of input usage for which $MRP < ARP$. This portion of the MRP curve shows the quantity of variable input that a profit-maximizing manager should hire at each price of the input.

Before concluding the discussion of input demand, we should note that when there is more than one variable input, the firm's demand function for a particular input is slightly different. For example, if the quantities of other inputs are also variable, when wages fall from w_1 to w_2 in Figure 12.13, the firm will use more labor but it may use more or less of the other variable inputs as well. For this reason, the MRP curve of labor may shift—either outward or inward—because the changed usage of these other inputs shifts the MP curve. Thus, the firm may use more than or less than L_2 units of labor at wage w_2, but not less than L_1. The firm's demand for any variable input is negatively sloped.

Nevertheless, two things are certain: (1) The firm will hire more labor when the wage falls, and (2) it will hire labor up to the quantity at which the wage equals the marginal revenue product, even though MRP may shift. Thus, for every variable input, the firm will hire the quantity of the input at which its MRP

[9]This result is demonstrated mathematically in the appendix to this chapter.

ILLUSTRATION 12.4

Are the Giants Subject to the Ups and Downs of the Markets?

In August 1997, executives from huge industrial firms, such as Mobil and Union Carbide, were in conference with a team of management consultants and, as reported in *The Wall Street Journal*, the mood was surprisingly somber.* "It's a fine summer day, the stock market is booming, and some of the companies represented here are posting stronger-than-expected profits. . . . They ought to be euphoric."

The director of the consultant group and the host of the meeting welcomed the executives by saying, "I feel like the prophet of doom. It's our belief that the downturn has started." For two days, the executives and their advisers had discussed what they expected in their industries over the next two years: "growing overcapacity, world-wide product gluts, price wars, shakeouts and consolidations." The problems seemed to stem from the investment, perhaps overinvestment, during the expansion, which appeared to many to have resulted in overcapacity.

The problem extended beyond the oil, chemical, paper, and other industries that process raw materials: "The global auto and airline industries are building capacity rapidly, and some experts expect shakeouts in them, too, by 1999. Already, U.S. retail space and semiconductor-manufacturing capacity are widely acknowledged to far exceed demand." A Union Carbide vice president cited a basic problem in chemicals: "The profitability that the industry sees in the good times has always led to overinvesting, and it has this time."

There was a new twist in this cycle, according to the *WSJ*: "More than in past cycles, this one is increasingly global." New factories were going up everywhere, especially in the emerging nations of Asia and Latin America. This was especially true in automaking: Latin America's auto production was expected to double between 1995 and 2000, and nearly double in Asia outside of Japan and South Korea. Industry experts expected a shakeout by the end of the century. The two largest airplane producers, Boeing and Europe's Airbus, responding to a record number of aircraft orders, were increasing production rates and "producing more than the market can absorb." Similar overinvestment was occurring in other industries.

The *WSJ* wondered, "Why don't many executives see capacity problems building up? One reason is ego. Companies figure that when the bloodbath is over, *they* will emerge the winners. Another reason is me-tooism, the hard mentality: When cash is strong the fad is to spend it." We might suggest an additional reason: They do see their own possible capacity problems building up, but they worry that if they are wrong and the boom continues, they may get left behind if they don't continue expanding.

The management consultants suggested some possible solutions at the meeting. Investments timed to match changes in demand, better management of working capital, and strong industrial marketing. All were rather nebulous. The head of strategic planning at Shell International Petroleum Corporation noted, "If we repeat some of the behaviors of the past, we might wind up giving it away to the marketplace again."

We would agree. We also believe the answer to the question in the title of this illustration is, "Yes."

*"Same Old Cycles: In Some Industries Executives Foresee Tough Times Ahead," *The Wall Street Journal*, Aug. 7, 1997.

equals its price. If, for example, the firm uses two variable inputs, denoted I and J, the firm will maximize profits by using both inputs at such levels that

$$MRP_I = P_I$$
$$MRP_J = P_J$$

Since the marginal product of either input shifts according to the level of usage of the other, these conditions must hold *simultaneously*.

12.7 SUMMARY

Perfectly competitive markets exist when there are a large number of buyers and sellers, identical products, unrestricted entry and exit by producers, complete knowledge, and prices freely determined by the interaction of supply and demand. While these conditions do not precisely describe real-world markets, many markets function in ways that can be explained by using the theory of perfect competition. Managers, who operate in markets where a large number of firms produce similar products and entry into the industry is not restricted, will find that the theory of perfect competition is applicable to their decisions concerning production levels and input usage, as well as for predicting market conditions.

The profit-maximizing decision for a manager can take either of two equivalent forms. The manager can choose the level of output that maximizes profit or the level of input usage that maximizes profit. The two approaches lead to identical levels of input usage, output, and profit.

Economic profit is the difference between total revenue and total economic cost. Normal profit is the opportunity cost of the owners' resources that are used by the firm. Normal profit plus explicit costs equal total economic cost. Thus when economic profit is zero, the firm is earning just enough revenue to pay all explicit costs and pay the owners of the firm a normal profit.

A manager operating a firm in a competitive market faces a perfectly elastic demand curve. The firm's demand curve is a horizontal line at the market-determined price. Since marginal revenue equals price for a perfectly competitive firm, the firm's demand is also simultaneously the marginal revenue curve under perfect competition.

In the short run, a manager chooses to produce that level of output where marginal revenue (price) equals marginal cost, as long as price exceeds average variable cost. When price is less than average variable cost, total revenue is less than total variable cost. If the firm produces, it would lose an amount equal to all its fixed costs plus some of its variable costs. Under these circumstances ($P < AVC$), the manager should shut down the firm and lose only fixed costs.

The supply curve for a perfectly competitive firm in the short run is the portion of the firm's marginal cost curve above minimum average variable cost. If all input prices are constant as industry output expands, the short-run supply curve for the industry is the horizontal summation of all the firms' marginal cost curves. If the industry's (although not the individual firm's) use of some inputs affects the prices of these inputs, industry supply is less elastic than this horizontal summation but is still positively sloped.

In managerial decision making, fixed costs don't matter. Fixed costs play no role in determining the profit-maximizing level of output. The shutdown rule involves comparing total revenue and total variable cost (or, equivalently, price and average variable cost). The optimal level of production is found by equating marginal revenue and marginal cost. Fixed costs have nothing to do with determining how much to produce or with the decision to shut down.

In the long run, the firm is in profit-maximizing equilibrium when MR (= P) equals long-run marginal cost (LMC). The industry is in long-run competitive equilibrium when economic profit is zero, eliminating any incentive for entry or exit, and all incumbent firms in the industry are in profit-maximizing equilibrium. Thus, industry equilibrium requires that all firms are satisfying the two conditions: $P = LMC$ and $P = LAC$. This occurs when the market-determined price is just equal to minimum long-run average cost.

The long-run industry supply curve for a competitive industry can be either upward-sloping in the case of an increasing-cost industry or horizontal in the case of a constant-cost industry. When industry output expands, the prices of inputs may be bid up, causing the minimum point on LAC to rise. Since long-run supply price equals minimum LAC, an upward shift in LAC due to rising input prices causes supply price to increase. This is why the industry supply curve is upward-sloping in the long run for an increasing-cost industry. If input prices are constant as industry output and input usage increase, minimum LAC remains constant and the long-run supply curve is perfectly elastic for the constant-cost industry.

When choosing the profit-maximizing level of labor usage to maximize the profit of the firm, the manager hires labor up to the point where the marginal revenue product of labor ($MRP = P \times MP_L$) equals the wage rate, which is the marginal cost when the price of labor is given to the firm. Using this rule, the demand for a single variable input by a competitive firm is the positive portion of the *MRP* curve over the range of input usage for which *ARP* is greater than *w*. The input demand curve gives the quantity of the variable input that the manager will hire at each price of the input.

It should be emphasized that the theory of perfect competition is not designed to describe specific real-world firms. It is a theoretical model that is frequently useful in explaining real-world behavior and in predicting the economic consequences of changes in the different variables contained in the model. It is also useful as a guide for managerial decision making.

In the next chapter, we will show how a manager can implement the theory developed in this chapter to make profit-maximizing decisions concerning the level of output and level of usage of variable inputs. You will see how to combine the statistical techniques of cost estimation with price forecasts and the decision-making rules developed in this chapter to make decisions about whether to produce or shut down, as well as the optimal level of production and input usage.

TECHNICAL PROBLEMS

1. The left-hand side of the following graph shows market demand and supply curves in a perfectly competitive market. Draw the demand facing a perfectly competitive firm selling in this market on the right-hand graph.

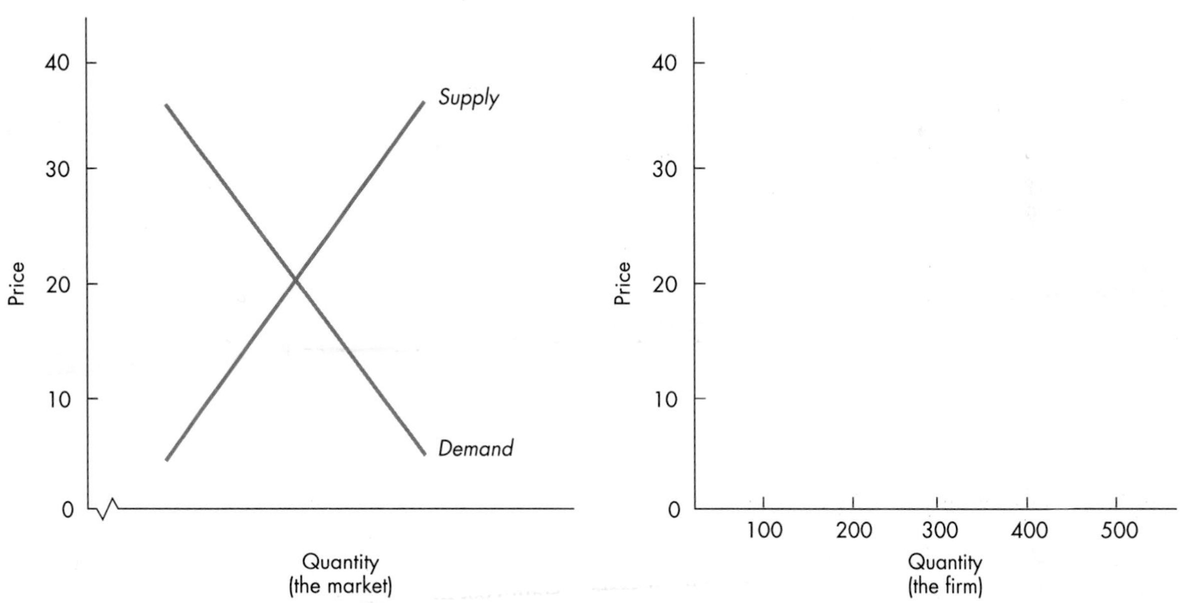

   a. What is the firm's demand elasticity at 200 units of output? At 400 units?
   b. What is the firm's marginal revenue from selling the 200th unit of output? From the 400th unit?

2. The following figure shows the marginal cost for a perfectly competitive firm and its demand and marginal revenue ($D = MR = P$).

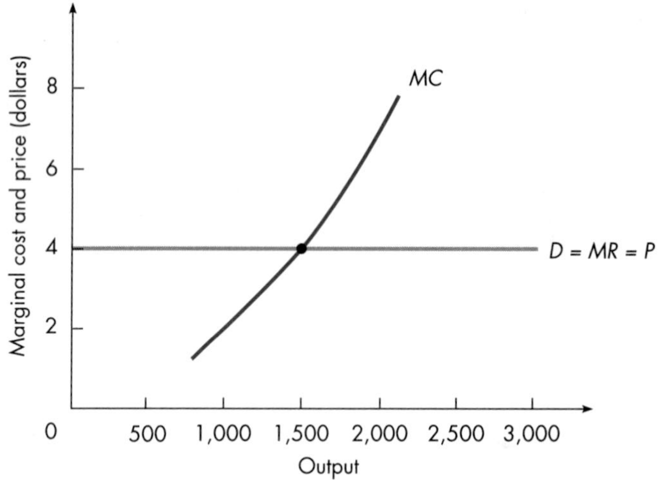

a. What output should the firm produce?

b. If the firm is producing 1,000 units of output, adding another unit of output would increase cost by $________ and revenue by $________. The firm's profit would ________ by $________.

c. If the firm is producing 2,000 units of output, taking away 1 unit of output would reduce cost by $________ and revenue by $________. The firm's profit would ________ by $________.

3. Answer the questions below using the cost curves for a perfectly competitive firm shown in the following graph:

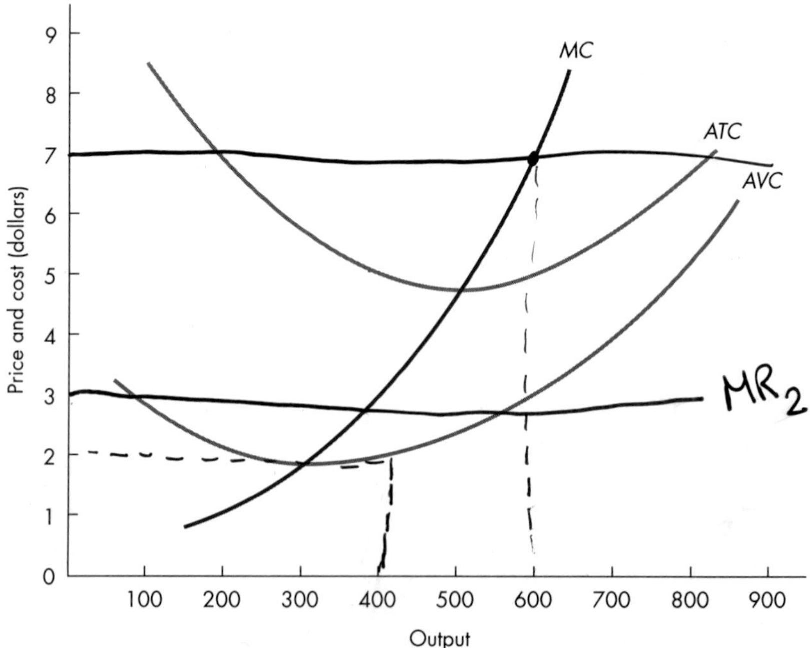

a. If price is $7 per unit of output, draw the marginal revenue curve. The manager should produce ________ units in order to maximize profit.
b. Since average total cost is $________ for this output, total cost is $________.
c. The firm makes a profit of $________.
d. Let price fall to $3, and draw the new marginal revenue curve. The manager should now produce ________ units in order to maximize profit.
e. Total revenue is now $________ and total cost is $________. The firm makes a loss of $________.
f. Total variable cost is $________, leaving $________ to apply to fixed cost.
g. If price falls below $________, the firm will produce zero output. Explain why.

4. In a perfectly competitive industry the market price is $12. A firm is currently producing 50 units of output; average total cost is $10, marginal cost is $15, and average variable cost is $7.
   a. Is the firm making the profit-maximizing decision? Why or why not? If not, what should the firm do?
   b. Consider another firm in a perfectly competitive industry that faces a market price of $25. This firm is producing 10,000 units of output, and average total cost, which at its minimum value, is $25. Answer part *a* for this firm.
5. Firm A and firm B both have total revenues of $100,000 and total fixed costs of $50,000; firm A has total variable costs of $80,000, while firm B has total variable costs of $110,000.
   a. How much profit or loss is each firm earning? Should firm A operate or shut down? What about firm B? Why?
   b. Firms C and D both have total revenues of $200,000 and total costs of $250,000; firm C has total fixed costs of $40,000, while firm D has total fixed costs of $70,000. How much profit or loss is each firm earning? Should firm C operate or shut down? What about firm D? Why?
6. The following graph shows a perfectly competitive firm's short-run cost structure:

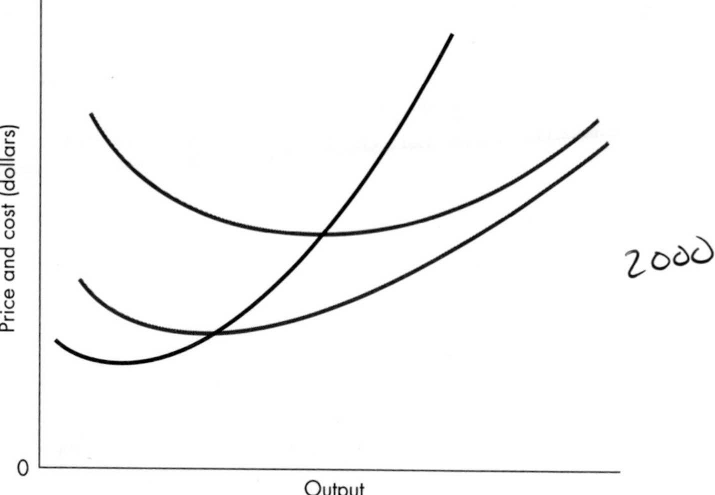

   a. Label the three curves.
   b. Show a price at which the firm would make economic profit. Show the quantity it would produce and the amount of economic profit that would be earned.
   c. Show a price at which the firm would continue to produce in the short run but would suffer losses. Show the output and losses at this price.
   d. Show a price at which the firm would not produce in the short run.

7. The following graph shows the short-run average variable cost and marginal cost curves for a perfectly competitive firm. There are 1,000 firms in the industry, and each has the same cost curves as this firm.

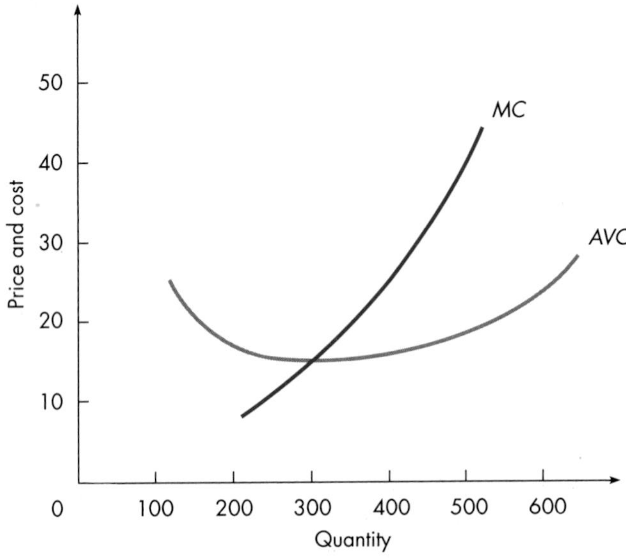

a. If the price of the product is $25, how much does each firm produce? What is the industry's total production?

b. Next let the price rise to $40. The industry has no effect on the prices of any inputs it uses. What is the new total production for the industry?

c. Answer part *b* under the assumption that the industry as a whole does affect the prices of some inputs by changing its output and hence input usage.

8. The following figure shows long-run average and marginal cost curves for a perfectly competitive firm. The price of the product is $40.

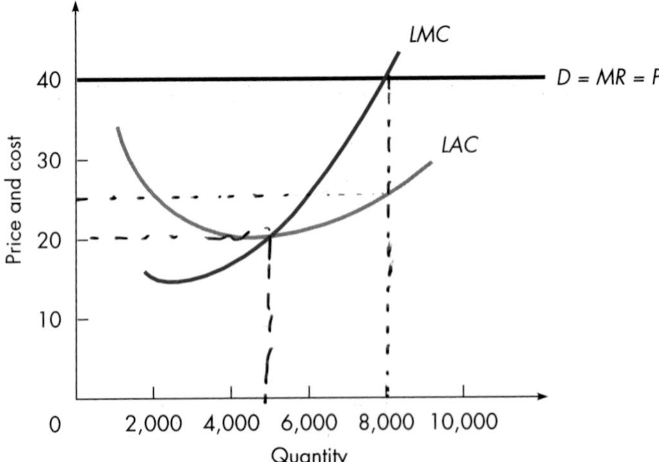

a. How much will the firm produce? What will be its economic profit?
b. When the industry attains long-run competitive equilibrium, what will be the price and the firm's output? What will be the firm's economic profit?

9. Describe a position of long-run competitive equilibrium for a perfectly competitive firm and industry.
a. How and why does such an equilibrium come about?
b. How would a manager of a perfectly competitive firm know when the industry is in equilibrium?

10. Suppose that a perfectly competitive industry is in long-run competitive equilibrium. Then the price of a substitute good (in consumption) decreases. What will happen in the short run to:
a. The market demand curve
b. The market supply curve
c. Market price
d. Market output
e. The firm's output
f. The firm's profit
What will happen in the long run?

11. A typical firm in a perfectly competitive market made positive economic profits last period. What do you expect will happen this period to:
a. The number of firms in the market
b. The market demand curve
c. The market supply curve
d. Market price
e. Market output
f. The firm's output
g. The firm's profit

12. The supply curve for an industry shows the relation between supply price and industry output.
a. The long-run competitive supply curve for a constant-cost industry is horizontal. Why is supply price constant?
b. The long-run competitive supply curve for an increasing-cost industry is upward-sloping. Why does supply price increase as industry production rises?

13. A manufacturing firm employs a superior plant manager to manage production at its plant. This plant manager is much more efficient than the typical plant manager employed at the rest of the firms in the industry, which is perfectly competitive. Typical plant managers make $5,000 per month in salary. By employing the superior plant manager, the firm faces the *LAC* and *LMC* curves shown in the following figure. In long-run equilibrium, the price of the product is $10.

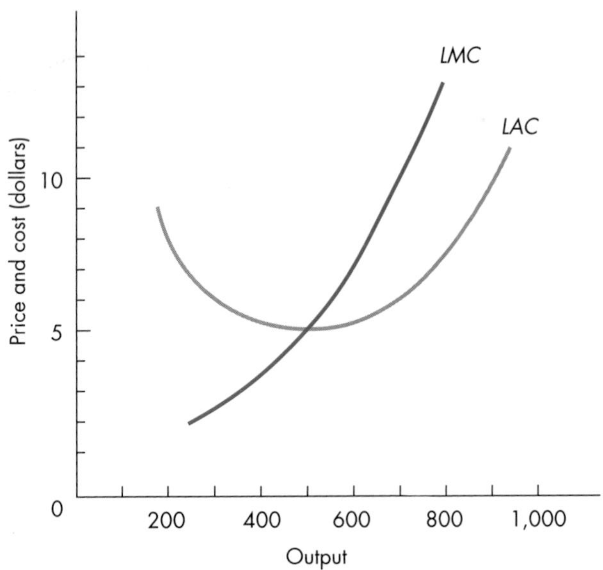

a. Minimum *LAC* for a firm with a typical plant manager is $______. The typical firm earns economic profit of $______.

b. The firm with the superior plant manager earns economic profit of $______.

c. The superior plant manager earns a salary of $______ per month, $______ of which is economic rent.

d. If the superior plant manager were also the owner of the manufacturing plant, how much profit would she earn? Explain.

14. Consider a perfectly competitive firm that has total fixed cost of $50 and faces a market-determined price of $2 per unit for its output. The wage rate is $10 per unit of labor, the only variable input. Using the following table, answer the questions below.

(1) Units of labor	(2) Output	(3) Marginal product	(4) Marginal revenue product	(5) Marginal cost	(6) Profit
1	5	____	____	____	____
2	15	____	____	____	____
3	30	____	____	____	____
4	50	____	____	____	____
5	65	____	____	____	____
6	77	____	____	____	____
7	86	____	____	____	____
8	94	____	____	____	____
9	98	____	____	____	____
10	96	____	____	____	____

a. Fill in the blanks in column 3 of the table by computing the marginal product of labor for each level of labor usage.
b. Fill in the blanks in column 4 of the table by computing the marginal revenue product for each level of labor usage.
c. How much labor should the manager hire in order to maximize profit? Why?
d. Fill in the blanks in column 5 of the table by computing marginal cost.
e. How many units of output should the manager produce in order to maximize profit? Why?
f. Fill in the blanks in column 6 with the profit earned at each level of labor usage.
g. Do your answers to parts *c* and *e* maximize profit? Does it matter whether the manager chooses labor usage or chooses output in order to maximize profit? Why?
h. How much labor should the manager hire when the wage rate is $20? How much profit is earned? Is marginal product greater or less than average product at this level of labor usage? Why does it matter?

15. The following graph shows the relevant portion of the marginal product curve for labor (the only variable input) used by a perfectly competitive firm.

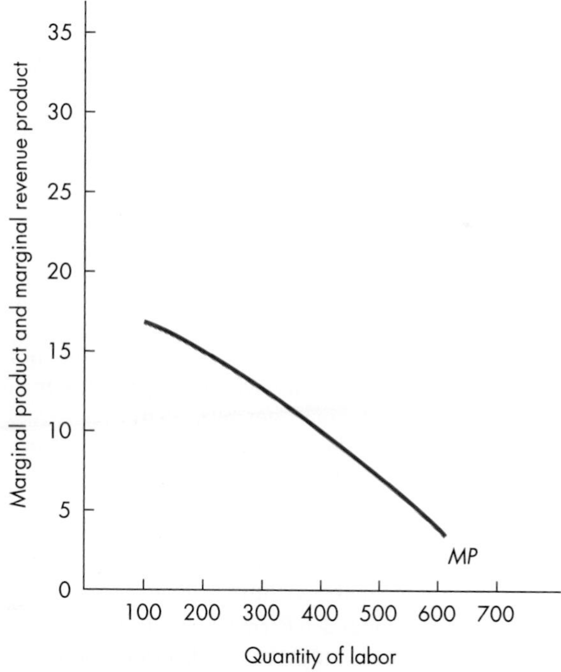

a. On the graph, draw the associated marginal revenue product curve over the relevant range of labor usage. The price of the product produced is $2 per unit.
b. At a wage rate of $30, how much labor will the firm hire? What if the wage rate falls to $20? What if the wage falls to $14?
c. Suppose the price of the product falls to $1. Draw the new *MRP* curve.
d. How much labor is hired now at each of the three wage rates?

APPLIED PROBLEMS

1. The MidNight Hour, a local nightclub, earned $100,000 in accounting profit last year. This year the owner, who had invested $1 million in the club, decided to close the club. What can you say about economic profit (and the rate of return) in the nightclub business?
2. In an article on the steel industry, *The Wall Street Journal* (July 18, 1996) noted that as steel prices were falling, steelmakers were not cutting production since "steelmakers can't afford to lose any sales because their costs, especially their fixed costs, are so high." What does this statement mean? Explain.
3. The manager of All City Realtors wants to hire some real estate agents to specialize in selling housing units acquired by the Resolution Trust Corporation (RTC) in its attempt to bail out the savings and loan industry. The commission paid by the RTC to the company to sell these homes is a flat rate of $2,000 per unit sold, rather than the customary commission that is based on the sale price of a home. The manager estimates the following marginal product schedule for real estate agents dealing in government-owned housing:

Number of real estate agents	Marginal product (number of additional units sold per year)	Marginal revenue product
1	20	_____
2	17	_____
3	15	_____
4	12	_____
5	8	_____
6	4	_____

   a. Construct the marginal revenue product schedule by filling in the blanks in the table above.
   b. If the manager of All City Realtors must pay a wage rate of $32,000 per year to get agents who will specialize in selling RTC housing, how many agents should the manager hire? Why?
   c. If the wage rate falls to $18,000 per year, how many agents should the manager hire?
   d. Suppose the RTC raises its commission to $3,000 per unit sold. Now what is the marginal revenue product for each real estate agent employed?
   e. Now that the RTC is paying $3,000 per unit sold, how many agents should the manager hire if the wage rate is $30,000?
4. HoneyBee Farms, a medium-size producer of honey, operates in a market that fits the competitive market definition relatively well. However, honey farmers are assisted by support prices above the price that would prevail in the absence of controls. The owner of HoneyBee Farms, as well as some other honey producers, complain that they can't make a profit even with these support prices. Explain why. Explain why even higher support prices would not help honey farmers in the long run.
5. Insurance agents receive a commission on the policies they sell. Many states regulate the rates that can be charged for insurance. Would higher or lower rates increase the incomes of agents? Explain, distinguishing between the short run and the long run.

6. If all the assumptions of perfect competition hold, why would firms in such an industry have little incentive to carry out technological change or much research and development? What conditions would encourage research and development in competitive industries?
7. At a recent board meeting, the president and CEO got into a heated argument about whether or not to shut down the firm's plant in Miami. The Miami plant currently loses $60,000 monthly. The president of the firm argued that the Miami plant should continue to operate, at least until a buyer is found for the production facility. The president's argument was based on the fact that the Miami plant's fixed costs are $68,000 per month. The CEO exploded over this point, castigating the president for considering fixed costs in making the shutdown decision. According to the CEO, "Everyone knows fixed costs don't matter!"
   a. Should the Miami plant be closed or continue to operate at a loss in the short run?
   b. How would you explain to the incorrect party that he or she is wrong?
8. Suppose you own a home remodeling company. You are currently earning short-run profits. The home remodeling industry is an increasing-cost industry. In the long run, what do you expect will happen to:
   a. Your firm's costs of production? Explain.
   b. The price you can charge for your remodeling services? Why?
   c. The rate of return in home remodeling? Why?
9. In January 1996, the New York City Parks Department doubled the annual fee for the hot-dog pushcart that had the exclusive license for the spot just south of the Metropolitan Museum of Art to $288,000. Why would anyone pay almost $300,000 for a pushcart license? Who is obtaining the economic rent for the obviously lucrative pushcart location? How much economic profit is the pushcart owner probably earning?
10. Many state governments are offering huge benefits to large corporations if the corporations agree to open new offices or manufacturing facilities in those states. The benefits offered include lump-sum cash payments, "forgivable" loans, free land for office sites, and lower taxes. In what sense are these benefits similar to economic rents for these firms? Other than the fortunate firms who receive these benefits, who else benefits from these payments?
11. Grocery stores and gasoline stations in a large city would appear to be an example of perfectly competitive markets—there are numerous sellers, each seller is relatively small, and the products sold are quite similar. How could we argue that these markets are not perfectly competitive (leaving out the assumption of perfect knowledge)? Could each firm face a demand curve that is *not* perfectly elastic? What rate of return do you expect grocery stores and gasoline stations to earn in the long run?

MATHEMATICAL APPENDIX Profit Maximization for a Perfectly Competitive Firm

This appendix describes a manager's choice of output and input usage in order to maximize profit for a perfectly competitive firm facing a given market-determined price for the product it sells. We examine the decision about the profit-maximizing output level first using the most general cost function and then using a quadratic cost function. Next we derive the profit-maximizing conditions when the manager chooses the level of usage of first one variable input and then two variable inputs.

The Firm Chooses the Level of Output

Assume that the firm is in the short run, so some costs are fixed. Let the market-determined price be $\overline{P}$. The firm's total revenue is

$$R(Q) = \overline{P}Q$$

The firm's profit function is

$$\pi = \overline{P}Q - TVC(Q) - TFC \tag{1}$$

where $TVC(Q)$ is total variable cost and TFC is total fixed cost.

The first-order condition for a maximum requires

$$\frac{d\pi}{dQ} = \overline{P} - \frac{dTVC}{dQ} = 0 \tag{2}$$

The second-order condition for a maximum is that at the equilibrium quantity

$$\frac{d^2\pi}{dQ^2} = -\frac{d^2TVC}{dQ^2} < 0 \tag{3}$$

Since, in equation (2), $dTVC/dQ$ is marginal cost (MC), choosing the quantity of output that maximizes profit requires that price equal marginal cost: $\overline{P} = MC$. The second-order condition shows that in profit-maximizing equilibrium marginal cost must be upward-sloping: $d^2TVC/dQ^2 > 0$. Equation (2) can be solved for the profit-maximizing output, Q^*.

If, at Q^*,

$$\pi = \overline{P}Q^* - TVC(Q^*) - TFC > 0$$

the firm makes an economic profit. If

$$\pi = \overline{P}Q^* - TVC(Q^*) - TFC < 0$$

the firm makes a loss. In this case the firm should produce Q^* rather than shutting down when

$$|\overline{P}Q^* - TVC(Q^*) - TFC| < TFC$$

which occurs if, at Q^*, price is greater than average variable cost:

$$\overline{P} > \frac{TVC(Q^*)}{Q^*} \tag{4}$$

The firm loses less than its fixed cost, which is the amount it would lose if it shuts down and produces nothing. If at Q^* price is less than average variable cost, the firm should shut down and produce nothing. It loses all its fixed cost rather than its fixed cost plus the amount of variable cost not covered by revenue.

Since the second-order condition in equation (3) requires that marginal cost be upward-sloping, the firm's short-run supply must be upward-sloping. The higher the price, the greater the equilibrium output at which price equals marginal cost. Since, from equation (4), the firm produces nothing if price falls below minimum average variable cost, the supply is zero at prices below minimum AVC.

For a less general approach, let the total variable cost function be the cubic function

$$TVC(Q) = aQ - bQ^2 + cQ^3$$

where a, b, and c are positive. We continue to assume that the market-determined price is $\overline{P}$. The profit function is

$$\begin{aligned} \pi &= \overline{P}Q - TVC(Q) - TFC \\ &= \overline{P}Q - aQ + bQ^2 - cQ^3 - TFC \end{aligned} \tag{5}$$

For profit maximization, differentiate equation (5) and set the derivative equal to zero:

$$\frac{d\pi}{dQ} = \overline{P} - (a - 2bQ + 3cQ^2) = 0 \tag{6}$$

Since $MC = dTVC(Q)/dQ = a - 2bQ + 3cQ^2$, price equals marginal cost in profit-maximizing equilibrium. The second-order condition for a maximum is

$$\frac{d^2\pi}{dQ^2} = 2b - 6cQ < 0 \tag{7}$$

or, solving equation (7) for Q, for a maximum it must be the case that

$$Q > \frac{b}{3c} \tag{8}$$

To obtain the profit-maximizing level of output, Q^*, solve the quadratic equation formed from equation (6):

$$(\overline{P} - a) - 2bQ + 3cQ^2 = 0$$

After solving such a quadratic equation, you will generally get two values for Q^*. The profit-maximizing Q^* will be the one at which the second-order condition in (8) holds, ensuring that this is the value of Q^* at which marginal cost is upward-sloping. This will be the larger of the two solutions. If total revenue exceeds total variable cost, i.e., if

$$\overline{P} > AVC(Q^*) = TVC(Q^*)/Q^* = a - bQ^* + cQ^{*2}$$

the firm produces Q^* and profit or loss is

$$\pi = \overline{P}Q^* - aQ^* + bQ^{*2} - cQ^{*3} - TFC$$

If $P < AVC(Q^*) = a - bQ^* + cQ^{*2}$ the firm shuts down, produces nothing, and loses its total fixed cost.

The Firm Chooses Input Usage

First we assume the firm chooses the level of usage of a single variable input, labor (L), in order to maximize profit. All other inputs ($\overline{K}$) are fixed in amount. The price of the product is $\overline{P}$. Let the production function be as derived for the short run in the Mathematical Appendix to Chapter 9:

$$Q = f(L, \overline{K}) = g(L)$$

The firm chooses L, so the following profit function is maximized:

$$\pi = \overline{P}g(L) - wL - TFC \tag{9}$$

where w is the wage paid to labor and TFC is the fixed payment to the fixed input. Profit maximization requires

$$\frac{d\pi}{dL} = \overline{P}\left[\frac{dQ}{dL}\right] - w = 0 \tag{10}$$

Since $dQ/dL = MP_L$ is the marginal product of labor, equation (10) can be expressed as

$$MP_L \times \overline{P} = \text{Marginal revenue product} = w$$

Equation (10) can be solved for L^*, then $Q^* = g(L^*)$.

If, at L^*, $MRP < ARP = \overline{P}g(L^*)/L^*$, total revenue will be greater than total variable cost ($PQ^* > wL^*$) and the firm will produce. Its profit or loss will be

$$\pi = \overline{P}g(L^*) - w - TFC$$

If, however, $MRP = w > \overline{P}Q^*/L^*$, total revenue will be less than total variable cost ($\overline{P}Q^* < wL^*$). In this case the firm would shut down and lose only its total fixed cost, rather than its total fixed cost plus the portion of total variable cost not covered by revenue.

Now assume that the firm uses two variable inputs, L and K, to produce Q and no inputs are fixed. The prices of L and K are, respectively, w and r. The production function is

$$Q = f(L, K)$$

The product price remains $\overline{P}$. The profit function is

$$\pi = \overline{P}f(L, K) - wL - rK$$

Since the firm chooses the levels of L and K to maximize profit, the first-order equilibrium conditions are

$$\overline{P}\frac{\partial Q}{\partial L} - w = 0 \tag{11a}$$

$$\overline{P}\frac{\partial Q}{\partial K} - r = 0 \tag{11b}$$

Equations (11a) and (11b) can be solved for the profit-maximizing levels of L^* and K^*; then the optimal level of output is $Q^* = f(L^*, K^*)$. This value of Q^* can be substituted into the above profit equation to find the maximum level of profit.

Equations (11a) and (11b) can be rewritten as

$$\overline{P}MP_L = MRP_L = w \tag{12a}$$

$$\overline{P}MP_K = MRP_K = r \tag{12b}$$

Thus in equilibrium the marginal revenue product of each input equals its price.

In Chapter 13 we will discuss in detail how a perfectly competitive firm, using actual estimates of the parameters of its cost function and product price forecasts, can implement the profit-maximizing decision and solve for the optimal value of output and profit. Also in that chapter we will show how a manager can use estimates of the parameters in the production function and price forecasts to implement the hiring decision and solve for the actual values of input usage that maximize the firm's profit.

CHAPTER 13

Profit Maximization in Perfectly Competitive Markets:

Implementation of the Theory

Although it is useful for managers to know the fundamentals of the theory of profit maximization, it is even more useful for them to know how to implement and use the theory to maximize their firms' profits. A manager should be able to use empirical estimates or forecasts of the relevant variables and equations to determine the actual values of the decision variables that maximize the firm's profit. As emphasized in Chapter 12, a manager can choose either the level of output or the level of input usage. The two approaches are equivalent because they both lead to the same levels of output, input usage, and profit. This chapter describes how to use empirical analysis to find the optimal level of output and inputs.

Using the statistical techniques for estimating demand, production, and cost functions, you will learn how to estimate or forecast the levels of output and input usage that maximize the firm's profit. You have spent a lot of time learning the techniques of estimating the various demand, production, and cost functions. Now you will learn how to use these empirical skills to answer an important question facing a manager: How can the theory of profit maximization be used in practice to make profit-maximizing decisions about production?

In the examples used here, the manager has complete information about most of the relevant variables and all the equations. In reality, managers will probably not have access to such ideal information. However, by showing how to make decisions about profit maximization under the most favorable circumstances, we can give you a feel for the way such decisions are made under conditions that are not so favorable—that is, when information is not complete.

We will first outline how managers can, in general, determine the optimizing conditions. This outline gives a pattern for situations in which numerical estimates of the variables and equations are available. Then we present examples of how a firm can use this approach to determine the optimal level of output and the optimal level of input usage. We demonstrate numerically that the two methods lead to the same results. We end with a discussion of how the presence of risk modifies the decision-making process.

13.1 IMPLEMENTING THE PROFIT-MAXIMIZING OUTPUT DECISION

In Chapter 12 we emphasized that a manager must answer two questions when choosing the level of output that maximizes profit. These two questions and the answers forthcoming from the theoretical analysis in Chapter 12 are summarized as follows:

1. Should the firm produce or shut down? *Produce as long as the market price is greater than or equal to minimum average variable cost*—$P \geq AVC_{min}$. *Shut down otherwise.*
2. If production occurs, how much should the firm produce? *Produce the output at which market price (which is marginal revenue) equals marginal cost*—$P = MC$.

It follows from these rules that to determine the optimal level of output, a manager must obtain estimates or forecasts of the market price of the good produced by the firm, the firm's average variable cost function, and the firm's marginal cost function. Based on the theoretical analysis in Chapter 12, the steps explained below can be followed to find the profit-maximizing rate of production and the level of profit the firm will earn.

Step 1: Forecast the price of the product

Output decisions are typically made for some period in the future: next week, next month, next quarter, and so on. Therefore, in order to decide whether or not to produce and how much to produce, a manager must obtain a forecast of the price at which the completed product can be sold. Remember that a perfectly competitive firm does not face a downward-sloping demand curve but simply takes the market price as given. We showed in Chapter 8 how to use two statistical techniques—time-series forecasting and econometric forecasting—to forecast the price of the product.

Step 2: Estimate average variable cost (*AVC*) and marginal cost (*MC*)

As emphasized in Chapter 11, the cubic specification is the appropriate form for estimating a family of short-run cost curves. Thus the manager could estimate the following average variable cost function:

$$AVC = a + bQ + cQ^2$$

As demonstrated in Chapter 11, the marginal cost function associated with this average variable cost function is

$$MC = a + 2bQ + 3cQ^2$$

Step 3: Check the shutdown rule

When P is less than AVC, the firm loses less money by shutting down than it would lose if it produced where $P = MC$. A manager can determine the price below which a firm should shut down by finding the *minimum* point on the AVC curve, AVC_{min}. As long as price is greater than (or equal to) AVC_{min}, the firm will produce rather than shut down.[1] Recall from Chapter 11 that the average variable cost curve reaches its minimum value at $Q_m = -b/2c$. The minimum value of average variable cost is then determined by substituting Q_m into the AVC function:

$$AVC_{min} = a + bQ_m + c(Q_m)^2$$

The firm should produce as long as $P \geq AVC_{min}$. If the forecasted price is greater than (or equal to) minimum average variable cost ($P \geq AVC_{min}$), the firm should produce the output level where $P = MC$. If the forecasted price is less than the minimum average variable cost ($P < AVC_{min}$), the firm should shut down in the short run, and it loses an amount equal to its total fixed costs.

Step 4: If $P \geq AVC_{min}$, find the output level where $P = MC$

A perfectly competitive firm should produce the level of output for which $P = MC$—if $P \geq AVC_{min}$. Thus, if the manager decides to produce in the short run, the manager maximizes profit by finding the output level for which $P = MC$. In the case of a cubic specification for cost, profit maximization or loss minimization requires that

$$P = MC = a + 2bQ + 3cQ^2$$

Solving this equation for Q^* gives the optimal output level for the firm—unless P is less than AVC, and then the optimal output level is zero.

Step 5: Computation of profit or loss

Once a manager determines how much to produce, the calculation of total profit or loss is straightforward. Profit (or loss) is equal to total revenue minus total cost. Total revenue for a competitive firm is price times quantity sold. Total cost is the sum of total variable cost and total fixed cost, where total variable cost is average variable cost times the number of units sold. Hence, total profit (loss) is

$$\begin{aligned}\pi &= TR - TC \\ &= (P \times Q^*) - [(AVC \times Q^*) + TFC] \\ &= (P - AVC)Q^* - TFC\end{aligned}$$

If $P < AVC_{min}$, the firm shuts down, and $\pi = -TFC$.

[1]When price exactly equals average variable cost ($P = AVC$), total revenue is just sufficient to cover total variable cost, and the firm loses an amount equal to total fixed cost. Losing an amount equal to total fixed cost is exactly what happens if the firm shuts down. Thus, when $P = AVC$ the firm is indifferent between producing or shutting down. As in Chapter 12, we continue to assume arbitrarily that the manager will choose to produce, rather than shut down, if price exactly equals average variable cost.

To illustrate how to implement these steps to find the profit-maximizing level of output and to forecast the profit of the firm, we now turn to a hypothetical firm that operates in a perfectly competitive market.

13.2 IMPLEMENTING THE PROFIT-MAXIMIZING OUTPUT DECISION: AN ILLUSTRATION

As an example, we use the output decision facing the manager of Beau Apparel, Inc., a clothing manufacturer that produces moderately priced men's shirts. Beau Apparel is only one of many firms that produce a fairly homogeneous product, and none of the firms in this moderate-price shirt market engages in any significant advertising. While the market for shirts does not exactly match all the conditions of perfect competition, it does, approximately, satisfy the conditions of a perfectly competitive industry. Consequently, the manager of Beau Apparel can employ the steps outlined above to find the level of shirt production that maximizes profit.

Price Forecasts

In mid-December 1998, the manager of Beau Apparel was preparing the firm's production plan for the first quarter of 1999. The manager wanted to obtain a forecast of the wholesale price of shirts for the first quarter of 1999. This price forecast would subsequently be used in making the production decision for Beau Apparel. Since the manufacturer sells shirts to retail clothing stores, the wholesale, rather than the retail, price is the relevant price.

The manager recognizes that in this particular segment of the shirt market, Beau Apparel is operating in a nearly perfectly competitive market. Consequently, the manager believed specifying a demand and supply model for the shirt market was appropriate. The manager specified the following demand and supply equations:

$$\text{Demand: } Q = a + bP + cM$$
$$\text{Supply: } Q = e + fP + gP_I$$

where Q represents both the quantity demanded and the quantity supplied (since they are the same in equilibrium), P is the wholesale price of a shirt (adjusted for the effects of inflation), M is per capita income, and P_I is the price of the variable input.[2]

Using quarterly data for the seven-year time period 1992(I) to 1998(IV), the manager estimated the demand and supply equations using the two-stage least-squares method of estimation to eliminate the simultaneous equations bias, as

[2]While there are usually many variable inputs used in production, it is not generally convenient (or necessary) to include in the supply equation the price of every one of the variable inputs employed by the firm. Instead, the effect of a change in input prices on supply can usually be adequately modeled by including the prices of only the most important inputs, where importance is determined by the share of the total cost attributable to a particular input. Alternatively, a weighted average of input prices can be used for P_I, where the weights are computed as the share of the total cost accounted for by each input.

discussed in Chapter 7. Both demand and supply were identified, and the estimated demand and supply equations were

$$\text{Demand: } Q = 125 - 2P + 0.0125M$$
$$\text{Supply: } Q = 250 + 8P - 3.125P_I$$

Each of the estimated coefficients had the expected sign and was statistically significant at the 5 percent significance level.

Before the estimated demand and supply equations can be used to forecast price in the first quarter of 1999, values for the exogenous variables, income and price of the variable input, must be forecast for the first quarter of 1999. To obtain the necessary forecasts for the exogenous variables, the manager purchased forecasts of per capita income and input prices from a large econometric forecasting firm. The forecast for the price of the variable input in the first quarter of 1999 was \$16.

In the case of the income forecast, the forecasting firm believed that future levels of per capita income depended crucially upon the outcome of a major domestic economic policy matter currently being addressed by the U.S. Congress. To reflect this uncertainty, the forecasting firm provided the manager of Beau Apparel with two different forecasts of income, each based on a different assumption about the outcome of the legislation pending in Congress. These income forecasts for the first quarter of 1999, which we shall refer to as the *low* and *high* forecasts, were

$$\text{High} = \$22{,}000$$
$$\text{Low} = \$14{,}000$$

When forecasting the price of shirts in the first quarter of 1999, the manager of Beau Apparel had two alternative values of $\hat{M}_{1999(I)}$, \$14,000 and \$22,000.

To obtain forecasts of the price of shirts, the manager next substituted the forecasted values of the exogenous variables into the estimated demand and supply functions. Using the high forecast for income, the demand and supply equations in the first quarter of 1999 are

$$\begin{aligned}\text{Demand: } Q_{1999(I)} &= 125 - 2P_{1999(I)} + 0.0125(22{,}000)\\ &= 400 - 2P_{1999(I)}\\ \text{Supply: } Q_{1999(I)} &= 250 + 8P_{1999(I)} - 3.125(16)\\ &= 200 + 8P_{1999(I)}\end{aligned}$$

To calculate the equilibrium price, the manager set quantity demanded equal to quantity supplied:

$$400 - 2P_{1999(I)} = 200 + 8P_{1999(I)}$$

to obtain

$$\hat{P}_{1999(I)} = 20$$

For the case of the high-income forecast ($22,000), the forecasted wholesale price of shirts in the first quarter of 1999 was $20 per unit.

In exactly the same way, the manager then calculated a forecast for product price using the low-income forecast ($14,000) and obtained a wholesale price of $10 per unit. Thus, the econometric method of forecasting generated two forecasts for the wholesale price of shirts in the first quarter of 1999, $10 and $20 per unit.

The manager decided to obtain one more price forecast by using a time-series model. Specifically, the manager specified a linear trend model with a dummy variable to correct for seasonal variation in shirt prices. The time-series model for shirt prices was

$$P_t = a + bt + cD_t$$

where P_t is the inflation-adjusted price of shirts in time period t, and D_t is a dummy variable to account for seasonal variations in the price of shirts. The dummy variable, D_t, equals 1 in the winter and summer quarters (I and III), when stores usually stock up shirts for the spring and fall buying seasons, and equals zero in the spring and fall quarters (II and IV), when stores are primarily concerned with selling the shirts they purchased in the winter and summer quarters.

The linear trend equation was estimated using quarterly data for the seven-year period 1992(I) through 1998(IV). Since the textile industry is an increasing-cost industry and textile demand had generally been increasing over the last seven years, the manager of Beau Apparel expected the estimated value of b to have a positive sign, indicating an upward trend in the price of shirts. The estimated value of c was expected to be positive, reflecting the higher wholesale prices during the winter and summer quarters. The estimated trend line was

$$P_t = 6.25 + 0.2759t + 0.75D_t$$

The estimated coefficients were each statistically significant at the 5 percent level and each coefficient had the expected sign.

To forecast the wholesale price for the first quarter of 1999, the manager substituted the values $t = 29$ and $D_t = 1$ [since 1999(I) corresponds to time period 29 and the first quarter is a winter quarter] into the estimated trend-line equation:

$$\begin{aligned} P_{1999(I)} &= \hat{P}_{29} = 6.25 + 0.2759(29) + 0.75(1) \\ &= 15 \end{aligned}$$

Thus, the time-series model generated a forecast of $15 for the first quarter of 1999. With this forecast, the manager of Beau Apparel had three forecasts of the wholesale price of shirts in the first quarter of 1999:

Econometric model (high) = $20
Time-series model (medium) = $15
Econometric model (low) = $10

Estimation of Average Variable Cost and Marginal Cost

The manager of Beau Apparel chose a cubic specification of short-run cost for estimating the average variable cost and the marginal cost curves. Using time-series data over the seven-year time period 1992(I) through 1998(IV), during which Beau Apparel had the same-size plant, the following average variable cost function was estimated:

$$AVC = 20 - 0.003Q + 0.00000025Q^2$$

All the estimated coefficients (20, − 0.003, and 0.00000025) had the required sign and were statistically significant. The estimated average cost function provided the information needed for making the decision to produce or shut down. We will return to this decision after we discuss how the manager of Beau Apparel estimated the marginal cost function.

As explained in Chapter 11 and as reviewed in the previous section, the parameter estimates for the average variable cost function can be used to obtain the estimated marginal cost function:

$$MC = a + 2bQ + 3cQ^2$$

where a, b, and c are the estimated parameters (coefficients) for the AVC function. The manager used the estimated coefficients of the average variable cost equation to obtain the corresponding marginal cost function. For the estimate of the average variable cost function given above, the corresponding marginal cost function for shirts was

$$\begin{aligned} MC &= 20 + 2(-0.003)Q + 3(0.00000025)Q^2 \\ &= 20 - 0.006Q + 0.00000075Q^2 \end{aligned}$$

After obtaining forecasts of price and estimates of the average variable cost and marginal cost curves, the manager was able to answer the two production questions: (1) Should the firm produce or shut down? And (2) if production is warranted, how much should the firm produce? We now can show how the manager of Beau Apparel made these two decisions and calculated the firm's forecasted profit.

The Shutdown Decision

Since the estimated average variable cost function for shirts was

$$AVC = 20 - 0.003Q + 0.00000025Q^2$$

AVC reaches its minimum value at

$$Q_m = \frac{-(-0.003)}{2(0.00000025)} = 6{,}000$$

Substituting this output level into the estimated average variable cost function, the value of average variable cost at its minimum point is

$$AVC_{\text{min}} = 20 - 0.003(6{,}000) + 0.00000025(6{,}000)^2 = 11$$

Thus, average variable cost reaches its minimum value of \$11 at 6,000 units of output.

The manager of Beau Apparel then compared this minimum average variable cost with the three price forecasts for the first quarter of 1999. For the high forecast, \$20,

$$\hat{P}_{1999(I)} = \$20 > \$11 = AVC_{min}$$

so the firm should produce in order to maximize profit or minimize loss. Likewise, with the time-series forecast, \$15,

$$\hat{P}_{1999(I)} = \$15 > \$11 = AVC_{min}$$

and the firm also should produce. However, if the market-determined price of shirts turned out to be equal to the low forecast, \$10, the firm should shut down (produce zero output) since

$$\hat{P}_{1999(I)} = \$10 < \$11 = AVC_{min}$$

In this case, total revenue would not cover all variable costs of production, and the firm would be better off shutting down and losing only its fixed costs. The manager, therefore, must determine only how much output to produce when price is either \$20 or \$15.

The Output Decision

Given the estimated marginal cost equation for Beau Apparel, profit maximization or loss minimization requires that

$$P = MC = 20 - 0.006Q + 0.00000075Q^2$$

The manager first considered the high forecast of wholesale shirt prices. After setting the \$20 forecasted price equal to estimated marginal cost, the optimal production of shirts when price is \$20 was found by solving

$$20 = 20 - 0.006Q + 0.00000075Q^2$$

Subtracting 20 from both sides of the equation and factoring out a Q term results in the following expression:

$$0 = Q(-0.006 + 0.00000075Q)$$

There are two solutions to this equation, since the right-hand side of the equation is zero if either $Q = 0$ or $Q = 8{,}000$. Since the manager of Beau Apparel had already determined that price was greater than AVC_{min} and production was warranted, the manager concluded that the profit-maximizing output level was 8,000 units.

Using the time-series price forecast of \$15, the manager again determined the optimal output by equating the forecasted price to estimated marginal cost:

$$15 = 20 - 0.006Q + 0.00000075Q^2$$

or

$$0.00000075Q^2 - 0.006Q + 5 = 0$$

The solution to this equation is not as simple as was the preceding case, because the left-hand side of the equation cannot be factored. To solve a quadratic equation that cannot be factored, the quadratic formula must be used:[3]

$$Q = \frac{-(-0.006) \pm \sqrt{(0.006)^2 - 4(0.00000075)5}}{2(0.00000075)} = \frac{0.006 \pm 0.004583}{0.0000015}$$

The two solutions for this quadratic equation are $Q = 945$ and $Q = 7{,}055$.

To determine which solution is optimal, the manager computed the average variable cost for each level of output:

$$AVC_{Q = 945} = 20 - 0.003(945) + 0.00000025(945)^2 = \$17.39$$
$$AVC_{Q = 7{,}055} = 20 - 0.003(7{,}055) + 0.00000025(7{,}055)^2 = \$11.28$$

Since the price forecast of \$15 is less than \$17.39, the manager would not produce the output level $Q = 945$. If the wholesale price is expected to be \$15, the manager would produce 7,055 units at which AVC is \$11.28. We now consider the amount of profit or loss that Beau Apparel would earn at each of the optimal levels of output.

Computation of Total Profit or Loss

Total revenue for a competitive firm is price times quantity sold. Total cost is the sum of total variable cost and total fixed cost, where total variable cost is average variable cost times the number of units sold. Hence, total profit (loss) is

$$\begin{aligned} \pi &= TR - TC \\ &= (P \times Q) - [(AVC \times Q) + TFC] \end{aligned}$$

The manager expects total fixed costs for the shirt division for 1999(I) to be \$30,000. The values for total revenue and total variable cost depend on the price forecast and corresponding optimal output. We now show how the manager of Beau Apparel computed profit or loss for each of the three forecasts of the wholesale price of shirts.

High-price forecast ($P = \$20$)

In this case, Beau Apparel's manager determined that the optimal level of production would be 8,000 units. The average variable cost when 8,000 units are produced is

$$AVC_{Q = 8{,}000} = 20 - 0.003(8{,}000) + 0.00000025(8{,}000)^2 = \$12$$

Economic profit when price is \$20 would be

$$\pi = (\$20 \times 8{,}000) - [(\$12 \times 8{,}000) + \$30{,}000] = \$34{,}000$$

---

[3]For an equation of the form $aX^2 + bX + c = 0$, the two solutions, X_1 and X_2, are

$$X_1, X_2 = \frac{-b \pm \sqrt{b^2 - 4ac}}{2a}$$

If the price of shirts is $20 per unit in the first quarter of 1999, Beau Apparel should produce 8,000 units to earn a profit of $34,000, which is the maximum profit possible given this price.

Middle-price forecast ($P = \$15$)

If the price of shirts is $15 in the first quarter of 1999, the optimal level of output is 7,055 units. The average variable cost is

$$AVC_{Q=7{,}055} = 20 - 0.003(7{,}055) + 0.00000025(7{,}055)^2 = \$11.28$$

Economic profit when price is $15 would be

$$\pi = (\$15 \times 7{,}055) - [(\$11.28 \times 7{,}055) + \$30{,}000] = -\$3{,}755$$

When the price of shirts is $15, the shirt division of Beau Apparel would be expected to suffer a *loss* of $3,755 in the first quarter of 1999. Note that the firm should continue to produce since this is the minimum loss possible when price is $15. If Beau Apparel shut down production when price is $15, the firm would lose an amount equal to the total fixed cost of $30,000—considerably more than the $3,755 the firm loses by producing 7,055 units.

Low-price forecast ($P = \$10$)

At a price of $10 per shirt, the firm would shut down and produce zero output ($Q = 0$). In this case, economic profit would be equal to $-TFC$:

$$\pi = (\$10 \times 0) - (0 + \$30{,}000) = -\$30{,}000$$

Beau Apparel would minimize loss by producing nothing and losing only its fixed costs of $30,000.

This extended example about Beau Apparel's production decision illustrates how the manager of a firm that sells in a perfectly competitive market can find the optimal level of output. Our purpose in using the three different price forecasts was to illustrate the decision-making rules developed in Chapter 12, where we showed that a firm makes one of the following choices in the shortrun:

1. Produce a positive level of output and earn an economic profit (if $P > AVC$ and $P > ATC$).
2. Produce a positive level of output and suffer an economic loss less than the amount of total fixed cost (if $AVC \leq P < ATC$).
3. Produce zero output and suffer an economic loss equal to total fixed cost (if $P < AVC$).

Graphical Illustration

We will now demonstrate that the numerical analysis of the firm's output decision is consistent with the graphical analysis in Chapter 12. The profit-maximizing and loss-minimizing decisions of Beau Apparel are shown graphically in Figure 13.1. The marginal, average variable, and average total cost curves are a graphical representation of those estimated previously:

$$AVC = 20 - 0.003Q + 0.00000025Q^2$$
$$MC = 20 - 0.006Q + 0.00000075Q^2$$
$$ATC = AVC + AFC = (20 - 0.003Q + 0.00000025Q^2) + \$30{,}000/Q$$

In Panel A, the product price is \$20 (= MR). As you can see in the graph, MC = \$20 at 8,000 units of output. At 8,000 units, AVC = \$12, as shown, and AFC = \$30,000/8,000 = \$3.75. Therefore ATC = \$12 + \$3.75 = \$15.75. Profit is (P − ATC) = (\$20 − \$15.75)8,000 = \$34,000, as derived above.

Panel B illustrates the loss-minimizing situation when $P = MR$ = \$15. As shown, MC = \$15 at 945 and 7,055 units of output. The lower output would not be chosen because price is less than average variable cost at this output. Thus the firm produces 7,055 units of output, where AVC is less than \$15. As shown in the graph, average total cost is greater than \$15 at every level of output, so Beau Apparel cannot make an economic profit. In the figure, at an output of 7,055, average variable cost is \$11.28, so total variable cost is \$79,580 (= \$11.28 × 7,055). The firm can use its total revenue of \$105,825 (= \$15 × 7,055) to pay all its variable cost and use the remainder, \$26,245, to pay part of its fixed cost. Therefore, Beau Apparel loses \$3,755 (= \$30,000 − \$26,245), the portion of total fixed cost not covered by revenue.

As the figure shows, average variable cost reaches its minimum at 6,000 units of output, where AVC = \$11. The firm would shut down and produce zero output if price falls below \$11. The Beau Apparel example follows the theoretical analysis set forth in Chapter 12.

13.3 IMPLEMENTATION OF THE PROFIT-MAXIMIZATION INPUT DECISION

Managers may choose the level of input usage, rather than output, to maximize the profit of the firm. This section illustrates how to find the optimal level of input usage for a firm in a perfectly competitive market. We consider the case of a single variable input.

To be consistent with the discussion in Chapter 12, we call the variable input labor, although the techniques shown here can be used for any variable input. As in the case of choosing output, the manager must answer two questions in order to find the level of input usage that maximizes profit. These two questions and the answers set forth in Chapter 12 are summarized as follows:

1. Should the firm produce or shut down? *Produce as long as the wage rate is less than or equal to the maximum value of average revenue product—*$w \leq ARP_{max}$. *Otherwise, shut down and hire no labor.*
2. If production occurs, how much labor should the firm hire? *Hire the amount of labor at which the wage rate equals the marginal revenue product—*$w = MRP$.

Recall from Chapter 12 that the marginal revenue product is the price of the product times the marginal product of labor:

$$MRP = P \times MP$$

FIGURE 13.1
Profit and Loss at Beau Apparel

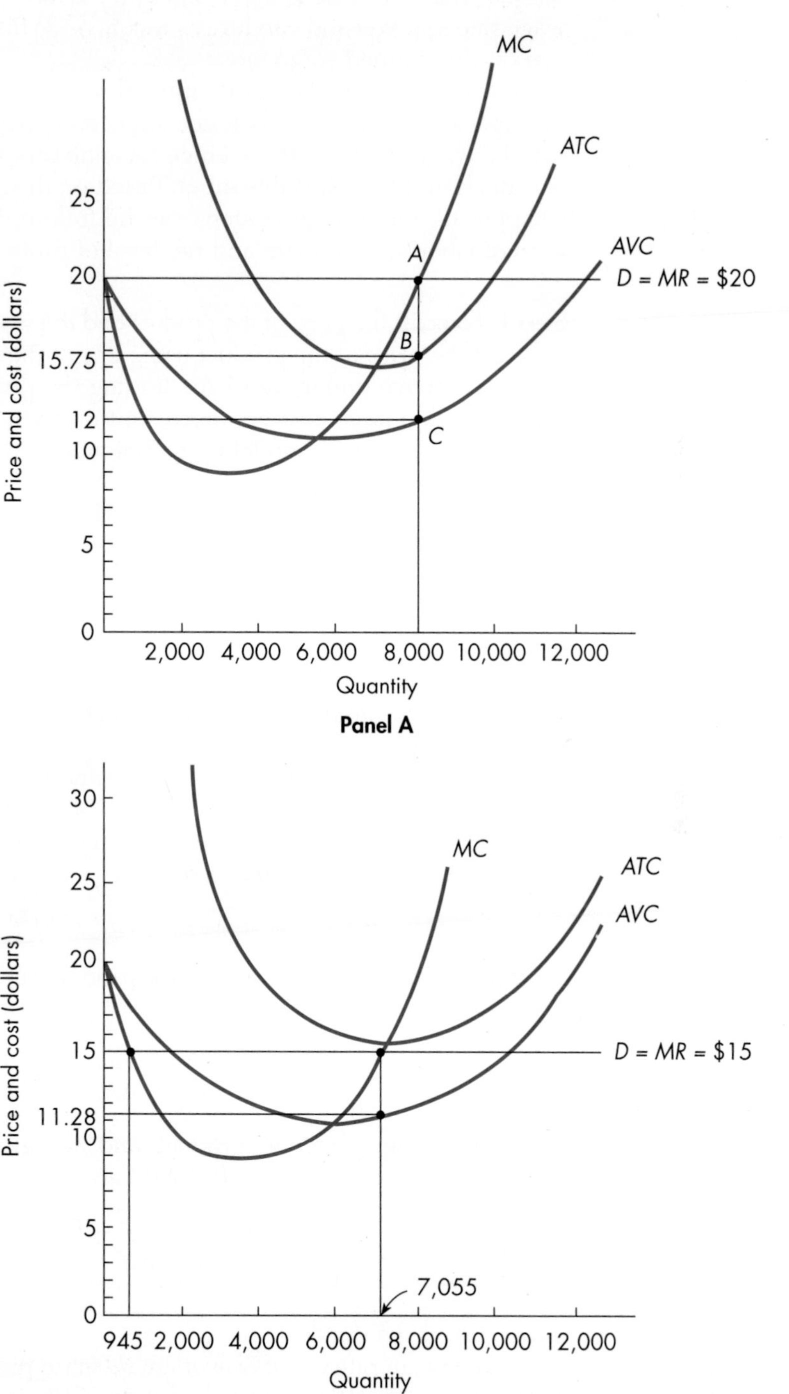

Because the wage rate is determined in the labor market, the manager treats the wage rate as given and can hire as much, or as little, labor as needed at the going market-determined wage rate.

In order to determine the optimal level of input usage from these rules, a manager must obtain estimates or forecasts of the market price of the firm's product, the wage rate, and the average revenue product and marginal revenue product functions of the variable input. Based on the theoretical analysis presented in Chapter 12, the following steps can be followed to find the profit-maximizing level of labor employment and the level of profit the firm will earn.

Step 1: Forecast the price of the product and the wage rate

Forecast the price of the product using one of the procedures from Chapter 8 and discussed above under step 1 for finding the profit-maximizing level of output. The wage rate must also be forecast either by using time-series methods or by applying econometric modeling techniques to the market for labor. In order to know how to model the supply of and demand for labor, you would need to take a course in labor economics. Most managers either use time-series techniques to forecast wages or purchase wage forecasts from econometric forecasting firms. Note that the product price must be forecasted regardless of whether the manager wishes to choose output or input usage to maximize profit but the wage rate is forecasted only when choosing input usage to maximize profit.

Step 2: Estimate average revenue product (*ARP*) and marginal revenue product (*MRP*)

To estimate the average revenue product and marginal revenue product functions of labor, the manager must specify and estimate a short-run production function. Following the procedure set forth in Chapter 11, the manager can specify a short-run cubic production function:

$$Q = AL^3 + BL^2$$

As shown in Chapter 11, the average product function and the marginal product function are

$$AP = AL^2 + BL$$
$$MP = 3AL^2 + 2BL$$

and the average revenue product and marginal revenue product functions ($ARP = P \times AP$ and $MRP = P \times MP$) are

$$ARP = P \times AP = PAL^2 + PBL$$
$$MRP = P \times MP = 3PAL^2 + 2PBL$$

Step 3: Check the shutdown rule

When the wage rate exceeds average revenue product ($w > ARP$), the firm loses less money by shutting down than it would lose if it produced where $w = MRP$. A manager can determine the wage above which a firm should shut down by finding the value of ARP at the *maximum* point on the average revenue product curve, ARP_{max}. To find ARP_{max}, the manager first finds the level of labor usage for which AP reaches its maximum value. Recall from Chapter 11 that AP reaches its maximum value at $L_a = -B/2A$. Thus,

$$ARP_{max} = A(L_a)^2 + BL_a$$
$$ARP_{max} = P \times AP_{max} = PA(L_a)^2 + PBL_a$$

The manager should produce as long as $w \leq ARP_{max}$.[4]

Step 4: If $w \leq ARP_{max}$, find the input level where $w = MRP$

In the case of a perfectly competitive firm, the manager should employ the amount of labor for which $w = MRP$—if $w \leq ARP_{max}$. Thus, if the decision is to produce in the short run, profit is maximized at the level of labor usage for which $w = MRP$. In the case of a cubic specification for the production function, profit maximization or loss minimization requires that

$$w = MRP = P \times MP = 3PAL^2 + 2PBL$$

Solving this equation for L^* gives the optimal level of labor usage for the firm—unless $w > ARP$, in which case the optimal level of labor to hire is zero.

Step 5: Computation of profit or loss

Once the profit-maximizing level of labor usage is determined, the calculation of total profit or loss can be easily accomplished. First, total revenue is computed by determining the level of output that is produced using the profit-maximizing amount of labor and multiplying this output by price. This level of output, which must also be the profit-maximizing output level, is found by substituting the profit-maximizing level of labor usage (L^*) into the production function:

$$Q^* = A(L^*)^3 + B(L^*)^2$$

Total revenue is equal to price times the profit-maximizing level of output:

$$TR = P \times Q^* = PA(L^*)^3 + PB(L^*)^2$$

Total variable cost is found by multiplying the wage rate by the profit-maximizing level of labor usage:

$$TVC = w \times L^*$$

Hence, total profit (loss) is $\pi = TR - TVC - TFC$. If $w > ARP_{max}$, the firm shuts down, and $\pi = -TFC$.

4 We will illustrate these steps, and let the manager choose labor usage to maximize profit by returning to our previous example.

---

[4]When the wage rate exactly equals average revenue product ($w = ARP$), total revenue is just sufficient to cover total variable cost, and the firm loses an amount equal to fixed cost. Just as in the case when price is exactly equal to AVC, the firm is indifferent between producing or shutting down. As before, we continue to assume arbitrarily that the manager will choose to produce, rather than shut down, if the wage rate exactly equals average revenue product.

13.4 IMPLEMENTING THE PROFIT-MAXIMIZING INPUT DECISION: AN ILLUSTRATION

We now return to the hypothetical textile firm, Beau Apparel, to show how the manager could maximize profit by choosing the optimal level of labor usage, instead of choosing the optimal level of output. As you will see, the resulting levels of output, profit, and labor employment are the same regardless of whether the manager chooses Q or L to maximize profit.

Price and Wage Forecasts

The manager of Beau Apparel wants to determine how much labor to hire in the first quarter of 1999. As discussed, the manager will need forecasts for the price of shirts and the wage rate in the first quarter of 1999. For this discussion, we will consider only the high-price forecast, $\hat{P}_{1999(I)} = \$20$. For the wage forecast, the manager purchased a high- and a low-wage forecast for the region in which the Beau Apparel plant is located from an econometric forecasting firm. The forecasted low-wage rate was \$16 per hour; $\hat{w}_{1999(I)} = \$16$. The forecasted high wage was $\hat{w}_{1999(I)} = \$30$.

Estimation of Average Revenue Product and Marginal Revenue Product

Using the 28 quarterly observations on output and labor usage, the following estimated production equation was obtained using the appropriate regression techniques:

$$Q = -0.051846L^3 + 0.53330L^2$$

where, in this case, for simplicity Q is expressed in units of 1,000, and L is expressed in thousands of hours. Both coefficients have the correct signs ($A < 0$ and $B > 0$), and both are statistically significant at the 5 percent level.

The manager used the production estimates to obtain the following equation for the average product of labor (Q/L):

$$AP = AL^2 + BL = -0.051846L^2 + 0.53330L$$

At the wholesale price forecast of \$20, the average revenue product function was obtained:

$$\begin{aligned} ARP = P \times AP &= 20 \times (-0.051846L^2 + 0.53330L) \\ &= -1.03690L^2 + 10.6660L \end{aligned}$$

The marginal product of labor for Beau Apparel was also computed using the parameter estimates for A and B from the cubic production function:

$$\begin{aligned} MP = 3AL^2 + 2BL &= 3(-0.051846)L^2 + 2(0.53330)L \\ &= -0.155538L^2 + 1.0666L \end{aligned}$$

At the wholesale price forecast of \$20, the manager computed the marginal revenue product function as follows:

FIGURE 13.2
The Profit-Maximizing Labor Usage for Beau Apparel

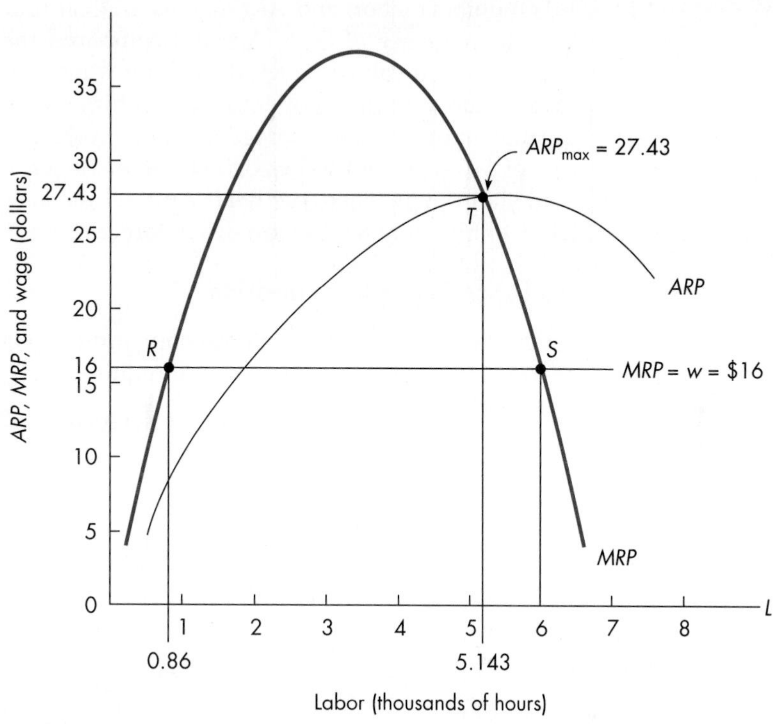

$$MRP = 20 \times MP = 20 \times (-0.155538L^2 + 1.0666L)$$
$$= -3.11076L^2 + 21.332L$$

Figure 13.2 shows the average revenue product (*ARP*) and the marginal revenue product curve (*MRP*). Note that *MRP* and *ARP* have the expected ∩-shape and *MRP* intersects *ARP* at *ARP*'s maximum value (compare Figures 12.13 and 13.2).

The Shutdown Decision

To find the maximum value of *ARP*, the maximum value of average product (AP_{max}) was calculated. The level of labor usage at which *AP* reaches its maximum value (L_a) was 5.143 [$= -B/2A = -0.5333/2(-0.051846)$]; thus the maximum value of the average product of labor was

$$AP_{max} = -0.051846(5.143)^2 + 0.5333(5.143)$$
$$= 1.3715$$

The maximum value of average revenue product was then calculated as

$$ARP_{max} = 20 \times 1.3715$$
$$= 27.43$$

In Figure 13.2, the maximum point on *ARP* (point *T*) occurs at 5,143 (= 5.143 × 1,000) units of labor, and *ARP* equals 27.43 at this level of labor usage.

The manager of Beau Apparel compared the two forecasted wage rates to this maximum value of *ARP*. If the high-wage forecast of $30 is correct, the manager would shut down operations and hire no labor since the wage rate exceeds the maximum value of average revenue product ($w > ARP$). If the low-wage forecast of $16 turns out to be correct, the manager would decide to produce rather than shut down. Thus, the Beau Apparel manager would determine how much labor to hire only for the low-wage forecast of $16.

The Labor Employment Decision

Given the estimated marginal revenue product equation for Beau Apparel, profit maximization or loss minimization requires that

$$w = \$16 = -3.11076L^2 + 21.332L$$

or

$$-3.11076L^2 + 21.332L - 16 = 0$$

As you can see in Figure 13.2, there are two points (*R* and *S*) where *MRP* equals $16. The solutions for these two levels of labor usage (L_1 and L_2) were obtained with the quadratic formula

$$L_1, L_2 = \frac{-21.332 \pm \sqrt{(21.3332)^2 - 4(-3.11076)(-16)}}{2(-3.11076)}$$

$$= \frac{-21.3332 \pm 16}{-6.222}$$

The two levels of labor usage that satisfy the condition that $MRP = \$16$ are

$$L_1 = \frac{-5.3332}{-6.222} = 0.86$$

and

$$L_2 = \frac{-37.3332}{-6.222} = 6.00$$

To determine which of these two levels of labor employment does indeed maximize profit (or minimize loss), a manager should compare the average revenue product at both levels of labor employment to the wage rate of $16. Only the level of labor usage for which *ARP* exceeds the wage rate will result in profit being maximized. The manager of Beau Apparel calculated the average revenue product for both $L = 0.86(860)$ and $L = 6(6{,}000)$:

$$ARP_{L=0.86} = -1.036920(0.86)^2 + 10.6660(0.86) = 8.41$$
$$ARP_{L=6} = -1.036920(6)^2 + 10.6660(6) = 26.60$$

Since $ARP < w$ for 860 units of labor, Beau Apparel would shut down rather than hire 860 hours of labor. For 6,000 units of labor, $ARP > w$. Thus, the profit-maximizing or loss-minimizing level of labor usage for the first quarter of 1999 is 6,000 hours.

Computation of Total Profit or Loss

When Beau Apparel employs 6,000 units of labor, the level of output is

$$Q = -0.051846(6)^3 + 0.5333(6)^2 = 8$$

The profit-maximizing level of output is 8,000 units. Total revenue is calculated by multiplying the output times the price:

$$TR = \$20 \times 8{,}000 = \$160{,}000$$

Total variable cost is \$96,000 ($= w \times L = 16 \times 6{,}000$), and total fixed cost is \$30,000, as before. Thus, Beau Apparel earns a profit of \$34,000:

$$\pi = \$160{,}000 - \$96{,}000 - \$30{,}000 = \$34{,}000$$

The Equivalence of Choosing Output or Input Usage

When the manager of Beau Apparel chose to employ 6,000 units of labor to maximize profit, the firm produced 8,000 units of output, which is the same output that was optimal when the manager set $P = \$20 = MC$ and chose Q rather than L to maximize profit. Because $MC = w/MP$ (as shown in Chapter 9) the marginal cost associated with using 6,000 units of labor is

$$MC = w/MP_{L = 6{,}000} = 16/0.80 = \$20$$

This means that when the manager of Beau Apparel chose either $Q = 8{,}000$ or $L = 6{,}000$, *both* profit-maximizing conditions were simultaneously satisfied.

$$P = MC_{Q = 8{,}000} \quad \text{and} \quad w = MRP_{L = 6{,}000}$$

Satisfying either one of these conditions results in satisfying the other condition. Note also that the profit is the same as that when the manager chose output to maximize profit:

$$\begin{aligned}\pi = PQ - wL - TFC &= (\$20 \times 8{,}000) - [(\$16 \times 6{,}000) + \$30{,}000] \\ &= \$34{,}000\end{aligned}$$

Before leaving the example of Beau Apparel, we should tell you that the equivalence of choosing either output or labor usage always holds when the functional forms of the cost and production equations are known exactly. When the cost curves and production curves must be estimated using regression analysis, the estimated coefficients usually differ from the true values of the parameters. Consequently, the error due to estimation will usually result in less than
 5 an exact equivalence between choosing Q and choosing L.[5]

[5]In the hypothetical example concerning Beau Apparel, we made certain the estimated values were in fact equal to the value of the underlying cost and production functions.

13.5 SUMMARY

This chapter illustrated how a manager can implement the theory of perfect competition to make profit-maximizing decisions. The manager can maximize profit by choosing either the level of production or the level of usage of the variable inputs. Both approaches lead to the same (maximum) profit for the firm or, in the case of short-run losses, the same (minimum) losses for the firm.

In the case of choosing output to maximize profit, the manager of a competitive firm makes one of the following choices in the short run:

1. If price is greater than average total cost, which implies that price is also greater than average variable cost, the manager will produce the level of output at which $P = MC$. The firm earns positive economic profit in this case.
2. If price is less than average total cost but greater than minimum average variable cost, the manager will produce the level of output at which $P = MC$. The firm makes a loss in this case, but a smaller loss than would occur if the firm produced nothing (shut down).
3. If price is less than minimum average variable cost, the manager will choose to produce nothing ($Q = 0$) and shut the firm down in the short run. The firm suffers a loss equal to its total fixed costs, but this is the smallest loss possible when $P < AVC$.

In order to implement the above decisions, the manager must have forecasts of the price of the product and estimates of the average variable cost and marginal cost functions. These estimates are obtained as explained in Chapters 8 and 11.

Once the required empirical work has been done, the manager compares the forecasted price ($\hat{P}$) with the estimated minimum value of average variable cost ($\widehat{AVC}_{min}$). If $\hat{P} \geq \widehat{AVC}_{min}$, the firm will produce a positive output. If $\hat{P} < \widehat{AVC}_{min}$, the manager will shut the firm down.

If the manager does decide to produce, the optimal level of output is determined by solving the following equation for Q:

$$\hat{P} = \widehat{MC}$$

Since marginal cost is U-shaped, $\hat{P} = \widehat{MC}$ at two levels of output. The optimal level of output is the one for which $\hat{P} > \widehat{AVC}$, which turns out to be the larger of the two values in every case.

In the case of choosing the level of variable inputs to maximize profit, we considered only the case of one variable input. For a single variable input, say, labor, the manager of a perfectly competitive firm maximizes profit by choosing the level of labor usage for which the marginal revenue product (MRP) is equal to the wage rate:

$$w = MRP$$

To obtain the estimated marginal revenue product equation, the manager must first estimate the MP equation. Then the estimated MP is multiplied by the forecasted price of the product to obtain

$$\widehat{MRP} = \hat{P} \times \widehat{MP}$$

The manager can use the methods of estimating production curves presented in Chapter 11. As noted, if a cubic equation is specified for either the cost or production function, then a cubic specification should be used to estimate the associated product or cost curves.

Since the marginal revenue product curve is $\cap$-shaped, the wage rate equals the marginal revenue product at two different levels of labor usage. The manager should choose the level of labor usage for which the average revenue product ($ARP = P \times AP$) exceeds the wage rate:

$$ARP > w$$

When $ARP > w$, total revenue will exceed total variable cost. When $ARP < w$, total revenue is less than total variable cost, and the manager should choose to hire no labor ($L = 0$) and shut down.

This chapter discussed only profit maximization in the short run. Long-run decision making involves making decisions about how much capital to employ. The decision to buy capital is an investment decision, which we will discuss in Chapter 19. We have now completed the analysis of perfectly competitive markets in which managers take the market-determined price as given. In Part VI of the text, firms with some degree of power to set the price of the product they sell will be examined. These firms have market power, and their profit-maximizing behavior differs from perfectly competitive firms in some rather interesting ways.

TECHNICAL PROBLEMS

1. In a perfectly competitive market, the manager of a firm will:
   a. Produce rather than shut down if the forecasted price of the product is greater than ________.
   b. Produce and make an economic profit if the forecasted price of the product is greater than ________.
   c. Produce at a loss if the forecasted price is less than ________ but greater than ________.
   d. Shut down if the forecasted price is less than ________.
   e. Minimize loss by producing the level of output where ________ equals ________ when forecasted price is greater than ________ but less than ________.
   f. Maximize profit by producing the level of output where ________ equals ________ when forecasted price is greater than ________.
2. Suppose that the manager of a firm operating in a perfectly competitive market has estimated the firm's average variable cost function to be

$$AVC = 10 - 0.03Q + 0.00005Q^2$$

   Total fixed cost is \$600.
   a. What is the corresponding marginal cost function?
   b. At what output is *AVC* at its minimum?
   c. What is the minimum value for *AVC*?

   If the forecasted price of the firm's output is \$10 per unit:
   d. How much output will the firm produce in the short run?
   e. How much profit (loss) will the firm earn?

   If the forecasted price is \$7 per unit:
   f. How much output will the firm produce in the short run?
   g. How much profit (loss) will the firm earn?

   If the forecasted price is \$5 per unit:
   h. How much output will the firm produce in the short run?
   i. How much profit (loss) will the firm earn?
3. Suppose the marginal cost function is estimated to be

$$MC = 80 - 0.1Q + 0.0001Q^2$$

   The price of the product is forecasted to be \$75.
   a. The average variable cost equation is *AVC* = ________.
   b. At what two levels of output does price equal marginal cost?
   c. What is average variable cost at the two levels of output in part *b?* Which of the two output levels is optimal? Explain.
4. Consider a firm that uses only one variable input, labor, to produce a good. The firm can hire all the labor it wishes for \$*w* per unit. In a perfectly competitive market, the manager of the firm will:
   a. Maximize profit or minimize loss by employing the amount of labor for which ________ equals ________ when the average revenue product of labor is ________ (greater, less) than the ________.
   b. Minimize loss by shutting down if, at the level of labor usage for which ________ equals ________, the wage rate is ________ (greater, less) than the average revenue product of labor.

5. A firm sells its product in a perfectly competitive market. The product is produced using only one variable input, labor. The wage rate is \$15 per unit of labor. The manager of the firm estimates the following cubic production function:

$$Q = -0.025L^3 + 1.45L^2$$

   a. Find the estimated average product equation.
   b. Find the estimated marginal product equation.
   c. If the forecasted price of the product is \$5, find the estimated marginal revenue product of labor function.
   d. What two levels of labor usage would the manager consider to be optimal? Which one maximizes profit (or minimizes loss)? How do you know?
   e. If total fixed costs are \$1,000, compute the profit and loss for this firm when it employs the optimal amount of labor.

APPLIED PROBLEMS

1. Suppose that you are the manager of a firm. If you wanted to determine the profit-maximizing level of output or input usage for your firm, how might you decide whether or not the competitive model is appropriate?
2. The production manager of the ABC Co., a perfectly competitive firm, has just returned from a trade convention. On the basis of the presentations there, he believes that market price next period will be somewhere between \$15 and \$25, with \$20 being the best guess.

   The firm's average variable cost function is

$$AVC = 30 - 0.01Q + 0.000001Q^2$$

   where AVC is dollars per unit, Q = number of units, and total fixed cost is \$10,000.
   a. How much output should the firm produce and how much profit (loss) will it earn if price is \$15? \$20? \$25?
   b. What is the shutdown price? How likely is it that the firm will have to shut down to minimize losses?
   c. If the manager's predictions are accurate, what is the range of expected profit?
3. During a coffee-room debate among several young M.B.A.s who had recently graduated, one of the young executives flatly stated, "The most this company can lose on its Brazilian division is the amount it has invested (its fixed costs)." Not everyone agreed with this statement. In what sense is this statement correct? Under what circumstances could it be false? Explain.
4. EverKleen Pool Services provides weekly pool maintenance in Atlanta. Dozens of firms provide this service. The service is standardized; each company cleans the pool and maintains the proper levels of chemicals in the water. The service is typically sold as a four-month summer contract. The market price for the four-month service contract is \$115.

   EverKleen Pool Services has fixed costs of \$3,500. The manager of EverKleen has estimated the following marginal cost function for EverKleen, using data for the last two years:

$$MC = 125 - 0.42Q + 0.0021Q^2$$

   where MC is measured in dollars, and Q is the number of pools serviced each summer. Each of the estimated coefficients is statistically significant at the 5 percent level.

a. Given the estimated marginal cost function, what is the average variable cost function for EverKleen?
b. At what output level does *AVC* reach its minimum value? What is the value of *AVC* at its minimum point?
c. Should the manager of EverKleen continue to operate, or should the firm shut down? Explain.
d. The manager of EverKleen finds two output levels that appear to be optimal. What are these levels of output and which one is actually optimal?
e. How much profit (or loss) can the manager of EverKleen Pool Services expect to earn?
f. Suppose EverKleen's fixed costs rise to $4,000. How does this affect the optimal level of output? Explain.

MATHEMATICAL APPENDIX

Profit-Maximizing Input Choice with a Cobb-Douglas Production Function

This appendix extends the analysis of a manager's choice of inputs to maximize the firm's profit to a Cobb-Douglas production function. The short-run Cobb-Douglas production function would have been a poor choice of specifications in the Beau Apparel example because the cost data suggested a U-shaped marginal cost curve, which then implied a ∩-shaped marginal product of labor curve. Thus, the cubic production function was the appropriate specification in the Beau Apparel example.

In cases where the sample data indicate only diminishing marginal product, a short-run Cobb-Douglas specification can be used to estimate the marginal product, average product, and marginal revenue product curves. We will now show how to use the Cobb-Douglas specification to find the profit-maximizing level of usage of a single variable input.

Recall from the appendix to Chapter 11 that for the Cobb-Douglas short-run production function, the total product function is

$$Q = \delta L^{\beta}$$

where δ is positive, and β is greater than zero but less than one ($0 < \beta < 1$). The marginal product of labor is

$$MP = \beta\delta L^{\beta-1}$$

and marginal product diminishes over all levels of labor usage. Once the manager obtains a forecast of the price of the product (P) and the wage rate (w) and estimates the marginal product equation, the profit-maximizing condition for the Cobb-Douglas specification is expressed as

$$MRP = P \times \beta\delta L^{\beta-1} = w$$

To find the profit-maximizing employment for labor, the manager simply solves this equation for L^* and checks to see that $w < ARP$ (i.e., shutdown is not warranted). To illustrate how this is done, let's look at an example.

Case Machine & Tool Company manufactures bearings that are widely used in oil field drilling equipment. The bearings are standardized and entry into the industry is unrestricted. Given the large number of firms producing these bearings, the manager of Case Machine & Tool views the market for bearings as perfectly competitive. The going price for the bearings has been $35 for the last two years and, for planning purposes, is not expected to change.

The primary variable input used in the manufacturing process is the labor of skilled machinists. The machinists earn $19.41 per hour. The manager estimates a short-run Cobb-Douglas production function of the form

$$Q = \delta L^{\beta}$$

Using 10 quarterly observations, the following log-linear form was estimated:

$$\ln Q = \ln \delta + \beta \ln L$$

where output (Q) was expressed in units of 1,000, and labor usage (L) was expressed in units of 1,000 hours. The estimation results were

$$\ln Q = 1.004 + 0.6 \ln L$$

The appropriate *t*-tests were performed, and the manager concluded that the estimate of β was significantly greater than zero but less than one.

Rewriting the estimated production function in its exponential form, the estimated empirical production function was

$$Q = 2.73L^{0.6}$$

From the estimated production function, the marginal and average product functions for labor were

$$MP = (0.6)(2.73)L^{0.6-1.0} = 1.638L^{-0.4}$$
$$AP = 2.73L^{-0.4}$$

Given the $35 price of bearings and a wage rate of $19.41, the profit-maximization condition ($P \times MP_L = w$) is

$$35 \times 1.638L^{-0.4} = 19.41$$

or

$$L^{-0.4} = 0.33856$$

Taking natural logarithms of both sides of the preceding equation,

$$-0.4 \ln L = -1.0830$$
$$\ln L = 2.708$$

and it follows that $L^* = 15$.* The profit-maximizing level of labor usage is 15,000 hours of machinist labor.

The firm would hire this amount of labor—15,000 units—only if the wage rate is less than the average revenue product of labor ($w < ARP$). In order to make sure $L = 15$ is indeed optimal, the manager substituted $L = 15$ into the estimated average product function

$$AP_{L=15} = 2.73(15)^{-0.4} = 0.9241$$

*Since natural logarithms were used, it follows that if ln $L = 2.708$, then $L = e^{\ln L} = e^{2.708} = 14.999$ (≈ 15).

Then the manager calculated ARP and compared ARP with the wage rate:

$$ARP = P \times AP = \$35 \times 0.9241 = \$32.34 > w = \$19.41$$

Since ARP exceeds the wage rate, the manager hired 15,000 units of labor rather than shut down.†

Using this optimal level of employment, the number of ball bearings produced by Case Machine & Tool is computed as

$$Q^* = 2.73(15)^{0.6} = 13.862$$

The profit-maximizing level of output is 13,862 units. Since the level of labor usage and wage rate are both known, the manager can calculate total variable cost:

$$TVC = w + L = \$19.41 \times 15{,}000 = \$291{,}150$$

If total fixed costs are $100,000, the profit earned by Case Machine & Tool Company is

$$P = (\$35 \times 13{,}862) - (\$291{,}150 + \$100{,}000) = \$94{,}020$$

We must emphasize once more that the choice between the cubic and the Cobb-Douglas specifications should be based on the nature of the data. If the data exhibit diminishing returns throughout the range of usage of the variable input, the Cobb-Douglas production function can be used to estimate the product curves. Alternatively, if the data indicate that marginal product at first rises, then falls, a cubic specification of the production function is a better choice than the Cobb-Douglas specification.

†This was the expected result since MP is always less than AP for a Cobb-Douglas. Thus, $P \times MP$ is always less than $P \times AP$, and $w(= MRP) < ARP$.

Part VI
Firms with Market Power

CHAPTER 14 **Managerial Decision Making for Firms with Market Power**

CHAPTER 15 **Oligopoly: Decision Making with Mutual Interdependence**

CHAPTER 16 **Profit Maximization for Firms with Market Power: Implementation of the Theory**

CHAPTER 17 **Multiple Plants, Markets, and Products**

CHAPTER 14

Managerial Decision Making for Firms with Market Power

The end of 1997 marked the third consecutive year of record corporate merger activity in the United States and abroad. The value of such transactions in the United States had increased 47 percent over the previous year. A very large percentage of these mergers and acquisitions were carried out by firms in the same industry. But spin-offs, in which firms sold branches that were primarily in other markets, also flourished. The result of this activity was increased market shares for a large percentage of the merged firms.

Regulators, politicians, and market analysts, not to mention competitors, were worried that these mergers and acquisitions were reducing competition and, hence, were giving the newly created firms too much power to affect market conditions. This was especially true in the case of the last merger in 1997 and the largest in history: the acquisition of MCI, the second-largest long-distance phone company, by WorldCom, the fourth largest, for $37 billion. The questions at the beginning of 1998 concerned the effect of these huge mergers and takeovers, which increased the relative size of the new firms, on prices. How much could the merged firms raise price because they were larger? Answering this and many other questions about firms that can affect market conditions requires an understanding of the behavior of firms with market power. **Market power** is the ability of a firm to raise price without losing all its sales. Stated alternatively, all firms with market power face downward-sloping demand for the products they sell. Firms with market power differ, of course, from perfectly competitive firms, discussed in Chapters 12 and 13, which face a market-determined price and

market power The ability of a firm to raise price without losing all its sales.

would not be able to sell anything if they raised price only slightly. All firms except perfect competitors have some market power.[1]

When firms with market power raise price, even though sales do not fall to zero, sales do, of course, decrease because of the law of demand. The effect of the change in price on the firm's sales depends to a large extent on the amount of its market power, which can differ greatly among firms. Firms with market power range in scope from virtual monopolies with a great deal of latitude over the prices they charge, such as Microsoft's Windows operating system for personal computers, to firms with a great deal of competition and only a small amount of market power, such as shoe stores or clothing stores in a large mall.

The primary focus of this chapter is to show how managers of firms with market power can choose price, output, and input usage so as to maximize the firm's profit. No matter how much market power a firm has, the primary objective of the manager is to maximize profit. As you would expect, the profit-maximization rule is to choose price and output so that the revenue from the last unit sold is equal to the marginal cost of producing and selling that unit. As we will discuss in the next chapter, complications can arise for managers when their demand and marginal revenue conditions depend on the decisions of rival firms. For the types of firms discussed in this chapter, however, the profit-maximizing decision is a straightforward application of the $MR = MC$ rule.

The first part of this chapter describes some ways of measuring market power that are more precise and concrete than terms such as "great deal" or "limited amount." We then discuss some of the determinants of the market power possessed by a firm and reasons why some firms have much more market power than others.

monopoly
A firm that produces a good for which there are no close substitutes in a market that other firms are prevented from entering because of a barrier to entry.

The major portion of the chapter is devoted to the theory of monopoly. A **monopoly** exists when a firm produces and sells a good or service for which there are no close substitutes and other firms are prevented by some type of entry barrier from entering the market. A monopoly, consequently, has more market power than any other type of firm. Although there are few true monopolies in real world markets—and most of these are subject to some form of government regulation—the theory of monopoly is important in managerial economics for two reasons. First, a lot of firms, while not meeting all the specifications of a monopoly, do have some of the characteristics. Many large and small firms possess a considerable amount of market power in the sense of having few close substitutes for the products they sell, and the monopoly model is useful for studying their behavior. Second, and perhaps more important, the theory of monopoly provides the basic analytical framework for the analysis of how managers of all firms with market power can make decisions to maximize their profit. As you will see in the next three chapters, theories that describe the

[1]Economists frequently use the terms "monopoly power" and "market power" interchangeably, both terms meaning the firm has the ability to raise price without losing all sales. In this text, we will always use the term "market power," instead of "monopoly power," because we do not want you to have the mistaken impression that only monopoly firms have market power. Monopolies, monopolistic competitors, and oligopolies all face downward-sloping demand curves and consequently have market power.

behavior of all types of firms in the range between perfect competitors and monopolies require only small modifications of the theory of pure monopoly. Therefore, managers of all types of firms will find monopoly theory useful for their own decision making.

monopolistic competition
A market consisting of a large number of firms selling a differentiated product with low barriers to entry.

We end this chapter with a fairly brief analysis of firms selling in markets under conditions of **monopolistic competition.** Under monopolistic competition, the market consists of a large number of relatively small firms that produce similar but slightly differentiated products and therefore have some, but not much, market power. Monopolistic competition is characterized by easy entry into and exit from the market. Most retail and wholesale firms and many small manufacturers are examples of monopolistic competition.

14.1 MEASUREMENT OF MARKET POWER

Even though we have not set forth a precise way to measure a firm's market power, you have probably figured out that the amount of market power is related to the availability of substitutes. The better the substitutes for the product sold by a firm, the less market power the firm posseses. However, there is no single measurement of market power that is totally acceptable to economists, policymakers, and the courts. Economists have come to rely on several measures of market power. These methods are widely used, frequently in antitrust cases that require objective measurement of market power.

Any of the methods of measuring the market power of a firm will fail to provide an accurate measure of market power if the scope of the market in which the firm competes has not been carefully defined. This section begins by discussing how to determine the proper market definition—identifying the products that compete with one another and the geographic area in which the competition occurs. Then we discuss some measures of market power.

Market Definition

market definition
The identification of the producers and products that compete for consumers in a particular geographic area.

A **market definition** identifies the producers and products or service types that compete in a particular geographic area, which is just large enough to include all competing sellers. As you can see by this definition of a market, properly defining a market requires considering the level of competition in both the product dimension and the geographic dimension of a market. Although the methodology of appropriately defining a market is primarily of interest to firms engaged in federal or state antitrust litigation—specifically cases involving illegal monopolization of a market or the impact of a proposed merger on the merged firm's market power—managers should know how to properly define the firm's market in order to measure correctly the firm's market power. We will now discuss some guidelines for determining the proper product and geographic dimensions of a market.

A properly defined market should include all the products or services that consumers perceive to be substitutes. A manager who fails to identify all the products that consumers see as substitutes for the firm's product will likely overestimate the firm's market power. The CEO of Coca-Cola would be foolish to view the company as a monopolist in the production of cola soft drinks and expect it to enjoy substantial market power. No doubt Coca-Cola's syrup formula is a closely guarded secret, but most soft-drink consumers consider rival brands of soft drinks, as well as a variety of noncarbonated drinks such as iced tea and Gatorade, as reasonable substitutes for Coca-Cola.

The geographic boundaries of a market should be just large enough to include all firms whose presence limits the ability of other firms to raise price without a substantial loss of sales. Two statistics provide guidelines for delineating the geographic dimensions of a market: (1) the percentage of sales to *buyers* outside the market, and (2) the percentage of sales from *sellers* outside the market. Both percentages will be small if the geographic boundary includes all active buyers and sellers. These two guidelines for determining the geographic dimensions of a market are sometimes referred to as LIFO and LOFI: little in from outside and little out from inside.

As mentioned earlier, economists have developed several measures of market power. We will discuss briefly only a few of the more important measures.

Elasticity of Demand

One approach to measuring how much market power a firm possesses is to measure the elasticity of the firm's demand curve. Recall from Chapter 3 that a firm's ability to raise price without suffering a substantial reduction in unit sales is inversely related to the demand elasticity. The less elastic is demand, the smaller the percentage reduction in quantity demanded associated with any particular price increase. The more elastic is demand, the larger the percentage decrease in unit sales associated with a given increase in price. Also recall from Chapter 3 that the elasticity of demand is greater (i.e., more elastic) the larger the number of substitutes available for a firm's product. As demand becomes less elastic, consumers view the product as having fewer good substitutes.

Although a firm's market power is greater the less elastic its demand, this does not mean a firm with market power chooses to produce on the inelastic portion of its demand. In other words, market power does not imply that a manager produces where $|E| < 1$; rather, the less elastic is demand, the greater the degree of market power. We will demonstrate later in this chapter that a monopolist always chooses to produce and sell on the elastic portion of its demand.

Relation The degree to which a firm possesses market power is inversely related to the elasticity of demand. The less (more) elastic the firm's demand, the greater (less) its degree of market power. The fewer the number of close substitutes consumers can find for a firm's product, the smaller the elasticity of demand and the greater the firm's market power. When demand is perfectly elastic (demand is horizontal), the firm possesses no market power.

Lerner index
A ratio that measures the proportionate amount by which price exceeds marginal cost: $\frac{P - MC}{P}$.

The Lerner Index

A closely related method of measuring the degree of market power is to measure the extent to which price deviates from the price that would exist under perfect competition. The **Lerner index,** named for Abba Lerner who popularized this measure, is a ratio that measures the proportionate amount by which price exceeds marginal cost:

$$\text{Lerner index} = \frac{P - MC}{P}$$

Since price equals marginal cost under perfect competition, the Lerner index equals zero under perfect competition. The higher the value of the Lerner index, the greater the degree of market power.

The Lerner index can be related to the elasticity of demand. In profit-maximizing equilibrium, marginal cost equals marginal revenue. Also recall from Chapter 3 that $MR = P(1 + 1/E)$. Thus, the Lerner index can be expressed as

$$\text{Lerner index} = \frac{P - MR}{P} = \frac{P - P(1 + \frac{1}{E})}{P} = 1 - (1 + \tfrac{1}{E})$$
$$= -\frac{1}{E}$$

In this form, it is easy to see that the less elastic is demand, the higher the Lerner index and the higher the degree of market power. The Lerner index is consistent with the above discussion showing that market power is inversely related to the elasticity of demand.

Relation The Lerner index, $\frac{P - MC}{P}$, measures the proportionate amount by which price exceeds marginal cost. Under perfect competition, the index is equal to zero, and the index increases in magnitude as market power increases. The Lerner index can be expressed as $-1/E$, which shows that the index, and market power, vary inversely with the elasticity of demand. The lower (higher) the elasticity of demand, the greater (smaller) the Lerner index and the degree of market power.

Cross-Price Elasticity of Demand

An indicator, though not strictly a measure, of market power is the cross-price elasticity of demand. Recall from Chapter 3 that cross-price elasticity measures the sensitivity of the quantity purchased of one good to a change in the price of another good. It indicates whether two goods are viewed by consumers as substitutes. A large, positive cross-price elasticity means that consumers consider the goods to be readily substitutable. Market power in this case is likely to be weak. If a firm produces a product for which there are no other products with a high (positive) cross-price elasticity, the firm is likely to possess a high degree of market power.

The cross-price elasticity of demand is often used in antitrust cases to help determine whether consumers of a particular firm's product perceive other products to be substitutes for that product. Using cross-price elasticities, antitrust officials try to determine which products compete with one another. For example, antitrust officials might wish to determine the degree of market power enjoyed

ILLUSTRATION 14.1

What Is the Definition of the Toy Market?

While the answer to this question doesn't seem important, it was quite important in early 1996 in a $5.2 billion bid by the largest toy maker, Mattel, for the second-largest toy maker, Hasbro. Hasbro, fearful of costly legal battles to win government approval of the merger, was hesitant about making the deal. According to *The Wall Street Journal,* Mattel, attempting to convince Hasbro that the FTC and the Justice Department would not find the merger to be anticompetitive, relied heavily on "cutting edge legal theories [that] . . . advocated a broader than traditional definition of the 'toy market,' assumed relative ease of entry for new industry competitors and generally claimed the existence of intense competition despite the huge gap between the second and third largest toy companies."*

Mattel's analysis predicted that the merger would create a firm with a 28 percent share of the $16.3 billion toy market. Hasbro worried that the proposed new firm would have a much larger share and would therefore be blocked by federal antitrust enforcement agencies. According to some observers, Hasbro was walking away from the deal because the company disagreed with Mattel's legal and political risk analysis. Several leading antitrust specialists agreed with Mattel's definition of the toy market. According to them, Mattel was relying "on the claim that video games, children's books and even some sporting goods should be included in any antitrust analysis." Under this scenario, the new company would have a share of 20 percent or less of such an expanded "toy" market. Antitrust experts also said that Mattel could argue that the industry offers relatively easy entry to new competitors. They pointed out that independents are often the ones that come up with surprise hits such as Cabbage Patch Kids. These analysts argued that the new company would have less market power under the expanded market definition, because of more intense competition, than would be the case under the more narrowly defined market.

A former top antitrust enforcer at the Justice Department, who wasn't working for either party, focused on a more reliable indicator of market power than share of the market. Noting that Mattel's expanded market definition seemed to track some of the more recent analyses of some federal antitrust regulators, he said, "To a certain extent there is some substitutability among traditional toys, some electronic games and perhaps other products designed for children of the same age . . . [which] should keep a lid on price increases." He asked rhetorically, "If the price of a particular doll or toy goes up 5 percent, for example, would consumers start buying other things?" Thus his focus was on elasticity and cross-price elasticity as being more reliable indicators of market power than share of a narrowly defined market.

This story illustrates three points. First, in practice, it is often difficult to define a firm's market, especially within a legal framework. Second, a firm's share of a narrowly defined market is generally not a good indicator of its market power. Third, elasticity and cross-price elasticity are better indicators of market power than is market share. It is, after all, the effect of price changes on sales that determines market power.

As a footnote, Hasbro's board rejected the offer and Mattel dropped it on February 2, 1996. Don't feel too sorry for Mattel's top executives, however. The *WSJ* noted that Mattel's top four executives "marched off with profits" after they sold stock in their company with an estimated value of $23.9 million.†

*"Mattel Practices Theories Preached in Attempt to Secure Bid," *The Wall Street Journal,* Jan. 30, 1996.

†"Mattel Officers Sold Stock after Hasbro Bid Ended," *The Wall Street Journal,* Mar. 6, 1996.

by Nike brand athletic shoes. Nike Corporation has spent a great deal of money advertising to establish a prominent position in the market for athletic shoes. To determine which other products compete with Nike, the cross-price elasticity of the quantity demanded of Nike shoes with respect to a change in the price of a rival's product can be calculated. Using such cross-price elasticities, antitrust officials can determine whether consumers view Nike as having any real competitors in the market for athletic shoes.

Relation If consumers view two goods to be substitutes, the cross-price elasticity of demand (E_{XY}) is positive. The higher the cross-price elasticity, the greater the perceived substitutability and the smaller the degree of market power possessed by the firms producing the two goods.

These are only a few of the measure of market power. The courts in antitrust cases and the Justice Department in merger and acquisition hearings sometimes use a combination of measures, including concentration ratios and share of the market. It is also not always clear just how high a cross elasticity or how low an elasticity constitutes "too much" market power. If you are ever involved in such a hearing, you should be aware of the problems in measuring market power. Illustration 14.1 shows the difficulty of determining what constitutes a market and what determines the amount of market power.

1

14.2 DETERMINANTS OF MARKET POWER

Entry or potential entry of new firms into a market can erode the market power of existing firms by increasing the number of substitutes. Therefore, as a general case, a firm can possess a high degree of market power only when strong barriers to the entry of new firms exist. A **strong barrier to entry** exists when it is difficult for new firms to enter a market where existing firms are making an economic profit. Strong barriers to entry hinder the introduction of new, substitute products and protect the profits of firms already in the market.

strong barrier to entry
A condition that makes it difficult for new firms to enter a market in which economic profits are being earned.

An example of a strong barrier to entry is a cable TV franchise granted by a city government to only one cable company. This fortunate company is protected from other firms' competing away any economic profits and is close to being a monopoly. Note that we said "close" to being a monopoly because the cable company has some outside competition even though it is the only cable company in town. Possible substitutes, though certainly not perfect ones, might be regular broadcast television, satellite dishes, radio, books and magazines, rental movies, and so on. Thus, the firm would be a monopoly if the cable TV market is the relevant market but not if the entertainment market is the relevant market. We should note that in cases in which a government body protects a firm from entry by other firms into a market, it typically regulates the protected firm.

Weak barriers to entry generally exist in most retail markets. Retail stores typically do not have much market power because entry by other firms into the market is easy and there are good substitutes for the products of firms selling in the market. The products are not perfect substitutes, as is the case for perfect competition, because other firms cannot sell identical products or sell in the same location. However, firms can produce close substitutes. Therefore, even though perfect competition would not exist in such markets because products are not perfect substitutes, no firm has much market power since it cannot raise its price much above its rivals' without a substantial loss of sales. Many types of barriers to entry exist, but we will discuss here only a few of the most common types.

Economies of Scale

An important barrier to entry is created when the long-run average cost curve of a firm decreases over a wide range of output, relative to the demand for the product. Consequently, a new firm that wishes to enter this type of market must enter on a large scale in order to keep its costs as low as the large-scale firm or firms already operating in the market. The necessity of entering on a large scale is usually not a barrier to entry by itself, but when it is coupled with relatively small product demand, a strong barrier to entry can be created.

Consider an industry where four existing firms each produce about 200,000 units annually to take advantage of substantial economies of scale. At the current price of the product, annual sales are running at about 800,000 units per year. While many entrepreneurs could obtain the financial backing to enter this industry with a large-scale plant capable of producing 200,000 units, there is no room in the industry for five large-scale producers without a significant decline in the price of the product. Even though a firm could enter the industry producing approximately 50,000 units annually, the per-unit production costs would be much higher than competitors' costs because of the substantial economies of scale. There just isn't room for a new firm to enter this industry on a scale big enough to enjoy costs as low as those of rivals. In such situations, economies of scale create a barrier to entry.

Barriers Created by Government

An obvious entry barrier is government. Licensing and franchises are ways monopolies are created by government decree. For example, licenses are granted to radio and television stations by the Federal Communications Commission (FCC), and only those stations possessing a license are allowed to operate. Governments also grant exclusive franchises for city, county, and state services. For example, local telephone and cable television utilities have a great deal of market power in that they are the only regional producers of the products. By law, no other producer can exist.

Another legal barrier to competition lies in the patent laws. These laws make it possible for a person to apply for and obtain the exclusive right to produce a certain commodity, or to produce a commodity by means of a specified process that provides an absolute cost advantage. Despite examples to the contrary, however, holding a patent on a product or production process may not be quite what it seems in many instances. A patent does not preclude the development of closely related substitute goods or closely allied production processes. International Business Machines (IBM) has the exclusive right to produce its patented computers, but many other computers are available and there is competition in the computer market.

Input Barriers

Historically, an important reason for market power has been the control of raw-material supplies. If one firm (or perhaps a few firms) controls all the known supply of a necessary ingredient for a particular product, the firm (or firms) can

ILLUSTRATION 14.2

Patents Are No Guarantee of Fat Monopoly Profits

As noted, holding a patent does not necessarily create substantial market power since a profitable product, even a patented one, will encourage potential rivals to develop close substitutes for the patented product or process. An illustration is provided by the introduction of a new substance named Simplesse, which was developed to replace fat in food.

It is no secret that fat is what gives many foods their taste; it makes Haagen-Dazs creamy and rich, Big Macs tasty, and real mayonnaise slippery. Dietary fat has been linked to heart disease, and many health-conscious Americans have reduced substantially their fat intakes. The new awareness of the ill effects of fat created a demand for substances to replace fat so that food manufacturers can produce tasty foods low in calories and cholesterol.

Simplesse, an engineered mixture of skim milk and whipped egg whites, was developed and patented by a Canadian firm that then sold the new product (patent and all) to NutraSweet. NutraSweet, a division of Monsanto Company, needed a new product to take the place of its sugar substitute, the 1969 patent of which expired in 1992. Consultants for NutraSweet predicted that Simplesse would generate more than $200 million in profits annually by 1992. In light of the lucrative market for fake fat and the protection of a patent, Simplesse seemed a sure bet. According to one executive at NutraSweet, "Simplesse is going to succeed because it's the best technology for getting the fat out of food." Unfortunately for NutraSweet, the patent on Simplesse failed to create the expected market power and accompanying profits.

According to *The Wall Street Journal*, a top executive at NutraSweet made a strategic error during the company's unveiling of Simplesse to the press. The overconfident executive boasted that Simplesse would not need approval by the Food and Drug Administration (FDA) because it was an all-natural substance. This statement irritated top administrators at the FDA. The FDA then spent two years reviewing Simplesse before it decided to approve its use in frozen desserts.

The delay imposed by the FDA approval process, coupled with NutraSweet's own internal difficulties in developing an imitation ice cream made with Simplesse, gave rival firms time to beat NutraSweet to the grocers' shelves with their own imitation ice cream. Kraft General Foods introduced the Sealtest Free brand and Dreyers/Edy's introduced the American Dream brand imitation ice cream.

By the time NutraSweet delivered its own product, called Simple Pleasures, to the grocers, the proliferation of other faux-fat ice creams had dramatically undercut NutraSweet. Even though the rival firms used only conventional gums, gels, and other ingredients to reduce the fat content of their brands of pseudo ice creams, NutraSweet failed to convince consumers of the value of using Simplesse as a fat replacer. As pointed out by Yves Coleon, the vice president of marketing at Haagen-Dazs, "The value of [NutraSweet's] fat substitute was diluted by competitive entries."

The *WSJ* reported that NutraSweet had been able to convince only four U.S. companies to use Simplesse in the production of their frozen desserts. Despite the superiority of Simplesse over currently available fat substitutes, many of the potentially large buyers of Simplesse have been working to invent their own substitute fat. In fact, Pfizer Incorporated and A. E. Staley Manufacturing Company produced FDA-approved substitutes for Simplesse.

The experience of NutraSweet with Simplesse illustrates how fleeting market power can be when profits create an incentive for rival firms to find a way to enter. Even the seemingly absolute protection afforded by patents can be quickly undermined by the development of close substitutes.

Source: "Maker of Simplesse Discovers Its Fake Fat Elicits Thin Demand," *The Wall Street Journal*, July 31, 1991.

refuse to sell that ingredient to other firms at a price low enough for them to compete. Since no others can produce the product, monopoly results. For many years the Aluminum Company of America (Alcoa) owned almost every source of bauxite, a necessary ingredient in the production of aluminum, in North America. The control of resource supply, coupled with certain patent rights, provided Alcoa with an absolute monopoly in aluminum production. It was only after World War II that the federal courts effectively broke Alcoa's monopoly in the aluminum industry. There have been other such historical examples, but at the present time there are few cases of firms with considerable market power because of exclusive control of a raw material.

Another frequently cited input barrier arises in capital markets. Established firms, perhaps because of a history of good earnings, are able to secure financing at a more favorable rate than new firms. Imagine how far a typical person would get by walking into a bank and requesting a loan for $100 million to start a mainframe computer company. Most bankers would take a very dim view of this new company's survival. Knowing that the new firm would be in the same market as IBM and other well-established companies, bankers would probably turn down the loan application. If the loan was made available, the interest rate for a new company would be above that paid by established firms. Capital markets pose a

barrier for new firms when a large investment is necessary to enter a market.

Brand Loyalties

On the demand side, older firms may have, over time, built up the allegiance of their customers. New firms can find this loyalty difficult to overcome. For example, no one knows what the service or repair policy of a new firm may be. The preference of buyers can also be influenced by a long successful advertising campaign; established brands, for instance, allow customers recourse if the product should be defective or fall short of its advertised promises. Although technical economies of scale may be insignificant, new firms might have considerable difficulty establishing a market organization and overcoming buyer preference for the products of older firms. A classic example of how loyalty preserves monopoly power can be found in the concentrated-lemon-juice market. ReaLemon lemon juice successfully developed such strong brand loyalties among consumers that rival brands evidently could not survive in the market. The situation was so serious that the courts forced ReaLemon to license its name to would-be competitors.

The role of advertising as a barrier to entry has long been a source of controversy. Some argue that advertising acts as a barrier to entry by strengthening buyer preferences for the products of established firms. On the other hand, consider the great difficulty of entering an established industry without access to advertising. A good way for an entrenched monopoly to discourage entry would be to get the government to prohibit advertising. The reputation of the old firm would enable it to continue its dominance. A new firm would have difficulty informing the public about the availability of a new product unless it was able to advertise. Thus advertising may be a way for a new firm to overcome the advantages of established firms. The effect of advertising on entry remains a point of disagreement among economists.

The purpose of this discussion is to expose you to several of the most common types of entry barriers and to illustrate the diversity of factors that hinder entry into a market and, consequently, foster market power. It is noteworthy that several of the barriers mentioned are somewhat influenced by the firm with market power. The control of inputs and the development of consumer loyalties are effective barriers essentially erected by firms already producing in the market. We will discuss other strategic barriers to entry, erected by existing firms, in the next chapter.

Despite the existence of barriers to entry, firms can lose and have lost their positions of extensive market power. Even quite strong barriers to entry can be overcome. A monopolist can become complacent in its protected position and allow inefficiencies to enter the production process. This raises the cost, and hence the price, and allows new, more efficient firms to enter the market. Some potential entrants are ingenious enough to find ways to lower cost, or (as noted above) get around patent protection, or overcome brand loyalty to the established firm. Thus barriers to entry cannot completely protect the established firm with great market power.

14.3 PROFIT MAXIMIZATION UNDER MONOPOLY: THE OUTPUT AND PRICE DECISIONS

We will now analyze the profit-maximizing decision of firms that are pure monopolies. Keep in mind that the fundamentals of this monopoly decision apply to a large extent to all firms with market power. The manager of a monopoly treats the market demand curve as the firm's demand curve. As was the case for perfect competition, we assume that the manager wishes to maximize profit. Thus, the manager of a monopoly firm chooses the point on the market demand curve that maximizes the profit of the firm. While the manager of a monopoly does, in fact, determine the price of the good, price cannot be chosen independent of output. The manager must choose price and output combinations that lie on the market demand curve.

In Figure 14.1, for example, if the manager wishes to charge a price of $14 per unit, the monopoly firm can sell (consumers will buy) only 700 units of the product. Alternatively, if the manager decides to sell 700 units, the highest price that can be charged for this output is $14. So, while the monopolist can choose both price and output, the two choices are not independent of one another.

In practice, some monopolists choose price and let market demand determine how many units will be sold, whereas other monopolists choose the level of output to produce and then sell that output at the highest price market demand allows. Consider your electric utility company. Electric utilities set the

FIGURE 14.1
Demand and Marginal Revenue Facing a Monopolist

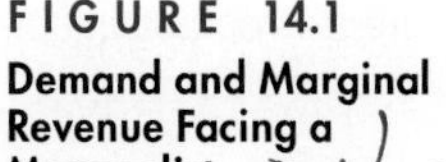

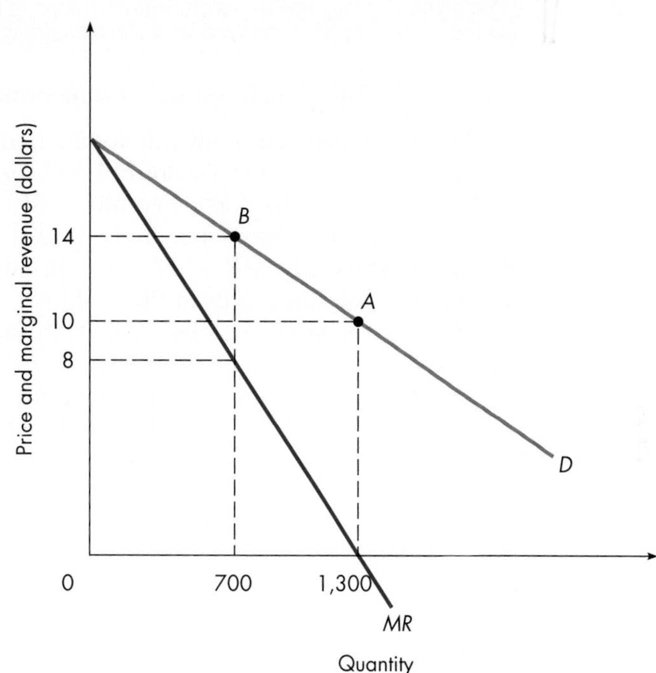

price of a unit of electricity, say, eight cents per kilowatt-hour, and then stand ready to supply as many kilowatt-hours as consumers wish to buy at that price. You can be sure that your electric company has estimated its demand function and knows approximately how much electricity will be demanded at various prices.

Alternatively, an automobile manufacturer might decide to produce 300,000 cars of a particular model in a given year. The manufacturer sells these cars at the highest possible price given the existing market demand. Again, you can be sure that the automobile manufacturer has estimated the demand for its cars and knows approximately the average price at which each car can be sold.

Given the demand curve facing a monopolist, choosing price to maximize profit is equivalent to choosing output to maximize profit. To be consistent with our discussion of profit maximization under perfect competition, we will view the monopolist as choosing *output* to maximize profit.

The basic principle of profit maximization—profit is maximized by producing and selling the output at which marginal cost equals marginal revenue—is the same for the monopoly as for the competitive firm. A manager can increase profit by expanding output as long as the marginal revenue from the expansion exceeds the marginal cost of expanding output. A manager would reduce output if marginal revenue is less than marginal cost. The fundamental difference for a monopolist is that marginal revenue is not equal to price.

Principle A monopolist chooses the point on the market demand curve that maximizes profit. If marginal revenue exceeds marginal cost, a profit-maximizing monopolist increases output. If marginal revenue is less than marginal cost, the monopolist does not produce these additional units.

Demand and Marginal Revenue for a Monopolist

A monopoly, facing a downward-sloping demand, must lower the price in order to sell more. As shown in Figure 14.1 and discussed in Chapter 3, marginal revenue is less than price for every unit sold except the first. You will recall that marginal revenue is the change in the firm's total revenue from an additional unit of sales; symbolically, $MR = \Delta TR/\Delta Q$. In Figure 14.1, if the firm sells 700 units at $14 each, you can see from the marginal revenue curve that the marginal or additional revenue from selling the 700th unit is $8. This means that reducing the price just enough to increase sales from 699 to 700 adds $8 to the firm's revenue, rather than the $14 price at which the 700th unit is sold. The reason is that in order to sell the 700th unit, the firm must reduce the price on the 699 units it could have sold at the slightly higher price.

Although we set forth a technical analysis of the relation between *MR* and *P* in Chapter 3, we can perhaps give you a bit more intuition about why *MR* is less than *P* with a hypothetical example. Suppose you manage a small appliance store that has been selling 20 radios a day at $50 apiece. You want to increase your sales of radios, so one day you reduce the price to $49. Sure enough, you sell 21 radios that day at the reduced price. So you sold one more at $49. You check the cash register and compare the receipts with those from previous days. You had been receiving $1,000 (= $50 × 20). Now you see that you have taken in $1029 (= $49 × 21) from selling radios. Your revenue increased by $29, but what happened to the $49 at which the additional radio was sold? Did someone steal $20 from the register? What happened was that, in order to sell the 21st radio, you had to take a $1 price reduction on the 20 you could have sold at $50. This $1 price reduction accounts for the "missing" $20.

Figure 14.1 illustrates the relation between demand and marginal revenue for a linear demand curve, as set forth in Chapter 3. When demand is linear, marginal revenue is twice as steep as demand and consequently lies halfway between demand and the vertical axis. When *MR* is positive, between zero and 1,300 units, demand is elastic. When *MR* is negative, above 1,300 units, demand is inelastic. When *MR* equals zero, at 1,300 units, demand is unitary elastic.

Relation The market demand curve is the demand curve for the monopolist. Because the monopolist must lower price in order to sell additional units of output, marginal revenue is less than price for all but the first unit of output sold. When marginal revenue is positive (negative), demand is elastic (inelastic). For a linear market demand, the monopolist's marginal revenue is also linear, with the same vertical intercept as demand, and is twice as steep.

Maximizing Profit at Southwest Leather Designs: An Example

Southwest Leather Designs specializes in the production of fashionable leather belts for women. Southwest's original designs are sometimes imitated by rival leather goods manufacturers, but the Southwest logo is a registered trademark

TABLE 14.1
Profit Maximization for Southwest Leather Designs

(1) Output (Q)	(2) Price (P)	(3) Total revenue ($TR = PQ$)	(4) Total cost (TC)	(5) Marginal revenue $\left(MR = \frac{\Delta TR}{\Delta Q}\right)$	(6) Marginal cost $\left(MC = \frac{\Delta TC}{\Delta Q}\right)$	(7) Profit (π)
0	$40.00	$ 0	$40,000	—	—	$−40,000
1,000	35.00	35,000	42,000	$35.00	$ 2.00	−7,000
2,000	32.50	65,000	43,500	30.00	1.50	21,500
3,000	28.00	84,000	45,500	19.00	2.00	38,500
4,000	25.00	100,000	48,500	16.00	3.00	51,500
5,000	21.50	107,500	52,500	7.50	4.00	55,000
6,000	18.92	113,520	57,500	6.02	5.00	56,020
7,000	17.00	119,000	63,750	5.48	6.25	55,250
8,000	15.35	122,800	73,750	3.80	10.00	49,050
9,000	14.00	126,000	86,250	3.20	12.50	39,750

that affords the company some protection from outright counterfeiting of its products. Consequently, Southwest Leather enjoys a degree of market power that would not be present if imitators could make identical copies of its belts, trademark and all.

Table 14.1 presents the demand and cost conditions faced by the manager of Southwest Leather Designs. Columns 1 and 2 give the demand schedule for 1,000 through 9,000 units of output (leather belts) in discrete intervals of 1,000. Column 3 shows the associated total revenue schedule (price times quantity). The total cost of producing each level of output is given in column 4. The manager computes profit or loss from producing and selling each level of output by subtracting total cost from total revenue. Profit is presented in column 7. Examination of the profit column indicates that the maximum profit ($56,020) occurs when Southwest Leather Designs sells 6,000 belts at a price of $18.92.

The manager of Southwest Leather Designs can reach the same conclusion using the marginal revenue–marginal cost approach. Marginal revenue and marginal cost are shown, respectively, in columns 5 and 6. The marginal revenue from selling additional leather belts exceeds the marginal cost of producing the additional belts until 6,000 units are sold. After 6,000 units the marginal revenue for each of the next 1,000 belts is $5.48 per belt while the marginal cost for each of the next 1,000 belts is $6.25 per belt. Clearly, increasing output and sales from 6,000 to 7,000 belts would lower profit. Thus profit must increase until 6,000 units are produced; then profit decreases thereafter. This is the same solution that was obtained by subtracting total cost from total revenue: an output of 6,000 belts maximizes profit.

The example in Table 14.1 is shown graphically in Figure 14.2. Since marginal revenue and marginal cost are per-unit changes in revenue and cost over discrete changes in output of 1,000 units, we plot these values in the middle of the 1,000-unit interval. For example, marginal revenue for the first 1,000 units sold is $35

FIGURE 14.2
Profit Maximization for Southwest Leather Designs: Choosing Output

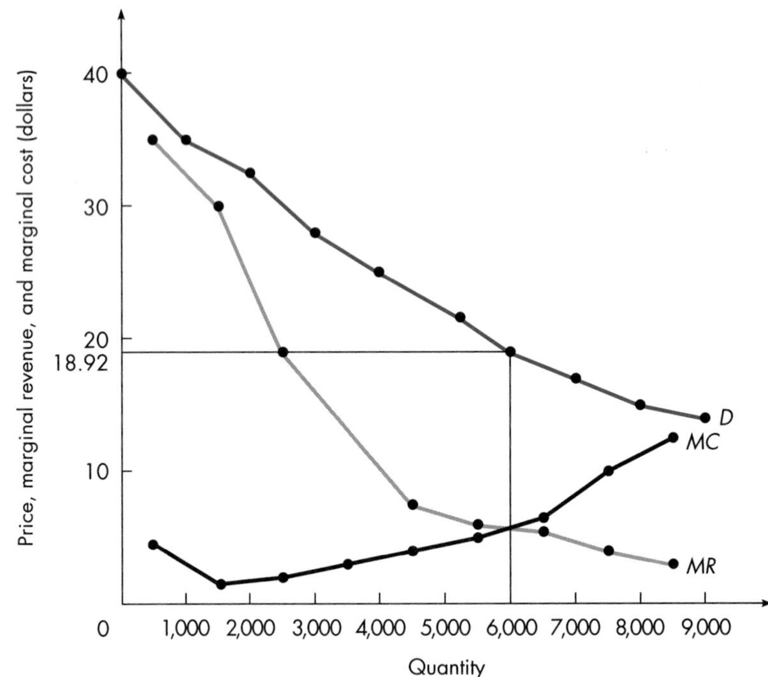

per unit for each of these 1,000 units. We plot this value of marginal revenue ($35) at 500 units of output. We do this at all levels of output for both marginal revenue and marginal cost.

In Figure 14.2, marginal revenue equals marginal cost at 6,000 units of output, which, as you saw from the table, is the profit-maximizing level of output. The demand curve shows that the price that Southwest Leather Designs will charge for the 6,000 belts is $18.92.

We turn now from a specific numerical example of profit maximization for a monopolist to a more general graphical analysis of a monopolist in the short run. In this case, we will assume for analytical convenience that output and price are

5 continuously divisible.

Short-Run Equilibrium: Profit Maximization or Loss Minimization

A monopolist, just as a perfect competitor, attains maximum profit by producing and selling the rate of output for which the positive difference between total revenue and total cost is greatest; or it attains a minimum loss by producing the rate of output for which the negative difference between total revenue and total cost is least. When price exceeds average variable cost, this condition occurs

FIGURE 14.3
Short-Run Profit-Maximizing Equilibrium under Monopoly

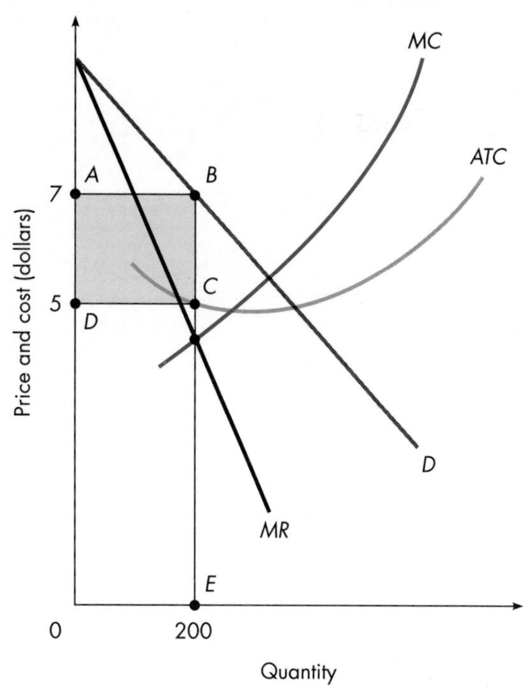

when marginal revenue equals marginal cost.[2] As was the case for the perfectly competitive firm, when price is less than average variable cost, the manager shuts down production in the short run. We will first discuss profit maximization and then loss minimization.

The position of short-run equilibrium is easily described graphically. Figure 14.3 shows the relevant cost and revenue curves for a monopolist. Since *AVC* and *AFC* are not necessary for exposition, they are omitted. Note that demand is the downward-sloping market demand curve. Marginal revenue is also downward-sloping and lies below the demand curve everywhere except at the vertical intercept. The short-run cost curves confronting a monopolist are derived in exactly the fashion described in Chapter 9 and have the typically assumed shapes. Figure 14.3 shows a situation where price exceeds average total cost, and thus the monopolist earns an economic profit.

The monopolist maximizes profit by producing 200 units of output where $MR = MC$. From the demand curve, the monopolist can (and will) charge $7 per unit. Total revenue is $1,400 (= $7 × 200), or the area of the rectangle 0*ABE*. The average total cost of producing 200 units of output is $5. Total cost of producing 200 units is $1,000 (= $5 × 200), or the area of the rectangle 0*DCE*. Economic

[2]This result is derived mathematically in the appendix to this chapter.

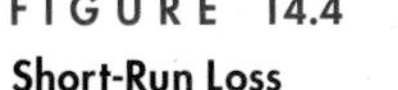

FIGURE 14.4

Short-Run Loss Minimization under Monopoly

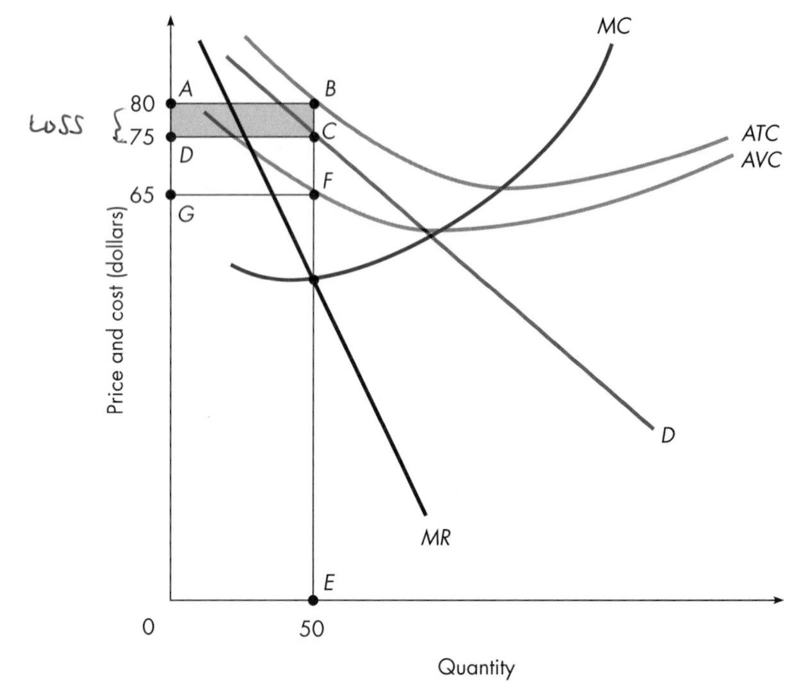

profit is *TR* minus *TC*, $400 (= $1,400 − $1,000), or the shaded area *ABCD*. Since price is greater than average total cost at the equilibrium output of 200 units, the monopolist earns an economic profit. This need not be the case, however.

People often have the idea that monopoly firms can always make a profit; if the firm is making losses, it can simply raise price until it makes a profit. It is, however, a misconception that all monopolies are ensured a profit. Figure 14.4 illustrates a monopolist that makes losses in the short run. Marginal cost equals marginal revenue at 50 units of output, which, from the demand curve, can be sold for $75 each. Total revenue, then, is $3,750 (= $75 × 50), or the area 0*DCE*. Since average total cost is $80 per unit, total cost is $4,000 (= $80 × 50), or the area 0*ABE*. Since total cost exceeds total revenue, the firm makes a loss of $250 (= $4,000 − $3,750), which is the shaded area *ABCD*.

Note that in Figure 14.4 the monopolist would produce rather than shut down in the short run since total revenue (area 0*DCE*) exceeds the total variable cost of $3,250 (= $65 × 50), or area 0*GFE*. After all variable costs have been covered, there is still some revenue, $500 (area *GDCF*), left over to apply to fixed cost. Since total fixed cost in this example is $750 (= $15 × 50), or area *ABFG*, the firm loses less by producing 50 units than by shutting down. If the monopolist shuts down, it would, of course, lose its entire fixed cost of $750.

If demand decreases so that it lies below *AVC* at every level of output and the monopolist could not cover all its variable cost at any price, the firm would shut down and lose only fixed cost. This is exactly the same shutdown rule as that of the perfect competitor.

We should note that a monopolist would never choose a situation in which it was producing and selling an output on the inelastic portion of its demand. When demand is inelastic, marginal revenue is negative. Since marginal cost is always positive, it must equal marginal revenue when the latter is also positive. Thus, the monopolist will always be on the elastic portion of demand.

In the short run, the primary difference between a monopoly and a perfect competitor lies in the slope of the demand curve. Either may earn a pure profit; either may incur a loss.

 6 7 8

Relations In the short run a monopoly will produce a positive output if some price on the demand curve exceeds average variable cost. It maximizes profit or minimizes loss by producing the quantity for which $MR = MC$. The price for that output is given by the demand curve. If the price exceeds average total cost, the firm makes a pure economic profit. If price is less than average total cost but exceeds average variable cost, the firm suffers an economic loss but continues to produce in the short run. If demand falls below average variable cost at every output, the firm shuts down in the short run and loses only its fixed cost. If the firm produces a positive output, equilibrium price exceeds marginal cost, since the monopolist's demand curve is above its marginal revenue curve at every output.

Long-Run Equilibrium

A monopoly exists if there is only one firm in the market. Among other things, this statement implies that entry into the market is closed. Thus, if a monopolist earns an economic profit in the short run, no new producer can enter the market in the hope of sharing whatever profit potential exists. Therefore, economic profit is not eliminated in the long run, as was the case under perfect competition. The monopolist will, however, make adjustments in plant size as demand conditions warrant, in order to maximize profit in the long run.

Clearly, in the long run, a monopolist would choose the plant size designed to produce the quantity at which long-run marginal cost equals marginal revenue. Profit would be equal to the product of output times the difference between price and long-run average cost:

$$\pi = P \times Q - LAC \times Q = Q\,(P - LAC)$$

New entrants cannot come into the industry and compete away profits—entry will not shift the demand curve facing the monopolist

Demand conditions may change for reasons other than the entry of new firms, and any such change in demand and marginal revenue causes a change in the optimal level of output in both the short run and the long run. Suppose demand does change, due perhaps to a change in consumer income. In the short run, the manager will adjust output to the level where the new marginal revenue curve intersects the short-run marginal cost curve (or it will shut down if $P < AVC$). This short-run adjustment in output is accomplished without the ben-

FIGURE 14.5
Long-Run Profit Maximization under Monopoly

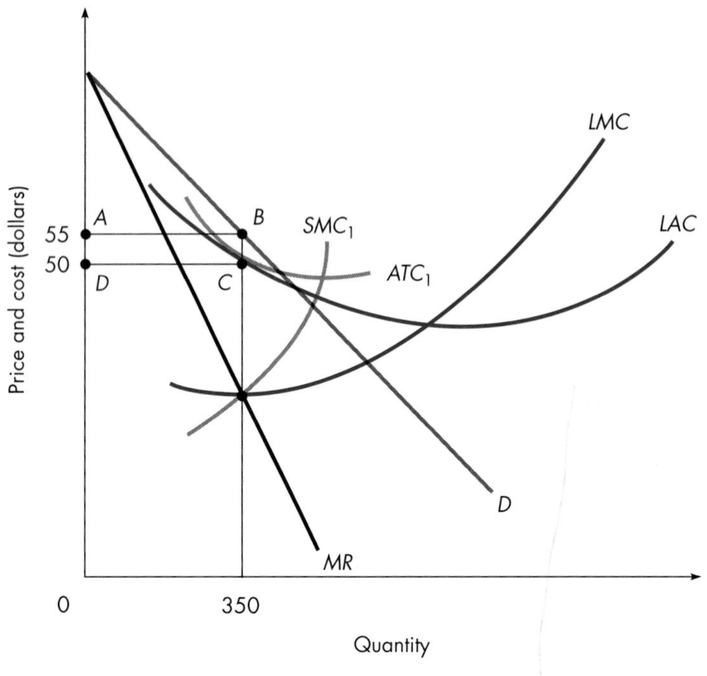

efit of being able to adjust the size of the plant to its optimal size. Recall from Chapter 10 that the plant size that minimizes the cost of production varies with the level of output. Hence, in the long run, the manager would adjust plant size to the level that minimizes the cost of producing the optimal level of output. If there is no plant size for which long-run average cost is less than price, the monopolist would not operate in the long run and would exit the industry.

Principle The manager of a monopoly firm maximizes profit in the long run by choosing to produce the level of output where marginal revenue equals long-run marginal cost ($MR = LMC$), unless price is less than long-run average cost ($P < LAC$), in which case the firm exits the industry. In the long run, the manager will adjust plant size to the optimal level; that is, the optimal plant is the one with the short-run average cost curve tangent to the long-run average cost at the profit-maximizing output level.

This principle is illustrated in Figure 14.5. The level of output that maximizes profit in the long run is 350 units, the point at which $MR = LMC$. In the long run, the manager adjusts plant size so that 350 units are produced at the lowest possible total cost. In Figure 14.5, the optimal plant size is the one with short-run average total cost and marginal cost curves labeled ATC_1 and SMC_1, respectively. Thus, the average cost of producing 350 units is \$50 per unit. The

ILLUSTRATION 14.3

Does High Market Power Mean High Prices and Profits?

Not necessarily, but it certainly can. Three major airports serve New York City: La Guardia, Newark, and JFK. La Guardia is the closest of the three to Manhattan. In 1996 *The Wall Street Journal* reported, "Largely because of a scarcity of slots—time periods for takeoff and landing—a total of 21 destinations, including Atlanta, are served by just one airline out of La Guardia. . . . This [scarcity of slots] effectively keeps upstarts out and ticket prices high."* Delta Airlines was the only airline between La Guardia and Atlanta at the time. Only USAir served Baltimore-Washington, Charlotte, and Kansas City. Only Delta served Cincinnati, and only Northwest flew nonstop to Detroit or Minneapolis–St. Paul. The president of an airline-consulting firm said, "There's virtually no competition at all." In a recent antitrust suit with ValuJet, Delta denied that it had a monopoly and stated, "There is no dangerous probability that Delta could successfully create a monopoly." The company noted that eight other large carriers fly from Atlanta and control slots at La Guardia, so they could easily enter if they "found the prospect attractive."

Nonetheless, the one-way fare between Atlanta and La Guardia was $200, compared with $132.60 for Atlanta to JFK and $130 for Atlanta to Newark. The cheapest round-trip fare between Atlanta and La Guardia was $398, compared with about $228 to the other airports where there was more competition. ValuJet claimed that Delta's yield per passenger-mile between Atlanta and La Guardia was 32 cents, or more than double its average throughout its domestic system. Delta claims that its average fares to La Guardia were skewed by the large number of business passengers who travel on short notice and thus pay more. ValuJet claimed that Delta conspired with another airline to keep it from obtaining 10 valuable slots at La Guardia, which it was on the verge of obtaining.

Whatever the merits of the case, Delta enjoyed considerable market power on the valuable La Guardia-to-Atlanta route, and it was using that market power to charge high prices and obtain a relatively high rate of return. Even potential competition was not keeping prices down. Because of its popularity and limited size, La Guardia was one of only four U.S. airports whose access was limited by the Federal Aviation Administration. As the *WSJ* noted, "For carriers, getting in is tough." So even though strong market power may be hard to come by, when you have it, it's profitable (usually).

*"Why It Costs So Much More to Fly into La Guardia," *The Wall Street Journal*, Nov. 30, 1995.

manager will sell the 350 units at a price of $55 in order to maximize profit. Long-run profit is $1,750 [$= Q \times (P - LAC) = 350 \times (\$55 - \$50)$], or the area *ABCD*. By the now familiar argument, this is the maximum profit possible under

the given revenue and cost conditions.

14.4 PROFIT-MAXIMIZING INPUT USAGE

Thus far we have analyzed monopoly profit maximization in terms of the output decision. As was the case for perfect competition, the manager can also maximize profit by choosing the optimal level of input usage. Choosing the optimal level of input usage results in exactly the same output, price, and profit level as choosing the optimal level of output would. We now discuss the monopoly firm's input decision assuming that there is only one variable input.

Marginal Revenue Product for a Monopolist

marginal revenue product (*MRP*) The additional revenue attributable to hiring one additional unit of the input, which is also equal to the product of marginal revenue times marginal product, $MRP = MR \times MP$.

The analytical principles underlying the input decision for the manager of a monopoly are the same as those for managers of perfectly competitive firms. But since price does not equal marginal revenue for a monopoly, $P \times MP$ is not the correct measure of the **marginal revenue product (*MRP*)**—the increase in revenue attributable to hiring an additional unit of the variable input. Suppose a monopolist employs an additional unit of labor, which causes output to increase by the amount of the marginal product of labor. To sell this larger output, the manager must reduce the price of the good. Each additional unit adds marginal revenue (*MR*) to total revenue. Thus the additional unit of labor adds to total revenue an amount equal to marginal revenue times the marginal product of labor:

$$MRP = \Delta TR/\Delta L = MR \times MP$$

For example, suppose hiring the tenth unit of labor increases output by 20 units ($MP = 20$). To sell these 20 additional units of output, the monopolist must lower price. Further suppose that marginal revenue is $5 per additional unit. Thus the additional revenue attributable to hiring the tenth unit of labor is the $5 additional revenue received on each of the 20 additional units of output produced and sold, or $100 (= $5 × 20). The marginal revenue product of the tenth unit of labor is $100.

Recall that in the case of perfect competition, marginal revenue product is measured by multiplying price (= *MR*) by the marginal product of labor. Also recall that *MRP* for a perfect competitor declines because marginal product declines. For a monopolist, marginal revenue product declines with increases in input usage not only because marginal product declines but also because marginal revenue declines as output is increased.

Marginal Revenue Product and the Hiring Decision

average revenue product (*ARP*) The ratio of total revenue to the total amount of the variable input hired, which is also equal to the product of price times average product of the variable input, $ARP = P \times AP$.

For the same reason that the *MRP* curve (over the relevant range) is the input demand curve for a perfectly competitive firm, the *MRP* curve (over the relevant range) is the input demand curve for a monopoly. We will establish the principle that the relevant range over which *MRP* serves as the monopolist's input demand curve is the downward-sloping, positive portion of *MRP* over which the **average revenue product (*ARP*)** of the variable input exceeds the marginal revenue product. As in the case of perfect competition, $ARP = TR/L = P \times AP$.

Figure 14.6 shows that the positive portion of *MRP* below *ARP* is the monopoly demand for a single variable input. The figure shows the relevant portion of the *MRP* curve for a monopolist employing labor as its only variable input. Suppose the wage rate is $45. In order to maximize profit, the manager should hire 400 units of labor at a wage rate of $45. To see why this is the optimal level of labor usage, suppose the manager hires only 300 units of labor. Hiring the 301st unit of labor adds slightly less than $58 to total revenue while adding only $45 to total cost. Clearly, hiring the 301st unit increases profit, in this case, $13

FIGURE 14.6
A Monopoly Firm's Demand for Labor

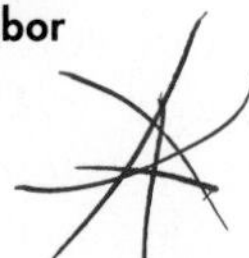

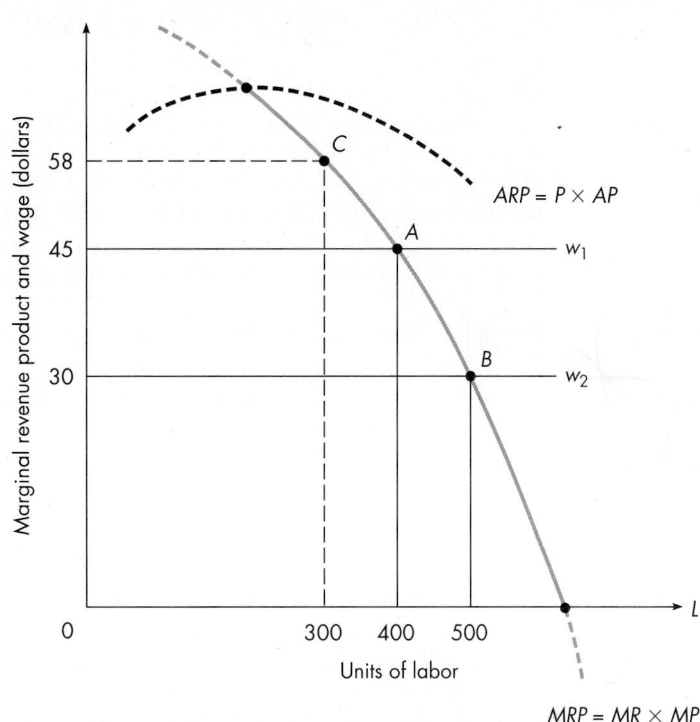

(= \$58 − \$45). The manager should continue to hire additional units of labor until $MRP = w_1 = \$45$ at point *A* in Figure 14.6. If the manager mistakenly hired more than 400 units, say, 500 units of labor, the additional revenue from hiring the last unit of labor (\$30 for the 500th unit) is less than the additional cost, \$45, and profit falls if the 500th worker is hired. Getting rid of the 500th worker lowers cost by \$45 but revenue falls by only \$30; thus, reducing labor by 1 unit increases profit by \$15. And each additional 1-unit reduction in labor similarly increases profit until labor usage is reduced down to the 400th worker.

If the wage rate falls to \$30 per unit (shown by the horizontal line w_2), the manager should hire 500 units of labor (point *B*) to maximize monopoly profit. Similarly, at a wage of \$58, the manager would hire 300 workers (point *C*). Thus, you can see that over the relevant range, the *MRP* curve is the monopolist's demand curve for a single variable input.

We now show that a monopolist would never choose a level of variable input usage at which the average revenue product is less than the marginal revenue product ($ARP < MRP$). If, at the level of input usage where $\text{MRP} = w$,

$$MRP > ARP$$

then

$$w > PQ/L$$

and

$$wL > PQ$$

which implies that total variable cost exceeds total revenue, and the profit-maximizing monopolist would hire zero units of the variable input and shut down. Hence, the relevant range over which the *MRP* curve is the input demand curve is the downward-sloping portion that lies below the *ARP* curve.

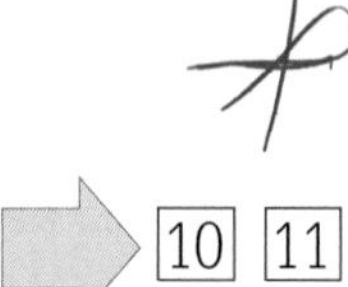

Principle When producing with a single variable input, a monopolist will maximize profit by employing that amount of the input for which marginal revenue product (*MRP*) equals the price of the input when input price is given. Consequently, the *MRP* curve, over the relevant range, is the monopolist's demand curve for the variable input when only one variable input is employed. The relevant range of the *MRP* curve is the downward-sloping, positive portion of *MRP* for which $ARP > MRP$.

Equivalence of Choosing Input Usage or Output to Maximize Profit

Recall that, for a perfect competitor, the profit-maximizing condition that the marginal revenue product of labor equals the wage rate ($MRP = w$) is equivalent to the profit-maximizing condition that product price equals marginal cost ($P = MC$). By "equivalent" we mean that regardless of whether the manager chooses Q or L to maximize profit, the resulting levels of output, labor usage, and profit are identical. We will now demonstrate that, for a monopolist, the profit-maximizing condition $MRP = w$ is equivalent to the profit-maximizing condition $MR = MC$.

Suppose the manager of a monopoly firm chooses the level of output to maximize profit. The optimal output for the monopolist is where

$$MR = MC$$

Recall from Chapter 9 that

$$MC = \frac{w}{MP}$$

where MP is the marginal product of labor and w is its price. Substituting this equation for marginal cost, the profit-maximizing condition $MR = MC$ can be expressed as

$$MR = \frac{w}{MP}$$

or

$$MR \times MP = w$$
$$MRP = w$$

Thus, you can see that the two profit-maximizing rules are equivalent: $MR = MC$ implies $MRP = w$, and vice versa.

Relation For a monopolist, the profit-maximizing condition that the marginal revenue product of the variable input must equal the price of the input ($MRP = w$) is equivalent to the profit-maximizing condition that marginal revenue must equal marginal cost ($MR = MC$). Thus, regardless of whether the manager chooses Q or L to maximize profit, the resulting levels of input usage, output, price, and profit are the same in either case.

We now illustrate the equivalency of maximizing profit by choosing either the level of output or input usage by returning to the numerical example involving Southwest Leather Designs. As you will see, the company earns exactly the same level of profit in either case.

Maximizing Profit at Southwest Leather Designs: The Input Choice

Table 14.2 presents the production function for Southwest Leather Designs in columns 1 and 2. Using this production function, we computed the marginal product of labor, which is given in column 4. The price and marginal revenue from Table 14.1 are reproduced in Table 14.2 as columns 3 and 5, respectively. The marginal revenue product for each level of labor usage is computed by multiplying marginal revenue by marginal product ($MRP = MR \times MP$). MRP is given in column 6. In order to determine the relevant range over which MRP is the monopolist's demand for labor, we also computed average revenue product by multiplying price by the average product of labor shown in column 7 ($ARP = P \times AP$), which is presented in column 8.

As we have shown, the monopolist's demand for labor is the positive portion of MRP over the range of labor usage for which $ARP > MRP$. Hence, the monopolist's demand for labor schedule in Table 14.2 is the MRP schedule for levels of labor usage of 220 units or more when $ARP > MRP$.

Figure 14.7 presents the demand for labor curve for Southwest Leather Designs. Since MRP is the per-unit change in revenue over discrete changes in labor usage, we plot the values of MRP in the middle of the interval of labor usage. For example, marginal revenue product for the 160 units of labor in the interval between 340 units and 500 units of labor is \$46.88. We plot this value of MRP (\$46.88) at 420 units of labor, which is the midpoint between 340 and 500 units (see point a in Figure 14.7).

The wage rate earned by leather workers is \$25. Using Figure 14.7, the manager of Southwest Leather Designs should hire 700 units of labor to maximize profit. The manager would not hire more than 700 units of labor because MRP is less than \$25 beyond 700 units and profit would decrease.

At 700 units of labor, you can see from the production function in Table 14.2 that 6,000 leather belts are produced, each of which can be sold for \$18.92. The total variable cost of producing the 6,000 leather belts is \$17,500 (= 700 × \$25). Total fixed cost is \$40,000, as you can see by looking at total cost when $Q = 0$ in Table 14.1. Total cost, then, is \$57,500 (= \$17,500 + \$40,000). Subtracting total cost from the total revenue of \$113,520 (= 6,000 × \$18.92), economic profit is

TABLE 14.2

The Hiring Decision for Southwest Leather Designs

(1) Labor (L)	(2) Output (Q)	(3) Price (P)	(4) Marginal product $\left(MP = \frac{\Delta Q}{\Delta L}\right)$	(5) Marginal revenue (MR)	(6) Marginal revenue product ($MRP = MR \cdot MP$)	(7) Average product $\left(AP = \frac{Q}{L}\right)$	(8) Average revenue product ($ARP = P \cdot AP$)
0	0	$40.00	—	—	—	—	—
80	1,000	35.00	12.50	$35.00	$437.50	12.50	$437.50
140	2,000	32.50	16.67	30.00	500.10	14.29	464.43
220	3,000	28.00	12.50	19.00	237.50	13.64	381.92
340	4,000	25.00	8.33	16.00	133.28	11.76	294.00
500	5,000	21.50	6.25	7.50	46.88	10.00	215.00
700	6,000	18.92	5.00	6.02	30.10	8.57	162.14
950	7,000	17.00	4.00	5.48	21.92	7.37	125.29
1,350	8,000	15.35	2.50	3.80	9.50	5.93	91.03
1,850	9,000	14.00	2.00	3.20	6.40	4.86	68.04

FIGURE 14.7

Profit Maximization for Southwest Leather Designs: The Hiring Decision

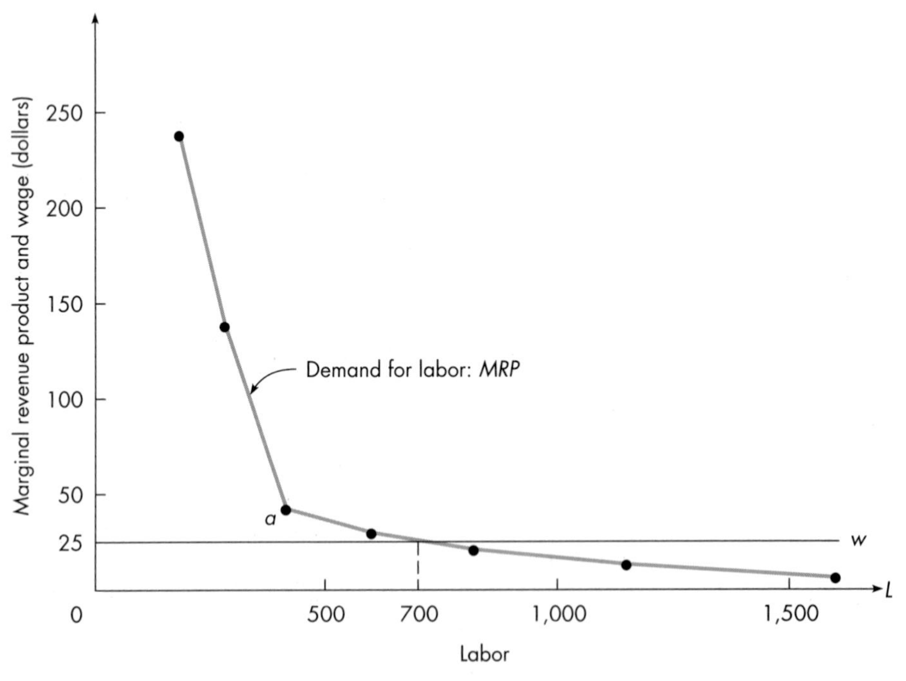

calculated to be \$56,020 (= \$113,520 − \$57,500). Thus, when the manager chooses the amount of labor to maximize profit, the firm produces 6,000 belts using 700 units of labor, sells them for \$18.92 each, and earns an economic profit of \$56,020. This is exactly the same result obtained from Table 14.1 when the manager chooses the level of output to maximize profit using the rule
12 13 $MR = MC$.

Input Demand: Several Variable Inputs

As was the case for perfect competition, the derivation of input demand curves is a bit more complicated when production involves more than one variable input. The *MRP* curve is no longer the demand for the productive service, because the inputs are interdependent in the productive process. A change in the price of any one input leads to a change not only in the usage of that input but also in the use of other inputs as well. Recall that the marginal product curve for an input is derived assuming the usage of all other inputs is held constant. Thus changes in the rates of usage of other inputs shift the *MRP* curve.

Nonetheless, the monopolist's demand for an input is still downward-sloping. And, most important, the monopolist still uses the amount of each variable input at which its marginal revenue product equals its price.[3] For instance, if the monopoly firm uses three variable inputs—V_1, V_2, and V_3 —which have given, market-determined prices—w_1, w_2, and w_3—the firm will maximize profit (or minimize loss) by employing each input so that

$$MRP_{V_1} = w_1$$
$$MRP_{V_2} = w_2$$
$$MRP_{V_3} = w_3$$

Since the inputs are interdependent in the production process, these conditions must hold simultaneously; the optimal levels of usage of the inputs must be determined simultaneously.

14.5 MONOPOLISTIC COMPETITION

As we pointed out at the beginning of this chapter, the general model of monopoly is useful in the analysis of firm behavior in other types of markets in which firms have some degree of market power but are not pure monopolies. Firms in such markets, facing downward-sloping demands, attempt to maximize profit in the same way a monopoly does: by setting $MR = MC$. In these intermediate markets, between firms with the most market power (monopoly) and firms with the least (perfect competition), certain complications arise for the profit-maximizing decision. We end this chapter with an analysis of the intermediate market structure in which firms have the least market power of all firms that are not perfect competitors: monopolistic competition.

[3] The mathematical derivation of this result is in the appendix to this chapter.

Monopolistically competitive markets are characterized by (1) a large number of relatively small firms, (2) products which are similar to, but somewhat different from, one another, and (3) unrestricted entry and exit of firms into and out of the market. The only difference between monopolistic competition and perfect competition is that under monopolistic competition firms produce a differentiated product. The major difference between monopolistic competition and monopoly is that under monopolistic competition firms can easily enter into and exit out of the market. Thus, as the name implies, monopolistic competition has characteristics of both monopoly and perfect competition.

Product differentiation under monopolistic competition prevents a firm's demand from becoming horizontal. Real or perceived differences between goods, though slight, will make them less than perfect substitutes. For example, gasoline stations in a particular city are good, but not perfect, substitutes for one another. Your car would run on gasoline from any gasoline station, but stations differ in location, and people's tastes differ—some people prefer Texaco, some prefer Exxon, some prefer the service at Joe's, others prefer Julie's service. And the differentiating characteristics go on and on. The most important point is that although the products are similar, they are differentiated, causing each firm to have a small amount of market power.

We will first set forth the theory of monopolistic competition in its original form, as developed by Edward Chamberlin in the 1930s.[4] Because each firm in the market sells a slightly differentiated product, it faces a downward-sloping demand curve, which is relatively elastic but not horizontal. Any firm could raise its price slightly without losing all its sales, or it could lower its price slightly without gaining the entire market. Under the original set of assumptions employed by Chamberlin, each firm's output is so small relative to the total sales in the market that the firm believes that its price and output decisions will go unnoticed by other firms in the market. It therefore acts independently.

As you will see, the theory of monopolistic competition is essentially a long-run theory; in the short run, there is virtually no difference between monopolistic competition and monopoly. In the long run, because of unrestricted entry into the market, the theory of monopolistic competition closely resembles the theory of perfect competition.

Short-Run Equilibrium

With the given demand, marginal revenue, and cost curves, a monopolistic competitor maximizes profit or minimizes loss by equating marginal revenue and marginal cost. Figure 14.8 illustrates the short-run, profit-maximizing equilibrium for a firm in a monopolistically competitive market. Profit is maximized by producing an output of Q and selling at price P.

In the situation illustrated, the firm will earn an economic profit, shown as the shaded area $PABC$. However, as was the case for perfect competition and

[4]E. H. Chamberlin, *The Theory of Monopolistic Competition* (Cambridge, Mass.: Harvard University Press, 1933).

FIGURE 14.8
Short-Run Profit Maximization under Monopolistic Competition

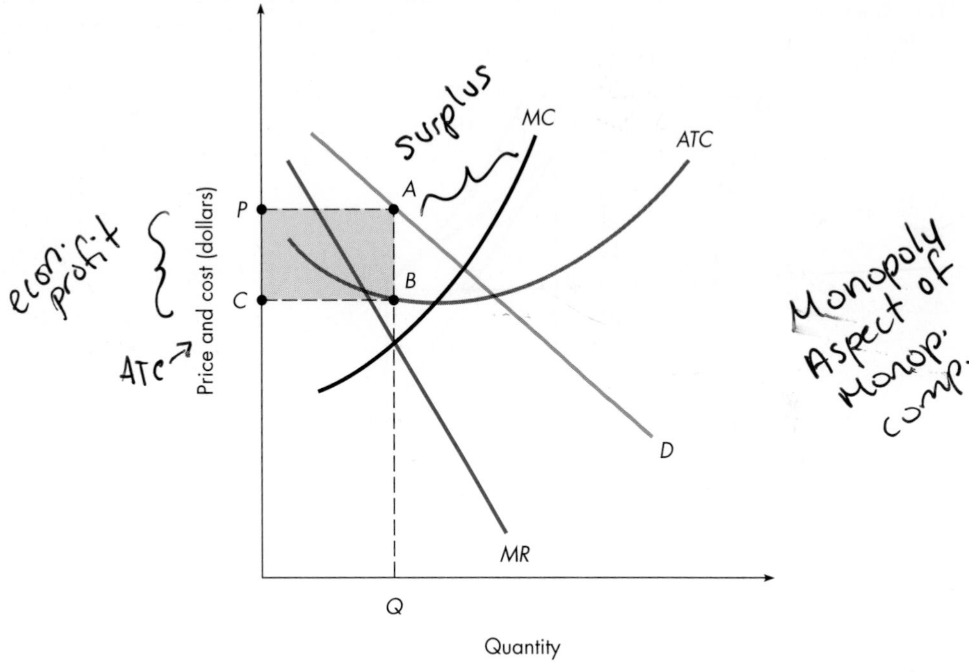

monopoly, in the short run the firm could operate with a loss, if the demand curves lies below *ATC* but above *AVC*. If the demand curve falls below *AVC*, the firm would shut down.

In its original form, there appears to be little competition in monopolistic competition as far as the short run is concerned. Indeed Figure 14.8 is identical to one illustrating short-run equilibrium for a monopoly. In the long run, however, a monopoly cannot be maintained if there is unrestricted entry into the market. If firms are earning economic profit in the short run, other firms will enter and produce the product, and they will continue to enter until all economic profits are eliminated.

Long-Run Equilibrium

While the short-run equilibrium for a firm under monopolistic competition is similar to that under monopoly, the long-run equilibrium is more closely related to the equilibrium position under perfect competition. Because of unrestricted entry, all economic profit must be eliminated in the long run, which occurs at an output at which price equals long-run average cost. This occurs when the firm's demand is tangent to long-run average cost. The only difference between this

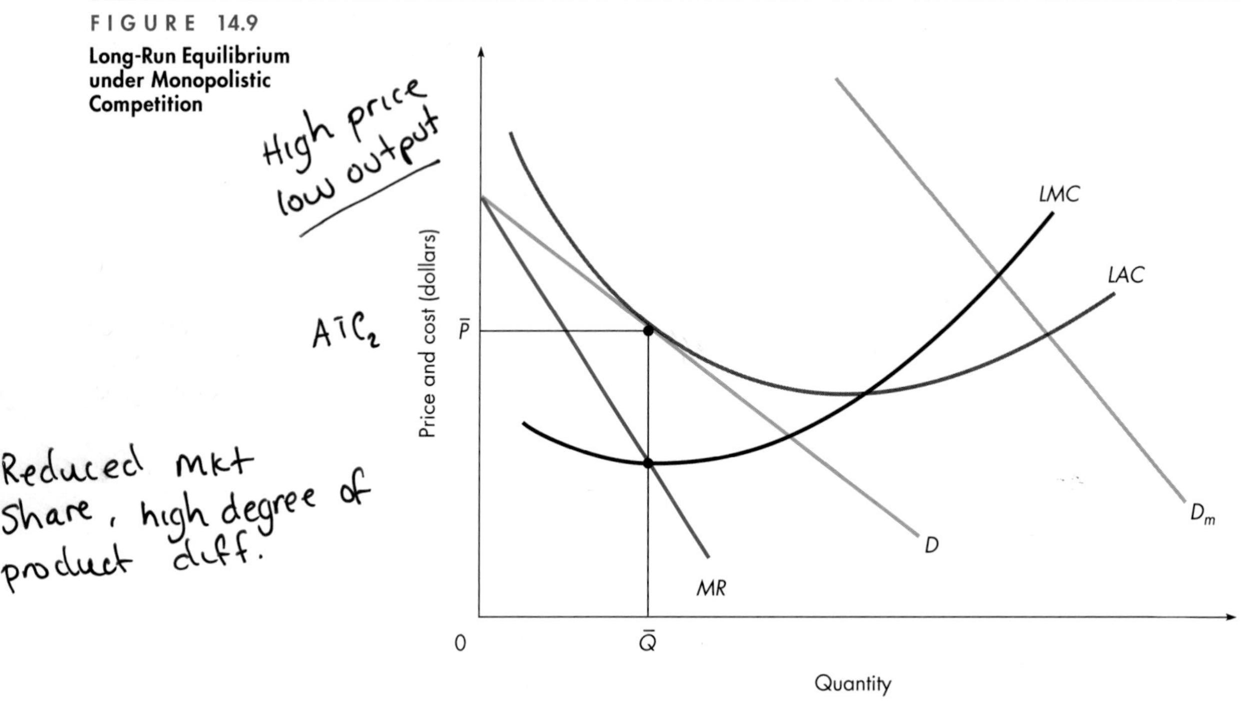

FIGURE 14.9
Long-Run Equilibrium under Monopolistic Competition

equilibrium and that for perfect competition is that, for a firm in a monopolistically competitive market, the tangency cannot occur at minimum average cost. Since the demand curve facing the firm is downward-sloping under monopolistic competition, the point of tangency must be on the downward-sloping range of long-run average cost. Thus, the long-run equilibrium output under monopolistic competition is less than that forthcoming under perfect competition in the long run.

This long-run result is shown in Figure 14.9. *LAC* and *LMC* are the long-run average and marginal cost curves for a typical monopolistically competitive firm. Suppose that the original demand curve is given by D_m. In this case the firm would be making substantial economic profits because demand lies above *LAC* over a wide range of output, and if this firm is making profits, one would expect that other firms in the market are also earning economic profits. These profits would then attract new firms into the market. While the new firms would not sell exactly the same products as existing firms, their products would be very similar. So as new firms enter, the number of substitutes would increase and the demand facing the typical firm would shift backward and probably become more elastic (though not perfectly elastic). Entry will continue as long as there is some economic profit being earned. Thus entry causes each firm's demand curve to shift backward until a demand curve such as *D* in Figure 14.9 is reached. This long-run demand curve, *D*, is tangent to *LAC* at a price of $\overline{P}$ and output of $\overline{Q}$.

In such an equilibrium either an increase or a decrease in price by the firm would lead to losses. No further entry would occur since there are no economic profits to be earned in this market.

If too many firms enter the market, each firm's demand curve would be pushed so far back that demand falls below *LAC*. Firms would be suffering losses and exit would take place. As this happened, the demand curve would be pushed back up to tangency with *LAC*. Free entry and exit under monopolistic competition must lead to a situation where demand is tangent to *LAC*—where price equals average cost—and no economic profit is earned, but the firms do earn a normal profit.

The equilibrium in Figure 14.9 must also be characterized by the intersection of *LMC* and *MR*. Only at output $\overline{Q}$ can the firm avoid a loss, so this output must be optimal. But the optimal output requires that marginal cost equal marginal revenue. Thus, at $\overline{Q}$, it must be the case that $MR = LMC$.

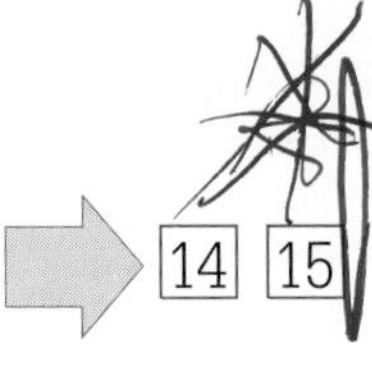

Relation Long-run equilibrium in a monopolistically competitive market is attained when the demand curve for each producer is tangent to the long-run average cost curve. Unrestricted entry
14 15 and exit lead to this equilibrium. At the equilibrium output, price equals long-run average cost and marginal revenue equals long-run marginal cost.

In closing our discussion of monopolistic competition, we briefly mention two points. First, according to the original model as set forth here, firms act independently when making decisions, ignoring the actions of other firms in the market. In reality firms may not act independently when faced with competition from closely related firms, possibly because of proximity; in fact, they may exhibit a great deal of interdependence and intense personal rivalry. We will address this possibility at more length in the next chapter. This change in assumptions will not alter the long-run, zero-profit conclusions of the theory, however.

Short of getting the government to prevent entry, there is nothing firms in a monopolistically competitive market can do about having their profits competed away. Even if the firms were to conspire to fix a price, new firms would enter. Each firm would find its demand decreased and its sales reduced until price equaled average cost and economic profits were zero, although possibly at a higher price than would occur in the absence of the price-fixing agreement.

Second, we have emphasized that, under monopolistic competition, profits are competed away in the long run. This is correct in general. But we do not mean to imply that there is no opportunity for astute managers to postpone this situation to the future by innovative decision making. Firms selling in monopolistically competitive markets can and do advertise and change product quality in an effort to lengthen the time period over which they earn economic profit. Those managers who are successful in their marketing strategy can sometimes earn profit for a long time. Some firms can reduce their cost. However, successful strategies can be imitated by competitors selling a product that is rather similar. Therefore, under monopolistic competition there is always a strong tendency for economic profit to be eliminated in the long run, no matter what strategies man-
16 agers undertake.

ILLUSTRATION 14.4

Can Monopolistic Competitors Protect Their Profits?

Only Time Will Tell

In May 1996, a *Wall Street Journal* article on apparel pricing began this way: "Remember all the nifty bargains you found shopping for clothes last year? So do retailers. And they vow never again. For two years, stores have countered slowing demand for apparel—from sweats to cocktail dresses—with constant discounting, trying to spur demand by giving up profits. Now, after one of their least profitable years, big apparel merchants are ruling out another avalanche of sales and markdowns. . . . They are deploying an array of merchandising gimmicks to wean shoppers off their addiction to deep discounts.*

Laura Bird, the author of the article, was not optimistic for the merchants: "There's just one catch: Shoppers' addiction to the steal lingers on." A customer of Marshall Field's said, "I know everyone has to make their money, but I just feel taken somehow when I pay full price." Another shopper agreed, "There are certain stores where I would feel horribly guilty buying anything at full price because everything eventually goes on sale." Said another shopper, "I'm more embarrassed when I pay full price."

To counter such feelings, the large fashion merchants were "conducting what amounts to a mass effort at behavior modification." One huge merchandiser was cutting the number of sales events by half at its department stores. Many retailers were trying to encourage full-price purchases by displaying fewer clothes. They believed that if there were only a few of something on the rack people would be more likely to pay full price. One retailer was planning to abandon high-low pricing and switch to everyday low prices, also called "value pricing," despite the fact that other large chains, such as Sears, had previously tried such a strategy with little success. According to the *WSJ*, "Retailers are dressing up modest discounts in other ways." For example, sales racks displayed signs with the sale price rather than "40% Off." Some were selling one item at full price with 50 percent off the second item. The result would be a fairly low 25 percent off for the two.

Nevertheless, as Bird stated, there was a lot of resistance on the part of consumers. But profits had been terrible for two years. And changing consumers' perception of what is and what isn't a bargain is a long-term process. Fashion retailers do have to reduce prices to clear out old merchandise and make room for the new. Otherwise, their inventories would be so small that they would lose sales by not having the goods on hand.

Did the new policy work? Possibly not as well as the retailers would have liked, but also a little better than customers would have preferred. As the 1996 Christmas shopping season got well under way with the huge post-Thanksgiving shopping weekend, *USA Today* ran a story entitled "Retailers Slow to Slash Prices in Robust Season."† The article began, "In spite of a wealth of sale items in stores, the holiday season is starting without the heavy discounts of a year ago. While merchants responded to last year's sluggish sales with deep markdowns, increased consumer spending and tighter retail inventories are expected to keep heavy price slashing in check." Retail sales were good, but many shoppers were still waiting for the big discounts.

One research analyst gave a reason for the general absence of large price decreases: "People are feeling that they don't have to buy at the lowest possible prices because there are a few more bucks in their pockets." It would appear that the rise in consumer income increased sales and slowed the return to extensive discounting.

There were some exceptions. The article mentioned big sales at some stores: Circuit City, Mervyn's, and Sears. However, two of the large chains noted above as wanting to reduce the number of sales events had scheduled 13 fewer promotion days for December than they had the year before and still expected a strong fourth quarter. One reason given was leaner inventories. As a whole most merchants were optimistic. By the 1997 Christmas shopping season most stores had returned to heavy discounting.

So sometimes good planning can help monopolistic competitors. But so does a little luck and a lot of economic prosperity.

*Laura Bird, "Apparel Stores Seek to Cure Shoppers Addicted to Discounts," *The Wall Street Journal,* May 29, 1996.

†"Retailers Slow to Slash Prices in Robust Season," *USA Today,* Dec. 4, 1996.

14.6 SUMMARY

A monopoly exists if a single firm produces and sells a good or service for which there are no close substitutes and new firms are prevented from entering the market in the long run. While these conditions are seldom met in the real world, many firms do have the power to make price and output decisions in essentially the same way that a monopolist chooses price and output to maximize profit. For this reason, managers can use the theory of monopoly as a guide to making pricing decisions when their firms face downward-sloping demand curves; that is, when their firms possess market power.

Market power is the ability of a firm to raise price without losing all its sales. Any firm that faces a downward-sloping demand curve has market power. In contrast, a perfectly competitive firm, facing a horizontal demand curve, has no market power—any increase in price causes sales to fall to zero. Market power gives a firm the ability to raise price above average cost and earn economic profit, demand and cost conditions permitting. In the long run, a firm with market power may be able to earn economic profit because entry of new firms is difficult. In order to be a true monopolist, there must be some barriers to entry to prevent rival firms from entering and competing away the monopolist's profit. Barriers to entry, therefore, must exist in order for a firm to be a monopoly in the long run. Barriers to entry include economies of scale, barriers created by government, input barriers, and barriers resulting from brand loyalties.

Market power is never absolute. There are always substitutes for a monopolist's product, even if imperfect. And even though monopolists have no *direct* competitors that sell an identical product, monopolists do compete indirectly with all goods and services for a place in the consumer's budget. Market power, then, is possessed not absolutely but, rather, to varying degrees. The degree to which a firm possesses market power is inversely related to the availability of close substitutes for the firm's product and, thus, can be measured (approximately) by the own-price and cross-price elasticities of demand.

The less elastic the demand for the monopolist's product, the less available are good substitutes and the greater its degree of market power. The degree to which consumers view another good to be a substitute for the monopolist's good can be measured by the cross-price elasticity of demand. The higher the (positive) cross-price elasticity, the greater the perceived substitutability and the smaller the degree of market power enjoyed by the monopolist. The Lerner index, $(P - MC)/P$, measures the proportionate amount by which monopoly price exceeds marginal cost (i.e., the competitive price level). The higher the Lerner index, the greater the degree of market power. Because the Lerner index can be shown to be equal to the inverse of the own-price elasticity of demand $(-1/E)$, it follows that the Lerner index will be high when consumers perceive few readily substitutable goods and $|E|$ is low.

As in the case of perfect competition, the profit-maximizing decision for a monopoly can take either of two equivalent forms. The manager can choose either output or input usage to maximize profit using the rule $MR = MC$ or $MRP = w$, respectively. The two rules lead to identical prices, outputs, input usage, and profits.

In the short run, the manager of a monopoly firm maximizes profit by producing and selling that level of output for which $MR = MC$, as long as $P > AVC$ for this output level. If $P < AVC$ for all output levels, the manager should shut down in the short run. Alternatively, the manager of a monopoly that produces using a single variable input can maximize profit by hiring the amount of labor for which $MRP = w$, as long as average revenue product exceeds marginal revenue product. If ARP is less than MRP, the manager should shut down.

In the long run, the manager should produce the output level for which $MR = LMC$ and adjust plant size so that the optimal plant is used to produce the profit-maximizing output. The optimal plant is the one associated with the short-run average cost curve that is tangent to long-run average cost at the profit-maximizing output. If $P < LAC$ for all levels of output, the monopolist exits the industry. In the long run when all inputs are variable, the manager can maximize profit by choosing the levels of all inputs so that their marginal revenue products all equal their respective input prices *simultaneously*.

Finally we briefly developed the theory of monopolistic competition. Of all firms with market power, a monopolistically competitive firm has the least. The barriers to entry are so low that it is easy for new firms to enter the market when economic profits are made by existing firms. As we showed, the key feature of monopolistic competition is that in the long run, the firm's economic profit is competed away even though each firm has some market power. The firm's demand curve is downward-sloping because each firm sells a product that is somewhat differentiated from that of every other firm in the market. In the short run, a monopolistic competitor simply acts like a monopoly. In the long run, the entry of new firms causes each firm's demand to become tangent to long-run average cost.

TECHNICAL PROBLEMS

1. Compare the market power of the following pairs of firms. Explain.
   a. Chase Manhattan Bank and the First National Bank of Pecos, Texas
   b. The "Big Three" U.S. auto manufacturers prior to the early 1970s and the same firms after the early 1970s
   c. A regional phone company and a regional electric company in the same area
2. Explain why input barriers to entry have probably declined in importance with the recent expansion of international markets.
3. Assume a monopoly has the following demand schedule:

Price	Quantity
$20	200
15	300
10	500
5	700

   a. Calculate total revenue at each P and Q combination.
   b. Calculate marginal revenue per unit for each decrease in price.
   c. For the change in price from $20 to $15, is demand elastic or inelastic? How much revenue does the firm lose from reducing the price on the 200 units it could have sold for $20? How much revenue does the firm gain from selling 100 more units at $15? Compare the two changes, then compare these changes with MR.
   d. Answer part *c* for the price change from $15 to $10.
4. The following graph shows demand and MR for a monopoly:

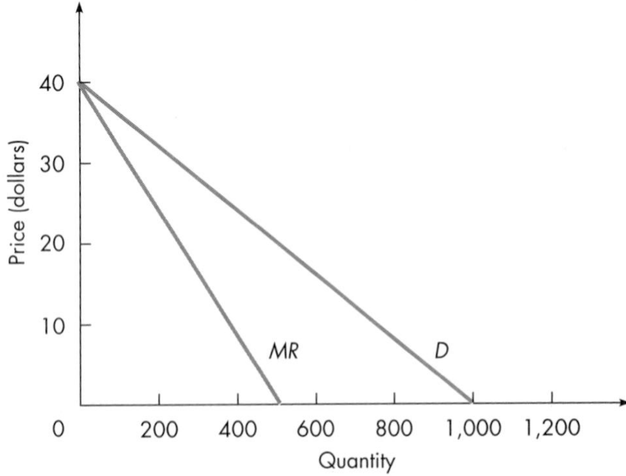

a. If the firm wants to sell 200 units, what price does it charge?
b. If the firm charges a price of $32.50, how much will it sell?
c. What is *MR* for parts *a* and *b*? Is demand elastic or inelastic?
d. If the firm charges $20, how much will it sell? What is demand elasticity?

5. A monopolist faces the following demand and cost schedules:

Price	Quantity	Total cost
$20	7	$36
19	8	45
18	9	54
17	10	63
16	11	72
15	12	81

a. How much output should the monopolist produce?
b. What price should the firm charge?
c. What is the maximum amount of profit that this firm can earn?

6. The following graph shows demand, *MR*, and cost curves for a monopoly in the short run:

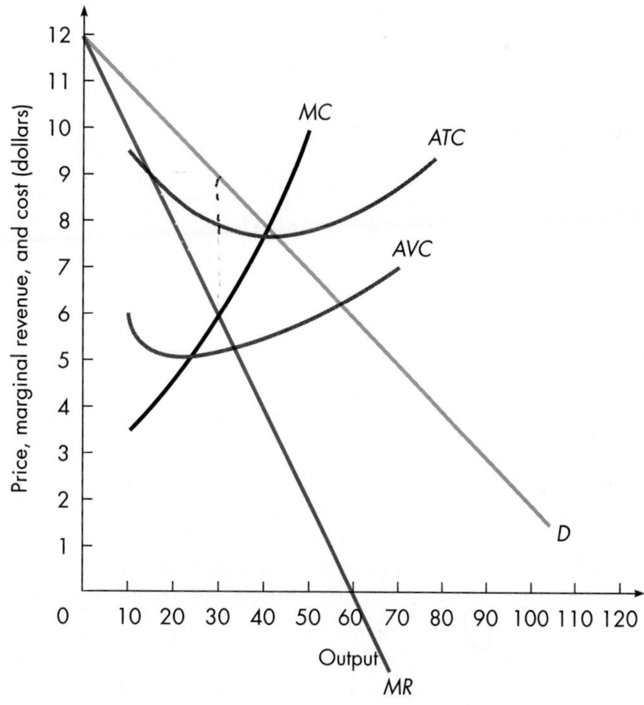

a. Profit is maximized at a price of $________.
b. The profit-maximizing level of output is ________.
c. At the optimal level of output, total revenue is $________, total cost is $________, and profit is $________.

7. Explain why the manager of a profit-maximizing monopoly always produces and sells on the elastic portion of the demand curve. If costs are zero, what output will the manager produce? Explain.

8. The following figure shows demand, marginal revenue, and short-run cost curves for a monopoly:

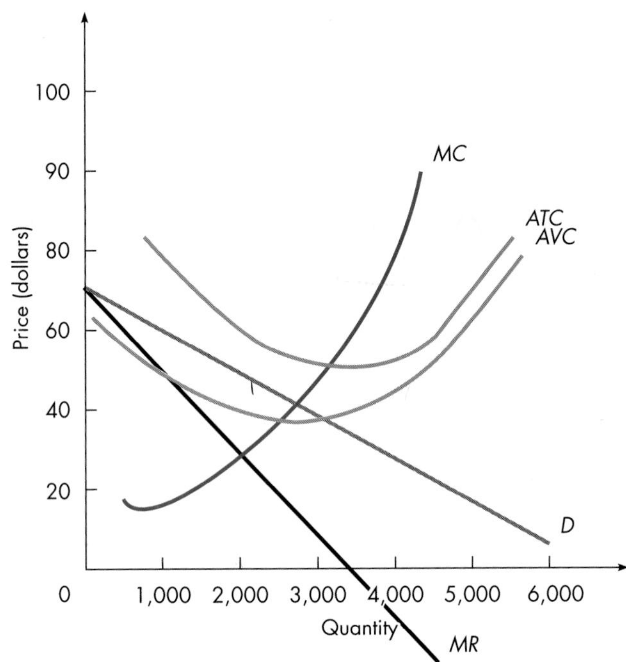

a. How much should the firm produce? What price should it charge?
b. What is the firm's profit (loss)?
c. What is total revenue? What is total variable cost?
d. If the firm shuts down in the short run, how much will it lose?

9. Consider a monopoly firm with the demand and cost curves shown in the graph. Assume that the firm is operating in the short run with the plant designed to produce 400 units of output optimally.

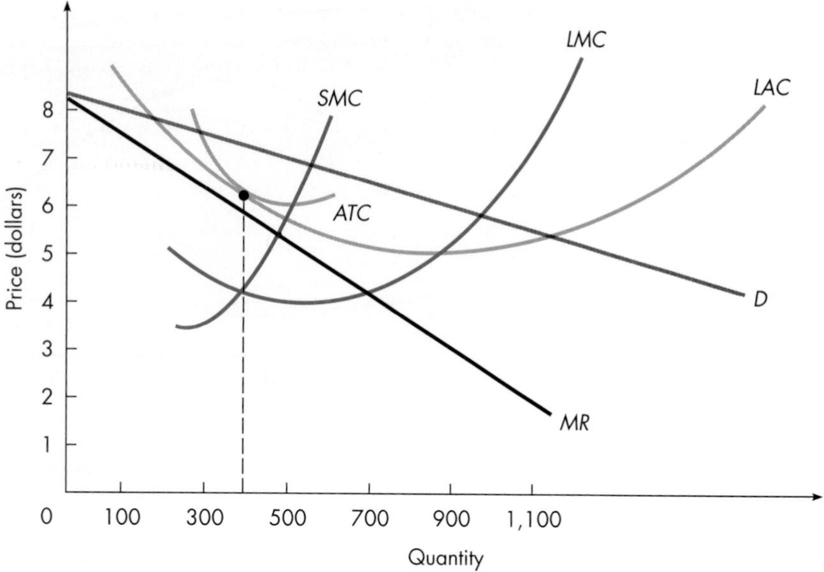

a. What output should be produced?
b. What will be the price?
c. How much profit is made?
d. If the firm can change plant size and move into the long run, what will be output and price?
e. Will profit increase? How do you know?
f. Draw in the new short-run average and marginal cost curves associated with the new plant size.

10. In the following table, columns 1 and 2 make up a portion of the production function of a monopolist using a single variable input, labor. Columns 2 and 3 make up the demand function facing the monopolist over this range of output.

(1) Labor	(2) Quantity	(3) Price
9	50	$21
10	100	20
11	140	19
12	170	18
13	190	17
14	205	16
15	215	15

a. Derive *MP*, *MR*, and *MRP* over this range.
b. If the wage rate is $60, how much labor would the manager hire? Why? What if the wage falls to $40?

11. The following figure shows the average revenue product and the marginal revenue product of labor for a monopoly:

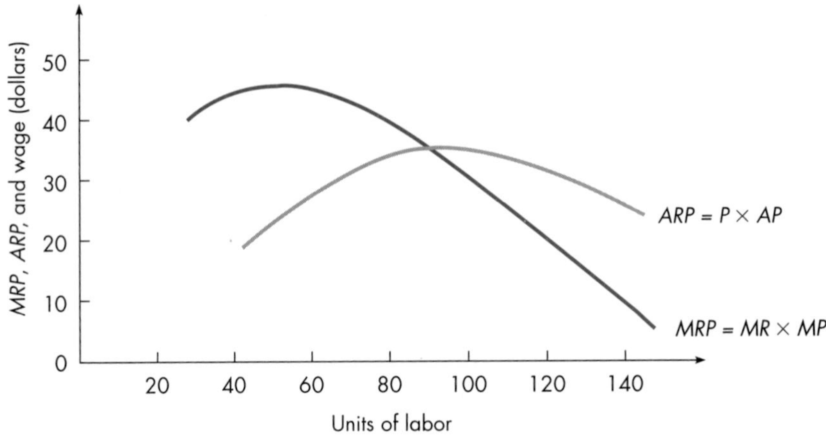

a. If the wage is \$20, how much labor would the firm hire?
b. If the wage is \$10, how much labor would the firm hire?
c. If the wage is \$40, how much labor would the firm hire?

12. A manager of a monopoly faces the demand schedule given in columns 2 and 3 of the table below. Column 1 shows the amount of the single variable input, labor, used to produce each of the output levels in the table. Total fixed cost is \$50, and the price of labor is \$5 per unit. Fill in the blanks in the table and answer the following questions.

(1) Labor usage	(2) Output	(3) Price	(4) Total revenue	(5) Marginal revenue	(6) Total variable cost	(7) Total cost	(8) Marginal cost	(9) Profit
0	0	\$8.00	____	—	____	____	—	____
8	10	7.50	____	____	____	____	____	____
12	20	7.00	____	____	____	____	____	____
17	30	6.50	____	____	____	____	____	____
24	40	6.00	____	____	____	____	____	____
33	50	5.50	____	____	____	____	____	____
44	60	5.00	____	____	____	____	____	____
57	70	4.50	____	____	____	____	____	____

a. In order to maximize profit, the manager should produce ________ units of output and charge a price of \$________. Explain why.
b. At the optimal level of output, the monopolist earns a (profit, loss) of \$________.
c. Examine the profit schedule in column 9. Does profit reach its maximum value at the level of output given in part *a*?

13. Suppose the manager in problem 12 decides to choose the level of input usage to maximize profit rather than choosing output to maximize profit. The same demand and production schedules from problem 12 are reproduced in the table below. Fixed cost and the wage rate are the same. Complete the table and answer the following questions.

(1) Labor usage	(2) Output	(3) Price	(4) Marginal product	(5) Average product	(6) Average revenue product	(7) Marginal revenue product
0	0	$8.00	—	—	—	—
8	10	7.50	____	____	____	____
12	20	7.00	____	____	____	____
17	30	6.50	____	____	____	____
24	40	6.00	____	____	____	____
33	50	5.50	____	____	____	____
44	60	5.00	____	____	____	____
57	70	4.50	____	____	____	____

a. In order to maximize profit, the manager should hire ____ units of labor. Explain.

b. This amount of labor will result in the production of ______ units of output, which can be sold at a price of $______. The firm earns a (profit, loss) of $______.

c. What does it mean to say that choosing output to maximize profit is equivalent to choosing labor usage to maximize profit? Use your results from this problem and problem 12 to illustrate this equivalency.

d. If the wage rate is $10, the manager should hire ______ units of labor. Explain.

e. If the wage rises to $15, the manager should hire ______ units of labor. The firm earns a (profit, loss) of $______. Explain.

14. Describe the features of monopolistic competition:
    a. How is it similar to monopoly?
    b. How is it similar to perfect competition?
    c. What are the characteristics of short-run equilibrium?
    d. What are the characteristics of long-run equilibrium?
    e. How is long-run equilibrium attained?

15. The following graph shows the long-run average and marginal cost curves for a monopolistically competitive firm:

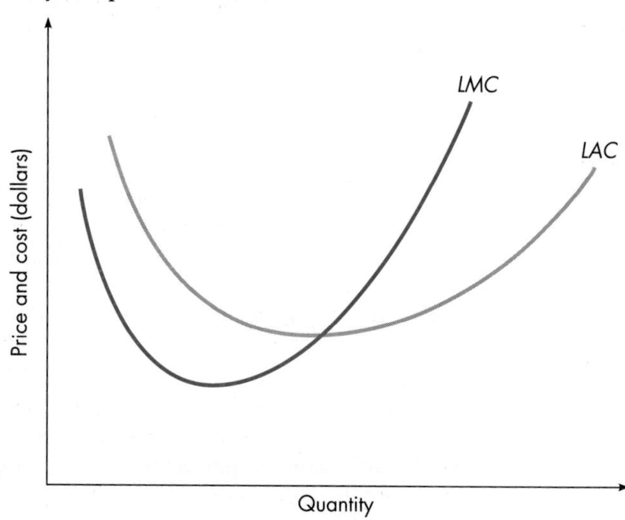

a. Assume the firm is in the short run and making profits. Draw in the demand and marginal revenue curves. Show output and price.
b. Now let the firm reach long-run equilibrium. Draw in precisely the new demand and marginal revenue curves. Show output and price.
c. Why must $MR = MC$ at *exactly* the same output at which LAC is tangent to demand?
d. Contrast this firm's output and price in long-run equilibrium with the price and output if this firm was a perfect competitor.

16. Why would a monopolistic competitor advertise while a perfect competitor would not?

APPLIED PROBLEMS

1. QuadPlex Cinema is the only movie theater in Idaho Falls. The nearest rival movie theater, the Cedar Bluff Twin, is 35 miles away in Pocatello. Thus QuadPlex Cinema possesses a degree of market power. Despite having market power, QuadPlex Cinema is currently suffering losses. In a conversation with the owners of QuadPlex, the manager of the movie theater made the following suggestions: "Since QuadPlex is a local monopoly, we should just increase ticket prices until we make enough profit."
   a. Comment on this strategy.
   b. How might the market power of QuadPlex Cinema be measured?
   c. What options should QuadPlex consider in the long run?
2. The *El Dorado Star* is the only newspaper in El Dorado, New Mexico. Certainly, the *Star* competes with *The Wall Street Journal, USA Today,* and *The New York Times* for national news reporting, but the *Star* offers readers stories of local interest, such as local news, weather, sporting events, and so on. The *El Dorado Star* faces the revenue and cost schedules shown in the table that follows:

Number of newspapers per day (Q)	Total revenue (including advertising revenues) per day (TR)	Total cost per day (TC)
0	$ 0	$2,000
1,000	1,500	2,100
2,000	2,500	2,200
3,000	3,000	2,360
4,000	3,250	2,520
5,000	3,450	2,700
6,000	3,625	2,890
7,000	3,725	3,090
8,000	3,625	3,310
9,000	3,475	3,550

   a. How many papers should the manager of the *El Dorado Star* print and sell daily?
   b. How much profit (or loss) will the *Star* earn?
   c. Graph the marginal revenue and marginal cost curves. Do these curves support your answer to part *a?* (*Hint:* Be sure to plot the values of MR and MC in the middle of the intervals over which they are computed.)

d. What is total fixed cost for the *El Dorado Star?* If total fixed cost increases to $5,000, how many papers should be printed and sold in the short run? What should the owners of the *Star* do in the long run?

3. *The Wall Street Journal* reported: "1991 was the worst year for housing starts since World War II. The nation's largest builders should feel truly grateful. For when it comes to home building, this isn't an equal opportunity recession." Why would the largest builders feel grateful? Why would small- and medium-size builders be saddened? (*Hint:* The savings-and-loan crisis had just occurred and banks and S&Ls were more reluctant to make construction loans.)
4. Tots-R-Us operates the only day-care center in an exclusive neighborhood just outside of Washington, D.C. Tots-R-Us is making substantial economic profit, but the owners know that new day-care centers will soon learn of this highly profitable market and attempt to enter the market. The owners decide to begin spending immediately a rather large sum on advertising designed to decrease elasticity. Should they wait until new firms actually enter? Explain how advertising can be employed to allow Tots-R-Us to keep price above average cost without encouraging entry.
5. Antitrust authorities at the Federal Trade Commission are reviewing your company's recent merger with a rival firm. The FTC is concerned that the merger of two rival firms in the same market will increase market power. A hearing is scheduled for your company to present arguments that your firm has not increased its market power through this merger. Can you do this? How? What evidence might you bring to the hearing?
6. In the mid-1990s firms competing in the same market were increasingly entering into joint ventures to develop new products and new technologies together. The *WSJ* reported that the Justice Department was generally looking on these ventures more favorably than it had a decade or so before. How would you explain this change in attitude?
7. You own a small bank in a state that is now considering allowing interstate banking. You oppose interstate banking because it will be possible for the very large money center banks in New York, Chicago, and San Francisco to open branches in your bank's geographic market area. While proponents of interstate banking point to the benefits to consumers of increased competition, you worry that economies of scale might ultimately force your now profitable bank out of business. Explain how economies of scale (if significant economies of scale do in fact exist) could result in your bank being forced out of business in the long run.
8. The Harley-Davidson motorcycle company, which had a copyright on the word "hog," applied for exclusive rights to its engine sound. Why would a company want copyrights on two such mundane things?
9. An industry said to be characterized by monopolistic competition is the apparel industry. Suppose you were hired as a consultant by a firm in this industry. How would you advise the firm as to the levels of output, price, input usage, and advertising? What problems might the firm encounter?
10. Some states have laws restricting the sale of many types of goods on Sunday. Consumers, by and large, oppose such laws because Sunday is a convenient time to shop. Retail sales organizations frequently support such laws. Discuss the reasons for merchants' supporting such laws. (This question somewhat anticipates material in the next chapter.)

11. Even if the firms in a monopolistically competitive market collude successfully and fix price, economic profit will still be competed away if there is unrestricted entry. Explain. Will price be higher or lower under such an agreement in long-run equilibrium than would be the case if firms didn't collude? Explain.
12. Suppose you own a medium-size clothing store that has the exclusive franchise in the city for the popular WaterPolo brand of men's shirts and slacks. You will check your competitors to see what they are charging for comparable items, but you obviously cannot estimate the demand for every item you sell. How could you tell if the price you are charging for specific WaterPolo items is too low or too high?

MATHEMATICAL APPENDIX Profit Maximization for a Monopoly

This appendix describes a manager's choice of output and price or input usage in order to maximize profit for a monopoly. First, we examine the decision about the profit-maximizing price and output using the most general demand and cost functions, then using a linear demand and cubic cost function. We also demonstrate that the profit-maximizing price and output are always on the elastic portion of demand. Next, we derive the profit-maximizing conditions when the manager chooses the level of usage of one variable input and then two variable inputs.

The Monopolist Chooses Output and Price

Assume that the firm is in the short run, so some costs are fixed. Let the inverse demand for a monopoly be

$$P = P(Q)$$

so total revenue is

$$R(Q) = P(Q)Q$$

The monopoly profit function is

$$\pi = R(Q) - TVC(Q) - TFC \tag{1}$$

where $TVC(Q)$ is total variable cost and TFC is total fixed cost.

The first-order condition for profit maximization requires

$$d\pi/dQ = dR/dQ - dTVC/dQ = 0 \tag{2}$$

The second-order condition for a maximum is that at the equilibrium quantity

$$d^2\pi/dQ^2 = d^2R/dQ^2 - d^2TVC/dQ^2 < 0$$

Since in equation (2) dR/dQ is marginal revenue and dC/dQ is marginal cost, choosing the quantity of output that maximizes profit requires that marginal revenue equal marginal cost: $MR = MC$. Solve equation (2) for the equilibrium output, Q^*, so the equilibrium price is $P^* = P(Q^*)$.

If

$$\pi = P(Q^*)Q^* - TVC(Q^*) - TFC > 0$$

the firm makes an economic profit. If

$$\pi = P(Q^*)Q^* - TVC(Q^*) - TFC < 0$$

the firm makes a loss. In this case the firm should produce Q^* rather than shutting down when

$$|P(Q^*)Q^* - TVC(Q^*) - TFC| < TFC$$

which occurs if, at Q^*, price is greater than average variable cost:

$$P(Q^*) > TVC(Q^*)/Q^*$$

The firm loses less than its total fixed cost, which is the amount it would lose if it shuts down and produces nothing. If at Q^* price is less than average variable cost, the firm should shut down and produce nothing. It loses all its fixed cost rather than its fixed cost plus the amount of variable cost not covered by revenue.

We next demonstrate that the profit-maximizing price and quantity must lie on the elastic portion of demand. Since

$$\begin{aligned} MR &= dR/dQ = P(Q) + Q(dP/dQ) \\ &= P[1 + (Q/P)(dP/dQ)] = P[1 + (1/E)] \end{aligned}$$

where E is the elasticity of demand, in equilibrium

$$MR = P[1 + 1/E] = MC \tag{3}$$

Since MC and P must be positive, $(1 + 1/E) > 0$, which, because $E < 0$, requires that E be greater than one in absolute value: $|E| > 1$. Thus in equilibrium P^* and Q^* must lie on the elastic portion of demand.

For a less general approach, assume that the inverse demand function is the linear function:

$$P(Q) = a - bQ$$

where a and b are positive. Let the total variable cost function be the cubic function,

$$TVC(Q) = dQ - eQ^2 + fQ^3$$

where d, e, and f are positive. The profit function is therefore

$$(4) \qquad \pi = PQ - TVC(Q) - TFC$$
$$= aQ - bQ^2 - dQ + eQ^2 - fQ^3 - TFC$$

For profit maximization, differentiate (4) and set it equal to zero:

$$(5) \qquad d\pi/dQ = (a - 2bQ) - (d - 2eQ + 3fQ^2) = 0$$

Since $MR = a - 2bq$, and $MC = d - 2eQ + 3fQ^2$, $MR = MC$ in profit-maximizing equilibrium. The second-order condition for a maximum is

$$(6) \qquad d^2\pi/dQ^2 = -2b + 2e - 6fQ < 0$$

or, solving equation (6) for Q, for a maximum, it must be the case that

$$(7) \qquad Q > (e - b)/3f$$

To obtain the profit-maximizing level of Q^*, solve the quadratic equation formed from equation (5):

$$(a - d) - (2b + 2e)Q - 3fQ^2 = 0$$

After solving such a quadratic equation, you will generally obtain two values for Q^*. The profit-maximizing Q^* will be the value at which the second-order condition in (7) holds, ensuring that this is the value of Q^* at which marginal cost crosses marginal revenue from below. This will be the larger of the two solutions in such problems. To obtain the equilibrium price, substitute Q^* into the inverse demand function:

$$P^* = a - bQ^*$$

If the total revenue exceeds total variable cost, i.e., if $P(Q^*) > TVC(Q^*)/Q^*$, then profit or loss is

$$\pi = aQ^* - bQ^{*2} - dQ^* + eQ^{*2} - fQ^{*3} - TFC$$

The Monopolist Chooses Input Usage

Now we assume that the manager chooses the level of usage of a single variable input, L, in order to maximize profit. All other inputs are fixed in amount. Let the production function be as derived for the short run in the Mathematical Appendix to Chapter 9:

$$Q = f(L, \bar{K}) = g(L)$$

The inverse demand function is

$$P = P(Q) = P[g(L)]$$

The firm chooses L so that the following profit function is maximized:

$$(8) \qquad \pi = P[g(L)]g(L) - wL - TFC$$

where w is the wage paid to labor and TFC is the fixed payment for the fixed inputs. Profit maximization requires

$$(9a) \qquad d\pi/dL = (dP/dQ)(dQ/dL)g(L) + P(dQ/dL) - w$$
$$= 0$$

or

$$(9b) \qquad (dQ/dL)[(dP/dQ)Q + P] = w$$

Since dQ/dL is marginal product and $[(dP/dQ)Q + P]$ is marginal revenue, equation (9b) can be expressed as

$$MP \times MR = \text{Marginal revenue product} = w$$

Equation (9a) or (9b) can be solved for L^*; then $Q^* = g(L^*)$ and $P^* = P(Q^*)$.

If, at L^*, $MRP < ARP = P[g(L^*)]/L^*$, the firm will produce and its profit or loss will be

$$\pi = P[g(L^*)]g(L^*) - wL^* - TFC$$

If, however, $MRP = w > P^*Q^*/L^*$, total revenue will be less than total variable cost; i.e., $wL^* > P^*Q^*$. In this case the firm would shut down and lose only its total fixed cost, rather than its total fixed cost plus the portion of total variable cost not covered by revenue.

Now assume that the firm uses two variable inputs, L and K, and no inputs are fixed. The prices of L and K are, respectively, w and r. The production function is

$$Q = f(L, K)$$

and the inverse demand function is

$$P = P(Q) = P[f(L, K)]$$

The profit function is now

$$\pi = f(L, K)P[f(L, K)] - wL - rK$$

Since the firm chooses the levels of L and K to maximize profit, the first-order equilibrium conditions are

$$P[f(L, K)](\partial Q/\partial L) + QdP/dQ(\partial Q/\partial L) - w = 0 \quad (10a)$$
$$P[f(L, K)](\partial Q/\partial K) + QdP/dQ(\partial Q/\partial K) - r = 0 \quad (10b)$$

Equations (10a) and (10b) can be solved for the optimal levels of L^* and K^*; then the optimal levels of output and price are $Q^* = f(L^*, K^*)$ and $P^* = P[f(L^*, K^*)]$. These values can be substituted into the above profit equation to find the maximum level of profit.

Equations (10a) and (10b) can be rewritten as

$$\partial Q/\partial L(P + QdP/dQ) = MP_L \times MR = MRP_L = w \quad (11a)$$
$$\partial Q/\partial K(P + QdP/dQ) = MP_K \times MR = MRP_K = r \quad (11b)$$

Thus in equilibrium the marginal revenue product of each input equals its price.

In Chapter 16 we will discuss in detail how a firm with market power, using actual estimates of the parameters in the demand and cost equations, can actually implement the profit-maximizing decision and solve for the optimal numerical values of price, output, and profit. Also in that chapter we will show how a manager can use estimates of the parameters in the production and demand functions in order to implement the hiring decision and solve for the profit-maximizing level of input usage. For this reason we have postponed the exercises usually in the appendix until that chapter.

CHAPTER 15

Oligopoly: Decision Making with Mutual Interdependence

We are now going to address some new types of business decision-making problems. These problems are more complex than those of a perfectly competitive firm, facing a given price, deciding on the level of output, or those of a monopolist, with a fixed demand, deciding on price and output. Consider these examples:

- American Airlines might be debating whether or not to reduce fares on all its European flights this summer. The reductions could substantially increase its profitable vacation-travel business. But if Delta, United, and other large overseas carriers match the reductions, a costly fare war could result, causing losses for all.
- Miller Lite may be preparing an expensive new advertising campaign. Its advertising agency says the new campaign should be extremely effective. But how will Bud Light react? Will it respond with an even-more-expensive advertising campaign of its own, or will it continue as is? Budweiser's response will have a huge effect on the profitability of Miller's decision.
- Pepsi could be preparing to introduce a new cola flavor. The new flavor is designed to appeal to the maturing baby boomers. Pepsi's marketing experts believe there will be a strong demand for the new flavor, but introducing it will be expensive. Does Coke already have a similar new flavor it could respond with? Some of Pepsi's older executives remember the debacle of its Pepsi Max and the colorless cola, Crystal Pepsi. What should Pepsi do?

- At a much smaller marketing level, Joe's Pizza, a successful local restaurant near the campus, wants to open a new restaurant in a recently developed suburban area. But will Pizza Hut or Domino's also come into the new suburb, which, for the next several years, will probably not be large enough to support more than one pizza place? During this period, Joe could lose a lot of money. What should Joe do?

Except for Joe's Pizza, these are the types of business decisions and decision-making processes that are discussed in *The Wall Street Journal* and other well-known business publications. They differ substantially from the previously developed theories of the firm in which firms took price or demand as given. In the above examples, managers have to make decisions under the assumption that their decisions will affect the sales of their rivals and that their rivals would themselves react. Depending on how their rivals react, their own sales will consequently be affected. But these managers do not know what their rivals will actually do.

Economists generally use the term oligopoly in reference to a market in which competition is characterized by personal competition or interaction. An **oligopoly** market consists of a few relatively large firms that have moderate to substantial market power and, most importantly, recognize their mutual interdependence. **Mutual interdependence** means that the actions of any one firm in the market will have an effect on the sales and revenues of other firms. Each firm knows that its actions or changes will have such an effect and that the other firms will, in response, take actions or make changes that will affect its sales. But no firm is really sure how the other firms will react.

oligopoly
A market consisting of a few relatively large firms, each with a substantial share of the market and all recognize their mutual interdependence.

mutual interdependence
Recognition by firms in the market that the actions of any one firm will have an effect on the other firms, which will react in turn.

This scenario applies to the above examples in which American Airlines considered how its rivals would react before it decided to reduce fares; Miller worried about Budweiser's reaction to an expanded advertising campaign; Pepsi didn't know what Coke would do if it introduced a new flavor or what the effect of Coke's reaction would be; and Joe considered what the pizza chains would do if Joe entered the new suburb. We will devote most of this chapter to analyzing how oligopolists make decisions when they are uncertain about the reaction of rivals and the effect of these reactions on their own sales.

Oligopolists differ in their characteristics, and oligopoly markets exhibit many different types of behavior patterns. Some oligopoly markets are intensely competitive; some are not. Firms in some markets cooperate with each other; in other markets, they do not. Some oligopoly markets are characterized by a great deal of price competition; some have little price competition, but firms compete fiercely with advertising or product development. Some markets use price competition some of the time but use advertising or product quality to compete at other times.

Some oligopolies, such as those in the steel, rubber, and aluminum markets, produce a homogeneous product and sell to other manufacturers; others, such as automobiles, soft drinks, and electronics, produce differentiated products and sell primarily to consumers. Strong barriers to the entry of new firms are prevalent in some oligopoly markets; in other markets, there are only moderate barriers.

The size of oligopolists ranges from huge international firms, selling in the world market, to relatively small firms selling in regional or even local markets. When people think of oligopolies, they typically think of the international giants, such as GM, Coke, and IBM. However, there are many smaller oligopolies, such as the few banks in a medium-size city, the two or three newspapers in a city, or the network TV stations in a particular area. Firms in markets such as these exhibit a great deal of mutual interdependence.

Actually, there is sometimes only a fine line distinguishing whether a market is classified as oligopolistic or as monopolistically competitive. All the restaurants in a city could be said to be in a monopolistically competitive market, but there may be a great deal of mutual interdependence among the few restaurants in a given area, causing these restaurants to behave as oligopolies.

Because oligopoly markets differ so greatly in their behavior patterns and in their overall characteristics, economists have not been able to develop a single general theory of oligopoly, unlike the case for the other three market structures we have analyzed. In our discussion of oligopoly markets, we will emphasize that the price and output decisions depend critically upon the assumptions made about the behavioral reactions of rival managers. Since many different assumptions can and have been made, many different solutions can and have been reached.

In spite of their inability to develop a general theory of oligopoly, economists do have a great deal to say about oligopoly behavior. They have developed many different oligopoly models designed to explain how firms attempt to maximize profits under different behavioral assumptions in markets characterized by mutual interdependence among firms. The discussion of oligopoly behavior in this chapter is designed to introduce you to and give you some insight into the way managers of firms in oligopoly markets make decisions.

We will use models of game theory to show some pitfalls that can occur, whereby perfectly rational behavior on the part of all firms can lead to lower than maximum profits for all. And we discuss some models showing how managers can adapt to and sometimes overcome these pitfalls. A rather large part of the analysis of oligopoly consists of the study of strategic behavior by the firms in the market. As you will see, the study of strategic behavior is similar to the study of players participating in a game of strategy, such as chess, poker, bridge, or checkers. This is why this important area of economic analysis is called game theory.

Because strategic behavior is so important in managerial decision making, it is also an important topic in managerial economics. In this text, however, we can only scratch the surface of the broad range of topics in this area. A complete treatment of game theory and strategic behavior would require several courses.

Keep in mind throughout the discussion that oligopolists have the same goal as perfect competitors and monopolists—to maximize profit. And, to maximize profit, the oligopolist tries to equate marginal revenue and marginal cost. But, as we will show, oligopolies face complications that competitors and monopolies do not face. These complications arise from the mutual interdependence among firms.

We cannot give you a straightforward solution to the problems of American Airlines, Miller, and Pepsi. We certainly cannot tell you how to solve similar types of problems that you may face in your managerial career. But we will give you some insight into how to address such problems, as well as a framework for developing your own techniques. And we will try to give you a feel for the way managers think in strategic business decisions.

15.1 CHARACTERISTICS OF OLIGOPOLY

In the introduction to this chapter we briefly mentioned the characteristics of oligopoly markets. As noted there, the nature of an oligopoly market cannot be described by a uniform set of characteristics that apply to each and every case of oligopoly. Certain characteristics are shared by all oligopolies; others may differ substantially from one oligopoly market to another. This section discusses these common and differing characteristics in a bit more detail.

Common Characteristics

As already noted, the key characteristic shared by all oligopolies is that the number of firms in a market is small enough that each firm recognizes its mutual interdependence with the other firms. This is by far the most important characteristic of oligopoly and the one that makes the analysis of oligopoly so complicated. Firms are uncertain how rivals will react to their actions, such as rivals' reactions to a price change. This uncertainty about competitors' reactions causes uncertainty about the oligopolist's demand and marginal revenue curves. (We will develop this point to a much greater extent in the next section.)

All oligopolies have a certain amount of market power. If an oligopolist raises its price, it generally won't lose all its sales; if it lowers its price, it won't gain the entire market. We should stress, however, that how much sales are increased or decreased after a price change depends upon the reactions of rival firms. Furthermore, the amount of market power can vary considerably among firms and depends, to some extent, on the strength of the barriers to entry into the market. Some oligopolies possess a large amount of market power; others may have a rather small amount.

Oligopoly markets are characterized by some barriers to entry, ranging from moderate to high. If oligopolies were not protected by some barriers, the market would become much more like perfect or monopolistic competition. Although entry barriers for oligopoly are not as strong as those for monopoly, they are quite similar in form. As in monopoly, economies of scale over a large range of output are probably the most important barrier in oligopoly markets. But in an oligopoly market the extent of these economies permits a few firms, rather than only one, to sell in the market without making losses. New firms would be forced to enter the market at a large size in order to compete with existing firms.

Other oligopoly entry barriers, similar to those for monopoly, are the control of an essential raw material and the possession of protective patents by a few firms. Some entry barriers are the direct result of the strategic behavior of the oligopolistic firms selling in the market. For example, brand loyalty can be an important barrier to entry in many, though not all, oligopoly markets. Buyer allegiance for durable goods can be built by establishing a reputation for service. Or, the allegiance of buyers can be built by a long, successful advertising campaign. (This type of allegiance is also probably more prevalent for durable goods.) New firms might have considerable difficulty establishing a market organization and overcoming buyer preferences for the established firms. Some barriers to entry arise because the pricing policy of established firms discourages the entry of new firms into the market. Such a policy is called entry limit pricing. Other oligopolies may increase their capacity or the size of their firms in order to discourage entry. We will discuss strategic entry deterrence at some length in this chapter.

Differing Characteristics

Oligopolies can be classified by the type of product produced. As mentioned above, in some oligopoly markets the products are homogeneous. Unless a buyer knows which firm sold the product, it would be impossible to determine the seller solely from the characteristics of the product itself. Other oligopoly markets are characterized by differentiated products. In varying degrees it is possible to determine who produced the product from the product itself or its package. The type of product produced can affect the oligopolist's strategic behavior.

Broadly speaking, economists refer to two contrasting patterns of behavior for oligopolists: cooperative or noncooperative. *Cooperative oligopolists* tend to follow changes made by rival firms. For example, if a rival raises price, a cooperative oligopolist would go along with the move and raise price also. *Noncooperative oligopolists,* on the other hand, do not accommodate such changes. If a rival firm raises price, other firms would keep prices low in order to attract sales away from the higher-price producer.

But oligopolists have ways other than price to compete. Some oligopolistic markets are characterized by a great deal of price competition. In others, firms don't compete extensively by price changes but instead compete with their advertising, product quality, and marketing strategies.

Because of these differences in oligopoly markets, there are four general oligopolistic market structures. These are (1) a few noncooperative firms producing a homogeneous product, (2) a few noncooperative firms producing related but differentiated products, (3) a few cooperative firms producing a homogeneous product, and (4) a few cooperative firms producing related but differentiated products. The price and output decisions of an oligopolist depend to a large extent on the market structure.

Oligopoly behavior is also determined by other factors. For example, if entry barriers are relatively moderate and new firms would find it fairly easy to enter, the gains from cooperation are small. High prices encourage new firms to enter the market. Prices in such oligopoly markets tend to be low, and cooperation tends to increase profit only minimally. When entry is extremely difficult, firms have a greater incentive to reach a cooperative agreement. Prices will tend to be higher in such markets.

The history of the industry and even the personalities of the top executives tend to affect oligopoly behavior. Over time firms learn something about how their rivals will react to changes. Some industries are characterized by a live-and-let-live attitude. In others, firms compete far more aggressively and competitively. As noted, in some markets competition takes the form of price cutting. In others, firms compete much more by advertising and marketing strategy.

Mutual Interdependence in Monopolistic Competition

In the introduction to this chapter, we mentioned briefly that in individual segments of monopolistically competitive markets firms may face the oligopoly mutual-interdependence problem. Firms in these small segments may have to worry a great deal about how close rivals will react to their moves. In the theory of monopolistic competition, as set forth in Chapter 14, monopolistic competitors act independently and in the short run behave like monopolists. This is a reasonable assumption under many circumstances. If there are many small shirt manufacturers producing similar but not identical apparel in a national market, each firm would probably believe, justifiably, that its own sales or pricing policy would have an insignificant effect on the total market. Similarly, no service station, grocery store, or restaurant in a large city would have much effect on its respective total citywide market.

However, in small segments of many markets, firms may believe, justifiably, that there is a great deal of mutual interdependence among firms within the same market segment. For example, the manager of an Exxon station on one corner of an intersection would know that if the station dropped its price it would have a substantial impact on the sales of the Chevron station across the street, and the Chevron manager would probably respond. But the Exxon manager would not know how the Chevron station would react. Chevron might exactly meet Exxon's new price, it might take an even larger price reduction, perhaps leading to a mutually ruinous price war, or it might cut price by a lesser amount.

If there were three or four bar and grill establishments across the street from a campus, one of them, Joe's Grill, knows that if it has a promotion of three beers for the price of one during happy hour, Jane's Bar and Grill next door would have to respond, perhaps by advertising four for the price of one. But Joe really doesn't know what Jane, or for that matter, the other bars, will do. In certain areas, the Albertson's grocery store puts the price charged by Kroger's or Appletree or another nearby grocery store on the same price marker as it posts its own price for certain products on the shelf—the competitor's price is obviously always higher when it is posted. This is intense personal rivalry and is indicative of a great deal of mutual interdependence.

In the above examples, Albertson's has no effect on stores in other parts of the city; Joe's price does not affect the sales at cocktail lounges in the large downtown hotels, and Exxon has little impact on gasoline sales along the interstate highway outside the city. Taken as a whole, the gasoline market, the bar and grill market, and the grocery market in the city are monopolistically competitive. But specific submarkets are quite oligopolistic in nature and exhibit the oligopoly characteristics discussed in the introduction. Firms in these types of submarkets can easily fit into one or another pattern of oligopoly behavior to be developed throughout the remainder of this chapter. We will not go into these patterns now because we will devote so much space to them later. But when you read about these oligopoly models, be aware that they can easily apply to firms that would seem to exhibit all the characteristics of monopolistic competition—with the strong exception of easy entry into the market.

15.2 THE PROBLEM WITH OLIGOPOLY DEMAND

We must emphasize that, in spite of the uncertainty about the reaction of rivals to a price change, managers of oligopolies should use the marginal revenue–marginal cost rule when making decisions. A firm should reduce price and increase output when marginal revenue exceeds marginal cost. It should increase price and reduce output when the marginal revenue from the last unit sold is less than the marginal cost of that unit. This is one of the most important rules of decision making, even when the market is characterized by uncertainty about the reaction of rivals.

The problem for an oligopolist is, of course, accurately forecasting its demand and marginal revenue if it changes its price. As emphasized, any change in price and output has a noticeable effect on the sales of other firms. These rivals may react by changing *their* prices and output, or they may not react at all. We begin our discussion of noncooperative oligopoly behavior with a hypothetical story to illustrate the problem with forecasting oligopoly demand.

An Example of the Problem

Suppose the marketing executives at Pepsi-Cola are meeting to decide whether or not the company should change the price of a six-pack of Pepsi. For several months both Pepsi and Coca-Cola have been charging the same price, $3, for a six-pack. Over that period, Pepsi has been selling, on average, 1 million six-packs a day. This is shown as point *C* in Figure 15.1. The question is, Should Pepsi change its price in an attempt to make more profit?

Some of the marketing vice presidents suggest raising the price of Pepsi to $4, because they believe that the sales of Pepsi will not decline much and the higher price will be more profitable. When questioned about how Coke will respond, they answer that Coke will probably raise its price to $4 also and, if in fact this is the case, Pepsi's sales will fall only to 800,000. There won't be much substitution away from Pepsi to Coke if Coke is selling at the same price. If these vice presidents are correct, the movement in Figure 15.1 will take place along

FIGURE 15.1
The Problem with Oligopoly Demand

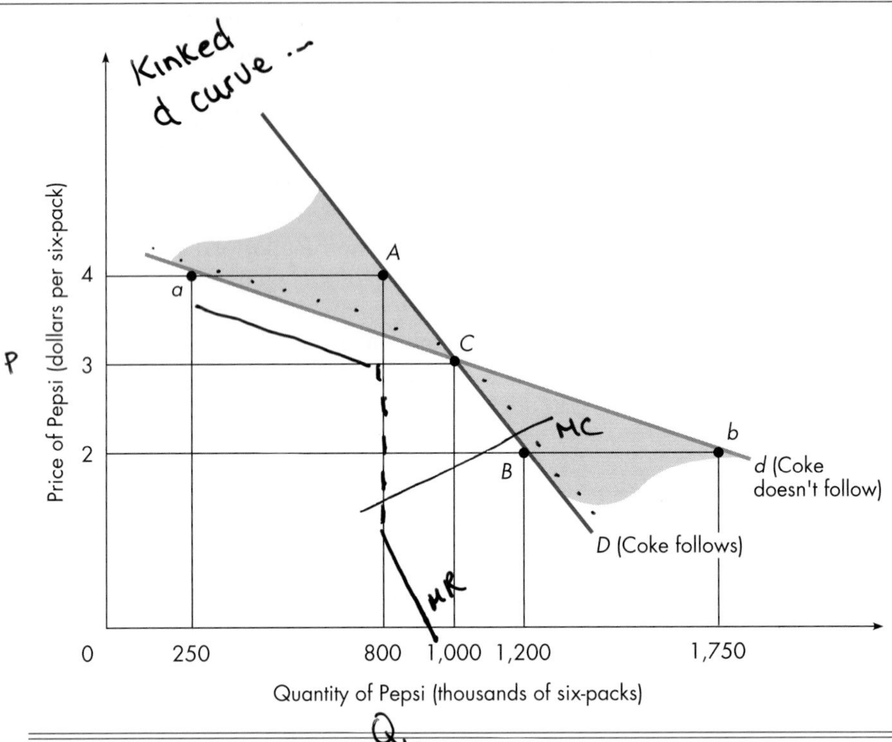

demand curve *D* (labeled "Coke follows" in the figure) from point *C* to point *A*. As you can see, the $1 price increase causes sales to fall by 200,000 six-packs.

Another group of vice presidents vehemently objects, saying that Coke would never follow the $1 price increase. If Coke keeps its price at $3, Pepsi will lose a huge amount of sales, probably falling to 250,000 six-packs. If this group is correct, the movement takes place along demand curve *d* (labeled "Coke doesn't follow" in the figure) from point *C* to point *a*. Under this assumption about Coke's response, sales fall by 750,000 six-packs to 250,000.

Because of the confusion about the effect of a $1 price increase, someone suggests a $1 price reduction, to $2. Again, one group argues that Coke, not wishing to lose a large share of the market, would immediately follow with a $1 price decrease of its own, and thus Pepsi would enjoy a sales increase of only 200,000, to 1,200,000 six-packs. If this is correct, the movement is along demand curve *D*, from point *C* to point *B*. Pepsi picks up some sales, but not many, when Coke responds with a lower price.

Then those who believe that Coke will not follow the price cut argue that the price reduction from $3 to $2 will increase Pepsi's sales by 750,000, to 1,750,000 six-packs. They maintain that the movement will take place along demand curve *d*, from point *C* to point *b*. Pepsi will take a huge share of Coke's market in this scenario.

After a considerable amount of arguing about which demand is the correct demand curve, a management trainee asks what would happen if Coke responds to Pepsi's price increase with less than a $1 increase of its own or to a price decrease with less than a $1 decrease of its own. Under these assumptions, couldn't Pepsi's actual demand be anywhere in the shaded area between demand curves *D* and *d*? Or, following up that question, the trainee asks whether it is possible that Coke would choose not to follow a price increase, hoping to pick up a lot of sales when Pepsi raises its price; but not wanting to lose a lot of sales if Pepsi lowers price, would Coke choose to follow a price decrease? Then wouldn't the demand curve for Pepsi be *d* for a price increase above $3 and *D* for a price decrease below $3. The meeting is adjourned when the senior marketing vice president announces that there will be no change in price anytime soon, unless of course, Coke changes its price, and then there will be another meeting.

So there is the oligopoly problem. The firm would like to know what its demand actually is so that it can maximize profits under those demand and marginal revenue conditions. However, it can't do this, because the actual demand depends crucially on what rivals will do, and there is a considerable amount of uncertainty about this response. Certainly, in the above example, the CEO of Pepsi could call the CEO of Coke and work out a pricing agreement between the two firms. But price fixing is illegal in the United States, and business executives

1 have been fined or even sent to prison for doing just that.

Price Rigidity under Oligopoly

Some economists have argued that the very nature of the oligopoly problem—the expected reaction of rivals—causes oligopoly markets to be characterized by a great deal of price rigidity. That is, prices under oligopoly would not be very responsive to changes in demand or cost conditions.

Many theories have been set forth to explain why prices are supposedly inflexible in an oligopoly market structure. The most frequently cited hypothesis takes the following form: If one oligopolist increases its price, competing oligopolists will hold their prices constant, so the oligopolistic firm that raises its price will lose considerable sales to rivals. On the other hand, if one oligopolist lowers its price, the rival firms, fearing substantial losses in sales, will also lower their prices. Thus, the oligopolist that lowers price will experience only an insignificant increase in sales, because of the price competition. (Remember the question asked by the Pepsi trainee, the question that broke up the meeting when the CEO decided not to change price: What happens if Coke follows a decrease in price but not an increase?)

The nature of the problem is shown in Figure 15.2. Suppose that a firm in a noncooperative oligopolistic market structure has been producing 400 units of output per period and selling them at $5 each. Its total revenue is therefore $2,000. Also suppose that the firm is considering changing its price.

The firm believes that if it increases its price to $6, its rivals will not change their prices and the firm will lose a great deal of sales to them after the price

FIGURE 15.2
Price Rigidity under Oligopoly

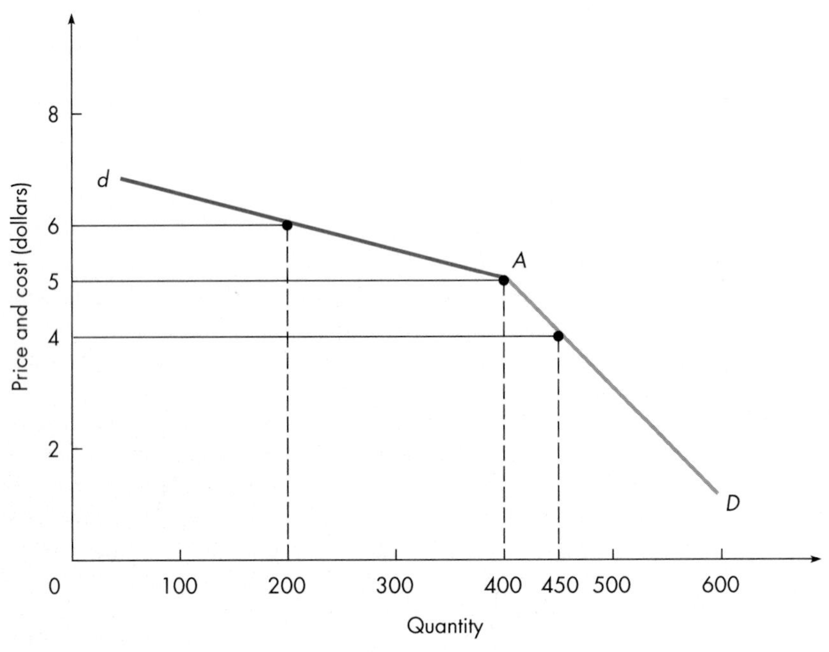

increase. Thus it thinks it will be able to sell only 200 units after raising its price to \$6. Its revenue would fall to \$1,200. For any price increase that is unmatched by the other firms, this firm's demand is segment *dA*, which is quite elastic, as is shown by the fall in revenue after the price increase. (Note that this is similar to the upper portion of demand *d* in Figure 15.1.)

But suppose the firm decreases price from \$5 to \$4. Now the firm expects its rivals to match the price decrease so as not to lose sales. Thus the firm would gain few additional sales from its rivals by decreasing price. Sales would increase some because of the downward-sloping market demand for the products of all the firms, but not by much. In the figure, sales increase only to 450 units when price is reduced to \$4. Thus revenue decreases to \$1,800. For any reduction in price from \$5, the firm's demand is the inelastic segment *AD,* when rivals match the decrease. Thus the firm expects revenue to decline if price is changed in any direction, under its assumption about its rivals' behavior. (Note that this segment is similar to the lower portion of demand *D* in Figure 15.1.)

If the preceding hypothesis is true, oligopolists would have little motivation to change prices. Thus oligopoly is sometimes claimed to be less adaptable than other market structures, since prices are rigid. This theory is sometimes used by economists to explain why oligopoly markets are characterized by "sticky" prices; however, the theory does not explain why price is where it is in the first place. It must, therefore, be regarded as an ex post rationalization of market behavior rather than an ex ante explanation of market behavior. Furthermore, there is a certain amount of contradictory empirical evidence. Several studies have shown that, in general, oligopoly markets are characterized by as many price changes as are both more competitive markets and markets characterized by monopoly.

Managers of oligopolies usually just have to live with the problem of oligopoly interdependence and the consequent uncertainty. Nonetheless, successful managers have obviously adapted quite well to this problem. Those who don't probably don't last very long. We cannot give you any hard-and-fast rule about how to adapt if you are placed in such a situation. We can, however, show you some of the ways that managers have come to grips with the oligopoly problem. The descriptions that follow are not meant as a blueprint for making decisions. They are designed to give you a feel for decision making under these conditions.
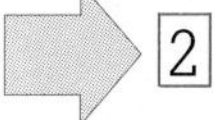
2 The art of strategic decision making is learned only from experience.

15.3 NONPRICE COMPETITION IN OLIGOPOLY MARKETS

Although the preceding discussion indicates that there is a certain amount of debate among economists as to the amount of price competition in oligopoly markets, most would agree that oligopoly is characterized by considerable nonprice competition, particularly when the product is differentiated. The alternative forms of nonprice competition are as diverse as the minds of inventive managers can make them. Yet there is one central feature: an oligopoly frequently attempts to attract customers to its own product (and, therefore, away from those of rivals) by some means other than a price differential.

Nonprice competition, therefore, involves differentiating a product, even when the product is fundamentally similar to those sold by competitors. It is obviously designed to make the product seem more useful or desirable to consumers. There are many ways of differentiating a product, but the two most important methods of nonprice competition are advertising and product quality.

Advertising

Obviously, a firm uses advertising to try to increase the demand for its product and probably make the demand less elastic. As you would expect, to maximize the *net* benefits from advertising, the firm should choose the amount of advertising at which the marginal revenue from the last unit of advertising equals the marginal cost of that unit.

This is certainly not the place to discuss how a firm should allocate dollars among the different advertising media (a constrained optimization problem) or how to design an advertising campaign. We are not qualified to discuss this aspect of advertising, which we leave to your marketing classes. We will, however, discuss why choosing the optimal amount of advertising is not always a simple, straightforward decision for an oligopolist.

The problem in making the advertising decision is the same as that involved in price-quantity choices: any firm's change in its advertising will probably have some effect on the sales of other firms. These firms may very well react with changes of their own, which could, in turn, cause the originating firm to react, and so on. Recall the hypothetical Miller-Budweiser example in the introduction to this chapter.

Nowhere is oligopoly interdependence so noticeable as in TV ads:

- Nissan advertises by showing that its sports sedan outperforms BMW and is $10,000 cheaper. BMW counters with ads showing that the BMW is much better and worth the premium price. Nissan counters with ads showing a boy doll, driving a Nissan, taking Barbie away from Ken, who obviously drives an inferior sports car.
- Bayer runs ads stating that only Bayer aspirin relieves pain and, unlike any other pain reliever, prevents heart attacks. Tylenol responds that aspirin upsets your stomach while Tylenol does not.
- Suscatal, a nutricional supplement, shows a handsome older couple coming up from the sea after spear fishing; they drink Suscatal, while another older, but less handsome, couple sit fully dressed under an umbrella drinking Ensure, a rival nutricional supplement, and looking on with envy. Ensure counters with an older Ensure drinker telling his young granddaughter he will be at her wedding. He drinks Ensure, not the other thing, and will consequently be around in 20 years.

We could just as easily have demonstrated the oligopoly interdependence problem with a story about Pepsi's advertising department meeting to discuss what Coke would do in response to a change in Pepsi's advertising, as we did with the marketing department and the price changes. Or perhaps Reebok would be debating what Nike will do in response to a new Reebok campaign or Ford and Chevrolet, Kellogg Cereal and Post Cereal, and on and on. Can't you imagine the Reebok advertising manager opening the meeting with, "Well, Nike has Michael Jordan and Tiger Woods, so let's counter with Troy Aikman and Drew Bledsoe. But they might come back with Ken Griffey Jr. and Roger Clemens; then what could we do . . . ?"

So oligopoly advertisers face the same problem as that discussed for price and quantity decisions: How will my rivals react, and how will I, in turn, respond to their reactions? Each firm has to take into account the reactions of other firms when making its decisions. As was the case for price, this interdependence complicates the advertising decision considerably.

Furthermore, as we will demonstrate in the next section, the advertising problem can become even more complicated. We will show how oligopoly firms, acting in their own self-interest, can be forced into a situation in which they advertise too much. That is, each firm in the market uses more advertising than would be the most profitable level. And no firm can afford to advertise any less.

Product Quality

As noted above, oligopolists can use product quality as a means of nonprice competition—that is, an oligopolist can differentiate its product from those of rival firms by making its product better. The change in quality can be real or perceived. It can take the form of a change in the actual product itself or in the service provided. Whatever the case, such decisions should be made employing the process of evaluating marginal revenue and marginal cost.

As was true for advertising and price, the firm must consider the reaction of its rivals to any quality changes. Some successful quality changes can be quickly noticed and copied. In other circumstances it may take competitors a great deal of time to emulate or otherwise react to the changes. In such cases the originating firm can enjoy profits while rivals try to respond. Quality changes that will be noticed by consumers but cannot be quickly copied by rivals are frequently attempted. A wine that is aged longer to give it a better taste, a few added inches between seats on an airplane, or fewer defective parts in a large shipment of equipment are quality changes not easily copied by rivals.

Product-quality competition is particularly intense in service oligopolies, where product quality is difficult to judge. Doctors and dentists, for instance, do not usually compete via the prices they charge patients, but the quality of their services and the waiting time in their offices vary a great deal.

The annual style change made by manufacturers of consumer durables is another method of product-quality competition. We see such changes in automobiles, household appliances, TVs, stereos, and sporting goods. Until the new models are put on the market, these style changes are closely guarded secrets. If other firms do not know what the new model is going to look like, it may take a year or more for rivals to copy it—if, in fact, the style change is successful.

We could go on with many other examples, but we are sure you have seen the point. The types of quality competition are practically as numerous as the oligopolistic industries themselves.

But oligopolists have ways of using product quality to differentiate their products other than by simply improving the real or perceived quality of the product. Products can be thought of as a collection of attributes or characteristics. For example, an automobile can be described by its engine size, brakes, transmission, suspension, fuel efficiency, tires, head and trunk room, number of doors, color, and so on. These product features can differ among products and can be altered by the manufacturers to differentiate their products from others. How a producer selects these attributes determines the quality and nature of the product and the product's substitutability with other products in the market. A manufacturer that produces an automobile with most of the attributes that characterize a Cadillac Sedan DeVille will make a car that is an unlikely substitute for a Ford Mustang.

To illustrate how product attributes can serve as a competitive tool, we consider another hypothetical example. The basic idea is captured by letting all the possible preferences a consumer may have for a particular attribute be measured along a scale with end points 0 and 1, as shown in Figure 15.3. Assume that this product attribute is sugar on breakfast cereal; 0 is cereal with no sugar, and 1 is cereal of virtually pure sugar cubes. The values 1/4, 1/2, and 3/4 mark equal-distance points along this scale. Suppose that those who buy breakfast cereal are uniformly distributed along this scale so that the number of individuals who want no sugar on their cereal is equal to the number who want their cereal half-sugared and is equal to the number who want all sugar.

FIGURE 15.3
Product Quality Measure

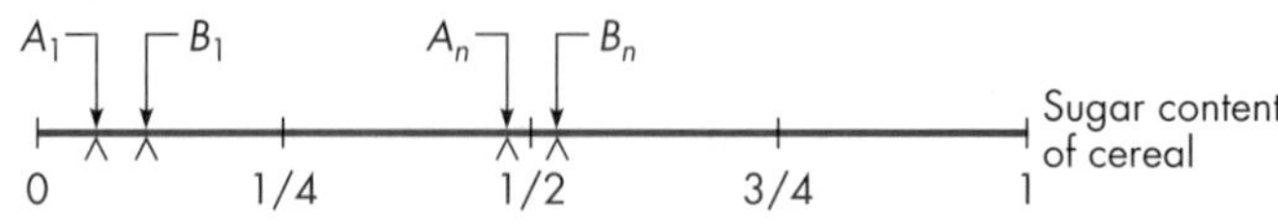

For the first firm that enters the cereal market, it does not matter how much sugar is put on its product. It is the only cereal consumers can buy. We arbitrarily locate firm A on the scale at A_1. Since sugar is expensive, firm A initially chooses a point on the lower end of the scale. We subscript the location because the firm may later want to change the sugar content of its cereal when other firms enter the market.

Rivalry begins when firm B decides to enter the market. The new seller knows the preferences of consumers, that is, the scale in Figure 15.3, and how much sugar A has on its product. The question is, How much sugar should B use to capture the largest share of the market? You can see in the figure that (with constant prices) firm B could capture most of the market by using a little more sugar than A. The best thing for B to do is enter with a product that is just to the right of A_1. We label this point B_1. Firm B captures all the market to the right of A_1 in sugar content.

Firm A will, of course, not tolerate this for long. Its market share has been reduced to an insignificant part of the total market. Only those buyers with preferences between 0 and A_1 remain loyal to A's cereal. The firm could lower price or think about countering B's product by putting more sugar on its cereal. It can regain much of its lost market by moving just to the right of B_1. But then B will move to the right of A again, and A will then move to the right of B a second time. The leapfrogging will continue until one firm drops out of the market or both firms end up with approximately equal market shares at the midpoint of the preference scale. After a large number of moves, firms will put approximately the same amount of sugar on their cereals and supply the amounts desired by the average buyer, that is, at A_n and B_n.

The situation gets more complicated when a third firm enters the market. With a little experimenting, you can discover that firms do not find an equilibrium; they continually change the amount of sugar on their cereals. This is not uncommon in the real world—think how many new and improved labels producers put on their products. Often these improvements are nothing more than a slight adjustment in a product attribute, a change the marketing personnel hope will place them near their rival but on the side of the preference scale that gives them the largest market share.

We have oversimplified things a great deal by allowing product differentiation for only one product variable and assuming price competition does not take place at the same time. Realistically, there are all sorts of ways attributes can be mixed. Discovering the attributes that capture the largest share of the market requires sophisticated marketing techniques and, at times, just plain luck. The point of the simple model, though, is that product differentiation is a tool that firms use to compete.

A recent method of oligopoly nonprice competition can be called, for want of a better name, competition by "doing the right thing." Over the past several years, many major corporations have seemingly discovered social consciousness. Companies tell us that they are becoming more careful in protecting the environment. McDonald's changed from styrofoam packaging to paper, because styrofoam wasn't sufficiently biodegradable. McDonald's has also established a "hire the handicapped" program. Major tuna sellers don't use tuna from fishing fleets that may inadvertently catch dolphin. How many commercials have you seen in which the company promises to donate money to some worthy cause for each of its products sold?

We do not mean to imply that all this socially conscious behavior is motivated solely by profits. But this behavior does convey an image of the product; using the product makes a statement about the user's social responsibility. The product is somehow better if it is produced in a socially responsible way. (Some problems in using this type of competition are discussed in Illustration 15.1.)

To summarize, we have shown that noncooperative oligopolists compete in many ways. They generally don't like price competition, but they use it. And they don't like nonprice competition much better, but they use it also. No matter what type of competition oligopolists use—price, advertising, or product quality—there is always the problem of mutual interdependence among firms and the resulting uncertainty.

Actually, we have barely touched upon the more specific ways oligopolists compete with one another. The methods employed depend on many factors: the structure of the market, the history of the industry, even the personalities of the managers. Not surprisingly, a huge number of competitive patterns are possible.

Our intent in this section was simply to show the general types of competition that have been used. We certainly would not be bold enough to try to tell you what you should do in specific situations. Managers learn by gaining experience and by keeping up to date by reading the major business and industry publications. Managing is best learned by doing.

15.4 GAME THEORY: STRATEGIC INTERACTION IN OLIGOPOLY MARKETS

strategic behavior Actions taken by firms to plan for and react to competition from rival firms.

You are certainly aware by now that managers of firms in oligopoly markets must think about and plan for the actions of other firms. Mutual interdependence requires strategic behavior. **Strategic behavior,** or *strategic interactions,* consists of the actions by firms to plan for and react to the actions of rival firms. Knowing about and anticipating potential moves and countermoves of the other firms are of critical importance to managers in oligopoly markets.

Perhaps you are thinking, "Sure, interdependence complicates decision making and makes it messy. So what do I as a manager do in such situations? How do I go about making strategic decisions?" We can't give you a set of rules to follow. The art of making strategic decisions is learned from experience.

ILLUSTRATION 15.1

Competition by Doing the Right Thing

As we mentioned, many large corporations have, over the last decade or two, seemingly discovered social consciousness. We gave a few examples in the text. How many commercials have you seen in which the corporation promises to donate money to some worthy cause? Sometimes it appears that beer manufacturers are more interested in promoting responsible drinking than in selling more beer. Soft-drink companies beg customers not to litter.

Why this sudden change? If a miraculous conversion seems rather unlikely, firm managers must believe that, given the current social climate, doing good will be good for business. *Newsweek* reported that the public is now paying more attention to corporate behavior.* A Roper poll found that 52 percent of a sample of U.S. consumers said they would pay 10 percent more for a socially responsible product and 67 percent said that when they shopped they were concerned about a company's social performance. (Remember the problem with consumer interviews, discussed in Chapter 7.) Whether or not these consumers told the truth, many corporations have used their social consciousness to try to increase sales or to charge more for their products. Doing good has been used, though not admitted, as a way to increase profits.

Some oligopolies that sell a differentiated product to consumers have tried to improve their image by informing people about their socially responsible behavior. This type of nonprice competition has overtones of both advertising and product-quality competition. The advertising conveys an image of the product; using the product makes a statement about the user's social responsibility. The image of corporate responsibility also is a way to change the quality of the product. The product is somehow "better" if it was produced in a socially responsible way.

We do not mean to imply that desirable behavior by corporations is solely motivated by profits, although *Newsweek* reported that some corporate observers were a bit skeptical about the motivations and about the long-term usefulness of such behavior, particularly as consumers' incomes fall in a recession. One skeptical corporate observer was Alex Taylor III, writing in *Fortune* about a well-known company that is widely known for trying to "do good": Ben & Jerry's Ice Cream.† Mr. Taylor notes that Ben & Jerry's pays farmers extra to supply them with milk that is free of a certain growth hormone. He reports that this socially beneficial action cost $375,000 last year, even though there is no conclusive evidence that the hormone is bad for people. And he reports other social actions of the firm, some of which harmed the company and some of which may have benefited it.

Mr. Taylor ends the article by stating that Ben & Jerry claim that their principles give them a competitive advantage that ensures additional profits but they offer no supporting evidence. He notes that their stockholders are not likely to agree. After hitting a high of $32 in August 1992, Ben & Jerry's stock has been trading around $13, and the company was expected to lose money in the first quarter of 1997. "As for dividends, to date they have been spiritual."

Judging from their advertising and ad hoc evidence, oligopolies appear to be the firms that are

game theory
A guideline or analytical tool for explaining and understanding behavior in strategic interactions.

We can, however, introduce you to a tool for thinking about strategic decision making: *game theory.* **Game theory** provides a useful guideline on how to behave in strategic situations involving interdependence. This theory was developed approximately 50 years ago in order to provide a systematic approach to strategic decision making. During the past 20 years it has become increasingly important to economists for analyzing oligopoly behavior. And it is also becoming more useful to managers in making business decisions.

most socially conscious. Clearly, perfect competitors would not tell consumers how much good they are doing. Because of homogeneous products, consumers wouldn't know whether they were buying from a socially conscious firm or not. A monopoly faces no good substitutes for its product and would not use this approach unless it was government-regulated and wanted to please the regulators. It would appear that, to a greater or lesser extent, many oligopolies undertake such activities as a market tactic to gain sales from competitors.

We end this illustration by noting the plight of a truly socially conscious firm owner who gains absolutely no economic benefit from his behavior. A California peach and grape orchard owner, David Mas Manumoto, told his story of "political correctness" in *USA Today.*[‡] According to Mr. Manumoto, "[I] farm organically, utilizing farm practices that sustain the land and air. [My] peach and grape farm is part of a renewable, natural system. [My] peaches are part of the environmental solution, not part of the problem. They don't add to landfills, compost piles love their peelings, and the trees provide habitat for wildlife. My produce is 'made in the USA' and grown by a minority (I'm Japanese-American) who employs 90 percent minorities. . . . [I don't] use toxic pesticides."

But the only benefit for Mr. Manumoto is "knowing my peaches are grown with a raised consciousness." As he notes, "The problem is that you won't think about this when you squeeze or smell my peaches in the grocery store. You won't ask the produce manager where the peaches came from or how they were grown. But you'll buy lots of peaches this summer because they're cheap."

Mr. Manumoto is a perfect competitor in the peach market. He sums up the problem of perfect competitors beautifully: "A simple law of economics drives agriculture: For us growers, there are just too damn many peaches out there. . . . Supply and demand deals a crushing blow to political correctness."

A perfectly competitive market doesn't value social responsibility. As you saw in Chapter 12, profits are driven to a normal return. Competitors who use socially responsible production methods that add to their cost will be driven out of business if other competitors in the market use the least-cost method of production.

As Mr. Manumoto states, "You can't fault me for wanting to make a profit. I can't farm very long just on social consciousness. . . . Until political correct0ness is valued more highly, price will still be the primary consideration when consumers decide to buy my peaches. What I believe in won't add much value in the marketplace."

So what does all this illustrate about "correct behavior" in management decisions? Very little. If you manage an oligopoly selling a differentiated product to consumers, you may or may not benefit from doing good and letting consumers know about it. Some have, some haven't. About all we can conclude is that if you are like Mr. Manumoto and run a firm that is highly competitive, you probably won't benefit. Do it if you want to, but be aware of the costs.

[*]"Doing the Right Thing," *Newsweek,* Jan. 7, 1991.

[†]"Yo Ben! Yo Jerry! It's Just Ice Cream!" *Fortune,* Apr. 28, 1997.

[‡]"Politically Correct Peaches Confront Law of Supply and Demand," *USA Today,* July 2, 1991.

A large part of oligopoly strategy is similar to strategy used in such games as poker and chess. Therefore, when economists analyze oligopoly behavior, they frequently treat oligopolists as though these firms were playing a game against rivals, which are also playing the same game against them. The objective of the game is similar to that in poker—make money—but in the case of oligopolies it is to make as much profit as possible under the given constraints. As you will see, sometimes the oligopolists in such a game actually find their profits reduced below the level they could have reached if they were not in the game, but they cannot withdraw from it without even worse consequences.

The outcome of the game and the amount earned generally depend on the assumptions made about the strategy of the participants and the method of playing the game. To introduce you to the concept of oligopoly games, we begin with the grandfather of most economic games, which doesn't involve oligopoly behavior at all. This game is called the *prisoner's dilemma.*

The Prisoner's Dilemma

The model of the prisoner's dilemma is best illustrated by the story for which it is named. Suppose that a crime is committed and two suspects are apprehended and questioned by the police. Unknown to the suspects, the police do not have enough evidence to convict them of a serious crime unless one of them confesses. So the police separate them and make each one an offer that is known to the other. The offer is this: If one suspect confesses to the crime and turns state's evidence, the one who confesses receives only a 1-year sentence, while the other (who does not confess) will get 12 years. If both prisoners confess, each receives a 6-year sentence. If neither confesses, both will receive 2-year sentences. Thus, each prisoner could receive 1 year, 2 years, 6 years, or 12 years, depending on what the other does.

Figure 15.4 shows the four possibilities. The upper-left and lower-right cells show the results if both, respectively, do not confess or do confess. The upper-right and lower-left cells show the consequences if one confesses and the other does not.

The problem for these suspects is that they are separated and cannot collude. If they could collude, neither would confess, and each would receive a 2-year sentence. Because they must make their decisions separately, the one who does not confess will get 12 years in prison if the other confesses.

The police have designed the situation so that each suspect will be induced to confess and spend 6 years in prison. To see this, put yourself in the shoes of suspect 2, who knows that suspect 1 has only two alternatives, confess or not confess. If suspect 1 does not confess, 2 receives the lighter sentence by confessing: one year, compared with two if not confessing. If suspect 1 confesses, 2 still receives a lighter sentence by confessing: 6 years compared with 12. Therefore, for suspect 2, confessing is better than not confessing—it gives the lighter sentence—no matter what suspect 1 does. You can see also that for suspect 1, confessing is better than not confessing no matter what suspect 2 does. So both will probably confess and end up with sentences of 6 years.

dominant strategy
A strategy that provides the best outcome no matter what decision a rival makes.

This situation illustrates the concept of a dominant strategy. In game theory a **dominant strategy** is the strategy that provides the best outcome no matter what decision a rival makes. For each suspect confessing is the dominant strategy.

Recall that the police designed the situation so that confessing was the best choice (the dominant strategy) no matter what the other suspect did. Sometimes, however, there is no dominant strategy. Suppose, for example, that each suspect

FIGURE 15.4
The Prisoner's Dilemma

		Suspect 1: Does not confess	Suspect 1: Confesses
Suspect 2	Does not confess	A 1: 2 years 2: 2 years	B 1: 1 year 2: 12 years
	Confesses	C 1: 12 years 2: 1 year	D 1: 6 years 2: 6 years

would go free if neither suspect confesses; both the sentences would be zero in cell A. Now you can see that, for each suspect, not confessing is better than confessing if the other does not confess (zero versus one year). Confessing remains the best choice if the other confesses.

There is still a high probability that both will confess and end up in cell D (no pun intended) serving 6 years. Again we put ourselves in the shoes of suspect 2, who knows that if suspect 1 does not confess, the *worst* thing that can happen to 2 is to confess and receive a one-year sentence. However, if suspect 1 confesses, the worst that 2 can expect is a 12-year sentence by not confessing, but by confessing, suspect 2 would receive only 6 years. Suspect 1 obviously faces the same alternatives. If each suspect chooses the alternative that minimizes the maximum possible sentence, a fairly likely possibility, each will confess and serve 6 years. In game theory a strategy that minimizes the worst possible outcome is called a **minimax strategy.**

minimax strategy
A strategy in game theory that involves minimizing the worst possible outcome.

In both examples, each suspect would be better off if both do not confess and both end up in cell A, rather than both confessing and ending in D. In the first example, confessing is the dominant strategy for each, so it is highly likely they will end in D. In the second example, the safest tactic, or the minimax strategy, is for both to confess and end up in D. And, in fact, the less each suspect knows about the other, the more likely that each will confess. That is, the less information these accused criminals have about the other, the less certainty they have about settling in cell A.

In closing this discussion of the prisoner's dilemma, we introduce a concept sometimes encountered in oligopoly theory—a credible threat. A **credible threat** means that one or more of the participants in a game believe that something bad will happen to them if they do something the other participants do not want them to do.

credible threat
A threat made by one party to a second party when the second party has reason to believe that if it does something, the threat will be carried out.

In the context of the prisoner's dilemma, suppose the two suspects belong to a gang. The gang has a rule that if a member cooperates with the police in a way that harms another member, serious consequences—injury or even death—will result. If both suspects believe that threat—if the threat is credible—the probability is higher that neither will confess, even if confessing is the dominant strategy. We will return to this concept in a less violent context later.

An Advertiser's Dilemma

We now turn from a dilemma that you are unlikely to face in the future—being a suspect in a crime—to a more business-oriented dilemma, which you are much more likely to face. Oligopolists frequently get trapped in such a dilemma in the case of both price and nonprice competition. We consider first a dilemma that can occur when oligopolies compete in the level of advertising purchased. To illustrate the problem, we return to the two firms we used to illustrate the difficulty of determining a firm's demand when it was uncertain about how its rival would respond to a change in price—Coke and Pepsi.

Suppose now that each firm is deciding how much to advertise but does not know how the other will respond to a change in its advertising budget. Suppose, for simplicity and illustrative purposes, that each firm is limited to only two choices of advertising—a large advertising budget or a small advertising budget. Each firm must make its choice with little knowledge about what the other will do. Each firm knows that the outcome, the amount of profit earned from its choice, will depend crucially on the choice of its rival.

Once again, let's consider Pepsi's alternatives. If Pepsi chooses a low level of advertising and Coke also chooses a low level, Pepsi knows that its profits will be large. The advertising of each firm attracts sales from the other but has a rather small effect on total soft-drink sales. That is, total soft-drink sales are relatively inelastic with respect to advertising. If Pepsi chooses a low level of advertising but Coke chooses a high level, total soft-drink sales will not increase much but Coke's advertising will attract a huge amount of sales away from Pepsi. Coke's profit will be quite high, but Pepsi will actually make a loss.

Alternatively, suppose Pepsi chooses a high advertising budget. If Coke chooses a low budget, Pepsi will take away a lot of Coke's sales; Pepsi will make a large profit, and Coke will make a loss. If Pepsi chooses a high level of advertising while Coke chooses a high advertising budget also, neither firm will increase its market share and neither will increase its sales or its revenue much. Both will experience high advertising costs, so both will make some profit but not nearly as much as would be the case for the firm that chooses the high budget when the other chooses the low budget.

The complete picture is illustrated in Figure 15.5, which shows the advertiser's dilemma. Pepsi's choices are shown along the top of the table and Coke's along the side of the table. The profits of Pepsi and Coke for each combination of advertising choices (in millions of dollars) are shown, respectively, as π_p and π_c in each cell. In cell A, when both companies choose a low budget, each earns a profit of $600 million. In cells B and C, the firm with the high budget increases its profit to $900 million while the firm with the low budget makes a loss of $400. If both choose a high budget and end up in cell D, each will earn a $200 million profit, which is much lower than would be the case if both choose a low budget.

Pepsi and Coke each know the limits on the choices of the other. Note that if Coke chooses low advertising, Pepsi is better off choosing high advertising: $900 profit compared with $600. If Coke chooses a high budget, Pepsi is also

FIGURE 15.5
An Advertiser's Dilemma

		Pepsi: Low budget	Pepsi: High budget
Coke	Low budget	A π_p = $600 π_c = $600	B π_p = $900 π_c = –$400
	High budget	C π_p = –$400 π_c = $900	D π_p = $200 π_c = $200

Profit in $1,000,000

better off choosing a high budget: $200 profit compared with a $400 loss with a low budget. The incentives facing Coke are identical.

For both firms, therefore, a high advertising budget is the dominant strategy. Each firm makes a choice and ends up in cell D, with lower profits than could be earned in cell A when they both choose a low budget. From each seller's perspective, there is too much advertising. Once the choice of a high budget is made, it is extremely difficult to get out of cell D and into cell A, where profits are higher. Neither firm has the incentive to reduce its advertising given the current choice of the other firm; it would move from a $200 profit to a $400 loss.

Nash equilibrium
Situation in which each participant in a game is choosing its best action given the action chosen by the other participants.

Such a situation is often referred to as a *Nash equilibrium,* named after the game theorist John F. Nash. A **Nash equilibrium** occurs when each participant in a game is choosing the best action possible, *given what action the other participants have chosen.* Therefore, no participant has any incentive to make a change. Thus this situation represents an equilibrium, as in the above dilemma, even though all could make a change and be better off. Note the difference between a Nash equilibrium and a dominant strategy: a dominant strategy is the strategy that leads to the best outcome no matter what the rival does; in a Nash equilibrium each party is making the best choice, given the choice of the rival. Neither has an incentive to change.

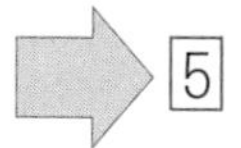 5

A Pricing Dilemma

Oligopolies may find themselves in similar dilemmas when making price decisions. Recall the previous example, in which Coke and Pepsi were trying to decide on a price, each knowing that its sales, and hence profits, depend on the price charged by the other firm. We illustrate how firms attempt to adapt in such a dilemma with the following example, using much smaller firms.

Pizza Palace and Pizza Castle are located practically side by side across the street from a major university. Since the products of the Palace and the Castle are practically identical, their primary means of competition is pricing. For illustrative purposes, suppose each restaurant can choose between only two prices for

FIGURE 15.6
A Pricing Dilemma

		Palace price: High ($10)	Palace price: Low ($6)
Castle price	High ($10)	A π_p = $1,000 π_c = $1,000	B π_p = $1,500 π_c = 0
	Low ($6)	C π_p = 0 π_c = $1,500	D π_p = $300 π_c = $300

its pizza: a high price of $10 and a low price of $6. Clearly the profit for each firm at each of the prices depends greatly on the price charged by the other firm.

Figure 15.6 illustrates the familiar dilemma in which the managers of Castle and Palace find themselves. Clearly, if both charge $10, each will do quite well, making $1,000 a week profit, as shown in cell A. If both lower their prices to $6, sales will increase some, each will probably maintain its market share, and, because of the lower price, the profit of each will fall to $300 a week, as shown in cell D. However, if either firm lowers its price to $6 while the other maintains its price at $10, the firm with the lower price will capture most of the other's business. The firm with the lower price will enjoy a $1,500 profit ($\pi_p$ in cell B or π_c in cell C), while the profits of the other fall to zero (π_c in cell B or π_p in cell C).

As Figure 15.6 shows, charging a low price is the dominant strategy for each. If, for example, Castle sets a high price, Palace earns $1,500 by charging a low price but only $1,000 with a high price. If Castle sets a low price, Palace makes zero profit with a high price but earns $300 with a low price. The same situation faces Castle. Therefore, both act rationally under the circumstances and, quite likely, end up in cell D, taking part in what their customers call a "price war." Both would be better off charging a high price and earning $1,000, but the low price for each is a Nash equilibrium, in which, given what the other is doing, neither firm has any incentive to change.

Obviously the best solution for the two firms would be that the Castle and the Palace merge or reach an agreement under which both charge $10. The U.S. Department of Justice probably would not actually prosecute two local pizza establishments for violation of antitrust laws if the firms cooperate and set price jointly. There may, however, be problems if one firm breaks or cheats on the agreement (a problem we will discuss later). More likely, if both set the high price, someone else will enter the market, charge a price lower than $10, and cause one or both to go out of business.

We have illustrated oligopolists' dilemmas for price and advertising. While these are the most familiar examples, similar dilemmas can arise in other forms of competition among oligopolies. Firms can introduce too many new models or put too many features on their products. In all such cases, firms would be better

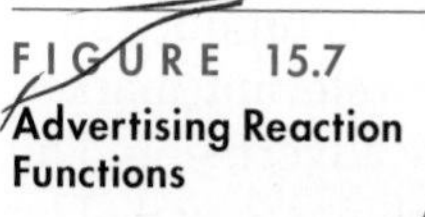

FIGURE 15.7
Advertising Reaction Functions

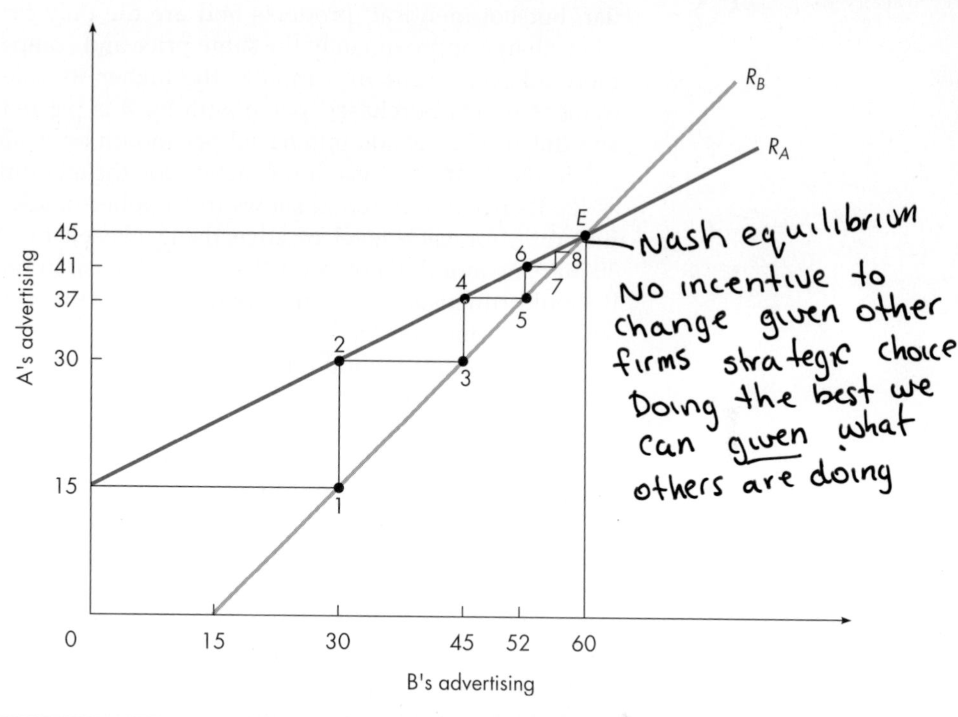

off if they cooperated and agreed to compete less even though such agreements are generally illegal and hard to maintain. In the absence of such an agreement, firms will likely end up in a situation involving too much competition for their own good, thus reaching an equilibrium such as the ones in cell D in the examples we discussed.

Reaction Functions

Thus far in this section we have assumed for simplicity that firms face only two alternatives and make a one-time decision, unaware of what a rival's decision will be. Once the decision is made, neither firm has an incentive to change if the other does not change. In the previous examples, cell D was the equilibrium situation. In practice, however, firms sometimes arrive at an equilibrium situation, which may or may not be optimal from the firms' point of view, by making a *series* of adjustments or changes in response to changes made by the rival firm. Economists have developed a tool, called **reaction functions,** to analyze and explain these adjustment paths.

reaction functions
Functions or curves that indicate the best (usually profit-maximizing) response to any changes made by a rival.

To illustrate the concept of reaction functions, we use an example of two oligopolists that compete with each other through advertising, although we could have chosen an example of pricing, output, or other nonprice competition. Figure 15.7 illustrates the process of adjustment.

Suppose there are two oligopolists, firms A and B. These firms produce similar, but not identical, products and are the only firms in the relevant market. They charge approximately the same price and compete only by advertising. The more ads each runs in a month, the higher its sales, other things equal. The number of ads purchased per month by B is plotted along the horizontal axis, and the number of ads purchased per month by A along the vertical axis.

In the figure, B's reaction function for the amount of ads run by A is shown as R_B. B's reaction function shows the number of ads for B that would maximize B's profit, for each level of advertising chosen by A. For example, if A runs 30 ads per month (shown on the vertical axis), in order to maximize B's profit, B should run 45 ads, shown as point 3 on R_B. Or if A runs 15 ads, B would run 30 ads, at point 1 on R_B.

The reaction function for A is R_A; it shows the level of advertising by A that maximizes A's profit for each possible level of B's advertising. For example, if B runs 45 ads, A should run 37 ads, at point 4. Both reaction functions are upward-sloping, indicating that the more ads used by one firm, the more ads the other should run in order to maximize its own profit.

We begin at the origin with neither firm advertising. Clearly, the optimal move for either firm is to run 15 ads if the other runs no ads. Arbitrarily, suppose A leads off and uses 15 ads. B sees this and counters by running 30 ads, point 1 on B's reaction curve. Now, 15 ads are no longer optimal for A, which then increases the number of ads to 30 (point 2 on R_A). Then B counters with 45 ads (at point 3), after which A increases to 37 ads (point 4).

You have the picture by now and should realize why these curves are called reaction functions. Firms B and A continue to react to one another's changes moving from 4 to 5 to 6 and so on until point *E* is reached. Firm B uses 60 ads and firm A uses 45 ads. This combination of advertising is a Nash equilibrium because neither firm has an incentive to change the number of ads. From B's reaction function, 60 ads are optimal when A uses 45 ads. From A's reaction function, 45 ads are optimal when B uses 60 ads. The firms will continue with the same levels of advertising until some exogenous change occurs and shifts one or both reaction functions.

We must emphasize that point *E* in the figure is a Nash equilibrium only because neither firm has any incentive to change if the other firm does not change. Point *E* is not necessarily the combination of advertising that maximizes the total or joint profit of the two firms. Joint profit maximization may very well occur when each firm uses considerably less advertising. Actually, point *E* in Figure 15.7 may well be similar to cell D in the diagram showing the advertiser's dilemma. Neither firm is making as much profit as would be possible if both firms cooperated and moved back to a position similar to cell A in the advertiser's dilemma diagram.

Although the final equilibrium using reaction functions may be similar to the final equilibrium in the advertiser's dilemma when high advertising is the dominant strategy, we wanted to show that the theory need not be based solely

8 on the assumption that each firm makes one once-and-for-all move simultaneously with the other firm.

Adapting to Mutual Interdependence

We have shown that individuals, rationally pursuing their own gains, can easily end up worse off than they would be if they were able to cooperate. The situation is analogous to dividing a pie. People are struggling to get a larger share of a pie, but in the struggle some of the pie gets knocked off the table and onto the floor, and they end up sharing a smaller pie. A solution preferred by all participants exists but is difficult to achieve. And, even if the preferred situation is attained, such as the results in cell A in the above dilemmas, players have a strong incentive to change their actions, which leads back to cell D. In fact, when the products are similar and oligopolists compete with price, the price can fall almost to the perfectly competitive level, which is great for consumers but bad for the oligopolists.

But the situation is not hopeless for oligopoly managers. Certainly, in the situations we used as examples, cooperation is difficult to attain without a binding agreement. These situations, however, involved a single, one-time decision. Most pricing, advertising, and other similar decisions are repeated. Firms that can set price and ad budgets monthly, weekly, or even daily are in what are called *repeated games.*

Firms in a repeated game can sometimes achieve cooperation, even though they cannot write contracts or even reach a verbal agreement. Over time, managers can learn how their rivals tend to behave in various situations, especially when there are relatively few firms in the market—two or three rather than eight or nine. As they learn patterns of behavior, repetition may make cooperation possible.

For example, suppose that firms in a market have been in the pricing dilemma for a period of time. Each manager knows that all are charging a price below the level that would give enhanced profits if all firms raised their prices. No firm has been willing to take the chance. Perhaps one bold manager believes, knowing that the others realize the problem they all face, that the others may be willing to follow a small price increase.

This manager, in effect, signals to the others, "I am willing to take this chance, knowing full well that if you do not follow I will drop my price again and everything will be the same." This behavior would not be possible in the single-decision games. Perhaps the price raiser simultaneously announces to the press that the industry is in trouble because of the "price war" and casually mentions that the war could get even worse. This may signal to the others that the manager who raised price will drop the price even more, in retaliation, if the others do not follow.

Will this strategy work? Economists can say only that sometimes it does, sometimes it doesn't. It is more likely to work if the price raiser's rivals believe its threat to lower price if the others do not follow, that is, if the threat is credible. Concern for the future can bring about cooperation. Also, as mentioned, the price-signaling strategy is more likely to work when there are few firms in the market.

Price signaling has, however, failed many times—for example, when the products are so differentiated that managers find it difficult to observe rivals' prices. Is a higher price the result of better quality? Or will firms break the tacit cooperation when business is bad? Will the higher price and higher profit bring about the entry of new firms into the market, causing profits to decline?

One conclusion generally agreed upon by game theorists is that the best strategy is cooperation with retaliation, sometimes called a *tit-for-tat strategy*: set a high price, but if the others lower price, lower your price. However, in experiments using people, usually students, sometimes the participants cooperate, sometimes they don't. The same can be said for real oligopolies.

We have included this brief discussion of game theory and strategic behavior to give you a feel for theories of strategic interaction. For one manager's view on how game theory can be used in real-world business decision making, see

9 Illustration 15.2.

15.5 STRATEGIC ENTRY DETERRENCE

strategic entry deterrence
Strategic behavior of established firms that creates barriers to the entry of new firms into the market.

Managers of firms in oligopoly markets sometimes use types of strategic behavior other than the types we discussed in the preceding section. One example, **strategic entry deterrence,** occurs when an established firm (or firms) takes actions designed to discourage or even prevent the entry of a new firm or firms into a market. This type of entry barrier differs somewhat from the previously discussed barriers to entry as those barriers are in large part technical in nature or, to some extent, beyond the control of the manager. For example, economies of scale over a large range of output, an important entry barrier, exist because of properties of the production function.

Strategic entry deterrence is the result of the *behavior* of established firms. A firm selling in a particular market may be making above-normal profit. The manager realizes that entry of new firms into that market will probably reduce, or possibly eliminate, that profit. The manager can, sometimes, take measures to reduce the probability of new firms entering. This section discusses four types of such strategic behavior: lowering prices, building excess capacity, producing multiple products, and developing new products. All of these are designed to discourage entry into the market.

Entry Limit Pricing

entry limit pricing
Strategy in which a firm sets a price lower than the short-run profit-maximizing price in order to prevent or discourage the entry of new firms into the market.

Under certain circumstances an oligopolist, or possibly a monopolist, may charge a price lower than the short-run profit-maximizing price in order to prevent or discourage new firms from entering the market. Such a strategy is called **entry limit pricing.** In order to practice entry limit pricing, an established firm must have a cost advantage over potential entrants into the market.

ILLUSTRATION 15.2

How Can Game Theory Be Used in Business Decision Making?

Answers from a Manager

"Game theory is hot . . . it's been used to analyze everything from the baseball strike to auctions at the FCC. . . . Why are 50-year-old ideas being used by companies to answer basic questions about pricing, investments in capacity, purchasing, and other matters?" So began an article in *The Wall Street Journal,* "Making Game Theory Work in Practice," by F. William Barnett, a partner in McKinsey's Dallas office.*

Mr. Barnett points out that game theory helps managers pay attention to interactions with competitors, customers, and suppliers and focus on how near-term actions promote long-term interests by influencing what the players do. After describing a version of the game that we referred to as the pricing dilemma, he notes that an equilibrium, such as the one we showed in cell D, is unattractive to all players. He warns, "But you have to know your industry inside-out before game theory is truly valuable . . . you will need to understand entry costs, demand functions, revenue structures, cost curves, etc. Without that understanding, the answer you get [from game theory] may be wrong."

Some rules of the road: Examine the number, concentration, and size distribution of the players. For example, industries with four or fewer players have the greatest potential for game theory, because (1) the competitors are large enough to benefit more from an improvement in general industry conditions than they would from improving their position at the expense of others (making the pie bigger rather than getting a bigger share of a smaller pie) and (2) with fewer competitors it is possible to think through the different combination of moves and countermoves.

Keep an eye out for strategies inherent in your market share. Small players can take advantage of larger companies, which are more concerned with maintaining the status quo. Barnett's example: Kiwi Airlines, with a small share of the market, was able to cut fares by up to 75 percent between Atlanta and Newark without a significant response from Delta and Continental. But, he notes, large players can create economies of scale or scope, such as frequent-flier programs, which are unattractive to small airlines.

Understand the nature of the buying decision. For example, if there are only a few deals in an industry each year, it is very hard to avoid aggressive competition. Scrutinize your competitors' cost and revenue structures. If competitors have a high proportion of fixed-to-variable cost, they will probably behave more aggressively than those whose production costs are more variable.

Examine the similarity of firms. When competitors have similar cost and revenue structures, they often behave similarly. The challenge is to find prices that create the largest markets, then use nonprice competition—distribution and service. Finally, analyze the nature of demand. The best chances to create value with less aggressive strategies are in markets with stable or moderately growing demand.

Mr. Barnett concludes, "Sometimes [game theory] can increase the size of the pie; on other occasions it can make your slice of the pie bigger; and sometimes it may even help you do both. But for those who misunderstand [the] fundamentals of their industry, game theory is better left to the theorists." As we said earlier, strategic decision making is best learned from experience.

*F. William Barnett, "Making Game Theory Work in Practice," *The Wall Street Journal*, Feb. 13, 1995.

An example of a situation in which an established firm might lower its price below the profit-maximizing level is illustrated in Figure 15.8. Panel B shows the demand and marginal revenue curves for an established firm, along with the firm's long-run average and marginal cost curves, LAC_0 and LMC_0. To maximize profit, this firm would produce 60,000 units of output, where marginal revenue

FIGURE 15.8
Entry Limit Pricing

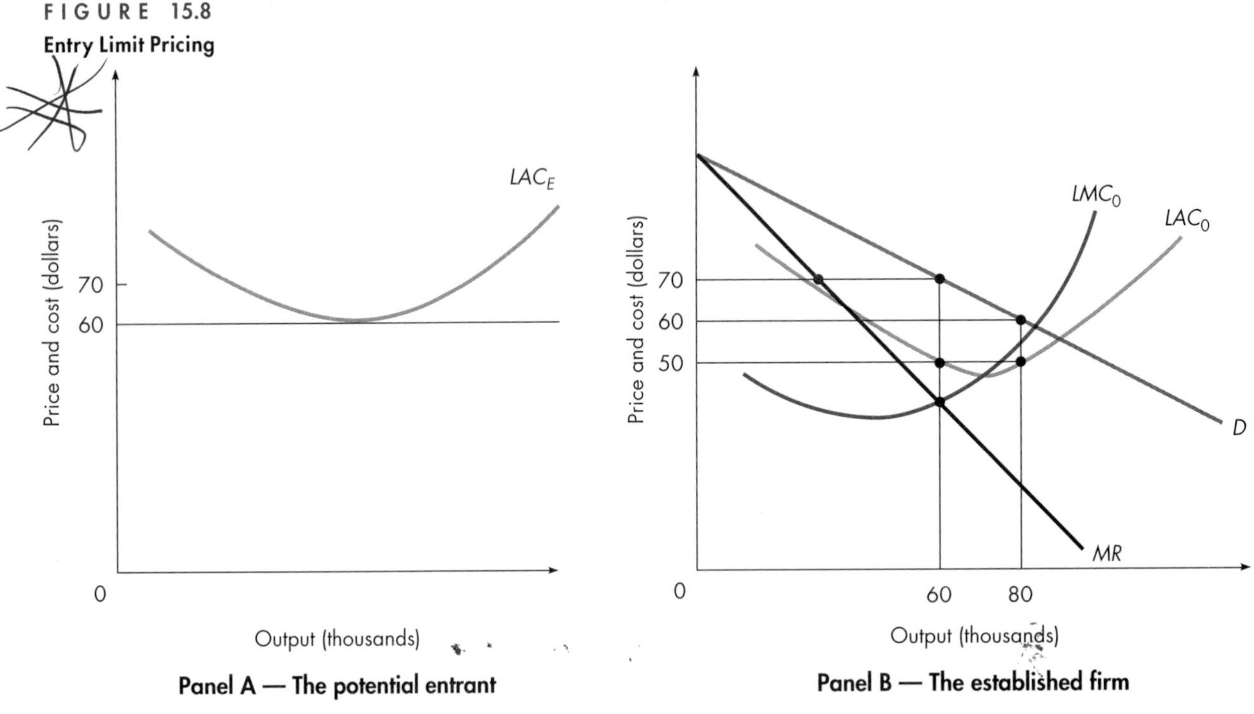

equals marginal cost, and set a price of \$70, from the demand curve. The firm's profit would be \$1,200,000 [= (\$70 − \$50) × 60,000].

The long-run average cost curve for a potential entrant into the market is shown as LAC_E in Panel A. If the established firm charges a price of \$70, this firm could enter the market, perhaps at a price a little lower than \$70, and make a profit. LAC_E is lower than \$70 over a broad range of output.

Note that the long-run average cost curve of the potential entrant is higher than the long-run average cost curve of the established firm; LAC_E reaches a minimum at \$60, while LAC_0 reaches its minimum at approximately \$45. Thus the established firm could charge a price slightly below the minimum long-run average cost of the potential entrant (\$60) but above its own long-run average cost and prevent the entry of the new firm, while continuing to make an economic profit.

Suppose, for example, that the established firm sets a price barely under \$60, and, from its demand, sells 80,000 units of output. The potential entrant could not cover its average cost at any level of output at this price. It would, therefore, be discouraged from entering the market, because if it did, it would make a loss. At the lower price, the established firm would sell 80,000 units of output and make less than the maximum profit of \$1,200,000. But, the firm would still make an economic profit of \$800,000 [= (\$60 − \$50) × 80,000].

This lower profit could, however, be higher than would be the case if the new firm had entered the market and taken away some of the sales of the established firm. Therefore, the firm is willing to sacrifice some immediate profit to prevent the entry of the new firm in order to earn a stream of lower, but protected, profits over a longer period of time. Of course, if the threat of entry is not great, the firm may not wish to sacrifice the stream of higher current profits. If entry is relatively easy, the firm may well be satisfied with lower profit. (In terms of the discussion in Chapter 1, the firm would compare the relative present values of the two choices.)

We should note that the ability to practice entry limit pricing depends on the established firm's having a cost advantage over potential entrants. If the established firm does not have a long-run average cost curve below that of the other firm, it could not lower its price below the minimum average cost of the potential entrant and continue to make an economic profit. Because the established firm shown in Figure 15.8 has a cost advantage, it can effectively block the entry of the other firm. Even though entry limit pricing is a form of strategic behavior, the feasibility of such behavior depends on technical conditions as well. Without a cost advantage, entry limit pricing is not feasible, and the firm would have to search for another way to impede entry—if that is possible.

Capacity Barriers to Entry

Under certain circumstances, it is possible for an established firm to discourage the entry of new firms into the market without actually decreasing the price it charges and consequently finding its profits reduced. The firm can maintain excess capacity, above the capacity it would normally build. The excess capacity signals to potential entrants that the established firm is prepared to increase its output by reducing its price if new firms prepare to enter the market.

The excess capacity makes the threat of a price reduction in the event of entry credible. The firm would already have the capacity of increasing production quickly in the face of entry. It would take much longer for a new firm to build a new factory in order to enter the market than it would for the established firm to gear up idle capacity. By the time the new entrant is ready for business, output in the market would be higher and price lower from the increased production. Thus new entrants would be discouraged. This is the nature of a **capacity barrier to entry.**

capacity barrier to entry
Strategy in which a firm holds excess capacity as a threat to potential entrants so that it is prepared to increase output and lower price if entry occurs.

Certainly holding idle capacity would add to a firm's costs, thereby reducing profits somewhat. However, compared with a pricing strategy that blocks entry, carrying idle capacity may be a less expensive (more profitable) way for a firm to hold its market share in the face of potential entry. The choice would depend on the expected relative stream of profit from excess capacity compared with the stream from entry limit pricing. If demand is not particularly elastic, a small increase in output would cause price to fall a great deal. In this case the required amount of idle capacity would be small, and excess capacity may be a less costly way to block entry. (We will discuss the dynamic aspects of this entry-blocking decision later in the text.)

Multiproduct Cost Barriers

The existence of economies of scope, discussed in Chapter 10, may enable a firm to make the entry of new competitors into the market more difficult. Recall that economies of scope means that producing two goods together is less costly (either in terms of total cost or per-unit cost) than producing the two goods separately. And it follows that producing three goods together is less costly than producing any other combinations of the goods. Therefore, if a firm produces two or more related goods together, it would have a cost advantage over any firm that produced the goods in another combination.

To show how economies of scope can act as an entry deterrent, we use the following simplified example: Suppose there are three related goods, X, Y, and Z, each of which has constant average costs of production of \$20:

$$c(X) = c(Y) = c(Z) = \$20$$

where $c(X)$, $c(Y)$, and $c(Z)$ denote *average* costs of production.[1] Thus, the price of each good would have to exceed \$20 in order to cover costs when the goods are produced separately.

Now suppose that if any two of the goods are produced together, the average cost of the pair of goods is \$34:

$$c(X, Y) = c(X, Z) = c(Y, Z) = \$34$$

In this case, a firm producing any pair of the goods must charge a price for each good that (on average) exceeds \$17 (= \$34/2) in order to cover costs. Note that we are not saying the *profit-maximizing* price for each good in a pair should be the same (\$17). Obviously demand conditions must also be considered. We simply want to point out that unless the *average* price of the two goods is at least \$17, then costs will not be covered by revenue. Since a firm producing a pair of goods has a lower per-unit cost for each good than it would if either good were produced separately, economies of scope exist.

Further suppose a firm that produces all three goods together has an average cost for the *triplet* of goods of \$48:

$$c(X, Y, Z) = \$48$$

This firm could sell the three goods at slightly under \$17 each (on average) and undersell any firms that are producing the three goods either separately or in pairs. If the price is just under \$17, the firm producing the three goods together would receive a revenue of just under \$51, which would more than cover its costs.

Certainly, the firm in the above example would not necessarily block the entry of new firms, nor would any established firm producing multiple products under economies of scope. A new firm could enter the markets with the same

[1]The assumption that all three goods have exactly the same average cost is made solely to simplify the discussion. The per-unit costs almost certainly would differ in a real-world situation, but the analysis would be the same. Similarly, the assumption that average costs are constant for all output levels is for the purpose of simplification and does not affect the analysis.

cost structure if it also produced all three products together. However, it is generally more costly to enter all three markets and produce all three products than it is to enter one or even two markets. For one thing, the initial capital cost would probably be considerably higher. It is harder for new firms to raise investment capital. Consequently, the large capital investment required would tend
11 to discourage some new firms from entering all three markets.

New Product Development as a Barrier to Entry

Sometimes established firms can block or at least discourage entry by producing substitutes for its own products. You might wonder why firms would want to produce substitutes that can take sales away from its own products. But managers may think someone else will introduce similar substitutes, and introducing your own substitutes is greatly preferred to seeing other firms introducing them.

Producing several related products crowds the market with choices. The wider the range of choices, the more substitutes there are for a given product. As you know, the more substitutes there are, the lower the demand and the greater the elasticity of demand for a product. This makes it more difficult for a new firm to find its own niche in the market, because the demand for its own products would be lower. Its price and sales would be lower than would be the case if the established firm had not introduced so many substitutes. It is therefore less likely under these conditions that new firms could cover their costs, so entry is discouraged.

There are many examples of oligopolists in consumer markets producing and selling a broad range of substitute products. Of course, we cannot say what their purpose in producing so many products actually is. Firms don't typically brag that they are trying to prevent new competition.

Nevertheless, the three largest breakfast cereal producers, General Mills, Kellogg, and Post, each produce a broad range of cereals. Some are aimed at children, some are aimed at adults, some are aimed at the health conscious, and so on. Coca-Cola sells regular Coke, Classic Coke, Diet Coke, Caffeine-Free Coke, and Cherry Coke. Pepsi has its own broad range of beverages. The major beer producers, primarily Budweiser and Miller, sell regular beer, light beer, dry beer, and nonalcoholic beer. Automobile manufacturers sell a large array of cars under the same brand name. The different models can vary widely in price and are designed to appeal to different segments of the market. We are sure that you can think of other producers that sell a range of substitutes for their own products.

We have touched upon some of the more important ways that established firms can discourage the entry of new firms into the market. Such strategic entry deterrence is limited only by the ingenuity of the managers. Quite possibly the most effective way a new firm can discourage entry, and the most beneficial for consumers, is to continue producing an excellent product that people like and carry out research and development that reduces costs, thereby enabling the firm to lower price over time. A good product at a low price with good service may very well be the best way to discourage entry (see Illustration 15.3).

ILLUSTRATION 15.3

Who Cares about a Little Bit of Sugar?

In the text, we presented an example of firms' using the amount of sugar on their cereal as a method of nonprice competition. The two firms ended up using about the same amount of sugar. We also described how firms can use multiple products (substitutes for their own products) as a barrier to entry. But they can also use multiple products as a method of nonprice competition against existing competitors. We will now describe how changing the amount of sugar was once used for this purpose.

You may be thinking, as the title of this illustration suggests, "Does anyone really care about how much sugar a company puts on its product?" Several years ago a lot of people cared. On Wednesday, July 10, 1985, Coca-Cola announced that it was bringing back its old Coke with a little less sugar, now called Classic Coke, after switching to a sweeter version almost three months before. ABC interrupted its soap opera, *General Hospital*, to break the news. Dan Rather, Peter Jennings, and Tom Brokaw had news stories on the CBS, ABC, and NBC evening news. ABC featured the story on *Nightline*. Senator David Pryor expressed jubilation on the Senate floor during a debate on South Africa. *Time* covered the story in a prominent article.*

The story actually began on April 23, 1985, when Coca-Cola announced that, after extensive testing, it was changing the flavor of Coke for the first time in its 99-year history. In essence, Coca-Cola had added a little more sugar to the recipe, making Coke taste much more like Pepsi, which celebrated the occasion by declaring a company holiday. No one actually knows, but Coke may well have "jumped" Pepsi in the sugar war, as described previously. Coke's advertising agency reported that two-thirds of the nation heard the news within 24 hours.

The change caused a national furor even though both firms already had several brands of soft drinks. Coke had merely tried to move its product closer to its largest competitor on the flavor spectrum. But people thought it was like tampering with a national institution. Coca-Cola received as many as 1,500 phone calls a day as well as a multitude of protesting letters. "Save Coke" clubs were formed. And all of this was after by far the most extensive market testing program in the company's history.

After almost three months of such protest, Coca-Cola decided to keep the new, sweeter Coke on the market but bring back the old flavor of Coke and call it Classic Coke. Some observers at the time thought it was one of the dumbest marketing moves in history. Some thought it was a giant hoax, claiming that Coke had planned all along to reintroduce the Classic Coke and reap the benefits of all the publicity. After all, Coke had Pepsi almost surrounded in the sugar battle.

Donald R. Keough, the president of Coca-Cola, denied the stories that the new Coke was a deliberate plot to create support for the old product, saying, "Some critics will say Coca-Cola has made a marketing mistake. Some cynics say that we planned the whole thing. The truth is, we're not that dumb, and we're not that smart."

There's an epilogue to this story: Twelve years later, in *U.S. News & World Report*, Maria Mallory noted that, in 1986, PepsiCo Chairman Roger Enrico flaunted his company's success in the book *The Other Guy Blinked: How Pepsi Won the Cola Wars*. She noted, "If Coca-Cola Chairman Robert C. Goizueta were a

15.6 COOPERATIVE OLIGOPOLY BEHAVIOR

Most of the discussion of oligopoly behavior thus far has concerned oligopolies that do not cooperate or collude. Oligopolies can compete in many ways—price, advertising, product quality, and so on. Although oligopolies do compete, they generally don't like doing so because of mutual interdependence and the related uncertainty. You have seen how noncooperating firms, under reasonable behavioral assumptions, can set prices too low or do too much advertising from their point of view. They make lower profits than they would if they were to cooperate.

vengeful kind of guy, he might retaliate today by writing a book of his own entitled *The Other Guy's Got His Eyes Sealed Shut.*"[†]

Mallory pointed out that in June 1997 Coke held its largest lead over Pepsi in decades: 32.9 percent of the U.S. market versus 22.8 percent for Pepsi. In 1985 Pepsi had a 25.8 percent market share compared with 31.2 percent for Coke. Overseas the news for Pepsi was grimmer. So after the sugar battle Coke must have done something right, Pepsi must have done something wrong, or both. According to Mallory's article the answer is probably "both."

The article did note that Pepsi was reorganizing its bottling operation in the image of Coca-Cola and was finally refocusing the company. But experts had begun "questioning the long-term strength of the Pepsi trademark." Marketing specialists believed that Pepsi's "brand equity" may have been eroding. A relatively new marketing concept, brand equity is a method of measuring the "financial valuation of a brand's reputation by translating consumer loyalty into dollars and cents." Alvin Schechter, a pioneer in brand valuations, stated: "When you talk about colas, which are essentially parity products, the emotional components are important." In other words, how do people feel about the product?

At the time Coke's brand equity was $43.4 billion versus $8.9 billion for Pepsi. And the growth in Pepsi's brand value had lagged behind Coke's, increasing 7 percent the past year compared with Coke's 11 percent. Mallory points out that brand equity, a measure of a product's connection with the consumer, can "carry the day when price wars rage, competition heats up, or economies turn cold."

Clearly, in 1985, Coke had felt compelled to change its age-old formula for a more Pepsi-like taste, so something happened since then. The article suggests some of the mistakes Pepsi made: two failed brand extensions, an ineffective advertising strategy, and too rapid expansion into the restaurant business. Coke's ad campaign co-opted much of Pepsi's "young and hip" attitude, and the company displayed "careful brand stewardship and operational savvy" to make overseas markets, where most of the growth potential was, pay off.

But the point of this story isn't to tell you what Coke did or what Pepsi did or didn't do. Coke is certainly not the only company that has attained strong brand equity or consumer loyalty when faced with strong competition. Mallory's article noted two other examples: Nike's ability to charge $150 for sneakers sporting a swoosh, and Marlboro's ability to survive a cigarette price war in 1993 because of its "strong cachet among consumers." Neither is Pepsi the only company that has made serious mistakes in the face of relentless competition. It would obviously be a mistake if your principal strategic decision is hoping your rival makes mistakes while you do nothing.

The Coke-Pepsi story illustrates the point we made at the end of the text sections on strategic behavior: Sometimes the best decision strategy is to sell a good product at a reasonable price, give good service, and, we might add, try to maintain consumer loyalty. This is a good strategy for many types of oligopolists, and for monopolistic competitors, faced by inevitable new entry, it is a good strategy for slowing down the consequent erosion of profits.

*"Coca-Cola's Big Fizzle," *Time,* June 22, 1995, pp. 48–52.
[†]Maria Mallory, "Pop Goes the Pepsi Generation," *U.S. News & World Report,* June 19, 1997, pp. 48–49.

As mentioned earlier, firms can move to a more profitable situation if they can reach implicit agreements to stop price cutting or reduce advertising expenditure. Firms do, at times, cooperate and reach agreements to raise price and reduce output or limit competition in other areas, even though explicit price fixing and other collusive behavior is illegal in the United States. Yet antitrust litigation still flourishes, indicating such behavior is still thought to exist.

This section extends the discussion of oligopoly cooperation. We will describe how firms attempt to make themselves better off by cooperative agreements, even though some of these agreements may be illegal. Such agreements are called *collusive agreements.* We will focus the analysis primarily on price agreements, even though the analysis can be extended to other forms of competition. We begin with the most extreme form of collusion: a price-fixing cartel.

Cartel Profit Maximization

cartel
A group of firms that agree to limit competitive forces in a market.

A **cartel** is a group of firms with the objective of limiting competitive forces within a market. It may take the form of open collusion, with the member firms entering into contracts about price and other market variables. Or the cartel may involve secret collusion among members with no explicit contract. One of the most famous cartels is OPEC (the Organization of Petroleum Exporting Countries), an association of some of the world's major oil-producing nations.

We first consider an *ideal* cartel. Suppose a group of firms producing a homogeneous commodity forms a cartel. A central management body is appointed, its function being to determine the uniform cartel price. The task, in theory, is relatively simple, as illustrated in Figure 15.9. Market demand for the homogeneous commodity is given by D, so marginal revenue is given by the dashed line MR. The marginal cost curve for the cartel, MC_C, must be determined by the management body of the cartel. As shown in Figure 15.10, the cartel marginal cost curve MC_C is simply the horizontal sum of the marginal cost curves of the two member firms A and B.[2] For example, the marginal cost of the cartel is $15 when the cartel produces a total of 450 units, which is the sum of 150 units produced by firm A and 300 units produced by firm B. Once the management group determines the cartel marginal cost curve (MC_C), the problem is the simple one of determining the price that maximizes cartel profit—the monopoly price. In Figure 15.9 marginal cost and marginal revenue intersect at A. This gives the level of output, Q, and the price, P, that maximizes total profit for the cartel.

Once the profit-maximizing price and output are determined, the problem confronting cartel management is how to allocate the output among the member firms. Two fundamental methods of allocation are possible: market sharing (or quotas) and nonprice competition.

There are several possible variants of market sharing or quotas. Indeed there is no uniform principle by which quotas can be determined. In practice, the bargaining ability of a firm and the importance of the firm to the cartel are likely to be extremely important elements in determining a quota. However, one method of allocating the market is to use either the relative sales of each firm in some precartel period or the productive capacity of the firm as a basis for allocating shares of the cartel sales. As a practical matter, the choice of which precartel

[2]Strictly speaking, the horizontal summing of the marginal cost curves of the member firms is the correct way to derive MC_C only when input prices remain constant as all firms increase their levels of input usage. Otherwise, allowance must be made for the increase in input price accompanying an increase in input usage. MC_C will be steeper than the horizontal sum of the individual marginal cost curves when input prices rise with increased input usage. (Recall the discussion of short-run supply in Chapter 12.)

FIGURE 15.9
Cartel Profit Maximization

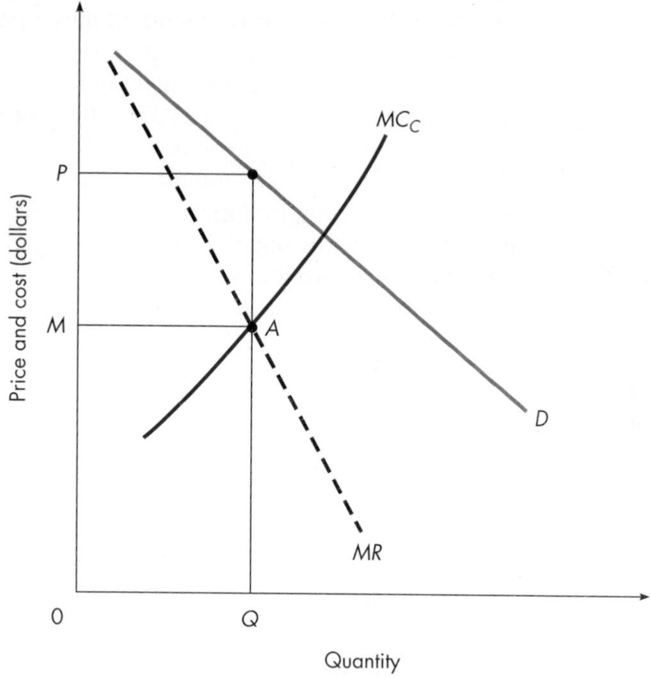

FIGURE 15.10
Derivation of Cartel Marginal Cost

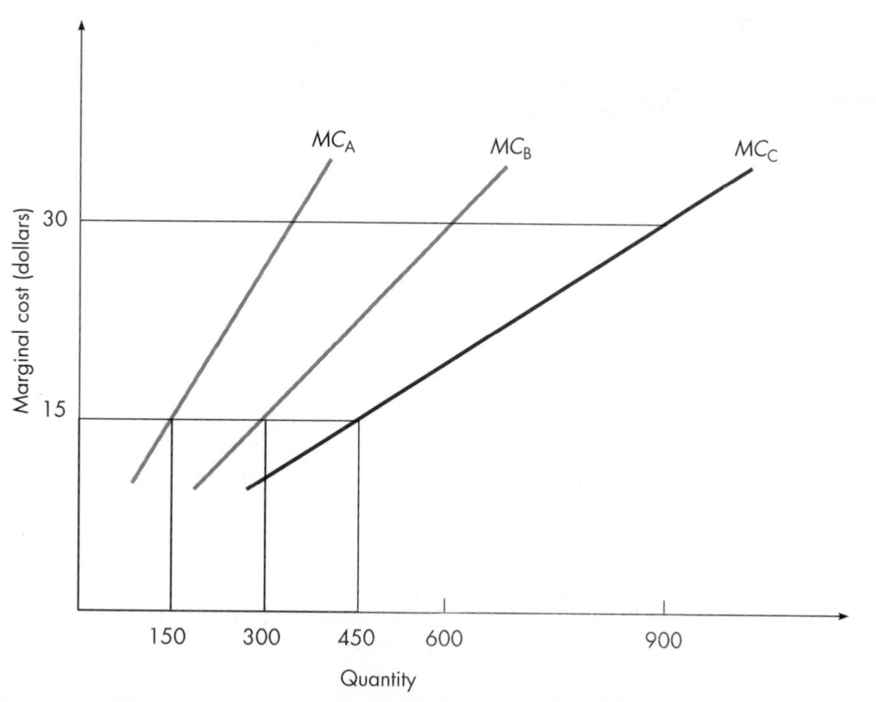

period or what measure of capacity to use is a matter of bargaining among the members. The most skillful bargainer is likely to come out best.

While market sharing or quota agreements may be difficult in practice, we can set forth some guidelines. If the cartel produces a homogeneous product, a reasonable objective for the cartel is to produce the optimal output at the minimum total cost. In this way, total cartel profit is maximized.

Minimum cartel cost is achieved when each firm produces that output for which its marginal cost equals the common cartel marginal cost and marginal revenue. Returning to Figure 15.9, each firm would produce the amount at which its marginal cost is equal to M. Summing to obtain MC_C, total cartel output will be Q, and total profit is maximized.

To reinforce this conclusion, suppose that two firms in the cartel are producing at different marginal costs; that is, assume

$$MC_1 > MC_2$$

for firms 1 and 2. In this case the cartel manager could transfer sales from the higher-cost firm 1 to the lower-cost firm 2. As long as the marginal cost of producing in firm 2 is lower, total cartel cost can be lowered by transferring production. For example, suppose MC_1 equals \$20 and MC_2 equals \$10. One unit of output taken away from firm 1 lowers the cartel's cost \$20. Producing that unit in firm 2 increases cartel cost by \$10. Thus the total cost of production falls \$10. And the cartel would continue taking output away from firm 1 and increasing the output of firm 2, thus lowering total cost, until $MC_1 = MC_2$. This equality would result because MC_1 would fall as the output of firm 1 decreases and MC_2 would increase as the output of firm 2 increases. Thus in equilibrium the marginal costs will be equal for all firms in the cartel.[3]

Principle In order to produce the profit-maximizing output at the minimum total cost, a cartel should allocate production among its various producers so that the marginal costs of all producers are equal. In profit-maximizing equilibrium, marginal revenue equals the common marginal cost.

The difficulty involved with this method of allocation is that, if firms differ in their cost structures, the lower-cost firms obtain the bulk of the market and therefore the bulk of the profits. To make this method of allocation acceptable to all members, a profit-sharing system, more or less independent of the sales quota, must be devised.

In some cases, it is easy for the member firms to agree upon the share of the market each is to have. This is illustrated in Figure 15.11 for an ideal situation. Suppose only two firms are in the market and they decide to divide the market evenly. The market demand curve is D, so the half-share curve for each firm is d, which lies halfway between D and the vertical axis. The marginal revenue curve for d is the line MR, the half-share marginal revenue for each firm. Suppose each firm has identical costs, represented by ATC and MC.

[3]This point is demonstrated mathematically in the appendix to this chapter.

FIGURE 15.11
Ideal Market Sharing

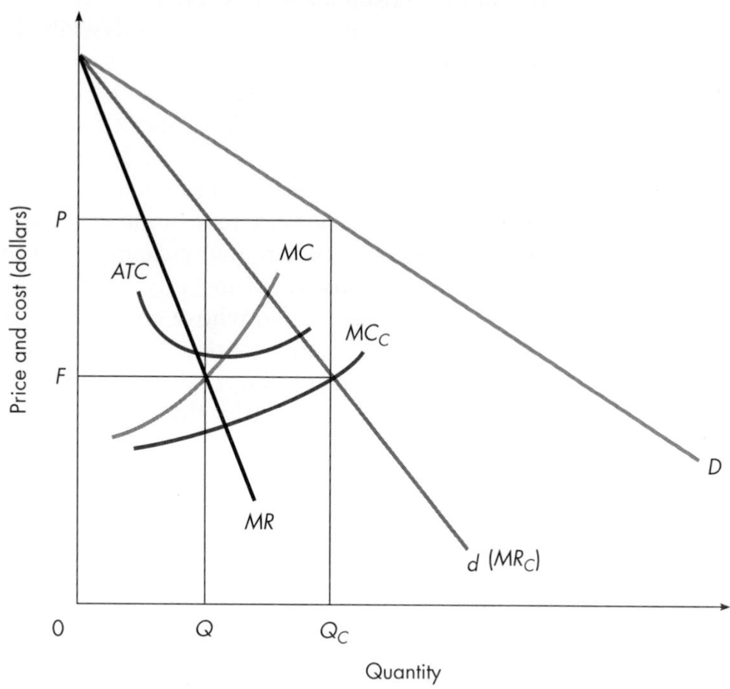

With these individual marginal revenue, marginal cost, and demand curves, each firm will decide to produce Q units of output, where MR and MC intersect. A uniform price of P is established on each firm's demand. At P a total output of Q_C is supplied (Q_C is twice Q, the output of each firm). This is a tenable solution because the market demand is consistent with the sale of Q_C units at a price of P.

To see this, let's approach the problem in another way. Suppose a cartel management group is formed and given the task of maximizing cartel profit. With the demand curve D, the cartel management views d as the marginal revenue curve (MR_C); d lies halfway between market demand, D, and the vertical axis. Next, summing the identical marginal cost curves, the manager obtains cartel marginal cost MC_C. The intersection of cartel marginal cost and cartel marginal revenue occurs at the level F, corresponding to output Q_C and price P. Since this is the same solution arrived at by the identical firms, the firms' decision to share the market equally is consistent with the objective of the cartel.

In this example we have assumed firms with identical cost functions. The solution is more complex when cost conditions differ, as noted above. Nonetheless, cartel profit is maximized when total cartel output is chosen so that market marginal revenue equals the horizontal sum of all firms' marginal costs—the cartel's marginal cost curve. Price is determined from the market demand curve at the chosen output. Output is allocated to the firms so that each firm's marginal cost equals market marginal revenue (which is also equal to the cartel's marginal cost) at the chosen level of output.

Ideal situations such as the one described above are rare. More likely, cost conditions will differ among firms. Yet another problem arises when firms produce a differentiated product. In such cases a cartel frequently allocates sales through nonprice competition. This type of allocation is generally associated with loose cartels.

In such cases, a uniform price is fixed and each firm is allowed to sell all it can at that price. The only requirement is that firms do not reduce price below the cartel price. There are many examples of this type of cartel organization in the United States today. For instance, in many localities both medical doctors and lawyers have associations whose code of ethics is frequently the basis of price agreement. The patient market, for example, is divided among the various doctors on the basis of nonprice competition: each patient selects the doctor of his or her choice. Similarly, the generally uniform prices of haircuts, major brands of gasoline, and movie tickets do not result from perfect competition within the market. Rather, they result from tacit, and sometimes open, agreement upon a price. The sellers compete with one another in various ways but not by price variations. This type of cartel arrangement is rather common in the sale of services.

We must reemphasize that the discussion of oligopoly cooperation thus far has focused primarily on the ideal system (from the viewpoint of the oligopolists) of cooperation. This shows what the rival firms would most like to do in overcoming the problems of mutual interdependence. In reality such arrangements are extremely difficult to carry out.

Even if such agreements were legal, firms frequently differ in the physical characteristics of the products sold, in their size, and in their cost structures. With differentiated products it is difficult to come up with a price, or set of prices, that maximizes cartel profits. Oligopolies selling in international markets face competition from firms in other countries, with whom it is hard to reach an agreement. Another problem arises from the inability to make contracts binding firms not to break the agreement that can be enforced by the courts. You may recall the discussion of why firms in price or advertising dilemmas were motivated, after coming to an implicit agreement not to cut price or increase advertising, to break the agreement and return to the less profitable situation. This is the major problem facing all cartels, both formal and informal. We now turn to
 12 a more extensive analysis of the problem of cheating.

The Problem of Cheating

Unless backed by strong enforcement mechanisms, cartel agreements are quite likely to collapse from internal pressure. That is, cartel members, particularly in times of weakened demand, have a strong incentive to cheat on the agreement in an effort to increase profits. A few large, geographically concentrated firms producing a relatively homogeneous commodity may form a successful cartel and maintain it, at least during prosperous times. But the greater the number of

FIGURE 15.12
The Incentive to Cheat

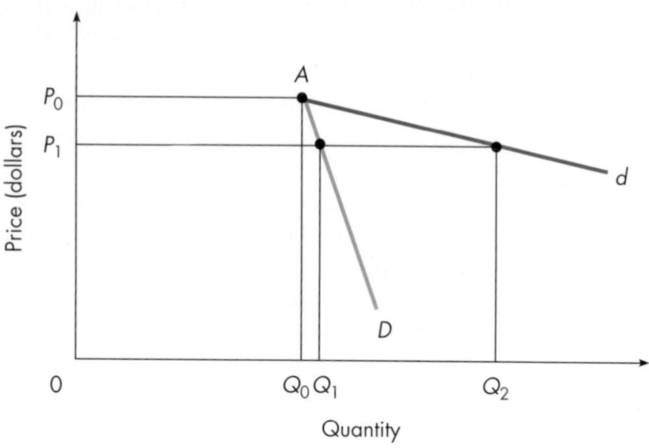

firms in the cartel, the more the products are differentiated, and the greater the geographical dispersion of the firms, the greater is the incentive to cheat on the cartel agreement. When profits are low or even negative, firms have an increased incentive to increase output and reduce price.

A typical cartel is characterized by a high (perhaps monopoly) price, a relatively low output, and a sales distribution that cause most firms to produce an output less than that associated with minimum long-run average cost. In this situation, any one firm, acting alone, can profit tremendously from secret price concessions leading to increased sales. As we will demonstrate, this incentive to cheat on the agreement typically causes the cartel to break up.

The incentive of a cartel member to cheat can be explained using the previously developed theory of sticky prices. Figure 15.12 shows the potential gain for a single member of the cartel. Assume the price is fixed at P_0; this particular cartel member sells Q_0, but output may vary among members.

The firm knows that if it reduces price slightly, say, to P_1, and other cartel members do not detect the reduced price, it can increase its own sales tremendously. In this case, the firm believes that an unmatched price reduction to P_1 would increase sales to Q_2, resulting in a substantial increase in profit. Thus the firm believes that the segment of its demand for an *undetected* price reduction is *Ad*.

This demand segment is quite elastic, because the firm knows that an unmatched price reduction would allow it to gain sales from the other, obedient members of the cartel. This situation is most likely when the number of members in the cartel is large and the product is differentiated.

But the price reduction is unlikely to go unmatched for very long. In the first place, even in a cartel with a large number of firms, other members are likely to notice their decreases in sales and find out that a rival has lowered price. A reasonable reaction would be to match the lower price. This would protect their market share and punish the cheater by reducing its sales. In most cartels that is the only means of enforcement. In the second place, if this firm has the incentive to reduce price and increase sales, so do all the other firms in the cartel. And this incentive is reinforced because every firm knows that every other firm has the same incentive. So there is the strong temptation to be the first to reduce price and gain at least a temporary increase in sales and profits before the others begin to cheat.

If rivals match the price cut or if they all cheat on the agreement, the firm's demand is the inelastic segment *AD.* Customers would have no reason to change sellers if they all sell at the lower price, P_1. Thus the firm's gain in sales is small; output increases from Q_0 to Q_1 rather than to Q_2. This increase is due mainly to increased total market sales because of the lower price charged by everyone in the cartel.

The increase in sales from Q_1 to Q_2 represents sales that would have been attracted away from rivals. A huge increase in the output of one firm while others are losing sales at the cartel price is, however, a strong signal of cheating. Rivals will suspect that someone has lowered the price. So a potentially large increase in sales from an undetected price cut is the incentive for cheating, but, at the same time, it is the signal to others that someone is cheating.

For these reasons, even strong cartels are likely to break up, particularly during times when the economy is weak. All have the incentive to cheat on the agreement, and firms frequently do.

Tacit Collusion

tacit collusion
Cooperation among firms that does not involve an explicit agreement.

A far less extreme form of cooperation among oligopoly firms is **tacit collusion**—agreement without explicit communication. We have mentioned this type of cooperation, within the context of the price and advertising dilemma, as a way for firms to move from a less profitable cell to one that is more profitable. There are many other types of tacit collusion that firms have tried.

For instance, the producers in a market may restrict their sales to specific geographical regions or countries without meeting and explicitly designating marketing areas on a map. One firm's market area is understood from the ongoing relations it has had with its rivals. As opposed to the formation of a cartel in an attempt to monopolize a market, tacit collusion is not per se (categorically) illegal. However, specific evidence of agreement would quickly tip the legal balance against accused participants.

Examples consistent with tacit collusion are evident among manufacturers of consumer durables. For instance, oligopolists will often act together (cooperatively) by changing their models annually at about the same time. Washing machines, refrigerators, cooking ranges, and lawn mowers have annual model changes that are announced by manufacturers at nearly the same time. Without any known agreement, there is a surprising amount of uniformity in such behavior. The same holds true for fashions, that is, when spring and fall designs are announced. Why do makers of soft drinks and beer all use the same-size cans and bottles (or makers of breakfast cereal package their products in similar-size boxes)? Certainly, all consumers do not have a preference for the 12-ounce size.

But, as far as anyone knows, cereal makers and bottlers have no explicit agreement that only certain container sizes are allowable.

Probably the strongest evidence consistent with tacit collusion is found in the prices oligopolists charge. Particularly in the service sector of the economy, there is surprising price uniformity, even though there is a wide variance in the quality of services. For instance, lawyers and real estate agents by and large charge the same prices for their services even though the quality of services varies from lawyer to lawyer and broker to broker. Explicit collusion is illegal in these industries and presumably does not take place, but a substantial amount of price uniformity exists.

Tacit collusion arises because of the consequences of noncooperation. Oligopolies usually know that they are caught in a prisoner's dilemma, even though they may not be familiar with the name. One prominent executive, caught in an advertising war, was quoted, "This is like an arms race between countries. Once you get in it, it is almost impossible to get out." Increased advertising, a lower price, or a new style may increase profit in the short run but may reduce profit in the long run when rivals have adapted. Therefore, whether or not a rival makes a change depends on the relative expected costs and benefits of making the change.

As we have noted, however, the situation is not necessarily hopeless. In many cases patterns of behavior are established among rivals. Oligopolists do, at times, cooperate because, given the expected reaction of rivals to one firm's attempt to raise profits, long-run profits are likely to be maximized by stable behavior. Oligopolists know this, but as we mentioned previously, sometimes tacit cooperation requires that one firm lead the others into a pattern of more stable behavior.

Price Leadership

price leadership
Practice in which one firm in an oligopoly market sets a price that the other firms match.

Another cooperative solution to the oligopoly problem is **price leadership.** This solution does not require open collusion, but the firms in the market must tacitly agree to the solution. Price leadership has been quite common in certain industries. It was characteristic of the steel industry some time ago. At times it has characterized the tire, oil, cigarette, and banking industries.

Any firm in an oligopoly market can be the price leader. While it is frequently the dominant firm in the market, it may be simply the firm with a reputation for good judgment. There could exist a situation in which the most efficient—the least-cost—firm is the price leader, even though this firm is not the largest. Or, in terms of the previous discussion, it could be the boldest or the one with a reputation of being trustworthy. In any case, the price leader sets a price that will maximize industry profits, and all firms in the industry compete for sales through advertising and other types of marketing. The price remains constant until the price leader changes the price or one or more other firms break away.

Possibly the simplest form of price leadership is *barometric* price leadership. In this case the price leader is a firm with a reputation for good decision making.

(In reality, most price leaders have been one of the larger firms.) The price leader acts as a barometer for prevailing market conditions and sets the price so as to maximize profits under these conditions. For example, if consumers' incomes increase (and the commodity in question is normal), the price leader would note an increase in demand and would respond by raising price. If all of the other firms in the industry follow with price increases, the result will be that the industry moves to a new position of equilibrium with a minimum of interfirm competition. It is important to note that, in this case, the price leader has no power to coerce the other firms into following its lead. Instead, the rival firms will follow this lead only as long as they believe that the price leader's behavior accurately and promptly reflects changes in market conditions.

A much more structured form of price leadership is *dominant-firm* price leadership. In this case, there is one firm in the oligopoly market that has the capability of becoming a monopoly. Hence the market is composed of one dominant firm and numerous small ones.

The dominant firm could possibly eliminate all its rivals by a price war. But in addition to being costly, this would establish the firm as a monopoly, with its attendant legal problems. Possibly a more desirable course of action for the dominant firm is to become the price leader and set the market price so as to maximize its own profit, at the same time letting the small firms sell all they wish at that price. Note that, given the size of the dominant firm, in this type of price leadership the price leader—the dominant firm—does have the ability to enforce the price it sets. It does not have to rely on its reputation or the trust of the smaller firms. The small firms, recognizing their position, will behave as do perfectly competitive firms. That is, they will regard their demand curve as a horizontal line at the price set by the dominant firm and sell that amount for which marginal cost equals price. Notice, however, that this does not necessarily entail the long-run, zero-profit solution for the smaller firms, because the dominant firm may set price above the (minimum) average cost of some firms.

There are many variations of dominant-firm price leadership. One may allow for the existence of two or more dominant firms, for product differentiation, for geographically separated sellers, for transportation costs, and so on. In all cases, however, the dominant firm is allowed to set price, since it controls such a large share of the market.

This completes our discussion of cooperative oligopoly behavior, although it by no means exhausts the topic. Methods of cooperation are diverse. Different types of cooperative behavior arise because of differences in products and markets, in the history of firms and industry, and in the personalities of managers.

Two fundamental themes are an integral part of all types of oligopoly cooperation. First, firms in an oligopoly market are strongly motivated to cooperate because of the problem of uncertainty about the reactions of rivals if firms do not cooperate. Competition of any type, as you have seen, lowers firms' profits. Second, once firms cooperate, there is a strong temptation for them to break the agreement. The cheating motive causes any type of agreement to become extremely fragile and likely to break down.

ILLUSTRATION 15.4

A Diamond (cartel) Is (not necessarily) Forever

For many years, the huge South African diamond colossus, De Beers Consolidated Mines Ltd., held a virtual monopoly of world diamond sales. At first its South African mines were practically the sole source of uncut diamonds. Then, as some other parts of the world began mining diamonds, De Beers responded by buying these "outside" diamonds and selling them through its Central Selling Organization (CSO), thereby limiting sales and controlling the price of diamonds. The company put strong pressure on dealers not to buy from other sources. This policy enabled De Beers to maintain its monopoly for several years. However, in September 1992, *Business Week* reported that De Beers was having trouble enforcing its agreements.* Its problems were primarily with Russia, the world's second-largest producer, but also, to a lesser extent, with producers from other countries.

At that time, top executives from De Beers were meeting with officials in Russia. At ceremonies marking the opening of the company's first Moscow office the company's deputy chairman toasted "the momentous event." *Business Week* pointed out, "Indeed it is. De Beers' efforts to strengthen its ties with the Russians came at a critical juncture. As the company faces its most dire business climate in a decade, its hammerlock on output and prices is loosening." Some suppliers were bypassing CSO and selling directly to dealers. De Beers executives were planning to spend $350 million during the year to buy up rogue supplies from Angola. "Beyond that, Russia's post-coup restructuring and its hunger for hard currency could lead to a breakup of its diamond industry, leaving the world awash in lustrous stones." Russian producers were already dumping some diamonds in violation of a 1990 agreement.

The new deal gave Russia $5 billion over five years in return for giving CSO exclusive rights to 95 percent of its uncut diamonds for export. But a London analyst believed at the time that Russia could be dumping up to 25 percent of its annual production. The deputy chairman of De Beers believed, however, that the Russians recognized that their own interests would be best served by maintaining the "well-being and stability of the industry" by relying on CSO's marketing clout. In other words, he thought the agreement would hold.

It didn't. On August 14, 1996, an article on De Beers in *The Wall Street Journal* began with these words: "Desperate for cash, Russia is flooding foreign markets with its diamonds, ignoring an informal agreement with the De Beers diamond-marketing cartel."† A De Beers executive admitted there "had been substantial leakages," and he was flying to Moscow for unscheduled talks. Russian sales had driven down diamond prices by around 3 percent over the previous few weeks. Dealers were saying that even with De Beers' huge share of the market, "without Russia . . . De Beers' elaborate hold over the market could crumble." But Russia appeared more interested in immediate revenue to shore up its treasury than in the long-term deal.

According to the managing director of an association of diamond dealers in Antwerp, "Nothing has changed, large quantities of Russian diamonds are still being sold independently. Russia needs the cash." Furthermore, a large Australian producer of low-quality diamonds had begun marketing diamonds on its own, and prices of these less expensive diamonds had fallen 10 to 20 percent. De Beers still sounded optimistic. The managing director of its Moscow office said, "Once a formal agreement is signed, we're hopeful of reducing the leakages." It should be noted that De Beers was still doing rather well. The *WSJ* mentioned that the company's earnings had risen 23 percent in the previous six months.

As this illustration emphasizes, it is very difficult to maintain cartel agreements. Cheating is almost always a problem. Also, it is even harder to maintain an agreement, formal or otherwise, when one of the parties to the agreement comes into bad times and desperately needs revenue in the short term. Such parties, whether countries or firms, are often willing to sacrifice long-term benefits for short-term gains.

*"Can De Beers Hold onto Its Hammerlock?" *Business Week*, Sept. 21, 1992.

†"Russia Bypasses Diamond Pact with De Beers," *The Wall Street Journal*, Aug. 14, 1996.

15.7 SUMMARY

This chapter has covered a huge amount of territory in a small amount of space. Managerial decision making in oligopoly markets is the most complex of all decision-making situations. We have treated oligopoly rather briefly, but not because economists do not have a great deal to say about it. They do, and they have said a great deal, much more than is discussed in this chapter. They just have not developed a definitive general theory of oligopoly. Mutual interdependence makes such a theory elusive at best and perhaps unattainable at worst.

We have emphasized that the primary feature differentiating oligopoly from the other market structures is that the *firms recognize their mutual interdependence.* In contrast to the other market structures, it is not sufficient for a firm in an oligopoly market to make its output and pricing decisions on the basis of its own demand and cost conditions. In addition, an oligopolist must consider the potential reactions of its rivals. In this chapter we discussed some possible ways in which the oligopoly firms could resolve this difficulty. However, as you have seen, the determination of the profit-maximizing levels of output and price for a specific firm becomes extremely difficult. Furthermore, oligopolistic firms frequently compete with one another on a non-price basis. Typically, the best solution for oligopolists is to collude with each other, but this is frequently impossible, illegal, or both.

The upshot of all this is that we cannot provide you with a simple profit-maximizing rule of the type described in Chapters 12 and 14. Nonetheless, we hope we have given you a feel for the problem of interdependence in managerial decision making. Our purpose was to provide a framework of analysis of how oligopolists have tried to cope with the problem and why they have succeeded or why they have failed. As discussed in Illustration 15.2, game theory, although it is a rather old concept, seems to hold some promise as a useful guide for decision making under interdependence. However, even several courses in game theory cannot teach you how to make such decisions; this type of decision making is best learned from experience. But a good economics foundation will make it easier for you to learn from experience.

TECHNICAL PROBLEMS

1. The following graph shows segments of Southwest Airlines' demand for round-trip tickets in the Houston-Atlanta city-pair market. Continental Airlines, the only other airline in this specific market, and Southwest Airlines both charge $200 per round-trip ticket.

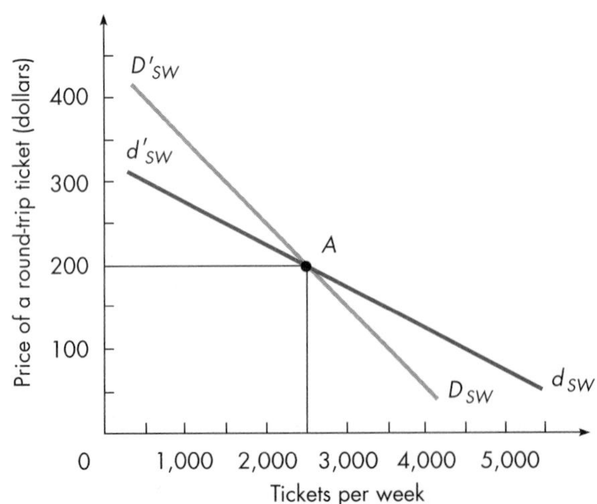

a. Managers at Southwest Airlines believe reducing ticket price to $100 when Continental Airlines also lowers its price to $100 will result in sales of ________ tickets per month. If Continental keeps its price at $200 when Southwest lowers its price to $100, Southwest can expect to sell ________ tickets per month.
b. If Southwest raises its price to $300 and Continental keeps its price constant at $200, Southwest will sell ________ tickets per month. If both airlines raise the price to $300, managers at Southwest Airlines can expect to sell ________ tickets per month.
c. Suppose Southwest lowers its price to $100, but Continental lowers its price only to $150. Where would Southwest's demand lie?
d. Which demand is more elastic, $D_{SW}D'_{SW}$ or $d_{SW}d'_{SW}$? Why?

2. The following graph shows what an oligopoly believes its demand curve looks like:

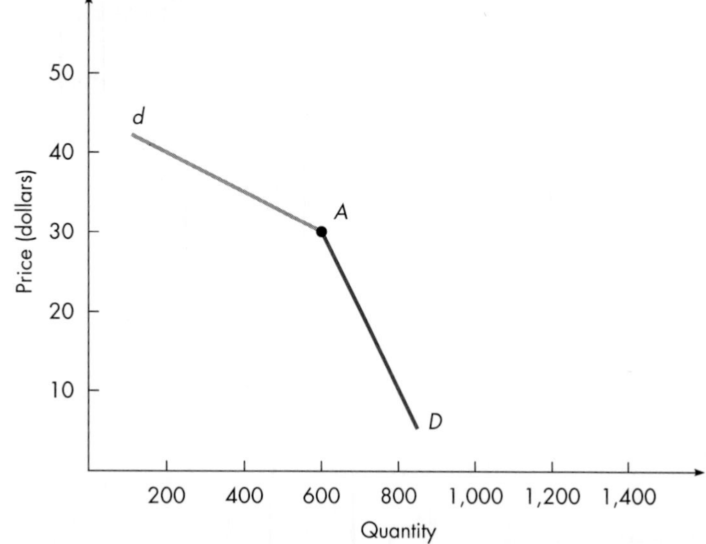

a. Suppose the firm is charging a price of $30 and selling 600 units of output? What is the arc demand elasticity for a $10 price increase?
b. Starting at the same original price and output, calculate the arc demand elasticity for a $10 price decrease.
c. What must be the firm's implicit assumptions about these two segments of demand?
d. Why might this firm be reluctant to change its price?
e. Why would the firm have set a price of $30 in the first place?

3. Are oligopolists that produce a differentiated product more or less likely to use nonprice competition than those that produce a homogeneous product? Explain.
4. On a 1-mile stretch of beach, sunbathers, swimmers, waders, etc., typically are spaced rather evenly. A mobile soft-drink stand is located near one end of the beach. Another mobile soft-drink stand comes onto the beach.
a. Where will the new stand probably locate? Why?

b. If so, where will the old stand move? Why?
c. After a period of time, where would you predict that the two stands will end up? What will be the share of business for the two stands?
d. If a third joins the other two, where will the three be located?

5. Two firms, A and B, do not practice price competition but do compete through product quality. Each can choose to produce a low-quality product or a high-quality product. Higher quality helps sales but costs more to produce. The following table shows the profit each firm would earn in each of the four possible high- or low-quality combinations:

		A: *Low quality*	A: *High quality*
B	*Low quality*	$\pi_A = \$200$ $\pi_B = \$200$	$\pi_A = \$400$ $\pi_B = \$0$
	High quality	$\pi_A = \$0$ $\pi_B = \$400$	$\pi_A = \$100$ $\pi_B = \$100$

a. For firm A is there a dominant strategy? If so, what is it? Why?
b. Answer the same question for firm B.
c. What will the two firms probably end up doing?

6. Two firms, C and D, compete by price. Each can choose either a low price or a high price. The following table shows the profit each would earn from each of the four possible high- or low-price combinations:

		C: *Low price*	C: *High price*
D	*Low price*	$\pi_C = \$500$ $\pi_D = \$500$	$\pi_C = \$300$ $\pi_D = \$1{,}200$
	High price	$\pi_C = \$1{,}200$ $\pi_D = \$300$	$\pi_C = \$800$ $\pi_D = \$800$

a. For firm C is there a dominant strategy? If so, what is it? Why?
b. Answer the same question for firm D.
c. What will the two firms probably end up doing?

7. This is a different type of pricing dilemma. The choices for the firms are not symmetric. There are two firms in the market, one large, firm L, and one small, firm S. The firms can choose a high price or a low price. The profits from each of the four possible combinations of choices are given in the following table:

		L: *Low price*	L: *High price*
S	*Low price*	$\pi_L = \$500$ $\pi_S = \$200$	$\pi_L = \$600$ $\pi_S = \$600$
	High price	$\pi_L = \$1{,}500$ $\pi_S = \$0$	$\pi_L = \$1{,}000$ $\pi_S = \$400$

a. Is there a dominant strategy for the small firm? If so, what is it? Why?
b. Is there a dominant strategy for the large firm? If so, why, or if not, why not?
c. If the large firm knows the profit of the small firm in each situation, what is the large firm likely to do? Why?
d. If the large firm follows a minimax strategy, what is it likely to do? Why?
e. In both *c* and *d* where will both firms end up? Why? Is this a Nash equilibrium? Why or why not?

8. The following graph shows the price reaction functions for two firms, A and B. A's reaction function shows the most profitable price for A to charge, on the vertical axis, for each of a range of prices that B charges, on the horizontal axis. B's reaction function shows the most profitable price for B, given A's price.

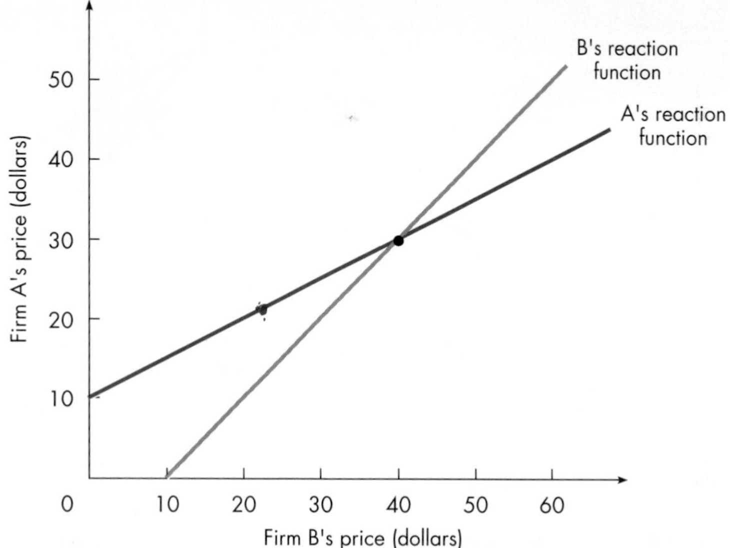

a. If A sets a price of $20, what will B do?
b. Then what will A do?
c. What price will the two firms likely end up charging? Is this a Nash equilibrium? Why or why not?

9. Assume several firms in an oligopoly market are charging a price lower than a price that would be more profitable. In each of the following situations explain why one condition would be more likely to lead to a tacit cooperative price agreement than the other:
a. Firms can change price fairly often as opposed to setting a once-and-for-all price.
b. There are 2 firms in the market rather than 10.
c. The products are very similar rather than differentiated.
d. There is 1 large firm in the market and 9 small firms, rather than 10 small- to medium-size firms.

10. The cost curves, demand, and marginal revenue for an established firm in the market are shown in Panel B below. The long-run average cost curve for a potential entrant is shown in Panel A.

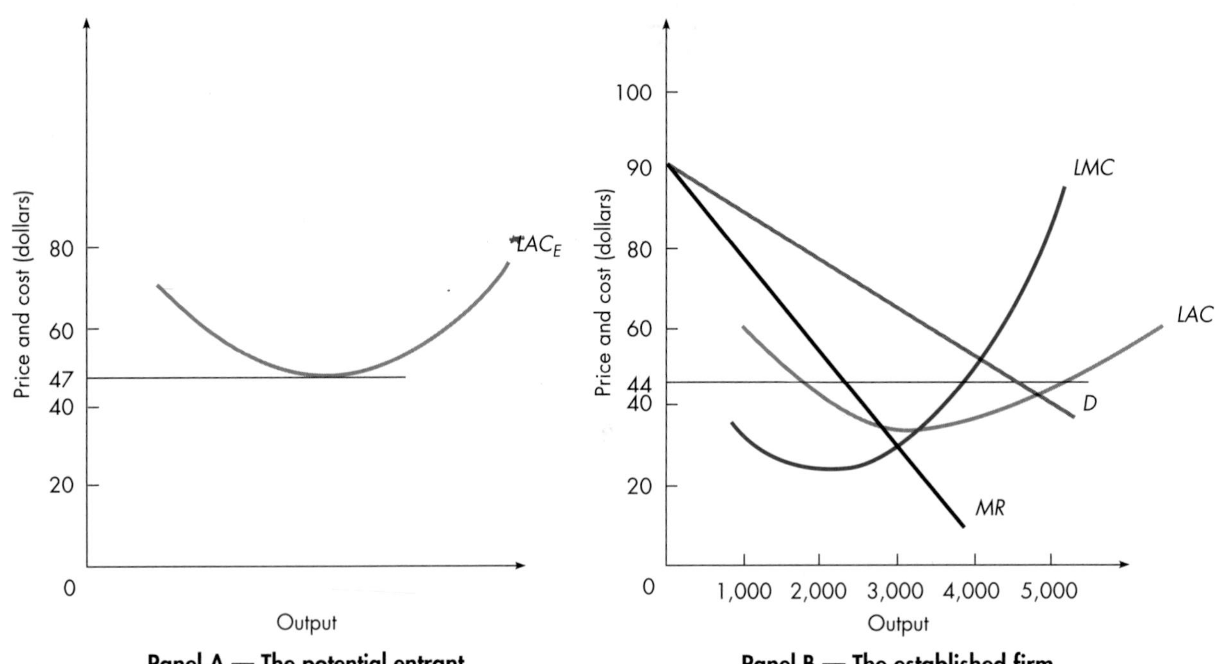

a. What are the profit-maximizing output and price if the established firm is not worried about entry? What is the maximum profit?
b. Below what price could the established firm prevent entry? Why?
c. If the established firm sets a price of $44, how much profit will it make? Will the new firm enter the market? Why or why not?
d. Would this firm's price prevent entry or not? What are conditions under which it would or would not?

11. A firm can produce two goods, X and Y, separately at a constant coverage cost of $C(X) = C(Y) = \$40$. If it produces the two goods together, the average cost of the pair of goods is $C(X, Y) = \$70$. This firm could set price below $________, discouraging the entry of a firm that makes only one of the goods, and still make a profit. Explain.

12. In the graph below, MC_1 and MC_2 are the marginal cost curves for two firms that have formed a cartel. D and MR represent market demand and market revenue, respectively, for the cartel, and MC_C is the cartel's marginal cost curve.

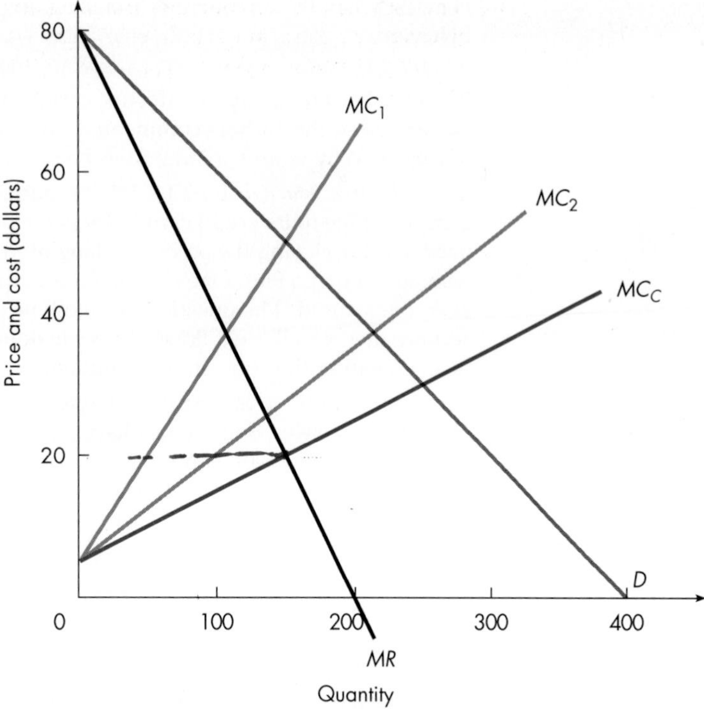

a. What is the profit-maximizing level of cartel output? How should it be allocated between the two firms? What price should the cartel set?
b. Suppose the firms are each producing and selling 75 units of output. What is marginal cost for each firm? Is this optimal? Why or why not? If not, what should the firms do instead?
c. Under what conditions might this cartel break up?

13. What is tacit collusion? How would the behavior of the firms differ from that of members of a cartel? Why would tacit collusion exist?

APPLIED PROBLEMS

1. In April 1997, McDonald's Corp. reduced the price of its Big Mac 75 percent, to 55 cents, if customers also purchased french fries and a soft drink. *The Wall Street Journal* reported that the company was hoping the novel promotion would revive its U.S. sales growth. It didn't. Within two weeks sales had fallen. Using your knowledge of game theory, what do you think disrupted McDonald's plans?
2. In January 1996, the well-known nationally syndicated columnist David Broder reported the findings of two academic political scientists. These scholars found that voters are quite turned off by "negative campaigns" of politicians. Many people went as far as not voting because of this. Nevertheless, the political scientists noted it is futile to urge candidates to stay positive. The damage from staying positive is

heaviest when the opponent is attacking. Explain the dilemma in terms of strategic behavior.

3. A *Wall Street Journal* article (February 10, 1995) on commodity cartels stated that it is very hard to set up an effective cartel and even harder to keep it going. Nevertheless, the authors commented, commodities are "particularly vulnerable" to cartels. Why would commodities be particularly vulnerable to cartels?
4. *The Wall Street Journal* (June 11, 1997) reported that Advanta Corp. was considering charging a fee to its credit card holders for periods during which the card is not used and for closing the account. Many of the larger credit card companies also wanted to charge fees. One consultant was quoted: "Everyone is considering it but everyone's afraid. The question is, who'll be daring and be second? If there's a second, then you'll see a flood of people doing it." Within the context of game theory, analyze the consultant's comments.
5. An applied problem in Chapter 14 asked this question. Now use the prisoner's dilemma to answer. Some states have had laws restricting the sale of most goods on Sunday. Consumers, by and large, oppose such laws because they find Sunday afternoon a convenient time to shop. Paradoxically, retail trade associations frequently support the laws. Discuss the reasons for merchants' supporting these laws.
6. MegaCorp is a large manufacturer of household robots used as mechanical servants for wealthy families. MegaCorp has considerable market power—it invented the household robot—but is facing some potential competition from some new firms. MegaCorp is considering using entry limit pricing, increasing its capacity, or simply maximizing profits until the new firms enter.
   a. What factors should the firm consider when making its plans? In your answer, discuss the length of the time horizon, the time new firms would require to enter the market, any possible cost advantage MegaCorp may have, the financial backing the new firms might have, brand loyalty of consumers, and any other factors you think may be relevant.
   b. Suppose MegaCorp decides it doesn't have a sufficient cost advantage to practice entry limit pricing, so it decides on a strategy of building excess capacity. Under what conditions might some new firms enter the market? What do you think may happen under this circumstance?
7. The Sweetbreath Company produces two rather successful mouthwashes: one is strong and has a medicinal taste, and the other is more gentle and has a sweet taste. Sweetbreath is thinking about introducing an intermediate brand of mouthwash that tastes like ice cream. Discuss the pros and cons for Sweetbreath's introducing a new product.
8. Suppose you are attempting to establish a price-fixing cartel in an industry.
   a. Would you prefer many or few firms? Why?
   b. How could you prevent cheating (price cutting) by cartel members? Why would members have an incentive to cheat?
   c. Would you keep substantial or very few records? What are the advantages and disadvantages of each approach?
   d. How could you prevent entry into the industry?
   e. How could government help you prevent entry and even cheating?
9. Many economists argue that more research, development, and innovation occur in the oligopolistic market structure than in any other. Why might this conclusion be true?

10. In light of the discussion about product quality as a form of nonprice competition, can you explain the common complaint that TV programs are all alike?

MATHEMATICAL APPENDIX Reaction Functions and Cartel Profit Maximization

A Quantity Reaction Function

The first model of oligopoly behavior was developed by Augustin Cournot in 1836. In this model there are two firms producing a homogeneous product. For simplicity, assume that the product can be produced at zero cost, so marginal cost is also zero. The demand for the product, Q, is linear with a horizontal (quantity) intercept of a and a vertical (price) intercept of b. Thus demand is

(1) $$Q = a - \frac{a}{b}P$$

The inverse demand is

(2) $$P = b - \frac{b}{a}Q$$

If a monopoly produces and sells this product, the firm would maximize the following profit function:

(3) $$PQ = \left(b - \frac{b}{a}Q\right)Q$$

Then, take the derivative and set it equal to zero:

$$\frac{d\pi}{dQ} = b - 2\frac{b}{a}Q = 0$$

Now solve for the level of output that maximizes profit:

$$Q^* = \frac{1}{2}a$$

To find the price that maximizes profit, substitute Q^* into inverse demand function (2):

$$P^* = b - \frac{b}{a}\left(\frac{a}{2}\right) = \frac{1}{2}b$$

Thus the monopoly would produce an output of half the horizontal demand intercept and set a price of half the price intercept. Notice that if the product is produced by a perfectly competitive industry, $P^* = MC = 0$ and $Q^* = a$.

Next let two firms produce the product. Each firm chooses its own output, assuming the output of the other firm is fixed. (This is often referred to as the *Cournot assumption.*) The market price is determined by the output of both firms:

$$P = b - \frac{b}{a}(Q) = b - \frac{b}{a}(Q_1 + Q_2)$$

where Q_1 and Q_2 are the outputs of firms 1 and 2, respectively. The profit functions for the firms are

$$\pi_1 = PQ_1 = \left[b - \frac{b}{a}(Q_1 + Q_2)\right]Q_1$$

and

$$\pi_2 = PQ_2 = \left[b - \frac{b}{a}(Q_1 + Q_2)\right]Q_2$$

Profit maximization for firm 1 requires

(4a) $$\frac{\partial \pi_1}{\partial Q_1} = b - 2\frac{b}{a}Q_1 - \frac{b}{a}Q_2 = 0$$

and for firm 2,

(4b) $$\frac{\partial \pi_2}{\partial Q_2} = b - 2\frac{b}{a}Q_2 - \frac{b}{a}Q_1 = 0$$

Reaction functions, showing the optimal output for the firm at each level of output of the other firm, are obtained from each firm's first-order conditions for profit maximization. Solve equations (4a) and (4b) for the reaction functions

$$Q_1 = \frac{1}{2}(a - Q_2)$$

$$Q_2 = \frac{1}{2}(a - Q_1)$$

The intersection of the reaction functions is found by substituting each reaction function into the other reaction function to obtain:

$$Q_1^* = \frac{1}{3}a \quad \text{and} \quad Q_2^* = \frac{1}{3}a$$

From the inverse demand function, the price is

$$P^* = b - \frac{b}{a}(Q_1^* + Q_2^*) = b - \frac{b}{a}\left(\frac{2}{3}a\right) = \frac{1}{3}b$$

As you can see, the price is lower than the monopoly price, $(1/3)b$ compared with $(1/2)b$, and the total output is higher, $(2/3)a$ compared with $(1/2)a$. But the price is higher in this situation than the price under competition, $(1/3)b$ compared with zero, and output is lower, $(2/3)a$ compared with a.

A Price Reaction Function

Assume there are two products, A and B, that are fairly close substitutes for one another. As before, the products are produced at zero cost. The linear demand functions for the two products are

(5a) $$Q_A = a - bP_A + cP_B$$

and

(5b) $$Q_B = d - eP_B + fP_A$$

where all parameters are positive.

First, for comparison, assume that a monopoly produces both products, so the profit function is

$$\pi = P_A(a - bP_A + cP_B) + P_B(d - eP_B + fP_A)$$

Monopoly profit maximization requires that both of the following conditions be simultaneously met:

(6a) $$\frac{\partial \pi}{\partial P_A} = a - 2bP_A + (c + f)P_B = 0$$

(6b) $$\frac{\partial \pi}{\partial P_B} = d - 2eP_B + (c + f)P_A = 0$$

Solving equations (6a) and (6b) by substitution or by Cramer's rule gives the following profit-maximizing prices:

(7a) $$P_A^* = \frac{2ae + d(c + f)}{4be - (c + f)^2}$$

(7b) $$P_B^* = \frac{2bd + a(c + f)}{4be - (c + f)^2}$$

Now assume that parameter values for the linear demand relations are $a = 40$, $b = 2$, $c = 0.4$, $d = 30$, $e = 1.5$, and $f = 0.5$, so the demand functions are

(8a) $$Q_A = 40 - 2P_A + 0.4P_B$$

(8b) $$Q_B = 30 - 1.5P_B + 0.5P_A$$

Substituting these parameter values into the above solutions for P_A and P_B [expressions (7a) and (7b), respectively] yields the following profit-maximizing prices:

$$P_A^* = \$13.14 \qquad \text{and} \qquad P_B^* = \$13.94$$

Then using these prices in demand functions (8a) and (8b) yields the profit-maximizing outputs for A and B:

$$Q_A^* = 19.30 \qquad \text{and} \qquad Q_B^* = 15.67$$

The firm's profit can be calculated as

$$\pi^* = P_A^*Q_A^* + P_B^*Q_B^* = (\$13.14)(19.3) + (\$13.94)(15.67)$$
$$= \$472.04$$

We now use these same parameter values to compare this monopoly solution to that of a two-firm oligopoly, or duopoly, that competes with price under the same demand and cost conditions. The profit functions for the two *separate* firms, A and B, are now

(9a) $$\pi_A = P_A(a - bP_A + cP_B)$$

(9b) $$\pi_B = P_B(d - eP_B + fP_A)$$

Each firm's first-order condition for profit maximization is

(10a) $$\frac{\partial \pi_A}{\partial P_A} = a - 2bP_A + cP_B = 0$$

(10b) $$\frac{\partial \pi_B}{\partial P_B} = d - 2eP_B + fP_A = 0$$

Solve equation (10a) for A's reaction function:

(11a) $$P_A = \frac{a}{2b} + \frac{c}{2b}P_B$$

and solve equation (10b) for B's reaction function:

(11b) $$P_B = \frac{d}{2e} + \frac{f}{2e}P_A$$

Substituting the values of the parameters in equations (8a) and (8b) into equations (11a) and (11b), results in the following equations for reaction functions:

$$P_A = \frac{40}{2 \cdot 2} + \frac{0.4}{2 \cdot 2}P_B = 10 + 0.1P_B$$

$$P_B = \frac{30}{2 \cdot 1.5} + \frac{0.5}{2 \cdot 1.5}P_A = 10 + 0.167P_A$$

These reaction functions are shown in the following graph, with P_A plotted on the vertical axis and P_B on the horizontal:

FIGURE 15A.1

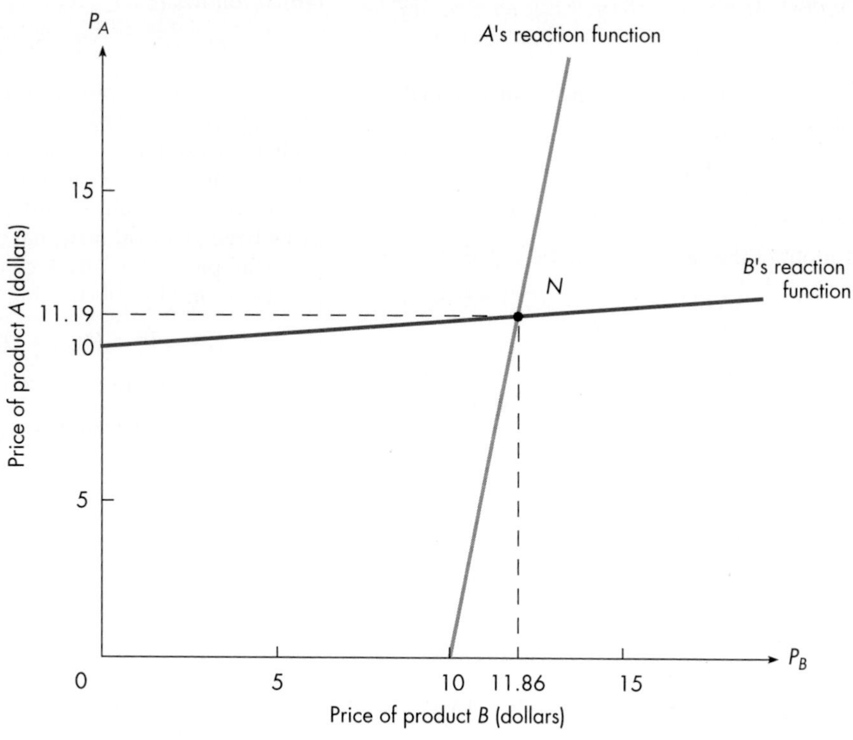

The point N, where the two reaction functions cross, is the Nash equilibrium. Each firm is doing the best it can, given what the other is doing. To obtain the Nash equilibrium, solve the two reaction functions simultaneously by substitution or by Cramer's rule to get

$$P_A^* = \$11.19 \qquad \text{and} \qquad P_B^* = \$11.86$$

Solve for Q_A^* and Q_B^* by substituting these prices into the demand functions:

$$Q_A^* = 40 - 2(\$11.19) + 0.4(\$11.86) = 22.36$$

$$Q_B^* = 30 - 1.5(\$11.86) + 0.5(\$11.19) = 17.80$$

Finally, profits for the two firms are

$$\pi_A^* = P_A^* Q_A^* = (\$11.19)(22.36) = \$250.21$$

$$\pi_B^* = P_B^* Q_B^* = (\$11.86)(17.80) = \$211.10$$

Total profit is

$$\pi_A^* + \pi_B^* = \$250.21 + \$211.10 = \$461.31$$

Comparing the duopoly situation with that in which a monopoly produces and sells the products, you can see that, under monopoly, prices are higher, sales are lower, and total profit is higher. A solution would be for the two firms to merge.

Profit Maximization for an Ideal Cartel

Firms A and B, producing a homogeneous good, form a cartel. Managers of the cartel wish to maximize the total profit of the cartel—the profit of firm A plus the profit of firm B. The managers must determine the price to charge, the total output for the cartel to produce, and how to divide total cartel output between the two firms.

Letting Q_A and Q_B denote the outputs of firms A and B, respectively, total cartel output can be expressed as $Q = Q_A + Q_B$, and the inverse market demand for the cartel's product is

(1) $$P = P(Q_A + Q_B) = P(Q)$$

Each firm's costs, which are not necessarily equal, are expressed as

(2a) $$C_A = C_A(Q_A)$$

(2b) $$C_B = C_B(Q_B)$$

The total profit of the cartel, π_C, can be expressed as

(3) $$\pi_C = P(Q_A + Q_B)(Q_A + Q_B) - C_A(Q_A) - C_B(Q_B) = P(Q)Q - C_A(Q_A) - C_B(Q_B)$$

Maximizing the cartel profit function (3) with respect to the two firms' outputs, Q_A and Q_B, results in the following first-order conditions:

(4a) $$\frac{\partial \pi_C}{\partial Q_A} = \frac{dP}{dQ}Q + P - \frac{dC_A}{dQ_A} = MR_C - MC_A = 0$$

(4b) $$\frac{\partial \pi_C}{\partial Q_B} = \frac{dP}{dQ}Q + P - \frac{dC_B}{dQ_B} = MR_C - MC_B = 0$$

From the profit-maximizing conditions (4a) and (4b), it follows that Q_A and Q_B must be chosen such that

(5) $$MR_C(Q_A^* + Q_B^*) = MC_A(Q_A^*) = MC_B(Q_B^*)$$

Notice that the optimal total cartel output, $Q_C^* = Q_A^* + Q_B^*$, must be divided between the two firms so that each firm produces at the same marginal cost, which must equal the cartel's marginal revenue, MR_C. The two firms do not equally share cartel output unless both firms have identical marginal cost functions.

The price the cartel charges to maximize cartel profit is found by substituting Q_C^* into equation (1):

(6) $$P^* = P(Q_A^* + Q_B^*) = P(Q_C^*)$$

Thus, the maximum cartel profit is

(7) $$\pi^* = P(Q_C^*)Q_C^* - C_A(Q_A^*) - C_B(Q_B^*)$$

MATHEMATICAL EXERCISES

1. Assume there are two goods, A and B; the demands for these goods are, respectively,

$$Q_A = 100 - 4P_A + 1.5P_B$$
$$Q_B = 120 - 2P_B + 0.5P_A$$

   Production cost is zero.

   a. Assume both goods are produced by a single firm. Derive the profit-maximizing prices and quantities of the two goods. What is total profit (i.e., total revenue)?
   b. Assume each good is produced by a separate firm.
      i. Derive the price reaction function for each firm.
      ii. What is the Nash equilibrium price and output for each firm?
      iii. What is total profit (revenue) for each?
      iv. Compare these results with those for production by a single firm.

2. Assume that two firms (A and B), producing a homogeneous good Q, form a cartel. The linear demand for the good is

$$P = 200 - 2(Q_A + Q_B)$$

   where Q_A and Q_B are the output levels of the two firms and $(Q_A + Q_B) = Q_C$. The cost functions of the two firms are

$$C_A = 2Q_A^2 \quad \text{and} \quad C_B = 3Q_B^2$$

   a. To maximize cartel profit, how much should each firm produce?
   b. What will be the profit-maximizing price?
   c. Calculate the maximum cartel profit.

CHAPTER 16

Profit Maximization for Firms with Market Power: Implementation of the Theory

Managers of firms that have some control over the price they charge should know the fundamentals of the theory of profit maximization by firms with market power. They should also know how to use empirical estimates of the demand for the firm's product and the cost equations for determining the price and level of output that maximize the firm's profit. This chapter describes how to use empirical analysis to find that optimal price and output.

In the examples used to demonstrate the process of implementing the profit-maximizing decision, we assume that a manager has accurate information about, and precise estimates of, all the relevant variables and equations. For most managers, such exact estimates would seldom be available at any reasonable cost. However, the assumption of complete and accurate information allows us to show how the profit-maximizing results are obtained under the best of circumstances. This process can then be adapted to situations in which less accurate information is available.

We devote most of this chapter to examining the price and output decision for a monopoly. However, as we stressed in Chapter 14, the decision-making process for a monopoly is applicable to any firm with market power, with perhaps a few modifications for changes in the form of the demand and marginal revenue functions to account for differences in the market structure. We will also set forth an alternative pricing rule that is sometimes used by managers who do not have good information about the demand for their product.

16.1 A GUIDE TO IMPLEMENTING THE PROFIT-MAXIMIZING PRICE AND OUTPUT DECISION

Recall from Chapter 14 that the profit-maximizing or loss-minimizing output for a monopoly, or for any firm with market power, is the output level at which marginal revenue equals marginal cost. Once the optimal level of output is determined, the manager finds the optimal price from the demand curve. The firm should produce in the short run if price is greater than average variable cost. The situation in which a monopoly produces in the short run and makes an economic profit is reviewed in Figure 16.1. The profit-maximizing level of output, Q^*, occurs at point A, where $MR = MC$. The profit-maximizing price, P^*, is found by locating the point on demand associated with Q^* units of output—point B in Figure 16.1. Since P^* exceeds average variable cost, the monopolist should produce rather than shut down. The maximum value of economic profit is calculated by multiplying the profit per unit, $P^* - ATC$, times the profit-maximizing level of output: $\pi^* = (P^* - ATC) \times Q^*$. The shaded area shown in the figure represents the maximum value of profit. On the basis of this theoretical analysis, we can summarize the process of finding Q^*, P^*, and π^* with the following step-by-step procedure:

Step 1: Estimate the demand equation

To determine the optimal level of output, the manager must estimate the marginal revenue function. Since marginal revenue is derived from the demand equation, the manager begins by estimating demand. In the case of a linear demand specification, the empirical demand function facing the monopolist can be written as

$$Q = a + bP + cM + dP_R$$

where Q is output, P is price, M is income, and P_R is the price of a good related in consumption. As discussed in Chapter 8, in order to obtain the estimated demand curve for the relevant time period, the manager must have forecasts for the values of the exogenous variables, M and P_R, for that time period. Once the empirical demand equation has been estimated, the forecasts of M and P_R (denoted $\hat{M}$ and $\hat{P}_R$) are substituted into the estimated demand equation, and the demand function is expressed as

$$Q = a' + bP$$

where $a' = a + c\hat{M} + d\hat{P}_R$.

Step 2: Find the inverse demand equation

Before we can derive the marginal revenue function from the demand function, the demand function must be expressed so that price is a function of quantity: $P = f(Q)$. This is accomplished by solving for P in the estimated demand equation in step 1:

FIGURE 16.1
Short-Run Profit Maximization for Monopoly

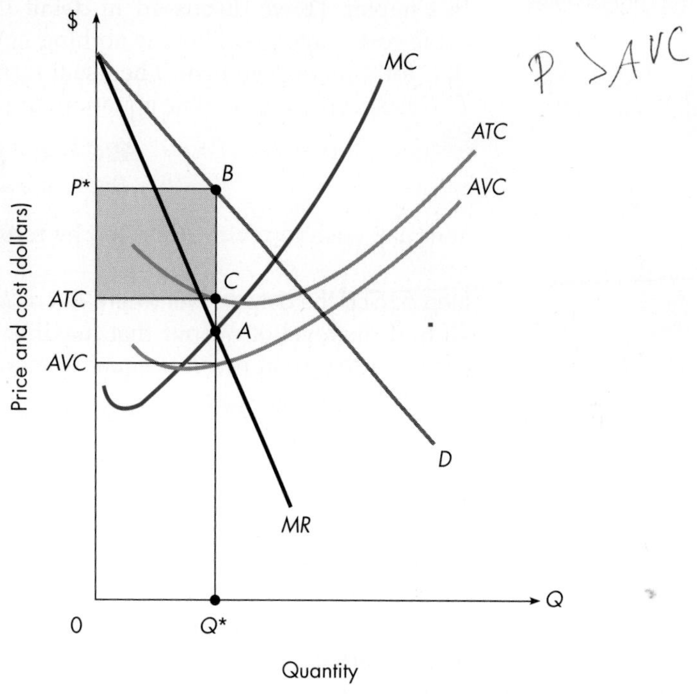

$$P = \frac{-a'}{b} + \frac{1}{b}Q$$
$$= A + BQ$$

where $A = \frac{-a'}{b}$ and $B = \frac{1}{b}$. This form of the demand equation is called the **inverse demand function.** Now the demand equation is expressed in a form that makes it possible to solve for marginal revenue in a straightforward manner.

inverse demand function
The demand function with demand price expressed as a function of output, $P = f(Q)$.

Step 3: Solve for marginal revenue

Now recall from Chapter 3 that when demand is expressed as $P = A + BQ$, marginal revenue is $MR = A + 2BQ$. Using the inverse demand function, we can write the marginal revenue function as

$$MR = A + 2BQ$$
$$= \frac{-a'}{b} + \frac{2}{b}Q$$

Step 4: Estimate average variable cost (*AVC*) and marginal cost (*MC*)

In Chapter 11 we discussed in detail the empirical techniques for estimating cubic cost functions. There is nothing new or different about estimating *MC* and *AVC* for a monopoly firm. The usual forms for the *AVC* and *MC* functions, when *TVC* is specified as a cubic equation, are

$$AVC = a + bQ + cQ^2$$
$$MC = a + 2bQ + 3cQ^2$$

You may wish to review this step by returning to Chapter 11 or to Chapter 13.

Step 5: Find the output level where *MR* = *MC*

To find the level of output that maximizes profit or minimizes losses, the manager sets marginal revenue equal to marginal cost and solves for *Q*:

$$MR = A + 2BQ = a + 2bQ + 3cQ^2 = MC$$

Solving this equation for Q^* gives the optimal level of output for the firm—unless *P* is less than *AVC*, and then the optimal level of output is zero.

Step 6: Find the optimal price

Once the optimal quantity, Q^*, has been found in step 5, the profit-maximizing price is found by substituting Q^* into the inverse demand equation to obtain the optimal price, P^*:

$$P^* = A + BQ^*$$

This price and output will be optimal only if price exceeds average variable cost.

Step 7: Check the shutdown rule

For any firm, with or without market power, if price is less than average variable cost, the firm will shut down ($Q^* = 0$) because it makes a smaller loss producing nothing than it would lose if it produced any positive amount of output. The manager calculates the average variable cost at Q^* units:

$$AVC^* = a + bQ^* + cQ^{*2}$$

If $P^* \geq AVC^*$, then the monopolist produces Q^* units of output and sells each unit of output for P^* dollars. If $P^* < AVC^*$, then the monopolist shuts down in the short run.

Step 8: Computation of profit or loss

To compute the profit or loss, the manager makes the same calculation regardless of whether the firm is a monopolist, oligopolist, or perfect competitor. Total profit or loss is

$$\begin{aligned}\pi^* &= TR - TC \\ &= (P^* \times Q^*) - [(AVC^* \times Q^*) + TFC]\end{aligned}$$

If $P < AVC$, the firm shuts down, and $\pi = -TFC$.

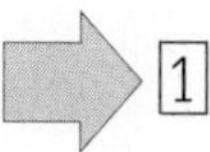

To illustrate how to implement these steps to find the profit-maximizing price and output level and to forecast profit, we now turn to a hypothetical firm that possesses a degree of market power.[1]

16.2 MAXIMIZING PROFIT AT AZTEC ELECTRONICS: AN EXAMPLE

By virtue of several patents, Aztec Electronics possesses substantial market power in the market for advanced stereo headphones. In December 1998, the manager of Aztec wished to determine the profit-maximizing price and output for its stereo headphones for 1999.

Estimation of Demand and Marginal Revenue

The demand for headphones was specified as a linear function of the price of headphones, the income of the buyers, and the price of stereo tuners (a complement good):

$$Q = f(P, M, P_R)$$

Using data available for the period 1988–1998, a linear form of the demand function was estimated. The resulting estimated demand function was

$$Q = 41{,}000 - 500P + 0.6M - 22.5P_R$$

where output (Q) is measured in units of sales, and average annual family income (M) and the two prices (P and P_R) are measured in dollars. Each estimated parameter has the expected sign and is statistically significant at the 5 percent level. The R^2 and F-statistics were both quite high, indicating the linear model specification does an excellent job of explaining the variation in quantity demanded.[2]

From an economic consulting firm, the manager obtained 1999 forecasts for income and the price of the complementary good (stereo tuners) as, respectively, \$45,000 and \$800. Using these values—$\hat{M} = 45{,}000$ and $\hat{P}_R = 800$—the estimated (forecasted) demand function in 1998 was

$$Q = 41{,}000 - 500P + 0.6(45{,}000) - 22.5(800) = 50{,}000 - 500P$$

The inverse demand function for the estimated (empirical) demand function was obtained by solving for P:

$$P = 100 - 0.002Q$$

[1] The monopolist can choose input usage rather than output in order to maximize profit.

[2] Recall from Chapter 7 that when a firm is a price-setting firm (i.e., possesses some degree of market power), the problem of simultaneity vanishes. Thus, the demand for a monopolist can be estimated using the standard method of least-squares estimation—two-stage least-squares is not necessary.

FIGURE 16.2
Demand and Marginal Revenue for Aztec Electronics

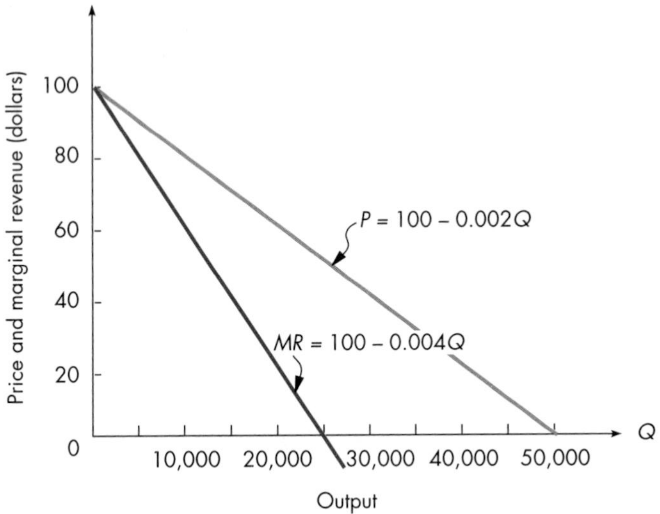

From the inverse demand function, the manager of Aztec Electronics obtained the estimated marginal revenue function:

$$MR = 100 - 0.004Q$$

We should note that if the parameters of the demand equation are statistically significant, so are the parameters of the marginal revenue equation.

Figure 16.2 illustrates the estimated linear demand and marginal revenue curves for Aztec Electronics.

Estimation of Average Variable Cost and Marginal Cost

The manager of Aztec Electronics obtained an estimate of the firm's average variable cost function using a short-run quadratic specification (as described in Chapter 11). The estimated average variable cost function was

$$AVC = 28 - 0.005Q + 0.000001Q^2$$

For this estimation, *AVC* was measured in dollar units, and Q was measured in units of sales. Given the estimated average variable cost function, the marginal cost function is

$$MC = 28 - 0.01Q + 0.000003Q^2$$

As you can see, the specification and estimation of cost functions is the same regardless of whether a firm is perfectly competitive or possesses a degree of market power.

The Output Decision

Once the manager of Aztec obtained estimates of the marginal revenue function and the marginal cost function, the determination of the optimal level of output was accomplished by equating the estimated marginal revenue equation with the estimated marginal cost equation and solving for Q^*. Setting MR equal to MC results in the following expression:

$$100 - 0.004Q = 28 - 0.01Q + 0.000003Q^2$$

Solving this equation for Q, the manager of Aztec finds two solutions: $Q = 6{,}000$ and $Q = -4{,}000$. Since $Q = -4{,}000$ is an irrelevant solution—negative outputs are impossible—the optimal level of output is $Q^* = 6{,}000$. That is, the profit-maximizing (or loss-minimizing) number of stereo headphones to produce and sell in 1999 is 6,000 units—if the firm chooses to produce rather than shut down.

The Pricing Decision

Once the manager of Aztec Electronics has found the optimal level of output, determining the profit-maximizing price is really nothing more than finding the price on the monopolist's demand curve that corresponds to the profit-maximizing level of output. The optimal output level, Q^*, is substituted into the inverse demand equation to obtain the optimal price. Substituting $Q^* = 6{,}000$ into the inverse demand function, the optimal price, P^*, is

$$P^* = 100 - 0.002(6{,}000) = \$88$$

Thus, Aztec will charge $88 for a set of headphones in 1999.

The Shutdown Decision

To see if Aztec Electronics should shut down production in 1999, the manager compared the optimal price of $88 to the average variable cost of producing 6,000 units. Average variable cost for 6,000 units was computed as

$$AVC^* = 28 - 0.005(6{,}000) + 0.000001(6{,}000)^2 = \$34$$

Since $88 is greater than $34, if these forecasts prove to be correct in 1999, all the variable costs will be covered and the manager should operate the plant rather than shut it down. Note that Aztec's expected total revenue in 1999 is $528,000 (= $88 × 6,000) and estimated total variable cost was $204,000 (= $34 × 6,000). Since total revenue exceeds total variable cost ($TR > TVC$), the manager would produce rather than shut down.

Computation of Total Profit or Loss

Computation of profit is a straightforward process once the manager has estimated total revenue and all costs. The manager of Aztec has already estimated price and average variable cost for 1999, but total fixed cost is needed to calculate total profit or loss. On the basis of 1998 data, the manager of Aztec Electronics

FIGURE 16.3
Profit Maximization at Aztec Electronics

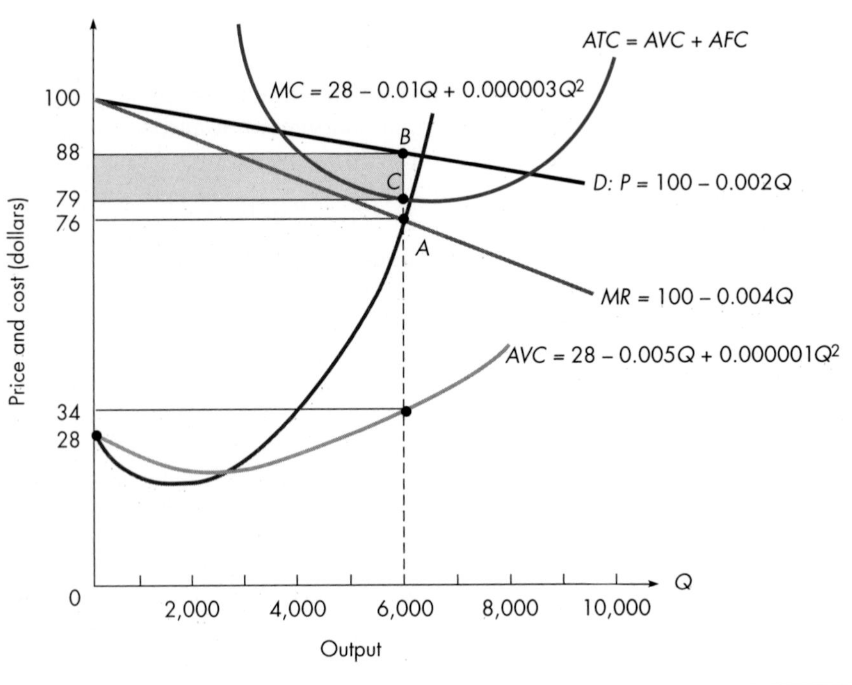

estimated that fixed costs would be \$270,000 in 1999. The profit for 1999 was calculated to be

$$\begin{aligned}\pi &= TR - TVC - TFC \\ &= \$528{,}000 - \$204{,}000 - \$270{,}000 \\ &= \$54{,}000\end{aligned}$$

Figure 16.3 shows the estimated equations for 1999 and the profit-maximizing price and output. At point A, $MR = MC$, and the profit-maximizing level of output is 6,000 units ($Q^* = 6{,}000$). At point B, the profit-maximizing price is \$88, the price at which 6,000 units can be sold. At point C, ATC is \$79, which was calculated as

$$\begin{aligned}ATC &= TC/Q = (\$204{,}000 + \$270{,}000) \,/\, 6{,}000 \\ &= \$79\end{aligned}$$

The total profit earned by Aztec is represented by the area of the shaded rectangle.

The Firm Makes a Loss

Now suppose that per capita income falls, causing the demand facing Aztec to fall to

$$P = 80 - 0.002Q$$

so marginal revenue is now

$$MR = 80 - 0.004Q$$

Average variable and marginal costs remain constant.

To determine the new level of output under the new estimated demand conditions, the manager equates the new estimated marginal revenue equation with the marginal cost equation and solves for Q^*:

$$80 - 0.004Q = 28 - 0.01Q + 0.000003Q^2$$

Again there are two solutions: $Q = -3{,}167$ and $Q = 5{,}283$. Ignoring the negative level of output, the optimal level is $Q^* = 5{,}283$. Substituting this value into the inverse demand function, the optimal price is

$$P^* = 80 - 0.002(5{,}283) = \$69.43$$

To determine whether to produce or shut down under the reduced-demand situation, the manager calculated the average variable cost at the new level of output and compared it with price:

$$AVC = 28 - 0.005(5{,}283) + 0.000001(5{,}283)^2 = \$29.49$$

Clearly if Aztec produces in 1999, total revenue will cover all of total variable cost since

$$P = \$69.43 > \$29.49 = AVC$$

Aztec's profit or loss is

$$\begin{aligned}\pi &= TR - TVC - TFC \\ &= \$69.43(5{,}283) - \$29.49(5{,}283) - \$270{,}000 \\ &= \$366{,}799 - \$155{,}796 - \$270{,}000 \\ &= -\$58{,}997\end{aligned}$$

Despite the predicted loss of \$58,997 in 1999, Aztec should continue producing. Losing \$58,997 is obviously better than shutting down and losing the entire fixed cost of \$270,000.

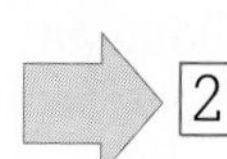

16.3 COST-PLUS PRICING: AN ALTERNATIVE PRICING RULE

It should be clear by now that the short-run pricing decision based upon the equality of marginal revenue and marginal cost yields the maximum profit (or minimum loss) for a firm. However, there is some evidence to suggest that many firms use some other types of rules to determine price and output, particularly when it is difficult to obtain an accurate estimate of their demand function. Examples of such cases might be when a firm's demand is a function of the prices and levels of advertising of several close rivals. One prominent alternative pricing technique is called **cost-plus pricing.** Firms using cost-plus pricing determine their price by setting price equal to average total cost plus a percentage of average total cost (*ATC*) as a markup.

cost-plus pricing
A method of determining price by setting price equal to average total cost plus a percentage of *ATC* as a markup.

The basic concept is deceptively simple. In cost-plus pricing, the firm determines its average total cost then adds a percentage markup (or margin). Thus, price is

$$P = ATC + (m \cdot ATC)$$
$$= (1 + m) \cdot ATC$$

where m is the markup on cost. For example, if the markup is 20 percent, price would be $1.2 \times ATC$.

This very basic description of cost-plus pricing glosses over two major difficulties. First, how does the firm determine average total cost? Second, how does the firm select the appropriate markup (or margin)?

Because costs vary with the level of output produced, determination of average cost requires that the firm first specify the level of output that will be produced. Obviously, a precise determination of this output would require consideration of the prevailing demand conditions—a feature not incorporated in cost-plus pricing. Instead, firms typically specify some standard volume of production, based on some assumption about the percentage of the firm's capacity that will be utilized. Furthermore, the costs used are derived from accounting data. As noted in earlier chapters, the use of accounting data may not be valid, since accounting costs do not always reflect opportunity costs. Also, such historical data would not reflect recent or potential changes in input prices.

Notwithstanding the difficulties involved in determining average cost, a potentially more troublesome problem is the selection of the markup percentage. While the firm might arbitrarily select some target rate of return on invested capital, recent empirical evidence suggests that firms use a more subjective approach. It appears that the markups for different products differ according to such factors as the degree of competitiveness in the market and the price elasticity of demand. Apparently, managers employ knowledge about the market to determine the markup that maximizes profits.

Cost-plus pricing has been criticized on two grounds. First, it employs average rather than marginal cost. As you know from Chapter 4, marginal (or incremental) cost rather than total cost should be used in making any optimizing decision. Second, cost-plus pricing does not incorporate a consideration of prevailing demand conditions. Using the $MR = MC$ pricing rule, demand conditions enter explicitly through the marginal revenue function, but cost-plus pricing does not embody this information.

Although these criticisms are valid, it should be noted that, *under certain circumstances,* cost-plus pricing may approximate $MR = MC$ pricing. Let us show you how this can occur. As was shown in an earlier chapter, marginal revenue may be written as

$$MR = P\left(1 + \frac{1}{E}\right)$$

where E is the own-price elasticity of demand. Setting marginal revenue equal to marginal cost, the optimization condition may be written as

$$P\left(1 + \frac{1}{E}\right) = MC$$

so

$$P = \left(\frac{E}{1 + E}\right) MC$$

If the firm has a horizontal average cost curve (e.g., if the firm's long-run cost relation is characterized by constant returns to scale), average cost is constant and is equal to marginal cost. In this case, the preceding condition can be expressed as

$$P = \left(\frac{E}{1 + E}\right) LAC$$

Note the similarity between this equation and the equation for cost-plus pricing, $P = (1 + m)LAC$. Setting these equations equal (i.e., assuming that cost-plus pricing is equivalent to $MR = MC$ pricing) and solving for m, the markup would be

$$m = -\frac{1}{1 + E}$$

That is, if firms are using cost-plus pricing as an approximation to pricing based on profit maximization, the markup would be determined by the price elasticity of demand—precisely the relation indicated in the empirical investigations mentioned earlier. While a firm with market power is limited to the elastic portion of the demand function (i.e., where $|E| > 1$), this formulation indicates that, as the demand curve becomes more elastic (i.e., as $|E|$ increases), the profit-maximizing markup decreases. For example, if $|E| = 2$, the profit-maximizing markup would be 100 percent. However, if the demand curve were more elastic, say, $|E| = 5$, the profit-maximizing markup would fall to 25 percent. The point is that if the firm's average cost is constant, cost-plus pricing *could* be equivalent to pricing based on profit maximization. Moreover, the size of the markup would depend on the own-price elasticity of demand, which of course depends upon the availability of good substitutes for the product. The easier it is for consumers to substitute, the lower the markup.

Relation When a manager practices cost-plus pricing, the price of the product is determined as

$$P = (1 + m)ATC$$

where m is the markup on average total cost (ATC). Cost-plus pricing is not, in general, equivalent to the profit-maximizing price determined by equating marginal revenue and marginal cost. In the special case in which the markup is related to the elasticity of demand as

$$m = -\frac{1}{1 + E}$$

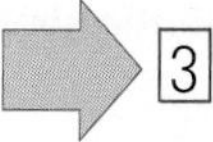 3

and when average cost is constant, cost-plus pricing is equivalent to pricing based on profit maximization.

16.4 SUMMARY

This chapter showed how a manager of a firm with market power can use estimates of demand and cost functions to make profit-maximizing decisions. The steps a manager follows to find the price and output that maximize profit or minimize losses are summarized below:

1. The demand curve facing the firm is estimated. Then the inverse demand function—which is used to derive the marginal revenue function—is derived.
2. The cost curves are estimated in order to estimate the marginal cost function facing the firm.
3. Set the estimated marginal revenue equal to the estimated marginal cost, and solve for the profit-maximizing level of output.
4. The profit-maximizing price is then found by substituting the optimal level of output into the inverse demand function.
5. The optimal price is then compared to average variable cost at the optimal output level to make sure the firm should actually produce. The firm should produce if $P \geq AVC$, and the firm should shut down if $P < AVC$.
6. The profit or loss earned by the firm is calculated by subtracting total cost from total revenue: $\pi = TR - TC = P \times Q - [(AVC \times Q) + TFC]$.

Sometimes it is difficult, or perhaps impossible, to estimate the demand conditions when there is mutual interdependence in a market. In such cases, the $MR = MC$ rule cannot be applied, and some managers resort to alternative pricing techniques. One such technique is cost-plus pricing, where the price charged represents a markup (margin) over average cost and is determined as follows:

$$P = (1 + m)ATC$$

Two problems exist with this approach: (1) The appropriate output level at which to measure ATC is unknown, and (2) the appropriate margin (m) is unknown. However, when the firm's cost curve is relatively flat, cost-plus pricing can approximate profit maximization if the markup is equal to $\frac{-1}{1+E}$, where E is the own-price elasticity of demand.

TECHNICAL PROBLEMS

1. The manager of a monopoly firm obtained the following estimate of the market demand function for its output:

$$Q = 2{,}600 - 100P + 0.2M - 500P_R$$

From an econometric forecasting firm, the manager obtained forecasts for the 1999 values of M and P_R as, respectively, \$20,000 and \$2. For 1999 what is:
   a. The forecasted demand function?
   b. The inverse demand function?
   c. The marginal revenue function?

2. For the firm in problem 1, the manager estimated the average variable cost function as

$$AVC = 20 - 0.07Q + 0.0001Q^2$$

where AVC was measured in dollars per unit and Q is the number of units sold.
   a. What is the estimated marginal cost function?
   b. What is the optimal level of production in 1999?
   c. What is the optimal price in 1999?
   d. Check to make sure that the firm should actually produce in the short run rather than shut down.

In addition, the manager expects fixed costs in 1999 to be $22,500.

e. What is the firm's expected profit or loss in 1999?

3. Cost-plus pricing is a method of price determination used predominantly by monopolistically competitive firms.
   a. Why is cost-plus pricing used mainly by monopolistic competitors and not often by monopolists?
   b. Under what condition(s) would cost-plus pricing be equivalent to profit-maximizing pricing, that is, $MR = MC$ pricing?
   c. If the condition(s) in part *b* are satisfied and if the own-price elasticity of demand facing the firm is -1.5, what is the profit-maximizing markup?
   d. What is the profit-maximizing markup if the own-price elasticity is equal to -3?

APPLIED PROBLEMS

1. The Ali Baba Co. is the only supplier of a particular type of Oriental carpet. The estimated demand for its carpets is

$$Q = 112{,}000 - 500P + 5M$$

where Q = number of carpets, P = price of carpets (dollars per unit), and M = consumers' income per capita.

The estimated average variable cost function for Ali Baba's carpets is

$$AVC = 200 - 0.012Q + 0.000002Q^2$$

Consumers' income per capita is expected to be $20,000 and total fixed cost is $100,000.

   a. How many carpets should the firm produce in order to maximize profit?
   b. What is the profit-maximizing price of carpets?
   c. What is the maximum amount of profit that the firm can earn selling carpets?
   d. Answer parts *a* through *c* if consumers' income per capita is expected to be $30,000 instead.

2. Dr. Leona Williams, a well-known plastic surgeon, has a reputation for being one of the best surgeons for reconstructive nose surgery. Dr. Williams enjoys a rather substantial degree of market power in this market. Dr. Williams has estimated demand for her work to be

$$Q = 480 - 0.2P$$

where Q is the number of nose operations performed monthly, and P is the price of a nose operation.

   a. What is the inverse demand function for Dr. Williams's services?
   b. What is the marginal revenue function?

The average variable cost function for reconstructive nose surgery is estimated to be

$$AVC = 2Q^2 - 15Q + 400$$

where AVC is average variable cost (measured in dollars), and Q is the number of operations per month. The doctor's fixed costs each month are $8,000.

   c. If the doctor wishes to maximize her profit, how many nose operations should she perform each month?
   d. What price should Dr. Williams charge to perform a nose operation?
   e. How much profit does she earn each month?

CHAPTER 17

Multiple Plants, Markets, and Products

Until now we have considered—at least implicitly—only a rather simple firm. This firm has a single plant in which it produces a single product that is sold in a single market. Although the simpler models give great insight into a firm's decision process, this is frequently not the type of situation faced by many real-world firms or corporations.

In this chapter, we will show how some complications, such as multiple plants, multiple markets, and multiple products, affect the profit-maximization conditions set forth in previous chapters. The discussion of each of these topics will of necessity be brief. It is not our intention to provide an exhaustive discussion of these complications. Rather, we want to show that these complications do not alter the principles of profit maximization already set forth: The firm continues to produce that output at which marginal revenue equals marginal cost or to choose the level of input usage at which marginal revenue product is equal to marginal cost of the input. The effect of these complications does, however, make the implementation of these principles somewhat more complex computationally: "The rule's the same, but the arithmetic's a little harder."

In this discussion, we limit our attention to firms with market power—monopoly, oligopoly, and monopolistic competition. Since we will be concerned with the firm's output and pricing decision in the short run, these market structures are analytically the same. Hence, in our discussion, we will normally consider a monopoly firm, but the conclusions also apply to monopolistic competition and oligopoly, with perhaps a few modifications.

We begin with a discussion of multiplant firms. This will be followed by a discussion of firms that sell in multiple markets and then a discussion of firms that produce multiple products. For clarity of exposition, we treat these extensions of the theory as separate topics without trying to integrate them. Keep in mind, however, that firms frequently fall into two or even all three of the categories.

17.1 MULTIPLANT FIRMS

A firm with market power often produces output in more than one plant. In this situation, it is likely that the various plants will have different cost conditions. The problem facing the firm is how to allocate the firm's desired level of production among these plants so that the total cost is minimized.

For simplicity, we assume there are only two plants, A and B. Suppose at the desired level of output, the following situation holds:

$$MC_A < MC_B$$

for the last unit of output produced in each plant. In this situation, the manager should transfer output from the higher-cost plant B to the lower cost plant A. If the last unit produced in plant B costs $10, but 1 more unit produced in plant A adds only $7 to A's cost, that unit should be transferred from B to A. The transfer results in a cost reduction of $3. In fact, output should be transferred from B to A until

$$MC_A = MC_B$$

Equality eventually occurs because of increasing marginal cost. As output is transferred out of B into A, the marginal cost in A rises, and the marginal cost in B falls. It is simple to see that exactly the opposite occurs in the case of

$$MC_A > MC_B$$

Output is taken out of plant A and produced in plant B until

$$MC_A = MC_B$$

The total output decision is easily determined. The horizontal summation of all plants' marginal cost curves is the firm's total marginal cost curve. This total marginal cost curve is equated to marginal revenue in order to determine the profit-maximizing output and price. This output is divided among the plants so that the marginal cost is equal for all plants.[1] The solution is identical to that for a cartel dividing production among firms.

The two-plant case is illustrated in Figure 17.1. Demand facing the firm is D, and marginal revenue is MR. The marginal cost curves for plants A and B are, respectively, MC_A and MC_B. The total marginal cost curve for the firm is the *horizontal summation* of MC_A and MC_B, labeled MC_T. Profit is maximized at that output level where MC_T equals marginal revenue, at an output of 175 units and a price of $45. Marginal cost at this output is $20. Equalization of marginal cost requires that plant A produce 50 units and plant B produce 125 units, which of

[1]For a mathematical demonstration, see the appendix to this chapter.

FIGURE 17.1
A Multiplant Firm

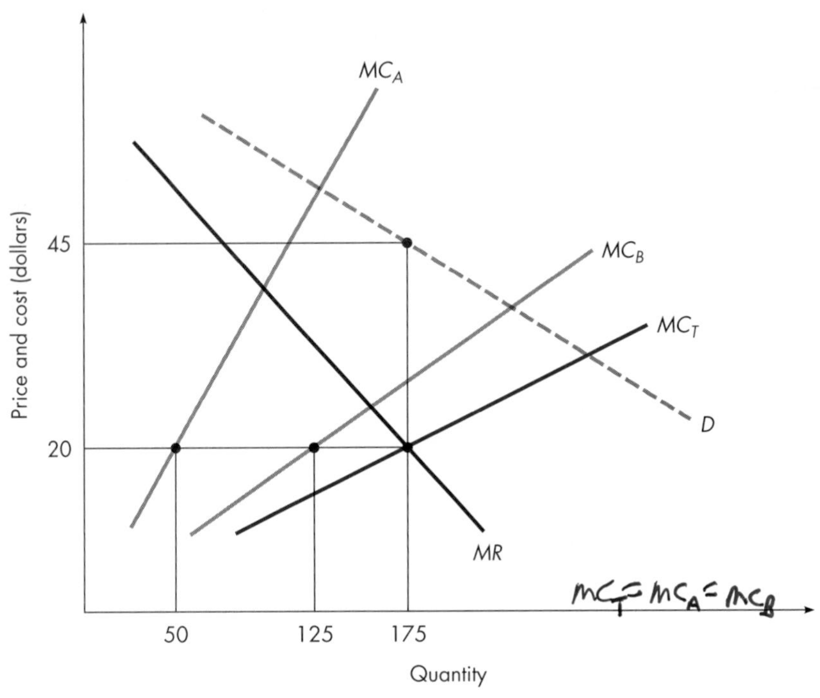

course sums to 175 since MC_T is the horizontal summation of MC_A and MC_B. This allocation equalizes marginal cost and consequently minimizes the total cost of producing 175 units.

To further illustrate the principle of optimally allocating output in a multiplant situation, we turn now to a numerical illustration. As you will see, the algebra is somewhat more complex than it is for the single-plant case, but the principle is the same: The manager maximizes profit by producing the output level for which marginal revenue equals marginal cost.

Principle For a firm that produces using two plants, A and B, with marginal costs MC_A and MC_B, respectively, the total cost of producing any given level of total output Q_T $(= Q_A + Q_B)$ is minimized when the manager allocates production between the two plants so that the marginal costs are equal:

$$MC_A = MC_B$$

Multiplant Production of Mercantile Enterprises

Mercantile Enterprises—a firm with some degree of market power—produces its product in two plants. Hence, when making production decisions, the manager of Mercantile must decide not only how much to produce but also how to allocate the desired production between the two plants.

The production engineering department of Mercantile was able to provide the manager with simple, linear estimates of the incremental (marginal) cost functions for the two plants:

$$MC_A = 28 + 0.04Q_A \quad \text{and} \quad MC_B = 16 + 0.02Q_B$$

Note that the estimated marginal cost function for plant A (a plant built in 1978) is higher for every output than that for plant B (a plant built in 1995); plant B is more efficient.

The equation for the total marginal cost function (the horizontal sum of MC_A and MC_B) can be derived algebraically using the following procedure. First, solve for both inverse marginal cost functions:

$$Q_A = 25MC_A - 700$$

and

$$Q_B = 50MC_B - 800$$

Next, Q_T (= $Q_A + Q_B$) is found by summing the two inverse marginal cost functions. Recall, however, that the horizontal summing process requires that $MC_A = MC_B = MC_T$ for all levels of total output Q_T. Thus, it follows that

$$Q_A = 25MC_T - 700$$

and

$$Q_B = 50MC_T - 800$$

Summing the two inverse marginal cost functions results in the inverse *total* marginal cost function:

$$Q_T = Q_A + Q_B = 75MC_T - 1{,}500$$

which, after taking the inverse to express marginal cost once again as a function of output, results in the total marginal cost function:

$$MC_T = 20 + 0.0133Q_T$$

The marginal cost functions for plants A and B and the associated total marginal cost function are shown in Panel A of Figure 17.2. The process of horizontal summation can be seen by noting that when MC = \$40, Q_A = 300 units (point *A*), Q_B = 1,200 units (point *B*), and $Q_T = Q_A + Q_B$ = 1,500 units (point *C*). Thus, if 1,500 units are to be produced, the manager should allocate production so that 300 units are produced in plant A and 1,200 units are produced in plant B. This allocation of production between the two plants minimizes the total cost of producing a total of 1,500 units.

Note that when Q_T is less than 600 units, plant A is shut down and only plant B is operated. Until Mercantile increases total production to 600 units or more (point *K*), the marginal cost of producing any output at all in plant A is greater than the marginal cost of producing additional units in plant B. For output levels in the zero to 600-unit range, MC_B is the relevant total marginal cost curve since

FIGURE 17.2

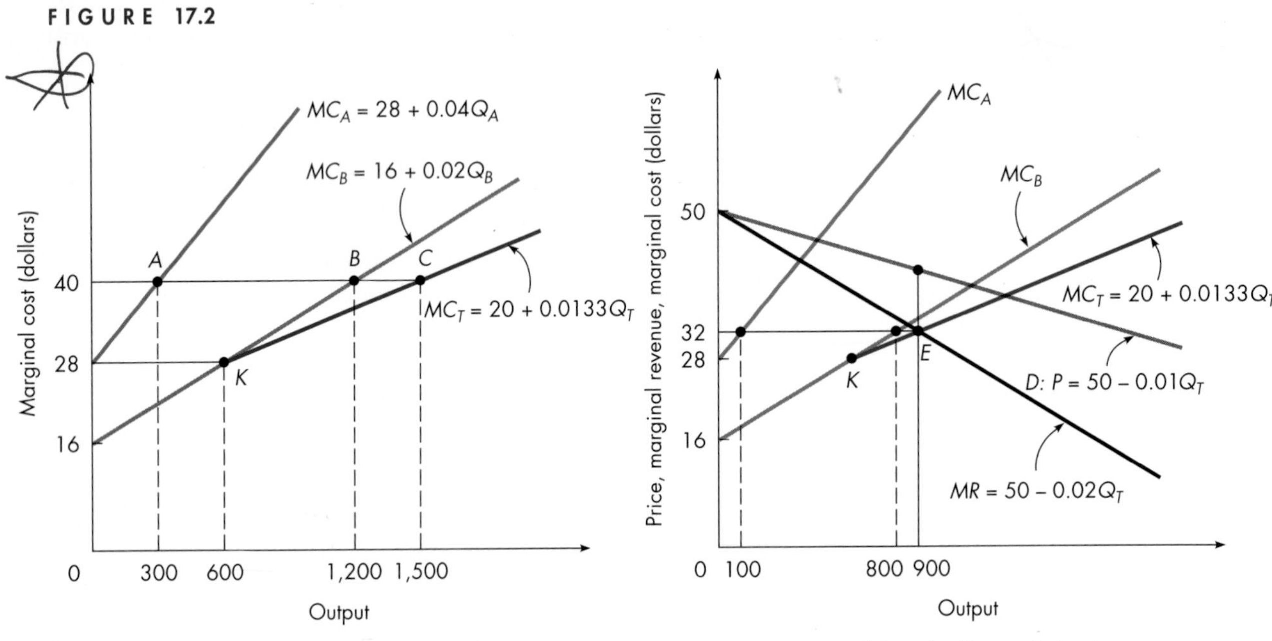

Panel A — Derivation of total marginal cost

Panel B — Profit maximization

$Q_A = 0$. For total output levels greater than 600 units, Mercantile Enterprises will operate *both* plants and MC_T is the total marginal cost function.

Suppose that the estimated demand curve for Mercantile's output is

$$Q_T = 5{,}000 - 100P$$

The inverse demand function is

$$P = 50 - 0.01Q_T$$

and marginal revenue is

$$MR = 50 - 0.02Q_T$$

Equating marginal revenue and total marginal cost,

$$50 - 0.02Q_T = 20 + 0.0133Q_T$$

and solving for Q_T, the profit-maximizing level of output for Mercantile Enterprises is $Q_T^* = 900$. At this output level, marginal revenue and total marginal cost are both \$32 at point E in Panel B of Figure 17.2. In order to minimize the cost of producing 900 units, the production of the 900 units should be allocated between plants A and B so that the marginal cost of the last unit produced in either plant is $32:

$$MC_A = 28 + 0.04Q_A = 32 \quad \text{and} \quad MC_B = 16 + 0.02Q_B = 32$$

Hence, for plant A, $Q_A^* = 100$, so 100 units will be produced in plant A. For plant B, $Q_B^* = 800$, so 800 units will be produced in plant B.

Now suppose that forecasted demand decreases and a new forecast of the demand for Mercantile's output is

$$Q_T = 4{,}000 - 100P$$

Given that the corresponding marginal revenue function is

$$MR = 40 - 0.02Q_T$$

the firm's profit-maximizing output (where $MR = MC_T$) declines to 600 units. At this output, marginal revenue and marginal cost are both $28. Equating MC_A and MC_B to $28, the manager found that for plant A, $Q_A^* = 0$, and for plant B, $Q_B^* = 600$. With the new (lower) forecast of demand, plant A will be shut down and all the output will be produced in plant B. As you can verify, if demand declines further, Mercantile would still produce, using only plant B. So for output levels of 600 or fewer units, the total marginal cost function is MC_B.

In effect, the total marginal cost function has a "kink" at point K in the figure. The kink at point K represents the total output level below which the high-cost plant is shut down. A kink occurs when marginal cost in the low-cost plant equals the minimum level of marginal cost in the high-cost plant, thereby making it optimal to begin producing with an additional plant.[2] The output at which the kink occurs is found by setting marginal cost in the *low*-cost plant equal to the minimum value of marginal cost in the *high*-cost plant:

$$MC_B = 28 = 16 + 0.02Q$$

so the high-cost plant begins operating when Q exceeds 600 units.

The preceding discussion and example show how a manager should allocate production between two plants to minimize the cost of producing the level of output that maximizes profit. The principle of equating marginal costs applies in exactly the same fashion to the case of three or more plants: Marginal cost is the same in all plants that produce. The only complication arises in the derivation of total marginal cost.

Once the total marginal cost function is derived, either by summing the individual plants' marginal cost curves graphically or by solving algebraically, the

[2]The low-cost (high-cost) plant is the plant with lowest (highest) marginal cost at $Q = 0$.

manager uses the total marginal cost function to find the profit-maximizing level of total output.

Principle A manager who has n plants that can produce output will maximize profit when the firm produces the level of total output and allocates that output among the n plants so that

$$MR = MC_T = MC_1 = \cdots = MC_n$$

17.2 FIRMS WITH MULTIPLE MARKETS—PRICE DISCRIMINATION

Thus far we have treated demand as simply the horizontal summation of the demands of all consumers, and every consumer is charged the same price for the product. But since consumers are different, their demands differ. At times, firms can take advantage of these differences in demand in order to increase their profit. Price discrimination is the method by which this is accomplished. **Price discrimination** means that the firm charges different consumers different prices for the same good (when there are no corresponding differences in costs). For example, price discrimination can occur when a firm charges different prices in its domestic and foreign markets or when a movie theater charges adults a higher price to see a movie than it charges children.

price discrimination Method in which firms charge different groups of customers different prices for the same good or service.

Certain conditions are necessary for the firm to be *able* to price-discriminate. First, the firm obviously must possess some market power. Economists normally think of price discrimination in the context of a monopoly firm, but since they have market power, monopolistic competitors and oligopolists may also be able to price-discriminate. Second, the demand functions for the individual consumers or groups of consumers must differ. As we will demonstrate later, this statement can be made more specific to require that the own-price elasticities must be different. Third, the different markets must be separable. The firm must be able to identify the individuals or groups of individuals and effectively separate them into submarkets. Finally, purchasers of the product must not be able to resell it to other customers. If consumers could buy and sell the product among themselves, there is no way that the firm could keep the submarkets separated. (A firm doesn't want the low-price buyers to sell its product to the high-price buyers.)

Normally, economists speak of three degrees of price discrimination. However, because we want to provide only a brief overview of price discrimination, we will limit our discussion to what is referred to as third-degree price discrimination. This is the form most commonly observed and is the form that best illustrates our primary concern in this section: profit maximization with multiple markets.

Allocation of Sales in Two Markets to Maximize Revenue

The analysis of price discrimination is a straightforward application of the $MR = MC$ rule. As a first step in that analysis, assume that a firm has two separate markets for its product. Demand conditions in each market are such that the marginal revenues from selling specified quantities are as given in Table 17.1. Assume also that the manager has decided to produce 12 units. How should the

TABLE 17.1
Allocation of Sales between Two Markets

Quantity	Marginal revenue in market 1	Order of sales	Marginal revenue in market 2	Order of sales
1	$45	(1)	$34	(3)
2	36	(2)	28	(5)
3	30	(4)	22	(7)
4	22	(6)	13	(10)
5	17	(8)	10	(12)
6	15	(9)	8	
7	10	(11)	7	
8	7		4	
9	4		2	
10	0		1	

manager allocate sales between the two markets in order to maximize the total revenue from the sale of 12 units? Clearly, revenue from selling the chosen level of output must be maximized if profit is to be maximized.

Consider the first unit; the firm can increase revenue by $45 by selling it in market 1 or by $34 by selling in market 2. Obviously, the firm will sell the first unit in market 1. The second unit is also sold in market 1 since its sale there increases revenue by $36, whereas it would increase revenue by only $34 in market 2. Since $34 can be gained in market 2 but only $30 in market 1, unit 3 is sold in market 2. Similar reasoning shows that the fourth unit goes to market 1 and the fifth to market 2. Since unit 6 adds $22 to revenue in either market, it makes no difference where it is sold; 6 and 7 go one to each market. Units 8 and 9 are sold in market 1 because they yield higher marginal revenue there; 10 goes to market 2 for the same reason. Unit 11 can go to either market, since the additional revenues are the same, and unit 12 goes to the other. Thus the 12 units will be divided so that the marginal revenue is the same for the last unit sold in each market; the firm sells 7 units in market 1 and 5 in market 2. Thus, the price-discriminating firm allocates a given output in such a way that the marginal revenues in each market are equal.[3]

The results from Table 17.1 indicate that a manager will maximize profit at a given level of output when that output is allocated in such a way that

$$MR_1 = MR_2$$

This condition should not be surprising since it is just another application of the principle of constrained optimization presented in Chapter 4. If a manager wants to maximize total revenue subject to the constraint that there is only a limited number of units to sell, the manager should allocate sales so that the

[3]For a mathematical demonstration, see the appendix to this chapter.

marginal revenues (marginal benefits) per unit are equal in the two markets. The marginal cost of selling 1 unit in market 1 is the 1 unit not available for sale in market 2 ($MC_1 = MC_2 = 1$ unit).

Principle A manager who wishes to maximize the total revenue from selling a given amount of output in two separate markets (*A* and *B*) should allocate sales between the two markets so that

$$MR_A = MR_B$$

and all units are sold.

Although the marginal revenues in the two markets are equal, the prices charged are not. The higher price will be charged in the market with the less elastic demand; the lower price will be charged in the market having the more elastic demand. In the more elastic market, price could be raised only at the expense of a large decrease in sales. In the less elastic market, higher prices bring less reduction in sales.

This assertion can be demonstrated as follows: Let the prices in the two markets be P_1 and P_2. Likewise, let E_1 and E_2 denote the respective own-price elasticities. As shown in Chapter 3, marginal revenue can be expressed as

$$MR = P\left(1 + \frac{1}{E}\right)$$

As shown above, managers will maximize revenue if they allocate output so that $MR_1 = MR_2$. That is,

$$MR_1 = P_1\left(1 + \frac{1}{E_1}\right) = P_2\left(1 + \frac{1}{E_2}\right) = MR_2$$

Since MR_1 and MR_2 must both be positive, E_1 and E_2 must both be greater (in absolute value) than one (i.e., demand must be elastic in each market). Assume that

$$P_1 < P_2$$

when $MR_1 = MR_2$. By manipulating the equation above,

$$\frac{P_1}{P_2} = \frac{\left(1 + \frac{1}{E_2}\right)}{\left(1 + \frac{1}{E_1}\right)} < 1$$

Therefore, since

$$\left(1 + \frac{1}{E_2}\right) < \left(1 + \frac{1}{E_1}\right)$$

it must be the case that

$$\left|\frac{1}{E_2}\right| > \left|\frac{1}{E_1}\right|$$

so that

$$|E_1| > |E_2|$$

The market with the lower price must have the higher elasticity at that price. Therefore, if a firm price-discriminates, it will always charge the lower price in the market having the more elastic demand curve.

Principle A manager who price-discriminates in two separate markets, A and B, will maximize total revenue for a given level of output by charging the lower price in the more elastic market and the higher price in the less elastic market. If $|E_A| > |E_B|$, then $P_A < P_B$.

Profit Maximization with Price Discrimination

Thus far we have assumed that the price-discriminating firm wishes to allocate a *given level of output* among its markets in order to maximize the revenue from selling that output. Now we discuss how a manager determines the profit-maximizing level of output and the prices to charge in the different markets.

As you probably expected, the manager maximizes profit by equating marginal revenue with marginal cost. The firm's marginal cost curve is no different from that of a nondiscriminating firm with market power. So the problem is to derive the marginal revenue curve.

With discrete data such as those in Table 17.1, we would simply increase sales as discussed above, then determine the total marginal revenue from the allocation of each unit of output to the market with the higher marginal revenue. Thus total marginal revenue from Table 17.1 would be \$45 for the first unit sold, \$36 for the second (both in market 1), \$34 for the third (in market 2), \$30 for the fourth, and so on.

For continuous demand and marginal revenue curves in each submarket, the total marginal revenue curve for a price-discriminating firm is simply the horizontal summation of the marginal revenues in each market. Assume that the firm sells in two markets, 1 and 2. The demand and marginal revenue curves in markets 1 and 2 are shown, respectively, as D_1 and MR_1 in Panel A of Figure 17.3 and as D_2 and MR_2 in Panel B. In Panel C of the figure, the total marginal revenue, MR_T, is the horizontal summation of MR_1 and MR_2.

From the above discussion, a manager will allocate any given output between the two markets so that MR_1 equals MR_2. For example, if the firm produces 300 units of output at which MR equals \$30, it will sell 100 units in market 1 and 200 in market 2. At 100 units of output (from Panel A), MR_1 equals \$30. At 200 units of output (from Panel B), MR_2 also equals \$30. Thus, no matter which market unit 300 is sold in, the firm's marginal revenue is \$30, as shown in Panel C. And this is the only allocation of 300 total units that equates the marginal

FIGURE 17.3

Deriving Total Marginal Revenue

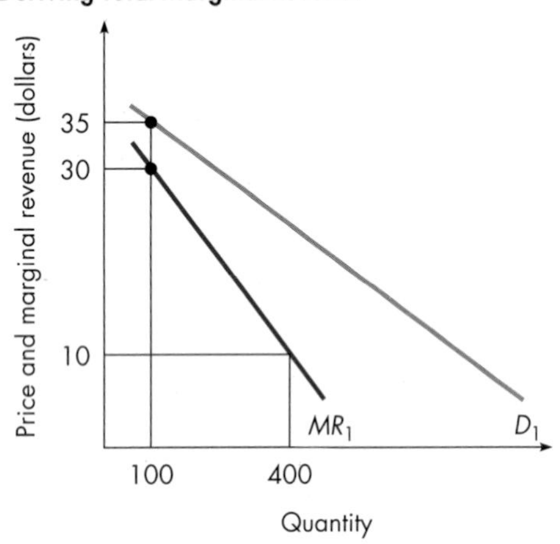

Panel A — Demand and marginal revenue: market 1

Panel B — Demand and marginal revenue: market 2

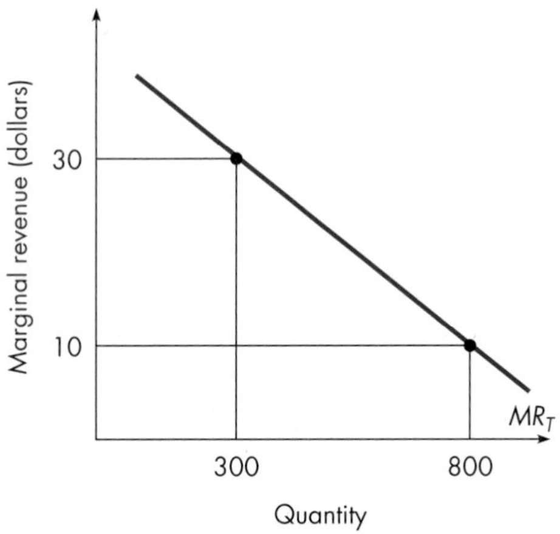

Panel C — Total marginal revenue

revenues in the two markets. Likewise, if the firm wants to sell 800 units, it will sell 400 in market 1 and 400 in market 2; as shown in the figure, the marginal revenue is \$10 in each market. Thus for 800 units of output the total marginal revenue is \$10. At every other output, the marginal revenue in Panel C (MR_T) is obtained in the same way.

For each level of output, the price in each market is given by the demand in that market. For example, if 300 units are sold, from D_1 the price of the 100 units sold in market 1 is \$35; from D_2 the price of the 200 units sold in market 2 is \$40.

FIGURE 17.4
Profit Maximization with Two Markets

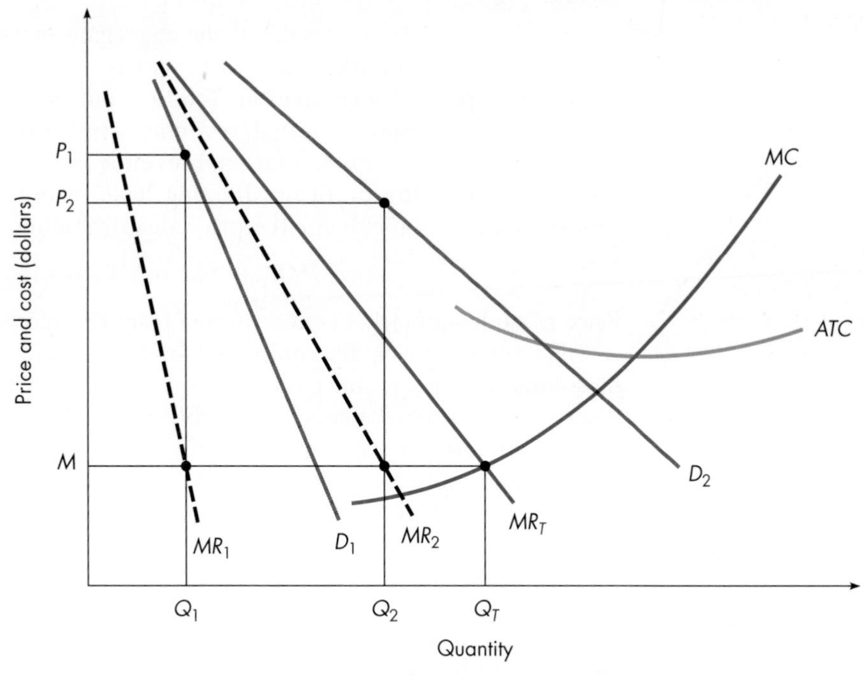

(The horizontal sum of D_1 and D_2 was not graphed since this curve is irrelevant for the price-discriminating firm.)

The only decision remaining is how much total output the firm should produce to maximize its profits. To see how this decision is made, consider Figure 17.4, in which all the relations are generalized graphically. Again the firm is selling a product in two markets: D_1 and MR_1 are demand and marginal revenue in market 1; D_2 and MR_2 are demand and marginal revenue in market 2. MR_T is the horizontal summation of the two marginal revenue curves. For convenience, all these curves are shown on the same graph, along with the firm's average cost (*ATC*) and marginal cost (*MC*) curves.

As always, the firm maximizes profit by producing the output at which total marginal revenue equals marginal cost. In this case, Q_T, where *MC* equals MR_T, is the total output. The marginal revenue and marginal cost are both equal to the dollar amount *M* in Figure 17.4.

The market allocation rule, previously determined, requires that marginal revenue be the same in each submarket. Since the total market marginal revenue is the added revenue from selling the last unit in either submarket, $MR_1 = MR_2 = M$. At a marginal revenue of *M*, the quantity sold in market 1 is Q_1, in market 2, Q_2. Since MR_T is the horizontal summation of MR_1 and MR_2, $Q_1 + Q_2 = Q_T$, the total output. Furthermore, from the relevant demand curves, the price associated with output Q_1 in market 1 is P_1, and the price associated with Q_2 in market 2 is P_2.

Summarizing these results, if the aggregate market for a firm's product can be divided into submarkets with different price elasticities, the firm can profitably practice price discrimination. Total output is determined by equating marginal cost with total marginal revenue. The output is allocated among the submarkets so as to equate marginal revenue in each submarket with total marginal revenue at the profit-maximizing level of output. With two markets, the profit-maximization rule for the price-discriminating firm is

$$MR_T = MC = MR_1 = MR_2$$

Price in each submarket is determined from the submarket demand curve.

Examples of price discrimination are not hard to find. Many drugstores offer discounts on drugs to persons 65 and over. Thus, the drugstores price-discriminate. Retired persons probably have a more elastic demand for drugs, because the market value of their time is lower. Retired persons would tend to shop around more for lower prices, and differences in price among different age groups can be explained by different price elasticities, resulting from different evaluations of time.

Movies, plays, concerts, and similar forms of entertainment practice price discrimination according to age. Generally, younger people pay lower prices. Supposedly, in such cases, younger people have more elastic demands for tickets, possibly because of the availability of more substitute forms of entertainment. (It is not correct to say that different ticket prices for afternoon and evening performances are evidence of price discrimination. These are different products in the eye of the consumer.)

Airlines frequently discriminate between vacation and business travel. Vacation travelers would have a more elastic demand than business travelers, probably because the value of time in business travel is greater. Other examples of price discrimination are electric companies that charge lower rates to industrial users than to households (although this may be, in part, due to differences in costs), and university bookstores that charge lower prices to faculty than to students. On the other hand, students frequently are charged a lower price for subscriptions to newspapers and magazines.

Manufacturers and sellers of durable goods, such as automobiles and large appliances, sometimes practice price discrimination also. Automobiles with exactly the same characteristics all have the same window or sticker price (excluding the shipping charge). But as you probably know, dealers generally discount these prices on many models. Except for extremely hot sellers, people seldom pay the listed price. However, everyone does not pay the same price for the same vehicle. Ms. Jones may pay a lower price than Mr. Smith because Ms. Jones is willing to bargain longer or possibly the dealer recognized that Mr. Smith is already sold on the car. Perhaps Mr. Smith came into the showroom, saw the list price, and said, "Wow, is that all you're charging for that great car?" In any case, Mr. Smith probably has the less elastic demand. We should note, however, that this is a slightly different form of price discrimination than that discussed above.

In this case the dealer treats each potential consumer as a separate market, and charges as much as the consumer is willing to pay, if possible.

In order to implement profit maximization with multiple markets, it would be necessary for the manager to estimate demand and marginal revenue functions for each of the markets. After summing to obtain a total marginal revenue function, total output would be that at which total marginal revenue is equal to marginal cost. Then, this output will be allocated to the various markets so that the marginal revenues are all equal to total marginal revenue at the profit-maximizing output. We illustrate this procedure with a simple algebraic example.

Multiple Market Pricing at Galactic Manufacturing

The manager of Galactic Manufacturing—a firm with substantial monopoly power—knows that the firm faces two distinct markets. Using the techniques described earlier in this text, the demand curves for these two markets were forecasted to be

$$\text{Mkt 1: } Q_1 = 1{,}000 - 20P_1 \qquad \text{and} \qquad \text{Mkt 2: } Q_2 = 500 - 5P_2$$

Solving for the inverse demand functions in the two markets,

$$\text{Mkt 1: } P_1 = 50 - 0.05Q_1 \qquad \text{and} \qquad \text{Mkt 2: } P_2 = 100 - 0.2Q_2$$

The marginal revenue functions associated with these inverse demand functions are

$$\text{Mkt 1: } MR_1 = 50 - 0.1Q_1 \qquad \text{and} \qquad \text{Mkt 2: } MR_2 = 100 - 0.4Q_2$$

To obtain the total marginal revenue function, $MR_T = f(Q_T)$, we follow steps identical to those employed in the algebraic derivation of the total marginal cost function. First, the inverse marginal revenue functions are obtained for both markets in which Galactic Manufacturing sells its product:

$$\text{Mkt 1: } Q_1 = 500 - 10MR_1 \qquad \text{and} \qquad \text{Mkt 2: } Q_2 = 250 - 2.5MR_2$$

For any given level of total output, $MR_1 = MR_2 = MR_T$; thus

$$\text{Mkt 1: } Q_1 = 500 - 10MR_T \qquad \text{and} \qquad \text{Mkt 2: } Q_2 = 250 - 2.5MR_T$$

Since $Q_T = Q_1 + Q_2$, the inverse of total marginal revenue is obtained by summing the two inverse marginal revenue curves to get

$$Q_T = Q_1 + Q_2 = 500 - 10MR_T + 250 - 2.5MR_T = 750 - 12.5MR_T$$

Taking the inverse, we obtain the total marginal revenue function facing Galactic Manufacturing:

$$MR_T = 60 - 0.08Q_T$$

Panel A of Figure 17.5 illustrates graphically the derivation of total marginal revenue for Galactic Manufacturing. Panel A shows graphs of the demand and

FIGURE 17.5
Multiple Market Pricing at Galactic Manufacturing

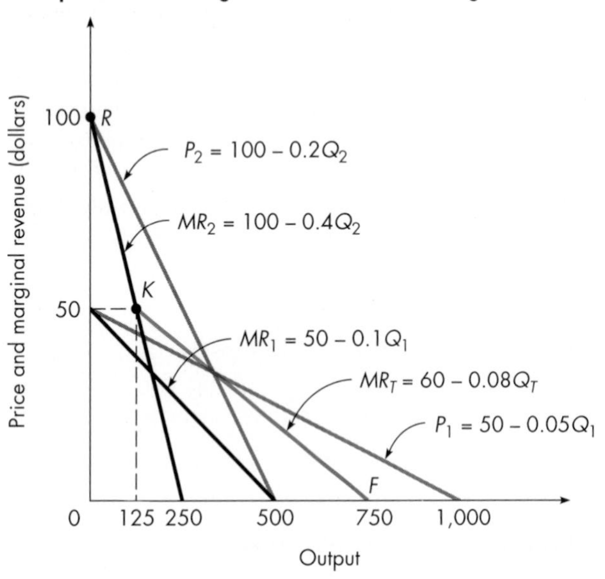

Panel A — Derivation of total marginal revenue

Panel B — Profit maximization

marginal revenue functions in markets 1 and 2. The total marginal revenue function is the line *RKF.* If total output is less than 125, every unit produced should be sold in market 2 in order to maximize revenue (for that output level) because MR_2 exceeds MR_1 until Galactic chooses to sell more than 125 units. Thus, total marginal revenue has a kink at 125 (point *K*), and MR_2 is the total marginal revenue function since $Q_1 = 0$ when total output is 125 units or less.

The manager of Galactic Manufacturing obtained from the engineering department an estimate of the firm's marginal cost function:

$$MC = 20 - 0.05Q + 0.0001Q^2$$

Equating estimated total marginal revenue and marginal cost,

$$60 - 0.08Q = 20 - 0.05Q + 0.0001Q^2$$

the manager of Galactic solved for Q using the quadratic formula and determined the profit-maximizing level of output to be 500. As you can see in Panel B of Figure 17.5, MR_T intersects MC at 500 units (point *E*). At 500 units of output, total marginal revenue and marginal cost both equal \$20. To find the optimal allocation of 500 units between the two markets, the manager allocates sales so that marginal revenues are equated across the two markets at a value of \$20. The manager must solve the following two equations:

$$\text{Mkt 1: } 20 = 50 - 0.1Q_1 \quad \text{and} \quad \text{Mkt 2: } 20 = 100 - 0.4Q_2$$

The solution is to sell 300 units in market 1 and 200 units in market 2. These points where $MR_1 = MR_2 = MR_T$ are shown in Panel B by points *C*, *D*, and *E*.

The manager determines the price to charge in the two markets by substituting the optimal quantities into the demand equations in each of the markets. The manager finds that profit is maximized by selling the 300 units of output in market 1 at a price of \$35 and the 200 units of output in market 2 at a price of \$60. Points *A* and *B* in Panel B show the optimal pricing solution for Galactic Manufacturing. By charging different prices in the separate markets, Galactic Manufacturing collects total revenues of \$10,500 (= \$35 × 300) in market 1 and \$12,000 (= \$60 × 200) in market 2, for a combined market total revenue of \$22,500 (= \$10,500 + \$12,000).

To verify that charging two (different) prices generates more revenue than charging a single price in both markets, we now calculate the total revenue Galactic could collect if it instead charged a single price to sell 500 units.[4] The price Galactic can charge to sell a total of 500 units is \$40, which is the price for 500 units obtained from the horizontally summed demand curves in markets 1 and 2. Mathematically, this price can be obtained from the price equation associated with MR_T:

$$P_T = 60 - 0.04Q_T = 60 - 0.04(500) = \$40$$

If Galactic charged all customers a single price of \$40, it would sell 500 units and generate just \$20,000 (= \$40 × 500) in total revenue—a reduction in revenue of \$2,500 compared with the revenue from charging different prices in the two market segments. We now summarize this discussion of pricing in multiple markets with a principle:

Principle A manager who wishes to sell output in *n* separate markets will maximize profit if the firm produces the level of total output and allocates that output among the *n* separate markets so that

$$MR_T = MR_1 = \cdots = MR_n = MC$$

The optimal prices to charge in each market are determined from the demand functions in each of the *n* markets.

17.3 FIRMS SELLING MULTIPLE PRODUCTS

Even the most cursory survey of firms operating in the United States shows that many firms produce several different products or at least several different models in their product lines. While in some cases a firm's products are unrelated, in most cases the products are related either in consumption or in production.

[4]Notice that 500 units is also the profit-maximizing output level when Galactic chooses to charge all buyers a single price. This is true because MR_T is the monopolist's marginal revenue curve when the two market demand curves are horizontally summed to construct the total demand facing the monopolist. In this example, the horizontal summation of the two demand equations is $P_T = 60 - 0.04Q_T$ and the associated marginal revenue is $MR_T = 60 - 0.08Q_T$.

ILLUSTRATION 17.1

Sometimes It's Hard to Price-Discriminate

In the theoretical discussion of price discrimination, we made two important points: (1) Firms must separate the markets according to demand elasticity, and (2) firms must be able to separate markets so as to keep buyers in the higher-price market from buying in the lower-price market. In some of the market examples we used, it was relatively easy to separate the markets. For example, at movie theaters it is fairly simple, and relatively inexpensive, to prevent an adult from entering the theater with a lower-priced child's ticket. In other cases of price discrimination, it is rather difficult or costly to separate the markets. If it is impossible or expensive to separate markets, price discrimination will not be profitable, and the monopolist will charge a single price to all customers.

One of the most frequently cited examples of a market in which separation is difficult is the airline market. It is no secret that airlines attempt to charge leisure fliers lower fares than business travelers. The story of such an attempt by Northwest Airlines illustrates the difficulty of separating markets.

The Wall Street Journal reported: "Northwest Airlines, seeking to entice families and groups of leisure travelers who often wait for deep fare cuts before flying, has introduced a permanent discount fare. The new supersaver fare will offer savings of 20 percent to 40 percent anytime *groups of two or more people* travel together." According to a Northwest vice president, "We're trying to decouple the leisure fares from the rest of the fare market by offering fares low enough so that it won't pay for them to wait for a special fare sale."

The *WSJ* noted that this change would be likely to stimulate family travel but would also eliminate the use of supersaver fares by business travelers. Previously, many business travelers purchased round-trip supersaver tickets when fares dropped below 50 percent, then threw away the return portion of the ticket or used it later. Northwest was planning to raise or do away with its other supersaver fares designed to attract leisure travelers. Most business travelers fly alone and would not be able to take advantage of the new, lower fares requiring groups of two or more. The Northwest executive also predicted that businesspeople would not abuse these tickets. Should the plan stick and spread, he said, it will allow airlines to maintain an attractive offering for the most price-sensitive travelers, while allowing the basic supersaver fares to continue rising along with business rates.

This reasoning was a bit optimistic on the part of the airline. The *WSJ* noted that groups of business travelers could work around the restrictions that currently applied to supersavers. The president of one travel agency said, "Groups of business people going to company meetings or conventions might be able to save thousands." One airline official expressed concern that travel agents would match travelers who did not know each other who were going to the same destination. Clearly there were many ways to defeat the airline's attempts to price-discriminate effectively.

But Northwest knew about the problems and tried to make the practice of cross-buying difficult. Travelers were required to book their flights together, check in together, and follow identical itineraries in order to qualify for the group discounts. The fares were nonrefundable, required a Saturday night stay, and had to be booked 14 days in advance—practices that business travelers typically would find difficult to accomplish. Of course, some of these restrictions designed to weed out business travelers could discourage many leisure travelers, the very people the new discounts were designed to attract. And obviously single leisure travelers would be left out.

As you can see, the problem of separating markets—preventing customers in the higher-price market from buying in the lower-price market—can be an extremely challenging task for the would-be price discriminator. For airlines, it would be much easier if passengers came with signs saying "business traveler" or "leisure traveler." As previously noted, in markets where separating the higher-price buyers from the lower-price buyers is too difficult or too expensive, price discrimination will not be profitable.

Source: Brett Pulley, "Northwest Cuts Fares to Boost Leisure Travel," *The Wall Street Journal*, Jan. 12, 1993.

When the products that a firm produces are related, the firm's output and pricing decision must incorporate the interrelations in order to maximize total profit.

Multiple Products Related in Consumption

Recall that the demand for a particular commodity depends not only on the price of the product itself but also on the prices of related commodities, incomes, tastes, and so on. For simplicity, we ignore the other factors and write one demand function as

$$Q_X = f(P_X, P_Y)$$

where Q_X is the quantity demanded of commodity X, P_X is the price of X, and P_Y is the price of a related commodity Y—either a substitute or complement.

In the discussion so far in the text, we have treated P_Y as if it were given to the firm. That is, we assumed P_Y to be a parameter determined outside the firm. Thus, the firm would maximize its profits by selecting the appropriate level of production and price for X. If, however, the firm in question produces *both* commodities X and Y, the price of the related commodity Y is no longer beyond the control of the manager.

In order to maximize profit, the levels of output and prices for the related commodities must be determined *jointly*. For a two-product firm, the profit-maximizing conditions remain the same:

$$MR_X = MC_X \qquad \text{and} \qquad MR_Y = MC_Y$$

However, the marginal revenue of X will depend on the quantities sold of both X and Y, as will the marginal revenue of Y. The interdependence of the two marginal revenues, MR_X and MR_Y, requires that the marginal conditions set forth above must be satisfied *simultaneously*. (Note that in this case the products are not related in production, so MC_X and MC_Y depend only upon, respectively, the output of X and the output of Y.) When products are used together, consumers typically buy them together, and these kinds of goods are **complements in consumption.** A different situation, **substitutes in consumption,** arises when a firm sells multiple products that are substitutes. Then buyers would purchase only one of the firm's products. In both cases, marginal revenues are interdependent.

complements in consumption
Products that are used together and purchased together.

substitutes in consumption
Products are substitutes and buyers purchase only one of the firm's products.

To show how a manager would maximize profit under these circumstances, we will use another hypothetical example. In this example we will look at a firm that produces products that are substitutes in consumption, but exactly the same technique applies for products that are complements in consumption.

Producing Multiple Products at Zicon Manufacturing

Zicon Manufacturing produces two types of automobile vacuum cleaners. One, which we denote as product X, plugs into the cigarette lighter receptacle; the other—product Y—has rechargeable batteries. Assuming that there is no relation between the two products other than the apparent substitutability in consumption, the manager of Zicon wanted to determine the profit-maximizing levels of production and price for the two products.

Using the techniques described in this text, the demand functions for the two products were forecasted to be

$$Q_X = 80{,}000 - 8{,}000P_X + 6{,}000P_Y \qquad \text{and} \qquad Q_Y = 40{,}000 - 4{,}000P_Y + 4{,}000P_X$$

Solving these two forecasted demand functions simultaneously, the manager obtained the following functions in which prices are a function of both quantities:[5]

$$P_X = 70 - 0.0005Q_X - 0.00075Q_Y \qquad \text{and} \qquad P_Y = 80 - 0.001Q_Y - 0.0005Q_X$$

The marginal revenue functions were[6]

$$MR_X = 70 - 0.001Q_X - 0.00075Q_Y \qquad \text{and} \qquad MR_Y = 80 - 0.002Q_Y - 0.0005Q_X$$

As noted earlier, MR_X is a function of both Q_X and Q_Y, as is MR_Y.

The production manager obtained estimates of the marginal cost functions:

$$MC_X = 10 + 0.0005Q_X \qquad \text{and} \qquad MC_Y = 20 + 0.00025Q_Y$$

To determine the output that will maximize profit, the manager of Zicon equated MR and MC for the two products:

$$70 - 0.001Q_X - 0.00075Q_Y = 10 + 0.0005Q_X$$
$$80 - 0.002Q_Y - 0.0005Q_X = 20 + 0.00025Q_Y$$

Solving these equations simultaneously for Q_X and Q_Y (following the approach in footnote 5), the profit-maximizing outputs were found to be $Q_X^* = 30{,}000$ and $Q_Y^* = 20{,}000$. Finally, using these outputs in the price functions, the manager of Zicon found that the profit-maximizing prices for X and Y were

$$P_X^* = 70 - 0.0005(30{,}000) - 0.00075(20{,}000) = \$40$$

and

$$P_Y^* = 80 - 0.001(20{,}000) - 0.0005(30{,}000) = \$45$$

From the preceding discussion and Illustration 17.2, the point we wish to stress is that if a firm produces products that are related in consumption, profit maximization requires that output levels and prices be determined jointly. Specifically, in such a firm, the profit-maximizing price for a particular commodity will be determined not only by the demand and cost conditions for that commodity but also by those of any related commodities the firm produces.

---

[5]One way to solve these two equations simultaneously is to use the method of substitution. First, solve one demand function for P_X in terms of Q_X and P_Y and the other demand function for P_Y in terms of Q_Y and P_X. Then substitute the equation for P_Y into the equation for P_X, and vice versa. These two equations can then be solved for P_X and P_Y in terms of Q_X and Q_Y.

[6]As noted several times, the marginal revenue curve associated with a straight-line demand curve has the same intercept and is twice as steep as the demand curve. The intercepts for MR_X and MR_Y are, respectively, $(70 - 0.00075Q_Y)$ and $(80 - 0.0005Q_X)$. Thus

$$MR_X = (70 - 0.00075Q_Y) - (2)(0.0005)Q_X = 70 - 0.00075Q_Y - 0.001Q_X$$

and

$$MR_Y = (80 - 0.0005Q_X) - (2)(0.001)Q_Y = 80 - 0.0005Q_X - 0.002Q_Y$$

ILLUSTRATION 17.2

Computer Printers and Replacement Cartridges: Pricing Multiple Products That Are Complements

When a firm sells two (or more) products that are related in consumption, as either substitutes or complements, the price of each good affects the demand for the other good. Therefore, a manager must account for this interdependence by choosing prices that result in equalization of marginal revenue and marginal cost for both goods *simultaneously.* While you may have found our discussion of this rule a bit tedious because of the messy algebra required to solve marginal conditions simultaneously, we want you to see that, messy or not, the rule can offer a manager a way to make sizable profits. Gillette, the manufacturer of razors and blades, understood this pricing relation and made a fortune nearly a half-century ago by setting a low price for razors to stimulate demand for its high-profit-margin blades.* Today, many multiproduct firms still can increase profits by making pricing decisions that account for product complementarities.

The Wall Street Journal recently reported that manufacturers of computer printers are enjoying exceptional profitability despite dramatically falling prices for computer printers.[†] Managers at companies such as Hewlett-Packard, Seiko-Epson, and Canon have exploited the multiproduct pricing rule for complements, discussed in this chapter, to make huge profits in the market for replacement printer cartridges—both ink-jet cartridges and laser toner cartridges. Computer printers enjoy nearly the same popularity as personal computers: over 100 million of them are in use worldwide. In the *WSJ* article, John B. Jones, Jr., an analyst at Salomon Brothers, estimated that H-P, which has about half of the entire printer market, earned an astonishing $3.4 billion worldwide on sales of ink-jet and laser replacement cartridges.

The strategy for making the replacement cartridge market enormously profitable is a straightforward application of some of the tools developed in managerial economics. First, since the two goods, printers and replacement cartridges, are complements produced by the multiproduct firms, the printer firms lower prices on the printers and raise prices on replacement cartridges. The *WSJ* reported that the profit margin on printers is just 30 percent while the profit margin on replacement cartridges is a whopping 70 percent. One H-P official, commenting on the firm's pricing policy for replacement cartridges, was quoted as saying, "We just charge what the market will bear." Of course this is true of any firm with market power, but H-P has cleverly boosted "what the market will bear" by lowering prices of its printers, the complement good.

A second part of the strategy for exploiting profits in the printer–replacement cartridge business involves securing profits over the long run by slowing or blocking entry of rivals into the replacement cartridge market. The large printer manufacturers now design their printer cartridges so that they are not simply plastic boxes with ink or toner in them. Purposely, engineers design the cartridges to include some or all of the printer-head technology required to make the printer work. In so doing, the printer cartridge can be covered by patents to prevent other companies from producing "clone" replacement cartridges. Clearly, this second part of the strategy is just as important as the first part, at least if long-run profitability is the manager's objective.

It is interesting to note that H-P, Canon, and Seiko-Epson are all suing Nu-Kote Holding, a Dallas supplier of generic replacement cartridges, for patent infringement. Nu-Kote, in turn, is suing the three manufacturers for allegedly colluding to keep replacement cartridge prices artificially high. It seems to us that Nu-Kote would be smart to spend its litigation resources winning the patent infringement case and let any alleged pricing conspiracy continue to prop up prices of its product.

*King Gillette invented the disposable razor blade but did not make much profit selling it. He sold the patent and the name, and it was the new owner who devised the strategy of setting a low price for razors and a high price for the blades. Using this now widely used pricing strategy, the new owner of Gillette was enormously successful.

[†]Lee Gomez, "Industry Focus: Computer-Printer Price Drop Isn't Starving Makers," *The Wall Street Journal*, Aug. 16, 1996.

Principle When a firm produces two products, X and Y, that are related in consumption either as substitutes or complements, the manager of the multiple-product firm maximizes profit by producing and selling the amounts of X and Y for which

$$MR_X = MC_X$$

and

$$MR_Y = MC_Y$$

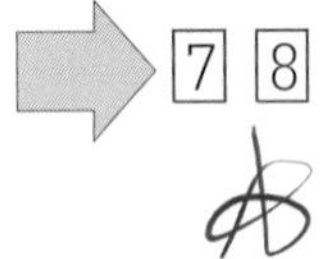

are *simultaneously* satisfied. The profit-maximizing prices, P_X and P_Y, are determined by substituting the optimal levels of X and Y into the demand functions and solving for P_X and P_Y.

Multiple Products That Are Substitutes in Production

substitutes in production
Goods, produced by the same firm, that compete for limited production facilities.

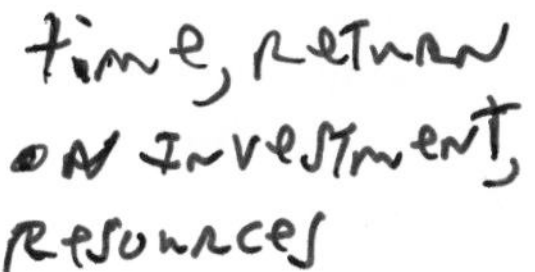

It is not uncommon for multiproduct firms to produce goods that are **substitutes in production.** This situation is often encountered when a firm produces several models of the same basic product. These different models compete for the limited production facilities of the firm and are therefore substitutes in the firm's production process. In the long run, the firm can adjust its production facility in order to produce the profit-maximizing level of each product. We will now demonstrate how a manager could determine the profit-maximizing number of total hours to operate a production facility (H_T^*) and the optimal allocation of hours between the production of good $X(H_X^*)$ and good $Y(H_Y^*)$.

The optimization condition for the allocation of the production facility between the production of X and Y is easy to demonstrate. A manager first must determine, for each of the two products X and Y, the additional revenue that can be generated by allocating to a good one more hour of the production facility. Consider production of good X. The amount of additional output of X that can be produced by using the facility one more hour in the production of X can be expressed as $\Delta X/\Delta H_X$, which is the marginal product for good X of one more hour of time spent producing X. The same relation holds for good Y. The marginal products of X and Y for extra hours of production time can be expressed as

$$\frac{\Delta X}{\Delta H_X} = MP_{H_X} \qquad \text{and} \qquad \frac{\Delta Y}{\Delta H_Y} = MP_{H_Y}$$

In order to determine the value to the firm of one more hour of time spent producing either good X or good Y, the manager must have estimates of marginal revenue for each good, MR_X and MR_Y. As shown in Chapter 14 for firms with market power, the marginal revenue product of an input measures the additional revenue the firm can earn by using 1 more unit of an input. For goods X and Y, the marginal revenue products are

$$MRP_X = \frac{\Delta TR}{\Delta H_X} = MR_X \times MP_{H_X} \qquad \text{and} \qquad MRP_Y = \frac{\Delta TR}{\Delta H_Y} = MR_Y \times MP_{H_Y}$$

For a given number of total hours of production facility time, the firm will maximize total revenue and profit by allocating the facility so that its marginal reve-

FIGURE 17.6
Profit-Maximizing Allocation of Production Facilities

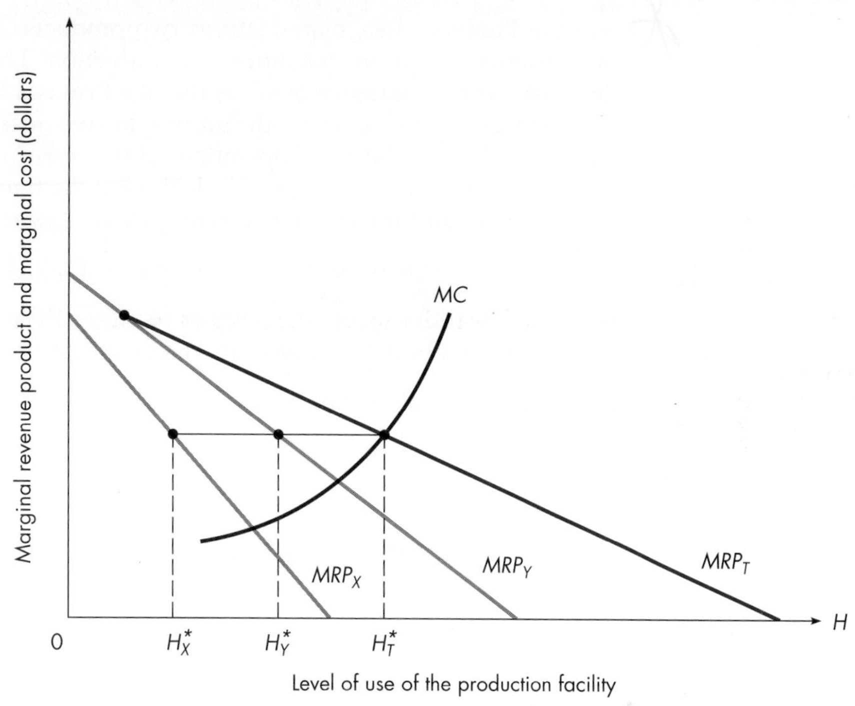

nue product in producing each good is the same:

$$MRP_X = MRP_Y$$

If the allocation of total hours were such that $MRP_X > MRP_Y$, total revenue could be increased by reallocating hours away from the production of Y to the production of X—increase H_X and decrease H_Y. This reallocation would reduce MRP_X and increase MRP_Y. Reallocation should continue until the marginal revenue products are equal, $MRP_X = MRP_Y$.

To find the optimal number of total hours to operate a facility (H_T^*), the *total* marginal revenue product curve (MPR_T) must be constructed by horizontally summing MRP_X and MRP_Y, as shown in Figure 17.6. The profit-maximizing condition is

$$MRP_T = MC = MRP_X = MRP_Y$$

Profits will be maximized when total marginal revenue product equals marginal cost and this production is allocated so that the marginal additions to revenue are the same for the two products. H_X^* is devoted to the production of X, H_Y^* is devoted to the production of Y, and $H_X^* + H_Y^* = H_T^*$. To see how this condition can be utilized, let's look at a simplified example.

Multiple-Product Production at Surefire Products

Surefire Products, Inc., manufactures two products, X and Y, that are unrelated in consumption but are substitutes in production. The manager can increase or decrease the total number of hours that the firm can use its production facilities. The manager wants to know the answer to two questions: (1) What is the optimal level of usage (hours of operation) of the plant? (2) How should the level of usage be allocated between the production of the two products?

The demand functions for the two products were forecasted to be

$$Q_X = 60 - 0.5P_X \quad \text{and} \quad Q_Y = 40 - 0.67P_Y$$

where the quantities were the number of units demanded per day and the prices were expressed in dollars per unit. The inverse demand functions were

$$P_X = 120 - 2Q_X \quad \text{and} \quad P_Y = 60 - 1.5Q_Y$$

From these inverse demand functions, the marginal revenue functions were

$$MR_X = 120 - 4Q_X \quad \text{and} \quad MR_Y = 60 - 3Q_Y$$

Discussions with the plant supervisor indicated that in one hour of production time either 2 units of X or 4 units of Y could be produced. In a sense, the production functions for the two products are

$$Q_X = 2H_X \quad \text{and} \quad Q_Y = 4H_Y$$

where H_X and H_Y denote, respectively, hours of assembly-line time in the production of X and Y. From the production functions, the marginal products are $MP_{H_X} = 2$ and $MP_{H_Y} = 4$.

Using the demand forecasts and the estimates of the production functions provided by the plant supervisor, estimates of the marginal revenue product of the production facility in the production of X and Y were

$$\begin{aligned} MRP_{H_X} &= MR_X \times MP_{H_X} = [120 - 4(2H_X)] \times (2) \\ &= 240 - 16H_X \end{aligned}$$

and

$$\begin{aligned} MRP_{H_Y} &= MR_Y \times MP_{H_Y} = [60 - 3(4H_Y)] \times (4) \\ &= 240 - 48H_Y \end{aligned}$$

To obtain the total marginal revenue product function, these two curves were summed horizontally, that is, these functions were inverted to find H_X and H_Y, the hours were summed ($H_T = H_X + H_Y$), then the inverse was taken once again. The resulting total MRP was

$$MRP_T = 240 - 12H_T$$

Working with the engineers for Surefire, the plant supervisor was able to come up with an estimate of the additional cost of operating the plant an addi-

FIGURE 17.7
Substitutes in Production at Surefire Products, Inc.

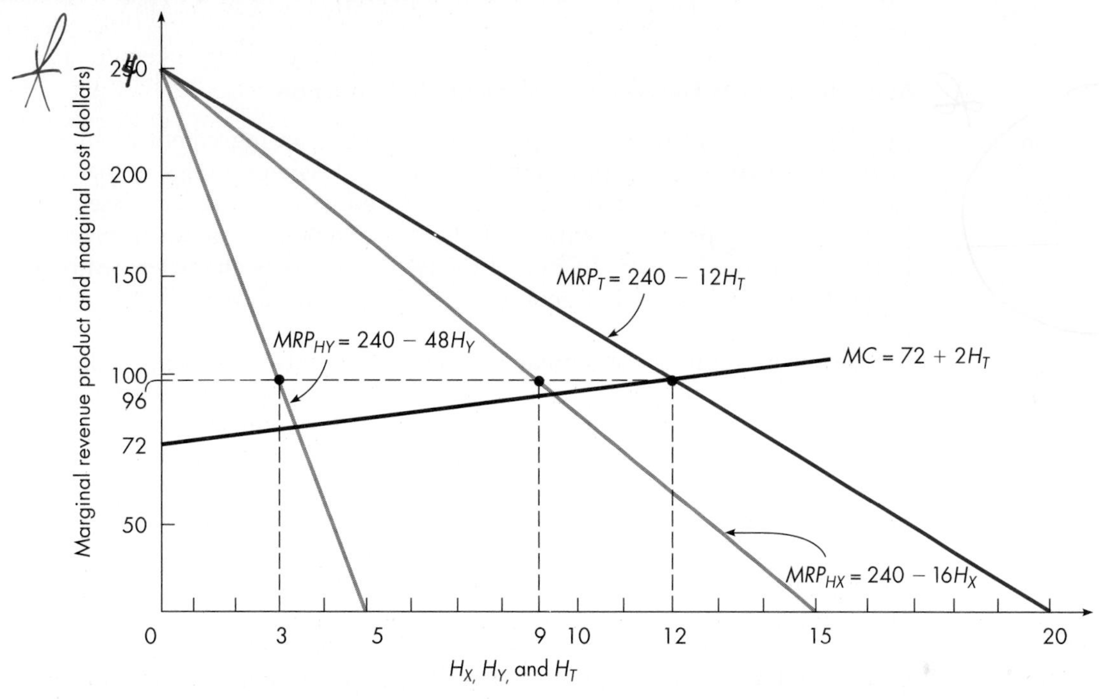

tional hour—an incremental (marginal) cost for usage of the plant. This estimate was

$$MC = 72 + 2H_T$$

Figure 17.7 shows MRP_X, MRP_Y, MRP_T, and MC for this example.

Equating the total marginal revenue product of an hour's usage of the plant with the marginal cost of an additional hour's usage,

$$240 - 12H_T = 72 + 2H_T$$

the manager then solved for H_T and found that the optimal level of usage of the plant was 12 hours per day. At this level of usage, $MRP_T = MC = \$96$. To allocate these hours between the production of X and Y, the marginal revenue products for the production facility in the production of X and Y must both be equal to \$96:

$$240 - 16H_X = 96 \quad \text{and} \quad 240 - 48H_Y = 96$$

Since $H_X^* = 9$ and $H_Y^* = 3$, the optimal allocation would be nine hours in the production of X and three hours in the production of Y. Figure 17.7 shows the profit-maximizing solution for Surefire Products.

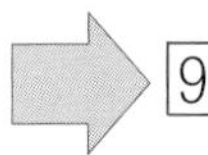

From the production functions, the quantity of X produced is 18 (= 2 × 9) units, and the quantity of Y produced is 12 (= 4 × 3) units. The prices are $P_X^* =$ \$84 [= 120 − 2(18)] and $P_Y^* =$ \$42 [= 60 − 1.5(12)].

Multiple Products That Are Complements in Production

complements in production
Two or more goods that are produced using a common input.

Complements in production typically occur when an ingredient input is used to produce two or more products. One of the classic examples is that of beef carcasses and hides. The food products produced with the beef carcasses and the leather products produced with the hides are complement goods in production. Furthermore, the joint production of the two products is characterized by fixed proportions—for each additional beef carcass produced, one additional hide is produced also.

Petroleum refining has similar characteristics. With an existing refinery and a given mix of input crude oils, production of an additional barrel of one of the lighter distillates, such as gasoline, requires that the refinery produce some additional amount of the heavy distillates, such as fuel oil. Complementarity in production can also be observed in mineral extraction. Frequently, two or more metals are found together in the same ore deposit. When the ore goes into the smelter, more than one metal is produced. For example, since nickel and zinc frequently are in the same deposit, the smelters are designed to produce both metals from the same ore.

Since complements in production frequently result when one raw material is used to produce two or more products, this type of joint production results in the products being produced in fixed proportions from the ingredient. When a firm produces products that are complements in production, the manager maximizes profit by choosing to produce the level of output of the joint product at which the joint marginal revenue (MR_J) equals the marginal cost:

$$MR_J = MC$$

The joint marginal revenue gives the additional revenue attributable to producing 1 more unit of the joint product—say, one more beef carcass or one more ton of mineral ore—from which two (or more) products will be forthcoming. In the case of complements in production, the relevant marginal revenue for decision making is the joint or combined additional revenue from selling the additional units of *both* products which come from 1 extra unit of the joint product. Once the profit-maximizing production level is determined, the prices for the individual products are taken from the individual demand curves.

While this decision-making procedure is just another application of the optimization theory developed in Chapter 4, it differs a bit from the other cases in this chapter, which involved horizontally summing either marginal cost curves or marginal revenues. In order to derive the joint marginal revenue, we sum the individual marginal revenue curves *vertically* over the range of production for which both individual marginal revenues are positive. Since the firm earns additional revenue from the sale of two products, for a given level of output of the

FIGURE 17.8
Profit Maximization with Joint Products

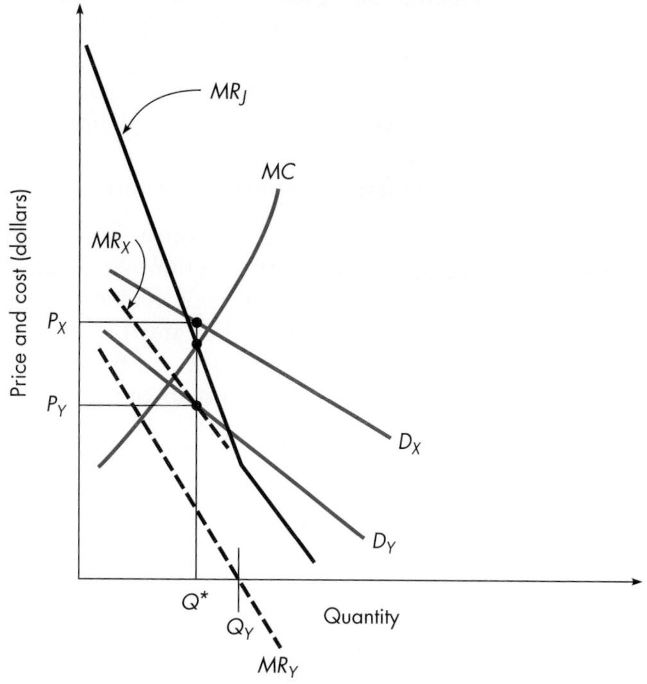

joint product, the total or joint marginal revenue is the sum of the marginal revenues from the two goods, MR_X and MR_Y. Thus, joint marginal revenue, MR_J, is obtained by vertically summing the individual marginal revenues over the range of outputs for which both MR_X and MR_Y are positive. When the marginal revenue of one of the goods becomes zero, as all marginal revenue curves will do at sufficiently high sales levels, that marginal revenue is set equal to zero and the vertical summation continues until all (or both in this case) marginal revenues are zero. At each point where one of the marginal revenue curves being vertically summed is equal to zero, a kink in the joint marginal revenue curve is created.

Figure 17.8 illustrates this vertical summation process for the case of two complement goods in production. In the figure, MR_Y becomes zero at an output denoted as Q_Y. For sales of commodity Y in excess of Q_Y, the marginal revenue for Y would be negative. Because no manager would wish to sell a unit of a product for which the marginal revenue is negative, the maximum amount of Y the firm will *sell* is Q_Y. Therefore, the marginal revenue curve for the joint product is the vertical sum of MR_X and MR_Y until MR_Y equals zero. For outputs in excess of Q_Y, the excess units of Y would be discarded, and only commodity X would be sold. Beyond Q_Y the joint marginal revenue curve corresponds to MR_X. The result is the kinked MR_J curve shown in the figure.

Figure 17.8 shows the profit-maximizing equilibrium situation for a firm producing joint products. The profit-maximizing condition stated above, $MR_J = MC$, determines the optimal level of production of the joint good, Q^* $(= Q_X^* = Q_Y^*)$. The profit-maximizing prices, P_X^* and P_Y^*, are found on the individual demand curves. To see how the firm can implement profit maximization with joint products, we turn to a stylized example.

Joint Products at ChemTech Corporation

ChemTech Corporation produces refined chemicals, and two of these chemicals are complements in production. As it refines the raw chemical input, the processes yield equal amounts of xylene and ylene, denoted, of course, as X and Y.[7] The manager of ChemTech must determine the profit-maximizing amounts of xylene and ylene to produce and the prices to charge.

The manager has forecasts of the demand functions for the two products:

$$Q_X = 285{,}000 - 1{,}000P_X \qquad \text{and} \qquad Q_Y = 150{,}000 - 2{,}000P_Y$$

where quantities are measured in 55-gallon drums and prices are in dollars per drum. The marginal revenue curves associated with these demand functions (derived from the inverse demand functions) are

$$MR_X = 285 - 0.002Q_X \qquad \text{and} \qquad MR_Y = 75 - 0.001Q_Y$$

Note that MR_Y is equal to zero at an output of 75,000 drums. Over the range of output from zero to 75,000 units, the joint marginal revenue function is the vertical summation of the two marginal revenue curves:

$$MR_J = 285 - 0.002Q + 75 - 0.001Q = 360 - 0.003Q$$

where Q is the sum of the two outputs, $Q_X + Q_Y$. For output levels greater than 75,000, the joint marginal revenue is the same as MR_X. The joint marginal revenue function for ChemTech is shown in Figure 17.9 as the line between A and C, with the kink at point B, where MR_Y becomes negative. If production of the joint product exceeds 75,000 drums, the production of ylene in excess of 75,000 drums will be destroyed, discarded, or disposed of somehow rather than sold.

The marginal cost function for refining the raw chemical input is estimated to be

$$MC = 10 + 0.002Q$$

where Q is the number of drums of joint product, $Q_X + Q_Y$. Equating marginal revenue and marginal cost for the joint product,

$$MR_J = MC$$
$$360 - 0.003Q = 10 + 0.002Q$$

Solving for the production level of the joint product, the profit-maximizing level of output is 70,000 drums. From the demand functions, the profit-maximizing

[7] In other words, to keep this example simple, one drum of raw chemical input yields one drum of xylene and one drum of ylene.

FIGURE 17.9
Complements in Production at ChemTech Corporation

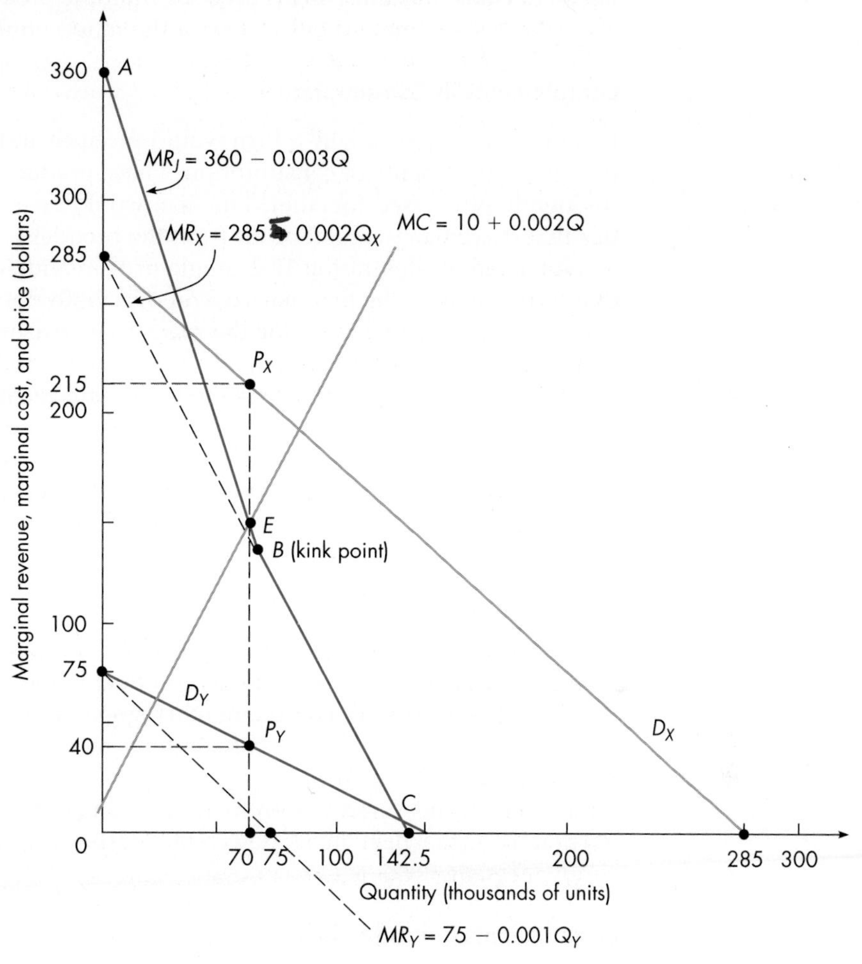

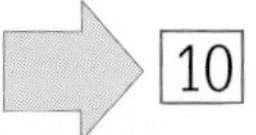

prices for xylene and ylene are \$215 per drum of xylene and \$40 per drum of ylene.[8] Using the profit-maximizing pricing decisions results in total revenue of \$17,850,000 [= (215 + 40) × 70,000].

17.4 WHY MULTIPLE PRODUCTS?

The preceding discussion simply assumed that firms produce not one but several products; then it described the conditions of production under several sets of product characteristics. No attempt was made to answer why firms would want

[8]The two demand functions, which can be derived from the marginal revenue functions, are $P_X^* = 285 - 0.001Q_X$ and $P_Y^* = 75 - 0.0005Q_Y$. Substituting 70,000 for Q_X and Q_Y in the two functions provides the profit-maximizing prices $P_X^* = \$215$ and $P_Y^* = \$40$.

to produce multiple products. In some cases the answer is obvious; in others it is not so obvious. Certainly firms produce multiple products for a multitude of reasons. We can summarize only a few of the most common reasons.

Complements in Consumption

It is rather easy to see why a firm would produce and sell two or more products that are complements in consumption. These products are used together and are frequently purchased together. The firm would be able to set prices and quantities that maximize the total profit from the products.

As noted in Illustration 17.2, single firms manufacture razors and the blades that fit the razors. The firm has control over both design and prices. It may well want to set a very low price for the razor to increase sales and extend the future market for its blades. It can also advertise the two together.

Another example is a firm such as Coleman, which produces several commodities that are complementary—tents, lanterns, stoves, ice chests, and so forth. Consumers of outdoor recreational equipment frequently wish to purchase this bundle of commodities. Therefore, we would expect the sales of, say, lanterns to depend to some extent on the price charged for goods that are used in conjunction, for example, tents, It follows that the price charged for tents would affect the profits of the division producing lanterns and those of the firm as a whole. Even if the goods were not purchased at the same time, buyer loyalty can carry over for the next purchase. A family that was well satisfied with a Coleman tent would be likely to choose a Coleman product when it purchased a stove.

Similar examples of complementary goods produced and sold by the same firm are golf clubs and golf balls, tennis rackets and tennis balls, and baseball equipment. In all such cases the firm will set output and price to maximize total profits rather than the profit from a single item. Therefore, as stressed in Section 17.3, the firm must determine output and price for all the products simultaneously.

Complements in Production

The discussion of complements in production in Section 17.3 deals specifically with the fixed proportions production of two or more products from the same ingredient input. We mentioned as examples the production of beef carcasses and hides, a refinery that produces several final products from crude oil, and a smelter that obtains different minerals from the same ore. But there are more subtle examples of complementarity in production for which the final products need not be produced in fixed proportions.

Less obvious examples arise from capital expenditures that contribute to the production of more than one product. Railroads, for instance, offer both freight and passenger transportation over the same tracks and between the same depots. These inputs are shared. The postal service shares its capital in sorting and delivering parcels and letters. In these instances, a single investment contributes to the production of more than one product. This is a common phenomenon among multiproduct firms.

ILLUSTRATION 17.3

Multiproduct Firms: Diversification to Reduce Risk

In our discussion of why firms diversify and produce several different products, we did not mention the problem of dealing with risk. It is a well-known theorem in portfolio theory that an investor can reduce the variability of a portfolio of investments by diversification—increasing the number of different types of investments. Many manufacturing firms try to follow this advice by increasing the number of different products they produce, particularly when the firms previously had "all their eggs in one basket" but the basket went into a slump. In this illustration, we show you how two market leaders in two vastly different industries added new products to their lines to reduce risk.

At the end of the cold war in the early 1990s many companies that had specialized in sales to the military experienced large declines in sales with the reduction of U.S. military expenditures. One such firm was the Canadian firm CAE Inc., the world's largest producer of aircraft simulators. The firm's traditional customers had been the military and the airline industry. Military sales had fallen, perhaps permanently, and airline sales had slumped. CAE was determined to become much less dependent on the military segment of its market.

The company was trying to capitalize on its most productive resource, expertise in high-tech simulation, to develop a host of novel products. According to CAE's president, "The markets we're now serving don't offer the growth we'd like to see. So we have to seek new products and new markets." Among the wide range of new products introduced were a simulator system for hospitals to train anesthetists without risking anyone's life, other types of simulators to train medical practitioners in emergency procedures, the first commercial version of a totally implantable artificial heart, a "telerobotic" that would allow a miner to perform work underground without leaving the surface, and a simulator to train refinery workers.

The goal of the company was to reverse a three-year decline in sales. All in all, CAE had about 20 major initiatives in new product areas. According to a senior vice president, the plan was showing promise: "Although the airline business has been slow over the last few years, our annual sales haven't been decreasing. We've managed to smooth it because we have a lot of different strengths to our bow."

In an entirely different industry, a leading toy manufacturer also reduced risk by increasing the number of products offered. During the 1980s, the conventional wisdom in the toy industry was that a firm should concentrate its marketing on a few major toys, in the hope of coming up with a roaring success that would carry the company with large profits. During that period, the fortunes of many toy companies rose and fell on mega-hits and mega-misses. In the early 1990s, Hasbro, the industry leader, began bucking that wisdom by diversifying. Hasbro had grown from a tiny firm to the largest toymaker by 1985 with blockbusters such as G.I. Joe. But its growth stalled in the late 1980s with a series of losers.

By 1992, Hasbro was no longer dependent on a handful of toys. Six years before, three toys had accounted for 45 percent of the company's sales. By 1992, no toy accounted for more than 5 percent. Even a major flop would not have hurt the overall profit picture much. An analyst at Salomon Brothers stated that Hasbro was "no longer like a traditional toy company where unpredictability is an issue, but they've become more like a consumer products franchise, where stability and dependability are key words."

Source: This illustration is based on Larry M. Greenberg, "Shrinking Aircraft Market Forces CAE to Branch Out," *The Wall Street Journal*, Aug. 24, 1993, and Joseph Pereira, "Hasbro Enjoys Life Off the Toy-Market Roller Coaster," *The Wall Street Journal*, May 5, 1992.

Whenever it is less costly to produce products together than to produce them separately, economies of scope exist. Recall from the discussion of economies of scope in Chapters 10 and 15 that multiproduct firms enjoy a cost advantage over single-product rivals when there are economies of scope in production. With economies of scope, not only does a multiproduct firm benefit from higher profits due to lower costs, but, as discussed in Chapter 15, the economies of scope can provide a barrier to entry that enhances market power and profit.

There are other examples of the production of goods that are complementary in production. But we can summarize the majority of such cases simply by saying that when such complementarity exists, it is less costly to produce the goods together than to produce them separately.

Substitution in Consumption and Production

One reason that many firms produce products that are good substitutes for other products they sell, even when these products compete for time and space on a firm's production facilities, was discussed at some length in Chapter 15. As noted there, a firm can sometimes block entry or gain a competitive advantage by introducing substitutes for its own product in the market. Such a maneuver is frequently preferred to seeing new entrants or old rivals introduce them. Producing related products crowds the market with choices. As the demand for each individual product decreases and becomes more elastic, a new firm finds it more difficult to enter that segment of the market because it would face a smaller demand.

Certainly not all firms that produce multiple products that are substitutes in consumption do so to strengthen their market power. Many oligopolists are caught in a product-quality dilemma, similar to the advertiser's dilemma discussed in Chapter 15. If they don't enter a particular segment of the market, they will lose a considerable market share to their rivals. It is possible that each of the oligopolists would be better off if each offered fewer products. In spite of this possible problem, producing a variety of differentiated yet similar products that are substitutes is simply another way that firms, particularly oligopolists, compete among themselves.

17.5 SUMMARY

In this chapter we have looked at a lot of special cases. While it might seem that we have introduced a lot of new conditions, we really have not. Essentially, all we have done is apply the basic principles of profit maximization to instances in which the firm has more than one plant or market or product. To show that the resulting roles for profit maximization have much in common, we review them here briefly.

1. Multiple plants

If a firm produces in two plants, A and B, it should allocate production between the two plants so that $MC_A = MC_B$. The optimal total output for the firm is that at which $MR = MC_T$. Hence, for profit maximization, the firm should produce the level of output and allocate the production of this output between the two plants so that

$$MR = MC_T = MC_A = MC_B$$

2. Multiple markets

If a firm sells in two distinct markets, 1 and 2, it should allocate output (sales) between the two markets such that $MR_1 = MR_2$. The optimal level of total output for the firm is that at which $MR_T = MC$. Hence, for profit maximization, the firm should produce the level of output and allocate the sales of this output between the two markets so that

$$MR_T = MC = MR_1 = MR_2$$

3. Multiple products/related in consumption
Defining the two products to be X and Y, the firm will produce and sell those levels of output for which

$$MR_X = MC_X \quad \text{and} \quad MR_Y = MC_Y$$

Since the products are related in consumption, MR_X is a function not only of Q_X but also of Q_Y, as is MR_Y. Therefore, the marginal conditions for the two products must be satisfied simultaneously.

4. Multiple products/substitutes in production
If a firm produces two products, X and Y, that compete for the firm's limited production facilities, the firm should allocate the production facility so that the marginal revenue product of the production facility is equal for the two products, $MRP_X = MRP_Y$. If in the long run the firm can vary its usage of or size of the production facility, the optimal level of usage of the facility is that at which $MRP_T = MC$. Hence, for profit maximization the firm should select the level of usage of its production facility and allocate this level of usage between the production of the two products so that

$$MRP_T = MC = MRP_X = MRP_Y$$

5. Multiple products/complements in production
When a firm produces goods that are complements in production and the two goods are produced in fixed proportions from the common input, the joint marginal revenue curve, MR_J, is the vertical summation of the two individual marginal revenue functions, MR_X and MR_Y, over the range of output for which both marginal revenues are positive. Beyond the output level where one of the marginal revenues becomes negative, the joint marginal revenue, MR_J, is the same as the marginal revenue for the other good.

To maximize profit, the manager produces the level of joint product where the joint marginal revenue equals marginal cost: $MR_J = MC$. If the profit-maximizing level of joint production exceeds the output where the MR_J kinks, then, for the good with negative marginal revenue, the units beyond the point of zero marginal revenue are disposed of rather than sold in the market. The profit-maximizing prices are found using the demand functions for the two goods.

Note, in particular, the similarities between Cases 1, 2, and 4. All of these are allocation problems, so they share a common solution. Cases 3 and 5 require only that the basic $MR = MC$ profit-maximization conditions be satisfied, but each situation requires a special treatment. In Case 3, the multiple $MR = MC$ conditions must be solved simultaneously. For Case 5, the marginal revenue curve for the multiple (joint) products is obtained not by a process of horizontal summation, the process applied in Cases 1, 2, and 4, but by a process of vertical summation.

The pricing and output decisions presented in this chapter represent some of the most challenging decisions facing managers in the "real world." By employing the powerful logic of marginal analysis, we showed how managers can make these decisions in a way that maximizes the profit, and value, of a firm.

TECHNICAL PROBLEMS

1. In the following graph, D represents the demand for dishwashers facing the Allclean Company. The firm manufactures dishwashers in two plants; MC_1 and MC_2 are their marginal cost curves.

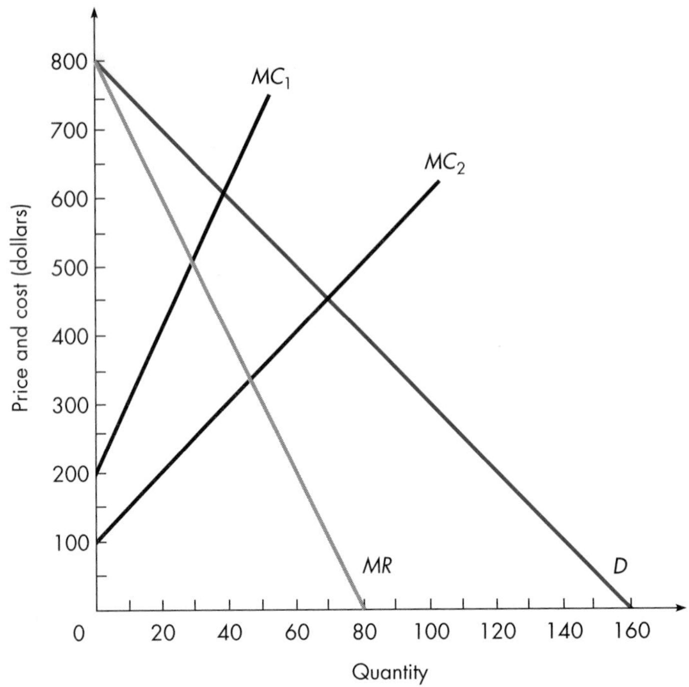

a. How many dishwashers should the firm produce?
b. What price should the firm set?
c. How should the output be allocated between the two plants so as to maximize profit?

2. Consider a firm that produces using two plants, A and B, with the following marginal cost functions:

$$MC_A = 10 + 0.01Q_A$$

$$MC_B = 4 + 0.03Q_B$$

a. Find the inverse marginal cost functions.
b. Set $MC_A = MC_T$ and $MC_B = MC_T$, and find the algebraic sum $Q_A + Q_B = Q_T$.
c. Take the inverse of the horizontal sum in part *b* to get the total marginal cost (MC_T) expressed as a function of total output (Q_T).
d. Beyond what level of output will the firm use both plants in production? (*Hint:* Find the output level where MC_T kinks.)
e. If the manager of this firm wished to produce 1,400 units at the least possible total cost, should 700 units be produced in each plant? Why or why not? If not, what should the allocation be?
f. Draw a graph of MC_A, MC_B, and MC_T. Check your algebraic derivation of total marginal cost with your graph. Check your answer to part *e*.

3. Suppose the firm in problem 2 faces the following demand function:

$$Q = 4{,}000 - 125P$$

a. Write the equation for the inverse demand function.
b. Find the marginal revenue function.

c. How much output should the manager produce to maximize profit? What price should be charged for the output?

d. How should the manager allocate production between plants A and B?

Now suppose demand decreases to $Q = 800 - 80P$.

e. How many units should the manager produce in order to maximize profit?

f. How should the manager allocate production between plants A and B?

4. A hotel serves both business and vacation travelers. In the following figure, D_B is the demand for business travelers and D_V is the demand for vacation travelers. The firm wishes to price-discriminate.

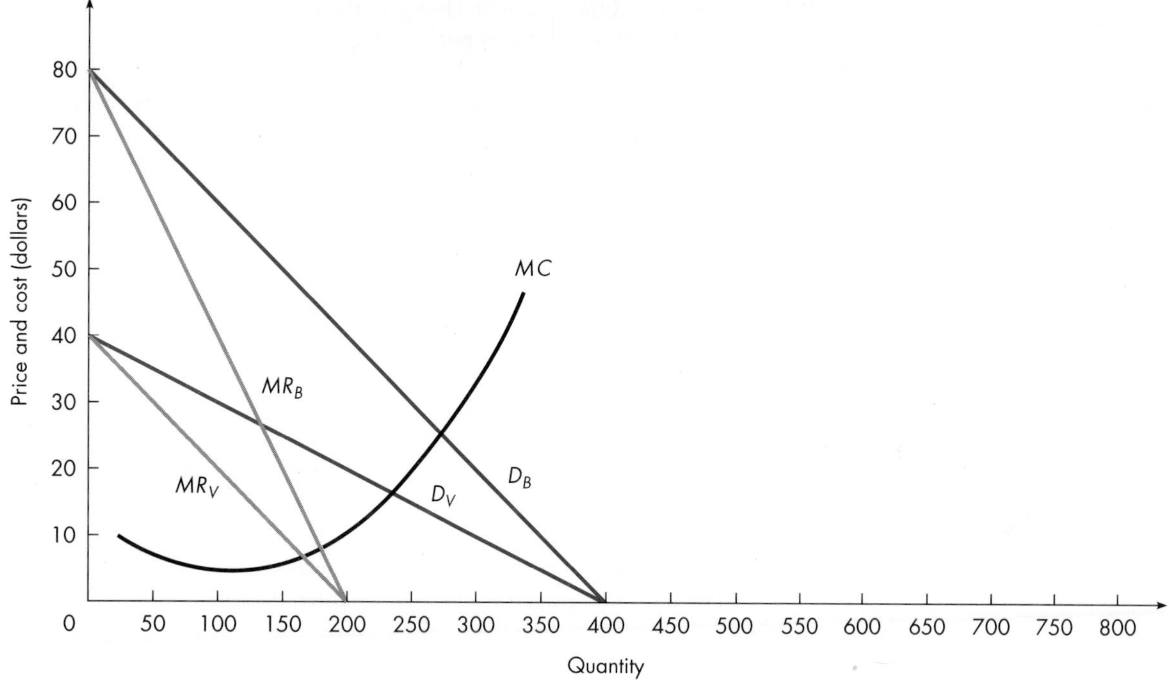

a. What is the profit-maximizing number of business travelers to serve? Vacation travelers?

b. What price should be charged to each? How much revenue is collected from each market?

c. If the hotel charged just one price to all travelers, what price would it be? How much revenue would the firm collect? Compare this revenue to that in part *b*.

5. A manager faces two separate markets. The estimated demand functions for the two markets are

$$Q_A = 1{,}600 - 80P_A$$

$$Q_B = 2{,}400 - 100P_B$$

a. Find the inverse marginal revenue functions.

b. Find the total marginal revenue functions.

c. Draw a graph of MR_A, MR_B, and MR_T. Check your algebraic derivation of total marginal revenue.

d. If the manager has a total of 650 units to sell, how should the 650 units be allocated to maximize total revenue?

6. Suppose the manager in problem 5 decides to price-discriminate. The marginal cost is estimated to be

$$MC = 4.5 + 0.005Q$$

a. How many units should the manager produce and sell?
b. How should the manager allocate the profit-maximizing output between the two markets?
c. What prices should the manager charge in the two markets?
d. Measured at the prices found in part *c*, which market has the more elastic demand?

7. How would the profit-maximizing decision for a firm that produces two products that are related in consumption differ from that for a firm whose two products are unrelated?
8. Look again at Zicon Manufacturing—a firm that produces products that are substitutes in consumption. Suppose that the production manager changed the estimates of the marginal cost functions to

$$MC_X = 20 + 0.00025Q_X \quad \text{and} \quad MC_Y = 16 + 0.0005Q_Y$$

Calculate the new profit-maximizing levels of output and price for the two products.

9. In the example dealing with the optimal usage of a production facility (Surefire Products, Inc.), suppose that the plant supervisor changes the estimate of the marginal cost for usage of the plant to

$$MC = 150 + 3H_T$$

a. What is the optimal level of usage for the plant (hours per day)?
b. How will this level of usage be allocated between the production of the two products?
c. What will be the daily outputs?
d. What prices will be charged?

10. Consider again the pricing and output decision facing the manager at ChemTech Corporation. New estimates for the demand for xylene and ylene are

$$Q_X = 200{,}000 - 1{,}000P_X \quad \text{and} \quad Q_Y = 180{,}000 - 2{,}000P_Y$$

The manager also reestimates marginal cost and finds the new marginal cost function to be

$$MC = 50 + 0.001Q$$

a. Find the equation for the joint marginal revenue function.
b. What is the profit-maximizing level of production for the joint product?
c. What prices should the manager charge for xylene and ylene in order to maximize profit?

A technological innovation in chemical processing reduces the marginal cost of production to

$$MC = 3.3 + 0.00005Q$$

d. What is the profit-maximizing level of production of xylene? Of ylene?
e. What are the profit-maximizing prices to charge for xylene and ylene?

APPLIED PROBLEMS

1. *The Financial Herald,* a weekly newspaper specializing in corporate financial news, is purchased by both businesspeople and students. A marketing research firm has estimated the two linear demand and marginal revenue functions shown in the figure below. MR_B is the estimated marginal revenue for the business readers, and MR_S is the estimated marginal revenue for the student readers. The production department at *The Financial Herald* estimates a linear marginal cost function for newspaper production, which is also graphed in the figure below. All quantities are in units of 1,000 per week.

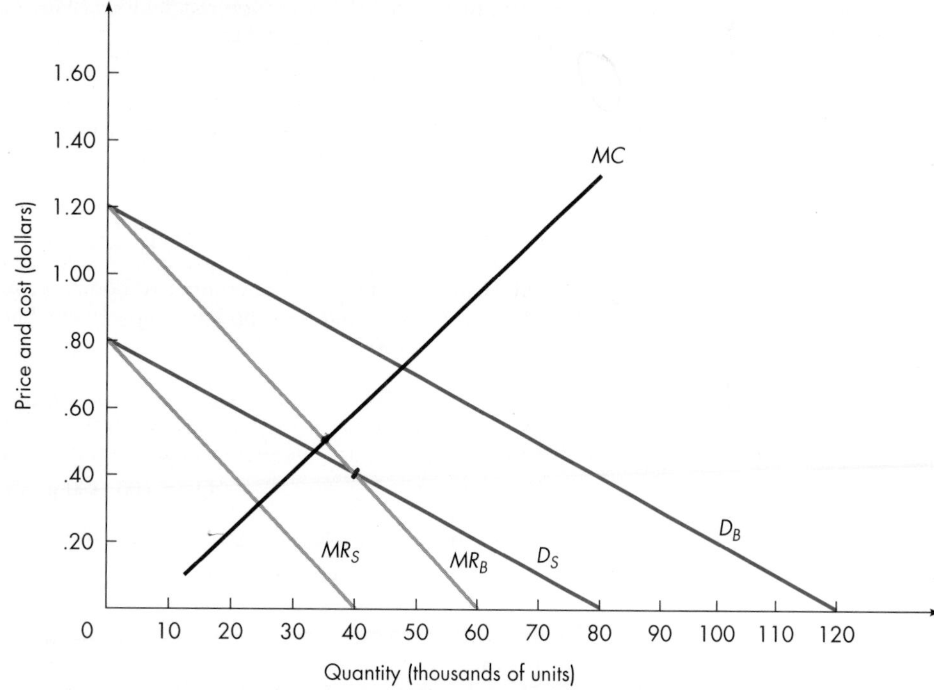

a. How many total copies should *The Financial Herald* print each week?
b. How many copies should be sold to business readers? How many copies should be sold to students?
c. What price should business readers be charged? What price should students be charged?

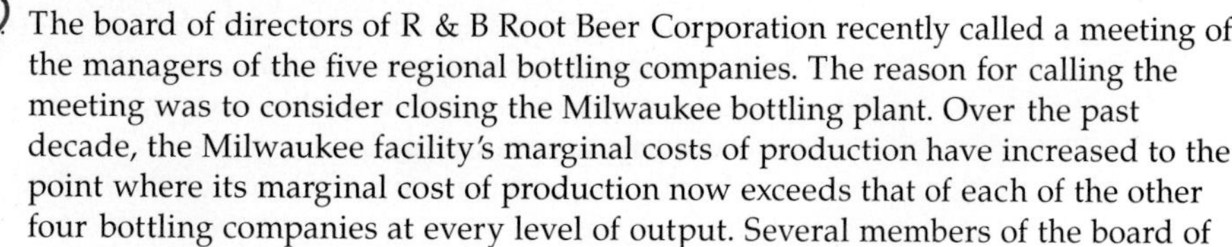

2. The board of directors of R & B Root Beer Corporation recently called a meeting of the managers of the five regional bottling companies. The reason for calling the meeting was to consider closing the Milwaukee bottling plant. Over the past decade, the Milwaukee facility's marginal costs of production have increased to the point where its marginal cost of production now exceeds that of each of the other four bottling companies at every level of output. Several members of the board of

directors and two of the managers favored closing the Milwaukee plant. The manager of the Milwaukee bottling plant pointed out that, while the Milwaukee plant is the oldest of the five, with the oldest capital equipment, it would be inefficient to close it given the current growth rate in sales. Only if sales fell by a rather substantial amount would it be profit-maximizing to shut the Milwaukee plant. Draw a graph and defend the manager of the Milwaukee plant.

3. Although there is relatively little difference in the cost of producing hardcover and paperback books, these books sell for very different prices. Explain this pricing behavior.

4. *The Wall Street Journal* once reported on dating services, noting that the fees were \$300 for men and \$250 for women. The owner of the service said that the difference in fees was to compensate for inequalities in pay scales for men and women. Can you suggest any alternative reasons for this difference?

5. In the mid-1980s, many observers of the automobile industry were saying that GM was producing cars that were too much alike. Many GM executives agreed. Why would this be a problem for GM?

6. Caytel Products manufactures two models of a particular product—the "good" model (G) and the "best" model (B). The two models are substitutes in production, and must share Caytel's production facilities. Caytel has determined that the production functions for the two models are

$$\text{Good Model: } Q_G = 4.0H_G$$
$$\text{Best Model: } Q_B = 4.0H_B$$

where H_G and H_B measure the number of hours per month Caytel's plant spends producing the good and best models, respectively. The demand functions for the two models are forecasted to be

$$Q_G = 4{,}000 - 256P_G$$

and

$$Q_B = 600 - 4P_B$$

The marginal cost of using Caytel's plant is estimated to be

$$MC = 5.0 + 0.05H, \text{ where } H = H_G + H_B$$

a. In order to maximize profit, how many hours per month should Caytel's plant operate?
b. How should the manager allocate production time between the good model and the best model?
c. How many units of the good model should be produced to maximize Caytel's profit? How many units of the best model?
d. What prices should Caytel charge for the two models?

7. Airlines practice price discrimination by charging leisure travelers and business travelers different prices. Different customers pay varying prices for essentially the same coach seat because some passengers qualify for discounts and others do not. Since the discounts are substantial in many cases, the customer who qualifies for a discount pays a significantly lower airfare.
a. Which group of customers tends to pay the higher price—business travelers or leisure travelers?

b. Why would business travelers generally have a different elasticity of demand for air travel than leisure travelers? Is the more elastic market paying the lower or higher price? Is this consistent with profit maximization?

Airlines rely on an assortment of restrictions that travelers must meet in order to qualify for the discounted fares. In effect, these restrictions roughly sort flyers into business travelers and leisure travelers.

c. Explain how each of the following restrictions sometimes used by airlines tends to separate business and leisure travelers.
   (1) Advance purchase requirements, which require payment at least 14 days before departure.
   (2) Weekend stay requirements, which require travelers to stay over a Saturday night before returning.
   (3) Time-of-day restrictions, which disallow discounts for travel during peak times of the day.

d. In each of the above cases, which group of passengers effectively pays a higher price for air travel? Is this consistent with profit maximization?

8. For many years American Express had charged a fee (generally higher than Visa or MasterCard) to each merchant accepting its credit cards. The fee was a percentage of each sale, and American Express charged all merchants the same fee. Many merchants who accepted American Express cards complained that the fee was too high; they discouraged customers from using the card, and some even stopped accepting the card. The president of the company's card division announced that American Express would lower its fees, but a merchant with a lower than industry average charge volume on American Express would get a lower fee than those with a higher than average charge volume. This was supposed to lower the fee the most on each transaction "where the value of accepting American Express is not present" (*The Wall Street Journal,* February 24, 1992).

   Is this price discrimination? If not, why not? If so, on what is American Express basing its discrimination?

9. A woman complained to "Dear Abby" that a laundry charged $1.25 each to launder and press her husband's shirts, but for her shirts—the same description, only smaller—the laundry charged $3.50. When asked why, the owner said, "Women's blouses cost more." Abby suggested sending all the shirts in one bundle and enclosing a note saying, "There are no blouses here—these are all shirts."
   a. Is the laundry practicing price discrimination, or is there really a $2.25 difference in cost?
   b. Assuming the laundry is engaging in price discrimination, why do men pay the lower price and women the higher?
   c. Could the laundry continue to separate markets if people followed Abby's advice? What about the policing costs associated with separating the markets?

10. A firm with two factories, one in Michigan and one in Texas, has decided that it should produce a total of 500 units in order to maximize profit. The firm is currently producing 200 units in the Michigan factory and 300 units in the Texas factory. At this allocation between plants, the last unit of output produced in Michigan added $5 to total cost, while the last unit of output produced in Texas added $3 to total cost.
   a. Is the firm maximizing profit? If so, why? If not, what should it do?
   b. If the firm produces 201 units in Michigan and 299 in Texas, what will be the increase (decrease) in the firm's total cost?

11. A bar offers female patrons a lower price for a drink than male patrons. The bar will maximize profit by selling a total of 200 drinks (a night). At the current prices, male customers buy 150 drinks, while female customers buy 50 drinks. At this allocation between markets, the marginal revenue from the last drink sold to a male customer is \$1.50, while the marginal revenue from the last drink sold to a female customer is \$0.50.
    a. What should the bar do about its pricing?
    b. If the bar sells 151 drinks to males and 49 to females, what will be the increase (decrease) in total revenue?

MATHEMATICAL APPENDIX — Derivation of Decision Rules

This Mathematical Appendix develops two of the most important decision rules employed in this chapter. We derive the profit-maximizing conditions for a multiplant firm and for a price-discriminating firm.

The Multiplant Firm's Allocation Decision

To maximize profit, a multiplant firm will produce the level of output at which the horizontal sum of each plant's marginal cost equals marginal revenue. Each plant will produce the output at which the marginal costs of all plants are equal.

Assume the firm has two plants, A and B, whose total cost functions are, respectively, $C_A(Q_A)$ and $C_B(Q_B)$. The firm's total revenue function is $R(Q_A + Q_B) = R(Q)$. Thus the firm's profit function is

$$\pi = R(Q) - C_A(Q_A) - C_B(Q_B)$$

Maximizing profit with respect to Q_A and Q_B requires

$$\frac{\partial \pi}{\partial Q_A} = \frac{dR}{dQ} - \frac{dC_A(Q_A)}{dQ_A} = 0$$

$$\frac{\partial \pi}{\partial Q_B} = \frac{dR}{dQ} - \frac{dC_B(Q_A)}{dQ_B} = 0$$

Combining these conditions, profit is maximized when

$$MR = MC_A = MC_B$$

Thus, MC must be the same in both plants and also equal to MR.

Price Discrimination in Multiple Markets

A price-discriminating manager maximizes profit at the level of output at which marginal revenue in each market equals marginal cost. The price in each market is given by the demand in that market.

Assume the firm sells its output in two markets. The demands in these markets are

$$P_1(Q_1) \quad \text{and} \quad P_2(Q_2)$$

Cost is a function of total output:

$$C = C(Q_1 + Q_2) = C(Q)$$

The firm maximizes profit,

$$\pi = P_1(Q_1)Q_1 + P_2(Q_2)Q_2 - C(Q)$$

with respect to the levels of output sold in the two markets.

Thus, the first-order conditions for profit maximization are

$$\frac{dP_1}{dQ_1}Q_1 + P_1 - \frac{dC}{dQ} = MR_1 - MC = 0$$

$$\frac{dP_2}{dQ_2}Q_2 + P_2 - \frac{dC}{dQ} = MR_2 - MC = 0$$

Thus, profit maximization requires that the marginal revenues in the two markets be equal and equal to marginal cost. Once Q_1^* and Q_2^* are determined, P_1^* and P_2^* are given by the demand functions.

Part VII
Risk and Uncertainty

CHAPTER 18

Decision Making under Risk and Uncertainty

All the analysis of managerial decision making up to this point in the text has been developed under the assumption that the manager knows with certainty the marginal benefits and marginal costs associated with a decision. While managers do have considerable information about the outcome for many decisions, they must frequently make decisions in situations in which the outcome of a decision cannot be known in advance. A manager may decide, for example, to invest in a new production facility with the expectation that the new technology and equipment will reduce production costs. Even after studying hundreds of technical reports, a manager may still not know with certainty the cost savings of the new plant until the plant is built and operating. In other words, the outcome of the decision to build the new plant is random because the reduction in costs (the outcome) is not known with certainty at the time of the decision. Another risky decision involves choosing the profit-maximizing production level or the price to charge when the marginal benefit and marginal cost can take on a range of values with differing probabilities.

In this chapter we present some basic rules that managers, and for that matter all decision makers, can and do use to help make decisions under conditions of risk and uncertainty. In the first section, we explain the difference between decision making under risk and decision making under uncertainty. The larger portion of this chapter is devoted to analyzing decisions under risk, rather than situations of uncertainty, because, as you will see, managers facing random benefits and costs are more often confronted with situations involving risk than uncertainty. As you will also see, the rules we present in this chapter for decision making under risk and uncertainty provide only guidelines for making decisions when outcomes are not certain, because no single rule for making such decisions is, or can be, universally employed by all managers at all times. Nevertheless, the rules presented give an overview of some of the helpful methods of analyzing risk and uncertainty.

Before plunging into our presentation of decision making under uncertainty and risk, we want to address a question that may be concerning you: Why do we devote such a large portion of this text to managerial decision making under certainty or complete information, knowing full well that a large proportion of managerial decisions are made with incomplete information—that is, under risk or uncertainty? There are two good reasons. First, the theory of optimization, weighing marginal benefits and marginal costs, as explained in Chapter 4 and applied throughout the text, provides the basic foundation for all decision making regardless of the amount of information available to a decision maker about the potential outcomes of various actions. In order to learn how to do something under less than ideal conditions, one must first learn how to do it under ideal conditions. Second, even though a decision maker does not have complete information about the marginal benefits and marginal costs of all levels of an activity or choice variable, the *MB*/*MC* rule from Chapter 4 is the most productive approach to profit-maximization decisions under many, if not most, relevant circumstances.

18.1 DISTINCTIONS BETWEEN RISK AND UNCERTAINTY

risk
A decision-making condition under which a manager can list all outcomes and assign probabilities to each outcome.

When the outcome of a decision is not known with certainty, a manager faces a decision-making problem under either conditions of risk or conditions of uncertainty. A decision is made under **risk** when a manager can make a list of all possible outcomes associated with a decision and assign a probability of occurrence to each one of the outcomes. The process of assigning probabilities to outcomes sometimes involves rather sophisticated analysis based upon the manager's extensive experience in similar situations or on other data. Probabilities assigned in this way are *objective probabilities.* In other circumstances, in which the manager has little experience with a particular decision situation and little or no relevant historical data, the probabilities assigned to the outcomes are derived in a subjective way and are called *subjective probabilities.* Subjective probabilities are based upon hunches, "gut feelings," or personal experiences rather than on scientific data.

An example of a decision made under risk might be the following: A manager decides to spend $1,000 on a magazine ad believing there are three possible outcomes for the ad: a 20 percent chance the ad will have only a small effect on sales, a 60 percent chance of a moderate effect, and a 20 percent chance of a very large effect. This decision is made under risk because the manager can list each potential outcome and determine the probability of each outcome occurring.

uncertainty
A decision-making condition under which a manager cannot list all possible outcomes and/or cannot assign probabilities to the various outcomes.

In contrast to risk, **uncertainty** exists when a decision maker cannot list all possible outcomes and/or cannot assign probabilities to the various outcomes. When faced with uncertainty, a manager would know only the different decision options available and the different possible *states of nature.* The states of nature are the future events or conditions that can influence the final outcome or payoff of a decision but cannot be controlled or affected by the manager. Even though both risk and uncertainty involve less than complete information, there is more information under risk than under uncertainty.

An example of a decision made under uncertainty would be, for a manager of a pharmaceutical company, the decision of whether or not to spend $3 million on the research and development of a new medication for high blood pressure. The payoff from the research and development spending will depend upon whether or not the President's new health plan imposes price regulations on new drugs. The two states of nature facing the manager in this problem are (1) government does impose price regulations or (2) government does *not* impose price regulations. While the manager knows the payoff that will occur under either state of nature, the manager has no idea of the probability that price regulations will be imposed on drug companies. Under such conditions, a decision is made under uncertainty.

This important distinction between conditions of uncertainty and conditions of risk will be followed throughout this chapter. The decision rules employed by managers when outcomes are not certain differ under conditions of uncertainty and conditions of risk.

18.2 MEASURING RISK WITH PROBABILITY DISTRIBUTIONS

Before we can discuss rules for decision making under risk, we must first discuss how risk can be measured. The most direct method of measuring risk involves the characteristics of a probability distribution of outcomes associated with a particular decision. This section will describe these characteristics.

Probability Distributions

probability distribution
A table or graph showing all possible outcomes or payoffs of a decision and the probabilities that each outcome will occur.

A **probability distribution** is a table or graph showing all possible outcomes (payoffs) for a decision and the probability that each outcome will occur. The probabilities can take values between 0 and 1, or, alternatively, they can be expressed as percentages between 0 and 100 percent.[1] If *all possible* outcomes are assigned probabilities, the probabilities must sum to 1 (or 100 percent); that is, the probability that some other outcome will occur is zero because there is no other possible outcome.

To illustrate a probability distribution, we assume that the director of advertising at a large corporation believes the firm's current advertising campaign may result in any one of five possible outcomes for corporate sales. The probability distribution for this advertising campaign is as follows:

[1]If the probability of an outcome is 1 (or 100 percent), the outcome is certain to occur and no risk exists. If the probability of an outcome is 0, then that particular outcome will not occur and need not be considered in decision making.

FIGURE 18.1
The Probability Distribution for Sales Following an Advertising Campaign

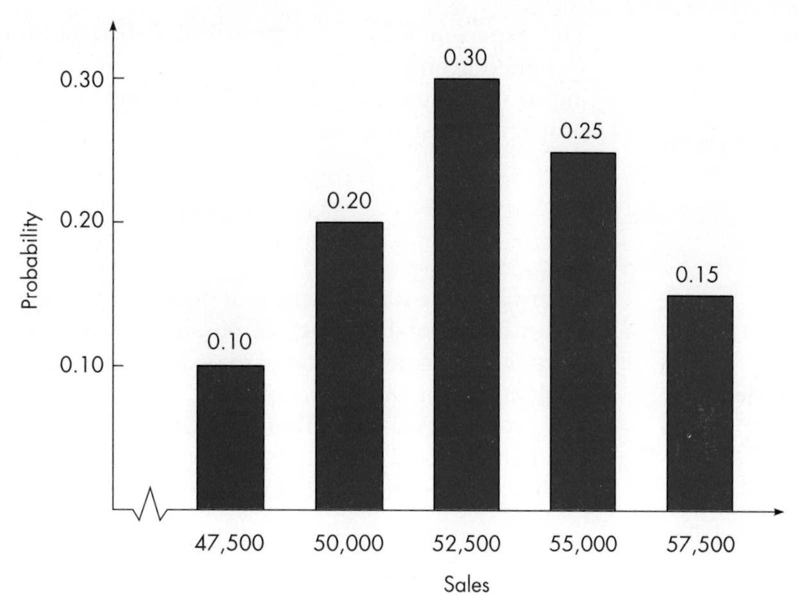

Outcome (sales)	Probability (percent)
47,500 units	10
50,000 units	20
52,500 units	30
55,000 units	25
57,500 units	15

Each outcome has a probability greater than 0 but less than 100 percent, and the sum of all probabilities is 100 percent (= 10 + 20 + 30 + 25 + 15). This probability distribution is represented graphically in Figure 18.1.

From a probability distribution (either in tabular or in graphical form), the riskiness of a decision is reflected by the variability of outcomes indicated by the different probabilities of occurrence. For decision-making purposes, managers often turn to mathematical properties of the probability distribution to facilitate a formal analysis of risk. The nature of risk can be summarized by examining the central tendency of the probability distribution, as measured by the expected value of the distribution, and by examining the dispersion of the distribution, as measured by the standard deviation and coefficient of variation. We discuss first the measure of central tendency of a probability distribution.

Expected Value of a Probability Distribution

expected value
The weighed average of the outcomes, with the probabilities of each outcome serving as the respective weights.

The **expected value** of a probability distribution of decision outcomes is the weighted average of the outcomes, with the probabilities of each outcome serving as the respective weights. The expected value of the various outcomes of a probability distribution is

$$E(X) = \text{Expected value of } X = \sum_{i=1}^{n} p_i X_i$$

where X_i is the ith outcome of a decision, p_i is the probability of the ith outcome, and n is the total number of possible outcomes in the probability distribution. Note that the computation of expected value requires the use of fractions or decimal values for the probabilities p_i, rather than percentages. The expected value of a probability distribution is often referred to as the **mean of the distribution.**

mean of the distribution
The expected value of the distribution.

The expected value of sales for the advertising campaign associated with the probability distribution shown in Figure 18.1 is

$$\begin{aligned} E(\text{sales}) &= (0.10)(47{,}500) + (0.20)(50{,}000) + (0.30)(52{,}500) + \\ &\quad (0.25)(55{,}000) + (0.15)(57{,}500) \\ &= 4{,}750 + 10{,}000 + 15{,}750 + 13{,}750 + 8{,}625 \\ &= 52{,}875 \end{aligned}$$

While the amount of actual sales that occur as a result of the advertising campaign is a random variable possibly taking values of 47,500, 50,000, 52,500, 55,000, or 57,500 units, the expected level of sales is 52,875 units. If only one of the five levels of sales can occur, the level that actually occurs will not equal the expected value of 52,875, but expected value does indicate what the *average* value of the outcomes would be if the risky decision were to be repeated a large number of times.

Dispersion of a Probability Distribution

variance
The dispersion of a distribution about its mean.

As you may recall from your statistics classes, probability distributions are generally characterized not only by the expected value (mean) but also by the variance. The **variance** of a probability distribution measures the dispersion of the distribution about its mean. Figure 18.2 shows the probability distributions for the profit outcomes of two different decisions, A and B. Both decisions, as illustrated in Figure 18.2, have identical expected profit levels but different variances. The larger variance associated with making decision B is reflected by a larger dispersion (a wider spread of values around the mean). Because distribution A is more compact (less spread out), A has a smaller variance.

The variance of a probability distribution of the outcomes of a given decision is frequently used to indicate the level or degree of risk associated with that

FIGURE 18.2
Two Probability Distributions with Identical Means but Different Variances

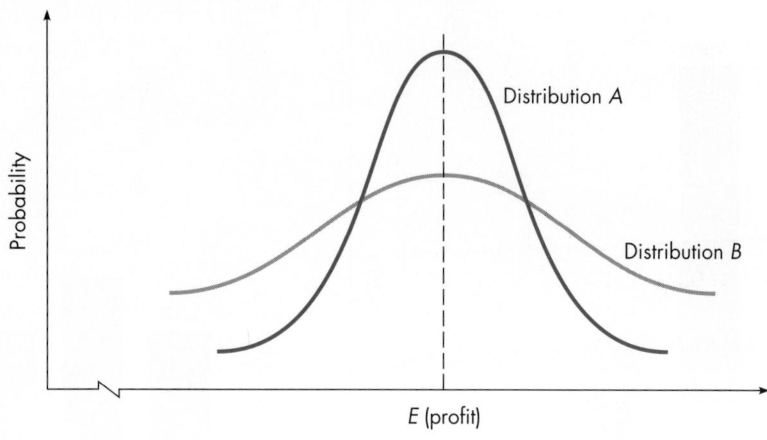

decision. If the expected values of two distributions are the same, the distribution with the higher variance is associated with the riskier decision. Thus in Figure 18.2, decision *B* has more risk than decision *A*. Furthermore, variance is often used to compare the riskiness of two decisions even though the expected values of the distributions differ.

Mathematically, the variance of a probability distribution of outcomes X_i, denoted by σ_x^2, is the probability-weighted sum of the squared deviations about the expected value of *X*:

$$\text{Variance }(X) = \sigma_x^2 = \sum_{i=1}^{n} p_i[X_i - E(X)]^2$$

As an example, consider the two distributions illustrated in Figure 18.3. As is evident from the graphs and demonstrated in the table below, the two distributions have the same mean, 50. Their variances differ, however. Decision *A* has a smaller variance than decision *B*, and it is therefore less risky. The calculation of the expected values and variance for each distribution are shown in the following table:

FIGURE 18.3
Probability Distributions with Different Variances

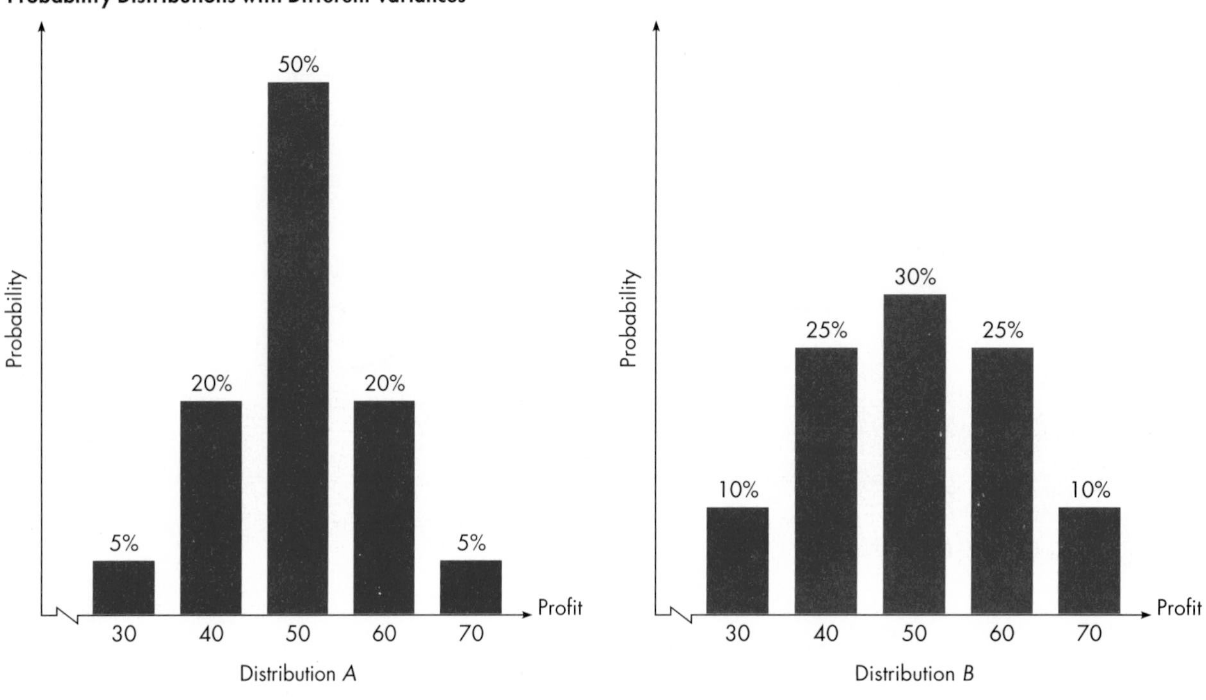

	Decision A			Decision B		
Profit (X_i)	Probability (p_i)	p_iX_i	$[X_i - E(X)]^2p_i$	Probability (p_i)	p_iX_i	$[X_i - E(X)]^2p_i$
30	0.05	1.5	20	0.10	3	40
40	0.20	8	20	0.25	10	25
50	0.50	25	0	0.30	15	0
60	0.20	12	20	0.25	15	25
70	0.05	3.5	20	0.10	7	40
		$E(X) = 50$	$\sigma_A^2 = 80$		$E(X) = 50$	$\sigma_B^2 = 130$

standard deviation The square root of the variance.

Because variance is a squared term, it is usually much larger than the mean. To avoid this scaling problem, the standard deviation of the probability distribution is more commonly used to measure dispersion. The **standard deviation** of a probability distribution, denoted by σ_x, is the square root of the variance:

$$\sigma_x = \sqrt{\text{Variance }(X)}$$

The standard deviations of the distributions illustrated in Figure 18.3 and in the above table are $\sigma_A = 8.94$ and $\sigma_B = 11.40$. As in the case of the variance of a probability distribution, the higher the standard deviation, the more risky the decision.

Managers can compare the riskiness of various decisions by comparing their standard deviations, as long as the expected values are of similar magnitudes. For example, if decisions *C* and *D* both have standard deviations of 52.5, the two decisions can be viewed as equally risky if their expected values are close to one another. If, however, the expected values of the distributions differ substantially in magnitude, it can be misleading to examine only the standard deviations. Suppose decision *C* has a mean outcome of $400 and decision *D* has a mean outcome of $5,000 but the standard deviations remain 52.5. The dispersion of outcomes for decision *D* is much smaller *relative to its mean value of $5,000* than is the dispersion of outcomes for decision *C relative to its mean value of $400.*

When the expected values of outcomes differ substantially, managers should measure the riskiness of a decision *relative* to its expected value. One such measure of relative risk is the coefficient of variation for the decision's distribution. The **coefficient of variation,** denoted by υ, is the standard deviation divided by the expected value of the probability distribution of decision outcomes:

coefficient of variation The standard deviation divided by the expected value of the probability distribution.

$$\upsilon = \frac{\text{Standard deviation}}{\text{Expected value}} = \frac{\sigma}{E(X)}$$

The coefficient of variation measures the level of risk *relative* to the mean of the probability distribution. In the preceding example, the two coefficients of variation are $\upsilon_C = 52.5/400 = 0.131$ and $\upsilon_D = 52.5/5{,}000 = 0.0105$.

18.3 DECISIONS UNDER RISK

Now that we have shown how to measure the risk associated with making a particular managerial decision, we will discuss how these measures of risk can help managers make decisions under conditions of risk. We now set forth three rules to guide managers making risky decisions.

Maximization of Expected Value

Information about the likelihood of the various possible outcomes, while quite helpful in making decisions, does not solve the manager's decision-making problem. How should a manager choose among various decisions when each decision has a variety of possible outcomes? One rule or solution to this problem, called the **expected value rule,** is to choose the decision with the highest expected value. The expected value rule is easy to apply. Unfortunately, this rule uses information about only one characteristic of the distribution of outcomes, the mean. It fails to incorporate the riskiness (dispersion) associated with the probability distribution of outcomes into the decision. Therefore, the expected value rule is not particularly useful in situations where the level of risk differs very much across decisions—unless the decision maker does not care about the level of risk associated with a decision and is concerned only with expected value. (Such a decision maker is called *risk neutral,* a concept we will discuss

expected value rule Choosing the decision with the highest expected value.

later in this chapter.) Also, the expected value rule is only useful to a manager when the decisions have *different* expected values. Of course, if decisions happen to have identical expected values, the expected value rule offers no guidance for choosing between them, and, considering only the mean, the manager would be indifferent to a choice among them. The expected value rule *cannot* be applied when decisions have identical expected values and *should not* be applied when decisions have different levels of risk, except in the circumstance noted above.

To illustrate the expected value rule (and other rules to be discussed later), consider the owner and manager of Chicago Rotisserie Chicken, who wants to decide where to open one new restaurant. Figure 18.4 shows the probability distributions of possible weekly profits if the manager decides to locate the new restaurant in either Atlanta (Panel A), Boston (Panel B), or Cleveland (Panel C). The expected values, standard deviations, and coefficients of variation for each distribution are displayed in each panel.

On the basis of past experience, the manager calculates that weekly profit in Atlanta will take one of four values: $3,000 or $4,000 per week each with a 30 percent chance of occurring, and $2,000 or $5,000 a week each with a 20 percent chance of occurring. The expected weekly profit in Atlanta is $3,500. If the manager decides to open a restaurant in Boston, the weekly profits may be any of six indicated values ranging from $1,000 to $6,000 weekly with the indicated probabilities and an expected value of $3,750. For Cleveland, the manager assigns a probability of 30 percent to weekly profits of $1,000 and $6,000 and a probability of 10 percent to each of the profits, $2,000, $3,000, $4,000, and $5,000, with an expected value of $3,500 for the distribution. If the manager is not concerned with risk (is risk neutral) and follows the expected value rule, the new restaurant will be opened in Boston, with the highest expected profit of $3,750. Note that if the manager had been choosing between only the Atlanta and Cleveland locations, the expected value rule could not have been applied because each has an expected value of $3,500. In such cases some other rule may be used.

Mean-Variance Analysis

Managers who choose among risky alternatives using the expected value rule are, in effect, ignoring risk (dispersion) and focusing exclusively on the mean outcome. An alternative method of making decisions under risk uses both the mean *and* the variance of the probability distribution, which incorporates information about the level of risk into the decisions. This method of decision making, commonly known as **mean-variance analysis,** employs both the mean and the variance (or standard deviation) to make decisions according to the rules listed below.

mean-variance analysis
Method of decision making that employs both the mean and the variance to make decisions.

Given two risky decisions (designated A and B), the *mean-variance rules* for decisions under risk are:

1. If decision A has a higher expected outcome *and* a lower variance than decision B, decision A should be made.

FIGURE 18.4
Probability Distributions for Weekly Profit at Three Restaurant Locations

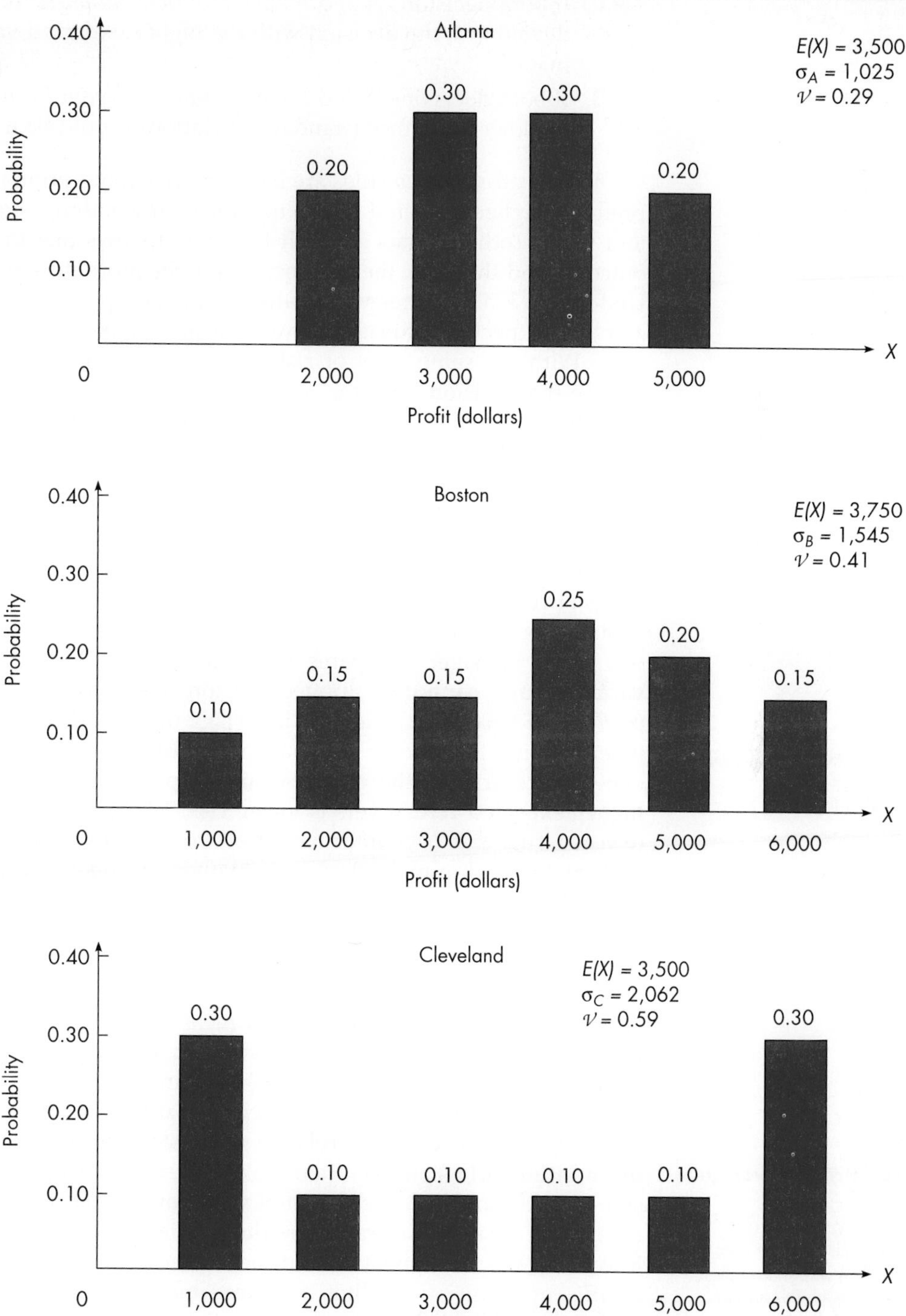

2. If both decisions *A* and *B* have identical *variances* (or standard deviations), the decision with the higher expected value should be made.
3. If both decisions *A* and *B* have identical *expected values,* the decision with the lower variance (standard deviation) should be made.

The mean-variance rules are based on the assumption that a decision maker prefers a higher expected return to a lower, other things equal, and a lower risk to a higher, other things equal. It therefore follows that the *higher* the expected outcome and the *lower* the variance (risk), the more desirable a decision will be. Under rule 1, a manager would always choose a particular decision if it has *both* a greater expected value *and* a lower variance than other decisions being considered. With the same level of risk, the second rule indicates managers should choose the decision with the higher expected value. Under rule 3, if the decisions have identical expected values, the manager chooses the less risky (lower standard deviation) decision.

Returning to the problem of Chicago Rotisserie Chicken, no location dominates both of the other locations in terms of any of the three rules of mean-variance analysis. Boston dominates Cleveland because it has both a higher expected value and a lower risk (rule 1). Atlanta also dominates Cleveland in terms of rule 3 because both locations have the same expected value ($3,500), but Atlanta has a lower standard deviation—less risk ($\sigma_A = 1{,}025 < 2{,}062 = \sigma_C$).

If the manager compares the Atlanta and Boston locations, the mean-variance rules cannot be applied. Boston has a higher weekly expected profit ($3,750 > $3,500), but Atlanta is less risky ($\sigma_A = 1{,}025 < 1{,}545 = \sigma_B$). Therefore, when making this choice, the manager must make a tradeoff between risk and expected return, so the choice would depend on the manager's valuation of higher expected return versus lower risk. We will now set forth an additional decision rule that uses information on both the expected value and dispersion and can be used to make decisions involving tradeoffs between expected return and risk.

Coefficient of Variation Analysis

As we noted in the discussion about measuring the riskiness of probability distributions, variance and standard deviation are measures of *absolute risk.* In contrast, the coefficient of variation $[\sigma/E(X)]$ measures risk *relative* to the expected value of the distribution. The coefficient of variation, therefore, allows managers to make decisions based on relative risk instead of absolute risk. The **coefficient of variation rule** states: "When making decisions under risk, choose the decision with the smallest coefficient of variation $[\sigma/E(X)]$." This rule takes into account both the expected value and the standard deviation of the distribution. The lower the standard deviation and the higher the expected value, the smaller the coefficient of variation. Thus a desired movement in either characteristic of a probability distribution moves the coefficient of variation in the desired direction.

coefficient of variation rule
Decision-making rule that the decision to be chosen is the one with the smallest coefficient of variation.

We return once more to the decision facing the manager of Chicago Rotisserie Chicken. The coefficients of variation for each of the possible location decisions are

$$\upsilon_{\text{Atlanta}} = 1{,}025/3{,}500 = 0.29$$
$$\upsilon_{\text{Boston}} = 1{,}545/3{,}750 = 0.41$$
$$\upsilon_{\text{Cleveland}} = 2{,}062/3{,}500 = 0.59$$

The location with the smallest coefficient of variation is Atlanta, which has a coefficient of 0.29. Notice that the choice between locating in either Atlanta or Boston, which could not be made using mean-variance rules, is now resolved using the coefficient of variation to make the decision. Atlanta wins over Boston with the smaller coefficient of variation ($0.29 < 0.41$), while Cleveland comes in last.

Which Rule Is Best?

At this point, you may be wondering which one of the three rules for making decisions under risk is the "correct" one. After all, the manager of Chicago Rotisserie Chicken either reached a different decision or reached no decision at all depending upon which rule was used. Using the expected value rule, Boston was the choice. Using the coefficient of variation rule, Atlanta was chosen. According to mean-variance analysis, Cleveland was out, but the decision between Atlanta and Boston could not be resolved using mean-variance analysis. If the decision rules do not all lead to the same conclusion, a manager must decide which rule to follow.

When a decision is to be made repeatedly, with identical probabilities each time, the expected value rule provides managers with the most reliable rule for maximizing (expected) profit. The average return of a given risky course of action repeated many times will approach the expected value of that action. Therefore, the average return of the course of action with the highest expected value will tend to be higher than the average return of any course of action with a lower expected value, when carried out a large number of times. Situations involving repeated decisions can arise, for example, when a manager must make the same risky decision once a month or even once every week. Or a manager at corporate headquarters may make a decision that directs activities of dozens, maybe even hundreds, of corporate offices in the country or around the world. When the risky decision is repeated many times, the manager at corporate headquarters believes strongly that each of the alternative decision choices will probably result in an average profit level that is equal to the expected value of profit, even though any one corporate office might experience either higher or lower returns. In practice, then, the expected value rule is justifiable when a decision will be repeated many times under identical circumstances.

When a manager makes a one-time decision under risk, there will not be any follow-up repetitions of the decision to "average out" a bad outcome (or a good outcome). Unfortunately, there is no best rule to follow when decisions are not repetitive. The rules we present for risky decision making should be used

Illustration 18.1

Lowering Risk by Diversification

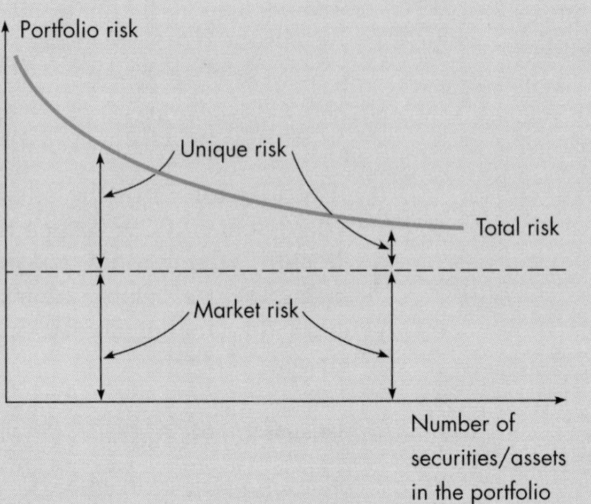

Although investors can't do much about the amount of risk associated with any specific project or investment, they do have some control over the amount of risk associated with their entire portfolio of investments. *The Wall Street Journal* (April 8, 1993) advised: "for anyone who doesn't need . . . money right away, this may be a good time to broaden your investment horizon. The best strategy, investment advisors say, is to diversify by spreading your money among a wide variety of stocks, bonds, real estate, cash, and other holdings."

The *WSJ* pointed out that you will have to expect the value of your holdings to fluctuate with changes in the economy or market conditions. The returns should comfortably beat those from CDs, and the ups and downs should be a lot smaller than if you simply put all your money in the stock market. One investment adviser stated, "Diversified portfolios of stocks and bonds had much less risk while providing nearly as much return as an all-stock portfolio during the past 15, 20, and 25 years." During the period since 1968, stocks soared in five years but were losing investments in six years. Investors who put a third of their money in stocks, a third in Treasury bonds, and a third in "cash equivalent" investments would have lost money in only four years, with the largest annual loss being less than 5 percent. The annual compound return over the 25 years in that investment would have been 9 percent, compared with 10.56 percent in an all-stock portfolio, 8.26 percent in all bonds, and 9.89 percent in 60 percent stock and 40 percent bonds. But the more diversified investment would have been less risky.

The theoretical arguments in the *WSJ* article are based on portfolio theory. The core of portfolio theory is deceptively simple: As more securities are added to an investor's portfolio, the portfolio risk (the standard deviation of portfolio returns) declines. A particular security or investment is subject to two types of risk: market risk and unique risk. Market risk is the risk faced due to economywide changes, such as economic fluctuations and fluctuations in the market rate of interest. Unique risk is the risk associated with the particular security or investment, such as fluctuations in the sales of a particular firm or region relative to the entire economy.

As different securities are added to a portfolio, the unique risk associated with a specific security is diversified away. That is, as more securities are added, the entire portfolio is less subject to the unique risk associated with a given stock. As the number of securities or assets is increased, unique risk decreases and the total risk of the portfolio (the standard deviation) approaches the market risk.

Source: Tom Herman, "The First Rollovers of Spring Bring Advice on Diversification," *The Wall Street Journal*, Apr. 8, 1993.

by managers to help *analyze* and *guide* the decision-making process. Ultimately, making decisions under risk (or uncertainty) is as much an art as it is a science.

The "art" of decision making under risk or uncertainty is closely associated with a decision maker's preferences with respect to risk taking. Managers can differ greatly in their willingness to take on risk in decision making. Some managers are quite cautious, while others may actually seek out high-risk situations. In the next section, we present a theory, not a rule, of decision making under risk that formally accounts for a manager's attitude toward risk. This theory, usually referred to as *expected utility theory,* postulates that managers make risky decisions with the objective of maximizing the expected *utility* of profit. The theory can, in some situations, provide a more powerful tool for making risky decisions than the rules presented in this section.

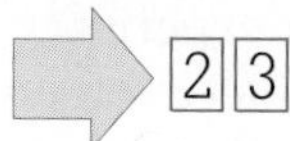

18.4 EXPECTED UTILITY: A THEORY OF DECISION MAKING UNDER RISK

expected utility theory
A theory of decision making under risk that accounts for a manager's attitude toward risk.

As we just mentioned, managers differ in their willingness to undertake risky decisions. Some managers avoid risk as much as possible, while other managers actually prefer more risk to less risk in decision making. To allow for different attitudes toward risk taking in decision making, modern decision theory treats managers as deriving utility or satisfaction from the profits earned by their firms. Just as consumers derived utility from the consumption of goods in Chapter 6, in **expected utility theory,** managers are assumed to derive utility from earning profits. Expected utility theory postulates that managers make risky decisions in a way that maximizes the expected utility of the profit outcomes. While expected utility theory does provide a tool for decisions under risk, the primary purpose of the theory, and the reason for presenting this theory here, is to explain why managers make the decisions they do make when risk is involved. We want to stress that expected utility theory is an economic model of how managers *actually* make decisions under risk, rather than a rule dictating how managers *should* make decisions under risk.

expected utility
The sum of the probability-weighted utilities of each possible profit outcome.

Suppose a manager is faced with a decision to undertake a risky project or, more generally, must make a decision to take an action that may generate a range of possible profit outcomes, $\pi_1, \pi_2, \ldots, \pi_n$, which the manager believes will occur with probabilities $p_1, p_2, \ldots, p_n$, respectively. The **expected utility** of this risky decision is the sum of the probability-weighted utilities of each possible profit outcome:

$$E[U(\pi)] = p_1U(\pi_1) + p_2U(\pi_2) + \ldots + p_nU(\pi_n)$$

where $U(\pi)$ is a utility function for profit that measures the utility associated with a particular level of profit. Notice that expected *utility* of profit is different from the concept of expected *profit,* which is the sum of the probability-weighted profits. In order to understand expected utility theory, you must understand how the manager's attitude toward risk is reflected in the manager's utility function for profit. We now discuss the concept of a manager's utility of profit and show how to derive a utility function for profit. Then we demonstrate how managers could employ expected utility of profit to make decisions under risk.

A Manager's Utility Function for Profit

Since expected utility theory is based on the idea that managers enjoy utility or satisfaction from earning profit, the nature of the relation between a manager's utility and the level of profit earned plays a crucial role in explaining how managers make decisions under risk. As we now show, the manager's attitude toward risk is determined by the manager's *marginal utility of profit.*

It would be extremely unusual for a manager *not* to experience a higher level of total utility as profit increases. Thus, the relation between an index of utility and the level of profit earned by a firm is assumed to be an upward-sloping curve. The amount by which total utility increases when the firm earns an additional dollar of profit is the **marginal utility of profit:**

marginal utility of profit
The amount by which total utility increases with an additional dollar of profit earned by a firm.

$$MU_{\text{profit}} = \Delta U(\pi)/\Delta\pi$$

where $U(\pi)$ is the manager's utility function for profit. The utility function for profit gives an index value to measure the level of utility experienced when a given amount of profit is earned. Suppose, for example, the marginal utility of profit is 8. This means a one dollar increase in profit earned by the firm causes the utility index of the manager to increase by 8 units. Studies of attitudes toward risk have found most business decision makers experience *diminishing marginal utility of profit.* Even though additional dollars of profit increase the level of total satisfaction, the additional utility from extra dollars of profit typically falls for most managers.

The shape of the utility curve for profit plays a pivotal role in expected utility theory because the shape of $U(\pi)$ determines the manager's attitude toward risk, which determines which choices a manager makes. Attitudes toward risk may be categorized as *risk averse, risk neutral,* or *risk loving.* People are said to be **risk averse** if, facing two risky decisions with equal expected profits, they choose the less risky decision. In contrast, someone choosing the more risky decision, when the expected profits are identical, is said to be **risk loving.** The third type of attitude toward risk arises for someone who is indifferent between risky situations when the expected profits are identical. In this last case, a manager ignores risk in decision making and is said to be **risk neutral.**

risk averse
Term describing a decision maker who makes the less risky of two decisions that have the same expected value.

risk loving
Term describing a decision maker who makes the riskier of two decisions that have the same expected value.

risk neutral
Term describing a decision maker who ignores risk in decision making and considers only expected values of decisions.

Figure 18.5 shows the shapes of the utility functions associated with the three types of risk preferences. Panel A illustrates a utility function for a risk-averse manager. The utility function for profit is upward-sloping, but its slope diminishes as profit rises, which corresponds to the case of diminishing marginal utility. When profit increases by \$50,000 from point *A* to point *B*, the manager experiences an increase in utility of 10 units. When profit falls by \$50,000 from point *A* to point *C*, utility falls by 15 units. A \$50,000 loss of profit creates a larger reduction in utility than a \$50,000 gain would add to utility. Consequently, risk-averse managers are more sensitive to a dollar of lost profit than to a dollar of gained profit and will place an emphasis in decision making on avoiding the risk of loss.

In panel B, the marginal utility of profit is constant ($\Delta U/\Delta\pi = 15/50 = 0.3$), and the loss of \$50,000 reduces utility by the same amount that a gain of \$50,000 increases it. In this case, a manager places the same emphasis on avoiding losses as on seeking gains. Managers are risk neutral when their utility functions for profit are linear or, equivalently, when the marginal utility of profit is constant.

Panel C shows a utility function for a manager who makes risky decisions in a risk-loving way. The extra utility from a \$50,000 increase in profit (20 units)

FIGURE 18.5
A Manager's Attitude toward Risk

Panel A — Risk averse: diminishing MU_{profit}

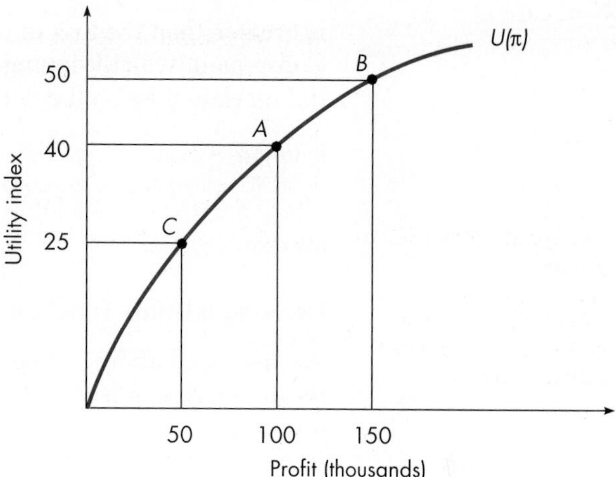

Panel B — Risk neutral: constant MU_{profit}

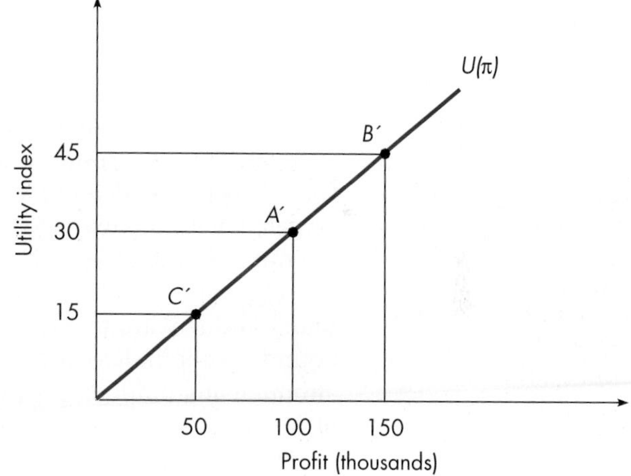

Panel C — Risk loving: increasing MU_{profit}

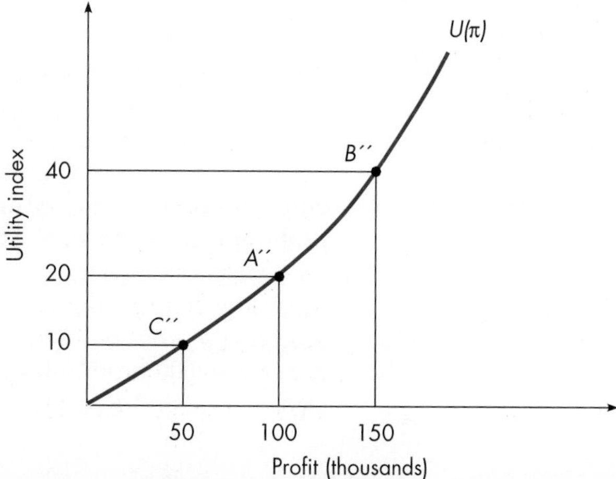

is greater than the loss in utility suffered when profit falls by $50,000 (10 units). Consequently, a risk-loving decision maker places a greater weight on the potential for gain than on the potential for loss. We have now developed the following:

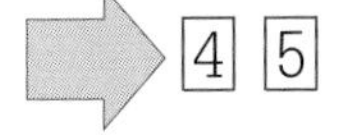

Relation A manager's attitude toward risky decisions can be related to his or her marginal utility of profit. Someone who experiences diminishing (increasing) marginal utility for profit will be a risk averse (risk loving) decision maker. Someone whose marginal utility of profit is constant is risk neutral.

Deriving a Utility Function for Profit

As discussed above, when managers make decisions to maximize expected utility under risk, it is the utility function for profit that determines which decision a manager chooses. We now show the steps a manager can follow to derive his or her own utility function for profit, $U(\pi)$. Recall that the utility function does not directly measure utility but does provide a number, or index value, and that it is the magnitude of this index that reflects the desirability of a particular profit outcome.

The process of deriving a utility function for profit is conceptually straightforward. It does, however, involve a substantial amount of subjective evaluation. To illustrate the procedure, we return to the decision problem facing the manager of Chicago Rotisserie Chicken (CRC). Recall that CRC must decide where to locate the next restaurant. The profit outcomes for the three locations range from $1,000 to $6,000 per week. Before the expected utilities of each location can be calculated, the manager must derive her utility function for profits covering the range $1,000 to $6,000.

The manager of CRC begins the process of deriving $U(\pi)$ by assigning minimum and maximum values that the index will be allowed to take. For the lower bound on the index, suppose the manager assigns a utility index value of 0—although any number, positive or negative, will do—to the lowest profit outcome of $1,000. For the upper bound, suppose a utility index value of 1 is assigned—any value greater than the value of the lower bound will do—to the highest profit outcome of $6,000. Again, we emphasize, choosing 0 and 1 for the upper and lower bounds is completely arbitrary, just as long as the upper bound is greater algebraically than the lower bound. For example, lower and upper bounds of −12 and 50 would also work just fine. Two points on the manager's utility function for profit are

$$U(\$1{,}000) = 0 \qquad \text{and} \qquad U(\$6{,}000) = 1$$

Next, a value of the utility index for each of the remaining possible profit outcomes between $1,000 and $6,000 must be determined. In this case, examining profit in increments of $1,000 is convenient. To find the value of the utility index for $5,000, the manager employs the following subjective analysis: The manager begins by considering two decision choices, A and B, where decision A involves receiving a profit of $5,000 with certainty and risky decision B involves receiving either a $6,000 profit with probability p or a $1,000 profit with probability $1 - p$. Decisions A and B are illustrated in Figure 18.6. Now the probability p that will

FIGURE 18.6
Finding a Certainty Equivalent for a Risky Decision

A	$p = 1$ →	Earn \$5,000 weekly profit	(Certainty equivalent)
B	p →	Earn \$6,000 weekly profit	(Risky decision)
	$1 - p$ →	Earn \$1,000 weekly profit	

make the manager indifferent between the two decisions A and B must be determined. This is a subjective determination, and any two managers will likely find different values of p depending upon their individual preferences for risk.

Suppose the manager of Chicago Rotisserie Chicken decides $p = 0.95$ makes decisions A and B equally desirable. In effect, the manager is saying that the expected utility of decision A equals the expected utility of decision B. Since the expected utilities of decisions A and B are equal, $E(U_A) = E(U_B)$:

$$1 \times U(\$5{,}000) = 0.95 \times U(\$6{,}000) + 0.05 \times U(\$1{,}000)$$

Only $U(\$5{,}000)$ is unknown in this equation, so the manager can solve for the utility index for \$5,000 of profit:

$$\begin{aligned} U(\$5{,}000) &= (0.95 \times 1) + (0.05 \times 0) \\ &= 0.95 \end{aligned}$$

certainty equivalent
The dollar amount that a manager would be just willing to trade for the opportunity to engage in a risky decision.

The utility index value of 0.95 is an indirect measure of the utility of \$5,000 of profit. This procedure establishes another point on the utility function for profit. The sum of \$5,000 is called the **certainty equivalent** of risky decision B because it is the dollar amount that the manager would be just willing to trade for the opportunity to engage in risky decision B. In other words, the manager is indifferent between having a profit of \$5,000 for sure or making a risky decision having a 95 percent chance of earning \$6,000 and a 5 percent chance of earning \$1,000. The utility indexes for \$4,000, \$3,000, and \$2,000 can be established in exactly the same way.

This procedure for finding a utility function for profit is called the *certainty equivalent method.* We now summarize the steps for finding a utility function for profit, $U(\pi)$, in a principle:

Principle To implement the certainty equivalent method of deriving a utility of profit function, the following steps can be employed:

1. Set the utility index equal to 1 for the highest possible profit (π_H) and 0 for the lowest possible profit (π_L).
2. Define a risky decision to have probability p_0 of profit outcome π_H and probability $(1 - p_0)$ of profit outcome π_L. For *each* possible profit outcome π_0 ($\pi_H < \pi_0 < \pi_L$), the

FIGURE 18.7
A Manager's Utility Function for Profit

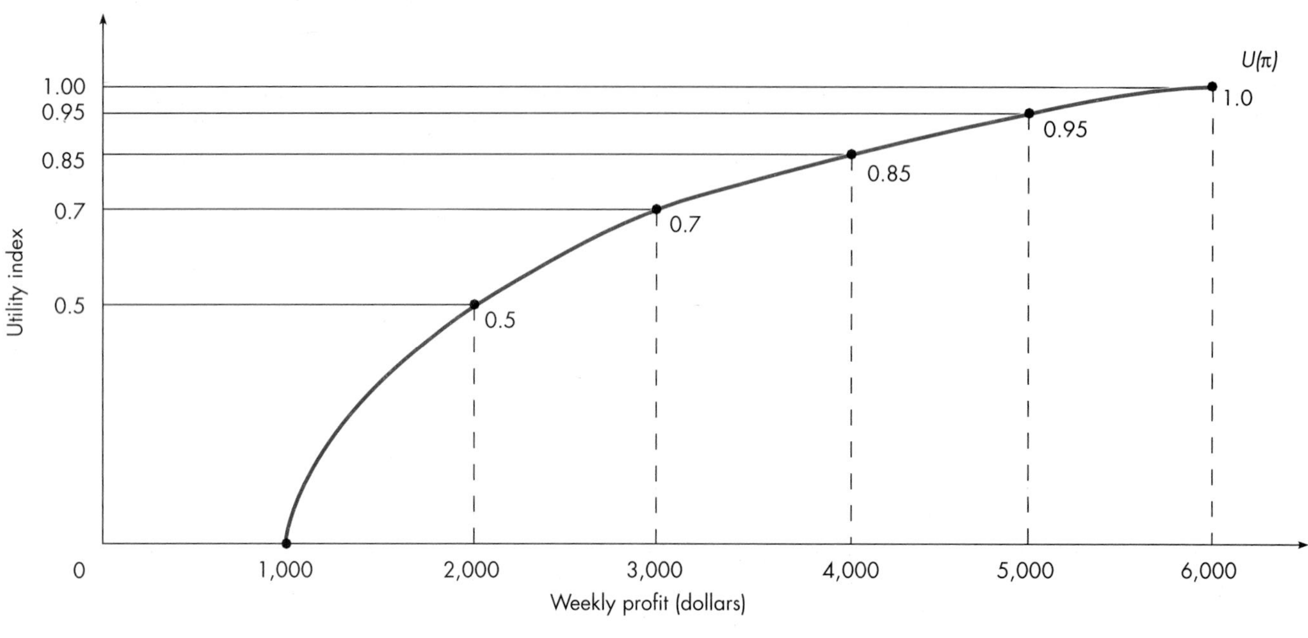

manager determines subjectively the probability p_0 that gives that risky decision the same expected utility as receiving π_0 with certainty:

$$p_0 U(\pi_H) + (1 - p_0)\, U(\pi_L) = U(\pi_0)$$

The certain sum π_0 is called the certainty equivalent of the risky decision.
Let the subjective probability p_0 serve as the utility index for measuring the level of satisfaction the manager enjoys when earning a profit of π_0.

Figure 18.7 illustrates the utility function for profit for the manager of Chicago Rotisserie Chicken. The marginal utility of profit diminishes over the entire range of possible profit outcomes ($1,000 to $6,000), and so this manager is a risk-averse decision maker.

Maximization of Expected Utility

When managers choose among risky decisions in accordance with expected utility theory, the decision with the greatest expected utility is chosen. Unlike maximization of expected profits, maximizing expected utility takes into consideration the manager's preferences for risk. As you will see in this example, maximizing expected utility can lead to a different decision than the one reached using the maximization of expected profit rule.

Return once more to the location decision facing Chicago Rotisserie Chicken. The manager calculates the expected utilities of the three risky location decisions using her own utility function for profit shown in Figure 18.7. The expected utilities for the three cities are calculated as follows:

Atlanta $E(U_A) = 0\ U(\$1{,}000) + 0.2\ U(\$2{,}000) + 0.3\ U(\$3{,}000) + 0.3\ U(\$4{,}000)$
$+ 0.2\ U(\$5{,}000) + 0\ U(\$6{,}000)$
$= 0 + (0.2)(0.5) + (0.3)(0.7) + (0.3)(0.85) + (0.2)(0.95) + 0$
$= 0.755$

Boston $E(U_B) = 0.1\ U(\$1{,}000) + 0.15\ U(\$2{,}000) + 0.15\ U(\$3{,}000)$
$+ 0.25\ U(\$4{,}000) + 0.2\ U(\$5{,}000) + 0.15\ U(\$6{,}000)$
$= (0.1)(0) + (0.15)(0.50) + (0.15)(0.7) + (0.25)(0.85) + (0.2)(0.95)$
$+ (0.15)(1)$
$= 0.733$

Cleveland $E(U_C) = 0.3\ U(\$1{,}000) + 0.1\ U(\$2{,}000) + 0.1\ U(\$3{,}000) + 0.1\ U(\$4{,}000)$
$+ 0.1\ U(\$5{,}000) + 0.3\ U(\$6{,}000)$
$= (0.3)(0) + (0.1)(0.5) + (0.1)(0.7) + (0.1)(0.85) + (0.1)(0.95)$
$+ (0.3)(1.0)$
$= 0.600$

In order to maximize the expected utility of profits, the manager of Chicago Rotisserie Chicken chooses to open its new restaurant in Atlanta. Even though Boston has the highest expected profit [$E(\pi) = \$3{,}750$], Boston also has the highest level of risk ($\sigma = 1{,}545$), and the risk-averse manager at CRC prefers to avoid the relatively high risk of locating the new restaurant in Boston. In this case of a risk-averse decision maker, the manager chooses the less risky Atlanta location over the more risky Cleveland location even though both locations have identical expected profit levels.

To show what a risk-neutral decision maker would do, we constructed a utility function for profit that exhibits constant marginal utility of profit, which, as we have explained, is the condition required for risk neutrality. This risk-neutral utility function is presented in columns 1 and 2 of Table 18.1. Marginal utility of profit, in column 3, is constant, as it must be for risk-neutral managers. From the table you can see that the expected utilities of profit for Atlanta, Boston, and Cleveland are 0.50, 0.55, and 0.50, respectively. For a risk-neutral decision maker, locating in Boston is the decision that maximizes expected utility. Recall that Boston also is the city with the maximum expected profit [$E(\pi) = \$3{,}750$]. This is not a coincidence. As we explained earlier, a risk-neutral decision maker ignores risk when making decisions and relies instead on expected profit to make decisions in risky situations. Under conditions of risk neutrality, a manager makes the same decision by maximizing either the expected value of profit, $E(\pi)$, or the expected utility of profit, $E[U(\pi)]$.[2]

[2]The appendix to this chapter demonstrates the equivalence for risk-neutral decision makers of maximizing expected profit and maximizing expected utility of profit.

TABLE 18.1
Expected Utility of Profit: A Risk Neutral Manager

(1)	(2)	(3)	(4)	(5) Probabilities	(6)	(7)	(8) Probability-weighted utility	(9)
Profit (π)	Utility [$U(\pi)$]	Marginal utility [$\Delta U(\pi)/\Delta\pi$]	Atlanta (P_A)	Boston (P_B)	Cleveland (P_C)	$P_A \times U$	$P_B \times U$	$P_C \times U$
$1,000	0	—	0	0.1	0.3	0	0	0
$2,000	0.2	0.0002	0.2	0.15	0.1	0.04	0.03	0.02
$3,000	0.4	0.0002	0.3	0.15	0.1	0.12	0.06	0.04
$4,000	0.6	0.0002	0.3	0.25	0.1	0.18	0.15	0.06
$5,000	0.8	0.0002	0.2	0.2	0.1	0.16	0.16	0.08
$6,000	1.0	0.0002	0	0.15	0.3	0	0.15	0.3
					Expected utility =	0.50	0.55	0.50

Table 18.2
Expected Utility of Profit: A Risk Loving Manager

(1)	(2)	(3)	(4)	(5) Probabilities	(6)	(7)	(8) Probability-weighted utility	(9)
Profit (π)	Utility [$U(\pi)$]	Marginal utility [$\Delta U(\pi)/\Delta\pi$]	Atlanta (P_A)	Boston (P_B)	Cleveland (P_C)	$P_A \times U$	$P_B \times U$	$P_C \times U$
$1,000	0	—	0	0.1	0.3	0	0	0
$2,000	0.08	0.00008	0.2	0.15	0.1	0.016	0.012	0.008
$3,000	0.2	0.00012	0.3	0.15	0.1	0.06	0.03	0.02
$4,000	0.38	0.00018	0.3	0.25	0.1	0.114	0.095	0.038
$5,000	0.63	0.00025	0.2	0.2	0.1	0.126	0.126	0.036
$6,000	1.0	0.00037	0	0.15	0.3	0	0.15	0.3
					Expected utility =	0.32	0.41	0.43

Finally, consider how a manager who is risk loving decides on a location for CRC's new restaurant. In Table 18.2, columns 1 and 2 show a utility function for profit for which marginal utility of profit is increasing. Column 3 shows the marginal utility of profit, which, as it must for a risk-loving manager, increases as profit increases. The expected utilities of profit outcomes for Atlanta, Boston, and Cleveland are 0.32, 0.41, and 0.43, respectively. In the case of a risk-loving decision maker, Cleveland is the decision that maximizes expected utility. If Atlanta and Cleveland were the only two sites being considered, then the risk-loving manager would choose Cleveland over Atlanta, a decision that is consistent with the definition of risk loving. We now summarize our discussion in the following principle:

Illustration 18.2

Floating Power Plants Lower Risks and Energize Developing Nations

Two crucial industries in developing countries are agriculture and manufacturing. A third-world nation cannot emerge from poverty without achieving a significant ability to feed itself and to manufacture both durable goods for consumption and capital goods for production. Neither of these two crucial industries can develop without energy. Domestically generated electricity can provide a versatile source of energy capable of meeting many of the most fundamental energy demands of a developing country.

A serious roadblock to construction of electric power plants in developing countries has been the risk of default on the financing required to purchase power plants. With prices beginning in the hundreds of millions of dollars, investors are understandably reluctant to lend these enormous amounts when repossession of the asset is, for all practical purposes, impossible. Donald Smith, president of Smith Cogeneration, found a solution to the problem of default risk: build floating power plants on huge barges that can be relocated in the event of a default.

The Wall Street Journal reported recently that Smith's idea of building power plants on barges has spawned a niche industry that "could become a significant portion of the world's [electricity] generating capacity." Nations such as the Dominican Republic, Ghana, India, and Haiti are signing agreements with producers of floating power plants that would not have been financed without the risk reduction created by the mobility of a floating platform. Indeed, the *WSJ* has estimated that the floating nature of the power plant not only makes financing possible but also probably "lower(s) the financing costs by two or three percentage points"—no small change on a half-a-billion-dollar loan.

This illustration highlights the importance of risk in decision making. If financial institutions were managed by risk-loving managers, land-based power plants would likely be common in developing nations. Apparently, developing nations can expect to generate most of their electricity on barges anchored in their harbors—evidence that large financial lenders are indeed risk-averse.

Source: William M. Bulkley, "Building Power Plants That Can Float," *The Wall Street Journal*, May 22, 1996.

Principle If a manager behaves according to expected utility theory, decisions are made to maximize the manager's expected utility of profits. Decisions made by maximizing expected utility of profit reflect the manager's risk-taking attitude and generally differ from decisions reached by decision rules that do not consider risk. In the case of a risk-neutral manager, the decisions are identical under either maximization of expected utility or maximization of expected profit.

18.5 FINDING THE OPTIMAL LEVEL OF A RISKY ACTIVITY

One of the most important tools for decision making is optimization theory. Chapter 4 presented the theory of optimization under conditions of complete information about marginal benefits and marginal costs. We will now show how optimization theory can be used in a straightforward manner in situations where the decision maker has incomplete information about the marginal benefits and marginal costs of an activity, but does have information on the *expected value* of marginal benefits and marginal costs for different levels of the activity. We will also discuss how regression estimates of the marginal benefits and costs of an activity generally meet all the criteria needed for finding the optimal level of the activity. As you will see, the rules you learned in Chapter 4 can easily be modified to handle situations involving risk.

Maximizing Expected Net Benefits

Recall from Chapter 4 that the optimal level of an activity is the level of activity that maximizes net benefit, where net benefit is the difference between total benefit and total cost ($NB = TB - TC$). When the activity varies continuously, the optimal level occurs where marginal benefit equals marginal cost ($MB = MC$). If the activity only varies discretely, the optimal level of activity is the last level of activity for which marginal benefit exceeds marginal cost ($MB > MC$).

For decision-making situations in which benefits and costs are random variables, net benefit is also a random variable. For each level of activity, the net benefit may take on a range of values in a random fashion, and there is a probability distribution for net benefit at each level of activity. Figure 18.8 shows the expected value of an activity, X, over a range of the activity and the probability distribution for three levels of activity, 100, 200, and 300. If the manager chooses 100 units of X, net benefit may take on a range of values as indicated by the bell-shaped probability distribution shown at 100 units of activity X. The expected value of net benefits at that level is $40,000. If the manager repeatedly chooses 100 units of activity X a large number of times, net benefit will, on average, equal $40,000. At an activity level of 200 units, the expected value of net benefits is $50,000. The **expected net benefit curve,** shown in Figure 18.8, represents the locus of expected values of net benefit for all relevant levels of activity X. The **optimal level of a risky activity** is the level that maximizes the *expected net benefit* of the activity. In Figure 18.8, a manager would choose 200 units of the activity since the expected value of net benefit is maximized at that level.

expected net benefit curve
The locus of expected values of net benefit for all relevant levels of activity X.

optimal level of a risky activity
The level of activity that maximizes the expected net benefit $E(NB)$ of the activity.

As long as the probability distribution for net benefit has the same variance at each level of activity—a topic we discuss further below—maximizing the expected net benefit is optimal regardless of whether the manager is risk neutral, risk loving, or risk averse. This is obvious for a risk-neutral manager who ignores risk and simply chooses the level of activity that maximizes expected net benefit.

A risk-loving manager wants to choose the level of activity that maximizes the probability of earning high returns. Since the variance is assumed constant at each activity level, the level with the highest expected return is associated with the greatest probability of achieving a high return. For example, suppose the manager wants to choose X in such a way as to maximize the probability of earning a net benefit of at least $60,000. As you can see in Figure 18.8, it is possible that net benefit might equal $60,000 or more at any of the possible activity

FIGURE 18.8
Probability Distributions for the Net Benefits Associated with a Risky Activity

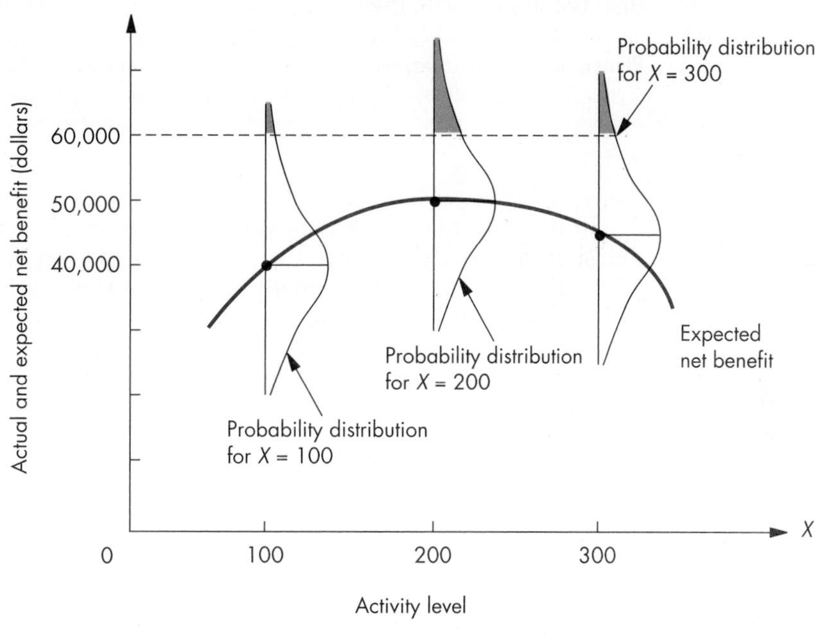

levels. But the activity level that maximizes the likelihood of at least a \$60,000 payoff (net benefit) is 200 units of the activity—as you see by comparing the shaded area above \$60,000 in each of the three probability distributions in Figure 18.8. If the risk-loving manager chooses an activity level of 100 or 300 units, the manager needlessly reduces the probability of earning \$60,000 or more. The probability of earning at least \$60,000 is highest at 200 units of the activity, the activity level with the maximum expected value.

Alternatively, suppose a risk-averse manager wants to choose the level of X that minimizes the probability of earning \$40,000 or less. As you can see from the figure, the probability distribution with the smallest portion lying below \$40,000 is that associated with 200 units of X. If this manager chooses 100 or 300 units of X, the probability of receiving \$40,000 or less is needlessly increased. Therefore, as long as the variance of net benefit is constant across activity levels, the manager should choose the activity level that maximizes the expected value of net benefit no matter what the attitude toward risk. We now summarize this discussion in a principle:

Principle When the variance of the probability distribution on net benefit is constant at all relevant levels of activity, the optimal level of a risky activity is the level of activity with the highest expected net benefit, regardless of whether the decision maker is risk neutral, risk loving, or risk averse.

In order to maximize the expected value of net benefits from an activity, a decision maker does not need to know the expected net benefits and the probability distribution on net benefit at each level of activity. For an activity that varies continuously, expected net benefit reaches its maximum value at the level of the activity at which the *expected* marginal benefit of the activity equals the *expected* marginal cost.[3] When the activity varies discretely, the expected value of net benefits is maximized at the last value of the activity for which expected marginal benefits exceed expected marginal cost.

Figure 18.9 shows the expected marginal benefit and expected marginal cost curves for activity X that correspond to the expected net benefit curve shown in Figure 18.8. The probability distributions of marginal benefit and marginal cost are shown for 100, 200, and 300 units of the activity. The two expected marginal curves in Figure 18.9 are derived from expected total benefit and expected total cost curves (not shown), which also are used to derive the expected net benefit curve in Figure 18.8. The decision maker, following the $E(MB) = E(MC)$ rule, would choose 200 units of activity for which expected marginal benefit equals expected marginal cost at \$20. Engaging in 200 units of activity X yields expected net benefit of \$50,000, the maximum point on the expected net benefit curve. If the manager repeatedly engages in 200 units of activity a large number of times, the actual net benefit incurred will vary randomly but the firm will *on average* earn \$50,000 net benefit.

Regression Analysis and Maximizing Expected Net Benefits

You might be a bit skeptical about whether a manager can actually use the analysis in this section to make decisions under risk, such as finding the level of sales, advertising, or input usage to maximize the expected value of profits. It appears at first that actually estimating expected marginal benefits and cost would pose an insurmountable problem. Fortunately, however, this task is rather simple.

You may recall from the discussion in Chapter 5 on basic estimation techniques that a regression equation such as $Y = a + bX$ shows the *average* or *expected value* of the dependent variable, Y, for a given level of the independent variable, X. We emphasized that the regression equation has a random error term to capture the effect of random influences on Y. Because the variation in Y is due to random effects as well as variation in X, the *exact* value of Y cannot be

[3]A mathematical proof of this statement is presented in the appendix of this chapter.

FIGURE 18.9
Expected Marginal Benefit and Expected Marginal Cost

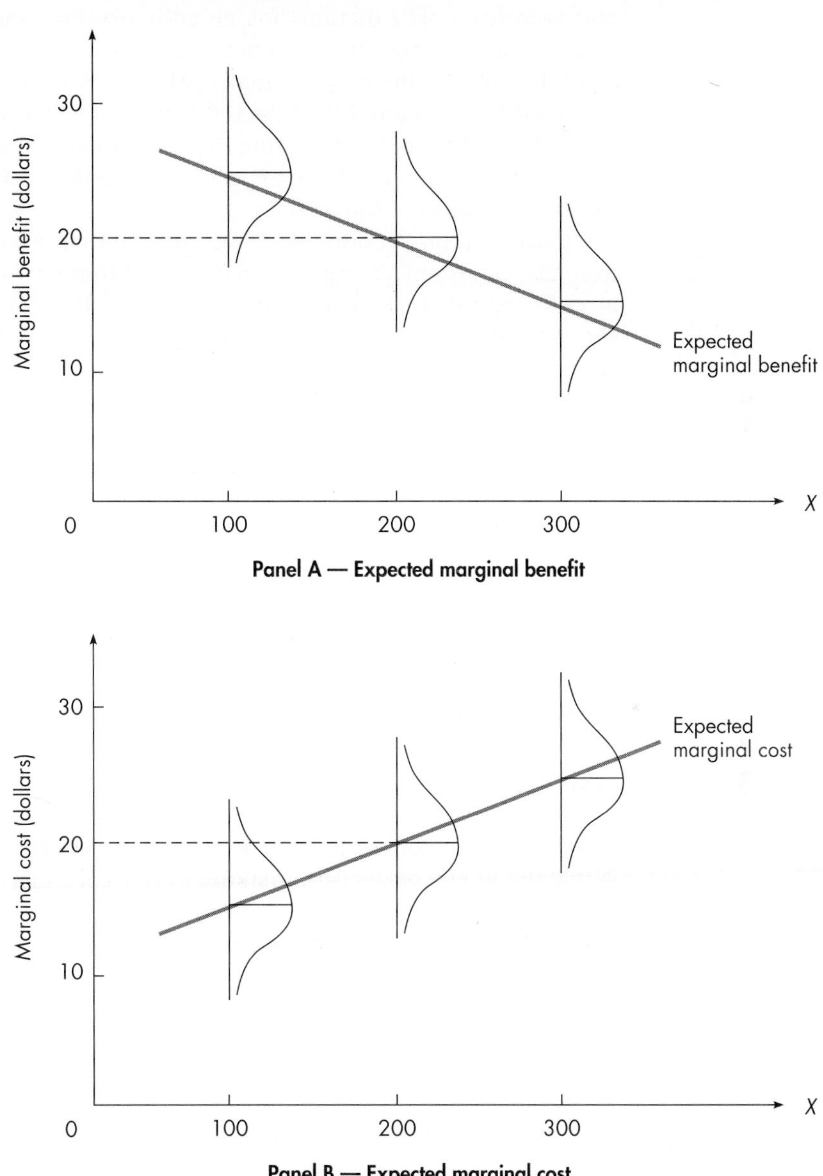

predicted. The value of Y predicted by the regression equation is the value Y would take, on average, after being observed a large number of times for a constant level of X. Thus, the predicted value of the dependent variable given by a regression equation is correctly interpreted as the expected value of the dependent variable Y for a given level of X.

We showed how to use regression analysis to estimate the marginal benefit and marginal cost functions for an activity—for example, a firm's output level. These estimated marginal functions can be interpreted to show the expected values for marginal benefit and marginal cost. We also showed how to derive the expected total benefit and expected total cost functions from the marginal functions. And, of course, subtracting expected total cost from expected total benefits at any level of activity gives expected net benefits—for example, expected profits—for that level of the activity.

Earlier in this section, we demonstrated that if the expected net benefit function has a constant variance, it makes no difference whether the decision maker is risk neutral, risk averse, or risk loving. In each case, the decision maker should choose the level of activity at which expected net benefit is maximized. The regression estimates of expected marginal benefit and expected marginal cost are generally assumed to have a constant variance at all levels of activity *X*.[4] When the expected marginal functions—*E*(*MB*) and *E*(*MC*)—have constant variances at all activity levels, the expected net benefit function—*E*(*NB*)—has a constant variance as well.[5] Therefore, equating the *estimated E*(*MB*) to the *estimated E*(*MC*) does indeed locate the level of activity that maximizes *E*(*NB*), no matter
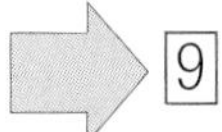
9 what the risk preference of the decision maker.

18.6 PROFIT MAXIMIZATION UNDER RISK: PERFECT COMPETITION

In this section, we show how the manager of a perfectly competitive firm can make the output decision when risk is involved. While the focus of this section is perfect competition, the approach set forth here can be readily extended to firms with market power. Recall from Chapter 12 that the manager of a perfectly competitive firm maximizes profit, under certainty, by choosing to produce the level of output for which the known price equals the known marginal cost. While the model of decision making under certainty is extremely useful in providing a manager with an understanding of how to use information about revenues and costs to maximize profit, we also want to apply the rules of decision making under risk, set forth in Section 18.5, to show how a manager can make decisions when risk is involved. In this section we focus on decisions made in the short-run period of production, but the techniques can be applied in identical fashion in the long run.

Assume that a manager can choose the level of output precisely; that is, output can be controlled and is known with certainty. For any chosen level of out-

[4]In regression analysis, researchers typically assume that the variance of the error term and, by implication, the variance of the dependent variable are constant for all values of the explanatory variables. However, when the problem of heteroscedasticity is encountered, the variance of the error term and the dependent variable are not constant. The appendix to Chapter 5 briefly discusses heteroscedasticity. Heteroscedasticity can usually be corrected using special estimation techniques typically taught in econometrics courses.

[5]Some rather unusual circumstances can occur under which the expected marginal functions *E*(*MB*) and *E*(*MC*) could have constant variances even though the expected total functions *E*(*TB*) and *E*(*TC*) and expected net benefit function *E*(*NB*) do not have constant variances. A discussion of these exceptions is beyond the scope of this text.

FIGURE 18.10
Probability Distribution for Price

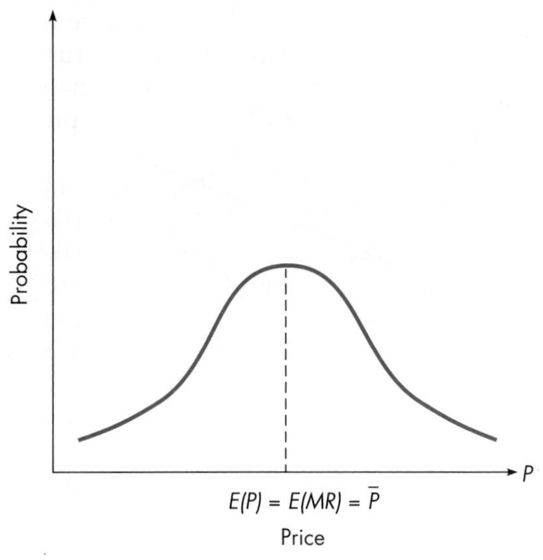

Panel A — Probability distribution for *P*

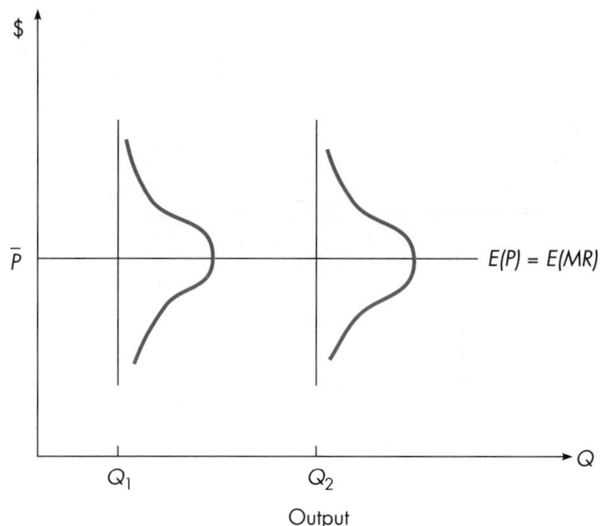

Panel B — The expected *MR* curve

put, however, the manager does not know with certainty either the revenue or the costs associated with that output level. On the revenue side, the manager does not know with certainty the price at which the product can be sold but does have a subjectively (or possibly objectively) determined probability distribution for price. Panel A of Figure 18.10 shows the probability distribution for product price. The expected value of price, $E(P)$, is also the expected marginal revenue for the perfectly competitive firm, $E(MR)$. Since a competitive firm can sell all the product it wishes at the going (expected) market price, the expected price (and expected marginal revenue) is constant for all levels of output. Panel B of Figure 18.10 illustrates how expected price and marginal revenue remain constant for all possible output levels. Regardless of whether the manager chooses to produce Q_1 units or Q_2 units—or any other level of output—the expected price is $\overline{P}$.

On the cost side, the manager does not know with certainty the costs that will be associated with any given level of output. In order to choose output—either under conditions of certainty or risk—the manager needs information about marginal cost. Panel A in Figure 18.11 shows a probability distribution for the possible marginal costs associated with the production of a particular level of output, Q_1. The expected marginal cost of producing Q_1 units is $\overline{MC}_1$, as shown in Panel B. Because the marginal cost of production increases at higher levels of production, the expected marginal cost will rise for higher output levels, as shown in Panel B. In Panel B, the probability distribution for marginal cost

FIGURE 18.11
Probability Distribution for Marginal Cost

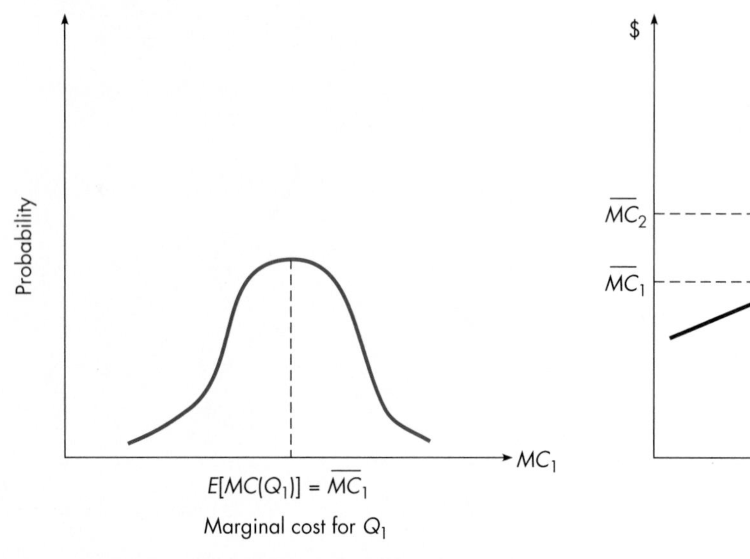

Panel A — Probability distribution for $MC(Q_1)$

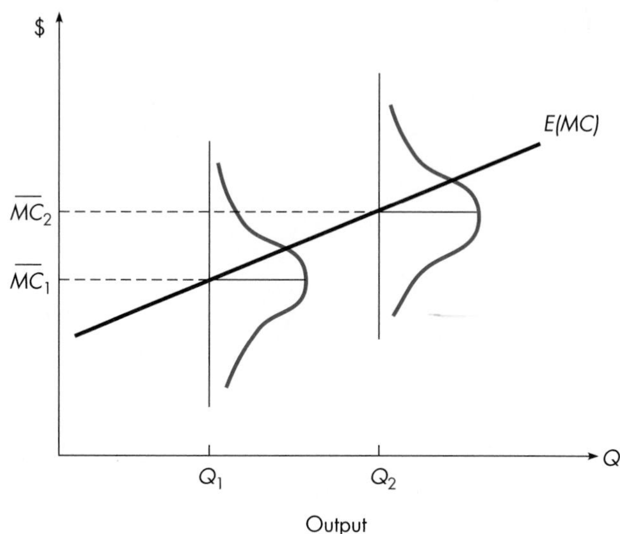

Panel B — The expected *MC* curve

has the same shape at different output levels, but the expected values of the probability distributions rise with higher production levels. In other words, the variance of marginal cost is constant across various output levels; only the expected marginal cost changes. For example, at Q_2 units of production, the expected marginal cost is $\overline{MC}_2$, which is higher than the expected marginal cost of producing Q_1 units.[6]

Recall from Section 18.5 that when the variance of net benefit is constant for all levels of activity, the optimal level of a risky activity is that level for which *expected* marginal benefit equals *expected* marginal cost—regardless of whether the decision maker is risk neutral, risk loving, or risk averse. According to this rule, the manager of a perfectly competitive firm, choosing output under conditions of risk, will maximize expected profit by choosing the level of output for which expected marginal revenue (expected price) equals expected marginal cost:

$$E(MR) = E(P) = E(MC)$$

[6]Recall from our discussion of regression analysis in Chapter 5 that the regression line gives the expected value of Y for a given level of X. As noted in Section 18.5, when regression analysis is used to estimate the marginal cost curve, the estimated marginal cost function actually gives the manager an estimate of the *expected* marginal cost of producing any given level of output.

FIGURE 18.12
Maximization of Expected Profit: $E(MR) = E(P) = E(MC)$

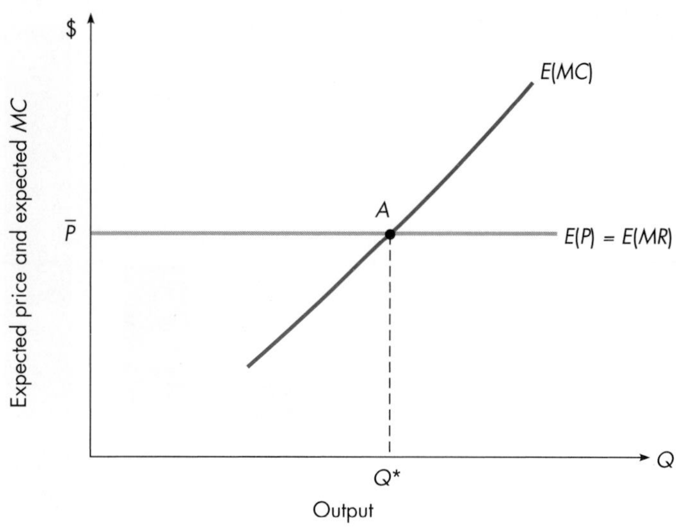

Since we are assuming the variance of price and marginal cost are constant for different outputs, the variance of net benefit (profit) is constant, and the above rule applies to all managers. Figure 18.12 shows the level of output that will maximize expected profit. At Q^* units of production, the expected price, $\overline{P}$, equals the expected marginal cost of producing Q^* units of output (point A). We can summarize our discussion of maximizing expected profit in a principle:

Principle When the variance of profit is constant for all levels of output, a manager of a perfectly competitive firm will choose the level of output that maximizes expected profit, regardless of whether the manager is risk averse, risk loving, or risk neutral. The level of output that maximizes expected profit is the output level for which $E(MR) = E(P) = E(MC)$.

Maximizing Expected Profit at Beau Apparel: An Example

Consider again the perfectly competitive manufacturer of men's shirts, Beau Apparel, which we introduced in Chapter 13. Suppose the manager of Beau Apparel did not know with certainty the price of men's shirts or the costs of production. The manager, who wanted to maximize expected profit, could choose the level of output of shirts with certainty and wished to maximize expected profit but had only a subjective idea about the probability distribution of prices in the first quarter of 1999. Figure 18.13 shows the probability distribution for price in 1999(I). From the figure, the expected price of shirts in 1999(I) is \$18:

$$E(P_{1999(\text{I})}) = (16 \times 0.1) + (17 \times 0.2) + (18 \times 0.4) + (19 \times 0.2) + (20 \times 0.1) = \$18$$

Thus, the expected marginal revenue for Beau Apparel was \$18, $E(MR_{1999(\text{I})}) = E(P_{1999(\text{I})})$.

FIGURE 18.13
Probability Distribution for Price in the First Quarter of 1999

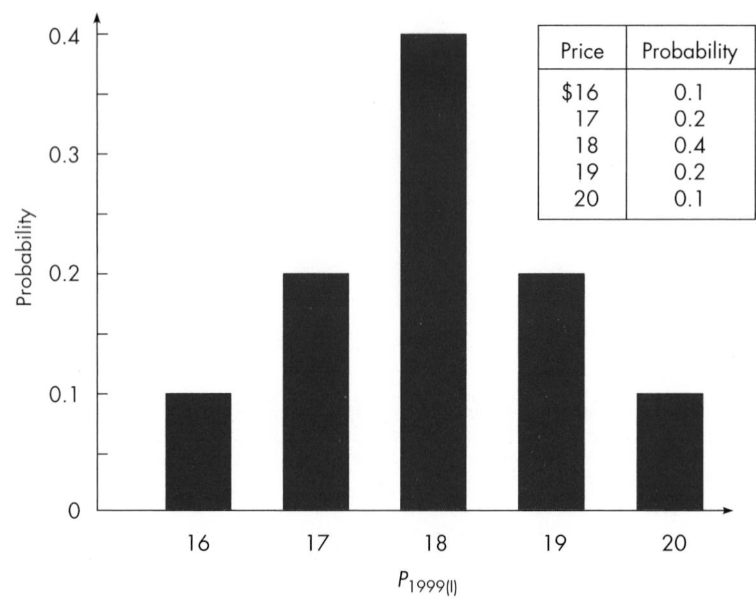

Price	Probability
$16	0.1
17	0.2
18	0.4
19	0.2
20	0.1

The manager used regression analysis to estimate the marginal and average variable cost functions. As stressed earlier in this chapter, the regression analysis of cost provides estimated equations for *expected* costs. Thus, the estimated marginal cost function is an estimate of the expected marginal cost for producing any given level of output. The previously estimated marginal cost function (in Section 13.2) is interpreted as the *expected* marginal cost function:

$$E(MC) = 20 - 0.006Q + 0.00000075Q^2$$

Similarly, the estimated average variable cost function is an estimate of the *expected* average variable cost for any given level of production. Fixed costs are known with certainty to be $30,000.

The manager of Beau Apparel maximizes the expected profit by choosing the level of output for which $E(MR) = E(P) = E(MC)$:

$$18 = 20 - 0.006Q + 0.00000075Q^2$$

Solving for Q using the quadratic formula, the manager found two solutions, $Q = 350$ and $Q = 7{,}650$. When 350 units are produced, the expected average variable cost would be greater than the expected price, and the firm should not produce:

$$E(AVC_{Q=350}) = 20 - 0.003(350) + 0.00000025(350)^2 = \$18.98 > \$18 = E(P_{1999(I)})$$

The level of output that maximizes the expected profit is 7,650 units because the expected average variable cost is less than the expected price of $18:

$$E(AVC_{Q=7,650}) = 20 - 0.003(7,650) + 0.00000025(7,650)^2 = \$11.68 < \$18$$

The manager did not know with certainty how much profit would actually be earned in the first quarter of 1999, but by choosing to produce 7,650 shirts, the expected profit is maximized. The expected profit in 1999(I) was calculated as follows:

$$E(\pi_{1999(I)}) = E(P_{1999(I)}) \times Q - E(AVC_{1999(I)}) \times Q - TFC$$

10 $$= (\$18 \times 7,650) - (\$11.68 \times 7,650) - \$30,000$$

$$= \$18,348$$

18.7 PROFIT MAXIMIZATION UNDER RISK: DUOPOLY

Recall that the most important characteristic of oligopoly, which also creates a serious problem for managers trying to maximize oligopoly profit, is the mutual interdependence that exists among firms. The manager of each oligopoly firm realizes that changes in the firm's own price and output will affect the demand (and profit) of all its rivals, and the managers of these rival firms will likely respond by adjusting their firms' prices and outputs, which in turn will affect the demand (and profit) of the firm that originated the price change. While managers can be rather certain that rivals will notice changes in price, they generally do not know with certainty how their rivals will react to the changes.

In Chapter 15, we illustrated the interdependence problem with an example of a manager considering a price change. The oligopoly firm faced two or more demands—and hence, two or more marginal revenue functions—depending upon how rival firms actually responded to the price change. At the extremes, the manager recognized two demand curves: one demand curve assuming that rivals follow the manager's price change, and the other demand curve assuming that rivals do not change their prices in response to a price change.

Which demand is the "correct" one for decision-making purposes? Clearly, there is no "correct" demand *before* the firm acts. A manager facing a risky demand situation cannot know what the true demand is until after the firm changes price or takes some other action and the rival firms have had time to react, if they so desire. In order to make plans, managers should have some idea about the way rivals will respond and, therefore, some idea about the firm's demand. The principles of decision making under risk give one possible method that a manager can use when there is incomplete information about how rivals will react to a price change. We will now show you a simple example to illustrate this approach, but we must emphasize that there are many other methods of approaching this problem.

Suppose Atlas Corporation and Butler Industries are the only two firms in a market producing close substitutes—a market structure called *duopoly*—and both firms are charging a price of \$40 ($P_A = P_B = \$40$). The manager of Atlas Corporation estimates its demand to be

$$Q_A = 6,000 - 300P_A + 225P_B$$

In the current situation, both firms are charging a price of \$40, and Atlas's sales are 3,000 [= 6,000 − (300 × 40) + (225 × 40)] units. The manager of Atlas Corporation does not believe selling 3,000 units at a price of \$40 is maximizing the firm's profit and so is considering a price change.

If Butler Corporation does not match Atlas's new price and continues to charge a price of \$40, then Atlas's demand when Butler does not follow a price change ($D_{\text{doesn't follow}}$) is

$$\begin{aligned} Q_A &= 6{,}000 + (225 \times 40) - 300P_A \\ &= 15{,}000 - 300P_A \end{aligned} \qquad (D_{\text{doesn't follow}})$$

Alternatively, if Butler Corporation exactly matches any price charged by Atlas ($P_A = P_B$), then Atlas faces the following demand:

$$\begin{aligned} Q_A &= 6{,}000 - 300P_A + 225P_A \\ &= 6{,}000 - 75P_A \end{aligned} \qquad (D_{\text{follows}})$$

The manager at Atlas believes there is a 40 percent probability that Butler will maintain a constant price of \$40 and believes there is a 60 percent probability that Butler will match any price change made by Atlas. For any price chosen by the manager at Atlas, the expected quantity demanded at each price, $E(Q_A)$, is

$$E(Q_A) = 0.4 \times (15{,}000 - 300P_A) + 0.6 \times (6{,}000 - 75P_A) = 9{,}600 - 165P_A$$

Note that if Atlas's manager is correct in assuming that Butler will make one of only two responses to a price change, then Atlas's actual sales after a price change will never equal the expected sales, $E(Q_A)$. The actual quantity sold will lie on one of the two demands, $D_{\text{doesn't follow}}$ or D_{follows}. If Atlas changes price a large number of times, the average level of sales will lie on the expected-quantity-demanded curve, $E(Q_A)$. Figure 18.14 shows the two demand curves facing the manager of Atlas Corporation, depending upon the price response from its rival. The expected quantity demanded, $E(Q_A)$, is shown by the dotted line between the two inverse demand curves.

In order to maximize *expected* profit, the manager at Atlas will decide how much to produce and what price to charge by equating *expected* marginal revenue and *expected* marginal cost. In order to obtain the expected marginal revenue function, the inverse function for $E(Q_A)$ must be found:[7]

$$P_A = [9{,}600 - E(Q_A)]/165 \approx 58 - 0.006E(Q_A)$$

The expected marginal revenue function is

$$E(MR) \approx 58 - 0.012E(Q_A)$$

[7]This is not an expected price. Alpha's manager chooses a given expected quantity from its expected quantity function and will charge exactly that price in order to maximize profit. In other words, the manager knows with certainty the price the firm will receive for each unit sold, but once the price has been chosen, the actual level of sales is the risky variable.

FIGURE 18.14
Duopoly Profit Maximization

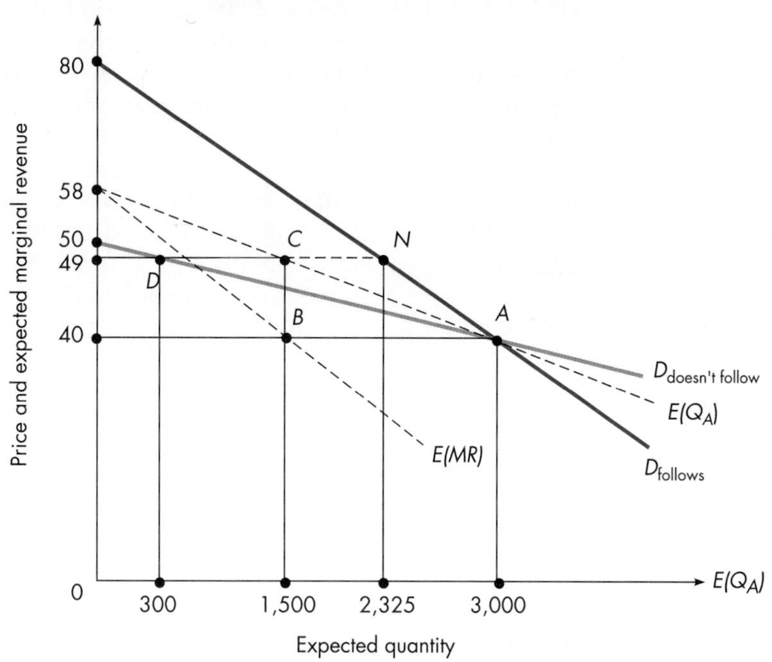

This function is the *expected* marginal revenue because once the manager chooses a price, the sales depend upon the reaction of the rival. Thus, marginal revenue also depends on the rival's reaction.

Atlas Corporation faces a constant marginal cost that is known with certainty to be equal to \$40. To find the level of output that maximizes expected profit, the manager at Atlas Corporation sets expected marginal revenue equal to marginal cost:

$$E(MR) = 58 - .012E(Q_A) = 40$$

and solves for $E(Q_A)$,

$$E(Q_A) = 1{,}500$$

Thus, the manager should choose the (certain) price that will generate expected sales of 1,500 units. This price is determined from the inverse function:

$$P_A = 58 - (0.006 \times 1{,}500) = \$49$$

The *actual* sales will be 300 [= 15,000 − (300 × 49)] units if Butler Corporation does not match Atlas's new price and keeps their price at \$40. The *actual* sales will be 2,325 [= 6,000 − (75 × 49)] units if Butler does match the price change and sets its own price at \$49.

Figure 18.14 illustrates this numerical example. When Atlas sets a price of \$40 (as does Butler), it sells 3,000 units (point *A*). The demand curves when Butler does and does not follow are, respectively, D_{follows} and $D_{\text{doesn't follow}}$. The expected sales at each price are given by the dashed inverse demand, $E(Q_A)$. The expected marginal revenue at any price on $E(Q_A)$ is given by the dashed line, $E(MR)$.

If the firm sets $E(MR) = MC = \$40$ (point *B*), expected sales are 1,500 units and the manager of Atlas sets a price of \$49, given by $E(Q_A)$ at point *C* in Figure 18.14. Atlas will sell 300 units if demand is actually $D_{\text{doesn't follow}}$ (point *D*) and 2,325 units if demand is actually D_{follows} (point *N*).

This simple example is not intended to demonstrate precisely how an oligopolist with incomplete information about its rivals' reaction to price changes actually makes its profit-maximizing decision. It is designed only to show how a manager can take risk into account in decision making. The actual process would probably be more complex. Nonetheless, a manager can use objectively or subjectively determined probabilities about demand in estimating rivals' reactions.

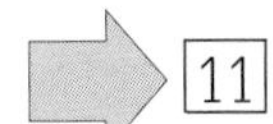
11

18.8 DECISIONS UNDER UNCERTAINTY

Practically all economic theories about behavior in the absence of complete information deal with risk rather than uncertainty. Furthermore, decision science has little guidance to offer managers making decisions when they have no idea about the likelihood of various states of nature occurring. This should not be too surprising, given the nebulous nature of uncertainty. We will, however, present four rather simple decision rules that can help managers make decisions under uncertainty.

The Maximax Criterion

maximax rule
Decision-making guide that calls for identifying the best outcome for each possible decision and choosing the decision with the maximum payoff of all the best outcomes.

For managers who tend to have an optimistic outlook on life, the **maximax rule** provides a guide for making decisions when uncertainty prevails. Under the maximax rule, a manager identifies for each possible decision the best outcome that could occur and then chooses the decision that would give the maximum payoff of all the best outcomes. Under this rule a manager ignores all possible outcomes except the best outcome from each decision.

To illustrate the application of this rule, suppose the management at Dura Plastic is considering changing the size (capacity) of its manufacturing plant. Management has narrowed the decision to three choices. The plant's capacity will be either (1) expanded by 20 percent, (2) maintained at the current capacity, or (3) reduced by 20 percent. The outcome of this decision depends crucially upon how the economy performs during the upcoming year. Thus the performance of the economy is the "state of nature" in this decision problem. Management envisions three possible states of nature occurring: (1) the economy enters a period of recovery, (2) economic stagnation sets in, or (3) the economy falls into a recession.

TABLE 18.3
The Payoff Matrix for Dura Plastic, Inc.

	States of nature		
Decisions	Recovery	Stagnation	Recession
Expand plant capacity by 20%	$5 million	−$1 million	−$3.0 million
Maintain same plant capacity	3 million	2 million	0.5 million
Reduce plant capacity by 20%	2 million	1 million	0.75 million

payoff matrix
A table with rows corresponding to various decisions and columns corresponding to various states of nature, with each cell giving the outcome or payoff associated with that decision and state of nature.

For each possible decision and state of nature, the managers determine the profit outcome, or payoff, shown in the *payoff matrix* in Table 18.3. A **payoff matrix** is a table with rows corresponding to the various decisions and columns corresponding to the various states of nature. Each cell in the payoff matrix in Table 18.3 gives the outcome (payoff) for each decision when a particular state of nature occurs. For example, if management chooses to expand the manufacturing plant by 20 percent and the economy enters a period of recovery, Dura Plastic is projected to earn profits of $5 million. Alternatively, if Dura Plastic expands plant capacity but the economy falls into a recession, it is projected that the company will lose $3 million. Since the managers do not know which state of nature will actually occur, or the probabilities of occurrence, the decision to alter plant capacity is made under conditions of uncertainty. In order to apply the maximax rule to this decision, management first identifies the best possible outcome for each of the three decisions. The best payoffs are:

$5 million for expand plant size by 20 percent
$3 million for maintain plant size
$2 million for reduce plant size by 20 percent

Each best payoff occurs if the economy recovers. Under the maximax rule management would decide to expand its plant.

While the maximax rule is simple to apply, it fails to consider "bad" outcomes in the decision-making process. The fact that two out of three states of nature result in losses when management decides to expand plant capacity, and neither of the other decisions would result in a loss, is overlooked when using the maximax criteria. Only managers with optimistic natures are likely to find the maximax rule to be a useful decision-making tool.

The Maximin Criterion

maximin rule
Decision-making guide that calls for identifying the worst outcome for each decision and choosing the decision with the maximum worst payoff.

For managers with a pessimistic outlook on business decisions, the *maximin rule* may be more suitable than the maximax rule. Under the **maximin rule,** the manager identifies the worst outcome for each decision and makes the decision associated with the maximum worst payoff. For Dura Plastic, the worst outcomes for each decision from Table 18.3 are:

−$3 million for expand plant size by 20 percent
$0.5 million for maintain plant size
$0.75 million for reduce plant size by 20 percent

TABLE 18.4
Potential Regret Matrix for Dura Plastic, Inc.

Decisions	States of nature		
	Recovery	Stagnation	Recession
Expand plant capacity by 20%	$0	$3 million	$3.75 million
Maintain same plant capacity	2 million	0	0.25 million
Reduce plant capacity by 20%	3 million	1 million	0

Using the maximin criterion, Dura Plastic would choose to reduce plant capacity by 20 percent. The maximin rule is also simple to follow, but it fails to consider any of the "good" outcomes.

Minimax Regret Criterion

potential regret
For a given decision and state of nature, the improvement in payoff the manager could have experienced had the decision been the best one when that state of nature actually occurs.

Managers concerned about their decisions not turning out to be the best *once the state of nature is known* (i.e., after the uncertainty is resolved) may make their decisions by minimizing the potential regret that may occur. The **potential regret** associated with a particular decision and state of nature is the improvement in payoff the manager could have experienced had the decision been the best one when that state of nature actually occurred. To illustrate, we calculate from Table 18.3 the potential regret associated with Dura Plastic's decision to maintain the same level of plant capacity if an economic recovery occurs. The best possible payoff when recovery occurs is $5 million, the payoff for expanding plant capacity. If a recovery does indeed happen and management chooses to maintain the same level of plant capacity, the payoff is only $3 million, and the manager experiences a regret of $2 million (= $5 − $3 million).

minimax regret rule
Decision-making guide that calls for determining the worst potential regret associated with each decision, then choosing the decision with the minimum worst potential regret.

Table 18.4 shows the potential regret for each combination of decision and state of nature. Note that every state of nature has a decision for which there is no potential regret. This occurs when the correct decision is made for that particular state of nature. To apply the **minimax regret rule,** which requires that managers make a decision with the minimum worst potential regret, management identifies the maximum possible potential regret for each decision from the matrix:

$3.75 million for expand plant size by 20 percent
$2 million for maintain plant size
$3 million for reduce plant size by 20 percent

Management chooses the decision with the lowest worst potential regret: maintain current plant capacity. For Dura Plastic, the minimax regret rule results in management's choosing to maintain the current plant capacity.

Equal Probability Criterion

In situations of uncertainty, managers have no information about the probable state of nature that will occur and sometimes simply assume that each state of nature is equally likely to occur. In terms of the Dura Plastic decision, management assumes each state of nature has a one-third probability of occurring. When managers assume each state of nature has an equal likelihood of occurring, the decision can be made by considering the *average* payoff for each equally possible state of nature. This approach to decision making is often referred to as the **equal probability rule.** To illustrate, the manager of Dura Plastic calculates the average payoff for each decision as follows:

equal probability rule
Decision-making guide that calls for assuming each state of nature is equally likely to occur, computing the average payoff for each equally likely possible state of nature, and choosing the decision with the highest average payoff.

\$0.33 million [= (5 + (−1) + (−3))/3] for expand plant size
\$1.83 million [= (3 + 2 + 0.5)/3] for maintain plant size
\$1.25 million [= (2 + 1 + 0.75)/3] for reduce plant size

Under the equal probability rule, the manager's decision is to maintain the current plant capacity since this decision has the maximum average return.

The four decision rules discussed here do not exhaust the possibilities for managers making decisions under uncertainty. We present these four rules primarily to give you a feel for decision making under uncertainty and to show the imprecise or "unscientific" nature of these rules. Recall that management could choose any of the courses of action depending upon which rule was chosen. These and other rules are meant only to be guidelines to decision making and are not substitutes for the experience and intuition of management.

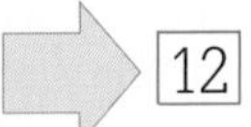

18.9 SUMMARY

When managers make choices or decisions under risk or uncertainty, they must somehow incorporate this risk into their decision-making process. This chapter presented some basic rules for managers to help them make decisions under conditions of risk and uncertainty. Conditions of *risk* occur when a manager must make a decision for which the outcome is not known with certainty. Under conditions of risk, the manager can make a list of all possible outcomes and assign probabilities to the various outcomes. *Uncertainty* exists when a decision maker cannot list all possible outcomes and/or cannot assign probabilities to the various outcomes.

In order to measure the risk associated with a decision, the manager can examine several characteristics of the probability distribution of outcomes for the decision. A probability distribution is a table or graph showing all possible outcomes (payoffs) for a decision and the probability that each outcome will occur. The various rules for making decisions under risk require information about several different characteristics of the probability distribution of outcomes: (1) the expected value (or mean) of the distribution, (2) the variance and standard deviation, and (3) the coefficient of variation.

The expected value (or mean) of a probability distribution is

$$E(X) = \text{Expected value of } X = \sum_{i=1}^{n} p_i X_i$$

where X_i is the ith outcome of a decision, p_i is the probability of the ith outcome, and n is the total number of possible outcomes in the probability distribution. The variance of a probability distribution measures the dispersion of the outcomes about the mean outcome. The variance is calculated as

$$\text{Variance } (X) = \sigma_x^2 = \sum_{i=1}^{n} p_i(X_i - E(X))^2$$

Because the variance is a squared term and usually much larger than the mean, the standard deviation is often used to measure the dispersion of a probability distribution:

TABLE 18.5

Summary of Decision Rules under Conditions of Risk

Rule	Description
Expected value rule	Choose the decision with the highest expected value.
Mean-variance rules	Given two risky decisions *A* and *B*: If decision *A* has a higher expected outcome *and* a lower variance than decision *B*, decision *A* should be made. If both decisions *A* and *B* have identical *variances* (or standard deviations), the decision with the higher expected value should be made. If both decisions *A* and *B* have identical *expected* values, the decision with the lower variance (standard deviation) should be made.
Coefficient of variation rule	Choose the decision with the smallest coefficient of variation.

$$\sigma_x = \sqrt{\text{Variance } (X)}$$

When the expected values of outcomes differ substantially, managers should measure riskiness of a decision relative to its expected value using the coefficient of variation:

$$\upsilon = \frac{\text{Standard deviation}}{\text{Expected value}} = \frac{\sigma_x}{E(X)}$$

The coefficient of variation measures the level of risk relative to the mean of the probability distribution.

When managers make decisions under risk they must incorporate the risk into their decision-making process. While there is no single decision rule that managers can follow to guarantee that profits are actually maximized, there are a number of decision rules that managers can use to help them make decisions under risk: (1) the expected value rule, (2) the mean-variance rules, and (3) the coefficient of variation rule. These three rules are summarized in Table 18.5. These rules can only guide managers in their analysis of risky decision making.

The actual decisions made by a manager will depend in large measure upon the manager's willingness to take on risk. Managers' propensity to take on risk can be classified in one of three categories: risk averse, risk loving, or risk neutral. These categories of risk preference are defined according to how that manager would choose between the following two alternatives:

A. Take a risky course of action with a known expected value and variance.
B. Receive the expected value of that course of action with certainty.

A *risk-averse* person would choose to receive with certainty the expected value of the risky course of action (alternative B). A *risk-loving* person would choose the risky course of action (alternative A). A *risk-neutral* person would be indifferent between the two alternative decisions.

Expected utility theory explains how managers can make decisions in risky situations. The theory postulates that managers make risky decisions with the objective of maximizing the expected utility of profit. The manager's attitude for risk is captured by the shape of the utility function for profit. If a manager experiences diminishing (increasing) marginal utility for profit, the manager is risk averse (risk loving). If marginal utility for profit is constant, the manager is risk neutral.

If a manager maximizes expected utility for profit, the decisions can differ from decisions reached using the three decision rules discussed for making risky decisions. However, in the case of a risk-neutral manager, the decisions are the same under maximization of expected profit and maximization of expected utility of profit. Consequently, a risk-neutral decision maker can follow the simple rule of maximizing the expected value of profit and simultaneously also be maximizing utility of profit.

When managers wish to find the optimal level of a risky activity, they follow the same rule no matter what their preference for risk. When the variance of the probability on net benefit is constant at all relevant levels of activity, the optimal level of a risky activity is the level of activity with the highest expected net benefit, regardless of whether the manager is risk neutral, risk loving, or risk averse. For activities that vary continuously, expected net benefit reaches its maximum value at the level of activity for which the expected marginal benefit equals the expected marginal cost:

$$E(MB) = E(MC)$$

TABLE 18.6
Summary of Decision Rules under Conditions of Uncertainty

Maximax rule	Identify the best outcome for each possible decision, and choose the decision with the maximum payoff.
Maximin rule	Identify the worst outcome for each decision, and choose the decision associated with the maximum worst payoff.
Minimax regret rule	Determine the worst potential regret associated with each decision, where the potential regret associated with any particular decision and state of nature is the improvement in payoff the manager could have experienced had the decision been the best one when that state of nature actually occurred. The manager chooses the decision with the minimum worst potential regret.
Equal probability rule	Assume each state of nature is equally likely to occur and compute the average payoff for each equally likely possible state of nature. Choose the decision with the highest average payoff.

When the activity varies discretely, the optimal level of activity occurs at the last level of activity for which $E(MB)$ exceeds $E(MC)$.

The expected marginal benefit and expected marginal cost curves can be obtained using the techniques of regression analysis presented in Chapter 5. As explained there, the predicted value of Y is correctly interpreted as the expected value of Y given a particular value of X. Thus, the optimal level of a risky activity can be found by equating marginal benefit and marginal cost curves that are estimated using regression analysis.

In the case of uncertainty, decision science can provide very little guidance to managers beyond offering them some simple decision rules to aid them in their analysis of uncertain situations. Four basic rules for decision making under uncertainty are presented in this chapter: (1) the maximax rule, (2) the maximin rule, (3) the minimax regret rule, and (4) the equal probability rule. Table 18.6 summarizes each of these rules.

TECHNICAL PROBLEMS

1. Consider the following two probability distributions for sales:

Sales (thousands of units)	Distribution 1 probability (percent)	Distribution 2 probability (percent)
50	10	10
60	20	15
70	40	20
80	20	30
90	10	25

   a. Graph the two distributions shown in the above table. What are the expected sales for the two probability distributions?
   b. Calculate the variance and standard deviation for both distributions. Which distribution is more risky?
   c. Calculate the coefficient of variation for both distributions. Which distribution is more risky relative to its mean?

2. A firm is making its production plans for next quarter, but the manager of the firm does not know what the price of the product will be next month. He believes that

there is a 40 percent probability the price will be \$15 and a 60 percent probability the price will be \$20. The manager must decide whether to produce 7,000 units or 8,000 units of output. The following table shows the four possible profit outcomes, depending on which output management chooses and which price actually occurs:

	Profit (loss) when price is	
	\$15	\$20
Option A: produce 7,100	−\$3,750	+\$31,770
Option B: produce 8,000	−8,000	+34,000

a. If the manager chooses the option with the higher expected profits, which output is chosen?
b. Which option is more risky?
c. What is the decision if the manager uses the mean-variance rules to decide between the two options?
d. What is the decision using the coefficient of variation rule?

3. Suppose in the above problem that the price probabilities are reversed: the manager expects a price of \$15 with a probability of 60 percent and a price of \$20 with a probability of 40 percent. Answer all parts of problem 2 under the assumption of these reversed probabilities. What would the probabilities have to be to make the expected values of the two options equal?
4. A manager's utility function for profit is $U(\pi) = 20\pi$, where π is the dollar amount of profit. The manager is considering a risky decision with the four possible profit outcomes shown below. The manager makes the following subjective assessments about the probability of each profit outcome:

Probability	Profit outcome
0.05	−\$10,000
0.45	−2,000
0.45	4,000
0.05	20,000

a. Calculate the expected profit.
b. Calculate the expected utility of profit.
c. The marginal utility of an extra dollar of profit is ________.
d. The manager is risk ________ because the marginal utility of profit is ________.

5. Suppose the manager of a firm has a utility function for profit of $U(\pi) = 20\ ln(\pi)$, where π is the dollar amount of profit. The manager is considering a risky project with the following profit payoffs and probabilities:

Probability	Profit outcome	Marginal utility of profit
0.05	\$1,000	—
0.15	2,000	________
0.30	3,000	________
0.50	4,000	________

a. Calculate the expected profit.
b. Calculate the expected utility of profit.
c. Fill in the blanks in the table showing the marginal utility of an additional $1,000 of profit.
d. The manager is risk ________ because the marginal utility of profit is ________.

6. Derive your own utility function for profit for the range of profits shown in the table below:

Profit outcome	Utility index	Marginal utility of profit
$1,000	0.0	—
2,000	________	________
3,000	________	________
3,200	________	________
4,000	1.0	________

a. Find the probability p that would make you indifferent between (i) accepting a risky project with probability p of making $4,000 and probability $1 - p$ of making a profit of $1,000 or (ii) making a profit of $2,000 with certainty. Write this probability in the correct blank in the table above.
b. Repeat part *a* for $3,000 and $3,200.
c. Compute the marginal utility of profit. (*Hint:* $MU_{\text{profit}} = \Delta\text{utility index}/\Delta\text{profit}$, and the denominator, Δprofit, is not constant in this table.)
d. Does your utility index indicate that you have a risk-averse, risk-neutral, or risk-loving attitude toward risk? Explain.

7. Suppose the manager in problem 4 can avoid the risky decision in that problem by choosing instead to receive with certainty a sum of money exactly equal to the expected profit of the risky decision in problem 4.
a. The utility of the expected profit is ________.
b. Compare the utility of the expected profit with the expected utility of the risky decision (which you calculated in part *b* of problem 4). Which decision yields the greatest expected utility for the manager?
c. Is your decision in part *b* consistent with the manager's attitude toward risk, as it is reflected by the utility function for profit? Explain.

8. The manager in problem 5 receives an offer from another party to buy the rights to the risky project described in that problem. This party offers the manager $3,200, which the manager believes will be paid with certainty.
a. The utility of $3,200 is ________.
b. Comparing the utility of $3,200 with the expected utility of the risky project (you calculated this for part *b* of problem 5), what should the manager do if the manager wishes to maximize expected utility of profit? Explain.
c. Is your decision in part *b* consistent with the manager's attitude toward risk as it is reflected by the utility function for profit? Explain.
d. Is the decision consistent with the mean-variance rules for decision making under risk? Explain.

9. The following table shows the expected marginal benefits and expected marginal costs associated with 100, 200, 300, and 400 units of an activity and the associated variances for each level of activity:

Activity level	Marginal benefit: Expected MB	Marginal benefit: Variance of MB	Marginal cost: Expected MC	Marginal cost: Variance of MC
100	$62	756	$50	336
200	58	756	55	336
300	52	756	56	336
400	46	756	60	336

a. If the decision maker is risk neutral, what level of the activity would be chosen?
b. How might the decision change (if it would change) if the manager is risk loving?
c. How might the decision change if the manager is risk averse?

10. The manager of a perfectly competitive firm must choose the profit-maximizing level of production without knowing with certainty the price of the product or the costs of production. The manager wishes to maximize expected profit given the following subjective probabilities for price:

Price	Probability
$15	0.20
16	0.30
17	0.30
18	0.20

The manager has estimated average variable cost using regression analysis, which assumes the variance of costs is constant at all levels of production. The estimated equation for average variable cost is

$$AVC = 20 - 0.025Q + 0.00002Q^2$$

The manager is certain that total fixed costs are $2,000.
a. The equation for expected marginal cost is $E(MC) =$ ________.
b. The expected price is $________.
c. The expected minimum average variable cost is $________. Should the manager produce or shut down?
d. A production level of ________ units maximizes expected profit.
e. Expected profit is $________.

11. A duopolist wants to raise price. The manager of the duopoly firm believes there is an 80 percent probability that its rival will match the firm's price increase and a 20 percent chance that it will leave its price unchanged. The rival is currently charging a price of $40. The manager estimates the firm's demand to be

$$Q = 8{,}000 - 280P + 200P_R$$

where P_R is the price charged by the rival firm. The manager faces constant marginal costs of $30.
a. Find the demand function for the situation in which (i) the rival firm does not match the price increase and (ii) the rival does match the price increase.
b. Find the expected demand function.
c. Write the equation for the expected marginal revenue function.
d. The manager should set a price of $________ to maximize expected profit.

e. While the amount of expected sales for the price set in part *d* is ______ units, the actual level of sales will be ______ units if the rival firm matches the manager's price increase or will be ______ units if the rival firm keeps its price at $40.

12. Suppose the manager in problem 2 has absolutely no idea about the probabilities of the two prices occurring. Which option would the manager choose under each of the following rules?
    a. Maximax rule
    b. Maximin rule
    c. Minimax regret rule
    d. Equal probability rule

APPLIED PROBLEMS

1. Consider a firm that is deciding whether to operate plants only in the United States or also in either Mexico or Canada or both. Congress is currently discussing an overseas investment in new capital (OINC) tax credit for U.S. firms that operate plants outside the country. If Congress passes OINC in 1999, management expects to do well if it is operating plants in Mexico and Canada. If OINC does not pass in 1999 and the firm does operate plants in Mexico and Canada, it will incur rather large losses. It is also possible that Congress will table OINC in 1999 and wait until 2000 to vote on it. The profit payoff matrix (profits in 1999) is shown below:

	States of nature		
	OINC passes	OINC fails	OINC stalls
Operate plants in U.S. only	$10 million	−$1 million	$2 million
Operate plants in U.S. and Mexico	15 million	−4 million	1.5 million
Operate plants in U.S., Mexico, and Canada	20 million	−6 million	4 million

   Assuming the managers of this firm have no idea about the likelihood of congressional action on OINC in 1999, what decision should the firm make using each of the following rules?
    a. Maximax rule
    b. Maximin rule
    c. Minimax regret rule
    d. Equal probability rule

2. Suppose your company's method of making decisions under risk is "making the best out of the worst possible outcome." What rule would you be forced to follow?
3. "A portfolio manager needs to pick winners—assets or securities with high expected returns and low risk." What is wrong with this statement?
4. Remox Corporation is a British firm that sells high-fashion sportswear in the United States. Congress is currently considering the imposition of a protective tariff on imported textiles. Remox is considering the possibility of moving 50 percent of its production to the United States to avoid the tariff. This would be accomplished by opening a plant in the United States. The table below lists the profit outcomes under various scenarios:

	Profit in 1999	
	No tariff	Tariff
Option A: Produce all output in Britain	$1,200,000	$ 800,000
Option B: Produce 50% in the United States	875,000	1,000,000

Remox hires a consulting firm to assess the probability that a tariff on imported textiles will in fact pass a congressional vote and not be vetoed by the President. The consultants forecast the following probabilities:

	Probability
Tariff will pass	30%
Tariff will fail	70

a. Compute the expected profits for both options.
b. Based upon the expected profit only, which option should Remox choose?
c. Compute the probabilities that would make Remox indifferent between options A and B using that rule.
d. Compute the standard deviations for options A and B facing Remox Corporation.
e. What decision would Remox make using the mean-variance rule?
f. What decision would Remox make using the coefficient of variation rule?

5. Using the information in problem 4, what decision would Remox make using each of the following rules if it had no idea of the probability of a tariff?
a. Maximax
b. Maximin
c. Minimax regret
d. Equal probability criterion
6. Return to problem 1 and suppose the managers of the firm decide on the following subjective probabilities of congressional action on OINC:

	Probability
OINC passes	40%
OINC fails	10
OINC stalls	50

a. Compute the expected profits for all three decisions.
b. Using the expected value rule, which option should the managers choose?
c. Compute the standard deviations for all three decisions. Using the mean-variance rule, does any one of the decisions dominate? If so, which one?
d. What decision would the firm make using the coefficient of variation rule?

7. The Pluto Corporation makes toy space vehicles. It has one close rival, Red Planet, Inc., which also makes toy space vehicles but of lower quality. Red Planet therefore generally charges a lower price than Pluto, but the toys are substitutes. Pluto's demand is estimated as

$$Q = 1{,}000 - 8P + 4P_R$$

where P_R is the price set by Red Planet. Currently Red Planet is selling its toys for $80. Pluto is charging $140 and selling 200 per period. Pluto's marginal cost is constant at $65.

a. What are Pluto's inverse demand and marginal revenue functions in this situation?
b. Is Pluto maximizing its profit?

Pluto's management is deciding whether or not to change price, but the manager is not certain about how Red Planet will respond. From past experience, it is believed that if Pluto changes, there is a 20 percent probability Red Planet will not change price, a 50 percent probability it will set its price at one-half of Pluto's price, and a 30 percent probability it will set its price at three-fourths of Pluto's price.

c. What is the expected demand function?
d. What is the inverse expected demand function? The expected marginal revenue function?
e. What price should Pluto set to maximize expected profits?
f. What are Pluto's expected sales at the profit-maximizing price?
g. What will Pluto's actual range of sales be at this price?

MATHEMATICAL APPENDIX Decisions under Risk

The Equivalence of Maximizing Expected Profit and Maximizing Expected Utility of Profit

As discussed, but not demonstrated, in this chapter, maximizing expected profit, $E(\pi)$, is equivalent to maximizing the expected utility of profit, $E[U(\pi)]$, when the manager or decision maker is risk neutral. We now demonstrate this result for a simple case where profit can take only two values: π_A, with probability p, and π_B, with probability $(1 - p)$. Thus, the expected profit in this case is

$$E(\pi) = p\pi_A + (1 - p)\pi_B \tag{1}$$

Recall that the utility function for profit is linear for risk-neutral decision makers. Thus, the utility function for profit, $U(\pi)$, can be expressed as

$$U(\pi) = a + b\pi \tag{2}$$

where $a \geq 0$ and $b > 0$. Using this expression for utility of profit, the *expected* utility of profit in the risky situation described above can be expressed as

$$E[U(\pi)] = pU(\pi_A) + (1 - p)U(\pi_B) \tag{3}$$

Using the linear utility function for profit (2), expected utility in equation (3) can be expressed as a linear function of $E(\pi)$:

$$\begin{aligned} E[U(\pi)] &= p[a + b\pi_A] + (1 - p)[a + b\pi_B] \\ &= a + b[p\pi_A + (1 - p)\pi_B] \\ &= a + bE(\pi) \end{aligned} \tag{4}$$

From expression (4), it follows immediately that maximizing $E[U(\pi)]$ requires maximizing $E(\pi)$. Thus, when the utility function for profit is linear—the decision maker is risk-neutral—maximizing expected profit and maximizing expected *utility* of profit are equivalent.

The Optimal Level of Activity under Risk

Suppose an activity, X, generates benefits and costs that are random, and the decision maker knows the probability distribution for the random benefits and costs. Since total benefit and total cost are random variables, net benefit is also a random variable.

$$NB = NB(X) = TB(X) - TC(X) \tag{5}$$

The summation rule for expected values—found in any textbook on statistics—states that the expected value of a sum (or difference) of independent random variables is equal to the sum (or difference) of the expected values. Applying this rule to net benefit in equation (5), the expected net benefit at any given level of activity X is equal to the difference between expected total benefit and expected total cost:

$$E(NB|X) = E(TB|X) - E(TC|X) \tag{6}$$

where $E(\bullet|X)$ denotes the expected value of benefits or costs *given* the level of activity X.

The first-order condition for a maximum of $E(NB|X)$ is

$$(7) \qquad \frac{d\,E(NB|X)}{dX} = \frac{d\,E(TB|X)}{dX} - \frac{d\,E(TC|X)}{dX} = 0$$

which can also be expressed as

$$(8) \qquad E\left(\frac{dTB}{dX}\right) - E\left(\frac{dTC}{dX}\right) = 0$$

and

$$(9) \qquad E(MB) = E(MC)$$

Thus, maximizing expected net benefit requires that the level of activity be chosen so that expected marginal benefit equals expected marginal cost.

CHAPTER 19

The Investment Decision

In this final chapter, we will address the question of how managers can make decisions about investment projects in order to maximize the value of the firm. Investment projects may involve purchasing new equipment for a plant, expanding the size of a production facility, adding a new product to the firm's product line, or even buying another firm.

Investment decisions involve cash flows over multiple periods of time in the future. These cash flows are inherently risky—they are obviously not known with certainty. To make investment decisions, managers must examine the present value of the stream of revenues and costs associated with the many investment projects available. As you will see, investment decision making requires using the analysis of present value presented in the appendix to Chapter 1, as well as the optimization theory from Chapter 4 and the risk analysis discussed in Chapter 18.

We begin the analysis of investment decisions by describing how managers can determine the value of a stream of risky cash flows received over a period of time. Then we develop the net present value rule for maximizing the value of a firm and apply it to the investment decision. As always, this analysis is an extension of the marginal benefit–marginal cost rule first set forth in Chapter 4. We discuss the various methods of finding the appropriate discount rate for making investment decisions. Next, we present some critiques and several alternative investment criteria—payback, return on investment, and the internal rate of return—that are sometimes used by managers to make investment decisions. Finally, we examine the manager's investment decision when the firm's investment funds are constrained by budgetary limits imposed either by banks or by the firm itself. This is the problem of capital rationing.

The topics covered in this chapter on investment decisions are covered in much greater detail in the finance courses you will take or may have already taken. Since investment decision making is a critical component of a manager's decision-making responsibilities, and since these decisions are typically made using the basic techniques of microeconomic analysis, managerial economics courses traditionally cover investment decision making. We follow tradition by including this chapter.

19.1 VALUING RISKY CASH FLOWS

The value of a *riskless* project (asset) is given by its present value. To obtain the present value of some specific project, j, the following valuation equation is used:

$$PV_j = \sum_{t=1}^{T} \frac{NCF_{j,t}}{(1 + r_t)^t}$$

where $NCF_{j,t}$ is the net cash flow generated by project j in year t and r_t is the riskless discount rate in year t (the interest rate on U.S. government securities).[1] We now examine the way this valuation equation changes when project j is a *risky* project.

Risky Cash Flows

When cash flows are risky, the numerator of the present value equation must change. The cash flows from project j are no longer known with certainty. Instead of a single, known value of $NCF_{j,t}$, there exists a probability distribution for the cash flow from project j in year t, an illustration of which is provided in Figure 19.1. Since the probability distribution for the *NCF* is known, the manager can calculate the expected value of the net cash flow in each time period t for project j, $E(NCF_{j,t})$. Recall from Chapter 18 that decisions involving risk may require calculating the expected value of random outcomes. For investment decisions, the manager is interested in the expected value of risky net cash flows.

A Discount Rate Reflecting Risk

Another change in the valuation equation must be made when risk is present. A change is required in the denominator. For the riskless project, the appropriate discount rate is the riskless rate. Since there is no question about the size of the cash flow, the only thing that matters is the time at which the cash flows are to be received (paid).

However, as is clear from Figure 19.1, the probability distribution for the cash flows from the risky project j has a positive variance. Because the variance is a measure of risk, the cash flows from this project are risky in the sense that the size of the cash flow varies randomly. The larger the variance (or standard deviation) of the cash flows from a project, the riskier the project.

[1]The appendix to Chapter 1 reviews the mathematics of present value calculations.

FIGURE 19.1
Cash Flows from a Risky Project

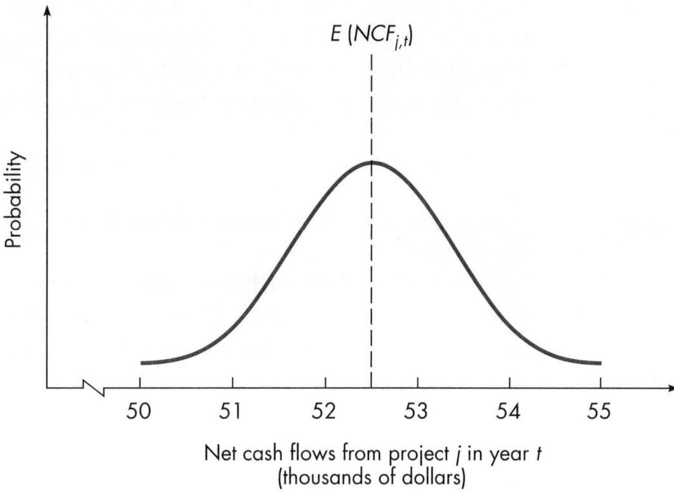

Since the risk associated with the variance in the probability distribution for cash flows is not accounted for in the numerator of the valuation equation (*NCF*), it must be accounted for in the denominator. Thus, this risk must be reflected in the discount rate used. The riskless rate is clearly not appropriate; neither is some common or general discount rate for risky projects. Project *j* has some level of risk associated with the probability distribution of its cash flows, and this risk is not necessarily the same as the risk for some other project *k*—even if the two projects have the same expected net cash flows. Therefore, there will exist a specific discount rate that reflects the risk associated with project *j*. We denote this specific discount rate for cash flows received (paid) from project *j* in year *t* as $r_{j,t}$.

Combining the discussions of uncertain cash flows and a risk-adjusted discount rate, it should be clear that, for a risky project *j*, the *expected* present value is

$$E(PV_j) = \sum_{t=1}^{T} \frac{E(NCF_{j,t})}{(1 + r_{j,t})^t}$$

Just as the present value equation provides the value of a riskless project, this equation can be used to value a risky project.

It should be clear now how a manager could estimate a probability distribution for cash flows from a project, then, using the appropriate discount rate, determine the expected net cash flows. Choosing the appropriate discount rate to reflect the riskiness of a project is not always a simple matter. We will now
1 discuss the problem of finding the appropriate discount rate.

19.2 THE APPROPRIATE DISCOUNT RATE FOR A RISKY PROJECT

To discount the expected net cash flows from a risky project j, a manager should use a discount rate that compensates the firm for bearing the additional risk. Thus, the discount rate should be higher than the riskless rate. The appropriate discount rate for cash flows from risky project j in year t could be expressed as

$$r_{j,t} = r_t + (\text{risk premium})_j$$

where r_t is the riskless rate and the second term is the appropriate risk premium for project j.[2]

We will now show how to determine the appropriate risk premium. Several methods exist. We will describe two that are used most often: risk-adjusted discount rates and the weighted average cost of capital. After defining and briefly discussing these two rules of thumb, we will present a simple numerical example to illustrate their use.

The Risk-Adjusted Discount Rate

risk-adjusted discount rate
The riskless rate plus a risk premium.

The preceding equation illustrates the discounting problem quite clearly: a risk premium must be attached to the riskless rate. The **risk-adjusted discount rate** approach does that directly, simply by adding a specific risk premium directly to the riskless rate. Apparently simple, the risk-adjusted discount rate methodology is complicated by an obvious problem: How does the manager determine the appropriate risk premium? Elegant mathematical formulas have been presented by Franco Modigliani and Merton Miller and by J. Miles and R. Ezzell. However, the risk-adjusted discount rates remain rules of thumb and are at the discretion of the manager.

The Weighted Average Cost of Capital

weighted average cost of capital
The rate at which the firm can borrow, weighted by the ratio of debt to net worth, plus the rate of return required by stockholders, weighted by the ratio of equity to net worth: $r_{WACC} = r_D[D/(D + E)] + r_E[E/(D + E)]$.

The weighted-average-cost-of-capital (WACC) approach to finding the appropriate risk premium reflects market conditions more than the risk-adjusted discount rate approach. In essence, the weighted-average-cost-of-capital method is based on the assumption that the appropriate discount rate for new projects is the interest rate currently paid by the firm in the market, that is, a weighted-average rate at which the firm can borrow funds and the rate of return required by the firm's shareholders. Following this approach, the **weighted average cost of capital** for a firm, denoted as r_{WACC}, is calculated as[3]

[2]The risk discussed here deals with variation in the size of the cash flow. It should not be confused with default (performance) risk, which is embedded in the numerator: $E(NCF)$ will incorporate any probabilities of default.

[3]This formula neglects corporate taxes. If corporate taxes were included

$$r_{WACC} = (1 - CTR)\left[r_D\left(\frac{D}{D + E}\right) + r_E\left(\frac{E}{D + E}\right)\right]$$

where CTR is the marginal corporate income tax rate.

$$r_{\text{WACC}} = r_D\left(\frac{D}{D+E}\right) + r_E\left(\frac{E}{D+E}\right)$$

where D and E are, respectively, the current market values of the firm's outstanding debt and equity and r_D and r_E are, respectively, the current rate at which the firm can borrow and the rate of return on equity required by the firm's shareholders to induce them to hold the shares of stock.

In the above equation, D plus E is the net worth of the firm. Thus the first term is the rate at which the firm can borrow, weighted by the proportion of net worth that is represented by debt. The second term is the rate of required return on equity, weighted by the proportion of net worth represented by equity. Hence the term, weighted average cost of capital.

The weighted-average-cost-of-capital approach is intuitively appealing, and, in some cases, it actually works. Specifically, the WACC approach is appropriate (1) if the project being considered is just like the rest of the firm, and (2) if the project is to be financed with the same mix of debt and equity prevailing in the rest of the firm. The WACC approach is not appropriate for projects that are more or less risky than the firm's existing portfolio of projects. Likewise, the WACC approach is not appropriate if acceptance of the project would cause the firm's debt/equity ratio to change.

Perhaps because it is more intuitively appealing than the risk-adjusted discount rate approach, the weighted-average-cost-of-capital approach is widely used. However, like the risk-adjusted discount rate, weighted average cost of capital is only a rule of thumb.

Estimating the Probability Distribution of Cash Flows and Discount Rates: A Numerical Example

We will now show how a firm can estimate a probability distribution for the cash flows from a project and determine the net cash flows. Suppose the managers of Zeus Manufacturing are considering the acquisition of machinery to produce a new product line. The machinery has a five-year time horizon. (At the end of the five years, the project has no scrap value.) The firm obtained low, best, and high estimates for the net cash flows from the project in each of its five years. The resulting table of outcomes is presented below:

	Net cash flow estimates ($, millions)		
Year	Low	Best	High
1	−2	0	4
2	1	3	5
3	4	5	6
4	4	5	6
5	2	4	5

Management subjectively assigned probabilities to these outcomes as low, 20 percent; best, 70 percent; high, 10 percent.

Using these probabilities, the expected net cash flow in year 1 is zero:

$$E(NCF_1) = (-2)(0.2) + (0)(0.7) + (4)(0.1)$$
$$= -0.4 + 0 + 0.4 = 0$$

Calculated in the same way, the expected net cash flows for years 2 through 5 are (in millions of dollars)

$$E(NCF_2) = 2.8$$
$$E(NCF_3) = 4.9$$
$$E(NCF_4) = 4.9$$
$$E(NCF_5) = 3.7$$

The managers of Zeus now want to determine the expected present value of this project. Their policy has been to attack a risk premium based on their evaluation of how risky the project is. The risk premiums they use are as follows:

Project riskiness	Risk premium (percent)
Low-risk project	3
Average-risk project	6
High-risk project	9

In their judgment, the project being considered is an average-risk project. Hence, the rates used to discount the expected cash flows are obtained by adding this risk premium to the riskless rate (the interest rate for U.S. government securities):

Years to maturity	Riskless rate (percent)	Risk premium (percent)	Risk-adjusted discount rate (percent)
1	5.75	6	11.75
2	6.00	6	12.00
3	6.25	6	12.25
4	6.50	6	12.50
5	6.75	6	12.75

Using these risk-adjusted discount rates, the expected present value of the project is

$$E(PV_j) = \frac{0}{(1.1175)} + \frac{2.8}{(1.12)^2} + \frac{4.9}{(1.1225)^3} + \frac{4.9}{(1.125)^4} + \frac{3.7}{(1.1275)^5}$$
$$= 0 + 2.232 + 3.464 + 3.059 + 2.031$$
$$= 10.786$$

That is, the expected present value of the new machinery is \$10,786,000, using a risk-adjusted discount rate.

Now suppose the managers of Zeus want to compare this expected present value with an expected present value calculated with a discount rate reflecting the WACC method. To calculate the weighted average cost of capital for Zeus Manufacturing, the managers first needed the current market value of Zeus's debt and equity. The market value of Zeus's equity was the easier of the two: there were 1,200,000 shares of stock currently selling at \$27.25 per share, so

$$E = 1{,}200{,}000 \times \$27.25 = \$32{,}700{,}000$$

Zeus had issued debt with a face value of \$95 million. Currently, these corporate bonds are being traded at 92 percent of their face (par) value, so

$$D = 0.92 \times \$95{,}000{,}000 = \$87{,}400{,}000$$

The managers also needed Zeus's current borrowing rate and the rate of return required by its shareholders. Using data on the general performance of the stock market and a subjective assessment of the riskiness of Zeus, the finance director estimated that Zeus's shareholders require a return of 18 percent:

$$r_E = 0.18$$

Using the market valuation of Zeus's debt issues and prevailing interest rates, the finance director calculated that the current yield on Zeus's debt—the interest rate Zeus would have to pay to borrow money today—is 7 percent:

$$r_D = 0.07$$

Hence, the weighted average cost of capital for Zeus Manufacturing is

$$\begin{aligned} r_{\text{WACC}} &= 0.07\left(\frac{87.4}{87.4 + 32.7}\right) + 0.18\left(\frac{32.7}{87.4 + 32.7}\right) \\ &= 0.05 + 0.05 = 0.10 \end{aligned}$$

Using this discount rate to discount the expected net cash flows of the project under consideration,

$$\begin{aligned} E(PV_j) &= \frac{0}{(1.1)} + \frac{2.8}{(1.1)^2} + \frac{4.9}{(1.1)^3} + \frac{4.9}{(1.1)^4} + \frac{3.7}{(1.1)^5} \\ &= 0 + 2.314 + 3.681 + 3.347 + 2.297 \\ &= 11.639 \end{aligned}$$

That is, the expected present value of the project is \$11,639,000, using a WACC discount rate. The latter method yields an expected present value for the project that is \$853,000 higher than the first method of calculation, because it discounts with a lower rate than the risk-adjusted rate.

19.3 MAKING INVESTMENT DECISIONS TO MAXIMIZE THE VALUE OF THE FIRM

As we demonstrated, present values are additive. The present value of the portfolio of two projects, A and B, is equal to the sum of the present values of projects A and B: $PV(A + B) = PV(A) + PV(B)$. Going a step further, a firm is really a portfolio of its projects (assets). As we emphasized in Chapter 1, the worth or the value of a firm, the price the firm would bring if it were sold, is the present value of the firm. The present value of the firm is the sum of the present values of all its projects or assets.

If, as noted in Chapter 1, the objective of management is to maximize the value of the firm, the following principle applies: The present value of a firm will increase if the present value of an additional project (the marginal benefit) exceeds the marginal cost of the project. If the present value of an additional project is less than its marginal cost, that project will decrease the present value of the firm. Therefore, the firm should undertake projects for which the present value is greater than the cost. It should reject projects for which the present value is less than the cost. This simple rule is the foundation of the theory of investment.

net present value (NPV)
The present value of an investment minus its cost.

We define **net present value (NPV)** as the present value of an investment minus the cost of the investment. Thus the general rule for a value-maximizing firm is summarized in the following

Principle The net present value rule for maximizing the value of the firm is to accept projects (acquire assets) for which the net present value is positive and reject projects for which the net present value is negative.

The Expected Net Present Value Rule for Investment

As we stressed in Section 19.2, the risk associated with a particular project can be accounted for by discounting the *expected* net cash flow using a discount rate that includes a risk premium. This modification results in an expected net present value rule for investment decision making. Accordingly, we define net present value of investment project j as[4]

$$E(NPV_j) = E(PV_j) - \text{Cost of investment project } j$$
$$= \sum_{t=1}^{T} \frac{E(NCF_{j,t})}{(1 + r_{jt})^t} - C_0$$

where the numerator is the expected value of the net cash flow in time period t, $r_{j,t}$ is the risk-adjusted discount rate for project j in time period t, and C_0 is the cost of the investment project.

The expected net present value rule for investment projects is to accept projects for which the expected net present value is positive and reject those for which the net present value is negative:

$$E(NPV_j) > 0 \ldots \text{Accept}$$
$$E(NPV_j) < 0 \ldots \text{Reject}$$

Implementation of the expected net present value rule is a straightforward application of the techniques we have described in this text:

[4]We consider a simple investment project for which the only outlay for the project occurs in the current period (C_0). However, it would not be difficult to generalize this expression to incorporate an investment project that requires outlays in future periods as well as the current period.

1. Forecast demand to obtain estimates of expected revenues from the project, $E(R_{j,t})$.
2. Forecast (estimate) costs to provide estimates of the expected future costs associated with the project, $E(C_{j,t})$.
3. Combine the expected revenues and costs to obtain estimates of expected net cash flows for the project:

$$E(NCF_{j,t}) = E(R_{j,t}) - E(C_{j,t})$$

4. Determine the appropriate discount rate, $r_{j,t}$.
5. Discount the expected net cash flows to obtain the expected present value of the project.
6. Subtract the current cost of the project to obtain expected net present value.

To show how this might be accomplished, we present the following example.

Investment Decision Making at Trenton Enterprises: An Example

The manager of Trenton Enterprises is considering purchasing a new production facility for a price of \$5.3 million. The manager expects to use the production facility for five years, then resell it. Investment analysts at Trenton determined expected revenues and costs and the expected resale value of the plant. Using these data, the manager obtained the following expected net cash flows for the firm's investment in a new production facility:

Year	Expected revenues*	Expected resale value*	Expected cost*	Expected net cash flow*
1	\$10.2	—	\$10.4	−\$0.2
2	10.2	—	10.4	−0.2
3	14.2	—	11.6	2.6
4	16.3	—	13.2	3.1
5	16.3	\$3.5	13.2	6.6

*In millions of dollars per year.

Using the weighted-average-cost-of-capital method of determining the appropriate discount rate, the manager obtained the following discount rates for each of the next five years:

Year	Discount rate (percent)
1	13.13
2	13.38
3	13.63
4	13.88
5	14.13

ILLUSTRATION 19.1

Do Income Taxes Affect Managerial Decision Making?

Throughout this text we have essentially ignored any effects of income taxes or corporate taxes in our analysis of managerial decision making. Excise taxes raise prices and decrease quantities sold, the extent of which depends on elasticity and the size of the tax. But we have not yet mentioned the effect of an income tax or corporate profit tax on price and sales, even though these are the taxes that are typically foremost in many people's minds. When we discussed managerial decision making and optimization, there was no reason to consider the effect of income taxes—until now.

To put things into perspective, we will quote briefly from a column by Michael Kinsley, in *The New Republic,* September 6, 1993. Mr. Kinsley was commenting on congressional and media debate over the effect on small businesses of President Clinton's proposal to increase tax rates for upper-income taxpayers. He pointed out that many politicians and small-business owners had been complaining that the higher taxes would put their businesses at a disadvantage when competing with foreign companies—presumably because of resulting price increases—and force them to eliminate jobs—presumably because of reduced production.

Mr. Kinsley commented, "Neither [complaint] makes economic sense. The income tax is levied on a businessperson's net profits. [The rate of the tax] has no effect on the question of how best to maximize those profits: how much to produce, what prices to charge, how many people to hire, etc. To be sure, higher tax rates can reduce the *incentive* to work and invest for small business people, like any other people."

Now we will take a look at these different effects to explain why we have ignored income taxes thus far. First, consider the effect on profit-maximizing decisions: output, price, and hiring. As we have emphasized throughout the text, profit is maximized in a given situation when price and output are chosen so that $MR = MC$ or when the usage of variable inputs is chosen so the MRP = Price of the input. Suppose a firm is choosing an output and price to maximize profit, but there is no income tax. If an income tax of t percent is levied, the firm would still choose the price and output that maximize profit—$MR = MC$—because the owners prefer to receive $(100 - t)$ percent of the maximum possible profit to $(100 - t)$ percent of any lower profit at which MR is not equal to MC. There is no incentive to change output, price, or, for that matter, the usage of any input. For example, suppose the income tax rate is 25 percent and the maximum before-tax profit is \$1 million. The firm pays \$250,000 in taxes and keeps \$750,000. If the tax rate rises to 35 percent, paying taxes of \$350,000 on the maximum before-tax profit of \$1 million and keeping \$650,000 is better than any alternative that would reduce before-tax profit.

Discounting each of the expected net cash flows by the appropriate discount rate and summing, the manager obtained the expected present value of the new plant:

Year	Expected net cash flow (\$, millions, per year)	Discount rate (percent)	Expected present value (\$, millions, per year)
1	−\$0.2	13.13	−\$0.18
2	−0.2	13.38	−0.16
3	2.6	13.63	1.77
4	3.1	13.88	1.84
5	6.6	14.13	3.41
		Total	\$6.68

Therefore, the reason that we have ignored the discussion of income taxes until now is that we have been concerned with the way firms maximize profit under given conditions and the tax rates have no effect on decision making under these circumstances. But now we are considering the investment decision, and, as Mr. Kinsley pointed out, taxes can have an effect on the incentives to work and invest. We will consider here only the effect on the incentive to invest and will ignore the incentive to work.

As we have stressed in this chapter, the *NPV* rule provides the foundation for investment decision making. If *E*(*PV*) is greater than the cost of a project, *E*(*NPV*) is positive and the project should be undertaken. But the return that investors are interested in is the after-tax expected net present value. In an extreme case, suppose there is a 99 percent tax on yearly cash flows. This would presumably reduce the after-tax *NPV* of most prospective investments below their costs and substantially reduce the number of investments with a positive *E*(*NPV*). Alternatively, when choosing price and quantity, an owner would prefer 1 percent of maximum profit over 1 percent of a lesser amount, as we discussed. So the tax would probably have a large effect on investment and no effect on price.

As the tax rate is reduced, the after-tax expected cash flows from investment projects would increase; and more and more projects would change from negative *E*(*NPV*) to positive *E*(*NPV*)—assuming the cost of the project does not change. However, since the cost of an investment can be a tax deduction when financed with retained earnings, the costs may change when the tax rate changes. Nonetheless, the basic conclusion is the same. Increases in the tax rate reduce investment by reducing after-tax expected net cash flows, and decreases in the tax rate increase investment by increasing after-tax expected net cash flows. There are some additional factors influencing *E*(*NPV*), so the extent of the effect on tax rates is basically an empirical question and depends to some extent on the characteristics of individual investors.

There is another way in which the tax structure, combined with inflation, may have a negative effect on investment. Under the present tax structure, nominal, not real, income is subject to taxation. Therefore, if someone purchases an asset and sells it later, all gains are subject to taxation, even though most, or even all, of the gain could be due to inflation. For example, suppose a firm purchases an asset for $100,000. The value of the asset increases during a year at the same rate as the rate of inflation, 5 percent. If the firm sells the asset for $105,000, realizing a net gain of $5,000 which, for sake of illustration, is taxed at a 34 percent rate, the after-tax return is $3,300. The firm, in real terms, has lost $1,700 (.34 × $5,000), because the $105,000 is worth only $100,000 in year-1 dollars. In order to receive $105,000 after inflation and taking taxes into account, the rate of return must be about 7.6 percent.

Subtracting the cost of the project, $5.3 million, from the expected present value of the project, $6.68 million, the expected net present value of the plant is $1.38 million. Since the expected net present value of the project is positive, the project should be undertaken.

As should be obvious, the discount rate plays a key role in determining the expected net present value and, therefore, in the investment decision. The expected net present value equation indicates the inverse relation between the expected net present value and the discount rate: As the discount rate rises, the expected net present value of the project will fall.

For example, consider a one-year investment project that currently costs $100,000 and will generate an expected net cash flow of $108,000 at the end of one year. With a risk-adjusted discount rate of 7 percent, the expected net present value of this project is $935. If the discount rate falls to 6 percent, the

FIGURE 19.2
An Expected Net Present Value Profile

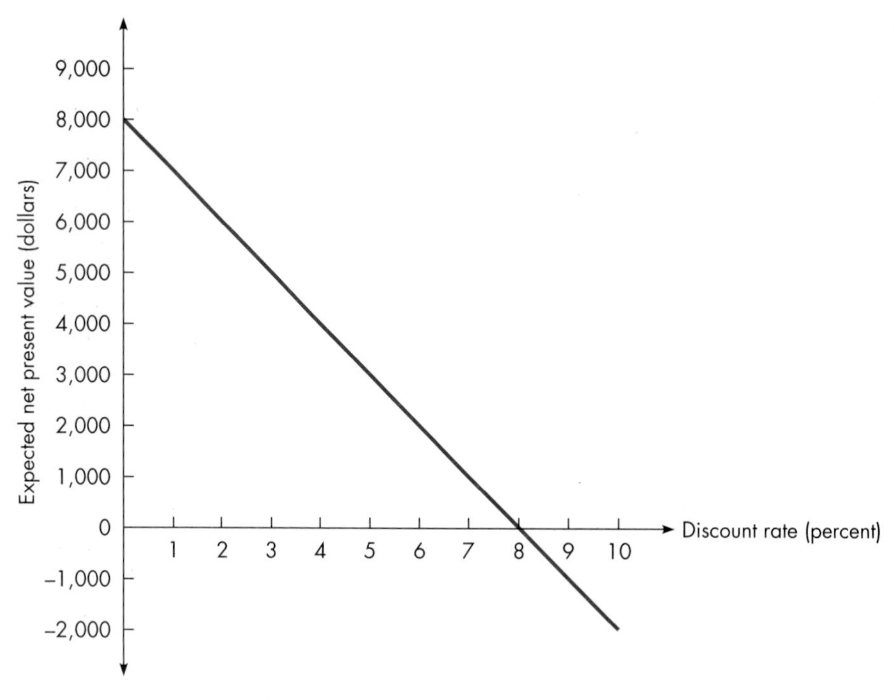

expected net present value of the project rises to $1,887. If the discount rate rises to 8 percent, the expected net present value of the project falls to zero. And if the discount rate rises further, to 9 percent, the net present value of the project becomes negative, −$917. This relation between the expected net present value of the project and the discount rate—sometimes referred to as the *expected net present value profile*—is illustrated in Figure 19.2. This profile clearly shows that the expected net present value falls as the discount rate rises.

Principle When evaluating risky investment projects, the firm should accept projects with a positive expected net present value and reject projects with a negative expected net present value.

19.4 ALTERNATIVES TO THE EXPECTED NET PRESENT VALUE RULE

Although economists would argue that the expected net present value rule is the correct investment criterion, it is not the only criterion available to managers. Three of the most widely cited are payback, return on investment, and internal rate of return. We will now discuss these alternative criteria to show how they compare with the net present value rule.

Payback Period

payback period
Time required for the firm to recover its initial investment.

The **payback period** for an investment project is the time required for the firm to recover its initial investment. For example, if a project costs $1 million and it is expected to return $250,000 per year, the payback period is four years; if expected returns are $500,000 per year, the payback period is two years.

Using the payback criterion, the payback period for the investment project is calculated and compared with some maximum payback period set by the firm. If the project's payback period is less than this maximum, the project is accepted.

For example, returning to Trenton Enterprises, suppose the manager has set the maximum payback period for investment projects as three years. The payback period for the previously discussed prospective production facility is calculated from the cumulative expected net cash flows from the project:

Year	Expected net cash flow*	Cumulative expected net cash flow*
1	−$0.2	−$0.2
2	−0.2	−0.4
3	2.6	2.2
4	3.1	5.3
5	6.6	11.9

*In millions of dollars.

The cumulative expected net cash flows equal (or exceed) the cost of the investment ($5.3 million) at the end of the fourth year. Hence, the payback period for this project is four years. And since the payback period is longer than the maximum set by the firm, the project would be judged unacceptable using this criterion.

As this example makes clear, the major problem with the payback criterion is that it can lead to the rejection of positive net present value projects—projects that will increase the value of the firm. Conversely, this rule could lead to accepting negative net present value projects.

As should be clear from the discussion to this point, the reason the payback rule can lead to this value-reducing situation is that the cash flows are not discounted. Hence, the payback criterion gives too much weight to near returns and too little weight to distant returns: with the payback rule, net cash flows received after the maximum payback period have no value. This criterion ignores the time value of money and the time pattern of the cash flows generated by the investment project.

One critic noted that a survey of investors revealed that many users of the payback criterion thought of the payback period as a measure of risk. He pointed out that gambling at the tables in Las Vegas may have a shorter payback period than purchasing a U.S. government security but that doesn't mean the crap tables
5 6 in Las Vegas are less risky than T-bills.

Return on Investment (*ROI*)

return on investment (*ROI*) Average return from an investment divided by the average investment in a project.

The average **return on an investment (*ROI*)** project is defined as average returns from the investment divided by the average investment in the project. Then, using the *ROI* criterion, the decision of whether or not to invest in the project is made by comparing the *ROI* for the project with the firm's target return.

For example, suppose Trenton Enterprises requires a rate of return on investment of 60 percent. The manager wanted to look at the prospective investment again with this criterion in mind. As shown in previous calculations, the cumulative net cash flows from the project amounted to \$11.9 million for the five years of the project's lifetime. Hence, the average net cash flow was \$11.9/5 = \$2.38 million. Dividing this average income by the amount the firm would invest in the project, \$5.3 million, the average return on the investment is

$$2.38/5.3 = 45\%$$

Since this *ROI* is less than the firm's target return of 60 percent, the project would be rejected using the rate of return on investment as the criterion.

As in the case of payback, the *ROI* criterion could result in positive net present value projects not being undertaken. And, also like the payback criterion, the problem with the return on investment criterion is that the cash flows are not discounted. However, unlike the payback criterion, which gives *too little* weight to distant cash flows, the *ROI* criterion gives distant cash flows *too much* weight. With the *ROI* criterion, distant cash flows are treated as equivalent to current cash flows.

Internal Rate of Return (*IRR*)

internal rate of return (*IRR*) The discount rate that makes the net present value of a project equal to zero.

The **internal rate of return (*IRR*)** for an investment project is the discount rate that makes the net present value of the project equal to zero. In order to understand the concept of the internal rate of return, consider again the single-period investment project we discussed earlier and illustrated in Figure 19.2:

Cost of investment	\$100,000
Net cash flow at end of year 1	\$108,000

The rate of return on this investment project is 8 percent:

$$\frac{108{,}000 - 100{,}000}{100{,}000} = 0.08 = 8\%$$

Hence, for this single-period investment project, we have a criterion that is equivalent to the net present value rule: Accept the project if the discount rate for the project is less than 8 percent; reject the project if the discount rate is more than 8 percent.

Indeed, for any single-period investment project, the *NPV* rule is implemented by comparing the project's rate of return with its discount rate:

$$\text{Rate of return} > \text{Discount rate} \rightarrow NPV > 0 \rightarrow \text{Accept project}$$
$$\text{Rate of return} < \text{Discount rate} \rightarrow NPV < 0 \rightarrow \text{Reject project}$$

From this, it follows that the internal rate of return on the project is 8 percent, which makes the net present value of the project equal to zero:

$$NPV = 0 \rightarrow \text{Rate of return} = \text{Discount rate}$$

For investment projects with longer lifetimes (multiple-period projects), the internal rate of return becomes more difficult to determine. Nonetheless, the definition of the internal rate of return (*IRR*) is simply a generalization of the preceding relation. However, solving for the *IRR* is not an easy arithmetic problem in such cases, since it involves solving for the discount rate at which the *NPV* of the project is zero. Operationally, that means that the equation

$$NPV = \sum_{t=1}^{T} \frac{NCF_t}{(1 + IRR)^t} - C_0 = 0$$

is solved for *IRR*. Given (1) the complexity of this solution and (2) the wide acceptance of the *IRR* criterion, it is probably not surprising that most business calculators are preprogrammed to calculate this value.

From the discussion of the single-period investment project, it should be clear that the investment criterion associated with the internal rate of return is to accept the project if the cost of capital to the firm is less than the *IRR* and reject the project if the cost of capital to the firm exceeds the *IRR*.

The *IRR* criterion can be illustrated graphically by looking at the net present value profile for an investment project. A generalized profile is presented in Figure 19.3. As long as the internal rate of return exceeds the discount rate—the opportunity cost of capital—the *NPV* of the project is positive and the project should be undertaken. However, if the *IRR* is less than the discount rate, the *NPV* of the project is negative and the project should be rejected.

As an example of the use of the internal rate of return as an investment criterion, we return once again to Trenton Enterprises and its investment decision. The manager determined that the cost to Trenton of raising additional capital is 13.5 percent. That is, to raise money to finance investment projects, Trenton will have to pay 13.5 percent annually. He then reevaluated the proposed acquisition of the facility by looking at the project's rate of return relative to Trenton's opportunity cost of capital.

The internal rate of return for the project is the single discount rate (the *IRR*) that would make the *NPV* of the project equal to zero. This is found by solving the following for the *IRR*:

$$NPV = \frac{-0.2}{(1 + IRR)} + \frac{-0.2}{(1 + IRR)^2} + \frac{2.6}{(1 + IRR)^3} + \frac{3.1}{(1 + IRR)^4} + \frac{6.6}{(1 + IRR)^5} - 5.3 = 0$$

FIGURE 19.3
A Generalized Net Present Value Profile

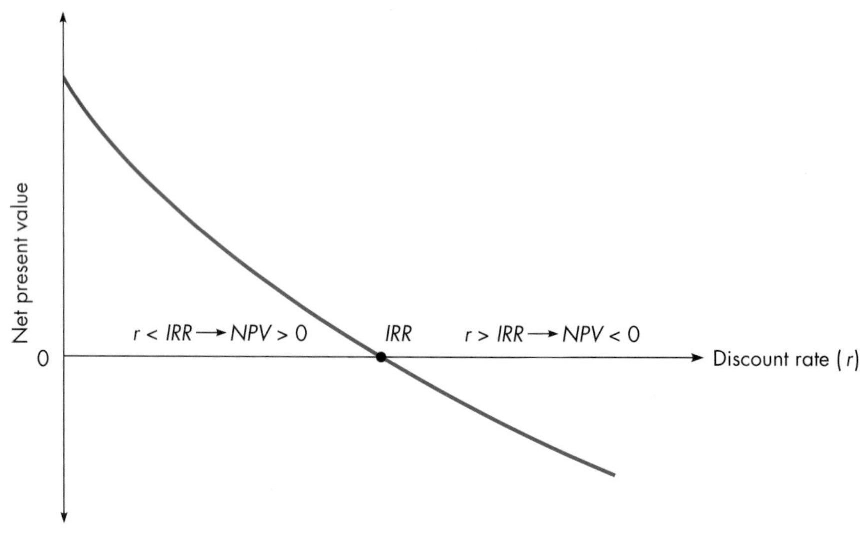

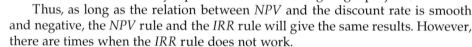

The resulting value for the *IRR* is 20.2 percent. Therefore, since the *IRR* for the project exceeded the firm's opportunity cost of capital, the project should be undertaken.

Note that, in contrast to the payback and return on investment criteria, the *IRR* criterion led to acceptance of the hypothetical investment project. In the context of this simple example it appears as though the *IRR* criterion and the *NPV* criterion are equivalent rules. And they are: as long as the *NPV* of the project declines smoothly as the discount rate rises—as is illustrated in Figure 19.3—the two criteria are functionally equivalent (for evaluating single projects).

Thus, as long as the relation between *NPV* and the discount rate is smooth

9 and negative, the *NPV* rule and the *IRR* rule will give the same results. However, there are times when the *IRR* rule does not work.

Nonequivalence of *IRR* and *NPV* Rules

If the net present value profile does not look like that in Figure 19.3, the *IRR* rule and *NPV* rule may no longer be equivalent. Most investment projects are like lending money; an original outflow is made in return for a stream of inflows thereby generating downsloping net present value profiles like that in Figure 19.3. However, this need not always be the case; it is not always the case that the largest expenditures on the project occur in the initial period. It is possible that the inflows occur earlier than the outflows—the investment project could look more like borrowing than lending. In this case the net present value profile would look like that illustrated in Panel A of Figure 19.4, where the discount rate, *r*, is plotted along the horizontal axis. Or it could be the case that the investment project will require net cash outflows both initially and in some subsequent pe-

FIGURE 19.4
Net Present Value Profiles That Do Not Decline Smoothly as the Discount Rate Rises

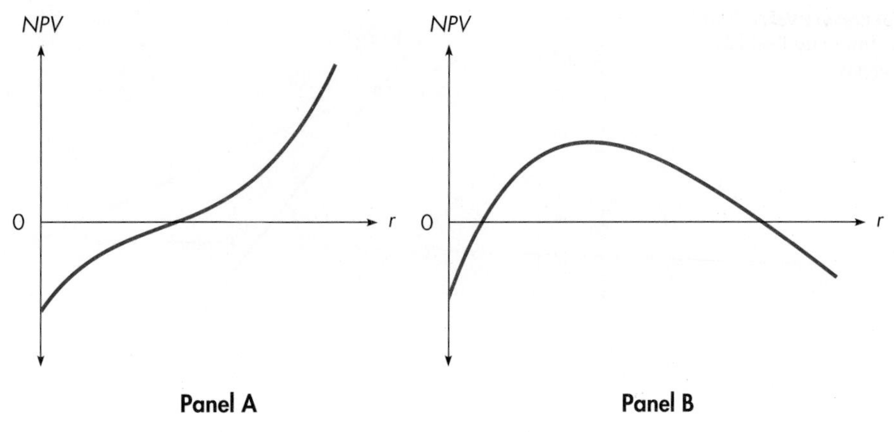

riod; for example, the project may require a retrofit at some date in the future. In this case, the net present value profile will look like that illustrated in Panel B of Figure 19.4. In either case, the *IRR* criterion is no longer equivalent to the *NPV* criterion.

Another case in which *IRR* and *NPV* rules do not necessarily provide the same recommendation occurs when the decision concerns mutually exclusive projects. Consider a firm deciding whether to replace or refit a machine—decisions that are clearly mutually exclusive. Suppose the net cash flows from these two projects are as presented in the following table:

	Refit	Replace
Current cost	$100,000	$250,000
Net cash flow, year 1	75,000	125,000
Net cash flow, year 2	50,000	175,000

Looking at the internal rates of return,

	Refit	Replace
IRR	17.5%	12.3%

it seems as if refitting is the better choice. And if the firm's cost of capital is greater than 12.3 percent but less than 17.5 percent, refitting is the correct decision. But suppose the firm's opportunity cost of capital is less than 12.3 percent. Is refitting always the best choice? Suppose the discount rate is 9 percent. Looking at the net present values using a 9 percent discount rate,

	Refit	Replace
NPV (r = 9%)	$10,900	$12,000

the choice is reversed; the better choice now is to replace the machine.

FIGURE 19.5
Net Present Value Profiles for Mutually Exclusive Projects

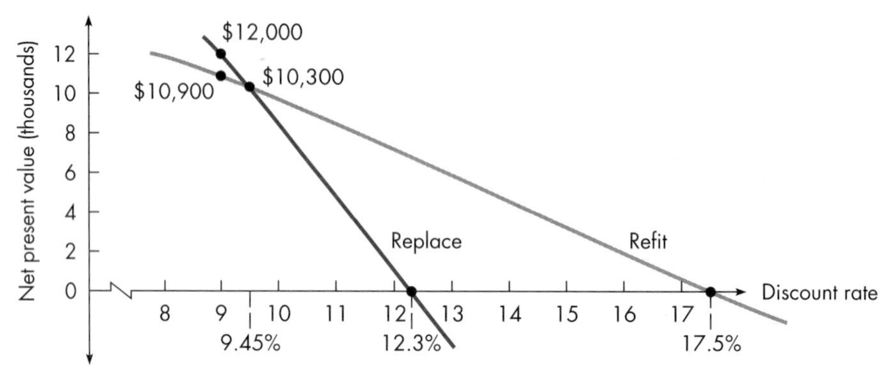

The reason for the inconsistency is illustrated in Figure 19.5. For discount rates in excess of 9.45 percent, the *IRR* criterion and the *NPV* criterion will be consistent. That is, with the discount rate in excess of 9.45 percent, the project with the higher *IRR* will have the higher *NPV*. However, for discount rates below 9.45 percent, the *IRR* is no longer a useful criterion. With a discount rate less than 9.45 percent, the project with the higher *IRR* has the lower *NPV*. And, with these lower discount rates, the *IRR* criterion would lead to selecting the project with the lower, not higher, *NPV*.

Finally, you may have noted a methodological difference. When we worked with net present value, we used different discount rates for different periods; payments received early were discounted at a different rate than those received late. The internal rate of return approach does not permit that differentiation. With the *IRR* approach, there is a single discount rate—payments received early are discounted using the same discount rate as those received late.

19.5 CAPITAL RATIONING

In the broadest perspective, capital rationing by the manager of a firm should not occur; there is no *external* constraint on a number of projects a firm can undertake. If the firm has available a project that will increase the value of the firm, the project should be undertaken. The capital constraint (the limit of available monies to finance the project) can always be eliminated by the credit market. If going to the credit market means that the firm will have to pay a higher and higher price for its capital (if the opportunity cost of capital is rising), the net present value of the project will decline. Indeed, if the opportunity cost of capital rises, some projects will no longer have a positive net present value. But in this case we are simply looking at the investment decision, not capital rationing.

From a more pragmatic perspective, most firms ration capital; most firms are subject to a constraint on the number of investment projects they can undertake. However, it is important to recognize that the constraint is, by and large, a *self-*

imposed constraint. For some reason, the managers must believe that they will be unable to fund all the investment projects available. And if this is the case, they need some way to determine which projects to undertake.

When confronted by this constraint, many managers first think of the internal rate of return as a means of ranking the competing projects. However, we hope we have convinced you of the problems involved in using the *IRR* to choose among competing projects.

Then why not just rank projects according to their net present values? Suppose the firm had available the three projects ranked below by their net present values:

Project	*NPV* ($, millions)	Rank
A	$10	1
B	7	2
C	5	3

Project *A* has the highest *NPV*. But if the combination of projects *B* and *C* costs less than *A* alone, it would be preferable to invest in the combination, since investing in both *B* and *C* would give a higher total *NPV* than would *A* alone. It is not sufficient to think simply about the project's net present value; a manager should think about the *NPV* per dollar spent on the project.

This shouldn't be at all surprising. This is a constrained optimization problem: the manager wants to maximize the value of the firm subject to the capital limitation. The rule for constrained optimization is to allocate so that the marginal benefit (the *NPV*) per dollar spent is equal among the competing activities. Hence, the most straightforward approach to the problem is to determine a **profitability index**—the ratio of the present value of the investment project to its cost. Presented below are additional data for the three projects introduced above:

profitability index
The ratio of the present value of an investment project to its cost.

Project	*NPV* ($, millions)	Cost ($, millions)	Present value ($, millions)	Profitability index
A	$10	$5	$15	3.0
B	7	3	10	3.3
C	5	3	8	2.7

Given the values of the profitability index, the firm would allocate the first $3 million to project *B*, since it has the largest ratio of marginal benefits to cost. The second project to be undertaken would be project *A*. Project *C* would be undertaken only if the capital constraint is lifted.

The profitability index is, however, not without its own limitations. This approach fails if there is more than one constraint, for example, if the capital constraint is imposed in more than one period. It is also unreliable when the projects are mutually exclusive or when one project is dependent on another's being undertaken. For such cases, more complicated techniques, including a linear programming approach, have been developed.

11 12

19.6 SUMMARY

The investment decision combines decision making over time and under conditions of risk. A fundamental problem faced by all firms making investment decisions is the valuation of risky net cash flows generated by risky projects, assets, or investments. When dealing with risky cash flows, a manager must consider the *expected present value* of the project:

$$E(PV_j) = \sum_{t=1}^{T} \frac{E(NCF_{j,t})}{(1 + r_{j,t})^t}$$

where $E(NCF_{j,t})$ is the expected net cash flow generated by this jth project in period t and $r_{j,t}$ is the discount rate in period t, which reflects the riskiness of project j.

The primary difficulty in evaluating the expected present value of a project is the determination of the appropriate discount rate for a risky project. Put another way, the problem is the determination of the *risk premium* for the jth project,

$$r_{j,t} = r_t + (\text{Risk premium})_j$$

We first considered two rules of thumb. With a *risk-adjusted discount rate,* some premium associated with the (total) variability in returns to the project is used. With the weighted-average-cost-of-capital approach, the firm's borrowing and equity costs are weighted by their relative shares to provide the discount rate for the firm:

$$r_{\text{WACC}} = r_D\left(\frac{D}{D+E}\right) + r_E\left(\frac{E}{D+E}\right)$$

The investment decision-making rule consistent with maximizing the value of the firm is simply the expected net present value rule. The expected net present value rule for investment projects is to accept those projects for which the expected net present value is positive and reject those for which the expected net present value is negative:

$$E(NPV_j) > 0 \ldots \text{ Accept}$$
$$E(NPV_j) < 0 \ldots \text{ Reject}$$

The expected net present value of a project is calculated as

$$\begin{aligned} E(NPV) &= E(PV) - \text{Cost of the project} \\ &= \sum_{t=1}^{T} \frac{E(NCF_t)}{(1 + r_t)^t} - C_0 \end{aligned}$$

where r_t is the risk-adjusted discount rate for the project in time period t.

To implement the expected net present value rule, the manager must (1) forecast revenues, (2) forecast (estimate) operating costs for the project, and (3) determine the appropriate discount rate for the project. Particular emphasis was placed on the relation between expected net present value and the discount rate, a relation depicted graphically by the expected net present value profile.

While the expected net present value rule is the theoretically and analytically correct investment criterion, other rules continue to be used. Two rules of thumb were considered:

- *The payback rule:* The payback period is the time required for the firm to recover its initial investment. The investment criterion is to accept only those projects that have a payback period less than some arbitrary maximum set by the firm.
- *The return on investment* (ROI) *rule:* The average return on investment is the ratio of average net cash flows to average investment. If the *ROI* for the project is larger than the firm's arbitrary target return, the investment project will be undertaken.

The primary shortcoming with these two ad hoc rules is that the net cash flows are not discounted; these rules ignore the time value of money. The payback rule gives too much weight to cash flows that will be received early; the *ROI* rule gives too much weight to distant cash flows. A preferable alternative investment criterion is the internal rate of return rule:

- *The internal rate of return* (IRR) *rule:* The *IRR* is the discount rate that makes the *NPV* of the investment project equal to zero. The project should be accepted if the *IRR* is greater than the firm's opportunity cost of capital.

As long as the expected net present value profile is a smooth, downward-sloping function, the *IRR* and expected *NPV* rules are functionally equivalent. However, the *IRR* rule can provide erroneous recommendations when mutually exclusive projects are considered. And the *IRR* methodology requires that all net cash flows be discounted at the same rate—early and late cash flows are discounted using the same discount rate.

The constraint of limited funding for investment

projects and the resulting capital rationing problem are, by and large, self-imposed by the management of the firm. Nonetheless, this is yet another constrained optimization problem: the solution must involve the ratio of marginal benefits to marginal costs (dollar expenditures). In this case, the profitability index is the ratio of the present value of the investment project (the marginal benefit from undertaking the project) to its cost. In order to maximize the value of the firm, managers will respond to the capital rationing problem by undertaking investment projects in the order of their profitability indexes.

TECHNICAL PROBLEMS

1. A manager is considering a risky investment project with a three-year life that will generate the following expected net cash flows:

Year	Expected net cash flow
1	$275,000
2	425,000
3	300,000

   The manager determines that the risk of the project is appropriately accounted for by a project-specific discount rate of 8.2 percent.
   a. Calculate the expected present value of the risky project.
   New information about the project causes the manager to revise upward to 9.2 percent the appropriate discount rate for the project.
   b. Calculate the expected present value of the risky project in light of this new information.
   c. Did the higher discount rate increase or decrease the expected present value of the project? Why?
2. Reconsider the example in Section 19.2 of Zeus Manufacturing's acquisition of a new machine. The old manager is fired, and a new manager is asked to evaluate the project. The new manager subjectively assigns different probabilities to the three outcomes: 10 percent chance of the low outcome, 60 percent chance of the best outcome, and 30 percent chance of the high outcome.
   a. Using the new probabilities and the net cash flow estimates presented in the example, calculate the new expected net cash flows for each of the five years.
   b. The new manager assesses the risk of the project to be low. Using the new risk-adjusted discount rates, calculate the expected present value of the project.
   c. The new manager also found that shareholders demand only a 14 percent return and Zeus would still have to pay 7 percent to borrow money. What is the new weighted average cost of capital? What is the expected present value using the new weighted average cost of capital?
3. Consider an investment project costing $162,500 that is expected to generate net cash flows of $100,000 in years 1 and 2.
   a. Calculate the expected *NPV* for this project using discount rates of 10 percent, 15 percent, and 20 percent.
   b. Sketch the expected *NPV* profile for this project.
4. Consider an investment project with the following expected net cash flows:

Year	Expected net cash flow
1	$20,000
2	15,000
3	10,000
4	10,000
5	5,000

The investment will cost the firm $45,000. The appropriate discount rate is 10 percent.

a. What is the expected net present value?

b. Should the firm undertake this project? Briefly explain.

c. Suppose the appropriate discount rate is 18 percent. What is the expected net present value now?

d. At 18 percent, will this investment project increase the present value of the firm?

e. Compute the expected net present value for the following discount rates:

Discount rate (percent)	*E(NPV)*
9.5	_______
11.0	_______
13.25	_______

5. Your supervisor has asked you to evaluate two potential investment projects. Both of these projects cost $2 million. The net cash flows from the two projects are presented below:

	Net cash flows ($, millions)	
Year	Project *A*	Project *B*
1	2	1.0
2	0	0.8
3	0	0.6
4	0	0.4

The firm's policy is that the maximum payback period for an investment project is two years.

a. Evaluate projects *A* and *B* using the criterion that two years is the maximum payback period.

b. Evaluate the two projects using the expected *NPV* criterion with a discount rate of 10 percent.

c. Compare the recommendations in parts *a* and *b*.

6. Reconsider the investment project in problem 4 using the 10 percent discount rate.

a. What is the payback period for this project?

b. If corporate policy is to accept only those projects with payback periods shorter than 30 months, will management accept this project?

c. Under what circumstances will management's decision under the payback rule be consistent with maximization of the firm's present value?

7. Explain why the payback rule gives too little weight to distant net cash flows and the *ROI* rule gives them too much weight.
8. Your firm has a target rate of return on investment of 35 percent. Using this criterion, you have been asked to evaluate two investment projects, both of which cost $20.5 million and have four-year lifetimes. The net cash flows from the two projects are provided below:

	Net cash flows ($, millions)	
Year	Project *A*	Project *B*
1	$10	$ 4
2	8	6
3	6	9
4	4	11

   a. Which, if either, of the two projects would be accepted using the *ROI* criterion?
   b. Reevaluate the two projects using the expected *NPV* criterion and a discount rate of 15 percent.
   c. Compare the two recommendations. What report would you forward on these two projects?
9. Calculate the internal rate of return (*IRR*) for the project in
   a. Problem 3.
   b. Problem 4.
10. In general, when would the *IRR* and the expected *NPV* rules give conflicting recommendations?
11. The capital rationing problem is, by and large, self-imposed. Explain why this is so. What could the management of a firm do to eliminate the constraint? Why do so many firms ration capital?
12. Your firm has available four investment projects, the cost and expected net present values of which are presented below:

Project	Expected *NPV*	Cost
A	$20	$10
B	17	10
C	12	5
D	8	5

   a. Calculate the profitability index for each of the projects.
   b. Which projects will be undertaken if the firm has an expenditure (funding) constraint of $5? $10? $15? $20?

APPLIED PROBLEMS

1. Consider a risky project under consideration by Sharp Investments that will produce a single net cash flow at the end of two years. The probability distribution for the net cash flow is:

Net cash flow ($, thousands)	Probability (percent)
25	5
30	5
35	20
40	30
45	30
50	10

a. Calculate the expected net cash flow for this project.

b. Suppose the interest rates on U.S. government securities are currently:

Maturity	Interest rate (percent)
6 months	6.0
1 year	6.5
2 years	7.0
3 years	7.78

Compare the expected value for this project using the appropriate risk-free interest rate. Is the risk-free rate the appropriate discount rate to use? Why or why not?

c. Suppose Sharp Investments' current borrowing rate is 8.5 percent and its current outstanding debt is $20 million. Shareholders expect to earn 10 percent on equity, which amounts, in total, to $40 million. Compute the weighted average cost of capital (r_{WACC}). Using r_{WACC} for the discount rate, compute the expected present value of this project.

2. The fact that you are attending a college or university indicates that you have made an investment decision. What kind of investment decision is this? What factors did you (at least implicitly) evaluate when making this decision? In what way would the decision to go to graduate school differ?

3. In this chapter we concentrated on investment projects, implicitly talking about investments in plant and equipment. However, the same techniques could be used to evaluate other investment projects, including new products.

   Down-Home Eatin' is considering the introduction of Diet Grits. The proposal is to test market the new project for one year in two regions—Macon, Georgia, and northwest Bergen County, New Jersey. If the test markets are successful, the product will be introduced nationwide.

   How would the investment decision be structured? What data are required to make the decision? How would the necessary data be obtained?

For problems 4 through 7, use the following data: Argonaut Enterprises had available four potential investment projects that would all begin in 1999. The characteristics of these projects are summarized in the table below:

Project:	*A*	*B*	*C*	*D*
Cost:	$123,000	$89,200	$56,600	$55,800
Net cash flow*				
1999	30,000	50,000	20,000	40,000
2000	30,000	50,000	20,000	20,000
2001	30,000	0	20,000	10,000
2002	30,000	0	20,000	0
Scrap or resale value at end of 2002:	50,000	0	10,000	0

*At year-end.

4. Evaluate these projects using the expected *NPV* criterion and a discount rate of 15 percent.
5. The expected *NPV* evaluation did not sit very well with the vice president for operations, for whom project *A* was a particular favorite. He argued that the discount rate used in the calculation of the net present values was too high. In response, the board of directors asked to see the internal rates of return for each of the projects. Provide these values and an evaluation based on these values.
6. The vice president for operations came back to the board of directors with another argument: He believes that the resale value for project *A* was underestimated and that the resale value should be $70,000 rather than $50,000. If this is true, should this project be undertaken, using 15 percent as the relevant discount rate? Use the net present value of the project to support your answer.
7. It turns out that project *B* also has a supporter. The director of new product development argues that the capital outlay necessary for project *B* is $86,800 rather than $89,200. If this is true, what would be the internal rate of return for project *B*? Would this project be undertaken, using 15 percent as the relevant opportunity cost of capital?

APPENDIX

Statistical Tables

STUDENT'S t-DISTRIBUTION

The table on page 725 provides critical values of the t-distribution at four levels of significance—0.10, 0.05, 0.02 and 0.01. It should be noted that these values are based on a two-tailed test for significance: a test to determine if an estimated coefficient is significantly different from zero. For a discussion of one-tailed hypothesis tests, a topic not covered in this text, the reader is referred to Terry Sincich, *A Course in Modern Business Statistics,* 2d ed. (New York: Dellen/Macmillan College Publishing, 1994).

To illustrate the use of this table, consider a multiple regression that uses 30 observations to estimate three coefficients, a, b, and c. Therefore, there are $30 - 3 = 27$ degrees of freedom. If the level of significance is chosen to be 0.05 (the confidence level is $0.95 = 1 - 0.05$), the critical t-value for the test of significance is found in the table to be 2.052. If a lower level of significance (a higher confidence level) is required, a researcher can use the 0.01 level of significance (0.99 level of confidence) to obtain a critical value of 2.771. Conversely, if a higher significance level (lower level of confidence) is acceptable, the researcher can use the 0.10 significance level (0.90 confidence level) to obtain a critical value of 1.703.

THE F-DISTRIBUTION

The table on pages 726–727 provides critical values of the F-distribution at 0.05 and 0.01 levels of significance (or the 0.95 and 0.99 levels of confidence, respectively). To illustrate how the table is used, consider a multiple regression that uses 30 observations to estimate three coefficients; that is, $n = 30$ and $k = 3$. The appropriate F-statistic has $k - 1$ degrees of freedom for the numerator and $n - k$ degrees of freedom for the denominator. Thus, in the example, there are 2 and 27 degrees of freedom. From the table the critical F-value corresponding to a 0.05 level of significance (or 0.95 level of confidence) is 3.35. If a 0.01 significance level is desired, the critical F-value is 5.49.

Critical *t*-Values

Degrees of freedom	Significance level 0.10	0.05	0.02	0.01
1	6.314	12.706	31.821	63.657
2	2.920	4.303	6.965	9.925
3	2.353	3.182	4.541	5.841
4	2.132	2.776	3.747	4.604
5	2.015	2.571	3.365	4.032
6	1.943	2.447	3.143	3.707
7	1.895	2.365	2.998	3.499
8	1.860	2.306	2.896	3.355
9	1.833	2.262	2.821	3.250
10	1.812	2.228	2.764	3.169
11	1.796	2.201	2.718	3.106
12	1.782	2.179	2.681	3.055
13	1.771	2.160	2.650	3.012
14	1.761	2.145	2.624	2.977
15	1.753	2.131	2.602	2.947
16	1.746	2.120	2.583	2.921
17	1.740	2.110	2.567	2.898
18	1.734	2.101	2.552	2.878
19	1.729	2.093	2.539	2.861
20	1.725	2.086	2.528	2.845
21	1.721	2.080	2.518	2.831
22	1.717	2.074	2.508	2.819
23	1.714	2.069	2.500	2.807
24	1.711	2.064	2.492	2.797
25	1.708	2.060	2.485	2.787
26	1.706	2.056	2.479	2.779
27	1.703	2.052	2.473	2.771
28	1.701	2.048	2.467	2.763
29	1.699	2.045	2.462	2.756
30	1.697	2.042	2.457	2.750
40	1.684	2.021	2.423	2.704
60	1.671	2.000	2.390	2.660
120	1.658	1.980	2.358	2.617
∞	1.645	1.960	2.326	2.576

Source: Adapted with permission from R. J. Wonnacott and T. H. Wonnacott, *Econometrics,* 2d ed., New York: John Wiley & Sons, 1979.

table t
compare
calculated t
tell u if coef. is sign.

Critical *F*-Values

Note: The values corresponding to a 0.05 significance level are printed in lightface type and the values corresponding to a 0.01 significance level are printed in boldface type.

Degrees of freedom for denominator $(n-k)$	Degrees of freedom for numerator $(k-1)$																			
	1	2	3	4	5	6	7	8	9	10	11	12	14	16	20	24	30	40	50	∞
1 . . .	161	200	216	225	230	234	237	239	241	242	243	244	245	246	248	249	250	251	252	254
	4052	**4999**	**5403**	**5625**	**5764**	**5859**	**5928**	**5981**	**6022**	**6056**	**6082**	**6106**	**6142**	**6169**	**6208**	**6234**	**6258**	**6286**	**6302**	**6366**
2 . . .	18.51	19.00	19.16	19.25	19.30	19.33	19.36	19.37	19.38	19.39	19.40	19.41	19.42	19.43	19.44	19.45	19.46	19.47	19.47	19.50
	98.49	**99.01**	**99.17**	**99.25**	**99.30**	**99.33**	**99.34**	**99.36**	**99.38**	**99.40**	**99.41**	**99.42**	**99.43**	**99.44**	**99.45**	**99.46**	**99.47**	**99.48**	**99.48**	**99.50**
3 . . .	10.13	9.55	9.28	9.12	9.01	8.94	8.88	8.84	8.81	8.78	8.76	8.74	8.71	8.69	8.66	8.64	8.62	8.60	8.58	8.53
	34.12	**30.81**	**29.46**	**28.71**	**28.24**	**27.91**	**27.67**	**27.49**	**27.34**	**27.23**	**27.13**	**27.05**	**26.92**	**26.83**	**26.69**	**26.60**	**26.50**	**26.41**	**26.30**	**26.12**
4 . . .	7.71	6.94	6.59	6.39	6.26	6.16	6.09	6.04	6.00	5.96	5.93	5.91	5.87	5.84	5.80	5.77	5.74	5.71	5.70	5.63
	21.20	**18.00**	**16.69**	**15.98**	**15.52**	**15.21**	**14.98**	**14.80**	**14.66**	**14.54**	**14.45**	**14.37**	**14.24**	**14.15**	**14.02**	**13.93**	**13.83**	**13.74**	**13.69**	**13.46**
5 . . .	6.61	5.79	5.41	5.19	5.05	4.95	4.88	4.82	4.78	4.74	4.70	4.68	4.64	4.60	4.56	4.53	4.50	4.46	4.44	4.36
	16.26	**13.27**	**12.06**	**11.39**	**10.97**	**10.67**	**10.45**	**10.27**	**10.15**	**10.05**	**9.96**	**9.89**	**9.77**	**9.68**	**9.55**	**9.47**	**9.38**	**9.29**	**9.24**	**9.02**
6 . . .	5.99	5.14	4.76	4.53	4.39	4.28	4.21	4.15	4.10	4.06	4.03	4.00	3.96	3.92	3.87	3.84	3.81	3.77	3.75	3.67
	13.74	**10.92**	**9.78**	**9.15**	**8.75**	**8.47**	**8.26**	**8.10**	**7.98**	**7.87**	**7.79**	**7.72**	**7.60**	**7.52**	**7.39**	**7.31**	**7.23**	**7.14**	**7.09**	**6.88**
7 . . .	5.59	4.74	4.35	4.12	3.97	3.87	3.79	3.73	3.68	3.63	3.60	3.57	3.52	3.49	3.44	3.41	3.38	3.34	3.32	3.23
	12.25	**9.55**	**8.45**	**7.85**	**7.46**	**7.19**	**7.00**	**6.84**	**6.71**	**6.62**	**6.54**	**6.47**	**6.35**	**6.27**	**6.15**	**6.07**	**5.98**	**5.90**	**5.85**	**5.65**
8 . . .	5.32	4.46	4.07	3.84	3.69	3.58	3.50	3.44	3.39	3.34	3.31	3.28	3.23	3.20	3.15	3.12	3.08	3.05	3.03	2.93
	11.26	**8.65**	**7.59**	**7.01**	**6.63**	**6.37**	**6.19**	**6.03**	**5.91**	**5.82**	**5.74**	**5.67**	**5.56**	**5.48**	**5.36**	**5.28**	**5.20**	**5.11**	**5.06**	**4.86**
9 . . .	5.12	4.26	3.86	3.63	3.48	3.37	3.29	3.23	3.18	3.13	3.10	3.07	3.02	2.98	2.93	2.90	2.86	2.82	2.80	2.71
	10.56	**8.02**	**6.99**	**6.42**	**6.06**	**5.80**	**5.62**	**5.47**	**5.35**	**5.26**	**5.18**	**5.11**	**5.00**	**4.92**	**4.80**	**4.73**	**4.64**	**4.56**	**4.51**	**4.31**
10 . . .	4.96	4.10	3.71	3.48	3.33	3.22	3.14	3.07	3.02	2.97	2.94	2.91	2.86	2.82	2.77	2.74	2.70	2.67	2.64	2.54
	10.04	**7.56**	**6.55**	**5.99**	**5.64**	**5.39**	**5.21**	**5.06**	**4.95**	**4.85**	**4.78**	**4.71**	**4.60**	**4.52**	**4.41**	**4.33**	**4.25**	**4.17**	**4.12**	**3.91**
11 . . .	4.84	3.98	3.59	3.36	3.20	3.09	3.01	2.95	2.90	2.86	2.82	2.79	2.74	2.70	2.65	2.61	2.57	2.53	2.50	2.40
	9.65	**7.20**	**6.22**	**5.67**	**5.32**	**5.07**	**4.88**	**4.74**	**4.63**	**4.54**	**4.46**	**4.40**	**4.29**	**4.21**	**4.10**	**4.02**	**3.94**	**3.86**	**3.80**	**3.60**
12 . . .	4.75	3.89	3.49	3.26	3.11	3.00	2.92	2.85	2.80	2.76	2.72	2.69	2.64	2.60	2.54	2.50	2.46	2.42	2.40	2.30
	9.33	**6.93**	**5.95**	**5.41**	**5.06**	**4.82**	**4.65**	**4.50**	**4.39**	**4.30**	**4.22**	**4.16**	**4.05**	**3.98**	**3.86**	**3.78**	**3.70**	**3.61**	**3.56**	**3.36**
13 . . .	4.67	3.80	3.41	3.18	3.02	2.92	2.84	2.77	2.72	2.67	2.63	2.60	2.55	2.51	2.46	2.42	2.38	2.34	2.32	2.21
	9.07	**6.70**	**5.74**	**5.20**	**4.86**	**4.62**	**4.44**	**4.30**	**4.19**	**4.10**	**4.02**	**3.96**	**3.85**	**3.78**	**3.67**	**3.59**	**3.51**	**3.42**	**3.37**	**3.16**
14 . . .	4.60	3.74	3.34	3.11	2.96	2.85	2.77	2.70	2.65	2.60	2.56	2.53	2.48	2.44	2.39	2.35	2.31	2.27	2.24	2.13
	8.86	**6.51**	**5.56**	**5.03**	**4.69**	**4.46**	**4.28**	**4.14**	**4.03**	**3.94**	**3.86**	**3.80**	**3.70**	**3.62**	**3.51**	**3.43**	**3.34**	**3.26**	**3.26**	**3.00**
15 . . .	4.54	3.68	3.29	3.06	2.90	2.79	2.70	2.64	2.59	2.55	2.51	2.48	2.43	2.39	2.33	2.29	2.25	2.21	2.18	2.07
	8.68	**6.36**	**5.42**	**4.89**	**4.56**	**4.32**	**4.14**	**4.00**	**3.89**	**3.80**	**3.73**	**3.67**	**3.56**	**3.48**	**3.36**	**3.29**	**3.20**	**3.12**	**3.07**	**2.87**
16 . . .	4.49	3.63	3.24	3.01	2.85	2.74	2.66	2.59	2.54	2.49	2.45	2.42	2.37	2.33	2.28	2.24	2.20	2.16	2.13	2.01
	8.53	**6.23**	**5.29**	**4.77**	**4.44**	**4.20**	**4.03**	**3.89**	**3.78**	**3.69**	**3.61**	**3.55**	**3.45**	**3.37**	**3.25**	**3.18**	**3.10**	**3.01**	**2.96**	**2.75**
17 . . .	4.45	3.59	3.20	2.96	2.81	2.70	2.62	2.55	2.50	2.45	2.41	2.38	2.33	2.29	2.23	2.19	2.15	2.11	2.08	1.96
	8.40	**6.11**	**5.18**	**4.67**	**4.34**	**4.10**	**3.93**	**3.79**	**3.68**	**3.59**	**3.52**	**3.45**	**3.35**	**3.27**	**3.16**	**3.08**	**3.00**	**2.92**	**2.86**	**2.65**

18 . . .	4.41	3.55	3.16	2.93	2.77	2.66	2.58	2.51	2.46	2.41	2.37	2.34	2.29	2.25	2.19	2.15	2.11	2.07	2.04	1.92
	8.28	**6.01**	**5.09**	**4.58**	**4.25**	**4.01**	**3.85**	**3.71**	**3.60**	**3.51**	**3.44**	**3.37**	**3.27**	**3.19**	**3.07**	**3.00**	**2.91**	**2.83**	**2.78**	**2.57**
19 . . .	4.38	3.52	3.13	2.90	2.74	2.63	2.55	2.48	2.43	2.38	2.34	2.31	2.26	2.21	2.15	2.11	2.07	2.02	2.00	1.88
	8.18	**5.93**	**5.01**	**4.50**	**4.17**	**3.94**	**3.77**	**3.63**	**3.52**	**3.43**	**3.36**	**3.30**	**3.19**	**3.12**	**3.00**	**2.92**	**2.84**	**2.76**	**2.70**	**2.49**
20 . . .	4.35	3.49	3.10	2.87	2.71	2.60	2.52	2.45	2.40	2.35	2.31	2.28	2.23	2.18	2.12	2.08	2.04	1.99	1.96	1.84
	8.10	**5.85**	**4.94**	**4.43**	**4.10**	**3.87**	**3.71**	**3.56**	**3.45**	**3.37**	**3.30**	**3.23**	**3.13**	**3.05**	**2.94**	**2.86**	**2.77**	**2.69**	**2.63**	**2.42**
21 . . .	4.32	3.47	3.07	2.84	2.68	2.57	2.49	2.42	2.37	2.32	2.28	2.25	2.20	2.15	2.09	2.05	2.00	1.96	1.93	1.81
	8.02	**5.78**	**4.87**	**4.37**	**4.04**	**3.81**	**3.65**	**3.51**	**3.40**	**3.31**	**3.24**	**3.17**	**3.07**	**2.99**	**2.88**	**2.80**	**2.72**	**2.63**	**2.58**	**2.36**
22 . . .	4.30	3.44	3.05	2.82	2.66	2.55	2.47	2.40	2.35	2.30	2.26	2.23	2.18	2.13	2.07	2.03	1.98	1.93	1.91	1.78
	7.94	**5.72**	**4.82**	**4.41**	**3.99**	**3.76**	**3.59**	**3.45**	**3.35**	**3.26**	**3.18**	**3.12**	**3.02**	**2.94**	**2.83**	**2.75**	**2.67**	**2.58**	**2.53**	**2.31**
23 . . .	4.28	3.42	3.03	2.80	2.64	2.53	2.45	2.38	2.32	2.28	2.24	2.20	2.14	2.10	2.04	2.00	1.96	1.91	1.88	1.76
	7.88	**5.66**	**4.76**	**4.26**	**3.94**	**3.71**	**3.54**	**3.41**	**3.30**	**3.21**	**3.14**	**3.07**	**2.97**	**2.89**	**2.78**	**2.70**	**2.62**	**2.53**	**2.48**	**2.26**
24 . . .	4.26	3.40	3.01	2.78	2.62	2.51	2.43	2.36	2.30	2.26	2.22	2.18	2.13	2.09	2.02	1.98	1.94	1.89	1.86	1.73
	7.82	**5.61**	**4.72**	**4.22**	**3.90**	**3.67**	**3.50**	**3.36**	**3.25**	**3.17**	**3.09**	**3.03**	**2.93**	**2.85**	**2.74**	**2.66**	**2.58**	**2.49**	**2.44**	**2.21**
25 . . .	4.24	3.38	2.99	2.76	2.60	2.49	2.41	2.34	2.28	2.24	2.20	2.16	2.11	2.06	2.00	1.96	1.92	1.87	1.84	1.71
	7.77	**5.57**	**4.68**	**4.18**	**3.86**	**3.63**	**3.46**	**3.32**	**3.21**	**3.13**	**3.05**	**2.99**	**2.89**	**2.81**	**2.70**	**2.62**	**2.54**	**2.45**	**2.40**	**2.17**
26 . . .	4.22	3.37	2.89	2.74	2.59	2.47	2.39	2.32	2.27	2.22	2.18	2.15	2.10	2.05	1.99	1.95	1.90	1.85	1.82	1.69
	7.72	**5.53**	**4.64**	**4.14**	**3.82**	**3.59**	**3.42**	**3.29**	**3.17**	**3.09**	**3.02**	**2.96**	**2.86**	**2.77**	**2.66**	**2.58**	**2.50**	**2.41**	**2.36**	**2.13**
27 . . .	4.21	3.35	2.96	2.73	2.57	2.46	2.37	2.30	2.25	2.20	2.16	2.13	2.08	2.03	1.97	1.93	1.88	1.84	1.80	1.67
	7.68	**5.49**	**4.60**	**4.11**	**3.79**	**3.56**	**3.39**	**3.26**	**3.14**	**3.06**	**2.98**	**2.93**	**2.83**	**2.74**	**2.63**	**2.55**	**2.47**	**2.38**	**2.33**	**2.10**
28 . . .	4.20	3.34	2.95	2.71	2.56	2.44	2.36	2.29	2.24	2.19	2.15	2.12	2.06	2.02	1.96	1.91	1.87	1.81	1.78	1.65
	7.64	**5.45**	**4.57**	**4.07**	**3.76**	**3.53**	**3.36**	**3.23**	**3.11**	**3.03**	**2.95**	**2.90**	**2.80**	**2.71**	**2.60**	**2.52**	**2.44**	**2.35**	**2.30**	**2.06**
29 . . .	4.18	3.33	2.93	2.70	2.54	2.43	2.35	2.28	2.22	2.18	2.14	2.10	2.05	2.00	1.94	1.90	1.85	1.80	1.77	1.64
	7.60	**5.52**	**4.54**	**4.04**	**3.73**	**3.50**	**3.33**	**3.20**	**3.08**	**3.00**	**2.92**	**2.87**	**2.77**	**2.68**	**2.57**	**2.49**	**2.41**	**2.32**	**2.27**	**2.03**
30 . . .	4.17	3.32	2.92	2.69	2.53	2.43	2.34	2.27	2.21	2.16	2.12	2.09	2.04	1.99	1.93	1.89	1.84	1.79	1.76	1.62
	7.56	**5.39**	**4.51**	**4.02**	**3.70**	**3.47**	**3.30**	**3.17**	**3.06**	**2.98**	**2.90**	**2.84**	**2.74**	**2.66**	**2.55**	**2.47**	**2.38**	**2.29**	**2.24**	**2.01**
40 . . .	4.08	3.23	2.84	2.61	2.45	2.34	2.25	2.18	2.12	2.08	2.04	2.00	1.95	1.90	1.84	1.79	1.74	1.69	1.66	1.51
	7.31	**5.18**	**4.31**	**3.83**	**3.51**	**3.29**	**3.12**	**2.99**	**2.88**	**2.80**	**2.73**	**2.66**	**2.56**	**2.49**	**2.37**	**2.29**	**2.20**	**2.11**	**2.05**	**1.81**
50 . . .	4.03	3.18	2.79	2.56	2.40	2.29	2.20	2.13	2.07	2.02	1.98	1.95	1.90	1.85	1.78	1.74	1.69	1.63	1.60	1.44
	7.17	**5.06**	**4.20**	**3.72**	**3.41**	**3.18**	**3.02**	**2.88**	**2.78**	**2.70**	**2.62**	**2.56**	**2.46**	**2.39**	**2.26**	**2.18**	**2.10**	**2.00**	**1.94**	**1.68**
60 . . .	4.00	3.15	2.76	2.52	2.37	2.25	2.17	2.10	2.04	1.99	1.95	1.92	1.86	1.81	1.75	1.70	1.65	1.59	1.56	1.39
	7.08	**4.98**	**4.13**	**3.65**	**3.34**	**3.12**	**2.95**	**2.82**	**2.72**	**2.63**	**2.56**	**2.50**	**2.40**	**2.32**	**2.20**	**2.12**	**2.03**	**1.93**	**1.87**	**1.60**
125 . . .	3.92	3.07	2.68	2.44	2.29	2.17	2.08	2.01	1.95	1.90	1.86	1.83	1.77	1.72	1.65	1.60	1.55	1.49	1.45	1.25
	6.84	**4.78**	**3.94**	**3.47**	**3.17**	**2.95**	**2.79**	**2.65**	**2.56**	**2.47**	**2.40**	**2.33**	**2.23**	**2.15**	**2.03**	**1.94**	**1.85**	**1.75**	**1.68**	**1.37**
∞ . . .	3.84	2.99	2.60	2.37	2.21	2.09	2.01	1.94	1.88	1.83	1.79	1.75	1.69	1.64	1.57	1.52	1.46	1.40	1.35	1.00
	6.64	**4.60**	**3.78**	**3.32**	**3.02**	**2.80**	**2.64**	**2.51**	**2.41**	**2.32**	**2.24**	**2.18**	**2.07**	**1.99**	**1.87**	**1.79**	**1.69**	**1.59**	**1.52**	**1.00**

Source: Adapted with permission from R. J. Wonnacott and T. H. Wonnacott, *Econometrics,* New York: John Wiley & Sons, 1970.

APPENDIX

Linear Programming

Linear programming is a mathematical technique used to determine the optimal solutions to certain specific problems. This tool is frequently used to find the least-cost combinations of inputs necessary to produce some desired level of output; that is, cost minimization problems. However, the same technique can be used to solve other types of optimization problems, such as the optimal level of inventory, the least-cost method of transporting commodities, and so on.

BASIC CONCEPTS

Let's begin with a practical problem: A firm produces two products, X_1 and X_2, which it can sell at fixed prices, P_1 and P_2. The production of X_1 and X_2 requires the use of three different types of machines, which can be used for eight hours a day. The firm currently owns three type-1 machines, two type-2 machines, and five type-3 machines. Therefore, given the daily capacity of each machine, the firm has available 24 type-1 machine-hours, 16 type-2 machine-hours, and 40 type-3 machine-hours per period. In the short run, the firm cannot buy or sell any machines; but it can employ various amounts of labor or other inputs at prevailing market prices.[1]

Since labor and other inputs are obtainable in unlimited supplies, the firm first calculates the gross profit on each product net of labor and other input costs from the market prices for X_1 and X_2. These net prices,

[1]Outputs and inputs are assumed to be infinitely divisible, and the outputs are produced according to fixed proportions, constant-returns-to-scale processes.

$$p_1 = P_1 - \text{Labor cost per unit of } X_1 - \text{Other costs per unit of } X_1$$
$$p_2 = P_2 - \text{Labor cost per unit of } X_2 - \text{Other costs per unit of } X_2$$

are the accountant's measure of gross profit. The problem for the firm is to choose the output combination that maximizes total (gross) profit.

To solve this problem, we must first know something about the actual productive capacity of each machine. Suppose that the number of type-1 machine-hours required per unit of X_1 is six, while only three type-1 machine-hours are required to produce a unit of X_2. Likewise, suppose each unit of X_1 requires two type-2 machine-hours and X_2 requires four hours per unit. Finally, suppose that eight type-3 machine-hours are required to produce a unit of either X_1 or X_2. Given the respective fixed quantities of machine-hours per period, these production relations may be written in the form of constraints:

$$6X_1 + 3X_2 \leq 24$$
$$2X_1 + 4X_2 \leq 16$$
$$8X_1 + 8X_2 \leq 40$$

which show the possible combinations of X_1 and X_2, given machine availability. For example, the first constraint indicates that if no X_2 is produced, the maximum daily production of X_1 is 4 units because each unit of X_1 requires 6 hours of a type-1 machine and only 24 hours of type-1 are available. Similarly from the first constraint, if 4 units of X_2 are produced, only 12 hours of type-1 machine time are left to produce X_1; thus, only 2 units of X_1 can be produced. The other two constraints are interpreted similarly. Thus, all three constraints put a limit on the combinations of X_1 and X_2 that the firm can produce daily.

Suppose that the net prices of X_1 and X_2 are \$12 and \$8 per unit, respectively. The problem facing the firm is to choose the combination of X_1 and X_2 (X_1 and X_2 are the *choice variables*) that maximizes total gross income:

$$\pi = 12X_1 + 8X_2$$

subject to the physical constraints imposed by the production processes and the limited availability of machines.

In general, we write this type of problem, a *linear program,* as

$$\begin{aligned} \max \pi &= p_1X_1 + p_2X_2 \\ \text{subject to } & a_{11}X_1 + a_{12}X_2 \leq r_1 \\ & a_{21}X_1 + a_{22}X_2 \leq r_2 \\ & a_{31}X_1 + a_{32}X_2 \leq r_3 \\ & X_1, X_2 \geq 0 \end{aligned}$$

where a_{ij} ($i = 1, 2, 3$; $j = 1, 2$) is the required number of type-i machine-hours per unit of output j and r_i represents the restrictions on the program—in our example, the fixed quantities of machine-hours available. Of course, it should be noted that there could be any number of choice variables and constraints in any given linear program.

FIGURE A.1
Linear Constraints

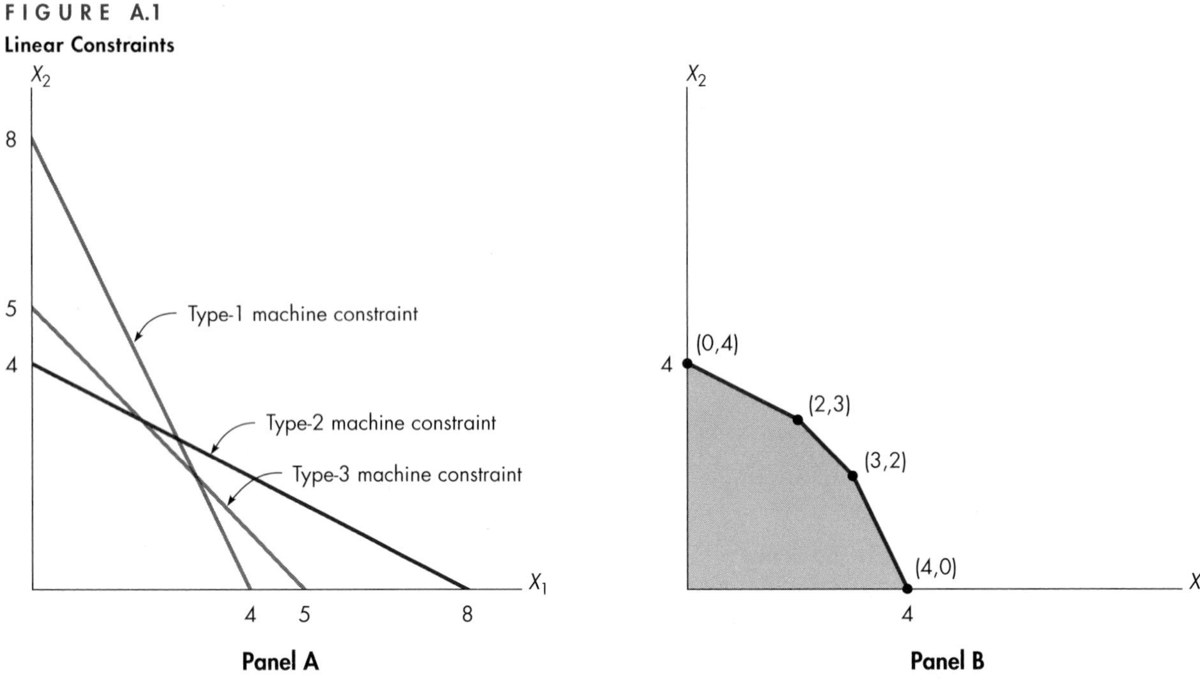

The first equation in the program, the total (gross) profit function, constitutes the objective function of the linear program; that is, it is the firm's *objective* to maximize total gross profits per production period. The three inequalities that follow are the *constraints* imposed on the linear program by the technological relation and the restrictions. Finally, by the last two inequalities ($X_1, X_2 \geq 0$), referred to as the *nonnegativity restrictions,* we impose the restriction that negative outputs are impossible. Therefore, there are three essential ingredients to every linear program: an objective function, a set of constraints, and a set of nonnegativity restrictions.

Returning to our specific example, we may write our problem in this general form:

$$\begin{aligned} \max \pi &= 12X_1 + 8X_2 \\ \text{subject to } 6X_1 + 3X_2 &\leq 24 \\ 2X_1 + 4X_2 &\leq 16 \\ 8X_1 + 8X_2 &\leq 40 \\ X_1, X_2 &\geq 0 \end{aligned}$$

Since our problem involves only two choice variables, X_1 and X_2, the linear program may be solved graphically. In Figure A.1 we plot X_1 along the horizontal axis and X_2 along the vertical axis. Because of the nonnegativity restrictions, we need concern ourselves only with the positive (nonnegative) quadrant.

To see what the constraints look like graphically, first treat them as equalities and plot them as straight lines as in Panel A. Since each constraint is of the "less-than-or-equal-to" type, only the points lying on the line or below it will satisfy the constraint. To satisfy all three constraints simultaneously, we can accept only those points that lie interior to all three constraint lines. The collection of all points that satisfy all three constraints simultaneously is called the *feasible region,* shown as the shaded region in Panel B. Each individual point in that region is known as *feasible solution.* It should be noted that the feasible region includes the points on the *boundary,* or the heavy line in Panel B. Note that in the present (two-dimensional) case, the corner points on the boundary are called *extreme points.* They occur either at the intersection of two constraints [(2, 3) and (3, 2)] or at the intersection of one constraint and one of the axes [(0, 4) and (4, 0)].

The feasible region contains all output combinations satisfying all three constraints and the nonnegativity restrictions. However, some of these points may entail a lower level of total profits than others. To maximize profits, we must consider the objective function. To plot the profit function in (X_1, X_2) space we rewrite it as

$$X_2 = \frac{\pi}{8} - \frac{3}{2}X_1$$

This equation represents a family of parallel straight lines corresponding to different levels of profits or values of π. Since each of these lines is associated with a specific value of π, they are sometimes called *isoprofit curves.* Three isoprofit curves are shown in Figure A.2 as dashed lines, labeled I, II, and III.

The firm's objective is, of course, to attain the highest possible isoprofit curve while still remaining in the feasible region. In Figure A.2, isoprofit curve II satisfies this objective. While isoprofit curve III represents the highest level of profits, the combinations of X_1 and X_2 on this line are not in the feasible region, so this level of profit cannot be attained. Combinations on isoprofit line I clearly lie in the feasible region; however, a higher level of profit can be reached. Isoprofit line II represents the highest possible profit level that still incorporates a point in the feasible region. It coincides with the output combination of 3 units of X_1 and 2 units of X_2. Thus, the point (3, 2) is the *optimal solution* to our linear program. Total profits for this optimal output combination can easily be obtained by using the values $X_1 = 3$ and $X_2 = 2$ in the objective function to yield the maximum profit, $\pi = \$52$ per production period.

Note that the optimal solution is an extreme point. In fact, the optimal solution to *any* linear program is always an extreme point. This fact will prove useful in developing a general solution methodology for linear programs.

GENERAL SOLUTION METHOD

With two choice variables, the graphical method provided an optimal solution with little difficulty. This situation holds regardless of the number of constraints; additional constraints simply increase the number of extreme points, not the dimension of the diagram. When there are more than three choice variables,

FIGURE A.2
An Optimal Solution

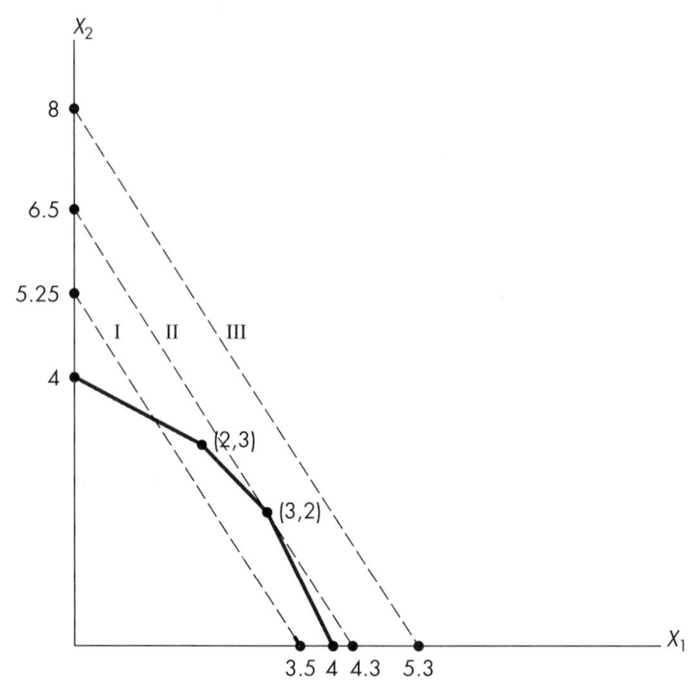

however, the graphical method becomes intractable, since we cannot draw a four-dimensional graph. Therefore, we need an analytical method to find the optimal solution to linear programs involving any number of choice variables.

As suggested above, the optimal solution of a linear program is one of the extreme points. Given a two-dimensional feasible region, it is relatively easy to find its extreme points, but finding them for the nongraphable n-variable case is more complex. Before considering the n-variable case, it will be instructive to return to our example. In Figure A.2, note that there are five extreme points—(0, 4), (2, 3), (3, 2), (4, 0), and (0, 0)—all of which can be placed in one of three general categories.

The first category consists of those extreme points occurring at the intersection of two constraints. In our example, these points are (3, 2) and (2, 3). While such points exactly fulfill two of the three constraints, the remaining constraint is inexactly fulfilled. Consider the output combination (3, 2). While the type-1 and type-3 machine constraints are exactly fulfilled, (3, 2) lies inside the type-2 machine constraint and hence there is *slack* (or underutilization) in the use of type-2 machines.

Extreme points in the second category, illustrated by (0, 4) and (4, 0), occur at the intersection of a constraint and one of the axes. Because they are located on only one of the constraints, these points exactly fulfill only one constraint;

therefore, at such points there will be slack in the two remaining constraints. Last, the third category of extreme points consists of a single output combination, the origin (0, 0), where there exists slack in all the constraints.

The point is that whenever the number of constraints exceeds the number of choice variables, every extreme point will involve slack in at least one of the constraints. Furthermore, as is evident from Panel A of Figure A.1, the magnitude of the slack in any particular constraint can be calculated. Therefore, when we choose a particular extreme point as the optimal solution, we are choosing not only the optimal output combination (X_1, X_2) but also the optimal amount of slack in at least one constraint. Let us consider these slacks explicitly and denote the slack in the ith constraint ($i = 1, 2, 3$ in our example) by S_i. We call these S_i's *slack variables.* Since we now explicitly consider the possible slack in each constraint, we can transform each inequality constraint into a strict equality by adding these S_i's to the left-hand side of the ith constraint.

Returning to our example and adding a slack variable to each constraint, we may rewrite our linear program as

$$\begin{aligned} \max \pi &= 12X_1 + 8X_2 \\ \text{subject to } 6X_1 + 3X_2 + S_1 &= 24 \\ 2X_1 + 4X_2 + S_2 &= 16 \\ 8X_1 + 8X_2 + S_3 &= 40 \\ X_1, X_2, S_1, S_2, S_3 &\geq 0 \end{aligned}$$

There are now five choice variables: X_1, X_2, S_1, S_2, and S_3. When $S_i > 0$, there is slack in the ith constraint (a *nonbinding* constraint); if $S_i = 0$, there is no slack and the ith constraint is exactly fulfilled (a *binding* constraint). Slack in a constraint for this particular problem could best be thought of as excess capacity or overcapitalization of a certain type of machine.

It is easy to determine the values of the slacks implied by each extreme point. If we start with the origin (0, 0), we substitute $X_1 = 0$ and $X_2 = 0$ into the transformed constraints and find that $S_1 = 24$, $S_2 = 16$, and $S_3 = 40$. Thus, the extreme point (0, 0) in output space can be mapped into *solution space* as the point

$$(X_1, X_2, S_1, S_2, S_3) = (0, 0, 24, 16, 40)$$

Similarly, we may map each extreme point in outer space into solution space. The results are presented in Table A.1.

From Table A.1 the profit contribution at each extreme point can be calculated by inserting the values for X_1 and X_2 into the objective function. The point that yields the maximum profit is the constrained profit-maximizing output point—the solution to our linear programming problem. The profit contributions of each point in solution space are shown in Table A.2. Again, we confirm that output combination (3, 2) is the profit-maximizing point. Note that $S_2 > 0$ at the optimum indicates that the constraint on the type-2 machine is nonbinding.

The procedure described above is used in solving more complex linear programming problems. Computer programs are available which find solution values for the variables at all extreme points, evaluate total profits at each potential

TABLE A.1

Extreme Points in Output Space

Output space (X_1, X_2)	Solution space $(X_1, X_2, S_1, S_2, S_3)$
(0,0)	(0, 0, 24, 16, 40)
(0,4)	(0, 4, 12, 0, 8)
(4,0)	(4, 0, 0, 8, 8)
(3,2)	(3, 2, 0, 2, 0)
(2,3)	(2, 3, 3, 0, 0)

TABLE A.2

Profit Contribution of Extreme Points

Solution at extreme point	Value of variable					Total profit contribution
	X_1	X_2	S_1	S_2	S_3	
(0,0)	0	0	24	16	40	0
(0,4)	0	4	12	0	8	32
(4,0)	4	0	0	8	8	48
(3,2)	3	2	0	2	0	52
(2,3)	2	3	3	0	0	48

extreme point, and then determine the extreme point at which the objective function is maximized.

THE DUAL IN LINEAR PROGRAMMING

For every maximization problem in linear programming there exists a symmetrical minimization problem and vice versa. The original programming problem is referred to as the *primal* program, and its symmetrical counterpart is referred to as the *dual* program. The concept of this duality is quite significant because the optimal values of the objective functions in the primal and in the dual are always identical. Therefore, the analyst can pick the program, the primal or the dual, that is easiest to solve.

The linear program we have been using as an illustration—our *primal*—is a maximization problem: we wish to maximize total (gross) profit subject to the constraints imposed by the technology and machine time availability:

Primal

$$\begin{aligned} \max \pi &= 12X_1 + 8X_2 \\ \text{subject to } 6X_1 + 3X_2 &\leq 24 \\ 2X_1 + 4X_2 &\leq 16 \\ 8X_1 + 8X_2 &\leq 40 \\ X_1, X_2 &\geq 0 \end{aligned}$$

Corresponding to this maximization problem there exists a *dual* minimization problem: minimize the (opportunity) cost of using available machine-hours for the three machines subject to the constraints imposed by the production process and (gross) profitability of the two outputs:

Dual

$$\begin{aligned} \min \pi^\circ &= 24y_1 + 16y_2 + 40y_3 \\ \text{subject to } 6y_1 + 2y_2 + 8y_3 &\geq 12 \\ 3y_1 + 4y_2 + 8y_3 &\geq 8 \\ y_1, y_2, y_3 &\geq 0 \end{aligned}$$

In the primal, the choice variables X_1 and X_2 are the output levels of the two products. In the dual, the choice variables y_1, y_2, and y_3 represent the shadow prices (or premiums) for the inputs. For example, the variable y_1 is the shadow price of using one hour of machine type-1, and since we have 24 type-1 hours, the total cost of using machine type-1 is $24y_1$. A shadow price can be viewed as the implicit value to the firm of having 1 more unit of the input; that is, the marginal profit contribution of the input. We then attempt to determine minimum values, or shadow prices, for each of the inputs, such that these shadow prices will be just sufficient to absorb the firm's total profit. In other words, we seek to assign values to each input so as to minimize the total inputted value of the firm's resources.

In the primal, the constraints reflected the fact that the total hours of each type of machine used in the production of X_1 and X_2 could not exceed the available number of hours of each type of machine. In the dual, the constraints state that the value assigned the inputs used in the production of 1 unit of X_1 or 1 unit of X_2 must not be less than the profit contribution provided by a unit of these products. Recall that \$12 is the (gross) profit per unit of X_1 and \$8 is the profit per unit of X_2. The constraints require that the shadow prices of the different types of machines times the hours of each type required to produce a unit of X_1 or X_2 must be greater than or equal to the gross (unit) profit of X_1 or X_2.

To solve the dual, we again introduce slack variables, which allow us to write the constraint inequalities as strict equalities. Notice that in constrained minimization problems the constraints are of the "greater than or equal to" variety. Therefore, we introduce slack variables to the left-hand side of the constraints with a negative sign. (These negative S_i's used in the solution of minimization programs are often referred to as *surplus* variables.) We can then write the dual program as:

$$\begin{aligned} \min \pi^\circ &= 24y_1 + 16y_2 + 40y_3 \\ \text{subject to } 6y_1 + 2y_2 + 8y_3 - S_1 &= 12 \\ 3y_1 + 4y_2 + 8y_3 - S_2 &= 8 \\ y_1, y_2, y_3, S_1, S_2 &\geq 0 \end{aligned}$$

Since there are three choice variables (y_1, y_2, and y_3), a graphical solution would require a three-dimensional figure. Instead of such a complex diagram let's use the general techniques described above to find the solution space, evaluate the objective function for each feasible solution, and find that solution which minimizes the objective function.

A general rule illustrated in Table A.1 is that the maximum number of nonzero values in any solution is equal to the number of constraints. (In Table A.1, the number of constraints is three; so the maximum number of nonzero values in any solution is three.) Since there are two constraints in this dual problem, a maximum of two nonzero-valued variables define any solution point. Therefore, we can solve for the solutions by setting three of the variables—y_1, y_2, y_3, S_1, S_2—equal to zero and solving the constraint equations for the values of the remaining two.

For example, we can set y_1, y_2, and y_3 equal to zero and solve for S_1 and S_2. Using the first constraint,

$$6 \times 0 + 2 \times 0 + 8 \times 0 - S_1 = 12$$

so $S_1 = -12$. Likewise, using the second constraint,

$$3 \times 0 + 4 \times 0 + 8 \times 0 - S_2 = 8$$

and $S_2 = -8$. However, since S_1 and S_2 cannot be negative, this solution is outside the feasible region. Alternatively, setting y_1, y_2, and S_1 equal to zero, $y_3 = 1.5$ and $S_2 = 4$. Since all the values in this solution are positive, the solution lies in the feasible region. All the potential solutions are presented in Table A.3.

It is apparent from the table that not all the solutions lie within the feasible region. Only solutions 3, 5, 7, 9, and 10 meet the nonnegativity restrictions; that is, these are the only feasible solutions.

Each of the feasible solutions is then used to calculate a corresponding value of the objective function. For example, using solution 3, the value of the objective function is

$$\pi^\circ = 24 \times 0 + 16 \times 0 + 40 \times 1.5 = 60$$

All these values are summarized in Table A.4.

With solution 9, the objective function—the total value inputed to the different types of machines—is minimized. As mentioned earlier, and confirmed in this example, the optimal value of the dual objective function is equal to the optimal value of the primal objective function (see Table A.2).

Note that at the optimum, the shadow price of type-2 machine-hours is zero. A zero shadow price implies that the input in question has a zero marginal value to the firm; adding another type-2 machine-hour adds nothing to the firm's maximum attainable profit. Thus, a zero shadow price for type-2 machines is consistent with our findings in the solution to the primal: the type-2 machine constraint is nonbinding. Excess capacity exists with respect to type-2 machines, so additional hours will not result in increased production of either X_1 or X_2. Analogously, we see that the shadow prices of type-1 and type-3 machines are positive. A positive shadow indicates that the fixed number of these machines' hours imposes a binding constraint on the firm and that, if an additional hour of type-1 (type-3) machine work is added, the firm can increase its total profit by $1.33 ($0.50).

TABLE A.3
Potential Solutions to Dual Problem

Solution number	Value of variable y_1	y_2	y_3	S_1	S_2	Feasible?
1	0	0	0	−12	−8	No
2	0	0	1	−4	0	No
3	0	0	1.5	0	4	Yes
4	0	2	0	−8	0	No
5	0	6	0	0	16	Yes
6	0	−2	2	0	0	No
7	2.66	0	0	4	0	Yes
8	2	0	0	0	−2	No
9	1.33	0	0.5	0	0	Yes
10	1.8	0.66	0	0	0	Yes

TABLE A.4
Value of Objective Function in Dual Problem

Solution	(y_1, y_2, y_3)	Value of objective function	(S_1, S_2)
3	(0,0,1.5)	60	(0,4)
5	(0,6,0)	96	(0,16)
7	(2.66,0,0)	64	(4,0)
9	(1.33,0,0.5)	52	(0,0)
10	(1.8,0.66,0)	53.75	(0,0)

The dual solution has thus far not indicated the optimal output combination (X_1, X_2); however, it does provide all the information we need to determine these optimal values. Note first that the solution to the dual tells us that the type-2 machine constraint is nonbinding. Furthermore, it tells us that, at the optimal output combination, $\pi = \pi^\circ = \$52$. Now consider the three constraints in the primal, which we rewrite here for convenience:

$$\begin{aligned} 6X_1 + 3X_2 + S_1 &= 24 \quad \text{type-1} \\ 2X_1 + 4X_2 + S_2 &= 16 \quad \text{type-2} \\ 8X_1 + 8X_2 + S_3 &= 40 \quad \text{type-3} \end{aligned}$$

From the solution to the dual we know that the type-1 and type-3 constraints are binding, because the dual found these inputs to have positive shadow prices. Accordingly, S_1 and S_3 equal zero in the primal program, and the binding constraints can be rewritten as

$$\begin{aligned} 6X_1 + 3X_2 &= 24 \\ 8X_1 + 8X_2 &= 40 \end{aligned}$$

These two equations may be solved simultaneously to determine the optimal output combination. In this example, the solution is $X_1 = 3$ and $X_2 = 2$, the same output combination that was obtained in the primal problem.

Let us stress the two major points of this discussion and example. First, the choice between solving the primal or the dual of a linear programming problem is arbitrary, since both yield the same optimal value for the objective function. Second, the optimal solution obtained from the dual provides the information necessary to obtain the solution for the primal and vice versa. Thus, as we mentioned at the outset, one can elect to solve either the primal or the dual, depending on which one is easier to solve.

ACTIVITY ANALYSIS: LINEAR PROGRAMMING AND PRODUCTION PLANNING FOR A SINGLE OUTPUT

As emphasized in Chapters 9 and 10, a decision problem faced by all firms is how to determine the least-cost combination of inputs needed to produce a particular product. If the production process satisfies certain regularity conditions, linear programming may be applied to solve the cost minimization problem.

Suppose that a firm produces a single product, Q, using two inputs, capital (K) and labor (L). As long as the production processes are subject to fixed proportions and constant returns to scale, we can characterize the relation between input usage and output as linear functions and thereby use linear programming to obtain a solution.

To illustrate how this is accomplished, consider the four production processes depicted in Figure A.3. Since production is characterized by fixed proportions, the relations between input usage and output are shown by a straight line from the origin. These lines are referred to as *activity rays*—hence the title *activity analysis*.

In Figure A.3, production process A requires 4 units of K and 4 units of L to produce 1 unit of Q. This requirement is illustrated by point A_1. Process B uses 4 units of L and 2 units of K to produce 1 unit of output. Similarly, process C uses 1.5 units of K and 5 units of L, while process D requires 8 units of L and 1 unit of K to produce 1 unit of output. These input-output relations are illustrated by B_1, C_1, and D_1, respectively. If we recall the definition of an isoquant, that is, different input combinations for which the level of output is constant, we can connect points A_1 through D_1 and derive an isoquant corresponding to a level of output equal to 1 unit of Q. In Figure A.3 this piecewise linear isoquant is labeled Q_1. With constant returns to scale, doubling the amount of both inputs employed results in output also doubling. In our graph, this doubling of inputs is illustrated by points A_2, B_2, C_2, and D_2. Connecting these points, we derive an isoquant corresponding to 2 units of output; it is labeled Q_2. Similarly, we may find isoquants Q_3 and Q_4 for 3 and 4 units of output, respectively.

Suppose that you are asked to determine the least-cost combination of L and K for an output level of 4 units when a unit of labor costs \$4 (say the hourly wage rate is \$4) and a unit of capital costs \$8 (say it costs \$8 to run a machine for one hour). This problem is simply a constrained minimization problem; that is, we want to minimize the total cost of producing 4 units of output. Accordingly,

FIGURE A.3
Piecewise Linear Isoquants

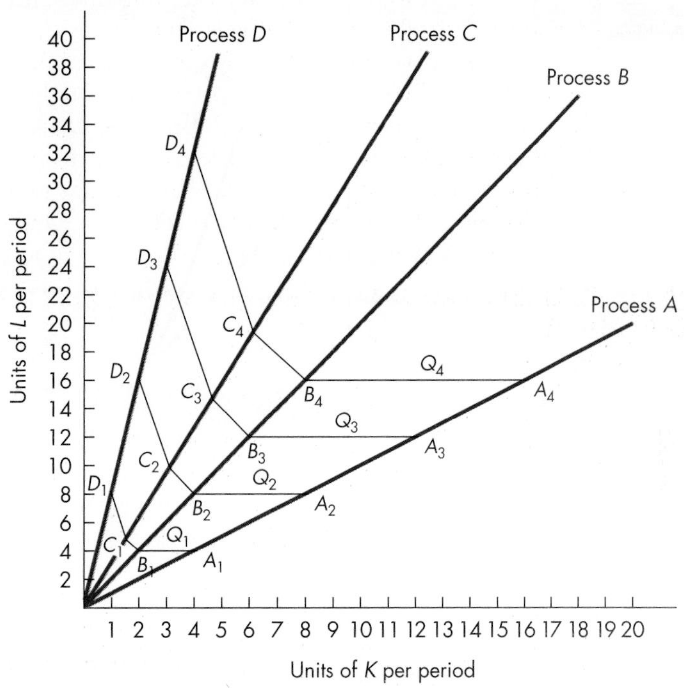

we may translate the problem into a linear programming problem. For illustrative purposes we will solve this program first graphically and then solve it using our general algebraic method developed above.

The isoquant for 4 units of output is reproduced in Figure A.4. Since we know the price of a unit of K is \$8 and the price of a unit of labor is \$4, we can plot on this graph a family of *isocost* curves corresponding to different levels of total cost. These curves are derived by solving the total cost function $C = 8K + 4L$ to obtain

$$L = \frac{C}{4} - 2K$$

Recall from Chapter 10 that we used a tangency rule to find the least-cost combination of inputs: we find the isocost curve that is just tangent to the isoquant and, therefore, the closest to the origin. At that point of tangency, corresponding to a particular combination of inputs, total cost of production is minimized. In linear programming, the same process is used.

In Figure A.4 isocost curves (I_1, I_2, I_3, I_4) are drawn through points B_4, C_4, D_4, and A_4. It is easy to see that isocost I_1 through point B_4 (8, 16) is closest to the origin and, therefore, represents the least cost possible of producing 4 units of output. If we use 8 units of K and 16 of L in our cost equation, we obtain a minimum total cost of production of \$128.

FIGURE A.4
Solution to Cost Minimization Problem

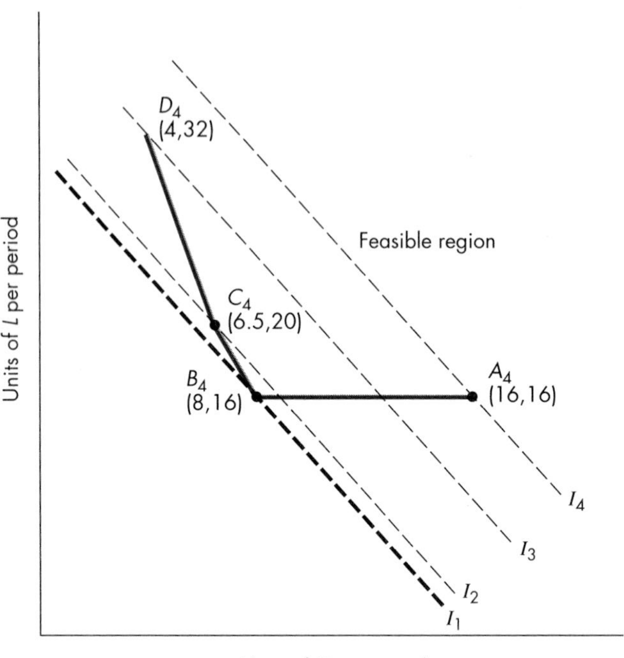

TABLE A.5
Total Cost at Extreme Points

Extreme point	Value of variable K	Value of variable L	Total cost
(4, 32)	4	32	$160
(6.5, 20)	6.5	20	132
(8, 16)	8	16	128
(16, 16)	16	16	192

We can use our algebraic method to solve the same problem. First note that there is only one constraint—the isoquant representing 4 units of output. Therefore, at the optimum there will be no slack or surplus in the constraint, and we can determine the solution simply by substituting the values for the extreme points into the cost function (our objective function in this program). The results are shown in Table A.5. Since our objective is to minimize total cost, we pick the input combination that does just that. Again we confirm our result from the graphical solution; the combination of 8 units of capital and 16 units of labor minimizes the total cost of producing 4 units of Q.

TECHNICAL PROBLEMS

1. Solve the following linear programming problem graphically:

$$\begin{aligned} \text{maximize } \pi &= 2X_1 + 3X_2 \\ \text{subject to } \quad X_1 &\leq 8 \\ X_2 &\leq 6 \\ X_1 + 4X_2 &\leq 16 \\ X_1, X_2 &\geq 0 \end{aligned}$$

2. In problem 1, how would the optimal solution change if the restrictions imposed (i.e., the r_i's) were all cut in half?
3. Solve the following linear programming problem using the general solution method:

$$\begin{aligned} \text{minimize } C &= 3X_1 + 4X_2 \\ \text{subject to } \quad X_1 + X_2 &\geq 2 \\ 2X_1 + 4X_2 &\geq 5 \\ X_1, X_2 &\geq 0 \end{aligned}$$

4. Form the dual to the linear programming problem presented in problem 3; then solve it to obtain the optimal values of X_1 and X_2.
5. Provide an explanation of the nonnegativity constraints for the problem of minimizing cost subject to a desired level of output.
6. Give some examples of managerial decisions for which linear programming can provide useful information. For each of these, suggest the type of analysis that would be employed.
7. Suppose you were hired by a firm that produces several products. This firm needs to know the amounts of the different products it should produce to maximize total profit. What information would you require? How would you analyze this problem?

ANSWERS TO TECHNICAL PROBLEMS

Chapter 1

1. *a.* Normal; accounting; economic
   b. total revenue; economic
   c. total economic cost; higher
   d. Economic
2. *a.* \$80,000; \$70,000; \$150,000
   b. \$25,000; \$70,000; 14
   c. \$95,000
   d. \$150,000
   e. −\$5,000
3. *a.* \$299,925; \$299,925
   b. \$310,522; \$310,522
4. *a.* smaller
   b. smaller

Chapter 2

1. *a.* 600 units of good A can be sold each month if P, M, P_B, $\mathcal{T}$, P_e, and N are all simultaneously equal to zero.
   b. −4. The slope parameter for a good's own price must be negative because the law of demand stipulates that quantity demanded and price of a good are inversely related.
   c. The slope parameter on M (−0.03) indicates that a \$1 increase in average household income, all else constant, will *decrease* sales of good A by 0.03 unit per month. (Or a \$1,000 increase in M will decrease Q_d by 30 units per month.) Good A is an inferior good because the slope coefficient on M is negative.
   d. Complements. The slope parameter on P_B is negative. A \$1 increase in the price of good B, all other factors constant, will cause the quantity demanded of good A to decrease by 12 units per month.
   e. These three slope parameters should all be positive, since each of the variables varies directly (rather than inversely) with quantity demanded. For tastes, note that the slope parameter e (= 15) is *not* restricted to the range 1 to 10 as is the value of the taste index $\mathcal{T}$.
   f. $Q_d = 600 - 4(5) - 0.03(25{,}000) - 12(40) + 15(6.5) + 6(5.25) + 1.5(2{,}000)$
   $= 2{,}479.0$ units of good A per month
2. *a.* $Q_d = 8{,}000 - 16P + 0.75(30{,}000) + 30(50) = 8{,}000 - 16P + 22{,}500 + 1{,}500 = 32{,}000 - 16P$
   b. Intercept parameter: If price were zero, consumers would take 32,000 units of the good for free. Slope parameter: A \$1 increase in price, all else constant, will cause consumers to buy 16 fewer units per period.
   c. The sketch plots price on the vertical axis and quantity demanded on the horizontal axis. Demand is a straight line that intersects the price axis at \$2,000 and the quantity demanded axis at 32,000 units.

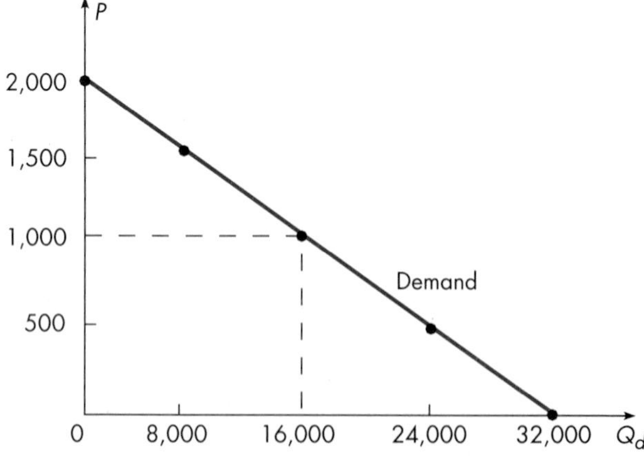

   d. When $P = \$1{,}000$, $Q_d = 32{,}000 - 16(1{,}000) = 16{,}000$ units. When $P = \$1{,}500$, $Q_d = 8{,}000$.

e. $P = 2{,}000 - 1/16Q_d$ or $P = 2{,}000 - 0.0625Q_d$. To calculate demand price: $P = 2{,}000 - 0.0625(24{,}000)$, and $P = \$500$. The maximum price consumers will pay to buy 24,000 units per period is $500.

3. (1) For a price of $2, the maximum amount of the good consumers are willing and able to buy is 35 units, or (2) the maximum price consumers will pay for 35 units of the good is $2.

4. a. $Q_d = 1{,}800 - 20P + 0.6(19{,}500) - 50(250) = 1{,}800 - 20P + 11{,}700 - 12{,}500 = 1{,}000 - 20P$

   b. D_3 is a line parallel to D_2 with a quantity intercept 300 units less than the quantity intercept for D_2, i.e., $1{,}000 - 300 = 700$; D_3: $Q_d = 700 - 20P$; $0.6 \times \Delta M = -300$, so $\Delta M = -500$ (if income falls to $19,000, then D_3 is the demand function).

5. Whenever the price of a good (P) changes, *quantity demanded* (Q_d) changes in the opposite direction. This results in a movement along a given demand curve. A change in quantity demanded due to a change in P is shown in the figure by a movement from A to B. When any one of the five demand-shifting variables changes in value, the demand curve shifts either leftward or rightward. The five demand-shifting variables that cause demand to shift are (1) consumer income (M), (2) price of related goods (P_R), (3) price expectations (P_e), (4) consumer tastes ($\mathcal{T}$), and (5) the number of consumers (N). A *change in demand* which can be caused only by a change in one of these five variables, is shown in the figure by the shift in D to D' or to D''.

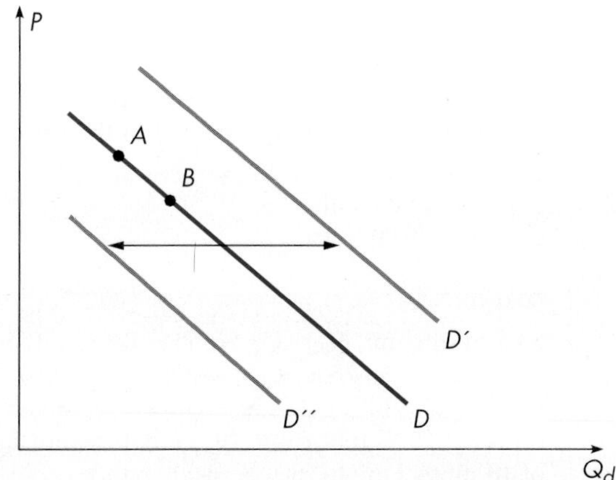

6. a. No change in demand. A change in price causes a change in *quantity* demanded, which is a movement along the demand curve.

   b. Demand increases.

   c. Demand decreases.

   d. Demand increases.

   e. Demand decreases.

   f. Demand decreases.

   g. Demand increases.

7. a. For P: A $1 increase in the price of the commodity, all else constant, will increase quantity supplied by 5 units per period.
   For P_I: A $1 increase in the price of a key input, all other factors affecting producers held constant, will decrease quantity supplied by 12 units per period.
   For F: If one more firm begins producing the commodity, all other things held constant, the quantity supplied of the commodity will increase by 10 units each period.

   b. $Q_s = 60 + 5P - 12(90) + 10(20) = 60 + 5P - 1{,}080 + 200 = -820 + 5P$

   c. The sketch plots price on the vertical axis and quantity supplied on the horizontal axis. Supply is a straight line that intersects the price axis at $164 and the quantity supplied axis at −820 units. Only the segment of the supply line at and above $P = \$164$ is economically meaningful. The price intercept of the supply curve, $164, is found by setting $Q_s = 0$ in the supply function and solving for P. Since the price intercept is $164, it follows that the price below which firms will quit producing the commodity is $164.

   d. $Q_s = -820 + 5(300) = 680$, and $Q_s = -820 + 5(500) = 1{,}680$

   e. Add 600 to the quantity intercept to get the new supply equation: $Q_s = (-820 + 600) + 5P \Rightarrow Q_s = -220 + 5P$. The new supply curve is linear and parallel to the supply curve in part *b*, and its quantity-supplied intercept is −220. $-12 \times \Delta P_I = 600$, so $\Delta P_I = 50$ (i.e., input price falls to $40 to get the new supply curve).

   f. To derive the inverse supply function, take the supply equation in part *b* and solve algebraically for P as a function of Q_s. The inverse supply equation is $P = 164 + 0.20Q$. Supply price for 680 units: $P = 164 + 0.20(680) = 300$. The minimum price producers will accept to produce 680 units per period is $300.

8. (1) For a price of $25, the maximum amount producers are willing to supply is 500 units, or (2) the minimum price producers will accept to produce 500 units is $25.
9. *a.* $Q_s = -30 + 20P_x$
   b. $Q_s' = -40 + 20P_x$. The graph is shown here as a dotted line.
   c. Since the coefficient on P_r is negative (−32), an increase in the price of the related good results in a reduction in the quantity supplied, all other things held constant. Therefore the related good is a substitute in production.

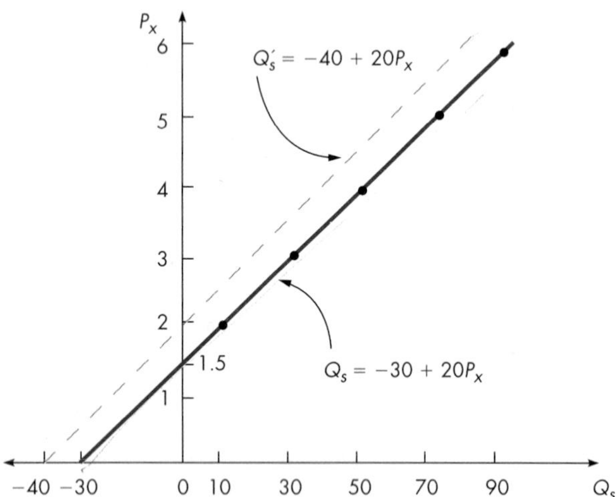

   d. The coefficients on each of the variables in the supply relation are interpreted as follows:
   P_x: A $1 increase in price results in 20 more units being supplied, *all other things remaining constant.*
   P_I: A $1 increase in the price of labor results in 10 fewer units being supplied, *all other things remaining constant.*
   T: A 1-unit increase in the technology index results in 6 more units being produced, *all other things remaining constant.*
   P_r: A $1 increase in the price of related good R results in 32 fewer units being produced, *all other things remaining constant.*
   P_e: A $1 increase in the expected future price of X: results in 20 fewer units of X being produced in the current period, *all other things remaining constant.*
   F: The addition of one more firm results in 5 more units being produced, *all other things remaining constant.*

10. Whenever the price of a good (P) changes, *quantity supplied* (Q_s) changes in the same direction. This results in a movement along a given supply curve. A change in quantity supplied due to a change in P is shown in the figure by a movement from A to B. When any one of the five supply-shifting variables changes value, the supply curve shifts either leftward or rightward. The five supply-shifting variables that cause supply to shift are (1) technology (T), (2) input prices, (P_I), (3) price of goods related in production (P_r), (4) price expectations (P_e), and (5) the number of firms producing the good (F). A *change in supply,* which can be caused only by a change in one of these five variables, is shown in the figure by the shift in S to S' or to S''.

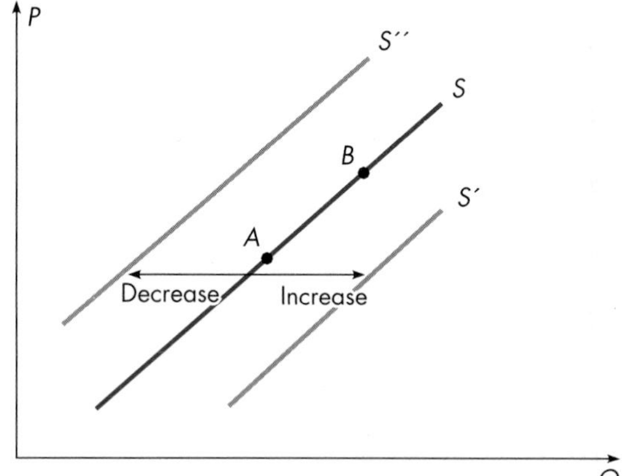

11. *a.* Supply is unchanged (quantity supplied decreases).
   b. Supply increases.
   c. Supply decreases.
   d. Supply increases.
   e. Supply decreases in the current period as managers hold back some current output for sale at the higher price expected in the future period.
12. *a.* supply; 15,000; fall
   b. demand; 78,000; rise
   c. $550
   d. 60,000
13. *a.* At equilibrium, $Q_d = Q_s$. So $50 - 8P = -17.5 + 6P$, and $P_E = \$3.75$ and $Q_E = 20$.
   b. When $P = \$2.75$, $Q_d = 50 - 8(2.75) = 28$ and $Q_s = -17.5 + 10(2.75) = 10$; there is a shortage of 18 units. Due to the excess demand,

consumers will bid up the price, decreasing quantity demanded and increasing quantity supplied. Consumers will bid up price until it reaches \$3.75, the price at which quantity demanded equals quantity supplied.

c. When $P = \$4.25$, $Q_d = 16$ and $Q_s = 25$; there is a surplus of 9 units. Producers will lower price in order to avoid accumulating unwanted inventories. The price will fall (reducing the excess supply) until equilibrium is attained at a price of \$3.75.

d. At equilibrium, $59 - 8P = -17.5 + 10P$; thus $P_E = \$4.25$ and $Q_E = 25$.

e. At equilibrium, $50 - 8P = -40 + 10P$; thus $P_E = \$5$ and $Q_E = 10$.

14. *a.* The increase in demand results in an increase in both P_E and Q_E.
   b. The increase in demand results in an increase in both P_E and Q_E.
   c. The decrease in supply results in an increase in P_E and a decrease in Q_E.
   d. The decrease in demand results in a decrease in both P_E and Q_E.
   e. The decrease in supply results in an increase in P_E and a decrease Q_E.
   f. The increase in demand results in an increase in both P_E and Q_E.
   g. The decrease in demand results in a decrease in both P_E and Q_E.
   h. The increase in supply results in a decrease in P_E and an increase Q_E.

15. *a.* By itself, event *a* would cause an increase in P_E and an increase in Q_E. By itself, event *h* would cause a decrease in P_E and an increase in Q_E. Since both events occur simultaneously, only Q_E is "pushed" in the same direction by both events. Therefore, Q_E is predicted to rise, but P_E is indeterminate because the two events "push" in opposite directions. This is the situation presented in Panel A of Figure 2.9.
   b. By itself, event *d* would cause a decrease in P_E and a decrease in Q_E. By itself, event *e* would cause an increase in P_E and a decrease in Q_E. Since both events occur simultaneously, only Q_E is "pushed" in the same direction by both events. Therefore, Q_E is predicted to fall, but P_E is indeterminate because the two events "push" in opposite directions. This is the situation presented in Panel D of Figure 2.9.
   c. P_E falls and Q_E is indeterminate. See Panel B of Figure 2.9.
   d. P_E rises and Q_E is indeterminate. See Panel C of Figure 2.9.

16. *a.* Good X is normal because when income (M) increases, *all other variables held constant,* quantity demanded (Q_d) increases (the coefficient on M is positive).
   b. Goods X and R are substitutes because when the price of the related good (P_R) increases, *all other variables constant,* quantity demanded (Q_d) increases (the coefficient on P_R is positive).
   c. $Q_d = 60 - 2P + 0.01(40{,}000) + 7(20) = 600 - 2P$
   d. $600 - 2P = -600 + 10P \Rightarrow P_E = \$100$ and $Q_E =$ 400 units
   e. Now $Q_d = 60 - 2P + 0.01(52{,}000) + 7(20) = 720 - 2P$. $P_E = \$110$ and $Q_E = 500$ units.
   f. Now $Q_d = 60 - 2P + 0.01(40{,}000) + 7(14) = 558 - 2P$. $P_E = \$96.50$ and $Q_E = 365$ units.
   g. At equilibrium, $600 - 2P = -360 + 10P$, and thus $P_E = \$80$ and $Q_E = 440$ units.

17. *a.* shortage; 59,000
   b. 19,000 = 60,000 − 41,000
   c. surplus; 15,000

18. *a.* $P_E = \$60$ and $Q_E = 400$ units.
   b. A shortage of 400 (= 600 − 200) units occurs.
   c. A price floor of \$50 has no effect on market price and output since market price (\$60) exceeds \$50. A floor price of \$70 results in a surplus of 200 (= 500 − 300) units.
   d. $P_E = \$65$ and $Q_E = 450$ units.
   e. $P_E = \$55$ and $Q_E = 550$ units.

Chapter 3

1. *a.* $E = -8\%/10\% = -0.8$
   b. inelastic (since $|-0.8| = 0.8 < 1$)
   c. less than (When $|E| < 1$, the numerator of E is less than the denominator.)

2. *a.* increase; 9 ($+30\%/\%\Delta P = -1.5 \Rightarrow \%\Delta P = 9\%$)
   b. reduced; 20 ($\%\Delta Q/6\% = -1.5 \Rightarrow \%\Delta Q = 20\%$)

3. *a.* quantity; price
   b. price; quantity
   c. neither
   d. same; dominant

4. *a.* decrease; fall
   b. increase; fall
   c. decrease; stays the same
   d. inelastic

e. unitary elastic
f. inelastic

5. To verify $E = -1$, just show $TR_f = TR_g$. $13 × 1,100 = $14,300 = $11 × 1,300

6. a. Coca-Cola. More substitutes are available for one brand than for the product group as a whole.
   b. business suits. Suits account for a larger share of a clothes shopper's budget than socks.
   c. Long-run demand for electricity is more elastic than short-run demand because homeowners and businesses can replace appliances and improve insulation given a longer period of time to adjust to a price increase.

7. a. $E = (\Delta Q/Q_{\text{midpoint}}) \div (\Delta P/P_{\text{midpoint}}) = (-400/1{,}600) \div (2/4) = -0.25 \div 0.50 = -0.5$
   b. $E = (\Delta Q/Q_{\text{midpoint}}) \div (\Delta P/P_{\text{midpoint}}) = (-200/300) \div (1/10.5) = -0.6667 \div 0.0952 = -7$
   c. $E = (\Delta Q/Q_{\text{midpoint}}) \div (\Delta P/P_{\text{midpoint}}) = (-400/1{,}200) \div (2/6) = -0.33 \div 0.33 = -1$

8. a. $E = P/(P - a) = 800/(800 - 1{,}000) = 800/-200 = -4$
   b. $E = 200/(200 - 1{,}000) = 200/-800 = -1/4 = -0.25$
   c. Demand will be unit elastic at a price of $500 since $E = 500/(500 - 1{,}000) = -1$.
   d. gets larger

9. a. $20
   b. $20
   c. $20
   d. −1. This is a special case where demand has a constant elasticity, $Q = aP^b$, where $a = 20$ and $b = -1$. Since TR is constant at all prices, demand is unitary elastic.

10. a. $E = (\Delta Q/Q_{\text{midpoint}}) \div (\Delta M/M_{\text{midpoint}}) = (-100/250) \div (4{,}000/32{,}000) = -0.40 \div 0.125 = -3.20$; inferior
    b. $E = (\Delta Q/Q_{\text{midpoint}}) \div (\Delta P_y/P_{y\text{ midpoint}}) = (270/375) \div (8/64) = 0.72 \div 0.125 = 5.76$; substitutes

11.

Price	Quantity demanded	Total revenue	Marginal revenue	Elasticity of demand	$MR = P(1 + 1/E)$*
$60	8	480	–	–	
50	16	800	40	−3.67	40 = 55(1 + 1/−3.67)
40	24	960	20	−1.80	20 = 45(1 + 1/−1.80)
30	32	960	0	−1.00	0 = 35(1 + 1/−1.00)
20	40	800	−20	−0.56	−20 = 25(1 + 1/−0.56)
10	48	480	−40	−0.27	−40 = 15(1 + 1/−0.27)

*The last column verifies the relation among MR, P, and E. Note that average P must be used.

12. a. At $P = \$0.20$, $E = 0.20/(0.20 - 0.8) = -0.33$. At $P = \$1$, $E = 1/(1 - 2) = -1$.
    b. For a small price increase at point A, TR is unchanged since demand is unitary elastic; $MR = 0$.
    c. For a small price decrease at point B, TR falls since demand is inelastic; $MR < 0$.

13. $Q_d = 2{,}400 - 200P$; $MR = 12 - 0.01Q$; $E = -1$ at $P = \$6$; $MR = 0$ at $Q_d = 1{,}200$ units.

Chapter 4

1. a. Constrained maximization subject to the cost constraint of the grant. The choice variables are the types of PCs. The objective is probably to maximize staff productivity.
   b. An unconstrained maximization problem with the objective of getting the most profit from advertising. The choice variables are the amounts to spend on each of the media.
   c. A constrained minimization problem with the objective of the lowest production cost subject to making the quota. The constraint is the quota. The choice variables are the levels of the three inputs.
   d. A constrained maximization problem. The objective is to get the maximum pleasure possible from the vacation within the budget of $2,000. The constraint is the budget. The choices are where to go and how long to stay.
   e. An unconstrained maximization problem. The objective is to obtain the highest net benefits, which are the value of sales of the new salesperson minus the cost of the interviewing process. The choice variable is how long to carry out the interview process or how many to interview.

2. a. marginal benefit, marginal cost
   b. marginal cost, marginal benefit
   c. marginal benefit, marginal cost
   d. net benefit

3.

X	TB	TC	NB	MB	MC
0	$ 0	$ 0	$ 0		
1	35	8	27	$35	$ 8
2	65	18	47	30	10
3	85	30	55	20	12
4	95	44	51	10	14
5	103	60	43	8	16
6	108	80	28	5	20

a. increases; $20
b. increases; $12; increases; 8

c. decreases; \$8
d. decreases; \$16; increases; \$8
e. 3; \$55

4. a. \$7; \$2
b. increase; \$5 (= \$7 − \$2)
c. \$4; \$6.50
d. increase; \$2.50
e. 140; \$5; \$5

5. increases; total; increases; total; increasing; increase; equal

6. a. \$47.50; \$42.50; greater; increases; \$5 (= \$47.50 − \$42.50)
b. \$40; \$50; less; increases; \$10 (= \$50 − \$40)
c. 200; \$45; \$45
d. \$9,500; \$8,500; \$1,000

7. "The optimal level of any activity is that level for which *total* benefit exceeds *total* cost by the greatest possible amount."

8. This statement is generally incorrect. At the optimal level of activity further increases in the activity cause total benefit to decrease *only* if MB is negative. Marginal benefit equals marginal cost at the optimal activity level. Since MC cannot be negative, MB cannot be negative at the optimal activity level, and thus total benefit cannot fall as activity increases beyond X^*. It is true (by definition) that net benefit *falls* as X increases beyond the optimal level of activity.

9. This is a two-variable unconstrained maximization problem, which requires

$$MB_A = 20A^* - 10B^* = \$40$$
$$\text{and} \quad MB_B = -6A^* + 30B^* = \$42$$

to be solved simultaneously for A^* and B^*. Using the MB_A equation to solve for A^* in terms of B^*,

$$20A^* = 40 + 10B^*, \quad \text{so } A^* = 2 + (1/2)B^*$$

Using this solution for A^* in the MB_B equation,

$$-6[2 + (1/2)B^*] + 30B^* = \$42$$
$$27B^* = 54, \quad \text{so } B^* = 2$$

Then using this solution for B^* in $A^* = 2 + (1/2)B^*$,

$$A^* = 2 + 1 = 3$$

10. a. Bad reasoning. What has already been paid for the room is a sunk cost and is irrelevant. Should weigh the expected marginal benefits and costs, then make the decision about whether or not to stay.
b. This person should ignore the investment, which is a sunk cost. Should compare expected benefits and costs. If net benefits seem to be higher doing something else, then close the business. If not, remain open.
c. What was paid for the clubs is a sunk cost no matter what is done. It should be ignored.
d. The yearly license fee would be a fixed cost if the business is continued. It should not affect the level of sales. Compare the expected net benefits of continuing with those to be expected in the best alternative.
e. See answer to *d*. Should continue the business if this is the best that can be done.

11. Compare the marginal benefit per dollar for each applicant: For Jane, $MB/P = 600/200 = 3$; for Joe, $MB/P = 450/150 = 3$; for Joan, $MB/P = 400/100 = 4$. Thus Joan ranks first, and Joe and Jane are tied for second.

12. a. greater than
b. less than
c. MB_A/P_A, MB_B/P_B.

13. Always compare MB_A/P_A and MB_B/P_B.
a. $\dfrac{MB_A}{P_A} = \dfrac{400}{20} = 20 < \dfrac{MB_B}{P_B} = \dfrac{600}{15} = 40$
Use more B and less A, keeping expenditure constant.
b. $\dfrac{MB_A}{P_A} = \dfrac{200}{20} = 10 = \dfrac{MB_B}{P_B} = \dfrac{300}{30} = 10$
Make no changes.
c. $\dfrac{MB_A}{P_A} = \dfrac{300}{20} = 15 > \dfrac{MB_B}{P_B} = \dfrac{400}{40} = 10$
A 1-unit reduction in B reduces cost by \$40, which can purchase 2 units of A at \$20. Total benefits will increase by 600 ($= \Delta A \times MB_A = 2 \times 300$) − 400 ($= \Delta B \times MB_B = 1 \times 400$) = 200.
d. In equilibrium $MB_A/P_A = MB_B/P_B$; then $250/20 = 12.5 = MB_B/40$, so MB_B must equal 500.

14. a. 10 + 2(22) + 3(14) = \$96
b. 10; \$20 (= 2 × 10)
c. The combination 1X, 4Y, 3Z is optimal when income is \$18. At this combination $MU_X/P_X = MU_Y/P_Y = MU_Z/P_Z$. The combination 2X, 2Y, 4Z is not optimal because $MU_Y/P_Y > MU_X/P_X = MU_Z/P_Z$. The decision maker should engage in more units of activity Y and fewer units of activities X and Z.

d. When income is \$33, the optimal combination is 5X, 5Y, 6Z. With two more dollars to spend (income = \$35), the decision maker can either increase activity X by 2 units or activity Y by 1 unit. Two more dollars spent on activity X increases benefit by \$9 (= \$5 + \$4), while two more dollars spent on activity Y increases benefit by only \$4. The optimal combination of activities is 7X, 5Y, 6Z.

15. a. The combination 3X, 2Y maximizes total benefit subject to a budget constraint of \$26.
    b. Total benefit of 3X, 2Y is \$262 (= \$72 + \$190).
    c. The combination 4X, 5Y is optimal when the budget constraint is \$58. Total benefit of 4X, 5Y is \$484 (= \$84 + \$400).

16. Compare MB_A/P_A and MB_B/P_B.
    a. $MB_A/P_A = 600/10 = 60 > MB_B/P_B = 300/10 = 30$
    One less B reduces benefits by 300. One-half unit of A adds (1/2)600 = 300. Cost falls by \$10 − \$5 = \$5.
    b. Since $P_A = P_B$, in equilibrium, where $MB_A/P_A = MB_B/P_B$, MB_A must equal MB_B.

Chapter 5

1. a. *W*; *R*
   b. *b*; *a*
   c. *a*
   d. *b*
2. Regression analysis chooses parameter values to fit a line to a particular data set. The best fit results when the parameter values minimize the sum of the squared errors, hence the name "least squares."
3. Tests for statistical significance must follow estimation of parameters because the estimates themselves are random variables that are not likely to be equal to the true value of the parameter. Testing for statistical significance allows a researcher to determine whether or not an estimate is far enough away from zero to conclude that the true value of the parameter is *not* equal to zero.
4. a. Correct; the smaller is $S_{\hat{b}}$, the smaller the dispersion of the parameter estimate around its true value.
   b. Incorrect; when an estimate is unbiased, the parameter estimate tends to equal the true value only *on average*.
   c. Correct; the t-ratio ($= \hat{b}/S_{\hat{b}}$) is indeed larger the smaller the standard error of $\hat{b}$.
5. a. 24
   b. 2.492; 2.064
   c. Yes, 2.492 > 2.064, so the estimate is significant at the 0.05 level.
   d. 0.02 (2.492 is the critical t for a 0.02 significance level); $b = 0$; zero; 95
   e. The hypothesis that $b = 0$ can be rejected with only a 5% chance of being wrong (i.e., making a Type I error).
   f. You can be 95% sure that if b is actually zero, the t-test will not reject the hypothesis that $b = 0$ (i.e., will *not* make a Type I error).
   g. The significance level gives the probability of making a Type I error, while the confidence level gives the probability of *not* making a Type I error. They mean the same thing since knowing one gives the same information as knowing the other.
6. a. $Y = 800 - 2.50X$
   b. The critical t for $n - k = 10 - 2 = 8$ degrees of freedom at the 0.01 level of significance is 3.355. The t-tests are:
   For $\hat{a}$: $t = 4.23 > 3.355$; $\hat{a}$ is statistically significant.
   For $\hat{b}$: $t = -2.94$. Since t is negative, $|t| = |-2.94| < 3.355$; $\hat{b}$ is *not* statistically significant.
   c. For $\hat{a}$ the exact level of significance is 0.0029, which means there is only a 0.29% chance that $a = 0$ with a t-ratio as large as 4.23. For $\hat{b}$ the *exact* significance is 0.0187, which means there is only a 1.87% chance that $b = 0$ with a t-ratio as large as −2.94.
   d. The critical F-statistic with $1(= k - 1)$ and 8 $(= n - k)$ degrees of freedom at the 1% significance level is 11.26. Since the F-statistic 8.747 is less than 11.26, the overall equation is *not* statistically significant at the 1% level of significance. The p-value for the F-statistic, 0.0182, shows that the equation is statistically significant at the 1.8% level.
   e. $\hat{Y} = 800 - 2.5(140) = 450$
   f. $R^2 = 0.5223$, so 52.23% of the total variation in Y is explained by the regression equation.
7. a. $n - k = 25 - 2 = 23$
   b. 2.069
   c. For $\hat{a}$: $t = 2.60 > 2.069$; statistically significant.
   For $\hat{b}$: $t = 2.78 > 2.069$; statistically significant.

d. The exact significance level for $\hat{a}$ is 0.0160, and the exact significance level for $\hat{b}$ is 0.0106. The exact confidence levels are 0.984 (98.4%) and 0.989 (98.9%), respectively. A *t*-test at the 95% confidence level understates the degree of confidence associated with $\hat{a}$ and $\hat{b}$.

e. $R^2 = 0.7482$ tells us that 74.82% of the total variation in Y is explained by the regression equation (i.e., by variation in X); and 25.18% of the variation in Y is unexplained.

f. $k - 1 = 2 - 1 = 1$ and $n - k = 23$, so at a 95% confidence level, the critical value of F is 4.28. The regression equation is statistically significant because the *F*-ratio (68.351) is greater than the critical value of *F*. The *p*-value on the *F*-statistic is less than 0.0001, so there is virtually no chance that the *F*-test is mistakenly indicating significance for the equation as a whole.

g. $325.24 + 0.8057(100) = 405.81$
$325.24 + 0.8057(0) = 325.24$

8. *a.* In a multiple regression model, the coefficients on the explanatory variables do *not* measure the percent of the total variation in Y explained by that explanatory variable. The coefficients measure the rate of change in Y as that explanatory variable changes, all *other* explanatory variables remaining constant.

b. This statement is correct because critical *t*-values get smaller as the number of degrees of freedom increases. See the *t*-table at the end of the textbook to verify this.

c. This statement is correct because R^2 equals 1.0 when $Y = \hat{Y}$ for all observations.

9. *a.* $n - k = 34 - 4 = 30$

b. 2.457

c. For $\hat{a}$: $t = 1.51 < 2.457$; *not* statistically significant at 2% level; exact significance = 14.13%.
For $\hat{b}$: $t = 6.09 > 2.457$; statistically significant at 2% level; exact significance < 0.01%.
For $\hat{c}$: $|t| = |-2.48| < 2.457$; statistically significant at 2% level; exact significance = 1.88%.
For $\hat{d}$: $t = 3.66 > 2.457$; statistically significant at 2% level; exact significance = 0.01%.

d. 31.79% of variation R is explained by the model. 68.21% of the variation is unexplained.

e. The critical F with $k - 1 = 4 - 1 = 3$ and $n - k = 30$ degrees of freedom and a significance level of 1% is 4.51. Since the *F*-ratio = 4.66 > 4.51, the overall regression equation is statistically significant at the 1% level of significance. The exact significance level for the *F*-statistic is 0.865%.

f. $12.6 + 22.0(10) - 4.1(5) + 16.3(30) = 701.1$
$12.6 + 22.0(0) - 4.1(0) + 16.3(0) = 12.6$

10. *a.* Take logarithms: $\ln Y = \ln a + b \ln R + c \ln S$.

b. The critical t for 60(= 63 − 3) degrees of freedom and a 5% level of significance is 2.000.
For $\ln \hat{a}$: $t = |-1.67| < 2.000$; *not* statistically significant; exact significance = 10%.
For $\hat{b}$: $t = 2.58 > 2.000$; statistically significant; exact significance = 1.23%.
For $\hat{c}$: $t = 3.06 > 2.000$; statistically significant; exact significance = 0.33%.

c. The critical F for $k - 1 = 2$ and $n - k = 60$ degrees of freedom and a 5% level of significance is 3.15. The *F*-ratio of 132.22 is greater than 3.15, so the overall equation is statistically significant at the 5% level. Since the *p*-value is less than 0.01%, the equation as a whole is extremely significant.

d. The model fits the data well, as 81.5% of the total variation in $\ln Y$ is explained by the model. Only 18.5% of the variation is not explained by the model.

e. Since $\ln a$ is estimated to be -1.386, $\hat{a}$ is equal to $e^{\hat{a}} = e^{-1.386} = 0.25$.

f. $\hat{Y} = 0.25(200)^{0.452}(1{,}500)^{0.30} = 24.6$ units per day

g. Estimated elasticity of $R = \%\Delta Y/\%\Delta R = \hat{b} = 0.452$
Estimated elasticity of $S = \%\Delta Y/\%\Delta S = \hat{c} = 0.30$

Chapter 6

1. *a.* Prefers Classic Coke to regular Pepsi.

b. Cannot say because the Ferrari obviously costs more. He might prefer the Ferrari but isn't willing or able to pay the higher price.

c. She clearly prefers the Ferrari because she is willing to pay the higher price.

d. Cannot say for sure. Can say, however, that James' and Jane's preferences are either (1) indifference between brands of colas—so they might flip a coin to choose a drink, or (2) they prefer the cola they chose.

2. a. Utility will be unchanged if the consumer exchanges 3 units of Y for 1 unit of X ($\Delta Y/\Delta X = -6/2 = -3$).
   b. Utility will be unchanged if the consumer exchanges 1/3 unit of X for 1 unit of Y ($\Delta X/\Delta Y = -1/3$).
   c. $MRS = -\Delta Y/\Delta X = 3$.
3. a. $MRS = -\Delta Y/\Delta X = -(-200/200) = 1$
   b. $MRS = -\Delta Y/\Delta X = -(-200/300) = 2/3$
   c. Extend tangent T to the two axes to obtain $MRS = -(-900/1{,}100) = 9/11 = 0.82$.
4. a. $\text{MRS} = -\Delta y/\Delta x = MU_x/MU_y = 2$. If $MU_x = 20$, $MU_y = 10$ since $20/10 = 2$.
   b. $MU_x/MU_y = 3$. If $MU_y = 3$, $MU_x = 9$ since $9/3 = 3$.
   c. As more X is added, MU_x decreases; as Y is reduced, MU_Y increases, so MRS decreases.
5. a. $Y = 10 - 1X$
   b. $Y = 10 - 2.5X$
   c. $Y = 5 - 0.5X$
   d. $Y = 4 - 0.5X$
   e. Given the vertical and horizontal intercepts of budget line LR, it follows that $P_y \times 10 = \$200$ and $P_x \times 4 = \$200$. Thus $P_y = \$20$ and $P_x = \$50$. For budget line LZ, if income is \$200, then $P_y \times 10 = \$200$ and $P_x \times 10 = \$200$ which means $P_y = \$20$ and $P_x = \$20$.
   f. Given the vertical and horizontal intercepts of budget line MN, it follows that income along MN can be calculated by either $4 \times P_y$ or $8 \times P_x$. Given $P_y = \$40$ and $P_x = \$20$, income can be calculated in either of two equivalent ways: $M = 4 \times \$40 = \$160$ or $M = 8 \times \$20 = \$160$. Similarly, for budget line KZ, $M = 5 \times P_y$ or $10 \times P_x$. Given $P_y = \$40$ and $P_x = \$20$, then income along KZ can be found either as $M = 5 \times \$40 = \$200$ or $M = 10 \times \$20 = \$200$.
6. a. $50 \times \$10 = \$500$
   b. $40 \times P_x = \$500$, thus $P_x = \$12.50$.
   c. For LZ: $12.50X + 10Y = 500$, or $Y = 50 - 1.25X$.
   d. The consumer will chose 20 units of X and 25 units of Y, where indifference curve II is tangent to budget line LZ. No other combination costing \$500 provides more utility than 20x, 25y.
   e. At the optimal choice, $MRS = P_X/P_Y = \$12.50/\$10 = 1.25$.
   f. At combination A: By the definition of MRS, the consumer can give up 1 unit of X in return for MRS more units of Y and the consumer's utility will not change. With market prices P_x and P_y, the consumer can buy P_x/P_y (= 1.25) more units of Y if 1 less unit of X is purchased and remain on the budget line. Visual inspection of the slopes of the indifference curve and budget line at point A shows that $P_x/P_y > MRS$ at combination A. The consumer can buy P_x/P_y more Y if 1 fewer unit of X is purchased, which is *more* Y than would be needed to remain indifferent. Therefore, giving up 1 unit of X to get MRS more units of Y must increase utility, and combination A would not be chosen by the consumer. At combination B: The consumer could trade (give up) MRS units of Y to get 1 more unit of X and the consumer's utility would be unchanged. The consumer must give up P_x/P_y units of Y to get 1 more unit of X and remain on the budget line. By visual inspection of slopes, $MRS > P_x/P_y$ at combination B. Thus, the consumer can buy 1 more X and give up only P_x/P_y units of Y, which is *less* than the loss of Y that would leave utility unchanged (i.e., MRS units of Y). Since the consumer gives up less Y than the amount that would leave the consumer indifferent, trading P_x/P_y units of Y for 1 more X must increase utility, and combination B would not be chosen by the consumer.
   g. $80 \times P_x = \$500$, thus $P_x = \$6.25$. The consumer will now choose 30 units of Y and 32 units of X ($\$10 \times 30 + \$6.25 \times 32 = \$500$), where indifference curve III is tangent to budget line LM.
   h. $MRS = P_x/P_y = \$6.25/\$10 = 0.625$.
7. a. $MRS = -\Delta Y/\Delta X = 2$. Utility will be unchanged if the consumer gives up 2 units of Y for 1 unit of X.
   b. Utility will be unchanged if the consumer gives up 1/2 unit of X for 1 unit of Y ($-\Delta X/\Delta Y = 1/2$).
   c. MRS = 2
   d. Market rate of exchange $= P_x/P_y = \$3/\$1 = 3$.
   e. No, the consumer is not making the utility-maximizing choice. At the current choice, $MRS = MU_x/MU_y < P_x/P_y$, so $MU_x/P_x < MU_y/P_y$. By spending one more dollar on Y and one less dollar on X, total expenditures will be unchanged, and utility will increase by ($MU_y/P_y - MU_x/P_x$). The consumer can increase utility by continuing to purchase more Y and less X (thus decreasing MU_y and increasing MU_x) until

the marginal utility per dollar is equal for the two goods, and the consumer obtains the maximum possible utility given a limited income.

8. *a.* $30 \times \$20 = \$600$.
   b. $P_y = \$20$.
   c. For *LZ*: $20X + 20Y = 600$, or $Y = 30 - X$.
   d. The consumer chooses 10*X* and 20*Y*. This combination lies on the highest indifference curve that can be attained given the budget line *LZ*.
   e. $MRS = 1 = P_x/P_y = \$20/\$20$
   f. At point *A*, $MRS > 1$. The consumer is willing to give up *more* than 1 unit of *Y* for 1 more unit of *X* and remain indifferent. The consumer can obtain 1 more unit of *X* in the marketplace by giving up exactly 1 unit of *Y*. Since the consumer gives up fewer units of *Y* than necessary to remain indifferent, the consumer must be better off when trading 1 *Y* for 1 more *X* at point *A*. At point *B*, $MRS < 1$. The consumer is willing to give up 1 unit of *X* in return for *less* than 1 unit more of *Y* and remain indifferent. In the market, the consumer can purchase exactly 1 more *Y* by giving up 1 *X*. By giving up 1 *X*, the consumer gets more *Y* than the amount necessary to leave him or her just indifferent, so the consumer must be better off at point *B* when giving up *X* for more *Y*.
   g. 15*X*, 10*Y*
   h. $P_y = \$30$
   i. $P_x = \$20$
   j. $MRS = 2/3 = P_x/P_y = \$20/\$30$
9. Since $MU_p/P_p < MU_s/P_s$, she should buy more salad and less pasta. The marginal utility per dollar is higher for salad.
10. *a.* 8*X*, 9*Y*, 6*Z*
    b. 5*X*, 6*Y*, 4*Z*
    c. 0*X*, 6*Y*, 4*Z*. Since the price of *X* is \$5 and income is \$38, the consumer can indeed *afford* to buy *X*. The consumer chooses not to purchase *X* because MU_x/P_x is so small relative to MU_y/P_y and MU_z/P_z that zero consumption of *X* maximizes utility subject to the budget constraint.
11. $P_y = \$4$, since $\$4 \times 250 = \$1{,}000$. Three price-quality combinations are $P_x = \$5$, $Q_x = 125$; $P_x = \$4$, $Q_x = 175$; $P_x = \$2.50$, $Q_x = 250$.
12. *a.* Yes, all income is spent and the marginal utility per dollar is the same for both goods.
    b. Purchasing power increases. He can buy the same combination of goods and have money left over. If both goods are normal, he will probably buy more of each.
    c. $MU_x/P_x = 30/\$15 = 2 > MU_y/P_y = 15/\$10 = 1.5$. He will trade some *Y* for some more *X*.
    d. In equilibrium, $P_x/P_y = \$15/\$10 = 1.5 = MRS = MU_x/MU_y$.
13. *a.* 300
    b. 125
    c. \$1,250
    d. −175 units of X; −75 units of X; −100 units of X
    e. normal
14. *a.* 50 units of *X*
    b. 80 units of *X*
    c. $80 \times \$25 = \$2{,}000$
    d. Total effect = +30 units of *X*
    Substitution effect = +40 units of *X*
    Income effect = −10 units of *X*
15. *a, b, c:* see figure below.

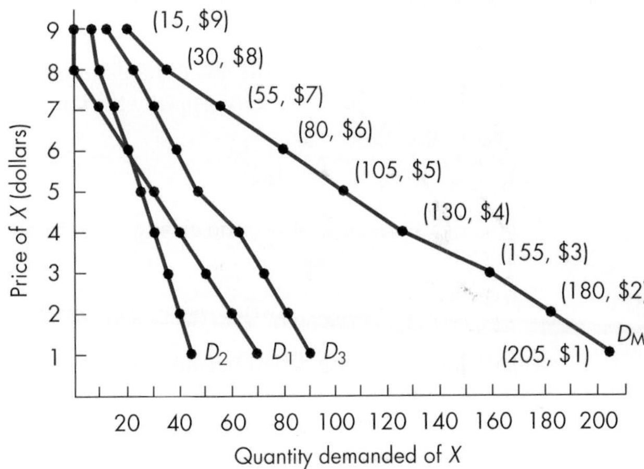

16. *a.* 8 hours, since $MB_{search} = 0$ for 8 hours or more of search.
    b. MC_{search} is a horizontal line at \$15.
    c. 5 hours; $MB_{search} = MC_{search}$
    d. 7 hours

Chapter 7

1. First, the sample may not be random. For example, a political opinion poll that interviews only in a predominantly Republican area will yield biased results. A second potential problem is response

bias. In a survey to see if people would buy handmade items from a charitable organization, for instance, some of those interviewed might answer "yes" even if they would not purchase such items. Finally, consumers may be unable to respond accurately. Most people, for example, don't know beforehand how their purchases of a particular good would change if the price increased by 5%.

2. *a.* X is an inferior good. A negative parameter estimate for income (−0.6) means the quantity of X demanded decreases (increases) when income increases (decreases).
   b. X and Z are substitutes. A positive parameter estimate for the price of $Z(4)$ means that the quantity of X demanded increases (decreases) when the price of Z increases (decreases).
   c. $\hat{Q} = 70 - 3.5(10) - 0.6(30) + 4(6) = 41.0$
   $\hat{E} = \hat{b}(P/Q) = -3.5(10/41) = -0.85$
   $\hat{E}_M = \hat{c}(M/Q) = -0.6(30/41) = -0.44$
   $\hat{E}_{XZ} = \hat{d}(P_z/Q) = 4(6/41) = 0.59$
3. *a.* X is a normal good since the estimated coefficient on ln M, the income elasticity, is positive (0.8).
   b. X and Y are complements since the estimated coefficient on ln P_y, the cross-price elasticity, is negative (−2.5).
   c. $\hat{Q} = 125{,}755P^{-1.65}M^{0.8}P_y^{-2.5}$ (*Note:* $125{,}755 = e^{11.74209}$.)
   d. For all values of P, M, P_y, the elasticity estimates are constant and equal to $\hat{E} = -1.65$; $\hat{E}_M = 0.8$; $\hat{E}_{XY} = -2.5$. Estimated Q: $\hat{Q} = 125{,}755(50)^{-1.65}(36{,}000)^{0.8}(25)^{-2.5} = 279.52$.
4. *a.* Demand is not identified because supply does not contain any exogenous variables.
   b. The supply equation contains no exogenous variables excluded from the demand equation, so the demand function is not identified.
   c. The demand function is not identified because the exogenous variable in supply is also an explanatory variable in the demand equation.
   d. Demand is identified because supply contains at least one (two in this case) exogenous variable that is not an explanatory variable in demand.
5. If a demand equation is not identified, there is no estimation technique (2SLS or otherwise) capable of estimating the parameters of the demand equation. 2SLS can be used only when the demand equation is identified.
6. Using OLS to estimate industry demand for price-taking firms when price is an endogenous variable results in a simultaneous equations bias for each of the estimated parameters of the demand equation. The most obvious problem with the OLS estimation results is the parameter estimate for copper price. The OLS estimate (−12.517) is much smaller in absolute value than the 2SLS estimate. Further, price does not appear to have a statistically significant effect on the quantity demanded of copper (p-value = 0.3936).
7. *a.* The quantity of copper demanded will decrease 2.96% if the price of copper increases 10%. [$\hat{E} = -0.296 = \%\Delta QC/10\% \Rightarrow \%\Delta QC = (-0.296)(10\%) = -2.96\%$]
   b. The quantity of copper demanded will decrease 9.165% if income decreases 5%. [$\hat{E}_M = 1.833 = \%\Delta QC/-5\% \Rightarrow \%\Delta QC = (1.833)(-5\%) = -9.165\%$]
   c. The quantity of copper demanded will increase 1.776% if the price of copper decreases 6%. [$\hat{E} = -0.296 = \%\Delta QC/-6\% \Rightarrow \%\Delta QC = (-0.296)(-6\%) = +1.776\%$]
   d. The quantity of copper demanded will decrease 3.0% if the price of aluminum decreases 10%. [$\hat{E}_{CA} = 0.30 = \%\Delta QC/-10\% \Rightarrow \%\Delta QC = (0.30)(-10\%) = -3.0\%$]
8. *a.* The theory of demand predicts that price and quantity demanded will be inversely related and that income and quantity demanded will be directly related for a normal good. The estimates of b and c thus are consistent with economic theory and imply that X is a normal good.
   b. A negative coefficient of the price of related good R means that the price of R and the quantity of X demanded are inversely related. In other words, X and R are complements.
   c. The p-values show all parameter estimates are significant at the 5% level, or better.
   d. $\hat{Q} = 68.38 - 6.50(225) + 0.13926(24{,}000) - 10.77(60) = 1{,}302$
   (1) $\hat{E} = \hat{b}(P/Q) = -6.50(225/1{,}302) = -1.12$
   (2) $\hat{E}_M = \hat{c}(M/Q) = (0.13926)(24{,}000/1{,}302) = 2.57$
   (3) $\hat{E}_{XR} = \hat{d}(P_R/Q) = (-10.77)(60/1{,}302) = -0.50$
9. *a.* $\ln Q = 6.77 - 1.68 \ln P - 0.82 \ln M + 1.35 \ln P_R$
   b. Yes, the sign of $\hat{b}$ is negative, indicating demand is downward-sloping.

c. Since the sign of $\hat{c}$ is negative, X is an inferior good. Goods X and R are substitutes since $\hat{d}$ is positive.
d. The p-values show that $\hat{b}$ and $\hat{c}$ are significant at the 5% level, while $\hat{a}$ and $\hat{d}$ are significant at the 10% level.
e. (1) $E = -1.68$; (2) $\hat{E}_{XY} = 1.35$; (3) $\hat{E}_M = -0.82$
f. increase; 8.2%
g. decrease; 16.8%
h. decrease; 6.75% (= 5% × 1.35)

Chapter 8

1. Forecasters using qualitative methods first collect data and get advice from other people. They then assign subjective weights to the available information to obtain a forecast. Statistical forecasting methods, on the other hand, employ explicit models that can be replicated. Other advantages of this method include standard methods of model evaluation and the ability to use the models in simulation techniques.
2. a. *$\hat{a}$: p*-value is 0.0498, so $\hat{a}$ is just barely significant at the 5% level of significance or the 95% level of confidence.
   $\hat{b}$: p-value is 0.0030, so $\hat{b}$ is highly significant. It is significant at the 0.3% level of significance or the 99.7% level of confidence. Conclusion: Sales exhibit a statistically significant positive trend over time (i.e., $\hat{b} > 0$ and p-value is very small). The model as a whole, as indicated by the extremely small p-value on the F-statistic, explains a statistically significant amount of the variation in sales.
   b. $Q_{2000} = 73.71460 + 3.7621(2{,}000) = 7{,}598$
   $Q_{2001} = 73.7146 + 3.7621(2{,}001) = 7{,}602$
   (*Note:* the "year 2000" problem is handled in trend analysis by using all four digits in the year when estimating the parameter values.)
   c. The farther the values of the variables in the forecast are from the mean values of the regression, the less precise the forecast will be. Thus the forecast for 2001 will be less precise than the forecast for 2000.
3. a. For a 99% confidence level with 31 (36 − 5) degrees of freedom, the critical value of t is about 2.750.
   For $\hat{a}$: $t = 7.16 > 2.744$; statistically significant at the 1% level.
   For $\hat{b}$: $t = 5.97 > 2.744$; statistically significant at the 1% level.
   For $\hat{c}_1$: $|t| = |-4.31| > 2.744$; statistically significant at the 1% level.
   For $\hat{c}_2$: $|t| = |-1.70| < 2.744$; *not* statistically significant at the 1% level.
   For $\hat{c}_3$: $|t| = |-8.22| > 2.744$; statistically significant at the 1% level.
   For a 99% confidence level (a 1% significance level) with 4 (= 5 − 1) and 31 (= 36 − 5) degrees of freedom, the critical value of F is (approximately) 4.02. The regression equation is statistically significant because the F-ratio (761.133) is greater than the critical value of F.
   In terms of p-values, all individual estimated coefficients except $\hat{c}_2$ are significant at much less than the 1% level of significance (or, equivalently, at much greater than the 99% level of confidence). While a t-test did not find significance for $\hat{c}_2$ at the 1% level, its p-value reveals an exact level of significance for $\hat{c}_2$ of 9.85%, suggesting slightly less than a 10% chance that there is no seasonal effect in the second quarter. The p-value for F shows the equation to be highly significant.
   b. The intercepts are 51.234 − 11.716 = 39.518 for the first quarter, 51.234 − 1.424 = 49.81 for the second quarter, 51.234 − 17.367 = 33.867 for the third quarter, and 51.234 for the fourth quarter. These intercept values imply that, after accounting for trend, sales in the first quarter, second quarter, and third quarter are lower than in the fourth quarter.
   c.
   $$Q_{1999(I)} = 51.234 + (3.127)(37) - 11.716 = 155.217$$
   $$Q_{1999(II)} = 51.234 + (3.127)(38) - 1.424 = 168.636$$
   $$Q_{1999(III)} = 51.234 + (3.127)(39) - 17.367 = 155.820$$
   $$Q_{1999(IV)} = 51.234 + (3.127)(40) = 176.314$$
4. a. Economic theory predicts that price and quantity demanded will be inversely related, income and quantity demanded will be positively related for a normal good, and the price of a complement and quantity demanded will be inversely related. The signs of the coefficients in the demand equation thus are consistent with economic theory and imply that X is a normal good and that X and R are complements. The signs of the coefficients in the supply equation are also consistent with economic theory because price and quantity

supplied are positively related, while input prices and quantity supplied are inversely related.

b. Demand Q2001(I) = 500 − 300*P* + 1(10,000) − 200(20) = 6,500 − 300*P*
Supply Q2001(I) = −400 + 200*P* − 100(6) = −1,000 + 200*P*
In equilibrium, 6,500 − 300*P* = −1,000 + 200*P* ⇒ *P* = \$15 ⇒ *Q* = 2,000.

c. For *M* = \$9,000:
Q2001(I) = 500 − 300*P* + 1(9,000) − 200(20) = 5,500 − 300*P*
In equilibrium, 5,500 − 300*P* = −1,000 + 200*P* ⇒ *P* = \$13 and *Q* = 1,600.
For *M* = \$12,000:
Q2001(I) = 500 − 300*P* + 1(12,000) − 200(20) = 8,500 − 300*P*
In equilibrium, 8,500 − 300*P* = −1,000 + 200*P* ⇒ *P* = \$19 and *Q* = 2,800.
Thus, increasing projected income in 2001(I) from \$9,000 to \$12,000 causes forecasted price to rise by \$6 (from \$13 to \$19) and forecasted sales to rise by 1,200 units (from 1,600 to 2,800).

5. The major shortcoming of time-series models is that they do not use a structural model that explains the economic determinants of a forecast. Instead, they assume that the future behavior of an economic variable can be predicted solely on the basis of past behavior.

6. First, the further in the future, the less reliable the forecast; parameter estimates become more uncertain as the variable values move further away from the regression mean values. For example, a researcher can provide a more reliable forecast of pencil sales in 2000 than in 2050. (After all, some people claim that personal computers eventually will make paper and pencil obsolete.) Incorrect specification is another potential problem because the exclusion of important explanatory variables or the choice of an inappropriate functional form will result in biased estimates and incorrect forecasts. A forecast of rail freight, for instance, would be misspecified if it omitted the prices of alternative means of transportation, such as air, truck, and barge freight. Finally, structural changes will undermine a forecast's accuracy. Unforeseen events can alter the underlying assumptions of a forecast and thus invalidate predictions based on the model. Suppose, for example, a consultant predicted that tourist expenditures in Key West would be \$100 million in 2000. A hurricane that devastated Key West in 1999 would make the forecast useless.

Chapter 9

1. This statement is not true in general. All technically efficient input combinations are not economically efficient. It is true, however, that all economically efficient input combinations are technically efficient.

2. *a.* Yes, both processes can be technically efficient. With variable proportions production, many different technically efficient input combinations can be employed to produce 1,000 units daily.
   b. Process 1, since the total cost of using process 1 (\$4,000) is less than the total cost of process 2 (\$4,100).
   c. Process 2, since the total cost of using process 2 (\$3,875) is less than the total cost of process 1 (\$4,000).

3. A manager's "plans" often involve changes in future levels of inputs that are, for now, fixed. In this sense, a manager's "plans" involve long-run production decisions. The day-to-day operation of the firm requires that the manager make production decisions without being able to change the usage of certain fixed inputs. In this sense, "operation" decisions are short-run production decisions.

4. *a.* Short-run decision. The drilling supervisor has just one rig (a fixed input) but plans to use more variable input (rig hands) to increase output (number of feet drilled per day).
   b. Long-run decision. Increasing the number of drill platforms involves changing the level of usage of an input that is fixed in the short-run period.
   c. Short-run decision. Production operation decisions are generally made with the understanding that at least some inputs cannot be changed during the production period.
   d. Long-run decision. Adding a new wing to a hospital represents a long-run increase in an input that is fixed in size in the short run.

5. Your table should look like this:

Labor	TP	AP	MP
0	0	—	—
1	40	40	40
2	88	44	48
3	138	46	50
4	176	44	38
5	200	40	24
6	210	35	10
7	203	29	−7
8	176	22	−27

6. The combination of 10*L* and 2*K* is not economically efficient because 314 units of output can be produced with just 8 units of labor (and 2*K*), which would represent a lower total cost of producing 314 units.

7. *a.* When capital is held constant at 2 units:

L	Q	AP	MP
1	120	120	120
2	260	130	140
3	360	120	100
4	430	107.5	70
5	480	96	50

When marginal product is greater than average product, average product is increasing. When marginal product is less than average product, average product is decreasing.

b.

	Marginal product of labor			
L	K = 1	K = 2	K = 3	K = 4
1	50	120	160	180
2	60	140	200	210
3	40	100	150	170
4	20	70	120	130
5	−10	50	80	100

As the capital stock increases for each level of labor usage, the marginal product of labor increases. The additional unit of labor is more productive because it has more capital with which to work.

8. *a.* Explicit costs = \$1,000 + \$500 + \$750 + \$400 = \$2,650; implicit costs = \$1,000

b. \$1,000 (Normal profit is simply the implicit cost of owner-supplied resources.)

9.

Q	TC	TFC	TVC	AFC	AVC	ATC	MC
100	260	200	60	2.00	0.60	2.60	0.60
200	290	200	90	1.00	0.45	1.45	0.30
300	350	200	150	0.67	0.50	1.17	0.60
400	420	200	220	0.50	0.55	1.05	0.70
500	560	200	360	0.40	0.72	1.12	1.40
600	860	200	660	0.33	1.10	1.43	3.00
700	1,320	200	1,120	0.29	1.60	1.89	4.60
800	2,040	200	1,840	0.25	2.30	2.55	7.20

10. If *AVC* is constant over a range of output, then *MC* is also constant and equal to *AVC*. *ATC*, however, would be decreasing over this range of output, since $ATC = AVC + AFC$, and *AFC* declines as output increases.

11. *a.* $MC = w/MP = \$60/12 = \$5$

b. $AVC = w/AP = \$60/30 = \$2$

c. $AP = 30 = Q/L = Q/20$, so $Q = (30)(20) = 600$

d. $AFC = TFC/Q = \$3{,}600/600 = \$6$; $ATC = AFC + AVC = \$6 + \$2 = \$8$

e. $MC = \$5 > AVC = \$2$; AVC is increasing. $MC = \$5 < ATC = \$8$; ATC is decreasing.

12. *a.*

L	Q	AP	MP	TFC	TVC
0	0	—	—	10,000	0
20	4,000	200	200	10,000	10,000
40	10,000	250	300	10,000	20,000
60	15,000	250	250	10,000	30,000
80	19,400	242.5	220	10,000	40,000
100	23,000	230	180	10,000	50,000

TC	AFC	AVC	ATC	MC
10,000	—	—	—	—
20,000	2.50	2.50	5.00	2.50
30,000	1.00	2.00	3.00	1.67
40,000	0.67	2.00	2.67	2.00
50,000	0.52	2.06	2.58	2.27
60,000	0.43	2.17	2.61	2.78

b. When *MC* is less than (greater than) *AVC*, *AVC* is decreasing (increasing). When *MC* is less than (greater than) *ATC*, *ATC* is decreasing (increasing).

c. When *AP* is increasing (decreasing), *AVC* is decreasing (increasing). When *MP* is increasing (decreasing), *MC* is decreasing (increasing).

13. *a.* *AVC* ($= w/AP$) reaches its minimum value when *AP* reaches its maximum, i.e., when $L = 80$.

b. When $L = 80$, $AP = Q/L = 250$, so $Q = (250)(80) = 20{,}000$.

c. $AVC = w/AP = \$2/250 = \$0.008$ or $AVC = TVC/Q = wL/Q = \$2(80)/20{,}000 = \$0.008$

d. When $L = 100$, *AP* appears to be approximately 240 and *MP* is 150. Output is $Q = AP \times L = 240(100) = 24{,}000$ units. $MC = w/MP = \$2/150 = \$0.0133$. $AVC = w/AP = \$2/240 = \$0.00833$ or $AVC = TVC/Q = wL/Q = \$2(100)/24{,}000 = \$0.00833$.

Chapter 10

1. *a.* 1/4

b. decrease; 1/4
c. 20

2. a. $K = 60 - 3/4L$; $37.50; $3,000
b. 40; 30; $3,000; $60 - 3/4(40) = 30\surd$
c. 90; 120; $K = 90 - 3/4L$; 60

3. a. less than; $6,000; $33.33
b. decreases; increases; total cost; output; less than; $5,000
c. minimizes; total; equal to
d. 20; 60; $4,000
e. $3,000. Although E costs less than C, E cannot produce the 2,500 units required by the manager.

4. Since MP_L/w = (= 25/25 = 1) is greater than MP_K/r (= 65/130 = 1/2), the manager is using too much capital and not enough labor. In order to produce efficiently, the manager should increase L and decrease K until $MP_L/w = MP_K/r$.

5. a. greater. The manager can increase spending on labor by $1, which causes output to rise by MP_L/w units. Since $MP_K/r < MP_L/w$, spending on capital must be decreased by *more* than $1 in order to keep output at the initial level of output represented by isoquant I. Hence it is possible to find another input combination that produces the level of output associated with isoquant I but costs less to obtain than combination A.

b. less. The manager can increase spending on capital by $1, which causes output to rise by MP_K/r units. Since $MP_L/w < MP_K/r$, spending on labor must be reduced by *more* than $1 to keep output at the level associated with isoquant I. Hence it is possible to find another input combination that produces the level of output associated with isoquant I but costs less to obtain than combination B.
c. When an isocost line parallel to LZ is constructed such that the new isocost curve is tangent to the Q_1 isoquant, the point of tangency occurs at approximately 200L and 200K.

6. In either case, minimizing cost or maximizing output, the optimal input combinations must satisfy the same condition that $MRTS = w/r$, or equivalently, the slope of the isoquant must equal the slope of the isocost curve. Since an expansion path is the locus of tangency points, the expansion path looks the same regardless of whether the manager is trying to minimize cost for a given output or maximize output for a given cost.

7. a. w = $25 (= $5,000/200)
b. 32; 12; $2,000
c. 60; 20; $3,500
d. 72; 32; $5,000
e. The expansion path is the curve passing through each of the tangency points.
f. $MRTS = 0.25$

8. a. 1.5
b. 3
c. less than; increasing

9.

Q	L	K	LTC	LAC	LMC
10	64	24	4,000	400	400
20	140	40	7,500	375	350
30	200	58	10,800	360	330
40	288	80	15,200	380	440
50	460	90	20,500	410	530

10. Economies of scale exist for 0 to 30 units of output; there are diseconomies of scale for 30 to 50 units of output.

11. SC = [($1,000 + $600) − 1,400]/1,400 = 0.143 > 0. Since $SC > 0$, there are economies of scope.

Chapter 11

1. In the theoretical analysis, a typical production function requires positive amounts of both inputs to produce output and exhibits a diminishing marginal rate of technical substitution ($MRTS$) as the firm uses more labor and less capital. A linear specification is not appropriate for estimating production functions because in this functional form output can be produced when either capital or labor is zero, and the $MRTS$ is constant at all levels of input usage ($MRTS = MP_L/MP_K = b/a$).

2. a. Yes, because $a(0)K = aL(0) = 0$.
b. $MP_L = aK$ and $MP_K = aL$. No, the marginal products are constant.
c. $MRTS = MP_L/MP_K = aK/aL = K/L$. As you move down the isoquant, K decreases and L increases, and thus $MRTS$ (= K/L) diminishes.

3. a. Total product: $Q = -0.002(10)^3L^3 + 6(10)^2L^2 = -2L^3 + 600L^2$
Letting $A = -2$ and $B = 600$,
$$AP = AL^2 + BL = -2L^2 + 600L$$
$$MP = 3AL^2 + 2BL = -6L^2 + 1{,}200L$$
b. $L_m = -B/3A = -600/-6 = 100$ units of labor
c. $AP_{10} = -2(10)^2 + 600(10) = 5{,}800$
$MP_{10} = -6(10)^2 + 1{,}200(10) = 11{,}400$

d. Total product: $Q = -0.002(20)3L^3 + 6(20)^2L^2 = -16L^3 + 2{,}400L^2$
Letting $A = -16$ and $B = 2{,}400$,
$AP = -16L^2 + 2{,}400L$
$MP = -48L^2 + 4{,}800L$

e. Marginal and average product increased for all levels of labor usage. When $K = 20$ and 10 units of labor are employed,
$AP_{10} = -16(10)^2 + 2{,}400(10) = 22{,}400$
$MP_{10} = -48(10)^2 + 4{,}800(10) = 43{,}200$
As expected, AP_{10} and MP_{10} are higher when $K = 20$ than when $K = 10$, $L_m = -B/3A = 2{,}400/48 = 50$.

4. *a.* $A = -0.002$ and $B = 0.40$
$TP = -0.002L^3 + 0.40L^2$
$AP = -0.002L^2 + 0.40L$
$MP = -0.006L^2 + 0.80L$

b. Yes, signs are correct. Both A and B are statistically significant at the 1 percent level of significance since both p-values are less than 0.01.

c. $L_a = -B/2A = -0.40/2(-0.002) = 100$ units of labor

d. $Q_{AP\ max} = -0.002(100)^3 + 0.40(100)^2 = -2{,}000 + 4{,}000 = 2{,}000$ units of output

e. $AP_{L=100} = -0.002(100)^2 + 0.40(100) = -20 + 40 = 20$
$AVC_{Q=2{,}000} = w/AP_{L=100} = \$200/20 = \$10$
$MP_{L=100} = -0.006(100)^2 + 0.80(100) = -60 + 80 = 20$
$MC_{Q=2{,}000} = w/MP_{L=100} = \$200/20 = \$10$

f. $TP = -0.002(120)^3 + 0.40(120)^2 = -3{,}456 + 5{,}760 = 2{,}304$
$AP_{L=120} = -0.002(120)^2 + 0.40(120) = -28.80 + 48 = 19.20$
$AVC_{Q2{,}304} = w/AP_{L=120} = \$200/19.20 = \$10.42$
$MP_{L=120} = -0.006(120)^2 + 0.80(120) = -86.40 + 96 = 9.60$
$MC_{Q=2{,}304} = w/MP_{L=120} = \$200/9.60 = \$20.83$

g. Repeat the procedure in parts *e* and *f* for all levels of output.

5. *a.* *Yes,* all three coefficients have the correct sign. All three coefficients are statistically significant at the 5% level of significance because all three p-values are less than 0.05.

b. $Q_m = -b/2c = 0.079952/2(0.000088) = 454.27$

c. $MC = a + 2bQ + 3cQ^2 = 30.420202 - 0.159904Q + 0.000264Q^2$

d. $MC_{700} = 30.420202 - 0.159904(700) + 0.000264(700)^2 = \$47.85$

e. $AVC = a + bQ + cQ^2 = 30.420202 - 0.079952Q + 0.000088Q^2$

f. $AVC_{700} = 30.420202 - 0.079952(700) + 0.000088(700)^2 = \$17.57$

Chapter 12

1. The firm's demand is a horizontal line at \$20, the price at which supply and demand intersect in the left-hand graph.
   a. The firm's demand is perfectly (or infinitely) elastic at every quantity.
   b. $MR = \$20$ at every level of output.

2. *a.* 1,500 units will maximize profit.
   b. \$2, \$4; increase, \$2
   c. \$7, \$4; increase, \$3

3. *a.* MR is a horizontal line at \$7; 600
   b. $ATC_{600} = \$5$; $TC_{600} = \$5 \times 600 = \$3{,}000$
   c. $TR_{600} = \$7 \times 600 = \$4{,}200$, so $\pi = TR - TC = \$4{,}200 - \$3{,}000 = \$1{,}200$
   d. MR curve is a horizontal line at \$3; 400
   e. $TR_{400} = \$3 \times 400 = \$1{,}200$; $TR_{400} = ATC_{400} \times 400 = \$5 \times 400 = \$2{,}000$; loss $= \$800$.
   f. $TVC_{400} = AVC_{400} \times 400 = \$2 \times 400 = \$800$; $TR - TVC = \$400$ to apply to fixed cost.
   g. \$1.90. When $P < 1.90$, the firm loses less by shutting down than it would lose if it produced where $MR = MC$.

4. *a.* The firm is not producing the profit-maximizing level of output. At the current level of output (50 units), P ($= MR$) $= \$12 < MC = \$15$. The firm can increase profit by producing less. The firm should reduce output until $P = MC$.
   b. When ATC is at its minimum point, $ATC = MC$. Thus, at the current level of output (10,000 units), P ($= \$25$) $= MC$ ($= \$25$). The firm is making the profit-maximizing decision; producing any other level of output would reduce the firm's profit.

5. *a.* For firm A, $\pi = TR - (TFC + TVC) = \$100{,}000 - (50{,}000 + 80{,}000) = -\$30{,}000$. For firm B, $\pi = \$100{,}000 - (50{,}000 + 110{,}000) = -\$60{,}000$. Although both firms have the same TR and the same TFC, firm A should operate in the short run and firm B should shut down. Firm A will lose less by operating (\$30,000) than by shutting down (\$50,000), while firm B will lose less by shutting down (\$50,000) than by operating (\$60,000).

b. Although both firms incur losses of $50,000, firm C should shut down and firm D should continue to operate in the short run. Firm C will lose less by shutting down ($40,000) than by operating ($50,000), while firm D will lose less by operating ($50,000) than by shutting down ($70,000). In both cases, as in all cases, variable cost, not fixed cost, is important in making the shutdown decision.

6. *a.*

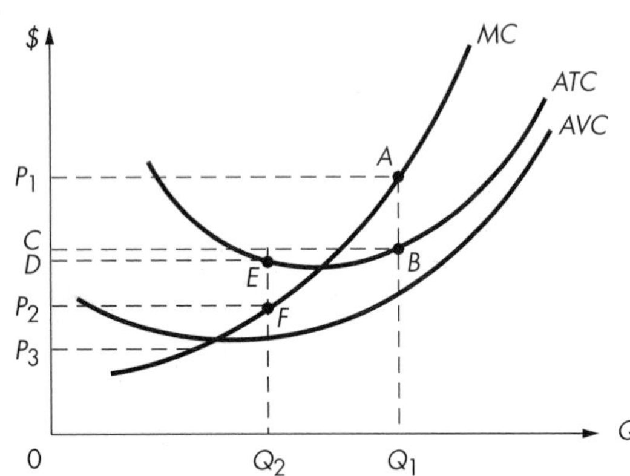

b. At price P_1 the firm will produce Q_1 units of output, earning economic profit equal to P_1ABC.

c. At price P_2 the firm will produce Q_2 units of output, incurring a loss equal to $DEFP_2$.

d. The firm will shut down if price is below minimum *AVC*, for example, P_3.

7. *a.* Demand = *MR* is a horizontal line at $25. $MR = MC$ at $Q = 400$. Industry output is $400 \times 1{,}000 = 400{,}000$.

b. Demand $= MR = MC$ at $Q = 500$. Industry output is $500 \times 1{,}000 = 500{,}000$.

c. If industry output affects some input prices, as all firms expand after the price increase, costs will increase, causing all firms' *MC* to shift upward. Each firm's output at $40 will be less than 500 but more than 400. Thus industry output will be between 400,000 and 500,000.

8. *a.* The firm's demand $= MR = P$ is a horizontal line at $40. The firm will produce 8,000 units of output where $MC = \$40$. Economic profit $= (P - LAC)Q = (\$40 - \$25)8{,}000 = \$120{,}000$.

b. $P =$ minimum $LAC = \$20$. Economic profit $= 0$.

9. A perfectly competitive firm in long-run equilibrium faces a market price just equal to the minimum *LAC* and earns exactly a normal profit.

a. If firms earn economic profits in the short run, other firms will enter the industry. Entry will increase market supply, thus reducing market price and each firm's profit until entry ceases. Short-run losses, on the other hand, lead to exit, reducing the losses of the remaining firms.

b. In long-run equilibrium, firms have no motive to enter or exit—economic profit is zero. Because profit is zero, price equals *LAC*. Because firms maximize profit, price equals *LMC*. Thus, in the long run a perfectly competitive firm produces the level of output at which *LAC* equals *LMC*, i.e., the level of output at which *LAC* is minimum.

10. *a.* If the price of a substitute good decreases, market demand will decrease.

b. Initially market supply will be unaffected.

c. Market supply is unchanged and market demand has decreased: market price will decrease.

d. Market output will decrease.

e. A profit-maximizing firm's output will decrease.

f. At the original price, economic profit was zero. Now the firm suffers economic losses.

In the long run, firms will exit in response to the losses. Exit will reduce market supply, thus increasing market price. Exit will continue until the market returns to equilibrium, i.e., until each firm earns only a normal return.

11. *a.* Economic profit will induce entry, thus increasing the number of firms in the market.

b. Entry will not affect the market demand curve.

c. An increase in the number of firms will increase market supply.

d. Market demand is unchanged and market supply has increased: market price will decrease.

e. Market output will increase.

f. When market price decreases, a profit-maximizing firm will reduce output.

g. The firm is producing less and receiving a lower price per unit—profit will fall.

12. *a.* Industry output does not affect any input prices and therefore does not affect costs. At each

point on long-run competitive supply, price equals each firm's minimum long-run average cost, which does not change as industry output changes.

b. As industry output increases, some input prices increase, which causes costs to increase. At each point on long-run competitive supply, price equals each firm's minimum long-run average cost, which rises as industry output increases, causing long-run competitive supply to be upward-sloping.

13. *a.* \$10; 0
b. zero
c. \$7,800; \$2,800 [= (\$10 − \$6) × 700 units]
d. If the superior manager also owned the firm, as firm owner she would earn only a normal profit but as manager she would earn economic rent of \$2,800. The wage of \$5,000 is an implicit cost or normal profit.

14. *a.* and *b.* Your table should be:

(1) Units of labor	(2) Output	(3) Marginal product	(4) *MRP*	(5) *MC* (= 10/*MP*)	(6) Profit
1	5	5	\$10	\$2	−\$50
2	15	10	20	1	−40
3	30	15	30	0.67	−20
4	50	20	40	0.50	10
5	65	15	30	0.67	30
6	77	12	24	0.83	44
7	86	9	18	1.11	52
8	94	8	16	1.25	58
9	98	4	8	2.50	56
10	96	−2	−4	—	42

c. Profit is maximized by hiring 8 units of labor. If more than 8*L* are hired, $MRP < w(= \$10)$ and profit falls. If fewer than 8*L* are hired, $MRP > w$ and increasing *L* will increase profit.
d. See column (5) of table above.
e. 94, because *MR* (= \$2) will be less than *MC* if output is increased by hiring the ninth worker.
f. See column (6) of table above.
g. 8*L* or 94*Q* both result in a maximum profit of \$58. It doesn't matter whether the manager chooses *L* or *Q* to maximize profit. $MR = MC$ and $MRP = w$ are equivalent rules for profit maximization.
h. 6*L*; $\pi = -\$16$; $MP_6 = 12 < 12.83 = AP_6$. If $AP < MP$, the firm would shut down in the short run.

15. *a.* See figure below:

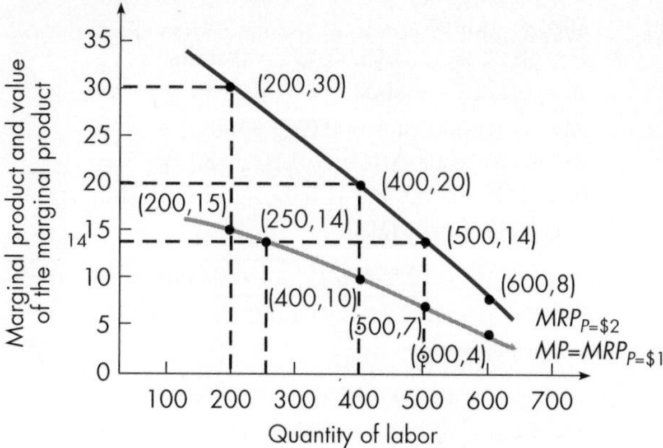

b. At $w = \$30$, the firm hires 200 units of labor. At $w = \$20$, the firm hires 400 units of labor. At $w = \$14$, the firm hires 500 units of labor.
c. Since $MRP = P \times MP$, when $P = \$1$, $MRP = MP$. Thus the *MP* curve is also the *MRP* curve.
d. At $w = \$30$ and $w = \$20$, the firm hires no labor. At $w = \$14$, $L = 250$.

Chapter 13

1. *a.* minimum *AVC*
b. *ATC*
c. *ATC*; minimum *AVC*
d. minimum *AVC*
e. *P*; *MC*; minimum *AVC*; *ATC*
f. *P*; *MC*; *ATC*

2. *a.* $MC = 10 + 2(-0.03)Q + 3(0.00005)Q^2 = 10 - 0.06Q + 0.00015Q^2$
b. $Q_{min} = -(-0.03)/2(0.00005) = 300$ units
c. $AVC_{min} = 10 - 0.03(300) + 0.00005(300)^2 = \$5.50$
d. $P = \$10 > AVC_{min} = \$5.50$; $MC = P$: $10 - 0.06Q + 0.00015Q^2 = 10$
$Q^* = 0.06/0.00015 = 400$ units
e. $AVC_{400} = 10 - 0.03(400) + 0.00005(400)^2 = \$6$; $TVC_{400} = AVC \times Q = \$6(400) = \$2{,}400$; $TR = P \times Q = \$10(400) = \$4{,}000$
$\pi = TR - TVC - TFC = \$4{,}000 - \$2{,}400 - \$600 = \$1{,}000$
f. $P = \$7 > AVC_{min} = \$5.50$; $MC = P$: $10 - 0.06Q + 0.00015Q^2 = 7$; solve $0.00015Q^2 - 0.06Q + 3 = 0$

$$Q^* = \frac{0.06 + \sqrt{0.0018}}{0.0003} = 341 \text{ units}$$

g. $AVC = 10 - 0.03(341) + 0.00005(341)^2 = \$5.58$
$\pi = TR - TVC - TFC = \$7(341) - \$5.58(341) - 600 = -\$116$
h. $P = \$5 < AVC = \$5.50$; $Q^* = 0$ units
i. $\pi = -TFC = -\$600$

3. a. $AVC = 0.000033Q^2 - 0.05Q + 80$
b. $MC = 75 \Rightarrow 0.0001Q^2 - 0.1Q + 80 = 75 \Rightarrow$ $0.0001Q^2 - 0.1Q + 5 = 0$. Solving with the quadratic formula:

$$Q_1, Q_2 = \frac{0.10 \pm \sqrt{0.1^2 - 4 \times 0.0001 \times 5}}{0.0002}$$

$Q_1 = 53$ and $Q_2 = 947$
c. $AVC_{Q=53} = 0.000033(53)^2 - 0.05(53) + 80 = \$77.44 > P = \$75 \Rightarrow$ shut down.
$AVC_{Q=947} = 0.000033(947)^2 - 0.05(947) + 80 = \$62.24 < P = \$75 \Rightarrow$ produce 947 units.

4. a. *MRP*; *w*; greater; wage
b. *MRP*; *w*; greater

5. a. $AP = -0.025L^2 + 1.45L$
b. $MP = -0.075L^2 + 2.90L$
c. $MRP = P \times MP = 5(-0.075L^2 + 2.90L) = -0.375L^2 + 14.5L$
d. Set *MRP* equal to *w* and solve for *L*:
$-0.375L^2 + 14.5L = 15$
$-0.375L^2 + 14.5L - 15 = 0$
Using the quadratic formula, the two values of *L* where $MRP = w$ are

$$L_1, L_2 = \frac{-14.5 \pm \sqrt{14.5^2 - (4)(-0.375)(-15)}}{2(-0.375)} = \frac{-14.5 \pm \sqrt{187.75}}{-0.75} = \frac{-14.5 \pm 13.7}{-0.75}$$

and $L_1 = 1.067$, $L_2 = 37.6$.
The profit-maximizing level of labor usage is 37.6 since $AP_{37.6} = 19.18 > 3.0 = MP_{37.6}$. L_1 is *not* profit maximizing because $AP < MP$, and the firm should shut down.
e. $\pi = PQ - wL - TFC$
First, compute $Q^* = -0.025(37.6)^3 + 1.45(37.6)^2 = 721$
$\pi = \$5 \times 721 - \$15 \times 37.6 - \$1{,}000 = 3{,}605 - 564 - 1{,}000 = \$2{,}041$

Chapter 14

1. a. Strangely enough, it may well be that the much smaller Texas bank has fewer good substitutes in its area than the huge Chase Manhattan Bank and hence has more market power. Chase Manhattan competes worldwide with many other large international banks.
b. There was not nearly as much foreign competition in the U.S. auto market prior to 1970. Thus the Big Three would have less market power now.
c. They probably have about the same market power, although the regional phone company may have better substitutes and hence less market power. Both are generally regulated.

2. As international markets have expanded, new sources of raw material have come onto the world market, making control of a raw material much more difficult for a single company.

3. a. and b.

P	*Q*	*TR* (= *PQ*)	*MR* (= Δ*TR*/Δ*Q*)
$20	200	$4,000	—
15	300	4,500	$500/100 = $5
10	500	5,000	500/200 = $2.50
5	700	3,500	−1,500/200 = −$7.50

c. Demand is elastic. $\$5 \times 200 = \$1{,}000$ lost revenue. $\$15 \times 100 = \$1{,}500$ added revenue. The added revenue is $500 more than the lost revenue. Divided by the added sales, $MR = \$500/100 = \$5$.
d. Demand is elastic. $\$5 \times 300 = \$1{,}500$ lost revenue. $\$10 \times 200 = \$2{,}000$ added revenue. The added revenue is $500 more than the lost revenue. Divided by the added sales, $MR = \$500/200 = \$2.50$.

4. a. $32.50
b. 200 units
c. $MR = \$25$; elastic
d. 500 units. Since $MR = 0$, $E = -1$

5. a. $Q^* = 9$. The ninth unit of output should be produced because it adds more to *TR* than to *TC* ($MR > MC$), but producing the tenth unit would decrease profit ($MC > MR$).
b. $P^* = \$18$
c. $\pi = (\$18)(9) - (\$54) = \$108$

6. a. $9
b. 30
c. $270; $240; $30

7. A profit-maximizing monopolist produces the level of output at which $MR = MC$. In general, $MC > 0$,

so $MR > 0$ also, and thus a monopolist operates in the elastic portion of the demand curve. A monopolist will never operate in the inelastic region of demand. When demand is inelastic, $MR < 0$, and by decreasing output the firm can increase TR, decrease TC, and thus increase profit. If costs were zero, then $MC = 0$ and a monopolist would produce the level of output at which $MR = 0$. Demand is of unitary elasticity when MR is zero and TR is at its maximum.

8. *a.* 2,000 units; $P = \$50$
   b. Profit $= (P - ATC)Q = (\$50 - \$60)2{,}000 = -\$20{,}000$
   c. $TR = \$50 \times 2{,}000 = \$100{,}000$; $TVC = AVC \times Q = \$40 \times 2{,}000 = \$80{,}000$
   d. It loses $TFC = TC - TVC = \$60 \times 2000 - \$80{,}000 = \$40{,}000$.
9. *a.* $Q^* = 500$ ($MR = SMC$)
   b. $P^* = \$7$
   c. $\pi = Q(P - ATC) = (500)(\$7 - 6) = \$500$
   d. $Q^* = 700$, $P^* = \$6.50$ ($MR = LMC$)
   e. When $Q = 500$, $MR > LMC$; as the firm increases output the addition to TR will exceed the addition to TC—profit will increase.
   f.

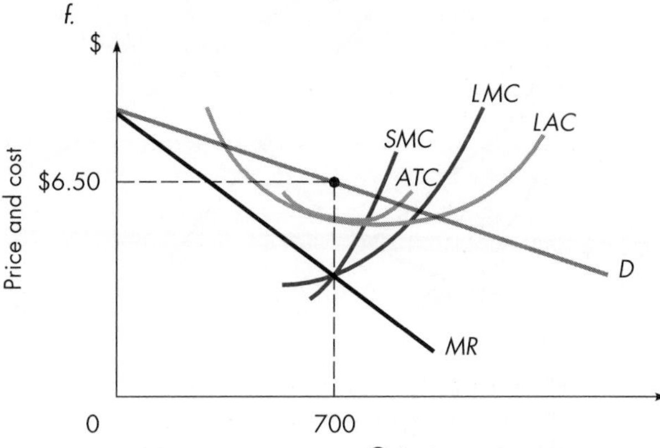

10.

L	Q	P	MP	MR	MRP
9	50	$21	—	—	—
10	100	20	50	19.00	950
11	140	19	40	16.50	660
12	170	18	30	13.33	400
13	190	17	20	8.50	170
14	205	16	15	3.33	50
15	215	15	10	−5.50	−55

   b. If the wage rate is \$60, the monopolist will employ 13 units of labor. Through the 13th unit, each unit of labor adds more to TR than to $TC(MRP > w)$; employing the 14th unit of labor would decrease profit ($MRP < w$). If the wage rate falls to \$40, the 14th unit of labor now adds more to TR than to TC and so should be hired. Regardless of the wage rate, no more than 14 units of labor will be employed—the firm will never hire a unit of labor with negative MP.

11. *a.* $L = 120$ at $\$20 = MRP$
    b. $L = 140$ at $\$10 = MRP$
    c. zero (At $\$40 = MRP$, ARP is less than MRP.)

12.

(1) Labor usage	(2) Output	(3) Price	(4) Total revenue	(5) Marginal revenue
0	0	$8.00	0	—
8	10	7.50	75	7.50
12	20	7.00	140	6.50
17	30	6.50	195	5.50
24	40	6.00	240	4.50
33	50	5.50	275	3.50
44	60	5.00	300	2.50
57	70	4.50	315	1.50

(6) Total variable cost	(7) Total cost	(8) Marginal cost	(9) Profit
0	50	—	−50
40	90	4	−15
60	110	2	30
85	135	2.50	60
120	170	3.50	70
165	215	4.50	60
220	270	5.50	30
285	335	6.50	−20

    a. 40; \$6. 40 units of output is the greatest amount of output for which $MR > MC$. If the manager increased output to 50 units, profit would fall because MR_{50} (= \$3.50) $< MC_{50}$ (= \$4.50).
    b. profit; \$70
    c. yes

13.

(1) Labor usage	(2) Output	(3) Price	(4) Marginal product
0	0	$8.00	—
8	10	7.50	1.25
12	20	7.00	2.50
17	30	6.50	2
24	40	6.00	1.43
33	50	5.50	1.11
44	60	5.00	0.91
57	70	4.50	0.77

(5) Average product	(6) Average revenue product	(7) Marginal revenue product
—	—	—
1.25	9.38	9.38
1.67	11.69	16.25
1.76	11.44	11
1.67	10.02	6.44
1.52	8.36	3.89
1.36	6.80	2.28
1.23	5.54	1.16

a. 24. Since $w = \$5$, 24 L is the last increment of labor for which $MRP_L > w$. For 33 L, $MRP_L < w$ and profit would fall.

b. 40; \$6; profit; $70 = TR - wL - TFC = 240 - 5(24) - 50$

c. Choosing either $L = 24$ or $Q = 40$ leads to exactly the same level of profit. The two rules ($MRP_L = w$ and $MR = MC$) lead to the same P^*, Q^*, and π^*.

d. 17. $MRP_L <$ \$10 if L is increased to 24 L.

e. 0; loss; \$50. Since $ARP_L < MRP_L$ at 17 L, the firm loses less by shutting down than by producing. If the manager did (mistakenly) hire 17 workers, $\pi = \$195 - \$15(17) - \$50 = \$-110$, which is a greater loss than would occur if the firm shuts down.

14. *a.* Monopolistic competition is similar to monopoly in that both types of firms have market power (face a downward-sloping demand). But the source of a monopolist's market power is the fact that the firm is the only seller in the market; a monopolistic competitor has market power because the firm produces a differentiated product—i.e., the products of rival firms are not perfect substitutes.

b. Monopolistic competition is similar to perfect competition in that there are many firms and unrestricted entry and exit in both types of markets.

c. In the short run, a monopolistic competitor produces the level of output at which $MR = SMC$, as long as price at that output is greater than or equal to AVC. If $P < AVC$, the firm will shut down. Monopolistic competitors, like all other firms, can earn positive, zero, or negative economic profit in the short run. Although the source of the firm's market power differs, the short-run analysis of monopolistic competition is identical to that of pure monopoly.

d. In the long run, a monopolistic competitor produces the level of output at which $MR = LMC$, charges the price associated with that level of output, and earns zero economic profit (i.e., $P = LAC$). Thus, in the long run, a monopolistic competitor's demand curve is tangent to its LAC curve.

e. Unrestricted entry and exit drive economic profit to zero in the long run in a monopolistically competitive market. If firms earn positive economic profit in the short run, the subsequent entry will increase the number of substitutes for a firm's product—the firm's demand will decrease and become more elastic. Entry will continue until economic profit is zero. Losses in the short run will lead to exit, which will reduce the number of substitutes for the remaining firms. Long-run equilibrium occurs when there is no incentive for entry or exit, i.e., when economic profit equals zero.

15. *a.* In the short run, with demand curve D_s and marginal revenue curve MR_s, the monopolistic competitor will produce Q_s and charge price P_s.

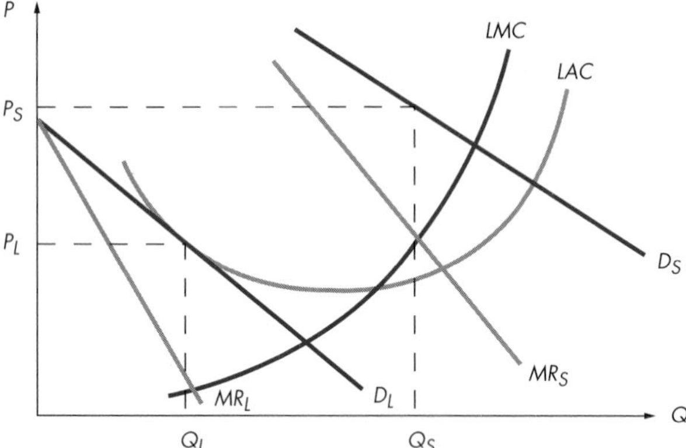

b. The long-run demand curve is D_L: the firm will produce Q_L and charge price P_L.

c. In order for the *firm* to be maximizing profit, MR_L must equal LMC. If $MR_L \neq LMC$ at the point of tangency, the firm will have an incentive to change its output, and thus the point where $P_L = LAC$ would not be equilibrium.

d. In the long run, for the monopolistically competitive firm, equilibrium price is higher ($P >$ min LAC) and output lower ($Q < Q_{\min LAC}$) than they are for a perfectly competitive firm.

16. In monopolistic competition, products have different characteristics—consumers can differentiate among the various brands.

Advertising these differences creates brand loyalty, thereby increasing demand and making it less elastic. For perfect competitors, goods are homogeneous. Advertising is a waste of money since consumers view all producers' output as perfect substitutes; that is, no brand loyalty can be generated by advertising.

Chapter 15

1. *a.* 3,500; 4,500
   b. 500; 1,500
   c. Southwest's demand would lie somewhere between D_{SW} and d_{SW}.
   d. $d_{SW}d'_{SW}$ is more elastic because sales increase or decrease more after a price change by Southwest when Continental keeps its price at $200 rather than matching Southwest's price change.
2. *a.* $E = \dfrac{\Delta Q/Q}{\Delta P/P} = \dfrac{(600 - 200)/(600 + 200)/2}{(40 - 30)/(40 + 30)/2} = -3.5$
   b. $E = \dfrac{\Delta Q/Q}{\Delta P/P} = \dfrac{(600 - 700)/(600 + 700)/2}{(30 - 20)/(30 + 20)/2} = -0.38$
   c. Rivals will not follow a price increase. Rivals will follow a price decrease.
   d. Demand is elastic for a price increase, so revenue would fall. Demand is inelastic for a price decrease, so revenue would also fall.
   e. There is no way of determining this from the theory.
3. Oligopolists producing a homogeneous product are less likely to engage in nonprice competition than oligopolists producing differentiated products. In the absence of product differentiation, prices must be the same across producers.
4. *a.* Probably next to the first stand, toward the longer end of the beach. It will get more business with this location.
   b. It will move just to the other side of the new stand, again toward the longer end of the beach, for the same reason as that given in part *a*.
   c. They will probably end up almost next to one another in the center. About half the business will go to each.
   d. It is difficult, if not impossible, to predict this from the theory.
5. *a.* The high-quality strategy dominates. No matter what B chooses, A makes more profit with the high quality.
   b. Same answer as that for firm A in part *a*.
   c. They will probably both choose high quality and end up earning $100 each.
6. *a.* The low-price strategy dominates. No matter what D chooses, C makes more profit with the low price.
   b. Same answer as that for firm C in part *a*.
   c. They will probably both choose the low price and end up earning $500 each.
7. *a.* For firm S, a low price dominates, because S makes more profit this way with either choice of L.
   b. Firm L has no dominant strategy. If S chooses high, L makes more with a low price. If S chooses low, L makes more with a high price.
   c. If L knows the results of each combination for S, L knows that the dominant strategy for S is a low price, which is what S would likely choose. Therefore, L would choose a high price, which is more profitable under this circumstance than a low price.
   d. For L, the worst thing that could happen is for S to choose a low price, so L would choose a high price at which it makes more profit.
   e. The firms will likely end up with S setting a low price and earning $600 while L sets a high price and earns $600 also. This is a Nash equilibrium because, given what the other is doing, any firm that changes would become worse off.
8. *a.* From B's reaction function, it will set a price of $30.
   b. From A's reaction function, it will set a price of $25.
   c. A price of $30 for A and $40 for B; this is a Nash equilibrium. Given what its rival is charging, this is the most profitable price for each.
9. *a.* Firms that can adjust price are more likely to cooperate. One firm can signal by raising price, since it knows that if the others don't follow, it would suffer reduced profit for only a short period, as it could soon lower its price.
   b. It is easier for 2 firms to reach a tacit agreement, or any other kind, than it is for 10.
   c. Agreements are harder with differentiated products because it is harder to establish a price that satisfies everyone.
   d. If the one large firm signals by raising price, the others realize that this firm could lower price

even more if they don't follow and they would be hurt more. But there are some alternative answers.

10. *a.* $MR = MC$ at an output of 3,000 with a price of \$60.
    Profit $= (P - LAC)Q = (\$60 - \$40)3{,}000 = \$60{,}000$.
    b. Below a price of \$47 the potential entrant would make a loss if it enters.
    c. At a price of \$44 profit is approximately $(P - LAC)Q \approx (\$44 - \$40) \times 4{,}500 \approx \$18{,}000$.
    d. Clearly entry limit pricing reduces profit. So the firm would compare the profit stream if it practiced entry limit pricing with the stream if it maximized profit during entry and then had reduced profit after entry occurred. It would weigh the costs and benefits. A shorter time horizon would, for example, reduce the probability of entry limit pricing.

11. Any price below \$40 would discourage entry by a single-product firm. At an average price a little below \$40 the firm's per-unit revenue would be above the average cost of $\$70/2 = \$35$.

12. *a.* $Q_T = 150$ (where $MR = MC_T$); $Q_1^* = 50$ and $Q_2^* = 100$ (where $MC_1 = MC_2$); $P^* = \$50$ (from the demand curve).
    b. When $Q_1 = Q_2 = 75$, $MC_1 \approx \$28 > MC_2 \approx \$17$. This is not the cost-minimizing allocation of cartel output; moving 1 unit of output from firm 1 to firm 2 will leave the cartel's output and total revenue unchanged but will decrease total cost and thus increase profit by \$11 (\$28 − \$17). The cartel should shift output from firm 1 to firm 2, keeping total output unchanged, until $MC_1 = MC_2$. Only when marginal cost is the same for both firms is cost minimized and thus profit maximized for a given level of cartel output.
    c. If one firm cheats on the price or if a new entrant comes in at a lower price.

13. Tacit collusion is unspoken cooperation among firms. The behavior of firms that tacitly collude can approximate the behavior of members of a cartel—pricing tends to be uniform among firms. Tacit collusion, often based on historical patterns of interaction among firms, exists when firms believe that profit will be maximized by stable behavior.

Chapter 16

1. *a.* $Q = 2{,}600 - 100P + 0.2M - 500P_R = 2{,}600 - 100P + 0.2(20{,}000) - 500(2) = 5{,}600 - 100P$
   b. $P = 56 - 0.01Q$
   c. $MR = 56 - 0.02Q$
2. *a.* $MC = 20 - 2(0.07)Q + 3(0.001)Q^2 = 20 - 0.14Q + 0.0003Q^2$
   b. Set $MR = MC$: $56 - 0.02Q = 20 - 0.14Q + 0.0003Q^2$. The solution is $Q^* = 600$ units.
   c. $P^* = 56 - 0.01Q^* = 56 - 0.01(600) = \$50$
   d. The firm should produce. For $Q^* = 600$, $AVC = 20 - 0.07(600) + 0.0001(600)^2 = \$14$, so $P^* = \$50 > AVC = \$14$.
   e. $TR = P^* \times Q^* = (\$50)(600) = \$30{,}000$; $TVC = AVC \times Q^* = \$14(600) = \$8{,}400$; $\pi = TR - (TVC + TFC) = \$30{,}000 - \$8{,}400 - \$22{,}500 = -\$900$
3. *a.* Demand is more easily estimated for a monopolist than for a monopolistically competitive firm.
   b. When LAC is constant and $m = -1/(1 + E)$.
   c. $m = -1/(1 + -1.5) = 2$, or 200% markup.
   d. $m = -1/(1 + -3) = 0.5$, or 50% markup.

Chapter 17

1. *a.* $MC \Rightarrow Q_T = 50$ dishwashers per week
   b. $P = \$550$ when $Q_T = 50$ (from the demand curve)
   c. $MR = MC_T = MC_1 = MC_2 \Rightarrow Q_1 = 10$ and $Q_2 = 40$

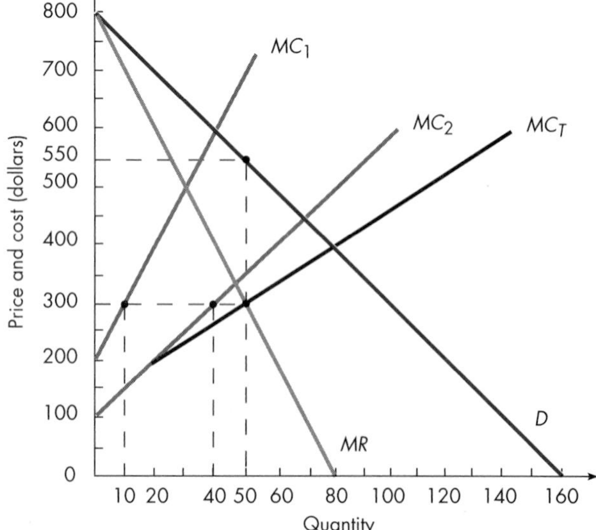

2. *a.* $Q_A = -1{,}000 + 100\ MC_A$
$Q_B = -133.33 + 33.33MC_B$
b. $Q_T = (-1{,}000 - 133.33) + (100 + 33.33)MC_T = -1{,}133.33 + 133.33MC_T$
c. $MC_T = 8.50 + 0.0075Q_T$
d. The output at which the kink occurs is found by setting MC in the *low*-cost plant equal to the minimum value of MC in the *high*-cost plant:

$$4 + 0.03Q = 10$$

So $Q = 200$ at the kink. At total output greater than 200 units both plants are used.
e. At 700 units in each plant, $MC_A = \$17 < MC_B = \$25$. Therefore, the manager should produce more in plant A and less in plant B, until $MC_A = MC_B$. To find equal values of $MC_A = MC_B$ that produce 1,400 units at least cost, substitute 1,400 into MC_T:

$$MC_T = 8.50 + 0.0075(1{,}400) = \$19$$

Now find Q_A and Q_B such that $MC_A = MC_B = \$19$. Use the inverse MC functions:
$Q_A = -1{,}000 + 100(19) = 900$
$Q_B = -133.33 + 33.33(19) = 500$
Note that $Q_A + Q_B = 1{,}400$.
f. See the figure below:

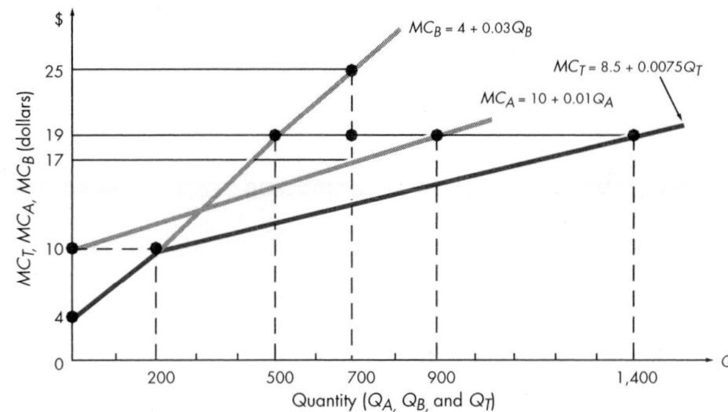

3. *a.* $P = 32 - 0.008Q$
b. $MR = 32 - 0.016Q$
c. Set $MR = MC_T$: $32 - 0.016Q = 8.5 + 0.0075Q \Rightarrow Q_T^* = 1{,}000$; $P^* = \$24 = 32 - 0.008(1{,}000)$
d. MC_T at 1,000 units = \$16. Set $MC_A = MC_B = 16$
$Q_A^* = -1{,}000 + 100(16) = 600$
$Q_B^* = -133.33 + 33.33(16) = 400$
Note: $Q_A^* + Q_B^* = Q_T^*$ $(600 + 400 = 1{,}000)$
e. $MC_T = MR$ at $Q_T < 200$, which is the kink in MC_T. Thus, only plant B should be operated; plant A shuts down. Set $MC_B = MR$ to find Q_B. To find MR, find inverse demand and apply the rule:
$P = 10 - 0.0125Q$
$MR = 10 - 0.025Q$
$MR = MC_B \Rightarrow 10 - 0.025Q_B = 4 + 0.03Q_B \Rightarrow Q_T^* = 109$ units
f. $Q_A = 0$ and $Q_B = 109$ (see part *e*).

4. *a.* Profit is maximized when $MR_T = MC = \$20$ at a total quantity $Q_T^* = 250$. For the business market: $MR_B = \$20 \Rightarrow Q_B = 150$ business travelers. For the vacation market: $MR_V = \$20 \Rightarrow Q_V = 100$ vacation travelers.
b. From their respective demand curves, $P_B = \$50$ and $P_V = \$30$. Revenue from vacation travelers is $\$3{,}000 = \$30 \times 100$, and revenue from business travelers is $\$7{,}500 = \$50 \times 150$. Combined total revenue is \$10,500.
c. You must construct the horizontal sum of the two demand curves and read off the price for 250 units. The precise answer is \$36.67, which you should be close to if your lines are carefully drawn. The total revenue when only a single price is charged is $\$9{,}167 = \$36.67 \times 250$.

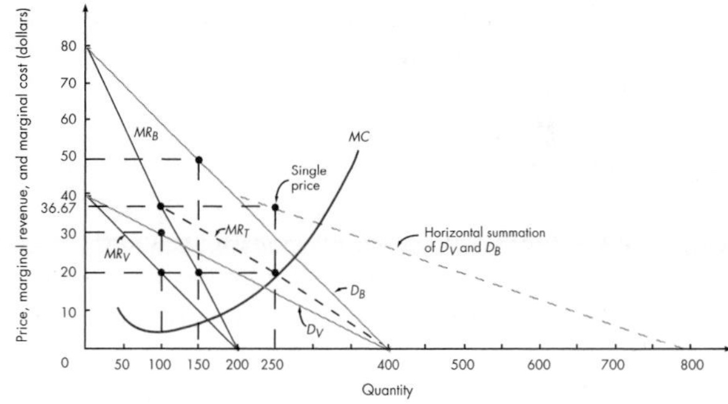

5. *a.* First find inverse demands:
$P_A = 20 - 0.0125Q_A$ $\qquad P_B = 24 - 0.01Q_B$
Then the marginal revenues are:
$MR_A = 20 - 0.025Q_A$ $\qquad MR_B = 24 - 0.02Q_B$
Finally take the inverses:
$Q_A = 800 - 40MR_A$ $\qquad Q_B = 1{,}200 - 50MR_B$
b. Set $MR_A = MR_B = MR_T$ and add Q_A and Q_B:
$Q_T = Q_A + Q_B = (800 - 40\ MR_T) + (1{,}200 - 50MR_T) = 2{,}000 - 90MR_T$
Next take the inverse to get $MR_T = f(Q_T)$:
$MR_T = 22.22 - 0.0111Q_T$
c. See figure below:

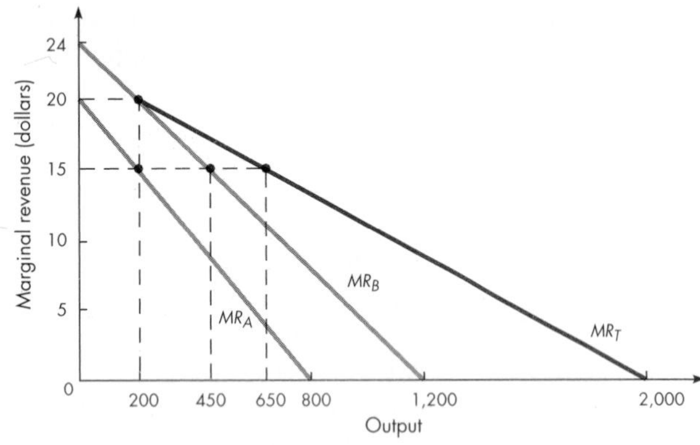

d. $MR_T = 22.22 - 0.0111(650) = \$15$
Setting $MR_A = MR_B = \$15$,
$Q_A = 800 - 40(15) = 200$
$Q_B = 1{,}200 - 50(15) = 450$
Note: $Q_A + Q_B = 200 + 450 = 650$.

6. a. Set $MR_T = MC$: $22.22 - 0.0111Q = 4.5 + 0.005Q \Rightarrow Q_T^* = 1{,}100$ units.
   b. At $Q_T^* = 1{,}100$, $MR_T = 10$, so the profit-maximizing allocation between the two markets is such that $MR_A = MR_B = 10$:
   $Q_A = 800 - 40(10) = 400$
   $Q_B = 1{,}200 - 50(10) = 700$
   Note: $Q_A^* + Q_B^* = Q_T^*$, or $400 + 700 = 1{,}100$
   c. $P_A^* = 20 - 0.0125Q_A^* = 20 - 0.0125(400) = \$15$
   $P_B^* = 24 - 0.01Q_B^* = 24 - 0.01(700) = \$17$
   d. $E_A = P/(P - a) = 15/(15 - 20) = -3$
   $E_B = P/(P - a) = 17/(17 - 24) = -2.43$
   Note: The higher price ($P_B = \$17$) is charged in the market with the less elastic demand ($E_B = -2.43$) in profit-maximizing equilibrium.

7. If a firm produces two products that are unrelated, then the marginal revenue function for each product depends only on the level of output of that product. In order to maximize profit, the firm will produce the level of output for each product at which $MR = MC$. If a firm produces two products that are related in consumption, the profit-maximizing rule is the same: Produce the level of output for each product at which $MR = MC$. But in this case, the marginal revenue function for each product depends on the levels of output of *both* products. The profit-maximizing levels of output for two products related in consumption thus must be determined jointly.

8. $MR_X = 70 - 0.001Q_X - 0.00075Q_Y = MC_X = 20 + 0.00025Q_X$
   $MR_Y = 80 - 0.002Q_Y - 0.0005Q_X = MC_Y = 16 + 0.0005Q_Y$
   Solving simultaneously, $Q_X = 28{,}000$ and $Q_Y = 20{,}000$
   $P_X = 70 - 0.0005(28{,}000) - 0.00075(20{,}000) = \$41$;
   $P_Y = 80 - 0.001(20{,}000) - 0.0005(28{,}000) = \$46$

9. a. $MRP_T = 240 - 12H_T = MC = 150 + 3H_T \Rightarrow H_T^* = 6$
   b. $H_T^* = 6 \Rightarrow MRP_T = MC = \$168$
   $MRP_X = \$168 \Rightarrow H_X^* = 4.5$
   $MRP_Y = \$168 \Rightarrow H_Y^* = 1.5$
   c. $Q_X^* = 2H_X = 9$; $Q_Y^* = 4H_Y = 6$
   d. $P_X^* = \$120 - 2(9) = \$102$;
   $P_Y^* = 60 - 1.5(6) = \$51$

10. a. $MR_J = 290 - 0.003Q = MR_X + MR_Y = 200 - 0.002Q_X + 90 - 0.001Q_Y$
    b. Setting $MR_J = MC$ and solving for $Q \Rightarrow Q^* =$ 60,000 drums of joint product.
    c. $P_X^* = 140 = 200 - 0.001(60{,}000)$; $P_Y^* = \$60 = 90 - 0.0005(60{,}000)$
    d. $Q_X^* = 94{,}000$ drums; $Q_Y^* = 90{,}000$ drums. *Note:* $MR_Y = 0$ at 90,000 drums.
    e. $P_X^* = \$106 = 200 - 0.001(94{,}000)$; $P_Y^* = \$45 = 90 - 0.0005(90{,}000)$

Chapter 18

1. a.

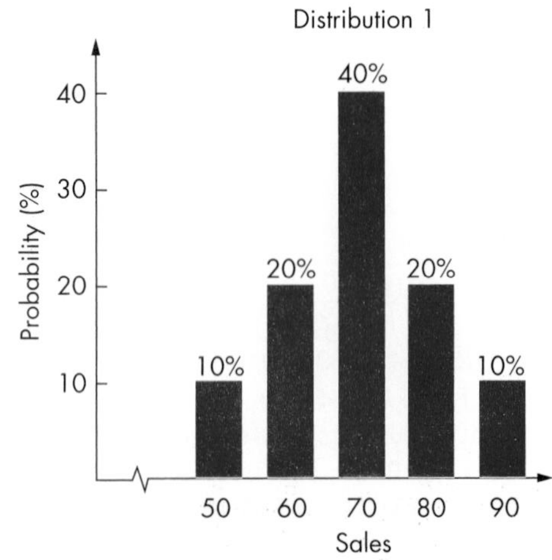

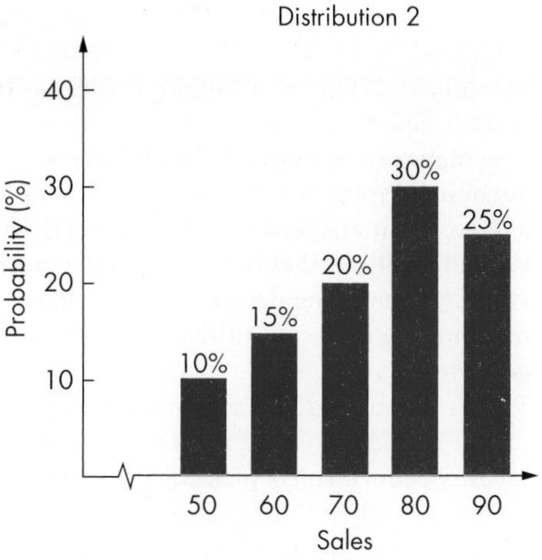

Distribution 2

Probability (%)

40
30
20
10

10% 15% 20% 30% 25%

50 60 70 80 90

Sales

E_1(sales) = (50)(0.10) + (60)(0.20) + (70)(0.40) + (80)(0.20) + (90)(0.10)
= 5 + 12 + 28 + 16 + 9 = 70 (70,000 units)

E_2(sales) = (50)(0.10) + (60)(0.15) + (70)(0.20) + (80)(0.30) + (90)(0.25)
= 5 + 9 + 14 + 24 + 22.5 = 74.5 (74,500 units)

b. Distribution 2 has a higher variance and thus is more risky than distribution 1:

Distribution 1

Sales (X_i)	Probability(P_i)	$[X_i - E(X)]^2$	$[X_i - E(X)]^2(P_i)$
50	0.10	400	40
60	0.20	100	20
70	0.40	0	0
80	0.20	100	20
90	0.10	400	40
			$\sigma^2 = 120$

Distribution 2

Sales (X_i)	Probability(P_i)	$[X_i - E(X)]^2$	$[X_i - E(X)]^2(P_i)$
50	0.10	600.25	60.0250
60	0.15	210.25	31.5375
70	0.20	20.25	4.0500
80	0.30	30.25	9.0750
90	0.25	240.25	60.0625
			$\sigma^2 = 164.75$

c. $\sigma_1 = \sqrt{120} = 10.95$
$\sigma_2 = \sqrt{164.75} = 12.84$
$\upsilon_1 = 10.95/70 = 0.16$
$\upsilon_2 = 12.84/74.5 = 0.17$

Distribution 1 has the smaller coefficient of variation (0.16 < 0.17), and thus distribution 1 is less risky relative to its mean than distribution 2.

2. *a.* Expected value of option A = 0.4(−\$3,750) + 0.6(\$31,770)= \$17,562.
Expected value of option B = 0.4(−\$8,000) + 0.6(\$34,000) = \$17,200.
Option A has the higher expected value.

b. Variance of option A = $0.4(-3{,}750 - 17{,}562)^2 + 0.6(31{,}770 - 17{,}562)^2 = 302{,}800{,}896$
Variance of option B = $0.4(-8{,}000 - 17{,}200)^2 + 0.6(34{,}000 - 17{,}200)^2 = 423{,}360{,}000$
$\sigma_A = \sqrt{302{,}800{,}896} = 17{,}401$
$\sigma_B = \sqrt{423{,}360{,}000} = 20{,}576$
Option B is more risky since its variance (or standard deviation) is higher than option A's variance.

c. Option A is chosen since it has a higher expected payoff and a lower variance.

d. $\upsilon_A = 17{,}401/17{,}562 = 0.99$
$\upsilon_B = 20{,}576/17{,}200 = 1.20$
Based on the coefficient of variation rule, option A is chosen.

3. *a.* Expected value of option A = 0.6(−\$3,750) + 0.4(\$31,770) = \$10,458
Expected value of option B = 0.6(−\$8,000) + 0.4(\$34,000) = \$8,800
Option A has the higher expected value and would thus be chosen if only expected value is used in decision making.

b. Variance of option A = $0.6(-3{,}750 - 10{,}458)^2 + 0.4(31{,}770 - 10{,}458)^2 = 302{,}800{,}896$
Variance of option B = $0.6(-8{,}000 - 8{,}800)^2 + 0.4(34{,}000 - 8{,}800)^2 = 423{,}360{,}000$
$\sigma_A = \sqrt{302{,}800{,}896} = 17{,}401$
$\sigma_B = \sqrt{423{,}360{,}000} = 20{,}576$
Option B is more risky since its variance (or standard deviation) is higher than option A's variance.

c. Option A is chosen since it has a higher expected payoff and a lower variance.

d. $\upsilon_A = 17{,}401/10{,}458 = 1.66$
$\upsilon_B = 20{,}576/8{,}800 = 2.34$
Based on the coefficient of variation rule, option A is chosen.

To find the probabilities that make the two expected values equal, solve the following for p:

$$p(-3{,}750) + (1 - p)(31{,}770) = p(-8{,}000) + (1 - p)(34{,}000)$$

After combining terms and simplifying:

$$p = 0.34$$

Thus, expected values are equal when the probability that price is \$15 equals 0.34, and the probability that price is \$20 equals 0.66.

4. *a.* $E(\pi) = 0.05(-\$10{,}000) + 0.45(-\$2{,}000) + 0.45(\$4{,}000) + 0.05(\$20{,}000) = \$1{,}400$
   b. $E[U(\pi)] = 0.05\ U(-\$10{,}000) + \cdots + 0.05\ U(\$20{,}000) = 0.05(-200{,}000) + \cdots + 0.05(400{,}000) = 28{,}000$
   c. $MU_{\text{profit}} = \Delta U/\Delta\pi = 20$ since $U(\pi)$ is linear.
   d. neutral; constant
5. *a.* $E(\pi) = \$3{,}250 = 0.05(\$1{,}000) + \cdots + 0.50(\$4{,}000)$
   b. $E[U(\pi)] = 160.69 = 0.05\ U(\$1{,}000) + \cdots + 0.05\ U(\$4{,}000)$
   c. 13.86; 8.11; 5.75 (in the three blanks)
   d. averse, decreasing
6. *a., b., c.* Professor Thomas derived his own utility index for this answer:

Profit outcome	Utility index	Marginal utility of profit
\$1,000	0.0	—
\$2,000	0.70	0.000700
\$3,000	0.90	0.000200
\$3,200	0.93	0.000150
\$4,000	1.0	0.000093

   d. Professor Thomas is risk averse because his marginal utility for profit is decreasing as profit rises.
7. *a.* $U[E(\pi)] = U(\$1{,}400) = 20(1{,}400) = 28{,}000$
   b. $U[E(\pi)] = 28{,}000 = E[U(\pi)]$. The two decisions yield the same expected utility since the expected utility of receiving \$1,400 with certainty is 28,000.
   c. You found the manager to be risk neutral in problem 4. You would expect two decisions with exactly the same expected value to yield exactly the same expected utility for risk-neutral decision makers because they ignore risk.
8. *a.* $U(\$3{,}200) = 161.42 = 20\ \ln(3{,}200)$
   b. The expected utility of receiving \$3,200 with certainty is 161.42. The expected utility of the project was calculated to be 160.69 in part *b* of Technical Problem 5. Thus, the manager maximizes expected utility by choosing to receive \$3,200 with certainty.
   c. The manager is shown to be risk averse in Technical Problem 5. By the definition of risk averse, the manager chooses the less risky of two alternatives that have the same expected value, which is the decision reached by maximizing expected utility of profit (thank goodness . . .).
   d. The decision made by maximizing expected utility would also have been reached using mean-variance rules; pick the decision with lower risk when the expected values are equal.
9. *a.* 200 units. This is the last level of activity for which $E(MB)$ exceeds $E(MC)$. Choosing 200 units maximizes expected net benefit.
   b. Since the variance is constant for both MB and MC, a risk-loving decision maker behaves just as a risk-neutral decision maker alsobehaves—200 units would be chosen.
   c. Since the variance is constant for both MB and MC, a risk-averse decision maker also behaves just as a risk-neutral decision maker behaves, and 200 units would be chosen.
10. *a.* $E(MC) = 20 - 0.05Q + 0.00006Q^2$
   b. $E(P) = \$16.50 = 0.20(15) + 0.30(16) + 0.30(17) + 0.20(18)$
   c. minimum AVC occurs at $Q = 625$; minimum $AVC = \$12.19$; the manager should produce since $E(P) > \$12.19$
   d. $Q^* = 756$
   e. $E(\pi) = \$1{,}001 = \$12{,}474 - \$9{,}473 - \$2{,}000$
11. *a.* (*does not match*): $Q = 8{,}000 - 280P + 200(40) = 16{,}000 - 280P$
   (*does match*): $Q = 8{,}000 - 280P + 200P = 8{,}000 - 80P$
   b. $E(Q) = 0.2(16{,}000 - 280P) + 0.8(8{,}000 - 80P) = 9{,}600 - 120P$
   c. $E(MR) = 80 - 1/60\ Q$
   d. \$55
   e. 3,000; 3,600[= 8,000 − 80(55)]; 600[= 16,000 − 280(55)]
12. *a.* Option B
   b. Option A
   c. Option A, because potential regret for A is \$2,230 while potential regret for B is \$2,270.
   d. Option A (\$14,020 > \$14,000).

Chapter 19

1. *a.* $E(PV) = \$854{,}014 = 275{,}000/1.082 + 425{,}000/1.171 + 300{,}000/1.267 = 254{,}159 + 363{,}023 + 236{,}832$
   b. $E(PV) = \$838{,}621 = 275{,}000/1.092 + 425{,}000/1.192 + 300{,}000/1.302 = 251{,}832 + 356{,}405 + 230{,}385$
   c. The higher discount rate decreased $E(PV)$ as it should to reflect the higher risk.
2. *a.* $E(NCF_1) = 1.00$; $E(NCF_2) = 3.40$; $E(NCF_3) = 5.20$; $E(NCF_4) = 5.20$; $E(NCF_5) = 4.10$
   b. $E(PV) = 13.961\ (\$13{,}961{,}000) = \dfrac{1.00}{(1.0875)} + \dfrac{3.40}{(1.090)^2} + \dfrac{5.20}{(1.0925)^3} + \dfrac{5.20}{(1.095)^4} + \dfrac{4.10}{(1.0975)^5}$
   c. $$r_{\text{WACC}} = 0.089 = r_e\left(\frac{E}{D+E}\right) + r_d\left(\frac{D}{D+E}\right) = 0.14\left(\frac{32.7}{87.4+32.7}\right) + 0.07\left(\frac{87.4}{87.4+32.7}\right)$$
   $$E(PV) = 14.183\ (\$14{,}183{,}000) = \frac{1.00}{(1.089)} + \frac{3.40}{(1.089)^2} + \frac{5.20}{(1.089)^3} + \frac{5.20}{(1.089)^4} + \frac{4.10}{(1.089)^5}$$
3. *a.* $r = 10\%$ $PV = \$100{,}000/1.1 + \$100{,}000/(1.1)^2 = \$173{,}554$
   $NPV = \$173{,}554 - 162{,}500 = \$11{,}054$
   $r = 15\%$ $PV = \$100{,}000/1.15 + \$100{,}000/(1.15)^2 = \$162{,}571$
   $NPV = \$162{,}571 - 162{,}500 = \$71$
   $r = 20\%$ $PV = \$100{,}000/1.2 + \$100{,}000/(1.2)^2 = \$152{,}777$
   $NPV = \$152{,}777 - 162{,}500 = -\$9{,}723$

   b.

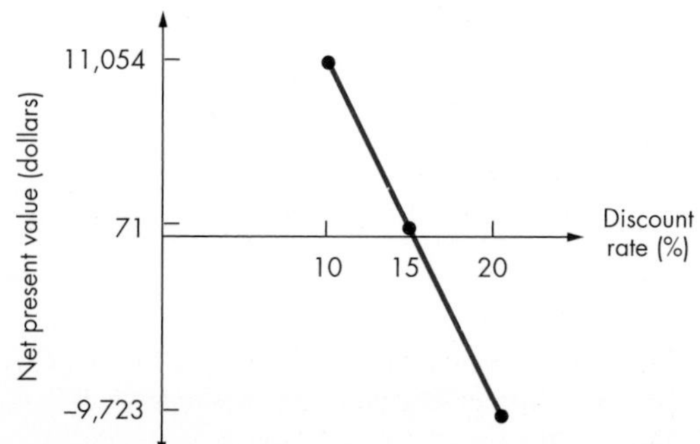

4. *a.* $$E(NPV) = \frac{20{,}000}{(1.10)} + \frac{15{,}000}{(1.10)^2} + \cdots + \frac{5{,}000}{(1.10)^5} - 45{,}000 = 18{,}181 + 12{,}396 + \cdots + 3{,}104 - 45{,}000 = 48{,}026 - 45{,}000 = 3{,}026$$
   b. Yes, because the expected net present value is positive. Thus this project will increase the present value of the firm.
   c. $$E(NPV) = \frac{20{,}000}{(1.18)} + \cdots + \frac{5{,}000}{(1.18)^5} - 45{,}000 = 41{,}151 - 45{,}000 = -3{,}848$$
   d. No. Since the expected net present value is negative, this project will decrease the present value of the firm.
   e.

Discount rate	*E(NPV)*
9.5 %	\$3,532
11.0 %	\$2,058
13.25%	\$ 0

5.

	Project A		Project B	
Year	*NCF* (\$, millions)	Cumulative *NCF* (\$, millions)	*NCF* (\$, millions)	Cumulative *NCF* (\$, millions)
1	2	2	1.0	1.0
2	0	2	0.8	1.8
3	0	2	0.6	2.4
4	0	2	0.4	2.8

   a. For project A, the cumulative *NCF* is equal to the cost of the project at the end of the first year, while the cumulative *NCF* from project B equals or exceeds cost in the third year. Using a maximum payback period of two years, project A is acceptable, while project B is not.
   b. *Project A:* $E(PV) = \$2.0/1.1 = \$1.82$; $E(NPV) = \$1.82 - 2.0 = -\$0.18$
   Project B: $E(PV) = \$1.0/1.1 + 0.8/(1.1)^2 + 0.6/(1.1)^3 + 0.4/(1.1)^4 = \$2.29$; $E(NPV) = \$2.29 - 2.0 = \$0.29$
   c. The recommendation is reversed under the expected *NPV* criterion: Reject project A, accept project B.
6. *a.* 3 years
   b. No
   c. When the appropriate discount rate exceeds 13.25%, $E(NPV)$ will be negative, and the payback rule leads to the same decision. [*Note:* $E(NPV) = 0$ at 13.25%.]
7. The payback rule gives too little weight to distant cash flows because any cash flows received after the maximum acceptable payback period are treated as though they have no value. The *ROI* rule, on the other hand, gives too much weight to

distant cash flows because the time value of money is ignored; cash flows in the future are treated as though they are equivalent to current cash flows.

8. *a.* *Project A:* Cumulative *NCFs* = \$10 + 8 + 6 + 4 = \$28; Average *NCF* = \$28/4 = \$7

   ROI = average *NCF*/average amount invested = \$7/\$20.5 = 34%

   Project B: Cumulative *NCFs* = \$4 + 6 + 9 + 11 = \$30; Average *NCF* = \$30/4 = \$7.5

   ROI = \$7.5/\$20.5 = 37%

   Using the *ROI* criterion with a target rate of return on investment of 35%, project A would be rejected and project B accepted.

   b. *Project A:* $E(PV) = \$10/1.15 + 8/(1.15)^2 + 6/(1.15)^3 + 4/(1.15)^4 = \$21.0$; $E(NPV) = \$21.0 - 20.5 = \$0.5$

   Project B: $E(PV) = \$4/1.15 + 6/(1.15)^2 + 9/(1.15)^3 + 11/(1.15)^4 = \$20.2$; $E(NPV) = \$20.2 - 20.5 = -\$0.3$

   c. The recommendation is reversed under the expected *NPV* criterion: Accept project A, reject project B. The *ROI* method treats current cash flows equivalently. The recommendation based on the expected *NPV* rule should be used because following the *ROI* criterion would reduce the value of the firm.

9. The *IRR* is the discount rate at which a project's *NPV* equals zero.

   a. $\$100{,}000/(1 + r) + \$100{,}000/(1 + r)^2 - \$162{,}500 = 0$

   Rearranging, $1.65r^2 + 2.25r - 0.375 = 0 \Rightarrow r = 15.034\%$.

   b. 13.25%; looking at the answer to part *e* in problem 4, note that $E(NPV) = 0$ when $IRR = 13.25\%$.

10. The *IRR* and *NPV* investment decision rules give conflicting recommendations when a project's *NPV* does not decline smoothly as the discount rate increases and when projects are mutually exclusive.

11. The capital rationing problem is largely self-imposed because the credit market should always be willing to finance a positive *NPV* project. Management could eliminate the constraint by going to the credit market and convincing creditors that, at the correct risk-adjusted discount rate and opportunity cost of capital, a project has a positive *NPV.* Firms may ration capital when it is actually other resources, such as managerial expertise, that are in short supply.

12. *a.*

Project	Expected *NPV*	Cost	*PV*	Profitability Index	Rank
A	20	10	30	3.0	2
B	17	10	27	2.7	3
C	12	5	17	3.4	1
D	8	5	13	2.6	4

b.

Expenditure constraint	Projects undertaken
5	C
10	C and D (or A)
15	C and A
20	C, A, and D

INDEX

D

E

Q

R